EIGHT IMPORTANT THINGS TO DO BEFORE INSTALLING WINDOWS XP

1. Check the Hardware Compatibility List at www.microsoft.com/hcl to see whether your computer and/or specific hardware is compatible with Windows XP.

2. (If upgrading an old computer) Record the names and model numbers of all your computer's hardware devices and their settings. You can get this information by opening Control Panel, System, Device Manager in Windows 9x and Me. You also can get this from the manuals with your equipment. (If all your devices are Plug and Play compatible, this step probably is not necessary.)

3. Check the hardware manufacturer's Web sites for updated Windows XP device drivers, and download them to a folder on the hard drive (or onto floppies or CD-Rs if you're going to reformat the hard disk during installation).

4. (If upgrading) Record your computer's network settings and Internet connection information, in case the upgrade process doesn't carry it over. You can get this information from the Network control panel and Dial-Up Networking in Windows 9x, Me, and NT, or from Network and Dial-Up Connections in Windows XP. Write down network protocol settings, connection telephone numbers, e-mail account settings (POP and SMTP settings), and anything else you can find. You also should record your computer's network name and workgroup or domain identification, which you can get from the Identification tab on the Network Control panel, or from Computer Properties.

5. Decide whether you want to upgrade your current OS to XP, or dual-boot it with 2000. (See Chapter 3 for details.) If you are going to dual-boot, create or find a new partition that does not have an OS on it. That partition will be the target for installing XP.

6. Decide which file system you want to use on the target partition, because the partition can be optionally reformatted (non-destructively) to NTFS during installation. If you are going to dual-boot, think about whether you want the preexisting operating system to have access to the target partition. It will need to be in a file system that is common to both (typically FAT32). (Chapters 3 and 31 discuss file system choices in detail.)

7. Be sure you have enough hard disk space on the target partition (minimum 1.5GB).

8. Back up your important data if you are upgrading.

Ten Steps to Making a Secure Internet Connection

If you'll be connecting to the Internet over your company's LAN or through a connection-sharing router, just set up your computer's network adapter as discussed in Chapter 16. The Network Setup Wizard will configure your Internet connection. If you're going to connect your computer directly, follow this quick-start guide, or see Chapter 8 for all the details.

If you're connecting via a dial-up modem:

1. First, install your modem. Then, click Start, My Computer, My Network Places, and View Network Connections.

2. Click Create a New Connection to start the New Connection Wizard. Click Next, and select Connect to the Internet. If you already have an ISP, choose Set Up My Connection Manually and follow the wizard's instructions to enter your ISP's setup and telephone information. Otherwise, let the wizard help you choose an ISP, or find one on your own, and let them walk you through the setup process.

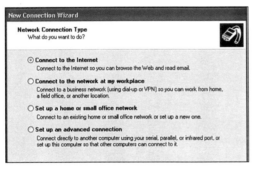

3. When the wizard is finished, a new connection icon will appear. It should say Firewalled to show you that Windows's Internet Connection Firewall is ready to protect you from hackers.

If you're connecting via "always-on" cable or DSL:

4. Get the hardware specified or provided by your ISP. Install the modem and/or LAN adapter according to the manufacturer's instructions.

5. Configure your new adapter using the settings provided by your ISP. Chapter 8 gives some pointers.

6. Click Start, My Computer, My Network Places, and View Network Connections. Find the icon for your new adapter or broadband connection, right-click it, and rename it Internet Connection.

7. If the icon doesn't say Firewalled, right-click it and select Properties. Select Advanced, and check Protect My Computer.

If you're connecting via DSL or cable requiring a sign-on:

8. Install and configure your modem and/or adapter. Then, click Start, My Computer, My Network Places, and View Network Connections. Click Create a New Connection to start the New Connection Wizard. Select Connect to the Internet, Set Up My Connection Manually, and Connect Using a Broadband Connection That Requires a User Name and Password. Follow the wizard's instructions to enter your username and password.

9. Be sure the resulting connection icon says Firewalled as discussed in step 7.

No matter how you connect:

10. The Internet Connection Firewall can't protect you from rogue programs downloaded or delivered by e-mail. Purchase or download a good antivirus program and *keep it up-to-date* by frequently checking for updates. Better yet, get an antivirus program that automatically checks for updates.

TEN IMPORTANT THINGS TO KNOW ABOUT THE NEW START MENU

The Start menu is the gateway to Windows XP. It packs a lot of power into a small space! This quick-reference map shows you how to navigate and customize it.

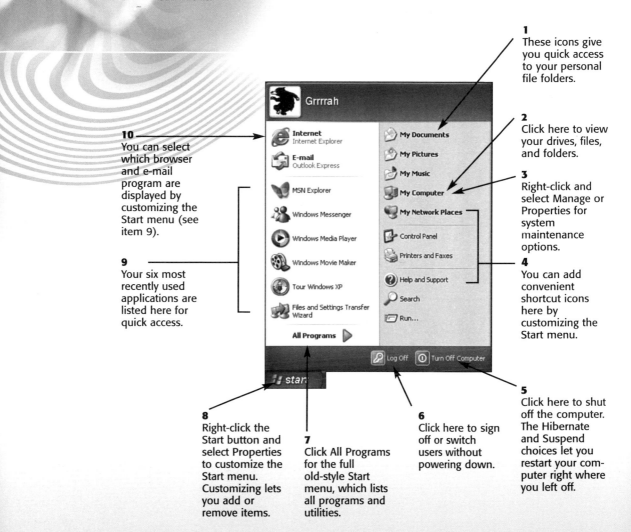

1
These icons give you quick access to your personal file folders.

2
Click here to view your drives, files, and folders.

3
Right-click and select Manage or Properties for system maintenance options.

4
You can add convenient shortcut icons here by customizing the Start menu.

5
Click here to shut off the computer. The Hibernate and Suspend choices let you restart your computer right where you left off.

6
Click here to sign off or switch users without powering down.

7
Click All Programs for the full old-style Start menu, which lists all programs and utilities.

8
Right-click the Start button and select Properties to customize the Start menu. Customizing lets you add or remove items.

9
Your six most recently used applications are listed here for quick access.

10
You can select which browser and e-mail program are displayed by customizing the Start menu (see item 9).

Nine Important Things to Do After Installing Windows XP

1. Set up accounts and passwords for all the people who will be using the computer. Chapter 28 tells how to do this.

2. Create a Password Recovery disk for the Administrator account at least, as described in Chapter 28.

3. Adjust the taskbar: Right-click on it and choose Properties. Click the Taskbar tab. Turn on Show Quick Launch if it's not on already. Turn on other toolbars if you want: Right-click the toolbar and choose Toolbars.

4. Adjust the Start menu: Right-click the Start button and choose Properties. Click the Start Menu tab. Choose Classic Start Menu if you want it to work like previous versions of Windows. Click the Customize button and then the Advanced tab to enable display of Printers and Faxes, My Network Places, and Administrative Tools. Turn on the list of most recently used documents if you like to easily get to your list on the Start Menu. Right-click the taskbar and choose Unlock if you want to be able to size up the taskbar to two or more lines of icons.

5. Adjust screen resolution and color depth by right-clicking on the desktop and choosing Properties, Settings. If screen elements are then too small, click the Advanced button, change the DPI settings, and adjust.

6. On a CRT, set the screen refresh rate to at least 72 Hertz by clicking the Monitor tab (in dialog box in the preceding step). This reduces eye fatigue and screen flicker.

7. On an LCD screen, set the refresh rate to 60 Hertz. Experiment with ClearType to see if you like its effect. Get there by Display Properties, Appearance, Effects, Use the Following Method to Smooth Edges of Screen Fonts, Clear Type.

8. Set desktop theme, screen saver, and appearance via the Display Properties dialog box. If you want the desktop to look and act like Windows 2000/Me/98, choose Windows Classic Style on the Appearance tab.

9. Put your favorite programs on the Quick Launch bar by dragging them from the Start menu or from their folders. To be safe, right-click+drag them to there, and choose Create Shortcuts Here.

SPECIAL EDITION
USING
Microsoft®
Windows XP
Professional Edition

Robert Cowart

Brian Knittel

201 W. 103rd Street
Indianapolis, Indiana 46290

CONTENTS AT A GLANCE

SPECIAL EDITION USING MICROSOFT® WINDOWS® XP PROFESSIONAL

Associate Publisher
Greg Wiegand

Executive Editor
Rick Kughen

Acquisitions Editor
Rick Kughen

Development Editor
Todd Brakke

Managing Editor
Thomas F. Hayes

Project Editor
Sheila Schroeder

Production Editor
Benjamin Berg

Indexer
Tina Trettin

Proofreaders
Harvey Stanbrough
Mary Ann Abramson

Technical Editors
Mark Reddin
David Eytchison
Doug Klippert
Terry W. Ogletree

Team Coordinator
Sharry Lee Gregory

Media Developer
Michael Hunter

Interior Designer
Ruth Harvey

Cover Designers
Dan Armstrong
Ruth Harvey

Page Layout
Scan Communications
Group, Inc.

Contents

ABOUT THE AUTHORS

Robert Cowart has written more than 35 books on computer programming and applications, with more than a dozen on Windows. His titles include *Windows NT Unleashed, Mastering Windows* (*3.0, 3.1, 95, 98,* and *Me*), *Windows NT Server Administrator's Bible, Windows NT Server 4.0: No Experience Required,* and *Special Edition Using Windows 2000 Professional.* Several of his books have been bestsellers in their categories, and have been translated into more than 20 languages. He has written on a wide range of computer-related topics for such magazines as *PC Week, PC World, PC Magazine, PC Tech Journal, Mac World,* and *Microsoft Systems Journal.* He has taught programming classes at the University of California Extension in San Francisco and has appeared as a special guest on the PBS TV series *Computer Chronicles,* CNN's *Headline News,* ZD-TV's *The Screen Savers,* and ABC's *World News Tonight with Peter Jennings.* He is president and co-founder of Brainsville.com, a company specializing in creating multimedia training courses. Robert resides in Berkeley, California.

In his spare time, he is involved in the music world, presenting chamber-music concerts and playing classical piano. He also is a teacher of the Transcendental Meditation technique.

Brian Knittel has been a software developer for more than 20 years. After doing graduate work in nuclear medicine and magnetic resonance imaging technologies, he began a career as an independent consultant. An eclectic mix of clients have led to long-term projects in medical documentation, workflow management, real-time industrial system control, and most importantly, 15 years of real-world experience with MS-DOS, Windows, and computer networking in the business world. Previously, he co-authored *Special Edition Using Microsoft Windows 2000 Professional* and contributed to several of Bob Cowart's other Windows books. Brian lives in Albany, California, halfway between the tidal wave zone and the earthquake fault. He spends his free time restoring antique computers (check out www.ibm1130.org) and trying to perfect his wood-fired pizza recipes.

ABOUT THE CONTRIBUTORS

Elaine Kreston has been a contributing author on other computer book titles, and is a creator and designer of Web sites. Her natural affinity for helping others solve computer problems was discovered while procrastinating from her real job, that of a professional cellist.

Mark Edward Soper has been a PC user for 18 years, and has been a computer trainer and technical writer since 1988. Author of more than 150 magazine articles and several books, including *The Complete Idiot's Guide to High-Speed Internet Connections* and *TechTV's Upgrading Your PC,* he also has written frequently about Windows from version 3.1 to Windows 2000. He lives in Evansville, Indiana, where he enjoys researching the history of transportation.

James Michael Stewart has been writing about Microsoft, the Internet, and certification for nearly seven years. Michael has contributed to more than 75 books in this area. His technical interests include IT certification, Windows, security, and the Internet. Michael also is an instructor at Networld+Interop. He spends his spare time learning to do everything, one hobby at a time.

Will Schmied (BSET, MCSE 2000, MCSA, CWNA, Server+, Network+, A+) is a freelance consultant and technical writer. Will contributed works to several of the Internet's largest IT websites, including `MCPMag.com`, `TCPMag.com`, `TechRepublic.com`, `CertCities.com`, `Cramsession.com`, `ISAServer.org`, and `MSExchange.org`. Will has also worked on books for several publishers, including Que, Osborne/McGraw Hill, and Syngress in addition to working on several print magazine articles.

Will holds a bachelors degree in engineering technology from Old Dominion University. He currently resides in Newport News, Virginia with his wife, Allison, their children, Christopher, Austin, Andrea, and Hannah and their pets, Peanut and Squeaky. When he's not busy playing with the latest in technologies, you can find him trying to improve his bowling average or logging some serious time on Dungeon Siege. You can visit Will at `www.netserveworld.com` or `www.soitslikethat.com`.

DEDICATION

In memory of all the victims of the World Trade Center and Pentagon attacks, near and far—Bob

To Dr. Bertram G. Katzung, who many years ago gave me support, encouragement, and the opportunity to begin my career in computing—Brian

ACKNOWLEDGMENTS

This book, as much as the product it covers, is the product of a team effort. We couldn't have produced this without the great team at Que, the assistance of contributing writers, the patience and support of our friends, and so . . .

We feel privileged to be part of the consistently professional *Special Edition Using* family. Producing these highly technical, state-of-the art books requires a dedicated and knowledge-able staff, and once again the staff at Que did an amazing job. Executive editor Rick Kughen has provided unflagging, cheerful support and guidance through our three *SE Using* volumes. Our development editor, Todd Brakke, pored over every word on every page of this volume and our equally weighty Windows XP Home Edition book and offered invaluable direction and tuning. This is a much better book than it could have been without him.

We'd like to acknowledge the efforts of our technical editors: Mark Reddin, Doug Klippert, and David Eytchison. Special thanks to Benjamin Berg for not only his ace copy editing, but for the technical know-how and eye for detail that he brought to the project. We also would like to thank the editorial, indexing, layout, art, proofing, and other production staff at Que—Tonya Simpson, Tina Trettin, and more. These folks labor away largely unseen and often unthanked. You did a marvelous job.

We'd like to thank Elaine Kreston, James Michael Stewart, and Mark Soper for their come-to-the-rescue aid in helping us get this book to press on time (more or less!); Norm Aleks for advice and insight into the world of Linux; and Eric Fitzgerald at Microsoft for clarify-ing the intricacies of Windows network security.

No book could make it to market without the real-world personal relationships developed between booksellers on the one hand, and the sales and marketing personnel back at the publishers. We've had the opportunity to meet sales and marketing folks in the computer publishing world, and know what a difficult job selling and keeping up with the thousands of computer titles can be. Thanks to all of you for your pivotal role in helping us pay our mortgages!

Finally, we should acknowledge those who made it possible for us to get through the months of writing. Bob first thanks his agent, Chris Van Buren, for standing by him with encouragement on down days and sharing his excitement after his successes. Many thanks for fighting for better contracts, keeping things in perspective, and phoning in long distance (even from Brazil!) for conference calls. And, as always, thanks to friends and family who, even though used to seeing him disappear for months on end, let him back in the fold when it's over. This goes for Elaine, in particular, whose daily support and patience made such a difference. Also, to Baxter the cat for her companionship.

Brian adds big dittos to Chris Van Buren and special thanks to Bryce Carter for guidance, and Norm Aleks for patience and support. Life will get back to normal soon . . . just in time to start another book or two.

WE WANT TO HEAR FROM YOU!

As the reader of this book, you are our most important critic and commentator. We value your opinion and want to know what we're doing right, what we could do better, what areas you'd like to see us publish in, and any other words of wisdom you're willing to pass our way.

As an associate publisher for Que, I welcome your comments. You can email or write me directly to let me know what you did or didn't like about this book—as well as what we can do to make our books better.

Please note that I cannot help you with technical problems related to the topic of this book. We do have a User Services group, however, where I will forward specific technical questions related to the book.

When you write, please be sure to include this book's title and author as well as your name, email address, and phone number. I will carefully review your comments and share them with the author and editors who worked on the book.

Email: feedback@quepublishing.com

Mail: Greg Wiegand
            Que Publishing
            201 West 103rd Street
            Indianapolis, IN 46290 USA

For more information about this book or another Que title, visit our Web site at www.quepublishing.com. Type the ISBN (excluding hyphens) or the title of a book in the Search field to find the page you're looking for.

INTRODUCTION

WELCOME

Thank you for purchasing or considering the purchase of *Special Edition Using Microsoft Windows XP Professional*. It's amazing the changes that 15 years can bring to a computer product such as Windows. When we wrote our first Windows book back in the mid-'80s, our publisher didn't even think the book would sell well enough to print more than 5,000 copies. Microsoft stock wasn't even a blip on most investors' radar screens. Boy, were they wrong! Who could have imagined that a little more than a decade later, anyone who hoped to get hired for even a temp job in a small office would need to know how to use Microsoft Windows, Office, and a PC. Fifteen Windows books later, we're still finding new and exciting stuff to tell our readers.

Some people (including the U.S. Department of Justice) claim Microsoft's predominance on the PC operating system arena was won unethically through monopolistic practices. Whether or not this is true (we try, almost successfully, to stay out of the politics in this book), we believe that Windows has earned its position today through reasons other than having a stranglehold on the market. Consider that Windows NT 3.1 had 5 million lines of code. Windows XP weighs in with more than 30 million. This represents a lot of work, by anyone's accounting. Who could have imagined in 1985 that any decent operating system a decade and half later must have support for so many technologies that didn't even exist at the time: CD-ROM, DVD, CD-R and CD-RW, Internet and intranet, MP3, MPEG, DV, USB, FireWire, APM, ACPI, RAID, UPS, PPOE, 802.11b, fault tolerance, disk encryption and compression . . . ? The list goes on. And could we have imagined that a Microsoft Certified System Engineer certificate (MCSE) could prove as lucrative as a medical or law degree?

Although rarely on the bleeding edge of technology, and often taking the role of the dictator, Bill Gates has at least been benevolent from the users' point of view. In 1981, when we were building our first computers, the operating system (CP/M) had to be modified in assembly language and recompiled, and hardware parts had to be soldered together to make almost any new addition (such as a video display terminal) work. Virtually nothing was standardized, with the end result being that computers remained out of reach for average folks.

Together, Microsoft, Intel, and IBM changed all that. Today, you can purchase a computer, printer, scanner, Zip drive, keyboard, modem, monitor, and video card over the Internet, plug them in, and install Windows, and they'll probably work together. The creation and adoption (and sometimes forcing) of hardware and software standards that have made the PC a household appliance the world over can largely be credited to Microsoft, like it or not. The unifying glue of this PC revolution has been Windows.

Yes, we all love to hate Windows, but it's here to stay. Linux is on the rise, but for most of us, at least for some time, Windows and Windows applications are "where it's at." And Windows XP ushers in truly significant changes to the landscape. That's why we were excited to write this book.

This book covers Windows XP as well as the latest upgrades to XP, which is called SP-1, or Service Pack 1. Service Pack 1 adds a bevy of new features and hardware support to Windows XP, as well as attempting to meet the demands of the U.S. Department of Justice for unbundling "middleware" programs such as Internet Explorer and Outlook Express.

WHY THIS BOOK?

We all know this book will make an effective doorstop in a few years. You probably have a few already. (We've even written a few!) If you think it contains more information than you need, just remember how helpful a good reference can be when you need it at the 11th hour. And we all know that computer technology changes so fast that it's sometimes easier just to blink and ignore a phase than to study up on it. Windows XP definitely is a significant upgrade in Windows technology—one you're going to need to understand. Microsoft has folded all of its operating systems into the Windows XP product line, so rest assured it will be around for some time.

On the surface, Windows XP might provide much of the same functionality as Windows 98 and Windows Me, but it's a completely different animal, and the differences are more than skin deep. From the way users sign on, to the new Start menu, to its day-to-day management tools, XP bears little resemblance to its predecessors. Don't let that worry you: In all ways, it's superior to any operating system Microsoft has ever produced.

Is Windows XP so easy to use that books are unnecessary? Unfortunately, no. True, as with other releases of Windows, online help is available. As has been the case ever since Windows 95, however, no printed documentation is available (to save Microsoft the cost), and the Help files are written by the Microsoft cronies. You won't find criticisms, complaints, workarounds, or talk of third-party programs there, let alone explanations of *why* you have to do things a certain way. For that, you need this book!

You might know that Windows XP comes in two versions: Home Edition and Professional. Other publishers have produced single volumes to cover both operating systems, but we think that will only end up confusing readers. Instead, we've produced two books, because we wanted you to have a book that addresses your specific needs. This book covers Windows XP Professional's more advanced management and networking features, and, while it anticipates that some home users will choose the Professional version, it also addresses the business and/or power user. Still, we assume you probably are not an engineer, and we'll do our best to speak in plain English and not snow you with unexplained jargon.

In this book's many pages, we focus not just on the gee-whiz side of the technology, but why you should care, what you can get from it, and what you can forget about. The lead author on this book has previously written 15 books about Windows, all in plain English (several bestsellers), designed for everyone from rank beginners to full-on system administrators deploying NT Server domains. The co-author has designed software and networks for more than 20 years. We work with and write about various versions of Windows year in and year out. We have a clear understanding of what confuses users and system administrators about installing, configuring, or using Windows, as well as (we hope) how to best convey the solutions to our readers.

This book grew out of our popular Windows 2000 book *(Special Edition Using Windows 2000 Professional)*, and like Windows XP itself, builds on the experience we gained with that operating system. We spent many months testing Windows XP betas through numerous builds, participating in the Microsoft beta newsgroups, documenting and working through bugs, and installing and reinstalling Windows XP on a variety of networks and computers. The result is what you hold in your hands.

While writing this book, we tried to stay vigilant of four cardinal rules:

- Keep it practical.
- Keep it accurate.
- Keep it concise.
- Keep it interesting, and even crack a joke or two.

We believe that you will find this to be the best book available on Windows XP Professional for the intermediate to advanced user. While writing it, we targeted an audience ranging from the power user at home or the office, to the support guru in a major corporation. Whether you use a Windows XP PC or support others who do, we firmly believe this book will address your questions and needs.

We're also willing to tell you what we don't cover. No book can do it all. As the title implies, this book is about Windows XP *Professional*. We don't cover setting up the Server versions of this operating system called Windows 2003 Server, Advanced Server, and Datacenter. However, we do tell you how to connect to and interact with these servers, and even other operating systems, including MacOS, Linux, and older variants of Windows, over a local area network. And, due to space limitations, there is only passing coverage of Windows XP's command-line utilities, batch file language, and Windows Script Host. For that (in spades!), watch for Brian's upcoming book *Windows XP Under the Hood*, to be published in June, 2002.

Also in summer 2002, look for Bob and Brian's *Platinum Edition Using Microsoft Windows XP*. That hefty tome will pick up where the *Special Edition Using Windows XP* book leaves off. If you think this book changed your life, just wait until you get your hands on the Platinum Edition.

We worked hard not to assume too much knowledge on your part, yet we didn't want to assume you aren't already experienced with Windows. The working assumption here is that you are already conversant at least with some form of Windows, preferably 9x, Me, or 2000, and possibly with NT 4. However, we provide a primer on the Windows XP interface (including video of it on the CD-ROM) because the look and feel of Windows XP is significantly different from its predecessors. Even when you've become a Windows XP pro, we think you'll find this book to be a valuable source of reference information in the future. Both the table of contents and the very complete index will provide easy means for locating information when you need it quickly.

How Our Book Is Organized

Although this book advances logically from beginning to end, it's written so that you can jump in at any location, quickly get the information you need, and get out. You don't have to read it from start to finish, nor do you need to work through complex tutorials.

This book is broken down into six major parts. Here's the skinny on each one:

Part I, "Introducing Windows XP Professional," introduces Windows XP and explains its features, new screen elements (GUI), and the design and architecture behind Windows XP. It then explains how to ready your hardware and software for installation of XP and describes the installation process itself.

Part II, "Getting Your Work Done," is, well, about getting your work done. Perhaps the bulk of readers will want to study and keep on hand this part as a reference guide. Here, we cover using the interface, running programs, organizing documents, sharing data between applications, and printing and faxing documents. We also cover how to best work with the increasingly popular plethora of digital imaging tools and formats encountered with digital photography and nonlinear video editing in your PC.

Part III, "Windows XP and the Internet," introduces you to Windows XP networking, Internet style. We start with Internet connection options and then move on to the supplied Internet tools. We provide in-depth coverage of Outlook Express for mail and newsgroups, Internet Explorer for Web surfing, and Windows Messenger for audio and videoconferencing. The final two chapters show you how to set up your own Web server, and how to diagnose Internet connection problems with utilities such as ping and ipconfig.

Part IV, "Networking," deals with networking on the LAN. Here, we explain the fundamentals of networking and, in case you don't have a corporate networking department to do this for you, we walk you through planning and installing a functional LAN in your home or office. We cover the use of a Windows XP network; give you a chapter on dial-up, remote, and portable networking; show how to internetwork with Unix and other operating systems; and finish up with crucial security tips and troubleshooting advice that the Windows Help files don't cover. This chapter also covers Windows XP's new Remote Desktop and Remote Assistance features, and shows you how to set up a secure, shared Internet connection for your LAN.

Part V, "System Configuration and Customization," covers system configuration and maintenance. We tell you how to work with Control Panel applets, provide tips and tricks for customizing the graphical user interface to maximize efficiency, manage your system fonts, and describe a variety of ways to upgrade your hardware and system software (including third-party programs) for maximum performance.

Part VI, "System Administration and Maintenance," dives even deeper into system administration and configuration, with coverage of supplied system administration tools such as the Microsoft Management Console (MMC) and its plug-ins. We also provide techniques for managing multiple users; means for managing the hard disk, including multiple file system formats such as FAT32 and NTFS; and details on setting up multiboot machines with Windows 9x, DOS, Linux, and Windows 2000. We cap off this part with coverage of the Windows Registry and a chapter on troubleshooting and repairing problems with your Windows XP installation.

Appendix A covers installation of Service Pack 1, and Appendix B covers in detail all the new and exciting features you'll find in SP1.

WHAT'S ON THE CD?

We've made a 45-minute CD-ROM–based video presentation, so not only can we tell you how to use and manage Windows XP, we can actually demonstrate specific skills so you can learn more quickly. We show you how to get around the new XP interface as well as how to set up a simple network—one of XP's great strengths. You'll want to be sure to check this out, and meet the authors.

CONVENTIONS USED IN THIS BOOK

Special conventions are used throughout this book to help you get the most from the book and from Windows XP Professional.

TEXT CONVENTIONS

Various typefaces in this book identify terms and other special objects. These special typefaces include the following:

Type	Meaning
Italic	New terms or phrases when initially defined.
`Monospace`	Information that appears in code or onscreen.
`Bold monospace`	Information you type.
Words separated by commas	All Windows book publishers struggle with how to represent command sequences when menus and dialog boxes are involved. In this book, we separate commands using a comma. Yeah, we know it's confusing, but this is traditionally how the Special Edition Using book series does it, and traditions die hard. So, for example, the instruction "Choose Edit, Cut" means that you should open the Edit menu and choose Cut. Another, more complex example would be "Click Start, Settings, Control Panel, System, Hardware, Device Manager."

Key combinations are represented with a plus sign. For example, if the text calls for you to press Ctrl+Alt+Delete, you would press the Ctrl, Alt, and Delete keys at the same time.

TIPS FROM THE WINDOWS PROS

Ever wonder how the experts get their work done better and faster than anyone else? Ever wonder how they became experts in the first place? You'll find out in these special sections throughout the book. We've spent a lot of time under the Windows hood, so to speak, getting dirty and learning what makes Windows XP tick. So, with the information we provide in these sections, you can roll up your shirt sleeves and dig in.

SPECIAL ELEMENTS

Throughout this book, you'll find Notes, Cautions, Sidebars, Cross-References, and Troubleshooting Tips. Often, you'll find just the tidbit you need to get through a rough day at the office or the one whiz-bang trick that will make you the office hero. You'll also find little nuggets of wisdom, humor, and lingo that you can use to amaze your friends and family, not to mention making you cocktail-party literate.

TIP FROM

Bob & Brian

> We specially designed these tips to showcase the best of the best. Just because you get your work done doesn't mean you're doing it in the fastest, easiest way possible. We'll show you how to maximize your Windows experience. Don't miss these tips!

NOTE

> Notes point out items that you should be aware of, but you can skip them if you're in a hurry. Generally, we've added notes as a way to give you some extra information on a topic without weighing you down.

CAUTION

> Pay attention to cautions! They could save you precious hours in lost work.

 We designed these elements to call attention to common pitfalls that you're likely to encounter. When you see a Troubleshooting note, you can flip to the end of the chapter to learn how to solve or avoid a problem.

CROSS-REFERENCES

Cross-references are designed to point you to other locations in this book (or other books in the Que family) that will provide supplemental or supporting information. Cross-references appear as follows:

→ For information on updating offline Web pages, **see** "Browsing Offline," **p. 299**.

Sidebars
Sidebars are designed to provide information that is ancillary to the topic being discussed. Read this information if you want to learn more details about an application or task.

INTRODUCING WINDOWS XP PROFESSIONAL

INTRODUCING WINDOWS XP PROFESSIONAL

In this chapter

1

AN OVERVIEW OF WINDOWS XP PROFESSIONAL

Windows XP Professional is the successor to Windows 2000 Professional, and takes its place as the corporate desktop and workstation version of Windows for the early 21st century. However, Windows XP Professional also is part of the first family of Windows to break down the long-standing barrier between home-oriented and business-oriented releases of Windows. The release of Windows XP in Home and Professional versions is a big move for Microsoft, which has offered separate home-oriented (Windows 3.x/9x/Me) and corporate-oriented (Windows NT/2000) versions with drastically different internal designs since 1993. The common code base of both versions of Windows XP also is a big benefit for both users and developers. It makes program and device driver development much easier, because device drivers and software programs need to be created just once, rather than twice.

The goal that Microsoft had in mind for Windows XP Professional was ambitious: to create a reliable, easy-to-use operating system whose features would provide complete corporate network and security features, while also including features popular with users who might have previously used Windows 9x or Windows Me. Windows XP Professional also is designed to provide application and hardware compatibility with products made for older versions of Windows, and even MS-DOS game and graphics applications.

It's a tough job, but Windows XP Professional meets these requirements quite well. Windows XP Professional combines the reliability and corporate networking/security features of Windows 2000 with improved versions of the multimedia and crash-recovery features that Windows 98 and Windows Me pioneered. To make it easier to move to Windows XP Professional, it's designed to work much better than Windows 2000 did with older Windows (and even DOS-based) software, while still supporting the latest productivity, educational, recreational, and gaming programs from Microsoft and other publishers.

What does the "XP" in Windows XP stand for? "Experience," and you will find that using Windows XP Professional will feel like a new experience thanks to its new Luna user interface. And, beneath the surface, there's a mixture of the new, the enhanced, and the tried-and-true features brought over from both Windows 2000 and Windows 9x/Me.

Originally code-named Whistler, Windows XP is the product of a development process that began with a consumer operating system code-named Neptune in late 1999 and a separate business-oriented operating system code-named Odyssey, which was planned as a successor to Windows 2000. In January 2000, Microsoft decided to integrate both Neptune and Odyssey into a single operating system family code-named Whistler, which you now know as Windows XP.

Windows XP has been in the public eye longer than any other Windows version during its development process, and the final product has received a great deal of user feedback, thanks to its unprecedented public beta-testing process. Although some pundits derided Microsoft for charging users for the "privilege" of using a beta product, the decision to allow users to try beta versions with the Windows XP Preview Program, starting in April 2001, has helped make Windows XP a better product. The public scrutiny of Windows XP

1

has forced controversial features such as Smart Tags (which added Microsoft-generated URLs to Web pages) to be dropped and others such as Hardware Activation (required before Windows XP can be used for the first time) to be modified in the favor of users.

A LITTLE WINDOWS HISTORY

As you surely know, Windows is a *graphical user interface (GUI)* and *operating system (OS)* that is the heart and soul of your computer. Although Windows was once a toy (I remember when people bought Windows mainly because of the graphical word processor and paint program it included), it's now an essential element in your computing experience.

When Windows first hit the market in 1985, it actually was a shell that sat upon the increasingly shaky foundations of MS-DOS. Early versions were frequently used as menuing systems for launching MS-DOS programs, because programs that actually required Windows were quite scarce for several years. In fact, to help promote Windows as a platform for programs, Microsoft distributed a "runtime" version of Windows with some of the early Windows-based programs such as Aldus PageMaker (now an Adobe product). Users who didn't have a full version of Windows needed to install the runtime version before using the program. The runtime version of Windows was launched when the application (such as PageMaker) was started and provided Windows menuing and print services, and closed when the application was closed.

Windows didn't really take off until the introduction of Windows 3.0 in 1990 (it could multitask both DOS and Windows programs if you used a 386 or 486 processor) and Windows 3.1 in 1992, which introduced TrueType scalable fonts. Windows for Workgroups 3.1 (1992) and 3.11 (1994) pioneered the built-in networking features that would typify all subsequent versions of Windows up to the present. Windows for Workgroups 3.11 was the last version of Windows to require that MS-DOS or a comparable text-based operating system be present at installation time.

Although Windows 95, Windows 98, and Windows Me no longer required MS-DOS, they still used an improved form of DOS for some operations. This dependence upon MS-DOS made for an increasingly unstable operating system because the management tricks necessary to keep MS-DOS, old 16-bit Windows applications, and new 32-bit Windows programs running on the same hardware at the same time led to frequent reboots and system lockups. Although many of the features pioneered by Windows 9x and Windows Me have been retained and enhanced in Windows XP, Windows XP is not a true descendent of DOS-based Windows.

Instead, the Windows XP family is the latest descendent of the "other" Windows family a family of Windows products that do not use MS-DOS as a foundation. Microsoft's development of a non–DOS-based operating system goes back to 1987 and the joint development (with IBM) of a Windows replacement called OS/2. OS/2 was aimed squarely at the emerging corporate network world then dominated by Novell and its NetWare network operating system.

1

Unlike NetWare, Microsoft and IBM's OS/2 was designed to handle both the server and the desktop side of network computing. Unfortunately for OS/2, the IBM-Microsoft partnership broke up in 1991 after a series of disagreements about the direction of OS/2. IBM kept OS/2, and Microsoft stuck with Windows. Microsoft had already begun the development of Windows NT in October 1988 with the hiring of Dave Cutler, who had developed the VMS (Virtual Memory System) operating system for Digital Equipment's (DEC) line of VAX multitasking and multiuser computers.

The development of Windows NT took several years: The first version to reach retail shelves, Windows NT 3.1, was introduced in mid-1993. Windows NT introduced several features common to all its successors, including Windows 2000 and Windows XP:

- Preemptive multitasking—The user doesn't need to wait for one task to finish before starting another one.
- Client/server model for computing—The operating system is divided into two parts, just as with mainframe systems.
- Dynamic disk caching/virtual memory—The operating system can use more than one drive as virtual memory (using disk space in place of RAM); desktop Windows versions up through Windows Me can use only one drive for virtual memory.
- Fault tolerance features—The capability to handle power outages and disk crashes.
- Capability to start and stop network services without rebooting.
- Fully 32-bit architecture—Windows NT and its successors are free from the limitations of 16-bit Windows (and MS-DOS!) instructions.
- Support for multiple file systems, including the old FAT16 file system used by MS-DOS and Windows 9x and the NTFS file system developed for Windows NT, which supports advanced security features, long filenames, and automatic error correction.

Windows NT 4.0, introduced in mid-1996, was modeled after the Windows 95 user interface (instead of the Windows 3.1 user interface used by earlier Windows NT versions), and provided crash protection superior to that of Windows 95. However, it lacked support for Plug and Play, the easy hardware installation feature introduced by Windows 95, and many Windows 95-compatible hardware devices wouldn't work with Windows NT 4.0.

Windows 2000, introduced in early 2000, was originally called NT 5.0 during its prerelease period, and began the NT family's move toward becoming more user-friendly. Many of Windows 2000's features have become part of Windows XP Professional, including Plug-and-Play hardware support, ACPI power management, support for USB and IEEE-1394 ports and devices, AGP video, Internet Connection Sharing, and enhanced system management. Windows 2000 also improved drive support by adding support for FAT32, the file system introduced by Windows 95 OSR 2.x that shatters the 2.1GB limit per drive letter imposed by FAT16. It also introduced a more advanced version of NTFS that supports file encryption, file compression, and support for mounting and dismounting drives to allow them to be accessed through folders on another drive. Windows XP also supports these file-system features of Windows 2000.

1

While Windows NT was being developed and improved, Microsoft was also developing its Windows 9x product family, which culminated in the release of Windows Me in 2000. Windows Me, like Windows 9x, is a hybrid operating system with some features inherited from MS-DOS as well as 32-bit code, so its internal architecture is nothing like Windows XP's. Instead, the most significant fact about Windows Me from a Windows XP Professional user's viewpoint is Windows Me's introduction of a wide variety of built-in multimedia and imaging features. Windows XP features, such as the Scanner and Camera Wizard, the slideshow features in the My Pictures folder, and Movie Maker, are all descended from Windows Me. Another significant feature of Windows XP that Windows Me pioneered is System Restore, which allows the user to get around tricky OS problems by resetting the system configuration to what it was on a previous day.

Like Windows 2000 before it, Windows XP is a highly extensible operating system. Windows XP uses a microkernel derived from Windows 2000, featuring an object-oriented, modular design that enables various types of services, file systems, and other subsystems to be attached to the core operating system, just as various types of hardware can be attached to a PC. The result is that Windows XP can emulate other operating systems and support applications originally designed for DOS, 16-bit Windows, older 32-bit Windows versions, POSIX-compliant Unix applications, and OS/2. Whereas Windows 2000 provided a "one-size-fits-all" approach to running older Windows programs, which didn't always work, Windows XP goes beyond Windows 2000 by providing a customizable emulation feature that enables you to select which version of Windows it should emulate to run a particular program. See Chapter 25, "Maintaining and Optimizing System Performance," for details.

Windows XP Professional can be fairly described as a combination of the security, stability, and corporate networking features of Windows 2000 and the multimedia, entertainment, and error-handling features of Windows Me.

WHAT'S NEW IN WINDOWS XP PROFESSIONAL?

Now that you know Windows XP's family history, you're ready to find out what new features Windows XP Professional brings to the Windows family. One of the questions people ask me as I write books about each new version of Windows is whether the new version is different enough to justify upgrading. The Windows XP family is a major upgrade from any previous version of Windows, and the jump from Windows 98 or Windows Me to Windows XP Professional is as massive a jump as the one from Windows 3.1 to Windows 95 was a few years ago. Windows XP Professional isn't just a much-improved version of the Windows 2000 family, preserving Windows 2000 Professional's corporate networking and security features, but is also a superset of Windows XP Home Edition, which integrates improved versions of multimedia and recreational features originally introduced by Windows 98 and Windows Me. Thus, whether you want an operating system ready for the corporate desktop or are looking to add multimedia and recreational features to your corporate operating system, Windows XP Professional can do the job. Thus, Windows XP Professional can be used to replace both Windows 2000 and the long-lived Windows 9x family on corporate desktops.

How big a change is Windows XP? Estimates are that by the time it was released, it contained about 40 million lines of code (see Table 1.1). That's more than one-third more code than its immediate predecessor, Windows 2000, and plenty of room for its new and enhanced features.

TABLE 1.1   LINES OF CODE COMPARISON

Operating System	Lines of Programming Code
Windows NT 3.1	6.5 million
Windows NT 3.5	10 million
Windows 95	10 million
Windows 98	13 million
NT 4	16.5 million
Windows 2000	~29 million
Windows 2000 Advanced Server	~33 million
Windows 2000 Datacenter	>40 million
Windows XP	~40 million

Windows XP is much bigger than Windows 2000 because it adds new multimedia and entertainment features absent from Windows 2000 Professional and because it also contains improvements to features carried over from Windows 2000.

Because Windows XP Professional offers so many improvements and new features when compared to Windows 98, Windows Me, and even Windows 2000, in this section we'll highlight some of the new and improved features and what each feature does. Table 1.2 highlights some of the key improvements found in Windows XP Professional and points you to the chapter in which it is covered.

TABLE 1.2   COVERAGE OF NEW AND IMPROVED WINDOWS XP PROFESSIONAL FEATURES

Feature	Covered in Chapter
New setup process	3
New interface: My Documents, My Pictures, My Music, custom toolbars, intelligent Menus, new help system, search function	4
Multimedia improvements: DVD, DirectX 8.1, image color management, scanner and digital camera support, Windows Movie Maker, Windows Media Player 8, CD burning, Web Publishing Wizard	4, 7, 13
Hardware support: Plug and Play, multiple monitors, FireWire	25
Active Directory	15
Enhanced Web browsing with IE 6	9

TABLE 1.2   CONTINUED

Feature	Covered in Chapter
Better e-mail and news reader with Outlook Express 6	10, 11
Improved mobile support and power management	18
New Microsoft Management Console (MMC)	27
Improved Installer/Remover	24
Kerberos security	17
Internet Connection Sharing	17
Fast User Switching	28
Windows Messenger, NetMeeting	12
Remote Assistance	33
Files and Settings Transfer Wizard	5
System Restore	27
Network Setup Wizard	16
System File Protection	33
Internet Connection Firewall	19
Credential Manager	16
Task Manager	27
Personalized Welcome Screen	28
Taskbar Grouping	23
File Management	4
Compatibility Mode	23
Dual View	27
ClearType	4
Windows Help	4
Device Driver Rollback	33
Network Bridging	17

INTERFACE IMPROVEMENTS

Although some might disagree, Windows XP really is the best-looking version of Windows ever, but the improvements are more than just skin deep. Windows XP takes full advantage of today's widespread support for high-resolution, 24-bit (16.8 million color) displays to provide subtle shading and animation effects to make working easier, but it also provides a more intelligent and customizable interface compared to previous Windows versions.

1

STARTUP AND START MENU IMPROVEMENTS

After you get to the splash screen, Windows XP Professional looks like no other Windows version. Before the splash screen loads, pressing F8 brings up a troubleshooting options menu that most closely resembles the one provided for Windows 2000, although Windows 9x/Me users will also find it familiar. This Advanced Options menu lets you boot into alternative modes such as "safe mode" to do troubleshooting (see Figure 1.1). Normal boot processes display a splash screen that is more compact than the previous full-screen one used by Windows 9x/Me and has an easy-to-see progress bar in the middle of the screen.

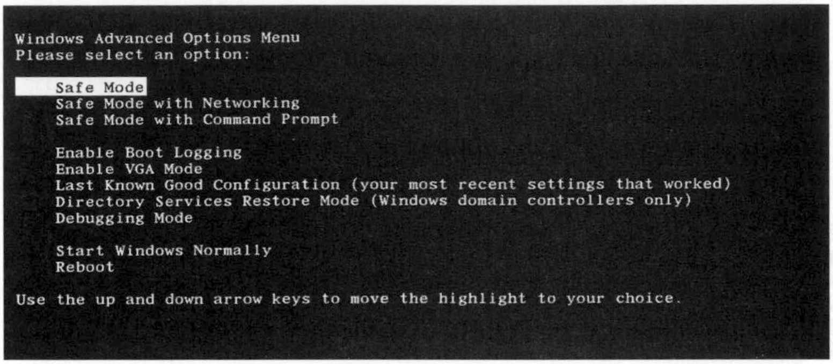

Figure 1.1
New startup options in Windows XP Professional offer various troubleshooting options if you simply press F8 at boot time.

```
Windows Advanced Options Menu
Please select an option:

    Safe Mode
    Safe Mode with Networking
    Safe Mode with Command Prompt

    Enable Boot Logging
    Enable VGA Mode
    Last Known Good Configuration (your most recent settings that worked)
    Directory Services Restore Mode (Windows domain controllers only)
    Debugging Mode

    Start Windows Normally
    Reboot

Use the up and down arrow keys to move the highlight to your choice.
```

NOTE

If you upgraded from an earlier version of Windows, your system will also display a "Return to OS Choices Menu" option after the "Reboot" option when looking at the troubleshooting options.

Windows XP shortens the startup time by using a technique called *prefetching*, which loads major portions of the operating system at the same time that devices are being initialized, rather than performing loading and device initialization in series, as with earlier versions of Windows. And, Windows XP learns which hardware and software you use during the first few times you boot your system, and moves the files used by your hardware and software to the fastest parts of your drive to further improve boot time.

If you're bringing up your system from a sleep mode, standby and hibernation are both much faster with Windows XP Professional. Newer notebook computers can restart from Standby, which shuts down power to peripherals but maintains power flowing to your RAM, in as little as two seconds. Hibernation, which stores the state of your system (open files and programs) on the hard disk before powering down, is also faster. Newer systems can emerge from Hibernation in as little as 20 to 30 seconds. After you've booted your system, the Windows XP Professional Start menu makes it easier to use the most popular programs. It shows you the major new features, and a link called All Programs displays the rest of the programs ready for your use.

If you need help through the Internet or e-mail, or with your system's configuration, the Start menu items Control Panel, Help and Support, Internet Explorer, and Outlook Express are all available as soon as you click the Start button.

Right-click on the taskbar, select Properties, Start Menu, and Customize and you can control the appearance of the Start menu and the programs and features that will be displayed (Figure 1.2).

Figure 1.2
Customize your Start menu by selecting the number of popular program shortcuts, icon sizes, and default Web browser and e-mail programs.

Select large icons for better visibility, or small icons to show more programs at a time. By default, the Start menu displays six programs you use most often, but you can set the number yourself or clear the list of programs. By default, Internet Explorer is displayed as the standard Web browser, and Outlook Express is the standard e-mail program, but you can remove them from the Start menu or choose alternatives you've installed.

Click Advanced to specify other Start menu features (see Figure 1.3), including

- Disabling features such as submenus opening when you pause over them
- Disabling the highlighting of newly installed programs until you run them for the first time
- Whether to display the Control Panel, Favorites menu, Help and Support, My Computer, My Documents, My Music, My Network Places, My Pictures, Network Connections, Printers and Faxes, Run command, Search, and System Administration tools

Figure 1.3
The Advanced dialog box lets you choose which Windows XP folders and tools to display on the Start menu, which display options to use, and other customizations.

You also can select whether to scroll the Programs menu, select how to display some menu items, and whether to display recently opened documents. Figure 1.4 shows a typical menu on a Windows XP Professional system.

Figure 1.4
The Windows XP Professional main menu on a typical system just after initial installation. As you use different programs, the contents of the lower left-hand side of the menu will vary.

As you can see in Figure 1.4, the menu also adapts to your recent selections, placing shortcuts to the last six programs you've run into the blank space at the left side of the Start menu, as discussed earlier in this section.

Windows XP also launches your favorite programs up to 50 percent faster after you've run them a few times. It stores information about frequently used programs for faster loading in the future.

The following is the rundown of a few other interface niceties that are new or improved, especially if you previously used Windows 9x or Windows Me:

- **New wizards**—Several new wizards have been added to simplify common tasks such as printing photos, copying photos to a CD-R or CD-RW drive, running older programs under Windows XP, and others.

- **Easier-to-use multiple-tab menus and properties sheets**—As you move your mouse from tab to tab, the tab currently under the mouse pointer is highlighted with a colored bar across the top of the tab. This feature makes it easier to click the correct tab on properties sheets such as the System properties and many others.

- **My Music**—A new My Music folder has been added for MP3 and WMA digital music files you download or create. You can play the music in this folder by clicking the Play All button, and shop for more music online. This complements the My Documents and My Pictures folders for unified storage of all types of media files.

- **Customizable toolbars**—You can drag toolbars, such as the Web address toolbar, around on the desktop or add them to the taskbar at the bottom of the screen. Additional personalized Start menu and taskbar settings are available from the Taskbar Properties dialog box shown in Figure 1.5 (right-click the Taskbar and choose Properties).

- **Media toolbar**—In all Explorer windows, you can add a Media toolbar. From this toolbar, you can easily choose music or radio stations to listen to while you work, and you can view current movie previews.

- **Taskbar icon grouping**—If you have multiple instances of the same program running (such as several Internet Explorer windows), Windows XP saves room in the taskbar by displaying a single icon for the program with a number listing how many instances are stored under the icon. Click on the icon and scroll to display the instance you want to display. You also can close an entire group of windows at the same time.

Figure 1.5
In this dialog box, you can choose new options for taskbar properties.

■ **Smarter Open dialog boxes**—Many dialog boxes, such as the ones you use to open and save files, now remember the most recently entered filenames. Open dialog boxes also sport an iconic representation of the common locations in a new left pane, called the *Places Bar* (see Figure 1.6). Not all applications support the Places Bar, but those that do make it easier to save files to different local or network drives.

Figure 1.6
New Open dialog boxes include the Places Bar at the left side of the window.

Places Bar

■ **Customizable Explorer toolbars**—The toolbars are customizable, just like in IE or Office.

■ **Improved topic-based help system in enhanced HTML**—The Windows XP Help and Support Center most closely resembles the hugely remodeled help system introduced in Windows Me. To save search time, major topics are displayed on the left side, and common tasks are listed on the right side. The index is a click away on the top of the screen, and a Favorites button makes it easy to collect help pages you use frequently, and display them instantly. Click the Home button to return to the main Help and Support Center menu at any time.

■ **New display options in Windows Explorer**—You can group related files in Windows Explorer with the Show in Groups option, view Thumbnails of picture files, use a Tiled view to combine large icons with file detail, and use Filmstrip view in picture folders to see a larger view of the selected picture and navigate with directional arrows to other pictures in the folder.

■ **New balloon help tips**—Novice users will appreciate the new balloon help tips that pop up, such as when you let your mouse pointer hover over certain icons, when network connections are made, reporting the connection speed, or to report immediate problems that require quick action (see Figure 1.7).

Figure 1.7
The Windows XP Help system makes it easy to move within the current topic or to switch to related topics, and balloon help pops up to provide immediate warnings.

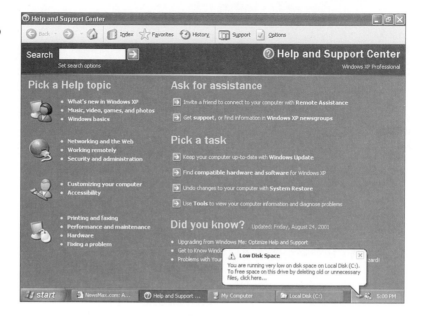

ENHANCED SEARCH FEATURE AND HISTORY

The Windows XP Search option is familiar to users of Windows 2000 and Windows Me, but is greatly enhanced compared to the Find feature used by Windows 9x; you can search from any and all Windows Explorer windows. When you search the Internet, the LAN, or your local hard disk, you use the same dialog box now. You can search for a file, folder, network computer, person, Web topic, help topic, or map. You can display a thumbnail view of search results to see what files or other items have been found. If the network you're on is using the MS Index Server, the discovered items are also ranked according to closeness of match, just like search engines do. A friendly animated dog provides minimal levels of entertainment during Search, but you can banish the dog off-screen by changing your search preferences.

Pressing the Windows key + F or choosing Search from the Start menu brings up the box you see in Figure 1.8. This integrated, easier-to-use search feature helps you find information on your computer, your network, or on the Web. Select the type of search you want to perform, enter all or part of the name, and start the search. If you search the Internet with plain-text questions, Windows XP will choose a search task and web site best suited to your search.

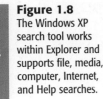

Figure 1.8
The Windows XP search tool works within Explorer and supports file, media, computer, Internet, and Help searches.

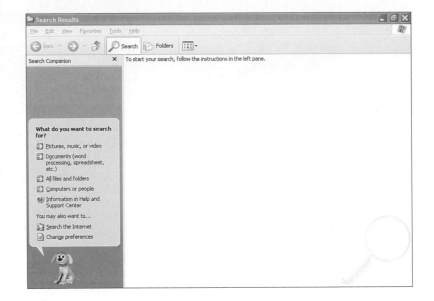

ENHANCED ACCESSIBILITY SUPPORT

Using computers is hard enough for those of us who have full mobility and physical abilities, considering how cryptic and idiosyncratic Windows is. For many folks, just the physical act of using a computer poses an additional challenge. Windows XP Professional provides the following accessibility features through the Accessibility Options icon in Control Panel:

- **Onscreen keyboard**—Allows text entry via the mouse
- **StickyKeys**—Allow keyboard combinations to be entered one keystroke at a time
- **FilterKeys**—Adjusts repeat rate and helps Windows ignore brief or repeated keystrokes
- **ToggleKeys**—Plays tones when keys such as Caps Lock are pressed
- **SoundSentry**—Displays your choice of visual alerts when your computer plays a sound
- **ShowSounds**—Provides captions for programs' speech and sounds
- **High-Contrast displays**—Choice of a variety of extra-large text sizes and high-contrast Windows desktops
- **Adjustable cursor blink rate and cursor width**—Makes it easier to find the text cursor onscreen
- **MouseKeys**—Enables the numeric keypad to run the mouse pointer
- **Serial keys**—Enables alternative keyboard and pointing devices to be attached through serial ports

1

The following accessibility features can be started from the Accessibility folder (Start, All Programs, Accessories, Accessibility) or by pressing the Windows key + U:

- **Magnifier**—Provides an enlarged view of the area under and near the mouse cursor
- **Narrator**—A simple text-to-speech program (English only) for onscreen events and typed characters
- **Onscreen keyboard**

INTERNET CONNECTIONS AND SOFTWARE

Windows XP Professional makes Internet use easier than ever. Its New Connection Wizard provides a one-stop interface for setting up Internet, home networking, direct serial/parallel/infrared connections (Direct Cable Connection for you Windows 9x fans), and remote office network connections through either dial-up or virtual private networking (VPN) connections. If you have an IEEE-1394 (FireWire) adapter, you also can use it for networking with this wizard.

Windows XP Professional also supports Internet Connection Sharing, using either a conventional modem (for the Internet) and a network card (for the rest of the network) or two network cards (the second one is for use with broadband connections) in the host system. And, if you're already running ICS on a Windows 9x/Me/2000 system, you can connect your Windows XP computer to it easily.

Internet Explorer 6.0, an improved version of the browser Microsoft has used to take over the browser market from one-time leader Netscape, is standard in retail and upgrade versions of Windows XP; hardware vendors who preinstall Windows XP on new computers can choose to omit it, although it's unlikely that most will. It now offers 128-bit encryption straight out of the box, meaning that you no longer need a strong encryption upgrade before you can go to some online banking, stock brokerage, or shopping sites.

Internet Explorer 6.0 is visually different than IE 5.5 in its icon display. For example, the Stop icon is now a red X in a page, rather than in a circle. The Favorites icon is a star instead of a folder. Beneath the surface, more significant differences include

- Integrated MSN Messenger support
- New Privacy tab in Internet Options to control cookies and personal data
- New Clear SSL State option on the Content tab to flush SSL (Secure Sockets Layer) certificates from the SSL cache for security
- Automatic resizing of images too large to be displayed in the browser window without scrolling
- Enhanced Internet setup options
- New Reset Web Settings option on the Programs tab

IE 6.0 also retains the integrated search tool used in previous versions of IE, integrates it with the Explorer Search tool, and offers a much wider variety of search engines from which to choose. IE's Search acts as a front end to popular search tools. Initially, it searches using the default search tool (MSN) or your preferred replacement (I like Google.com). After completing that search, you can send the search to other major search engines, one at a time. Type in two or more words, and the Search tool treats it as a phrase to get you more accurate results in most cases and fewer non-relevant hits. You can remove IE 6.0 from your system if you absolutely prefer another browser, but even if you're more of a Netscape or Opera fan, you'll probably want to keep IE 6.0 around for its tight integration to Windows Update, the online feature Microsoft uses to keep Windows up to date.

Windows XP Professional provides these enhancements and brand-new features to its networking and Internet feature set:

- An integrated Internet Connection Firewall—This feature, which is controlled from the network connection properties sheet, helps protect your connection from hacking by outside users, and is especially useful for full-time, always-on broadband connections such as cable modem, DSL, and LAN-based.

- Automatic adjustment of receive window size to achieve better performance on ICS when a dial-up connection is being shared.

- Support for Point-to-Point Protocol over Ethernet (PPPoE), an increasingly popular connection method for broadband modems.

- A protocol stack that supports IP version 6, which enables Windows XP to be used to develop applications that will support IP v6 when it is introduced (IPv6 will use a larger universe of IP addresses and have other benefits).

HARDWARE IMPROVEMENTS

Although Windows XP Professional is built upon the foundation of the "all-business" Windows NT 4.0 and Windows 2000 versions, it is still designed to be a replacement for the consumer operating systems (Windows 9x/Me). Therefore, Microsoft is determined to support a much broader range of hardware in Windows XP than in previous versions. Windows XP ships with drivers for hundreds of hardware devices not supported by Windows 2000, making it easier to install a broad range of hardware with Windows XP than with Windows 2000.

Drivers for many popular devices are supplied on the Windows XP Professional CD-ROM or are available from the vendor; Windows XP Professional will check Microsoft's Windows Update Web site for new drivers if it doesn't locate the right driver for your hardware. Both Windows XP Professional and Home Edition use the same Windows driver model (WDM) technology originally developed for hardware drivers in Windows 98/Me/2000. Thanks to the widespread preinstallation of Windows XP on new PCs, however, users should have a wider assortment of drivers to choose from initially than Windows 2000 users did.

If you can't get a Windows XP-specific driver for your hardware, most Windows 2000 device drivers will work with Windows XP Professional. And, because Windows XP Professional and Windows XP Home Edition share a common code base and have common multimedia and imaging features, the same device drivers will work on either version.

In the meantime, if you have rare, discontinued, or otherwise nonstandard hardware, be sure to check Microsoft's Hardware Compatibility List at www.microsoft.com/hcl before upgrading.

→ To learn more about hardware support issues, **see** Chapter 2, "Getting Your Hardware and Software Ready for Windows XP."

The following is the lowdown on the newly added hardware support, help, and troubleshooting:

- The Device Manager can be launched as a part of the Microsoft Management Console (MMC) and offers online help, more ways to view devices, and easier driver updates.

- The Add Hardware Wizard has been enhanced to make installing drivers for new hardware easier and more reliable, and to make it harder to install drivers for "phantom" devices not already installed in or connected to your system.

- The Scanner and Camera Wizard introduced in Windows Me has been included and now supports flash memory card readers used by digital cameras, using a new technology called Windows Imaging Architecture (WIA). WIA is a Component Object Model (COM)-based architecture that incorporates device drivers supplied by the manufacturer and imaging applications supplied by third-party software vendors into its design. WIA supports both older TWAIN-based imaging devices as well as newer imaging devices supported specifically by WIA drivers.

- Enhanced audio playback is supported with separate volume controls for each speaker in a multichannel configuration, Acoustic Echo Cancellation (AEC) to improve signal processing with USB microphones in particular, and Global Effects (GFX) to add support for newer USB-based audio technologies such as USB array microphones.

- DirectX 8.1 is included for full support of the newest 3D games and multimedia programs. It supports USB, digital joysticks, more realistic 3D graphics effects, and better sound than previous DirectX versions.

- After you install a third-party DVD decoder, you can use the Windows Media Player as your DVD playback program.

- Support for both CD-R and CD-RW drives without the need to install third-party software for both data storage and music CD copying.

- An enhanced version of multiple-monitor support called Dualview, which enables separate video displays on multi-monitor video cards and the built-in screen and external video ports of notebook computers.

- Improved power management, with support for wake-on-event, an improved user interface, and support for power management in applications.

1

PLUG AND PLAY AND OTHER GOODIES

Windows XP Professional supports *Plug and Play (PnP)*, meaning you can add new stuff to your computer, such as a printer, video card, USB port, and so on, and Windows will attempt to automatically assign it resources and add drivers. It does so, assuming the add-on hardware is Plug and Play compatible and the computer's BIOS is Plug and Play compliant. Windows XP Professional's version of Plug and Play works better than the Windows 9x/Me flavor, locating new hardware faster and mapping more PCI-based hardware to the same IRQ than Windows 9x/Me could do. This reduces hardware conflicts considerably.

Windows XP Professional also supports ACPI's enhancements to Plug and Play, USB devices, IEEE-1394 (FireWire/i.Link) devices, AGP video cards, DVD, and CD-ROM drives on a par with Windows 98/Me and Windows 2000.

New hardware supported in Windows XP Professional includes

- Portable audio players
- CD-R and CD-RW drives

Windows XP Professional offers wizards to make copying files to these devices very easy.

FILE SYSTEM IMPROVEMENTS

Realizing the inherent security and efficiency limitations in the old DOS (FAT 16) file system, Microsoft has developed two improved file systems over the last several years—FAT32 and NTFS. NTFS was introduced with NT 3.1; FAT32, with Windows 98. Each has its strengths and weaknesses. FAT32's big advantage is that it's highly compatible with FAT16 yet supports larger disk drive partitions and divides the drive into smaller clusters than FAT16, thus economizing on disk space. However, it's not nearly as secure as NTFS.

Microsoft's updates and tweaks to NTFS in NT 4 service packs pushed NTFS's security even further, and Windows XP Professional uses the same enhanced NTFS 5.0 version originally introduced with Windows 2000. Now file caching for networked and shared drives is an option, and 128-bit file and folder encryption is built in. Caching speeds up access to the files as well and allows users to work with them offline.

> **NOTE**
>
> You can still use FAT16 and FAT32 file systems with Windows XP Professional, but you might want to convert to NTFS either during the installation process or later for more efficient and more secure file storage. You can convert either FAT file system to NTFS, but you cannot convert FAT16 to FAT32 with Windows XP (as you could with Windows 98/Me).

MORE STABILITY

Windows XP Professional inherits its stability in performance from Windows NT and Windows 2000. What makes the Windows NT/2000/XP family more stable than consumer Windows (3.x/9x/Me)?

Windows XP Professional is more stable than Windows 9x/Me (not to mention old Windows 3.1!) because its internal design protects the system kernel, which is the core of the operating system. Windows XP Professional's system kernel never interfaces directly with applications or hardware, which could corrupt the kernel and crash the system. Instead, applications and hardware make requests to subsystems, which then request attention from the kernel.

Windows XP Professional's stability also comes from its use of *preemptive multitasking*, which uses a scheduler to tell each program running how much CPU time it can use. Windows XP Professional divides tasks into four priority rankings and provides the most CPU time to real-time processes, followed by high-priority processes, normal priority tasks, and, finally, idle tasks. While Windows 9x and Me also support preemptive multitasking, their reliance on old 16-bit code made multitasking a much riskier process.

To make multitasking work even better, Windows XP Professional also uses *multithreading*, which enables a single program to be divided up into separate *threads* (or subprocesses) which can be managed and run separately for greater efficiency.

Finally, Windows XP Professional is more stable because it prevents "DLL Hell," that all-too-common problem for Windows 9x/Me users who installed different programs that used different versions of the same DLL (Dynamic Link Library) program files. When programs used the wrong DLL files, they crashed, and sometimes took the whole operating system down with them. Microsoft has been aware of "DLL Hell" for some time, but fixes to this problem have been slow in coming.

Windows 98 Second Edition provided for a feature called "side-by-side DLLs." This allowed a developer to use the particular version of DLLs required by a particular program without overwriting system DLLs (those stored in the \Windows\System folder). This feature worked *only* on Windows 98SE and only if the program developer took advantage of the feature.

Windows 2000 introduced Windows File Protection, which restored system files automatically if they were overwritten by an application when you installed it or ran it. This protected Windows from crashing, but didn't do a thing about a program which needed a particular system file version to run. Microsoft's solution in Windows XP is called *Fusion*, which allows programs to install whatever system files (DLLs and others) they need, and redirects any files which would replace system files to the program's own folder. When such a program is run, Windows XP creates a memory-protected virtual machine to run the program with its own DLLs. The end result is that even if two or more programs are running at the same time, using different versions of DLL or other system files that would "break" the system in past versions of Windows, both programs will now run properly. No other programs can touch the area of memory granted to each program. Nor can that program or other programs gain access to the area of memory in which the basics of the operating system are running. This prevents the kinds of crashing well-known to Windows 9x/Me users.

Other Windows XP features that promote stability include

- **Shutdown Event Tracker**—This optional feature can be enabled to allow you to enter the reasons for a shutdown or restart of Windows XP and takes a detailed technical snapshot of the system's condition. The snapshot records the processes running on the system, system resource usage, pagefiles, and drives. You can use this information to determine causes for problems and their solutions. The Shutdown Event Tracker can be enabled via Group Policy by editing the Local Group Policy for the computer. This is a safer and more effective way to change this item than via Registry editing.

- **Easier shutdown of unresponsive applications**—You no longer need to open the Task Manager to shut down a program that's no longer responding; just click on the window (which states if the program is not responding) and click the Close button, just as with a normally-responding application.

- **Windows Driver Protection**—This feature prevents installation of defective drivers and provides an online link for more information and possible updates. It also blocks defective drivers that are installed via Registry keys or the CreateService API set.

- **Device Driver Rollback**—You can return to the previous version of a device driver with all devices except printers. This feature is accessed through the Driver tab of a device's properties sheet in Device Manager.

- **Automatic updates**—Provides background updates for Windows with the ability to resume an interrupted download. You can choose whether or not to install the update once it's been downloaded.

- **Dynamic updates**—This setup option, if selected, checks for newer drivers and fixes online than those available on the Windows XP CD-ROM, assuring you of an up-to-date version of Windows when first installed. A Dynamic Update package is available for network administrators to assure that all users get updated files when they install Windows XP in a corporate environment.

- **New Shadow Copy feature in Backup**—The Windows XP Backup program can back up open files and create volume snapshots while users are working. This prevents open files from being skipped during a backup.

- **Enhanced Last Known Good Configuration**—The Windows XP version of this startup option restores the device drivers used by the last known good configuration as well as the registry information. This enables you to recover from defective device drivers without the need to reinstall the originals.

- **Automated System Recovery (ASR)**—ASR enables the Windows XP Professional backup tool can back up applications, the current condition of the system, and critical boot and partition files and restore them. ASR replaces the Emergency Repair Disk used by Windows NT 4.0 and Windows 2000, and supports PnP devices.

- **Enhanced System Restore feature**—Originally developed for Windows Me, System Restore (which enables a user to return the system to a preset past condition) has many enhancements in Windows XP, including better performance and better use of disk space, support for NTFS compression, warning messages when disk space is running out, and the ability to remove all but the latest restore point to save disk space.

- **Better error handling**—Windows XP's error messages are easier to understand than those in previous versions of Windows, and provide better help for recovering from the error without rebooting the system. Also, Windows XP has a new Online Crash Analysis feature that logs details about a shutdown or "blue screen" crash to a file. When you restart the system, you can open an Internet connection and send the log to Microsoft Product Support Services for help within 24 hours. A companion Web site (oca.microsoft.com) allows you to check the status of your report.

IMPROVED SYSTEM MANAGEMENT

Now let's look briefly at what Windows XP Professional has to offer you as a manager of either a single computer or hundreds of machines in a large office setting. Will your work life really be less complicated, and should your company's operating costs be lower? Most likely, because Windows XP Professional provides you with centralized control over all the PCs in your organization. You'll also be able to use a new class of applications that are easier to deploy, more manageable, and more reliable. As a result, you will be able to provide better service with less hassle. Following are a few examples of Windows XP Professional's features that can improve an IT administrator's work life.

The most important management tool in Windows XP Professional is called the Microsoft Management Console (MMC) or Computer Management.

Computer Management provides a single interface for managing hardware (System Tools), drives (storage), and services such as indexing. It replaces the hodgepodge of programs and features found in Windows 9x and Me with a single interface (see Figure 1.9). It's also extensible with new "snap-in" modules provided by Microsoft or other companies.

Figure 1.9
Windows XP Professional's Computer Management tool offers many different system services under one roof, and accepts plug-in modules.

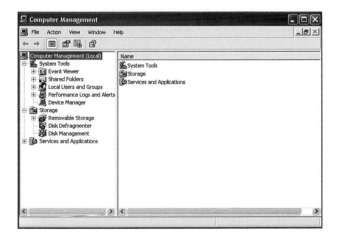

The Microsoft Management Console is a one-stop shop that you can use from your own desk to do the following:

- Check the status of remote machine
- Automatically install new applications
- Upgrade old applications
- Repair damaged applications
- Manage devices
- Manage security
- Prepare new hard drives for use

In addition to MMC, an improvement to the Windows Management Architecture alerts administrators to possible impending hardware or software problems. Microsoft has implemented industry standards called WBEM (Web-based Enterprise Management) and WMI (Windows Management Instructions) that empower help-desk teams to diagnose problems using a variety of third-party management tools. These tools gather information about a workstation to aid in diagnosing problems.

Another big area of annoyance for administrators is keeping track of updates for deployment across a whole sea of users. This is version control management. Management tools have been added to Windows XP Professional to help in service-pack slipstreaming, so a company can keep one master image of the operating system on a network and deploy it to individual PCs as necessary.

Windows XP Professional also uses the Windows Update feature introduced by Windows 98, enabling managers and users to keep their systems up-to-date via a simple connection to the Web. Just click Start, All Programs, and choose Windows Update. Windows Update now supports both individual users with automatic gathering of device information and immediate downloads and corporate users, who can manually specify the updates needed and download an assembled package of desired updates.

The Windows XP Control Panel now offers a choice of Classic View (resembling its default in previous Windows versions) or the new default, Category View. Category View groups Control Panel options by typical uses in a task-centric approach, and provides quick links to other related Control Panel options in its Other Places window (see Figure 1.10).

Figure 1.10
The default Category View of Windows XP's Control Panel is designed to display the most common tasks.

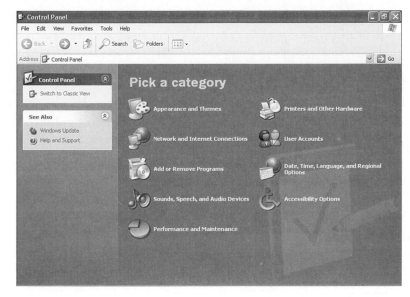

NEW AND IMPROVED WIZARDS

Windows XP Professional features improved versions of wizards originally found in Windows 9x, Windows Me, or Windows 2000, including

- **Network Connection Wizard**—This wizard lets you start up network connections on-the-fly, whether in the office or at home (phoning into the Internet via your ISP), creating a Virtual Private Networking (VPN) connection to a LAN in another location, or whatever. The Network Connection Wizard is also used to set up direct connections to other computers, directly through infrared, parallel, or serial connections (see Figure 1.11). Note that infrared connections between computers are now supported for an ad hoc instant (slow-speed) cable-less LAN.

Figure 1.11
You can use the Network Connection Wizard to create several different types of connections.

- **Add Printer Wizard**—This wizard makes it easy to set up and connect to local and network printers, even from an application, right from the Print dialog box (see Figure 1.12). No more fishing around for the Printers folder. The wizard automatically tries to determine the make and model of your printer without forcing you to scroll through a list of options.

- **Files and Settings Transfer Wizard**—This wizard helps you move settings for Internet Explorer, Outlook Express, desktop and display, dial-up connections, and document folders (such as My Documents and My Pictures) to a different computer running any 32-bit version of Windows; you can also use it to transfer settings from your old computer to a computer running Windows XP. While you still need to install matching applications on the target computer, this wizard saves valuable setup time and helps you get back to work faster with your new system.

Figure 1.12
You can choose or create a new printer without opening the Printers Control Panel.

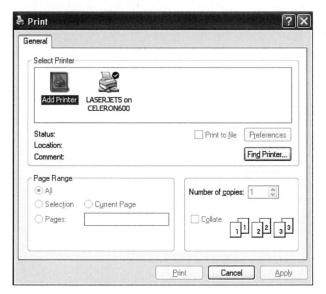

WHAT IS NOT IN WINDOWS XP PROFESSIONAL

Windows XP Professional is almost completely a superset of Windows XP Home Edition. In other words, virtually every feature found in Windows XP Home Edition is also part of Windows XP Professional. Thus, it's no longer necessary to decide between multimedia features and corporate networking as you would with Windows Me and Windows 2000 Professional.

About the only major feature missing from Windows XP Professional is Windows XP Home Edition's simplified user configuration. Because Windows XP Professional is designed for corporate networking it uses, as you learned earlier in this chapter, corporate-style security settings which are much more comprehensive than those used by Windows XP Home Edition. Otherwise, every feature in Windows XP Home Edition is present in Windows XP Professional.

Like Windows 2000 Professional, Windows XP Professional is limited to ten simultaneous connections when it's used as a Web server, and it supports either one or two processors. You will need to use Windows 2003 Server (the server family based on Windows XP) when available if you need support for more users or more processors.

DIFFERENCES BETWEEN WINDOWS XP HOME EDITION, WINDOWS XP PROFESSIONAL, 64-BIT, AND SERVER VERSIONS OF WINDOWS XP

Windows XP comes in two distinct varieties for 32-bit processors:

- Home Edition
- Professional

Although both versions contain the same integrated applications and multimedia features, Windows XP Professional also includes corporate network support, backup, and security features similar to those found in Windows 2000 Professional.

The new 64-bit Itanium processor from Intel has its own 64-bit versions of Windows XP. Windows XP 64-bit Edition is the workstation version, shipping at the same time as 32-bit versions of Windows XP. It supports up to 16GB of physical RAM and up to eight terabytes (8TB) of virtual memory, and takes full advantage of the superior floating-point performance of the Itanium processor. The recommended hardware platform is an 800MHz or faster Itanium processor with 1GB of RAM onboard; one or two Itanium processors can be used. Windows XP 64-bit Edition can run 32-bit Windows programs in a subsystem. The user interface is very similar to Windows XP Professional but the features will vary.

The first server version of Windows XP, Windows Advanced Server Limited Edition, is available from hardware OEMs of Itanium-based servers such as HP, IBM, and Compaq before the official release of Windows XP. Free upgrades will be available to Windows 2003 Server (the name for XP-based server products) to users who license the product.

Both 64-bit versions use an emulation layer called WOW64 to run Win32-based applications, although for best performance, Microsoft recommends using 32-bit software on 32-bit Windows systems. The emulation feature allows organizations to use their Itanium-based systems with existing Windows applications until 64-bit versions are created internally or purchased from software vendors.

What about 32-bit server versions of Windows XP? Microsoft plans multiple server editions of Windows XP, although the products will be called Microsoft Windows 2003 Server when they are introduced; previously, the server products were referred to as Windows 2002 Server. The editions will differ based on differences in the total amount of memory used by each version, the number of processors supported, and the number of domains that can be controlled.

Table 1.3 compares Windows XP Home Edition and Windows XP Professional to other versions of Windows.

TABLE 1.3 VARIOUS CAPABILITIES OF WINDOWS XP HOME EDITION AS COMPARED TO EARLIER VERSIONS OF WINDOWS

Feature	Windows 9x/Me	Windows NT 3.xx	Windows NT 4 Workstation	Windows NT 4 Server	Windows 2000 Professional	Windows 2000 Server	Windows 2000 Advanced Server	Windows 2000 Datacenter Server	Win XP Home	Win XP Pro
Virtual memory management (paging file on hard disk)	Yes	Yes	Yes	Yes	Yes	Yes	Yes	Yes	Yes	Yes
Multitasking type	Preemptive	Preemptive	Preemptive	Preemptive	Preemptive	Preemptive	Preemptive	Preemptive	Preemptive	Preemptive
Multithreading	Yes	Yes	Yes	Yes	No	Yes	Yes	Yes	Yes	Yes
Number of CPUs (maximum)	1	2 native, 4 with OEM-modified HAL	2	4	2	4	8	32	1	2
Maximum RAM supported					4GB	4GB	64GB	64GB	64GB	64GB
Access security	No	Yes	Yes	Yes	Yes	Yes	Yes	Yes	No	Yes
Kerberos security	No	No	No	No	Yes	Yes	Yes	Yes	No	Yes
Runs real-mode device drivers	Yes	No	No	No	No	No	No	No	No	Yes
Runs 16-bit DOS and Windows applications	Yes	Yes	Yes	Yes	Yes	Yes	Yes	Yes	Yes	Yes
Runs 32-bit Windows applications	Yes	Yes	Yes	Yes	Yes	Yes	Yes	Yes	Yes	Yes
Runs OS/2 applications	No	Yes	Yes	Yes	Yes	Yes	Yes	Yes	Yes	Yes

Feature	Windows 9x/Me	Windows NT 3.xx	Windows NT 4 Workstation	Windows NT 4 Server	Windows 2000 Professional	Windows 2000 Server	Windows 2000 Advanced Server	2000 Datacenter Server	Win XP Home	Win XP Pro
Runs POSIX applications	No	Yes	Yes	Yes	Yes	Yes	Yes	Yes	Yes	Yes
Supports DOS FAT16	Yes	Yes	Yes	Yes	Yes	Yes	Yes	Yes	Yes	Yes
Support DOS FAT32	95 OSR2 and 98/Me only	No	No	No	Yes	Yes	Yes	Yes	Yes	Yes
Supports OS/2 HPFS	No	Yes	No	No	No	No	No	No	No	No
Supports NTFS	No	Yes	Yes	Yes	Yes	Yes	Yes	Yes	Yes	Yes
Supports disk compression	Yes	No	Yes	Yes	Yes	Yes	Yes	Yes	Yes	Yes
File encryption	No	No	No	No	Yes	Yes	Yes	Yes	Yes	Yes
RAID support/ levels	No	Yes	No	Yes	No	Yes	Yes	Yes	No	Yes
Built-in networking	Yes	Yes	Yes	Yes	Yes	Yes	Yes	Yes	Yes	Yes
Built-in e-mail	Yes	Yes	Yes	Yes	Yes	Yes	Yes	Yes	Yes	Yes
Minimum Intel CPU required	386	386	Pentium	Pentium	Pentium	Pentium	Pentium	Pentium	Pentium	Pentium
Supports RISC chips	No	Yes/MIPS R4000 Alpha	Yes/ R4000 Alpha	Yes/ R4000 Alpha	Yes/ DEC Alpha	Yes/ DEC Alpha	Yes/ DEC Alpha	Yes/ DEC Alpha	No	No
Supports Active Directory	Planned	No	No	No	Yes	Yes	Yes	Yes	No	Yes

1

TABLE 1.3 CONTINUED

Feature	Windows 9x/Me	Windows NT 3.xx	Windows NT 4 Workstation	Windows NT 4 Server	Windows 2000 Professional	Windows 2000 Server	Windows 2000 Advanced Server	Windows 2000 Datacenter Server	Win XP Home	Win XP Pro
Supports clustering	No	No	No	Yes, only in Enterprise Edition				Yes	No	No
Supports load balancing	No	No	No	No	No	No	Yes	Yes	No	No
Supports Novell NDS	No	No	Yes	Yes	Yes	Yes	Yes	Yes	No	Yes
Includes Web server/Maximum number of connections	Yes/10	No/unlim	Yes/10	Yes/unlim	Yes/10	Yes/unlim	Yes/unlim	Yes/unlim	No	Yes/10

How Does Windows XP Professional Compare to Unix and Linux?

Windows XP's kernel, like Windows 2000's, has its roots in Unix. Unix is a very popular multitasking operating system developed at Bell Labs in the early 1970s. It was designed by programmers for programmers. In fact, the language C was developed just to write Unix. Even though Unix has become a friendlier operating system with the addition of Windows-like interfaces such as MOTIF, it's still relatively user-unfriendly, requiring cryptic commands much like DOS.

Unix

Because it is written in C, Unix can run on any computer that has a C compiler, making it quite portable. AT&T gave away the Unix source code to universities and licensed it to several companies during its early years. AT&T no longer owns Unix; the Unix trademark is now owned by OpenGroup, though the source code is owned by the Santa Cruz Operation (SCO).

Unfortunately, to avoid even the licensing fees to AT&T, Unix lookalikes sprung up over the years. Without the proper license, these versions could not call themselves Unix, only Unix-like. And as these clones proliferated, cross-compatibility became an issue. More than a handful of versions (dialects) of Unix have appeared, the primary contenders being AT&T's own, known as System V, and another developed at the University of California at Berkeley, known as BSD4.x, x being a number from 1 to 3. Other popular brands of Unix these days are HP-UX from HP, AIX from IBM, Solaris from Sun, and SCO's version, UnixWare.

In 1984, industry experts were brought together to create guidelines and standards for Unix clones, in hopes of creating a more coherent market. The result was a single Unix specification, which includes a requirement for POSIX (Portable Operating System Interface for Unix) compliance. Accepted by the IEEE and ISO, POSIX is a standard that makes porting applications and other code between variants of UNIX as simple as recompiling the source code.

NOTE

> Another popular version of Unix that runs on the PC platform is called FreeBSD. Briefly, FreeBSD 4.x is a Unix-like operating system based on U.C. Berkeley's 4.4BSD-lite release for the Intel 386 platform. It is also based indirectly on William Jolitz's port of U.C. Berkeley's Net/2 to the Intel 386, known as 386BSD, though very little of the 386BSD code remains. You can find a fuller description of what FreeBSD is and how it can work for you at www.freebsd.com.

Unix has been the predominant operating system for workstations connected to servers, mostly because of its multiuser capabilities and its rock-solid performance. Windows NT and its successors, Windows 2000 and Windows XP, have been making inroads due to the extensive number of development tools and applications for the Windows platform. However, the low-cost Unix variant called Linux is revitalizing Unix across all platforms.

LINUX

Linux is a Unix lookalike. Linux isn't a port of a preexisting operating system, but rather it was written from the ground up by Linus Torvalds, a Finnish-born computer scientist who wanted to develop a Unix-like operating system for computer students to run on low-cost Intel computers. Torvalds wrote the kernel with the help of a handful of computer programmers. Like all variants of Unix, Linux has many of the features of NT/Windows 2000/Windows XP, such as true multitasking, virtual memory, shared libraries, intelligent memory management, and TCP/IP networking.

Linux is an open system, and programmers worldwide are invited to participate in its building and refinement. Unlike other flavors of Unix that were based on licensed source code, Linux is based on Minix, which mimics Unix in a way that does not infringe on the Unix license. That's why Linux distributions are practically free.

NOTE

> Actually, the term Linux pertains only to the kernel. What people have come to refer to as Linux is actually a collection of separate pieces of code, the majority of which are GNU. It was not until Linux came together with GNU that the full power of the Linux OS (what GNU enthusiasts would called GNU Linux) crystallized.

The several popularly distributed Linux versions are differentiated mostly by the selection of tools and utilities bundled with them. The most popular package at this point is Red Hat Linux. If you want to go it alone, you can acquire Linux for free, but buying some commercially bundled packages makes the job of installation and support easier because you get support. Technically, the distribution of the software must be free, in accordance with the GNU General Public License (GPL) agreement governing the distribution of Linux and the collected modules that accompany it.

Linux is now running on a wide variety of systems, including Sun JavaStations, the IBM RS/6000, and the Alpha chip originally developed by DEC and later sold by Compaq, MIPS, SPARC, Open VMS, Digital Unix, and other platforms.

WINDOWS APPLICATION COMPATIBILITY WITH LINUX

IT professionals willing to get under the hood and poke around and learn Linux's ways are impressed with its solidity. Though Linux is not commonly used as a business productivity workstation, it is being embraced by some for back-end Web servers or transaction servers where reliability is a high priority.

WINE, a DOS, Windows 3.1, and 32-bit Windows emulator, is a popular program used by a number of vendors to move their Windows programs to the Linux platform. For more information, see the WINE Web site at www.winehq.com. However, even the most recent versions of WINE are limited, especially in their multimedia support. To get full Linux and full Windows XP support on a single system, set up a dual-boot system. The only reliable way to run Windows programs on a Linux system is to dual-boot.

→ To learn more about dual-booting Linux, **see** "Windows XP and Linux," **p. 1111**.

Mainstream applications for Linux have taken a long time to arrive, but Corel's WordPerfect Office 2000 for Linux and Sun's StarOffice 5.2 provide powerful office suites with many of the features of recent Microsoft Office releases. CorelDRAW for Linux includes Linux-compatible versions of CorelDRAW 9 and PhotoPaint 9, and there are, of course, many downloadable freeware and shareware programs for Linux available online.

Microsoft, of course, doesn't want to develop Linux versions of either its programming languages or applications such as Office, for obvious reasons.

Obviously, as a capitalistic enterprise, Linux doesn't cut it for the entrepreneur, unless he or she is willing to look at the world through a radically new set of glasses. Giving away your software doesn't net you much. Then again, people are giving away PCs to sell the advertising, so go figure. The world of computing might be changing more than we know. But because applications developers for the Linux environment are supposed to distribute their source code along with the applications, this is a daunting shift of worldview for a behemoth such as Microsoft, which works overtime to protect its intellectual property. The upshot is that you're out of luck if you want to run Word, Excel, or Access, Internet Explorer, or any other Microsoft programs on a Linux box.

WINDOWS XP VERSUS LINUX

Trying to compare Windows XP versus Linux is difficult for several reasons, including

- Windows XP requires a relatively recent computer with at least 128MB of RAM to function, while Linux can run successfully on even 486-based systems long obsolete for use with Windows
- Windows XP is available in just two versions (Home Edition and Professional), while Linux is available in numerous distributions
- Windows XP is primarily a GUI-based operating system, while Linux is primarily command-line driven (although KDE and Gnome, the two most common GUIs, are increasingly popular)

Although Linux has made great strides in so-called "back end" uses such as Web servers, network servers, and embedded devices, Windows XP is a better choice for desktops for several reasons, including

- Journaling file system for higher reliability and crash recovery.
- Compatibility testing and guarantees for operating system and applications.
- Wide availability of commercial applications at retail and online stores.
- Clustering and base-load balancing.
- Long-term roadmap of operating system deployment plans.
- Larger hard disks and maximum file sizes. Linux's maximum file size is 2 Gigabytes; Windows XP's limit is 18.4 quintillion bytes (Petabytes).

- "Synchronous I/O," which allows smoother running in Windows XP when multiple threads are being processed and waiting for input or output. It improves SMP scalability as well.

- Consistent GUI across all tools—Linux has no single standard GUI at present.

- A single version which can be installed for most major languages and countries.

- Dedicated support network, with close to one-half million Microsoft-certified trained professionals and engineers.

We believe that the entire Linux/Windows controversy comes down to this: Microsoft offers lots and lots of powerful stuff (which you can use to build very sophisticated software) from the C++ compiler, to the component-nature of Excel and other apps, to the ASP scripting language, COM, and so on. These tools let you leverage everything Microsoft offers to make very powerful applications. As people used to say in the sixties and seventies, nobody ever lost his job buying IBM. Now it's safe to say nobody ever lost his job buying Microsoft. True, you're locked into Windows because the stuff you build on Windows systems can't be ported to Unix variants, but that's the price you pay for the tools, the user base, and the support and training. Although increasing support options are available for Linux (see `www.linuxcare.com`), enterprise-level support for Linux is still not as widespread as for Windows.

Linux might be a decent choice for the small-business owners or IS professionals who need to build low-cost servers for Web, e-mail, or file sharing. This operating system is designed for those uses, and the popular Red Hat and Caldera Linux packages make installation relatively painless (not as easy as Windows XP Professional, though, mind you). If you're thinking of using Linux on your desktop PC, beware—you might be biting off more than you can chew. The manuals that come with Linux—even the commercial versions—are dense. It is not always headache-free. But if you have a good understanding of computer technology and insist on switching from Windows to something more stable and more flexible, Linux might be the choice for you. If nothing else, using Linux will be a learning experience. However, for the foreseeable future, Linux will be primarily a server and embedded-device operating system, rather than a desktop operating system.

WINDOWS XP PROFESSIONAL ON THE CORPORATE NETWORK

Windows XP Professional, because it's designed as a replacement for Windows 2000 Professional, is designed to work well on corporate networks. Thus, it contains all the network and security features of Windows 2000 Professional, including

- Support for IP Security (IPSec) to protect data being transmitted across VPNs

- Kerberos v5 support for authentication

- Group Policy settings for administering networks and users

- Offline viewing of network data when not connected to the network

- Synchronization of local and network files

- Remote access configuration wizard
- Microsoft and Novell NetWare network clients
- Support for Active Directory (Microsoft's directory service feature which helps to manage users and resources on large networks)
- Disk quotas to prevent a few storage-hog users from running the server out of space
- Internet Information Services, including FTP, FrontPage 2000 Server Extensions, SMTP (Simple Mail Transport Protocol) service, World Wide Web service, the management snap-in for the Microsoft Management Console, remote deployment support, and documentation
- Fax services for sending and receiving faxes
- Simple Network Management Protocol (SNMP) support
- Print services for Unix

NEW NETWORKING FEATURES

Windows XP also adds many new network features especially designed to make corporate networking easier and more reliable, including

- Networking has been integrated into the Task Manager to display real-time network usage and connection-speed information.
- An enhanced Netdiag.exe command-line diagnostics tool is provided on the Windows XP CD-ROM.
- An enhanced version of Network Driver Interface Specification (NDIS), version 5.1, with support for PnP and Power Event Notification, send cancellation, better statistics capability, and better performance.
- A new version of the Windows Telephony API (TAPI), version 3.1, with support for H.323-compatible IP telephony and IP multicast A/V conferencing, recording of streaming A/V data for playback, USB phones, automatic discovery of telephony servers, and support for H.323 services such as call hold, call transfer, call diversion, call pack, and call pickup.
- Support for newer network devices, including HomePNA phoneline networks, USB-connected network devices, software-based (also called controllerless or "Winmodem") modems, and infrared-enabled cell phones (as modems).
- Support for Universal Plug and Play (UPnP) devices on a network, and use of UPnP to detect Internet Connection Sharing (ICS) hosts on a network.
- Network bridging—One computer can run two different types of networks (such as Fast Ethernet and IEEE 802.11b [Wi-Fi] wireless Ethernet) and act as a connection between them. You need a network card for each network type you're bridging.
- Auto-configuration of IEEE 802.11b Wi-Fi networks—Wi-Fi (wireless Ethernet) networks are harder to configure than wired networks such as Fast Ethernet, because you must synchronize the card to the wireless access point that allows your PC to talk to others. Windows XP Professional detects the correct settings automatically.

- Ability to store and recall settings of various wireless networks the user has connected to in the past for automatic configuration when the same network is encountered again. This feature simplifies moving between multiple wireless networks, such as home and office or different offices.

- An enhanced Connection Manager with new management options, split tunneling (secure VPN and public Internet access at the same time), Favorites feature for storing connection settings for different locations (useful for business travelers), client-side logging for troubleshooting, and support for ICS.

- The enhanced Network Troubleshooter feature, available from the left-hand menu of the Network Connections menu, provides one-stop access to network-related tools in the Help and Support center. You can start Ping and Net View commands to diagnose and check Internet and LAN connections, as well as run troubleshooters for Internet Connection Sharing, Modems, and other home and corporate network configurations. A new Network Diagnostics tool scans the network and tests your network card. As shown in Figure 1.13, at the end of the testing process, it displays the results of its tests for Internet service settings, computer information, and network adapters (including modems).

- Support for encrypted folders with multiple users.

- Remote desktop support via Remote Desktop Protocol (RDP), enabling users to access their computers remotely from anywhere with network access, including other offices, at home, or airport kiosks.

- Improved Group Policy feature with hundreds of new policies provided, making it easier to choose a pre-defined policy instead of needing to modify one.

Figure 1.13
The Network Diagnostics tool displays the configuration of both hardware and software components on your network.

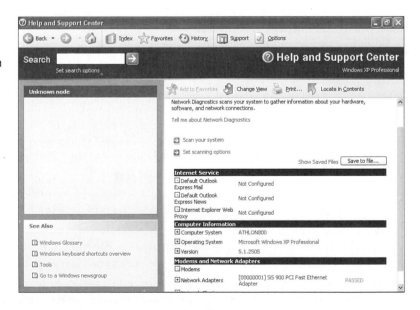

- Remote Assistance to allow network or Internet-based help desk personnel to view a user's display and provide training or technical assistance. This feature can be centrally enabled or disabled as desired.

IMPROVED NETWORK SECURITY

Windows XP Professional, like Windows NT 4.0 and Windows 2000, is a high-security operating system designed for corporate networks. While many of its security features are carryovers from its predecessors, Windows XP Professional also features new and enhanced tools for network security, including

- Standard access control list settings, standard security groups, and predefined security templates offering Basic, Compatible, Secure and Highly Secure group policies—All of these security settings can be modified as needed, and can be controlled with tools such as the Microsoft Management Console or those provided with the optional Windows XP Professional Resource Kit.

- Default guest-level access for network, Internet access, and simple security (non-domain) networks—This feature limits the ability of intruders to gain access to private information.

- Limited access for users who don't password-protect their accounts—User accounts without passwords can't be used for any purpose other than to logon to their own systems; remote logons are no longer permitted.

- Support for the Encrypted File System (EFS)—You can encrypt data with your choice of the expanded Data Encryption Standard (DESX) or Triple-DES (3DES), and all contents of an encrypted folder are also encrypted. Encryption also works with offline files and folders and with Web folders, and is designed to be managed through Group Policy and command-line programs.

- User certificates are stored in a subfolder of each user's Documents and Settings folder, and private keys are stored in a different subfolder. Private keys are automatically encrypted when stored.

- A Credential Manager Key Ring feature which stores multiple credentials (username/password) used on the system. As you navigate from one secured network to another, the correct credential to log in is selected automatically, based on criteria such as the server name and domain name. This feature also works with Remote Access and Virtual Private Networking.

- Support for digitally signed software—This feature allows an administrator to block unsigned or unapproved ActiveX controls from running a system, prevent Windows Installer from installing unsigned or unapproved programs, and prevent unsigned Visual Basic Scripts from being run.

- Built-in support for smart card authentication

Windows XP Professional builds on the already-strong corporate network features of Windows 2000 Professional to provide more powerful and easier corporate networking, security, and management.

CHAPTER 2

GETTING YOUR HARDWARE AND SOFTWARE READY FOR WINDOWS XP

In this chapter

GENERAL CONSIDERATIONS

So much for the hype about Windows XP, all its new features, and some of the details of its design and architecture you learned about in Chapter 1, "Introducing Windows XP Professional." So, the question at this point is, "Are you really going to install it?" If you are, you should go ahead and read this chapter and the next one. In this chapter, I'll coach you on preparing for the installation and checking your hardware and software requirements; then I'll discuss some compatibility issues that might affect your product-purchasing decisions. The next chapter covers more specific installation issues, such as choosing disk formats, upgrading versus installing fresh, and dual-booting. I'll also walk you through the setup procedure.

Of course, if Windows XP Professional is already installed on your PC, you can probably skip Chapter 3, "Installing Windows XP Professional." You should at least, however, take a brief look at this one because it includes some discussion that might affect software and hardware installation decisions you might make when using Windows XP Professional in the future. Understanding what you can do with, and shouldn't expect from, an operating system is always good background material when you use as complex a tool as a computer on a regular basis. Pay particular attention to the section about RAM and hard disk upgrades, how to access the online Hardware Compatibility List (HCL), and how to find the Windows XP-approved applications list at `Microsoft.com`.

As you'll learn in the next chapter, the Windows XP Setup program automatically checks your hardware and software and reports any potential conflicts. Using it is one way to find out whether your system is ready for prime time. It can be annoying, however, to find out something is amiss at midnight when you're doing an installation, especially when you could have purchased RAM or some other installation prerequisite the previous day when you were out at the computer store. Likewise, you don't want to be technically capable of running Windows XP Professional only to experience disappointing performance. To help you prevent such calamity or surprise, the first part of this chapter will cover hardware compatibility issues.

In general, I'll say this about Windows XP hardware compatibility. Microsoft's goal was for 90 percent of systems sold since January 2000 to have a "positive upgrade experience." Microsoft defines a positive upgrade experience as everything working without any issues at all. This is a significantly high figure. The remaining ten percent may have a speed bump along the way, not necessarily a computer that doesn't boot. Generally, these speed bumps are devices in, or attached to, your PC that might not have a driver that tells Windows XP how to use it; or maybe there's an application or two on your system that doesn't run.

NOTE
> You might be able to obtain a "preflight" CD from retail stores to check your current system's compatibility with Windows XP or download a compatibility checker from the Microsoft Web site. Check the Windows XP Web site (`www.microsoft.com/windowsxp`) for details.

HARDWARE REQUIREMENTS

Let's start with the basics. The principal (and minimal) hardware requirements for running Windows XP Professional are as follows:

Windows XP Professional Minimum

Pentium 233 (or equivalent) or higher CPU (Pentium III or 4, or equivalent such as AMD Duron or Athlon recommended).

64MB RAM (128MB recommended); 4GB of RAM maximum)

At least 1.5GB of free disk space

Super VGA (800×600 resolution) or higher video adapter and monitor with 16-bit or higher color depth

Keyboard

Mouse or compatible pointing device

CD-ROM (12x minimum speed) or DVD drive

These are Microsoft's suggested minimums, and not necessarily what will provide satisfactory or exceptional performance. Some users have reported that they have installed on lesser machines. Microsoft tries to quote minimum requirements that will provide performance the average user can live with. I have installed XP on a little Sony VAIO n505VE which has an Intel Celeron II 333MHz processor, and it works like a champ. Although Microsoft doesn't specifically mention it, you'll want at least 4MB of video RAM to allow your system to choose 24-bit (16.8 million colors) color depths at 1024×768 resolutions, and a sound card to work with Windows Media Player.

Table 2.1 compares system requirements for popular operating systems.

TABLE 2.1   HARDWARE REQUIREMENTS BY OPERATING SYSTEM

Operating System	CPU (Minimum Required/ Recommended)	Memory (Minimum Required/ Recommended)	Disk space (Minimum Required/ Recommended)
Windows 98	P133 MMX/PII-300	16MB/64MB	300MB
Windows NT 4.0 Workstation	P133/P166	16MB/32MB	110MB
Windows NT 4.0 Server	P133/P166	32MB/64MB	200MB
Windows 2000 Professional	P133/PII-300	64MB/128MB	650MB/500MB
Windows 2000 Server	P133/PII-300	64MB/128MB	850MB/1GB
Novell NetWare 5	386	64MB/256MB	500MB/1GB

continues

TABLE 2.1   CONTINUED

Operating System	CPU (Minimum Required/ Recommended)	Memory (Minimum Required/ Recommended)	Disk space (Minimum Required/ Recommended)
Red Hat Linux 5.2 Server	P166	16MB	1.6GB
Windows XP Professional	P233/PII300+	64/128MB	1.5GB
Windows XP Home Edition	P233/PII300+	64/128MB	1.5GB

Surprised that you can run this operating system on a machine that's only a 233MHz Pentium? By today's standards, that's a pokey old processor. I've actually heard of people running Windows NT on 33MHz machines with decent performance, assuming the system had enough RAM. But with over 30 million lines of programming code in Windows XP (NT had only 5 million), some additional horsepower is clearly a good idea for XP.

TIP FROM

Bob & Brian

> With the plummeting prices of CPUs these days, there's scant disincentive to upgrading your CPU and motherboard or just getting a whole new system for Windows XP. The price wars between Intel and AMD might be brutal on the corporate battlefield, but the consumer is clearly the winner. 700–900MHz-class desktop clone computers with 20GB or larger hard disks and 128MB of RAM are easily available for around $500 to $700.

Anyway, based on what you can get for a song these days, you shouldn't have any difficulty hustling up the bucks to buy a machine that will run Windows XP adequately. Almost a decade ago when I was writing about Windows NT 3.1, the cost of admission was significantly higher; you had to be on the bleeding edge of computing to build a quality NT-style workstation.

As a consultant, I get more phone calls and e-mails asking what kind of computer to buy than on any other topic. Despite the rapid de-escalation in prices and apparent exponential increase in computing speed, putting together a machine to run Windows XP Professional successfully for your needs might not be as easy as you think. Whenever I build a new system, I'm surprised by twists I hadn't considered, new hardware standards I didn't know even existed, and so on. You probably know the story.

If you're a power-user type or hardware jock running the PCs at your company, you probably spend your coffee breaks poring over magazines like *Killer PC* or belong to the Captain Number Crunch fan club. You can find some blindingly fast stuff, such as accelerated 3D AGP video cards, ATA 100 drive arrays, new kinds of high-speed RAM, and so on. As much fun as it is for speed freaks, a screamer PC that will take the computing Grand Prix doesn't necessarily a good XP box make. And as much as everyone is hoping that Windows XP will broaden hardware and application compatibility over the annoying confines that Windows NT and Windows 2000 suffered, it's still a protected and somewhat picky system. Hardware that purrs away happily under Windows 9x might not necessarily cut it under Windows XP. Before you go cutting purchase orders and checks for your personal PC or 20 for the office, look a little further by at least skimming through this chapter.

OPTION 1: USING WHAT YOU'VE GOT: ENSURING COMPATIBILITY VIA THE HCL

You can take three basic approaches to ensure hardware compatibility. The first is relatively simple and may prevent your having to purchase anything new. Microsoft has done most of the compatibility testing for you already and posted that information in its Hardware Compatibility List (HCL). You can view the HCL by opening the Hcl.txt file in the Support folder on the XP CD, although the Web-based list will be more up to date.

`http://www.microsoft.com/hcl/`

In either case, if your hardware isn't listed, the setup process might not be successful. To see the most recent version of this list, visit the site. There's a link to the site from the Windows XP Setup CD-ROM. Just insert the Setup CD and click on Visit the Compatibility Web Site.

TIP FROM

Bob

& Brian

> To find general information about Windows XP Professional, including compatibility, check out the following:
>
> `http://www.microsoft.com/WindowsXP/`

The HCL site has an interactive list displaying hardware compatibility for all Microsoft operating systems. Figure 2.1 shows the result of my search for display cards.

Figure 2.1
Use the online Microsoft Hardware Compatibility List to check on your hardware before you either purchase or decide to upgrade to Windows XP.

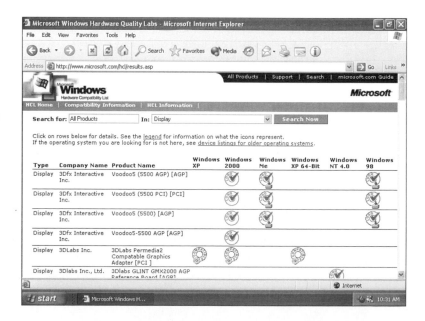

2

The interface is a little Spartan, and the first field you fill in is not explained. The upside is that you can type a word to narrow the search, such as Presario or SCSI, and then choose the subcategory of hardware you want the site to search, such as system/mobile uniprocessor (that means *laptop computer* in layman's terms) or Printer. Then click Search Now. You might have to try several approaches to find the item you want. The list is quite large, so keep trying with a slightly different approach if your item doesn't come up the first time. Scroll to the right to see additional operating systems such as Windows 98 or Windows Me. Also, be sure to click Legend to learn what the icons represent. The check mark in a bullseye reading "Logo" indicates the product meets requirements for the Windows Logo program, the highest level of hardware compatibility. If the Logo icon also displays a drive icon, you can download a compatible driver by clicking on the icon. If the Logo icon also displays a CD icon, the Windows CD-ROM has the driver needed for the device. A bullseye reading "Compatible" indicates the device will work with Windows, although the device doesn't meet all the requirements for the Windows Logo program; the Windows CD-ROM contains a compatible driver.

⚠ *For a complete list of URLs related to upgrading to Windows XP, see "Compatibility and Upgrade Help," in the "Troubleshooting" section at the end of this chapter.*

Don't know what's in your system or not sure if you thought of everything that might conflict with Windows XP Professional? No problem. You can run the Windows XP Compatibility Tool (testing program) from the CD. This program detects your hardware and verifies compatibility. Insert the CD (you'll have to borrow one from someone who has it, if you don't want to purchase it just to find out), and choose Perform Additional Tasks from the main menu. Then choose Check System Compatibility. When you run the program, a report is generated telling you whether your computer cuts the mustard. The test is discussed in Chapter 3.

NOTE

> If you forget to run the test in advance, don't worry; you'll still get the report. Why? It's run automatically when you activate the Setup program to install XP. It's just nice to do it in advance so you are aware of contingency problems well ahead of time. (The Setup program and some examples of reports are covered in Chapter 3.)

What do you do if some component of your system (or your entire computer) doesn't rank high enough to appear and isn't listed in the compatibility list? Well, you can wing it and see how things work out. Just install XP onto the computer in a separate directory or disk partition (dual-boot); then see what happens. If this approach doesn't work, you can revert to using your old operating system, having only lost an hour's time. You should also approach the hardware manufacturer and ask whether a Windows XP driver is available for the component. (How to set up a dual-booting arrangement is discussed in Chapter 3.)

TIP FROM

Bob & Brian

> Some people say that you don't need to ensure availability of drivers for Plug and Play devices. Although the idea was that all officially sanctioned Plug and Play devices (bearing the PnP logo) are automatically supported by Windows, this isn't always true.

> Check carefully to see that any new PnP device you're considering comes with drivers for, or has been tested with, Windows 2000 Professional or XP. If the box says "Designed for Microsoft Windows 2000" or "Designed for Microsoft Windows XP" and bears the Windows 2000 and/or XP logo, you're probably home free. Since Windows 2000 and XP are built on the same base code, drivers for one might work with the other in some cases.

OPTION 2: CHOOSING A WINDOWS XP-READY PC

It isn't a bad idea to just bite the bullet and shell out for a new machine once every two years or so. I'm a holdout myself, even though I'm a techno-junkie. The bottom line is that I'm cheap, so I try to squeeze out every last CPU cycle from my computers and keep them running for a very long time. I'm still using an old machine based on Intel's 386 processor (which is two generations removed from the original Pentium) running DOS as a router to the Internet. Clearly, I don't like to participate in the "throw-away society's" idea of planned obsolescence. But every time I upgrade to a new computer, I notice a significant number of niceties across the board, for example, quicker response; more inclusive power management so my system uses less power when it's idle (and cuts my utility bills!); reduced energy consumption due to lower chip count (which also cuts my utility bills!); more hardware setting options; a faster DVD drive with support for CD-ROM media; high-speed ports such as USB and FireWire (also known as i.Link and IEEE 1394b) that work with the newest scanners, printers, and drives; faster video display; and so on.

If you have decided to start fresh and purchase new PCs for your personal or corporate arsenal, let me suggest an easier way to choose them than to check each piece against the HCL. Just as with the individual hardware item listings in the HCL, Microsoft's testing lab awards the "Windows-Ready PC" merit badge to computers that meet their requirements.

To see a list of XP-ready computers, check this site:

http://www.microsoft.com/windowsxp/ready/

You'll find a mixture of major-brand and budget vendors listed, so you have a lot of choices if you decide to buy a new PC with a Windows XP logo on it. It will take awhile for them to show up. My recent purchase was guaranteed to run Windows 2000, though, and that was enough for me. Sure enough, it installed and booted Windows XP just fine.

WHAT YOU GET WITH A WINDOWS XP-READY PC

When you purchase a Microsoft-sanctioned Windows XP computer, you get more than you asked for, but I guess that's capitalism and, besides, with "bloatware" being so prevalent these days, it's better to prepare for the coming need for bigger and faster everything.

A Windows XP–ready PC will meet or more often than not exceed the requirements listed in Table 2.2.

TABLE 2.2 WINDOWS XP-READY PC REQUIREMENTS[1]	
Feature	**Requirements**
Operating system	It comes preinstalled with Windows XP.
RAM	Includes at least 128MB of RAM.
XP Logo rating	It bears the "Designed for Windows XP" logo.
Power Management	Supports Advanced Configuration and Power Interface (ACPI) for laptops to increase battery life, among other benefits.
CPU	Desktop and laptop machines come with at least a 266MHz Pentium III processor or equivalent.
Other	USB ports, CD-R or CD-RW drive, Wake-On LAN network interface card. Preferably no parallel or serial ports. Possibly a microphone and Web camera, and an IEEE-1394 (FireWire) port.

[1]*The requirements listed in Table 2.2 are preferred. They exceed the minimum requirements to run Windows XP. See the beginning of this chapter for the minimum requirements.*

Notice that, depending on when you buy it, an XP-ready PC might have Windows Me, Windows 2000, or Windows XP as its operating system. In any case, XP-ready machines are fully capable of being upgraded to Windows XP if they include one of the other Windows versions.

OPTION 3: UPGRADING YOUR COMPUTER

Don't want to purchase a whole new computer, but your hardware isn't all on the HCL? Or do you have some old, stodgy disk drive, SCSI controller, video adapter, motherboard, or some other piece of gear that you want to upgrade anyway? You're not alone. The PC upgrade business is booming, as evidenced by the pages and pages of ads in the backs of computer rags and the popularity of computer "swap meets," where precious little swapping is going on except that of hardware components for the hard-earned green stuff. If only my co-author and I had written Scott Mueller's book, *Upgrading and Repairing PCs*, we would be very happy authors. It's perennially one of the best-selling computer books.

Buy It or Build It?

I have a word of caution about the "building your own" mindset. I started in PCs back before IBM got into the fray, and in those days, you had no choice but to build your own microcomputer. Lots of the building required using a soldering iron, too (and close proximity to the freezer to thrust burned fingers into).

The notion of a completely packaged PC ready to go was sort of disgusting to hobbyists, of course, at least at first. I've been through about 20 PCs so far. After my first few fully integrated (packaged) systems, it started to dawn on me that I didn't have to spend half my time under the hood, and I could really get some work done. I was pretty much hooked, even though I get stung by the upgrade bug once in a while, adding peripherals, hard drives, scanners, CD-RW drives, video cameras, and backup devices.

Overall, though, my advice is this: If you think you're going to save a lot of time and money while building yourself a better mousetrap than you can get from some serious vendor or systems integration house, "fo 'get about it!" as Crazy Eddie says. Any company worth its salt has engineers and testers whose job is to iron out the software and hardware incompatibilities that you don't want to lose sleep over.

If you want to upgrade what you have, that's not necessarily terrible, but if you want to build a new system from the ground up, I advise against it. Save yourself some agony, and buy a computer from a reputable dealer, preferably someone who will guarantee it to work with the operating system you have in mind. Especially when you're dealing with local clone builders, you should get that guarantee in writing. Get as much in the box as you can, including video, audio, modem, network card, CD-ROM/DVD/CD-R/CD-RW, hard disk, floppy drive, USB, and serial and parallel ports. The basic system with keyboard, mouse, and drives should all work and boot.

The next few sections describe upgrading your PC for operation under Windows XP Professional in case you're the incurable upgrader type and want to take that route.

2

PREPARING YOUR HARDWARE FOR WINDOWS XP

The amount of hardware upgrading you might need to make to prepare your system for Windows XP Professional depends in great measure on how close your system is to the minimum hardware requirements discussed earlier in the chapter. Because Windows XP's user-friendly multimedia and system protection features demand more computer power than previous versions of Windows, a system which barely exceeds the minimum hardware requirements for CPU, memory, video, and hard disk space can make running Windows XP an ordeal instead of a pleasure. I've had slow machines with small hard drives and fast machines with large hard drives; faster and larger is better, both for you and for Windows XP.

THE MOTHERBOARD AND CPU

So, you want a general upgrade to the performance of your system? The cheapest upgrade you can make is probably to add more RAM (see below). But if your wallet allows, and you want to get to the core of your system for a serious upgrade, start with the motherboard. Don't bother upgrading just your CPU without upgrading the motherboard too. While CPU upgrade kits are available to allow some older systems to use newer processors, recent changes in CPU speeds, physical packaging, and electrical requirements mean you're much better off upgrading both the motherboard and the CPU if you need a speed boost. Even if you're considering a RAM upgrade, do the motherboard/CPU upgrade *first* because a new motherboard often uses a better, faster type of RAM than your current system does. Motherboard improvements roll down the pike every few months, and adding a new CPU to an old design isn't going to net you much.

Motherboards are pretty cheap—typically around $100–$150 even for a good one, such as an Intel, Supermicro, Abit, or ASUS (this price is sans CPU); figure anywhere from $75 to $200 bucks more for the CPU, depending upon how close to the 2.0GHz and above "bleeding edge" you want to go). Don't get a motherboard from a company that doesn't put its name on the board, doesn't have a good Web site for technical support, or doesn't have a phone number. It's not worth saving a few bucks. Also, check the Microsoft HCL, of course, to see whether it's been tested. Get a board with the latest system memory (PC2700

DDR SDRAM, PC2100 DDR SDRAM or PC133 SDRAM), and a chipset that was designed to make it work optimally with the CPU you selected. (See the next section to learn about the importance of chipsets.)

Ideally, you'll want a modern motherboard with a fast CPU. So, get your hands on a motherboard that supports the ACPI power management scheme (not just APM) *and* a reasonably quick processor (in the 800 to 1GHz range), such as a Celeron, Pentium III, Pentium 4, AMD Athlon (with the Thunderbird core), Athlon 4, or AMD Duron. It should have a 100 or 133MHz or faster internal bus (called the "front-side bus" or FSB), support for ATA-100 hard drives and AGP graphics, a flashable (upgradable) BIOS for later upgrading, and it should be designed around the processor you have in mind. Preferably, it should come with the CPU installed. Installing a CPU isn't that difficult, but if you don't do it right, the CPU can overheat and croak.

TIP FROM

Bob
& Brian

> Some processors—such as the Intel Celeron, Pentium III, and AMD Athlon—are available in both slot-based and socket-based types. The slot-based processors are out-of-date for new motherboard/CPU purchases. Buy socketed processors and motherboards that match and your ability to move up the computer ladder to faster processors later is more likely than with the older slot-based processors.

Virtually all new motherboards are of the "ATX" format. These motherboards don't fit in the older AT-style cases and don't work with the AT power supplies either. ATX power supplies work hand-in-hand with the ACPI chipset and operating system, allowing the software to control the power states of the PC, including sleep, suspend, soft power down and up, and so on. There are some AT-style boards available still, but I suggest getting a new case and power supply and opting for the ATX version of whatever motherboard you're considering. A new case and power supply shouldn't cost you more than about $60.

When you install Windows XP on an ACPI-based system, you might need to update the ACPI BIOS to get the full benefits of Plug and Play and power management. If you don't do the update, you might have any of the following problems:

- You can't install Windows XP because of an ACPI BIOS error.
- After you install Windows XP, power management or Plug and Play functionality is not present.
- After you install Windows XP, power management or Plug and Play functionality is present but doesn't work correctly.

To obtain an update that should prevent these problems, contact your computer's manufacturer. Actually it's a good idea to contact the manufacturer (or check their Web site) even before you install XP. If you can get the latest BIOS update, the XP installation will go more smoothly and the ACPI features such as power management are more likely to work properly once XP is installed. BIOS upgrades are available for many laptops as well as for desktop computers.

CAUTION

> Now listen up. This one is really important. Be aware that installing an incorrect BIOS update may cause serious damage to your computer system. It's mandatory that you obtain the correct version of BIOS for your motherboard model from the manufacturer. Computer manufacturers may offer several different BIOS versions for different models. *Do not* download a version of BIOS that is *not* specified for your specific motherboard model. Installing an incorrect BIOS update may cause serious damage to your computer system. Contact your computer or motherboard manufacturer to ensure you have the most current BIOS version.

TIP FROM

Bob & Brian

> Many motherboard manufacturers provide an easy way to download a BIOS upgrade and install it via their Web pages. Also, on some motherboards, you have to enable BIOS upgrading by changing a jumper setting. I suggest that you disable the jumper when you're not upgrading to prevent viruses or some runaway program from messing with your BIOS settings.

TIP FROM

Bob & Brian

> Check the Web site www.motherboards.org for in-depth information about the latest motherboards, chipsets, types of RAM, and much more. You can even find information on building your own computer. It's a pretty amazing site.
>
> If you really want to delve into the research, check the Usenet newsgroups. Point your newsreader to
>
>   alt.comp.periphs.mainboard
>
> You can find many other motherboard groups as well, addressing specific brands, but this is the place to start. You'll have your reading cut out for you. If you prefer to use a Web browser to search newsgroups, send your browser to groups.google.com.

If you're going to be running applications that can actually benefit from multiple processors (check with the software vendor because not all applications do), then you should consider going full bore with a dual-processor motherboard. Although Intel's processors were the only players in this game until mid-2001, AMD's Athlon MP now provides you with a cost-effective choice.

NOTE

> Only XP Professional will run with dual CPUs, incidentally. XP Home will not. Check with the maker of a dual-CPU motherboard to ensure it will run with XP, if in doubt. Also, if you want to run with the new Intel Itanium processor, you need a special 64-bit Itanium version of XP Professional.

Suffice it to say that older systems based on 386, 486, and early Pentium processors are now out of the picture. If you want to keep these machines in service, put less-demanding versions of Windows on them, and network them as clients into your Windows XP or 2000 LAN.

THE IMPORTANCE OF THE CHIPSET

Keep in mind that the CPU is only a very small part of the overall design of a motherboard and computer. Many people ask me about upgrading their computers by simply dropping in a (relatively) expensive CPU chip or going through all kinds of machinations to speed-double the chip, and so forth. Just like you don't become Arnold Schwarzenegger or Rambo by getting a brain transplant, you can't create a supercomputer just by upgrading the CPU. Efficiency of the CPU is interdependent with several variables, such as the support chipset and the internal system bus speed. In fact, contrary to popular belief, the efficiency of the computer is more affected by the chipset than by any other factor—not the CPU nor the video nor the hard disk.

The CPU can be changed. The memory can be upgraded. The hard disk can be swapped. But the motherboard has been designed around the capabilities of the chipset, and until you change the motherboard, your PC will function largely the same. You cannot upgrade the chipset on a motherboard; you have to replace the board. Desirable chipsets support the following features:

- Advanced memory types—SDRAM, DDR SDRAM, RDRAM.
- Error-checking and correction—ECC memory uses parity-checked or special ECC modules, which are more expensive than ordinary memory; recommended for servers or mission-critical workstations.
- Hardware monitoring and management—Support for S.M.A.R.T. hard disks (drives that can alert you to impending failure), compatibility with system management standards such as DMI (Desktop Management Interface) and SNMP (Simple Network Management Protocol), and on-board monitoring of processor temperature and fan RPMs.
- Fast (800MHz to 1GHz or above) processors—Intel Pentium III and Celeron, Intel Pentium 4, AMD Athlon and Duron.
- Fast memory bus (FSB) speeds—PC133 (SDRAM), PC2100 (DDR SDRAM), Rambus 800MHz (RDRAM).
- PCI bus sync—Synchronous or asynchronous to memory bus speed.
- PCI bus type—32-bit or 64-bit (for servers and technical workstations).
- SMP capability—Single, dual, trio, or quad CPU support.
- AGP 4x or faster slot—For fastest video.
- Four or more USB ports—Enables use of more USB devices and allows each device to run faster (due to less contention with other devices).
- Support for built-in PCI EIDE controller running at ATA/100; RAID support enables faster or more reliable operation.

You can see that the chipset is at the very heart of much of what the computer does. Because it cannot be upgraded, though, there isn't much talk about it, and people tend to forget about its centrality. Equally important to the overall design of the chipset is how well the

CPU and chipset engineers communicated during the design of the chipset. Doing your homework on the latest chipsets and their compatibility/performance with specific CPUs will serve you well.

SLOTS

When you're scoping out a motherboard, think about how many slots you will need for plug-in boards (which can include cards for your sound, video, modem, and so on). More and more hardware is built onto the main boards now because very large-scale integration chips (VLSI) make it possible; therefore, you'll tend to need fewer slots than in the past. Often network support, audio, and even AGP video are built into the motherboard. If you want to use your own sound card and special super-duper video adapter, you can save a few bucks by getting the "bare-bones" version of a motherboard that does not include sound or video on it. However, if you want to avoid the hassle and keep more slots available for your other boards, buy the motherboard with this stuff integrated on it (such as on-board audio, which provides lower-cost—and lower-performance—audio capability that should suit your needs, unless you need high-end workstation performance, performing video capture or editing sound files). For one thing, all the parts are guaranteed to work together. If you think you'll want to add your own boards for the motherboard-included functions, make sure you can turn them off (usually with jumpers or software settings in the BIOS).

As of this writing, most motherboards were strong in PCI slots and have phased out ISA slots. Few have even one ISA slot these days. And most motherboards now have an AGP (Accelerated Graphics Port) slot for plugging in a fast video card. AGP is based on the PCI bus but fine-tuned for the needs of high-performance 3D graphics.

RAM

Like other versions of Windows NT, Windows XP Pro uses the memory it finds in the system intelligently. And it loves memory! The cheapest and easiest upgrade you can make to your PC is to add RAM. If your computer seems to "hit the hard disk" (that is, you have a delay in activity and you hear some clickity-click sounds in the computer and see the disk access light on the front of your system flash annoyingly) every time you click something or move the mouse around, Windows is doing way too much disk swapping (accessing data from your hard drive rather than system memory). You should be able to quickly switch among 5 to 10 programs without a lot of wait or noise from your PC. Go get some new memory that matches the kind of board you have (read the motherboard or your PC's manual), and *carefully* install the memory. Unplug the computer. Open the case, and find the RAM slots. Touch the metal case with your other hand before inserting the RAM. (RAM chips are very susceptible to damage by static electricity.) Get the fastest kind of memory that your motherboard can take advantage of.

Modern motherboards automatically detect memory you install (no switch setting is necessary), and Windows XP reads this setting and uses it as necessary. In general, the more memory you have installed, the better. Microsoft suggests 128MB for decent system performance. If you're running lots and lots of programs at once, I even suggest more on the order of 256MB to 512MB, but I've found 128MB adequate for even running 10 or more programs, while many folder windows were open, along with a couple of browser windows.

I'm writing this chapter on a PII 300 with 128MB laptop, and it's plenty zippy. I typically have more than 10 programs and/or windows open, playing MP3 files, checking e-mail in the background, and browsing the Web. Another machine of mine has only 64MB and does a fair bit more disk swapping. At this point, memory is so inexpensive that there is no reason not to upgrade if you need to.

 If you can't seem to get your newly installed RAM to be detected, see "RAM Not Recognized" in the "Troubleshooting" section at the end of this chapter.

HARD DISK

You need approximately 1.5GB of free hard disk space just to install Windows XP. This amount is just a little indication of Windows XP's storage hunger. With bloatware on the rise (programmers figure why bother making programs fast and tight with storage being so cheap, I guess), it behooves you to have lots of storage space. Like upgrading RAM, upgrading the hard disk is easy these days—even on the pocket book. Get down to Costco, or check www.buycomp.com for the latest prices on hard disks. They are continuing to plummet. For less than a couple hundred dollars, you can get a hard disk up to 60GB or more in size. The 1.5GB you need for the installation will look like nothing.

As with RAM, modern motherboards autodetect and configure hard disks when you insert them. Installing the current crop of EIDE (sometimes called ATA) drives has become very easy. The biggest nuisances with drive upgrades are figuring out whether to ditch the old one or keep it, deciding which drive will be the boot drive, and figuring out how to back up and restore. The EIDE spec allows for four drives, one of which is probably your CD-ROM. That typically leaves room for three, unless you have a CD-RW or another type of removable-media drive (such as a Zip or SuperDisk drive) in the box. There are too many options to cover here, but the easiest upgrade path is to make the new drive a "slave" on the primary IDE channel. Make sure to set jumpers on the drives' circuit as necessary, and ensure that you have the necessary cables to hook up the drives. Jumper your boot drive as *master* and the secondary drive as *slave*.

→ To learn more details about multibooting schemes, **see** Chapter 31, "Multibooting Windows XP with Other Operating Systems."

TIP FROM

Bob & Brian

If you want to install another hard disk (instead of removing the one you already have) and both of your IDE cables already have two drives connected, you can add additional ATA/IDE ports with an Ultra ATA/100 adapter card from Maxtor (www.maxtor.com), SIIG (www.siig.com), or Promise Technologies (www.promise.com). All you need is an empty PCI slot to add support for up to four more IDE/ATA drives.

If you have no more 3.5-inch drive bays for your hard disk, but you have an empty 5.25-inch drive bay (the drive bay size used by CD-ROM drives), use the adapter kit packaged with some retail-boxed drives, or purchase a separate kit from a computer store. The kit has spacers and screws to allow your small drive to fit into the larger bay.

Unlike NT, Windows XP can be installed on large removable media. The Setup program doesn't look to determine whether the target volume is removable. The %SystemRoot% (WINNT) folder is typically on a fixed hard disk, but it could be on a removable disk, such as a Jaz drive. One application would be to install, say, Linux on one removable drive, Windows NT 4 on another, Windows 98 on a third, and so on.

→ To learn more details about multibooting schemes, **see** Chapter 31, "Multibooting Windows XP with Other Operating Systems."

NOTE

Some computer jocks building high-performance systems such as big servers use SCSI drives. These require a special SCSI controller card. Note that even with Ultra2/Wide SCSI and a high-spindle-speed (10,000 RPM) drive, you'll only get 80MB/sec transfer rates—slower than today's fastest ATA drives. (The older Fast-Wide SCSI and Ultra-SCSI are only 20MB/sec.) So the advantages of SCSI over ATA are a thing of the past.

If what you're after is performance for, say, non-linear video editing workstations, or high-speed servers, I'd opt for multiple ATA/100 drives connected via a RAID 0 arrangement. Some motherboards, such as those from Abit, offer an on-board RAID controller that lets you gang up two ATA/100 drives to work in tandem, essentially doubling your hard drive data transfer rate. Promise (http://www.promise.com) makes a plug-in board called the FastTrak 100 that allows RAID arrangement using up to four additional drives to your computer.

MONITOR/VIDEO CARD SUPPORT

Because a doggy, older video card can bring even a snappy system to a crawl when you scroll the screen or move a window around, you'll want to find yourself a fast AGP card if your motherboard has an AGP slot. Microsoft has made the move to support video as nicely in Windows XP Professional as it did in the 9x platform, even more so in some ways. You have the option of connecting up to ten monitors, for example, and using them together. You should check your video cards' specs and the HCL to see whether they will work in multi-monitor arrangements before purchasing, though.

Virtually any Super VGA–compatible video card will work with Windows XP, but if you're thinking about upgrading for more speed or features, get an AGP board that has the bells and whistles you want—TV out, video capture, a fast 3D chipset for games, whatever; any recent motherboard which doesn't have on-board video will have an AGP slot. Decide the resolution you want to use, and make sure the card supports the number of colors you'll need at that resolution; if you choose a video card with at least 16MB of RAM, you can handle resolutions up to 1,600×1,280 with 24-bit (16.8 million) color. If you have a 17-inch CRT or 15-inch LCD monitor, you'll want to be running at 1024×768 resolution. Make sure the board can run at 72Hz refresh rate at the color depth and resolution you desire, too, so you won't see flicker on your CRT screen (LCD monitors don't require a high refresh rate). P.S. Your monitor needs to be able to do it, too. Check the monitor specs. Some older monitors can't run at, say, 1024×768 while refreshing at 72Hz.

If you're looking for a new monitor for use with Windows XP, keep in mind that 15-inch LCD panels have about the same usable screen space as 17-inch conventional monitors.

TIP FROM

Bob & Brian

> Many users who are in the market for a new monitor are buying LCD panels instead of conventional glass-tube CRTs. If you're shopping for a new monitor, keep these differences between LCD and CRT monitors in mind.
>
> Laptop and other flat-panel screens look very good at only one resolution—the so-called "native resolution." Other resolutions can be displayed, but they tend to look blocky. Some LCDs look better than others in nonnative resolutions due to built-in antialiasing firmware. If you plan to switch resolutions (as with DOS-based graphics software or for previewing Web pages you're building), check the quality of the LCD panel at different resolutions. And, unlike standard CRT monitors, LCD monitors look best at low refresh rates. If you buy an LCD monitor, be sure to set the refresh rate to 60Hz. It will probably look clearer that way. You don't have to worry about flicker on an LCD monitor; it's not an issue, and any advertising about high refresh capabilities of an LCD monitor is bogus and misleading. The pixels are transistors and simply don't flicker because they don't have to be refreshed in order to stay on.
>
> You'll still pay 2–3 times more for an LCD panel than for a CRT, but if you're crowded for space on your desk, they're great.

Windows XP comes with a large complement of 32-bit driver support for many devices, including a wide variety of video cards. It's quite likely that your card is going to be recognized, but you should check with the HCL just to make sure.

PLUG AND PLAY ITEMS

Plug and Play (or *PnP*, as it is commonly abbreviated) has brought a new level of sophistication to the PC. Much of the headache of PC upgrades stemmed from internal conflicts between plug-in boards and peripheral devices that were not easily detected by the operating system and too difficult for users to configure. Installing even a simple modem was often an exercise in failure for many users as they struggled to determine and set the board's jumpers, dip switches, or software settings to use an available IRQ (Interrupt Request). With PnP, you just plug in a board, screen, printer, scanner, or other peripheral, and reboot.

PnP doesn't always work as advertised, but most of the time it does, and it's a big step in the right direction. NT-based platforms began supporting PnP with Windows 2000. Now with XP, PnP installations are easier than ever. If XP can't find a driver when you install a device, the Windows Update site will be queried. There are currently more than 5,000 drivers on the Windows update site. Chances are good the system will automatically find a driver for you somewhere.

NOTE

> The pivotal question to ask when wondering whether your hardware is XP-compatible is whether the manufacturer or Microsoft supplies a Windows 2000 driver for it. Windows 2000 and XP rely on what is called the Windows Driver Model (WDM). (In addition to WDM, Windows 98 also supported older 16-bit drivers, but Windows 2000

and Windows XP don't.) The bottom line is that if there is a Windows 2000 driver for a piece of your hardware, it will probably work okay in XP.

Microsoft has been very busy testing existing hardware with XP, and in cases where a driver won't work with XP, rather than causing a system crash, XP utilizes a trick called "defective driver blocking." DDB prevents problem drivers from ruining a user's system. When an acceptable driver for a detected hardware device can't be found, you'll see a window that lets you offer feedback to Microsoft, such as "Hey, the driver for my _____ didn't work." If and when a driver for that device is developed, an AutoUpdate notification will pop up and offer it to you. If by fluke a bad driver is actually loaded, it shouldn't cause your system not to boot. Instead, the system should boot into "Safe Mode," where you can remove the driver so that the system will boot normally.

For more information about Safe Mode, see Chapter 33, "Troubleshooting and Repairing Windows XP."

For more information about removing devices and drivers, see Chapter 30, "Installing and Replacing Hardware."

TIP FROM

Bob & Brian

To be permitted to display the "Windows 2000-compatible," "Windows Me compatible," or "Windows XP compatible" logo, hardware and software must be PnP-capable. Look for this logo or the Plug and Play moniker when buying.

PREPARING YOUR SOFTWARE FOR WINDOWS XP

In preparation for upgrading to or installing Windows XP fresh, you need to consider software compatibility issues. Chapter 1, "Introducing Windows XP Professional," described how Windows XP is largely backward-compatible with DOS, Windows 3.x, Windows 9x, and Windows 2000 applications. Windows 2000's support for older programs, was, well, not so great. In fact, during the development of Windows 2000, application compatibility (especially for consumer end-users) was almost an afterthought. The focus for Windows 2000 was the corporate user. As a result, numerous consumer-oriented applications, such as games, failed to run on Windows 2000, leaving many power users and home consumers in the lurch.

Windows XP Professional is designed to work with both corporate users and home users' applications. To ensure expanded software compatibility, Microsoft set up an Application Compatibility Experience group shortly after the XP project began in December 1999. This group consisted of more than 200 testers, developers, and program managers who tested applications in a variety of scenarios (clean installs, migrations, upgrades) using various hardware configurations.

The result is that your existing software, whether Windows 98, Windows NT, Windows 2000, or even DOS and Windows 3.x, will likely run under XP. Even older games should run. As an example, SoundBlaster-compatible sound works in DOS boxes under Windows

XP. This means you can spend your lunch hour playing games like DOOM and Castle Wolfenstein in Windows XP—in a window or in full screen mode. As with the hardware compatibility notifications previously described, for programs that don't run, application fixes can be shipped dynamically to customers automatically, via AutoUpdate and Windows Update, after XP is installed.

TIP FROM

Bob & Brian

> Although discussed more in Chapter 3, it is worth mentioning that XP Home Edition will support upgrades from Windows 98, 98 SE, and Millennium Edition (Me), but not from Windows 95, NT 4.0 Workstation, or Windows 2000 Professional. Users of Windows XP Professional can also upgrade from Windows 95, NT 4.0 Workstation, and Windows 2000 Professional. The moral is that if you want to upgrade rather than to dual-boot, and you're running Windows 95, NT 4.0 Workstation, or Windows 2000 Professional, you'll need to purchase Windows XP Professional.

The good news is that Windows XP (both Home and Professional) will be highly compatible with many DOS and Windows 3.x applications, and with virtually all 32-bit programs that were designed for Windows 9x, Me, NT, and 2000. In addition, all your software (especially 3.x software) will benefit from having a face-lift—nicer borders, more options in the dialog boxes, smoother functioning, an increased capability to work with larger files, and so forth.

For programs that are quirky, you may have to resort to the new Windows XP compatibility modes. Windows XP's programmers have supposedly pinpointed more than 150 areas where apps from earlier versions of Windows might fail. They've created fixes for these problems and supplied XP with "compatibility modes" that let you fake out the offending application, running it in such a way that it believes it's running under Windows 95, or Windows 98, Me, NT 4, or 2000. The fixes can be applied to an application shortcut so that it always works properly when executed. This was mentioned in Chapter 1. For some apps, you may be alerted that there's a downloadable patch for the application (this may happen also when installing Windows XP, as described in Chapter 3).

While Windows XP is designed to run most older applications and games, this backward compatibility doesn't apply to utility programs which must work at a very deep level with the operating system and hardware. Programs such as older versions of disk-repair utilities such as Norton Utilities; anti-virus programs such as Norton Antivirus and McAfee Virus Scan; and system-management utilities such as Norton System Works, Ontrack System Suite, and others might not be compatible with Windows XP, because of differences in how Windows XP handles internal programs, memory, and drives compared to earlier Windows versions. If you're wondering if a particular disk, anti-virus, or system utility works with Windows XP, contact the vendor before you run the program.

To avoid problems that can be caused by running programs that are not designed with Windows XP in mind (and can't be tamed by the compatibility options built in to Windows XP), Windows XP will block programs from running if they won't work. Windows XP also features a new technology called AppsHelp which is triggered when problematic programs try to run. Thus, Windows XP is designed to achieve the twin goals of making your older software work while protecting your system from any problems that some older programs can cause.

In general, if you have your arsenal of programs chugging away under Windows 9x, Me, NT, or 2000 successfully, your applications will upgrade to Windows XP with only minor incident. Setup's compatibility testing program will alert you about any needs or incompatibilities. If you want to better understand the vagaries and nuances of Windows XP's application restrictions, read on.

CLASSES OF PROGRAMS

You are probably aware of a distinction to be made between types of programs. Most programs folks use on a daily basis are called *productivity applications* or simply *applications*. They include programs such as Microsoft Word, Microsoft Access, Adobe Photoshop, DreamWeaver and other Web page editors, CAD-CAM programs, video and sound editing programs—just to name a few of the thousands that are available. Typically, such programs help you produce documents in a certain line of work. These applications run at the highest level of the computer system, well on top of the operating system, and don't get down into the nitty-gritty of it.

By contrast, *utilities* are programs that try to get down deeper into the operating system and are used to manage the computer. Programs such as virus eradicators, hard disk partitioning and image backup tools, hard disk organizers, user interface tweakers, and power management tools fall into this class of programs. Norton System Works, Ontrack Partition Magic, and McAfee Anti-virus are examples.

Even though most people don't typically distinguish between utilities and applications and simply use the word *application* (or just *program*) to refer to any program, technically, they are different. As you'll see, it's very likely that your existing *applications* are going to work under Windows XP Professional. However, it's far less likely that the system or disk utilities you want to bring over from less-empowered iterations of Windows will work without being updated.

TIP FROM

Bob
& Brian

> If you have a program that uses 16-bit drivers, you need to get 32-bit drivers from the software vendor to ensure that the program functions properly after the upgrade to Windows XP.

LEGIT APIS VERSUS HARDWARE TWIDDLING

As you might recall from Chapter 1's brief discussion of the XP architecture, when applications need help from the operating system to, say, print or write a file to disk or accept keyboard input, the environment subsystem passes the request to the Executive. The NT Executive runs in protected mode so that applications (or utilities) can't threaten the stability of the system. The requests that applications make are known as *API calls*. (API stands for *application programming interface*.) APIs are built into each environment subsystem and make up a set of tricks or canned functions the programmer can call upon.

The NT Executive, kernel, and hardware abstraction layer (HAL) take care of the rest of the work after the request is made. Recall also that the non-Win32 environment subsystems turn their calls over to the Win32 subsystem, which then routes them to the Executive. Thus, the environment subsystems have to translate native Windows 3.x, OS/2, and DOS calls into Win32 calls, which are then passed to the Executive using API calls the Executive understands. A lot of interpreting goes on, and lots of middle management.

For general applications, all this is just peachy because most applications just want traditional access to hardware: keyboard input, screen output, printing, and reading and writing data files on disk. APIs are a great help here, as is the Executive, because applications programmers don't have to handle the drudgery of system housekeeping on their own. The existence of an API makes writing Windows programs much easier.

As you might have suspected, any program or utility that wants to work directly with hardware, or makes calls that would otherwise be trapped because they don't exist in the Windows XP environment subsystems, will fail or will likely be crippled in some way. Typically, Windows XP shuts them down after generating an error message of some sort, possibly asking if you want to try a solution on the Windows Update Web site. Exceptions are legitimate calls to COM and LPT (serial and parallel) ports made by DOS programs in the course of traditional procedures such as dialing a modem or printing a document. Many DOS communications programs expect to access the serial port UART (the chip that runs the serial port) directly, for example. NT "virtualizes" the PC serial and parallel ports in the 16-bit subsystem, intercepting the request and sending it through the Executive as legitimate. The port is emulated in software, basically, and the DOS program is none the wiser. DOS programs that try anything more sophisticated, such as writing to the hard disk tracks or doing fancy stuff with the ports, screen, or keyboard, will be trapped.

In Windows 3.x, API end runs often were neither perceived nor prevented, resulting in system breaches and crashes. This was particularly a problem with DOS programs because they assumed they had control of the entire computer (DOS isn't a multitasking operating system). Windows 3.x allowed this use, so games and utilities programmers took advantage of this "feature" to write some pretty audacious programs. DOS-based viruses are a good case in point. Viruses make a hobby of fiddling with the innards of your operating system (typically by altering data on the hard disk), with insidious effects. Windows 3.x couldn't prevent such security breaches because it had no way of knowing they were occurring. Windows XP (and 2000) are much better at preventing them. The BIOSs of modern PCs can also detect attempts to futz with the boot tracks of the hard disk, too, though the feature can be defeated through disabling the antivirus or write-protect boot sector setting in the BIOS Setup utility.

Windows 9x and Windows Me were somewhat better at protection than 3.x, though not by a great margin. Portions of the *kernel* were protected, and if a program acted improperly, you stood a better chance of being able to kill it without bringing down the whole operating system. The designers of Windows 9x and Me achieved a higher degree of hardware isolation by virtualizing all the hardware, the same approach used in NT, 2000, and XP. Every physical piece of hardware in the computer is accessed only by *virtual device drivers* (called *VxDs* in Windows lingo). When an application wants to use device, it asks the operating system for it via the API call. Then the operating system validates the request and passes it along to the device driver, which in turn handles the actual communication with the device.

As with previous Windows versions, Windows XP allows the user to define certain characteristics for running DOS programs, through PIFs (Program Information Files). PIFs allow you to set default properties for MS-DOS programs, such as font size, screen colors, and memory allocation.

HARDWARE-BASED DEVICE-PROTECTION CAPABILITIES

Intel and compatible CPUs have capabilities that come to the rescue, to some degree, in helping prevent hardware access breaches, yet still handle the request. The CPU works in concert with the operating system to achieve the desired result. When a DOS program running in Windows tries to access hardware, Windows maps the DOS API call to the Win32 API. This procedure is fine until a direct call to hardware is attempted. An intelligent feature built in to Intel 386 and subsequent chips (up to and including the Pentium 4 as well as compatible processors such as the AMD K6 family, Athlon and Duron), called the *I/O permission bitmap*, comes to the rescue by noticing this request and putting up a red flag.

When an application is run, Windows XP detects what type of program it is—whether DOS, Windows 3.x, 32-bit Windows, or OS/2. When the VDM (virtual DOS machine) for a DOS program is set up, it provides all the basic services of a PC, and it also creates an I/O permission bitmap for the application. The bitmap is essentially a table with entries for each of the computer's internal ports (there are many, used for different things, such as the system clock, network boards, and so on), and it shows which, if any, of the ports allow direct access. If the DOS program tries to access hardware outside this accepted list of virtualized hardware, the red flag goes up, Windows XP notices it, and the program is terminated, typically accompanied by an entry in the system error logs.

WHY SHOULD YOU CARE?

Enough theory. What does this mean to you and to your application choices? Most of your older software will probably run fine after the upgrade. But if you're upgrading from Windows 3.x or 9x and you've been running older 16-bit programs, especially hard disk utilities, you might have some trouble.

CAUTION

Even though you might be able to run some of your older programs such as disk utilities that interact directly with your computer's hard disk by forcing the issue with the XP compatibility modes, it doesn't mean that it's advisable. Windows 3.x programs, for example, don't know about long filenames and can truncate long filenames or at least not display them or accept them in dialog boxes, which can be annoying. Running such programs is not recommended, and I suggest you put them in cryogenic suspension. With XP, the upgrade might be significantly easier than Windows 2000 was (or might have been), but that doesn't mean you should necessarily be cheap and not upgrade to the XP versions of your favorite apps when you get the chance.

As mentioned, Setup examines the applications you have installed and attempts to warn you of incompatibilities. In some cases, you'll just be told to bag the program. In other cases, you'll be prompted to contact the maker for updates, called *upgrade packs*, or to insert the disks with upgrade packs on them at the appropriate time.

WINDOWS XP-APPROVED APPLICATIONS

So, which programs are really ready for Windows XP? The logo requirements for "Windows XP-Ready Software" are similar to those discussed previously for hardware. Just check the product's packaging or the Web page description of the product you're thinking of purchasing. If it's Windows 2000-compatible, chances are good that it will run under Windows XP, but that's not guaranteed. I suggest you contact the maker or check a few sites on the Web first.

TROUBLESHOOTING

RAM NOT RECOGNIZED

I've added RAM to my computer, and it doesn't seem to show up.

You must check several things when adding RAM to ensure that it shows up correctly in Windows. If the BIOS detects the RAM, you can be assured that it will be detected in Windows, so don't worry about any settings within Windows per se. Just do what is necessary for the computer to report the correct amount of total RAM when it is booting within the BIOS. Older machines used to require switch settings or BIOS setting adjustments when you added RAM, but virtually all new computers do not. Of course, you can and should always consult the manual supplied with your computer when performing a RAM upgrade. Follow this checklist:

- Be sure you purchased the correct type, form factors, and capacity of RAM.
- Be sure the RAM is the correct speed for the computer.
- Double-check that the RAM is inserted correctly and firmly seated in the computer. With the power off, try removing and reinserting it.
- Be sure you inserted the RAM in the correct slot. Most computers have a few slots for RAM. Many motherboards require that RAM slots be filled in a specific order, or autodetection of RAM will not work.
- If it's still a no-go, remove the RAM (turn off the power first, of course), carefully package the RAM in an antistatic bag, and return it to the dealer to be tested.

COMPATIBILITY AND UPGRADE HELP

Where can I learn more about compatibility and upgrade options for my Windows XP computer?

Microsoft maintains several resources for Windows XP. You can check the following:

- The Microsoft Deployment Resources Web site includes operating system migration guides, pointers to training resources, and a strategic upgrade white paper. You can find this information at the following address:

  http://www.microsoft.com/windowsxp/pro/techinfo/deployment/default.asp

- The Hardware Compatibility List provides quick access to compatibility information for a variety of equipment vendors, computer systems, and specific peripherals by name and type. It's located at this address:

  `http://www.microsoft.com/hcl`

- Microsoft's Windows XP Expert Zone features columns, tips, and XP newsgroups. It's located at this address:

  `http://www.microsoft.com/windowsxp/expertzone/default.asp`

- The Windows XP Professional site is located at this address:

  `http://www.microsoft.com/windowsxp/pro/default.asp`

- Microsoft's "Windows XP Ready" program can help you find workstations and servers that are 100 percent Windows XP-compatible. Check with your PC vendor to see whether existing products can be retrofitted to comply with Microsoft's specifications. Go to the following address:

  `http://www.microsoft.com/windowsxp/ready`

TIPS FROM THE WINDOWS PROS: SHOPPING FOR THE RIGHT HARDWARE AND SOFTWARE

Many people ask how I decide what hardware and software to purchase or discard when preparing for an operating system upgrade such as Windows XP. Here are some personal notes.

When I want to use one of my old utilities or applications for my Windows XP machine, I first check to see whether what I want to do is already covered by some other program. A better mousetrap is always around. Consider zip utilities, for example. I used to use DOS-based zip programs; then I moved on to WinZip. Under Windows 98, I used Windows 98 Plus!, which includes native support for zip in the GUI, so I could zip and unzip right in the Explorer interface. When I upgraded to Windows 2000 Professional and I was wondering what to use, I popped onto the Web and did a search or two and came across Turbo Zip. I think the link said something about working with NT, so I gave it a shot. Now I'm using Turbo Zip. It works fine under NT and Windows 2000 Professional. Although Windows XP has native compression included, like Windows 98 Plus! and Windows Me, you might want to use WinZip or Turbo Zip if you are familiar with them and like them.

As for productivity applications, I'm game to try anything I was using under Windows 98 and Me: Photoshop, Adaptec Easy CD Creator, CoolEdit 96, Excel 97, Word 97, Ulead Media Studio Pro, RealJukebox MP3 player, FrontPage Express, CuteFTP, ThumbsPlus, even some 3.x applications such as Collage Image Capture (for capturing screen shots for this book). I trust that Windows XP will alert me if the application isn't safe to use.

If I hear that a 32-bit version of a previously 16-bit application is available and will run faster (I usually assume it will at least have some nifty new features, such as better Save As and Open dialog boxes, support for more file formats, or something) then I'll spring for it if the price isn't too outrageous or if an upgrade option is available.

I used to hang with Netscape Navigator, but frankly I like Internet Explorer better mostly because I love the F11 feature that increases the browser size to the full screen so that I can see the maximum amount of text at one time. Also, because I use Outlook Express for my mail, and they are integrated pretty nicely, I go for the package. (Microsoft got me on this one, sorry to say.)

A few years ago, after first starting to use Windows 95, it took me several months to get used to using the desktop and the taskbar. But soon I was converted. Anyone upgrading from Windows 3.x will probably go through the same confusion at first. Whereas my home base had been the 3.x Program Manager and File Manager, I quickly became addicted to dropping folders and documents right on the desktop, dragging files to a floppy drive on the desktop, and so forth. The Windows XP interface is better-looking and has more features than the Windows 9x interface also familiar to Windows Me, NT, and 2000 users, and offers even more file-management features. It's getting easier and easier to copy files around, drop them in e-mail, or view a slide show of images from my digital camera using thumbnails in an Explorer window. The need for many of the shell add-ons that I once used in earlier Windows has vaporized.

When it comes to hardware, although I'm an experimenter and always want to try out the latest gizmos, I'm hard-core practical. Got that from my parents, I guess. Trying out new hardware and returning it aren't nearly as easy as deciding not to purchase software after trying the demo for free. As the saying goes, "Learn from other people's mistakes because you won't live long enough to make them all yourself." Too bad you can't try hardware for free; shipping charges, restocking fees, and hassles with sales people are too much for me to worry about. I don't buy new hardware unless it's on the Microsoft HCL for the operating system that I'll be using with the system. It's that easy. I have too much weird off-brand hardware sitting in closets around my office or that I've donated to local community groups just because it didn't work with my operating system. Before I purchase, I also look around to see what the most popular item in a niche is. I bought a PalmPilot even though the CE devices have broader functionality, for example. Buying mainstream means I'll have more add-on products, supplies, cables, media, drivers, and online support from users. That support is worth the extra few dollars or loss of bleeding-edge features any day.

And finally, I usually go for version 2.0. If a product catches on and has industrywide support, I'll go for it, but not until then. I never bought a Sony Beta VCR, a nine-track tape player, or an Atari or Timex-Sinclair computer. My newest computers are a Socket A-based 1GHz AMD Athlon uniprocessor on an ASUS motherboard, and an HP 1GHz Pentium III laptop. I checked the newsgroups and various Web sites before shelling out for the Athlon and didn't push it to beyond 1GHz, even though I could have overclocked the CPU to squeeze out a tad more performance. I didn't go with multiprocessors or UltraWide SCSI. Internal timing in CPUs and computers that are pushing the outside of the envelope can be problematic, so why push it?

CHAPTER 3

INSTALLING WINDOWS XP PROFESSIONAL

In this chapter

CHOOSING AN UPGRADE PATH

This chapter describes the variety of installation options available for Windows XP Professional. Even if your system is already installed, you might be interested in reading through this chapter for some helpful information about dual-booting various operating systems and working with multiple formats of disk partitions (FAT, FAT32, and NTFS). For information on partitions, see the "Disk Partitioning Tips" later this chapter.

Due to improvements and standardization in user interfaces and to Microsoft-imposed installation procedures for Windows programs, setup of application programs nowadays is typically a piece of cake and self-explanatory. Likewise, installation of all newer Windows versions has grown increasingly automated. Installing Windows XP is usually a fairly simple process, but it will take an hour or more to complete.

This chapter covers the installation issues you will need to ponder under different scenarios. I'll walk you through a typical installation, but if you've installed any Windows product since Windows 98 you shouldn't be surprised by anything. I'll also describe the basic decision tree you'll have to mull over before committing to Windows XP and the path you'll follow to get it up and running. Along the way, I'll discuss why you might make one choice over another and what to do when the process goes awry.

There are two primary installation scenarios: clean installation or upgrade installation. A clean installation is performed onto a new/formatted empty hard drive or to overwrite an existing OS. An upgrade installation retains existing settings and applications. In addition to the type of installation to perform, you must also address the issues of multi-booting and selecting a file system.

I'll tell you what to expect when upgrading. Look for the section that applies to you. Also, check the general discussions about dual-booting and upgrading your file system because they apply in all cases. You'll find a more in-depth discussion of multi-booting in Chapter 31, "Multibooting Windows XP with Other Operating Systems."

NOTE

> In addition to this chapter, you should also read two informative text files found on the Windows XP CD. The first is the file Read1st.txt, which you'll find on the root directory of the CD. This file contains last-minute installation information Microsoft didn't publish until it released the final version of Windows XP. The second is the file PRO1.txt, which is found in the SETUPTXT folder of the CD. This file contains detailed release notes covering topics such as installation, customization, and startup.

As mentioned in Chapter 1, "Introducing Windows XP Professional," Windows XP also supports installation capabilities attractive to the IS professional, such as *push* installations and automated installations that require no user intervention. For more information about these kinds of sophisticated deployment processes and automated installation tools, you should seek the aid of Microsoft's Windows XP Resource Kit. There, you'll find instructions for creating automated installation scripts. I've provided a short overview of automated installations at the end of this chapter.

CLEAN INSTALLATION VERSUS UPGRADE

Let's talk about installing Windows XP. The next major question you must ask is whether to upgrade from an existing operating system or install fresh. Windows XP Professional supports upgrading from the following operating systems:

- Windows 98, OSR2, Second Edition (SE), Millennium Edition (Me)
- Windows NT 4.0 Workstation (with Service Packs)
- Windows 2000 Professional (with Service Packs)

NOTE

Windows XP Home edition can be upgraded to Windows XP Professional edition.

3

If your system is running any other OS not included in this list (such as Windows 95, Windows NT Server, Windows 2000 Server, or even Windows 3.x), you must perform a clean install. Clean installs do not retain any settings or applications. All settings must be re-configured and all applications must be re-installed after the clean installation of Windows XP is complete.

Most Windows veterans know by now that doing a fresh installation is usually the most beneficial approach in the long run, even though it means more work up front installing applications and reentering personal settings, remote access and networking details, and so forth. You probably have some seat-of-the-pants experiences with Windows operating systems becoming polluted over time by wacko applications that mysteriously trash the Registry or erase or overwrite important files, like .DLL files, that Windows needs to operate properly.

With a clean installation, such worries are forgotten. It's like selling off that lemon of a car you've been wrestling with for the last five years. And yes, you'll lose lots of settings that are annoying to input again, such as Internet dial-up and TCP/IP settings, e-mail accounts, address books, and so forth. You should attempt to back up as much important data as you can, such as your address books, e-mail, personal documents, and so on, before performing a clean installation over an existing OS. Windows XP is somewhat self-healing. Because system files and DLLs are protected against trampling, you're going to have a more sturdy system in the long run anyway. If your system is acting a little wonky already anyway (unexpected crashes, for example), it's better to do a clean installation. A clean installation will reformat your boot partition (that's the one where Windows lives) and will just edit your system partition (that's the one that boots the system and displays the boot menu). In those cases where the boot and system partitions are the same, the partition will be reformatted.

When you choose to upgrade over an existing operating system, you also run the possibility that some applications won't work properly afterward because they aren't fully compatible with Windows XP. Fortunately, Windows XP is even more backward-compatible than Windows 2000, especially with its Windows Compatibility Mode.

NOTE

> Windows Compatibility Mode is a nifty new feature that enables Windows XP to support a wider range of software products than Windows 95 and Windows NT combined. A compatibility mode is simply a designation for a software platform emulation environment. In other words, when an application is launched with compatibility mode enabled, a virtual machine representing that application's native environment (Windows 95, Windows 98, Windows NT, or Windows 2000) is created in such a way that the application is fooled into thinking that it is the only application present on the computer system running its preferred OS. More details on working with applications is discussed in Chapter 23, "Tweaking the GUI." By the way, for DOS executables the Properties dialog box is much different than for those of Windows executables. To learn more about tweaking the DOS environment, see "Configuring the Program Environment" in Chapter 25.

Table 3.1 compares performing a clean installation versus upgrading your existing Windows installation.

TABLE 3.1 CLEAN INSTALLATION VERSUS UPGRADING

Perform a New Installation When You Can Answer "Yes" to Any of the Following:	Consider Upgrading When You Can Answer "Yes" to All the Following:
You've just purchased a new hard disk or reformatted it.	Your current operating system supports upgrading.
The operating system you have on your computer isn't among those on the upgrade list.	You want to fully replace your previous Windows operating system with Windows XP.
Your computer has an operating system already, but you're ready to kill it and start fresh with Windows XP.	You want to keep your existing files and preferences.
You want to create a dual-boot configuration with Windows XP and your current system. (Note that Microsoft recommends using two partitions to do so.)	You're ready to chance that in some rare cases, applications or hardware won't immediately work as they did under the old operating system.

NOTE

In any case, installing a "new" or "clean" version of Windows XP does not mean that the drive on which you are installing XP will be reformatted. The XP installer won't format the drive unless you direct it to do so. You can place a new or clean Windows XP installation on a drive (in this case, we'll assume it's the C: drive) even if the C: drive already has Windows 98 installed on it. To do this, install XP in a different directory. When the XP installation is complete, delete Windows 98, because running two operating systems in the same partition is not recommended. Ideally, however, if you plan to keep your original operating system intact, you'll want to install XP into another partition.

DUAL-BOOTING VERSUS SINGLE BOOTING

In addition to the upgrade/fresh installation issue, you also must consider the dual or multi-boot issue. Dual-booting is a scheme that lets you keep your old operating system and install Windows XP as a clean installation. Windows XP can be installed onto any hard disk volume or partition within a computer; it is not limited or restricted to drive C as is Windows 9x. Thus, by adding a new hard drive and installing Windows XP onto it, you'll retain your original, pre-existing OS. When you boot up, you are given a choice of operating system to start.

NOTE

Notice in this book that we use the term "dual-booting" often. This usually refers to having only two OSes on the same system. We use this term since most multiple OS scenarios employ only two OSes. But we could have just as easily substituted the term "multi-booting" to include those systems with two or more OSes. So, when you see "dual-booting" don't limit your thinking to only two OSes.

Windows XP officially supports dual-booting with any Microsoft Windows operating systems as well as MS-DOS and OS/2. You can multi-boot almost any OS that uses FAT or NTFS file systems on the boot drive. That includes Linux (notice that Microsoft doesn't tout that feature loudly?). With the aid of third-party partition managers, you are able to multi-boot Windows XP with any OS in existence.

NOTE

Third-party partition or multi-boot managers include PartitionMagic from Power Quest (www.powerquest.com) and System Commander from V Communications (www.v-com.com).

PROS OF DUAL-BOOTING

There are lots of reasons for setting up a dual- or multi-booting computer, especially if you are in the business of testing computers or you run a wide variety of software and hardware on your computers. Personally, of the five computers in my office, four of them are dual-booting. The following are a few thoughts about dual-booting that you might want to consider before making the decision:

- I multi-boot on a couple of my machines because I run lots of Windows tools, hardware-specific programs like video editing programs, CD-writers or rewriters, and so on. Also, I'm always testing new programs. No matter how much I would prefer to run just a single operating system, sometimes I need to run other versions of Windows to get a driver or some application to work. So, it makes sense for me to multi-boot.

- If you're a gamer, chances are you need MS-DOS, Windows 9x, or Windows 2000 just to get certain games to run or even some joysticks or control devices. Most games will function under Windows XP, but you may discover a few cases where things are not exactly as you'd expect. If you can't live without a game, then create a multi-boot system including the alternate OS needed for your game-du-jour. For the full scoop on compatibility with your favorite games, check with some gaming magazines or the makers of the games in question. Configuring game controllers is covered in Chapter 24, "Configuration via Control Panel Applets."

- If you're regularly testing or running lots of different kinds of software and own an abundance of hardware, or you're a new hardware junkie like me, being stuck with just a single operating system is like being in jail. Choose to multi-boot, even though this choice can cause some headaches, as described in the following section.

- If you have doubts about compatibility with your hardware or software and don't want to jeopardize your existing operating system, use a dual-boot arrangement for a while and see what you think. If you become confident that XP is going to work for you, you can either perform an upgrade installation over your existing operating system or move over into using XP only. (That is, you can migrate your data and applications into your XP setup.) If you decide to upgrade over your old OS rather than migrate into the clean XP, you can then remove the clean XP test system to free up disk space. If you decide XP doesn't cut the mustard, you can remove it. Regardless of how you do the eventual upgrade, this kind of approach gives you the time to test things out. You'll eventually end up with a single OS in the long run, one you're happy with.

TIP FROM

Bob & Brian

> There is an alternative to dual- or multi-booting that makes installing multiple OSes on your computer easier, although not quite as quick or responsive. A program called Virtual PC lets you install and run multiple operating systems at the same time. One host operating system runs the secondary operating systems within it. For example, you could have Windows Me be the host to run Windows XP. You boot up Windows Me, run the Virtual PC program, and then tell Virtual PC to boot up Windows XP. You end up having Windows Me and Windows XP running at the same time. It's pretty impressive. Use of virtual computers is covered in Chapter 31.

CONS OF DUAL-BOOTING

Dual or multi-booting isn't always as simple or attractive as it might seem at first. You must understand the limitations and requirements of making your computer a home for more than one operating system. Operating systems are, for the most part, egotistical and stingy. They don't always coexist on the same computer peaceably. Therefore, you should be aware of a few points before deciding to dual-boot your machine:

■ You must reinstall many applications, particularly ones that make Registry entries, such as Office, or ones that put portions of themselves (for example, DLL files) in the operating system directory. You must run the Setup routines for each such program once for each operating system. Your applications should still work in both environments, and contrary to what you might think, you don't have to duplicate all the files on disk if you install them into the same directories under each operating system. Still, you must go through the process of installation again.

■ Some applications that run in both environments just don't behave properly or cooperate as you would hope. This is especially true of ones that share the same data files or futz with the Registry. If a program itself tweaks the Registry or alerts your data files to what operating system has been working with it, and then you reboot in the other operating system (each operating system has its own Registry files, remember), unexpected incompatibilities can crop up.

> **NOTE**
>
> Some programs are, obviously, less picky because they are not as integrated into the operating system. Netscape seems to live quite peaceably in a multi-boot arrangement, mail and all.

■ Any application that relies on the operating systems' rights settings, user identities, or multiple profiles will likely not interrelate properly between the operating systems. As you probably know, Windows XP, Windows 98/SE/Me, Windows NT, and Windows 2000 can be set up with multiple-user settings stored on the same machine. Applications that take advantage of these settings often store individual settings in the Registry and in folders such as Windows\profiles or C:\windows\application data or, in the case of Windows 2000 and Windows XP, C:\documents and settings. In any case, because applications sometimes look to the operating system for information about a user's individual settings, whether it's gleaned from the Registry or user-specific folders such as the Desktop folder, things can go mighty awry if you're hoping to run certain applications under either operating system, and you're not a bit crafty. One way to live with this situation is to focus on using one operating system and use the other only when some application or hardware refuses to run in your primary OS.

■ Upgrading to Windows XP pulls in all (or as much as possible) of the preexisting settings, such as e-mail accounts, LAN settings and dial-up connections, machine user accounts, and so on. If you dual-boot, you have to create them from scratch for the new operating system.

■ Security is a biggie. Is security an issue for you? Do you need to keep prying eyes at bay? Unless you're going to set up a separate partition or drive with NTFS and encryption on it, you're increasing the chances of security breaches by dual-booting. Drive, volume, partition, and file security are minimal under any OS using FAT16 or FAT32 partitions (including Windows 9x/Me), since these can be altered by anyone who can boot the system in DOS or a DOS-based operating system. If you want to dual-boot and still have some decent security, then you should install Windows XP on a second drive, formatted in NTFS; alternatively, you can create an NTFS partition on your main drive and install into it. Use the NTFS partition for your Windows XP files and encrypt sensitive data files. When installing, you are given the option of converting to NTFS. (Encryption can be performed after Windows XP is installed.)

→ To learn more details about file and folder encryption, **see** "Encryption," **p. 1009**.

■ The only Microsoft operating systems that read NTFS partitions are Windows NT, Windows 2000, and Windows XP. If you want to multi-boot and gain the advantages of NTFS, remember that you can't access any data files on the NTFS partitions when you're running DOS, Windows 3.x, or Windows 9x/SE/Me. (Linux, however, can read and write to NTFS partitions.)

PRECAUTIONS WHEN DUAL-BOOTING

If, after reading the pros and cons, you think you want to set up a dual-boot system, consider the following precautions in addition to those listed previously. This part is going to take a little studying, so put on your thinking cap.

■ Although it's possible to install multiple OSes into the same partition on your hard drive, don't do it. However, many of the Windows operating systems, specifically Windows 95 and 98/SE/Me as well as Windows 2000 and Windows XP share similar common directory names (such as \Windows, \Program Files, and \Documents and Settings). Installing a new OS into the same partition as an existing OS runs the risk of overwriting important files. This is true, even if you select to use a different primary folder name. I highly recommend installing each OS into its own partition (with the possible exception of DOS). You make this choice when installing Windows XP through the "advanced" options during the initial phase of setup. Most other OSes (especially Windows NT and Windows 2000) offer similar options.

■ Microsoft doesn't suggest mixing file systems in dual-boot arrangements because it complicates matters. To quote the documentation, ". . . such a configuration introduces additional complexity into the choice of file systems." Microsoft's warning is probably just an admonition against burdening the operating system and your applications with multiple file systems *and* multiple operating systems on the same machine.

Admittedly, mixing them does complicate things. If you want to play it safe, go with the lowest common denominator of file systems for the operating systems you're installing. Typically, it is FAT or FAT32. (See the "Choosing a File System: FAT, FAT32, or NTFS?" section later in this chapter.)

- Installation order is important in some cases. To set up a dual-boot configuration between MS-DOS/Windows 3.x or Windows 95 with Windows XP, you should install Windows XP last. Otherwise, important files needed to start Windows XP could be overwritten by the other operating systems. For dual-booting between Windows 98/SE/Me, Windows NT, Windows 2000, and Windows XP, installation order is irrelevant.

- To set up a dual-boot configuration between MS-DOS/Windows 3.x or Windows 95 with Windows XP, the primary partition (that is, the one you boot from) must be formatted as FAT. If you're dual-booting Windows 95 OSR2, Windows 98, Windows NT, or Windows 2000 with Windows XP, the primary partition must be FAT or FAT32, not NTFS. These two rules make sense because, without third-party drivers, Windows 9x/SE/Me can't read or exist with NTFS, and Windows 95 can't read either NTFS or FAT32.

- There is more than one version of NTFS. Windows XP and Windows 2000 both use NTFS v5. Windows NT 4.0 right out of the box uses NTFS v4. But Windows NT 4.0 can be upgraded to use NTFS v5 by installing Service Pack 4. This becomes important when you attempt to dual-boot with Windows NT 4.0 (without Service Pack 4) and Window XP. The NT OS will be unable to access files on the Windows XP NTFS formatted partitions. Your only options are to apply SP4 to NT or use FAT.

- You can install Windows XP on a compressed drive if that drive was compressed using the NTFS disk compression utility, but not if made with DoubleSpace or DriveSpace or some other disk compressor such as Stacker. If you're going to dual-boot with Windows 9x, remember that Windows XP Professional won't see the compressed DoubleSpace and DriveSpace partitions, and any NTFS partitions, compressed or not, will be invisible to Windows 9x without third-party drivers.

- Sometimes an operating system reconfigures your hardware through software settings. Suppose you install some new hardware and run Windows 98. That operating system will detect it and might do some software setting on the hardware that works with Windows 98 but which conflicts with Windows XP. This problem should be rare because most hardware these days is Plug and Play-compatible and should be configurable on-the-fly as the operating system boots up. But be aware of the possibility. A good example is that two operating systems might have different video display drivers for the same video adapter, causing you to have to manually adjust the screen size and orientation when you switch between them.

3

PRECAUTIONS WHEN DUAL-BOOTING WINDOWS NT AND WINDOWS XP

You must follow some weird rules when dual-booting Windows NT (3 or 4) and Windows XP. Mostly, they have bearing on which file systems you can use. For folks testing Windows XP while keeping the tried and true Windows NT 4 around, they can pose a bit of an annoyance. Here's the list:

- You should upgrade to at least NT 4.0 Service Pack 4 if you want to dual-boot with Windows XP sharing NTFS partitions. Upgrade first and then install Windows XP; or your NT 4 system will not boot.

- Computers dual-booting Windows NT and Windows XP must have different computer names under each boot configuration if the computers are connected to an NT domain. Otherwise, the domain controller is given conflicting information about the workstation, and it deals with these two types of workstations in slightly different ways (for example, security tokens).

NOTE

> Dual-booting with Windows 2000 does not encounter these issues since it shares the same version of NTFS that Windows XP uses. For more detailed information about configuring your computer to dual-boot, see Chapter 31, which is devoted to this topic.

CHOOSING A FILE SYSTEM: FAT, FAT32, OR NTFS?

The next major consideration on the pre-installation agenda is determining what type of file system you intend to use. The rules and regulations discussed in the preceding section might have narrowed down this choice for you. Still, you'll likely want to read about the pros and cons of the various file-keeping schemes in use on Windows XP machines and consider a few details on how they influence your installation.

NOTE

> Windows XP doesn't know about compressed drives such as those created with DriveSpace or DoubleSpace. You have to decompress them before installing to Windows XP. Decompressing is a real pain if your disk space is totally packed (because as your files decompress, they fill up even more space on an already cramped drive). You might have to decompress in stages, moving data off the hard disk to backup media or another drive.

As mentioned in the preceding sections on dual-booting Windows XP and a second operating system, it's a good idea to think about what file system you're going to use, preferably before installing Windows XP. Although you can use utilities in Windows XP and external utilities such as PartitionMagic to convert partitions between file systems after the fact, forethought and advance partition preparation are the better path. Let's do a little review of file systems you can use and advantages of each.

A file system is a scheme by which data files and directories (folders) are stored and retrieved on a floppy disk or hard disk. Tape and other media have file systems as well, but here I'm talking only about hard disks. Windows XP supports three file systems: the NT File System (NTFS) or one of the file allocation table file systems (FAT or FAT32).

A Brief History of File Systems

In the beginning, there was FAT, and it was good. FAT is the system that DOS uses; it's been around for a long time, since the early '80s. FAT stands for File Allocation Table. A file allocation table is basically a table of contents of the disk that the operating system uses to look up the location of a file, even if the file is broken up in pieces (sectors) scattered across the disk's surface. The FAT scheme brought relatively simple, reliable, and efficient floppy and small hard disk storage to the PC. It's also the scheme that, unlike the Macintosh file system, brought the confining 8.3 file-naming convention that many of us learned to live with and hate. For example, myletter.doc is an example of the longest-possible 8.3 filename.

When NT 3.x appeared, it included NTFS as an acknowledgment of the shortcomings of the FAT system, including a hard drive partition size limit of 2 gigabytes (GB). NTFS provided long filenames, more security and fault tolerance, better disk compression, support for hard disks up to 2 terabytes (that's big), and support for advanced multiple-disk arrangements such as striping and mirroring (RAID). Also, as drives become larger, efficiency of disk storage doesn't fall off under NTFS as it does with FAT.

Windows 95 brought long filenames to FAT through some sleight of hand, but still the system was not good at dealing with the newer large drives and wasted a bunch of space on them when it stored tiny files. So, to both provide good backward compatibility with FAT disks and still offer support for large drives, Windows 95 OSR2 and Windows 98 both included a new file system called FAT32. Essentially a beefed up FAT file system, FAT32 isn't as robust as NTFS, and it's not compatible with NTFS. The FAT32 system eliminated the 2GB upper limit on partition size support (it also can run as high as 2TB) and increased effective storage capacity by lowering the cluster size on large drives. NT 4 can't read or work with FAT32, nor can DOS and Windows 3.x. However, both Windows 2000 and Windows XP support FAT32.

NOTE

Clusters are the smallest amount of space that can be used to store information on a hard disk. On smallish drives, the cluster size is also pretty small, so storing dinky files that are only, say, 1KB in size is pretty efficient (there is little wasted space). But on today's huge drives, under the FAT scheme, the cluster would necessarily be much larger (this is a limitation of the FAT system, not the drive). You end up donating serious amounts of space to no good cause. The bottom line is that FAT32 and NTFS get you more bang for your hard disk buck, because lowering the cluster size allows for more efficient use of space, especially on larger drives.

The bottom line? As with Windows NT and Windows 2000, NTFS is the recommended file system for use with Windows XP. NTFS v5 has all the basic capabilities of FAT as well as all the advantages of FAT32 file systems. The weird thing is that now you have to think about three different file systems when considering dual-booting. When you consider that you have at least nine Microsoft operating systems to choose from and three file systems, the combinations get complex. Therefore, understanding the limitations of each is important.

TIP FROM

Bob
& Brian

> You can convert an existing partition to NTFS during setup, but if you want to wait, you can convert it later by using a command-line utility called convert.exe (see "Convert" in Chapter 29). Another approach is to use PartitionMagic, which is discussed later in this chapter.

One of the prime points to remember is that if you're dual-booting, only Windows NT, Windows 2000, and Windows XP systems can read NTFS partitions. If you don't care about accessing the NTFS partition from, say, Windows 98, this is not a big deal. It simply does not appear in Windows Explorer and is not available from your applications. This is the main reason Microsoft doesn't want you to mix file systems; it simply confuses people.

When you're running partitions larger than 32GB, you should really format them as NTFS. If you choose to use FAT, anything over 2GB should be formatted FAT32.

NOTE

> File systems are terribly complex and a subject far beyond what I can cover in a Windows book. For the most part, you don't need to know more than what is presented here, unless you are naturally inclined to learn everything you can about complex topics (don't worry, you are not alone). In that case, I recommend that you pick up a copy of *Upgrading and Repairing PCs, 13th Edition*, by Scott Mueller (also published by Que).

DISK PARTITIONING TIPS

In case you don't know, disk partitioning is a scheme by which you can have a single hard disk look like multiple hard disks to the operating system. If you partition a disk into, say, two partitions, the operating system displays disks C and D rather than just C. You split up the space on the drive between the partitions based on your needs.

One of the most notable needs for disk partitioning was to accommodate operating systems that imposed limitations on the size of partitions. As hard disks grew in size, partitioning was required in order to use the entire disk. Because FAT had a limitation of 2GB, users relied on partitioning or other software driver schemes to get around this imposed top end. Another common reason for partitioning is for running dissimilar operating systems, ones that cannot read from or write to a common file system. Because each partition can have its own disk format, this could often circumambulate such requirements. One partition could be FAT, another NTFS, and another HPFS (for OS/2), and so on. Any hard disk can contain up to four primary partitions.

Only primary partitions can be marked active. An active primary partition is where the computer's BIOS looks for a bootable operating system when powered on. In addition to primary partitions, there are extended partitions. A system can have up to four primary partitions or a maximum of three primary partitions and a single extended partition. The extended partition is a bit different than a primary partition. First, extended partitions cannot be marked active. Second, extended partitions must be divided into logical drives. Only primary partitions and logical drives can be formatted and assigned a drive letter. To total number of primary partitions plus logical drives cannot exceed 32 for a single hard drive.

For examples of these issues, see Figure 3.1. Disk 0 has a single primary partition (C), and an extended partition. The extended partition contains two logical drives (D and G) and 1.86GB of free space. The extended partition is highlighted with a thick border; that's how you distinguish it from primary partitions. This extended partition could contain another 29 logical drives before reaching the 32 division maximum per drive. Disk 1 consists of a single primary partition (F) and 15.11GB of free space. This free space could be used to create up to 3 additional primary partitions, or up to 2 additional primary partitions and an extended partition containing logical drives. Drive 2 consists of a single primary partition (E).

Figure 3.1
Disk Management viewed through Computer Management, showing drive partitioning.

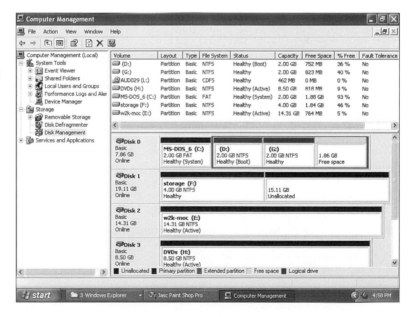

In most cases, you'll rarely need to divide a drive into more than 4 sections. And then, that may only occur when you need to divide a large drive into FAT partitions (because each partition cannot be larger than 2GB). The tools you use to create partitions will manage the division classification for you. If you use FDISK, you'll be a bit more aware of the presence of extended partitions and logical drives. If you use the Windows NT, Windows 2000, or Windows XP drive tools (such as the Disk Management tool) you'll see extended partitions and logical drives labeled, but the OS manages when these need to be created.

Some people use partitions for dividing up their data rather than for accommodating different file systems. You might want a partition to organize information—for example, one for backup data, one for documents and data files, one for applications only, or for the operating system only. Then you can more easily design your backup strategy.

> **NOTE**
>
> When you do a new installation of Windows XP, the Setup program looks around and automatically selects an appropriate disk partition as the destination based on size and format. You can override the choice by clicking the Advanced Options button during Setup, though.

If you're going to dual-boot, you should install on a separate partition. Either create one or use one that is already present. The reason for using a separate partition for each operating system is to prevent Setup from overwriting important files belonging to the other operating system. If you have unpartitioned (different from unused) space on your disk, Setup can create a partition during installation.

If you intend to dual-boot Windows 9x and Windows XP, Windows 9x should be on the first partition. In general computer terms, this means the boot drive. In Windows NT speak, this is the system partition.

→ If you're considering creating a system that is bootable in more than one operating system,
see "Dual-Booting Versus Single Booting," **p. 75**.

The exact options you have during Setup change depending on your existing hard disk configuration. You might have as many as four options when partitioning your hard disk:

- If you have adequate unpartitioned space, you can create a new Windows XP partition in that space and install Windows XP in it.

- If the hard disk is unpartitioned (no partitions at all—freshly formatted) you can create and size the Windows XP partition.

- If the disk does have an existing partition, but you don't care what's in it, Setup lets you delete the partition and create a new one of your chosen format for installing Windows XP. Beware, though; deleting an existing partition destroys *every file* on the partition.

- If the existing partition is large enough, it's actually possible to put Windows XP on it. Contrary to what the Microsoft documentation says, installing on an existing partition doesn't overwrite all data on that partition. If you choose a directory separate from the existing operating system (for example, install into C:\winxp), Setup leaves any existing C:\windows directory alone. But don't forget, the \Program Files and \Documents and Settings folders may be altered by the new OS so that the pre-existing OS can't access the data stored there. Things can get kind of funky with other possible file collisions, too. You can dual-boot, but you might have to reinstall your applications. The better approach is to play it safe and create a new partition to install into.

TIP FROM

Bob & Brian

Don't even try to install Windows XP on a partition that is less than 1GB. Although Windows XP only requires 650MB (only!), I think creating a 2GB partition is more reasonable. If you are upgrading you'll need an extra 300MB to store the recovery files, and Setup won't allow you to start the process with less than 1GB of free space. You'll want (and need) the additional free space later for future additions and modifications to the operating system.

FILE SYSTEM CONVERSION LIMITATIONS

This section lists a few ridiculous warnings and limitations—ridiculous because these steps are not required if you use PartitionMagic. Due to limitations of Setup and Microsoft's supplied disk tools (FDISK, for example), you should be aware of these issues. First, most conversions between file systems are multi-step processes involving backing up and then restoring the partitions after reformatting.

For example, although converting *to* NTFS during installation is easy, if you change your mind and want to revert to FAT, you have to back up all your files on the NTFS partition, reformat the partition as FAT (which erases all the files), and then restore the files from backup. The same is true of converting a FAT partition to FAT32. One workaround is to use the FAT32 converter in Windows 98 or 95 OSR2. Each of these operating systems has a tool that performs such a conversion quite easily.

Second, you can't restore an NTFS v4 (file system from NT 4) partition after you convert it to NTFS v5 (file system from Windows XP, Windows 2000, and Windows NT 4.0 SP4+). There's no easy way out on that score. There is support for NTFS v5 file formats via tools like PartitionMagic to do this, though.

GETTING YOUR NETWORK INFORMATION TOGETHER

As part of the installation procedure, you are asked details about your network connection (assuming you're going to run the computer in question on a local area network; if it's not, just skip over this part).

You must supply the following information:

- Is the computer going to join a domain or a workgroup? You can answer Workgroup if you don't know and later change to a domain. Ask someone who knows. If you select the Domain option, you'll have to ask your network administrator to create a new *computer account* to allow you to join that domain or to edit your existing account to reflect the new computer name.

→ To learn more information about networking settings, **see** "Setting Your Computer Identification," **p. 531**, and "Adding Network Clients, Services, and Protocols," **p. 523**.

N O T E

> A computer account is a specific type of account that a Windows NT, Windows 2000 Server, or .NET Server administrator makes to allow a given computer to join the domain. In a domain, both computers and users have accounts on the server. A domain client is a system that is a member of a centrally controlled and secured network environment.

- Are you already part of a network? If so, collect the following information, scribble it down on a piece of paper, and keep the paper handy:

Name of your computer

Name of the workgroup or domain

IP address (if your network doesn't have a DHCP server)

It's Backup Time!

Okay, so you're ready to do the installation. Need I say it? If you're upgrading from a previous version, Setup is supposed to let you back out and restore your system to its previous state if you panic in the middle. I've actually backed out of Setup a few times successfully, but that doesn't mean it will always work. Setup does lots of stuff to your operating system and hard disk files, and particularly if it bombs halfway through the process, things could get sticky. So ask yourself, "Do I have important data on my computer?" If so, back it up before you start your installation. Can you afford the downtime incurred should you need to reinstall your applications and operating system? If not, back them up, too.

Windows XP does bring a new feature to the table when you are upgrading from Windows 9x/SE/Me. This new feature is the ability to uninstall Windows XP and return to the previous OS. During the initial stages of the upgrade installation, a complete backup of the existing 9x OS is created (about 300MB of stuff). This backup is performed automatically to protect users. There are advanced command-line startup options that can be used to disable this activity, but if you are smart enough to figure out how to do that, you are smart enough to make your own backup. Plus, this backup feature not only allows you to roll back but it protects you during installation. If the upgrade install fails, the system will return to the previous OS automatically. After about 60 days or so, you will be prompted whether to retain or delete this backup archive of the previous OS. This backup procedure consumes about 300MB of space, so if your destination partition does not have around 1GB of free space the Setup routine will terminate before even getting started. This backup protection is only used for Windows 9x/SE/Me; it is not available for upgrades from Windows NT or Windows 2000.

Backing Up to a Disk Image

One technique I like for doing serious backups is to make a disk image of my main hard drive. With a disk image, if the drive dies or I have some other catastrophe, such as a new operating system installation going south, I can just restore the drive to its previous state, boot tracks, operating system, data, and applications, all in one fell swoop. I use a program called DriveImage from PowerQuest for this task, though some people swear by a competing product called Norton Ghost. Either one is a powerful tool for making backups and recovering from a dead operating system. These programs work by copying your hard disk sector by sector and storing the whole image in a single huge file on another drive. The large file they create contains all the necessary information to replace the data in the original tracks and sectors.

If you have a CD-writer, you can use a CD-R as the backup medium. If you have a CD-RW drive, it can provide a very cost efficient (though slow) means of backing up and restoring. It also works with a second hard disk in the computer, a second partition on a hard disk, and removable media such as Zip or Jaz drives. Another approach is to store an image on a hard disk across the LAN on another workstation, though recovering from the remote station is a little more complex than from a local drive.

3

If you must back up data only and don't care about reinstalling your applications or operating system (this backup approach is easier, of course), you can use some backup program or you can simply copy the files onto other drives using Windows Explorer or some other utility. How you back up your files depends on your current operating system. If you're running Windows 9x/SE/Me/NT/2000, one obvious approach is to employ the Windows Backup program (by choosing Start, Programs, Accessories, System Tools, Backup). You might have to install it if it's not there. To do so, open the Control Panel, choose Add/Remove Programs, and then select Windows Setup. Remember, in Windows NT, you need a tape drive installed for the Backup tool to work. All other Windows versions of Backup can store the backup files to any writable media. If you're in doubt about the use of the Backup program, check the Windows Help system.

→ To learn more details about backup strategies, **see** "Backup Tools and Strategies," **p. 1023**.

Okay, enough for the safety speech. You are old enough to know whether you put on your parachute before you jump out of the plane.

CLEAN INSTALLATION PROCEDURE

The three basic types of clean installation procedures are as follows:

- Install on a brand new disk or computer system
- Erase the disk, format it, and install
- Install into a new directory for dual-booting (see the multi-boot discussion earlier in this chapter)

If you intend to use either of the first two methods, make sure you are equipped to boot your computer from the CD-ROM. Most of today's breeds of computers support booting from the CD-ROM drive. Doing so might require changing the drive boot order in the BIOS or CMOS, but try it first without. With no floppy disk inserted and a clean hard disk, the CD-ROM drive should be tried next. The Windows XP CD-ROM is bootable and should run the Setup program automatically.

The Windows XP setup procedure can also be launched using the five setup boot floppies. On an older computer, you might have to ensure you can boot into DOS from a floppy. People preparing to set up Windows on older computers often overlook this point. They wipe the hard disk and then boot up with a floppy only to find the CD-ROM drive isn't recognized, so they can't run the Setup program on the CD. If you have the boot floppy for Windows XP, your CD-ROM drive will mostly likely be recognized upon booting, assuming your CD-ROM drive is among those supported. If you have misplaced your floppies or they were not included with your Windows XP CD, check out the "Making Replacement Startup Floppies" section later this chapter.

 If you can't get DOS to recognize your CD-ROM drive, see "My Existing OS Won't Recognize the CD-ROM Drive" in the "Troubleshooting" section at the end of this chapter.

NOTE

> Remember to check Chapter 2, "Getting Your Hardware and Software Ready for Windows XP Professional," to ensure that your hardware components meet the minimum requirements to run Windows XP.

Installation takes 60–90 minutes depending on the speed of your machine. Refer to the following sections if you have questions about the steps of the process. The process is fairly similar for each category of installation, with the addition of the software compatibility report when you're upgrading from an older operating system.

TYPICAL CLEAN SETUP PROCEDURE

If you're installing into an empty partition, and you can boot an operating system that is supported for the purpose of Setup (Windows 9x/SE/Me/NT/2000), just boot up, insert the CD, and choose Install Windows XP from the resulting dialog box. Then, you can follow the installation step-by-step procedure below.

If Windows doesn't automatically detect the CD when you insert it, you must run the Setup program, setup.exe, manually from the Start, Run dialog box. Once the Setup routine has started, you can follow the installation step-by-step procedure below.

Another method of kick-starting the installation of Windows XP can be performed from any OS which has access to the CD. If the OS is a non-Windows non-32-bit OS, then execute \i386\winnt.exe. If the existing OS is a 32-bit Windows OS, then execute \i386\winnt32.exe. If you are able to use the winnt32 launch tool, you can follow the typical installation step-by-step procedure below.

If your computer has a blank hard disk, or your current operating system isn't supported, the process is different. You will need to start the installation by using Setup floppy disks or by booting from the Windows XP CD (this approach works only if your computer is newer, and you can boot from the CD-ROM drive). Setup automatically runs if you boot from the CD-ROM.

→ If you need to create Setup floppy disks, see the "Making Startup Floppies" section later in this chapter.

Yet another setup initiation method involves the network. To initiate a network installation, you must have a network share of the distribution CD or a copy of the CD on a hard drive. The destination system must have network access and the user account must have at least read access to the installation files. Setup is initiated by executing winnt or winnt32 from the network share (the same 16-bit and 32-bit rules apply). For example, from the Start, Run command type a path of \\<servername>\<sharename>\i386\winnt. Setup will recognize an over-the-network installation and will automatically copy all files from the network share to the local system before the first reboot.

If you used the winnt launch tool, used the boot floppies to initiate setup, or were able to start from a bootable CD your installation varies from the typical installation step-by-step procedure as follows:

1. A text-only step wizard is launched.
2. Verify that the displayed path is the correct location of the Windows XP source files. Press Enter.
3. Setup copies numerous files to the hard drive of the computer; this may take a few minutes. Once complete, the system reboots.
4. Once the system reboots, the Setup Wizard continues.
5. Jump to step 15 of the following typical installation step-by-step procedure to continue.

The typical clean installation step-by-step procedure is as follows:

1. The Windows Setup Wizard appears. Using the Installation Type pull-down list, select New Installation. (Note: Upgrading is discussed later in this chapter).
2. Click Next. The License Agreement page appears.

NOTE

> Corporate attorneys know that people don't read these software agreements. I've even heard reports of software in which the agreements make you promise not to write a review of the software without alerting the manufacturer first. I'm sure some interesting, precedent-setting cases will occur in upcoming years.

3. Read the agreement then select the "I accept this agreement" radio button.

4. Click Next. The Your Product Key page appears.

5. Type in your 25-digit Product Key.

6. Click Next. The Setup Options page appears.

7. Click the Advanced Options button.

8. Verify that the path for the location of the source files is correct (it should be <cd-rom drive letter>:\i386, or if you are installing over a network this would be \\<servername>\<sharename>\i386).

9. If you wish, change the name of the main Windows directory.

10. To force Setup to duplicate all necessary files to the hard drive before initiating the installation procedure, mark the Copy all installation files from the Setup CD check box.

NOTE

> Copying all the Setup files to the hard disk has two advantages. First, you can save yourself some time because the file copying and decompressing process is faster from the hard disk than from a CD-ROM drive. Second, the next time Windows XP needs access to Setup files (when you add new hardware, for example), you won't have to insert the CD-ROM. Just browse to the correct directory. Copying the more than 6,000 files (yes, that's thousand, amounting to about 450MB) from the CD takes about 15 minutes on a reasonably fast system.

11. To be able to select the partition to install Windows XP into (that is, other than drive C), mark the I want to choose the install drive letter and partition during Setup checkbox.

12. Click OK. Click Next. The Performing Dynamic Update page appears.

13. If your system has Internet access on the pre-existing OS, you can optionally select to download the latest setup files for Windows XP at this time. Mark the Yes radio button. If your system does not currently have Internet access, select No, click Next, and then skip to step 15.

14. Click Next. The setup routine attempts to contact the Microsoft download site and retrieve any new Setup files. Once this is completed, the setup routine reboots the system automatically.

15. Once the system reboots, the Welcome to Setup text-only screen prompts you to install Windows XP, repair an existing installation, or exit Setup. Press Enter to continue with setup.

16. Your drives will be examined and the partition manager is displayed. This tool is used to select the installation partition for Windows XP. If the partition already exists, use the arrow keys to select it, then skip to step 25.

TIP FROM

Bob & Brian

If you want to install Windows XP into a separate partition, make sure the partition is preexisting or that you have some unpartitioned space on your hard drive. Sorry to state the obvious, but Setup doesn't let you change the *size* of existing partitions on-the-fly, even though it does convert from FAT to NTFS and does create NTFS partitions from an unpartitioned space.

If you have a large hard disk all in one partition (typical with today's cheap drives as they come from the factory) and want to split it, use a utility program such as FDISK, NT's Disk Administrator tool, 2000's Computer Management tool, or PartitionMagic (I highly recommend PartitionMagic). If you want to install into an NTFS partition, remember that FDISK can't create NTFS partitions. As a workaround, you either have to convert the target partition to NTFS during or after Setup or use a utility such as PartitionMagic that can make or convert FAT partitions to NTFS. Note that the NTFS partition does not have to be formatted in advance of your running Setup; as long as it exists as a partition, Setup will offer to format it for you.

The main advantage of having multiple partitions on a hard disk these days is to support different file system formats. You can use FAT or FAT32 on one partition to run DOS or Windows 9x, for example, and use an NTFS partition for Windows XP.

TIP FROM

Bob & Brian

FDISK is often the tool of choice for ex-DOS users when managing drive partitions. This tool works great as long as you are working with all primary partitions or only FAT, FAT32, and OS/2's HPFS. FDISK is not even able to recognize NTFS-formatted extended partitions. So, if you need to delete such a partition, you either need to have access to a Windows NT, Windows 2000, or Windows XP OS on the same system as the hard drive in question, and boot into the setup routines of one of these three OSes to use the text-based partition configuration tool, or use a third party tool. I've already mentioned PartitionMagic, but there is another tool you may want to look at: DELPART. DELPART is a DOS based tool from Windows NT 3.51; you can find it floating around the Internet with a quick search on "delpart". This tool can delete any and all partitions on a hard drive, thus making way for easy re-partitioning and new OS installation. This is a tool I always keep handy.

3

17. If an existing partition must be deleted to create unpartitioned space where you want to install Windows XP, go on to step 18. Otherwise, skip to step 21.

18. Use the arrow keys to select the partition to delete, then press D.

19. If the selected partition is a system partition, you must press Enter to confirm the deletion of a system partition.

20. Press L to confirm deletion of the partition. (Yes, this is a valid extra step to make sure you are aware that you are deleting a partition.)

21. To create a new partition out of unpartitioned space, use the arrow keys to select the unpartitioned space, then press C.

22. Type in the size of the partition you wish to create out of the unpartitioned space. The default size listed is the maximum size that can be created. Once you have typed in a number, press Enter.

23. Use the arrow keys to select the newly created partition.

24. Press Enter to install Windows XP into the selected partition.

25. Select the file system to format the partition. If the partition is already properly formatted with NTFS v5, another option of "Leave the current file system intact (no changes)" is available. If this option is available, select it and press Enter. Then skip to step 28.

26. Use the arrow keys to select the NTFS file system (not the one with (Quick) next to it).

NOTE

> By the way, the Quick options for both NTFS and FAT are only there when you are converting or over-formatting a partition which already has been formatted. It's a way to save time, especially if you are formatting a 2GB or larger drive. I recommend staying away from the Quick format and letting the Setup Wizard perform a full format on the destination partition. It will take a little longer, but it will ensure a properly formatted drive.

→ If you want to know more information about deciding whether you should change file systems, **see** "Choosing a File System: FAT, FAT32, or NTFS?" **p. 80**. Also, Chapters 29 and 31 contain additional information about file systems and formats.

27. Press Enter to initiate formatting. The progress of the formatting action is displayed.

28. When formatting is complete, files are copied to the destination partition. This can take 10 minutes.

29. When the file copy procedure completes, the system automatically reboots.

30. After it's rebooted, Setup launches a basic Windows GUI environment. After performing numerous operations (this could take about 10 minutes or more), the Setup Wizard appears displaying the Regional and Language Options page. The defaults are for English and a US keyboard; if you require other settings click on the Customize or Details buttons to change them.

If the Windows installer crashes during the installation, see "Windows Crashes During Installation" in the "Troubleshooting" section at the end of this chapter.

31. Click Next. The Personalize Your Software page appears.

32. Type in your name and a company name if appropriate.

33. Click Next. The Computer Name and Administrator Password page appears.

34. Type in a meaningful computer name for this system in the Computer name field, such as `wxp-181`. WXP-181 in my naming convention tells me that the system is running Windows XP and has an IP address of 172.16.1.181. All of the systems on my network use the same first three values in the four part IP address.

> **NOTE**
>
> Choose a computer name that is unique. It must differ from any other computer, workgroup, or domain names on the network. You'll probably want to enter your name or a name of your own choosing, though Setup supplies some cryptic name for you. You might want to coordinate naming your computer with your LAN administrator, if you have one.

35. Type in and confirm a password for the administrator account.

> **CAUTION**
>
> You definitely should assign a password for the administrator account. If you leave this field blank, anyone can get into the system settings by just entering Administrator as the username and pressing Enter with no password.
>
> An Administrator account is set up automatically during each installation, just as in NT/2000. The Administrator account is assigned full rights, allowing the administrator to create user passwords, set up new accounts, and mess with all the computer's settings as a manager. When you specify a password for the administrator, enter it, write it down somewhere safe, and remember it!

36. Click Next. If you have a modem present on your system, the Modem Dialing Information page appears. Type in your area code, and then click Next.

37. The Date and Time Settings page appears. Set the date and time and select a time zone.

38. Click Next. If a network interface is detected, the system installs networking components, and then the Networking Settings page appears. If no network interface is installed in your system, skip to step 46.

39. If you are connected to a Microsoft network which uses DHCP to assign TCP/IP address configuration settings for clients, select the Typical settings radio button, click Next, and then skip to step 46. DHCP or Dynamic Host Configuration Protocol is a networking service operating from a Windows Server system which can provide clients with IP configuration upon bootup.

40. If you are connected to a network of any other configuration, select the Custom settings radio button, and then click Next.

N O T E

> Select the Custom settings option if you want to manually configure network clients, services, and protocols. But do so only if you're an expert in these matters and know that the typical settings won't cut it. You'll probably be fine with the default settings, and you can change them later if not.

41. The Networking Components page appears. To alter the TCP/IP settings on this system, click to select the Internet Protocol (TCP/IP) item from the list of components, and then click the Properties button.

42. The Internet Protocol (TCP/IP) Properties dialog box appears. Select the Use the Following IP Address radio button. Fill in the IP address, subnet mask, and default gateway (if available).

43. If you need to use DNS, select the Use the Following DNS Server Addresses radio button and fill in the IP addresses of one or two DNS servers.

44. Click OK. You are returned to the Networking Components page.

45. Click Next. The Workgroup or Computer Domain page appears.

N O T E

> During Setup, you must join either a workgroup or a domain. If your system is a stand-alone system, you must join a workgroup. If your system is the first or only system within a workgroup, providing a name in the field on the Workgroup or Computer Domain page will create the workgroup. Being a member of a workgroup offers you nothing as a standalone system, but it is still a requirement of setup.
>
> A workgroup is a more casual collection of connected computers than is a domain. Any computer can join a workgroup. To join a workgroup on the LAN, you just supply the workgroup name. All computers set for the same workgroup name can share files, printers, and other resources. The Setup program suggests a name, but if you already have a workgroup in your office, use that name.
>
> A domain is a collection of computers that an administrator creates. Domains offer more security and control than workgroups do. Ask your system administrator if you don't know the domain settings. He or she has to create a computer account for you before you can join the domain. If you're upgrading from Windows NT, your existing computer account is used to identify you. If you have the right privileges already, you can create the account during the Setup process, but you have to enter the username and password that match the entry in the domain controller (server) for the preexisting account. A wizard for Network Identification will walk you through joining a domain. If you run into trouble joining a domain (the network server doesn't allow it), join a workgroup first, and join the domain later.

46. If this system is not on a network or is a member of a non-domain network, select the No radio button and provide a name of a workgroup. The default name of Workgroup is often sufficient.

47. If this system is to be a member of a domain, select the Yes radio button and provide the name of the domain.

48. Click Next.

49. If you selected to join a domain, you will be prompted for the name and password of an administrator level account within the domain. Provide this information and click OK.

50. Setup will proceed with installing the OS using the settings you've just provided. This may take 20 minutes or more.

51. If any issues or problems were encountered during the installation, a pop-up dialog box appears. If you want to view the log file of errors now click Yes. If not, click No. You can always view this information by reading the setuperr.log file later with any text editor, such as Notepad or WordPad.

52. At this point, the Setup process is complete and the system needs to be rebooted. This may occur automatically or you may be prompted to confirm the reboot.

53. Window XP is booted, but there are still several steps remaining before you can gain access.

54. The Welcome to Microsoft Windows XP screen appears, accompanied by an animated wizard. You must wait until it is through "talking" to you. Then, click Next.

55. Setup checks your system for Internet connectivity. No matter what Setup determines, you must indicate whether the system gains Internet access through a local network (the Yes radio button) or must establish a dial-up connection (the No radio button). I assume you have a cable modem or a connection over a network, so select Yes.

56. Click Next. The Ready to activate Windows screen appears.

57. Unless you have a specific reason not to, select the Yes, Activate Windows Over the Internet Now radio button.

> **NOTE**
>
> In an effort to curb software piracy, Microsoft has implemented a new scheme to prevent unauthorized installations of Windows XP. After installing Windows XP, you must activate it within 30 days. When you activate Windows XP, your product key is filed into a database along with hardware identifiers from your computer. Activation prevents the same product key from being used numerous times. Microsoft claims the hardware identifiers cannot be used to trace a specific computer and that the activation process is fully anonymous. If you fail to activate within the time limit, the system fails to function until activation is completed.
>
> Activation can occur over the telephone if you do not have an Internet connection. The phone numbers to call are listed on the activation screen and in the readme file on the distribution CD.
>
> If you choose to skip activation during setup, an activation command is added to the top of the All Programs list within the Start menu.

58. Click Next. The Ready to register with Microsoft screen appears.

59. Unless you want to offer private information to Microsoft, select the No, Not At This Time radio button.

> **NOTE**
>
> Registration is a separate and distinct process from activation. Activation is mandatory for a functioning OS past the 30-day grace period. Registration is voluntary. You should register if you want to get junk snail mail and e-mail from Microsoft, because Microsoft uses this information to focus product marketing.

60. Click Next. The Will you be sharing this computer with other users screen appears.

61. If you want to maintain unique user accounts for each person who will use this system, select Yes. If you select no, Windows XP is configured to log in automatically with the administrator account each time the computer boots. If you select No, skip to step 64.

> **NOTE**
>
> Selecting not to create unique user accounts for each person does not mean you cannot switch to this in the future. However, if you select No, you must initially log in to the system with the Administrator account. Once you've logged on, you can create other local user accounts or configure the system to log on to a domain and use domain user accounts. Network logon is discussed in Part IV. See Chapter 28 for details on creating user accounts.

62. Click Next. The Who will use this computer? screen appears.

63. Type in the names of up to six users for this system, one in each field.

64. Click Next. The Thank you! page appears; click Finish.

65. The Windows XP Welcome screen appears with the names of the user accounts created in step 63 listed in a column on the right ready for logon. If you selected No in step 61, you'll be automatically logged on as the administrator and presented the Windows XP desktop.

The final step necessary to complete the installation of Windows XP is to log in. If you don't already know how to log in to Windows XP, jump over to Chapter 4 and check out the "Logging into Windows XP" section.

 If Windows refuses to boot after the installation is complete, see "Windows XP Fails to Boot After Installation" in the "Troubleshooting" section at the end of this chapter.

UPGRADING OVER AN EXISTING OPERATING SYSTEM

If you're upgrading rather than performing a clean installation, the process is a bit different. Setup checks on the advisability of upgrading and asks a few more questions. This section provides a few points concerning the upgrade or dual-boot with preexisting operating systems. The steps included here are for upgrading over Windows 98 SE. Similar steps apply to the other operating systems.

CAUTION

> Let me add an additional note about network connections when you're upgrading. If you're upgrading a Windows 9x/SE/Me/NT/2000 system that's a member of a Windows NT or Windows 2000 domain, you must check a few things in advance, or you'll end up wasting some time. Ideally, you should make sure the Windows 9x machine is connected to the domain and working properly because the user profile for the upgraded workstation needs to be stored on the domain controller.
>
> If the domain isn't available during setup, the user's preferences are placed in a local user account on the workstation computer, and you have to copy the profile to the domain profile after joining the domain. So, to avoid that situation, follow these steps:
>
> 1. Ensure that the computer's workgroup is set to the domain you participate in by choosing Start, Settings, Control Panel, Network (on Windows 9x/SE/Me systems). Then select the Identification tab, and verify the workgroup.
> 2. Create a computer account on the domain server if it doesn't exist already. The computer must have access to the domain during setup.
> 3. Upgrade the system to Windows XP.
>
> If you don't follow these steps, you'll have to copy the profile to the domain later. To do so, choose Control Panel, System, User Profiles, Copy.

3

To begin the upgrade process, follow these steps:

1. Start the Setup program as discussed in the clean install section. The Windows Setup Wizard appears. Using the Installation Type pull-down list, select Upgrade.
2. Click Next. The License Agreement page appears.
3. Read the agreement then select the I accept this agreement radio button.
4. Click Next. The Your Product Key page appears.
5. Type in your 25-digit Product Key.
6. Click Next. The Performing Dynamic Update page appears.
7. If your system has Internet access from the pre-existing OS, you can optionally select to download the latest setup files for Windows XP at this time. Mark the Yes radio button. If your system does not currently have Internet access, select No, click Next, and then skip to step 9.
8. Click Next. The Setup routine will attempt to contact the Microsoft download site and retrieve new Setup files.
9. The Provide Compatible Names page may appear. If you have local names which conflict with existing network names, you'll be prompted to change them. This dialog box automatically provides alternative names by adding a dash and a number to the end of the duplicate. Click Next to accept the suggested changes. You can alter a name change by selecting it in the list and clicking the Change button.
10. The Network Connection Status page appears. Select the appropriate radio button that matches the network connectivity of this system. The options are: This computer is

offline; It connects directly to a local area network; and It connects to a remote network through a modem or other connection. The default selection represents the status that setup detected from your existing OS. I assume you have direct LAN connection (the middle radio button), select it, then click Next. If your system is offline or connected through a modem or some other connection, you might see other setup wizard screens prompting for related configuration details.

11. The Join a Domain page appears. If the current OS is a member of a domain, the default setting of this page will be Yes, Use This Domain with the name of the domain in the text field. If no domain is used by the existing OS, the No, Skip This Step option is selected. You can change the default on this page and even define a different domain to join. I assume you will accept the default of the same domain as the current OS. Click Next.

12. If a computer account is not already present in the domain for the new OS, Setup prompts you whether to create an account. Click Yes. You must provide the username and password of an Administrative level user account in the domain, and then click OK. You'll need to confirm that the provided user account has permissions to create new computer accounts in the domain; click Yes.

13. Setup prepares the Upgrade Report.

UPGRADE REPORT

After you supply your product key, Setup creates an upgrade report summarizing everything that might not work with Windows XP and giving you a chance to access update files that hardware or software vendors might have available (check their Web sites). If you don't have upgrade files for the listed items, you might skate by anyway.

The upgrade report is a pretty spiffy HTML-based dialog box that details what might not work anymore if you go ahead with the installation. It has a link to the Windows XP Hardware Compatibility List (HCL) for easily checking to see whether the Brand X video card you just bought really won't work or if the compatibility test was just out of date. Do check the list, assuming your computer is on the Internet.

Although your list might be long, it might not be catastrophic news. Most of the stuff my systems showed didn't end up causing problems. For example, I know that the video card I have is supported, as is the Epson printer. Both were listed as potentially problematic. Most of the other things such as shares, Recycle Bin, backup files, and DOS startup file issues were no big deal. The new operating system takes care of most of these issues, mostly due to Plug and Play and good hardware detection during Setup. Plus, I probably did have some old junk in my AUTOEXEC.BAT and CONFIG.SYS files that's no longer valuable. The DOS exceptions were Sound Blaster drivers that DOS-based games used—the kinds of things that most Windows XP users are not going to worry about.

If you see anything listed about your video card, disk controller, sound card, or tape backup, you might want to check on those items a little more closely and download a driver update pack from the manufacturer before you update. Basically, you should take seriously anything that might suggest incompatibility that will prevent basic operation or bootability of the system, and you can acknowledge but not sweat the rest.

TIP FROM

> If you just want to run the upgrade report and not execute the complete Setup program, insert the installation CD in the CD-ROM drive, or connect over the LAN to the CD. If the Welcome to Microsoft Windows XP splash screen appears, click Check System Compatibility, and then Check My System Automatically. Follow the wizard's prompts to perform an upgrade or XP compatibility test. If the splash screen does not appear or you are working from DOS, issue the following command:
>
> ```
> winnt32 /checkupgradeonly
> ```
>
> This command generates just the report.

You can just follow the rest of the instructions as they come up on the screen. Your computer might have to restart several times in the process. If the computer seems to be stuck, wait several minutes to ensure it's really stopped functioning properly. Then reboot it. Windows XP uses an "intelligent" Setup feature that should restart where it left off. Eventually, after much spinning of the hard disks, the system will boot up into Windows XP. But before you are granted access to the new system, there are still the issues of activation, registration, and user accounts to deal with. Jump to step 54 in the typical clean installation step-by-step (earlier in this chapter), to complete the installation procedure.

If Windows refuses to boot after the installation is complete, see "Windows XP Fails to Boot After Installation" in the "Troubleshooting" section at the end of this chapter.

MAKING STARTUP FLOPPIES

Windows XP Setup can be launched from floppy disks but not by default. Unlike Windows 2000, the Setup CD-ROM does not contain the utility program needed to create setup floppy disks. You can download the utility, makeboot.exe, from the Microsoft Web site at `http://support.microsoft.com/default.aspx?scid=kb;EN-US;q310994`.

After you've downloaded the appropriate file for your version and language of Windows XP, simply double-click it to begin the diskette creation process. You will need to have six 3 1/2 inch empty, formatted floppy disks ready. You might want to label the first disk Windows XP Setup Boot Disk and the remaining disks Windows XP Setup Disk #2 through #6.

Once you have created your Windows XP Setup disks, you can use them to perform a clean installation of Windows XP only; you cannot use them for performing upgrade installations. The setup disks will load the drivers required to allow you to gain access to your non-bootable CD-ROM so that you can commence the installation of Windows XP.

TROUBLESHOOTING

Windows XP and the setup process itself are very resilient. I've performed dozens of installations while writing this book and I've yet to have a failed install. In general, as each new generation of Microsoft OS hits the streets, there are fewer installation problems. I remember the days of installing Windows NT 4.0, which had problems more often than not. I probably spent upwards of two days on a single system once just to get the main OS installed! Anyway, just because it is much improved over previous OSes doesn't mean that the Windows XP installation procedure can't experience problems when you perform the install. There are several common causes of problems and several common problems. In the next sections I tackle each of these and provide you with realistic solutions.

WINDOWS CRASHES DURING INSTALLATION

I tried to install Windows XP, but it crashes while installing.

The trick with any Windows Setup is to get it to complete without crashing or freaking out about some setting you try to make during the process. Hold off doing anything fancy—stuff like network settings, screen savers, video display settings, and so on—until well after you have finished the installation. Just get through the installation as simply as possible, and then poke around and tweak up your settings later.

→ To learn more details about recovering a trashed installation of Windows XP, **see** "The Recovery Console," **p. 1157**.

Windows Setup is intelligent. It keeps tabs on where in the process things stalled. Simply restarting Setup should result in it picking up where it left off. This, at least, is some consolation. Next time around, keep it simple, and get by with as few settings as possible. Just make the necessary ones. Sometimes a machine will hang when you're playing with the Regional settings, language, or something you can easily change later. Also, avoid the Advanced settings if you don't need them.

At a certain stage, Setup switches from character-based screens to graphical screens (GUI mode). If, at this point, Setup crashes, your video display card might not be compatible with Windows XP. Make sure you checked your system's innards against the Hardware Compatibility List. Also, ensure that you meet the minimum requirements in terms of RAM and hard disk space. Most of the causes of installation problems are directly related to non-HCL compliant hardware.

MY EXISTING OS WON'T RECOGNIZE THE CD-ROM DRIVE

I can't get my existing OS to recognize my CD-ROM drive, so I can't install Windows XP.

The following are a few other workarounds for those weird occasions when you just can't get DOS to recognize your CD-ROM drive:

■ Create the Setup floppy disks needed to start the installation. See the section "Making Startup Floppies," earlier in this chapter.

- Create an Emergency Startup Disk (ESD) from Windows 98. As of Windows 98, popular CD-ROM drivers are dumped on the ESDs when you create them by choosing Control Panel, Add/Remove Programs, Startup Disk.

- Use an old DOS startup disk with installable device drivers for the CD-ROM drive on it as stipulated in the AUTOEXEC.BAT and CONFIG.SYS files on the floppy. Creating such a disk typically takes a little knowledge of MSCDEX command-line arguments, and you need the driver supplied with the CD-ROM drive.

- Using your existing operating system or a floppy disk with network client software on it, connect to the network and run Setup from a remote CD-ROM drive. This process can take some work if you have to boot in DOS, however. You must know lots of network settings and use the command line to get them going. Your network administrator might have to tell you the exact path of the setup command. You're looking for the file winnt.exe or winnt32.exe from the i386 directory of the distribution files.

- Another solution is to copy all the appropriate CD-ROM files to your hard disk one way or another (even lap-linking between two computers is an approach I've used successfully). You need all the files in the root directory of the CD and everything in the I386 folder. When files are on the hard disk, switch to the folder you stored the file in, and run winnt.exe or winnt32.exe.

WINDOWS XP FAILS TO BOOT AFTER INSTALLATION

I got through the installation, but Windows XP won't boot now.

You can take several steps when an installation doesn't seem to have worked out. As I mentioned in the first troubleshooting tip, you can try to determine when Setup failed. If, by observation, you can determine the point at which it failed, you might be able to avoid whatever it was you did the first time around. Restart Setup, and see whether reinstalling will help.

While you're installing again, note that Setup asks whether you want to load any SCSI drivers at a certain point. At about this point, you can opt not to install support for power management. Try opting out of the power management. You can install it later by choosing Control Panel, Add New Hardware. Sometimes power management can cause problems on a machine that doesn't support it correctly, or doesn't support it at all.

TIPS FROM THE WINDOWS PROS: AUTOMATING SETUP

If you intend to install Windows XP on a bevy of computers, answering all of its installation questions repeatedly can prove an exercise in inefficiency. Instead, you can create a special script to automate the process. The Setup Manager Wizard helps you design the script, or you can base yours on the example supplied on the Windows XP CD.

The script you create is called an *answer file*, and it is used to install Windows XP in so-called *unattended mode*. In this mode, nobody needs to interact with the computer during installation. The script simply supplies the answers that you would normally have to enter from the keyboard, such as acceptance of the license agreement, workgroup and computer name, network details, and so on. The script can fully automate or only partially automate the Setup process. For example, you might want to supply defaults for the user but let him or her change them. A script can additionally stipulate the creation of special folders, execution of programs upon completion of Setup, location of Setup files, and more.

Of course, creating answer files makes sense only when you're installing Windows XP on multiple computers with a hardware complement that you know will install Windows XP properly; otherwise, you can waste even more time trying to troubleshoot what happened in your absence that caused a failed or broken installation. As you know, sometimes unexpected developments occur during Setup that might require intervention. The Setup routine is fairly successful at detecting hardware when doing installations, so it's worth a try if you're deploying a large number of machines. In most cases, the time spent creating an answer file for automated unattended setup will become cost effective when you must install three or more systems.

Performing unattended setups is a fairly advanced topic. I would need to devote several chapters to it in order to give it reasonable coverage. Instead of listing step-by-step information here, I prefer to point you to the best reference available on the subject—namely Microsoft itself. The Windows XP Resource Kit has complete and exhaustive information about automating installation. Plus, if you check out the text, html, and Word doc files on the distribution CD (don't forget to check the support subdirectory), you'll find a fairly useful description there too.

In addition to the script-based answer file method of installation automation, there is another type of automated install for Windows XP. IntelliMirror for Windows XP (available on the Windows XP Server product) has a tool called RIS or Remote Installation Services. This is a nifty tool that can create clones of existing systems or create new systems from the original distribution files. Clients are installed over the network. The clients are booted using a special NIC or a RIS boot disk. The system image is pushed to the client over the network. The whole process of RIS can be automated so no human interaction is required between powering on the client and logging in after the install completes. RIS is another level of complexity beyond the answer file installation method. Deployment of RIS usually becomes cost effective for 30 or so systems. Complete details about RIS and installing Windows XP is found in the Windows XP and Windows 2003 Server Resource Kits.

PART II

GETTING YOUR WORK DONE

CHAPTER 4

USING THE WINDOWS XP INTERFACE

In this chapter

WHO SHOULD READ THIS CHAPTER?

Before going on in this book, make sure you've read the introduction and installed Windows XP correctly onto your computer (installation is explained in Chapter 3, "Installing Windows XP Professional"). When those hurdles are completed, return here to learn about the user interface. Many might wonder why an advanced book such as this would include coverage of something as basic as the user interface. This is a decision that was primarily driven by the knowledge that many users of Windows XP Professional will be upgrading from Windows 9x, NT, and even 2000. For those users, savvy as they may be with Windows concepts, the Windows XP interface is different enough that they'll need a roadmap to get started. Once you are familiar with it, you'll wonder how you ever got around in those old clunky environments. In addition to just the new look of Windows XP, many new functions are woven into the fabric of the new user interface (UI). We don't want you to miss out on them! We've also included some UI tips and tricks you might not have known about. So even if you consider yourself a Windows veteran, at least take the time to skim through this chapter before you move on.

NOTE

> Upgrading may not be just for the fun of it. Microsoft stopped offering support for MS-DOS, Windows 1.0-3.x, Windows for Workgroups, and Windows 95 on December 31, 2001. Support for Windows 98 (OSR2, and SE), Me, and Windows NT 4 Workstation will be dropped on June 30, 2003. When Microsoft says it will be dropping support, that means the Microsoft technical support system will not respond to calls or e-mail with questions regarding these operating systems. So, upgrade or be left in the dust.

Don't just take our word for it. Experiment with the new UI as you read this chapter. We've found that nothing can substitute for direct hands-on operation to get an understanding and a feel for the new user environment. Most of the information in this chapter is not of a level or type that may damage your system, but whenever caution is needed we'll be sure to spell it out clearly.

We won't be able to cover everything about the new environment in this chapter, but we do a good job of covering the important aspects and those of interest to most readers. If you run across a button or command that you don't recognize, don't be afraid to explore the Windows Help service for details and instructions. The XP Help system is much improved over its predecessors and actually includes meaningful content.

→ For those looking for ways to tweak and customize the new GUI, take a look at Chapter 23, "Tweaking the GUI," **p. 773**.

If at any time you desire to put this book down and walk away from your system, jump to the "Exiting Windows Gracefully" section near the end of this chapter to find out how to log off with aplomb.

LOGGING IN TO WINDOWS XP

At this point, you should have Windows XP Professional installed. But before you explore the OS, you have to log in. There are often several steps required before you gain access to your system. First, the OS must be installed—that was covered back in Chapter 3. Second, you must power up the system if it is not already. Booting can take several minutes depending on the installed components and network membership. Be sure that all bootable CDs are removed from the CD drives and that no floppies or Zip/Jaz disks are present in their respective drives (you want to allow the system to boot from the hard drive, not to attempt a boot from some other media).

Once the system is fully booted, you need to log on. Depending on which logon mode the system is using, you need to either click on a username/icon on the Welcome screen, or press Ctrl+Alt+Del to provide logon credentials to gain access to the system. If your system was a network member before an upgrade install, or you altered the default settings of the network components during a manual or unattended installation, you'll need to use the secure logon, which is covered in the section, "Using the Classic Logon." Otherwise, Windows XP presents you with the Welcome screen for one click access to the desktop.

LOGGING ON FROM THE WELCOME SCREEN

If you see the Welcome screen, just click on your user account to log on. The Welcome screen presents a list of available user accounts that can be employed to access this system. If a password is associated with a selected account, you will be prompted to provide it. If you need a hint (and a hint is defined), click the question mark.

Every time you boot your system, you must log in. Also, any time you return to your system after another user has logged off, you must log in. The Welcome screen is the default logon mode for Windows XP. In this mode, the screen lists all local user accounts available for accessing this system. This mode offers no real logon security; it is simply a means by which the system maintains unique user environments (that is, profiles) that it can easily switch between. (As mentioned in Chapter 1, even running applications are maintained in memory as users sign in and out.) If passwords are defined for an account, they are requested.

USING THE CLASSIC LOGON

The classic logon mechanism accessed by pressing Ctrl+Alt+Del from the Welcome screen is a secure logon method for accessing the machine you're using on a domain. Keep in mind that the logon credentials required for a secure logon are *username*, *password*, and *logon location*. The logon location is either local (indicated by the computer name) or domain. If your system is a member of a workgroup, you will log in locally. We'll talk more about the issues of networking, workgroups, and domains in later chapters (see Part IV).

If you don't have a user account with which to log in, go to the secure logon screen and log on using the Administrator account (if you know the password). Keep in mind that to log on as the system administrator, you *must* use the secure logon screen. If you want to create other user accounts (either for yourself or others), see the section "Working with User Accounts," later in this chapter.

The classic logon method is labeled as secure for two specific reasons. First, you must always provide a password. Even though a blank password can be assigned, thus making an insecure account, the password field must be addressed at logon. Second, you must provide a valid username. By default, the last username to successfully log on will be displayed, but that's the only user account name you get to see, unlike the Welcome logon screen which openly displays the names of all defined user accounts.

If you see a Press CTRL-ALT-DEL to logon message, follow these steps:

1. Press Ctrl+Alt+Del. The Log On to Windows dialog box appears.

2. In the User name field, type in your user account name.

3. If your computer is not part of a network and you did not upgrade a system that had local user accounts with passwords, then you can ignore the password field. If you are a member of a network domain or using an account upgraded from a previous system, you'll need to provide the password you used to log in before you upgraded to Windows XP. If you've forgotten your password, talk with your network administrator or jump to Chapter 28, "Managing Users," or Chapter 33, "Troubleshooting and Repairing Windows XP."

4. The logon location will be the same as the last successful user logon. If you are not sure what this was, click Options to reveal the Location pull-down list. Select the domain or local computer name (for standalone or workgroup).

5. Click OK to continue.

NOTE

> Those of you unfamiliar with processes involved in using a networked OS (like Windows XP) are no doubt finding much of this material, like managing accounts, or having to log on to your computer using an account, new to you. All you need to know for now is the following:
>
> - A domain is a logical collection of computers who are all members of the same network. A domain is centrally controlled—which means one (or few) server(s) define the domain, control access to resources, and verify your identity at logon (a.k.a. credential authorization).
> - The Administrator is a default user account on every Windows NT, 2000, and XP system which has full and unrestricted access to the system. The Administrator account is typically used to configure hardware and software, install new applications, and define user access to resources.
>
> If you'd like to know more about domains, please see Part IV where networking is discussed, and if you'd like to know more about the Administrator account take a look at Chapter 28.

CHANGING THE DEFAULT LOGON MODE

Changing the default Logon mode requires the following steps (note: this action can only be performed if the computer is not a domain member):

1. Click the Start button, and then click on Control Panel. The Control Panel appears.

2. In Category mode or Classic mode, click User Accounts. The User Accounts interface appears. If the User Accounts interface does not appear, your system probably is configured as a domain client.

> **NOTE**
>
> The layout and presentation of many aspects of Windows XP is different from any previous Microsoft OS. The default setting is to use the new XP layout, but if you prefer the more familiar look and feel of previous versions of Windows, look for options that let you display windows and dialog boxes like the Control Panel in "Classic mode." This most often means returning to a Windows 2000 or Windows Me layout. The main difference between the two is that the Category mode displays links only to common actions that it has grouped into categories, whereas (in the case of the Control Panel) Classic mode displays *all* of the individual Control Panel applets.

3. Click on Change the Way Users Log On or Off. The Select Logon and Logoff options page appears, as shown in Figure 4.1.

Figure 4.1
The Select logon and logoff options page of the User Accounts interface.

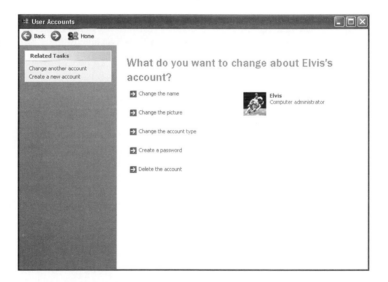

4. If you leave the Use the Welcome Screen box checked, the system will continue to use the Welcome logon screen in which you just choose an account by selecting it from the list of accounts available to that machine. If you uncheck the box, the system will use the classic logon method, in which you must type in the account to which you want to log in.

5. If you leave the Use the Welcome Screen check box checked, an additional check box of Use Fast User Switching is available. This lets users quickly log on and off, while keeping their programs actively running and operating in the background. It's an easy and efficient way for people to share a computer.

6. Click OK to save your changes and close the Select logon and logoff options.

7. Click the Red X button on the title bar to close the User Accounts interface and then do the same to close the Control Panel.

Your changes will take effect the next time you log out and log back in.

After you've logged in, it's time to explore the user interface, or as Microsoft likes to call it, the *user experience*.

WORKING WITH USER ACCOUNTS

During the installation of Windows XP, you defined a password for the Administrator account. If you also defined additional user accounts during that process, Windows considers these accounts to be equal to the Administrator account. If you performed an upgrade install on a system with pre-existing user accounts, any pre-existing accounts were retained, and their access levels were converted into their XP equivalents. There are three types of local accounts available on Windows XP Pro:

NOTE

If you purchase a system with XP pre-installed, the system will prompt you for a few specifics, such as a computer name and an administrator password, during the first bootup.

- **Computer administrator**—Can create, change, and delete user accounts; can make system level changes; can install programs; and can access all files

- **Standard**—Can make basic changes to computer settings, can install hardware and software if the installation does not affect restricted settings, and can access only personal files

- **Limited**—A restricted user with only minimal system access and no ability to alter system configuration

If your system is connected to a network, then when you are logged in to the domain you will be using a domain-level user account.

There is always at least one user account on Windows XP—namely the Administrator account. This account is always protected by a password. There is also another default account, the Guest account. This account has restricted system access and can be disabled, so it may not always be available for use as a login. Plus, even if it is enabled, you won't be able to make any system changes or even create other user accounts under its security restrictions.

When performing normal tasks on your system, you should always log in with a standard user account instead of the Administrator account or any account with computer administrator level access. Why? Because it's too easy to make a system level change that damages or significantly alters your system. By removing your ability to make sweeping changes you'll limit your exposure to this risk.

CREATING NEW USER ACCOUNTS

User account management is performed by the Administrator or any other user account with computer administrator level access. This access includes creating new users and altering the settings on existing users. Lets explore new user creation first:

1. Open the Control Panel by clicking on the Start menu, then clicking on Control Panel. The Control Panel appears.
2. Click on User Accounts. The User Accounts interface appears (see Figure 4.2).

Figure 4.2
The User Accounts interface.

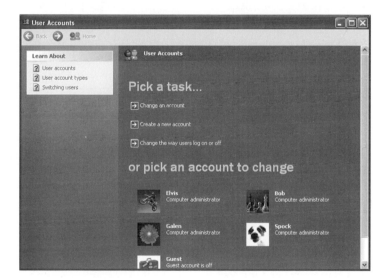

3. Click Create a New Account.
4. The first prompt is for the name of the user account. Type a name into the field (for example, Joe or lab1user), and then click Next. Your account name may consist of upper- and lowercase letters, numbers, and symbols except for /\[]":;|<>+=,?*. The account name can be up to 20 characters long.
5. The second prompt is to select the access level for the account. Select the Standard radio button, and then click Create Account.
6. You'll be returned to the User Accounts interface. The newly created user account will appear in the list of user accounts at the bottom on this window.

MODIFYING AN EXISTING ACCOUNT

After you create an account, there are several changes you can make to it that tailor it to that user's needs. To alter the settings on an existing account from the User Accounts interface

1. With the User Accounts window open (as described in the previous section), click Change an Account.

2. Click on the name/icon of the account to alter.

3. A menu of options for this account is displayed (see Figure 4.3).

Figure 4.3
The alter user account menu.

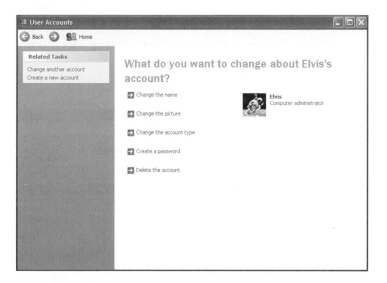

4

For a standard account, these include

- Change the name
- Change the picture
- Change the account type
- Create a password
- Delete the account

Click on one of these selections and follow the prompts to make the desired change to the selected account.

4. Once you complete altering the current account, click the Back button. This returns you to the account to change selection list. If you wish to alter a different account, go back to step 2.

5. If you are finished altering accounts, click the Back button again to return to the User Accounts interface.

6. Go ahead and click the X button to close the User Accounts windows, and then do the same for the Control Panel.

Using Passwords

By default, new accounts do not have passwords. After you define a password for an account, you are prompted for that password whenever you attempt to log on with that user account, whether through the Welcome screen or Ctrl+Alt+Del. Through the Welcome screen, if you forget your password, click on the ? button to obtain a hint (if you defined one when you created the password). The password hint is not accessible through the Ctrl+Alt+Del logon mode.

You'll want to create a unique user account for every user of this system. Plus, be sure to grant computer administrator access only to those users who actually need it, in other words, those users who will be installing a lot of hardware and software and performing systemwide configuration changes. Plus, if anyone is concerned about other users snooping into their stuff, define passwords for each user account. Password-protected user accounts are a necessity in office environments, but even if you're using Windows XP Professional at home, it might be a blessing there, too.

NOTE

> There is a lot more to working with user accounts than what is described here. For more exhaustive coverage of user account management, please see Chapter 28, "Managing Users."

4

When you first log on to Windows XP, you are deposited directly into your so-called Windows XP *user experience*. This consists of a desktop with a recycle bin and a taskbar with a Start menu and a clock/icon tray. Microsoft has finally provided a clean, elegant first logon screen. It's up to you to populate your desktop and customize your environment to fit your needs, habits, and desires. This could be a little disconcerting at first if you are a veteran Windows user. You'll wonder where the icons such as My Computer, Internet Explorer, and Network Neighborhood are. Don't worry, you'll figure out other ways to get to these, and you can add them to the desktop later. But for now you can access them through the Start menu.

Using Windows XP—the User Experience

Windows XP has a familiar yet different user interface. Most of the visual aspects of the desktop environment have been updated, but you'll find most of the tools and applications you remember from Windows 9x and Windows 2000 right where you expect. The new interface or user experience is called Luna. Luna includes visual updates and improvements to all native dialog boxes, displays, windows, and interfaces. Most notably these changes are seen on the Start menu, the taskbar, the Explorer, and the Control Panel. If you want the older stylings of previous Windows versions (mainly Windows 2000 era visual stylings), revert to the "classic" style. However, we highly recommend giving the new look and feel a try for a week or so. We did, and we love it.

Microsoft's visual palette has moved from a flat gray to include brilliant blues and subtle off-whites. In addition, Microsoft has rounded the corners of windows, added 3D icons, and added *action centers* (that is, tasks and commands focused on content) everywhere. The result is not only eye-pleasing, but elegantly simple to work with. But even with all the enhancements, everything still seems to have a similar function or placement to that of Windows 2000 and not too different from Windows 9x or Me. Thus, you'll easily leverage your existing experience and expertise in navigating and operating Windows XP. After a few days, you'll soon forget how you got by without all these useful improvements.

NOTE

> For a nearly exhaustive list of keyboard shortcuts for navigating and controlling aspects of Windows XP, check out the "Windows keyboard shortcuts overview" document, available through the Help and Support Center. Just click Start, Help; type in the title in the Search field; and then click the green arrow. It should appear under Full-text Search Matches, so click on that button in the Search Results to get to it.

However, Windows is more than just an operating system and graphical user interface. Like other versions of Windows, Windows XP includes a broad collection of useful programs, from a simple arithmetic calculator to fancy system and network management tools. This list also includes a word-processing program called WordPad, a drawing program called Paint, Internet Explorer for cruising the Web, Outlook Express for e-mail, MovieMaker for creating digital movies, NetMeeting for video and telephone conferencing over the Internet, CD burning software that lets you create your own CDs, a DVD playback tool, utilities for keeping your hard disk in good working order, and a data-backup program—just to name a few.

PARTS OF THE WINDOWS XP SCREEN

At this point, you should be booted and signed in. After you've logged in, Windows XP deposits you in its basic environment (called the *desktop*). You'll probably notice two things almost immediately: first, the taskbar at the bottom of the screen, and second, an empty (or nearly so) desktop (see Figure 4.4). The taskbar is the central control mechanism for the Windows XP user experience. It hosts the Start menu, the Quick Launch bar, active program buttons, the system tray, and the clock. The only item that is present on your desktop is the Recycle Bin, although if you purchased a computer system with XP pre-installed, you might see other icons as well. Notice that it's now located by default in the bottom right corner. (That's awfully Macintosh-ish, don't you think?)

NOTE

> If you or someone else has used your Windows XP setup already, it's possible that some open windows will come up on the screen automatically when Windows boots (starts up). It's also possible that you'll see more icons on the Desktop than what's shown in Figure 4.4, depending on the options chosen when Windows XP was installed, whether other applications were loaded before upgrading, and whether custom shortcuts to the desktop have been defined.

Figure 4.4
The default desktop with the Start menu open.

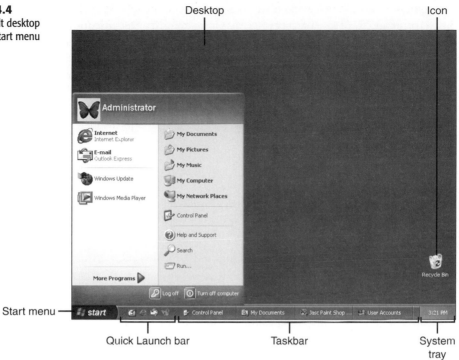

Desktop

Icon

Start menu

Quick Launch bar

Taskbar

System tray

4

There are three primary areas of the screen to explore: the desktop, icons, and the taskbar. All you really must know to use Windows XP's interface are these essential building blocks and how to manipulate a window and its commands. If you've been using Windows 3.x, 9x, NT, or 2000, then you already know the latter. You just need to be brought up to speed on the advanced XP interface specifics. As mentioned in the introduction, for the purposes of this book, we assume that you have basic Windows proficiency and have been using Windows 9x, NT, or 2000. Therefore, we skip subjects such as how to click using the mouse, what double-clicking is, and how to scroll a window. (If you need this level of hand-holding, you may want to find a beginner's book, such as *Easy Windows XP*, instead.)

THE DESKTOP

Let's start with the desktop. This is your home base while doing your work in Windows. It is always on the screen as the backdrop (whether you see it or not) and you can deposit files and folders right on it for storage. It's analogous to a real desktop in this way. It also serves as a handy temporary holding area for files you might be copying from, say, a floppy disk to a hard disk folder. The *Recycle Bin* holds deleted work objects such as files and folders until you empty it (with caveats). Just as in previous versions of Windows (or the Mac for that matter, if you're coming from that background), you'll do all your work in Windows XP using graphical representations of your files and applications (called *icons*).

All the desktop icons you are familiar with from Windows 9x and 2000 have been moved to the Start menu. You can gain access to My Computer, My Documents, and My Network Places with a simple click on the Start button. If you revert to the previous Windows 2000 Start menu (called classic), then these items reappear on the desktop (see Chapter 23's section titled "Start Menu Pizzazz!"). In either case, you control which icons or shortcuts appear on your desktop.

You can add icons and shortcuts to your desktop to you heart's content. However, Windows XP doesn't want to let things stay cluttered. So, if you fail to use any of the items on your desktop for more than 60 days, the Desktop Cleanup Wizard is launched automatically to prod you into removing unused items or moving them into the Unused Desktop Shortcuts folder. This folder appears on the desktop automatically after the Desktop Cleanup wizard is used to remove unused shortcuts. When the Desktop Cleanup Wizard launches, just follow the wizard's prompts to select which icons to remove (or, more specifically, move into the Unused Desktop Shortcuts folder).

The Recycle Bin

The Recycle Bin acts a bit like the waste paper basket at the side of your desk. After you throw something into it, it's basically trash to be thrown out, however you can still retrieve items from it if you get there before the cleaning staff takes empties it and throws it away for good. Within Windows XP, the Recycle Bin holds those files you've deleted using Windows Explorer, My Computer, or the Open/Save As dialog boxes. It does not capture files deleted by third-party tools, files deleted from floppies or network drives, files removed with an uninstall program or from DOS boxes, and DOS files running in a DOS box.

The Recycle Bin has limited storage capacity. By default, it retains deleted files that total up to 10% of the total capacity of each hard drive on your computer. When the maximum size of the Recycle Bin is reached, the oldest files are permanently removed from the hard drive to make room for newly deleted files. The size of the Recycle Bin can be customized as a percentage across all drives or as a unique size on each individual volume. The Recycle Bin is customized through its Properties dialog box (see Figure 4.5). The configuration options are discussed in Chapter 23, "Tweaking the GUI," but if you want to get there now, just right-click over the Recycle Bin icon and select Properties from the pop-up menu.

After a file is removed from the Recycle Bin, it cannot be recovered using native tools. You must restore the files from a backup, use a third-party recover tool (which often needs to be in place before the file is deleted), or live without the lost files. If you don't want your excess trash sitting around, you can also configure the system to bypass the Recycle Bin entirely so that it permanently deletes files immediately instead of granting you a recovery period.

To restore a file still retained in the Recycle Bin, double-click the desktop icon to open the Recycle Bin, locate and select the file to restore, and then issue the Restore command from the File menu or the Recycle Bin Tasks list (see Figure 4.6). The file/folder(s) will be returned to its original location.

Figure 4.5
The Recycle Bin
Properties dialog box.

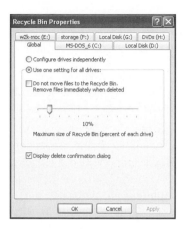

Figure 4.6
Restoring a file from
the Recycle Bin.

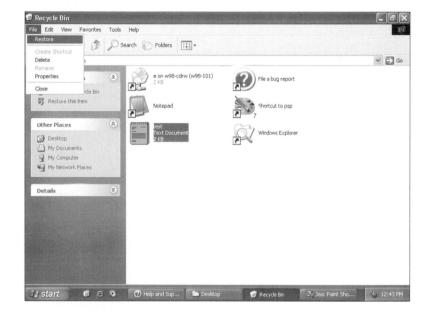

You can also manually empty the Recycle Bin. This is often a useful activity before defragmenting your hard drive or just wanting to permanently delete files and folders. The Empty Recycle Bin command, found in the right-click pop-up menu for the icon, the File menu (be sure no items are selected, otherwise the File menu's context changes to file/folder restore operations), and the Recycle Bin Tasks list of the Recycle Bin interface, is used to clear out all files being retained.

NOTE

> Don't try moving program files unless you know that they have not registered them-selves with the operating system and they can harmlessly be moved around between folders. If you must move applications, use a tool specifically designed for this. The tool MagicMover from PowerQuest, a program bundled with PartitionMagic (see www.powerquest.com), was able to perform this task for Windows 2000 systems. PowerQuest has released an updated version of PartitionMagic that does support Windows XP.

ICONS

As you almost certainly know, the small graphical representations of your programs and files are called *icons*. Windows XP uses icons to represent folders, documents, programs, and groups of settings (such as dial-up connections). Graphically, icons got a 3D facelift in Windows XP, even when compared to their Windows 2000 counterparts. In most cases, the default icon displayed for an object somewhat represents the function of that object.

NOTE

> In recent versions of Windows Microsoft has begun using the term "folder" instead of "directory". They want to focus your thoughts toward the idea of your files being stored on the hard drive in a manner similar to that of a filing cabinet for manila fold-ers. While we think this analogy is helpful, we don't always stick to Microsoft-speak. So, if you see "folder" or "directory" anywhere in this book, keep in mind we consider them to be the same thing.

Icons are either objects themselves or they are shortcuts. A shortcut is a means to gain access to an object from multiple locations throughout the environment. Shortcuts are the preferred mechanism by which access to the same object is achieved from multiple loca-tions, rather than making duplicate copies of the original object or application. Duplicating the object often causes version problems, such as never knowing which one has your most recent changes, and difficulties in upgrading or replacing applications. Shortcuts eliminate these issues and take up less space. You could have thousands of shortcuts pointing to the same application or document and still save drive space!

Additionally, a shortcut can define alternative launching parameters, such as default directo-ries, command line parameters, compatibility mode, and so on. To alter the settings of a shortcut, just right-click and select Properties from the pop-up menu.

NOTE

> Compatibility mode is a nifty new feature that enables Windows XP to support a wider range of software products than Windows 95 and Windows NT combined. A compatibility mode is simply a designation for a software platform emulation envi-ronment. In other words, when an application is launched with compatibility mode enabled, a virtual machine representing that application's native environment (Windows 95, Windows 98, Windows NT, or Windows 2000) is created in such a way

that the application is fooled into thinking that it is the only application present on the computer system running its preferred OS.

Don't fret that I didn't include MS-DOS or Windows 16-bit (Windows 3.x) applications in that list of environments. Those are already automatically launched into their own virtual machine. That is discussed in Chapter 23, "Tweaking the GUI."

DIALOG BOX CHANGES

The Open and Save dialog boxes (a.k.a. file or browse dialog boxes) for most applications still offer the same shortcuts and controls as those of Windows 9x, Me, and 2000. This typically includes a shortcut menu to History, Desktop, My Documents, My Computer, and My Network Places. You'll also still find the Look In pull-down list with quick selections for local drives, user home directories, shared folders, and more. Not all applications that function on Windows XP will offer a fully enhanced file dialog box.

Many dialog boxes have tabs. These often appear at the top of a dialog box, like the tabs for General and Sharing shown in Figure 4.7. Tabs are used to offer multiple pages or displays of controls within a single smaller window. Many of the configuration settings dialog boxes have tabs, so watch for them. To select another tab, just click on it. In some cases, tabs are easy to miss. The new color scheme and display enhancements don't always direct your eyes to tabs.

Figure 4.7
A properties dialog box containing tabs you can click to see additional settings.

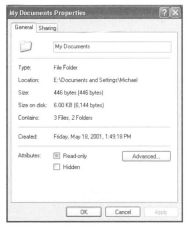

MY COMPUTER AND WINDOWS EXPLORER

My Computer and Windows Explorer are still present with many of the same functions and features as in previous versions of Windows, but a few interesting enhancements have been made. Yes, Windows Explorer is still hidden away in the Accessories area of the Start menu. Microsoft wants to draw your attention away from how files are managed on the hard drive and to direct your attention to how documents are arranged within your personal folders (such as My Documents, My Pictures, and so on). My Computer and Windows Explorer are used to access the folder structure of your hard drives to locate files. Through these tools you can move, copy, delete, rename, create new, and more.

TIP FROM

Bob & Brian

> Surprisingly, Windows XP still includes a Program Manager from the days of Windows 3.x. It's there for full backward compatibility for applications. If you want to work with it, just execute `Progman.exe` in the Start, Run box. Keep in mind that File Manager doesn't work with long filenames. Also, it doesn't have the capability to exploit the advances in the interface, such as links to the Web, and lacks flexibility in cutting, copying, and pasting objects between locations, including networked workstations.

WEBVIEW

WebView is Microsoft's attempt to make your local content integrate as seamlessly as possible with Internet-based content. This integration offers the benefits of more information displayed within the interface by default and quick access to common activities. For example, a single click can initiate a file or folder rename, a move or copy, or even the deletion of a selected item (or items).

NOTE

> In the chapters on using the Internet (Chapters 8–14), we'll cover the ins and outs of getting connected, browsing the Web, using search engines, creating and serving Web pages, and using e-mail, newsgroups, and so forth. However, what's relevant here is how the Windows XP WebView affects how you work with files and folders.

The WebView display option for Windows Explorer and My Computer has been greatly improved. No longer a direct annoyance, WebView finally offers useful information, true content-directed capabilities, and easier data object manipulation. What does this all mean? Well, it means that doing the things you normally do with files and folders will be easier than ever before. Basically, WebView transforms the interfaces of your file and folder utilities into more Web-like mechanisms. They offer graphical representations of objects, they display more details about the selected objects, and most of the functions or commands are single-click activated.

Figure 4.8 shows Windows Explorer in WebView. WebView gives you access to common tasks related to files and folders. In addition to the list of quick access tasks, WebView displays a quick access panel that allows you to jump quickly to other resource locations. The Details section displays basic information about a selected item, such as

- The selected item's name and type (such as document, folder, application, and so on)
- The date on which it was most recently modified
- Its size, author, and other item-specific information

Much of this information also appears in a ToolTip when the mouse cursor is placed over an object.

Figure 4.8
Windows Explorer in
WebView.

Some of the key WebView effects integrated into Windows XP include

- Your desktop is "active." It can display Web page information (such as your home page) or streaming data gathered from the Internet, such as news, weather reports, traffic reports, stock tickers, and so on.

- My Computer and Windows Explorer have Back, Forward, Search, and History buttons, just like a Web browser.

- The toolbars in folder and Explorer windows are customizable and have address lines, just like a browser. You can type in a Web address, hit Enter (or click Go), and the window will adjust appropriately to display the content. If you enter a Web address, that page will display. If you enter a drive letter (C:, for example), its contents will be displayed.

- Every folder on your system can be customized with a background color, picture, hot links, instructions, and so forth. Basic customizations are made without knowledge of HTML coding, through a wizard.

- Many of the Windows preset folders already have hot links to relevant sites, help files, and troubleshooting tools.

- WebView can be fully customized with unique icons for each folder and file, different display layouts for each folder, and thumbnails of album art on music files.

- Windows XP is able to navigate the contents of compressed archives, such as zip files, without a third party utility. Archive files act like compressed folders.

There are many more features and options in the interface, but we'll get to those in the sections on customizing with the Control Panel, as well as in the Windows Explorer and My Computer coverage. Also, Chapter 23, "Tweaking the GUI," covers even more ways to change the interface.

WebView is enabled by default on Windows XP. But, if you decide you would rather live without WebView, it is not difficult to return to the Classic style of Windows 2000's interfaces. WebView is enabled and disabled through the Folder Options Control Panel applet, by choosing Tools, Folder Options from any My Computer or Windows Explorer window. As shown in Figure 4.9, WebView is enabled or disabled on the General tab of the Folder Options Control Panel applet. This is a systemwide change. Once WebView is disabled, it is disabled on all Windows Explorer and My Computer windows.

Figure 4.9
The General tab of the Folder Options Control Panel applet.

If you're the controlling type, you might want to fine-tune other aspects of your folders' behavior. Go back to the Folder Options applet, and then select the View tab. You'll see a bevy of options that affect how folders and their contents are displayed. Change any settings you like. (Some of these are pretty technical, though. If you don't understand a setting, don't touch it.) We'll check out most of these in Chapter 23.

SELECTING SEVERAL ITEMS

On most lists, especially within My Computer and Windows Explorer, not to mention the file and browser dialog boxes, you can select multiple items at once to save time. The normal rules of selection apply:

■ Draw a box around them by clicking and holding over empty space near the first item then drag across and over the desired selections until all are highlighted and/or contained within the selection box, and then release the mouse button.

- Select the first of the items, hold down the Ctrl key, and click to select each additional object you want to work with. Use this technique to select a bunch of noncontiguous items.

- Select the first of the items, hold down the Shift key, and click the last item. This selects the entire *range* of objects between the starting and ending points.

After several items are selected (they will be highlighted), right-clicking any one of the objects will bring up the Cut, Copy, Paste menu. The option you choose will apply to *all* the selected items. Also, clicking anywhere outside of the selected items will deselect them all, and Ctrl-clicking (or pointing) to one selected object will deselect it.

TIP FROM

Bob
& Brian

Take a look at the Edit menu in any folder window. There are two commands at the bottom of the menu: Select All and Invert Selection. These can be useful when you want to select a group of files. Suppose you want to select all but two files; select the two you don't want and then choose Edit, Invert Selection.

Drag-and-drop support is implemented uniformly across the Windows XP interface. In general, if you want something placed somewhere else, you can drag it from the source to the destination. For example, you can drag items from the Search box into a folder or onto the desktop, or you can add a picture attachment to an e-mail you're composing by dragging the picture file into the new e-mail's window. Also, the destination folder does not have to be open in a window. Items dropped onto a closed folder icon are added to that folder. You can also drag-and-drop items via the taskbar by dragging an item over an application button and waiting a second for that application to be brought to the forefront. You can also drop items into the Start menu to add them to the listings, or drop items over desktop icons to open them with the application onto which you drop the item (assuming the application supports the object's file type).

Arranging your screen so you can see source and destination is graphically lovely and intuitively reassuring, because you can see the results of the process. However, it's not always the easiest. Once you get familiar with the interface, you'll want to try the Cut, Copy, and Paste methods of moving files and folders.

CAUTION

Don't try moving program files unless you know they have not registered themselves with the operating system and they can harmlessly be moved around between folders. If you must move applications, use a tool specifically designed for this, such as MagicMover from PowerQuest, a program bundled with PartitionMagic (see www.powerquest.com).

4

PUTTING ITEMS ON THE DESKTOP

The Desktop is a convenient location for either permanent or temporary storage of items. Many folks use the Desktop as a home for often-used documents and program shortcuts. I'm quite fond of using the Desktop as an intermediary holding tank when moving items between drives, computers, or to and from floppy disks. It's particularly good for pulling found items out of a Search window or other folder while awaiting final relocation elsewhere.

Here are some quick notes about use of the Desktop that you should know about. For starters, you can send a shortcut of an object to the Desktop very easily by right-clicking it and choosing Send To, Desktop (thus creating the shortcut).

Second, remember that the Desktop is nothing magical. Actually, it's just another folder with a few additional properties, prime among them is active Internet-based information, such as stock tickers, weather, and the like. Also, each user on the machine can have his/her own Desktop setup, with icons, background colors, screen saver, and such.

The major feature of the Desktop is that whatever you put on it is always available by minimizing or closing open windows or more easily by clicking the Show Desktop button on the Quick Launch bar. Keep in mind that some items cannot be moved onto the Desktop—only their shortcuts can. (For example, if you try dragging a Control Panel applet to the Desktop, you'll see a message stating that you cannot copy or move the item to this location.)

If you must be able to access a Control Panel applet from the Desktop, the answer is clear in this case because you don't really have a choice. Just create a shortcut to the applet and place it on the Desktop. However, in other cases when you're copying and moving items around, particularly when using the right-click method, you'll be presented with the options of copying, moving, or creating a shortcut to the item. What's the best choice?

Here are a few reminders about shortcuts. Remember that they work just as well as the objects they point to (for example, the program or document file), yet take up much less space on the hard disk. For this reason, they're generally a good idea. What's more, you can have as many shortcuts scattered about for a given object as you want. Therefore, for a program or folder you use a lot, put its shortcuts wherever you need them—put one on the Desktop, one on the Quick Launch bar, one on the Start menu, and another in a folder of your favorite programs on the Desktop.

Make up shortcuts for other objects you use a lot, such as folders, disk drives, network drives and printers, and Web links. From Internet Explorer, for example, drag the little blue E icon that precedes a URL in the address bar out to the Desktop to save it as a shortcut. Clicking it will bring up the Web page.

CAUTION

> Remember that shortcuts are not the item they point to. They're aliases only. Therefore, copying a document's shortcut to a floppy or a network drive or adding it as an attachment to an email doesn't copy the document itself. If you want to send a document to some colleagues, don't make the mistake of sending them the shortcut unless it's something they'll have access to over the LAN or Web. If it's a shortcut to, say, a word-processing document or folder, they'll have nothing to open.

The link between shortcuts and the objects they point to can be broken. This happens typically when the true object is erased or moved. Clicking the shortcut can result in an error message. In Windows 2000 and in Windows XP, this problem is addressed in an ingenious way. Shortcuts automatically adjusted when linked objects are moved. The operating system keeps track of all shortcuts and attempts to prevent breakage. Shortcut "healing" is built into Windows XP for those situations where the automated recover mechanism fails.

If you're in doubt about the nature of a given shortcut, try looking at its properties. You may find it telling, or at least interesting. Right-click the shortcut and choose Properties. Clicking on Find Target will locate the object the shortcut links to and will display it in a folder window.

TIP FROM

Bob & Brian

> To quickly bring up the Properties dialog box for most objects in the Windows GUI, you can highlight the object and press Alt+Enter.

SAVING FILES ON THE DESKTOP FROM A PROGRAM

Because the desktop is a convenient place to plop files and folders, modern applications' Save As boxes list the desktop as a destination option. Even if the app's dialog box doesn't have the desktop icon in the left pane, the drop-down list at the top of the box will have it. If you are using a very old legacy application (such as those for Windows 3.x), you may need to manually locate the desktop folder within the file system. It's located on the same drive as the main Windows directory, in \Documents and Settings\<username>\Desktop (where <username> is the name of the user account).

Locating the desktop in a Windows 3.x program's Save As box is a pain, because long filenames will be truncated to 8.3-style names and have ~ marks imposed on them. Here's how that works: For 16-bit programs, Windows removes spaces, shortens long names to six characters, and inserts a ~ character and then a number. If two files have the same first six characters (for example, Bob's resume and Bob's resume revised), the number is incremented for the second file. Therefore, those files appear as bobres~1 and bobres~2.

NOTE

> The location of the desktop folder for a user will not be on the local machine if
> *IntelliMirror* is being used on a network using Windows 2000 or Windows 2003 Server
> in such a way that the user's desktop will follow him or her from workstation to work-
> station. In this case, the desktop will be in a folder on the server and will be more diffi-
> cult to locate from an old-style Save As dialog box. Just use another folder to save the
> file and then move it to the desktop using My Computer or Windows Explorer.

PROPERTIES AND THE RIGHT-CLICK

Ever since Windows 95, a common theme that unites items within Windows is the aspect
called *properties*. Properties are pervasive throughout Windows 9x, Windows NT 4,
Windows 2000, and now Windows XP. The Properties dialog boxes provide a means for
making changes to the behavior, appearance, security level, ownership, and other aspects of
objects throughout the operating system. Object properties apply to everything from individual files to folders, printers, peripherals, screen appearance, the computer itself, or a network or workgroup. All these items have property sheets that allow you to easily change
various settings. For example, you might want to alter whether a printer is the default printer or whether a folder on your hard disk is shared for use by coworkers on the LAN.

A typical set of properties is shown in Figure 4.10, which displays the properties for the D:
drive (hard disk) on a computer. Notice that there are several tab pages on this dialog box.
Some property dialogs only have a single page, whereas others may have many.

Figure 4.10
A typical Properties
dialog box for a
hard disk.

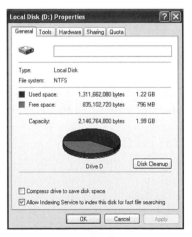

Property sheets are very useful and often serve as shortcuts for modifying settings that otherwise would take you into the Control Panel or through some other circuitous route. With
some document files (for example, Word files), you can examine many settings that apply to
the file, such as the creation date, author, editing history, and so forth. A typical printer's
property sheet contains security, color management, location, name, and share status information. You can even change your screen colors, display resolution, screen savers, and more

by right-clicking over the desktop and clicking Properties from the pop-up menu. This opens the Display applet without having to traverse the Control Panel.

Although everyday users might not have need for property sheets, power users certainly will. As you use property sheets, you'll also become familiar with and accustomed to another aspect of the Windows XP interface: the right-click. Until Windows 9x, the left (primary) mouse button was the one you did all your work with unless you were using a program that specifically utilized the other buttons, such as some art programs. However, Windows 9x instituted the use of the right-click to bring up various "context-sensitive" menus in programs and throughout the interface. These have been incorporated into Windows XP.

Here are some typical uses of right-click context menus:

- Sharing a folder on the network
- Changing the name of your hard disk and checking its free space
- Changing a program's icon
- Creating a new folder
- Setting the desktop's colors, background, screen saver, and so on
- Adjusting the date and time of the clock quickly
- Closing an application by right-clicking on its icon in the taskbar and choosing Close
- Displaying a font's technical details
- Renaming an object
- Accessing an object's Properties dialog box

As an example of the right-click, simply get to an empty place on the Desktop and right-click on it. Right by the cursor, you'll see a menu that looks like the one shown in Figure 4.11. Notice that you can slide up and down the menu to make choices. Choose Properties down at the bottom of the list. You'll see the Properties settings for the your desktop (as well as general video display, screen saver, and other related items). By the way, many menus (Start, menu bar, pop-up, and so on) have commands with a small arrow to one side. If you highlight one of these commands, a submenu will fly open, hence the term *fly-open menu*.

Here are some other examples of useful right-click activities:

- Right-clicking on any window's title bar produces a menu containing the Restore, Move, Size, Minimize, Maximize, and Close commands.
- Right-clicking on and dragging an icon from the Explorer or a folder onto the desktop reveals a pop-up menu with the options Copy Here, Move Here, Create Shortcuts Here, and Cancel.
- In many applications, selecting text and then right-clicking produces an edit menu at the cursor location that lets you choose Cut, Copy, or Paste.

4

Figure 4.11
An example of a right-click menu, this one from an empty location on the desktop. Notice how it contains fly-open menus.

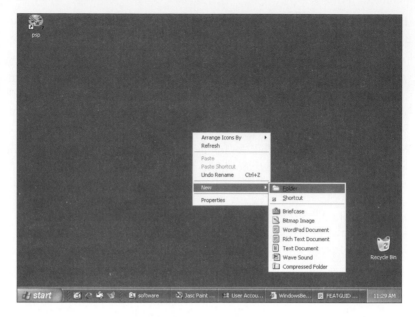

- Right-clicking an empty area of the taskbar gives you a menu that lets you manage the display of all the windows you have open. For example, you can tile all open windows or set the properties of the taskbar. (The taskbar is discussed in more detail later in this chapter.)

- In the Explorer, right-clicking on a file lets you work with it in various ways, depending on the file type. You can open the document, send it to an e-mail recipient, run a program, install or set up a utility such as a screen saver, play a sound file, and so forth.

If you want to use Windows most efficiently, make a habit of right-clicking on objects to see what pops up. You may be surprised to see how much time you save with the resulting shortcuts.

NOTE

Starting with this chapter, we're going to assume that you understand the choice between single-click mode and double-click mode. Some of the figures in the book might have icons, files, or other object names underlined, whereas other may not, based on what mode the computer was set in when the screen shots were grabbed. Don't let it throw you. When we say "double-click something," we mean run it or open it by whatever technique is applicable based on your click setting. Also, when we say "click on it," that means select it. Remember that if you have single-clicking turned on, just hover the pointer over (that is, point to) the item to select it. Generally, we will be working from the defaults set by Microsoft.

USING THE FOLDERS BAR (A.K.A. WINDOWS EXPLORER)

For a bird's-eye view of your computer, turning on the Folders bar is the way to go. It makes copying, moving, and examining all the contents of your computer easier than navigating up and down the directory tree through folders. If you're doing housekeeping, copying and moving items around from one folder to another or across the network, or hopping back and forth between viewing Web pages and your local hard disk, mastering this view will serve you well.

You probably remember that the folder view was introduced with Windows 95 in the form of Windows Explorer, and although it's still in XP under that name, it's not featured as much as it used to be. This is because the functionality of Windows Explorer can be added to all folder windows (such as My Computer) simply by clicking on the Folders button in the toolbar. The Folder View paradigm affords significant power and flexibility in file and folder control, and has been adopted by Microsoft and other software makers for other classes of programs. For example, right-click on My Computer and choose Manage. The resulting application (Computer Management) uses the same approach, as do many Web pages.

For everyday file and folder management, I prefer Folder View over the usual folder system, which can clutter your screen with numerous overlapping windows when you have lots of them open. Instead, with Folder View (call it Windows Explorer, if you wish), whether you want to examine the Control Panel, the local area network, the Internet, your hard disk, or the Recycle Bin, it can all be done with a minimum of effort from the Explorer. Folder View also makes copying and moving files between far-flung folders and drives a snap.

To recap, you can get to the Windows Explorer in two ways:

- Open My Computer (or any folder) and choose View, Explorer Bar, Folders (or easier yet, click on the Folders button in the toolbar).
- Click Start, All Programs, Accessories, Windows Explorer.

Figure 4.12 shows the folders that appear on my own computer in Folder View.

TIP FROM

Bob & Brian

As an easy way into Windows Explorer, I always keep a shortcut to it on the Quick Launch bar or on the Desktop (see Chapter 23 for how to use the Quick Launch bar). Another trick is to right-click the Start button and choose Explore. This brings up the Windows Explorer, too.

Figure 4.12
The basic Windows Explorer screen, showing the computer's major components on the left and the contents on the right.

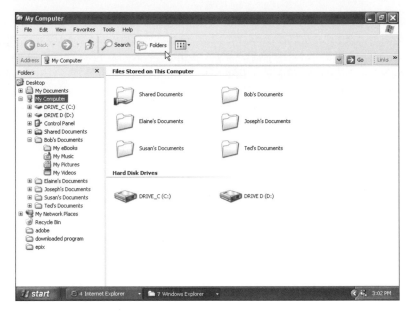

DISPLAYING THE CONTENTS OF YOUR COMPUTER

When you use Folder View (or run Windows Explorer), all the objects constituting your computer appear in the list on the left. Some of those objects have a plus sign (+) next to them, which means the object is collapsed; it contains subitems that aren't currently showing. For example, the hard disk drives (C: and D:) shown in Figure 4.12 are collapsed. So are My Network Places and My Documents.

Click an item in the left pane to see its contents in the right pane. If the item has a plus sign, click it to open up the sublevels in the left pane, showing you the relationship of the folders and other items in a tree arrangement. In the figure, you can see that the Bob's Documents folder has been opened in this way. Notice that the + is replaced with a minus (-) sign, indicating that the object's display has been expanded. Clicking the minus sign causes that branch to collapse.

If you open a local disk drive or disk across the network, you can quickly get a graphical representation of the disk's folder layout. Then, click a folder to see its contents. By right-clicking on disks, folders, or files, you can examine and set properties for them. The straight lines connecting folders indicate how they're related. If you have more folders than can be seen at one time, the window will have a scrollbar that you can use to scroll the tree up and down.

Notice that there are two scrollbars—one for the left pane and one for the right. These scroll independently of one another—a feature that can be very useful when you're copying items from one folder or drive to another.

WORKING WITH OBJECTS IN FOLDER VIEW

Working with folders and files in this view is simple. As explained previously, you just click an item in the left pane, and its contents appear in the right pane. Choose the view (Large Icons, Small Icons, and so on) for the right pane using either the toolbar's View button or the View menu. In Details view, you can sort the items by clicking the column headings.

When they're displayed, you can drag items to other destinations, such as a local hard disk, a floppy drive, or a networked drive. You can drag and drop files, run programs, open documents that have a program association, and use right-click menu options for various objects. For example, you can right-click files or folders and choose Send To, 3 1/2 Floppy to copy items to a floppy disk. I use the Send To, Mail Recipient option all the time, to send attachments to people via e-mail.

With a typical hard disk containing many files, when its folders are all listed in the left pane, some will be offscreen. Because the two panes have independent scrollbars, dragging items between distant folders is not a problem. Here's the game plan:

1. Be sure the source and destination folders are open and visible in the left pane, even if you have to scroll the pane up and down. For example, a network drive should be expanded, with its folders showing (using and mapping network drives are covered in Chapter 17).

2. Click the source folder in the left pane. Now its contents appear to the right.

3. Scroll the left pane up or down to expose the destination folder. (Click only the scrollbar, not a folder in the left pane; if you do, it will change the displayed items on the right side.)

4. In the right pane, locate and drag the items over to the left, landing on the destination folder. The folder must be highlighted; otherwise, you've aimed wrong.

This technique will suffice most of the time. Sometimes it's too much of a nuisance to align everything for dragging. In that case, use the cut/copy-and-paste technique discussed earlier in the chapter. Remember, you can copy and paste across your home LAN as well as between your local drives.

Here are a few tips when selecting folders:

- Only one folder can be selected at a time in the left pane. If you want to select multiple folders, click the parent folder (such as the drive icon) and select the folders in the right pane. Use the same techniques described earlier for making multiple selections.

- When a folder is selected in the left pane, its name becomes highlighted. This is a reminder of which folder's contents are showing in the right pane.

- You can jump quickly to a folder's name by typing its first letter on the keyboard. If there's more than one folder with the same first letter, each press of the key will advance to the next choice.

- The fastest way to collapse all the branches of a given drive is to click that drive's plus sign.

- You can quickly rearrange a drive's folder structure in the left pane by dragging folders around. You can't drag disk drives, but you can create shortcuts for them (for example, a network drive) by dragging them to, say, the Desktop.

- If a folder has subfolders, those will appear in the right pane as folder icons. Clicking one of those will open it as though you had clicked that subfolder in the left pane.

- When dragging items to collapsed folders (ones with a plus sign), hovering the pointer over the folder for a second will open it.

- You can use the right-click-drag technique when dragging items if you want the option of clearly choosing Copy, Move, or Create Shortcut when you drop the item on the target.

- To create a new folder, in the left pane, click the folder under which you want to create the new folder. Right-click in the right pane and choose New, Folder.

- Delete a folder by right-clicking on it and choosing Delete. You'll be asked to confirm.

CAUTION

> Although powerful, the Folder View is also dangerous. It makes accidental rearrangement of your hard disk's folders extremely easy. When selecting folders, be careful to not accidentally drag them! The icons are small, and this is easy to do accidentally, especially over in the left pane. A little flick of the wrist and a click of the mouse, and you've dragged one folder on top of another folder. This makes it a subfolder of the target. Remember, the left pane is "live" too. Rearranging the directory tree could make programs and files hard to find and even make some programs not work. If you think you've accidentally dragged a folder (its subfolders will go, too) into the wrong place, open the Edit menu. The first choice will probably read Undo Move. Choose it, and the folders or files you dragged will be returned to their previous locations.

THE TASKBAR, THE START MENU, AND OTHER TOOLS

The taskbar is the command center for your user environment under Windows XP. With few or no desktop icons after initial setup, everything you do within Windows XP has to start with the taskbar. The taskbar (refer to Figure 4.4) is host to several other highly useful tools, such as the Start menu, the Quick Launch bar, the open application buttons, and the system tray.

The Start menu is the control center for Windows XP. Most native applications and installed applications will have an icon within the Start menu used to launch or access them. The Start menu has two columns of access elements. The left column includes Internet and E-mail access on top and a list of most recently used applications on bottom. By default, it displays the six most recently accessed applications. A fresh installation of Windows XP will include pre-stocked items in this list, such as Windows Media Player, MSN Explorer, Windows Movie Maker, Tour Windows XP, and Files and Settings Transfer Wizard. This leaves room for only a single recently accessed application. These prestocked items will eventually disappear, but that can take up to 60 days. You can forcibly remove them one at a time by issuing the Remove from This List command from the right-click pop-up menu.

At the bottom of the left column is All Programs, which is an access point to the rest of the Start menu. Those of you from Windows 9x/Me/NT/2000 will recognize this as the Programs section of their Start menus. The Start menu's right column lists My Documents, My Recent Documents, My Pictures, My Music, My Computer, My Network Places, Control Panel, Printers and Faxes, Help and Support, Search, and Run. Below both columns are the Log Off and Shut Down buttons. Log Off is used to either fully log off the system or switch user contexts. The Shut Down command is used to power down (turn off), restart, or hibernate the computer.

TIP FROM

Bob
& Brian

> Pressing Ctrl+Esc or the Windows key opens the Start menu as though you clicked the Start button. Once open, navigate using the arrow keys. The Enter key is used to launch or access the selected item.

The top-level of the Start menu is managed by the system itself; you don't get to change what is displayed there, other than launching applications so they show up in the most-recently used (MRU) list.

It should be obvious that clicking on any of the items listed on the Start menu either launches an application or opens a new dialog box or menu. Most of the items on the top-level of the Start menu are discussed later in this chapter.

The organization of the All Programs section of the Start menu can be altered as you see fit. This is done through a series of drag-and-drop operations. New items are added to the Start menu by dragging the item from My Computer or Windows Explorer over the Start menu button, then over All Programs, and then to the location where you wish to drop it. The Start menu can even be manipulated from as a set of files and shortcuts through My Computer or Windows Explorer. You'll need to go to the system root (usually C:, but it could be anything on multi-boot systems), and drill down through to \Documents and Settings\<username>\Start Menu\Programs (where <username> is the name of the user account whose Start menu you wish to modify).

The area immediately to the right of the Start menu is the Quick Launch Bar. Microsoft sticks links to Internet Explorer and Windows Media Player here by default, as well as the Show Desktop tool, which minimizes all open windows. You can add your own link just by dragging and dropping an application icon over this area. The Quick Launch Bar is not enabled by default. To enable this handy tool, open Taskbar and Start Menu Properties, select the Taskbar tab, and then mark the Show Quick Launch check box.

To the far right on the taskbar is the *system tray*. Some services, OS functions, and applications place icons into this area. These icons provide both instant access to functions and settings as well as status displays. For example, when working on a portable system, a battery will appear in the system tray that indicates how much juice is left. The clock is also located in the system tray.

4

Between the Quick Launch Bar and the system tray are the active application buttons. These are grouped by similarity, not by order of launch. Plus, if the taskbar becomes crowded, multiple instances of similar applications will be cascaded into a single button.

NOTE

> You can reposition the taskbar on the right, left, or top of the screen. Just click any part of the taskbar other than a button and drag it to the edge of your choice. The Taskbar and Start Menu Properties dialog box includes a locking option to prevent the taskbar from being moved accidentally. Be sure to deselect this option before attempting to relocate the taskbar (right-click the taskbar and clear the check mark next to the Lock the Taskbar option).

You can further control and modify the taskbar and Start menu through their Properties dialog boxes.

→ For more information on customizing the taskbar and Start menu, **see** Chapter 23, "Tweaking the GUI."

RUNNING YOUR APPLICATIONS

If you're just upgrading from Windows 9x, you already know how to run applications, how to switch between them, and how to manage them. But, if you are new to Windows OSes, here is a quick how-to guide.

HOW TO LAUNCH YOUR APPS

Applications are launched under Windows XP in a number of different ways, as is the case with many other things in Windows. You'll probably end up employing the technique that best fits the occasion. To run an application, perform one of the following tasks (ranked in order of ease of use):

- Use the Start button to find the desired application from the resulting menus.
- Drag an application shortcut to the Quick Launch bar at the bottom of the screen and click it to run.
- Open My Computer or Windows Explorer, browse through your folders to find the application's icon, and double-click it.
- Run the old-style Windows 3.x Program Manager, open the group that contains the application's icon, and double-click it. To open Program Manager, execute `progman` from the Run command.
- Find the application using the Start, Search command and double-click it.
- Enter command names from the command prompt (click Start, All Programs, Accessories, Command Prompt to open the command prompt window). You must know the exact name and most likely the folder in which it's stored.
- Press Ctrl+Alt+Del to launch the Task Manager. Click on New Task and then type in the executable filename for the program (for example, `word.exe`).

An alternative approach is to open a document that's associated with a given application—this is a trick to open the application:

- Locate a document that was created with the application in question and double-click it. This runs the application and loads the document into it. With some applications, you can then close the document and open a new one if you need to.

- Right-click on the desktop or in a folder and choose New. Then choose a document type from the resulting menu. This creates a new document of the type you desire, which, when double-clicked, will run the application.

Here's how to open an existing document in an application (ranked in order of ease of use):

- Click Start, Documents and look among the most recently edited documents. Clicking one will open the document in the appropriate application.

- Use the Start, Search command to locate the document.

- Run the application that created the document and check the document's MRU (most recently used) list on the File menu. It may be there. If so, click it.

In the name of expediency, we're not going to cover all these options. Once you get the hang of the most common approaches, you'll understand how to use the others. Notice that some of the approaches are "application centric," whereas others are "document centric." An application-centric person thinks, "I'll run Word so I can write up that trip expense report." A document-centric person thinks, "I have to work on that company manual. I'll look for it and double-click it."

RUNNING PROGRAMS FROM THE START BUTTON

The most popular way to run your applications is with the Start button, which is located down in the lower-left corner of your screen. When you install a new program, the program's name is usually added somewhere to the Start button's All Programs menu lists. If you've recently used an application, Windows XP may list it in the recently used list on the top-level Start menu area. Sometimes you'll have to "drill down" a level or two to find a certain program, because software makers sometimes like to store their applications under their company names (for example, RealNetworks creates a group called Real, which you have to open to run RealPlayer or RealJukebox). Then you just find your way to the program's name, choose it, and the program runs. Suppose you want to run the calculator. Here are the steps to follow:

1. Click the Start button.
2. Point to All Programs.
3. Point to Accessories, and then choose Calculator.

Note that all selections with an arrow pointing to the right of the name have submenus—meaning that they'll open when you click them or hover the pointer over them. There may be several levels of submenus. For example, to see the System Tools submenu, you have to go through All Programs, Accessories, System Tools.

TIP FROM
Bob & Brian

> Sometimes, spotting a program in a list is a visual hassle. Press the first letter of the program you're looking for and the cursor jumps to it. If there are multiple items starting with that letter, each keypress advances one item in the list. Also, pressing the right-arrow key opens a submenu. The Enter key executes the highlighted program. Items in the lists are ordered alphabetically, although folders appear first, in order, with programs after that.

Often you'll accidentally open a list that you don't want to look at (say, the Games submenu). Just move the pointer to the one you want and wait a second, or press the Esc key. Each press of Esc closes one level of any open lists. To close down all open lists, just click anywhere else on the screen, such as on the desktop or another window. All open Start button lists go away.

 If a shortcut on your Start menu doesn't work, see "Shortcut Doesn't Work" in the "Troubleshooting" section at the end of this chapter.

RUNNING A PROGRAM FROM MY COMPUTER OR WINDOWS EXPLORER

If you're a power user, chances are good you'll be sleuthing around on your hard disk using either the My Computer approach or the Windows Explorer. I certainly have programs floating around on my hard disk that do not appear in my Start button program menus, and I have to execute them directly. In general, the rule for running programs without the Start menu is this: If you can find and display the program's icon, just double-click it. It should run.

TIP FROM
Bob & Brian

> Just as in Windows 2000 and Windows Me, the differences between My Computer and Windows Explorer within Windows XP are more cosmetic than functional. In fact, simply by changing the defaults of the display mode (WebView or classic), the same view (that is, the same layout, panes, and details) is obtainable using either interface. To alter the views, use the View menu (or the toolbar buttons).

TIP FROM
Bob & Brian

> Right-clicking My Computer and choosing Manage launches a powerful computer manager program called *Computer Management.* This is covered in Chapter 27, "System Utilities."

TIP FROM
Bob & Brian

> My Network Places is a version of the My Computer interface that is used to gain access to network resources. Overall, it's used in the same manner as My Computer. The only difference is that you must be on a network and someone must grant you access to shared resources on other systems for this tool to be of any use. Thus, we've left the discussion of this tool to Part IV, "Networking."

Getting to a program you want is often a little convoluted, but it's not too difficult to grasp. Plus, if you understand the DOS directory tree structure or you've used a Mac, you already know more about XP than you think. Double-click a drive to open it, and then double-click a directory to open it. Then double-click the program you want to run. Figure 4.13 shows a typical directory listing for My Computer.

Figure 4.13
A typical directory as shown in My Computer.

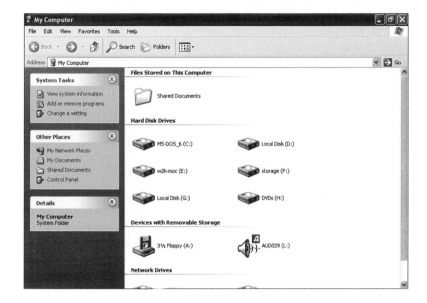

Here are some notes to remember:

- Get to the Desktop quickly by clicking the Show Desktop icon in the Quick Launch bar (just to the right of the Start Button).

- Folders are listed first, followed by files. Double-clicking a folder will reveal its contents.

- If you want to see more folders on the screen at once to help in your search, you have several options. The View menu or the View button on the toolbar can be used to change view options. The Titles view shows large icons with titles and other descriptors. The Icons view uses small icons with only the object name. The Thumbnails view displays images extracted from the file objects themselves—this view is most useful for graphic files. The List view displays everything in a column by its object name only. The Details view offers the most comprehensive information about file system objects in a multi-column display with object names, object type, size, modified date, comments, and so on.

TIP FROM

Bob & Brian

> Pressing Backspace while in any folder window will move you up one level in the directory tree. Also, the Back and Forward buttons work just like they do in a Web browser—they'll move you forward and back through folders you've already visited.

Of course, many of the files you'll find in your folders are *not* programs. They're documents or support files. To easily find the applications, choose the Details view and then click the column head for Type. This sorts the listing by type, making it easy to find applications in the list (which carry an "Application" label).

NOTE

> Applications, registered file types, and certain system files will not have their file extensions (a period and three letter label that follows the file name) displayed by default. "Hidden" system files and directories will be invisible, too. This choice was made to prevent cluttering the display with files that perform duties for the operating system but not directly for users. It also prevents meddling with files that could cripple applications and documents, or even the system at large. Personally, I like seeing as many details about files as possible, so when I first install a system, I change the default settings to show me every file on my system. This is done through the View tab of the Folder Options applet accessed through the My Computer or Windows Explorer Tools menu or the Control Panel.

RUNNING APPLICATIONS WITH THE SEARCH COMMAND

One of the first rules of organization is to know where things are, and how to keep them in their rightful places. The Search command from the Start menu is a tool often used in this mission. It is invaluable for those of us who are too lazy to *get* organized—just do a search for that file you know you stored *somewhere*, but couldn't remember where to save your life. Yes, indeed, it's a wonderful tool for the absent-minded. If you're interested in organizing your "stuff" (the lexicon's term *du jour* for anything in your computer), you must find it first. The Search command offers major assistance to the sleuth.

The Search tool found at the top level of the Start menu is a powerful tool for locating files, folders, computers, people, and even Internet resources (see Figure 4.14). (Press F3 or Windows-F as shortcuts to the Search tool.) The first page of the search tool prompts you to select the type of search to perform. The options include Pictures, music, or video; Documents; All files and folders; and Printers, computers, and people. You can limit your search to the local system or include anywhere within your reach over the network. It always helps to know the exact name of the object you are looking for, but even if you only know part of it, the Search tool quickly locates all of the possibilities.

You can use standard DOS-style wildcards in your searches for files. For example, the * character substitutes for a character string of any length and ? replaces one character. Once a list of possible suspects is returned, click on one to open it in its respective application.

Figure 4.14
The Search tool window with results from a "*.txt" search.

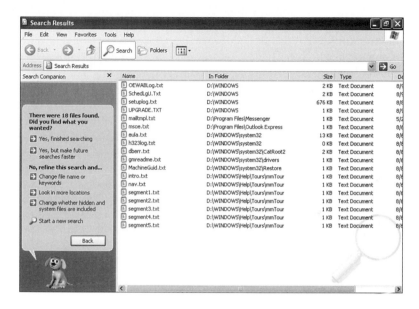

Once an item is listed in the search results, it is accessed by double-clicking on it. If it is an application, it will be launched. If it is a data file, it will be opened within its associated application. If it is a Web URL, your Web browser will be launched to view it. If it is a media file, the correct player will be launched to playback or display it. The Search tool can be used to execute a program that you can't seem to find in the Start menu, can't find anywhere on the system using My Computer, and which won't execute from the Run command. Also keep in mind that applications that won't execute from the Run command are outside of the paths known to Windows XP. Paths is an environment variable (see Chapter 24, "Configuration via Control Panel Applets") which defines all common locations where Windows will search for executables or other necessary files. If it lies outside the path, then Windows XP can't find it without help.

When using Search's All files and folders, be sure to pay attention to the Look In selection. By default, Search will look on all local hard drives. If you want to limit the search to a single drive or want to search over the network, you'll need to alter this setting. Fortunately, there is a pull-down list with all the common options plus Browse. The Browse selection is used to select any folder or drive anywhere within your reach over the network or locally.

USING MY DOCUMENTS, MY PICTURES, AND MY MUSIC

Windows XP is designed to help you focus on your creative tasks rather than the underlying OS which supports the tools and files. Part of this includes the My Documents, My Pictures, and My Music Start menu items. These links also appear on most file or browse windows as well as within My Computer and Windows Explorer. These three My labeled elements always link you back to a standard location where your personal data files are stored.

The My Documents folder is the master folder for all of your personal data files. This is the default storage location whenever you save a new document or data file. This is also where the My Music and My Pictures subfolders reside. These folders are provided to you to simplify the storage and retrieval of your most intimate file-stored creations. Clicking on one of these Start menu links will open a My Computer window.

TIP FROM

Bob

& Brian

My Documents is not the same as My Recent Documents. My Recent Documents is a quick-access list of the 15 most recently accessed resources. This included documents, music files, image files, archive files, and even (sometimes) programs. If you ever want to clear out the list of recently accessed documents, the Clear List button beside the check box does just that.

USING THE HELP SYSTEM

We've yet to advance our computing systems to the level displayed in Star Trek where officers command an action and it takes place. When you want your computer to do something, you need to tell it what to do. Often, you have to explain in great detail at every step exactly what actions to take or not to take. The Windows XP Help system is designed to aid you in finding out what everything within the environment can and cannot do as well as teaching you how to perform the activity you need for work or play.

The Help system is accessed by clicking on the Help and Support item on the top level of the Start menu. The Help system offers a wide range of options from a search routine, to topic-organized texts, to task-assisting walk-throughs, to Internet updated dynamic content help (see Figure 4.15). The Help system also includes access to a full index, a history list, and a favorites list. It operates in much the same way as a Web browser—using hyperlinks, back and forward buttons, and the ability to return to the start of the system using the Home button. When searching for material, you can use Boolean rules to fine-tune your keyword search phrases (AND, OR, NOT, and NEAR). This is definitely a tool that is worth your effort to explore and to consult in times of trouble or confusion.

Figure 4.15
The Help and Support Center interface.

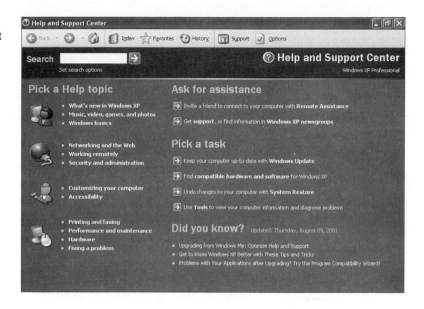

EXITING WINDOWS GRACEFULLY

When you've finished a Windows XP session, you should properly shut down or log off to ensure that your work is saved and that no damage is done to the operating system. Shall we reiterate? Shutting down properly is very important. You can lose your work or otherwise foul up Windows settings if you don't shut down before turning off your computer. If multiple people share the computer, you should at least log off when you're finished so that others can log on. Logging off protects your work and settings from prying eyes. When you shut down, Windows does some housekeeping, closes all open files, prompts you to save any unsaved work files, and alerts the network that you and your shared resources are no longer available for consultation.

There are several ways to shut down the computer, all or only some of which might apply to your machine. Newer machines will have more shutdown features because they're likely to have advanced power management built into them via ACPI.

Here are the steps for correctly exiting Windows:

1. Close any programs that you have running. (This can almost always be done from each program's File, Exit menu or by clicking the program's close button.) If you forget to close programs before issuing the Logout or Shut Down command, Windows will attempt to close them for you. If you haven't saved your work, you'll typically be prompted to do so. Some programs, such as DOS programs, you'll have to manually close. Windows will alert you if it can't automatically close an open program. Quit the DOS program and type exit at the DOS prompt, if necessary. If you are just switching user context, your open application's status is saved so you can quickly return to it later.

2. Click Start, Turn Off Computer. You'll see the dialog box shown in Figure 4.16.

4

Figure 4.16
The Turn off computer selection dialog box.

3. Click on the desired option.

Here are some points to consider:

■ The Hibernate option records the current state of the system to disk, and then shuts down the computer. Once the power is turned back on, the system reboots. If you log back in as the same user who initiated the hibernation, the system returns to its exact state at the moment of hibernation.

■ If your computer has *Advanced Power Manager (APM)* or *Advanced Configuration and Power Interface (ACPI)* built in, you will see the Standby option instead of Hibernate. (Standby is explained later in this section.) This will certainly be the case with PCs fitted with ATX motherboards (as opposed to the older AT-style PC) and power supplies. The ATX motherboards have standby capability that Windows XP should recognize and utilize. If your system isn't ACPI enabled, you won't see the Standby option.

■ If you have an APM or ACPI system and want to Hibernate your system rather than put it on Standby, you can access this option by pressing and holding Shift. This action changes the Standby button to Hibernate. Be sure to hold the Shift key down while you click the Hibernate button.

■ If you want to log off, use the Log Off command button from the Start menu instead of the Turn Off Computer command button (first click Cancel on the Turn Off Computer dialog box). There are no logoff options offered in the Turn Off Computer dialog box.

■ If you attempt to shut down the computer while another user's desktop is still active (that is, Switch User was employed and at least one other user is still logged on), you'll see a warning message stating that performing a shutdown could result in data loss along with the options to continue with shutdown (Yes) or abort (No).

TIP FROM

Bob & Brian

> Logging off clears personal settings from memory and puts the computer in a neutral state, waiting for another user to log on. However, it doesn't bring the system to its knees. Logging off will not stop running services, which can include Web services, file sharing, print sharing, UPS support, and scheduled tasks. When the Log Off command button is clicked on the Start menu, you are offered two options: Switch User or Log Off. The latter exits you from the system and closes all applications. The former retains your environment while allowing another user to gain access to their desktop.

Standby puts the computer in a suspended state, letting you quickly come right back to where you were working before you suspended the PC. This means you don't have to exit all your applications before turning off your computer. You only have to choose Standby. This also saves energy, because the hard drives, CPU, CPU fan, some internal electronics, and possibly the power supply and fan will go into a low-power state. Your monitor, if Energy Star compliant, should also go into a frugal state of energy consumption. When you want to start up again, a quick press of the power switch (on some computers a keypress on the keyboard or a jiggle of the mouse will do) should start up the system right where you left off. Make sure to press the power button for just a second or so. Anything more than four seconds on most modern computers in a standby state will cause the computer to completely power down.

Be aware that Standby will hold your system state only so long as the computer has power. If the power fails, everything stored in the computer's RAM will be lost. You'll end up doing a cold boot when the power is restored or, if it's a laptop with a dead battery, when you hook your AC adapter up to your laptop again. The moral is to be cautious when using Standby. You should save your work before going into Standby mode, if not close important documents.

One of the most welcome features of recent versions of Windows, including Windows XP, is *hibernation*. Like standby mode, hibernation lets you pause your work and resume later, without laboriously shutting down and reopening all your applications and files. But unlike Standby, Hibernate isn't volatile. If the AC power fails or batteries run flat, it doesn't matter because Hibernate stores the "system state" on a portion of the hard disk rather than keeping the system RAM alive in a low-power state. After storing the system state to the hard disk, the computer fully shuts down. When restarted, a little internal flag tells the boot loader that the system has been stored on disk, and it's reloaded into memory.

Hibernation requires as much free hard disk space as you have RAM in your PC. If you have 128MB of RAM, you'll need 128MB of free disk space for hibernation to work. If Hibernate is not an option on your Shut Down menu, enable it through the Power Options in Control Panel. The dialog box reports the amount of disk space needed for your system in case you're unaware of the amount of RAM in your system.

When you choose Hibernate from the shutdown menu, Windows XP has to create a fairly large file on disk. In my case, for example, it's 256MB in size. On a 1GHz Intel Pentium III, the entire process takes about 15 seconds. Restarting takes about the same amount of time. Remember, if you're going to put a laptop running on batteries to sleep for more than a few hours, use Hibernate or just do a complete shutdown, closing your applications and documents. That way, if the batteries run out, you won't lose your work.

DEALING WITH A CRASHED APPLICATION OR OPERATING SYSTEM

Even though Windows XP is fairly immune to crashing, the applications that run on it are not necessarily so robust. Not to be cynical, but many IS professionals don't consider any version of Windows worth their trouble until version 2 or a couple of service packs hit the

4

streets, because they know bugs tend to be prevalent in first-release software. With an operating system as complex as Windows XP, we bet there are a few gotchas lurking.

 If your system is still stuck but you can get the Task Manager up, see "Forcing Your Computer to Shut Down" in the "Troubleshooting" section at the end of this chapter.

 If your laptop computer won't shut down no matter what you do, see "Ctrl+Alt+Delete Doesn't Work" in the "Troubleshooting" section at the end of this chapter.

My point here is that you're going to bump into some unstable behavior from time to time. If you notice that a program's not responding, you may have a crash on your hands. To gracefully survive a crash, possibly even without losing any of your data, try the following steps:

1. Try pressing Esc. Some programs get stuck in the middle of a process and Esc can sometimes get them back on track. For example, if you accidentally pressed Alt, this activates the menus. A press of Esc will get you out of that loop. If you've opened a menu, two presses of Esc or a click within the application's window may be required to return to normal operation.

2. Windows XP has greatly improved application-management facilities. In most cases, even after an application has crashed, you should still be able to minimize, maximize, move, resize, and close its window.

3. Can you switch to the app to bring its window up front? First try clicking any portion of the window. If that doesn't work, click its button in the taskbar. Still no? Try using successive presses of Alt+Tab. If you get the window open and responding, try to save any unfinished work in the app and then try to close it by clicking the close button or selecting the File, Exit.

4. If that doesn't work, try right-clicking the program's button in the taskbar and choosing Close from the pop-up menu.

5. If that doesn't work, press Ctrl+Shift+Esc to launch the Task Manager. Notice the list of running applications. Does the one in question say "Not responding" next to it? If so, click it and then click End Task.

6. If Task Manager reports that you don't have sufficient access to terminate the task, you must reboot the system. First, attempt a graceful shutdown using the Turn Off Computer command. However, if that fails (that is, it hangs on the hung application or it never seems to complete the shutdown process), you'll need to resort to power cycling. Once the system reboots you should be back to normal.

TROUBLESHOOTING

SHORTCUT DOESN'T WORK

I click a shortcut somewhere in my Start menu and nothing happens or I get an error message.

Windows isn't smart enough, or, to put it another way, it would be too much software overhead for the OS to keep track of all the shortcuts and update them, as necessary, when the files they point to are moved or deleted. A system that's been in use for some time will certainly have "dead" shortcuts, just as Web pages have broken links floating around. When you click a shortcut icon anywhere in the system—be it the Start menus, the desktop, or in a folder—and you get an error message about the program file, click OK and let Windows take a stab at solving the problem by searching for the application. If it's found, Windows XP "heals" the shortcut so that it will work again next time you use it.

If that doesn't work, trying searching yourself using Start, Search. See whether you can track down the runaway application. If you're successful, you'll probably be best off erasing the bad shortcut and creating a new one that points to the correct location. You can create a new shortcut by right-clicking the app's icon and choosing Create Shortcut. Then drag, copy, or move the shortcut to wherever you want, such as onto the Start button.

Another good trick to help you sort out a bad shortcut or to follow where its trail is leading is to right-click the icon and choose Properties, Find Target.

TIP FROM

Bob & Brian

> Remember, moving folders containing applications (for example, Office might be in `C:\Program Files\MSOffice`) is a *really* bad idea. Once installed, many programs want to stay where they were put.

FORCING YOUR COMPUTER TO SHUT DOWN

The system is acting sluggish, nonresponsive, or otherwise weird.

If your system is really acting erratically or stuck in some serious way and you've already killed any unresponsive programs, press Ctrl+Alt+Delete. This should bring up the Task Manager (Ctrl+Shift+Esc will too). Click the Shut Down menu, and then select Turn off. If you get this far, there's hope for a graceful exit. You might have to wait a minute or so for the turn off command to take effect. If you're prompted to shut down some programs or save documents, do so. Hope for a speedy shutdown. Then reboot.

CTRL+ALT+DELETE DOESN'T WORK

Even Ctrl+Alt+Delete doesn't do anything.

If Turn off doesn't work, it's time to power-cycle the computer. Press the power switch to turn off the machine. On a machine with APM or ACPI support (one that can perform a soft power down), this may require holding the power button in for more than four seconds. You could lose some work, but what else are you going to do? Sometimes it happens. This is one good reason for saving your work regularly, and looking for options in your programs that perform autosaving. As writers, we set our AutoSave function in MS Word to save every five minutes. That way, we can recover from a system crash and only lose up to five minutes of work instead of everything.

Incidentally, while extremely rare, I've known laptops to not even respond to any form of command or power button when the operating system was fully hung. I've even had to remove any AC connection, fully remove the main battery, wait a few seconds, and then reinsert the battery and reboot. Removal of the battery is important; otherwise, the battery keeps the computer in the same stuck state, thinking it's just in standby mode.

TIPS FROM THE WINDOWS PROS: WORKING EFFICIENTLY

The interface is your portal into the operating system and therefore into your computer. You're likely to be using it every day, so it behooves you to "work the system" as effectively and efficiently as possible. As writers and programmers on deadlines, we're using our computers at breakneck speed most of the time. Cutting corners on how you control the system interface saves you literally hundreds of miles of mousing around on your desktop over the course of a few years. Here are our top time-saving and motion-saving tips for using Windows XP:

- To get to the desktop (minimize all open windows), press the Windows key and M at the same time. To reverse the effect, press Shift+Windows+M. This is a real time-saver. If you prefer the mouse, click the Show Desktop button in the Quick Launch Bar. It does the same thing.

- Change between apps with Alt+Tab. Aiming for an application's little button on the taskbar is a hassle. You'll get tendonitis doing that all day.

- Buy an ergonomic keyboard, split in the middle. Try not to rest your wrists on a hard surface. Cut a mouse pad in half and use Velcro, tape, or glue to affix it to the palm rest in front of the keys, if you're a "leaner."

- Double-click a window's title bar to make it go full screen. Editing in little windows on the screen is a hassle and requires unnecessary scrolling.

- To close a program or window, press Alt+F4. It's that easy. Alternatively, right-click its button on the taskbar and choose Close. Aiming for that little X in the upper-right corner takes too much mouse movement.

- Put all your favorite applications, dial-up connections, folders, and documents on the Quick Launch bar. Forget about the Start button. You can put about 20 things down there on the Quick Launch bar for easy one-click access. Use it. When an item falls out of use, erase the shortcut. They're only shortcuts, so it doesn't matter if you erase them.

- If there are too many items within the Quick Launch bar to be displayed within the current area, two little arrows (>>) will be displayed. This indicates that other Quick Launch icons are present but are currently hidden from view. To see the hidden icons, click on the double arrow to see a pop-up menu or click and drag the edge of the main toolbar area (just to the right of the Quick Launch bar) to expand the space available for the Quick Launch bar.

- Those little double arrows appear in many locations throughout the user experience. You'll see them on the Quick Launch bar, the system tray, the WebView details pane, ends of toolbars, and more. They simply indicate that either more data is available but it's currently hidden from view, or that all data is currently displayed but it can be hidden or reduced in size. In some cases, the double arrows are a toggle between minimum and expanded views, while at other times, the double arrows will display the hidden items when clicked but will return to their previous display once you make a selection or click somewhere else.

- Use Standby and Hibernate! Don't boot up every time you turn on your computer. It's a waste of valuable time. Keep your favorite programs open: e-mail, word processor, picture viewer, Web browser, spreadsheet, whatever. Yes, do save your work, maybe even close your document, but leave the apps open and keep the machine in standby or hibernate mode.

- If you use a laptop in the office, get a good external keyboard to work with it. Your hands will probably be happier, and you'll type faster. Also, get a pointing device that works best for you. Those "pointing stick" mice are not for everyone. Try a few different pointing devices and come up with one that works best for you.

- Discover and use right-click shortcuts whenever possible. For example, in Outlook Express, you can easily copy the name and e-mail address of someone from the Address Book and paste them into an e-mail. People are always asking me for e-mail addresses of mutual friends or colleagues. I click on a person's entry in the Address Book and press Ctrl+C (for copy); then I switch back to the e-mail I'm writing and press Ctrl+V (paste). Then Ctrl+Enter, and the e-mail is sent.

- Also in Outlook Express, you can reply to an e-mail with Ctrl+R. Forward one with Ctrl+F. Send a message you've just written by pressing Ctrl+Enter. Send and receive all mail with Ctrl+M.

- In Internet Explorer, use the F11 toggle to go full screen. This gets all the other junk off the screen. Also, use the Search panel to do your Web searches (opened by clicking the magnifying glass search toolbar button). You can easily check search results without having to use the Back button. And speaking of the Back button, don't bother moving the mouse up there to click Back. Just press Alt+left arrow. The left- and right-arrow buttons with Alt are the same as the Back and Forward buttons.

- In most Microsoft applications, including Outlook Express and Internet Explorer, F5 is the "refresh" key. In OE, for example, pressing F5 sends and receives all your mail, so long as the Inbox is highlighted. In IE, it refreshes the page. In Windows Explorer, it updates the listing in a window (to reflect the results of a file move, for example). Remember F5!

- In Word, Excel, and many other apps, Ctrl+F6 is the key that switches between open windows within the same app. No need to click on the Window menu in the app and choose the document in question. Just cycle through them with Ctrl+F6.

4

■ In whatever apps you use most, look for shortcut keys or macros you can use or create to avoid unnecessary repetitious work. Most of us type the same words again and again. (See, there I go.) As writers, for example, we have macros programmed in MS Word for common words such as *Windows 2000 Professional*, *Control Panel*, *desktop*, *folders*, and so on. Bob has created a slew of editing macros that perform tasks such as "delete to the end of line" (Ctrl+P), "delete line" (Ctrl+Y), and so on. In Word, press Alt+T+A and check out the AutoCorrect and AutoText features.

→ **See** Chapter 23, "Tweaking the GUI," to add more time-saving tricks to your arsenal.

4

CHAPTER 5

USING THE SIMPLE SUPPLIED APPLICATIONS

In this chapter

A SEA OF FREEBIES

Although you no doubt have collected your own arsenal of workhorse programs to assist you in your daily chores, Windows XP Professional, like past versions of Windows, comes replete with numerous freebie utility programs to handle common, everyday tasks. These utility programs range from the bizarre to the useful—from pinball and solitaire to audio CD and DVD movie players, word processing programs, and a calculator, to name but a few. Whether they are intended for entertainment or as daily helpmates for such tasks as jotting down simple notes or making quick calculations, none of these programs requires a degree in rocket science to figure out. They are fairly self-explanatory, and it's possible you've used them before in their previous versions. Therefore, this chapter covers them only briefly, suggests a few tips, and leaves the rest to you and the Windows Help file.

Because many of the accessory programs fall into discrete categories, such as communications, multimedia entertainment, or system tools, look to relevant sections of this book to find coverage of such tools. This chapter covers the more basic, yet still quite useful, tools that don't fit neatly into a pigeonhole.

TIP FROM

Bob
& Brian

> Windows XP comes with a bunch of games (FreeCell, Minesweeper, Pinball, Solitaire, Hearts, Internet Backgammon, Internet Checkers, Internet Hearts, Internet Reversi, Internet Spades, and Spider Solitaire). You can get to these from Start, All Programs, Games. If some of these are missing from your Windows XP installation, you can load them by using Add or Remove Programs in Control Panel. (Control Panel is covered in Chapter 24, "Configuration via Control Panel Applets"). After you select Add or Remove Programs, choose Windows Components (on the left side of the dialog box), then highlight Accessories and Utilities and click Details. Then click Games and click Details. Then check the games you want.
>
> This book doesn't cover the specifics of each of these games because you can probably figure them out yourself—and you probably ought to be getting some work done at the office (except for lunchtime and breaks). Click Help in each game for game rules and guidance. If you like games, you might check them out.

NOTEPAD

Notepad has been around since Windows 3.0. It's a simple, no-frills text editor that does no fancy formatting (though it does enable you to change the display font) and is popular for composing "clean" ASCII (.TXT) files. I use Notepad for jotting down quick notes. You could say Notepad is a *text editor*, whereas WordPad (see the "WordPad" section later in this chapter) is a *word processor*. Unlike WordPad, Notepad cannot view or edit Microsoft Word (.DOC) or Rich Text Format (.RTF) files. It's a perfect tool to call up whenever you need to view a simple README.TXT file or fine-tune some program code (programmers like this tool).

TIP FROM

Bob

& Brian

Here's a quick way to create a Notepad file. Just right-click the desktop or a folder, choose New, Text document. Then type in the name for your document and press Enter. Now press Enter or double-click the icon, and the new Notepad file opens. This is a good technique for taking down a quick memo, making notes about a phone call, or keeping a to-do list on your desktop.

Text-only files contain text characters and nothing else—no character formatting such as italics, bold, underlining, or paragraph formatting information such as line spacing, and definitely no graphics. Sometimes such files are called ASCII files, plain ASCII files, or simply *text files*. As of Notepad version 5 (included in Windows 2000; the notepad version in Windows XP is version 5.1), the Save As dialog box allows you to save in several text-only file types listed in the Encoding pull-down menu: ANSI, Unicode, UTF-8, and Unicode big endian. These formats provide you with greater flexibility when you're working with documents that use different character sets. The default is ANSI, and unless you are inserting non-U.S. characters, you should use this format when you save files.

ASCII, ANSI, and Unicode—Alphabet Soup Anyone?

ASCII stands for American Standard Code for Information Interchange. Standard ASCII is a 7-bit character-encoding scheme used to represent 128 characters (upper- and lowercase letters, the numbers 0 through 9, punctuation marks, and special control characters) used in U.S. English. Most current Intel-based systems support the use of extended (or "high") ASCII, which is an 8-bit system. The 8th bit allows an additional 128 special symbol characters, foreign-language letters, and graphic symbols to be represented. Even with 8 bits, ASCII is not capable of representing all the combinations of letters and diacritical marks that are used in the Roman alphabet. DOS uses a superset of ASCII called *extended ASCII* or *high ASCII*. A more universal standard is the ISO Latin-1 set of characters, which is used by many operating systems, as well as Web browsers.

ANSI stands for the American National Standards Institute. Windows uses the ANSI character set, which is very similar to ASCII. Windows 3.x and Windows 95 support the ANSI character set, which includes 256 characters, numbered 0 to 255. Values 0 to 127 are the same as in the ASCII character set. Values 128 to 255 are similar to the ISO Latin-1 character set but naturally have extensions and incompatibilities.

Unicode, which uses 16 bits, goes beyond ASCII and ANSI. Developed by the Unicode Consortium between 1988 and 1991, Unicode enables almost all the written languages of the world to be represented using a single character set. Using Unicode, 65,536 possible characters can be represented, approximately 39,000 of which have now been assigned, 21,000 of them being used for Chinese ideographs.

Although they're visually boring and lackluster, text files do have some important advantages over formatted text documents. Most importantly, they are the lowest common denominator for exchanging text between different programs and even between different types of computers. Literally any kind of word processor and many other types of programs, from email tools to databases, can share textual information using simple text files, regardless of computer type or operating system. To be sure your recipients using other kinds of computers can read a text email attachment or a text file on a disk, stick with the simple text files such as the ones Notepad creates.

5

Source code used to generate computer programs is often stored as text files, too. Because files are clean, without extraneous codes for formatting, program *compilers* (software that converts the source code into a working program) are not confused. Good examples of simple ASCII program code or configuration file code are found in the WIN.INI, SYS.INI, PROTO-COL.INI, BOOT.INI, CONFIG.SYS, and AUTOEXEC.BAT files. These files, found in many Windows computers, control various aspects of Windows, all of which can be edited with Notepad. HTML code for Web pages is another example. You can safely edit HTML in Notepad.

Windows recognizes any file with a .TXT extension as a text file and opens it in Notepad when you click it. For this reason, README files supplied with programs—even some supplied with Windows—are stored as .TXT files. Take a look around on the Windows XP Professional CD, and you'll find some pithy files about setup, networking, and so on. After you open them in Notepad, turn on the word wrap feature (by choosing Format, Word Wrap) to view the document correctly.

→ To learn more about Word Wrap, **see** "Running Notepad," **p. 153**.

NOTEPAD'S LIMITATIONS

As I mentioned previously, Notepad does no formatting. In fact, it doesn't even wrap lines of text to fill the window unless you tell it to. Notepad can't properly render or print formatted documents created with WordPad, Microsoft Word for Windows, WordPerfect, or any other fancy word processor (unless you saved files you create with those programs as ASCII or ANSI text files). You can open these document types, but they look like gibberish. Also, it doesn't have any fancy pagination options, though it does print with headers and footers via the Page Setup dialog box. Although you can change the font in Notepad 5, font information isn't stored in the file. Font choice is a personal preference for viewing and printing, and applies to all files you open in Notepad.

TIP FROM

Bob
& Brian

Be careful about opening formatted text files with Notepad. Typically, this will take a little doing, because when you use the File, Open command, the box defaults to ".txt" files. But you could enter the entire name of a preexisting file that you wanted to examine, such as a `mydocument.doc` or `mydocument.rtf`. A formatted file will probably appear as gibberish in Notepad. Nonetheless, if you accidentally save the file, the formatting is stripped out of it, and the file can become useless. I don't recommend using Notepad to view a file unless you have no other software tool suitable for the purpose, because it's hard to read the file and you can easily damage it.

If you want to examine executable files or initialization or control files used by programs, I suggest a file viewer intended for this purpose, such as FVIEW. Many utility programs for this purpose are available on the Web or at software stores. One such program is called QuickView Plus. It's a full version of the quick viewers supplied with Windows 9x. It's available from Jasc Software (`http://www.jasc.com`). QuickView Plus is also useful for viewing the contents of temporary files which may contain a version of a document you were working on when your system locked up.

Notepad files used to be limited in size to about 50KB. That's no longer the case. Even very large files can be loaded into Notepad 5.1.

RUNNING NOTEPAD

To run Notepad, click Start, More Programs (or just Programs, depending on how you have your taskbar settings), Accessories, Notepad. Notepad then appears on your screen (see Figure 5.1). When it does, you can just type away.

Figure 5.1
You can use Notepad to edit simple text. I've entered some text already.

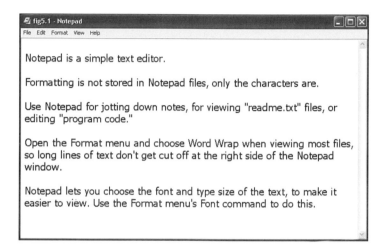

Of course, you can choose File, New to start a new file at any time. If you've made changes in the current file and haven't saved them, Notepad asks if you want to save it before creating the new file. You use the standard File, Open and File, Save As commands. You can only have one document open at a time in Notepad.

TIP FROM

Although you can have only one file open in a particular Notepad *window* at a time, you can have multiple Notepad windows running. This enables you to cut, copy, and paste text between windows or perform visual file comparisons.

You should turn on word wrap when you enter text unless you're entering program code that is line oriented. When you do, by choosing Format, Word Wrap, the text wraps within the constraints of the window. If you resize the window, the text rewraps to fit the available space. Note that the word wrap setting doesn't affect the text file itself. That is, Notepad doesn't insert line feeds or carriage returns at the points where the lines wrap.

As with most Windows text programs, the keys shown in Table 5.1 have the effects shown here.

TABLE 5.1   KEYS IN NOTEPAD

Key	Moves Insertion Point To
Home	Start of the line
End	End of the line
PgUp	Up one window
PgDn	Down one window
Ctrl+Left Arrow	Start of previous word
Ctrl+Right Arrow	Start of next word
Ctrl+Home	Start of the file
Ctrl+End	End of the file
F5 (particular to Notepad)	Inserts the time and date
Ctrl+Backspace	Deletes a word to the left
Del	Deletes letter right
Backspace	Deletes letter left

 If you can't see all the text in a Notepad window, see "My Text Is Chopped Off" in the "Troubleshooting" section at the end of this chapter.

SETTING MARGINS AND ADDING HEADERS AND FOOTERS

Despite the paucity of formatting options for onscreen display, you can format printed output to some degree. Use the File, Page Setup command to establish headers and footers. ¹ Enter your desired footing and heading text. Margin changes and header and footer settings aren't visible onscreen but do print. You can also include the special codes shown in Table 5.2 in the header and footer fields. You can enter these codes alone or within a text string.

TABLE 5.2   FORMATTING CODES FOR NOTEPAD

Code	Effect
&d	Includes the current date
&p	Includes the page number
&f	Includes the filename
&l	Forces subsequent text to left-align at the margin
&r	Forces subsequent text to right-align at the margin
&c	Centers the subsequent text
&t	Includes the time of the printing

Here are a couple examples to help you take advantage of these formatting codes. To print the time and filename at the top of each page, add this to the header field in the Page Setup menu as shown in Figure 5.2:

```
Printed at &t  Filename is &f
```

If the time the document was printed was 10:30 a.m. and the filename was README.TXT, the header will appear like this when the document is printed:

```
Printed at 10:30 Filename is Readme.txt
```

By default, &p (page number) is used in the footer field as shown in Figure 5.2, so the page number will print at the bottom of each page unless you add or remove footer codes.

Figure 5.2
Adding Header and Footer codes to identify printouts from Notepad.

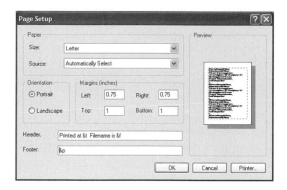

When you print a document, Notepad lets you choose the page range, the number of copies, and the printer to which the job is sent. See Chapter 6, "Printing and Faxing with Windows XP," for more details.

NOTE

You won't be able to select which page(s) to print with Notepad unless the document has had page breaks inserted in it by its creator. For example, the .TXT documents on the Windows XP CD-ROM can only be printed in their entirety.

5

WORDPAD

For more capable word processing than Notepad can accomplish, you can use WordPad. Though it's not Word or WordPerfect, it works fine for most everyday writing chores. It includes most of the formatting tools people need for typical writing projects, and the price is right. You can edit documents of virtually any length, it supports drag-and-drop editing, and it can accept graphics pasted to it from the Windows Clipboard. WordPad supports the following:

- Standard character formatting with font, style, and size
- Standard paragraph formatting with changing line spacing, indents and margins, bullets, justification, and right and left alignment
- Adjustable tab stops

- Search and replace
- Headers and footers
- Pagination control
- Insert and edit graphics
- Undo
- Print preview

It doesn't do tables, columns, indexes, master documents, outline view, legal line numbering, or anything really groovy, though. Go get Word or WordPerfect if you have that level of needs.

SAVE AND OPEN OPTIONS

WordPad can save and open files in several formats:

- **Rich Text Format**—This choice is the default. The Rich Text Format is used more and more as a common format for exchanging documents between word processors, though few, if any, use it as their primary format (it's sort of like an Esperanto for word processors). The Rich Text Format preserves the appearance as well as the content of your document. Graphics and other objects can be saved in the file along with the text but might be lost when you open the file with another application. To learn more about how to insert graphics into a WordPad document so that the graphic will be stored in the document, see "Adding Graphics to a WordPad Document" later in this chapter.

- **Text Files**—See the discussion of text files earlier in the chapter in the section covering Notepad.

- **Unicode**—See the discussion of Unicode earlier in the chapter in the section covering Notepad.

WordPad also can open the following document types (although it must save changes to these files as .RTF, Text, or Unicode documents):

- **Word for Windows**—This choice opens documents stored in the format used by Microsoft Word for Windows, version 6.0 and Microsoft Word 95 (.DOC). If you have any version of Microsoft Word installed, incidentally, double-clicking a .DOC file opens it in Word, not WordPad.

- **Windows Write**—This choice opens documents stored in the .WRI format used by Windows Write, the simple word processor supplied with Windows 3.x. This feature enables you to read README.WRI files supplied with some older Windows applications.

- **Text Documents—MS-DOS Format**—This choice opens text documents stored with the MS-DOS version of the ASCII character set.

WordPad correctly opens even incorrectly named (wrong extension) RTF and Word 6 files if you select the All Documents option in the Files of Type area in the Open dialog box or type the document's full name. If WordPad doesn't detect a file's format, it opens it as a text-only file. Note that if a document contains formatting information created by another application it will likely appear as garbage characters mixed with the document's normal text.

RUNNING WORDPAD AND EDITING WITH WORDPAD

To run WordPad, choose Start, All Programs, Accessories, WordPad. The WordPad window then comes up. Figure 5.3 shows an example of a Notepad file which has been edited with WordPad.

Figure 5.3
WordPad includes moderately sophisticated word processing features. Use the View menu to activate the toolbar and ruler bar shown here.

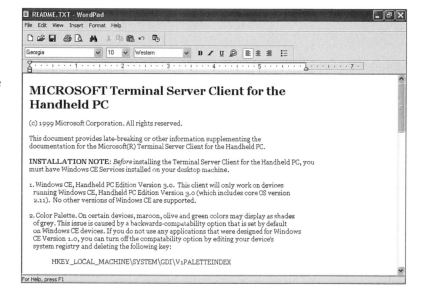

As with most Windows programs these days, you don't have to memorize what each button on the toolbar does. Just position the mouse pointer over the button and a pop-up screen tip will appear on the status bar at the bottom of the screen.

When you're doing lots of editing and formatting in WordPad, check the View menu. You can turn on as many of the toolbars as you need to quickly change formatting, tab locations, and so on. A check mark next to a bar's name means it's on. They are toggle settings.

You can drag and drop or "tear off" the various toolbars. Just position the mouse pointer over the far left edge of any bar (don't click a button); then drag the bar where you want it.

Editing is simple in this program and complies with Windows standards and then adds a few rules of its own. I'll outline them very quickly. Just enter your text as usual. Lines of text occur automatically and are readjusted if you resize the window, change the margins, or change the font size. You can move the cursor around with a click of the mouse or by using the control codes listed for Notepad in Table 5.1.

You can double-click a word to select the whole word. To select the entire document quickly (select all), move the cursor to the left edge of the document until the arrow changes direction, and then Ctrl+click. To select an arbitrary area, click and drag the pointer over the text. Release when the text is highlighted. You can also select areas of text by pressing Shift and using the arrow keys. The spot where you first click (beginning of the selection) is called the *anchor point*. You can triple-click to select a paragraph. After text is selected, you can format it with the toolbars and format menu commands.

To move blocks of text, either select the text and use Cut, Copy, and Paste from the Edit menu, or drag it with the mouse to the new location and drop it.

TIP FROM

Bob

& Brian

> To insert characters that aren't available on your keyboard, such as ™, ®, or ©, use the Character Map accessory, covered later in this chapter in the section "Character Map."

WordPad handles each paragraph as a separate entity, each with its own formatting information, such as tab stops. To apply changes to multiple paragraphs, select them first.

To undo the last command, choose Edit, Undo; click the Undo button (the curving arrow) on the toolbar; or press Ctrl+Z.

Undo can undo the following errors: block deletions, anything removed by pressing Del or Backspace (as a unit), blocks replaced by typing, new text typed (back to the last time you issued a command), and character and paragraph formatting changes (if you select the Undo command immediately after making the change).

ADDING GRAPHICS TO A WORDPAD DOCUMENT

You can insert a graphic—and other *OLE* objects—into a WordPad document in one of three ways: by pasting the graphic from the clipboard, by creating the object from scratch as you insert it, or by inserting an existing object stored in a disk file. The basic steps required are similar for either method, but they vary slightly in detail.

- Select Edit, Paste to insert a graphic you've put on the system Clipboard.
- Select Insert, New Object to create a new graphic using another program or an existing file. In the Insert Object dialog box, choose the type of graphic object you want from the list, and click OK. At the insertion point, an area opens for the graphic. You create the graphic in the second program and then exit the graphics program using the appropriate command (typically Exit and Return) and return to WordPad.
- Click the graphic, and then drag the picture's handles (the small black squares along the edges) to resize the image.

After you've pasted the graphic, you have only crude control over positioning it where you want it in the document. You can't move a graphic around with the mouse, and no menu command is available for this purpose. Instead, you must push the picture around in your document with ordinary typing, the Backspace key, or the Tab key, or you can cut and paste it into a new location.

TIP FROM

When you insert an existing object from a file, the Insert Object dialog box offers a Link check box. If you check this box, any changes to the source file are reflected in the WordPad file. This is called Object Linking and Embedding (OLE), and is different than the usual Cut, Copy, and Paste commands. It's not used very often, so it's not covered in this book. For more information about OLE, check the Windows Help system, and search for linking and embedding.

If you want to retrieve the document with graphics intact on another computer, I recommend using the Edit, Paste method if you can do so. Documents created with the Insert, New Object method that used an existing graphic didn't store the object inside the document file, but used a pointer to it. When the document was retrieved from another system, it would have a framing box instead of the actual graphic.

DISPLAY OPTIONS

A few WordPad preferences affect viewing of files. You can check the View, Options dialog box to see them. All the tab pages except General Options in the Options dialog box pertain to the various types of documents that WordPad can open: Text Only, Rich Text Format, Word for Windows, Windows Write, and Embedded. Each of these pages offers identical choices. These settings affect display only; none of these choices affect the way your document prints.

⚠ *If you have trouble inserting tab stops where you want them, see "Adding and Modifying Tab Stops" in the "Troubleshooting" section at the end of this chapter.*

PAINT

5

Paint is a simple drawing program that creates and edits bitmapped images in a variety of formats. Using free-form drawing tools, text, and special effects, you can create projects such as invitations, maps, signs, and wallpaper for your desktop. and you can edit images linked into documents created by other programs (see Chapter 4 for more details about linking and embedding).

Let me explain why Paint is called a bitmapped image editor. Your computer's screen is divided into very small dots (*pixels* or *pels*) that are controlled by the smallest division of computer information—bits. A *bitmap* is a collection of bits of information that creates an image when assigned (*mapped*) to dots on the screen. This bitmap is similar to one of those giant electronic billboards in Times Square, New York, that can display the score, a message, or even a picture by turning on and off specific light bulbs in the grid.

Being a bitmapped drawing program, rather than an object-oriented drawing program like Adobe Illustrator or CorelDraw, Paint has some significant limitations to keep in mind—also some advantages. After you paint a shape, you can't move it independently. You can use the computer to remove an area of the painting and place it somewhere else—as if you were cutting out a piece of the canvas and pasting it elsewhere. But all the dots in the area get moved, not just the ones in the shape you're interested in.

Windows XP Professional doesn't come with an object-oriented graphics program. Simple object-oriented graphics modules are included in some word processors and spreadsheets.

An addition to Paint that appeared in the Windows 2000 version and carries over to Windows XP is the capability to save files in JPG and GIF formats in addition to the usual bitmapped (BMP) formats. You can also edit and save files in the TIF and PNG files formats. Table 5.3 lists and briefly breaks down each of these picture formats.

TABLE 5.3   FILE FORMATS SUPPORTED BY MICROSOFT PAINT

File Format	Full Name	Typical Use
BMP	Bit-Mapped Picture	BMP files store graphics in a format called DIB. They tend to be large in file size, and are used by Windows for features things such as screen wallpaper.
JPG	Joint Photographic Experts Group	Highly compressed means of storing graphics files, and often compress to about 5% of uncompressed size. This is a "lossy" format, meaning that some of the detail is lost as a sacrifice for small sized files. Often used on the Web or for storing photos from digital cameras.
GIF	Graphics Interchange Format	Often used on Web pages for logos or other images with limited color (256 maximum) graphics. Like JPG, GIF files can be stored with compression, making them very efficient in terms of storage space and e-mail or Web transmission. GIF files discard color data rather than image detail.
PNG	Portable Network Graphics	A relatively new format similar to GIF and created by the World Wide Web Consortium (W3C) as a freely-usable, unlicensed format for storing graphics and photos. Browser support for PNG remains spotty at this time, even with the newest Microsoft and Netscape versions. See `http://www.libpng.org/pub/png/pngapbr.html` for details.
TIF	Tagged Image File Format	This is one of the most widely upported and cross-platform file formats for images on PCs (including Macs). These files are not used on the Web. Web browsers can't display them, and they are often large. Digital cameras sometimes store highest quality, uncompressed images in TIF format. Because TIF files use lossless compression (no visual data is ever lost), this format is recommended for archival storage of image data.

5

If what you want to do is edit photo images (typically JPG, TIF, or GIF) created with a digital camera or scanner, you should use another program such as Adobe Photoshop, Adobe Elements, or PhotoDeluxe, Paint Shop Pro, Kai Photo Soap, or another of the many popular programs designed specifically for photos. Microsoft Office comes with a photo editor, called Microsoft Photo Editor, that can do the job, too.

TIP FROM

Using the Image Preview feature (discussed in Chapter 7, "Multimedia and Imaging") you can view, rotate, and perform basic tasks with image documents. You can transfer pictures to your computer from a digital camera or scanner, view your pictures in a slideshow, and annotate your fax documents. The Photo Printing Wizard, in Windows XP, can walk you through the process of printing your digital photos or scanned images. We cover that in Chapter 7, also.

STARTING A NEW IMAGE

To bring up Paint, choose Start, All Programs, Accessories, Paint. When the Paint window appears, maximize it. Figure 5.4 shows the Paint window and its component parts. I've loaded a BMP-file photograph into the program by double-clicking on a BMP file I found using the Search tool. (See Chapter 4 and Chapter 9 for discussion of the Search tool.)

Figure 5.4
The Paint window.

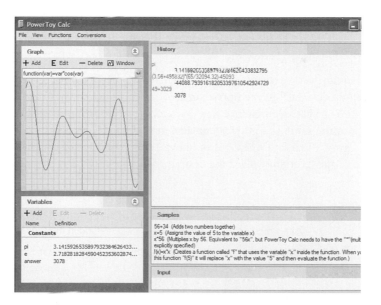

WORK AREA, TOOLBOX, TOOL OPTIONS, COLOR PALETTE

You create the drawing in the central area (or *work area*). Down the left side, the *Toolbox* holds a set of tool buttons for painting, drawing, coloring, and selecting. You choose colors from the *Color Box* at the bottom of the window. The status bar offers help messages on menu choices and displays the coordinates of the mouse pointer.

The object is to choose a tool and start fiddling around. You'll soon learn which tool does what. Hovering your mouse pointer over a tool displays some pop-up text with the tool's name. Some of the tools are a little difficult to figure out, but if you open Help and look up the tool, you can find descriptions there for each of them.

When you start a new picture, you must attend to a few details; then you can get on with painting.

1. If a picture is open, choose File, New to erase the previous image (if you need to have more than one graphic file open at a time with Paint, just start a new copy of Paint).

2. Choose Image, Attributes to set the picture size and whether it's color or black and white.

You can alter the size of the overall canvas when you're painting, so don't lose any sleep over perfecting it before you start. An image prints smaller on paper than it appears onscreen because the printer's resolution is much higher (each dot is smaller). So if you're aiming to print out your creation, you might want to do a little experimentation.

Setting the printed size of your image is easy. You used to have to calculate it based on the resolution of your printer and the pixel size of the image. Now you can just choose Image, Attributes and set the size in inches (or cm, or pixels, if you wish). You can check that the size looks about right at any time, by choosing File, Print Preview. Remember, though, that if your picture is wider than it is tall, and if it's printed width is more than about 8 inches, you need to change the page orientation for printing from Portrait to Landscape. To do so, just choose File, Page Setup, and select the appropriate button.

The maximum picture size is limited by available memory and color setting. Black-and-white pictures use far less memory than color pictures do, so they can be much larger. Paint lets you know if you set a picture size that's too large to fit in memory. A black-and-white image is not the same as a grayscale image, in which you can paint with 16 or more separate shades of gray. Black and white has only two colors—black and white. Duh. To create a grayscale image, you must place the desired shades of gray on the palette.

TIP FROM

Bob

& Brian

You can resize a picture with the mouse by dragging the handles on the edges of the white workspace; however, the direct entry method in the dialog box is more accurate.

WORKING WITH THE PAINTING TOOLS

Before beginning to use a tool, you set the color to paint with. You need to set two colors: background and foreground. One of the most fundamental techniques to learn is selecting a color to paint with. In Paint, you control both foreground and background colors independently.

The foreground or drawing color is the main color you paint with. For example, when you add strokes with Paint's paintbrush, draw lines or shapes, or even when you type text, these items appear in the currently selected foreground color. The term *background color* is somewhat different. Many of the tools (such as the Brush, Pencil, and the Shape tools) let you paint with the so-called background color just as you would with the foreground color. All you have to do is hold down the right mouse button instead of the left one as you paint. The background color also determines the fill color for circles, squares, and other enclosed shapes; the fill color inside text frames; and the color with which you erase existing parts of the picture. If you select a section of the picture and drag it to another location, the resulting "hole" is filled with the background color. You can change the background color as many times as you like.

An alternative technique for selecting colors is using the Eyedropper tool, which lets you "suck up" a color that already appears in the picture. That color becomes the new foreground or background color for use with any of the painting tools.

TIP FROM

Bob & Brian

> You can start a new picture with a certain color as the "canvas." Before you paint anything on the picture, choose the desired background color, and click anywhere over the work area with the Paint Can tool.

After you have the colors selected, you can use the tools to draw:

1. Click the tool you want to use to select it.
2. Position the pointer in the work area where you want to start painting, selecting, or erasing, and then click and hold the mouse button.
3. Drag to paint, select, or erase. Release the mouse button when you are through.

Some tools (for example, the polygon tool) require multiple clicks. When some of the tools are selected, the area below the grid of buttons provides options for the selected tool. The options are different for each tool.

UNDOING MISTAKES

Every addition you make to an image eventually melds into the picture and can't be undone. However, the program does keep track of the three most recent additions, allowing you some small degree of rethinking. Each time you make a new change, Paint "forgets" the fourth most recent change, and it becomes permanent.

To undo a change, press the fairly-universal Undo command key, Ctrl+Z, or choose Edit, Undo. You can undo an undo by choosing Edit, Repeat.

5

TIP FROM

Bob & Brian

> Use the Save As option on the File menu to save your work periodically under a differ-
> ent filename to give yourself additional margin for changes. If you make a serious error
> you can't undo, you can then open the most recently saved or an earlier version of
> your work and continue on from that version.

OPENING AN EXISTING PICTURE

You might often use Paint simply as a viewer of BMP files. Web browsers do not open BMP
files for display, so when you double-click a BMP, it runs Paint (unless the system association for BMP files has been set to another program) and opens the file.

To see the maximum image amount at once, choose View, View Bitmap. All the other screen
elements, including the title bar, menu bar, and scrollbars, disappear. Clicking anywhere on
the screen or pressing any key returns you to the working screen.

 *If you have opened a photographic picture for work in Paint, and it looks splotchy and uneven, see
"Photos Look Terrible in Paint" in the "Troubleshooting" section at the end of this chapter.*

ZOOMING IN FOR DETAIL WORK

One of the best features of Paint is pixel editing. You can zoom in closely to edit a picture,
dot by dot, and can choose from five magnification levels: normal, 2×, 4×, 6×, and 8×(800).
Figure 5.5 shows a detail of a full-face portrait, showing only the person's eye. This is at
highest magnification, 8×(800). In Paint, you can use any of the standard painting tools at
any magnification level. Use the Pencil tool to best change the color of one dot at a time.
This feature is most useful when you have a little touchup to do (such as photo retouching),
but you can't seem to control the mouse well enough to do it in normal view.

Figure 5.5
An image magnified
for pixel editing.

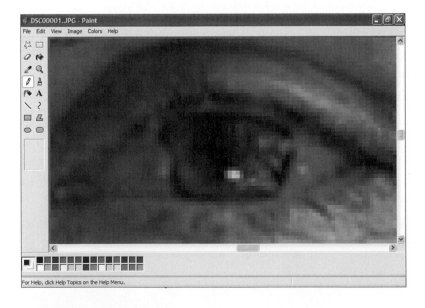

SAVING YOUR WORK

You can choose from several BMP formats for saving Paint files; the variations pertain to the number of colors stored in the file. Normally, you can just let Paint choose the correct format for you, but sometimes knowing which format to use comes in handy.

The following are the available BMP formats and their descriptions:

- **Monochrome bitmap**—Use when you have only two colors (black and white) in your picture.

- **16-color bitmap**—Use when you have 16 colors or fewer in your picture.

- **256-color bitmap**—Use when you have more than 16 and fewer than 257 colors in your picture.

- **24-bit bitmap**—Use when you have more than 256 colors in the picture.

Use the lowest possible setting, based on the number of colors with which you have been painting. The more colors you save, the larger the file. However, saving a picture with a format that has fewer colors might ruin it, causing it to lose detail. You can also save in a variety of other formats, as mentioned earlier. As a rule, save your image in a format that in which your target audience (or program) uses to view it. For example, if you intend to send an image to someone in email or put it on a Web page, stick with GIF, JPG, or PNG. These are the most universal image formats.

TIP FROM

Bob
& Brian

> When a picture is displayed in the Paint window, you can set it to be the wallpaper on the computer's desktop. Just choose File, Set as Background (tiled) or Set as Background (centered), depending on how you want it displayed. For large pictures, I would choose Centered.

CALCULATOR

The Calculator is a quick and dirty onscreen version of two traditional pocket calculators: a standard no-brainer calculator and a more complex scientific calculator used by statisticians, engineers, computer programmers, and business professionals. They are good for adding up your lunch bill, a list of inventory items, or the mortgage payment on your office building. But neither calculator sports a running tape that you can use to backtrack through your calculations.

To run the Calculator, choose Start, All Programs, Accessories, Calculator. A reasonable facsimile of a hand-held calculator then appears on your screen, as shown in Figure 5.6. You can switch between modes by choosing View, Standard or View, Scientific. The program always remembers which type was used last and comes up in that mode.

Figure 5.6
The Scientific Calculator is the often-unseen mode that the Windows Calculator can appear in. Many additional functions appear in this mode.

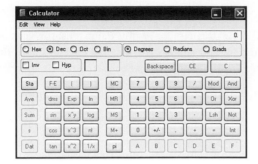

TIP FROM

To quickly see a little help about any Calculator button, right-click the button, and choose What's This?

TIP FROM

To add a series of numbers or to find their mean, use the statistical functions on the Scientific Calculator. This way, you can see all the numbers in a list before you perform the calculation instead of having to enter them one at a time. And don't let the idea of statistics make you nervous; the technique is very simple.

Most of the operations on the Standard Calculator are self-explanatory, but a couple of them—square roots and percentages—are just a bit tricky. Check the Help file for more information. Table 5.4 provides a quick reference chart of keyboard shortcuts.

TABLE 5.4 KEYBOARD SHORTCUTS FOR THE CALCULATOR

Button	Key	Button	Key	Button	Key
%	%	cos	o	MR	Ctrl+R
(	(	Dat	Ins	MS	Ctrl+M
)	)	Dec	F6	n!	!
*	*	Deg	F2	Not	~
+	+	dms	m	Oct	F7
+/-	F9	Dword	F2	Or	|
-	-	Qword	F12	PI	p
.	. or ,	Exp	x	Rad	F3
/	/	F-E	v	s	Ctrl+D
0 to 9	0 to	Grad	F4	sin	s
1/x	r	Hex	F5	SQRT	@
=	= or Enter	Hypo	h	Sta	Ctrl+S

TABLE 5.4   KEYBOARD SHORTCUTS FOR THE CALCULATOR

Button	Key	Button	Key	Button	Key
A to F	A to F	Int	;	Sum	Ctrl+T
And	&	Inv	I	tan	t
Ave	Ctrl+A	In	n	Word	F3
Bin	F8	log	l	Xor	^
Byte	F4	LSH	<	x^2	@
Back	Backspace	M+	Ctrl+P	x^3	#
C	Esc	MC	Ctrl+L	x^y	y
CE	Del	Mod	%		

COPYING YOUR RESULTS TO AND FROM OTHER DOCUMENTS

You can prepare a complex equation in a text editor such as Notepad and then copy it to the Calculator for execution. For example, you can enter the following in Notepad:

((2+8)+16)/14=

or

(2+(8+16))/14=

Mind your parentheses, and make sure to include the equal sign, or click = on the calculator after you paste in the equation; otherwise, the result will not appear. You can omit the parentheses if you use extra equal signs, like this:

2+8=+16=/14=

Some special characters can be included in your equations to activate various Calculator functions, as shown in Table 5.5.

TABLE 5.5   SPECIAL CALCULATOR FUNCTIONS

Special Character	Function
:e	If the Calculator is set to the decimal system, this sequence indicates that the following digits are the exponent of a number expressed in scientific notation; for example, 1.01:e100 appears in the Calculator as 1.01e+100.
:p	Adds the number currently displayed to the number in memory.
:c	Clears the Calculator's memory.
\	Places the number currently displayed into the Statistics box, which must already be open.
:m	Stores the number currently displayed in the Calculator's memory.
:q	Clears the Calculator.
:r	Displays the number stored in the Calculator's memory.

5

You can copy information to and from the Calculator using the Windows Clipboard.
Just use the standard Windows Copy and Paste commands.

POWER CALCULATOR

If you're really into calculators, you might want to download the Power Calculator, which is
free from Microsoft. It's part of the Windows XP PowerToys. You can download it from

`http://www.microsoft.com/WINDOWSXP/home/downloads/powertoys.asp.`

With this PowerToy, you can graph and evaluate functions as well as perform many different types of conversions such as length, mass, time, velocity, and temperature. Figure 5.7
shows the calculator.

Figure 5.7
Power Calculator is a
tool in the Windows
XP Power Toys, a free
download.

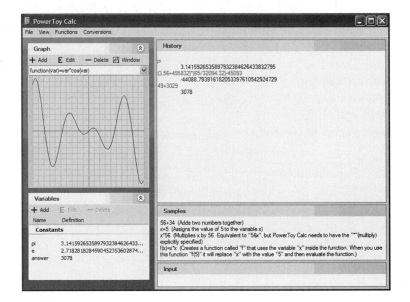

NOTE

See the discussion on page 788 in Chapter 23 for more information about installing the
PowerToys.

CHARACTER MAP

Character Map is a utility program that lets you examine every character in a given font and
choose and easily insert into your documents special characters, such as trademark (™ and
®) and copyright symbols (©), foreign currency symbols and accented letters (such as ¥)
and nonalphabetic symbols (such as fractions, $3/4$), DOS line-drawing characters (+), items

from specialized fonts such as Symbol and Wingdings, or the common arrow symbols ($\uparrow$, $\downarrow$, $\leftarrow$, and $\rightarrow$). Some fonts include characters not mapped to the keyboard. Character Map lets you choose them, too, from its graphical display. The Program Map displays Unicode, DOS, and Windows fonts' characters.

Character Map for Windows XP Professional is larger and updated from the one in Windows 98. Now you can choose the character set, rearrange the items in a font (such as grouping all currency types together) to eliminate hunting, and search for a given character.

Character Map works through the Windows Clipboard. You simply choose a character you want to use, click Copy, and it moves onto the Clipboard. Switch to your destination application (typically a word processing file), position the cursor, and choose Paste.

USING CHARACTER MAP

To run Character Map, follow these steps:

1. Choose Start, All Programs, Accessories, System Tools, Character Map. When the window appears, check the Advanced View box to see more. The window then appears with all the characters included in the currently selected font displayed.

2. Choose the font you want to work with from the Font list.

3. By default, the Character Set is Unicode. This means all the characters necessary for most of the world's languages are displayed. To narrow down the selection, choose a language from the drop-down list.

4. To examine an individual character, click a character box, and hold down the mouse button to magnify it. You can accomplish the same thing with the keyboard by moving to the character using the arrow keys (see Figure 5.8).

5. Double-click a character to select it, transferring it to the Characters to Copy box. Alternatively, after you've highlighted a character, you can click the Select button or press Alt+S to place it in the Characters to Copy box. You can keep adding characters to the copy box if you want to paste several into your document at once.

6. Click the Copy button to place everything from the Characters to Copy box onto the Windows Clipboard.

7. Switch to your destination application, and use the Paste command (typically on the application's Edit menu) to insert the characters into your document. In some cases, you might then have to select the inserted characters and format them in the correct font, or the characters won't appear as you expected. You can, of course, change the size and style as you like.

TIP FROM

Bob & Brian

> If you know the Unicode number of the item to which you want to jump, type it into the Go to Unicode field. The display scrolls as necessary, and the desired character is then highlighted, ready for copying.

5

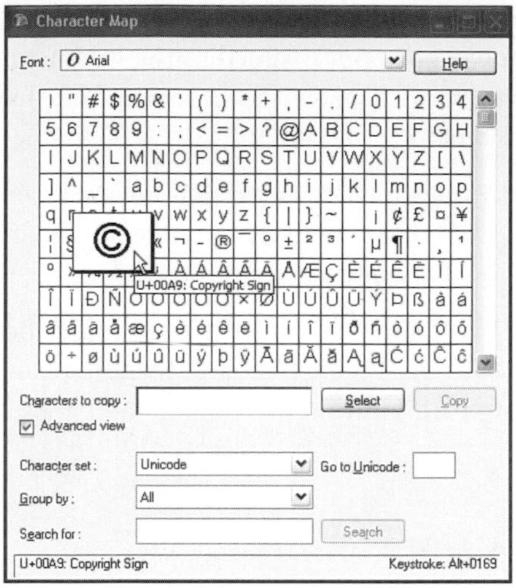

Figure 5.8
Character Map with Advanced options showing. You can double-click a character to put it in the copy list.

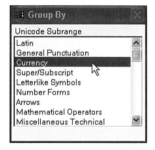

CHOOSING FROM A UNICODE SUBRANGE

A useful feature of Character Map lets you choose a subrange from the Unicode. Unicode was designed intelligently with characters grouped in sets. You can choose a subset of a font's characters to help you locate a specific symbol. To check out this feature, open the Group By list, and choose Unicode Subrange. When you choose this option, a box like the one in Figure 5.9 pops up.

Figure 5.9
Choosing a subset of a font from which to select a character.

Click the subgroup that you think will contain the character you're looking for. Good examples are currency or arrows. Make sure to open the Group By list again, and choose All when you want to see all the characters again.

ENTERING ALTERNATIVE CHARACTERS FROM THE KEYBOARD

At the bottom right side of the Character Map dialog box is a line that reads

```
Keystroke:
```

For nonkeyboard keys (typically, in English, anything past the ~ character), clicking a character reveals a code on this line—for example, Alt+1060. This line tells you the code you can enter from the keyboard to quickly pop this character into a document. Of course, you must be using the font in question. For example, say you want to enter the registered trademark symbol (®) into a Windows application document. Note that with a standard text font such as Arial or Times New Roman selected in Character Map, the program lists the keystrokes for this symbol as Alt+0174. Here's how to enter the character from the keyboard:

1. Press Num Lock to turn on the numeric keypad on your keyboard (the Num Lock light should be on).

2. Press and hold Alt, and then press 0+1+7+4 (that is, type the 0, 1, 7, and 4 keys individually, in succession) on the number pad. (You must use the number pad keys, not the standard number keys. On a laptop, you must activate the number pad using whatever special function key arrangement your laptop uses.) When you release the Alt key, the registered trademark symbol should appear in the document.

TIP FROM

Bob & Brian

> Not all programs accept input this way. If this approach doesn't work with a program, you'll have to resort to the standard means of putting characters into the Clipboard explained previously.

VOLUME CONTROL

The Volume Control accessory is basically a no-brainer. It provides a pop-up volume control sporting balance, mute, and other controls for your audio subsystem. Whether you're playing radio stations from the Web, CDs from your CD drive, listening to TV if you have a TV tuner card, doing online conferencing with NetMeeting, or recording sound files, you need access to these controls from time to time. Of course, if you don't have a working sound card installed, this accessory isn't available, or at least it won't do anything. A little known fact for many people is that this accessory has two sets of controls—one for recording and one for playback.

1. To open the volume controls, choose Start, All Programs, Accessories, Entertainment, Volume Control. A shortcut is to double-click the little speaker icon in the system tray on the Windows XP taskbar.

NOTE

> If the speaker icon isn't visible, open the Sounds and Audio Devices icon in Control Panel and click the box labeled Place Volume Icon in the Taskbar. Click Apply.

Your sound system's capabilities and possible changes that past users have made to the application's settings determine the format of the volume controls you see. On one of my computers the controls look like what you see in Figure 5.10.

Figure 5.10
The basic volume controls for setting playback volume. Another set is available for record levels.

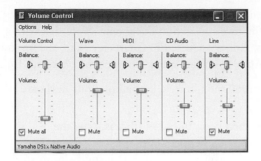

2. You can alter any volume control's setting by dragging the volume up or down. Change the balance between right and left channels by dragging the Balance sliders left or right. Mute any source input by checking the Mute box in its column.

3. Controls for some input sources are probably not showing. Check out the Options, Properties command. It offers options for turning on various volume controls and possibly special features. Figure 5.11 shows an example. Because audio controls operate differently for different sound cards, check out any Help files that might be available from your audio controls.

Figure 5.11
The Properties dialog box for typical volume controls.

If you are doing any sound recording, be sure to see the recording controls, too. Open the Properties dialog box, and choose Recording.

TIP FROM

Bob & Brian

Sometimes you want to see the playback and the recording controls at one time. To do so, run the Volume Control application twice. Set one for playback and the other one to record. Then adjust them onscreen so that you can see each side-by-side.

NOTE

> Some sliders in one module are linked to sliders in other modules. Adjusting the Volume setting on one affects Volume settings on the other mixers. For example, adjusting the playback volume in Media Player or your audio CD player or MP3 player will typically alter the "Wave" or the master Volume control slider position on the system Volume Controls.

To quickly adjust or mute the sound output from your system, or to adjust the master volume level (useful when the phone rings), click the little speaker icon in the system tray, near the clock, as shown in Figure 5.12. If the speaker icon isn't showing, then you have to turn it on. To turn it on, click Start, Control Panel, Sounds Speech and Audio Devices; click Sounds and Audio Devices, then turn on 'Place volume icon in the taskbar notification area' and OK the dialog box.

Figure 5.12
Quickly setting the master output volume.

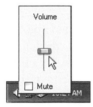

⚠ *If your system suddenly doesn't have any sound at all, see "No Sound" in the "Troubleshooting" section at the end of this chapter.*

If you are using a sound card with support for more than two speakers, open the Sounds and Audio Devices icon in Control Panel and click the Advanced button in the Speaker Settings section of the Volume tab to select the speaker or headset type you're using to ensure correct operation of your speakers.

WORKING WITH THE WINDOWS CLIPBOARD

Although not an application per se, the Clipboard is an integral part of Windows, and is typically used when working with applications. Chapter 4 introduced the Clipboard indirectly, explaining how to cut, copy, and paste items, particularly files and folders within the Windows GUI.

Because transferring data between applications and documents is such a common task, this chapter offers some additional detail on the techniques you can use to facilitate the process.

The most basic sort of information sharing relies on the Windows Clipboard. As you're probably well aware, you can cut, copy, and paste information from one application to another with relative abandon—assuming both applications allow you to work with the kind of information you're transferring (text, graphics, or musical notes, for example).

Almost all Windows applications use the Clipboard for everyday, on-the-fly data-transfer operations. The Clipboard lets you move text, graphics, spreadsheet cells, portions of multimedia files, and OLE objects from one location to another. It supports both 16-bit and 32-bit Windows programs and can even move text to and from non-Windows programs, within the constraints I explain later in this chapter.

Information cut or copied to the Clipboard goes into system memory (RAM and virtual memory), waiting there until you paste it to a new location elsewhere in the same document or in another document. Even then the data remains on the Clipboard until it's replaced by new cut or copied information or until you exit Windows. The upshot of this arrangement is that you can paste the same information as many times as needed, into as many different locations in your documents as necessary.

Want to know what information currently resides on the Clipboard? Run the ClipBook Viewer utility that comes with Windows XP to view the Clipboard contents as well as to store Clipboard information on disk (in CLP files or ClipBooks) for later retrieval. You won't find that program on your All Programs menus, but if you Click Start, Run, and enter `clipbrd`, it should come up. Double-click on the Clipboard's title bar (which is probably minimized at the bottom of the Clipbook Viewer window), and you can see what's in the Clipboard at any given time. Though you may seldom use it, the Clipbook Viewer can be used to share Clipboard contents over the local area network. It's a little tricky to do so, however, and rarely used. Figure 5.13 shows an example of some text on the Clipboard.

Figure 5.13
Checking the contents of the Clipboard using the Clipbook Viewer application.

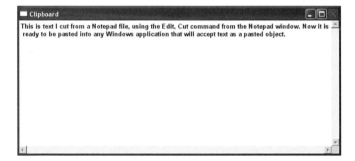

5

NOTE

> Some Windows applications maintain their own independent Clipboard-like storage areas for cut or copied data. These proprietary clipboards overcome some of the weaknesses of the main Windows Clipboard. For example, whereas the Windows Clipboard can hold only one chunk of cut or copied data at a time, Microsoft Office 2000/XP has its own "clipboard" that stores up to 12 chunks. In Office 2000/XP apps, a special toolbar pops up as the Office clipboard fills up. The toolbar displays each chunk of data with an icon identifying the data's source application, and you can paste the chunks in any order you need them into your Office 2000/XP documents.

COPYING, CUTTING, AND PASTING IN WINDOWS APPLICATIONS

Windows XP maintains time-honored Windows standards (most of them date all the way back to Windows 2.0) for selecting, cutting, copying, and pasting information. This section offers a brief review of the techniques you need. In summary, four steps are required to transfer data from one place to another via the Clipboard:

1. Select the data. The techniques required to select data depend on the type of information in question and the application you're using. If you're working with text, you can drag across the characters to be selected, or, if you prefer a keyboard approach, hold down the Shift key while you use arrow keys and other cursor movement keys to expand or reduce the selection. Many programs let you select entire lines or paragraphs using techniques such as clicking or double-clicking in the left margin. Selected text appears in reverse colors.

   With graphics and other non-text information, selection techniques vary, but you typically just click on the item you want to select, Shift+click to select a series of adjacent items, or drag over adjacent items to select them together. In many applications you can also Ctrl+click to select nonadjacent items. You can usually tell that an item has been selected by the appearance of an outline or small rectangles on its perimeter.

2. Cut or copy that data to place it on the Clipboard. Choose Edit, Copy to place the selected data on the Clipboard without disturbing the original. You can also choose Edit, Cut to put the information on the Clipboard and remove it from the source document. As mentioned in Chapter 4, many applications let you right-click over the selection and choose Copy or Cut from the shortcut menu that pops up. With the keyboard, the standard shortcuts are Ctrl+X for Cut and Ctrl+C for Copy; however, some applications don't abide by these conventions.

3. Identify the destination for the information by selecting the destination document and, if appropriate, navigating to a specific location in that document.

4. Paste the data into the destination document. With the mouse, choose Edit, Paste or choose Paste from the shortcut menu. Using the keyboard, pressing Ctrl+V does the trick, except in the odd, nonstandard application. With any of these techniques, the contents of the Clipboard will appear in the new location.

 If the Paste command fails to paste the data into the destination document, see "Paste Command Doesn't Work" in the "Troubleshooting" section at the end of this chapter.

 If the pasted data doesn't look like you expected, see "Pasted Data Doesn't Look Right" in the "Troubleshooting" section at the end of the chapter.

NOTE

> Almost all Windows applications have Cut, Copy, and Paste commands on their Edit menus, but that doesn't mean these commands are always available. If you haven't selected anything to be cut or copied, for example, the Cut and Copy commands will be inactive—they appear grayed out on the Edit menu and you can't choose them. For its part, the Paste command can be grayed out even if data is currently on the Clipboard. This happens when the application doesn't recognize the data format in which the Clipboard data is stored.

5

NOTE

Many Windows applications place cut or copied information onto the Clipboard in multiple formats. For example, suppose you copy some text from Microsoft Word. When the copy operation is complete, the Clipboard will contain at least four representations of that same text: a "plain text" (nonformatted) version, a version in the Rich Text format, a version in HTML, and a picture (an image of the text stored as a line, or *vector*, graphic). When you paste, the destination application communicates with the Clipboard to decide which format to use. In some cases, the application also has a command that lets you take manual control and decide the right format for yourself. At any rate, the availability of all these formats means that you have a better chance of successfully pasting the data into the destination document.

USING THE SEARCH APPLET

One of the first rules of organization is to know where things are, and how to keep them in their rightful places. The Search command (or Companion, as it's now called), found in the Start menu or the toolbar in any folder, is a tool often used in this mission. We think of the Search Companion as a supplied application, since it has grown into something formidable, despite the impression the cute little animated Search Assistant gives. Although we mentioned it briefly in Chapter 4 as a way to find and run programs, we wanted to cover this powerful feature more thoroughly in general terms here.

As we mentioned in Chapter 1, Windows XP's Search feature is new and wholly superior to anything in any version of Windows to date. In Windows 9x and NT 4, Search was called *Find*. The name has changed, as has the functionality of the look of the window. The Search Companion can find a needle in a haystack, and it doesn't much matter where the haystack is or what else is in it. The Search window will find people, computers, Web pages, files, folders, and programs. It will look on the Web, on the local machine, or across the intranet (LAN). In the context of this chapter, let's focus on searching for your multimedia files, document files, and folders, however. In the chapters covering network issues (Part IV) and the Web section (Part III), we'll cover searching out other kinds of information.

Just click Start and choose Search (or as a shortcut I use all the time on 104-key keyboards, press Windows+F). This will bring up the Search Companion window, as shown in Figure 5.14. Notice that this is essentially an Explorer window, but with a Search panel on the left side. By default, you have a little Search Companion there to help entertain you while a search is going on, in the form of a dog. He does tricks, and occasionally makes noise as he scratches himself, so don't be alarmed. You can choose another Search Companion, make him perform a trick, or turn him off by double-clicking on him and choosing from a menu.

Like a Web page, the Search Companion has links and Back buttons to move from page to page. In the previous versions of Search or Find, you filled in boxes more like a traditional dialog box, but no longer. It's all HTML-based now and very Webby-looking. There are numerous pages and links within the Search window to explore.

Figure 5.14
The new Search Companion is multi-talented. Use it to seek out multimedia files, documents, folders, people, computers, and other stuff.

→ To see some searching in action, **see** the video CD-ROM included with this book, Lesson 1, in which Bob takes you on a tour of the Windows interface.

Let's try a simple search for files on the computer. This is the most frequent kind of search, (outside of Web surfing). Suppose I wanted to search for any music on my computer that was by Beethoven.

Notice that I found three files, as indicated in Figure 5.15. After a search is complete (this could take some time as Windows searches through all your hard disk files, but the doggie sure looks cute turning those book pages), the found files are listed to the right. You are asked by the Search Companion whether you are finished searching. If you are satisfied, click Yes; the Search Companion disappears and is replaced by the normal view of an Explorer window, yet the found files remain in the right pane for you to work with as you will (copy, cut, open, run, edit, and so on) by clicking or right-clicking on them.

If you are not satisfied with the results of the search (either no hits, or too many hits), notice the several options:

- **Change the file name or keywords**—This is the most likely thing to do. You may have spelled the file or other item incorrectly. Use a smaller amount of the file name, don't specify the extension, or try a different spelling if you don't know how it's spelled. Maybe specify just the extension, such as *.tif.

- **Look in more locations**—Well, this is not likely going to help much, since normally a search is conducted on all your local hard disks. But it may be worth a try. Click this to see what options you have. Click the check mark in the resulting box to open a list of places you can look in. Then click Browse . . . to open a box that lets you look all around your system, including on the local area network.

5

Figure 5.15
Here I've searched for all music with Beethoven in the file name. I'm also showing you the result of the search.

■ **Change whether hidden and system files are included**—There are numerous files on your computer that are normally "hidden" so that you (or someone else) doesn't mess with them and mangle your operating system. If you're searching for DLL files or some other system-related things, you can choose this option. You won't need it for sleuthing out typical documents and programs, though.

You get the idea with the multimedia files. If you're a worker bee who doesn't have time for photos, videos, and MP3 music files, you're probably looking for those business reports you've been slaving over and are freaking out about whether your computer ate them. This happens to me all the time, especially since today's programs want to put your files in weird places that never see the light of day (like somewhere inside of My Documents under some strange user name). So, you'll want to experiment with conducting another search, this time for Documents (this is the second option listed when you first bring up the Search Companion. Notice that it offers two criteria categories for searching—file name and when it was modified. Actually, this makes a lot of sense, since people generally remember at least a little bit about their work-related documents this way, at least I do. "Gee, I worked on that thing two days ago, and I probably would have called it something like Bob's Pleading with the IRS for Mercy." So I click on Within the Last Week and in the document name area I type in **IRS**. The results are good (see Figure 5.16). (I've hit the Back button, so you can see both the results and the search criteria.)

Searching for Text Within a Document

Now for something a little more complicated. Suppose I wanted to find any files that I've modified in the last week, are related to this book, and also contain the word "Passport" in them. This is a real need for me, since I'm working on the Passport topic, and don't want to repeat myself in the chapter I'm writing now. Can the Search Companion help me? Yup. Here's how:

1. I run the Search Companion.

2. I choose to search for Documents.

3. I click on Within the Last Week for the last time it was modified.

4. I enter the file name **ch*.doc**, since I know that all my chapter files start with the letters "ch" and are Word or WordPad files (so they end with ".doc").

5. I click on Use advanced search options. The box changes a bit to show some advanced settings. I enter **Passport** in the lower area of the box (see Figure 5.17).

Figure 5.16
Here I've done a search for that file I hope will keep me out of debtor's prison. I used the "time modified" and "file name" criteria, together.

TIP FROM

Bob & Brian

When specifying file and folder names during searches of the hard disk, note that the asterisk "*" is a "DOS wildcard" that replaces any number of characters. The ? replaces one character).

LOOKING FOR ANY KIND OF FILE

If you're looking more generally for files or folders (that are not documents or multimedia files), choose the All Files and Folders option from the first page of the Search Companion. He'll now look through more of your folders. This will result in a more exhaustive search, because every file and folder will be examined, not just those that are popular document types.

5

Figure 5.17
Here I've searched for all files in the past month that start with "ch" and end with .doc (Word or WordPad files) and have the word "Passport" within the file.

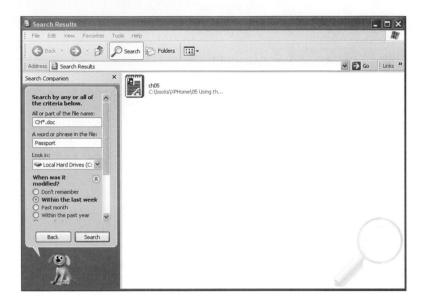

NARROWING THE SEARCH

Just as with the Find box in Windows 9x and NT, you have to be a bit crafty when filtering the search. If you enter a long filename with spaces between the words, the search will likely end up becoming too broad. For example, if you entered

```
Annual Report 2
```

in the Search For area, the result would be any file with the word *Annual*, *Report*, or *2* in any part of its name. This is annoying. Also, using quotes around the string, as when conducting a Web search, doesn't help either, unfortunately. I was trying to find a folder called Ch 3 and the only way to exactly find it was to enter Ch*3 as the criterion. So keep in mind that you should use DOS-style wildcards when searching for items that contains spaces in their names.

Experiment with other aspects of the Search box, such as searching the Internet or turning on the Indexing Service. The Indexing Service was introduced in Windows 2000 Professional. This tool scans files and folders on your hard disk and builds a database of the words it finds in those documents. This database helps speed up file and directory searches when you're looking for words within files or keywords in file descriptions. The database also helps the Internet Information Services Web server perform Web site searches. To turn it on, do this:

1. From the first page of the Search Companion click on Change Preferences.
2. Then choose With Indexing Service (for faster local searches).
3. Click Back.
4. Begin your search.

The Indexing Service can index the following types of documents in several languages:

- Text
- HTML

- Microsoft Office 95 and later
- Internet mail and news
- Any other document for which a document filter is available

The Indexing Service is designed to run continuously and requires little maintenance. After it's set up, all operations are automatic, including index creation, index updating, and crash recovery if there's a power failure.

→ To learn more about the Windows Indexing service, **see** "Indexing," **p. 1018**.

TIP FROM

Bob
& Brian

> You can save any search you have conducted by choosing File, Save Search. It will prompt you to save the search in My Documents and will suggest a file name for it such as "Files named CH05.doc". When you want to re-run the search, open the folder where you stored the file and double-click it. It will open in the Search Companion. Then click the Search button.

TROUBLESHOOTING

MY TEXT IS CHOPPED OFF

I can't see all the text in a Notepad window. Where did it go?

You must manually turn on word wrap to get the text in a file to wrap around within the window. By default, word wrap is turned off, which can be annoying. The good news is that word wrap is now a persistent setting. After you turn it on and then close Notepad, it should be on the next time you run it. If you need to edit program code, make sure to turn it off, or your program lines will wrap, making editing and analysis of code more confusing.

If you still can't see enough text, remember that Notepad 5.1 now supports font changing for display. Change the display font from the Format menu. Choosing a monospaced font (for example, Courier) might help you line up columns. Choosing a smaller font and/or a proportional font (for example, Times) crams more text into the window.

ADDING AND MODIFYING TAB STOPS

Inserting and adjusting tab stops in WordPad is a pain. Is there an easy way?

You can easily insert and adjust tabs in WordPad by clicking in the ruler area. Choose View, Ruler to turn on the ruler. Then click in the ruler area where you want to insert a tab stop. You can drag the cursor left and right to see a vertical rule to align the stop. To kill a tab stop, drag it out of the ruler area into the document.

PHOTOS LOOK TERRIBLE IN PAINT

I've opened a photo in Paint, and it looks terrible. Why?

You probably have your display set to too few colors. When too few colors are available to the video display, it "bands" the colors, making photos look like a topographic map. Each sharp delineation between similar colors in the picture is called a *band*, for obvious reasons. Normally, the colors would blend together evenly. But if the video display's driver is set to 16, or even 256 colors, this is too few to render most photographic images properly.

Typically, photos have well over 256 colors. You need thousands (or millions) of colors to display an attractive photograph. As I said earlier, to edit photos in any professional manner, you should use a program designed for photographic retouching. Still, you can cut and paste, do some pixel editing, add text and so forth, with Paint. First, however, check your display settings by right-clicking the desktop, choosing Properties, and then Settings. Make sure you have your system set to run in 16-bit color or higher.

No Sound

I'm adjusting the volume control from the system tray icon, but I just don't get any sound.

Total loss of sound can be caused by myriad goofs, settings, hardware conflicts, or program malfunctions. Troubleshooting your sound system isn't always easy as a result. One tip is in order here: If you're using a laptop computer, ask yourself whether the sound stopped working after you hibernated or suspended the system. I've noticed this problem on several laptops, and this bug might not have been worked out of Windows XP Professional for your sound chip set. Try rebooting the computer, and see whether the sound comes back to life. Another thing to look for is a manual volume control on the computer. Many laptops have a control you can turn or push, that's often found along the right- or left-hand side of the computer itself. Such settings override any settings within Windows. If you have a set of powered speakers attached to your computer, make sure they are plugged into power, and are turned on. I often forget to do this, and then wonder why I have no sound. You should consult other chapters in this book that deal with the Control Panel and the Device Manager for serious problems. If none of the above remedies work, then you might have a bad sound card, or it might need a new device driver.

Paste Command Doesn't Work

I'm sure I placed information on the Clipboard but the Paste command won't work.

The problem is that the destination document doesn't recognize the format of your Clipboard data. You may be able to work around this obstacle by first pasting the data into another application that does accept the information and then copying and pasting from this way-station app into the intended destination document. Alternatively, try saving the selected information to disk in a file format that the destination app can import.

Pasted Data Doesn't Look Right

My pasted data sometimes looks quite different in the destination document than it did in the original.

You might be able to get better results by pasting the data in another format, if the destination application allows this. Look for a command in the destination app such as Edit, Paste Special that lets you select from all the Clipboard formats the application recognizes. Try each format in turn to see which gives the best results.

CHAPTER **6**

PRINTING AND FAXING

In this chapter

WINDOWS XP PRINTING PRIMER

During Windows setup, a printer might have been detected and installed automatically, eliminating the need for you to install a printer manually. In this case, a default printer is already installed, and printing should be fairly effortless from your Windows applications. You can just print without worrying about anything more than turning on the printer, checking that it has paper, and choosing the File, Print command from whatever programs you use.

If you didn't have your printer on or connected during setup, or it isn't a Plug and Play printer, this process might not have happened successfully, however. Sometimes simply plugging in a new printer or having Windows do a scan for new hardware is enough to get things rolling. I'll talk about installation procedures later, but regardless of your current state of printer connectedness, as a user of Windows XP, you should know how to control your print jobs, print to network-based printers, and share your printer for others to use. This chapter covers these topics.

When you print from an application, the application passes the data stream off to Windows, which in turn *spools* the data to a specified printer. Spooling is the process of temporarily stuffing onto the hard disk the data to be transmitted to the printer, and then delivering it at the relatively slow pace with which that printer can receive it. Spooling lets you get back to work with your program sooner. Windows passes the stored information from the queue through a *driver* program, which sends the printer the specific codes and commands it needs to *render*, or draw, your document. Meanwhile, additional documents can be added to a printer's queue, either from the same computer or from users across the LAN.

THE PRINTERS AND FAXES FOLDER

Windows gives you control over the printing system through the Printers and Faxes folder, shown in Figure 6.1. You can add printers, check the status of the queue, and manage print jobs by clicking Start, Control Panel, Printers and Other Hardware, Printers and Faxes.

TIP FROM

Bob & Brian

6

> If you use Printers and Faxes frequently, you can add it to your Start Menu. Right-click the Start button and select Properties. View the Start Menu tab and click Customize. Select the Advanced tab, and check Printers and Faxes under Start Menu Items. Customizing the Start Menu is discussed in more detail in Chapter 23 under "Start Menu Pizzazz!"

After you open the folder, you can view the Task menu for a particular printer by clicking that printer's icon.

The print spooler system takes control of all printing jobs, whether from Win32, Win16, OS/2, POSIX, or DOS applications. In cases of trouble (for example, ink or paper outage or paper jams), it also issues error or other appropriate messages to print job originators.

Figure 6.1
The Printers and Faxes folder is the starting point for printer setup and management. Open it from the Control Panel item Printers and Other Hardware.

NOTE

I'll refer to the spooling and other printer management capabilities of Windows XP's GUI, taken as a whole, as *Print Manager*.

TIP FROM

Bob & Brian

If you use the Print Manager a lot and find it cumbersome to bring up, add it to your Start menu by right-clicking the Start button and selecting Properties. Choose the Start Menu tab and click Customize. Choose the Advanced tab and locate Printers under Show These Items on the Start Menu. Check Printers and click OK twice. Now, you can access Printers and Faxes from your Start Menu right under Control Panel.

The Print Manager in Windows XP has the following features:

- It lets you easily add, modify, and remove printers right from the Printers and Faxes folder by using the Add Printer Wizard.

- The intuitive user interface uses simple icons to represent printers that are installed (available to print to) on the workstation. You don't need to worry about the relationships of printer drivers, connections, and physical printers. You can simply add a printer and set its properties. After it is added, it appears as a named printer in the Printers and Faxes folder.

- Thanks to Windows XP's *multithreading* and *preemptive multitasking*, 32-bit programs tend to print quite smoothly. Most applications let you start printing and immediately go back to work, while spooling and printing occurs in the background. (This isn't true for older 16-bit programs, which usually tie up the given application until output to the spooler is completed.)

- Multiple applications can send print jobs to the same printer, whether local or across the LAN. Additional documents are simply added to the queue and are printed in turn.

- Default settings for such options as number of copies, paper tray, page orientation, and so forth can be automatically used during print jobs, so you don't have to manually set them each time.

6

- You can easily view the document name, status, owner, page count, size, time of submission, paper source and orientation, number of copies, and destination port of jobs. You also can pause, resume, restart, and cancel jobs; plus, you can rearrange the order of the print queue. In addition, you can temporarily pause or resume printing without causing printer time-out problems.

- You can set color profiles for color printers, ensuring accuracy of output color. Associating the correct color profile with all your publishing tools helps to ensure consistent color application throughout the publishing process.

LAN users can take advantage of the more advanced features:

- Browsing for LAN-based printers to which to connect has been made very simple.

- You can easily share a printer over the LAN by modifying a few settings on the printer's Properties sheet. Your printer then acts as a print server for other computers. Shared printers can be given a meaningful name and comment, such as *LaserJet in Ted's Office*, which identifies them to LAN-based users surfing for a printer.

- Groups of users (administrators, guests, and so forth) can be assigned rights for printing, sharing, and queue management.

- The priority level of a print job can be increased or decreased.

- You can set printer properties, such as times of day when a network printer is available for use.

- In a busy LAN environment, you can attach a group (pool) of printers to a queue, so that output goes to the first available printer, and a notification is sent to you when the job is finished.

→ To learn more about using a printer on the network, **see** "Using Printers on the Network," **p. 568**.

- The system can track the use of network print servers locally or remotely for later review or for billing purposes.

- With the Web printer feature (Internet Printing Protocol, or IPP), printers can be shared securely over the Internet, without using *Virtual Private Networking (VPN)*.

→ To learn more about IPP, **see** "Traditional Versus Web Sharing," **p. 546**.

INSTALLING AND CONFIGURING A PRINTER

If your printer is already installed and operational at this point, you can skip this section and skim ahead for others that may be of interest. However, if you need to install a new printer, modify or customize your current installation, or add additional printers to your setup, read on.

You might want to add a printer in a few different instances, not all of which are obvious:

- You're connecting a new physical printer directly to your computer (obvious).

- You're connecting a new physical printer to the network (obvious).

- You want to print to formatted disk files that can later be sent to a particular type of printer (not so obvious).

- You want to set up multiple printer configurations (preferences) for a single physical printer, so that you can switch among them without having to change your printer setup before each print job (timesaving idea).

TIP FROM

Bob & Brian

> As discussed in Chapter 2, "Getting Your Hardware and Software Ready for Windows XP Professional," and Chapter 3, "Installing Windows XP Professional," before you buy a new piece of hardware, it's always a good idea to check the Microsoft Hardware Compatibility List (HCL) on the Web, or use the compatibility tool on the Windows XP CD. You should at least check with the manufacturer or check the printer's manual to ensure that it's compatible with Windows XP or Windows 2000.

The basic game plan for installing and configuring a printer is as follows:

- Read the printer's installation manual and follow the instructions for Windows XP or Windows 2000. Some printer manufacturers ask you to install their driver software *before* you plug in and turn on the printer for the first time. *Heed their advice!*

- Plug it in. Many newer printers are detected when you simply plug them into the parallel or USB port. Your printer might be found and then configure itself fairly automatically. If it does, you can skip on down to "Printing from Windows Applications," later in this chapter.

- If the printer doesn't configure itself, you can run the Add New Printer Wizard (or use a setup program, if one is supplied with your printer). We'll go over this procedure in detail in the next section.

At this point, you should have a functioning printer. You might want to make alterations and customizations to the printer setup, though. For example, you can do the following:

- Choose the default printer if you have more than one printer installed.

- Set job defaults pertaining to paper tray, two-sided printing, scaling, type of paper feed, halftone imaging, printer setup information (such as a PostScript "preamble"), and paper orientation.

- Check and possibly alter device-specific settings such as DPI (dots per inch), memory settings, and font substitution.

- Share the printer, and specify its share name so that other network users can use your printer from afar.

- Declare a separator file, usually one page long, that prints between each print job with the user's name, date and so on. (These are handy on busy networked printers so users can find their own output among stacks of printouts.)

- Arrange security for the printer by setting permissions (if you have Computer Administrator privileges).

6

NOTE

> Printer security issues such as setting permission, conducting printer access auditing, and setting ownership are covered in Chapter 17.

How you go about adding the printer depends on how you'll be connecting to it:

- To use a printer that's physically attached to another computer on your network, you still need to set up a printer icon on your own computer. This is called installing a *network printer*, as opposed to a *local printer*.

NOTE

> On a Windows XP Workgroup network, Windows automatically locates and installs icons for all the shared printers on your LAN without you needing to do anything. You can disable this behavior—open My Computer, select Tools, Folder Options, and select the View tab. You can check or uncheck "Automatically search for network folders and printers." You can also add networked printers manually using the procedures described under "Using Printers on the Network" in Chapter 17.

→ For detailed instructions on installing a network printer, **see** "Installing Network Printers," **p. 569**.

- A printer that's physically connected to the network wiring itself and not cabled to another computer is called "local printer on a network port" . . . just to make things confusing . . . We'll cover the installation of these in Chapter 17 as well.
- Most of us just connect our printer directly to our computer using a USB or parallel printer cable. Installing a local printer is covered in the next section.

INSTALLING A LOCAL PRINTER

Installing a local printer is a bit more complex than connecting to an existing network printer. For starters, unless Windows finds the printer automatically (via Plug and Play), you have to specify the location where the printer is physically connected, what you want to name it, and a few other pieces of information.

The procedures vary, depending on how the printer is connected to your computer:

- Parallel printer port
- USB/FireWire (IEEE 1394)
- Infrared

TIP FROM

Bob & Brian

> You must be logged on as a member of the Administrators group to add a local printer to a computer.

Here's the basic game plan, which works with most printers:

1. Read the printer's installation instructions for specific Windows XP or Windows 2000 instructions. You may be instructed to install software *before* connecting the printer to your computer for the first time. This is especially important if your printer connects via USB.

2. Connect the printer to the appropriate port on your computer according to the printer manufacturer's instructions.

3. Read the description that applies to the kind of connection your printer uses and proceed as directed:

Parallel Port	Connect the printer to your computer (typically you don't have to shut down the computer to attach parallel devices, though doing so might be a good idea). Windows might detect and install the printer. If it doesn't, open the Printers and Faxes folder, and select Add New Printer to start the wizard. Now click Next. Click Local Printer, and turn on Automatically Detect My Printer. Then click Next again to startthe Found New Hardware Wizard. Follow the instructions on the screen to finish installing the printer. The printer icon is then added to your Printers and Faxes folder.
USB or FireWire	Just connect the printer's cable to your computer. Windows will detect it and automatically start the Found New Hardware Wizard. Because USB and FireWire are hot-pluggable, you don't need to shut down or restart your computer. Simply follow the instructions on the screen to finish installing the printer. The printer icon is then added to your Printers and Faxes folder.
Infrared	Be sure your printer is turned on and within range of your computer's infrared eye. Also, make sure your infrared service is installed properly. Windows might detect the printer automatically and create an icon for it. If not, see Chapter 18, "Windows Unplugged: Remote and Mobile Networking," for more information on infrared printers.

If Windows can't detect the make and model of your printer, it will ask you to assist in selecting the appropriate type. If you can't find your printer's make and model in the list of choices, see step 5 in the next section.

IF THE PRINTER ISN'T FOUND OR IS ON A SERIAL (COM) PORT

If your printer isn't found using the options in the preceding section, or if the printer is connected via a COM port, you have to fake out Plug and Play and go the manual route. To do so, just follow these steps:

1. Open the Printers and Faxes folder, and run the Add New Printer Wizard again.

2. Click Next.

3. Click Local Printer, make sure that Automatically Detect My Printer is *not* checked, and then click Next.

4. Select the port the printer is connected to in the resulting dialog. Figure 6.2 shows the port dialog box; the options and what they mean are as follows:

Options	Notes
LPT1:, LPT2:, LPT3:	The most common setting is LPT1 because most PC-type printers hook up to the LPT1 parallel port.
COM1:, COM2:, COM3:, COM4:	If you know your printer is of the serial variety, it's probably connected to the COM1 port. If COM1 is tied up for use with some other device, such as a modem, use COM2. If you choose a COM port, click Settings to check the communications settings in the resulting dialog box. Set the baud rate, data bits, parity, start and stop bits, and flow control to match those of the printer being attached. Refer to the printer's manual to determine what the settings should be.
File	This is for printing to a disk file instead of to the printer. Later, the file can be sent directly to the printer or sent to someone on floppy disk or over a modem. When you print to this printer name, you are prompted to enter a filename. (See the section "Printing to Disk Option.")
Create a New Port	Create a New Port is used to make connections to printers that are directly connected to your LAN and are to be controlled by your computer. Its use is covered in Chapter 17.

5. Select the manufacturer and model of your printer in the next dialog, as shown in Figure 6.3. You can quickly jump to a manufacturer's name by pressing the first letter of the name, such as E for Epson. Then use the up- and down-arrow keys to home in on the correct one.

If you can't find the appropriate model, you have two choices: You can choose a similar compatible model, and risk getting less-than-perfect output, or you can get the correct driver. If you have an Internet connection, click Windows Update to see if Microsoft has a driver available. Otherwise, get the manufacturer's driver on a floppy disk or CD-ROM or download it via the Internet, and then click Have Disk. Locate the driver (look for an INF file, the standard type for driver setup programs) and click OK.

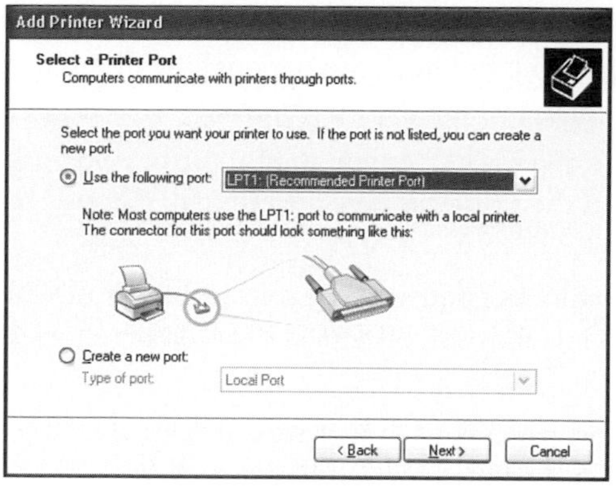

Figure 6.2
Choosing the port for a printer. Ninety-nine percent of the time it is LPT1.

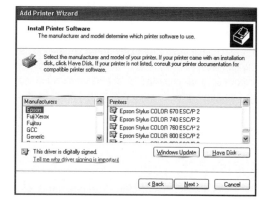

→ For more information on dealing with unlisted printers, see the next section, "What to Do if Your Printer Isn't Listed."

Figure 6.3
Choose the make and model of your printer here.

If the wizard finds that the appropriate driver is already installed on your machine, you can elect to keep it or replace it. It's up to you. If you think the replacement will be newer, go for it. By contrast, if no driver is listed on the machine, you may be prompted to install it or insert a disk, such as the Windows XP setup disk.

6. Name the printer. The name will appear in LAN-based users' browse boxes if you decide to share this printer. Some computers have trouble with filenames longer than 31 characters if you share the printer, so keep the name short and sweet.

7. Set whether you want this printer to be your default printer.

8. Click Next. Choose whether you want to share the printer on the LAN. If not, skip to step 10. If so, click Share As and enter a name for sharing—this name will also be visible to network users. If you're connected to any old DOS and 16-bit Windows computers, you might want to limit this name to 12 characters because that's the maximum length those users can see.

→ To learn more about sharing your printer on a network, **see** "Sharing Printers," **p. 589**.

9. Click Next. Now you can fill in additional information about the printer that people can see when browsing for a printer over the LAN, such as where it is and anything

6

else, like a cute joke or something goofy. Something like Joe's Laser Printer in Room 23 would be useful. Although these fields are optional, by filling in the location, you at least let users know where to pick up their documents.

10. Click Next. You then are asked whether you want to print a test page. Doing so is a good way to confirm that the printer is now operational. Choose Yes or No, and then click Next.

11. Assuming that everything looks good, be sure your printer is turned on and ready to print and click Finish. Some files will be copied between directories. You might be asked to insert disks again.

12. If you chose to print a test page, your printer should start up and print a single page. You will be asked whether it printed okay. If it did, click Yes and you're finished. If it didn't print correctly, click Troubleshoot, and follow the wizard's instructions to identify the problem.

When you're finished, the icon for the printer appears in your Printers and Faxes folder.

TIP FROM

Bob & Brian

> If you're going to share the printer with LAN users running Windows 95, 98, Me, or NT 4 on Intel or Alpha platforms, they'll need different printer drivers than Windows XP and 2000 machines do. You can install the drivers appropriate to their operating systems on your computer so they don't have to hunt around for driver files or so that they're not prompted to insert disks into their machines when they try to connect to your printer. You can do so by opening the Properties sheet for the printer, clicking the Sharing tab, and then clicking Additional Drivers.

→ For more details about sharing printers for use by workstations running other operating systems, **see** "Installing Extra Printer Drivers," **p. 590**.

WHAT TO DO IF YOUR PRINTER ISN'T LISTED

If your printer isn't detected with Plug and Play, and isn't listed in the selection list, you'll have to find a driver elsewhere.

First of all, your printer probably came with a floppy disk or CD-ROM with driver software. On the printer manufacturer selection dialog (Figure 6.5, shown later), click Have Disk and then click Browse to find the Windows XP or Windows 2000 driver files for your printer. Select the appropriate INF file and click OK.

If you can't find the disk or it doesn't contain a Windows XP or 2000 compatible driver, don't worry; there's still hope.

Many off-brand printers or models are designed to be compatible with one of the popular printer types, such as the Apple LaserWriters, Hewlett-Packard LaserJets, or one of the Epson series. Also, many printer models are very similar and can use the same driver.

Make your first stop Microsoft's online Hardware Compatibility List to see whether the printer in question has been tested with Windows XP or 2000. If it has, check the Microsoft drivers site, call the manufacturer, or check the manufacturer's Web site for the latest driver and download it. If the printer isn't on the HCL, determine whether the printer has a compatibility mode in which it can emulate a particular brand and model of printer that is. For example, some offbeat printers have an HP LaserJet compatibility mode.

Next, you can search for drivers on the Web. We're compiling a list of driver support sites that you can find at

http://www.helpwinxp.com

Assuming that you have obtained a printer driver, follow these instructions to install it:

1. Open the Printers and Faxes folder, and run the Add Printer Wizard.
2. Click Next, choose Local Printer, and then turn off the check box for autodetect.
3. Choose the correct port, and click Next.
4. Click Have Disk.

TIP FROM

Bob & Brian

If you're online, you can click the Windows Update button to query the Microsoft site for additions to the list of printers that are supported. If your printer isn't already on the standard list, connect to the Internet, and try this approach. Your printer driver might be newly available over the Net from Microsoft.

5. Click the Have Disk button. You're now prompted to insert a disk in drive A:. Insert the disk, or click Browse to get to a disk or network volume that contains the driver. The wizard is looking for a file with an .INF extension, which is the standard file extension for manufacturer-supplied driver files.
6. Click OK. You might have to choose a driver from a list if multiple options exist.
7. Continue through the wizard dialog boxes as explained previously.

CHANGING A PRINTER'S PROPERTIES

Each printer driver has a Properties sheet of associated settings (typically enough to choke a horse). The basic settings are covered in this chapter, whereas you'll find those relating to network printer sharing in Chapter 17, "Using a Windows XP Network."

Printer drivers dictate, among other things, the particular options available on their Properties sheet. Because of the variations possible, the following sections describe the gist of these options without necessarily going into detail about each printer type.

The settings pertaining to a printer are called properties. When you add a printer, the wizard dumps the icon for it in the Printers and Faxes folder, and it's ready to roll. At that point, you can alter its properties or accept the default properties. If you are logged on with Administrator privileges, or if the administrator has given you the correct privilege, you can then alter the properties as follows:

6

1. Open the Printers and Faxes folder by clicking Start, Control Panel, Printers and Other Hardware, View Installed Printers or Faxes.

2. Select the printer's icon and choose Set Printer Properties from the task list. Or, right-click the printer icon and select Properties. The printer's Properties dialog box then appears, as shown in Figure 6.4.

Figure 6.4
A typical printer's Properties dialog box. The settings available vary between printers. Some have more or fewer tabs.

3. Change any of the text boxes as you see fit. (Their significance was explained earlier in this chapter.)

Any printer's Properties sheet can have as many as eight tabs: General, Sharing, Ports, Advanced, Color Management, Security, Device Settings, and Utilities. Table 6.1 shows the general breakdown. Keep in mind that the tabs can vary depending on the capabilities of your printer.

TABLE 6.1   PROPERTIES SHEET TABS

Tab	What It Controls
General	This tab lists the name, location, model number, and features of the printer. From this tab, you can print a test page. You also can set default printing preferences, including the paper size, page orientation, paper source, pages per sheet (for brochure printing), affecting all print jobs. (You should rely on your application's Print Setup commands to control an individual print job's choice of paper orientation, paper source, and so on, which will override these settings.) Some color printers may have settings for paper quality, color control, and other utilities on this tab.
Sharing (see Chapter 17 for more)	On this tab, you can alter whether theprinter is shared and what the share name is. You also can set drivers for other operating systems by using the Additional Drivers button.
Ports	On this tab, you can add and delete ports; set time-out for LPT ports; and set baud rate, data bits, parity, stop bits, and flow control for serial ports.

TABLE 6.1 CONTINUED	
Tab	**What It Controls**
Advanced	This tab controls time availability, printer priority, driver file changes, spooling options, and advanced printing features such as booklet printing and page ordering. The first two settings are pertinent to larger networks and should be handled by a server administrator. The Advanced settings vary from printer to printer, depending on its capabilities. Booklet printing is worth looking into if you do lots of desktop publishing. Using this option, you can print pages laid out for stapling together small pamphlets.
Color Management	On this tab, you can set optional color profiles on color printers, if this capability is supported. (See "Color Management" later in this chapter.)
Security	If you have disabled Simple File Sharing (discussed in Chapters 16 and 18), this tab will appear to let you set who has access to print, manage printers, or manage documents from this printer.
Device Settings	The settings on this tab vary greatly between printers. For example, you can set paper size in each tray, set the amount of RAM in the printer, and substitute fonts.
Utilities	This tab contains options for nozzle cleaning, head cleaning, head alignment, and so on, depending on printer driver and printer type.

I discuss the most important of the settings in more detail in the next section.

TIP FROM

Each time you add a printer, Windows creates an icon for it in the Printers and Faxes folder. Although each is called a printer, it is actually a "virtual" printer, much the way a shortcut represents a document or application in the GUI. A given physical printer can have multiple icons, each with different default settings. For example, one could be set to print in landscape orientation on legal-size paper, whereas another printer would default to portrait orientation with letter-size paper. Of course, you can always adjust these settings when you go to print a document, but that can get tedious. With multiple printer icons, you can choose a setup by just selecting the appropriate printer icon.

TIP FROM

To assign a printer to an infrared port, select the Ports tab. Make sure the port selected under Print to the Following Port(s) is the infrared (IR) port. Setup and use of the infrared port are covered in Chapter 18, "Windows Unplugged: Remote and Mobile Networking."

6

→ For more details about printer sharing, printer pooling, port creation and deletion, and other server-related printing issues, **see** Chapter 17.

COMMENTS ABOUT VARIOUS SETTINGS

Table 6.2 describes the most common settings from the Properties dialog box for both PostScript and HP-compatible printers.

TABLE 6.2 THE OPTIONS IN THE BASIC SETUP DIALOG BOX

Option	Description
2 Sides	This option enables or disables double-sided printing for printers that support this feature.
Configure Port, LPT Port Timeout	This option specifies the amount of time that will elapse before you are notified that the printer or plotter is not responding. If printing from your application regularly results in an error message about transmission problems, and retrying seems to work, you should increase the setting. The maximum is 999,999 seconds.
Configure Port, Serial Port Settings	Settings here pertain to the serial port's communications settings, such as baud rate and parity. The serial port's baud rate, data bits, parity, stop bits, and flow control must match that of the printer's, or you're in for some garbage printouts. If you have trouble, check the printer's DIP switch or software settings and the printer manual to ensure that the settings agree.
Default Datatype	This setting usually doesn't need changing. The default is RAW. A very specialized application might ask you to create a printer with another data type setting for use when printing its documents. The EMF data types can result in faster transmission over slow networks (for example by modem).
Enable Advanced Printing Features	When this option is checked, metafile spooling is turned on, and options such as Page Order, Booklet Printing, and Pages Per Sheet may be available, depending on your printer. For normal printing, you should leave the advanced printing feature set to the default (Enabled). If compatibility problems occur, you can disable the feature.
Enable Bidirectional Support	This option lets the computer query the printer for setings and status information.
Font Cartridges	For this option, you choose the names of the cartridges that are physically installed in the printer. You can select only two.
Font Substitution	TrueType Font Substitution Table: Used for PostScript printers to declare when internal fonts should be used in place of downloading TrueType fonts to speed up printing. See Chapter 26, "Font Management," for more details on font substitution.
Form-to-Tray Assignment	For this option, you click a source, such as a lower tray, and then choose a form name to match with the source. When you choose a form name (such as A4 Small) at print time, the printer driver tells the printer which tray to switch to. You don't have to think about it. You can repeat the process for each form name you want to set up.

6

TABLE 6.2 CONTINUED	
Option	**Description**
Hold Mismatched Documents	This option directs the spooler to check the printer's form setup and match it to the document setup before sending documents to the print device. If the information does not match, the document is held in the queue. A mismatched document in the queue does not prevent cor- rectly matched documents from printing.
Keep Printed Documents	This option specifies that the spooler should not delete documents after they are printed. This way, a document can be resubmitted to the printer from the printer queue instead of from the program, which is faster.
New Driver	Use this button to install an updated driver for the printer. It runs the Add Printer Driver Wizard.
Orientation	This option sets the page orientation. Normal orientation is Portrait, which, like a portrait of the Mona Lisa, is taller than it is wide. Landscape, like a landscape painting, is the opposite. Rotated Landscape means a 90-degree counterclockwise rotation of the printout.
Page Order	This option determines the order in which documents are printed. Front to Back prints the document so that page 1 is on top of the stack. Back to Front prints the document so that page 1 is on the bottom of the stack.
Page Protect	If turned on, this option tells the printer to forcibly reserve enough memory to store a full page image; some intense graphics pages otherwise might not be able to print if the printer gives too much memory over to downloaded fonts and macros.
Print Directly to the Printer	This option prevents documents sent to the printer from being spooled. Thus, printing doesn't happen in the background; instead, the computer is tied up until the print job is completed. There's virtually no practical reason for tying up your computer this way, unless your printer and Windows are having difficulty communicating or you find that printing performance (page per minute throughput) increases significantly when this option is enabled. When a printer is shared over the network, this option isn't available.
Print Spooled Documents First	This option specifies that the spooler should favor documents that have completed spooling when deciding which document to print next, even if the completed documents are a lower priority than documents that are still spooling.
Printer Memory	This option specifies how much memory the printer has installed.

6

TABLE 6.2   CONTINUED

Option	Description
Printing Defaults	You click this option to view or change the default document properties for all users of the selected printer. If you share your local printer, these settings are the default document properties for other users.
Priority	Printers can have a priority setting from 1 to 99. The default setting is 1. Print jobs sent to a printer that has a priority level of 2 always print before a job sent to a printer with a level 1 setting if both setups use the same physical printer.
Resolution	Some printers can render graphics in more than one resolution. The higher the resolution, the longer printing takes, so you can save time by choosing a lower resolution. For finished, high-quality work, you should choose the highest resolution. (On some printers, this choice is limited by the amount of memory in the printer.)
Separator File	A preassigned file can be printed between jobs, usually just to place an identification page listing the user, job ID, date, time, number of pages, and so forth. Files also can be used to switch a printer between PostScript and PCL (HP) mode for printers that can run in both modes.
Use Printer Halftoning	Halftoning is a process that converts shades of gray or colors to patterns of black and white dots. A newspaper photo is an example of halftoning. When the arrangement of dots (pixels) on the page is varied, a photographic image can be simulated with only black and white dots. Because virtually no black-and-white printers and typesetters can print shades of gray, halftoning is the closest you get to realistic photographic effects. Normally, Windows processes the halftoning of graphics printouts. Only printers that can do halftoning offer halftone options.

6

NOTE

If you can't figure out what an option does, you can always click the Help button in the upper-right corner of the Properties dialog box and then click an option. A description of the option should appear.

TIP FROM

Bob & Brian

You can access the Printing Defaults tab through two paths: one by choosing Printing Defaults from the Advanced tab and the other by choosing Printing Preferences from the General tab. What's the difference? Printing Defaults are the baseline settings offered to each user. Printing Preferences hold your own personal preferences, overriding the Printing Defaults (but are not forced on other users of that printer).

TIP FROM
*Bob
& Brian*

Another set of properties is available for shared printers. To locate it, right-click an empty spot within the Printers and Faxes folder, and choose Server Properties. The Server Properties list ports and show the collective list of all installed drivers in use. Here, you can define forms and set events and notifications. The last tab is covered in Chapter 17 because it's a network topic.

REMOVING A PRINTER FROM THE PRINTERS AND FAXES FOLDER

You might want to remove a printer setup for several reasons:

- The physical printer has been removed from service.
- You don't want to use a particular network printer anymore.
- You had several definitions of a physical printer using different default settings, and you want to remove one of them.
- You have a nonfunctioning or improperly functioning printer setup and want to remove it and start over by running the Add Printer Wizard.

In any of these cases, the approach is the same:

1. Be sure you are logged on with Administrator privileges.
2. Open the Printers and Faxes folder.
3. Be sure nothing is in the print queue. You have to clear the queue for the printer before deleting it. If you don't, Windows will try to delete all jobs in the queue for you, but it unfortunately isn't always successful.
4. Select the printer icon you want to kill, and choose File, Delete (or press the Del key).
5. Depending on whether the printer is local or remote, you see one of two different dialog boxes. One asks whether you want to delete the printer; the other asks whether you want to delete the connection to the printer. In either case, click Yes. The printer icon or window disappears from the Printers and Faxes folder.

TIP FROM
*Bob
& Brian*

The removal process removes only the virtual printer setup from the Registry for the currently logged-in user. The related driver file and font files are not deleted from the disk. Therefore, if you ever want to re-create the printer, you don't have to insert disks or respond to prompts for the location of driver files.

PRINTING FROM WINDOWS APPLICATIONS

When you print from 16-bit or 32-bit Windows applications, the internal Print Manager kicks in and spools the print job for you, adding it to the queue for the selected printer. The spooler then feeds the file to the assigned printer(s), coordinating the flow of data and keeping you informed of the progress. Jobs are queued up and listed in the given printer's window, from which their status can be observed; they can be rearranged, deleted, and so forth. All the rights and privileges assigned to you, as the user, are applicable, potentially allowing you to alter the queue (as discussed later in this chapter), rearranging, deleting, pausing, or restarting print jobs.

If the application doesn't provide for a specific printer (typically through a Print Setup dialog box), then the default printer is used. You can set the default printer from the Printers and Faxes folder by right-clicking a printer and choosing Set as Default Printer.

Printing from DOS Applications

If you choose a default printer that your DOS application can't support, your printouts might be garbled. For example, if you're running WordPerfect 5.1 for DOS and have it installed for an Apple LaserWriter, but the default Windows printer is set to an Epson inkjet, your printouts will be nothing but a listing of PostScript commands. Make sure your non-Windows applications and your default printer are in accord before you try to print.

Furthermore, a DOS application will try to print to a DOS LPT port, usually LPT1, regardless of what port your default printer is installed on. If your printer is out there somewhere on a LAN, nothing will come out! To direct a DOS program's output to a network printer, issue the command

```
net use lpt1: \\server\sharename
```

from the Command Prompt window.

→   For more information about the net use command, **see** "Mapping Drives with net use," **p. 598**.

PRE-PRINTING CHECKLIST

To print from Windows applications, follow these steps:

1. Check to see that the printer and page settings are correct and the right printer is chosen for your output. Some applications provide a Printer Setup or other option on their File menu for this task. Recall that settings you make from such a box override the default settings made from the printer's Properties sheet. If the application has a Print Preview command, use it to check that the formatting of the document is acceptable.

2. Select File, Print from the application's window, and fill in whatever information is asked of you. Figure 6.5 shows the Print dialog for WordPad. (Print dialogs for other applications may differ.) Notice that you can just click a printer's icon to choose it. When you do, its printer driver kicks in, changing the options on the tabs. You can also find a printer on the LAN or print to a file, using their respective buttons. Two other tabs, Layout and Paper/Quality, could be useful. For advanced options such as halftoning and color matching, select the Layout tab and click Advanced.

3. Click OK (or otherwise confirm printing). The data is sent to the spooler, which writes it in a file and then begins printing it. If an error occurs—a port conflict, the printer is out of paper, or whatever—Windows will display a message indicating what the problem is, as shown in Figure 6.6.

Figure 6.5
Preparing to print a typical file.

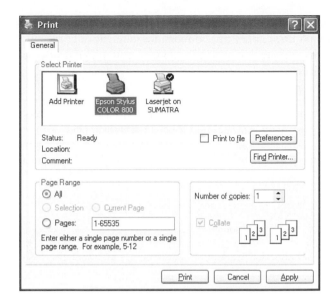

Figure 6.6
Typical error message resulting from a printer problem.

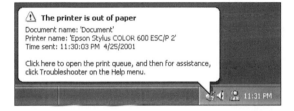

You can attempt to fix the problem by checking the cable connection, the paper supply, and so forth. Then click Retry. If you run into more serious trouble, you can run the Troubleshooting Wizard from the Help menu.

For most users, following these steps is all you'll ever need to do to print. The remainder of this chapter deals mostly with how to work with the printer queues of your own workstation printer or of network printers, and how to alter, pause, delete, or restart print jobs.

 If you receive printer errors when attempting to print a document, see "Printer Errors" in the "Troubleshooting" section at the end of this chapter.

 If nothing happens when you send a print job to the printer, see "Nothing Happens" in the "Troubleshooting" section at the end of this chapter.

PRINTING BY DRAGGING FILES INTO THE PRINT MANAGER

As a shortcut to printing a document, you can simply drag the icon of the document you want to print either onto an icon of a printer or into the printer's open window (from the Printers and Faxes folder). You can drag the file from Explorer right onto the chosen printer's icon or open window to see it added to the print queue for that printer.

When you drop the document, Windows realizes you want to print it, and the file is loaded into the source application, the Print command is automatically executed, and the file is spooled to the Print Manager. Figure 6.7 shows an example of dropping a Word document on a PostScript printer.

TIP FROM

Documents must have associations linking the filename extension (for example, .doc or .bmp) to the application that handles that file type; otherwise, printing by dragging them to Print Manager doesn't work. Also, you obviously don't have the option of setting printing options when you print this way. All the defaults are used.

→ For more information about file associations, **see** "Setting Folder Options," **p. 796**.

Figure 6.7
You can print a document or a number of documents by dragging them onto a destination printer in the Printers and Faxes folder. The files must have application associations.

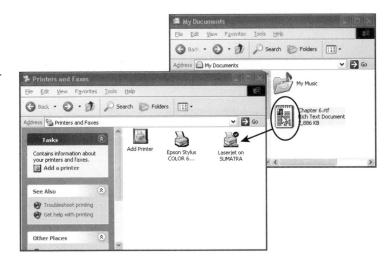

⚠ *If you're having trouble printing, you're getting "garbage" printouts, or you're getting only partial pages, see "Printer Produces Garbled Text" in the "Troubleshooting" section at the end of this chapter.*

⚠ *If only half of the page prints correctly before the printer starts printing garbage text, see "Only Half of the Page Prints Correctly" in the "Troubleshooting" section at the end of this chapter.*

PRINTING OFFLINE

If your printer is disconnected, you can still queue up documents for printing. You might want to do this while traveling, for instance, if you have a laptop and don't want to drag a 50-pound laser printer along in your carry-on luggage.

If you try this, however, you'll quickly find that the Print Manager will beep, pop up messages to tell you about the missing printer, and otherwise make your life miserable. You can silence it by right-clicking the printer's icon in the Printers and Faxes folder and selecting Use Printer Offline.

Windows will now quietly and compliantly queue up anything you "print." (Just don't forget that you've done this or nothing will print even when you've reconnected your printer. You'll end up yelling at your nonresponsive printer, when it's only doing what it was told).

When you've reconnected the printer, uncheck Use Printer Offline (with the same steps used above) and the output will flow forth. It's a nifty feature, but only available for local printers, not networked printers.

WORKING WITH THE PRINTER QUEUE

After you or other users on the network have sent print jobs to a given printer, anyone with rights to manage the queue can work with it. If nothing else, it's often useful to observe the queue to check its progress. This way, you can better choose which printer to print to, or whether some intervention is necessary, such as adding more paper. By simply opening the Printers and Faxes folder, you can see the basic state of each printer's queue, assuming you display the window contents in Details view.

For each printer, the window displays the status of the printer (in the title bar) and the documents that are queued up, including their sizes, status, owner, pages, date submitted, and so on.

TIP FROM

Bob & Brian

> You can drag a printer's icon from the Printers and Faxes window to your desktop, for easy access. Click Yes when Windows asks if you want to create a shortcut.

Figure 6.8 shows a sample printer's folder with a print queue and related information.

Figure 6.8
A printer's folder showing several print jobs pending.

TIP FROM

Bob & Brian

> When print jobs are pending for a workstation, an icon appears in the system tray, near the clock. You can hover the mouse pointer over it to see the number of documents waiting to print. Right-click it to choose a printer's queue to examine in a window.

To keep network traffic down to a dull roar, Windows doesn't poll the network constantly to check the state of the queue. If you are printing to a network printer and want to check the current state of affairs on the network printer, choose View, Refresh or press F5 to immediately update the queue information.

TIP FROM

By default, all users can pause, resume, restart, and cancel printing of their own documents. However, to manage documents printed by other users, your system administrator must give you the Manage Documents permission.

→ To learn more details about managing print jobs as a system administrator, **see** "Tracking Printer Users," **p. 592**.

DELETING A FILE FROM THE QUEUE

After sending a document to the queue, you might reconsider printing it, or you might want to re-edit the file and print it again later. If so, you can simply remove the file from the queue. To do so, right-click the document and choose Cancel, or choose Document, Cancel from the menu. The document is then removed from the printer's window.

If you're trying to delete the job that's printing, you might have some trouble. At the very least, the system might take some time to respond. Sometimes canceling a laser printer's job while it's printing in graphics mode necessitates resetting the printer to clear its buffer. To reset, either turn the printer off and then on, or use the Reset option (if it's available).

NOTE

Because print jobs are spooled to the hard disk, they can survive powering down Windows XP. Any documents already in the queue when the system goes down, whether due to an intentional shutdown or a power outage, reappear in the queue when you power up.

CANCELING ALL PENDING PRINT JOBS ON A GIVEN PRINTER

Assuming you have been given the privilege, you can cancel *all* the print jobs on a printer. In the Printers and Faxes folder, right-click the printer, and choose Cancel All Documents. A confirmation dialog appears to confirm this action.

PAUSING, RESUMING, AND RESTARTING THE PRINTING PROCESS

If you need to, you can pause the printing process for a particular printer or even just a single document print job. This capability can be useful in case you have second thoughts about a print job, want to give other jobs a chance to print first, or you just want to adjust or quiet the printer for some reason.

To pause a print job, right-click it and choose Pause. Pretty simple. The word Paused then appears on the document's line. The printing might not stop immediately because your printer might have a buffer that holds data in preparation for printing. The printing stops when the buffer is empty. When you're ready to resume printing, just right-click the job in question, and choose Resume.

TIP FROM

Bob
& Brian

> Pausing a document lets other documents later in the queue proceed to print, essentially moving them ahead in line. You can achieve the same effect by rearranging the queue, as explained in the section titled "Rearranging the Queue Order."

In some situations, you might need to pause all the jobs on your printer, such as to add paper to it, to alter the printer settings, or just to shut up the printer for a bit while you take a phone call. To pause all jobs, open the Printer's window and choose Printer, Pause Printing. You have to choose the command again to resume printing, and the check mark on the menu goes away.

Should you need to (due to a paper jam or other botch), you can restart a printing document from the beginning. Just right-click the document, and choose Restart.

REARRANGING THE QUEUE ORDER

When you have several items on the queue, you might want to rearrange the order in which they're slated for printing. Perhaps a print job's priority has increased because you need it for an urgent meeting, or you have to get a letter to the post office. Whatever the reason, as long as a given document hasn't yet started to print you can easily rearrange its position in the print queue like this:

1. Click the file you want to move, and keep the mouse button pressed.
2. Drag the file up or down to its new location. A solid line moves to indicate where the document will be inserted when you release the mouse button.
3. When you release the mouse button, your file is inserted in the queue, pushing the other files down a notch.

VIEWING AND ALTERING DOCUMENT PROPERTIES

Like everything in Windows, each document in the printer queue has its own properties. For a more detailed view of information pertaining to each document, you can open the Properties sheet for it by right-clicking it and choosing Properties. You can change only two settings from the resulting dialog box (see Figure 6.9):

- The print priority. Documents with higher priority numbers get printed ahead of documents with lower numbers.
- The time of day when the document can be printed

6

NOTE

> As a shortcut, you can open a document's properties by just double-clicking it.

Figure 6.9
Altering the properties for a print job on the queue.

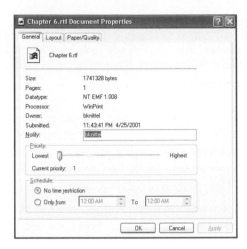

PRINTING TO DISK OPTION

Sometimes printing to a disk file rather than to a printer can be useful. What does printing to a disk file mean? It means that the same data that normally would be sent to the printer is shunted to a disk file, either locally or on the network. The file isn't a copy of the file you were printing; it contains all the special formatting codes that control your printer. Codes that change fonts, print graphics, set margins, break pages, and add attributes such as underline, bold, and so on are all included in this type of file. Print files destined for PostScript printers typically include their PostScript preamble, too. The primary use of print-to-disk files is to send documents as formatted using PostScript to a service bureau for professional printing.

In some applications, this choice is available in the Print dialog box. If it isn't, you should modify the printer's configuration to print to a file rather than to a port. Then, whenever you use that printer, it will use all the usual settings for the driver but send the data to a file of your choice instead of to the printer port. Just follow these steps:

1. In the Printers and Faxes folder, right-click the printer's icon, and choose Properties.

2. Click Ports.

3. Set the port to File, and close the dialog box.

    The next time you or another local or network user prints to that printer, you'll be prompted to enter a filename, as you can see in Figure 6.10. You should specify the full path with the filename. The file will be stored on the machine where the print job originated.

TIP FROM

Bob & Brian

> If you want to create an encapsulated PostScript file (.EPS), you can print to a printer that uses a PostScript driver (the Apple LaserWriter or the QMS PS-810, for example) or set up a phony printer that uses such a driver. No physical printer is needed. Then you can modify the properties of the printer via the Properties, Details, Job Defaults, Options dialog box to set an encapsulated PostScript filename.

Figure 6.10
Enter the full path and filename for the printer output file.

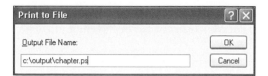

COLOR MANAGEMENT

Color management is the process of producing accurate, consistent color among a variety of input and output devices. In Windows, the color management system (CMS) maps colors between devices such as scanners, monitors, and printers; transforms colors from one color space to another (for example, RGB to CMYK); and adjusts tints displayed or printed for correctness. For most of us, this kind of precision isn't very important, but for graphic artists and designers, it's an essential part of preparing proofs and professional output.

Just like a printer needs a printer driver or a scanner needs a TWAIN driver, each piece of hardware needs its own color *profile*. A profile is a file made by the hardware manufacturer (or Microsoft) specifically for the device, and it contains information about the color characteristics of the hardware. You simply associate the profile with the device via the device's Properties sheet, and the color system does the rest. Only if a device supports color management does its Properties sheet have a Color tab on it, however.

Even though some profiles are included with Windows XP, you might need to obtain a profile for your particular hardware. Check with the manufacturer. You can use the following procedure to add a color profile to a printer:

1. If you obtain a custom color-profile file from your manufacturer, copy it to *%systemroot%*\system32\spool\drivers\color where *%systemroot%* is your Windows folder.

2. Open the Printers and Faxes folder by selecting Start, Control Panel, Printers and Other Hardware, Printers and Faxes.

3. Right-click the printer that you want to associate with a color profile, click Properties, and then click the Color Management tab. Notice that the tab has two settings: Automatic and Manual. Normally, Windows uses the Automatic setting, in which case it assigns a color profile to the printer from those it has on hand. If you want to override the default, click Manual.

4. Click Add to open the Add Profile Association dialog box.

5. Locate the new color profile you want to associate with the printer. You can right-click a profile and choose Properties to read more about the profile. Because the filenames are cryptic, this is the only way to figure out what device a color profile is for.

6. Click the new profile, and then click Add. Keep in mind that you can associate any number of profiles with a given piece of gear. Only one can be active at a time, however. After you open the profile list, select Manual and click the one you want to activate. For sophisticated setups, you may have reason for multiple profiles, but it's not likely that many users who are not designers or artists will bother.

6

You can use the same approach to add profiles for other hardware pieces, such as displays and scanners. Just bring up the Color Management tab of each item through its Properties sheet.

NOTE

> For a video display, open the Settings tab, click Advanced, and then click the Color Management tab.

FAXING

If your computer has a modem installed, you can use it to send and receive faxes. Windows XP comes with fax software built in.

To send a fax from Windows XP, just write a document using your favorite application, choose the Fax icon from the printer folder, and print. Windows asks for the appropriate fax phone number and makes the call—no paper is involved. You can also send scanned images. The fax service can even add a cover sheet to your document on the way out. To receive faxes, your modem can be set to answer calls. When a fax arrives, you can view its image on screen or print it, or even have it printed automatically.

Third-party Fax software such as Symantec's WinFax Pro has more bells and whistles, and can provide fax services for the whole network, but the basic version that comes with Windows will take care of most home and small office users' needs. Windows XP faxing can't be shared among a number of users on the LAN the same way you can share regular printers, though. If you want to provide a shared fax modem for your LAN, you should look for a third-party product. See the note below for some links.

NOTE

> I should tell you that while computer-based faxing is great for documents you're typing up in your word processor, it's not so great for handwritten documents (which you'll need to scan and then "print"). There's still a lot to be said for inexpensive dedicated fax machines, at least for sending.

INSTALLING THE FAX SERVICE

All you need to get started faxing is a fax device, such as a fax modem; it cannot be just a plain data modem. Because all modems sold these days have fax capability, the odds are slim that you'll have to buy a replacement. There also are some combination scanner/printer/faxing machines that can serve as a Windows Fax device.

In this day of Plug and Play, installing a modem or attaching a fax device will probably prompt Windows into installing the fax service and a fax printer. If, for some reason, Windows doesn't sense that you've attached a fax modem even when you reboot, you can use the Add/Remove Hardware Wizard. (See Chapter 30, "Installing and Replacing Hardware," for coverage of the Add/Remove Hardware applet and the Modem applet, both in the Control Panel.)

NOTE

> For more information on modem compatibility with faxes, see the Microsoft Windows Hardware Compatibility List at the Microsoft Web site (`http://www.microsoft.com/hcl`).

When a functioning fax modem or multifunction printer has been installed, check to see if a Fax icon has appeared in your Printers and Faxes folder (you get there from Start, Control Panel, Printers and Other Hardware). If it's not there, you'll need to install the fax service by following these steps:

1. Log on as a Computer Administrator user.
2. Open the Printers and Faxes folder by clicking Start, Printers and Faxes. If this isn't on your Start menu, click Control Panel, Printers and Other Hardware, and then View Installed Printers or Fax Printers.
3. Click Install a Local Fax Printer in the Printer Tasks list.
4. You may need to insert your Windows XP installation disc if Windows needs to copy the Fax service files.

NOTE

> If you have a functioning fax modem installed but the Fax icon doesn't appear in Printers and Faxes, or if you inadvertently delete the Fax icon from that folder later on, select Set Up Faxing or Add a Local Fax Printer from the Printer Tasks menu.

When the fax service has been installed, a Fax icon will appear in your Printers and Faxes folder, and a set of Fax management programs will be installed under Start, More Programs, Accessories, Communications, Fax. Table 6.3 lists these commands and their purposes.

TABLE 6.3   FAX-RELATED COMMANDS

Command	Action
Fax Console	Displays a queue of outgoing faxes and lists received faxes.
Fax Cover Page Editor	Lets you design custom cover pages for your faxes.
Send a Fax . . .	Used by itself, sends only a cover page. Invoked by applications to send whole documents.

In addition, there is a Fax Configuration Wizard that asks you for setup information to be used in cover sheets and selects devices to be used for sending and receiving faxes, and a more sophisticated setup program called the Fax Service Manager. We'll discuss all of these programs in the following sections.

6

GETTING SET UP

After you install your fax hardware, you can get started by entering your fax-related settings using the Fax Configuration Wizard (see Figure 6.11). Open it by clicking Start, More Programs, Accessories, Communications, Fax, Fax Configuration Wizard.

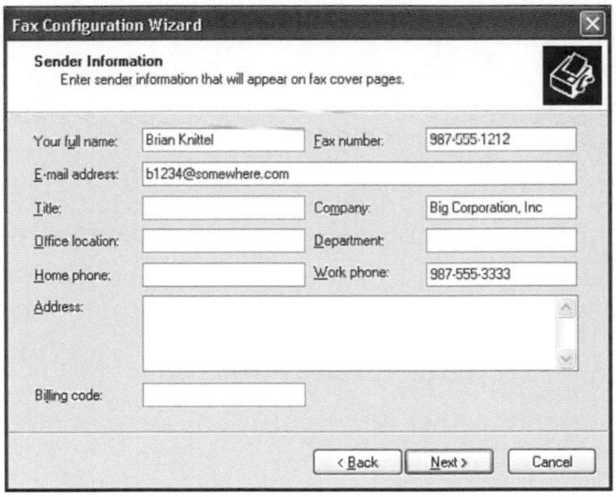

Figure 6.11
The Fax Configuration Wizard sets up your cover page particulars.

1. Enter the relevant information into the User Information tab. You can skip the stuff that is not relevant. This data will be printed on your cover pages. Click Next.

2. Select the modem(s) and/or other fax device(s) you wish to use. If there are more than one, you can prioritize them with the arrow buttons. Click Next when done.

3. Enter an identifying string (TSID) for your fax transmissions. This is displayed by receiving fax machines. Enter up to 20 characters and click Next.

4. If you'd like to receive faxes automatically, check the box corresponding to your fax modem. If you do, your modem will answer any incoming calls on its line (you can select the number of rings before it answers). If you leave the box unchecked, your computer won't be able to receive faxes. If you decide to receive faxes, enter a Called Station Identifier—this will be displayed on a sender's fax machine. Click Next.

5. If you chose to receive faxes, indicate what you'd like done with them as they arrive. You can choose to print them by checking "Print it on" and selecting a printer, and/or you can save a copy of the fax in a designated folder.

6. Finally, click Finish.

> **NOTE**
>
> There is one other configuration option you might want to set. By default, Windows will save its own copy of each fax it sends and receives. To alter this, open the Printers and Faxes folder, right-click the Fax icon, select Properties, and view the Archives tab. Here, you can select where and whether to store copies of incoming and outgoing faxes.

If you can't get your fax printer installed, see "Fax Printer Can't Be Added" in the "Troubleshooting" section at the end of this chapter.

IMPORTING FAXES FROM WINDOWS 9X/ME

If you used Personal Fax for Windows in Windows 95, 98, or Me, and you want access to the archived faxes you sent and received with it, you can import these faxes into the new Fax service. Follow these steps:

1. Open the Printers and Faxes folder and double-click the Fax icon. This opens the Fax Console.

2. Select File, Import, and then select either Sent Faxes or Received Faxes.

3. In the Browse dialog, locate the folder containing your sent or received faxes. When you have selected the folder, click OK.

4. The imported faxes are not deleted from their original location. If the import is successful and you're happy with the new setup, you can delete the old archives later on to recover disk space.

SENDING A FAX

The Fax service should now be running and your fax printer installed. You should now be ready to send a fax. To do so, just follow these steps:

1. Open the document you want to send.

2. Choose File, Print. From the standard Print dialog box, choose the Fax icon as the printer. Set up the particulars as necessary (page range, and so on), and click OK.

3. The Send Fax Wizard then begins and walks you through the process of preparing the fax. (If you haven't run the Fax Configuration Wizard yet, you'll get the pleasure of going through it now.)

4. Fill in the recipient and dialing information as prompted, as shown in Figure 6.12. You can add multiple names to the list. If you have fax numbers in your address book, you can use it as a source for your list. If you set up your area code and Dialing Rules when you installed your modem, just enter the fax recipient's area code and number. If you didn't, uncheck Dialing Rules and enter the recipient's number including a 1 and area code if needed. Click the Add button to add the first recipient, and repeat the process for each additional recipient. (This way, you can do a bulk faxing if you need to. This feature is one of the true advantages of faxing with a computer rather than a hardware fax machine.) When you've entered all of the recipients, click Next.

→ Windows can automatically manage area codes and special features like outside-line access by setting up Dialing Rules. This is really handy when you're on the road. For more information, **see** "Dialing Rules," **p. 831**.

5. If you'd like to add a cover page to your fax, check Select a Cover Page and choose one of the predefined formats from the drop-down list. Enter the subject and any notes you want to appear on the cover page. If you'd like to alter your personal information, click Sender Info.

6

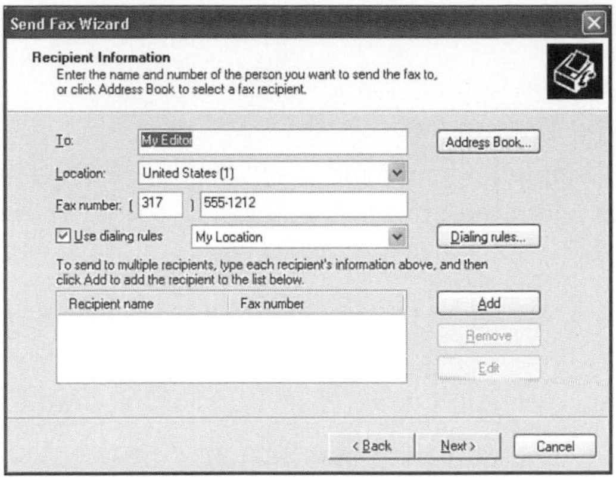

Figure 6.12
Adding recipients to
the fax transmission
list.

6. Click Next. Choose when you'd like to send the fax. Typically, it is Now, but the When Discount Rates Apply option is interesting. (See the description of Fax Service Management in the following section to see how to set the timing.) Alternatively, you can specify a time in the next 24 hours.

7. Click Next If you'd like to be notified if the fax is successfully sent or fails to go out, choose the desired notification method, then click Next.

Windows then will prepare the print job for faxing. You can follow its progress by watching the Fax Console, which I'll discuss in the next section.

TIP FROM

Bob
& Brian

You can send a quick note via fax without using a word processor at all. Just click Start, All Programs, Accessories, Fax, Send A Fax. This sends a cover sheet only, and you can type your message into the Send Fax Wizard's Note field.

FAX MANAGEMENT UTILITIES

For detailed control of how the Fax service sends and receives faxes, and to set up shared cover sheets that can be used by all of the computer's users, there's a management tool called Fax Console.

To run it, double-click the Fax icon in Printers and Faxes, or choose Start, More Programs, Accessories, Communications, Fax, Fax Console.

You then see the window shown in Figure 6.13.

Poke around in this application to familiarize yourself with it. As you can see, you can browse through outgoing and received faxes by opening their Explorer folder views. The most important use of Fax Console is to delete outgoing faxes if you change your mind. To do this, just highlight the entry in the Outbox listing and press the Del key.

Figure 6.13
Fax Console lets you
manage outgoing and
received faxes.

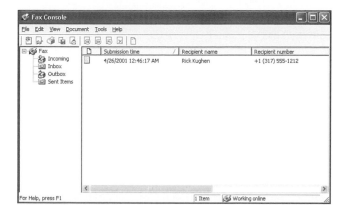

The Tools menu also offers several management options, as listed in Table 6.4

TABLE 6.4   FAX CONSOLE TOOLS

Tools Menu Item	Lets You . . .
Sender Information	change your contact information used on cover sheets
Personal Cover Pages	edit personal cover sheets not shared with other users of your computer
Fax Printers Status	(not terribly useful)
Configure Fax	Run the Fax Configuraion Wizard again
Fax Printer Configuration	Edit Fax Printer Properties
Fax Monitor	Monitor the progress of outgoing faxes

COVER SHEETS

Windows XP comes with several fax cover sheet forms predefined for typical business use:
Generic, Confidential, Urgent, and so on. You can modify these cover sheets using the Fax
Cover Page editor from the Fax menu or from Fax Console, as noted in Table 6.4. I can't go
into much detail on this program, except to give you few hints:

- From the Fax Console, select Tools, Personal Cover Pages to start the Cover Page
  Editor. You can select an existing cover sheet, or you can click New to create a new one.

- It's easiest to start with one of the predefined cover sheets and modify it as desired.
  Click New to start the Cover Sheet Editor. Use File, Open and browse to one of the
  files in this spectacularly-named folder: \Documents and Settings\All Users\
  Application Data\Microsoft\Windows NT\MSFax\Common Coverpages.

- Use the text button (labeled "ab|") and graphics button to draw items that never
  change, such as a confidentiality clause. Use the Insert menu to drop in information
  specified when each fax is sent, such as the recipient name.

6

■ When you've finished editing, use Save, or Save As to store the personalized cover sheet in My Documents\Fax\Personal Coverpages.

INCOMING FAXES

When you configure the Fax system to receive faxes, it will answer incoming calls on your Fax modem.

Each fax is converted to a file using the TIF file format when it arrives. Because TIF is a nonproprietary format, you can view or edit it with almost any graphics program. However, using the Windows Picture and Fax is easy enough.

There are two ways to set up the fax service for receiving faxes: It can answer your modem's phone line whenever it rings, or you can do a one-time receive.

To set up auto-answering, follow these steps:

1. Log on as a Computer Administrator user.
2. Open the Printers and Faxes folder, right-click the Fax icon, and select Properties.
3. Select your fax modem on the Devices tab and click Properties.
4. View the Receive tab. Check Enable Device To Receive. You can enable auto-printing here qas well, as I'll discuss later in this section.

If you don't want the fax modem to answer every call, you can enable a one-time receipt this way:

1. Open the Printers and Faxes folder.
2. Wait for the phone line to ring, or use a telephone handset to call the sender and him to press the Start button on his fax machine.
3. Double-click the Fax icon to open the Fax Console, and choose File, Receive A Fax Now.

If your system refuses to receive incoming faxes, see "Cannot Receive a Fax" in the "Troubleshooting" section at the end of this chapter.

TIP FROM

As long as the fax service is running, and you have enabled your fax modem to receive faxes, the fax icon appears in the system tray. Double-clicking it brings up the Fax Monitor.

By default, incoming faxes are converted to TIF files and are dumped into the Fax Console's Inbox. But you can configure a fax setup to actually print your documents on paper as they come in. To shunt all incoming faxes to a physical printer for automatic printing, follow these steps:

1. Log on as a Computer Administrator user.

2. Open the Printers and Faxes folder, right-click the Fax icon, and select Properties.

3. Select your fax modem on the Devices tab and click Properties.

4. View the Receive tab. Check the Print and/or Save a copy options, as shown in Figure 6.14, and click OK. Use Save a Copy only to store an *extra* copy of received faxes, as they'll also be stored in the Fax console's inbox.

Figure 6.14
Use this dialog box to configure automatic printing of received faxes. You can have incoming faxes printed automatically, and/or store a copy in a folder.

VIEWING RECEIVED FAXES

As I mentioned in the previous section, you can configure the fax service to automatically print incoming faxes. You can also view them on your monitor at any time.

There are two ways to view faxes. First, you can use the Fax Console, shown previously in Figure 6.13. There are three ways to open the Fax console:

- If the Fax Monitor icon appears in the Notification area of your task bar, right-click it and select Fax Console

- Select Start, All Programs, Accessories, Communications, Fax, Fax Console

- Use a shortcut created by right-clicking and dragging the Fax Console menu item to your Start Menu or desktop

In the Fax Console window's left pane, select Incoming to view received faxes, or Sent Items to view faxes you've sent. Double-click any item in the right pane to display the fax with the Windows Picture and Fax viewer.

The Picture and Fax Viewer tool sports a toolbar across the bottom. Figure 6.15 shows the functions of the most important toolbar buttons. You can print the fax with the small Printer icon.

6

Figure 6.15
The Picture and Fax Viewer toolbar lets you flip through the pages of a received fax, as well as rotate, scale, and print it.

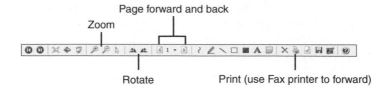

Page forward and back

Zoom

Rotate

Print (use Fax printer to forward)

TIP FROM

Bob
& Brian

> To forward a received or sent fax to another recipient, view the fax, click the Print button, and use the use the Photo Printing Wizard's instructions to print the fax images through your Fax printer.

Another way to view received faxes is to open the received fax folder directly. By default, the folder—get ready for this—is \Documents and Settings\All Users\Application Data\Microsoft\Windows NT\MSFax\Inbox. Double-click on any listed file to display the fax. If you receive a lot of faxes, you can create a shortcut to this folder.

Fax Resolutions

With all the talk about digital cameras, scanners, and cameras these days (and their respective resolutions), you might be wondering about fax resolution. Here's the skinny on that: The standard resolution for faxes is 3.85 scan lines/mm (approximately 98dpi vertically) with 1728 pixels across a standard scan line of 215mm (approximately 204dpi horizontally).

An additional, popular setting on many fax machines is called "fine" resolution. This setting scans 7.7 lines per millimeter (approximately 196dpi vertically) with the same resolution horizontally as with the normal setting.

Can some fax machines go higher? Yes. Many so-called Group III fax machines use nonstandard frames to negotiate higher resolutions. Some go as high as 300×300dpi (similar to older laser printers) and even 400×400dpi, but have to be talking with other fax machines made by the same manufacturer for this scheme to work. Manufacturers are working to set standards to support this level of resolution between machines of dissimilar manufacture.

The resolution you get on your printouts or as viewed on your computer screen depends on many factors. First, the screen resolution depends on the resolution of the source fax machine or computer. Second, it depends on the group of fax your system is employing and, finally, on the resolution of your display or printer. If what you intend to send someone is a high-resolution picture, you should always try to acquire a good color or grayscale scan of the image. Then you can attach it to an e-mail as a GIF, TIF, or JPEG file. Generally speaking, it will look better than sending it as a fax.

Sending Faxes over the Internet

The problem with sending faxes is that you don't always have a phone line available (as when you are in an office connected to the Internet via a LAN), or you don't want to pay for long-distance phone calls or high per-page charges to use a hotel fax machine. The problem with receiving faxes is that you aren't always there to receive the fax when it comes in. Isn't there a way to send faxes over the Internet?

Internet faxing is in development as of this writing, and there are various ways of both sending and receiving faxes using the Internet. If you're using an e-mail program capable of faxing (such as newer versions of Microsoft Outlook), you can configure it to send and receive faxes. Several services (commercial as well as free) offer to accept e-mail messages and fax them to the specified phone number. Some even let you fax from portable, wireless devices such as Palm Pilots.

The following are some links to information about e-mail–based faxing services:

```
http://www.j2.com
http://www.efax.com/
```

You can read a FAQ about this topic, courtesy of savetz@rahul.net (Kevin M. Savetz) at this address:

```
ftp://rtfm.mit.edu/pub/usenet/news.answers/internet-services/fax-faq
```

TROUBLESHOOTING

PRINTER ERRORS

I receive error messages when I try to print. What's wrong?

When an error occurs during a print job, Windows tries to determine the cause. If the printer is out of paper, you might see a Paper Out message in the status area. At other times, the message is ambiguous, and the word Error might appear in the status area. Add paper; make sure that the printer is turned on, online, and correctly connected; and make sure that the settings (particularly the driver) are correct for that printer.

NOTHING HAPPENS

I try to print, but nothing happens. How do I proceed?

If your print jobs never make it out the other end of the printer, work through this checklist:

- First, ask yourself whether you printed to the correct printer. Check to see whether your default printer is the one from which you are expecting output. If you're on a LAN, you can easily switch default printers and then forget that you made the switch.

- Check the settings in the Print dialog box carefully before you print. Is there something to print? Do you have to select some portion of your document first?

- Next, check to see whether the printer you've chosen is actually powered up, online, and ready to roll.

- If you're using a network printer, is the station serving the printer powered up and ready to serve print jobs?

- Then check the cabling. Is it tight?

- Does the printer need ink, toner, or paper? Are any error lights or other indicators on the printer itself flashing or otherwise indicating an error, such as a paper jam?

PRINTER PRODUCES GARBLED TEXT

When I print, the printout contains a lot of garbled text.

If you're getting garbage characters in your printouts, check the following:

- You might have the wrong driver installed. Run the print test page and see whether it works. Open the Printers and Faxes folder (by choosing Start, Control Panel, Printers and Other Hardware, Printers and Faxes), open the printer's Properties sheet, and print a test page. If that works, then you're halfway home. If it doesn't, try removing the printer and reinstalling it. Right-click the printer icon in the Printers and Faxes folder, and choose Delete. Then add the printer again, and try printing.

- If the printer uses plug-in font cartridges, you also might have the wrong font cartridge installed in the printer, or your text might be formatted with the wrong font.

- Some printers have emulation modes that might conflict with one another. Check the manual. You may think you're printing to a PostScript printer, but the printer could be in an HP emulation mode; in this case, your driver is sending PostScript, and the printer is expecting PCL.

ONLY HALF OF THE PAGE PRINTS CORRECTLY

My printer prints about half of a page, and then it starts printing garbage.

This problem is a rare occurrence nowadays, but it's still possible if you're running a printer off a serial port. If your printer regularly prints about the same amount of text or graphics and then flips out, suspect a buffer-related problem. On serial printers, buffer problems can often be traced to cables that do not have all the serial-port conductors (wires), or they're not in the correct order. Make sure the cable is the correct kind for the printer.

FAX PRINTER CAN'T BE ADDED

I can't add a fax printer.

If you're are unable to add a fax printer, you might not have sufficient user rights. See your system or fax server administrator. Also, be sure that your modem is fax-capable.

CANNOT RECEIVE A FAX

My system can't receive a fax. What's wrong with it?

Here's a quick checklist of common stumbling blocks:

- Have you plugged in the phone line properly?

- Is your modem installed and working properly?

- Is it a true fax modem, not just a data modem?

- Did you enable fax reception via the Fax Configuration Wizard (the default setting is off)?

- Is another device (for example, an answering machine) picking up the phone before your fax modem is? Check the ring settings for the fax modem and/or answering machines. Consider using the option that lets you screen for a fax first and then activate it manually (see the faxing section earlier in the chapter).

- If your computer goes into standby mode and doesn't wake up to receive incoming faxes, you might need to turn on an option in the computer's BIOS to "wake on ring." This option wakes up the computer any time it senses the ringer voltage on the phone line. If a fax is coming in, it takes the call. If it's not a fax, the computer goes back to sleep.

TIPS FROM THE WINDOWS PROS: CHOOSING A PRINTER NAME

Windows XP supports the use of long printer names. With this capability, you can create printer names that contain spaces and special characters. However, if you share a printer over a network, some clients do not recognize or correctly handle the long names, and users may experience problems printing. Also, some programs cannot print to printers with names longer than 32 characters.

For printers that are shared, the entire qualified name (including the server name, \\PRINTER2\PSCRIPT, for example) must be fewer than 32 characters.

- If you share a printer with a variety of clients on a network, use 31 or fewer characters for printer names, and do not include spaces or special characters in these names.
- If you share a printer with MS-DOS computers, do not use more than eight characters for the printer's share name. You can lengthen the name by adding a period followed by no more than three characters, but you cannot use spaces in the name.

6

MULTIMEDIA AND IMAGING

In this chapter

MULTIMEDIA, IMAGING, AND WINDOWS

When Windows was first developed in the mid-1980s, none of the hardware we use today to capture and transform still and video images was available. However, as time passed, still photographers and, more recently, videographers, have discovered the computer and its capability to edit, transform, organize, and store their work.

Whether you're a serious photographer with a portfolio that rivals Ansel Adams, a videographer inspired by Stanley Kubrick, or just a casual camera user who's looking for a way to organize company photos, Windows XP contains built-in tools and features that are designed to make the marriage of images and pixels a happy one. Even if you plan to replace the multimedia and imaging tools in Windows XP with higher-powered third-party solutions, Windows XP's architecture makes it easier to use the tools you want to work with the photos and video you love to create.

Some of the imaging and multimedia tools built in to Windows XP are improved versions of those originally designed for Windows Me, whereas others are brand new. Windows XP Professional has every one of the imaging and multimedia tools found in Windows XP Home Edition, so you no longer need to sacrifice imaging and multimedia performance for the stability and security of a corporate operating system. With Windows XP Professional, multimedia and imaging work as well in the office as they do at home.

HOW WINDOWS IMAGE ACQUISITION WORKS

Windows XP works with virtually any type of imaging device you can connect to your computer, including

- Scanners
- Digital cameras
- Web cameras
- DV camcorders

How does Windows XP interface with these devices to capture photos or video? Windows XP uses a technology called Windows Image Acquisition (WIA), originally introduced with Windows Me, which provides a standard method for all types of imaging devices to communicate with Windows. WIA is based on the Windows Driver Model (WDM) architecture for device drivers introduced with Windows 98.

WIA is designed to go beyond what's been possible with older types of imaging hardware/software interfaces, such as TWAIN and ISIS. If you've used scanners or digital cameras before, you might be familiar with TWAIN (developed by the TWAIN Working Group; www.twain.org), which has been used by most flatbed scanners and some digital cameras to communicate between a host application (such as Adobe Photoshop or other image editors) and the imaging device. TWAIN drivers are available for both Windows and Macs. A similar interface preferred by some scanner and imaging-device vendors is Pixel Translation's Image and Scanner Interface Specification (ISIS; see www.pixtran.com for more information). ISIS supports Windows applications.

Although WIA-compatible scanners and digital cameras show up in a program's image acquisition menus just as TWAIN and ISIS-compatible devices do, there are major differences between WIA and TWAIN, the more common scanner and camera interface software:

- WIA is activated immediately when a supported device is connected to the computer or turned on. For example, when you attach your digital camera to your computer and turn it on in Connect mode, WIA immediately brings up a menu of choices for working with your camera's images or starts your preferred application. This makes image transfer easier, even for inexperienced computer users.

- TWAIN and ISIS rely on your application's File, Acquire menu option to scan or retrieve pictures. This makes image transfers more difficult for inexperienced users.

- WIA can offer users a choice of options: copying, viewing, or editing pictures, whereas TWAIN is designed for users who want to edit pictures before saving them.

- WIA supports all types of imaging devices, including video, whereas TWAIN is designed for still image cameras and scanners only.

- WIA provides a universal interface for all types of imaging devices, whereas the details of TWAIN support vary a great deal from device to device.

WIA supports connections through all common port types, including USB and IEEE-1394 (FireWire) as well as SCSI, parallel, serial, and infrared (IR), and works through the Scanner and Camera Wizard, Windows Explorer My Pictures folder, image-editing programs such as Adobe Photoshop, and authoring programs such as Microsoft Word and PowerPoint. WIA also supports scripting with Visual Basic and other scripting languages, so you can develop custom applications.

Although this chapter focuses on XP's built-in WIA support for imaging devices, you might still prefer to use TWAIN or other device-specific support for your imaging device if WIA doesn't support all its functions.

What's Built in to Windows XP for Photographs?

Like digital photography? Own a scanner? Windows XP supports the immense popularity of digital photography and scanning with the following features:

- **Scanner and Camera Wizard**—Provides a unified interface for working with all types of digital imaging devices, including digital cameras, flash memory card readers, scanners, Web cameras, and DV camcorders with still image options.

- **Imaging preview**—See your pictures within Windows Explorer.

- **My Pictures folder**—Provides sorting, organizing, e-mail, Web site publishing, slideshow, and screen saver options for your digital and scanned photos.

- **New Photo Printing Wizard**—High-quality printing using templates for layout.

- **Integrated CD burning**—Create your own CD-R or CD-RW image archive.

7

No matter where your digital images come from, these features can help you have more fun and get more use from your photographs. In the following sections, you'll learn how each of these features works.

USING THE SCANNER AND CAMERA WIZARD

Windows XP's Scanner and Camera Wizard, originally introduced with Windows Me, provides a unified interface for transferring pictures from your imaging devices to your computer, your network, or to the World Wide Web.

If you have more than one imaging device supported by Windows XP, the Camera and Scanner Wizard displays all supported devices when you launch it from the Start menu (click Start, All Programs, Camera and Scanner Wizard the first time you use it) and allows you to choose the one you want to use (see Figure 7.1). Web cameras, scanners, digital cameras, and card readers are some of the devices the Scanner and Camera Wizard can recognize. The wizard also starts automatically when you press the Scan button on a supported scanner, skipping the dialog box shown in Figure 7.1. In these cases, the wizard skips the Choose Device dialog box and opens the scanner.

Figure 7.1
Click the device you want to use, and click Properties to configure it or OK to capture pictures.

If the Scanner and Camera Wizard is not available on your system, no supported imaging devices have been installed, although you can launch the applet manually through the Control Panel.

TIP FROM

Bob & Brian

If you have a choice between a USB-based scanner and other interface types such as SCSI and parallel, choose USB. The Scanner and Camera Wizard automatically detects and uses many USB devices, but it might not work with other interface types unless specific Windows XP–compatible drivers are available. If you set up other scanner types with Windows XP/2000 drivers, you might need to use the scanner's own TWAIN interface to scan photos and other media.

USING THE SCANNER AND CAMERA WIZARD WITH A SCANNER

To start the wizard with your scanner, you can push the Scan button on your scanner; open the Scanner and Camera Wizard and choose the scanner from the Scanner and Camera Wizard menu (refer to Figure 7.1); or use the image acquisition feature from within your favorite photo editor or paint program. Image acquisition is located in the File menu of most applications.

When the wizard starts, click Next to continue. Follow this procedure to scan your pictures:

1. On the Choose Scanning Preferences screen, select the picture type and select Preview to prescan your picture with default settings. With some scanners, you might need to press the Scan button to perform the preview (see Figure 7.2).

Figure 7.2
The preview scan has been completed. Use the Custom Settings button to adjust resolution, brightness, and contrast.

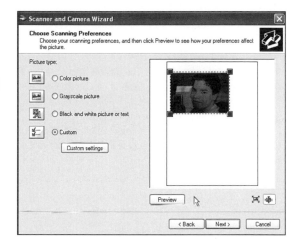

TIP FROM

If you place only one photo on your scanner, the wizard automatically selects it for you, as seen in Figure 7.2. Adjust the scan boundaries by dragging the corners only if you want to crop the photo during the scan. If you place more than one picture on the scanner, you will need to adjust the scan boundaries manually to scan each photo.

2. Click Custom Settings to adjust the contrast, brightness, and resolution for the scan (I recommend 75dpi for scans you plan to use in slideshows, and 150–300 dpi for scans you want to print). Click OK to return to the Choose Scanning Preferences screen, and click Next to scan the picture with the settings you've chosen.

3. On the Picture Name and Destination screen, enter a name for the group of pictures you're scanning, select a file format (BMP, JPG, TIF, and PNG are the options), and select a location. The default location is a subfolder beneath the My Pictures folder (see Figure 7.3). Click Next to scan your picture and save it. Each picture is numbered as it is scanned and saved.

7

Figure 7.3
Select a group name, file type, and location for your pictures.

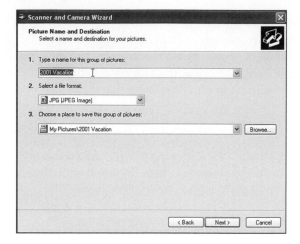

TIP FROM

Which file format should you choose? The default, JPEG, creates very small file sizes but does so by discarding fine image detail; it can be used on Web pages. Unless you're short on disk space, I recommend TIF, which creates large file sizes but retains all picture detail. Use BMP if you're saving files for use on the Windows desktop. PNG files also can be used on Web pages. If you save the file in one format and need to convert it into another later, retrieve the file into Windows Paint and save it in the format you need.

4. After the picture is scanned, the Other Options screen appears (see Figure 7.4). You can choose to publish your pictures online, order prints from a photo printing Web site, or finish working with the pictures. You also can use the Back button to return to previous menus so you can scan more pictures.

Figure 7.4
To learn more about Windows XP's picture tools, click the `working with pictures` link.

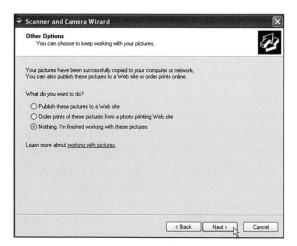

5. Click Next, and the Scanner and Camera Wizard provides an onscreen report of the number of pictures copied (scanned) and their location. Click the link provided to open the folder.

→ For details about the My Pictures folder, **see** "Viewing Images," **p. 230**.

USING THE SCANNER AND CAMERA WIZARD WITH A DIGITAL CAMERA

Start the Camera and Scanner Wizard to retrieve pictures from your digital camera:

1. Connect your device and turn it on.

2. Click Start, All Programs, Accessories, Camera and Scanner Wizard.

3. If you have more than one imaging device, select your digital camera from the opening menu shown in Figure 7.1, and click OK.

4. If you have only a digital camera, after the wizard locates your device, the opening screen of the wizard appears, as shown in Figure 7.5. To continue, click Next.

Figure 7.5
The Camera and Scanner Wizard identifies your digital camera and offers you the option to work directly from the camera or use the default wizard interface.

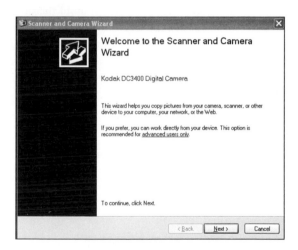

5. By default, all pictures are selected for copying to your computer. To skip a picture, clear the check mark. To rotate it or see its properties, click the buttons below the picture area (see Figure 7.6).

7

Figure 7.6
The second and third pictures will not be copied because the user has cleared the check marks. The currently selected picture has a heavy border around it.

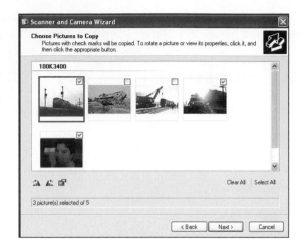

6. On the next screen, you can supply a name for the group of pictures (replace the default "Picture" with your own name) and specify where to store the pictures. If you use the default location (a folder beneath the My Pictures folder), you can use My Picture's multimedia and printing enhancements. You also can have the wizard delete the pictures from your device to free up space after copying them to your system.

7. The wizard displays each picture while it copies the selected pictures and provides a status display onscreen, shown in Figure 7.7.

Figure 7.7
The wizard displays the progress of the copying task.

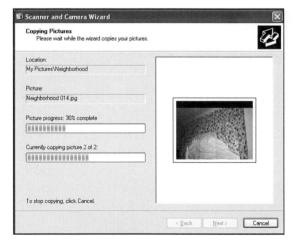

8. If you chose to delete the pictures from your imaging device, the wizard will also delete them and inform you of its progress.

9. When the pictures have been copied, you can choose to publish your pictures online, order prints from a photo printing Web site, or finish working with the pictures. You

also can use the Back button to return to previous menus so you can copy pictures you skipped (refer to Figure 7.4).

10. Click Next, and the Scanner and Camera Wizard provides an onscreen report of the number of pictures copied and their location. Click the link provided to open the folder.

→ For details about the My Pictures folder, **see** "Viewing Images," **p. 230**.

USING A CARD READER

Windows XP has built-in support for popular flash memory card readers, and automatically detects card readers and flash memory cards with pictures when you plug them in. When you plug a flash memory card containing pictures into your card reader, you can choose from several actions (see Figure 7.8):

- **Start the Scanner and Camera Wizard**—The wizard works with flash memory cards the same way it does with digital cameras. For more information, see "Using the Scanner and Camera Wizard with a Digital Camera," earlier in this chapter.

Figure 7.8
When you insert a flash memory card containing photos into your card reader, Windows XP displays options to help you copy, view, and print your photos.

- **View a slideshow**—This displays each picture onscreen for a few seconds and continues until you press the Esc key. For more information about slideshows, see "Using Slideshow," later in this chapter.

- **Print pictures directly from the media with the Photo Printing Wizard**—For more information about printing, see "Using the Photo Printing Wizard," later in this chapter.

- **Open folder to view files**—This option starts the Windows Explorer. For more information about using this option, see "Using Windows Explorer to View Your Photos," later in this chapter.

- **Take no action**—Select this option to leave the contents of the flash memory card alone until you decide what you want to do.

7

Check Always Do the Selected Action after you choose an action if you want to make that action the default.

TIP FROM

*Bob
& Brian*

> Use the Always Do the Selected Action option only if you're sure you always want to perform the same task with your pictures. If you leave this box unchecked, you can choose the task you want every time you insert your flash memory card. It takes only a couple of mouse clicks, so my advice is to keep your freedom and don't choose a default action to perform.

VIEWING IMAGES

Windows XP provides you with two ways to view your pictures:

- Through Windows Explorer
- As a slideshow

Which one is better for you? That depends on whether you're looking for immediate gratification or for long-term storage and enjoyment of your pictures. The following sections explain how to use both options.

USING WINDOWS EXPLORER TO VIEW YOUR PHOTOS

If you select the Windows Explorer option when you read the photos from your flash memory card, view pictures stored in My Pictures folder or a subfolder, or view the contents of a folder containing photos, Windows Explorer activates several special features designed to make working with your image files easier.

Instead of the normal large icons display of files, Windows Explorer switches to a special Filmstrip display option, which uses a large window on the right side of the screen to display the selected picture and shows other pictures in smaller size below navigation and image-rotation buttons (see Figure 7.9). You can use the navigation buttons to select which photo to display, or click on the photo you want to see in the large view.

TIP FROM

*Bob
& Brian*

> If the filmstrip view isn't selected automatically, click the View tool or the View menu and select Filmstrip. If Filmstrip isn't available because the images are not the correct type or the folder has a mixture of image files and other files, Filmstrip won't be listed as an option. Therefore, if you want to be sure Filmstrip view is available as an option, store your photos in a separate folder from other documents.

Figure 7.9
The filmstrip view is used automatically by Windows XP when you view a folder containing photos.

The File menu in Explorer also changes when you select a photo, providing the following options:

- **Preview**—Opens the photo in the Windows Picture and Fax Viewer
- **Edit**—Opens the photo in an image editor
- **Print**—Opens the photo printing wizard
- **Refresh thumbnail**—Generates a new thumbnail preview of the picture (useful if you've edited the picture)
- **Rotate clockwise/counter-clockwise**—Rotates the picture in 90-degree increments
- **Set As Desktop Background**—Puts your digital masterpiece on the Windows desktop
- **Open with**—Selects another program to open this picture
- **Send to**—Sends photo to a compressed folder, removable-media drive, or My Documents folder; creates a desktop shortcut; or provides other destinations
- **Properties**—Displays file properties

TIP FROM

Bob & Brian

By default, the Edit menu in Explorer uses Windows Paint to edit photos. If you prefer another image editor (and who wouldn't?), right-click a photo and select Open With. Windows XP will display Paint and Windows Picture and Fax Viewer, as well as Choose Program. Click Choose Program and select the program you want to use if it's listed, or click Browse to locate the program you prefer. To keep this choice for all files of the same type, check the Always Use the Selected Program box. You also can search the Web for a suitable program. Click OK when you're finished.

7

USING SLIDESHOW

Making a slideshow of your pictures once required you to fire up a program such as PowerPoint and click and paste your way through your digital stack of photos. If all you want to do is view your photos onscreen, you no longer need any third-party software: Just select the slideshow option when it's available within a folder or from the card reader's menu.

Windows XP's slideshow option is very simple: It sequences the images in a folder with five seconds per photo and continues to show the pictures in a loop until you press the Esc key on your keyboard.

An onscreen toolbar lets you play, pause, move to the previous photo or next photo, or exit the show. You also can use the keyboard commands in Table 7.1 to control the show.

TABLE 7.1 SLIDESHOW CONTROL KEYS

Action Desired	Keys to Press
Go to the previous picture in the folder	Left arrow or Page Up or up arrow
Go to the next picture in the folder	Right arrow or Page Down or down arrow
Rotate picture 90 degrees clockwise	Ctrl+K
Rotate picture 90 degrees counterclockwise	Ctrl+L
Play or pause the slide show	Spacebar (press once to pause, again to play)
Go to the next picture	Enter
Exit the show	Esc
Hide or display toolbar	Tab on or off (toggle)

TIP FROM

If you don't want to display all the images in a folder during your slideshow, just select the ones you want to view with Ctrl+Click or Shift+Click, and then click the Slideshow button on the left side of the Explorer screen or choose Slideshow from the menu. Only the slides you've selected will be displayed.

USING YOUR OWN PHOTOS AS A SCREEN SAVER

Want to show off the pictures of your spouse or kids but you've run out of room on your desk? You can use the pictures you scan or copy from a digital camera to create a screen saver.

To set up your favorite pictures as a screen saver, create a folder with Windows Explorer and copy the pictures you want to use to that folder. Then, open the Display properties sheet in

Control Panel, select the Screen Saver tab, select My Pictures Slideshow, and select the folder containing your pictures. You can display each picture for up to three minutes (the minimum is six seconds) and use anywhere from 25% to 100% of the screen. You can stretch small pictures to fit, show filenames, enable transition effects, and use the keyboard to scroll through pictures. Nobody else has a screen saver like it!

USING THE PHOTO PRINTING WIZARD

Windows XP's Slideshow feature can show you your digital photos immediately. How about instant prints from your digital photos? Thanks to the brand-new Photo Printing Wizard, you can have pictures as fast as your printer can produce them, and get them in a variety of sizes.

You can start the Photo Printing Wizard from

- The flash memory card opening menu
- The Picture Tasks menu in a photo folder
- The pull-down menu in a photo folder
- The File and Folder tasks menu in a regular folder

When the wizard starts, here's how to use it:

1. The Photo Printing Wizard displays its opening screen. Click Next to continue.
2. The Picture Selection screen lets you select the pictures you want to print. Clear or add check marks to select the pictures you want to print, and click Next to continue.
3. On the Printing Options screen, select the printer you want to use (if you have more than one printer). Click the Properties button to select the paper type, print quality, and other document properties (see Figure 7.10). Click the Advanced button to adjust the number of copies to print and other advanced printer features. Click OK to return to the Printing Options menu, and then click Next.

Figure 7.10
For best results in photo printing, choose the paper type you're using from the list of paper types.

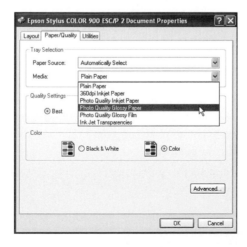

7

TIP FROM

Bob
& Brian

If you haven't used your inkjet printer for several days, or your printouts are of poor quality, you should click the Utilities tab (if available) and run your printer's head cleaning or nozzle test options with plain paper inserted in your printer (take out the photo paper until you're ready to print a good print). Head and nozzle clogs will ruin your printout and waste expensive photo paper, and most recent printers also offer a cleaning routine on this tab. If your printer doesn't have a menu option for head cleaning, check the instruction manual for the correct method to use. You might need to press buttons on the printer to activate a built-in head-cleaning routine.

4. Use the Layout selection screen to select how your photos should be laid out on the photo paper. Select from full-page; contact sheets; or sizes such as 3.5×5, 4×6, 5×7, and 8×10, and wallets. The preview shows you how your pictures will be laid out on each page. If you select a size that allows for multiple photos on a page, each image will be laid out once unless you specify a larger number (see Figure 7.11). Click Next to print your photos.

Figure 7.11
Select the layout you want, and the print preview displays your photos accordingly.

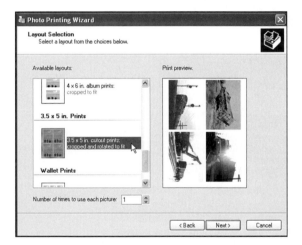

COPYING YOUR PICTURES TO A CD-RW DRIVE

CD-RW drives, which can use either rewritable CD-RW media or recordable CD-R media, have become some of the hottest peripheral options on the market. Previous versions of Windows couldn't use these drives until you installed CD-mastering software, but Windows XP has built-in features that enable you to use a supported CD-RW drive as soon as you install or connect it and turn on your computer.

When Windows XP detects a supported CD-RW, the Picture Tasks menu lists Copy to CD as an option. Here's how to use it:

1. If you want to copy only some of the pictures in your folder, select the pictures you want to copy and click Copy to CD.

2. To copy all photos in the folder to CD, don't select any pictures first. Click Copy all items to CD.

3. The pictures are copied to the CD-RW folder.

4. Repeat steps 1–3 for other folders that contain pictures you want to add to the CD.

5. Click My Computer in the Other Places menu.

6. Double-click the CD drive where you will store your pictures.

7. The folders you are going to copy are displayed under Files Ready to Be Written to the CD. If you've used the CD for other pictures previously, they also will be listed (see Figure 7.12).

Figure 7.12
Displaying the files to be written to the CD and those already on the CD with Thumbnail view.

TIP FROM

Bob & Brian

To see a small preview of your picture files as shown in Figure 7.12, select Thumbnails from the View menu or View tool instead of the default Icons view. This provides you with an easy way to be sure you're copying only the pictures you want.

8. Click Write These Files to the CD from the CD Writing Tasks menu at the left side of the screen, and the CD Writing Wizard opens.

9. Enter the name of the CD on the opening screen. If you want to create just one CD, select Close the Wizard. Otherwise, click Next to continue.

10. If your pictures were stored in a folder, the wizard creates a folder on the CD for the pictures. While the wizard writes the files to the CD, it displays a progress indicator onscreen (see Figure 7.13).

7

Figure 7.13
The CD Writing Wizard provides you constant updates on its progress in creating your CD.

11. The system ejects your CD after copying your picture(s). Click Yes to create another CD if you want or close the wizard. If you elected to close the wizard in step 9, the wizard closes automatically.

TIP FROM

If your CD-RW drive doesn't offer buffer underrun protection features such as BURNProof, be sure you're not running other programs while you make your CD. A buffer underrun (the drive running out of data to write to the CD) will ruin the CD. Use the Task Manager (press Ctrl+Alt+Del to display it) or the taskbar to see the programs that are running. Close other programs before writing your CD to help assure a successful burn.

If you are still having problems making a CD successfully, adjust the speed used by your drive to record data. Open My Computer, right-click the drive, and click the Recording tab. Select the next lower speed than the fastest speed listed and try the recording again (see Figure 7.14).

Figure 7.14
Selecting a lower write speed on a CD-RW drive that lacks buffer-underrun protection.

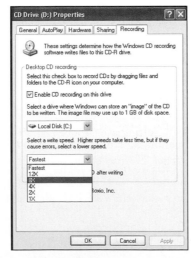

7

Your photo folders act as regular folders after they've been copied to the CD. If you want to use the special imaging features such as slideshow or photo printing discussed earlier in this chapter, select a file in the folder, open the File menu, and select Preview. The picture is loaded into the Windows Picture and Fax Viewer, which has buttons for photo printing, slideshows, image rotation, editing, and other imaging options. You can use the Forward and Back buttons to select other files in the folder.

TIP FROM

Bob & Brian

> If you start the copy-to-CD process and discover you're out of media, don't panic. Windows XP stores your pictures in a temporary folder and will remind you to finish the copy process with a pop-up balloon-help message coming out of the system tray. Click on the message when you have more media, and follow the prompts onscreen to complete the copy process or discard the temporary files.

WORKING WITH YOUR PICTURES ONLINE

Windows XP offers two online options that help you distribute your images to other offices:

- **Publish Photos to the Web**—Use this option to create an online photo album you can access from any location with Internet access.
- **Ordering Prints Online**—Get better prints for less cost than using your inkjet printer and its expensive cartridges.

PUBLISHING YOUR PHOTOS TO THE WEB

When you open a folder containing photos, one of the File and Folder Tasks available in the left side of your screen is Publish This Folder/File to the Web. Here's how to use this feature to make your pictures available on the Web:

1. If you want to publish only some of your photos, select them first, and then click Publish. Otherwise, click Publish.
2. The Web Publishing Wizard starts and connects to the Internet (if you're not already connected). Click Next to continue.
3. Files that will be published are check-marked. Add or remove check marks if desired, and then click Next.
4. Select a service provider from those listed, such as MSN and Xdrive. If you select MSN and you don't have a .NET Passport yet, you must complete the .NET Passport wizard that appears and continue. See "Getting a Passport to Microsoft Country" in Chapter 9 for details.
5. On the File Destination screen, select the destination folder you want to use, or create a new folder. Click Next to continue.
6. On the Adjust picture size dialog box, you can choose to resize your pictures to fit a Small (640×480; default), Medium (800×600), or Large (1024×768) browser window. Clear the check box to leave your photos at their original size.

7

TIP FROM

Bob & Brian

> The most common screen size today is 800×600. If you want to create a fast-loading Web page that maximizes screen area for most users, select Medium. However, if your company has standardized on 17-inch or larger CRTs or 15-inch or larger LCD panels, choose Large, because these monitor sizes are a good match for 1024×768 or higher resolutions.

7. Click Next to publish your photos to your chosen provider. If you are publishing only a few pictures or have a broadband (cable modem, DSL, two-way wireless or satellite, or T1) connection, the copying process can take only a few seconds. If you are using an analog (56Kbps or slower) modem or are copying many pictures, the process could take several minutes.

TIP FROM

Bob & Brian

> Photos stored in the JPEG (.JPG) format use less disk space and can be published faster than other types of photos. JPEG photos can also be viewed over the Web by standard browsers without using special software. If you plan to publish your photos to the Web, save a copy of each photo as a JPEG file.

8. At the end of the process, a URL for your pictures is displayed and a matching shortcut is added to your My Network Places folder. Close the wizard and your site is displayed.

9. If you carry your computer with you to meetings, just set up an Internet connection when you arrive, and click on the shortcut in My Network Places to display your pictures. To display the photos from other Web browsers, enter the URL provided, and provide the username and password assigned by your provider.

TIP FROM

Bob & Brian

> The Web Publishing Wizard's not the way to go if you're trying to share pictures with other users when you're not present. If you want to share your photos with everyone in your organization, talk to your company's IT managers about setting up a Web page on the company intranet. You can use any Web-publishing program to create customized pages that also can contain company contact information, the company logo, and other content not available with Microsoft's Web Publishing Wizard.

ORDERING PRINTS ONLINE

Inkjet printers are great for printing the occasional snapshot or Web page, but corporate bean counters are likely to start throwing things if you try to turn your high-cost-per-page printer into a high-volume photo producer. Save money and get more options with the Online Prints Ordering Wizard.

To use the wizard, follow these steps:

1. Click Order Prints Online from the Picture Tasks menu.

2. When the opening screen of the Online Print Ordering Wizard appears, click Next to continue.

3. Select the pictures you want to use for reprints.

4. Select the service from those listed (see Figure 7.15).

Figure 7.15
Choosing a printing company for reprints of your digital images.

5. Complete the order form that the vendor provides and enter your payment and shipping information when prompted. Depending on the vendor you choose, you can order prints, enlargements, gifts, and novelty items (such as mugs, t-shirts, jigsaw puzzles, and mousepads) from your pictures.

TIP FROM

Bob
& Brian

Digital pictures printed by an online vendor are higher quality than those you can produce with your inkjet printer, but the quality of the images you send to the vendor affect the prints you'll get back. For best results:

- Scan your prints at 150dpi for snapshots; use 300dpi if you're scanning only part of a picture.

- Scan 35mm slides and negatives (which are much smaller than prints) at 1350dpi or higher for 4×6-inch prints.

- Use a two-megapixel digital camera (1536×1024) or greater resolution for 4×6-inch or larger prints, and set the camera to use the highest quality and highest resolution. The minimum camera resolution recommended for 4×6-inch prints is 640×480 (the "VGA" setting on some cameras); remember, more pixels in the original image means better quality in the final print.

- The digital still mode on most DV camcorders is usually not nearly high enough quality for printing, although the results will look acceptable onscreen.

- Order just a few digital prints from a new vendor and evaluate the quality before you place a big order.

7

GOING BEYOND WINDOWS XP'S BUILT-IN IMAGING TOOLS

Windows XP's imaging tools make it easy to get digital images into your computer and keep them organized, but unless you're a perfect photographer, some of those images will need cropping, color-correcting, and other enhancements that Windows XP's tools don't offer.

Because WIA-compatible devices can be used from the Acquire menu of your favorite image editor, just as TWAIN-compatible digital cameras and scanners can be, you can use virtually any third-party photo-editing program you prefer to acquire your pictures, or retrieve them from a photo folder for editing after you copy them to your system with the Camera and Scanner Wizard or other Windows XP tool.

My favorite is Adobe Photoshop (www.adobe.com), which is immensely powerful, offering layers, automation, and many different ways to control brightness, contrast, and image appearance, but is also quite expensive. If you're on a budget, some capable alternatives include Jasc Software's Paint Shop Pro (www.jasc.com) and Corel PhotoPaint (www.corel.com), which is part of CorelDRAW and is also available separately in various editions.

In addition to the product sites listed above, check out these online resources:

- **Imaging Resource** (www.imaging-resource.com)—Covers the gamut of imaging hardware and software products, and has the unique "Comparometer" feature, which compares the actual output of any two digital cameras from their huge database.
- **DPReview** (www.dpreview.com)—The interactive buying guide helps you get the digital camera that matches the features you want, and its unique Timeline shows you when the camera you own was introduced.
- **FocalFix** (www.focalfix.com)—The new name for Focus Online, where readers review their favorite products.
- **John Cowley's Lonestardigital.com**—A long name for a great site with product reviews and tutorials on both digital imaging hardware and software.

WHAT'S BUILT IN TO WINDOWS XP FOR VIDEO?

If you prefer moving images to stills, Windows XP provides a video-friendly environment. By using the Windows Movie Maker program, Windows XP can capture video from

- Web cameras
- DV camcorders
- Analog camcorders
- VHS and other video players

Windows Movie Maker can then be used to edit your video into movies, which you then can save to your hard disk, removable-media drive, or CD for playback on systems through Windows Media Player.

The editing process that Windows Movie Maker and other digital video editing programs use is often referred to as *non-linear editing*, because you can arrange different digital movie sources in any order, and don't need to physically cut or damage video tape or film to edit your movies.

The Hardware You Need

You will need a video capture card or USB device to capture video from an analog camcorder or video tape player. Some video cards, such as the All-in-Wonder series from ATI, have TV-in jacks that also can be used for analog video capture. If your Web camera is supported by Windows XP, you can use it for video capture without any additional hardware.

You will need a supported IEEE-1394 (FireWire) port or add-on card to capture video from a DV camcorder, and Windows XP also must have support for the DV camcorder if you want to interface directly with Windows Movie Maker.

TIP FROM

Bob

& Brian

> If Windows Movie Maker doesn't support your video hardware but it can be used with third-party software, capture your data with third-party software and save it in a Windows Movie-Maker–compatible format, such as .mpeg, .mpg, .m1v, .mp2, .mpa, .mpe, .asf, .avi, or .wmv. You can import these types of files into Windows Movie Maker.

Video Capture with Microsoft Movie Maker

The first time you attach a supported DV camcorder to your Windows XP system and turn it on, WIA displays the menu shown in Figure 7.16. You can start Windows Movie Maker or take no action. To make Windows Movie Maker the default action, select it, and then checkmark the Always Perform the Selected Action box below the displayed options.

Figure 7.16
Digital video device actions in Windows XP.

7

When you select Windows Movie Maker, the Windows Movie Maker opening screen is displayed briefly. Then, if your digital video or audio source is already running, the Record dialog box is displayed. If you need to select a recording source, click File, Record. Use the Record dialog box to set the source, select the recording time limit, and choose the recording quality you want for your movies (see Figure 7.17).

Figure 7.17
Setting up the source device and quality for your movies. Artwork courtesy Ian Soper.

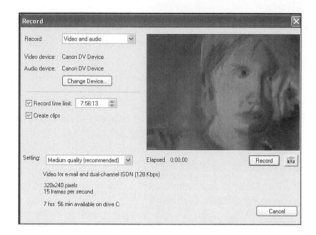

Table 7.2 lists the technical details for the three standard quality settings available with Windows Movie Maker. Note that the higher the quality, the more disk space is used (and the greater the connection speed required to avoid dropping frames when viewing).

TABLE 7.2 WINDOWS MOVIE MAKER STANDARD QUALITY SETTINGS

Quality Setting	Window Dimensions (pixels)	Frame Rate (FPS)	Bandwidth Needed (Kbps)	Best Use
Low	176×144	15	56	Dial-up
Medium	320×240	15	128	ISDN
High	320×240	30	256	Broadband

Select Other to choose settings for connections as low as 28.8Kbps, higher broadband connections, color PDA devices, and DV camcorder playback.

TIP FROM

Bob & Brian

If you are creating digital video for distribution over your company's high-speed network, choose High quality or even faster options from the Other menu. Use Low quality if the content will be hosted on a Web site where users might be using analog modems for access. The default, Medium, is a good choice for content that will be accessed by a variety of connection speeds.

Click Record to start recording from your device; click Stop when you're finished. After you click Stop, the Save Windows Media File dialog box is displayed, showing you any previously saved video files. Enter the name of your file and click Save to save the file to your hard drive in the My Videos folder (a subfolder of My Documents).

Each file you save is referred to as a *collection* of one or more clips in Windows Movie Maker.

SPLITTING AND COMBINING CLIPS

Movie clips frequently are too long or too short, or contain material you'd like to use in different places in your movie. To combine two or more clips into a single larger clip, follow this procedure:

1. Switch to the collection containing the clips you want to combine.
2. Make a copy of each clip you want to combine with Edit, Copy, and Edit, Paste.
3. Select the copied clips with Shift+click or Ctrl+click.
4. Click Clip, Combine from the top-level menu (see Figure 7.18).
5. The combined clips become part of the first clip you selected to combine.

Figure 7.18
Clips 2(1) and 4(1) will be combined into a single clip.

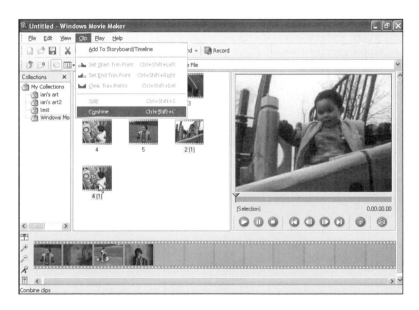

To split a clip into two clips, follow this procedure:

1. Switch to the collection containing the clips you want to split.
2. Make a copy of each clip you want to split with Edit, Copy, and Edit, Paste for safety's sake; this way, if you decide later you don't like the results of combining clips, you will have the original clips to work with.

7

3. Drag the playback indicator to the position in the clip where you want the split to take place.

4. Click Clip, Split. The beginning of the original file replaces the original file. The end of the original file is stored under a new name (the original clip's name plus a number in parentheses).

TURNING YOUR VIDEO CLIPS INTO A SIMPLE MOVIE

You can create a simple movie by dragging your movie clips into the Windows Movie Maker storyboard, which is the filmstrip-like area at the bottom of the screen. Although several empty frames are displayed in the storyboard, the clips you drag to the storyboard are positioned left to right (you can change the order later).

If you want to add the Windows Movie Maker sample files to your movie for practice, click File, Import, and select the sample files. They'll be added to a My Collections folder called Windows Movie Maker Sample File. Figure 7.19 shows the storyboard area after adding various clips from DV video I captured and some of the Windows sample clips.

Figure 7.19
A simple movie built from various video clips displayed in storyboard view. Paintings courtesy of Ian Soper.

To play only the currently selected video clip, click the triangular Play button beneath the preview window. To play the entire storyboard, click Play, Play Entire Storyboard/Timeline from the top-level menu. Use the keys in Table 7.3 to control playback.

TABLE 7.3   WINDOWS MOVIE MAKER PLAYBACK CONTROL KEYS

Key	Action
Spacebar	Toggles pause/playback
Period	Stop playback

Key	Action
TABLE 7.3 **CONTINUED**	
Alt+Left arrow	Display previous frame
Alt+Right arrow	Display next frame
Alt+Ctrl+Left arrow	Moves to previous clip
Alt+Ctrl+Right arrow	Moves to next clip
Alt+Enter	Toggles full-screen display

EDITING YOUR MOVIE

After you drag your video clips to the storyboard, you can use various tools to adjust the length of each clip, the order of your clips, and the transitions between each clip.

To change the length of each clip and transitions between clips, you must use timeline view; click View, Timeline. The timeline replaces the storyboard at the bottom of your screen. To change the order of clips, I recommend switching to storyboard view; click View, Storyboard.

To adjust the length of each clip

1. Switch to timeline view if necessary.
2. Click the clip in the timeline.
3. To delete the end of the clip, move the trim handle at the start of the clip to the right to the point where you want the clip to start. To delete the end of the clip, drag the trim handle at the end of the clip to the left until you reach the point where you want the clip to end.

TIP FROM

If you're trying to shorten the end of a video clip, play the video clip from start to finish to preview it, and then play it again and stop it at the point where you want to cut it. A vertical line in the timeline shows the playback location. Move the trim handle at the end of the clip until it is lined up with the vertical line.

To move a clip from one position to another, you can use either drag and drop or cut and paste. If you prefer cut and paste

1. Switch to storyboard view (not required, but easier to use than timeline view).
2. Click the clip in the storyboard.
3. Click Edit.
4. Select Cut.
5. In the timeline, click the clip that will be behind the moved clip when you paste it in.
6. Click Edit, Paste.

7

To create a transition effect from one scene to another

1. Switch to timeline view if necessary.

2. Zoom in with magnifying-glass zoom control at the left of the timeline.

3. Click the clip that you plan to use to end the transition.

4. Drag it to the left so it overlaps the timeline space used by the preceding clip (see Figure 7.20).

Figure 7.20
The highlighted clip (clip #2) has transitions from the clip in front of it and behind it on the timeline, as shown by the overlaps with clips #1 and #3.

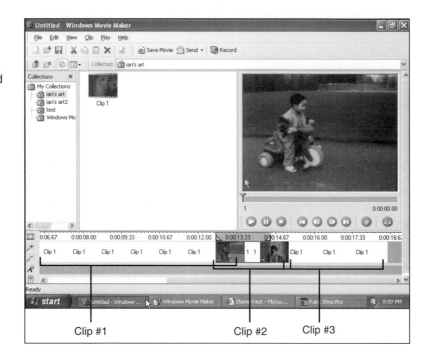

ADDING NARRATION TO YOUR MOVIE

You can record narration for your movie when the movie is in timeline mode if you have a microphone attached to your computer. To record narration

1. Select Timeline mode.

2. Click File, Record Narration.

3. The Record Narration Track dialog box appears (see Figure 7.21). The default audio device and input source are listed. To change the defaults, click Change and select alternative devices.

Figure 7.21
The Record Narration Track dialog box is used to select the recording devices and level for your narration.

4. If the movie already contains a soundtrack you want to replace, click Mute Video Soundtrack.

5. Adjust the recording level as desired, and click Record to begin.

The narration is saved as a .WAV file when you stop the recording, and is automatically added to your movie.

CAUTION

As you use Windows Movie Maker, during both video capture and audio recording you will see indicators of how much time you can record (refer to Figures 7.17 and 7.21). The amount of time you have to record is directly related to how much free hard disk space you have. If you're short of space and don't want to reduce quality (which uses less disk space), put in a requisition for a larger hard drive; 100GB 7,200 RPM IDE drives are now available for less than $300.

ADDING TITLES TO YOUR MOVIE

Although Windows Movie Maker doesn't have built-in titling features, you can create screens you can use for titles in any program that can create .bmp, .jpg, .gif, or .dib files, such as Windows Paint or most third-party imaging programs.

Your title slides should be the pixel size of the movie captures you've created or higher. Medium quality movies use a 320×240 pixel window, so a title slide should be the same size or have the same proportions (a 4:3 ratio).

CAUTION

If you want to make your title slide(s) blend in better with your movie, you can disable Create Clip during Record and use the Take Picture option to grab some images you can use for backgrounds. You can add text over these images, and then use Movie Maker to place them as desired in your movie.

Still images you import into your movie have a default length of five seconds.

7

SAVING YOUR PROJECT AND YOUR MOVIE

There are two ways to save your work in Windows Movie Maker. To save the various parts of your movie (the clips on the timeline and the storyboard), click File, Save Project. By default, your Windows Movie Maker Project (.MSWMM) file will be saved to the My Videos folder. Give your project a name, and save it.

You should save your projects frequently during the creation and editing process. If you don't, and a system lockup or power outage takes place, your clips will remain, but the structure and timing of your film will be lost, and it will be back to the digital cutting room to start over.

Here's how to save your movie:

1. Click File, Save Movie.
2. Set the Playback quality as desired and see the on-disk size of your movie and the estimated length of time that different Internet connections will require to download the file (see Figure 7.22). The estimated time is provided for your convenience if you are planning to use the video online or in a video e-mail.

Figure 7.22
The Save Movie dialog box helps you balance quality and download speed considerations.

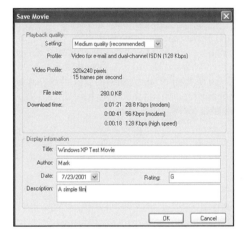

3. Click OK when you've described the film and selected the quality option you want to use.

CAUTION

Because Windows Movie Maker lets you save your movie at your choice of quality settings, you should use the highest-quality recording options possible when you create source material. Then, after you save your movie at the quality level matching the original material, you can save it again at a lower quality if you need to optimize the movie for limited-bandwidth viewing. However, if you start out with low-quality content, you can't add quality during the save process. Amateur-level digital camcorders and Microsoft Movie Maker use lossy compression techniques to create content and, after detail is discarded, it can't be re-created.

4. Enter the filename; use the Create New Folder button if you want to set up a special location for your movie. Click Save to save your movie as a Windows Media Video file (.WMV).

5. A moving-bar meter informs you of the process. After the movie is saved, click Yes to view it immediately. Windows Media Player loads the movie and plays it for you.

GETTING YOUR MOVIE TO THE MASSES

After you've saved your movie, you can send it to a Web site, attach it to e-mail, or store it on recordable or rewritable CDs.

From within Movie Maker, click File, Send Movie To if you want to e-mail your movie to a friend as an attachment (they'll need Windows Media Player to view it) or to publish your movie on a Web site using the same Web Publishing Wizard discussed earlier. From a My Videos folder, click E-mail This File or Publish This File to the Web to start the same processes.

After you've stored your movie in a folder, you can copy it to a CD for safekeeping. Click the Copy to CD option under the Video Tasks menu to start the process. If you plan to make additional changes to your movie, you should copy your project file as well as your movie. As Figure 7.23 shows, project files use a movie reel icon, while movie files use the first frame of the movie for the icon.

Figure 7.23
Selecting the "chapter 7" project file and movie files for copying to a CD.

Click My Computer to continue the process, and follow the procedure as described earlier in "Copying Your Pictures to a CD-RW Drive."

BEYOND WINDOWS MOVIE MAKER

Windows Movie Maker provides an enjoyable way to experiment with simple digital movie editing, but you might want to try more powerful editing programs, especially if you want to export movies to video tape, work with custom transitions, or create higher-resolution, better-quality films. You now can buy some video editors in versions that work with DVD-R recorders and that also create various movie formats, including DVD, on recordable CDs.

Some of the more popular low-priced video-editing programs on the market include Ulead's Video Studio 5.0, MGI's VideoWave 4, and Dazzle's DV-Editor SE. Some IEEE-1394 DV capture cards, TV capture cards, and VGA/TV capture cards also include various video editing programs, including the ones just mentioned.

More powerful DV-editing programs you might consider include Adobe's Premiere 6.0, which can be paired with Adobe AfterEffects for exciting special effects. To get more information about

- Video Studio 5.0 and VideoStudio 5.0 DVD Edition, see www.ulead.com
- VideoWave 4, see www.mgisoft.com
- Dazzle's lineup of digital video editing programs and hardware, see www.dazzle.com

HELP SITES AND RESOURCES FOR DIGITAL VIDEO

In addition to the product Web sites listed above, check out these resources:

- **Digital Video Magazine**—Look for the big "DV" on the cover for news, reviews, and tips for great digital video. The Web companion to the magazine is located at www.dv.com.

- **VideoMaker Magazine**—Get advice on good videographic techniques as well as buyer's guides and reviews. The Web companion to the magazine is located at www.videomaker.com.

- **CodecCentral**—The first stop if you're looking for the last word on streaming media compression algorithms (codecs) and technologies for video and Web animations. Find it online at www.icanstream.tv/CodecCentral.

WINDOWS MEDIA PLAYER

The Windows Media Player, which can be used to play music and video files (including Windows Movie Maker productions) from online sources and local drives and create digitized versions of music CDs, has been extensively retooled for the release of Windows XP. Windows Media Player 8 has a brand-new user interface, as shown in Figure 7.24, to support its many new and enhanced features.

Figure 7.24
Windows Media Player 8 defaults to the Media Guide view when you have a working Internet connection, providing links to popular audio and video content.

MEDIA TYPES COMPATIBLE WITH MEDIA PLAYER

Windows Media Player can play the file types shown in Table 7.4.

TABLE 7.4   WINDOWS MEDIA PLAYER–SUPPORTED FILE TYPES

File Type	Filename Extension
Music CD (CD audio)	.cda
Intel Indeo video	.ivf
Audio Interchange File Format (digitized sound)	.aif, .aifc, .aiff
Windows Media (audio and video)	.asf, .asx, .wax, .wm, .wma, .wmd, .wmv, .wvx, .wmp, .wmx
Windows audio and video	.avi, .wav
Windows Media Player skins	.wmz, .wms
MPEG (Motion Picture Experts Group) video	.mpeg, .mpg, .m1v, .mp2, .mpa, .mpe, .mp2v, .mp2
AU (UNIX audio)	.au, .snd
MP3 (digital audio)	.mp3, .m3u
DVD video	.vob

 To play back DVD video and .mp2v files, you must install a hardware or software DVD decoder on your system first.

7

MAJOR FEATURES OF MEDIA PLAYER

The major features of Media Player are accessible from the mode selection buttons on the left side of the default (full-view) display. Here's what they do:

- **Now Playing**—After you select online or locally stored content for playback, the Now Playing window displays a list of the content you're playing. An optional Visualizations feature can be used to display album art (when available) or various animated abstractions that change in response to the music. Open the top-level View menu to enable other features such as titles, lyrics, graphic equalizer, video settings, and others. Figure 7.25 shows Media Player with a typical selection of Now Playing options.

Figure 7.25
The Now Playing mode of Windows Media Player with visualization, playlist, and graphic equalizer options enabled.

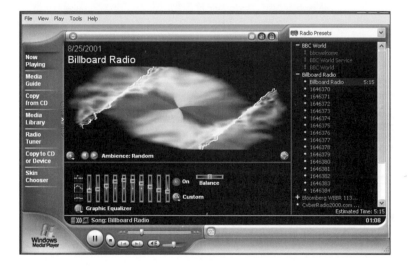

- **Media Guide**—As shown in Figure 7.24, this option enables you to select from a wide variety of online content.
- **Copy from CD**—Click this button to copy all or selected tracks from your favorite music CDs to the My Music folder on your system.

TIP FROM

Bob & Brian

> When you copy music, Windows Media Player, by default, prevents copied tracks from being played on any other computer. If you want to disable this feature so you can move copied music from one PC to another, check the box labeled Do Not Protect Content in the dialog box that appears when you click Copy Music.

7

- **Media Library**—Use this feature to organize and locate your favorite media types you've downloaded or created with Copy from CD. As you download and create music, Media Player automatically creates album and artist information for audio and video content. You also can view content by type and by genre.

- **Radio Tuner**—Use this feature to connect with the wide world of Internet radio. Featured stations offer a wide variety of music formats, and you also can locate stations by format or by searching for keywords. The Today's Hits section highlights the top pop, *Billboard Magazine*, R&B, and country hits.

- **Copy to CD or Device**—After you download or convert music tracks to WMA format, use this feature to transfer your music mix to either writable CDs (CD-R or CD-RW media) or to WMA-compatible portable audio players.

TIP FROM

Bob & Brian

> Be sure you fill your CD with all the music you want to play. Unlike conventional CD-mastering programs or Windows XP's Copy to CD feature in other parts of the operating system, Windows Media Player's Copy to CD feature closes the CD (so it no longer can accept data) after you copy your selected music to it, even if you use only a small portion of the CD. Why? Standalone CD players are designed to handle single-session CDs and won't work if you add music later. If you want to create a CD for playback on your computer, use Windows Explorer's Copy to CD feature instead, which will allow you to copy music over several sessions.

- **Skin Chooser**—If you're tired of the default Windows Media Player full view as seen in Figure 7.24, use this option to select a completely new look (called a skin) for the Media Player. From artistic to sci-fi, from minimalist to charming, Media Player provides lots of choices by default. Click More Skins to see downloadable options available on Microsoft's Web site. Click Apply Skin to use the selected skin; a Return to Full Mode button lets you switch back whenever you want. Figure 7.26 shows the Media Player in its Windows XP skin.

Figure 7.26
The Windows XP skin for Media Player features a visualization window and the most commonly used control buttons.

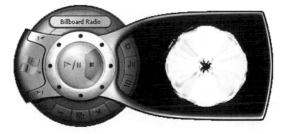

7

CUSTOMIZING MEDIA PLAYER

In addition to changing its default playback mode and appearance, you can adjust many other features of Windows Media Player.

Use the View menu to adjust menu bar and taskbar options when Media Player is in full mode (the default is to auto-hide the menu bar when the mouse is in the user interface, as shown in Figure 7.24) and to see statistics for your average connection speed. You can adjust the default for the connection speed in the Tools menu.

Use the Tools menu's Options selection to adjust most of the defaults for Media Player, including the following:

- **Player tab**—Select how often to check for Media Player updates, Internet options such as media licensing, and general player settings.

TIP FROM

Bob
& Brian

> Do you want to play a favorite tune and automatically add it to your Media Library? Check the Add Items to Media Library when Played box in the Player settings section of the Player tab.

- **Copy Music**—Adjusts the default location and bit-rate used to copy music. Also allows you to compare WMA to other formats and to download the optional MP3 Creation Pack for Windows XP, which will enable you to create MP3 files with Windows Media Player 8.

- **Devices**—Configures playback and copying settings for CD-RW, CD, and portable audio players. With CD-ROM and similar optical drives, you can select analog or digital copying and playback, and whether or not to enable error correction. With portable audio players, you can specify the quality level to use for copying music. With CD-RW drives, you can specify where to store CD images, the recording speed, and whether to eject the CD after recording.

- **Performance**—Configures the connection speed, network buffering settings, and video acceleration used for Internet content.

- **Media Library**—Configures access rights for the library and specifies whether to automatically add purchased music to the Media Library.

- **Visualizations**—Adds and configures visualizations; you can set the screen size and off-screen buffer size for each collection to match your screen resolution or the preferred window size you use for Media Player.

- **File Types**—Configures which file types compatible with Media Player will use Media Player as the default player program.

7

TIP FROM

Bob & Brian

> If you prefer a program such as WinAmp (which can rip MP3s from your music CDs as well as play them), clear the check box for MP3 Format Sound. Then, your preferred MP3 program can be used instead of Media Player to work with MP3 files.

- **Network**—Configures network protocols, TCP port numbers, and proxy settings to be used for streaming media. Use this menu to manually configure Media Player if your corporate network prevents Media Player from working when using its normal settings.

TIP FROM

Bob & Brian

> Contact your network administrator for help in configuring this tab, because the allowable settings can vary from network to network.

Click Apply when you are finished making changes, and then click OK to exit the Options menu.

TROUBLESHOOTING

SCANNER NOT RECOGNIZED BY SCANNER AND CAMERA WIZARD

My scanner was working fine with Windows Me, but Windows XP won't list it in the Scanner and Camera Wizard. What do I do?

The Scanner and Camera Wizard is certainly a convenient way to use your scanner, but it's not the only way. Before you try the scanner again, be sure you install Windows XP-compatible drivers for your scanner. You might be able to use Windows 2000-compatible drivers if you can't get Windows XP drivers yet. Install the latest drivers available (you might need to restart your computer afterward) and try the Wizard again. Windows Update is a great way to get new drivers.

Next, see if you can use the scanner with its own TWAIN or ISIS driver. If you can, you don't need to use the Scanner and Camera Wizard. Remember to use the Scan button on the scanner if it has one; some scanners require you to push this button to start the scanning process.

Contact the scanner vendor for help if you're still unable to use the scanner with either the wizard or its own scanning software.

POOR PRINT QUALITY WITH DIGITAL PHOTOS

My digital photos look terrific onscreen, but are poor quality when I print them.

There are three major factors which control digital photo quality:

- Camera settings
- Printer settings
- Paper type

Get any of these wrong, and you won't get the print quality you want.

Your digital camera should be set for its highest quality and resolution settings, especially if it's a two-megapixel or lower resolution camera. Highest quality uses less compression to avoid loss of fine detail (more space is used on the flash memory card per picture than with lower quality settings) and highest resolution uses all the pixels to make the picture (again, requiring more space on the flash memory card per picture). If you use your camera to create pictures for use on the Web, the lower-quality and lower-resolution settings are fine, but printed pictures need the best quality available. Remember that your monitor needs just 96 dots to make an inch, while most inkjet printers put 600 to 1,200 dots into the same inch. So, a picture that's just right to fit on the screen doesn't have enough detail to print well.

Similarly, the printer should be set for the best quality setting that matches the paper type. If you're planning to print "knock-em-dead" digital masterpieces, be sure to use photo-quality paper and set the printer's options accordingly. Just want a quick snapshot for the refrigerator? Use plain paper and set the printer for plain paper. Mismatch print type and paper type and you're sure to have problems, because inkjet printers calculate how much ink to use and how to put it on the paper according to the options you select.

Remember, high-quality printing takes time; several minutes for an 8×10-inch enlargement on photo paper with high quality settings is typical.

TIP FROM

Bob
& Brian

> If you've been using lower-quality and lower-resolution modes on your digital camera to jam more pictures into your flash memory card storage, that's false economy that leads to poor-quality pictures, especially for printing. With the explosion in the popularity of digital cameras, the per-MB price of flash memory cards is dropping. Camera vendors include very small flash memory cards to hold down the selling price of the camera, but you can almost always use a much larger media size.
>
> Check your camera maker's Web site or a leading flash media web site such as Lexar Media (www.lexarmedia.com) to find out what sizes of digital media you can use. If you're responsible for a prolonged shoot away from the office or home, consider picking up multiple flash memory cards (so you have lots of digital "film" and don't run out) or the IBM Microdrive (also sold by Iomega) if your camera is compatible with it (find out at www.iomega.com/support/documents/10870.html). The Microdrive's capacity (340MB or 1GB) beats the biggest Compact Flash memory cards and provides hundreds of shots.

Can't Control DV Camcorder in Windows Movie Maker

My DV camcorder is detected by Windows Movie Maker, but the only way I can capture video is by using the camera's own controls to advance the tape. What should I do?

Some DV camcorders work better with Movie Maker than others. If you can capture video by controlling the camera yourself but not with Movie Maker's onscreen buttons, check with the camera vendor for updated driver software. Otherwise, keep doing what you're doing. Remember that you can always cut extraneous information from a scene with the editing features in Movie Maker.

Tips from the Windows Pros: Archiving Your Company's History

If you've been chosen to create an archive of your company's history (or your family's, for that matter), you might need to add a few hardware and software tools to your system to do the job right.

Color photos in particular are frequently affected by fading and color shift as well as the usual photographic problems of poor cropping and exposure. You don't need to buy Adobe Photoshop to fix these kinds of problems. However, if you're not satisfied with the photo editor bundled with your scanner and you're on a budget, try Jasc's Paint Shop Pro (www.jasc.com). Paint Shop Pro (around $100–$110) is a very powerful choice that will leave you some money for the rest of your gear.

As you saw earlier in this chapter, a CD-RW drive is a terrific way to store digital photos. Be sure the drive you buy has at least a 12x speed rating for writing CD-R media (a better choice for long-term storage than erasable CD-RW media) and has a buffer-underrun prevention feature such as BURNProof. Go for an internal IDE/ATAPI drive to get the most bang for the buck; USB 1.1-compatible drives are easy to move around, but are too slow for big archiving jobs. You'll find plenty of choices starting at around $100 to $150. If you're planning to incorporate digital video into the mix, you might also want to consider an IEEE-1394–compatible CD-RW drive. It connects through the same port used by DV camcorders, and you can move it around to any machine with an IEEE-1394 card or port. Because IEEE-1394 has a high bandwidth (up to 400Mbps or 50MBps), it's a much better choice than USB 1.1 for fast data transfer.

Until the 1970s, the most popular way to take color photos was 35mm slide film, and most flatbed scanners either can't scan slides or use clumsy adapters that don't provide high enough scanning resolution to pull fine detail from slides. If the boss hands you some Carousel trays of slides for the archive, you need a real slide scanner to do the job right.

A high-quality slide scanner should scan with a resolution of at least 2,700 dpi to allow you to get great prints from the tiny 35mm slide. And, if black and white or color prints have gotten lost but you have the negatives, slide scanners can scan them as well. You can spend as little as $500 to as much as $1,000 or more for a slide scanner, but be sure the one you

7

buy has a feature called Digital ICE (developed by Applied Science Fiction, Inc—www.asf.com). Digital ICE removes dust and scratches from scans of less-than-perfect slides and negatives. Because most slides and negatives get dirty and scratched over time, Digital ICE is the way to go for scanners. It really works, and saves hours of retouching time (time you can't afford to spend anyway) afterward. Some of the better slide/negative scanners with Digital ICE on-board include

- Nikon Coolscan IV ED (around $900—includes the latest version of Digital ICE)
- Canon CanoScan FS4000US (around $1,000—uses a Canon-designed feature called FARE, which is similar to Digital ICE)
- Minolta Dimage Scan Elite (around $800–$900)

TIP FROM

Bob & Brian

> Before you buy *any* scanner, take a good look at the archival materials you're being asked to preserve. Use a flatbed scanner for black-and-white or color prints, and don't overlook the historical value of stock certificates, matchbook covers, postcards, personalized pens, and so on. You can scan anything that fits on the scanner, even if it's not completely flat.
>
> If your company history goes back far enough that some photos are actually large negatives (bigger than 35mm) or lantern slides, you need to buy a flatbed scanner with a special transparency adapter lid (which also can be added to some mid-range or high-end scanners) or internal compartment. Some mid-line scanners can handle transparencies and negatives up to 4×5 inches, but if you have larger-format materials, you need a scanner that can scan up to 8×10 negatives. Some of the better choices with built-in transparency handling up to 8×10 size include Epson's 1600 Professional (www.epson.com—around $900) and Microtek's ScanMaker 8700 (www.microtekusa.com—around $900). These scanners can also handle normal prints, so you get two for the price of one.

Finally, you need a way to view and organize your pictures after you've scanned them. Although the My Pictures folder has some built-in tricks (as described earlier in this chapter), third-party software will help you view and locate pictures stored in any folder and on any type of media. Here are a few programs that you should consider:

- MediaTracer 5.0 (www.mediatracer.com)
- Gazo (www.gazomania.com)
- ACDSee (www.acdsystems.com)

You can find other choices at

directory.google.com/Top/Computers/Software/Graphics/Image_Cataloguing/

WINDOWS XP AND THE INTERNET

INTERNET AND TCP/IP CONNECTION OPTIONS

In this chapter

8

GOING WORLD WIDE

Hooking up to the Internet used to be a privilege afforded only to universities and corporations. Now, it's an essential part of owning and using any PC. In this chapter, you will find information about choosing an Internet service provider (ISP), making the connection through a modem or other link, and installing and configuring your system.

This chapter tells how to connect a single computer to the Internet. You can take one of several routes:

- If your computer is part of an existing local area network (LAN) with Internet access, you can skip this chapter entirely because Internet access will come along as part of your Windows XP installation. In fact, if you are part of a corporate LAN, it is probably a violation of your company's security policy to establish your own independent connection. (If it's not, it should be!)

- If you are setting up a LAN for your home or office, you can provide Internet access to the entire LAN through one connection. You should read Chapter 19, "Connecting Your LAN to the Internet," and decide whether you want to connect your LAN. Use the instructions in this chapter to set up the one connection; Chapter 19 will tell you how to share it with the rest of your workgroup.

- If you want to use your existing ISP account and connection technology, you can skip the introductory sections of this chapter and go right down to "Installing a Modem in Windows XP," or, for broadband connections, "Installing a Network Adapter."

- If you need to make a clean start with the Internet, read on!

CONNECTION TECHNOLOGIES

Not long ago, you had one choice to make for your Internet connection: which brand of modem to buy. Now, options abound, and you can choose among several technologies, speeds, and types of Internet service providers. A huge technology shift is taking place, as high-speed digital (*broadband*) connection services are being deployed worldwide.

Let's take a look at the basic Internet connection technologies appropriate for an individual user or workgroup. After describing each one, I'll show you roughly what they cost to set up and use.

ANALOG MODEM

Standard, tried-and-true dial-up modem service requires only a telephone line and a modem in your computer. The connection is made when your computer dials a local access number provided by your Internet service provider (ISP). The downside is that this ties up a telephone line while you're online. Furthermore, if you have call waiting, the "beep" that occurs when someone calls while you're online can make the modem drop its connection. To avoid these hassles, many people order an additional line just for the modem, and this adds to the monthly expense.

8

NOTE

Some modems and ISPs provide a service called Internet Call Waiting. The modem detects the call-waiting beep and notifies you via a pop-up window that a call is coming in; you can ignore it or suspend your Internet connection for a time while you take the call. This requires a modem supporting the V.92 standard and a participating ISP. The service costs upward of $8 per month, if it's even available, so it's not a big win as far as I can see.

Modems transmit data at a top speed of 33Kbps and can receive data at up to 56Kbps (56 thousand bits per second). In real life, you will usually obtain download speeds of 40 to 50Kbps. This speed is adequate for general Web surfing—that is, reading text and viewing pictures. However, you will find it woefully inadequate for viewing video or for voice communication.

To use standard dial-up service, you'll need a modem and a telephone cable. Modems come in internal, external, USB, and PC-Card varieties from dozens of manufacturers. Most computers made for home use come with one pre-installed. On business computers, they're usually an extra-cost item.

ISDN

Integrated Services Digital Network (ISDN) is a special digital-only telephone service that can carry two independent voice or data conversations over one telephone wire. ISDN service is actually a different type of telephony; you can't plug ordinary telephones into an ISDN line. ISDN modems can carry data at 64 or 128Kbps, depending on whether you use one or two of its channels to connect to your ISP. Until broadband came along, that was pretty impressive. IDSN still is a good interim solution if you need higher speed than an analog modem can provide, and DSL and cable aren't yet available.

To use ISDN service, you'll need an internal or external ISDN modem, or an ISDN router device and a network adapter. Your ISP can help you choose compatible equipment. In addition, you'll need the ISDN telephone line wired into your home or office.

DSL

Digital Subscriber Line (DSL) service sends a high-speed digital data signal over the same wires used by your telephone line, while that line is simultaneously used for standard telephone service. This means that you can get DSL service installed without needing an extra telephone line. The most common DSL service is called *asymmetric* because it receives data at 128Kbps to 1200Kbps and sends at a lower rate. (This is fine, because most Web surfing involves sending out a very small request and receiving a large amount of data back.)

NOTE

DSL varieties include Asymmetric, Symmetric, High-Speed, and DSL-over-an-ISDN-line, so you'll see the acronyms *SDSL, ADSL, HDSL,* and *IDSL,* or the collective *xDSL*. As far as I'm concerned these distinctions are unimportant, so I'll just call it DSL.

8

DSL service is not available everywhere yet, but it's spreading rapidly. However, DSL has at least one Achilles heel in that its availability is restricted by your distance from the telephone company's central office, and isn't available when the distance is more than a couple miles (as the wires run, not as the crow flies). DSL's reach can be extended by optical fiber lines and special equipment, but this is expensive for the telephone companies to install. DSL might never make it into rural areas.

NOTE

U.S. readers can see reviews of various DSL providers and check for DSL service availability at `http://www.dslreports.com`.

DSL modems come in two varieties: External units connect to your computer through a network adapter or a USB cable. Internal units plug right into your computer. If your ISP uses external adapters, before you buy a network adapter, check with your DSL provider as they often include one in their installation kit. Also, before you decide to pay extra to get service for multiple computers, read Chapter 19 to see how you can share a single connection with all of your computers.

CABLE MODEM

Cable modem Internet service is provided by your local television cable company, which sends high-speed data signals out through the same distribution system it uses to carry high-quality TV signals.

Cable modem service has none of the distance limitations of ISDN or DSL. However, one criticism of cable service is that data speeds tend to drop during high-use times like the early evening, because everyone in a given neighborhood is sharing a single network "pipe."

NOTE

You can find a quirky and fascinating Web site devoted to high-speed Internet access, especially via cable, at `http://www.teleport.com/~samc/cable1.html`.

→ For more information on ISDN, xDSL, and cable modem service, **see** Chapter 19, "Connecting Your LAN to the Internet." That chapter describes these technologies with a focus on using them to connect a LAN to the Internet, but you still might find the information helpful.

Cable modems generally are external devices that connect to your computer through a network adapter or a USB cable. Before you buy a network adapter, though, check with your ISP as they may include one in their installation kit. Some ISPs charge extra to lease you the modem. Since cable modems cost $150 and up, leasing one might not be a bad idea, at least for the first few months. Also, before you decide to pay extra to get service for multiple computers, read Chapter 19 to see how you can share a single connection with all of your computers. This is especially important for cable users. Multiple-computer cable service has some serious problems that I'll discuss in Chapter 19.

SATELLITE SERVICE

Satellite Internet service uses microwave signals and small (roughly two-foot diameter) dish antennas to connect to an orbiting communication satellite. There are two types of satellite service: *unidirectional*, which receives high-speed data through the dish but transmits by modem over a phone line, and *bidirectional*, which uses the satellite dish for both sending and receiving. Bidirectional service is the way to go! It's currently available in most parts of the world.

Satellite's big advantage is that it's available wherever there's a good view of the southern sky (in the northern hemisphere), or northern sky (in the southern hemisphere). The disadvantages are that installation requires both a rocket scientist and a carpenter, the equipment and service plans can be expensive, and the system suffers from the same slowdowns that affect cable service.

NOTE

In the US, check out www.starband.com and www.direcpc.com. In Australia, check www.telstra.com. In Europe, Southern Africa, the Middle East, the Indian subcontinent, and Southeast Asia see www.europestar.com. Satellite services are often resold through regional companies.

Satellite service requires you to purchase a receiving dish antenna, a receiver, and a USB or network adapter to connect the setup to your computer. These devices will all be furnished by your ISP. For one-way satellite service, you'll also need to have a phone line near your computer.

TIP FROM

Bob
& Brian

To get the full scoop on satellite and wireless Internet service, check out *The Complete Idiot's Guide to High-Speed Internet Connections* by Mark Soper, published by Que.

WIRELESS

In some major metropolitan areas, wireless Internet service is available through a regional network of small radio transmitters/receivers. Cell phone companies are getting into this in a big way, so it's going to spread rapidly. The wireless modem connects to a small whip or dish antenna, and data transfer rates typically are more than 1Mbps using setups with fixed antennae.

NOTE

Check www.sprintbroadband.com for more information.

Wireless is similar to satellite service. You'll have to purchase a receiving dish antenna, a receiver, and a USB or network adapter to connect the setup to your computer. These devices will all be furnished by your ISP. You'll also have to pay for professional installation.

CHOOSING A TECHNOLOGY

With all the options potentially available to Windows users for Internet access, making a choice that fits your needs and limitations can become a bit confusing. You should research the options provided by local and national ISPs, and then start narrowing them down. Table 8.1 summarizes the costs and speeds of the different ways for a single computer user to access the Internet. The prices shown are typical costs for the service in question after applying the usual discounts and special offers.

TABLE 8.1   INTERNET CONNECTION OPTIONS FOR THE INDIVIDUAL USER

Method	Approximate Cost, $ per month	Approximate Setup and Equipment Cost	Time Limits in Hours	Availability	Download Speed
Analog Modem	$0* to 25	$50	10 to unlimited	Worldwide	33 to 56Kbps
ISDN	$40 plus ISDN toll charges	$300	10 to unlimited	Limited, unlikely to expand	64 to 128Kbps
DSL	$40 and up	$100	Unlimited	Limited but growing	312Kbps to 6Mbps
Cable Modem	$40	$100	Unlimited	Limited but growing	1 to 10Mbps
Satellite	$50 and up	$450–800	25 and up	Almost worldwide	400Kbps

There are some "free" ISP's; I'll discuss them later in this chapter.

Remember that you have three or four costs to factor in:

- The cost of hardware required to make the connection
- The cost of installation and setup
- The monthly ISP cost for Internet service
- The cost of telephone or ISDN lines, if you order a separate line just for Internet access

Try to estimate how long you'll keep the service, and amortize the startup and equipment costs over that time frame when comparing technologies. If you are going to share the connection among several computers, plan to be downloading lots of large files, or will be playing games online, a faster service might make more sense, even if it's a bit more expensive.

CHOOSING AN INTERNET SERVICE PROVIDER

Several different kinds of businesses offer Internet connections, including large companies with access points in many cities, smaller local or regional Internet service providers, and online information services that provide TCP/IP connections to the Internet along with their own proprietary information sources (I'm talking about AOL here, of course).

You might notice that Windows XP comes with pre-installed software to use Microsoft's MSN service. The Connection Setup Wizard (which we'll discuss below) may try to steer you to an ISP that paid Microsoft to be listed. And, your computer reseller may have installed icons for other preferred services. Remember, you don't *have* to use any of these providers. Windows has all the software it needs to connect to any ISP except AOL, and AOL is easy to add on, if that's the way you want to go. Do your own research to find the best fit for you.

The following are a few points to consider in choosing an ISP:

- Does the ISP offer the connection technology you want?
- Can you have multiple e-mail accounts for family members or employees? If so, how many?
- For dial-up access, check whether your modem uses the V.90, K56-Flex, or X2 protocol. Does the ISP support your modem?
- Does the ISP provide you with a news server so you can interact with Internet newsgroups?

→ To learn more about Newsgroups, **see** Chapter 11, "Reading Newsgroups with Outlook Express."

- What is the charge for connect time? Some ISPs offer unlimited usage per day. Others charge by the hour or have a limit on continuous connect time.
- Does the ISP have local (that is, free) phone numbers in the areas you live, work, and visit? If not, figure in the toll charges when you're comparing prices.
- Can you get a discount by signing up for a year or longer term contract?

If you have access to the Web, try checking the page www.thelist.com. You'll learn a lot about comparative pricing and features offered by ISPs, along with links to their pages for opening an account. Another good site is www.boardwatch.com.

Finally, you should know that there some ISPs that give you free dialup Internet access. These providers install software on your computer that displays a small window of advertising the entire time you're connected. If you're pinching pennies, this isn't a terrible way to go. You might check out http://www.freedomlist.com/ for a list of free (and cheap) ISPs in your area.

TIP FROM

Bob

& Brian

> In my opinion, getting good customer service is more important than saving a few dollars a month. As you narrow down your list of potential ISPs, call their customer support telephone number and see how long it takes to get to talk to a human being. This experience can be very illuminating.

8

TRAVEL CONSIDERATIONS

If you're a frequent traveler and have a laptop or other device with which you want to connect to the Internet while on the road, remember that broadband service is wired into place. In other words it doesn't provide for access when you travel or roam about town unlike many national dial-up ISPs that offer roaming. However, some broadband ISPs include a standard modem dial-up account at no extra charge just to compensate for this factor.

If you want Internet connectivity when you travel, consider these options:

- For occasional or personal travel, you can forgo national access. Just find an Internet cafe or get Internet access at your hotel.

- If you want to use your own computer for occasional travel, you can always place a long-distance call to your own ISP. Subtract the cost from the money you might save using a less expensive local ISP, versus the higher prices of a national ISP, to see which solution would be best.

- If you travel frequently, choose a national ISP with local access numbers in the places you visit frequently or toll-free access with an acceptable surcharge.

At the end of this chapter, I'll give you some advice about getting Internet access while traveling overseas.

AOL

If you're a current dial-up AOL user you know how painfully slow it is at accessing non-AOL Internet Web sites (or maybe you don't—maybe you think everyone suffers this way!). You should know that you can get a fast broadband connection or even standard dial-up service, which gives you fast Internet access, and still allows for use of AOL for e-mail and their exclusive content.

RELYING ON THE INTERNET CONNECTION WIZARD

Windows XP includes an Internet Connection Wizard that can connect via modem to a toll-free line operated by Microsoft, offer you a choice of ISPs, and sign you up for service, without your having to lift much more than a finger.

Before you let the wizard narrow the range of choices for you, remember that its range of choices is narrow to begin with. You'll probably want to do some research on your own. Then you can use the wizard to see if it recommends your ultimate choice. If it does, you can let it help you set up the account.

8

CHOOSING EQUIPMENT

You'll need to purchase equipment compatible with the particular type of Internet service you'll be using. If you're going to use dial-up service, your computer probably came with a modem pre-installed so you don't have any choices to make. If you are going to buy new connection hardware, here are some points to consider:

- Most broadband services require specific hardware that your ISP provides (you can sometimes buy a DSL or cable modem independently, but be sure it's going to be compatible with the equipment your ISP uses). In addition, broadband modems connect via USB or through an Ethernet network adapter. If your service needs a network adapter, be sure it's Windows XP-compatible.

- If you're going to share your Internet connection with other computers via a LAN, please read chapter 19 before making any hardware purchases, as there are some nifty special hardware setups you might want to consider.

- Above all, be sure any hardware that you have to plug directly into the computer (modem or LAN adapter) appears on the Windows XP Hardware Compatibility List. Check `http://www.microsoft.com/hcl` before you buy.

- For dial-up service, choose a modem that is compatible with the fastest service level provided by your ISP. They should be using V.90 modems for 56Kbps service. If your ISP still uses X2 or K6Flex modems, they're way behind the times. Some ISPs support the new V.92 call-waiting protocol. If you have a modem that supports this feature, ask prospective ISPs if they support it and if there's an additional charge.

ORDERING THE SERVICE

Ordering standard dial-up modem Internet service is really quite simple. Just call the ISP, talk to the sales department, and ask the sales representative to mail or fax you instructions for configuring Windows XP. In fact, it's easy enough that they may just talk you through it over the phone.

Ordering ISDN service is quite a different matter. The most difficult part is getting the ISDN telephone line ordered and installed correctly because ISDN service has a bewildering number of options, all specified in telephone-companyese. What you probably want is standard "2B+D, two data and voice" service with no extra-cost features.

TIP FROM

Bob & Brian

> Your best bet is to have your ISP order an ISDN line for you. If they won't, some ISDN modem manufacturers—for example, 3COM—will order your ISDN service for you.

Ordering cable, DSL, or satellite service is also quite easy because the ISP will take care of all the details for you. The provider first checks to see whether your neighborhood qualifies for the service. It calls you back with the news, and then schedules an installation appointment. Getting DSL installers to actually show up, though, can be a nightmare. But don't let me discourage you from trying. The service is really nice.

After the service is installed, you're ready to configure your Windows XP computer. I'll discuss modems first, and then we'll cover setup of broadband equipment.

INSTALLING THE HARDWARE

No matter what kind of Internet connection you'll be using, you'll need a modem, a network adapter, or some other sort of connection hardware. If you're lucky, your computer came with this preinstalled and you can just skip ahead to "Configuring your Internet Connection."

Otherwise, you'll be adding some hardware. For most types of high-speed service your ISP will either come install everything for you, or they'll give you detailed instructions. For the basic service types, I'll give you some generic installation instructions in the next few sections. Your connection hardware may come with detailed instructions. If it does, by all means follow those.

INSTALLING A MODEM IN WINDOWS XP

Installing a modem is a pretty painless process these days. If you had to undergo the experience in the mid '90s, you might remember worrying about interrupt conflicts, having to set jumpers, and needing to navigate the computer's setup screen. Plug and Play has pretty much eliminated this mess. Your modem should come with straightforward installation instructions. Follow those and you'll be online in no time.

For an internal modem, they'll have you pop open your PC's case and insert the modem card into a free expansion slot inside the computer. For an external modem it's a more simple matter of cabling it to a USB or serial port on your PC. (Don't forget to connect the power supply and turn it on.) A PC card modem simply plugs into your portable.

→ For more information about installing new hardware, **see** Chapter 30, "Installing and Replacing Hardware." From that point, here's what you'll need to do. These procedures apply to analog modems as well as external ISDN modems.

If your modem is Plug and Play (PnP) compatible, Windows XP should automatically detect it when you turn on your computer and log in using a Computer Administrator account, or the Administrator account itself.

→ For more details on Administrator privileges, **see** "Guest and Administrator Accounts," **p. 951**. If Windows XP cannot find a set of drivers that match your brand and model of modem, you might be asked to insert a CD or floppy disk that the modem manufacturer should have provided with your modem.

8

If you're using an older modem, you might need to add it to the configuration manually by following these steps:

1. Choose Start, Control Panel, Network and Internet Connections, Phone and Modem Options.

2. Select the Modems tab, as shown in Figure 8.1.

Figure 8.1
The Modems tab identifies the modems currently installed in your system.

3. If Windows has already detected your modem, its name will appear in the Modems tab. If the correct modem type is listed, skip to step 8. If the wrong modem type is listed, skip down to the next section, "Changing the Modem Type."

   If no modem is listed, click the Add button to run the Install New Hardware Wizard.

4. Click Next to have Windows locate the COM port and determine the type of modem you have. If this is successful, Windows will tell you. In this case, continue with step 7.

5. If Windows detects your modem incorrectly and doesn't offer you the chance to correct the mistake, skip down to step 7, and then correct the problem using the instructions in the next section. If you are given the opportunity, though, click Change and locate the manufacturer and model of your modem in the dialog box. If you find the correct make and model, select them and click OK. If your modem came with a driver diskette for Windows XP or 2000, click Have Disk, and locate the installation file for the modem.

   If your modem isn't listed, you might try selecting a similar model by the same manufacturer. Or, you might be able to download the proper driver from Windows Update or from the modem manufacturer (using another computer, of course!).

6. After you select the modem type, click OK and then Next.

7. Click Finish to complete the installation. The modem then appears in the list of installed modems in the Phone and Modem Options dialog box.

8. Select the Dialing Rules tab.

9. Select New Location, and click Edit.

10. Enter the General tab information for your current location, as shown in Figure 8.2.

Figure 8.2
In the Edit Location dialog box, you can record the dialing instructions for your current location. The important settings are Country, Area Code Access for an outside line, and Disable Call Waiting.

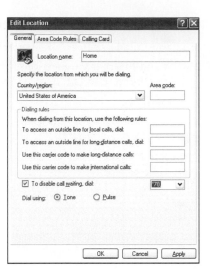

11. Enter a name for your location—for example, home, the name of your city, or another name that will distinguish the current telephone dialing properties. Set the country, area code, and dialing rules information.

    If your telephone system, for example, requires you to dial a 9 to make an outside local call, enter 9 in the box labeled To Access An Outside Line For Local Calls, Dial. Make a corresponding entry for long-distance access.

    If your telephone line has call waiting, check To Disable Call Waiting, and choose the appropriate disable code.

    I'm going to assume that your ISP access number will be a local call in the same area code. If this is not the case, you might want to fill in the Area Code Rules table for the ISP access number. (If you don't know the number yet, don't worry; you can come back and fix it later.)

12. Click OK.

Now your modem is installed, and you can continue with "Configuring Your Internet Connection," later in this chapter.

CHANGING THE MODEM TYPE

If Windows incorrectly determines your modem type, you can change it by selecting the appropriate line in the Modem list (see Figure 8.1) and clicking Properties. Then

1. Select the Driver tab and click Update Driver.

2. Check Install from a List and click Next.

3. Check Don't Search, and click Next.

4. Uncheck Show Compatible Hardware, and either select your modem make and model, or click Have Disk and locate the proper .INF setup file. Click Next, and then Finish.

INSTALLING MULTIPLE MODEMS

Windows XP supports *modem aggregation* (also called *Multilink* or *Multilink PPP*), making several simultaneous connections to your ISP to increase the total speed of your transfers. This process is tricky; it requires multiple modems and an ISP that supports synchronization of multiple modems, or a compatible setup on your corporate LAN.

You'll see this possibility mentioned in many Windows books, but to be honest, it's an obnoxious technology and one you can ignore if you can wait for DSL or cable service. It requires two telephone lines, two modems, and manual management on your part. It's a little bit like riding two skateboards at once: It might work, but why not just buy a bike?

ISDN modems, on the other hand, can make two concurrent connections and do not require the addition of a second line or modem. The two channels are built into one modem, and you can take advantage of this to get extra speed, as long as you're willing to pay the extra charges imposed by your ISP and telephone company. ISDN channel aggregation is discussed later in this chapter, under "Using Multiple Modems or ISDN Channels."

INSTALLING INTERNAL ISDN ADAPTERS

Internal ISDN modems or adapters are treated by Windows as network adapters, not modems. Plug and Play adapters should be set up automatically the first time you log in after installing the adapter. Log in as an administrator to be sure that you have sufficient privileges to install hardware drivers.

For older non-Plug and Play adapters, you must get up-to-date Windows XP drivers from the manufacturer's Web site, along with installation instructions (but, if your ISDN adapter is that old, don't count on finding any).

Modern ISDN driver software may be able to get the ISDN line's telephone number and other necessary information right over the line from the phone company, but you may be prompted for setup information. In this case you'll need the SPID (Service Profile Identification, a number assigned by the telephone company), directory number, and switch-type information provided by your telephone company.

INSTALLING A NETWORK ADAPTER

Some DSL and cable modems use a USB connection and can just be plugged into your computer this way.

However, most DSL and cable service providers require an Ethernet network adapter for use by their modems. If you're lucky, they'll supply and install this for you. You won't have to lift a finger, in fact, as long as the installer is familiar with Windows XP. You will just need to log in using the Administrator account, and supervise while the installer does his or her stuff.

8

TIP FROM

Bob & Brian

> If a professional installer configures your computer or adds software to it, be sure to take thorough notes of what he or she does. Don't hesitate to ask questions—you have a right to know exactly what they're doing. And, be sure to test the setup before the installer leaves.

If you want to purchase or install the network adapter yourself, install it according to the manufacturer's instructions. This process should involve no more than inserting the card into your computer, powering up, and logging on as an administrator. The Plug and Play system should take care of the rest for you.

After installation, confirm that the network adapter is installed and functioning by following these steps:

1. Click Start, right-click My Computer, and then select Manage.
2. Select the Device Manager in the left pane. The list in the right pane should show only "first-level" items. Under Network Adapters, you should see no items listed with an exclamation mark icon superimposed.

If the network adapter appears and is marked with a yellow exclamation point, follow the network card troubleshooting instructions in Chapter 22, "Troubleshooting Your Network." For DSL service, you might be provided with filters—devices to plug into your telephone jacks. Alternately, the service installer might connect your telephone line to a device called a *splitter* outside the house, and will install a wire to bring the DSL signal to your computer. These devices separate the high-frequency DSL carrier signal from the normal telephone signal. The phone line will be connected to a DSL modem, which will then plug into a USB port or a LAN adapter on your computer.

CAUTION

> After a LAN adapter or USB connection is made, you *must* enable the Internet Connection Firewall to protect your computer against hackers. Please follow the instructions under "Enabling the Internet Connection Firewall" later in this chapter to ensure that the Firewall is enabled on your Internet connection. You can read more about firewalls and network security in Chapter 21, "Network Security."

INSTALLING A SATELLITE OR WIRELESS CONNECTION

Installing satellite or wireless modems is not terribly tricky, but the procedure is very specific to the type of hardware you're using. Unfortunately, I have to leave you at the mercy of the manufacturer's instruction manual.

One bit of advice I can give: Installing a satellite dish is difficult, and it's best to hire a professional dish installer for this task. (Our executive editor, Rick Kughen, didn't have the benefit of this sage advice when he installed his, and his conclusion is "About halfway through the ordeal, I decided that I really wished I had paid the $199 installation fee.")

CAUTION

> After your satellite connection is set up, you *must* enable the Internet Connection Firewall to protect your computer against hackers. Please follow the instructions under "Enabling the Internet Connection Firewall" later in this chapter to insure that the Firewall is enabled on your Internet connection. You can read more about firewalls and network security in Chapter 21.

8

CONFIGURING YOUR INTERNET CONNECTION

Now that your modem is installed and ready to go, it's time to head off to see the wizard. The Internet Connection Wizard, that is.

TIP FROM

Bob & Brian

> Have your Windows XP Installation CD handy. The wizard might need to install some Windows files to set up your Internet connection.

The Internet Connection Wizard runs the first time you try to open Internet Explorer. You can also fire it up at any time by clicking Start, All Programs, Accessories, Communications, Internet Connection Wizard. You'll then see the wizard shown in Figure 8.3.

Figure 8.3
The Internet Connection Wizard has three starting paths, depending on whether you want Microsoft to suggest an ISP.

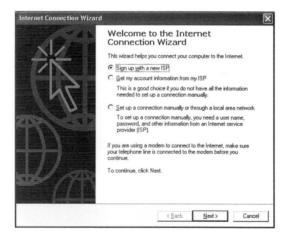

Now, your path from here depends on whether you

- Want Microsoft to give you a list of suggested ISPs
- Already have an existing ISP account
- Want to enter all your ISP's information manually

The first two choices are for analog modem or ISDN access only. If you take this route, go on to "Using a Referral ISP."

Otherwise, skip to "Making and Ending a Dial-Up Connection," or "Configuring a High-Speed Connection," later in this chapter.

USING A REFERRAL ISP

If you want the wizard to help you choose an ISP, select Sign Up with a New ISP, and click Next. Windows then makes a toll-free call to Microsoft's ISP referral server and downloads a list of ISPs in your area.

Internet Explorer then displays a list of available ISPs in your area. You can follow the onscreen instructions to establish an account with one of them, if you choose. If you choose not to, or if none are available, you are given the chance to manually configure an ISP account.

TRANSFERRING AN EXISTING ACCOUNT TO THIS COMPUTER

If you have an existing dial-up account with an Internet service provider, choose the wizard's Get My Account Information . . . option, and click Next.

Windows then dials the Microsoft referral service to see whether your current ISP is known. If you are using one of the listed ISPs, simply follow the instructions shown to retrieve the proper account settings. Otherwise, indicate that you want to perform a manual Internet account setup, and click Next.

MANUALLY CONFIGURING AN ISP ACCOUNT

If you want to enter your own ISP account information, select Set Up A Connection Manually . . . on the wizard's first screen, and click Next. Select I Connect Through a Phone Line and Modem, and click Next. You'll then need to complete three dialog boxes using the information provided by your ISP.

The first (shown in Figure 8.4) asks for the local access telephone number for your ISP.

Figure 8.4
In the manual Internet account connection information dialog, enter the local access number for your ISP.

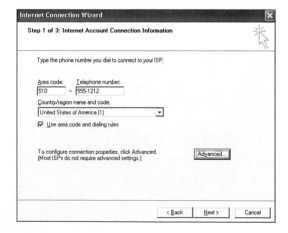

CAUTION

Be sure to use a local number. Your ISP will not help pay your phone bill if you choose a toll number by mistake!

Proceed as follows:

1. Enter the local access number for your ISP, including area code and telephone number. You should also be sure to check Use Area Code and Dialing Rules.

    In the unlikely event that your ISP has provided you with a list of DNS server addresses and has indicated that they will *not* be sent to your computer automatically each time you connect to the Internet, click the Advanced button. Otherwise, click Next and skip ahead to step 2.

    Select the Addresses tab and manually enter the DNS server addresses, as shown in Figure 8.5. Then click Next to proceed.

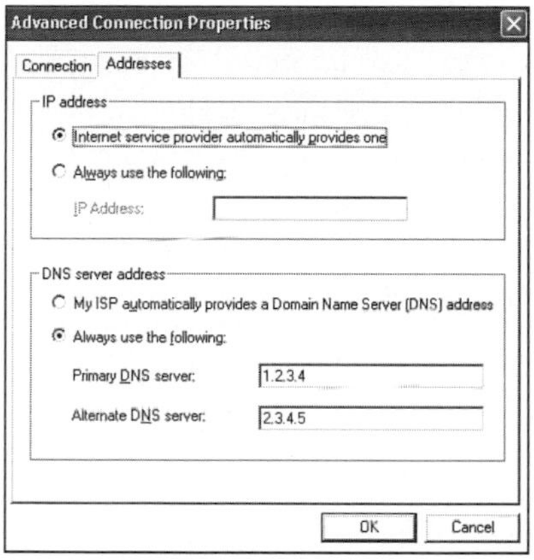

Figure 8.5
In the Advanced Connection Properties dialog box, you can enter your ISP's DNS addresses, if necessary.

2. Enter the username and password provided by your ISP in the Internet Account Logon Information dialog box. Click Next.

3. The wizard next asks you to give a name to the connection information being saved (see Figure 8.6). This name is displayed as part of the sentence `Connecting xxx`, so I like to use the name of the ISP rather than the default name `Connection to 555-1212` that Windows provides. You can change it as you see fit and then click Next.

4. The wizard will then want to immediately dial your ISP. Uncheck To Begin Browsing Immediately . . . if you do not want to dial immediately. Click Finish to finish the configuration wizard.

That's it. Your connection is ready to use. If you have no other LAN or dial-up connections, you can simply fire up Internet Explorer to automatically dial. You can choose Start, Control Panel, Network and Internet Connections to use or modify your dial-up configuration at any time.

8

Figure 8.6
Here, you can name the Internet dial-up connection. Use the name of your ISP.

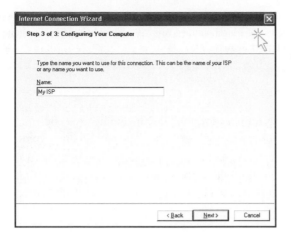

If you have several ISP accounts, ISP access numbers for different cities, or both personal and business dial-up connections, you can add additional connections by opening Start, Control Panel, Network and Internet Connections, Network Connections. Use the Make New Connection Wizard to add new Internet connections.

TIP FROM

Bob
& Brian

> If you find yourself frequently having to dig into Network Connections to get to a connection icon, you can make a desktop or quick-launch shortcut for it. Right-click and drag the connection icon from Network Connections to the desktop or Quick Launch bar and choose Create Shortcut Here from the shortcut menu that appears when you release the right mouse button.

NOTE

> For maximum protection against hackers, I suggest that you read Chapter 21 on network security. But at the very least, follow the steps in the next section to enable the Internet Connection Firewall, following the instructions in the next section.

ADJUSTING DIAL-UP CONNECTION PROPERTIES

As configured by the wizard, your dial-up connection is properly set up for most Internet service providers. It's unlikely that you would need to change any of these settings, but just in case, and because I know you're curious, I will walk you through the various settings and properties that are part of a dial-up connection. I'll explain dial-up connection properties in detail in Chapter 18, "Windows Unplugged: Remote and Portable Networking."

You can view a connection's properties by selecting Start, Control Panel, Network and Internet Connections, Network Connections. This will display all dial-up connections you've configured (see Figure 8.7). Right-click the icon for your dial-up connection and select Properties. You'll see five tabs as shown in Figure 8.8, which I will run through in the order in which they appear. Only a few settings ever need to be changed for an ISP connection. Here is a list of the ones that you might want to check if you encounter problems dialing in to your ISP:

- The General tab contains modem properties and the ISP telephone number. If you have multiple modems, you can choose which of one or more of these modems will be used for this particular connection.

- Using the Configure button for the modem, you can set the maximum speed used to communicate from the computer to the modem. For external modems—if you don't have a special-purpose high-speed serial port—you might want to reduce this speed from the default 115200 to 57600.

Figure 8.7
Network Connections shows icons for each of your dial-up accounts and high-speed links.

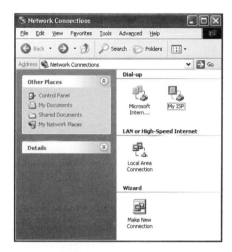

Figure 8.8
A dial-up connection's Properties page let you change dialing rules, set network parameters, and enable the Internet Connection Firewall.

■ Using the Alternates button for the telephone number, you can add multiple telephone numbers for your ISP, which will be automatically tried, in turn, if the first doesn't answer.

■ On the Options tab, you can change the time between redial attempts if the connection fails.

  • You can select a time to wait before hanging up the line when no activity occurs. By doing so, you can help cut costs if you pay an hourly rate to your ISP by having your computer disconnect itself from the Internet if it detects that you've not been using your connection for a set amount of time.

  • To maintain a permanent or *nailed-up* dial-up connection, check Redial If Line Is Dropped and set the disconnect time to Never. (Do this only with the agreement of your ISP.)

■ The Security tab controls whether your password can be sent in unencrypted form. It's okay to send your ISP password unsecured. *Don't* check Automatically Use My Windows Login Name and Password if you use a commercial ISP. That's only for connections to corporate networks.

■ The Networking tab determines which network components are accessible to the Internet connection. If you're dialing in to a standard ISP, you should leave File and Printer Sharing . . . unchecked. You'll learn more about that in Chapter 21.

■ On the Advanced tab, you can share this dial-up connection automatically with other users on a LAN. (You'll learn more details on that in Chapter 19). You can also enable Windows XP's Internet Connection Firewall, which protects your computer from hackers while you're connected. You *should* check Protect My Computer . . . .

Click OK to save your changes.

CONFIGURING A HIGH-SPEED CONNECTION

If you're using an Ethernet network adapter to connect your computer to a DSL or cable Internet service, the installer will probably set up your computer for you. "Self-install" providers will give you a set of instructions specific to your service. I can only give you a general idea of what's required.

Most DSL and some cable Internet providers use a connection scheme called *PPPoE (Point-to-Point Protocol over Ethernet)*. This is a technology that works a lot like a standard dial-up connection, but it takes place through the DSL circuit or TV cable rather than over a voice connection. Windows XP has PPPoE software built-in, but the setup process will vary from provider to provider. The setup process will involve installing and configuring a network adapter to connect to the modem, or plugging in a USB-based modem, and then setting up a dial-up connection with the Connect Using a Broadband Connection That Requires a User Name and Password option.

On the other hand, if you have "always-on" DSL or cable service, your ISP will provide different installation instructions. You'll most likely perform these steps:

1. In the Internet Connection Wizard, select Set Up a Connection Manually . . ., and click Next.

2. Check I Connect Through a Local Area Network and click Next.

3. Uncheck Automatic Discovery of a Proxy Server, click Next, and then Finish. These steps tell Windows it doesn't need to dial a modem connection.

Now you might need to configure the Ethernet card using information specified by your ISP. Your ISP will tell you whether your network card must be manually configured or whether the DHCP protocol is available through its service.

NOTE

Installing a network adapter to connect to a broadband modem doesn't give you a local area network—it's just a way of connecting to the modem. If you want to set up a LAN in addition to an Internet connection, please see Chapter 19.

SETTING UP DYNAMIC IP ADDRESSING

If your ISP uses the DHCP protocol to configure client network adapters, you might need to set your computer name before the connection will work. To do this

1. Click Start and right-click My Computer. Select Properties.

2. Select the Computer Name tab and click Change.

3. Enter the computer name as supplied by your ISP, as shown in Figure 8.9

Figure 8.9
Specify a required computer name in the Computer Name Changes dialog.

4. Click More, and enter the domain name specified by your ISP, as shown in Figure 8.10.

Figure 8.10
Enter your ISP's full domain name in the DNS suffix dialog box.

When you close all of these dialog boxes by clicking OK, you will need to let Windows restart.

CAUTION

> You *must* enable the Internet Connection Firewall to protect your computer against hackers. Please follow the instructions under "Enabling the Internet Connection Firewall" later in this chapter.

SETTING UP A FIXED IP ADDRESS

If you need to manually configure your LAN adapter for a fixed IP address, follow these steps:

1. Choose Start, Control Panel, Network and Internet Connections, Network Connections.

2. Right-click the Local Area Connection icon, and select Properties. View the General tab, as shown in Figure 8.11.

3. Select Internet Protocol and click the Properties button.

4. Select Use the Following IP Address, and enter the IP address, Subnet mask, and Default gateway information provided by your ISP, as shown in Figure 8.12.

Figure 8.11
Select Internet Protocol and click Properties to set the LAN adapter's IP address and network information.

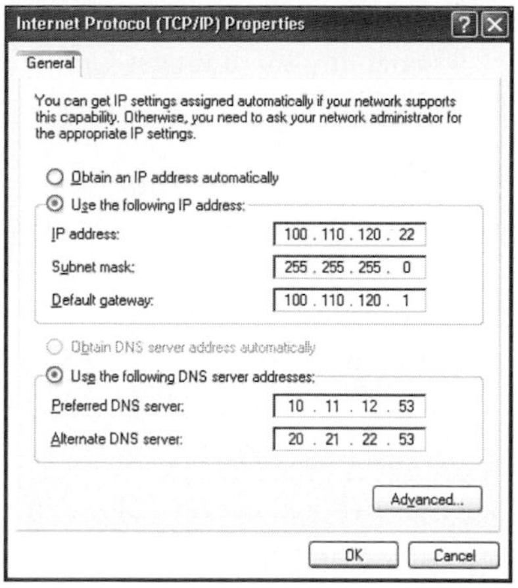

Figure 8.12
Here, you can add the network address, subnet mask, and DNS information supplied by your ISP.

TIP FROM

Bob & Brian

> When you're entering TCP/IP dotted-decimal numbers like 1.2.3.4, the spacebar advances the cursor across the periods. This technique is much easier than using the mouse to change fields.

5. Select Use the Following DNS Server Addresses, and enter the two DNS addresses provided by your ISP.

6. Click OK to return to the Local Area Connection Properties dialog. Select the Advanced tab.

7. Check Protect My Computer and Network . . . and click OK.

CAUTION

> It is very important that you enable Protect My Computer, to prevent Internet hackers from attacking your computer.

ENABLING THE INTERNET CONNECTION FIREWALL

Windows XP includes a new feature that protects your computer from hacking via the Internet, called the Internet Connection Firewall. In networking terminology, a firewall is a program that prevents undesired network traffic from reaching your computer.

→ To learn more about firewalls, **see** Chapter 21, "Network Security."

8

Hacking is a very serious problem, especially with fast, always-on broadband connections, but you can virtually eliminate the risk by enabling the Internet Connection Firewall. You need the firewall if you

- Use a dial-up connection to reach your ISP
- Connect to an ISP with a cable modem, DSL line, satellite, or other connection made directly to your computer

You do *not* want to enable the firewall if you reach the Internet over a LAN connection, where the actual Internet connection is made via a router or on a *different* computer.

After you've configured and tested your Internet connection, follow these steps to enable the Firewall:

1. Click Start, Control Panel, Network and Internet Connections, Network Connections (see Figure 8.7).
2. If you use dial-up Internet, right-click your ISP's dial-up connection. If you use a broadband connection with a LAN adapter, right-click the Local Area Connection icon. If your broadband connection uses a USB adapter, right-click the appropriate connection icon. In any case, select Properties.
3. Select the Advanced tab.
4. Check Protect my computer . . . and click OK.

This simple step can save you untold grief!

TIP FROM

Bob
& Brian

> You can easily tell that the firewall is enabled on a given connection. Windows displays a small padlock and uses the word "Firewalled" under the connection icon.
>
> —Padlock

NOTE

> If you run Personal Web Services or other Internet servers on your computer, you'll need to tell the Firewall to allow incoming Web connections to your computer. See Chapter 21 for instructions on doing this.

MAKING AND ENDING A DIAL-UP CONNECTION

If you use a dial-up connection with an analog modem or ISDN line, after you've set up an icon for your ISP, making the connection is a snap:

1. Select (double-click) the connection icon in Network Connections.

2. When Windows displays a connection dialog box (see Figure 8.13), enter the login name and password assigned by your ISP. If you're the only one using your PC (or you don't care who uses your account) check Save Password so that you won't need to retype it every time you dial.

TIP FROM

Bob
& Brian

> You can put Network Connections on your Start menu for quick access. To do this, right-click the Start button. Choose Properties, Customize, Advanced tab. Select Network Connections under Show These Items on the Start Menu.

Figure 8.13
When you want to initiate a dial-up connection, enter your user ID and password, and check Save Password to simplify connecting in the future.

3. Check that the phone number is correct, including area code and any required prefix numbers. You might need to correct your current location (Dialing From) and/or the Dialing Rules if the prefix or area code isn't correct.

4. If you want other users of your computer to be able to use this same ISP account and password, or if you are going to use Internet Connection Sharing to share this connection, check Save this user name . . . and check Any User Connects.

5. Select Dial to make the connection.

Windows then dials your ISP and establishes the connection; if it works, a connection icon will appear in the notification area with a temporary note indicating the connection (see Figure 8.14).

 If your modem doesn't attempt to connect to your ISP, see "Modem Didn't Dial ISP" in the Troubleshooting section at the end of this chapter.

If the connection fails, Windows displays a (usually) sensible message explaining why: there was no dial tone because your modem in unplugged, there was no answer at the ISP or the line is busy, or you user ID and password failed. In the last case, you'll get three tries to enter the correct information before Windows hangs up the phone.

Figure 8.14

 If the modem dials, but fails to establish a connection, see "Modem Dialed ISP but the Connection Failed" in the Troubleshooting section at the end of this chapter.

(Of course, if you use a dedicated, always-on Internet connection, you won't have to fool with dialing and hanging up connections at all. To be honest, I don't know which I like more about my DSL connection—its lickety-split speed or the fact that I don't have to wait for a modem connection to be made.)

After your connection is made, you should be able to browse Web sites, check your e-mail, and so on.

 If your Internet connection seems to be working but you can't view any web pages, see "Can't Reach Any Web Sites" in the Troubleshooting section at the end of this chapter.

CHECKING THE CONNECTION STATUS

The notification area connection icon shows two tiny computer screens, which are normally black. They flicker when data activity occurs on the dial-up connection, momentarily turning green to show that the modem is active. The two indicators represent data you're sending and data returned from your ISP, respectively. This icon is actually a decent troubleshooting tool because you can immediately see whether modem activity is taking place.

If you let your mouse cursor hover over the connection icon, a small pop-up window shows the number of bytes transmitted and received over the current connection.

If you right-click the connection icon, a pop-up menu appears. This menu contains the following options:

- Disconnect—Hang up the connection
- Status—View the Connection Status dialog
- Open Network and Dial-Up Connections—Bring up the whole dial-up networking control panel

Choosing Status from this menu opens the Status dialog box, as shown in Figure 8.15. The dialog displays the number of bytes transmitted and received during the connection and the number of transmission errors detected; it also has buttons to let you disconnect or adjust the connection properties.

Figure 8.15
In this dialog box, you can see connection statistics, such as the length of time you've been connected and the number of bytes sent and received.

HANGING UP A DIAL-UP CONNECTION

After you finish with your Internet connection, simply right-click the connection icon in your tasktray, and select Disconnect. Windows will hang up the dial-up connection and remove the icon from the tasktray in a few seconds.

USING MULTIPLE MODEMS OR ISDN CHANNELS

If you chose ISDN Internet service, your primary reason for doing so was probably its ability to use both ISDN channels simultaneously to get full 128Kbps throughput. You have to arrange for this "two channel" service with your ISP, and there may be additional costs, but it's a great way to get extra speed when DSL or cable Internet service isn't available. Combining two distinct connections into one big data pipe is called *Multilinking*. You can also use multiple analog modems to connect to some ISPs to get a similar rate boost, although this ties up multiple telephone lines, and more importantly, few ISPs support Multilink analog connections.

The procedure for setting up a two-channel call depends on what type of modem you have. If you're using an external ISDN modem connected through a serial cable (or an ISDN router connected to a network adapter) you'll have to follow the setup instructions provided by the modem manufacturer. With some modems, you specify the telephone number something like this: "5551212+5551212", which instructs the modem to dial your ISP's modem bank at 555-1212 for the first channel, and then to dial the same number again to establish the second channel. You'll have to find out how it's done for your particular modem. Your ISP will help you set this up.

TIP FROM

Bob
& Brian

> If you have to pay your telephone company or your ISP an extra fee for a two-channel data call, you might want to set up two connection icons in Windows: one configured for a single channel call, and one for a two-channel call, so you can choose between speed and expense.
>
> You also might be able to set an ISDN modem or router to automatically add or drop the second data channel based on how much data you're transferring.

8

However, if you use an internal ISDN modem, or you want to use multiple analog modems, you have to instruct Windows to set up the second channel. To do this, view the icon for your Internet connection, right-click it, and select Properties. You'll see two entries under "Connect using", as shown in Figure 8.16. Check the boxes next to both of the ISDN modem's channels (next to both analog modem entries). Check All Devices Call the Same Numbers, and then click OK.

Figure 8.16
To establish a 128Kbps ISDN connection, check both channels under Connect Using.

Now, when you use this icon to call your ISP, Windows will use both data channels to make the connection. You can create an additional icon with just one channel checked if you want to have the option of using a single channel to save on connection charges.

CHANGING THE DEFAULT CONNECTION

If you don't establish a connection manually before using an Internet program like Internet Explorer, Windows will go ahead and dial your ISP automatically when you start these programs. If you don't want Windows to dial automatically, or if you have defined multiple dial-up connections, you can tell Windows which, if any, of the connections you want it to dial automatically.

To change the default settings, follow these steps:

1. Open the Control Panel, select Network and Internet Connections, and click Internet Options. Alternatively, within Internet Explorer, you can choose Tools, Internet Options.

2. Select the Connections tab, and highlight the dial-up connection you want to use for Internet browsing (see Figure 8.17).

Figure 8.17
In the Internet Properties dialog box, you can specify which dial-up connection to use automatically when an Internet application is started.

3. If you use a standalone computer or a portable computer that sometimes has Internet access via a LAN, select Dial Whenever a Network Connection Is Not Present.

   If you want to use the modem connection even while you're connected to a LAN, you can select Always Dial My Default Connection.

   Finally, if you don't want Windows to dial automatically at all but prefer to make your connection manually, you can choose Never Dial a Connection.

4. If you have actually changed the default dial-up connection, click Set Default.

5. Click OK.

MANAGING MULTIPLE INTERNET CONNECTIONS

Life would be so simple if computers and people just stayed put, but that's not the way the world works anymore. Portable computers now account for more than half of the computers sold in the United States. Managing Internet connections from multiple locations can be a little tricky.

I'll talk a bit more about the ins and outs of traveling with your computer in Chapter 18, where the topic is remote networking.

The issue comes up with plain Internet connectivity as well, so let me share some tips:

- If you use a LAN Internet connection in the office and a modem connection elsewhere, bring up the Connections tab of the Internet Properties dialog box, and choose Dial Whenever a Network Connection Is Not Present, as I discussed in the previous section, "Changing the Default Connection."

- If you use different LAN connections in different locations, see "Multiple LAN Connections" in Chapter 18.

8

- If you use a dial-up Internet service provider with different local access numbers in different locations, life is a bit more difficult. It would be great if Windows would let you associate a distinct dial-up number with each dialing location, but it doesn't—dialing locations just adjust the area code and dialing prefixes.

  The solution is to make separate connection icons for each location's access number. After you set up and test one connection, right-click its icon and select Create Copy. Rename the icon using the alternate city in the name; for example, I might name my icons "My ISP Berkeley," "My ISP Freestone," and so on. Finally, open the Properties page for the new icon, and set the appropriate local access number and dialing location.

  In this case, it's best to tell Windows never to automatically dial a connection (as shown earlier in "Changing the Default Connection") because it will not know which of several connections is the right one to use; it might dial a long-distance number without you noticing.

TROUBLESHOOTING

MODEM DIDN'T DIAL ISP

When I attempted to make a connection to my ISP, the modem didn't make an audible attempt to connect.

There are four possible problems here:

- Your phone line may not be correctly plugged into the modem. Be sure the phone cable is plugged into the correct jack on the modem.

- The phone line may not be working. Try an extension phone in the same wall jack to see if there's a dial tone.

- The modem may be working but its speaker volume may be turned down. (This has fooled me more than once!) Some external modems have volume knobs. You can set the volume on an internal modem by opening Control Panel, Phone and Modem Options. View the Modems tab and select Properties. Select the Modem tab and adjust the volume control.

- There may be a hardware problem with the modem. Open the Modem properties as described in the previous paragraph. View the Diagnostics tab and click Query Modem. After 5 to 15 seconds, you should see some entries in the "Command / Response" list. If an error message appears instead, your modem is not working properly. If it's an external modem, be sure it's powered up. If it's an internal modem, see Chapter 30. Try to update the modem's driver software.

MODEM DIALED ISP BUT THE CONNECTION FAILED

When I attempted to make a connection to my ISP, the modem made the call, but the Internet connection still failed.

Windows should indicate what sort of problem was encountered. You may have typed your account name and password incorrectly. Try one or two more times. If it still doesn't work, a call to your ISP is the best next step. Your ISP may require you to enter the account name information in an unintuitive way (Earthlink, for example, requires you put "ELN\" before your account name.) Their customer support people will help you straighten this out.

CAN'T REACH ANY WEB SITES

My Internet connection seems to be established correctly but I can't reach any Web sites.

Troubleshooting connection problems is such a large topic that an entire chapter is devoted to it. If you're having trouble, turn to Chapter 14, "Troubleshooting Your Internet Connection," for the nitty-gritty details.

TIPS FROM THE WINDOWS PROS: STAYING CONNECTED WHILE TRAVELING ABROAD

As I said earlier, you can choose an ISP with regional local access numbers to let you connect without toll charges wheresoever you roam in your home country. But what about when you travel overseas?

Actually, you usually don't have to go far to find an Internet terminal. You can rent PCs with Internet connections for roughly $1 to $10 per hour almost anywhere. Listings of Internet cafés and computer parlors are now a required element in guide books (for example, the fantastic *Rough Guide* series), and tourism information centers in most towns can direct you to the nearest rental centers.

If you want to connect your own computer, however, connecting is a bit more difficult. The following are some tips I've picked up in travels through Mexico, Australia, and Europe:

- Do your research before you leave. Search the Internet to find at least one Internet location and/or ISP in each area you'll be visiting. Print these pages and bring them along, being sure to get the local address and telephone number. You might find a more convenient location or better service after you arrive, but this way you have a place to start.

- Most Internet cafés won't let you hook up your own computer. Some will. You can find Kinko's Copy centers, for example, in many large cities in North America, Europe, and Asia; they're outfitted with fast computers, fast connections, and at least one bay with an Ethernet cable that you can use to connect your own laptop. Bring a PCMCIA Ethernet card, and you're set. (You will have to configure it using the Local Area Connection icon in Network and Dial-Up Connections, as you'll learn in Chapter 16, using the settings provided by the rental center.)

- Bring some formatted floppy disks with you. If you need to transfer files and can't hook up your own computer, you can at least use the floppy disks.

- If you normally receive e-mail through a POP mail server at your ISP, use one of the free e-mail services such as Hotmail or Yahoo! Mail to view your home e-mail via the Web while you're traveling. Use a different password, not your regular password, for the free account. Set up the free service to fetch mail from your ISP, using what is called *external* or POP mail. Set the mail service to "leave mail on the server" so you can filter through your mail the normal way when you get home. Delete the free account, or change its password, when you return home.

  These steps will (a) let you read your mail from virtually any Internet terminal in the world and (b) protect your real mail password from unscrupulous types who might be monitoring the network traffic in the places you visit.

- If you're staying a reasonable length of time in one country, you can sign up for a month of Internet service. For example, in Australia, I used `ozemail.com`, which gave me local access numbers all over the Australian continent. A month's service cost only $17, with no setup fee. After I found an adapter for Australia's curious telephone jacks, I was all set.

- If you do use a foreign ISP, configure your e-mail software to use the foreign ISP's outgoing mail (SMTP) server, but keep your incoming POP server pointed to your home ISP. (This step is important because most ISPs' mail servers won't accept mail from dial-up users outside their own networks. You need to use *their* SMTP server to *send* mail, and *your* home POP server to *pick up* mail.)

- Get power plug adapters and telephone plug adapters from a travel store, telephone accessory store, or international appliance store before you leave, if you can.

CHAPTER 9

BROWSING THE WORLD WIDE WEB WITH INTERNET EXPLORER

In this chapter

ORIGINS AND DEVELOPMENT OF THE WORLD WIDE WEB

The World Wide Web (also called WWW or the Web) has worked its way into virtually every aspect of modern life, an astounding fact considering that just a short decade ago it was nothing more than an idea living inside a computer scientist's head. That scientist was Tim Berners-Lee, who, while working at the European Laboratory for Particle Physics (or CERN, from its original name, *Conseil Européen pour la Recherche Nucléaire*), needed to devise a way in which scientific data could easily be shared simultaneously with physicists around the world. Along with Robert Cailliau, he designed the first Web browser in 1990 to allow scientists to access information remotely without the need to reformat the data.

This new communications technology developed by Berners-Lee and Cailliau transmitted data to viewers via the Internet, which by the early 1990s already existed as a global network linking numerous educational and government institutions worldwide. The Internet served for decades as a means for exchanging electronic mail (e-mail), transferring files, and holding virtual conversations in newsgroups, although data shared online was typically static and text only. The new idea provided data in hypertext format, which made it easier for far-removed scientists to view the electronic library at CERN's information server. The hypertext data could even incorporate graphics and other file formats, a practice virtually unknown to Internet users of the time.

Despite a relatively small initial audience, the hypertext concept quickly caught on and by 1993 more than 50 hypertext information servers were available on the Internet. That year also saw the development of Mosaic, the first modern and truly user-friendly hypertext browser. Mosaic was produced by the National Center for Supercomputing Applications (NCSA) at the University of Illinois with versions for the X Window System, PC, and Macintosh. Mosaic served as the basis for a number of browsers produced by commercial software developers, with Netscape Navigator and Microsoft Internet Explorer eventually becoming Mosaic's best-known offspring.

The world was eager when the first commercial Web sites began appearing in 1994. President Bill Clinton and Vice President Al Gore had already popularized the idea of an "information superhighway" during their 1992 political campaign, and by the next year it seemed that everyone wanted to get online and see what this new World Wide Web of information had to offer. A high level of media coverage meant that by 1995 most of the general public knew what the World Wide Web was, and they wanted to be part of it.

The rest, as they say, is history. In its current form, the Web exists on hundreds of thousands of servers around the world. The system of naming and addressing Web sites is implemented by a number of private registrars contracted by the United States Government. Today you can go shopping, play games, conduct research, download tax forms, check the status of a shipment, find directions to a new restaurant, get advice, or just plain goof off on the World Wide Web.

The hypertext concept has grown as well, even outside the confines of the Internet. These days, Microsoft structures much of the Windows interface in a Hypertext Markup Language (HTML) format. This makes interfacing with the Web more seamless and allows you to use the same program—in this case, Internet Explorer 6—to browse the World Wide Web, your company's intranet, the contents of your own computer, the online Help system, Control Panel, and other network resources.

What's New in Internet Explorer 6?

If you have used Internet Explorer 5, IE6 will be very familiar to you. Some of its new features are behind-the-scenes, not readily apparent but designed to make IE run more smoothly. Others are enhancements that you will see:

- The Integrated Web searching tool formerly called the Search Assistant has been spiffed up and is now called the Search Companion. You'll notice some changes in the interface, but it works essentially the same way. (See Effectively Searching the Web, later in this chapter.)

- The Media button on the Explorer Bar is new. Click on it to bring up the Radio Guide and your music and video folders in a side-pane. The media player control buttons are also included in the pane for ease of use.

- A new pop-up menu for images makes it simpler to save or e-mail them. (For more about this tool, see Dealing with Multimedia Browsing and Downloading, later in this chapter.

- Playback support for Flash and Shockwave files is built into IE6.

The Department of Justice Consent Decree has brought about some changes in the way that middleware applications are handled. You can now configure your computer to show only Microsoft middleware applications (Outlook Express, Internet Explorer, and so on), to show only non-Microsoft middleware applications (Netscape Navigator, Eudora, and so forth), or some combination of both. See Appendix B for more information on how SP1 brings these changes to your Windows XP computer.

Internet Explorer 6 Quick Tour

Web browsers have become so ubiquitous that we'll assume here that you are already comfortable with the basics of Web browsing. And because many Windows XP elements such as Windows Explorer, the Control Panel, and My Network Places use the background code of IE6, you are probably already familiar with the location of common toolbar buttons, menus, and other screen elements.

Still, IE6 does have some new features, so an overview of how to use some of them is provided here. This overview will be especially useful if you are switching from an even earlier version of Internet Explorer or another Web browser such as Netscape Navigator.

➔ You must have a connection to the Internet configured on your computer before you can connect to the Web. **See** "Configuring your Internet Connection," **p. 275**.

You can begin browsing the Internet by launching Internet Explorer from the Start Menu.

If you connect to the Internet via a dial-up connection, you may be prompted to connect. When the connection is established, Internet Explorer probably opens, by default, to the MSN (The Microsoft Network) home page, as shown in Figure 9.1. Some PC manufacturers—such as Compaq—customize IE before delivery so that you see their home page instead.

➔ To change the home page so that you see a personal favorite when IE opens, **see** "Customizing the Browser and Setting Internet Options," **p. 310**.

Figure 9.1
Internet Explorer opens with MSN, the default home page, displayed.

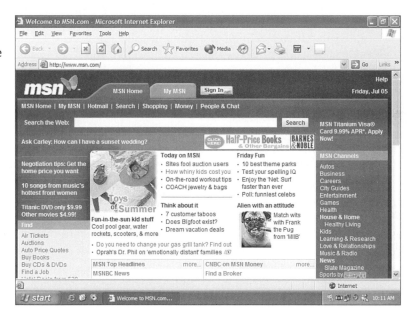

⚠ *Did a Web page freeze your browser? See "Internet Explorer Crashes on Certain Web Pages" in the "Troubleshooting" section at the end of the chapter.*

As you probably know, Web pages change frequently, so the page you see will almost certainly look different from Figure 9.1. The general layout of the IE6 window might also be somewhat different from what is shown here, although if you have performed a standard installation of Windows XP and have not done any customizations, it should look like this.

TIP FROM

Bob & Brian

> Want even more space to view Web pages? Press F11 to change the view to get rid of some screen elements and make more room for Web documents. If you don't like what you see, press F11 again to toggle back.

Consider creating buttons for the Web pages you visit most frequently on the Links bar. To see the Links bar more fully, you must first unlock the toolbars, by going to View, Toolbars, and unchecking "Lock the Toolbars." Then, click and drag the Links bar to a more visible position on the screen. It should look something like Figure 9.2. Before you customize the Links bar, keep these tips in mind:

■ The Customize Links button merely takes you to a Microsoft-hosted Web page that provides instructions on how to do what is already described here. Consider removing that button to make room for your own favorites.

Drag a Web site icon from the Address bar

Figure 9.2
The Links bar is a handy place to store your most frequently visited Web sites.

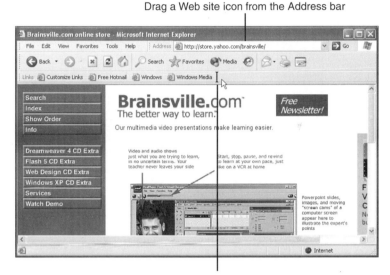

Drop it onto your Links bar by positioning the I-beam cursor where you'd like the new Link to appear.

■ You can remove unwanted Links buttons by right-clicking them and choosing Delete from the menu that appears.

■ Make space for more Links by right-clicking an existing Links button and choosing Rename from the menu that appears. Type in a shorter name or abbreviation and click OK.

■ To save more room, reduce the length of your Address bar and move it to share a "line" with another toolbar. (The main toolbar, on the top line, is a good place for the address bar.) Experiment with the placement of all the toolbars so that you have as much space as possible to view Web pages.

■ The easiest way to add a Web page to the Links bar is to drag the icon for the page from the Address bar and drop it onto the Links bar. Figure 9.2 demonstrates this technique.

As you probably know, you can navigate around the Internet by typing Web addresses into the Address bar or by clicking hyperlinks on a page. The mouse pointer changes from an arrow into a hand whenever it is over a link. Among the most useful features of the IE6 interface are the Back and Forward buttons. When you click the Back button, you return to the previously visited page. Clicking Forward moves you ahead once again. (To move around even faster, Alt + back arrow and Alt + forward arrow have the same function, and if you have a new mouse, it may have special Back and Forward buttons on it.)

 Are you frustrated because Internet Explorer tells you that a site you visit often is unavailable? See "What Happened to the Web Site?" in the "Troubleshooting" section at the end of this chapter.

Notice that next to both the Back and Forward buttons are downward-pointing arrows. If you have been browsing through several Web pages, click the down arrow next to the Back button. A menu similar to that shown in Figure 9.3 should appear showing a backward progression of the Web pages you have visited. Click a listing to move back several pages simultaneously rather than one at a time.

Figure 9.3
To move several Web pages instead of to the previous one, click the down arrow next to the Back button.

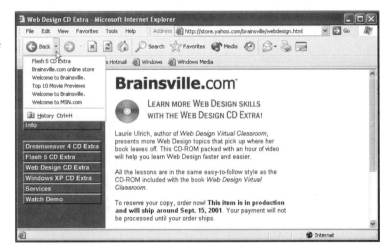

ENTERING URLs

Every Web document you view in IE6 is identified by a unique address called a *Uniform Resource Locator (URL)*. When you visit a Web page, for example, the URL for that page appears in the Address bar of Internet Explorer. URLs for links usually also appear in the status bar when you hover the mouse pointer over a hyperlink, although more and more Web site designers are setting up scripts so that an advertisement or other message appears in the status bar instead.

URLs are broken down into three main components. To illustrate, consider these URLs:

`http://www.quepublishing.com/`

`http://www.irs.treas.gov/prod/forms_pubs/forms.html`

`http://www.zen-satsang.org/calmain.htm`

`http://store.yahoo.com/brainsville/index.html`

Each of the listed addresses conforms to this scheme:

protocol://*domain*/*path*

The protocol for all World Wide Web documents is `http`, short for *Hypertext Transfer Protocol*. The protocol is followed by a colon, two forward slashes and the domain name. The domain often—but not always—starts with www. Following the domain is the path to a specific document file. You may notice that the first URL listed here does not actually show a path; this is usually okay because Internet Explorer automatically looks for a file called `default.htm`, `index.htm`, `home.html`, or something along those lines in the root directory of the domain.

TIP FROM

Bob & Brian

> If you get an error message when trying to visit a URL, remove the path from the address and try again. Although the exact link may have changed, it's quite possible that the main page for the site still exists and that you will be able to find the information you seek there.

9

When you type a URL into the IE Address bar, a built-in feature automatically reviews your browsing history and presents a number of possible matches. A list appears directly under the Address bar and shrinks as you type more characters, narrowing the search. If you see a desired URL appear in the list, click it to go directly to that page. This feature, called AutoComplete, can save keystrokes, but it can also be incriminating if others use your computer and user profile. I mean, do you really want your boss or a coworker to know you visited `howtomakebandanasfrombananas.com`? AutoComplete works with Web form data as well, which means that others could see your user IDs, passwords, and other sensitive data for various sites.

If you are concerned about others viewing your data, disable AutoComplete by doing the following:

1. Choose Tools, Internet Options.
2. Click the Content tab to bring it to the front, and then click AutoComplete.
3. Remove check marks next to the items you do not want affected by AutoComplete.
4. You can further safeguard existing information by clicking either of the two Clear buttons in the AutoComplete Settings dialog box. Click OK when you are finished.
5. To prevent existing Web URLs from being compromised, select the General tab in the Internet Options dialog box, and click Clear History. Click OK to finish.

NOTE

> If no one else has access to your Windows XP user profile or you really don't care who sees where you've been browsing, AutoComplete doesn't present a security problem. In this case, you should be able to safely leave the feature enabled.

BROWSING OFFLINE

If you have a permanent Internet connection that is never interrupted or shut off, consider yourself fortunate. A permanent connection—such as what you might have through your company's network—allows you a great deal of flexibility in terms of what and when you download from the World Wide Web.

Alas, not all users have this sort of flexibility in their daily computing, so IE offers you the ability to download Web pages into a cache for offline viewing. This feature can be useful in a variety of situations. For example, you can set up IE to download specific Web sites in the background every time you go online. You can also download Web sites onto your portable computer so that you can view them later—while you're on the plane, for example.

TIP FROM

Bob & Brian

> Internet Explorer works just fine whether or not an Internet connection is available. However, if no connection is available, it can view only files stored on the local computer or other available network resources. The IE6 status bar displays this icon when you are working offline.

The process of downloading a Web site for offline browsing is fairly simple. Your first step, obviously, is to browse to the Web site you want to make available offline. For best results, open the main or index page of the Web site first. Now try the following:

1. Choose Favorites, Add to Favorites.
2. In the Add Favorite dialog box, place a check mark next to Make Available Offline, as shown in Figure 9.4. You can also change the name so that you will be able to easily identify the page. The name entered here is what will be shown in your Favorites list.

Figure 9.4
In this dialog box, you can select this Web page for offline viewing and choose how this Web page will appear offline.

3. To set up offline browsing options, click Customize to start the Offline Favorite Wizard. Click Next in the introductory dialog box to open the window shown in Figure 9.5. Depending on the layout of the site, this screen could contain the most important options that you will set.

Figure 9.5
Here, you can choose how many link levels you want to make available offline.

4. Usually, you will want to choose Yes when asked whether you want to download pages that are linked to the one you are making available offline. For example, if the main page is a list of news stories, the next level of links probably contains the actual stories. Viewing a list of headlines won't do you much good without also being able to read the stories!

5. If you chose Yes in the preceding step, select the number of levels you want to download. The exact number will depend on the layout of the site.

TIP FROM

Bob

& Brian

> If you aren't sure how many levels to download, cancel this process, and browse the Web site to get a feel for it. Too many levels could result in a lot of unwanted content, and too few will leave you frustrated, trying to click links that are unavailable.

9

6. Click Next after you have chosen how many link levels you want to download. In the next window, you must choose between downloading the pages manually or automatically. If you will browse offline only occasionally—say, on a laptop—choose the first option, Only when I Choose Synchronize from the Tools Menu, and skip to step 8. Otherwise, select the second option, I Would Like to Create a New Schedule, and click Next to create a schedule for downloads.

7. Select a schedule to synchronize the download process. You may want to set a schedule that will download the pages when the computer is least likely to be in use. You can also choose to have the computer automatically connect to the Internet for you if the computer is not connected at synchronization time.

8. Click Next when you are finished setting your schedule. If the Web site requires a user-name and password, you must enter it in the last window of the wizard. Click Finish. If the Add Favorite dialog box is still open, click OK to close it.

VIEWING PAGES OFFLINE

Now that you've set up a schedule and have downloaded some pages for offline viewing, you are ready to actually read them offline. To do so:

1. Open Internet Explorer.

2. If you are prompted to establish an Internet connection, click the Cancel button. Internet Explorer may load a copy of your home page from cache, so it could appear as if you are online even though you are not. On the other hand, IE may open with a message that says "The page cannot be displayed." If so, go to File and click Work Offline.

3. To view a synchronized offline page you have set up and downloaded, click Favorites and choose the page's listing from the Favorites menu. You can view the page and click links that have been downloaded.

4. Notice that if you move the mouse pointer over a link that has not been downloaded, this "not available" symbol will appear.

If you click a link that has not been downloaded, you will be asked whether you want to connect or remain in offline mode. If you do not or cannot connect, you cannot open the link.

DEALING WITH MULTIMEDIA BROWSING AND DOWNLOADING

When the World Wide Web first debuted as a method for sharing scientific data among physicists, the hypertext format of the data was specifically chosen to lend itself to sharing information in many different formats. For early Internet users, the ability to download pictures and other graphics in conjunction with Web pages was both exciting and profound.

Today, Web pages with pictures in them are commonplace. Web developers continue to push the multimedia horizon, with many sites now featuring audio and video. You can even listen to radio stations and watch other broadcasts live over the Web.

In addition to multimedia-rich Web sites, you'll find that the Web is a good place to download software. You can find many places to download freeware, shareware, software updates, and sites to purchase and download full versions of programs.

IMAGES

Believe it or not, graphics-rich Web sites used to be controversial. Some people believed that graphics would put too much of a strain on the bandwidth capacity of the Internet, but those gloom-and-doom predictions have not come to pass. Backbone improvements have helped the Net keep pace with the ever-growing appetite for multimedia on the Web, and images are now both commonplace and expected.

Internet Explorer supports three basic graphics formats used in Web pages:

- **JPEG**—Short for Joint Photographic Experts Group, this format allows pictures to be compressed significantly (reducing download time and bandwidth, but also image quality) so it is used often for photos on Web pages.
- **GIF**—Short for Graphical Interchange Format, this format is often used for buttons and other simple icons used on Web pages.
- **PNG**—Short for Portable Network Graphics, was developed to help images load faster and to enable them to look the same on different platforms.

The exact format used for each image is not apparent when you view the page. Usually, the specific format used is not important unless you plan to copy the graphics and use them for some other purpose. For Web use, the formats are essentially interchangeable.

By default, IE6 displays graphics used in Web pages. Although the idea of disabling this feature to allow speedier downloads might seem appealing, many Web pages now rely so heavily on graphics that they do not include text links. This means you cannot navigate the site without the images. Don't disable this feature unless you deem it absolutely necessary.

What if some graphics on a page open, but others don't? See "Some Graphics Don't Appear" in the "Troubleshooting" section at the end of the chapter.

You can do a variety of things with online graphics. You will notice a new feature in IE6: When you mouse-over a graphic, a pop-up window will appear. Click the appropriate icon if you'd like to save the image to your hard drive, print it, e-mail it, or just open the My Pictures folder. If you find this toolbar annoying, disable it by going to Tools, Internet Options. Under the Advanced tab, scroll down to Multimedia and deselect Enable Image Toolbar. Click OK to save and close the window.

You'll also notice a little square with four arrows on it, in the lower right-hand corner of some pictures. This only happens on pictures that, if shown full size, wouldn't fit on the screen. IE6 thoughtfully auto-sizes such pictures so that you can see the whole image at once. Click on the little box and the image will scale up to its full size, in higher resolution. Once full size, click on the little box again, and the image you're viewing returns to the compressed size.

CAUTION

> Before you use any graphics you find on the Web, check the Web site for a copyright statement or other information about terms of use. You should obtain permission before you use any copyrighted material.

AUDIO AND VIDEO

A growing number of Web sites offer audio or video content in addition to standard text and graphics. The terms *audio* and *video* when used in conjunction with Web content can mean a few different things:

- Basic audio files—such as MIDI music files—that play in the background while you view a Web page.
- Video files on Web sites that download and play automatically or play when you click a Play button.
- Video media that plays using the Windows Media Player.
- Animated GIFs that give the appearance of a video signal but with a significantly reduced bandwidth requirement. They display a series of static GIF frames that simulate video and are often used in logos.
- Flash movies that also appear to be video but are actually vector-based instructions requiring very little bandwidth. Vector-based simply means that they have small mathematical descriptions (much the same way fonts do in Windows) that can be manipulated to animate the objects.
- Streaming audio or video that you choose to open and listen to or watch.

You might have noticed that, when you visit certain Web sites, a song starts to play while you read the page. Audio isn't nearly as common as graphics in Web pages because some people find it annoying. If you come across a Web page that contains a song you would rather not hear, the most obvious solution is to simply turn your speaker volume down or mute the Windows volume control. If you're listening to music on your computer (such as from a CD or MP3 file) and don't want to can your entire audio experience by turning off the speakers, see the note below.

→ To disable audio, video, or other multimedia from automatically downloading when you visit a Web site, **see** "Customizing the Browser and Setting Internet Options," **p. 310**. By disabling these "features," you also might notice that Web pages will load faster. Note that some Web pages use media playback programs that IE settings won't touch. For example, if a page has a RealMedia or QuickTime sound or video file in it, auto-playback of those files will commence regardless of IE settings.

Likewise, some Web sites contain video files and animations set to download and play automatically. MPEG and AVI video files are usually very large, and if you have restricted bandwidth capacity, you might want to consider disabling them.

Web-based video seems to be improving almost daily, but most broadcasts are still lower in quality than that produced by a plain old television set. Whereas a broadcast TV signal typically delivers about 30 frames per second (fps), typical Web-based streaming videos provide just 5 to 15fps. In contrast to streaming, many sites will give you the option of downloading a video clip before playing it. Usually the clip in this format is much larger and of a higher quality than the streaming video. Once the entire clip has been downloaded, it can be played and may appear as a high-quality image, depending on how it was produced. Playback will typically be in the Windows Media Player, QuickTime Player, or RealPlayer. The ranges of file sizes, frame sizes, and compression techniques all of which affect the quality of the picture, abounds. Unlike the TV standard we are all accustomed to, the Web is the wild, wild West of video non-standards.

→ To learn more about using the Windows XP audio controls, **see** "Volume Control," **p. 171**.

MPEG, AVI, AND WMV VIDEOS

By default, MPEG, AVI, and WMV (Windows Media Video) files are played using Windows Media Player. Windows Media formats are sort of the new kid on the block and are Microsoft's attempt to be a big player in the Internet multimedia market. Just as movies encoded in Apple's QuickTime format or RealNetworks' RealPlayer format require those companies' proprietary player, Microsoft's proprietary format only plays in their player.

→ Windows Media Player is covered in depth in Chapter 7, but because how you deal with online video is relevant to mastering Web browsing, I'll briefly mention its use in this context. Be sure to check Chapter 7 for more about the Media Player.

Snarfed Media Associations

When you install players such as RealPlayer, they want to alter your file associations. Each of the popular media players (QuickTime player, RealPlayer, or Windows Media Player) is engaged in a war of kidnapping your filename associations and wants to become your player of choice. They do this in hopes of garnering your business (that is, your money) one way or another. They do this either by selling you upgrades to the fancier model of the player or by selling advertisements that show up in their content—or both. These incentives behoove them to offer a quick means to reclaim any file associations that have been hijacked by another player. You don't have to play their game, though. You can always change those associations back to the player of your choice.

The easiest way to reset media file association is through the preferences dialog box for the media player in question. In Windows Media Player, for example, choose Tools, Options, File Types, and check off the file types (such as MPEG and "video file") you want played by Media Player. Some players try to reclaim associations each time you run them, which can be really annoying. Be aware, though, that not all players can play all the popular file formats. You'll need RealPlayer for Real format and QuickTime for QuickTime. Windows However, Media Player plays the greatest number of audio and video formats, by far.

Most Web pages featuring videos online will give you links for Real, QuickTime, or Media Player, letting you choose, such as the one in Figure 9.6. Some sites will give you links for downloading MPEG or AVI files. These don't stream, and must first download. Depending on your connection speed, downloading could take awhile. These files tend to be very large. Just be prepared for a long download, especially if using a dial-up connection.

Figure 9.6
Choose the target player of your choice, and connection speed, from the drop-down list.

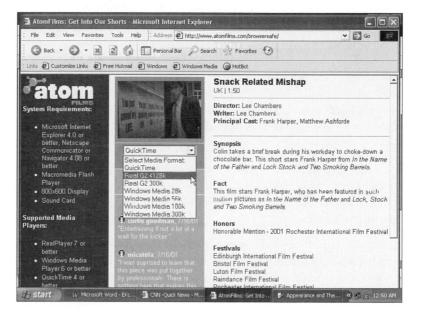

You might notice that Media Player opens as soon as you click the link. Earlier versions of Media Player (prior to ver. 8) would remain blank, however, until the entire file was downloaded. Now with some types of files such as .MWV (Windows Media Video), movies can start playing more quickly even though they are not technically streaming. (See the next section to read about streaming). Instead, they are doing a *progressive download*. This is less reliable than streaming, but at least you don't have to wait until the movie is completely downloaded before you start seeing it. It might hang up a few times, though, if your connection speed is slow. QuickTime movies have had this feature for some time. Now Media Player does too.

If you click on the Media button in the toolbar, a miniature version of the Media Player will open in the left pane of your IE window, along with a bunch of links for supposedly

9

interesting media. When you click on a Web page link for an audio or video file, you'll be asked if you want it to play in this tiny Media Player or you'd rather it open in a regular Media Player window. The choice is up to you. The advantage of its opening in the small window is that it lets you neatly play some tunes, or movie trailers or whatever, over in the left pane while you continue your Web surfing.

STREAMING BROADCASTS

As mentioned earlier, another type of sound or video you might play over the Internet is *streaming audio* or *streaming video*. Streaming audio/video is a format in which a signal "plays" over your Internet connection starting after a few seconds after you click, instead of playing from a file that was first downloaded to your hard drive.

When you first click a streaming signal, a portion of the signal is buffered in *RAM* on your computer. This buffer helps provide a steady feed if connection quality wavers. If the signal is received faster than it can be played, the additional data is buffered. However, if your connection deteriorates significantly, the video may not play smoothly. Streaming broadcasts are not written to the disk, so retrieving the signal later from your own PC will be impossible.

Although the minimum requirement of many streaming audio signals is typically 56K these days, a quicker connection is desirable. A lower speed delivers a lower-quality broadcast, skipping and jumping of video, or stopping altogether.

Streaming audio signals are often used to play various types of audio signals over the Web. For example, most online music retailers offer you the ability to listen to sample audio tracks from many of the CDs they sell. Also, you can listen to many radio stations and programs—such as those on National Public Radio (www.npr.org)—over your Internet connection instead of a radio.

Streaming video is used by a number of information providers to send newscasts and other broadcasts across the Web. Many news sites, such as www.cnn.com, allow you to watch news stories online. You'll notice that you can continue to surf the Web while a current audio or video is playing.

MSN (windowsmedia.msn.com) provides links to a number of online video resources, streaming and otherwise.

To access streaming audio or video signals, you need to have an appropriate plug-in program for IE6, such as the RealPlayer 8 from Real Broadcast Network (www.real.com), QuickTime from Apple (www.apple.com/quicktime/), or Windows Media Player 8.0, included with Windows XP. After you have downloaded and installed the appropriate streaming player (following the installation instructions provided by the player's publisher), you can access the streaming signals over the Web.

Although the Windows Media Player can handle many formats, most broadcasts require a specific player. Check the Web site that hosts the streaming media you want to play for specific requirements. Some Web sites offer a choice of player formats, and often, the Web site will have a convenient link for downloading the necessary freeware. RealPlayer is a common application used for streaming audio, and QuickTime is used by many streaming video providers.

Although the look may be different due to custom "skins" used on flashier sites, the basic functions are similar. You'll be able to tell whether it's Windows Media Player, Real Player, QuickTime, or another player if you look closely. Sometimes you'll have to wait for the file to download, and sometimes it will stream right away. QuickTime gives you the choice to download the entire file first so you can avoid glitches when you watch it. Notice that the play slider can go at a different rate than the progress bar, which indicates how much of the file has been downloaded. When it's downloaded, you can play the clip easily again and again without interruption. Note that the Windows Media Player can be encoded right into a Web page these days, so the video might just play with little ado when you hit a particular URL.

→ To learn about downloading programs from the Web, **see** "Downloading Programs," **p. 309**.

To use a streaming media player, follow these steps:

1. Locate a link to an audio clip or video signal you want to access, and click it.

2. Your streaming media player should open automatically. RealPlayer, Windows Media Player, and Apple QuickTime include standard Play, Pause, and Stop buttons.

3. When you are finished listening to the streaming signal, click the Close (x) button for the player.

When you access a streaming signal from the Web, notice the bandwidth requirements. Many signal providers provide scaling of signals from as low as 14.4Kbps up to 300Kbps and higher. Choosing a signal that is scaled higher will only provide a higher quality broadcast if your connection can handle it. If you choose a larger signal than you have bandwidth for, the signal will arrive too fragmented to use. For example, suppose you use a dial-up connection that typically runs at 24Kbps to 26Kbps, and the broadcaster offers signals in either 14.4 or 28.8 flavors. Although you might be tempted to opt for the 28.8Kbps signal because your connection is *almost* up to it, you will probably find that the 14.4Kbps broadcast provides a more usable signal.

MP3 Audio

MP3 is an audio file format whose name refers to files using MPEG Audio Layer 3, an encoding scheme for audio tracks. MP3 files are small (about one-twelfth the size of CD audio tracks) but they maintain a high sound quality. One minute of CD-quality MP3 music requires only 1MB of storage space.

Controversy has surrounded MP3 since its introduction. The small size of MP3 files makes it easier for people to slide behind copyright laws, pirate music, and illegally distribute it over the Internet. These days, authorities are working on ways of controlling this. However, this had only lead to Napster spinoffs that are harder to control and much more difficult to track down or prosecute. It will be interesting to see how the Justice Department handles the impending and unavoidable new age of intellectual property protection.

The bottom line is this: Distributing or downloading MP3 files from any artist without permission is, well, technically, a violation of the law. Although there are artists (particularly new artists) who willingly provide audio tracks for free download as a means for building a fan base, many MP3 sites contain audio files that have been pirated. If you have questions about the legality of MP3 files you find on the Internet, you'll have to be the judge. Probably the most ethical thing for you to do is not to download them, but I don't want to sound like a prude. As I say, it's a brave new world out there in copyright protection. I believe that free music on the Web probably drives the purchase of new CDs and of concert ticket sales. I'm a musician myself, and while I would want my music (and my books) protected, I wouldn't mind more people becoming acquainted with my works, either. It could pay off in the long run. In any case, you might want to be careful about sharing your MP3s of other people's music on the Web, since it could be a little bit dicey, legally.

The MP3 format has become extremely popular, with tiny portable players available that can contain endless hours of music. It is possible to load all of your music into your computer, and create your very own jukebox. Software is available at `www.real.com/jukebox`. MP3 files can be played by many different applications, including Windows Media Player, RealPlayer, and QuickTime. A number of consumer electronics companies are also now producing devices that allow you to play MP3 files away from your computer. Samsung makes a single device (called a Digimax) that functions as three: a digital camera, a PC camera to use for video conferencing, and an MP3 player. A wide variety of MP3 players are available, with varying storage capacities—some units as small as a pen. You can transfer MP3 files to the player's storage via a Universal Serial Bus (USB), parallel, or serial port connection.

For a good resource, free downloads, and to learn a bit more about the MP3 format, go to `www.mp3.com`. MSN also provides links to some free MP3 downloads at `windowsmedia.microsoft.com/music/`. After you have downloaded an MP3 file, you can play it using the Windows Media Player, RealPlayer, QuickTime, or any other MP3-compatible player.

TIP FROM

Bob
& Brian

> Sound quality is affected not only by your hardware, but also by the player application. Experiment with several different programs to find the one that works best for you.

When you click a Web page link for an MP3 file, your default MP3 application will probably open. It may or may not be the application you want to use. Also, the MP3 file will be inconveniently saved in IE's cache. You can exercise more control over the process by following these steps:

1. When you see a link for an MP3 file, right-click the link and choose Save Target As.

2. Select the location in which you'd like to save the file download.

3. When the download is complete, open the desired player application manually, and choose File, Open to listen to the file. If you click Open in the File Download dialog box, your default MP3 player will open.

TIP FROM

Bob
& Brian

> Another new kid on the block, incidentally, is called MP3 Pro. This is an audio format that uses half the storage space per minute, allegedly without reducing quality.

9

DOWNLOADING PROGRAMS

Although the World Wide Web is most often thought of as a source of information and entertainment, it is also an excellent place to obtain new software or updates for existing programs.

You can find numerous excellent resources for downloading free or trial versions of software. Good sources are www.tucows.com and www.download.cnet.com. It is necessary to follow the specific instructions for installation provided by the software publisher (and offered on most download sites), but when you're downloading, these general rules apply:

- Some Web sites require you to choose from a number of "mirror sites" for your download. Mirror sites are servers in different parts of the world that have the same files on them. The redundancy prevents traffic jams on a single server when many people hit it for the same program downloads. You are asked to select a location that is geographically close to you, but you're usually free to choose any site you want. The closer ones are sometimes faster, but not always. Sometimes I'll download from a mirror site in another country whose citizens are sleeping, and I get quicker downloads.

- To begin the download, typically you just click on a link that says something like "Download Now." This should open a dialog box asking you if you want to Open or Save the file. Choose to Save. Select a location that you will remember for saving the download files —it is a good idea to create a "downloads" folder. Within the Downloads file, I create a new folder with the name of the program, then switch to that and save the program there. This way, all my downloads are organized, and I know where each one is.

- Check with your network administrator before installing any new software to find out what your company policies are.

- Scan all downloads with virus-scanning software before you install them.

- Many downloads come in a compressed .ZIP format. If you download such a file, you can run it easily in XP, because ZIP files are supported without having to install a Zip program such as WinZIP or TurboZIP. Just double-click the Zip file and it will open in a folder window. Then, examine the contents. You'll probably double-click the installer or Setup program to begin installing the program into XP.

TIP FROM

Bob & Brian

> Downloads are fastest when Internet traffic is low, such as late at night. If you are given a choice of mirror sites for a download, keep in mind the local time for each site and choose a server located where current traffic is likely to be lower.

During the download process, a window appears showing the download progress and an estimation of the time remaining in the download. The estimates are helpful, but due to fluctuating transfer speeds, these estimates can be extremely unreliable. You might want to watch the window for a moment to see if the estimate changes in your favor. If you can't wait that long, click Cancel and try again later.

In addition to downloading new software, you can also download updates to software you already own. Check the manufacturer's Web site from time to time to see whether new updates, patches, or bug fixes are available (this is especially important for entertainment software). Another great source of information on software updates is the Versions! Web site (www.versions.com).

TIP FROM

Bob & Brian

> Create a Software folder in your Favorites list, and add to it the manufacturers' Web sites for software you own. Doing so will make it easier to periodically check for updates.

TIP FROM

Bob & Brian

> Downloading a program, and there is no choice for Windows XP as your operating system? Choose Windows 2000 instead.

CUSTOMIZING THE BROWSER AND SETTING INTERNET OPTIONS

One of the most important features of Internet Explorer is the capability to tailor it to your own specific needs. Every user sets up IE differently based on programs used, favorite Web sites, bandwidth capability, security needs, and so on.

You can make most customizations in the Internet Options dialog box, which you can access either through the Windows Control Panel or by choosing Tools, Internet Options in IE6. The dialog box contains seven tabs, each holding a number of unique preference settings. Figure 9.7 shows the General tab.

Figure 9.7
On the General tab, you can set general preferences for your home page, temporary cache files, history, and browser view options.

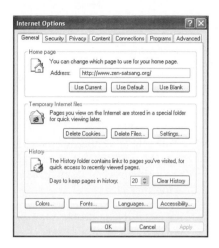

9

Check each tab in the dialog box to customize your own IE6 settings. Table 9.1 describes some of the key preference settings you can change.

TABLE 9.1   IMPORTANT INTERNET OPTIONS

Tab	Option	Description
General	Home Page	The home page is the first page that appears when you open Internet Explorer. It is probably set to MSN or has been customized by your PC's manufacturer. Consider changing this page to your company's home page or something else you find more useful.
	Temporary Internet Files	When you view a Web page, the files for the page are saved on your hard drive as Temporary Internet Files (also called cache). You can clear all files from the cache or change the amount of disk space they are allowed to consume.
	History	A record of the Web sites you have visited is maintained by IE6. You can change the length of time these records are kept or clear the history altogether.
	Colors, Fonts, and so on	You can customize default colors, fonts, languages, and set accessibility options here.
Security	Zones and Levels	You can set security options for IE6. See "Setting Security and Privacy Preferences" later in this chapter.
Privacy	Settings and Web Sites	This area allows you to determine how and under what conditions cookies are sent. See "Setting Security and Privacy Preferences" later in this chapter.

continues

TABLE 9.1   IMPORTANT INTERNET OPTIONS

Tab	Option	Description
Content	Content Advisor	You can control the capability to view objectionable content on your computer. See "Controlling Objectionable Content" later in this chapter.
	Certificates	When a Web page tries to run a script or install a piece of software on your computer, you can accept certificates from the publisher to authenticate their identity and trustworthiness. See "Setting Security Preferences" later in this chapter.
	AutoComplete	You can enable or disable AutoComplete when typing Web URLs, e-mail addresses, or form data.
	My Profile	You can create a profile for yourself in the Microsoft Address Book.
Connections		You can set up preferences for your Internet connection, whether it be through a dial-up or network connection.
Programs		You can select default programs for various actions. See "Setting Default Mail, News, and HTML Editor Programs" next.
Advanced		You can set various (but obscure) options for browsing, multimedia, printing Web pages, searching from the address bar, and security.
	Multimedia	This is where you can disable automatic downloading of graphics, videos, audio, and more.

SETTING DEFAULT MAIL, NEWS, AND HTML EDITOR PROGRAMS

Using the Programs tab of the Internet Options dialog box, you can decide some default programs for a variety of Internet-related tasks. If you have not installed any other Internet software packages, you probably won't have too many choices here, but if you use different programs, these options can be useful. Figure 9.8 shows the default program settings you can make on the Programs tab, and Table 9.2 describes the various options you can set.

Figure 9.8
On the Programs tab, you can choose the default programs for the various Internet tasks you perform.

TABLE 9.2   DEFAULT INTERNET PROGRAMS

Program	Description
HTML Editor	If you are a Web developer, make sure the correct editor is listed here. This will simplify editing during your testing process. The list might include Word, Notepad, FrontPage, or another installed editor.
E-mail	This program will open when you click the Mail button on the IE6 toolbar or when you click an e-mail link on a Web page.
Newsgroups	If you link to or open a newsgroup URL, the reader listed here will open.
Internet Call	Microsoft NetMeeting is the default Internet Call client, but if you have another call program, you can select it here.
Calendar	If you have a calendar program such as Outlook, you can set it here.
Contact List	The default list is the Microsoft Address Book. You should set this to the Address Book used by your favorite e-mail and calendar program.

 E-mail links in Web pages can cause many frustrations. See "E-mail Link Troubles" in the "Troubleshooting" section at the end of the chapter.

SETTING SECURITY AND PRIVACY PREFERENCES

In many ways, the World Wide Web is a safer place than the "real" world, but it does present its own unique dangers as well. The greatest hazards involve sensitive and private information about you or your company being compromised, or in having your computer infected with a software virus. IE6 incorporates a number of security features to protect you from these hazards, and those features can be customized to suit your own needs, browsing habits, and company policies.

Begin by opening the Internet Options dialog box from the IE6 Tools menu, and click the Security tab to bring it to the front. Click Default Level in the lower-right corner of the dialog box to show the slider as seen in Figure 9.9 that allows you to set a security level for each zone.

Figure 9.9
On the Security tab, you can customize security settings for various Web zones.

Click to customize individual settings

Select a zone here to change its settings

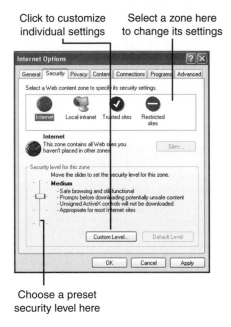

Choose a preset security level here

You first need to select a zone for which you want to customize settings. The four zones are shown in Figure 9.9.

Internet	This zone applies to all resources outside your LAN or intranet.
Local Intranet	This zone applies to pages available on your company's intranet. They are usually more trustworthy and can justify less restrictive settings.
Trusted Sites	You manually designate these sites as trusted. To designate a trusted site, browse to the site, open this dialog box, select the Trusted Sites zone, and click Sites. Here, you can add the site to your Trusted Sites zone list. Trusted sites usually allow lighter security.
Restricted Sites	Designated in the same manner as Trusted Sites, Web sites listed here are ones you specifically find untrustworthy. They should have the strictest security settings.

CAUTION

> Before you designate a Web page as trusted, try to remember that even the most diligently maintained sites can be compromised. Recent "hacker" attacks at Web sites of the FBI, U.S. Army, and others make the practice of designating any Web site as "trustworthy" questionable.

Each zone has its own security preferences, which you set. The easiest way to set preferences is to choose one of the four basic levels offered in the dialog box. The default level is Medium, and for most Web users, this setting works best because it provides a good balance of security and usability. The High setting offers the greatest possible security, but you might find that the level is so restrictive that it's difficult to browse your favorite Web sites.

Likewise, the Low and Medium-Low levels make browsing much easier because you aren't presented with dialog boxes and warnings every time a potentially hazardous activity begins. Because these two levels leave too many doors open to virus infection and other dangers, they are not advisable in most situations.

Besides setting a basic security level, you can customize individual settings. First, choose a basic level (such as Medium), and then try these steps:

1. Click Custom Level to open the Security Settings dialog box, as shown in Figure 9.10.
2. Browse through the list of options, and apply custom settings as you see fit.
3. Click OK when you're finished. A warning dialog box appears, asking whether you really want to apply the changes. Choose Yes.

Figure 9.10
You can scroll through this list to make custom security setting changes.

The items in the Security Settings dialog box that most deserve your attention are those pertaining to ActiveX controls and Java applets. Review these settings carefully, especially those for ActiveX controls, because of the unique hazards they can present. The ActiveX standard contains loopholes, so unsigned controls can run virtually any OLE-compliant operation on your system. Java, on the other hand, is relatively—but not entirely—secure.

You should also consider what level of cookie security you are willing to live with. A *cookie* is a small text file that some Web sites can leave on your computer in cache. Because cookies are text only, they cannot contain a virus or other harmful content. However, they can contain personal information such as a record of Web pages you have visited, how long you spent at a page, how many times you have visited, personal preferences for a Web page, and even user IDs and passwords. It is for these reasons that cookies are regarded by many people as an invasion of privacy.

You can disable cookies, or you can choose to have IE prompt you every time a site attempts to leave a cookie in your cache. However, keep in mind that some Web sites make such heavy use of cookies that you could find it difficult—if not impossible—to browse the Web normally.

To set your cookie preferences, go to Tools, Internet Options, and click on the Privacy tab. The Settings area enables you to determine how and under what conditions cookies are sent. Choose a level you are comfortable with, or click the Advanced button to always accept, block, or prompt you before enabling first-party or third-party cookies. (For more on first-party and third-party cookies, see "Getting a Passport to Microsoft Country" later in this chapter.)

There might be certain Web sites for which you'd like to override your other cookies settings. If so, go to the Web Sites area of the Privacy tab and click the Edit button. In the text box, enter a complete Web site address, and enter it carefully. Then click the Block or Allow button to specify Web sites for which you want to never or always allow cookies.

TIP FROM

Bob & Brian

A major security hole in IE involves the option Allow Paste Operations via Script, which is enabled in all security levels but High. It allows any Web site to see the contents of your Windows Clipboard via a scripted Paste operation. If you have been working with sensitive information in another program and used a Copy or Cut command, that information could be compromised by unscrupulous Webmasters. To be on the safe side, change this setting to Disable or Prompt no matter which security level you use.

USING ENCRYPTION

The Advanced tab of the Internet Options dialog box has a number of other security settings that deserve your attention. In particular, most of the security settings here deal with *certificates*. Certificates can be saved on your computer and serve to authenticate your identity or the identity of the server you are connected to. They also provide for secure encrypted communication over secure Web connections.

IE supports *Secure Socket Layer (SSL) encryption* technology developed by Netscape. It supports 128-bit encrypted SSL sessions, the highest level of data encryption available in the online world. SSL encryption works using a pair of encryption keys, one public and one private. One key is needed to decrypt the other. Certificates facilitate this use by including the following information:

- The issuing authority, such as VeriSign
- The identity of the person or organization for whom the certificate is issued
- The public key
- Time stamps

Thus, the certificate provides and authenticates the basis for an encrypted session. The identity is reverified, the private key is shared, and encryption is enabled.

Another encryption protocol supported by IE is *Private Communication Technology (PCT)*, developed by Microsoft. PCT is similar to SSL encryption, except that it uses a separate key for identity authentication and data encryption. Thus, in theory, PCT should provide slightly enhanced security versus SSL.

Again, encryption protocols can be enabled or disabled on the Advanced tab of the Internet Options dialog box. If you disable a protocol, any page you try to access on a secure server that uses that protocol will not open in IE.

→ Learn how to obtain a digital certificate for yourself in "Sending and Receiving Secure Messages," **p. 345**.

CONTROLLING OBJECTIONABLE CONTENT

The World Wide Web holds the most diverse range of information and content of any library in the world. That diverse range includes a great deal of material that you might deem objectionable, and there is no perfect way of protecting yourself from it short of never going online. However, Internet Explorer incorporates a feature called the Content Advisor, a tool to help you screen out many of the things you or the other people using your computer would rather not see.

The Content Advisor evaluates Web content based on a rating system. The included rating system is developed by RSACi (Recreational Software Advisory Council on the Internet), but you can add others if you want.

You must enable the Content Advisor manually, but after it is set up, the Advisor can be password-protected so that only you can adjust the settings. To enable the Content Advisor, open the Internet Options dialog box, and perform the following:

1. Click the Content tab to bring it to the front, and click Enable to open the Content Advisor dialog box.

2. The Content Advisor dialog box contains four tabs, as shown in Figure 9.11. On the Ratings tab, you can move the slider back and forth to set a rating level in each of the four categories presented.

Figure 9.11
On the Ratings tab, you can move the slider back and forth to change the rating level.

3. Click the Approved Sites tab to bring it to the front. List specific Web sites here to control access to them. Click Always to make it easily acceptable, or click Never to restrict access.

4. On the General tab, choose whether unrated sites can be viewed. Keep in mind that many objectionable sites will not be rated. You can also set a password to let people view unrated or restricted sites on a case-by-case basis, or you can add another rating system here.

5. Click the Advanced tab. If you plan to use a ratings bureau or PICSRules file you obtain from the Internet, your ISP, or another source, add it here. Click OK when you're finished.

RSACi and other organizations provide content rating systems based on the PICS (Platform for Internet Content Selection) system developed by the World Wide Web Consortium, or W3C (www.w3.org/PICS/). They work using meta tags in the code of a Web page. The tags are usually generated by the rating organization after a site developer follows a brief rating procedure. Developers can then place the PICS meta tag in the header of their HTML code, where it is identified by IE's Content Advisor when you try to open the page. The tag identifies the types and levels of content contained in the site, and the Content Advisor allows or disallows the site based on the content settings you have chosen. If you want to screen Web sites using a system other than RSACi's, you must install an appropriate PICSRules file provided by the rating organization.

Of course, rating is voluntary. Developers set the rating levels in the meta tags based on their own evaluation of the site content, so you never really get a surefire guarantee that the tag accurately represents the site. RSACi periodically audits rated sites, and Web developers generally *try* to rate their sites as accurately as possible. It is a voluntary system, after all, and providing inaccurate ratings defeats the purpose of voluntary rating in the first place.

OTHER INTERNET SETTINGS

Several other settings deserve your attention. On the Content tab of the Internet Options dialog box, check the AutoComplete option to make sure it does not contain information that you are concerned about being compromised. AutoComplete makes it easier to fill in data fields on forms and URLs in the Address bar, but if other people use your user identity, they could end up seeing your personal information because of these settings.

One setting you probably should *not* enable is the Print Background Colors and Images option. If a Web page uses anything but a plain white background, a printed copy of it will waste a considerable amount of printer ink and probably be harder to read.

Review the Search settings on the Advanced tab. In earlier versions of Internet Explorer, if you wanted to visit a Web site with a fairly simple URL like www.quehelp.com, all you had to type was **quehelp** and press Enter. Internet Explorer would assume the missing www. and .com and fill it in for you. But now, if you type only **quehelp** in the Address bar, IE6 opens a Search window in the Explorer bar. In theory, this is supposed to make searching easier, but if you've been using IE for a while, you might find it annoying.

TIP FROM

Bob
& Brian

> If you type Ctrl+Enter after typing a word in the Address bar, IE6 will assume that it is preceded by www. and followed by .com to create a URL.

You cannot completely restore the previous function of "assuming" the missing bits of the URL, but you can modify the way in which this feature works by altering settings under the Advanced tab. The different search options will have the following results:

- **Display results and go to the most likely site**—The default setting, this opens the Explorer bar search window. In some cases, the "most likely" site will also appear in the main window, but it may or may not be what you were hoping for.

- **Do not search from the Address bar**—No search is made of any kind. Typing a single word in the Address bar will generally result in a Page not available error.

- **Just display the results in the main window**—No attempt is made to find a close match, nor is the Explorer bar opened. A search engine will open in the main window.

- **Just go to the most likely site**—In theory, this setting should work as in previous IE versions, but in practice it does not. It first looks for a match within the Microsoft Web domain and then tries to find a match at large. Select this option, and then type **quehelp** in the Address bar to see what we mean.

Under Security, check Empty Temporary Internet Files Folder When Browser Is Closed to discard cache files you don't want others to see. This setting can also be useful if disk space is limited, but you shouldn't use it if you want to be able to view pages in offline mode later.

EFFECTIVELY SEARCHING THE WEB

You've probably heard that you can find virtually anything on the Web, and if you've spent much time online, you're probably left wondering where it all is. Finding information on the World Wide Web is a fine art, but Internet Explorer 6 makes the process much simpler than it used to be.

The new Search Companion (formerly Search Assistant) in IE6 can be a great help. Click the Search button on the IE toolbar to open the Search Companion in the Explorer bar on the left side of Internet Explorer, as shown in Figure 9.12.

Figure 9.12
The Search Companion opens and allows you to search for several different kinds of information.

To begin searching, enter a word, phrase, or even a question in the search text box, and click the Search button. If you type a single word—such as `antiques`—the search probably will yield a list of results too big to be useful. Using more words, and more descriptive words, will narrow your search. You probably will get better results by searching for "`antique furniture`" or "`antique French furniture`" instead. Search results are displayed in the main IE window, 15 at a time. You can click directly on a search result to link to that site, or you can click Next to see the next 15 results.

An advantage to using the Search Companion instead of the browser to go to individual search engines is its capability to easily search through several search engines for a single topic.

Notice that the Search Companion gives you more options and suggestions for helping you find what you're looking for. You can click on the options to Automatically Send Your Search to Other Search Engines or to Highlight Words on the Results Page, which is handy to locate the exact word you're looking for or to do a search within a page to which you navigated. When you click the option to go to other search engines, you will see a short list from which to choose. Click on one of them to conduct your search at that site. If you would like to reset your preferences so that the Search Companion always visits your favorite site first, click Change Preferences on the main Search Companion screen, and then click Change Internet Search Behavior. Select a default search engine from the list, and click OK.

To start a new search, click on Start a New Search, near the bottom of the Search Companion pane. If you'd like to go back to a previous option in the Search Companion, click the Back button near the bottom of the Search Companion pane. Clicking the Back button in the main IE window, however, will take you to the previous Web page.

The Search Companion will search for files and other resources on the local computer or network as well. Click Search This Computer for Files in the Search Companion pane to select categories for the local search. To return to Web searching, click Search the Internet.

When you're finished searching, close the Search Companion to get it out of the way. To revisit a previous search, click on the History button on the IE toolbar, and go to the search folders. Depending on the search engines you used, you could find information in folders labeled search.msn, search.yahoo, and northernlight. Another way to find previous search results is by clicking the Search button at the top of the History pane and entering a word to search among the pages you've visited recently.

As helpful as the Search Companion can be, when you've become familiar with the Internet, you are likely to discover your own favorite search engine. You could set the Search Companion to use it, as explained above, or you could add it to your Links bar for easy access. Many search engines have advanced options that allow you to perform a more directed search.

Try these helpful search engines, directly from a Web page:

- www.hotbot.com (includes a drop-down list for more effective searching)
- www.google.com (has a Web Directory that works much like Yellow Pages do in a phone book, and "Google Groups," which searches newsgroups)
- www.northernlight.com (categorizes search results into folders for ease in refining your search)

MSN EXPLORER BROWSER—THE TOUCHY-FEELY ALTERNATIVE TO IE

In addition to Internet Explorer, Microsoft has included its new breed of Web browser in the XP package. Dubbed MSN Explorer, it is more personalized than IE6: To use it, you must have a Microsoft Passport or Hotmail address, which is covered in the next section.

Begin by opening MSN Explorer from the Start menu; click the butterfly icon. If you are online, a wizard will guide you through the procedure to set up MSN Explorer. You will need to do this only once: Signing on in the future will be simpler and can be automated.

After you are signed in to MSN Explorer, you will see a window similar to Figure 9.13. Notice that it is already customized somewhat, giving you a personal greeting tailored to your time zone. Information about the city in which you live (according to the ZIP code you gave when you signed up for Hotmail) is also prominent. The toolbar shows how many new Hotmail messages are waiting for you. Simply click the mail button to display your Web-based Hotmail inbox. If you have MSN Messenger buddies, a number next to the icon will show you how many of them are online. By clicking the icon, a drop-down list appears with Messenger options to connect you with your buddies.

The downside to all this customization is that you cannot choose your own home page in MSN Explorer. The home page is permanently set to http://www.msn.com, although you can personalize it by choosing the MSN features and news you want to see. In addition, if you are frustrated that a significant portion of the main MSN Explorer screen is used for tool and navigation bars, you can make a bit more room for viewing Web pages by minimizing the one on the left (see Figure 9.13).

Figure 9.13
MSN Explorer–a
new browser with
a new look.

Click here to change your settings

There are 32 new e-mail messages

Click here to sign off or switch users

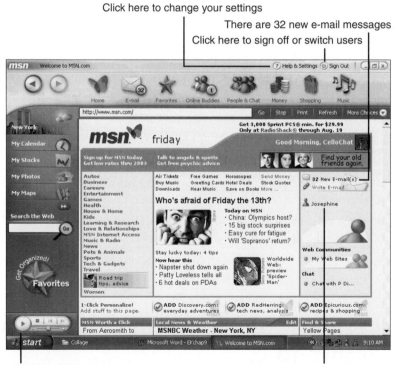

Integrated Media Player

There is one buddy online

Fans of Internet Explorer who open multiple IE windows while surfing the Web might be frustrated with the multiple-window format that MSN Explorer uses. The easiest way to open up additional windows is to type Ctrl+N within MSN Explorer. Or, you can click More Choices to the right of the address bar and select New Window from the drop-down list. Each new window that opens will be in a different format from the main MSN Explorer window—the My Stuff and main toolbars will not appear, leaving more room to view Web pages. It's all connected, more so than in other programs: Closing the main MSN Explorer window will close all its subwindows.

MSN Explorer does have its advantages: With personalized content and the possibilities of multiple users on a single computer, you can sign on and be sure to see all the information that you want to see. This includes e-mail, an integrated calendar, your MSN buddy list, favorite Web sites, stock quotes, and more. Because the information is Web-based, it is particularly handy when traveling. You can sign on to MSN Explorer from any computer and have all your personalized settings at your disposal. The information about your home town will make it easier to keep in touch, get local weather forecasts and news, and possibly alleviate homesickness.

To add a user, click Add New User from the opening screen of MSN Explorer. (You will need to sign out if you are already signed in.) Each User chooses a unique picture, which is used as an identifying icon, making it easier to see who's who.

Getting a Passport to Microsoft Country

Using MSN Explorer is only one reason to get a Microsoft Passport. These days, Microsoft requires the use of the Passport to use several of their sites and services, including MSN Calendar, MSN Messenger, MSN Communities, MSN Wallet, and more. If you already have a Hotmail or MSN e-mail address, you already have a Passport. If not, you can get a Microsoft Passport simply by signing up for a free Hotmail address at www.hotmail.com. Parents may be comforted to learn that a Kids Passport is also available, which can help parents protect the online identity of their children.

However, some might be understandably concerned that Passport is yet another way Microsoft is trying to invade our space and privacy to increase its profits. You can minimize the effect by entering the bare minimum of personal information when you sign up for a Passport. We were able to sign up using a single letter for a first name and last name. You also must enter a birth year and a ZIP code, but the Microsoft stormtroopers are not going to knock down your door in the middle of the night if you don't enter it truthfully. Personally, I'd avoid using Microsoft Wallet—I just don't want my credit card information floating around, regardless of how secure Microsoft says it is.

9

HEY, WHO'S AFRAID OF MICROSOFT PASSPORT?

The Microsoft Passport is a simple way of making it easy to sign on and purchase items and services from a growing number of sites affiliated with (read "owned by") Microsoft. Because people are so darned tired of having to remember tens of passwords (maybe even hundreds if you're a Web addict like me), the idea of using a simple MS Passport that stores your username, password, credit card, info, and so forth, and promises to effortlessly log you on at all kinds of Web sites and services might sound pretty alluring. I mean, I forget my passwords all the time, don't you? In fact, I keep a Notepad file on my computer of nothing but my passwords and other such stuff. If I don't have access to this file when I'm travelling and I want to, say, purchase a plane ticket, I'm out of luck, because I can't remember how to log in to Travelocity. (Of course, I keep this file in an encrypted file folder running under Windows XP, so it's not going to be easy for someone to liquidate my IRA. After the "substantial penalty for early withdrawal," it's not going to amount to that much anyway!)

But I'll suggest to you that Passport isn't all it's cracked up to be. In fact, it's a lot less. In fact, if you were concerned about cookies, you'll really be scared of Passport. As mentioned earlier, there are these things called cookies, which are small text files stored locally on your computer used to store a bit of info about you. When you go to a Web site that uses cookies, the Web server and your computer agree to exchange a little information, based on what you do on the Web site. Suppose you set up an account at Jack's Pizza with your name and address, or just that you like pepperoni pizza. Only the information you give to that site, along with possibly when you viewed the site, what you purchased, and what server you were coming in from, will be stored in the cookie. The idea is to make it easier for the site to recognize you the next time you visit. This is why you can go to some sites and the Web page says "Hi Karen!" It simply looks in your cookie directory on your hard disk (the cookie jar) and looks for the one it stored there. It opens the cookie, and sees that your name is Karen (because you typed that into its site the last time you visited), and then displays it. It also knows that last time, you bought an extra-large pepperoni pizza and a bag of fries. This time it automatically suggests an extra-large pepperoni pizza and fries. Neat. Convenient. It's like going into your favorite restaurant, and the waiter knows what you like.

The important point to remember is this: The agreement is that this information is transacted only between you and the Web site you're visiting. You have some privacy of information. Jack's Pizza's Web server is not talking to Jill's Soda Pop Company's Web server and then generating e-mail to you trying to sell you a soda to wash your pizza down with. (Okay, so maybe you want a soda with your pizza, so not a bad idea. But it can get out of hand. Keep reading.)

The idea of Passport is totally different. Although it contends otherwise, I don't think Microsoft is just trying to offer a better user experience on the Web by offering you a Passport to keep your passwords and stuff all tidy. With Passport, you sign on in one place, essentially Microsoft, even if you're clicking the Sign in Through Passport link on your favorite Web site. Really, you're signing in at Microsoft's Passport, which in turn links you back to the site you wanted. Then you start hopping around between sites. Although most of the Passport sites are now MS sites like Hotmail, they hope to entice other vendors to become Passport enabled. (With any luck on Microsoft's site, Jack and Jill will both fall down this slippery slope.) When that happens, the Web servers are linked to one another. Garnering lots of valuable customer information (such as your buying patterns, net worth, geographical location, age, sex, hobbies, medical history, and other such private info) can be more and more easily aggregated into one large database. Do you think that kind of information is valuable? You bet it is, and Microsoft knows it!

Let's consider some examples. Log in to Microsoft's Investor site (`http://www.investor.com`) and look in the upper-right corner. There's a logon button for Passport. Now, I'm not saying this is happening now, but it's possible. Suppose you're buying a house, refinancing your current one, or buying a new car through a Passport-affiliated site. It is possible using today's technology that the selling agent can determine your net worth by checking your portfolio on Investor.com and bargain harder with you. This kind of thing actually happened with Amazon, which raised its prices on DVDs for people who regularly bought DVDs from them. The practice was based only on cookies (and was stopped, by the way, after customers discovered what was going on).

If you want to read that story, here's a brief quote and URL: "Amazon customers on DVD Talk reported that certain DVDs had three different prices, depending on which so-called cookie a customer received from Amazon. `http://news.cnet.com/news/0-1007-200-2703210.html?tag=st.ne.1002.tgif.ni`.

But in essence, the idea of cookies being private is being circumnavigated by the Passport. What's particularly scary about all this is that there is one entry point (or gatekeeper) to all Passport sites—Microsoft. Over time, look to see more and more sites (and even IE itself) incorporating Passport. I think we should be wary of the aggregation of information about us, and allowing that information to be passed around freely between corporations. Even umpteen-page-long privacy statements can't protect you when a Web company goes bankrupt and the court orders sale of its valuable database with your buying patterns or other private information in it.

TROUBLESHOOTING

WEB PAGE ERRORS

An error occurs when I try to visit a specific Web page.

Try clicking the Refresh button to reload the page. If you still don't have any luck, remove the path information (that would be everything after the domain name) from the URL in the Address bar, and press Enter.

E-MAIL LINK TROUBLES

When I click an e-mail link, Outlook Express opens, but I prefer a different e-mail program.

Choose Tools, Internet Options to open the Internet Options dialog box, and change the default mail program on the Programs tab. You should be able to select any installed e-mail client (such as Outlook, Outlook Express, Eudora, Netscape Mail, and so on) here.

SOME GRAPHICS DON'T APPEAR

Some pictures on a page don't open.

If the Web page contains many pictures—say, a dozen or more—the graphics at the bottom of the page often do not open. Right-click the placeholder boxes for the images that didn't download, and choose Show Picture from the menu that appears.

INTERNET EXPLORER CRASHES ON CERTAIN WEB PAGES

A Web page freezes Internet Explorer.

Some Web pages contain poorly developed scripts or ones that needlessly strain your Internet connection. Scripts that try to detect the brand and version of browser you are using frequently cause this problem. Click the Stop button on the IE toolbar, and close and reopen the program if necessary. You can try disabling most scripting operations in the Security settings dialog box, but doing so might cause the offending Web page not to display properly.

WHAT HAPPENED TO THE WEB SITE?

I get a lot of Page not available *errors, even on major commercial sites.*

The most obvious suggestion is to check your Internet connection. Your server may also be having a temporary problem, or high Internet traffic is preventing your access. But another thing you should consider is whether the page you are trying to visit is on a secure Web server. Choose Tools, Internet Options, and click the Advanced tab to bring it to the front. Scroll down to the group of security settings, and see whether any of the encryption protocols supported by IE are disabled. If, for example, you are trying to visit a page that uses PCT encryption but Use PCT 1.0 is disabled, that page will not open.

TIPS FROM THE WINDOWS PROS: FINDING AND USING PDF DOCUMENTS ON THE WORLD WIDE WEB

Perhaps you saw the photograph on the cover of *Time* magazine a few years ago of Bill Gates in a forest, sitting atop a tree-sized stack of papers while holding a single compact disk in his hand, suggesting that digital information storage could save trees. It can, but it isn't easy.

The problem with digital documents is that, even with the best available technology, they are still not as easy to read as a paper book. Computer monitors put considerably more strain on your eyes, and even laptop PCs can be too bulky or clumsy to carry with you to a comfortable reading location. Furthermore, current digital storage technologies have a shorter shelf life than paper. Most CDs begin to deteriorate and lose their data after 10 to 20 years, but properly stored paper can last for centuries.

Still, digital documents have many advantages. First and foremost is cost: A single compact disc can contain hundreds of books yet cost less than $1 to manufacture. Printing the same amount of data on paper would cost hundreds, if not thousands, of dollars. Electronic books can be searched quickly, efficiently, and more thoroughly than printed ones. And, of course, digital documents are much easier to distribute.

One of the most popular methods for producing and distributing electronic books online is via PDF (Portable Document Format) files. PDF documents can be read using the Adobe Acrobat Reader, a free program offered by Adobe Systems, Inc. (www.adobe.com). PDF books can have the appearance and properties of a paper book but without the paper. They also have the advantage of being compatible across many platforms, with versions of the Reader software available for Windows, Macintosh, OS/2, and various incarnations of Unix. A PDF document link on a Web page is usually identified by the PDF icon.

PDF is used for a wide range of documents:

- It is used for government documents such as tax forms and educational materials.
- Technology companies such as Intel distribute technical documents and white papers in PDF.
- Private and commercial publishers produce and distribute electronic libraries of PDF books both on CD and the Web.
- News agencies produce PDF weather maps and other news material.

You can obtain the Acrobat Reader from many sources. If you own any other Adobe software—such as Photoshop or PhotoDeluxe—the reader is probably already installed on your computer. Look for a program group called Adobe or Adobe Acrobat in your Start menu. You can also download it for free from the Adobe Web site.

Even if you find Adobe Acrobat on your computer, it's best to download the latest version of the Acrobat Reader. Later versions integrate nicely with Internet Explorer to read PDF documents directly over the Web, and include the Find feature. When you're choosing the version to download, click the box next to "Include option for searching PDF files and accessibility support." The file size is just a little larger, but the additional features are well worth it. Some features are dependent on the writer of the PDF file. For example, "bookmarks" only work with PDF documents that have been indexed.

Acrobat Reader works as a plug-in for Internet Explorer. When you click a link for a PDF document, it opens Acrobat Reader within IE, but the tool bars and menu will change, as you can see in Figure 9.14. Just click the back button to bring you back to the Web page you were viewing.

Figure 9.14
PDF files can be viewed within a Web page.

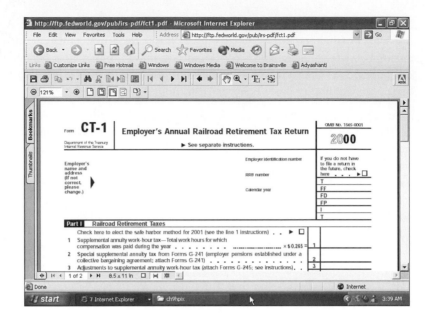

It is not uncommon to have problems with this whole procedure, although it does run more smoothly with the latest version. If you have trouble reading PDF documents over the Web, first save the PDF document to your hard drive. Instead of clicking the PDF link to open the file in a browser, right-click it and choose Save Target As from the shortcut menu that appears. After saving the document to the location you choose, open it manually using Acrobat Reader outside the IE session. Saving the PDF document in this manner has the added advantage of making the document easily available to you for future reference, and available offline.

CHAPTER **10**

SENDING E-MAIL WITH OUTLOOK EXPRESS

In this chapter

CHOOSING AN E-MAIL CLIENT

From the start, the Internet has been touted as a means for enhancing human communications, and among the many communication tools available in the online world, few have had the impact of electronic mail (e-mail).

To fully understand the nature of e-mail, you should keep in mind that, at its most basic level, it is simply a way for users to send messages to each other over a network. This network could be a local area network (LAN) run by your company using MS Exchange Server software. In this situation, the network server manages all message traffic. The server can also act as a gateway to other servers, allowing you to send mail beyond the local network. If you have an e-mail account with an Internet service provider (ISP) or other Internet-based service, the provider's server acts as your gateway to other mail servers across the Internet.

E-mail has been criticized by some as diminishing the art of written communication by making letter writing into a less formal exchange. You may or may not agree, but if your daily work requires you to use a computer, chances are you are also expected to use e-mail for much of your business communication.

Given that e-mail is here to stay, you must decide which e-mail client you plan to use for reading, composing, and sending messages. You have a number of options available to you, and which one you ultimately choose will depend not only on your personal preferences but also professional needs.

Windows XP includes an excellent e-mail client called Outlook Express 6 (OE6), which is actually a companion program to Internet Explorer 6 (IE6). It is a multifeatured program designed to appeal to a variety of e-mail users, but it isn't for everyone. OE6 can also function as a newsgroup client, making it a "one-stop" program if you routinely communicate via e-mail and use newsgroups.

→ To learn more about using Outlook Express to read newsgroups, **see** Chapter 11, "Reading Newsgroups with Outlook Express."

Outlook Express is relatively compact as Windows applications go. If you want an efficient program that can handle your e-mail needs without a lot of extra fluff, OE6 is a pretty good choice. However, it does lack a few features that you might want or need, so read the next couple of sections to find out if you should be using a different client.

> **NOTE**
>
> This discussion assumes you have a choice in e-mail clients. If you're using Windows XP in an office environment, check with your company's Information Systems (IS) manager to find out whether you must use one specific client.

WHAT IF YOU LIKE OUTLOOK 97, 98, OR 2000?

If you use Microsoft's Office suite, you're probably familiar with Outlook. Outlook is the primary communications tool included in the Office package, and many professional PC users like it. However, don't be misled by the name similarity between Outlook and Outlook

Express. OE6 is not a "lite" version of Outlook; these two applications are actually quite different. Aside from the name and a few basic interface similarities, the only thing they have in common is the capability to handle e-mail.

Outlook includes many features that Outlook Express does not, such as the following:

- A personal calendar
- An electronic journal
- Fax capability
- Compatibility with Microsoft Exchange Server

In addition, Outlook's system of managing personal contacts is far more advanced than that of Outlook Express. If the ability to integrate a heavy e-mail load with your personal scheduler on a daily basis is important to you, Outlook is the clear choice.

If you are already using Outlook and like the Calendar and Journal, stick with it. Furthermore, if your company's network or workgroup uses Exchange Server for mail services, Outlook is the only fully compatible upgrade to that system. Outlook is also Messaging Application Programming Interface (MAPI) capable, which means it can share mail with other MAPI-capable programs on your system. Outlook Express is not MAPI-capable. Because Outlook is bigger than OE, it requires more disk space, more RAM, and slightly more patience on the part of the user. If you find that you don't use Outlook for anything but e-mail, you might be better served by Outlook Express.

OTHER E-MAIL CLIENTS

Microsoft isn't the only company producing high-quality e-mail clients. One of the most popular alternatives is Eudora Pro from Qualcomm (www.eudora.com). Eudora offers an excellent package of mail management and filtering features, as well as compatibility with the latest Internet mail standards. Like Outlook Express, it is considerably more compact than Outlook, but it does not incorporate a newsgroup reader. Some unique Eudora features include the following:

- Voice messaging capability
- Integrated McAfee VirusScan protection for viruses propagated in mail attachments
- Built-in compression agent to shorten download times on slow dial-up connections

A free version of Eudora called Eudora Light is available, but it lacks so many of the features available in the identically priced Outlook Express that, at this point, it isn't worth your consideration.

Another popular e-mail client is Netscape Messenger, which comes as part of the Netscape Communicator package and is available as freeware. Messenger is comparable to Outlook Express in terms of mail management and newsgroup capability, and its interface is clean and uncluttered.

10

Numerous other e-mail clients exist, but we can only mention a few. You can find a more complete list of e-mail clients online in the Yahoo! directory. To find it, surf to

`http://dir.yahoo.com/Computers_and_Internet/Software/Internet/Electronic_Mail/`

OUTLOOK EXPRESS QUICK TOUR

Because covering the many different e-mail clients that are available would be beyond the scope of this book, we will assume that you have chosen Outlook Express 6. It comes free with Windows XP and will meet many of your electronic mail needs.

Outlook Express is installed during a clean installation of Windows XP, so it should be ready to open. You can launch it by clicking the Outlook Express icon near the top of the Start menu, next to "E-mail."

NOTE

In Windows, there is something called your "default e-mail program." This is the program used to generate e-mail from other programs. For example, it will be used if you click a link in IE to send an e-mail to someone. As installed, Windows XP assumes that OE is your default e-mail program. If you upgraded your previous version of Windows to XP, and had been using another e-mail program such as Outlook or Eudora for e-mail, that program will be your default e-mail program instead. Still, this does not mean it will necessarily appear at the top of the Start menu next to "E-mail." This setting should automatically show your default e-mail client. If not, you can simply change it by right-clicking the Start button, choosing Properties, clicking Start menu, then the Customize button, and then changing the E-mail drop-down list to the program of your choice. If you don't see the program you expected, then it's not installed into XP.

→ If you have not yet set up an Internet connection, you will need to do so. The New Connection Wizard will pop up to guide you through the process. Refer to Chapter 8, "Internet and TCP/IP Connection Options," for more information.

If you are online, and you already have an e-mail account set up, OE automatically checks for new mail when you open the program. If you don't yet have an account set up, when you open OE for the first time the (poorly-named) Internet Connection Wizard opens to help you set up a mail account. For now, click Cancel to close this screen and take a look at Outlook Express. I'll talk about setting up your account(s) in the next section, "Setting Up an E-mail Account." The OE window will appear as in Figure 10.1.

→ If you haven't yet set up an account, **see** "Setting Up an E-mail Account," **p. 334**.

If this is the first time you've opened OE6, notice that you have one unread mail message. Click the link to go to your Inbox and read the message, which is actually just a welcome letter from Microsoft.

TIP FROM

Bob & Brian

You'll probably find that you spend more time in the Inbox than in any other place in Outlook Express. For that reason, on the default OE startup screen, place a check mark next to When Outlook Express Starts, Go Directly to My Inbox.

Figure 10.1
The opening view of Outlook Express is not very useful. You can configure the program to open directly to the Inbox instead.

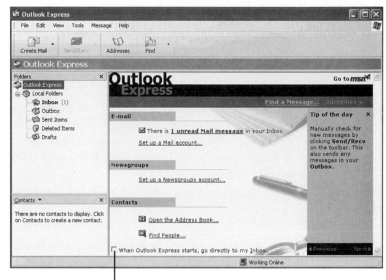

Place a checkmark here

When the Inbox opens, as shown in Figure 10.2, you'll see that the right side of the window is divided. The upper half is a list of messages in your Inbox, with unread messages shown in boldface. The lower half is the Preview Pane, which shows a preview of whichever message is selected above. You can use the scrollbar to read more of the message.

Figure 10.2
The Inbox includes a list of new messages and a Preview Pane that you can use to read them. The Folders list can serve as a directory to virtually all Outlook Express resources.

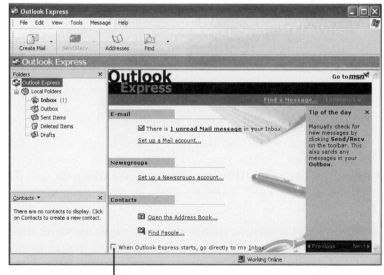

Place a checkmark here

10

The Preview Pane is useful, but some people don't like it. To open a message in a separate window, double-click it. If you always prefer to read mail in this manner, you can hide the Preview Pane to make more room to view the list of Inbox messages. To hide that pane or make a variety of other adjustments to the Outlook Express interface, try these steps:

1. Choose View, Layout.

2. In the Window Layout Properties dialog, select or deselect the screen elements you want to show or hide. We suggest you deselect the Folder Bar (duplicated with more clarity in the Folder List), as well as the Preview Pane if you don't plan to use it. You may also want to deselect the Contacts pane, since OE can be set to auto-complete an address that is in your Address Book.

3. Experiment with the settings, and click OK when you have OE6 looking the way you want it.

Take a look at the other screen elements. The Folders list shown in Figure 10.2 is handy because you can use it to quickly jump to any part of Outlook Express, including news-groups if you have an account set up.

 Does Outlook Express always seem to check for new mail at the wrong time? See "Making OE6 Less Automated" in the "Troubleshooting" section at the end of the chapter.

SETTING UP AN E-MAIL ACCOUNT

Before you can send or receive electronic mail, you need to have an e-mail account. There is a good possibility that your account has already been configured by your company's IS department or that some software from your ISP took care of it for you. Otherwise, you'll have to set it up yourself.

You can set up an account directly from Outlook Express by following the instructions listed here. These steps also work for setting up a second or third account or mail identity on the same machine.

1. In Outlook Express, choose Tools, Accounts.

2. In the Internet Accounts dialog (see Figure 10.3), click the Mail tab to bring it to the front.

3. Click Add, Mail.

4. The Internet Connection Wizard opens to a dialog asking for your display name. This is the name that other people will see when you send them mail, so choose carefully. Click Next after you've entered a name.

5. The next wizard box asks for your e-mail account address, which should have been provided by your company or ISP. Click Next after you've entered the address.

6. You must enter the types and names of your e-mail servers in the next dialog, which is shown in Figure 10.4. Again, this information is provided by your company or ISP. See the next section for an explanation of the different server types.

Figure 10.3
You can review your
e-mail accounts here
or add a new one.

Click the Mail tab

Click here to add an account

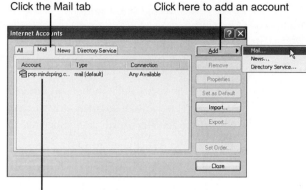

Only one e-mail account has been configured

Figure 10.4
You can enter the
types and names of
your e-mail servers
here.

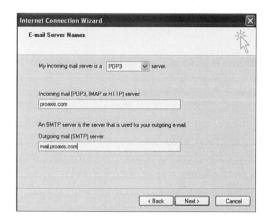

7. The next dialog asks for your login name and password. Do not check the option Remember Password if other people have access to your computer. Check the SPA (Secure Password Authentication) option if required by your e-mail provider; then click Next. Click Finish in the final dialog. Your new account should now be listed in the Internet Accounts dialog.

NOTE

Secure Password Authentication (SPA) is used by some e-mail services to prevent unauthorized users from getting or sending your e-mail. When you attempt to receive your mail in OE, a screen will pop up asking for you to enter a username and password. Both Outlook Express and MS Outlook have this feature. Most e-mail (POP) servers do not use this feature, so you should probably leave it turned off.

The only other piece of information that Outlook Express needs is which network or dial-up connection it should use when sending and receiving mail. You probably don't need to select this connection because OE6 automatically assigns your default connection to all mail accounts.

→ If you don't have a connection set up, **see** "Configuring Your Internet Connection," **p. 275**.

 If you routinely encounter server errors when sending or receiving mail, see "Missing Mail Servers" in the "Troubleshooting" section at the end of the chapter.

WHAT ARE POP, IMAP, SMTP, AND HTTP?

You've probably noticed the veritable alphabet soup of acronyms that exist for the many different kinds of e-mail servers. Unlike so many other cryptic terms thrown around in the PC world, these acronyms are actually worth remembering.

First, a basic understanding of how e-mail flows across networks (including the Internet) is important. Usually, when you send a message, Outlook Express transfers it to a *Simple Mail Transfer Protocol (SMTP)* server. An SMTP server is controlled by the sender, meaning that it waits for you to push mail through it. After you send the message to your SMTP server using OE6's Send/Recv or Send All command, no other interaction is required to deliver the message to its final destination.

NOTE

The Send command must be used in the main program, not just in an individual e-mail. Otherwise, the mail you've written will simply pile up in your Outbox. You can click on the Outbox in the Folder list to see if there are messages waiting to be sent. If so, click the Send/Recv button on the toolbar.

Mail sent to your computer doesn't just go from the sender to your PC. Since your PC is likely not always online, and certainly not always ready to receive e-mail, messages must go to an interim server (usually maintained through your Internet service provider). To receive mail, you probably use either a *Post Office Protocol (POP)* or *Internet Message Access Protocol (IMAP)* server. POP and IMAP differ in that POP servers forward all messages directly to your local machine, whereas IMAP servers maintain the messages on the server until you delete them. When you check for mail on an IMAP server, a list of message headers is downloaded, but the actual message bodies stay on the server (like newsgroup messages, as explained in the next chapter). An IMAP server comes in handy if you travel a lot and want to be able to check messages on the road with your laptop or PDA, but don't want to remove them from the server until you can download the mail to a more permanent location on your home desktop.

Another type of e-mail server is a *Hypertext Transfer Protocol (HTTP)* server, such as those offered by Yahoo!, Hotmail, and others. An HTTP mail account is useful for those who wish to travel light because it is not necessary to take a computer or software with you. You can access your HTTP account using a Web browser on any computer with access to the Internet, and generally the only information you will need to provide is your login name and password. Outlook Express can also be used to read and send mail using an HTTP account.

 Having trouble with a stubborn account password dialog? See "Password Trouble" in the "Troubleshooting" section at the end of the chapter.

SETTING UP AN HTTP MAIL ACCOUNT

HTTP mail accounts have their advantages. They are free, and it is possible to access these accounts on the road from any computer with Internet access. These accounts have limits to the server space they'll allow you to use for free (6MB on Yahoo!, 2MB on Hotmail), so don't use your HTTP e-mail address for receiving large quantities of mail or file attachments, and delete old mail regularly. It is possible to purchase more server space from these companies, but they still limit the size of attachments allowed. When your mailbox fills up, messages will be bounced back to the sender.

There are many free e-mail providers. Two of the most popular are at www.yahoo.com and www.hotmail.com. To find others, do an online search for "free e-mail," and you'll see a seemingly limitless list. Alternatively, go to this site that lists the top five free e-mail providers:

http://www.iopus.com/guides/bestpopsmtp.htm

Be prepared to provide information such as your name and geographic location. You will also be asked for your age, but testing has shown that you can pretty much enter anything you want into that field.

When your new account is configured, you can use it directly from the Web or add it to OE as described in the previous section, "Setting Up an E-mail Account." You enter the HTTP server address in the same location where you would otherwise enter the POP or IMAP server address. In terms of downloading and deleting messages, HTTP mail accounts work in a similar manner to IMAP accounts.

TIP FROM

Bob & Brian

> You can always check your HTTP account from another computer by visiting its Web site and entering your username and password. If you are checking mail when you are not at your own computer, it is a good idea to leave the messages you receive on the server so that they will still be available for download later using OE6.

One point to keep in mind about most free HTTP mail accounts is that although they can be helpful when you're traveling, you must use your account periodically to keep it active. For example, you need to log on to your Hotmail account at least once during the first 30 days of membership and once every 90 days beyond that.

READING AND PROCESSING INCOMING MESSAGES

After you have an account set up, you are ready to begin downloading and reading mail. To get started, open Outlook Express, and go to the Inbox. By default, Outlook Express automatically checks for new mail when it first opens. If your installation is configured otherwise, click the Send/Recv button on the toolbar. As your mail is coming in, a dialog box appears indicating which account is being checked, and shows the progress of the sending and receiving. It will also tell you how many messages are being transferred. New messages will then appear in your inbox, as shown in Figure 10.5.

Figure 10.5
The Inbox has seven new messages.

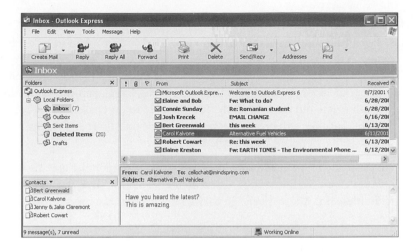

TIP FROM

Bob & Brian

If you receive a message from someone you plan to communicate with regularly, right-click his or her name in the message header, and choose Add Sender to Address Book. By doing so, you add the person to your contacts list so that sending him or her mail in the future will be easier.

When you reply to a message, you need to be wary of a few things. First, note that if the incoming message was sent to a group of people, clicking the Reply button will send your message to the single person who sent it to you; clicking Reply All will send your message to the entire list of people who received the original message. Although this can be a helpful tool when communicating with a group of people, it could get you in trouble if you think you are writing to a specific person and accidentally click the Reply All button. Before you send any message, make sure the correct person or persons are listed in the To: and Cc: fields. Anyone listed in those two fields will receive a copy of the message as well as a list of the other recipients and their e-mail addresses, so make sure you aren't airing your dirty laundry any more publicly than you intended. The section "Creating and Sending New Mail" discusses addressing messages more thoroughly.

The rest of the reply process is fairly straightforward. You just type in your own text and click Send on the toolbar when you are ready to deliver the message. By default, Outlook Express automatically places the text of the original message in the reply.

When you're composing your reply, you should keep in mind these important points:

■ Consider editing the quoted text in the reply by cutting it down to the text you actually intend to respond to. Most people don't appreciate reading four pages of quoted text followed at long last by "Me too."

■ Include enough of the original text to help the recipient understand exactly what you are replying to. If the recipient doesn't read your reply for several days, he or she might not remember what his or her original statements were.

- Breaking up quoted text with your own inserted comments is usually acceptable, but make sure it is obvious which words are yours. Figure 10.6 illustrates this reply technique.

Figure 10.6
Quoted text and reply text are interspersed throughout the message, but there is little doubt as to who wrote what.

Text of original message

Your reply

DELETING MESSAGES

How and when messages are deleted depends on what kind of mail server you use. If you receive mail from a POP server, deleted messages remain in the OE6 Deleted Items folder indefinitely, similar to "deleted" files in the Windows Recycle Bin.

You can permanently delete them by right-clicking the Deleted Items folder and choosing Empty 'Deleted Items' Folder from the shortcut menu that appears. If you have an IMAP mail server, the Deleted Items folder is emptied automatically when you log off the mail server.

You can change the way Outlook Express handles items in the Deleted Items folder. To do so, choose Tools, Options, and select the Maintenance tab to customize when and how mail messages are deleted.

CREATING AND SENDING NEW MAIL

The process of creating and sending new mail is almost as easy as receiving it. To open a New Message composition window, click the Create Mail button on the OE6 toolbar.

NOTE

You might find it helpful to have OE spell-check your e-mail before sending it. OE does have a spelling checker, but it is only available if you also have Microsoft Word, Excel, or PowerPoint installed on your computer. Once enabled, you can click the Spelling icon in the message window when composing a message. Adjust your spelling options by going to Tools, Accounts, and clicking on the Spelling tab.

Addressing messages properly is extremely important. A single misplaced character, or an extra one, in an e-mail address can send the message to the wrong person or to no one at all. A typical e-mail address looks like this:

bob@mcp.com

TIP FROM

Some mail servers are case sensitive. If you're not sure, just type the whole address in lowercase letters.

Notice that OE6 has two address fields that appear by default, To: and Cc:. Cc: is short for Carbon Copy or, these days when that messy blue paper is nearly extinct, Courtesy Copy. The address field is the only required field when sending e-mail; all the others, including the subject and even the message body, can be blank. The To: field usually contains the e-mail address of the primary recipient, although it can contain more than one address, as shown in Figure 10.7. You separate multiple addresses with a semicolon (;).

To send e-mail to several people without allowing its recipients to see the names or e-mail addresses of others who also received it, enter addresses in the Bcc: field (Blind Carbon/Courtesy Copy). In an e-mail window, choose View and select Show All Headers. The Bcc: field will now appear in the e-mail window.

Figure 10.7
A new message with an attachment has been addressed to several people.

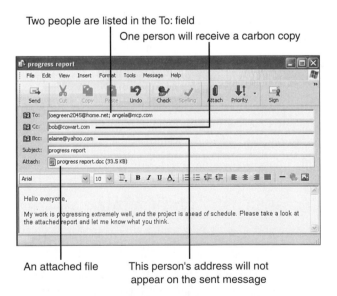

Two people are listed in the To: field
One person will receive a carbon copy

An attached file
This person's address will not appear on the sent message

When you are finished composing the message, just click Send on the toolbar. If you do not want your message sent right away, choose File, Send Later. The message is then sent to the Outbox folder and will be sent to your mail server the next time the Send command is given.

If you don't like the name that is being assigned to your outgoing mail, see "Identity Crisis" in the "Troubleshooting" section at the end of the chapter.

SENDING AND RECEIVING ATTACHMENTS

Of the many features that make e-mail a versatile method for communication, perhaps the most useful is the capability to send files along with an e-mail message. You can attach any electronic file stored on disk to an e-mail message in Outlook Express and then send it to someone else.

NOTE

Some e-mail accounts do not allow you to send or receive file attachments with messages. Others, particularly HTTP accounts, limit the number and size of attachments allowed. Check with your account provider to find out whether you have this capability. Also, make sure that the recipient has the capability to receive attachments.

Attaching a file to an outgoing message is easy. In the message composition window, click the Attach button on the toolbar, and locate the file you want to send in the Insert Attachment dialog. After you have selected the file, click Attach. The file attachment should appe   1 the header information, as shown earlier in Figure 10.7.

10

Bef   you send any attached files, consider the bandwidth it will require. Even if you have a very fast network or Internet connection, if the recipient connects to the Internet via a dial-up modem, downloading the attachment could take a long time. In general, you should avoid sending any attachments that are larger than one or two megabytes unless you are sure the recipient can handle them or knows in advance that they're about to receive some rather large files. It's best to ask your recipient first. Many mail servers (especially Web-based accounts) limit the total amount of space a person can use, and many also set a limit to the size of attachments allowed (often capping the attachment size at 1MB).

One more thing: If you or the recipient uses a 56Kbps or slower Internet connection, it is usually a good idea to compress large attachments before you send them. Simply right-click on the document(s) you wish to send, choose Send To, and then Compressed (zipped) Folder. Attach the compressed version to your e-mail.

To open an attachment in a message you receive, right-click the attachment (listed in the header) and choose Save As to save it to disk, or simply open it. If the attachment is a picture file, it often appears in the body of the message as well.

GUARDING YOURSELF AGAINST E-MAIL VIRUSES

Computer viruses often propagate themselves through e-mail attachments. Hackers seem to get their jollies out of slowing down the Internet or bringing corporate business to a crawl. One way to do this seems to be targeting the most popular e-mail programs, such as Outlook and Outlook Express. As a result, the bulk of e-mail–borne contagion exists in the form of attachments whose payloads sneak through weaknesses in those two programs. Personally, I think that both these programs are excellent e-mail clients, so I don't suggest changing your e-mail program just to avoid the onslaughts of malicious Internet hackers.

As you might suspect, Microsoft doesn't want to lose customers either, so it makes a point of looking for viruses and posting critical updates to its site for easy download. A good approach is to run a Windows System Update regularly.

In addition, security has been improved in OE6 to specifically combat this problem. By going to Tools, Options and clicking the Security tab, you'll notice the addition of Virus Protection since the previous version of OE. By default, OE6 will warn you if another program attempts to send a message to contacts in your Address Book. As you might have heard, this is a common way for viruses to spread. I recommend that you keep this option selected.

OE also has an option that deals with attachments. However, if you click the box next to Do Not Allow Attachments to Be Saved or Opened That Could Potentially Be a Virus, your ability to access any attachment to e-mail in OE will be quite limited. If you're diligent about it, a better way of dealing with the possibility of attachment-borne viruses is to carefully look over your incoming e-mail before opening any attachment by following the tips below. I've found that when enabling the automatic feature in OE6, even the most innocuous attachments are prevented from opening. (You can regain access to these attachments simply by returning to the Security dialog box and deselecting this option.)

Yet another option is to download and use one of many available anti-virus programs. http://www.mcafee.com is a reliable source, and its Web site is another good place to check for the latest discovered viruses and how to protect your computer from them.

Contrary to popular belief, simply downloading an infected attachment virtually never harms your computer. With few exceptions, it is only if you open an attached executable file that there could be dire consequences. If possible, save the file attachment on a separate disk, and then scan it with antivirus software.

Be especially wary of

- Attachments you weren't expecting (even from people you know). If in doubt, write back to the sender and ask if they intended to send you the attachment. Their computer may have a virus they are unaware of. Ask if the attachment is safe, and if they've run it on their computer.

- Executable attachments (filenames ending in .exe, .vbs, or .js). Be aware that sometimes filenames are misleading on purpose. For example, you might see an attachment such as party.jpg.vbs. This is not a picture. The final extension is the one that counts.

- E-mails with cryptic or odd subjects and messages, such as "I Luv U," "Here's that document you requested," or "CHECK THIS OUT!!!"

- Anything that comes from a source you are unfamiliar with.

SETTING UP A SIGNATURE

If you use e-mail for much of your personal and business communication, you may like to "sign" outgoing messages with an electronic signature file. These signatures frequently include additional information about you, such as an address, title, phone number, company name, Web URL, or a witty quote. Outlook Express makes it easy to set up a standard signature that will be included in every message you compose. You can configure your own signature by following these steps:

1. Choose Tools, Options. Click the Signatures tab to bring it to the front.

2. Click New to begin typing a new signature. Type your signature information as shown in Figure 10.8.

3. If you have multiple e-mail accounts, click Advanced and select the account or accounts you want this signature to be used with.

4. Place a check mark next to Add Signatures to All Outgoing Messages to enable this feature. Notice that, by default, your signatures will not be added to replies and forwards. Click OK when you're finished.

TIP FROM

Bob
& Brian

> Consider creating several signatures, with varying levels of personal information. You can then choose a signature in the message window by selecting Insert, Signature.

10

Figure 10.8
You can create a standard signature for your outgoing messages here.

REQUESTING RECEIPTS

It is possible for OE to send a request along with e-mail you send, asking the recipient to simply click a box to notify you that your e-mail message has been read. This is called a "read receipt." When typing a message, go to Tools, Request Read Receipt. If there is not already a check mark next to it, click on Request Read Receipt.

Note that this is a request only: The recipient has the option of refusing to send the receipt. Still, it is a helpful tool: If you don't get a receipt, you can follow-up with another e-mail or a phone call.

If you intend to request a read receipt every time you send e-mail, you can change your settings to make it simple. In OE, go to Tools, Options, and click on the Receipts tab. Click the box at the top of the window that says "Request a read receipt for all sent messages." Consider this carefully; your Inbox could get filled quickly with read receipts, and the significance of receipts could be diluted (and recipients irritated) if a request is attached even to the messages of minor importance that you send. In addition, this window allows you to select your preference for returning read receipts. If you find the pop-up windows to be annoying, choose an option to "never" or "always" send a receipt when requested.

FORMATTING OPTIONS FOR MAIL

A simple way to enrich e-mail is to apply message formatting using HTML code, the same type of code used to construct Web pages. HTML is the default format for new messages you create in OE6, although replies are typically formatted in whatever manner they were originally sent to you.

Applying special formatting to HTML messages is easy. Outlook Express provides a formatting toolbar similar to what you would see in a word processing program, where you can choose such formatting options as bold, italic, and so on. You also can give HTML messages graphic backgrounds by choosing one of several varieties of "stationery" provided by OE6. To do this, choose Format, Apply Stationery. You can even generate e-mail that looks much like a Web page, complete with pictures (and, heaven forbid, banner ads), as well as links.

→ **See** the "Tips from the Windows Pros" section at the end of this chapter for details on how to create Web-page–like HTML e-mail.

CAUTION

Although you don't have to worry about accidentally generating malicious HTML-formatted e-mail, you might want to know that HTML e-mail can carry scripts that might damage your system, or invade your privacy. Some viruses (such as the infamous bubbleboy virus) have used HTML mail to propagate. Also, HTML e-mails can be used to track how people view their e-mail. For example, some e-mails have links to pictures in them that automatically download from the Internet when you click on the message. These links can be used by advertisers (if they care to notice) to track when you've opened an e-mail. They can also track how often you read that e-mail. Some people consider this a breach of privacy.

One problem with HTML messages is that not all modern e-mail clients can view them properly. Messages formatted in this manner may appear with a huge quantity of gibberish at the end of the message if the recipient doesn't have an HTML-compatible client. Likewise, mailing lists usually cannot handle HTML formatting in messages that are sent to them.

There are two types of plain text message formatting available. Until a few years ago, all e-mail was formatted as simple text, with no special characters or fancy formatting. These early e-mails utilized a message format called *uuencode*, short for Unix-to-Unix encode. You don't need to be running UNIX to read uuencoded messages, though; virtually any e-mail client you are likely to encounter—including OE6—can read and send messages in this format.

To address the shortcomings of ASCII-based uuencode e-mail, the *Multipurpose Internet Mail Extensions (MIME)* specification was developed. MIME, which is supported by most modern e-mail clients, allows the use of graphics, file attachments, and some special non-ASCII characters in e-mail messages.

Most mailing lists and users in general can handle MIME messages. To change the default sending formats for outgoing messages, open the Options dialog in OE6. On the Send tab, choose HTML or Plain Text. If you choose Plain Text, your default message format will actually be MIME. If you want to change to uuencode, click the Plain Text Settings button, and choose the appropriate options in the dialog that appears.

TIP FROM

> If you happen to know that your recipient is using some truly ancient technology to download and read e-mail, such as Telnet and a text reader, send messages to that person uuencoded.

10

Is the formatting of your outgoing messages creating discontent among your recipients? See "Recipients Don't Like My Mail Formatting" in the "Troubleshooting" section at the end of the chapter.

SENDING AND RECEIVING SECURE MESSAGES

E-mail has fast become an essential method of communication, but for some uses, it might not be secure enough. Hiding or falsifying one's identity on the Internet is easy enough that some unscrupulous person could be masquerading as you or one of your associates. To combat this problem, several companies offer *digital IDs* that help verify the identity of the sender.

Another threat to the privacy of e-mail is the possibility that messages will be intercepted and read by others (think digital wiretapping). Sending *encrypted* e-mail will prevent your mail from being read by anyone on the way to your intended recipient.

A digital ID is made up of a private key, a public key, and a digital signature. When you digitally sign a message, two of these three things are added to your e-mail: a public key and your digital signature. This is called a *certificate*. The private key stays with you.

When you send secure mail, recipients use your digital signature to verify your identity. They use your public key to send encrypted e-mail to you. When you receive the encrypted e-mail, you use your private key to decrypt the message.

The mechanics of how this works are elaborate and a topic that can entertain the most advanced cryptologists and software engineers. What's important is that in order to send or receive secure mail, you will need to have a digital ID. To encrypt messages you send, your Address Book must contain a digital ID for each recipient.

You can obtain a digital ID for yourself by following these steps:

1. In OE, choose Tools, Options.

2. On the Security tab, click Get Digital ID, as shown in Figure 10.9. Choosing this option will launch your browser and automatically go to a Microsoft Web page that contains links to various certification authorities. Among those listed are VeriSign, GlobalSign, and Thawte Certification.

3. Select one of these companies and go to its Web site. Follow the instructions provided there to obtain and install a digital ID.

Figure 10.9
Get a Digital ID, and adjust your security preferences, on the Security tab of the Options dialog box.

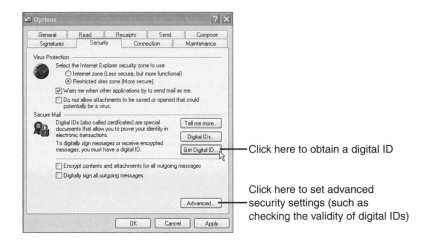

Click here to obtain a digital ID

Click here to set advanced security settings (such as checking the validity of digital IDs)

When you have a digital ID, it is simple to add it to a message. To do so

1. Open OE and click Create Mail.

2. In the new mail window, go to Tools and click Digitally Sign.

3. Compose and send your message.

Outlook Express will automatically add your digital ID to your e-mail account when you send your first digitally signed message, by searching your computer for a valid digital ID which matches the e-mail address from which you are sending. If more than one valid digital ID is found, you must choose which ID to add to that e-mail account. Also note that if you have more than one e-mail account, you will need to have a different digital ID for each account from which you want to send secure e-mail.

NOTE

When sending secure e-mail, your reply address must match the account from which you send digitally signed e-mail. If you have set up a different reply address (on the General tab of your account properties dialog box), message recipients won't be able to use your ID to reply with encrypted e-mail.

When others send digitally signed e-mail to you, messages are marked with a red seal in the message header. Outlook Express shows you an explanatory message about digital signatures before displaying the message. If you are online, you can check the validity of the digital ID of the sending party. To do this, choose Tools, Options, Security tab, Advanced, Check for revoked Digital IDs, Only when online.

USING THE ADDRESS BOOK

You don't have to communicate via e-mail for very long before you mistype someone's address. Suddenly, spelling has become more important than ever before. Your local mail carrier can direct your parcel to you when the label is misspelled, tattered, and torn, but e-mail with a misspelled address just gets bounced back to you. E-mail addresses can also be cryptic and long, and some are even case sensitive. The Address Book feature in Outlook Express is a big help with all of this.

Before going through the inner workings of the Address Book, keep in mind that this single feature goes by two different names within OE6. Sometimes it is called the Address Book, and other times it is called the Contacts list.

You can open the Address Book in its own window by choosing Tools, Address Book, or by clicking the Address Book icon in the toolbar.

 If you have too many unwanted entries in your Address Book, see "Thinning Your Contacts List" in the "Troubleshooting" section at the end of the chapter.

ADDING, EDITING, AND REMOVING ENTRIES

By default, OE adds an entry to your address book whenever you reply to an e-mail you've received. This is an easy way to fatten up your address book quickly. Before your Address Book grows to an unmanageable size, you may want to turn off that feature (see the Troubleshooting notes at the end of this chapter). If you do this, you'll need to know how to add contacts in other ways. A fool-proof way to add someone to your Address Book is by doing the following:

1. Open a message sent to you by someone you want to add to the Address Book.

2. Right-click the individual's name or e-mail address in the message header, and choose Add to Address Book.

3. A Properties sheet opens for the entry, but don't close it yet. Click the Name tab to bring it to the front, as shown in Figure 10.10. If the person uses a nickname, you might need to edit the name entries on this tab so that they are displayed correctly in your Contacts list. Pay special attention to the Display field.

4. Review all the other tabs in the Properties sheet, and enter any other information about this person you feel appropriate. Click OK when you're finished.

You also can add someone to your address book the old-fashioned way—that is, manually from a business card or other source. In Outlook Express, click on the Addresses icon. This will open up the Address Book. Click on the New icon, and select New Contact. The Properties window, described previously, will open for you to enter information.

Figure 10.10
Go through all the tabs on the Properties sheet, and enter any information about this contact you feel appropriate.

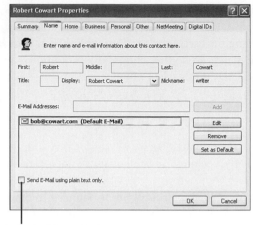

Click here to indicate this contact
prefers to receive plain text messages

To edit a contact later, click on the Addresses icon to open the Address Book. Select the contact that you wish to edit by double-clicking that person's name. The Properties window will now open with a summary of that person's contact information. To change or add information, you need to click on one of the other tabs along the top of the window—the information can not be changed on the Summary tab.

You might find duplicate listings or unwanted contacts in your Address Book. Deleting a contact is simple: Just highlight the entry and click Delete. Be certain you've selected the correct contact, since this action can not be undone.

CREATING DISTRIBUTION LISTS

Sending a single e-mail message to several people is not unusual. However, entering multiple addresses can get tiresome, especially if you frequently send messages to the same group of people.

To simplify this task, you can create *distribution lists* in the OE6 Address Book. You can group many people into a single list, and when you want to send a message to the group, you simply choose the distribution listing from your Address Book. Distribution lists can be created for co-workers, customers, friends and family, or any other group you communicate with. To create a list, just follow these steps:

1. Open the Address Book.
2. Click New, and select New Group from the menu that appears.
3. On the Group tab of the Properties dialog that opens, type a descriptive name. For example, consider using the name of your department at work.
4. Click Select Members. In the Select Group Members dialog, pick a name from your Address Book, and click Select. Repeat until you have selected all the names you want in the distribution list.

5. Click OK when you are finished selecting names from the Address Book. As you can see in Figure 10.11, each member is listed under Group Members. Check the Group Details tab to see whether you should enter any information there, and click OK when you're finished.

Figure 10.11
A distribution list has been created for sending group e-mails.

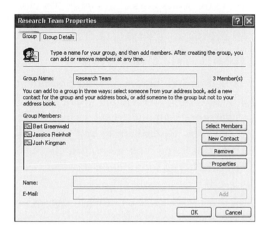

A listing for the group then appears in your Address Book. When you are composing e-mail for the group, simply select the group name from your Address Book to automatically send the message to all group members. To delete a group, highlight the group name and click Delete. Note that this deletes the group, but not the group's members, from your Address Book.

FINDING PEOPLE WHO AREN'T IN YOUR ADDRESS BOOK

A number of people-search directories exist on the Internet to help you locate individuals. Outlook Express does a good job of integrating these search engines into the program, making it easy for you to search for people and add them to your Contacts list.

TIP FROM

Bob & Brian

No matter how obscure a name may seem, you would be amazed at how many other people in the world share it. When you locate someone in an online directory, first send that person an e-mail inquiry to confirm that he or she is indeed the person you are seeking *before* you share any sensitive information with him or her. Unfortunately, you'll also find that the information given by some online directories is frustratingly out of date. (So much for the speed of the Internet.) If you suspect the information is not current, try a different search engine.

To find people who aren't in your Address Book, follow these steps:

1. Open the Address Book. Click Find People on the Address Book toolbar.

2. In the Find People dialog, click the drop-down arrow next to Look in, and select a directory service. No single directory is ideal, so you might need to try searching through several directories before you find the person you are looking for.

3. Click Find Now. A search of the directory service you selected in step 2 is conducted, and results are displayed. If the person is not found, a dialog tells you so. Try another directory or a different spelling for the name.

4. After you have located the person you are looking for, select his or her listing, and click Add to Address Book. Click Close when you are finished searching.

HANDLING UNIQUE MAIL SITUATIONS

Outlook Express 6 has features that go well beyond the most common e-mail-related tasks of reading and composing mail, addressing and sending messages, or using the Address Book. For example, you may have more than one e-mail account. You can set preferences for these accounts, choose to keep them separate, or to bring them all into the same OE Inbox. You'll also learn ways to organize and filter your mail, check your mail while traveling, and how to make an alternate backup location for the mail you want to save and protect. In this section, we'll describe these more advanced situations and capabilities. Even if you don't intend to use these features, skim through the sections just so you know what features are available. Once you know what features are built in, you might want to come back and try them out later.

MODIFYING AN EXISTING E-MAIL ACCOUNT

After setting up an e-mail account or two, you may find that you'd like to change a few things, such as the server name, password, connection preference, and more. To do this, go to Tools, Accounts, click the mail tab, and click Properties. Poke around in here to see all the characteristics that you can change.

Under the General tab, you can change how your name will appear on outgoing mail. Whatever you enter in the Name box will be what the recipient sees. Think about whether you'd like your e-mail to be listed in recipients' inboxes in a casual or formal way, or even with your business name instead. (In other words, enter "Bob Cowart" or "Mr. Robert Cowart" or "Bob's Car Care.")

You might want to send mail from one e-mail address, but have replies go to a different e-mail address (when recipients click Reply.) To do this, enter the outgoing e-mail address in the E-mail address box, and the alternate e-mail address in the Reply address box.

Some e-mail accounts (University accounts, for example) require you to connect to the Internet using a specific connection in order to access your e-mail. If you need to change the connection used for an account, open the Internet Accounts dialog and follow these steps:

1. Click the Mail tab to bring it to the front, and select the account you want to change. Click the Properties button on the right side of the dialog.

2. Click the Connection tab. If you need to use a specific connection, place a check mark next to Always Connect to This Account Using, and select a connection from the drop-down menu.

3. Click OK and Close to exit all the open dialogs.

HANDLING MULTIPLE E-MAIL ACCOUNTS FOR THE SAME USER

Increasingly, individuals have more than one e-mail account. Outlook Express can be configured to handle multiple e-mail accounts, even if they are on separate servers. For example, I have four e-mail accounts, one from each of my Internet service providers. I can pull all my e-mail into one inbox by setting up the various accounts under a single user identity. When I click on Send/Receive Mail on the OE toolbar, OE goes out and pulls in all the new mail from all four accounts automatically. It's just that simple. How do you set up your system so it can do this? Read on.

Each e-mail account needs to be set up and configured in Outlook Express as explained earlier in this chapter. Simply set up an account for each e-mail address and server you have, using the information provided by each ISP (or e-mail account, if a single ISP has given you multiple e-mail accounts).

Normally, OE6 checks all accounts when looking for new mail, even if they use different servers. Sending and receiving e-mail from different accounts will normally happen automatically and without impediments. You connect to the Internet (whether by dialup service or over your LAN or cable/DSL modem), click Send/Receive, and OE will try to access each server one after another, using the currently active Internet connection. However, there are a couple instances where this gets more complicated:

- If you have specified that an account must use a specific connection, you will see a dialog box when you try to use that account on another connection. Here, you must decide whether you want to switch connections or try to locate the server on the current connection.

- Some services require that you be actually dialed in to their Internet connection service before you can send e-mail through their SMTP (mail sending) service. This is to prevent "spoofing" or "spamming" by non-paying users who jam up SMTP servers sending their unwelcome advertisements. It's sort of like hijacking the US Postal Service to send free bulk mail. Such services check to see that you are connected to the Internet through them, and logged in. Once you are, you can send mail through that account. Sometimes such services will let you *receive* mail regardless of how you are connected to the Net, because that doesn't infringe on their services. It is typically only the *sending* that is restricted. If a unique connection is needed for a given e-mail account, then you must specify this in the account's properties dialogs. Click on the Connection tab and choose the Always Connect to This Account Using option. Then, choose which connection the account in question should use.

10

You can set up an unlimited number of e-mail accounts in OE6. You can even set up multiple accounts using the same e-mail address and server information. Each account can serve as a separate identity for you.

When you compose a new mail message, it is automatically addressed for your default mail account. The default account can be set in the Internet Accounts dialog. You can change the account used for an individual message manually, as follows:

1. Click Create Mail in Outlook Express to begin composing a new message.

2. In the New Message window, select an identity from the drop-down menu next to From: in the header, as shown in Figure 10.12. The identity used here appears on your outgoing mail and also determines the Reply to: address used if the recipient replies.

Figure 10.12
You can choose an identity for your new message here.

⚡ *Does Outlook Express check for new mail in some of your accounts but not in others? See "Checking Mail in Multiple Accounts" in the "Troubleshooting" section at the end of the chapter.*

ORGANIZING YOUR MAIL

You don't have to receive very much mail to realize that your Inbox can get cluttered in a hurry. The best way to save important mail and stay organized is to organize your mail into folders, just like files are organized on your hard drive.

The process of creating folders and storing messages in them is quite simple:

1. Right-click the Inbox in the OE6 Folder list, and choose New Folder. The Create Folder dialog opens.

2. Type a descriptive name for your folder under Folder Name. Look at the folder list in the lower half of the dialog to make sure that the correct parent folder is selected.

3. Click OK to create the folder.

The new folder appears in the OE6 Folder list under the parent folder. You can simply drag and drop messages from the message list to the designated storage or project folder.

CAUTION

> Compacting messages in the background automatically can be dangerous, so we choose to turn off this option. To do so, go to Tools, Options, and click the Maintenance tab. Uncheck Compact Messages in the Background. The reason this can be dangerous is because if the computer crashes or the phone connection is interrupted when message compaction is in progress, it can kill the crucial folders.dbx file or corrupt the entire message store. In addition, you may notice a significant drop in the computer's performance each time background compacting begins.
>
> It is important to compact folders regularly, however. By choosing a time to clean them up manually, you can minimize the risk of corruption while compacting. Go to File, Folder, and select Compact All Folders. Compacting folders can take several minutes. It is best not to use your computer during this time. If an error occurs, such as "cannot compact, folder in use", close OE, wait a moment, reopen OE, and restart the process.

FILTERING YOUR MAIL

Many e-mail users—especially those who subscribe to mailing lists—receive dozens or even hundreds of messages per day. Wading through all this mail for the really important stuff can be challenging (to say the least), so OE6 includes a mail filtering feature similar to Outlook's Inbox Rules that helps you direct certain kinds of mail to specific locations. For example, you might want to direct all mail from a list you are subscribed to into a special folder where it can be read later.

You can even use mail filters to delete mail you don't want to see at all. Mail can be filtered by content, subject, or sender information. If you are frequently being bothered by someone, you can simply set up OE6 to send all messages from that person to the Deleted Items folder.

To set up a filter:

1. In Outlook Express, choose Tools and select Message Rules, Mail. You will see the window shown in Figure 10.13. If there are already one or more Mail Rules set up, the Message Rules dialog opens first. In that case, click New to get to the New Mail Rule window, or Modify to change an existing rule.

2. Select a condition from box 1 of the New Mail Rule dialog. Place a check mark next to the condition or conditions you want to apply.

3. Select an action in box 2. This action will happen if the condition specified in box 1 is met.

4. Follow the instructions in box 3. They will be specific to the conditions and actions you set in boxes 1 and 2. As you can see in Figure 10.13, we have set up a rule that automatically files certain incoming messages in a specific folder. The reply states that we are away from the office until a certain date.

5. Check the description in box 3 to make sure the correct action will take place. Name the rule in box 4, and click OK when you are finished.

The rule then appears in the Message Rules dialog with a check mark next to it. You can open this dialog at any time to edit, disable (by clearing the check box), or remove any rules.

10

Figure 10.13
You can create mail rules to filter your mail and automate certain tasks.

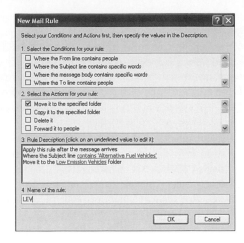

TIP FROM

Bob & Brian

An "out of office" auto reply rule can be created in mail rules to automatically respond to all incoming messages, stating that we are away from the office until a certain date. Although this can be useful, do not enable such a rule if you are subscribed to any mailing lists. (For more on mailing lists, see "What About Mailing Lists?" in Chapter 11.)

To block mail from a specific sender, you can use the Blocked Senders tab of the Message Rules dialog. You can open this tab directly by choosing Tools, Message Rules, Blocked Senders List in Outlook Express. Click Add in the dialog, and type the person's e-mail address in the Add Sender dialog. After you add the address, that person's name appears in your Blocked Senders list. Notice that you can opt to block newsgroup messages from that person as well.

CHECKING YOUR MESSAGES WHILE TRAVELING

Before leaving on a trip, consider setting up a message rule in Outlook Express to forward all incoming messages to your HTTP mail account (such as Hotmail or Yahoo!). That way, you can read all of your mail on the road, regardless of which of your addresses to which the messages are sent. Of course, in order for this method to work, your computer must remain on while you are away, and OE must be set to check for new messages regularly. This is not the best idea, environmentally speaking, but there are conditions where it will work with no wasted energy, such as if your office computer will be in use by others in your absence.

A better way to check e-mail while away from your computer is to set up POP mail in your HTTP mail account. At your HTTP account online, go to options (or something similar) to enter your POP server settings. Some servers let you differentiate between different mail accounts with color coding of messages. Once this is set up, simply click on the online Inbox or, in some cases, Check Other Mail.

BACKING UP OUTLOOK EXPRESS DATA

One of the unique aspects of electronic mail is that it can serve as a permanent record of your communications. Mail that seems insignificant now may be invaluable in the future, and many people back up all their correspondence on a regular basis to ensure that a record is kept for all time. You can save copies of individual messages by choosing Save As from the File menu in the message window. Choosing this option opens a standard Windows Save dialog, where you can choose a location and name for the file. It is saved with the .EML extension.

In addition, you might want to use a backup procedure regularly to store messages elsewhere and remove them from OE. If you receive and send thousands of messages a year, removing them and storing them elsewhere (yearly or quarterly) will help keep Outlook Express running efficiently and will free up space on your hard drive.

BACKING UP ALL YOUR OUTLOOK EXPRESS MESSAGES

The easiest and perhaps safest way to back up your mail is to make a backup copy of your entire Outlook Express e-mail message files. (It's complicated to backup and restore just individual folders). To begin, make a backup copy of all of your OE messages.

1. In OE, go to Tools, Options, and click the Maintenance tab.
2. Click the Store Folder button.
3. Copy the folder location that appears in the box (highlight the entire line and then press Ctrl+C).
4. Click Cancel twice to close the dialog boxes.
5. From the Start menu, click Run, press Ctrl+V (to paste the folder location into the Run dialog box), and click OK. This opens the mail folder in a new window.
6. On that window, open the Edit menu, and click Select All.
7. Open the Edit menu and click Copy.
8. Close the window.
9. Create a new folder on your hard drive or alternate back-up drive, and name it (Bob's E-mail Backup, for example).
10. Open the new folder, choose Edit, Paste. All the mail files will be copied into the new folder, leaving the originals in place.
11. Close the window.

TIP FROM

Bob
& Brian

> You might want to make one backup folder on your hard drive, and another on a CD-R or Zip disk.

BACKING UP THE OUTLOOK EXPRESS ADDRESS BOOK

The next thing you'll want to back up is your all-important Address Book. If you have any significant number of addresses, and especially mailing-list groups, losing your address book do to a reinstallation of Windows or a hard disk crash, you'll be glad you did. There are two ways you can do this. Firstly, you can sleuth out the location of the single .WAB (Windows Address Book) file that is used by OE6 for each user that logs onto on an XP system, and then back up the file somewhere safe. This takes a little digging, though. Also not that this technique backs up the address books belonging to other "identities" that you have created in your OE, too.

As an alternative, there is a menu command in OE that lets you back up (or, more accurately, *export)* any identity's address book. When you export, though, it's not in the native .WAB format, so pulling the data back into a system you're restoring is as simple as just copying in the .WAB file. You export in comma separated value (CSV) format, typically.

Let's look at the first technique. The individual data for each logged-in user on the XP system is stored in a unique .WAB file. The file can be found in a As mentioned above, this .WAB file contains all the address book data for all of that user's e-mail Identities.

The path for this file will look something like this:

```
D:\Documents and Settings\Owner\Application Data\Microsoft\Address Book
➥\Owner.wab
```

To find the place where your address book is stored in your computer, you'll have to be crafty, because the location normally is hidden by XP. Here's one way to do that:

1. Go to the Start menu and choose Search.
2. Click All Files and Folders.
3. Enter ***.wab** in the first text box.
4. Click More Advanced Options at the bottom of the Search Companion window.
5. Place a check mark in the box next to Search Hidden Files and Folders by clicking the box, because Application Data is hidden by default.
6. Click Search.

You will see a file for each XP system user. Make a backup copy of your address book, preferably on a separate drive or CD-R. By saving it in this way, it will be easier to load the data back into OE in the same format.

To restore the data, you have two options. First, simply copy and paste your saved address book to the location you found by the method above. Or, choose File, Import, Address Book, and specify the file location.

Here's the second approach to backing up address book data that I described above. If it is important to you to segregate the Address Book data of individual OE identities, or if you want to pull your address book data into another program, such as Excel, ACT, and so on, you will need to export Address Book data while logged in to a specific Identity. When the

.WAB file becomes disassociated from the user identities, the data can be exported only as a single file—not folder by folder. It gets a bit messy, because this process converts the file to a comma-separated values file and chooses which fields to export and import. (You also have the option of exporting to Microsoft Exchange Personal Address Book format, if you intend to use another program that reads that format.)

To export your OE address book in this way, go to the File menu and click Export, Address Book. Choose Text File (Comma-Separated Values), and click Export. Browse to the folder you created for mail backup, enter something like **Bob's address book backup**, and click Save. Click Next, and mark the boxes for each field you want to export. (If in doubt, select all fields.) Click Finish, and then click OK, and Close.

BACKING UP MAIL AND NEWSGROUP ACCOUNT INFORMATION

To copy your Outlook Express mail accounts, go to Tools in OE, and click Accounts. Go to the Mail or Newsgroup tab, select the account that you want to back up, and click Export. In the Save In box, find the mail backup folder that you created and click Save. Repeat for each account you want to save, and close the window when you're finished.

IMPORTING OUTLOOK EXPRESS DATA

Before restoring data, you might need to re-create identities. After the identities are established, repeat each step for each identity.

To import your OE e-mail messages from your backup folder, follow these steps:

1. Open OE, go to the File menu, click Import, and then click Messages.
2. In the box that appears, select an e-mail program from which to import, and click Next.
3. Click Import Mail from a Store Directory, and click OK.
4. Browse to your mail backup folder and click OK, and Next.
5. Choose All Folders, click Next, and click Finish.

Importing other data is done in a similar way. To import the Address Book as saved in a CSV file:

1. Go to the OE file menu, click Import, and click Other Address Book.
2. Click Text File (Comma Separated Values), and then click Import.
3. Browse to your mail backup folder, choose the address book *.csv file, and click Open.
4. Click Next, Finish, OK, and then Close.

Mail and News Accounts can be imported in this way:

1. Go to Tools, Accounts.
2. Click the Mail or News tab, and click Import.
3. In the Look In box, find the backup folder.

4. Click the account that you wish to import, and click Open.

5. Repeat for each account, and then click Close.

TIP FROM

Bob & Brian

> There are several methods of backing up and restoring data. For other options, go to these Web sites, current at the time of this writing. If no longer available, perform a search by entering `OE backup restore` in the window of a search engine such as www.hotbot.com.
>
> Answers to dozens of questions about OE:
>
> `http://www.chasms.com/mskb/mskbol.htm`
>
> How to back up and restore mail folders:
>
> `http://support.microsoft.com/default.aspx?scid=kb;`
> `EN-US;q270670`
>
> Advanced backup instructions here. Caution: Some of these tips advise you to modify the system Registry. Always back up your Registry files before modifying them. If you don't know how to do this, read about it first in Chapter 32, "The Registry."
>
> `http://www.tomsterdam.com/`

TIP FROM

Bob & Brian

> To make the process easier, there is software available that will back up files for you with a single click (after you've set up your preferences). An added perk is its capability to synchronize OE message folders on multiple computers. The program even includes a system that will remind you to back up files regularly.
>
> One of these programs, Express Assist, is available for downloading here:
>
> `http://www.ajsystems.com/oexhome.html`

DEALING WITH SPAM

A hot topic in e-mail circles today is the subject of commercial advertisements mass-delivered via electronic mail. This type of unsolicited mail is generally referred to as *Spam*, a name attributed in Internet lore to a Monty Python musical skit pertaining to the pink meat product of the same name. This type of mail is so offensive to some people that a few states have even enacted laws against it.

Some groups are also working with the U.S. Federal Government to ban unsolicited electronic mail and place identification requirements on people and organizations who send advertisements via e-mail. Countless anti-Spam organizations exist, with one of the foremost being CAUCE, the Coalition Against Unsolicited Commercial E-mail (www.cauce.org).

The real problem with Spam is that scam operations are rampant and difficult to detect. Spam also has an impact on Internet traffic, requiring a considerable amount of bandwidth that many people feel would be better used for other purposes.

If you have been online for very long, you've almost certainly received some Spam yourself. You can protect yourself from receiving a lot of Spam by taking some basic precautionary measures:

- Avoid giving out your e-mail address whenever possible. Some Web sites funnel you through pointless registration procedures that do little else than collect e-mail addresses.

- If you post to newsgroups periodically, alter your Reply to: e-mail address for your news account in such a way that "spam bots" searching newsgroups for e-mail addresses will not be able to send you mail correctly. Many people put "Nospam" or other phrase in front of their address (nospambob@mcp.com), a modification that will be easy for humans to correct when sending you a valid reply.

- Don't register with too many online directories. Some directories can be used as e-mail address archives for spammers. The trade-off is that someone looking for you will have a harder time.

Alas, no matter how careful you are, some spam will get through. Many spams contain instructions for getting yourself removed from their lists. Beware that following their instructions may result in even more spam, because some unscrupulous spammers use this trick to find active addresses. To avoid this, simply delete the messages.

You can also check with your local, state, or federal laws from time to time to find out whether there are regulations against spam that apply to your account. If so, you may have legal recourse against spammers. The CAUCE organization mentioned earlier is a good starting point to search online for information about laws in your area.

NOTE

If you're concerned about e-mail viruses and spam spreading throughout your office network, wreaking havoc and slowing down the system, you'll want to consider antivirus and content-filtering software designed for businesses. These software packages can be costly, but well worth it to companies that have been spared a nasty virus or have seen productivity increase when there is less spam to deal with.

Antivirus software offers an additional level of protection beyond the virus protection provided with XP, and it can often repair infected files in addition to identifying and blocking viruses in attached files. Content filters go further, by scanning e-mail for specific words, attachment names, and scripting commands. A content filter can be set to block or track messages with specified characteristics.

Consider using one of these products:

- eSafe Mail (www.ealaddin.com/esafe)
- ScanMail 3 for Microsoft Exchange and ScanMail eManager (www.antivirus.com/download/)
- Tumbleweed Messaging Management System (www.tumbleweed.com)
- Norton AntiVirus 2.5 for Microsoft Exchange (http://enterprisesecurity.symantec.com/content/productlink.cfm#0)
- McAfee GroupShield and WebShield for SMTP (www.mcafeeb2b.com)

TROUBLESHOOTING

PASSWORD TROUBLE

The server will not accept my password.

Many e-mail servers are case sensitive. If the Caps Lock key on your keyboard is on, it could cause the password to be entered in the wrong case. Sometimes an inadvertent space can be the culprit as well. This is true even if you have configured Outlook Express to remember your e-mail address so that you don't have to type it in every time you check mail.

IDENTITY CRISIS

I don't like the name Outlook Express is using to identify me in outgoing messages.

The name Outlook Express uses could be indicative of several things. First, if you have multiple accounts or identities configured in Outlook Express, make sure that you are selecting the desired one in the From: field when you send the messages. You can also open the Internet Accounts dialog and check the Properties sheet for your e-mail address(es). The Name field under User Information on the General tab is the name used to identify you on outgoing mail.

CHECKING MAIL IN MULTIPLE ACCOUNTS

I have several mail accounts, but OE6 doesn't check all of them when I click Send/Recv.

Open the Properties sheet for each of your mail accounts in the Internet Accounts dialog. On the General tab is an option labeled Include This Account When Receiving Mail or Synchronizing. Make sure a check mark appears next to this option for each of your mail accounts.

THINNING YOUR CONTACTS LIST

Several people in my Contacts List shouldn't be there, including spammers.

By default, OE6 adds an entry to the Address Book for every source to which you reply. You can disable this feature by opening the Options dialog in the Tools menu. On the Send tab, disable the option labeled Automatically Put People I Reply to in My Address Book. Then, to remove unwanted entries from your Address Book, highlight the contact and click Delete.

RECIPIENTS DON'T LIKE MY MAIL FORMATTING

People on my mailing list are sending me hate mail because of machine characters or strange attachments that accompany each of my posts.

HTML messages are not compatible with most electronic mailing lists. Change your default mail-sending format to Plain Text on the Send tab of the OE6 Options dialog.

Alternatively, you can have OE remind you of specific people in your address book that request Plain Text messages. Open the Address Book and click on the name of a person who requests Plain Text mail. Click on the Name tab, and put a check mark in the box next to

"Send E-Mail using plain text only." When you try to send HTML e-mail to this person, a reminder window will pop up asking if you'd like OE to reformat the e-mail to Plain Text.

MISSING MAIL SERVERS

When I try to go online and check mail, an error occurs stating that the server could not be found.

Assuming that the server information for your account is correct, you probably have a problem with your connection. OE6 should automatically dial a connection if one is not present, but if it doesn't, open the Internet Properties icon in the Windows Control Panel. On the Connection tab, select the option Dial Whenever a Network Connection Is Not Present, and click OK to close the dialog.

MAKING OE6 LESS AUTOMATED

I want/don't want Outlook Express to automatically check for mail periodically.

Go to the General tab of the Options dialog. If the option Check for New Messages Every XX Minutes is checked, OE6 automatically checks for new mail at the specified interval. Just below that option, you can also specify whether you want OE6 to automatically dial a connection at this time.

MISSING OE FOLDERS

My Outlook Express folders seem to have disappeared.

They might be still on disk, just not in Outlook Express anymore. Use these steps:

1. In OE, choose Tools, Options, Maintenance, and click Store Folder to locate the location of the store folder. Select the whole path of the store location and press Ctrl+C to copy it.

2. Click Start, Run, and then press Ctrl+V to paste in the name of the store file location. This opens a window with all your message store files in it.

3. Rename the folders.dbx file to folders.xxx. (You might need system administrator privileges to do this.)

4. Restart OE. Your folders should reappear, but all folders will now be on the same level instead of appearing as subfolders. Reorganize the folder structure by dragging and dropping. Check your message rules for any rules that move messages into folders to be certain that the destination folder is correct. Also, check other settings such as your Identities, Signatures, and Newsgroup Synchronization.

TIPS FROM THE WINDOWS PROS: CREATING FORMATTED E-MAIL

So you know a lot about e-mail. What about the fancy-looking messages you get in your Inbox—the ones that look like Web pages? This type of e-mail is created with HTML formatting.

And how do you create fancy HTML e-mail messages, anyway? In its simplest form, HTML mail lets you format the font and other goodies like color and background. Well, we already talked about stationery. So you know that this is HTML mail. You can also use the Insert Picture button on the OE toolbar to insert an image. But your ability to design a document with much control is still quite limited.

If you want to create more elaborate e-mail, with tables, text that wraps around pictures, and lots of links in it, you'll probably want to use a Web-design program such as FrontPage or DreamWeaver. After you've designed a page there

1. Start a new e-mail in OE.
2. Select and copy the new page you designed in your Web design program and paste into the new e-mail you're constructing. As you paste in the text and images, they should appear in your e-mail.
3. Adjust as necessary.

Test the look of the e-mail you created by sending the sample mail to yourself; see how it looks when you open it. Make sure to test it by sending it to another computer, too. That way you can determine if there are any missing images. Your test can be deceptive if you send and receive from the same computer, since the images you use are already on the source computer. If the images are missing from the e-mail, they are still likely to show up if you use the source computer for testing it, simply because they are being called up from your local hard drive.

To keep your e-mail easy to read, keep the page fairly narrow. Also, don't expect your message to display with as much predictably as it does in a Web browser since HTML-capable e-mail programs just aren't as polished in their ability to render HTML. It's a good idea to check your mail in various e-mail clients first to get an idea of how it will look to a variety of readers.

Much spam HTML e-mail only downloads the HTML code and the text portion into OE. The rest of the images are not loaded in until you look at the mail (assuming you are online at the time). When you click on the mail to read it, the images stream in because the HTML code in the message "points" to the image sources, which are out on Web servers somewhere across the Internet. This is an acceptable way to construct your HTML mail, but it assumes your readers are online. If you want to be sure people can read your mail offline, then you should include the images in the e-mail itself. However, this does make the file larger, and can slow down the transfer time. Make sure to keep your images relatively small and compressed (as a rule, your images shouldn't exceed about 25KB). Use a program such as Fireworks, FrontPage, or Photoshop to optimize photos and other images for transmission over the Web.

TIP FROM

Bob & Brian

> There are some folks whose programs cannot read HTML mail. In the subject line of HTML mail, I like to include the words "HTML version" so people will know not to bother reading it if their e-mail program isn't HTML-savvy. Then I send another message that is plain text, with subject line that includes the words "Plain text version."

CHAPTER 11

READING NEWSGROUPS WITH OUTLOOK EXPRESS

In this chapter

NEWSGROUPS AND THE INTERNET

With the overwhelming and still growing popularity of the World Wide Web since its inception in the early 1990s, you might easily forget that the Internet was around for more than two decades before the first Web page saw the light of a cathode ray tube. Before the inception of the Web, people used the Internet to access newsgroups. Newsgroups began in 1979 as a forum in which Unix users could communicate with each other, and the concept grew steadily from there into what is now a global assemblage of people sharing information on virtually every topic imaginable.

Originally, news servers exchanged articles using Unix-to-Unix Copy Protocol (UUCP), which involves direct modem dial-up over long-distance phone lines. In 1986, the Network News Transport Protocol (NNTP) was released, allowing news to be transported via TCP/IP connection over the Internet. Most modern newsgroups use the NNTP protocol, and it is the only news protocol supported by Outlook Express.

Newsgroups are scattered on servers around the world, and the rough network used to carry newsgroup bandwidth is generally referred to as *Usenet*. We're not implying, however, that some authority provides oversight of Usenet. "Usenet is not a democracy" is one of the first statements you will read in virtually any primer or Frequently Asked Questions list (FAQ) on the subject, alluding to the virtual anarchy in which this medium exists. Usenet has become so large and diverse that a simple definition cannot possibly do justice.

What we can do, however, is roughly describe the types of newsgroups and news servers that you can access using Outlook Express 6 (OE6). Basically, the administrator of your news server determines which news feeds you will have access to. Feeds are passed along to the server from adjacent servers, providing a decidedly decentralized structure to Usenet. Each server maintains a list of message IDs to ensure that new articles are received at a given server only once. An individual server can control which feeds it propagates, although the interconnectivity of Usenet servers ensures that a lone server has little or no control of the overall distribution. Thus, the authority of a news server is generally limited to what clients (that would be you) can access and what kind of material those clients can post. Likewise, the decentralization of servers means that an article you post may take hours—or even days—to circulate among all other news servers.

> **NOTE**
>
> The terms *newsgroup* and *Usenet* are used almost interchangeably in today's online world, but it is useful to know that *newsgroup* refers to individual groups, whereas *Usenet* refers to the entire network of groups as a whole.

WHAT ABOUT MAILING LISTS?

Are newsgroups the same as mailing lists, or *listservs*, as some people call them? No. So here's a little digression about those, just to make the distinction. The very openness that makes newsgroups desirable has its drawbacks: privacy and security are almost nonexistent. Mailing list posts are less public because usually the only people who can read them are other list members, and lists are generally less susceptible to spam and objectionable material. Furthermore, mailing list traffic comes into your e-mail reader (your inbox in OE), making lists easier to deal with for some people.

Mailing lists are simple; you send a message to the list address, which is then forwarded to every other list member. Every time another member posts a message to the list, you receive a copy. The list is managed by a list administrator who often, but not always, works directly with the mail server hosting the list. Often the administrator can be reached via the e-mail address `listproc` or `majordomo` followed by @ and the name of the domain server.

Virtually any topic imaginable has a mailing list. If you want to find one to join, a good place to start would be Vivian Neou's mailing list search directory, available online at `www.catalog.com/vivian/`.

Lists vary widely in terms of message volume, ranging anywhere from only a few messages per month up to hundreds of posts each day. Many lists let you opt to receive one or two daily list compilations rather than a string of individual posts. These compilations are called *digests* and are especially useful with high-volume lists.

USING MAILING LISTS

Before you join and start to participate in mailing lists, you need to keep two main issues in mind: security and netiquette. Security is largely determined by the list administrator, so you should check list policies for concerns before you join. You should also exercise caution when posting sensitive information to a list because, generally speaking, you won't know who is actually subscribed.

Netiquette is a little trickier. You've probably already read volumes on such topics as flame wars and the public airing of private laundry, but you should be aware of some issues unique to mailing lists:

- Don't post attachments. Most mailing lists, especially those offering a Digest mode, forbid file attachments, and for good reason. If you want to send a file to someone, do it off list.

- Send posts in plain text format. HTML formatting can wreak havoc on recipients' systems. Check with the list administrator to find out whether MIME or uuencode plain text formatting is best.

- Read and save the FAQ. Every list has a different procedure for subscribing, unsubscribing, switching to digest mode, or changing various other options. This information is usually contained in a list FAQ, which should also include guidance regarding list content and rules.

- Be conscious of the reply procedures for your list. Some mailing lists are configured so that a Reply action goes only to the original sender, and you must click Reply All to post a reply to the list. But with other lists, clicking Reply sends your response directly to the list. Again, double-check your list's FAQ to find out the correct procedure.

11

■ Do not use an "Out of Office" auto-reply rule for your Inbox. Automatic replies to incoming messages can cause destructive feedback loops in lists that you are subscribed to. (Since every incoming message from the list triggers a response from Outlook Express, those responses go back to the mailing list, generating more list traffic that will be sent to your account, resulting in more auto replies, and so on.) If you feel that you must use such a rule, unsubscribe or suspend your mailing lists before enabling it.

TIP FROM

Bob & Brian

> Because mailing lists can dump dozens—or even hundreds—of posts into your e-mail account daily, set up a separate folder in OE for each mailing list, and use Message Rules to direct incoming messages to that folder. (For more on Rules, see Chapter 10, "Sending E-mail with Outlook Express.")

→ Spam is a fact of life in both mailing lists and newsgroups. To learn more about spam, **see** "Avoiding Spam," **p. 377**.

LOCATING NEWS SERVERS

Many ISPs and companies provide news server accounts to their Internet users, but you still might find yourself looking for a server on your own. This might be the case even if you have a news account available to you; some service providers censor the news content that is available, and if you want uncensored news, you must rely on a different source.

Censorship, Big Brother, and NNTP Servers

News feeds are censored for a variety of reasons. For example, your company's server might restrict feeds from `alt.`, `rec.`, and `talk.` groups to reduce the number of work hours lost to employee abuse or simply to reduce bandwidth. Many other servers restrict feeds that contain pornographic content for both legal and moral reasons.

Even if your news server provides a relatively unrestricted news feed, you should exercise care when deciding which articles you download from the server. Virtually all servers maintain logs of the activities of each login account. This means that your service provider can track which articles you download, and in most cases these logs can be subpoenaed and used against you in court.

In other words, Big Brother might be watching you download porn, bomb-making instructions, and bootleg copies of the latest Hollywood blockbuster. Be especially paranoid if you access a company news server; hours spent receiving otherwise legal content such as fruit cake recipes, Bill Gates jokes, and the like could still land you in hot water if the boss is logging your online activities.

Many news servers are available through virtually any Internet connection, but you'll pay for that connection. Typically, monthly charges for a personal news server account range from $10 to $20 per month and get higher for corporate or higher bandwidth accounts. If you plan to use newsgroups frequently, you might want to factor in this cost when you're shopping for an ISP. You can find a good list of commercial news servers in the Yahoo! directory at

```
http://dir.yahoo.com/Business_and_Economy/Business_to_Business/Communications_
and_Networking/Internet_and_World_Wide_Web/Usenet_Servers/Commercial/
```

However, if you have an Internet connection and would simply like a different news server, you can find a list of free news servers available online: the list of free servers can change daily.

`http://freenews.maxbaud.net/newspage.html?date=today`

 If Outlook Express has trouble locating your news server, see "No News Server Connection" in the "Troubleshooting" section at the end of this chapter.

A free alternative to commercial news servers is a Web-based news service, such as the one created by deja.com. An advantage of using a Web-based news service is that a search brings back results from many newsgroups, not only one. It's a terrific way to find expert postings on just about anything from open-heart surgery, to child adoption, to what people think of the new car you're considering buying. However, messages are not brought into your news client program (such as OE) for reference offline. Deja was bought out and redesigned by Google awhile back, so until recently, you couldn't post new messages to Usenet, but now you can again. Just go to `http://www.google.com` and click the "Google Groups" option, or go directly to `http://groups.google.com/`.

 If you cannot locate a particular newsgroup on your news server, see "Newsgroup Isn't Available on News Server" in the "Troubleshooting" section at the end of this chapter.

SETTING UP A NEWSGROUP ACCOUNT IN OUTLOOK EXPRESS

Outlook Express 6 (OE6) is included free with XP and serves quite well as a news reader. If you already use OE6 for e-mail services, you're probably already familiar with the basics of using this program. If not, you may benefit from a quick review of Chapter 10, "Sending E-mail with Outlook Express," which will help you master the fundamentals of using OE6.

You first must set up a news account in OE6. You might do so at the same time you set up an e-mail account, but if not, you can configure it any time. Before you can configure your news account, you need to obtain a news server address, which should look something like this:

`news.domainname.com`

Your company might also have a news server account with a commercial provider. You can configure multiple server accounts in OE6, just as you can set up multiple e-mail accounts.

As mentioned earlier, a news server provides you with news feeds from other news servers. Which feeds are available to you depends on decisions made by your server's administrator. For example, some news servers restrict feeds for all `alt.` (alternative) newsgroups because some of them contain highly objectionable material.

→ If you do not have a news server you can access, **see** "Locating News Servers," **p. 366**.

To set up your account in Outlook Express, follow these steps:

1. Open Outlook Express, and choose Tools, Accounts to open the Internet Accounts dialog. Click the News tab to bring it to the front, and then select Add, News.

2. Follow the instructions in the Internet Connection Wizard for inputting your display name and e-mail address (the wizard may provide this information for you).

3. Type the name of your news (NNTP) server, as shown in Figure 11.1.

4. Click Next, and then click Finish.

Figure 11.1
You enter the name of your news server here. If you use multiple news servers, you must set up an individual account for each one.

Type your NNTP server name here

DOWNLOADING THE NEWSGROUP LIST

After you have configured Outlook Express for your news server, your next step is to download a list of newsgroups from the server. Depending on how many groups the server allows access to, this list could contain more than 75,000 newsgroups. In reality, most servers list less than half that number.

Why aren't they all listed? As you've already seen, some content might be censored by the server's administrator. In many cases, though, it is a much more practical matter: New groups are created so frequently that your server simply might not be aware of them. If you become aware of a newsgroup you would like to join, but it is not currently available on your server, try dropping an e-mail message to the administrator and ask for the group to be added. Assuming the group falls within the administrator's guidelines for acceptable content, adding the group will take only a few seconds.

To begin downloading your server's list, follow these steps:

1. Click the listing for your news account in the OE6 Folders list, as shown in Figure 11.2.

2. A message appears stating that you are not currently subscribed to any newsgroups and asking whether you would like to view the list. Click Yes.

3. If this is the first time you have viewed the list, a dialog appears, as shown in Figure 11.2. Depending on the size of the list and the speed of your connection, downloading could take several minutes. You probably have time to go get another cup of coffee. When the process is finished, the list is downloaded, and you are ready to locate and subscribe to newsgroups.

Figure 11.2
The list of newsgroups downloads from your news server.

TIP FROM

Bob
& Brian

Although new newsgroups are created daily, the list that has been downloaded to your computer is static and doesn't show new groups. To make sure you have a current list, click Reset List in the Newsgroup Subscriptions dialog periodically.

FINDING AND READING NEWSGROUPS

Usually, when you read a newsgroup, you must first subscribe to it. A subscription simply means you've placed a bookmark of sorts in Outlook Express for that group, making it easy to return to and follow conversations whenever you are using OE6.

Before you can subscribe to a newsgroup, you need to find one that piques your interest. Searching for a group in your downloaded list is fairly simple in OE6 (see Figure 11.3). If the list isn't already open, you can open it by clicking your news account in the Folders list. If the list doesn't open automatically, you can click the Newsgroups button on the toolbar.

As you type a word in the Display Newsgroups Which Contain field (Figure 11.3), the list of newsgroups shrinks. You can experiment by typing a keyword you are interested in, pausing after each keystroke.

Figure 11.3
You can begin typing a word to search the newsgroup list. The list automatically gets smaller as you type, showing only those groups with names that match what you typed.

Type a word here

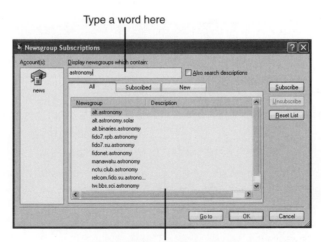

The list shows only groups with names that match what you typed

Newsgroups are usually—but not always—named descriptively. In Figure 11.3, you can see the option to search newsgroup descriptions as well as their names, but very few groups actually have descriptions listed in this window.

TIP FROM

Bob & Brian

> If you don't find a newsgroup that interests you, try a search at http://groups.google.com/ or another Web source to see whether other groups not currently available on your news server exist. There is no such thing as a "complete" list of newsgroups, so a search of several different resources will yield the best results.

SUBSCRIBING TO NEWSGROUPS

OE6 does not require you to subscribe to a group to view its contents. You can simply select a group from the list and click Go To to see messages posted to the group, but you might find it easier to manage the process by simply subscribing anyway. Subscribing to a newsgroup does not require any great level of commitment on your part because you can always unsubscribe with just two mouse clicks.

When you find a newsgroup you want to subscribe to, do the following:

1. Click once on the newsgroup name to select it, and then click the Subscribe button. An icon should appear next to the group name, as shown in Figure 11.4.

2. Click Go To at the bottom of the Newsgroup Subscriptions window. The window closes, and the 300 most recent posts are downloaded to your computer.

Actually, only the message headers are downloaded, and they appear listed in the OE6 window. The message contents are not downloaded until you choose to view a specific message.

Figure 11.4
You can select a newsgroup and subscribe to it here. When you click Go To, this window automatically closes.

This icon indicates that you have subscribed

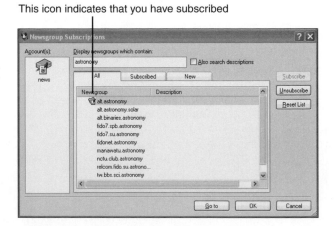

MANAGING YOUR SUBSCRIPTIONS

Newsgroups you are subscribed to are listed in the OE6 Folders list, under the news account listing, as shown in Figure 11.5. If you have multiple news server accounts, individual subscriptions are listed as subfolders under the server you used to subscribe to them.

Figure 11.5
Subscribed news-groups are shown in the Folders list.

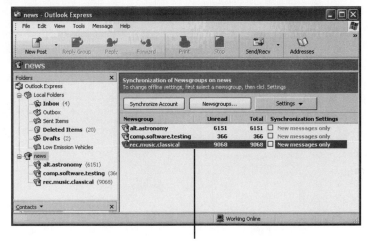

This group contains 9,068 messages

When you click a newsgroup's listing in the Folders list, the 300 most recent headers are downloaded.

→ If you want to change the number of headers shown, **see** "Customizing Outlook Express for Newsgroups," **p. 379**.

If you decide that you don't want to remain subscribed to a group, unsubscribing is easy. Just right-click the group's listing in the Folders list, and choose Unsubscribe from the shortcut menu that appears.

READING AND POSTING MESSAGES TO A NEWSGROUP

As you learned previously, when you first access a newsgroup using OE6, only the first 300 message headers are downloaded. You can download additional headers by clicking Tools, Get Next 300 Headers.

If you want to read a message, you need to manually open it. If you are using the Preview Pane, all you have to do is click once on the message header to cause it to download. If you are not using the Preview Pane, you can double-click a message to open it in a separate message window.

→ To learn how to show or hide the Preview Pane, **see** "Outlook Express Quick Tour," **p. 332**.

As you peruse the list of messages in the group, you need to understand the concept of *discussion threads*. A thread occurs when someone responds to a message. Others respond to the response, and this conversation becomes its own discussion thread. Messages that are part of a thread have a plus (+) sign next to them, and you can click this icon to expand a list of other messages in the thread. Figure 11.6 shows several expanded threads.

Figure 11.6
Threaded messages.

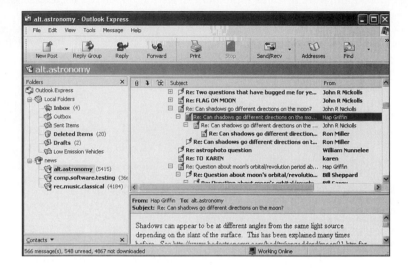

Posting messages to a newsgroup is quite simple. Perhaps the easiest way to post is to reply to an existing message. This process works much the same as replying to regular e-mail, except that you must take extra care to ensure that your reply is going to the right place. Notice that the toolbar has a new button—the Reply Group button—as shown in Figure 11.7.

Figure 11.7
You must choose your reply mode carefully.

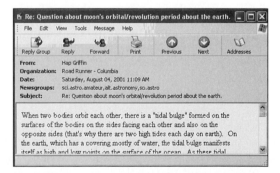

Each reply button serves a unique purpose:

Reply Group	Sends a reply back to the group
Reply	Sends a reply only to the original sender
Forward	Forwards the message to a third party

One aspect to watch carefully is that messages you post to a newsgroup are relevant. If the newsgroup is moderated, someone reviews all posts and removes those posts that are deemed inappropriate. Look for a newsgroup FAQ (Frequently Asked Questions) for more information on netiquette and any rules that might apply to the groups you are subscribed to.

CAUTION

Information posted in newsgroups can be viewed by anyone, and we do mean *anyone!* Never post personal or sensitive information in a newsgroup.

NOTE

The default news message format is Plain Text. You should maintain this setting to ensure that your message can be read by other news readers.

MANAGING MESSAGES

By default, OE6 deletes messages from your computer five days after you download them, but you can change this option easily. Likewise, you can also set up Outlook Express to delete read messages every time you leave the group. You can review these settings by choosing Tools, Options. In the Options dialog, click the Maintenance tab to bring it to the front, as shown in Figure 11.8.

 If a message you read earlier becomes unavailable, see "Message No Longer Available" in the "Troubleshooting" section at the end of this chapter.

 If you're not sure which messages have been read and which haven't, see "Which Ones Are New?" in the "Troubleshooting" section at the end of the chapter.

11

Figure 11.8
You can review your message management settings here.

Adjust the length of time
read messages are saved

If you want to maintain a record of the messages in your newsgroup, remove the check marks next to each Delete option shown in Figure 11.8. Messages remain in OE6 indefinitely if you deselect both of these options, but keep in mind that if the group has high traffic, these messages could eventually eat up a lot of disk space.

The better option is to save individual messages that you want to maintain. To do so, create a new folder for storing news messages under Local Folders in the OE6 Folders list, and then drag any messages you want to save into the folder. You can also drag and drop newsgroup messages to any of your e-mail folders, but you might find it easier to keep newsgroup and e-mail correspondence separate.

READING NEWS OFFLINE

In Chapter 9, "Browsing the World Wide Web with Internet Explorer," you learned that you can download Web pages for offline viewing. You can do the same with newsgroup messages, a capability that makes especially good sense if you must limit your Internet connection time or will be traveling with your laptop. OE6 calls this feature *synchronizing*.

> **N O T E**
>
> Before you synchronize a newsgroup for offline viewing, check the size of the messages you will download. Some people post pictures and other large files into newsgroups, and they can add significantly to download time.

To begin downloading a newsgroup for offline viewing, click your news server account in the Folders list. A list of the groups you are subscribed to then appears, as shown in Figure 11.9. Now follow these steps:

1. Select the newsgroup(s) you want to synchronize, and review the synchronization settings. By default, only new messages will be synchronized, but you can change this setting by clicking the Settings button and choosing another option.

2. Place a check mark in the box(es) under Synchronization settings, as shown in Figure 11.9.

3. Click Synchronize Account. Messages are downloaded based on the synchronization settings you choose. Keep in mind that if you choose to synchronize all messages, the download could take awhile.

When the download is complete, you can get offline to read the downloaded messages. If you try to open a message that isn't available offline, a warning advises you of this fact.

 If, after you synchronize a newsgroup, some messages are not available, see "Some Messages Are Unavailable After Synchronizing" in the "Troubleshooting" section at the end of this chapter.

Figure 11.9
You synchronize messages for offline viewing by choosing options as shown here.

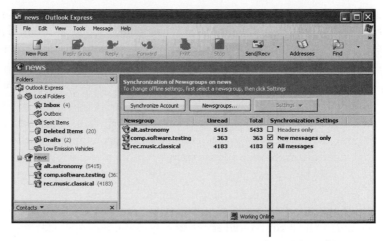

Place a check mark here for groups you want to synchronize

You also can select individual messages for offline reading. Choosing particular messages may be a better course of action, especially if the newsgroup has thousands of messages and you want to download only the first few. Select several message headers in the newsgroup by Ctrl+clicking or Shift+clicking. Then right-click the selection and choose Download Message Later from the menu that appears. When you later choose Synchronize Account from the server account window shown in Figure 11.9, only the selected messages are downloaded. Note that if you select to download all messages in your synchronization settings, all messages will be downloaded, not only the ones you selected.

NEWSGROUP SAFETY

It is no secret that many potential hazards exist in the online world, and nowhere is this more evident than in Usenet. Objectionable Web pages get all the media attention, but nowhere is objectionable—and often illegal—content more readily available than in newsgroups. You can avoid most objectionable content simply by staying away from certain newsgroups, but you might still find the need to filter some of the content you receive.

Besides objectionable content, you must also consider that you become more vulnerable to victimization (or, for that matter, prosecution) when you participate in newsgroups unless you take some basic precautions. Remember, anyone in the world who has access to an Internet connection can see what you post in a newsgroup.

FILTERING UNWANTED MESSAGES

OE6 enables you to set up some message rules to filter certain messages. You can set up this feature, which is similar to mail message rules, as follows:

1. In Outlook Express, choose Tools, Message Rules, News.

2. In the New News Rule dialog, choose conditions for your rule in box 1. As you can see in Figure 11.10, you can select more than one condition. In this case, we're looking for messages in the alt.astronomy newsgroup that contain the word *Hubble* in the subject line.

3. In box 2, choose what you want to happen to messages that meet your conditions. In this case, matching messages will be highlighted in yellow. If the condition were looking for objectionable material, we would probably choose to delete it instead.

4. In box 3, review the rule description and enter any required information. For example, you will probably have to specify words or other pieces of information pertaining to the conditions you set.

5. Click OK when you're finished, and click OK in the Message Rules dialog to close it.

You can modify or disable a rule at any time by using the Tools, Message Rules, News command.

→ You can also filter news by restricting senders. To learn how, **see** "Filtering Your Mail," **p. 353**.

Figure 11.10
You can create rules for filtering your news messages here. Be sure to look through each box for relevant information.

PROTECTING YOUR IDENTITY

Besides objectionable content, the other great hazard involved with using newsgroups is the threat to your identity and personal information. You can avoid having personal information compromised on Usenet by simply not posting it. Don't post your home address or phone number, age (especially if you are young), or financial information (such as a credit card number).

You also can hide your identity if you do not want to reveal it. Outlook Express identifies you in all outgoing posts by whatever username you entered when you configured the account. If you are concerned about protecting your identity in newsgroups, consider changing the username for your news account to a nickname that your friends or associates will recognize but strangers won't. Figure 11.11, in the next section, shows such a nickname in use.

Of course, there are limits to how much anonymity can be provided by simply changing the username and e-mail address for your news account in OE6. Any message you post to a newsgroup can be easily traced back to your server, and your server maintains transaction logs that allow your real identity to be ascertained.

A better way to protect your identity is by signing up for a Web-based e-mail account, such as those available at Yahoo! or Hotmail, and register for a rather bland address. When you do this, limit the amount of information that you give.

Using a *pseudonymous remailer* can be an even more secure solution. A pseudonymous remailer is a server that assigns you an ID based on a proprietary scheme, and you send and receive through the server. However, finding a remailer may be challenging because of their tendency to have a short lifespan, perhaps because of their low profitability. Also, some remailers require you to use a specific news application, and it never seems to be OE.

At the time of this printing, it was possible to find a list of pseudonymous remailers, and FAQs, online at the following site:

`http://www.andrebacard.com/remail.html`

Some remailer choices include: `www.ziplip.com`, `www.securenym.net`, `www.cyberpass.net`, and `www.hushmail.com`.

Avoiding Spam

One of the most pervasive threats to your identity that exists in Usenet is spam (see "Dealing with Spam" in Chapter 13 for more information).

Programs called *spambots* do nothing but scan Usenet message headers for e-mail addresses. These addresses are compiled and sold to companies that send out unsolicited advertisements via e-mail. If you post frequently to newsgroups, your e-mail address could get "vacuumed" in this manner, resulting in a greater volume of spam in your Inbox.

Fortunately, spambots aren't intelligent, so defeating them is relatively simple. The most common tactic is to add a word to your e-mail address that actual human beings will recognize as an anti-spam measure. It would look something like this:

`bob@nospam_mcp.com`

A person who wants to respond to you can easily remove the "nospam_" from your e-mail address, but most spambots won't be able to recognize it, and the spam that was meant for you will end up bouncing back to the sender. There are rumors that some spambots might have become savvy to this technique, and can remove text such as "nospam" from an e-mail address. You might want to try another approach, if you find that nospam isn't working. Use something odd such as

`bob@myhatmcp.com`

In your postings, you can say "to respond to me, just remove myhat and use the remaining address."

You can change your reply address by clicking Tools, Accounts to open the Internet Accounts dialog. Then click the News tab, select your news account, and click Properties. Type the modified e-mail address in the Reply Address text box, as shown in Figure 11.11, and click OK to close the dialog.

Figure 11.11
You can type a modified identity and reply address in this dialog to avoid spam and protect your identity somewhat in Usenet.

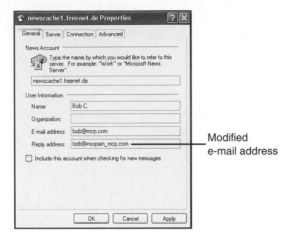

Modified
e-mail address

NOTE

> Outlook Express probably will show you a warning that the Reply To address is not valid. Click Yes to use the modified address despite the apparent problem.

RESPONDING TO ANONYMOUS POSTERS

You're not the only person trying to remain anonymous in Usenet. Trying to respond to a message you read can cause you a few problems, especially if you are trying to respond directly to the poster.

Obviously, there are different levels of anonymity. If the person is simply using a nickname, you should be able to respond to him or her normally. But if that person is also trying to conceal his or her e-mail address, responding can get trickier. If an error message is returned to you when you try to send someone e-mail (often called a *bounce*), check that person's e-mail address to see whether he or she is using an anti-spam scheme as shown here:

bob@nospam_mcp.com

People who use this naming scheme usually have something in their signature files that says "To reply, remove 'nospam_' from the domain" or something to that effect.

If the e-mail address is obviously not valid, and no clues to the individual's real address exist, your last resort may be to post to the newsgroup. But don't use this situation as an excuse to share a private response in a public forum. A typical response would look something like this:

```
Attn: bob@nospam_mcp.com
I wish to send you a response. Please contact me directly at rick@mcp.com.
```

This message should get the individual's attention. If not, there's not much else you can do.

CUSTOMIZING OUTLOOK EXPRESS FOR NEWSGROUPS

Outlook Express 6 comes with a fairly good package of preset options for reading and participating in newsgroups. Still, what works for the "average" user might not suit you. You can customize virtually every aspect of news reading in this program by reviewing the various settings available to you. To do so, follow these steps:

1. In OE6, choose Tools, Options.

2. Click the General tab to bring it to the front, and then remove the check mark next to Notify Me If There Are Any New Newsgroups if you already plan to reset your group list periodically without input from OE6.

3. Click the Read tab, as shown in Figure 11.12. OE6 automatically downloads the first 300 headers at a time, but you can change that number here. You also might want to check the option Mark All Messages as Read When Exiting a Newsgroup. If you routinely ignore some posts in the group, selecting this option will help you determine which messages are actually new the next time you open the group.

Figure 11.12
You can set the number of message headers that will be downloaded when you open a group here.

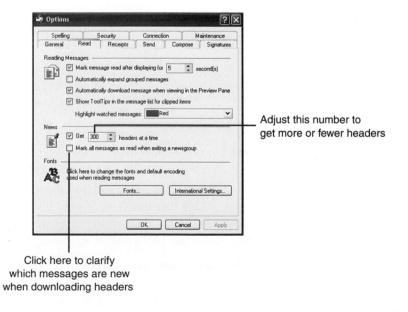

Adjust this number to get more or fewer headers

Click here to clarify which messages are new when downloading headers

4. Switch to the Send tab to make your default news-sending format HTML if you like, but doing so is not recommended because most news readers can't read HTML formatting.

5. Click the Signatures tab to bring it to the front, and create a new signature to be used exclusively with newsgroups. Your news signature could include instructions for removing anti-spam measures from your e-mail address. After you have created the new signature, click the Advanced button to open the dialog shown in Figure 11.13. Here, you can select your news account to "assign" the signature to it. After you have assigned a signature, it will be used only with that account.

Figure 11.13
You can assign a specific signature to your news account here.

Place a check mark here
to assign a signature

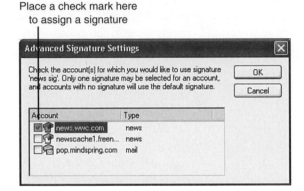

6. On the Maintenance tab, check the two news-related Delete options if you want to save disk space.

→ To learn more about setting the Delete options, **see** "Managing Messages," **p. 373**.

7. Click OK to close the dialog and save your settings changes.

TROUBLESHOOTING

NEWSGROUP ISN'T AVAILABLE ON NEWS SERVER

A newsgroup I want to access isn't available on my server.

Click Reset List in the Newsgroup Subscriptions window. The newsgroup may be new and simply not shown in your current list. If the group still isn't there, try contacting the ISP or other service that hosts the list and ask that service to add it. Often new groups simply go unnoticed because so many of them are out there. Many news servers are willing to respond to such a request, unless they have a rule restricting or censoring the particular group.

Try paying for an alternative dedicated news server that does carry the newsgroup you're interested in.

SOME MESSAGES ARE UNAVAILABLE AFTER SYNCHRONIZING

I tried to synchronize the group, but some messages I click aren't available.

Obviously, you should first check that the settings for the group are correct. If the group isn't set to All Messages, and the Synchronize check box isn't checked, this could easily explain the missing message bodies. Another possibility is that the message was removed from the host server sometime after the header list was distributed. It can take up to 72 hours after a message is physically removed before it disappears from the header list.

News servers only have so much disk space. To allow them to continually add incoming files to their lists, they must continually discard old files. If your server is missing a few articles you may "ask" for a repost of the incomplete files, but while the poster is expected to service reasonable repost requests there is no requirement to do so. Sometimes a regular poster might not service repost requests at all, but will instead indicate an FTP, ICQ, or IRQ service where you can pick up missing files. And in many cases a repost request will be answered by a person who just happens to have downloaded the same file set and is willing to help support the group.

Finally, if you are doing everything right and your server is not gathering all the articles that were posted, consider informing your ISP's support desk of the problem. It does not do any good to complain to everyone else in the newsgroup if you are not telling the few people who are actually paid to help you. Servers and the connecting routers are sensitive electronic equipment and their only guarantee is that they will fail at some point. Help your ISP monitor the network.

If your server is very poorly connected and misses a lot of articles, as I stated above, you should consider hiring a dedicated news service as a secondary server.

MESSAGE NO LONGER AVAILABLE

A message I read earlier is no longer available.

The default settings in Outlook Express delete read messages five days after you have downloaded them. You can change this option on the Maintenance tab of the OE Options dialog.

WHICH ONES ARE NEW?

I can't tell which messages are new.

Open the Options dialog by choosing Tools, Options. On the Read tab, place a check mark next to Mark All Messages as Read When Exiting a Newsgroup.

NO NEWS SERVER CONNECTION

Outlook Express cannot locate my news server.

Do you need to use a separate Internet connection to access the news server? If so, choose Tools, Accounts, and then click the News tab in the Internet Accounts dialog. Look at what is listed under Connection next to your news account listing. If it says Any Available, click Properties and select the Connection tab. Place a check mark next to Always Connect to This Account Using, and select the appropriate connection from the drop-down list.

TIPS FROM THE WINDOWS PROS: NEWSGROUPS . . . FOR MORE THAN JUST NEWS

Newsgroups began innocently enough as forums for university, government, and science research folks to find and offer various kinds of support and share info over the precursor to the 'Net. However, it didn't take long for Usenet to explode as a means of online recreation. Today, no matter how obscure you think your hobby or personal interest may be, a newsgroup is probably already dedicated to it. And one of the great advantages of newsgroups is the fact that files can be easily attached to posts. Attachments can be in the form of pictures, sound files, movies, text documents, programs, or anything else imaginable. In this respect, newsgroups really shine when compared to mailing lists; most mailing lists strictly forbid attachments, but in Usenet they are welcome.

Newsgroups with the word *binaries* in their address are good places to find attachments. The word Binary refers to a non-text attachment, some kind of a data or program file. Naturally, you need to exercise some care before you download any messages with large attachments. First, ask yourself whether you have enough bandwidth to download the message. The OE6 message list doesn't show a paper clip icon until you've downloaded a message with an attachment, but it does tell you the size of each individual message, as shown in Figure 11.14. It is a fair assumption that a large file size would indicate the presence of an attachment.

Figure 11.14
This newsgroup contains several messages that might contain large attachments.

The paper clip icon appears here when a message with an attachment has been downloaded

Note the message size here

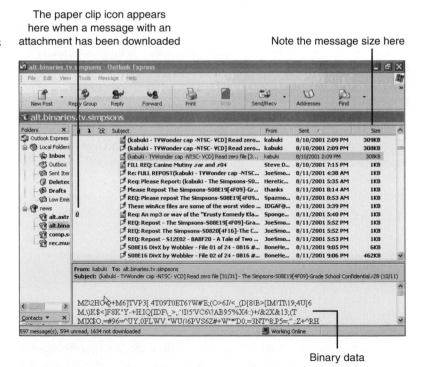

Binary data

After you have determined that you can handle the message download, you should also keep virus safety in mind. If the attachment is a standard multimedia format, such as JPEG, WAV, GIF, MP3, or AVI, it should be safe. But if the attachment is an unknown format or is an executable program (.EXE and .VBS are common extensions for these), you should follow your standard anti-virus procedures.

Large news attachments are posted as multi-part files, to get around the message-size limitations of news servers. These postings break up the large attachment over several consecutive posts. You can usually identify these types of posts by the Subject field, which identifies the message as part of a series. For example, you might see something like, "xfiles.avi (1/3), xfiles.avi (2/3) . . . ," and so on.

Multi-part attachments only open properly if downloaded and then combined together. Your first step is to identify each part of the series; if you miss even one portion of the series, it will not open properly. Use Ctrl+click and/or Shift+click to select each member of the series. After you've selected all of them, right-click the series, and choose Combine and Decode from the shortcut menu, as shown in Figure 11.15.

Figure 11.15
You must be sure you select every member of a multipart attachment series before attempting the download.

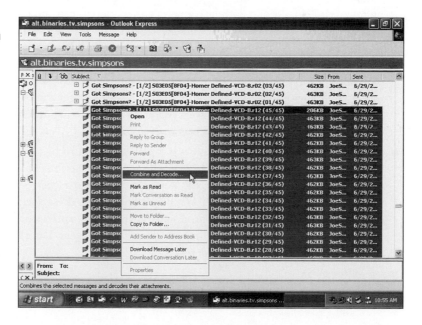

You are next presented with a dialog box asking you to put the series members in order. They should be in numeric order, starting with part one at the top of the list. Use the Move Up and Move Down buttons to place them in the correct order. Depending on the size of the multipart attachment, the download may take some time. When it is complete, a message window opens with a single attachment listed. This doesn't make much sense, since it looks as though you're going to send the file to someone. But typically you want to save it to your hard disk. So just right-click on that file icon in the attachment line, and choose Save As. Then save the file with the name and location you wish.

Multimedia attachments in Usenet can be a lot of fun. For example, the group `alt.bina-ries.tv.simpsons` usually contains WAV and AVI files of popular sound bites and catch-phrases—or even an entire episode—from the television series *The Simpsons*. If you save downloaded WAV files in the \WINNT\Media folder of your hard drive, you can later assign those sounds to various Windows events. Wouldn't Windows be more enjoyable if each critical stop were accompanied by Bart Simpson's "Aye Carumba" rather than the monotonous Chord.wav?

Another gem to be on the lookout for in Usenet is MP3 music. MP3 files offer CD-quality music, but because they use about one-twelfth the storage space, they can be transported efficiently over the Internet. You probably know about MP3s from all the hoopla about Napster, but you may not have known that MP3s were also available over newsgroups. Look for any newsgroup with *mp3* in the address, but watch out for those bootlegs!

If you become a serious newsgroup junkie, especially if you're into downloading (or upload-ing) large files, you'll have some boning up to do:

- Check out the news stuff at Deja.com or Google.com (they're actually the same compa-ny now), and correspond with heavy news posters on your group of choice. When you post large files, split them up into smaller chunks. In OE, choose Tools, Accounts. Click the News tab and Choose the news server you use. Click Properties, and the Advanced tab. Notice the setting there for Posting: Break Apart Messages Larger Than ____KB. This specifies to break up large messages, so that each part is smaller than the file size indicated. Some older servers cannot handle messages larger than 64 KB. By breaking large messages into smaller messages, you ensure that the messages are transmitted and received correctly. Make sure this option is selected.

- Second, if you are seriously into newsgroups, you'll want to bag OE and use it only for your e-mail. Download and get familiar with one of the serious programs designed for news, such as Xnews (`download.com`), News Rover (`download.com`), or Agent (`forteinc.com/agent/index.htm`). Among other benefits, these specialized products automate the process of finding, grouping, downloading, and decoding file attachments split across multiple messages. They are serious time savers. Here's a list of URLs for a couple other alternative newsreaders:

- NewsRover ($)
  `http://www.newsrover.com/`
- Newsbin Pro ($) and "classic" Newsbin (free)
  `http://www.newsbin.com/`
- Newgrabber ($)
  `http://www.news-grabber.com`
- Gravity ($)
  `http://www.microplanet.com/`

11

Figure 11.16 shows an example of Xnews.

 Some news readers, such as Agent-MP3, are specifically made to search Usenet and quickly find all the MP3 files.

Figure 11.16
Xnews makes downloading, combining, and decoding multipart news messages far less laborious than OE does.

Indicates missing
attachments

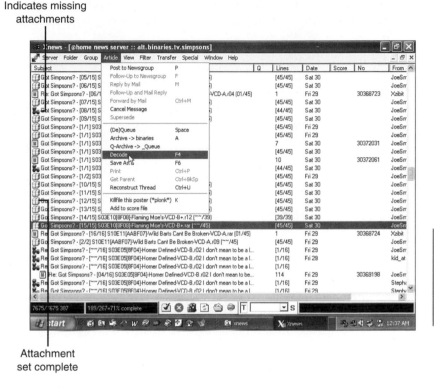

Attachment
set complete

Notice how the icons on the left indicate whether all the portions of a message are on the server. If the block icon is full, all the pieces of an attachment are present, and you can begin downloading. If not, skip it, and try to find it on another news server, or ask the poster to repost that portion. This saves you from having to visually examine and count to be sure all the attachments are there. Also, assuming the postings are named correctly, Xnews doesn't require you to rearrange them before downloading and decoding. It does so automagically.

CHAPTER 12

CHATTING AND CONFERENCING WITH WINDOWS MESSENGER

In this chapter

AN OVERVIEW OF WINDOWS MESSENGER

Windows Messenger is an online, real-time communication program that lets you talk with friends and coworkers across the house or across the world, over the Internet. For starters, Windows Messenger lets you keep a list of *contacts*—coworkers or friends you're interested in communicating with—and lets you know which are online at any given time. When they're online, you can type messages which appear instantly on your contacts' screens.

Depending on your interest and the speed of your Internet connection you can also communicate by voice, and even use two-way video so you can see as well as talk to each other. You can share a virtual electronic "whiteboard" or chalkboard to make collaborative drawings, or work interactively with a program, using a feature called Application Sharing. All of these capabilities are part of Windows Messenger.

NOTE   Many businesses use NetMeeting, an older Microsoft program with these same features. If your organization uses NetMeeting, see "What About NetMeeting?" later in this chapter.

Messaging has become very popular in the business world as a way to communicate with coworkers, to reduce travel costs through videoconferencing, and to give demonstrations and customer support. It can connect the office and wired-network world with specially enabled cell phones and wireless personal organizers. And, messaging also is a great way to stay in touch with friends and family.

Before we get into these details, though, we should talk a bit about the whole phenomenon of messaging itself.

WHAT IS MESSAGING, ANYWAY?

Messaging fills a niche somewhere between e-mail and the telephone. Like e-mail, it can travel anywhere around the globe, essentially for free. Unlike e-mail, though, it requires you and the person you're communicating with to be online at the same time. Like the telephone, it's immediate, interactive, and conversational. But unlike the telephone, it doesn't have to occupy your full attention—with it, you can carry on several conversations at once, or you can divide your attention between a conversation and other work.

Messaging has been around since the early 1980s when the first computer networks and "bulletin board" computer systems appeared. When the Internet became a public phenomenon, programs like IRC (Internet Relay Chat) and ICQ ("I seek you") became popular. But messaging really took off as America Online soared in popularity, and today millions of people, both AOL subscribers and non-subscribers alike use AOL's "Instant Messenger" service. Microsoft, which may join revolutions late but always brings bigger guns, came up with several attempts to move into the field: Microsoft Chat, then NetMeeting, and now Windows Messenger.

That brings us to the topic of competition and business practices, and I need to mention that the storm of controversy that has surrounded Microsoft for the past several years is threatening to blow Microsoft Messenger right off of your desktop. U.S. court rulings might force Microsoft to remove Messenger from Windows XP entirely, or may give computer sellers the option of removing it and replacing it with other programs such as AOL Instant Messenger. At the time this book was published, it wasn't clear what would happen. If you find that Messenger doesn't appear where I say it will on your computer's screen and menus, you've been caught in this storm. If this is the case, you can try any alternate software you've been given, or, you can download Windows Messenger from the Microsoft Web site at www.microsoft.com. In fact, even if Messenger is pre-installed on your computer, you may want to investigate other chat software anyway. Windows Messenger is a great program, but the choice is, and should be, yours.

That's enough of that. This chapter is about Windows Messenger, and so far I've talked about nothing but other programs. Let's get on with the show.

NOTE

> Windows Messenger used to be called Microsoft Messenger. My guess is that pretty soon it will be renamed .NET Messenger, as Microsoft's technology development department has been almost as busy as its legal department lately, and is advancing a whole raft of new products named ".NET this-or-that." Whatever it's called, I'm getting tired of typing it, so for the rest of this chapter I'll call it just plain old Messenger.

WHAT WINDOWS MESSENGER CAN AND CAN'T DO

Messenger has several options for communicating. You can choose any or all of them, so you can start out with the simple stuff and work your way up, if you want. With Messenger and an Internet connection, you can

- Type text messages.
- Communicate with voice and video even over a dial-up Internet connection. (It's not quite TV quality but you can, say, stick your tongue out at someone, and within a few seconds, they'll more likely than not be able to tell.) Over a cable or DSL connection or a corporate LAN, you can get up to 15 video frames per second, which is nearly TV quality, with excellent voice quality.
- Receive video and sound even if you don't have a camera or microphone of your own.
- Transfer pictures and files of any type.
- Collaboratively draw on a shared "whiteboard," which can be saved or printed out for permanent storage.
- Collaborate on a single application, or even share your entire screen with another. The desktop-sharing feature lets multiple people collaborate on, say, a word processing document, each being able to see the contents of a shared window, grab the cursor, and make edits. It's great for training and demonstrations too.

12

Although Messenger lets you communicate with several people at a time with text chat (as many as you want, actually), it does *not* have a group videoconference conference feature that lets several people participate in one collective voice or video conversation. For that, you'll need to turn to third-party software like CU-See-Me.

Also, in my experience, Messenger isn't perfect. I've found it to be picky and unpredictable: Sometimes the audio comes through, and sometimes it doesn't. Connections can drop out at random intervals. Audio "echoing" occurs sometimes, as well as other irritating sound glitches. But when it works, it works very well, and after all, it's free. If you look at it as a super CB radio rather than as a telephone, you should have a great time with it.

NOTE

Messenger uses the newly developed SIP Protocol (Session Initiation Protocol) for voice and video. SIP provides a standard way for messaging, telephony (voice), and video programs to communicate. Unfortunately, hardware-based Internet connection sharing routers may not be able to manage SIP data, so voice and video chat won't work if either you or your contact use one of these devices. Check with your router's manufacturer to see if they offer SIP support. Windows Internet Connection Sharing software doesn't have this limitation: It's "SIP aware."

SYSTEMS REQUIREMENTS AND PLATFORM COMPATIBILITY

For text messaging alone, there are no special requirements beyond having an Internet connection. To use the audio and video features of Messenger, your computer must meet the following minimum hardware requirements:

- The most current Windows Messenger version is available only for the 32-bit Windows platform, so you can't communicate with people using Linux or other operating systems. Messenger runs on only Windows 95, 98, Me, 2000, XP, and NT4, and it's not available on the 64-bit (Itanium) version of Windows XP. At the time this book was published, Macintosh support was limited to MSN Messenger version 2, which uses different audio and video protocols, so only text-chat communication is possible with Mac users. Hopefully, this will be rectified soon. Mac users should check www.microsoft.com/mac for developments.

- Any computer capable of running Windows XP has enough memory and processing power for Messenger. If the people you communicate with use an earlier version of Windows, they will need a 133MHz Pentium or better processor with 32MB of RAM or more. They'll also need to download the latest version of Messenger from www.microsoft.com. They should also be able to use Windows Update to get it.

- For text communication only, any connection speed is fine. If you want to use voice or video, you'll need a 33,600bps or faster modem, ISDN, DSL, cable, or LAN Internet connection. The faster the better.

- To establish voice or video connections, you need a sound card, a microphone, and speakers. A sound card is required for both audio and video support. Without a sound card, you can only use text chat and desktop sharing.

12

■ To transmit video with your calls, you need a video capture card or camera that provides a Video for Windows capture driver. Any recent USB- or FireWire-connected camera should meet this requirement. Older parallel-port cameras are very unlikely to have compatible drivers (see the manufacturer's Web site).

TIP FROM

Bob & Brian

Owing to the growing use of Messenger, NetMeeting, and other videoconferencing software, numerous companies now sell inexpensive add-on products such as cameras, microphones, headsets, video cards, and software additions. For example, I got a free color video camera as a bonus for buying a $99 hard drive!

TIP FROM

Bob & Brian

You should install any new audio or video hardware, and, if necessary, update your audio and video device drivers, *before* you run Messenger for the first time, if possible. Getting it to recognize newly installed hardware isn't always effortless.

Before we go any further, I should warn you that Messenger's voice and video communication will not work properly if you use a shared Internet connection made through a cable/DSL Sharing Router device, as described in Chapter 19, "Connecting Your LAN to the Internet." Messenger may also be blocked by firewall software or hardware. This can be a problem for corporate users wishing to communicate with others outside the company.

If this is the case, you will be able to communicate with text chat, but you will not be able to use voice, video, or desktop sharing. The technical reason is that the protocols used by Messenger aren't compatible with the Network Address Translation (NAT) mechanism that the connection sharing devices use. Yes, it's a drag, but I think it's a small price to pay for the additional protection from hackers that the NAT mechanism provides. I'll discuss this in more detail in Chapter 18 and in the "Troubleshooting" section at the end of this chapter.

On the other hand, voice and video should work with the Internet Connection Sharing and Internet Connection Firewall systems built into Windows XP, because these programs are "Messenger-aware."

With Whom Can I Communicate?

Messenger works with the .NET Passport system which was described in Chapter 9. You can only chat or voice/videoconference with people who have registered for a Passport. As mentioned in Chapter 9, you don't need to use Microsoft's Hotmail or MSN service, but you both need to register with Microsoft. Remember, if you're concerned about privacy, you can submit the absolute minimum of information when you register—only your e-mail address is really required. (Of course, without your name on file, others can't search for you by name if they want to chat you up. They'll need to know your e-mail address.)

The type of messaging you can use is limited by what equipment you and your contact(s) have in common. At the very least, you can always type text messages back and forth.

12

Obviously, if you don't have a camera attached to your computer you can't send video, but if your contacts do, you can still receive video when you chat with them, and vice versa. You'll need a microphone and speakers or a headset if you want to communicate by voice.

Text messaging may be the slowest way to communicate but at least it's a guaranteed thing. Personally, I find that I use it more than voice or video, by far. It's the least obtrusive form of Messenger communication—I can have a chat window or two open and pop off questions and answers while I continue to work on my projects.

GETTING STARTED WITH WINDOWS MESSENGER

To fire up Messenger, look at the bottom-right corner of your screen for the tiny Messenger icon —it looks like two tiny people—in the Notification area, as shown in Figure 12.1.

Figure 12.1
Double-click the little people to start Messenger.

If this icon doesn't appear in your Notification area, click Start, All Programs, and see if Windows Messenger appears in the menu. If it does, click it. (If it isn't listed, Windows Messenger might not be installed on your computer as a result of a decision by your organization, your computer manufacturer or by the U.S. courts—see the note in the beginning of this chapter.)

The first time you start Messenger, you'll see a blank window that says "Click Here to Sign In." Click there, and Messenger will walk you through a setup wizard to gather your personal information. You'll want to be sure you're connected to the Internet before proceeding.

SIGNING IN WITH YOUR .NET PASSPORT

If you haven't already signed up for a Passport, you'll have to do that now. Messenger will walk you through the .NET Passport Wizard to get this set up.

→ To learn about Passport and the .NET Passport Wizard, **see** "Getting a Passport to Microsoft Country," **p. 323**.

To link up with Passport, you'll have to provide an e-mail address. You can use your current e-mail address, or you can set up a Microsoft Hotmail or MSN e-mail address. If you have already set up a Passport, you'll only need to enter your e-mail address and password, following the .NET Passport Wizard's instructions. Then whenever you log on, Windows will use this Passport automatically.

NOTE

> You can change the Passport associated with your Windows user account (and the e-mail address it's linked to) from the User Accounts control panel. To do this, click Start, Control Panel, User Accounts. Click on your account's icon, and then click Change My .NET Passport.

SIGNING IN TO MESSENGER

When the Passport setup process is finished, or if you had already set up your Passport earlier, Messenger will ask you to sign in, as shown in Figure 12.2. It may seem odd that you have to sign in to Windows, and then sign in to Messenger separately. The reason the process is separate is so you can choose whether or not you want to be available to others who might want to use Messenger to contact you.

Figure 12.2
The Messenger Sign In screen asks for your Passport password. You can also choose to have Messenger sign in automatically when you log on to Windows XP.

By default, Windows will display your Passport e-mail address. If you happen to have multiple passports, you can select an alternate one from the drop-down list, or you can just type in a different e-mail address.

You can also choose to have Messenger sign on automatically when you log on to Windows. If you always want Messenger active and available when you're using your computer, check Sign Me In Automatically. You can always change this selection later on.

Finally, enter your Passport password and click OK.

 If Messenger can't sign in, see "Messenger Gives Connection Error When I Sign In" in the "Troubleshooting" section at the end of this chapter.

When you've signed on to Windows Messenger, you'll see a screen similar to the one shown in Figure 12.3. The Messenger screen shows you your current passport account or the name you want to display to others (I'll show you how to change this later in the chapter). If your passport is linked to a Microsoft Hotmail account, you'll see a notice telling you whether you have any new Hotmail messages. You can click this entry to open a Hotmail window.

Finally, the window shows you which of your contacts are presently online and which are not.

Figure 12.3
The Messenger screen shows you who's online and who's not.

NOTE

> If you have installed the Messenger add-in pack, located at http://messenger.microsoft.com/download/addin.asp, then you will receive visual and audible indication of new mail in your MSN or Hotmail account.

ADDING CONTACTS

A Messenger Contact is a person whom you've identified as someone you want to be able to chat with. Before you can communicate with Messenger, you'll need to add your coworkers, colleagues, clients, friends, or family to your Messenger contact list.

To add a contact, click the Add a Contact button at the bottom of the Messenger window or click Tools, Add a Contact. Windows will ask you whether you want to select a contact by their e-mail address (if you know their Passport sign-in name), or whether you want to search for them by name. Right now you can only search through the Hotmail member directory, your own personal Address Book, or Active Directory on corporate networks, but Microsoft may add other search directories later on. Select a method, and click Next.

In the next step, enter the person's e-mail address or Passport sign in name and click Next, or fill out the search form, which is shown in Figure 12.4. Fill in as much information as you can to help narrow things down, select the desired directory under Search For This Person At, and then click Next.

After a moment, Windows will show you a list of matching names and locations. If you don't see the desired name listed, select Back and change some of your selection criteria. If you do see the entry for your contact, select it and click Next.

As a matter of privacy, your new contact will be notified that you have added them to your contact list. Likewise, you'll be notified if others add you to their contact list. (For your own privacy, if you want to you can block them from knowing if you're online and from sending you messages. I'll show you how in the next section.)

Figure 12.4
To search for a contact in the Hotmail directory or your Address book, fill in as much information as you can.

Your first job then, before you can use Messenger, is to add contacts. Of course, you may first have to encourage your colleagues and friends to sign up for a Microsoft Passport in order to have anyone to chat with. (This, I'm sure, is part of Microsoft's Grand Plan.)

When contacts are added to your list, you'll receive notification when any of them sign in, as shown in Figure 12.5. If you find this annoying, you can disable notifications using the Preferences settings, which I'll discuss in the next section.

Figure 12.5
When your contacts sign in, you'll receive notification.

SETTING MESSENGER OPTIONS AND PREFERENCES

Messenger has the potential to intrude upon your workday and upon your privacy. You can control how much information about you is revealed, and what ways Messenger is allowed to notify and interact with you. In this section, I'll cover the Messenger options including its privacy settings. Remember that if you use Hotmail, you'll also need to configure your Hotmail privacy settings (such as whether or not your name is listed in the Member directory) on the Hotmail site.

To change Messenger options, click Tools and Options, and then view the six options tabs. I'll go through them in turn.

PERSONAL INFORMATION

The Personal tab (see Figure 12.6) lets you choose the name others see when you're signed in to Messenger. By default this is your Passport name; that is, your e-mail address. For privacy reasons, you want to change this to your name or nickname.

Figure 12.6
The Personal tab lets you change your displayed name and some other preferences.

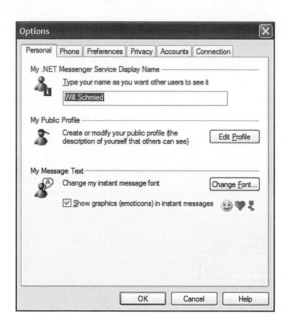

If your Passport is linked to a Microsoft Hotmail account, you can also choose whether or not Windows automatically supplies Hotmail with your Passport when you ask Messenger to read mail. If you're concerned that others might be reading your e-mail if you step away from your computer for a while, check this box. Finally, you can select the font used to display chat messages, and can enable or disable the automatic display of "smilies" or emoticons. With graphics enabled, if your friend types :) you'll see A.

PHONE CONTACT INFORMATION

The Phone tab lets you enter home and work telephone numbers that your contacts will be able to view. If you're using Messenger for business purposes, you'll probably want to enter your work telephone number here. Otherwise, I suggest leaving this page blank. You can always give out your phone number later on if you think it's appropriate.

MESSENGER PREFERENCES

The Preferences tab, shown in Figure 12.7, lets you control how Messenger starts, and how and when it's allowed to alert (or you might say "annoy") you as contacts and messages come and go. The options you are most likely to want to think about changing are

- **Run This Program When Windows Starts**—This is enabled by default. Uncheck to prevent Messenger from starting up automatically. (Automatic sign-in must be changed separately, from the Sign In window. To change that setting, click File, Sign Out, and then File, Sign In.)

- **Show Me as Away**—If your computer sits idle for 20 minutes, by default your contacts will see a notification that you're "away." This is another privacy issue. You can change the time, or block the message entirely by unchecking this option.

- **Alerts**—You can enable or disable pop-up messages and sounds for when contacts sign on and off or send messages with the options in the Alerts section. If you have installed the Messenger add-in pack, you can also control the alerts for new mail.

- **File Transfer**—This lets you change the folder where any files your contacts send you land. The default folder is My Received Files inside My Documents.

Figure 12.7
The Preferences tab lets you change Messenger startup, alert, and file transfer options.

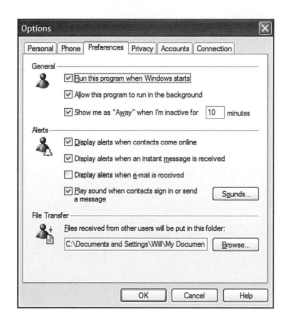

PRIVACY OPTIONS

The Privacy tab lets you choose to prevent specific contacts, or all unknown contacts, from seeing your status and from sending you messages. Additionally, you can also check on who has added you to their contact list, configure an alert to occur when someone adds you to their contact list, configure security for your Passport by instructing Messenger to always prompt you for your password, and lastly hide your tabs if you were using a public computer. All of these options have been provided to allow you to control the amount of security you feel you need.

Figure 12.8 shows the Privacy tab's Allow and Block lists. By default all of your contacts and "All Other Users" are in the Allow List, which lets them see when you sign in and out, and lets them send you messages. You can move individual contacts over to the Block List to shut them out. Move an entry by selecting it in one list or the other, and clicking Allow or Block.

You also can move the All Other Users entry to the Block list. All Other Users applies to people who have added you to their contact list but whom you haven't yet added to yours. In other words, these are unverified strangers. In the figure, I've moved it to the Block side to show how it looks, but unless you're *very* concerned about privacy you probably don't need to do this.

Figure 12.8
The Privacy tab lets you control who knows you're online.

ACCOUNTS

The Accounts tab allows you to configure a Messenger account and a communications service account, such as an internal system that supports SIP or Microsoft Exchange Server.

CONNECTION OPTIONS

The Connection tab can normally be ignored. If, however, your computer is on a network that uses a SOCKS or Web proxy server, you might need to make entries here in order to use Messenger. Your ISP or network administrator will tell you if you need to do this.

Finally, when you've enlisted your friends, signed in to Messenger, and gone over your privacy options, you're ready to chat.

CHATTING WITH TEXT

To chat with one of your contacts, they have to be signed on. That is, they have to appear in the Online list in the Messenger window. To start up a conversation with one of your contacts, double-click his/her name in the Online list, or click Actions, Send an Instant Message and select his/her name from the drop-down list.

When you do this, a text chat conversation window appears, as shown in Figure 12.9. Enter your message in the bottom part of the window, and press Enter, or click Send to send the message to your friend. The first message you send will start the conversation.

Figure 12.9
The Conversation window lets you carry on a text conversation.

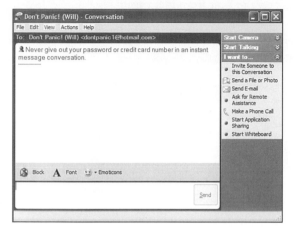

If someone starts a conversation with you, a notification will appear as shown in Figure 12.10. Click it to open the Conversation window and begin chatting. You can also open the window by clicking on the new button that appears in your taskbar.

Figure 12.10
When someone starts up a conversation with you, a notification will appear. Click it to open up the Conversation window.

The messages you type to each other will appear in the upper part of the window, as shown in Figure 12.11. This is pretty much all there is to know about text chat. Before we move on to other topics, though, there are a few tips:

- Unless you're certain of the identity of the person you're chatting with, don't give out any personal information, especially your telephone number, social security number, credit card info, and so on.

- You can save the text of your conversation by clicking File, Save As.

- You can change the size of the displayed text with View, Text Size.

- You can instantly add the person you're talking with to your Block list by clicking the Block icon or selecting File, Block. This is handy if someone contacts you out of the blue and you don't care to hear from them again.

Figure 12.11
As you chat, your messages scroll up in the Conversation window.

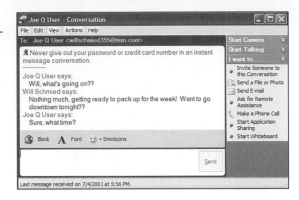

CHAT ETIQUETTE

Online chatting has an etiquette all its own. In face to face conversations, whether we realize it or not, facial expressions and body language communicate almost as much as the words we use. When we're using text chat, many of those emotional cues are missing. Sometimes it's hard to tell from a written message whether a person is joking, angry, sad, or sarcastic, and misunderstandings can follow.

One way to help with this is to spice up your text chat with the popular little punctuation-mark faces called emoticons or smilies. A wry comment might sound too sharp in written form, but if it's followed by a winking smiley face signified by ;-), the reader knows the remark was made in jest. Some of the most popular emoticons are listed in Table 12.1. (If they don't make sense, try rotating the page 90° to the right.)

TABLE 12.1	BASIC EMOTICONS
:-)	I meant that in the nicest possible way
;-)	Wink! Wink!
:-O	Horrors!

Messenger knows more than 30 others. To see the full list, click Help in the Messenger window, choose Help Topics, and search for *emoticons*.

Because we tend to type these messages off the top of our head and fire them off instantly, rather than considering them the way we do when writing a letter, it's especially important to think about how your remarks will be perceived. And before you write anything that could come back to haunt you, remember that these chat messages can be saved as files, and they could conceivably reappear as Exhibit A in court someday.

MY STATUS, OR OUT TO LUNCH AND BACK AGAIN

If you're signed in to Messenger but are planning on stepping away from your computer for a while, you can tell Messenger so that it can tell your contacts. This is the polite thing to do—otherwise, if someone tries to contact you while you're away, they'll think you're ignoring them when you don't respond.

To change your status, click File, My Status in the Messenger window, or click the Messenger icon in the Notification area and select My Status. Choose one of the messages, as shown in Figure 12.12. When you select one of the away messages, it will appear in your friends' contacts lists, as shown in Figure 12.12. This lets them know not to expect an immediate reply from you.

Figure 12.12
When you select a status message (left), it appears on your friends' contact lists (right).

Change your status back to Online when you're ready to be contacted again.

SIGNING OUT

If you're finished with Messenger, if you don't want to be disturbed at all, or if you don't want anyone to know you're your computer, you can sign off from Messenger completely. However, just closing the Messenger window *does not sign you out*. Messenger will stay active—you can still see the little person icon in the Notification area.

To sign out completely, choose File, Sign out in the Messenger window, or right-click the Messenger icon in the Notification area and select Sign Out. Now, you're signed out and no one can contact you. You can sign on again by double-clicking the Messenger notification icon.

You can also completely close Messenger by right-clicking the Messenger notification icon and selecting Exit.

12

GROUP CHAT

Messenger will let you open several Conversation windows at once and carry on several separate conversations. Sometimes, though, you'll want to have a conversation with several people together. Like conference-calling on the telephone, group chat lets everyone in the conversation see what anyone types. It's great for discussing anything from dinner plans to business proposals.

To set up a group conversation, set up a chat connection to one person. Then, click on the Invite icon in the Conversation window, just under the scrolling conversation text. Choose To Join This Conversation, and select another of your online contacts. They'll be invited to join the conversation. You can add as many people as you want by extending additional invitations.

You can't remove someone from the group, but individuals can leave the group at any time by closing their Conversation window.

SENDING AND RECEIVING FILES

While you're chatting with someone, you can easily transfer files back and forth using Messenger. You can use this to exchange documents, pictures, movie files, or anything else you please.

To send a file to a person you're chatting with, you can drag the file from the desktop or Explorer to the Conversation window. Or, you can click Send A File on the right side of the Conversation window, or select File, Send a File or Photo. In this case, a file selection dialog will appear. Locate the file and click Open to send it. Your friend will have to permit the file to be sent, and then the file will be transferred.

If someone attempts to send you a file, a message will appear in your Conversation window as shown in Figure 12.13. You can click on Accept or Decline. A pop-up message will warn you that you should check files from unknown sources with a virus scanner. I'll emphasize that warning here:

CAUTION

> Don't accept files from people you don't know! Don't accept executable program files with extensions ending in .exe, .wsh, .com, .vbs, or .bat unless you are *certain* that they're safe. You should scan any files you receive with a virus checker before opening them, in any case.

You can explore the folder into which received files arrive by clicking File, Open Received Files. By default, files received by Messenger are placed in My Received Files inside My Documents, but you can change this location using Tools, Options, Preferences.

12

Figure 12.13
If someone attempts to send you a file, you can accept or decline the transfer.

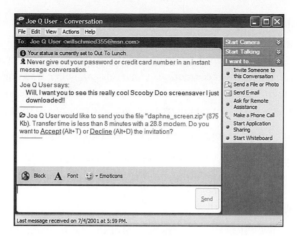

COMMUNICATING WITH VOICE

If you and one of your friends have computers outfitted with a sound card, speakers, and a microphone, you can converse over your LAN or Internet connection.

Now, before you get too excited about this, take note that AT&T and the other telephone carriers haven't sued Microsoft over this intrusion into their territory. Why? Internet voice chat isn't quite up to telephone quality standards. Over a dial-up Internet connection, you may find that the sound is choppy, that you miss phrases, or that the sound connection doesn't work at all. Over a high-speed Internet connection, it's better, but still far from perfect. Still, it's nearly free, and when it works, it's fun. On a corporate network or office LAN, the quality can be very good.

To use voice chat, as I mentioned, your computer will have to be outfitted with sound hardware (most are, these days), and you'll need speakers and a microphone that's compatible with your sound card. Your local computer store can show you what you need. You'll have even better luck if you use a headset designed for computer use, with an earphone and microphone that hangs in front of your mouth.

NOTE

> The voice transmission system used by the version of Messenger in Windows XP is not compatible with older versions of Messenger. Your contacts may have to upgrade their copy of Messenger if they're not using Windows XP. They should check for updates at www.windowsupdate.com or www.microsoft.com.

Before you try to use voice chat for the first time, you should check out your sound equipment using the Audio and Video Tuning Wizard.

12

TUNING UP AUDIO HARDWARE

Getting your microphone and speaker volume controls set up correctly is an important factor in being able to use Messenger for voice communication. If your microphone isn't set up correctly or its volume control is incorrect, your friends may hear horrendous noise or nothing at all. If your speakers are set too high, they may feed back into the microphone causing weird echoes. Messenger can help you check this out before you try to make your first call.

Click Tools, Audio and Video Tuning Wizard in the Messenger menu, then follow these steps:

1. Be sure to close any programs that use sound or video, such as Windows Media Player. Be sure your speakers and microphone (and camera, if you have one) are plugged in. Then click Next.

2. If you have a video camera or video capture hardware installed, the wizard will ask you to adjust your picture. I'll talk about this later in the chapter. You can skip this part now by clicking Next until you get to the screen that discusses speaker placement.

3. Read the instructions about proper speaker and microphone placement and click Next.

4. Select the microphone and speakers you're currently using, if you have multiple sets. If you are *not* using headphones, uncheck I Am Using Headphones. Then click Next.

5. Click the button marked Click to Test Speakers and adjust the volume slider (indicated in Figure 12.14) until you can hear the sound clearly. Then click Stop, and Next.

Figure 12.14
Test and adjust your speaker volume here.

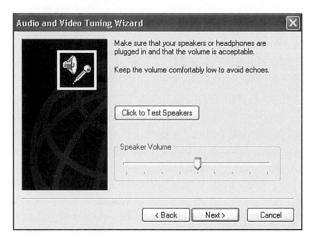

6. Read into the microphone in a normal speaking voice, and move the microphone until the indicator touches the yellow region at times while you're talking (see Figure 12.15). Windows will adjust the volume control automatically. When the level is correct, click Next, and then Finish to end the wizard.

 If the green, yellow, and red microphone indicator bar doesn't appear when you speak, see "No Sound Picked Up from Microphone" in the "Troubleshooting" section at the end of this chapter.

When your speaker and microphone volume have been adjusted, you're ready to call someone.

Figure 12.15
Adjust the microphone until the indicator bar touches the yellow region while you're speaking.

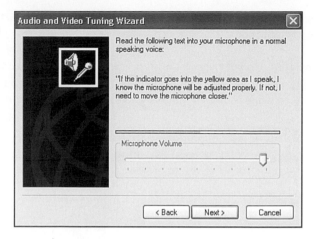

CHATTING BY VOICE

If your and your contact's computers are both equipped with a microphone and speakers, or preferably combination headsets that contain a built-in microphone, you can use Messenger to converse for free. The quality of this type of voice connection can vary, and never equals real telephone quality, but it usually works. And, if your Internet or network connection is fast enough, it can save some serious long-distance money.

TIP FROM

Bob & Brian

Be sure you use the Audio/Video Tuning Wizard to get your speaker and microphone volume set correctly *before* you make a call, as I discussed in the previous section. This step may save you some frustration later on. If the sound doesn't work at least you'll know it's Messenger and not your hardware.

NOTE

The versions of Messenger supplied with previous versions of Windows supported the Net2Phone service that links your computer through the Internet to the regular telephone system, so you could call *anyone* from your computer. Net2Phone is not built in to the Messenger service provided with Windows XP. You can still investigate net2phone at www.net2phone.com. There's a charge for this service, but it's still less expensive than regular long distance.

To use voice chat, you'll need to have your coworker, relative, or friend already listed as a contact in Messenger. Use the instructions I gave earlier in the chapter to add contacts. And, your contact has to be online.

There are two ways you can initiate a voice call:

- You can click the large Actions, Start a Voice Conversation. All of your online contacts are listed there. Select your friend's name and choose Computer. This opens up a Conversation window and starts up a voice chat connection.

■ If you already have a Conversation (chat) window open, you can select Start Talking on the right side of the window.

This sends an "invitation" to your contact to start voice chat. They'll need to accept the invitation by clicking on the word Accept in their chat window, as shown in Figure 12.16. Likewise, if one of your friends invites you to start voice chat, you'll see the same message.

Figure 12.16
An invitation to start voice chat requires you to click Accept or Decline.

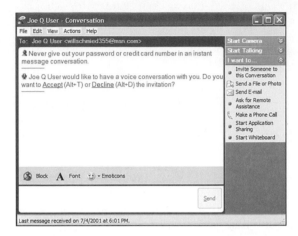

When the invitee clicks Accept, the voice conversation is started. The screen changes to show a speaker volume control, and a microphone mute button, as shown in Figure 12.17. You can use these to adjust the incoming sound, and to temporarily mute your microphone as you see fit.

Figure 12.17
When you have begun voice chat, sound controls appear in the Conversation window.

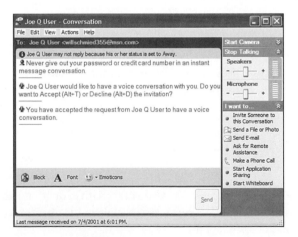

You can continue to use text chat in the Conversation window, if you wish. In fact, you may need to if the audio connection doesn't work smoothly.

 If the voice connection doesn't work for you, see "Voice Chat Doesn't Work" in the "Troubleshooting" section at the end of this chapter.

When you're finished chatting (or give up trying), you can click Stop Talking on the right side of the Conversation window, or you can just close the window entirely.

COMMUNICATING WITH VIDEO

If your computer has a "Web" camera installed, or if you have video capture hardware connected to a video camera, you can send pictures of your smiling self while you chat. Likewise, if your contact has a camera, you'll be able to see them while you chat. It's pretty nifty. It's just like the futuristic Videophone service that the telephone company promised (but never delivered) way back in the 1960s!

NOTE

> The video and voice transmission system used by the version of Messenger in Windows XP is not compatible with older versions of Messenger. Your friends may have to upgrade their copy of Messenger if they're not using Windows XP. They should check for updates at www.windowsupdate.com or www.microsoft.com.

Video chat is an extension of voice chat, so all of the caveats and setup instructions I gave in the previous section apply to video chat. Remember, you don't need a camera yourself to accept video chat calls. You only need to worry about this section if you want to send video.

TIP FROM

Bob & Brian

> I suggest that you use voice chat by itself a few times to get the hang of it before trying video. Video is slower and more troublesome, so you'll have better luck with audio the first time around.

TUNING VIDEO HARDWARE

Before you try to use video chat, you'll need to set up your Web camera or video camera according to the manufacturer's instructions. I prefer the little eyeball-sized cameras that connect through your computer's USB port. You can pick these up for $25 to $40 at office supply stores. Chapter 30 has some tips on adding and replacing hardware, if you haven't already installed the camera.

When the camera's installed, follow these steps:

1. Open Messenger and click Tools, Audio and Video Tuning Wizard. Click Next.
2. If you have more than one video input device installed, select the one you'd like to use. Click Next.
3. The Wizard will activate your camera and display your picture. Adjust the picture as needed. Center your face in the image, adjust the lighting, focus, brightness or anything else needed to get a good picture.

12

4. Click Next to proceed through the Audio tune-up portion of the Wizard, as I discussed earlier in the chapter.

When you know your picture and audio equipment are adjusted correctly, you can try to contact a friend.

CHATTING WITH PICTURES AND VOICE

The procedure for setting up a video connection is similar to the one used for voice chat. Your contact will have to be online first, of course. Click Actions, Start a Video Conversation to initiate a video connection with your friend. Alternatively, you can click the Start Camera button if you already have an open Conversation window.

Windows will inform your contact that you wish to begin a video and voice conversation. They'll have to click Accept or Decline, just as with a voice conversation.

 If the video connection can't be established, see "Video Chat Doesn't Work" in the "Troubleshooting" section at the end of this chapter.

When the connection has been made, a video window appears on the right side of the Conversation window, with sound controls underneath, as shown in Figure 12.18. By default, your own picture will appear in the lower right-hand corner of the video window. You can turn this screen-in-screen display off, and also temporarily stop sending a picture to your friend, by clicking on the Options menu just below the video screen.

Figure 12.18
With a video connection, you can see your own picture as well as your friend's. Click the Options button to change this display setup.

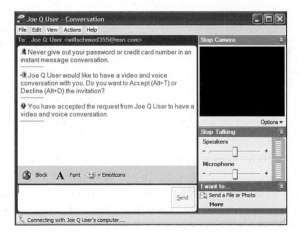

To end a video connection, click Stop Camera, or close the Conversation window.

CONFERENCING OPTIONS

Messenger provides a few features of the old NetMeeting program that are very useful for collaborating with another user, or for business presentations. From the Messenger Tools menu, you can select Send An Invitation . . .

- To Start Application Sharing. Application Sharing lets you and your contact both view the window of a program running on your computer. You can both use your mouse and keyboard to control the application. This is helpful for training, software demonstrations, or just plain collaboration on a project.

- To Start Remote Assistance. Remote Assistance, which I will discuss in more detail in Chapter 18, lets someone else view and manipulate your entire screen. Remote Assistance is great when you need help configuring or using Windows; a friend, coworker, or support person can show you what to do, or can just go ahead an fix problems for you.

- To Start Whiteboard. The Whiteboard is a drawing application that lets both you and your contact draw on a window. You can then save or print the results of your efforts.

Remote Assistance is covered in Chapter 18, "Windows Unplugged: Remote and Mobile Networking." I'll briefly discuss Application Sharing and the Whiteboard in the next two sections.

APPLICATION SHARING

If you want a friend, coworker, or consultant to help you work with a Windows program (such as Excel, WordPerfect, or Netscape Navigator) or even to help set up Windows itself, you can issue them an invitation to *share* the application or desktop. Application Sharing displays your program's window or your entire screen on your friend's computer. Either of you can take control of the program to make changes with the mouse and keyboard.

> **NOTE**
>
> Application Sharing is virtually identical to the Remote Assistance feature. Application Sharing is based on older technology. It's slower to use than Remote Assistance, but it does offer you a bit of privacy when you only want to share one application window— your contact won't be able to see the rest of your desktop unless you explicitly share it.

To use Application Sharing, Click Actions, Start Application Sharing. To Start Application Sharing, and select a name from the list of online contacts (or, click Other and enter their Passport address).

Windows will display a "Do you want to Accept" message in the other user's Conversation window. When they click Accept, Application Sharing will start up.

When the connection is established, you will see two new pages open, as shown in Figure 12.19 and Figure 12.20. In Figure 12.19, clicking App Sharing will open the Sharing page (see Figure 12.20) if it is not already open. From the Sharing page you can select a window name and click Share to share it, or select the Desktop to share all applications at once. Shared windows appear on your friend's screen, as shown in Figure 12.21. If you click on the Whiteboard button in Figure 12.19, you will start and share the Whiteboard application.

Figure 12.19
The Whiteboard button.

Figure 12.20
Share individual applications or the entire Windows desktop.

Figure 12.21
When someone shares an application with you, their application appears on your screen.

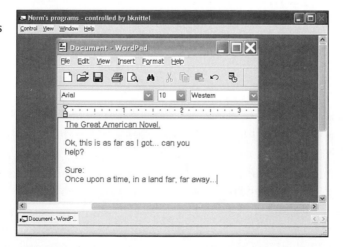

When you first share an application or the desktop, your contact will be able to see the shared window(s), but not change anything. If you want to let them actually manipulate the program you're sharing, click the Allow Control button in the Sharing dialog. If you want to work with an application someone has shared with you, click Control, Request Control. When you have control, you can use your mouse and keyboard to make changes in the shared program.

Normally, when the remote user requests to take control of the application, Windows asks the program's owner if this is okay. You can let your friend have control at will by checking the Automatically Accept Requests for Control button, which you can see in Figure 12.20. You can take control back at any time by pressing the Esc key.

TIP FROM

Bob
& Brian

> Application Sharing works best if the person who is sharing an application has their desktop resolution set to the same or a lower value than the person who's being invited to collaborate.

WHITEBOARD

When people started using computer conferencing to replace face-to-face meetings, everyone was happy about the travel money they saved, but noticed that it was tough to really interact. Some of the most productive parts of meetings occur at the chalkboard, where you can write down brainstorming ideas or sketch out ideas and get immediate feedback. To give the same sort of shared writing tool to online meetings, Messenger includes a "virtual chalkboard" called the Whiteboard that lets you and your chat partner draw on a common screen, as shown in Figure 12.22.

Figure 12.22
Whiteboard lets the members of a conversation draw on a common window.

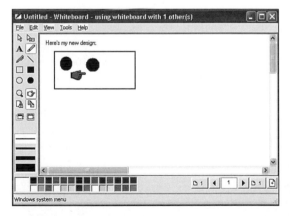

To start up the Whiteboard, you can select Tools, Send an Invitation, To Start Whiteboard in the Messenger window, or if you're already chatting with someone, you can click the Invite button and select To Start Whiteboard in the conversation window.

Whiteboard is similar to Windows Paint, but I don't have enough space in this book to go into any further detail. I'll leave it to you investigate its menus and drawing tools.

WHAT ABOUT NETMEETING?

As I mentioned at the beginning of this chapter, Messenger is meant as a replacement for Microsoft's previous chat/voice/video conferencing program called NetMeeting. If you or your organization prefers to use NetMeeting, you'll be happy to know that even though it doesn't appear on the Start menu, it's still present on your Windows XP computer. (The Whiteboard and Application Sharing features in Messenger use parts of NetMeeting, in fact.) If you want to continue to use NetMeeting, just follow these steps to create a shortcut for it:

1. Right-click on the desktop and select New, Shortcut.
2. Click the Browse button, and browse in turn into My Computer, the drive containing Windows, the Program Files folder, and the NetMeeting folder. Select conf, click OK, and then click Next.
3. Enter "NetMeeting" as the name of the shortcut and click Finish. A NetMeeting shortcut will appear on your desktop.
4. You can drag the shortcut from your desktop to your Quick Launch bar, or into your Start Menu. I suggest that you drag it to the Start button and hold it there. When the Start Menu opens, drag it to All Programs, Accessories, and Communication before letting it go.

When you start NetMeeting for the first time, it will walk you through its setup wizard. You'll need to enter personal information (only as much as you want to), and run the Audio/Video Tuneup Wizard. When this is done, you're ready to go on the air.

One significant difference between this version of NetMeeting and versions you may have used in the past is that the Directory system is gone. You no longer can log on to the ILS (Internet Locator Service) or a corporate directory server to search for chat buddies. NetMeeting now uses the same contact list that Windows Messenger uses. So, you have only two ways to choose a partner for chatting and conferencing: You can select from your list of MS Messenger contacts, or you can directly enter the IP address of someone else running NetMeeting. Of course, this makes NetMeeting more difficult to use, and that's probably intentional ("You will use Messenger. Resistance is futile").

TROUBLESHOOTING

MESSENGER GIVES CONNECTION ERROR WHEN I SIGN IN

When I click Sign In, I get an error message saying Messenger can't connect.

Be sure you're connected to the Internet when you try to sign on with Messenger. If your computer connects to the Internet through a network with a firewall (in a business environment), you may need to contact your network administrator for help.

No Sound Picked Up from Microphone

When I speak into the microphone, the green, yellow, and red indicator bar doesn't appear. Or, when I use voice chat, my friend doesn't hear any sound.

First, be sure that your microphone is plugged into the correct jack on your computer or sound card. There are usually three jacks: Line Out, Line In, and Mic. You want to plug into the Mic jack. Be sure that you're using a microphone designed for computer use.

If you have multiple sound cards or sound input devices, be sure you've selected the device that your microphone is actually plugged into.

If that doesn't help, click Start, Control Panel, Sounds Speech and Audio Devices, and Adjust the System Volume. Select the Audio tab, and click Volume in the Sound Recording section. Be sure that the Microphone volume slider is moved up and the Select button under it is checked.

Voice Chat Doesn't Work

When I initiate or accept a voice conversation, the connection fails with an error message, or I hear no sound.

If Windows displays an error message, the message may tell you what the problem is. In particular, you probably can't use voice chat if you or your friend uses a hardware Internet connection sharing router (residential gateway) for your Internet connection. These hardware devices don't pass the data connections properly. Check with the device's manufacturer to see if they have an upgrade that will allow it to pass the SIP protocol.

If there is no clear indication of what the problem is, the next thing to do is to see if your friend is hearing anything. Use the text chat window to ask them what they hear, while you speak. Check your screen's microphone indicator be sure that it's lighting up while you speak. If it doesn't, your microphone is probably not connected. If it does, have them check their speakers and volume settings. If you or your friend still don't hear anything, try disconnecting and starting the connection again. That sometimes fixes the problem.

Video Chat Doesn't Work

When I initiate or accept a video and voice connection, the connection fails with an error message, or I see no picture.

Video connections are even more troublesome than audio connections. There's so much more data to send that any little bit getting lost along the way can foul up the whole process.

First, check the comments in the previous "Troubleshooting" note, "Voice Chat Doesn't Work." Get the audio portion working before you try video.

If you get a good audio connection but still don't get a video connection, be sure that each person with a camera can see themselves in the lower right-hand corner of the Conversation Window's video area. If they don't, the camera is at fault. If the see-myself area is working but the other user isn't receiving video, disconnect and try making the connection again.

TIPS FROM THE WINDOWS PROS: EXTENDING YOUR CHAT COMMUNITY

If you spend a lot of time working at your computer, you may find that messaging is a powerful and effective tool for communicating with colleagues, clients, family, and friends. Messaging is much more immediate than e-mail, yet much less intrusive and demanding than the telephone. I use messaging on a daily basis to keep in touch with friends and colleagues all over the country.

Although messaging is free, it costs the providers big money to develop and run. Why do they pay to make this a free service? Well, if you haven't noticed yet, these services are tied into their manufacturers' other ventures. For example, AOL Instant Messenger (IM) displays an unobtrusive but constant parade of advertisements for AOL and other products. Microsoft's Messenger forces you to sign up for Passport and not so subtly steers you toward using Hotmail, MSN, and other Microsoft services, where you'll again be barraged with advertising that Microsoft collects on.

There's absolutely nothing wrong with this, in itself. The problem is that the messaging companies want you all to themselves, and have steadfastly refused to let their systems interoperate. Microsoft did make headlines by trying to make Messenger work with AOL's IM for a while (perhaps to lure away its users?). AOL modified their software to block Messenger users, and Microsoft fixed that until AOL changed their software yet again; lawsuits followed and it all got very ugly. The bottom line is that AOL Instant Messenger, Windows Messenger, and ICQ don't work together, so their users are in separate, non-communicating camps.

I've found that my contacts fall into all three camps. Since I want to be available to all of the, I've found it best to use all three programs. The programs are small and unobtrusive, so it's really no burden on my computer or desktop to do this. If you want to really take best advantage of messaging, you can try this too.

Here are some tips to help you get set up:

- You can download AOL Instant Messenger from www.aol.com. It also comes as part of the full Netscape browser program; if you download Netscape Communicator you can elect to install IM. IM's advantage is its huge community, and the ability to search for chat pals by areas of interest, should you want to.

- The ICQ program is now owned by America Online, but its community is totally separate from AOL. ICQ's advantage is its extreme configurability, as well as its search-for-a-pal features. You can download it at www.icq.com.

- Take steps to protect your privacy. Think twice about listing your e-mail address, telephone number, or full name in any of these service's directories. I prefer to contact others directly and give them my chat identification info, rather than making it public.

- On the same note, you can configure these programs to prevent unknown people from contacting you without your permission. It's your computer, your time, and your connection, so you should be in control of who uses it.

CHAPTER 13

HOSTING WEB PAGES WITH INTERNET INFORMATION SERVICES

In this chapter

OVERVIEW OF INTERNET INFORMATION SERVICES

Internet Information Services (IIS) is a collection of programs that make up Microsoft's industrial-strength IIS Web server platform. It's included for free as part of Windows XP Professional. Besides the basic Web (HTTP) server, add-ons include a File Transfer Protocol (FTP) server, an Indexing Service for site content searching, FrontPage and Visual InterDev publishing extensions, the ASP script processor, support for sophisticated multitier online transaction services, and a Simple Mail Transfer Protocol (SMTP) mail delivery server. In short, IIS is the Mother of All Web Servers.

> **CAUTION**
>
> If you are part of a corporate network, before you go any further, check with your network administrators because policies may prohibit you from setting up a Web site on your own. Many legitimate security concerns are involved, and in some companies, you could be fired for violating established security policies. Check first if you're not sure what's permitted.

While I'm on the subject of warnings, I'll give one more that's important enough that I'll repeat it later in the chapter:

> **CAUTION**
>
> Installing Internet Information Services might sound like fun, but don't install it unless you're really sure you need it and are willing to keep up with its frequent bug fixes and maintenance alerts. IIS has been Microsoft's biggest source of strange and dangerous security flaws. All sophisticated services come with a measure of risk, and IIS is very sophisticated.
>
> Microsoft has produced some tools to help you keep up to date on IIS security. Visit www.microsoft.com/technet. At the left, click Security. Then, in the tree view in the left panel, open Security, and select Tools and Checklists. Read about the IIS Lockdown Tool, Hfnetchk, and the Microsoft Personal Security Advisor.

WHAT DOES A WEB SERVER DO?

You're probably familiar by now with using a Web browser to view documents over the World Wide Web (WWW or Web), but you might not have seen what happens on the other side, from the server's point of view. I'll take you on a brief tour here. If you already are familiar with the function of Web servers, you can skip on down to "IIS Services and Requirements."

In the most basic sense, a Web server works like a call desk librarian: When you request a book by name, the librarian looks up the book's location, fetches the desired tome, passes it across the counter, and goes on to the next patron as quickly as possible. If the desired book is not in the shelves, the librarian will say so and again go on to the next client. The interactions are brief and involve no interpretation of the content—that is, the content of the book—passing back and forth.

The roles of a Web server and Web browser are very similar. A Web browser sends a short request message to a Web server. The request is a text string, mostly just the Uniform Resource Locator (URL) that you typed in or clicked. The server turns this virtual name into a real or physical filename and passes the appropriate HTML, image, or other type of file back across the Internet. When the URL refers to an executable program or a script file, instead of returning the file itself, a Web server runs the program and passes back whatever the program generates as its response.

A FOLDER BY ANY OTHER NAME IS . . . A VIRTUAL FOLDER

The translation of the URL filename into a physical filename is generally straightforward. When you set up your Web site, you'll specify which directory contains the documents that you want to publish. The Web site has a *home directory*, which is the starting point for the translation of URL names into filenames. For example, if the home directory is `c:\inetpub\wwwroot`, then the URL filename

`/index.html`

returns the file

`c:\inetpub\wwwroot\index.html`

Any file or folder inside this home directory is available to Web browsers. For example, the URL

`/sales/catalog.html`

would return the file

`c:\inetpub\wwwroot\sales\catalog.html`

You can also add other folders on your computer to this mapping, even if they aren't in the home directory or its subfolders. They are called *virtual directories* because to Web visitors, they appear to be part of the home directory structure, but they aren't physically. You could instruct IIS to share folder `c:\partlist` with the virtual URL name of `/parts`, so that the URL

`/parts/index.html`

would return the file

`c:\partlist\index.html`

When IIS is installed, adding a virtual folder to your Web site is a piece of cake: This process is integrated right into Explorer and is just a right-click away.

Web servers can also use a process called *redirection*, where the server is told to make virtual directory whose content is stored on another Web server. When one user requests a file in a redirected virtual directory, the Web server tells the browser program to go fetch the file from the other server. Redirection is useful when you rearrange your site—it lets visitors using an old URL obtain the files they want even though they're stored in a new location.

13

DEFAULT DOCUMENTS—WHEN "NOTHING" JUST ISN'T ENOUGH

In Web-speak, a *home page* is a URL that lists a server name but no filename, like "www.brainsville.com." So what does an empty or home page URL map to? For example, what file does www.brainsville.com refer to? You might guess that it corresponds to just the name of the server's home directory:

```
c:\inetpub\wwwroot
```

Indeed, it does, but this doesn't tell the server what content to return. The Web server has to look for a *default document*, the file that is to be returned whenever a URL names a folder but not a full filename. IIS looks first for a script file named default.asp. Failing that, default.html or default.htm will do. If a file by one of these names exists, it's returned as the content for this folder. If no default document can be found and "directory browsing" has been enabled for the folder, IIS simply returns a listing of all the files in the folder. Otherwise, it gives up and returns an error message.

MIMEs MAKE IT HAPPEN

Web browsers must be told how to interpret the content returned by the server. They don't know in advance whether they're going to get HTML text, a Microsoft Word document, an image, or something else. Whereas Windows determines a file's type from the end of its filename—for example, .doc or .html—that system isn't used by other operating systems, so a standardized naming scheme was developed for the Web. Web browsers get file type information from the Content-type field returned in the response header. This information is called a file's *MIME type*.

> **NOTE**
>
> MIME stands for Multipurpose Internet Mail Extensions. Prior to MIME, there was no standardized way to encode or name message content other than plain ASCII text.

MIME type names are agreed-upon Internet standards, and it's the Web server's job to know how to label each of the files it shares. When it's sending out files, IIS uses the Windows File Types Registry to map file types like .doc and .html into MIME types, and you can add to the list any special types of files you share.

TO RUN OR NOT TO RUN

When a URL refers to a program file, a Web server either can send you the program file itself, which you can save or run on *your* computer, or it can run the program on *its* side and return the program's output to you. Whereas Web pages stored in HTML files are *static*, and only change when their owner edits them, *dynamic* Web created by programs are generated from scratch every time they're viewed, and thus can contain interactive, up-to-the minute information. Programs on the server's side can do virtually anything: search libraries, access your bank account, buy airline tickets, or move robots on the moon, and then return the results to you as a Web page. In fact, this flexibility is *the* crucial feature that made the World Wide Web cause such a sensation and made the Internet explode into a global phenomenon.

These programs are generically called *CGI (Common Gateway Interface)* programs, or *server-side scripts*, when written in a language such as ASP, Perl, JavaScript, VBScript, or another interpreted language supported by the Web server. Useful CGI programs and scripts can be created with programming know-how, or can be purchased or downloaded from the Net. For IIS, the distinction between "send the program file itself" and "run the program and return the output" is made by changing a Web folder's *read*, *script*, and *execute* attributes. Folders with the read attribute treat scripts and executable programs as data to be returned directly. With the script or execute attribute, scripts and programs, respectively, are run on the server, and their output is sent back to the person visiting your site.

Just to reassure you, you don't need to take advantage of all this complexity if you just want to publish some simple Web pages and make files available to Web visitors. IIS can publish Web pages out-of-the box with no programming.

IIS SERVICES AND REQUIREMENTS

IIS version 5.1 is included with Windows XP Professional, but not Windows XP Home Edition. Version 5.1 has some minor improvements over version 5.0, which ships with Windows 2000. IIS 6.0 will ship with the forthcoming Windows 2003 Server products. At any rate, the version of IIS in Windows XP Professional has the same capabilities as its server-based brethren, with two major differences.

First, the license agreement for Windows XP Professional restricts the use of your computer and any services it hosts to a maximum of 10 concurrent connections.

Second, the software does not support multiple, separate Web sites hosted by one computer (that is, it does not support multiple *virtual domains*).

The bottom line is that it's legal to use Professional only for a low-volume site. Practically speaking, unless you're selling Viagra online or you get listed on Yahoo!'s Cool Site of the Day, you probably don't have to worry about this point.

DO YOU *REALLY* WANT TO DO THIS?

Before going any further, I should say: If you can get the hosting services you need from your Internet service provider (ISP), your corporate IS department, or just about anyone else, you might not want to bother with setting up your own Web server! There's no glory in hosting your own Web site, just hard work. Web servers at an ISP will have faster connections to the Internet, are probably backed up every night, *and* some poor soul with a pager tied around his neck is probably on call 24×7 in case something goes wrong with the server. With low-volume Web sites to be had for as little as $5 U.S. a month, including domain name service (DNS), mailboxes, FTP, and FrontPage support, taking this project on yourself hardly seems worthwhile.

13

Hosting a public World Wide Web site requires domain name service, which Windows XP Professional alone doesn't provide. Therefore, if you want your site to be accessible as www.mysite.com, you still need someone else or an add-on product to provide DNS support. This support alone can cost nearly as much as a full-service Web site package, although there are free and discounted DNS services too.

On the other hand, you might want to install IIS if you

- Want to host in-house communication within your company or workgroup.

- Want to share files or your printer over the Internet using Web Sharing.

- Develop custom Web programs or scripts, or use CGI programs that an ISP can't or won't provide.

- Want to write and preview Web pages and applications before deploying them to an online site.

- Think that a chance to participate in this global Internet thing is just too cool to pass by. (I have to admit that this was the reason *I* set up a Web server.)

Whatever your reason, IIS installed in all its glory will give you plenty to chew on.

IIS COMPONENTS

IIS is a collection of several independent components, which together provide a full range of Web services. You can install any or all of them.

- **World Wide Web (HTTP) Service**—The WWW service is the basic component that lets your computer host Web pages. The WWW server supports server-side Java, JavaScript, and ASP scripting. You can add third-party support for Perl, databases, and a host of other services. It's the full-blown IIS 5.1 package except for the limit of 10 connections; also, this version doesn't let you host multiple Web sites—for example, for different domain names—as the Server version does.

  The WWW service gives you Internet Printing capability. The Internet Printing Protocol (IPP) lets you manage and print to your Windows printer from anywhere on the Internet. IPP can be used from Windows 95, 98, Me, NT, XP, and 2000.

- **File Transfer Protocol (FTP) Server**—FTP lets remote users send and/or retrieve files from specified directories on your computer. FTP is a good interplatform file transfer system but poses some security risks, which we'll discuss in the next section.

- **FrontPage 2000 Server Extensions**—The FrontPage Extensions allow you to post Web pages and graphics to your server directly from the FrontPage design program as well as Word 2000 and 2002. This capability greatly simplifies the process of copying a set of related files (a web) to the server's "online" directories. The Extensions also add searching and form-posting services to the WWW service, which you can include in your pages. The Extensions obey Windows file security, so you can control who has permission to update files on various parts of your Web site.

> **NOTE**
>
> While the FrontPage program has progressed beyond the 2000 edition, the server component is still named FrontPage 2000 Server Extensions. Don't worry; it's up-to-date.

The Extensions also enable Web Sharing, which lets you share files with your printer via the Internet with a high degree of security. Web Sharing lets Internet Explorer versions 5 and higher treat Web folders like regular Windows shared folders. You can view, copy, rename, and delete files over the Internet just as if you were using a local area network (LAN).

If your computer is permanently accessible via the Internet, these two features alone are a good enough reason to install IIS.

- **Internet Information Services Snap-in**—This management tool permits you to configure and manage IIS from Administrative Tools on the Start menu, or from the Microsoft Management Console (MMC).

- **Visual InterDev RAD Remote Deployment Support**—Visual InterDev is Microsoft's software development system for sophisticated Web-based services that access corporate database and multitier transactional systems. The Remote Deployment Support service lets VID developers install and test software on-the-fly.

- **SMTP Service**—SMTP (Simple Mail Transfer Protocol) is the foundation for virtually all e-mail exchange on the Internet. The SMTP Service provided with Windows XP is designed to permit IIS and Windows Scripting Host applications to send mail. It is, however, only a delivery system and doesn't provide mailboxes or a Post Office Protocol (POP) service, so it's only half of what you need to host your own email system.

- **Indexing Service**—The Microsoft Indexing Service automatically builds a database of your Web site's content and gives visitors a way to search for documents by keywords and phrases. It understands Microsoft file formats such as RTF and Word Document format, so searches can locate text in these documents as well as plain text and HTML files. It also respects Windows file and folder security and doesn't list files a remote visitor doesn't have permission to view. The Indexing Service also assists when you choose Search for Files and Folders.

> **NOTE**
>
> Indexing Service is installed by default on Windows XP and it's technically not a subcomponent of IIS. I've listed it here because it works hand-in-hand with IIS.

13

Extensive online documentation is also available. It's helpful, but IIS is a very big program. If you're going to get serious about Web site management and development using IIS, you might want to look at the following books:

- *Active Server Pages 3.0 by Example*, published by Que
- *Active Server Pages 3.0 from Scratch*, published by Que
- *Microsoft IIS 5 Administration*, published by Sams

Before You Get Started

All IIS services require you to have a network using the TCP/IP protocol. These days, it would be very surprising if you did *not* because the Internet is everywhere, and you probably wouldn't be reading this book if you weren't either getting connected or already connected to it.

If you only want to make Web pages available to others in your company, your computer only needs to be connected to a local area network. If you want to publish Web pages on the Internet at large—that is, be part of the World Wide Web—you need a full-time Internet connection as well. If your site is available only a few hours a day while you're dialed in to your ISP, then few people will ever be able to see it. This kind of dedicated service is much less expensive today than it was only a few years ago, and can be had in some areas of the U.S. for under $50 a month. (You can read about Internet connectivity in Chapter 8, "Internet and TCP/IP Connection Options," and Chapter 19, "Connecting Your LAN to the Internet.") For global availability, you'll also need Domain Name Service, which I'll discuss in the next section.

TIP FROM

Bob
& Brian

> IIS requires *lots* of memory. Don't even think of installing it in your system unless you have 128MB of memory or more. (I advise having at least 256MB; you and Windows XP will both be much happier.)

Finally, your computer should use NTFS-formatted disks so that Windows can use its file security features to protect both your programs and web data.

→ If you want to learn more details about choosing the best file system (NTFS, FAT32, or FAT) for your Windows XP Professional installation, **see** "Choosing a File System: FAT, FAT32, or NTFS?," **p. 80**.

CAUTION

> If you share Web data from a FAT-formatted drive, a simple mistake in configuration could let anyone be able to write over your files. And if you use the FTP service, FAT is absolutely unacceptable.

Name Service

If you plan to use IIS just to develop and test Web pages, or if you want to share pages on a home, office, or corporate network, you don't have to worry about your computer being visible to the Internet at large. But if you want to host a public Web site with Windows XP Professional, you need the following:

- A static, or permanent, IP address and Internet connection, as opposed to the dynamic, or temporary, number you get when using a dial-up connection to an ISP
- An entry in the Internet's Domain Name Service so that people can find your site using a standard name like www.myfamouswebsite.com

Without both of these elements, you're a moving target, and nobody will be able to find or use your Web site on a consistent basis. Getting them set up is beyond the scope of this book, but here are a few hints:

- If you are part of a company network already connected to the Internet, your computer's network name may already be registered on the Internet.

- If you use a permanent Internet connection like a cable modem, DSL service, satellite, or other dedicated link, you *might* get a permanent IP address from your Internet provider, or you can ask for one. (Some providers won't do this, and some will levy an additional charge.)

- Your ISP may provide you free domain name service, or you might be able to buy this type of service from a commercial Web site provider for about $5 U.S. a month. If you have the technical know-how, check out the free DNS service provided by www.granitecanyon.com.

  You also have to register your domain name with an Internet registry service. The original Internet registrar www.networksolutions.com charges $70 for the first two years. I found registry service for $8 per year, with free DNS included, at www.stargateinc.com. It pays to shop around. The only worry with the discounters is that there's no telling if they will still be online next year. If they shut down, you may have a big problem getting your domain name transferred to another registrar.

- If your network has Windows .NET, 2000, or Windows NT Server, your network administrator can set up domain name service for you because a DNS server is included with the Server versions.

If you use a shared Internet connection, even if it has a static IP address, you'll also need to configure the sharing software or hardware to direct incoming Web site requests to the computer that's actually running IIS. I'll discuss this later in the chapter, under "Configuring Shared Connections."

DETERMINING WHICH IIS SERVICES YOU NEED

IIS is a bulky and sophisticated suite of programs. Although they're not more difficult than they need to be, considering what they do, they're also not "entry-level" programs. They require forethought and oversight to make them useful and to manage the security risk that comes with global accessibility. Two familiar laws of nature come into play here:

13

> As the number of components in a system increases, the number of ways it can fail grows exponentially.
>
> Anything that can go wrong will.

Applied to IIS, these laws mean that you should not install what you don't need. This is not information to dismiss out of hand. This is a very serious concern: Most of the security problems that were identified in Windows over the last several years were found in IIS and its accessory programs. The problem is that bugs in IIS can let random outside people examine—or worse, modify—files on your computer. The less of IIS you activate, the less of a chance some not-yet-identified security flaw will catch you by surprise.

Enough lecturing, now: What do you need?

WORLD WIDE WEB

The World Wide Web service delivers static and dynamic Web pages and also offers file and document pickup (via Web pages or directory listings), database interactivity, and just about any other sort of information sharing. This is the core of IIS. If you can't or don't want to use a commercial or other hosting service for your pages, or if you want to host Web pages, develop Web applications, or share folders using the Web model, you should install the WWW service.

FRONTPAGE 2000 EXTENSIONS

You should install the FrontPage 2000 Extensions if you want to do any of the following:

- Use FrontPage (any version) or Microsoft Office to develop Web pages
- Use your WWW service to use FrontPage's searching or form extensions
- Copy files to and from your computer via the Internet, using Internet Explorer and Web Sharing

The Extensions provide a way for Web-enabled applications to *publish*, or deliver, the composed HTML file and graphics to the Web server's online folders. Thus, the author doesn't have to manually drag files into the WWW folders or use the evil FTP service to copy them there. FrontPage Extensions also provide HTML Form processing services, in the form of some special CGI (Common Gateway Interface, or Web server extension) programs that can record or e-mail form responses, as well as index or searching services that let Web site viewers search your Web site for keywords or phrases. They also include as standard equipment a CGI-based Web page system to manage your printers.

NOTE

If you want to learn more information about using the FrontPage extensions, I recommend that you pick up a copy of *Special Edition Using Microsoft FrontPage 2002*, published by Que.

TIP FROM

Bob & Brian

If you use Microsoft Office 2000 or XP for collaborative projects, you might want to use the Office Server Extensions in addition to or instead of the FrontPage Extensions. The Office Server Extensions provide all the functions of the FrontPage extensions, with additional services for Office users. You can get them with the *Microsoft Office XP Pro SE or Developer editions*. For more information see
http://support.microsoft.com/support/kb/articles/Q235/0/27.asp.

FTP

FTP allows remote users to retrieve or deliver files to your computer. FTP, which is one of the original Internet applications, is available on virtually every Internet-connected system, from mainframe to Macintosh to PC, so it's really handy for file transfers between Windows and non-Windows computers. But the decision to install FTP should not be made lightly because FTP can create some severe security risks.

FTP permits two types of access: *anonymous* and *authenticated.* Anonymous access doesn't require a password and should be used to share folders for file-pickup only; you should *never* allow users from the Internet at large to write files to your computer (lest you find one day that someone has made your computer one of the Internet's prime repositories and distributors of pornography).

You can allow remote users to deliver files to your computer using *authenticated* access, but FTP doesn't encrypt passwords sent over the Internet, so this method is a security risk. The login name and password used are exposed while they are in transit over the Internet.

In most cases, if you only want to distribute files to the general public, you don't need to install FTP. The World Wide Web service can do the job nicely. The only two reasons to install FTP are as follows:

- You need to let remote users pick up files from your computer, and their computers might not have Web browser software.
- You need to let remote users deliver files to your computer, and their computers aren't running Windows.

If you decide to install FTP, you must understand the security consequences and take great care configuring the service and the folders it makes public. We'll discuss the risks and configuration issues in excruciating detail later. You might want to read that discussion before you make your decision.

SMTP MAIL

The SMTP Mail service provided with IIS is required to send e-mail from Web pages, ASP scripts, and FrontPage or Office Server Extensions. If you want to send mail from your Web server applications, you should install SMTP.

As a mail system, though, the SMTP service unfortunately doesn't provide you with mailboxes or any of the other user-side services that an e-mail system needs. If you want to host your own e-mail system, you need to purchase an add-on e-mail server such as Microsoft Exchange Server or download a free or shareware mail server system.

OTHER COMPONENTS

With the exception of the Visual InterDev RAD Remote Deployment service, the other components of IIS, such as online documentation and the Management Snap-In, are all handy to have. As Martha Stewart would say, "They are *good* things." I recommend installing them, and we'll go over their use later.

13

The RAD Remote Deployment service is a testing tool that's only useful if you are a Visual InterDev developer. Everyone else should skip installing it.

There is also an option for installing a Scripts directory. If you currently use or develop CGI programs or scripts, install the Scripts directory. Otherwise, follow the "if you don't need it, don't install it" rule and leave it out for now. You can always install it later on if you decide you want to develop script programs.

INSTALLING IIS

After you've decided which IIS services to install, you'll need to log on as Administrator or as a Computer Administrator user. Then follow these steps:

1. Click Start, Control Panel, Add or Remove Programs. Select Add/Remove Windows Components from the left pane.

2. Scroll down the Components list and check Internet Information Services (IIS). Click Details, and deselect any components you have chosen not to install. The following list provides some recommendations for installing IIS:

Component	Should You Install?
Common Files	required
Documentation	yes
File Transfer Protocol (FTP) Server	probably not
FrontPage 2000 Server Extensions	yes
Internet Information Services Snap-In	yes
SMTP Service	optional
Visual InterDev RAD Remote Deployment	optional
World Wide Web Service	required

If you select World Wide Web Service and click Details, you can make additional selections:

Component	Should You Install?
Printers virtual directory	yes
Remote Desktop Web Connection	yes
Scripts Virtual Directory	optional
World Wide Web Service	required

If you change your mind about using any of these services, you can always select Add or Remove Windows Components again later on.

13

NOTE

> If you had FrontPage Extensions installed under an earlier version of Windows that you upgraded to Windows XP, you must still manually choose to install the FrontPage Extensions, and reconfigure them afterward. They are not automatically upgraded and configured.

3. If you want to search the IIS online documentation or want to use site-searching for your own content, be sure that the Indexing Service is also installed. It's listed just above Internet Information Services in the Windows component list.

4. When you've selected all of the desired IIS components, click Next to complete the Windows Components Wizard. You may be asked to insert your Windows XP Installation CD-ROM.

When the installation procedure is finished, if you want to use the site-searching capabilities of the Windows Indexing service, you'll need to enable the service by following these steps:

1. Click Start, right-click My Computer, and select Manage.

2. Open Services and Applications.

3. Right-click Indexing Service.

4. Select Start.

5. When Windows asks if you want the service to start automatically, click Yes.

The Indexing Service builds a database of its default content directories, which include the IIS online documentation and your Web site's home and virtual directories. (It also indexes your own Documents and Settings folder but doesn't make this information available to Internet visitors.) The indexing process will take several minutes, during which you can tour the major components of IIS.

TAKING A QUICK TOUR

After you've installed IIS, you can take a quick tour of the major components that have been put into place. To do so, first start Internet Explorer, and enter the URL `//localhost`. Localhost is shorthand for "the IP address of this machine" and will display Internet Explorer's default installation Web page. You will see the default page shown in Figure 13.1. Internet Explorer will also fire up the online documentation for IIS in a separate browser window.

13

Figure 13.1
IIS serves you a welcome page when first installed. A remote browser, using your real IP address rather than localhost, would see a plain "Under construction" page.

Congratulations! You now have your own Web server. Let's take a look at the built-in pages. If you find them as handy as I did, you might want to add them to your Favorites folder. (You learned how to use Internet Explorer's Favorites folder in Chapter 9, "Browsing the World Wide Web with Internet Explorer.")

ONLINE DOCUMENTATION

Typing `http://localhost/iishelp` in the Address bar displays the IIS Online documentation, which has a built-in search and indexing feature. Check this documentation for the latest IIS news, release notes, and detailed instructions. (This documentation is a good place to spend a couple of hours.)

PRINTER MANAGER

If you chose the "Printers virtual directory" when you installed IIS, you now have a nifty Web-based printer management console. When you type `http://localhost/Printers` in the Address bar, note that your installed printer(s) and any pending print jobs are listed on the page. Other users on your network can view and use your shared printers by entering the URL `http://machine/Printers`, replacing the word *machine* with your computer's actual network identification name, its domain name, or its DNS name—for example, `judy.mycompany.com/Printers`. Because this page uses Windows user-level security, you must view it with Internet Explorer, and you may not be able to manage the printer if you don't have adequate permissions.

If you are viewing this page from a different Windows XP computer or from a Windows 9x or NT 4 computer with the Internet Printing Protocol add-on (it's available from `www.windowsupdate.com`), you can also select Connect and install this printer as a remote printer. You'll learn about Web printing in Chapter 18, "Windows Unplugged: Remote and Mobile Networking."

SETTING UP A SIMPLE WEB SITE

Right out of the box, IIS is ready to serve up static Web pages and images. If you have files from an existing Web site, or if you can create and edit HTML files yourself, you can simply copy them into the home directory c:\inetpub\wwwroot and any subfolders you want to create. The default page name is initially default.htm, so give this name to your home page file.

With no further administration or fuss, other users on your network and/or on the Internet can view your Web site, using your computer's Internet domain name or, on a Windows LAN, by viewing http://machinename, where machinename is the Windows name of your computer. (You can find that name by right-clicking My Computer, selecting Properties, and viewing the Network Identification tab.)

You can also use Notepad, FrontPage, FrontPage Express, Microsoft Word, or other editors like DreamWeaver to create Web pages. If you're the impatient type, as I am, you can just follow these steps to build a *really* quick and dirty home page, just to prove to yourself that you really do have a Web server up and running:

1. Select Start, Programs, Accessories, Notepad.

2. Type the following text:
   ```
   <HTML>
   <HEAD>
   <TITLE>This is My Home Page</title>
   </HEAD>
   <BODY>
   <P>Welcome to my completely spiffy new website, hosted by Windows XP!
   </BODY>
   </HTML>
   ```
   Be especially careful to get the angle brackets (< and >) right and to use the forward slash (/), not the backslash (\).

3. Select File, Save As, and enter c:\inetpub\wwwroot\default.htm as the filename. Click OK.

4. View http:\\localhost in Internet Explorer.

Now you have your very own home page. It's not much to look at, but now you can say you've coded Web pages by hand. This will impress people. When you're finished, you can create or copy other HTML documents and images into the wwwroot folder.

IIS can deliver more than static Web pages. I'll talk about dynamic Web pages and scripting in the "Tips for the Windows Pros" section at the end of this chapter.

If you are new to Web page building and want to learn how to populate the Web site you just created, skip back to Chapter 17 for the basics. If you've already built a site and are now interested in publishing it to the Web, stay here.

13

NOTE

If you are a Web development professional or want to become one, we recommend the following books as great starting places for learning more:

- *Special Edition Using Microsoft FrontPage 2002*, published by Que
- *Special Edition Using HTML 4.0*, also published by Que

TIP FROM

Don't put anything into your Web folders that you don't want to be seen all over the world. Just because *your* pages don't link to a given file doesn't mean that someone *else* won't publish a Web page linking to it.

MANAGING YOUR SITE WITH THE COMPUTER MANAGEMENT CONSOLE

If you want detailed control over access rights in your Web folders, or you have installed the FTP or SMTP services, you should take a look at the Internet Information Services management plug-in. There are three ways to get to it:

- Click Start, right-click My Computer, and select Manage. Under Services and Applications, select Internet Information Services.
- Open Control Panel and select Performance and Maintenance, Administrative Tools, Internet Information Services.
- If you've customized your Start menu so it displays Administrative Tools, just click Start, All Programs, Administrative Tools, Internet Information Services.

Open the Internet Information Services item, and then the entry for your computer, and under this you'll see entries for the specific services you installed: Web Sites, FTP Sites, if you installed the FTP service, and Default SMTP Virtual Server, if you installed the SMTP service. Figure 13.2 shows the manager window with all three services installed.

In this Explorer-like view of the IIS components, you can take complete control of IIS's behavior, down to its treatment of individual files. To get a feel of what is possible, you should look at the Web server's configuration settings. To view them, right-click the Default Web Site entry in the left pane and select Properties. You then are presented with a complex dialog box with eight tabs (see Figure 13.3).

13

Figure 13.2
The Computer Management console contains management tools for the FTP server, Web server, and SMTP server.

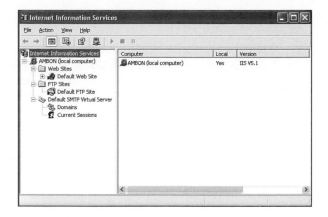

Figure 13.3
On the Default Web Site Properties dialog box, you can control the behavior of the Web server.

As I said earlier, IIS is a complicated program and there are *many* settings. In my experience, you'll only need to consider a few of them, and it's quite likely that you won't need to make any changes at all. I'll go through some of the more important settings in Table 13.1.

TABLE 13.1   IIS WEB SITE CONFIGURATION SETTINGS

Tab	Setting	Value
Web Site	Enable Logging	Lets you keep a record of all Web site visits. I'll discuss this later in the chapter.
	TCP Port	You can change the TCP Port of your Web site from the usual 80 to another value; this is usually only done if you host several different Web servers. 8080 is a common alternate port number.

continues

TABLE 13.1   CONTINUED

Tab	Setting	Value
Home Directory	Local Path	Sets the home or "starting point" directory for the folders displayed on your Web site. The home directory should be on a disk partition formatted with NTFS. You'll only need to change this if the default folder is on a drive using FAT formatting and you can't update the drive.
Documents	Default Document	Lets you select the names IIS tries when looking for a "default document" to return for a URL that names a folder but not a specific document.
HTTP Headers	File Types	Lets you specify MIME Types for file types not already registered with Windows.
Server Extensions	Settings	Specifies e-mail address and server information for e-mail sent by the FrontPage extensions and scripts.

If you plan to use the FrontPage Server extensions to process forms, or if you plan to send e-mail from forms or scripts, you'll need to make the following settings:

1. Select the Server Extensions tab, and under Performance, select the approximate number of pages you expect to have on your Web site: fewer than 100; 100 to 1,000; or more than 1,000.

2. If you plan to use form and e-mail processing with ASP scripts, FrontPage Extensions, and/or Mailing List services with the Office Server Extensions, select Specify How Mail Should Be Sent Settings, and make the following entries:

   Web server's mail address: Enter the e-mail address that you want mail sent by your Web site (such as responses from forms) to appear to come from. I use something like "webmaster@mydomain.com"; you'd want to use your own e-mail address.

   Contact address: Enter the e-mail address that people should use to report trouble with your Web site. This will appear on error message Web pages generated by Front Page. I use "webmaster@mydomain.com" for this also.

   SMTP Mail Server: Enter the name of your network's or your ISP's SMTP mail receiver, often something like smtp.myisp.com. This is the mail server that will process your outgoing mail.

3. Click OK to close the dialog box.

You also can manage the settings for specific folders listed under the Default Web Site entry, by right-clicking them and choosing Properties. On the Documents tab, you can specify that a given document or folder is to be obtained from a different URL on a different Web server, using a process called *redirection*. Complex CGI programs called *ASP applications* are configured here as well.

SHARING FOLDERS WITH WEB SHARING

If you want to add to your Web site a folder that is not inside `c:\inetpub\wwwroot`, you can add it as a virtual folder through the Internet Information Services management tool, which I described in the previous section, or through a shortcut feature called Web Sharing.

You can set up Web Sharing using Windows Explorer. It provides a quick and easy way to make a folder available to others through your computer's Web server. To do this, right-click a folder in the Explorer display, and select Properties. You'll see a new tab called Web Sharing—this appears when you've installed IIS. Select the Web Sharing tab, and select Share This Folder. The virtual directory or Edit Directory dialog appears, as shown in Figure 13.4.

Figure 13.4
Here, you can set alias properties for a new virtual directory. The Alias name is the URL name this folder will have.

Enter the URL name you want to use for this folder, and change the Access and Application Permissions check boxes if necessary. For a folder that will hold Web pages and images, check Read. If this folder will also contain scripts and/or CGI programs that you want to have run by the server, check Scripts or Execute (Including Scripts). If you want to let remote users see the contents of the directory in the absence of a default document, check Directory Browsing.

TIP FROM

The best practice is *not* to enable the Scripts or Execute permissions unless you know you require them.

TIP FROM

Bob & Brian

To minimize the number of folders requiring Scripts and Execute permissions, use the preinstalled Scripts folder for your scripts and CGI programs.

Remember that Windows file permissions will be in force as well as the permissions you set for Web sharing. If you use Simple File Sharing, you should only use Web sharing on folders that are in your Shared Documents file, so that outside visitors can read the files. If you are on a Windows domain network or are not using Simple File Sharing, you'll need to be sure that you give read permission to the shared folder to Everyone or to IUSR_*xxxx*, where *xxxx* is the name of your computer. Simple File Sharing and file permissions are discussed in Chapter 28, "Managing Users."

Managing the FTP Server

If you have installed the FTP service, open the Internet Information Services management tool as described in the previous section, right-click Default FTP Site, and select Properties.

To establish a secure server, make the following settings:

■ On the FTP Site tab, be sure to check Enable Logging (see the "Log Files" section).

■ On the Home Directory tab, you can specify the folder in which FTP looks for files.

CAUTION

The FTP folder should be stored on a disk partition that uses the NTFS format. You should *not* use the same disk partition that your Windows folder is on. Software bugs are a fact of life, and bugs in FTP could have very serious consequences. (They've been found before, and bugs are likely to still exist.) Protect yourself by setting up a separate partition just for FTP data. See Chapter 29, "Managing the Hard Disk," for information on disk partitions.

■ On the Security Accounts tab, you'll have to decide whether or not to permit access based on account names and passwords. Remember that FTP sends passwords without encryption, so permitting password-controlled access is a security risk. With anonymous access, where passwords are not required, you should let people pick up but not send you files. If you really do need to let people send you files with FTP, you'll have to use password control. Here's are the specific things you'll need to do:

• If you will use FTP to let people pick up files only, check Allow Anonymous Connections and check Allow Only Anonymous Connections. Be sure that Write permission is *not* checked on the Home Directory tab or any of its subfolders.

• If you want to let people send you files, you should uncheck Allow Anonymous Connections and uncheck Allow Only Anonymous Connections. Select only specific directories to give Write permission. In addition, you should use

NTFS-formatted disks, disable Simple File Sharing so you can make user-specific file security settings, and set appropriate user-specific permissions on the folders shared by your FTP server.

■ On the Messages tab, under Welcome, enter a greeting followed by a warning of this sort:

```
All access to this server is logged. Access to this server is
allowed by permission only and unauthorized use will be prosecuted.
```

(You might want to consult your attorney to choose the proper wording!)

You can view and disconnect current FTP site visitors from the FTP Site tab of the Default FTP Properties dialog by clicking Current Sessions. You can use Disconnect to remove any of them if, for some reason, you need to terminate their activity on your computer.

MANAGING THE SMTP SERVER

If you've installed the SMTP mail delivery service component, you'll need to take a moment to configure it so it can deliver mail generated by your Web sites.

Open the Internet Information Services manager as discussed earlier in this chapter (Start, Control Panel, Performance and Maintenance, Administrative Tools, Internet Information Services will do it). Open the Default SMTP Virtual Server entry. Right-click Default SMTP Virtual Server and select Properties, to display the configuration dialog shown in Figure 13.5.

Figure 13.5
Managing the SMTP Server.

There are four settings that you should consider:

■ **Relaying**—Relaying is the process of receiving mail from the outside world, and then sending it on to recipients in the outside world. Mail servers that do this are quickly exploited by people who send "spam," or junk e-mail. To avoid this, by default, your mail server will not accept outgoing mail from any other computer. If you want it to deliver mail for other computers on your network, you'll have to tell it which computers are allowed to relay. On the Access tab, click Relay, and then Add. Select Group of Computers and enter your computer's IP address and subnet mask. Click OK to close the Add box. This will make the server relay mail for computers on your network but no others.

- **Message Size**—On the Messages tab, you can configure the maximum message size and maximum number of messages that someone can send at once. You can uncheck all of the "Limit" boxes if you trust the users on your network not to send spam.

- **Delivery**—By default, the SMTP server will attempt to deliver all mail to all recipients by itself. If you want to give this job to your ISP's mail server, you can tell SMTP to send all mail to a "smart host" for delivery. To do this, on the Delivery tab, click Advanced. Under Smart Host enter the name of your ISP's SMTP server. If you have to authenticate with the server to send mail, click on the Outbound Security button to enter the required name and password.

- **Receiving domains**—If you want this SMTP server to receive mail, you'll have to tell it what domains are "local." Mail addressed to any other domains is considered "outside" mail and will be sent out to the Internet. As I mentioned, Windows XP Professional doesn't come with any means of delivering mail that the SMTP service receives. If you devise one, you'll need to configure the local domain list. On the Internet Information Services manager window, select Domains in the left pane. Right-click the default name that appears in the right pane and select Rename. Change the name to your desired domain name, such as "mycompany.com". This way any mail received for "somebody@mycompany.com" will be stored rather than sent back out again. You can add additional domains by right-clicking Domains and selecting New, Domain.

LOG FILES

By default, IIS services create log files in the Windows directory, usually in \Windows\System32\LogFiles. The Web service log files are in subfolder W3SVC1 and are named ex*yymmdd*.log, where *yymmdd* are digits indicating the current date. A new log file is created on any day on which Web server activity occurs.

The FTP service follows a similar format, storing its log files in \Winnt\System32\LogFiles\MSFTPSVC1.

You can change the period for changing log files from daily to hourly, weekly, or monthly, or you can base this change on the log file growing to a certain size. To do so, you use the Default Web or FTP Site Properties dialogs. Just locate the Enable Logging check box, and click the Properties button next to it.

The log files are plain ASCII text files that contain a line for each file or page retrieved from the Web server. Each line contains the time, the browser's IP address, the HTTP method used (usually GET), and the URL requested.

If you are interested in analyzing the use of your Web site, several free or shareware analysis tools are available. Of course, you also can hire hugely expensive consultants for intense analysis of your Web server activity logs for marketing research, but this in-depth analysis is probably more than you want.

ENABLING SITE SEARCHING USING THE INDEXING SERVICE

CAUTION

> While using the Indexing Service can provide great benefits to those using your Web site, it can also provide an open door inviting unscrupulous visitors to perform various nasty things to your Web server and possibly portions of your internal network. Ensure that you are have the most up-to-date security patches and hot fixes on your Web server by visiting the Windows Update Web site. For more information on the specific Security Bulletin relating to the Windows XP Indexing Service, see http://www.microsoft.com/technet/security/bulletin/ms02-018.asp.

If you want to let remote browsers search your Web site for documents of interest, you can install and configure the Indexing Service. This service periodically scours selected Web-shared folders and documents and maintains a list of all the words it finds in them. It actually maintains two separate indexes: one of your whole hard disk, for your use alone, and another of the Web folders for Internet searching. It's also sophisticated enough not to show results for documents Web visitors don't have permission to download. To install this service, follow these steps:

1. Right-click My Computer and choose Manage. From the Computer Management console, open Services and Applications, and then the Indexing Service section.

2. Right-click Web, and select Properties.

3. Select the Generation tab to bring it to the front (see Figure 13.6), and make the following choices:

   - Check Index Files with Unknown Extensions to include more than the expected .html and .txt files in the index. If you check this option, the Indexing Service will attempt to make sense of every file it finds in your Web folders.

   - Check Generate Abstracts. This option increases the size of the index in a large Web site but lets the search results return not only a filename but a paragraph or so of text from the beginning of each matching file. You can set the maximum size of this abstract if you want or leave the default setting of 320 characters.

4. Click OK. The Indexing Service updates the index automatically.

By default, the Indexing Service includes the IIS documentation in its index. You might find this information useful, but visitors to your Web site probably won't. You can open the Directories pane and remove the IIS documentation by selecting all the folders except \inetpub\wwwroot and any virtual folders you have added, double-clicking them in the right-hand pane, and checking No for Include in Index?

13

Figure 13.6
You can index generation properties for the Web index. Here, you can select the level of detail you want to include in the index.

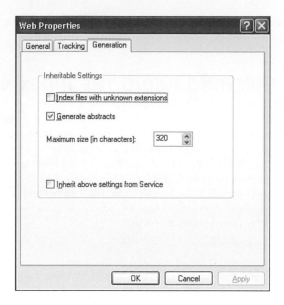

When you specify a folder, all its subfolders are included as well. You can prevent them from being included by specifying a subfolder and marking No under Include in Index.

Enabling the Indexing service only prepares a database of all the words and documents in your site. It doesn't automatically provide your Web pages with a search feature. For that, you'll have to use a Web page editor that can work with the Indexing service through the FrontPage extensions. Microsoft's FrontPage editor, not surprisingly, can do this.

CONFIGURING SHARED CONNECTIONS

If your computer uses a shared Internet connection, that is, one provided by Internet Connection Sharing or a connection-sharing router device, you'll have to set up the sharing service to direct incoming Web server requests to your computers. Otherwise, they'll stop at the connection sharing computer or router; it won't know what network computer they're intended for.

Connection forwarding is described in Chapter 19, "Connecting Your LAN to the Internet." You'll need to forward port 80, the HTTP service, from the connection sharing machine to your computer. With Microsoft's Internet Connection Sharing service on a computer running Windows XP, you can simply specify your computer's name as the target of the forwarded requests.

If you use a connection sharing device, however, you'll have to specify your computer's IP address on your LAN. This is often a number like 192.168.something.something. In this case, you can't use automatic IP address assignment (the DHCP) because your computer's address could change from day to day, and the forwarded requests would end up going to the wrong computer. You'll need to specify the IP address and other network information when you set up the Internet Protocol (TCP/IP) properties for your computer's Local Area Connection. You can read more about configuring IP address information in Chapter 16, "Creating a Windows XP Pro Network."

SECURITY ISSUES FOR INTERNET SERVICES

Simply stated, if your computer is connected to the Internet, it's exposed to millions of people who can reach it in milliseconds from anywhere in the world, many of whom have nothing better to do than to try to break into and damage your computer. Consider your connection to the Internet like the door to your house, and it's in a rough neighborhood: Don't leave the door unlocked.

Dealing with security is a little bit scary, but you can take a few steps to ensure your safety.

→ For a more detailed discussion of keeping your network safe from prying eyes, **see** "Network Security," **p. 727**.

KEEPING UP TO DATE

First and foremost, you'll need to keep up on bug fixes and security updates released by Microsoft. Since IIS has full access to your computer, and it's in contact with the rest of the world, it's critical that you keep it up to date. You should be sure that your computer is set up to receive updates automatically from Microsoft. You also need to subscribe to the Microsoft security bulletin service so you hear about problems as soon as they're discovered. Sometimes they describe interim precautionary measures you can take before bug fixes are released. You can sign up at http://www.microsoft.com/security. Click on Bulletins.

FILE SECURITY

Your server's file system contributes to the security of data on it. You can do the following:

- Use NTFS for any drives containing folders you share using IIS.

- By default, Windows puts the Web and FTP data directories on the same drive as Windows. For maximum safety, set up a different drive or partition and use that for your IIS data. You can change the location of the Web and FTP home directories on the Properties pages of these services in the Internet Information Services management tool as I described earlier in the chapter.

- If you grant Write permission to any of your Web or FTP folders, you should not use Simple File Sharing. Instead, you should use full user-level security and carefully review and adjust the permissions settings in your \inetpub folder and all of its subfolders. By default, Windows assigns new folders Full Control permissions to the Everyone group. Examine folders you create under the \inetpub folder to be sure that only authorized users can read and write files there. The user name IUSR_*xxxx*, where *xxxx* is your computer's name, is used for anonymous users, so IUSR_*xxxx* needs read permission in any folder that contains public pages.

→ For information on Simple File Sharing and folder permissions, **see** "Managing Users," **p. 949**.

- Store executable and scripts files in a separate folder from Web pages so that they can be executed but not read. *Never* check both write and script permissions on the same folder: This would let outside people send program scripts to your computer and then run them.

AUTHENTICATION

If you want to implement user restrictions to limit access to files or folders in your Web site, the Directory Security tab in the IIS Computer Management plug-in (which you open by right-clicking Default Web Site and choosing Properties) lets you permit or prevent Basic Authentication from being used to view protected Web pages.

Basic Authentication transmits unencrypted usernames and passwords across the Internet. This is a bad thing.

But you get a significant trade-off here. If you don't allow Basic Authentication, no Web browser other than Internet Explorer can view the protected pages. If you do allow Basic Authentication, usernames and passwords are transmitted across the Internet without encryption, which is a significant security risk.

My recommendation is that you *not* permit Basic authentication. These passwords aren't just for a Web page, remember; they're your Windows XP usernames and passwords, the keys to your computer and network domain.

CONFIGURING YOUR SERVER

My computer management philosophy is "keep it simple." The fewer services you run, the less likely that one will be configured incorrectly and become a security liability. Use care in configuring and managing your server. Be sure to read Chapter 21, "Network Security," for the scoop on securing your computer and network. Here are some additional tips:

- Install and run only the services you actually need and use.
- Set up a separate disk partition, formatted with the NTFS disk format, and put your \inetpub folder there.
- Enable auditing of access failures and privilege violations.

→ For instructions on auditing access failures, **see** "Tightening Local Security Policy," **p. 749**.

- Back up your system frequently. Include the Registry in your backups, for example, by checking System State in the Backup System Tool or the equivalent in another program.
- Run virus checks regularly.
- Keep track of the services that should be running on your computer, and watch out for unknown services that may have been installed by rogue software or unauthorized users.

Troubleshooting

Check to See Whether IIS Is Working

I cannot access my IIS server from another computer.

Go to the computer running IIS, start Internet Explorer, and view the address `http://localhost`. If you see a Web page, then IIS is functioning. If you don't, try restarting it following the instructions in the next troubleshooting tip.

Server Doesn't Respond to Requests

A Web browser locates my computer, but the status stays at `Contacting Server` *or* `Waiting for Response`*. No Web page is returned.*

Use the Internet Services Management tool to stop and restart the IIS Server. Open the Management tool, or locate Internet Information Services in Computer Management. Right-click Restart IIS. Then select Restart Internet Services on *machinename* and click OK.

Hyperlinks Return Gibberish

When I click on my links, my browser shows a screen full of random letters and numbers.

Check the file-type to MIME-type mappings on the server and the MIME-type to application viewer on the browser. You can choose File, Save As to save the seemingly senseless information to a file with the appropriate name (for example, XXXX.GIF if you think you have downloaded a GIF file) and try to view it by double-clicking the file in Explorer. If it displays correctly there, then the only problem is the MIME-type mapping.

Browser Doesn't Show Modified Web Page

I have modified a file on my Web site, but the browser still gets the old version.

Click Refresh on the browser. If that trick doesn't work, shut down the browser, restart it, and try again. It's usually the browser's fault. If you still get the wrong version, confirm that you are viewing the correct virtual directory.

Tips from the Windows Pros: Scripting for Interactive Sites

As I said earlier in the chapter, the idea of using programs to generate Web pages on-the-fly was the real spark that turned the Internet into a global phenomenon. (You can thank Tim Berners-Lee at the European Organization for Nuclear Research for this—check out www.cern.org and click on "Where the Web Was Born" for the story!)

The original server-side programs were complex and difficult to write and debug, however, until bright people developed scripting languages for Web servers. Scripting systems put most of the complex stuff into one program that was provided with the Web server. Then, users could write short, easy to manage programs, or scripts, that leverage the power in the main program to do all sorts of interesting and interactive things.

The most common scripting language is Perl, which is very popular in the Unix and Linux world. Perl can be added to IIS so that you can take advantage of the huge pool of already-written Perl programs that are available for free on the Internet. If you know Perl or want to learn, you can download a free Windows version at www.activestate.com. These folks give away Windows versions of Python and TCL as well, two other popular scripting programs, and have a huge library of documentation and free scripts.

Microsoft came up with a scripting system called ASP, which stands for Active Server Pages. (Everything at Microsoft was "Active-something-or-other" for a while there. Now it's .NET this and .NET that.) You can choose what programming language you want use inside: the default is a dialect of Visual Basic, but you can also use JavaScript, Perl, or other languages, if you install the appropriate interpreter programs.

The cool thing about ASP is that you can mix HTML and your chosen script language in the same file. You can use HTML to manage the formatting and static part of the page, and scripting to generate the dynamic part, and it's all there in one place.

ASP scripts can take full advantage of Microsoft COM and ActiveX programming objects. These objects provide a way for scripts to perform very complex functions such as manipulating databases and sending e-mail. You can find loads of useful pre-written ASP scripts on the Internet. For example, check out http://www.zdnet.com/devhead/resources/scriptlibrary/, and click on "ASP" on the left-hand side. Also, take a look at Microsoft's Developer's Web site at msdn.microsoft.com.

As an example of what ASP scripting can do, use Notepad to create a file named time.asp in c:\inetpub\wwwroot, with this inside:

```
<HTML>
<HEAD>
<TITLE>What time is it?</TITLE>
</head>
<BODY>
You viewed this web page at
<% response.write time() %>,
<% response.write date() %>.
</BODY>
</HTML>
```

Then you can view http://localhost/time.asp in Internet Explorer.

Here's what's happening: IIS copies most of the file literally. But stuff in between <% and %> is treated as *script* code, which are commands written in Visual Basic or JavaScript. In this case, VBScript commands insert the time and date into the HTML file at the server, before it's sent to your browser. To see what I mean, right-click the displayed page in Internet Explorer and select View Source. You'll see what the ASP script generated and send to you.

CHAPTER **14**

TROUBLESHOOTING YOUR INTERNET CONNECTION

In this chapter

IT'S GREAT WHEN IT WORKS, BUT...

Browsing the Internet is great fun—and very useful, too. In fact, watch as I instantly transfer millions of dollars from my secret Swiss bank account to . . . . Wait a minute, what's a 404 Server Not Found Error? What's going on? Did the modem disconnect? Is the IRS closing in on me? Help! *Where's my money?!*

If you've used the Internet for any length of time, this scene may seem all too familiar—except for the bit about the Swiss bank account (a guy can dream, can't he?). Connecting to the Internet and using the Web is an amazingly user-friendly experience, yet we can't escape the basic fact that it's a staggeringly complex system. If something goes wrong at any step along the way between your fingertips and a server somewhere off in cyberspace, the whole system comes to a crashing halt. Where do you begin to find and fix the problem?

In this chapter, I'll show you the basic strategies to use when tracking down Internet problems, and then I'll briefly discuss some of the diagnostic tools available to help you pinpoint the trouble.

TIP FROM

Bob
& Brian

> Experiment with the diagnostic tools when your network and Internet connection are operating correctly to learn how the programs work and what sort of output you should expect. This way, as we'll discuss in the next section, if you run into trouble later, you can compare the results to what you saw when things were working.

BEFORE YOU RUN INTO TROUBLE

The best tool to have on hand when you're diagnosing Internet problems is information about what you should expect when your connection is *working*.

It's very helpful to collect correct output of the TCP/IP diagnostic programs, which I'll discuss later in this chapter, and store the copies in a notebook for reference purposes. You can use the PrntScrn key to take snapshots of the output and setup windows, and then paste the pictures into a WordPad document as a super-fast way of recording this stuff.

Here are some things to record:

- The output of `tracert` to a sample Web site. Tracert is a tool that records all the intermediate steps that Internet data takes getting from your computer to a site out on the Net. Knowing what the route looks like when things are working can help you tell whether a problem is in your computer or out somewhere on the Internet, beyond your control.

- The output of `ipconfig /all` on each of your computers, while you're connected to the Internet. Ipconfig lists all of your networking settings so you can check for mistakes.

14

- The network hardware and protocol configuration dialog boxes in Network Connections, as pictures snapped with PrntScrn. If you have a network or a network adapter that you use for a broadband cable or DSL Internet connection, it's handy to record the setup information in case you need to reenter it at a later date. You might need to do that if you replace your network adapter, for example.

- The configuration of any routers or network connection equipment. If you have an Internet connection sharing device, it's a good idea to record its correct settings in case they are accidentally changed, or if you update or replace the device.

- The settings for any dial-up connections used. Many ISPs talk you through their setup, and it's important to record the setup information in case you need to reconstruct it someday.

- Diagrams showing network cabling, hubs, routers, and computers. If your three-year-old is a budding network installer and rewires your computer, it's handy to have a diagram of the correct setup to help you get the all the wiring spaghetti back in order.

In a business setting, documentation of your LAN configuration is a "due diligence" issue—it's not optional. Keep it up-to-date, and if you use an outside contractor for network installation or management, be sure that your contract requires good documentation.

This way, you'll be armed with supportive information if a problem does occur.

TROUBLESHOOTING

Troubleshooting is a real detective's art, and it's based more on methodical tracking down of potential suspect problems than intuition. Because a functioning computer and Internet connection depend on a whole chain of correctly functioning hardware and software components, if something goes wrong, what you have to do is go through each in turn, asking "Is this the component that's causing the problem?"

To that end, Figures 14.1 and 14.2 show flowcharts to help direct you to the problem. The first chart is for dial-up connections to an ISP, and the second is for LAN connections. If you're having Internet connection trouble, follow the appropriate flowchart. The endpoints in each flowchart suggest places to look for trouble. I'll discuss these in the sections that follow.

IDENTIFYING SOFTWARE CONFIGURATION PROBLEMS

Software configuration problems can easily be the cause of Internet connection problems, and it's fairly easy to determine that this is the problem—you can't make any Internet connection whatsoever, although the Device Manager says your network card or modem seems to be working correctly. The potential problems depend on the type of Internet connection you use.

14

Figure 14.1
Flowchart for diagnosing dial-up Internet connection problems.

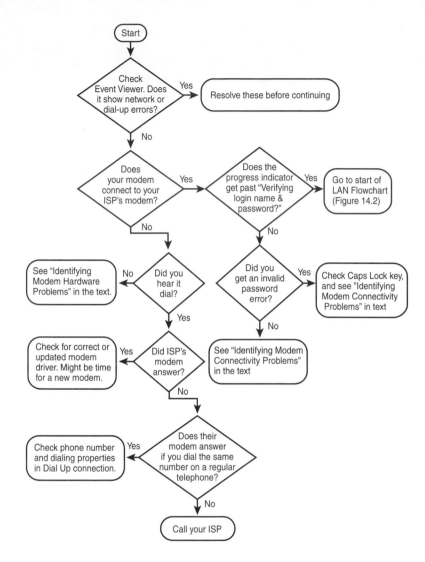

TROUBLESHOOTING A DIAL-UP CONNECTION

If your modem appears to connect to your ISP but, even though connected, you still can't access any Web pages or Internet services, here are some steps you can take:

1. In Internet Explorer, select Tools, Internet Options. Select the Connections tab. Be sure you have selected the correct dial-up connection. Click LAN Options and be sure that Use a Proxy Server is not checked, as shown in Figure 14.3.

14

Figure 14.2
Flowchart for diagnosing wired or LAN connection problems.

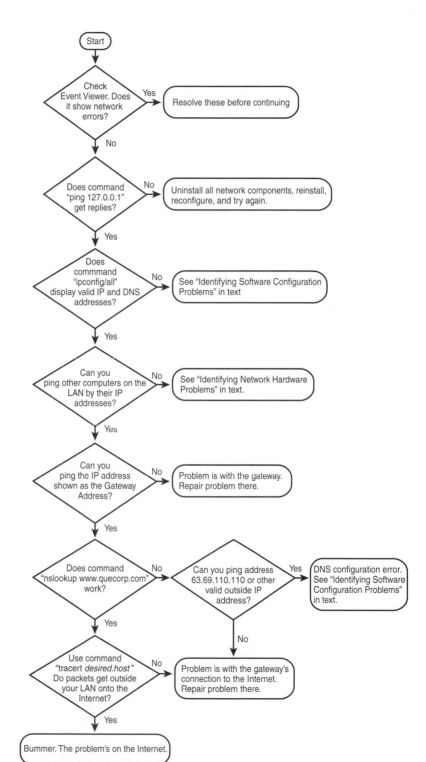

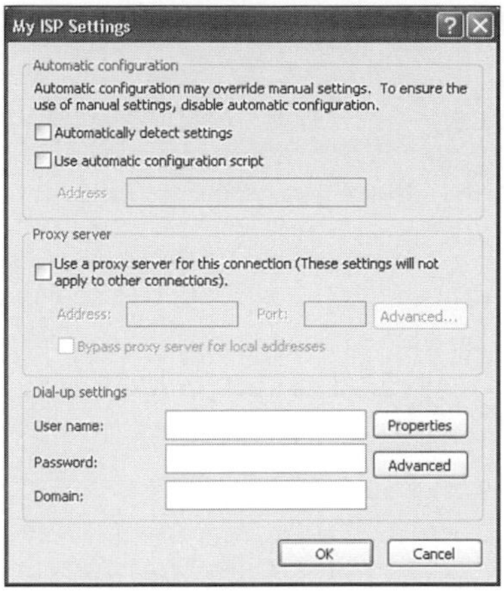

Figure 14.3
For a dial-up Internet connection, Proxy Server should not be checked.

2. Click Start, Connect To, and right-click your Dial-Up connection. Select Properties, and view the Networking tab. The type of dial-up server should be PPP, and under Components Used By This Connection, only Internet Protocol and QoS Packet Scheduler should be checked, as shown in Figure 14.4.

Figure 14.4
For a dial-up Internet connection, only Internet Protocol and QoS Packet Scheduler should be checked.

3. On the Security tab of your connection's Properties sheet (refer to step 2), be sure that Validate My Identity is set to Allow Unsecured Password for an ISP, or Require Secured Password if you're connecting to your office LAN.

If none of these steps identifies a problem, it's time to call your ISP for assistance. You might have to spend a half hour listening to really bad music on hold, but at this point, it's their job to help you get online and they should help you cheerfully and expertly (otherwise, you should get a new ISP).

TROUBLESHOOTING A CABLE OR DSL MODEM CONNECTION

If your computer connects to a cable or DSL modem, you may have one or two network cards installed in your computer, depending on whether you're sharing the high-speed connection on your LAN.

Here's how to check for the proper settings:

1. In a command prompt window, type `ipconfig /all`. Be sure that your IP address and DNS information for the network card that connects to your high-speed modem is accurate. Your ISP's tech support people can help you confirm this.

2. If your DSL provider requires you to "sign on" before using the Internet, you'll be using a sort of "dial-up" connection, except that the connection is made digitally over the DSL network. You will have set up a connection using "Connect using a broadband connection that requires a user name and password" as described in Chapter 8.

   If this is the case, and if you use a LAN adapter to connect to your DSL modem, this LAN adapter will have an IP address that is used *only* to communicate with your DSL modem. Be sure to check with your ISP to be certain that this computer-to-modem connection is configured correctly; if it's not, you won't be able to make the connection to your ISP.

   Then, be sure to use the Connection icon to connect to your ISP. You can get to it quickly using Start, Connect To.

   When the logon process has completed, ipconfig should show a dial-up connection with a different IP address. This is your real, public Internet address for the duration of the call.

3. If you're sharing a high-speed connection to a LAN using two network cards in your computer, be sure that you've enabled sharing on the correct connection! The connection to check as "shared" is the one that connects to your high-speed DSL or cable modem. The LAN-side connection is not the shared connection and should have an IP address of `192.168.0.1`. Internet Connection Sharing is described in Chapter 18.

TROUBLESHOOTING A LAN CONNECTION

If you connect to the Internet via a connection on your LAN, the first question is, can you communicate with other computers on your LAN? To test this, you should use the `ping` command.

Open a Command Prompt window and test the gateway address shown by ipconfig, for example

```
ping 192.168.0.1
```

This tests the connection to the computer sharing its Internet connection. If this doesn't work, you have a LAN problem that you'll need to fix first.

If you can communicate with other computers on the LAN but not the Internet, can anyone else on your LAN access the Internet? If no one can, the problem is in your LAN's connection

14

to the Net. If your LAN uses Internet connection sharing, go to the sharing computer and start diagnosing the problem there. Otherwise, follow these steps:

1. Open a command prompt window and type `ipconfig /all` to view your TCP/IP settings. The output will appear similar to that shown in Listing 14.1.

LISTING 14.1 OUTPUT FROM THE `ipconfig /all` COMMAND

```
Windows IP Configuration
        Host Name . . . . . . . . . . . . : ambon

        Primary Dns Suffix  . . . . . . . :
        Node Type . . . . . . . . . . . . : Unknown
        IP Routing Enabled. . . . . . . . : No
        WINS Proxy Enabled. . . . . . . . : No
Ethernet adapter Local Area Connection:
        Connection-specific DNS Suffix  . : mycompany.com
        Description . . . . . . . . . . . : Realtek RTL8139 Family PCI Fast
    Ethernet NIC
        Physical Address. . . . . . . . . : 00-C0-CA-14-09-7F
        Dhcp Enabled. . . . . . . . . . . : Yes
        Autoconfiguration Enabled . . . . : Yes
        IP Address. . . . . . . . . . . . : 192.168.0.102
        Subnet Mask . . . . . . . . . . . : 255.255.255.0
        Default Gateway . . . . . . . . . : 192.168.0.1
        DHCP Server . . . . . . . . . . . : 192.168.0.1
        DNS Servers . . . . . . . . . . . : 192.168.0.4
                                            207.155.183.72
                                            206.173.119.72
        Lease Obtained. . . . . . . . . . : Sunday, August 19, 2001 5:57:56 PM
        Lease Expires . . . . . . . . . . : Monday, August 20, 2001 5:57:56 PM
```

Check the following:

- The DNS suffix search list and/or the connection-specific DNS suffix should be set correctly for your ISP's domain name (or your company's domain name).

- The IP address should be appropriate for your LAN. If you're using Internet Connection Sharing, the number will be 192.168.0.*xxx*. If you're using a hardware connection sharing device, the number may be different.

- If your IP address appears to be 169.254.0.*xxx*, the sharing computer was not running the connection-sharing service when you booted up your computer. Get it started and then skip to step 2.

- The default gateway address should be the IP address of your router or 192.168.0.1 (if you're using a shared Internet connection).

  The default gateway address and your IP address should be identical for the first few sets of numbers, corresponding to those parts of the subnet mask that are set to 255.

- If your computer gets its IP address information automatically, DHCP Enabled should be set to Yes. If your computer has its IP address information entered manually, no DHCP server should be listed.

14

- If you're using Connection Sharing, the DNS server address will be `192.168.0.1`. Otherwise, the DNS server numbers should be those provided by your ISP or network administrator.

  If your computer gets its settings automatically or uses a shared connection, continue with the next two steps.

2. Be sure the master router or sharing computer is running. In Network Connections, click your Local Area Connection icon and select Repair This Connection from the task list. This may solve the problem.

3. Repeat the `ipconfig` command and see whether the correct information appears now. If it does, you're all set. If not, the master computer or the router is not supplying the information th at I described above, and needs to be set correctly before you can proceed.

These steps should take care of any software configuration problems, and there isn't much more that could be causing a problem, as long as your network hardware is functioning correctly. If none of these steps indicates or solves the problem, check that your network or modem hardware is functioning correctly.

IDENTIFYING NETWORK HARDWARE PROBLEMS

If you suspect hardware as the source of your Internet connection problems, check the following:

- On the Start menu, right-click My Computer and select Manage to open Computer Management. Select Device Manager. Look for any yellow exclamation point (!) icons in the device list; if your network adapter is marked with this trouble indicator, you'll have to solve the hardware problem before continuing. See Chapter 25, "Maintaining and Optimizing System Performance," for hardware troubleshooting tips.

- Still in Computer Management, check the Event Viewer for an informative error message that may indicate a hardware problem.

- Use ipconfig to check that all the computers on your LAN have the same network mask value and similar but distinct IP addresses.

- If your LAN has indicator lights on the network cards and/or hubs, open a command prompt window and type `ping -t x.x.x.x`, where `x.x.x.x` is your network's Default Gateway Address. This forces your computer to transmit data once per second. Confirm that the indicator lights blink on your LAN adapter and the hub, if you have one. This test may point out a cabling problem.

- If your hub or LAN card's indicator doesn't flash, you may have a bad LAN adapter, the wrong driver may be installed, or you may have configured the card incorrectly. You can stop the Ping test by pressing Ctrl+C when you're finished checking.

14

IDENTIFYING MODEM HARDWARE PROBLEMS

Modems can have a greater variety of problems than network adapters. Here are a few steps you can take to determine what the problem might be:

1. Before getting too frustrated, check the obvious one more time: Is a functioning telephone line connected to the right socket on the modem? Unless you're using an ISDN modem, it also doesn't hurt to plug in an extension phone and listen as the modem dials and your ISP answers. You must somehow put the extension on the "line" side of the modem, though, because most modems disable the "telephone" jack when dialing.

   If dialing was actually taking place but you couldn't hear it, run the Phone and Modem Options (open the Control Panel and select Network Connections). Select the Modems tab, select Properties, and then turn up the speaker volume.

   If you have a voicemail system that uses a stutter dial tone to indicate that you have messages waiting, your modem may not dial when the stutter is active. In this same Control Panel dialog, you can disable Wait for Dial Tone Before Dialing.

2. If you have an external analog or ISDN modem, be sure that it's plugged in and turned on. When you attempt to make a connection, watch for flickering in the Send Data LEDs. If you don't see flickering, your modem cable might not be installed correctly.

3. Check the Event Viewer for informative error messages that may indicate a hardware problem.

4. In the Start menu, right-click My Computer, select Manage, and select Device Manager. Look for any yellow exclamation point (!) icons in the device list; if a modem or port is marked with this trouble indicator, you'll have to solve the hardware problem before continuing. See Chapter 25 for hardware troubleshooting tips.

> **NOTE**
>
> If you'd like to learn more about troubleshooting hardware conflicts, I recommend that you pick up a copy of Scott Mueller's *Upgrading and Repairing PCs, 13th Edition*, published by Que.

5. In the Dial-Up Connection's Properties Option tab, check Prompt for Phone Number and try to make the connection. This will show you the actual number being dialed. Verify that the call waiting code, outside line access codes, and area code are correct. These are set on the connection's General tab and in the Phone and Modem Options control panel (on the Dialing Rules dialog box, select the proper location and click Edit).

6. If you have an analog or ISDN modem, and dialing is taking place but no connection is made, in the Device Manager or Control Panel Phone and Modem Properties, view the modem's Properties dialog. Select the Diagnostics tab, and check Append to Log. Close the dialog, and try to make the connection again. Go back to the Properties dialog, and select View Log. This log may indicate what is happening with the modem. Be sure to uncheck Append to Log when you're finished or the file that stores this information could grow to enormous proportions.

7. Try reducing the Maximum Port Speed (computer-to-modem connection speed) setting in Modem Properties to 19200. If this solves your problem, you need a new modem, or, if you have an external serial modem, a higher-quality serial port card.

IDENTIFYING MODEM CONNECTIVITY PROBLEMS

Modems are much more reliable these days than they were in the 1980s and 1990s. Still, compatibility problems and trouble due to poor telephone line quality still occur from time to time. If your modem fails to make a connection, or disconnects by itself, here are a few things to look for:

- If the ISP's modem answers but you don't establish a connection, your modem may be incompatible; call your ISP for assistance.

- If your modem disconnects and you are told that there was a problem with your username or password, try to connect again and check these entries carefully. If you try two or three times and still can't connect, contact your ISP for help. I've known them to disable accounts for various reasons, from non-payment to, well, no reason at all.

- Create and view a log file of modem activity and look for error messages indicating a protocol negotiation error. Your ISP can assist with this as well.

- If your modem makes screeching sounds for about 15 seconds and hangs up, your modem is probably incompatible with the equipment used at your ISP, and one of you needs to get an updated modem. Before you buy a new one, note that some modems can be updated via software. Check the manufacturer's Web site for information.

- If your connection works but the modem disconnects after a certain amount of time, there are two possible causes. If your connection was sitting idle, you may have run into the Windows inactivity timer. View the dial-up connection's properties in Network Connections and select the Options tab. Check the entry Idle Time Before Hanging Up. Increase the time (or stay busier!). You might enable the modem log and see whether it provides an explanation if this recurs. Your ISP may also have set up their equipment to disconnect you after a certain period of inactivity.

- If you don't think that idle time was the cause, your connection may have been interrupted by call waiting. On the connection's General tab, check Use Dialing Rules and select Rules and Edit. Verify that you've chosen to disable call waiting and have selected the proper call waiting turn off setting (for example, *70). Some newer modems are able to cope with call waiting, and even alert you to a call coming in. If you really rely on call waiting, it might be time for an upgrade. Although, in this case, you'd probably be better suited switching to a cable or DSL connection if one is available to you.

- If none of these are the cause, you may simply have a scratchy telephone line or a flagging older modem. This is an annoying problem and difficult to diagnose. Try changing modems.

If your modem is making contact with your ISP, but despite a solid modem connection you still can't use the Internet, see the next section for tips on diagnosing Internet connectivity problems.

14

TROUBLESHOOTING INTERNET PROBLEMS WITH WINDOWS TCP/IP UTILITIES

If you think you are connected to your ISP but still can't communicate, you can use some of the command-line tools provided with Windows XP to trace TCP/IP problems. (TCP/IP is the network language or *protocol* used by the Internet; see Chapter 14 for an introduction to networking and protocols.)

To run the command-line utilities, open a Command Prompt box with Start, More Programs, Accessories, Command Prompt. Then type in the commands as I'll describe them below. If you're not familiar with command-line utilities you can launch Windows Help (Start, Help and Support), and search for the command names, such as "ping" and "tracert." You can also open a Command Prompt window and type the command name followed by /?, as in

```
Ping /?
```

Now, let's go through some of the Windows XP TCP/IP diagnostic and command-line utilities.

NOTE

> If you're a Unix devotee, you'll find these utilities very familiar, if not identical, to their Unix counterparts. If you're new to TCP/IP networking or debugging, you might find these utilities a little unfriendly. (Welcome to the world of networking!)

IPCONFIG

Ipconfig is one of the most useful command-line utilities available with Windows XP, because it displays the current IP address information for each of your computer's network adapters and active dial-up connections. On networks that assign addresses automatically, ipconfig provides the only way to find out what your computer's IP address is, should you ever need to know it.

After opening a command prompt window, typing the command

```
ipconfig
```

returns the following information (of course the IP, subnet, and gateway information ipconfig provides will be different for your computer, and you might see a dial-up connection listed rather than a LAN adapter):

```
Windows IP Configuration
Ethernet adapter Local Area Connection:

        Connection-specific DNS Suffix  . : mycompany.com
        IP Address. . . . . . . . . . . . : 202.201.200.166
        Subnet Mask . . . . . . . . . . . : 255.255.255.224
        Default Gateway . . . . . . . . . : 202.201.200.190
```

If you type the command

```
Ipconfig /all
```

14

Windows displays additional information about your DNS settings, including

Host name	The name you gave your computer.
Primary DNS suffix	The Internet domain to which your computer primarily belongs. (You might temporarily belong to others as well while using a dial-up connection.) This might be blank; tis not a problem.
Node type	The method that Windows uses to locate other computers on your LAN when you use Windows Networking. This should be Hybrid if you have a Windows XP Server or a WINS server on your LAN; otherwise, the node type should say Broadcast.
DNS suffix search list	Alternative domain names used if you type just part of a host name and the default domain does not provide a match.
Connection-specific DNS suffix	The domain name for this particular connection. This is most applicable to dial-up connections.
DHCP enabled	If set to Yes, this adapter is set to receive its IP address automatically. If set to No, the address was set manually.
DNS servers	IP addresses of domain name servers.

Ipconfig displays most of the information in the Network and Dial-Up Connection Properties dialog box, but it shows their real-world values. This makes it an invaluable "first stop" when troubleshooting any network problem. If you determine that an Internet connection problem lies in your equipment somewhere (because you cannot access *any* Internet destinations), typing ipconfig /all will tell you whether your network setup is correct. You'll want this information at hand before calling your ISP for assistance.

ping

If you try to browse the Internet or share files with other computers on your LAN and get no response, it could be because the other computer isn't getting your data or isn't responding. After ipconfig, ping is the most useful tool to determine where your Internet connection or your network has stopped working.

TIP FROM

Bob
& Brian

> You can type ping *x.x.x.x*, replacing *x.x.x.x* with the default gateway address or the address of any other operational computer on the Internet or on your network, if you have one, and in an instant know whether your dial-up or high-speed modem, computer, network hardware, and cabling are operating properly. If echoes come back, the physical part of your network is functioning properly. If they don't, you can use tracert and other tools explained later in this chapter to see why.

14

Here's how it works:

1. The `ping` command sends a few packets of data to any computer you specify.
2. The other computer should immediately send these packets right back to you.
3. Then, ping lets you know whether the packets come back.

Therefore, ping tests the low-level communication between two computers. If ping works, you know that your network wiring, TCP/IP software, and any routers in between you and the other computer are working. Ping takes several options that can customize the type and amount of output it reports back to you. There are three especially useful variations of these options, the first two of which are

```
C:\> ping hostname
```

and

```
C:\> ping nnn.nnn.nnn.nnn
```

These variations transmit four packets to the host or IP address you specify and tell you whether they return. This command returns the following information:

```
C:\> ping www.mycompany.com
Pinging sumatra.mycompany.com [202.222.132.163] with 32 bytes of data:
Reply from 202.222.132.163: bytes=32 time<10ms TTL=32
Reply from 202.222.132.163: bytes=32 time<10ms TTL=32
Reply from 202.222.132.163: bytes=32 time<10ms TTL=32
Reply from 202.222.132.163: bytes=32 time<10ms TTL=32
```

In this example, the fact that the packets returned tells us that the computer can communicate with www.mycompany.com. It also tells us that everything in between is working as well.

NOTE

> It's not uncommon for one packet of the four to be lost; when the Internet gets congested, sometimes ping packets are discarded as unimportant. If *any* come back, the intervening networks are working.

Another useful variation is to add the `-t` option. This makes ping run endlessly, once per second, until you press Ctrl+C. This is especially helpful if you're looking at indicator lights on your network hub, changing cables, and so on. The endless testing lets you just watch the screen to see whether any changes you make cause a difference.

Ping is a great quick test of connectivity to any location. If the ping test fails, use tracert or pathping to tell you where the problem is. Ping is a good quick tool to use to discover whether an Internet site is alive. (However, some large companies have made their servers not respond to ping tests at all. `ping www.microsoft.com` doesn't work, ever, even with a good Internet connection. Guess Microsoft got tired of being the first site everyone thought of to test their Internet connections.)

tracert

Tracert is similar to ping: It sends packets to a remote host and sees whether packets return. However, tracert adds a wrinkle: It checks the connectivity to each individual router in the path between you and the remote host. (Routers are the devices that connect one network to another. The Internet itself is the conglomeration of a few million networks all connected by routers). If your computer and Internet connection are working but you still can't reach some or all Internet sites, tracert can help you find out where the blockage is.

In tracert's output, the address it tests first is your local network's gateway (if you connect to the Internet via a high-speed connection or a LAN) or the modem-answering equipment at your ISP's office (if you're using a dial-up connection). If this first address responds, you know your modem, LAN, or broadband connection is working. If the connection stops after two or three routers, the problem is in your ISP's network. If the problem occurs farther out, there may be an Internet outage somewhere else in the country.

Here's an example that shows the route between my network and the Web server www.ricochet.net. Typing

```
C:\> tracert www.ricochet.net
```

returns the following:

```
Tracing route to www.metricom.com [204.179.107.3]
over a maximum of 30 hops:

1    <10 ms    <10 ms    <10 ms   190.mycompany.com [202.201.200.190]
2    <10 ms    <10 ms     10 ms   129.mycompany.com [202.201.200.129]
3     20 ms     20 ms     20 ms   w001.z216112073.sjc-ca.dsl.cnc.net
                                  ➥[216.112.73.1]
4     10 ms     10 ms     10 ms   206.83.66.153
5     10 ms     10 ms     10 ms   rt001f0801.sjc-ca.concentric.net
                                  [ic:ccc][206.83.90.161]
6     10 ms     20 ms     20 ms   us-ca-sjc-core2-f5-0.rtr.
                                  ➥concentric.net [205.158.11.133]
7     10 ms     20 ms     10 ms   us-ca-sjc-core1-g4-0-0.rtr.
                                  ➥concentric.net [205.158.10.2]
8     10 ms     20 ms     20 ms   us-ca-pa-core1-a9-0d1.rtr.
                                  ➥concentric.net [205.158.11.14]
9     10 ms     20 ms     20 ms   ATM2-0-0.br2.pao1.
                                  ➥ALTER.NET [137.39.23.189]
10    10 ms     20 ms     20 ms   125.ATM3-0.XR1.PAO1.
                                  ➥ALTER.NET [152.63.49.170]
11    10 ms     10 ms     20 ms   289.at-1-0-0.XR3.SCL1.
                                  ➥ALTER.NET [152.63.49.98]
12    20 ms     20 ms     20 ms   295.ATM8-0-0.GW2.SCL1.
                                  ➥ALTER.NET [152.63.48.113]
13    20 ms     20 ms     20 ms   2250-gw.customer.
                                  ➥ALTER.NET [157.130.193.14]
14    41 ms     30 ms     20 ms   www.metricom.com
                                  ➥[204.179.107.3]

Trace complete.
```

14

You can see that between my computer and this Web server, data passes through 13 intermediate routers, owned by two ISPs. (Try this particular test yourself and you'll see that Ricochet has gone out of business!)

TIP FROM

Bob
& Brian

> When your Internet connection is working, run tracert to trace the path between your computer and a few Internet hosts. Print and save the listings. Someday when you're having Internet problems, you can use these listings as a baseline reference. It's very helpful to know whether packets are stopping in your LAN, in your ISP's network, or beyond when you pick up the phone to yell about it.

I should point out a couple of tracert's oddities. First, notice in the example that I typed www.ricochet.net, but tracert printed www.metricom.com. That's not unusual. Web servers sometimes have many alternative names. Tracert starts with a reverse name lookup to find the *canonical* (primary) name for a given IP address.

There's another glitch you might run into. For security reasons, many organizations use firewall software or devices, which block tracert packets at the firewall between their LAN and the Internet. In these instances, tracert will never reach its intended destination even when regular communications are working correctly. Instead, you'll see an endless list that looks like this:

```
14      *       *       *       Request timed out.
15      *       *       *       Request timed out.
16      *       *       *       Request timed out.
```

This continues up to tracert's limit of 30 probes. Just press Ctrl+C to cancel the test if this happens. If tracert was able to reach routers outside your own LAN or PC, your equipment's fine and that's all you can hope for.

pathping

Pathping is relatively new to Windows's toolkit, having first appeared in Windows 2000. It provides the function of tracert and adds a more intensive network traffic test.

Pathping performs the route-tracing function faster than tracert because it sends only one packet per hop, compared to tracert's three.

Then, after determining the route, pathping does a punishing test of network traffic at each router by sending 100 ping packets to each router in the path between you and the host you're testing. It measures the number of lost packets and the average round trip time for each hop, and it displays the results in a table.

The results tell you which routers along the way are experiencing congestion, because they will not be able to return every echo packet they're sent, and they may take some time to do it. Performing the pathping test can take quite a while. Fortunately, you can cancel the test by pressing Ctrl+C, or you can specify command-line options to shorten the test. A reasonably quick test of the path to a site, say www.quecorp.com, can be performed using just 10 queries instead of the default 100, using this command:

```
pathping -q 100 www.quecorp.com
```

You can type

```
pathping /?
```

to get a full description of the command line options.

route

Most of us have at most one modem or one LAN adapter through which we make our Internet and other network connections, but Windows Networking components are sophisticated enough to handle multiple LAN and dial-up adapters in one computer. When multiple connections are made, Windows has to know which connections to use to speak with another remote computer. For the TCP/IP or Internet Protocol (IP) data, this information comes from the *routing table*. This table stores lists of IP addresses and subnets (blocks of IP addresses) as well as indicates which adapter (or *interface*) Windows used to reach each of them.

Now, this is getting into some hardcore networking that only a few readers will be interested in; please don't think that you'll need to know about this tool (there will be *no* quiz next Friday). I'm discussing this only to get the details down for those few people who have a complex network setup and only need to know how to go to this information. You don't have to worry about routing unless one of the following scenarios is true:

- You use a dial-up connection *and* a LAN adapter simultaneously.
- You use multiple LAN adapters.
- You use Virtual Private Networking connections, as discussed in Chapter 18, "Windows Unplugged: Remote and Mobile Networking."

If you have trouble reaching an Internet destination and fall into any of these three categories, type route at the command line. You'll be shown a table that looks something like this:

```
===========================================================================
Interface List
0x1 ........................ MS TCP Loopback interface
0x2 ...0e c3 24 1f 09 3f ...... NDIS 5.0 driver
===========================================================================
===========================================================================
Active Routes:
Network Destination        Netmask          Gateway       Interface  Metric
        0.0.0.0          0.0.0.0  202.201.200.190  202.201.200.166       1
      127.0.0.0        255.0.0.0        127.0.0.1        127.0.0.1       1
  202.201.200.160  255.255.255.224  202.201.200.166  202.201.200.166       1
```

14

```
      202.201.200.166   255.255.255.255         127.0.0.1         127.0.0.1        1
      202.201.200.255   255.255.255.255   202.201.200.166   202.201.200.166        1
            224.0.0.0         224.0.0.0   202.201.200.166   202.201.200.166        1
      255.255.255.255   255.255.255.255   202.201.200.166   202.201.200.166        1
Default Gateway:      202.201.200.190
========================================================================
Persistent Routes:
  None
```

There's a lot of information here, but for our purposes, we can boil it down to this: The entry for network destination `0.0.0.0` is the effective gateway address for general Internet destinations. This *can* be different from your LAN's specified default gateway, especially while a dial-up or VPN connection is active. That, in turn, may mean that you can't get to the Internet. If you have multiple LAN adapters, the issues are more complicated. Contact your network administrator for assistance.

→ If the gateway address is incorrect after you've made a dial-up connection, **see** "Routing Issues," **p. 637**.

WEB-BASED UTILITIES

Besides the utilities provided with Windows XP, there are some third-party tools that you can use to help diagnose your connection and gather Internet information. I'll describe three Web-based utilities and one commercial software package.

SPEED CHECK

Ever wondered how to find the real-world transfer rate of your Internet connection? Intel Corporation has a nifty Web-based program to measure transfer speeds using a Java applet. Check out `www.intel.com/home/club/dcalc.htm`.

WHOIS DATABASE

Anyone registering an Internet domain name is required to file contact information with his or her Internet registry. This is public information, and you can use it to find out how to contact the owners of a domain whose customers have sent spam mail or with whom you have other concerns.

The `.com`, `.edu`, and `.org` domains all register with the U.S. InterNIC, which is managed by Network Solutions, Inc. You can look up domain contact information online using the "whois" service. Whois is a registered network protocol like finger. Although there are whois lookup programs out there, the simplest way to get at the InterNIC registry is through the following Web page:

`www.networksolutions.com/cgi-bin/whois/whois`

Links on that page lead you to similar lookup pages for the U.S. government and military domains (`.gov` and `.mil`) and for European and Asian/Pacific IP address registries.

14

Reverse Tracert

As I discussed earlier, the tracert program investigates the path that data you send through the Internet takes to reach another location. Interestingly, data coming back to you can take a different path. Users of older satellite Internet service know this already as their outbound data goes through a modem, while incoming data arrives by satellite. It turns out that this can happen even with standard Internet service, depending on the way your ISP has set up its own internal network.

It's handy to know how the path data takes coming to you. If you record this information while your Internet connection is working, then if you run into trouble you can have a friend perform a tracert to you (you'll need to give him or her your IP address, which you can find using the `ipconfig` command). If the results differ you may be able to tell whether the problem is with your computer, your ISP, or the Internet.

You can visit `http://www.traceroute.org` for a list of hundreds of Web servers that can perform a traceroute test from their site to you. Don't be surprised if the test results take a while to appear as these tests typically take a minute or more.

WS_Ping Pro Pack

If you want to be really well equipped to handle Internet and general networking problems, you can buy third-party utilities that are really much easier to use than the standard ones built into Windows. I really like WS_Ping ProPack from Ipswitch Software (`www.ipswitch.com`). This one utility packs almost all the TCP/IP tools into one graphical interface and adds other features such as whois for domain registration lookups, SNMP probing, and network scanning. The registration fee is $37.50 U.S. for a single-user license. I rarely use or like add-ons like this, but I use this program every few days for one reason or another, and it quickly made my "must have" list.

Tips from the Windows Pros: Pinging with Larger Packets

I have a DSL connection in my office, and one night it appeared that my Internet connection had stopped working. After a closer look, I saw that only downstream communication was affected, meaning my browser could contact Web sites, but information from the Web wasn't reaching my computer.

I first tried pinging my ISP at the gateway address of my DSL modem. It worked just fine. In fact, I could ping any site in the entire Internet but still could not view a single Web page. I called my Internet service provider and they found out that pings from their network into my LAN worked, too. The guy I spoke to suggested that I must have a software problem.

14

That didn't make sense to me, especially because everything was working fine just minutes before. Then I had a hunch. Ping, by default, sends very small packets: 32 bytes each, plus a few bytes of IP packet packaging. Requests for Web pages are very small, too (maybe 100 bytes). However, responses from Web servers are big and come in the largest packets possible—about 1500 bytes each. This meant the problem might not be the direction the data was taking. Instead, it could be the size of the data that was causing the problem.

I vaguely remembered that ping has a bunch of command-line options, so I looked up "ping" in Windows Help and saw that I could increase the size of its packets with the `-l` option. Typing

```
ping -l 300 www.someplace.com
```

tells ping to send 300-byte packets. Aha! I found that only about 50 percent of these packets made the roundtrip. When I sent 500-byte packets, the success rate dropped to 10 percent. When I called tech support with this news, the guy at my ISP tried the same test, and got the same result when he tried to ping my computer from his network.

It turned out that there was a bad connection in the telephone wiring down the street from my office. The connection had suddenly failed, making it difficult for the modem to send more than a few bytes at a time without interference. They fixed the problem a few days later.

The moral of this story is to be familiar with your friendly neighborhood command-line utilities.

14

PART IV

NETWORKING

OVERVIEW OF WINDOWS XP NETWORKING

In this chapter

15

NETWORK CONCEPTS

A revolution is going on now, and it compares to the one Johannes Gutenberg started in 1456 when he pioneered the use of movable type. The ability to print in quantity made it possible for the first time for the common man to gain knowledge by himself. This new revolution is based on global connectivity, and its impact is on our ability to *disseminate* information by ourselves. We now take it for granted that we can share information, preach, publish, talk, and touch the rest of the world through our computers. Networks have radically changed the way the world communicates.

Networks aren't limited to just the work environment anymore. Many homes with a computer quickly end up with two or more, and it's not long before it seems sensible to tie them together with a network. So, whether or not you have one now, a network is probably in your future. In this chapter, you'll learn how networking works and how Windows XP provides the tools to help you become part of the connected world.

NOTE

> This chapter is designed to provide some basic networking concepts. If you have been networking computers for some time, feel free to skip ahead. If you are new to networking, stick around. This chapter will help get you pointed in the right direction.

WHY YOU REALLY NEED A NETWORK

I probably don't have to convince you of the value of tying your computers together with a network, even if you have only two. With a network, you can do the following:

- Use any printer attached to any computer.
- Share files, that is, get at files stored on one computer from another. At home, having this capability might mean you can finish that letter you were writing yesterday using your kids' computer because they're now using yours to manage their stock portfolios. In the office, a network lets workers share information quickly and facilitates the creation of a centralized documentation system.
- Share CD-ROMs.
- Back up networked computers with one common backup system—for example, a tape drive.
- Use network-enabled application software, such as databases, workgroup scheduling and calendar programs, and e-mail. Network-enabled software is designed to give multiple users simultaneous access to information that is updated in real-time.
- Share a single Internet connection among several computers, saving on telephone lines and connection costs.
- Play multi-user games within your home or office, or across the Internet.

A network can justify its cost with printer or Internet connection sharing alone. But how hard is it to put together?

15

No Longer a Dark Art

It doesn't seem possible that it was only 12 years ago that I installed my first network in a client's office. Installing it was nerve-wracking because it had cost my client thousands of dollars in hardware and software above the cost of the computers alone, and although he didn't know, I had never installed networking software or a file server before. Networking was reputed to be a costly, mystical, and dark art, and I soon found that this reputation was well-deserved. The network eventually worked. For several thousand dollars, my client got 10 computers that could read and write to the same database file.

Now a network card can cost less than a movie, you can buy network cables at the corner hardware store, and first-class networking software is, well, nearly free—it's free if you were going to buy Windows anyway. And you can probably take it for granted that you should be able to just plug and play.

In the next few chapters, you'll learn how to use Windows networking to connect to the computer in your basement, to the rest of your office workgroup, or to a worldwide corporate enterprise. You may still need to learn an incantation or two, but fear not, they're no longer in Latin.

One other point: I'll be using the word *resource* frequently in this chapter. By *resource*, I mean a shared folder or printer on someone else's computer, which you can access through the LAN.

Network Neighborhoods

Windows XP has, right out of the box, all the software you need to communicate and share information with other computers. Windows XP Professional can fill several roles, depending on the way it's connected to other computers. It can be any of the following:

- A standalone computer working in complete isolation. An example might be a simple home computer.

- A standalone computer connected to others via a modem. An example is a laptop computer with a modem used to connect to an office or to the Internet. This computer works in isolation some of the time but can socialize when needed. You can think of this type as a *remote workstation*.

- A member of a small workgroup of computers with no central "server." An example might be a computer in a small office or home office, one of say 2 to 10. The computers share resources with each other but are essentially independent. This computer is a *peer* in what is called a *peer-to-peer* network; no one computer has an intrinsically special role in making the network work. All the participants are on equal footing; they are peers. Not all the computers need to use Windows XP either; Windows XP can peer with older versions of Windows and other operating systems such as Linux.

- A member of a group of computers working under the stewardship of a central server. This computer is probably one of a group of a dozen or more. The designated master computer or server contains, at least, centralized username and password information, which it passes out as a service to the other computers on the network. These other computers are the *clients* in a *client/server* network. Windows XP Professional can be the client of a Windows .NET or 2000 Server or a Novell NetWare server.

- A member of a client/server network that is in turn connected to other networks. An example is a computer in a branch office of a large company. This computer is participating in an *enterprise* network, where special consideration has to be made to management, security, and the allocation of resources of many, many computers and people spread out over a wide geographical area.

Windows XP Professional has all the stuff to participate in any of these network environments. The one thing it can't do is take the central, or server, role of a client/server or enterprise network. The reason for this is that Windows XP Pro doesn't have the ability to act as a centralized user/password database. For that, you need at least one computer running Windows XP Server or one of its more upscale versions: Advanced Server, Enterprise Server, or Data Center.

Also, Windows XP Professional file sharing service can make a network connection with at most 10 other computers. If you need to share a network resource (such a printer or file folder) with more than 10 computers, you'll need Windows XP Server.

In the next few chapters, you'll learn how to configure and tune up Windows XP in each of these environments. If you already understand how networks work, you can skip ahead to "The Many Faces of Windows XP" later in this chapter. If not, check out the following sections for an introduction to the concepts and terms you should know.

NETWORK FORM AND FUNCTION

What makes a network tick? Let's start by looking at Figure 15.1, the first sort of network you probably built.

Figure 15.1
Did your first network look like this?

Don't laugh! A tin can telephone has many of the attributes of a computer network. The basis of a network is a *physical transport*: a means of carrying raw information (for example, words) over a physical medium (string) between hardware interfaces (cans). When you first used a tin can phone, you found out right away that you couldn't speak at the same time as the person on the other end, so you had to work out a *protocol* to coordinate your conversation: You probably said "over" after you spoke. Finally, you found that there's a limit to how long the string could be for the phone to work. If the string was too long, you couldn't hear.

Computer networks have these components and limitations, too. The raw information in a network is digital data (bits), carried over a physical medium (usually wires or optical fibers, but also radio waves) between hardware interfaces (network adapters plugged into your computer), according to a mutually agreed-upon protocol to coordinate the computers' conversations. Although a tin can network probably isn't too particular about the type of can you use, a computer network is because the endpoints have to use the same sort of electrical or optical signals.

SIZE MATTERS

A computer network is often called a *local area network*, or *LAN*. A LAN is a group of computers connected by a physical medium that supports a relatively high rate of data transmission, say 1 million bits per second (Mbps) or more, in relatively close proximity, say within one building, all able to communicate directly with each other. Imagine 10 cans on strings, all tied together in the center. Typical LANs transmit data at 10 or 100 Mbps. This is fast enough that loading and saving large word processing documents to a remote computer isn't noticeably slower than using your own hard drive.

The electrical nature of LAN communication limits the physical distance allowed between computers to at most a few hundred yards. LANs can be extended much farther using optical fiber cables, which carry data as pulses of light, to connect groups of computers sharing a more traditional (and inexpensive) electrical connection. You might hear this arrangement called a *campus network* or *metropolitan area network*.

A *wide area network*, or *WAN*, is a group of two or more LANs tied together over even longer distances. Historically, these connections were much slower, between 56 thousand bits per second (Kbps) and 1Mbps because long-distance connections were extremely expensive. (A 56Kbps connection between San Francisco and Chicago [with a guaranteed throughput of only 16Kbps] cost about $2,500 per month in 1996.) Now that the telecommunications companies have installed optical fiber cables all over the country, even WAN connections can be as fast as LAN connections these days. Using the Internet, a 400Kbps connection between any two points in the U.S. can be made for as little as $400 per month.

In addition to your data, LANs carry quite a bit of "chatter" as the member computers broadcast questions, asking for the location of needed resources, and as servers broadcast announcements of the services they provide. This communications overhead could use up most of the carrying capacity of a slow WAN connection, so special devices called *routers* examine and make decisions about the data to be sent back and forth between the disparate geographical areas.

As I mentioned earlier, one of the main distinctions of a server-based network is a centralized username/password database. To let users continue working if the long-distance connection fails, and to provide speedier logon checks, builders of WAN networks usually install a server at each geographic location. Windows XP Server lets administrators add or alter user information at any location, and the server automatically copies the changes to all the other servers. For large enterprises, this one feature alone makes it worth the extra bucks.

NETWORK CONNECTION TECHNOLOGIES

As you know, a LAN consists of a group of computers connected together using some sort of electrical medium. You can choose from several different electrical media. They differ in the way they format and electrically represent the data sent between computers.

Network devices have to use some standardized way of organizing the data signals they transmit between computers. You might have heard of some of these already:

- *Ethernet* was developed by Xerox, Intel, and Digital Equipment Corporation. Ethernet has grown so popular and common that you hardly need to use the word anymore: Most networks are Ethernet networks.

- *Asynchronous Transfer Mode, or ATM,* is a networking technology widely used in the telecommunications and Internet industries for very high-speed backbone networks. *Backbone* is a term for an ultra-fast connection between the separate parts or sites of a large network. For example, it might refer to the set of links between major network sites of a corporation, the national network of a telephone carrier, or the high-speed Internet links between major ISPs. ATM also is used by some Internet service providers to route data to DSL (Digital Subscriber Line) modems. However, ATM is only rarely used to connect directly to individual user's computers, except for some very specialized graphics workstations and other ultra-high-tech situations.

Other technologies are waning in popularity and you won't be hearing of them again, so don't feel any need to memorize:

- *ARCnet, AppleTalk,* and *StarLan* were early network technologies but are hardly used now because they are so much slower than modern technologies. AppleTalk is still occasionally used to connect older Macintoshes to printers.

- *Token ring* was developed by IBM and is still used in businesses that are "blue" to the core, but nobody else in his right mind would install it now because it's slower and much more expensive than Ethernet.

If you're constructing your own network, you'll likely use Ethernet in one form or another. The choice you'll have to make is which kind of physical medium to use.

PHYSICAL MEDIA

The signals transmitted across a LAN are generated and interpreted by electronics in each computer. Some computers have built-in network interfaces; otherwise, each computer in a LAN needs a *network interface card*, or *NIC*. I may also refer to them as *network cards*.

These electrical signals have to be carried from computer to computer somehow. The original design for Ethernet used a *very* expensive 1/2-inch thick cable that could carry a 10Mbps Ethernet signal up to 500 meters. (It was named 10BASE5 for reasons that only make sense to an engineer).

15

Today's network interface cards are designed to use one of several inexpensive varieties of network cabling, or use radio waves to avoid the need for wiring altogether. In the following sections, I'll list the various types of media you're likely to encounter.

THIN ETHERNET, OR THINNET

Thin Ethernet uses coaxial cable similar to television cable. It is also called 10BASE2 Ethernet, which indicates that the network runs at 10Mbps and has a maximum wiring length of 200 meters or 660 feet. Thin Ethernet cables end in distinctive twist-on connectors called bayonet connectors, or BNC.

Thin Ethernet wiring runs from computer to computer in a daisy-chain fashion called a *bus* network, as shown in Figure 15.2.

Figure 15.2
Thin Ethernet network cabling runs from computer to computer in a single unbroken line called a bus.

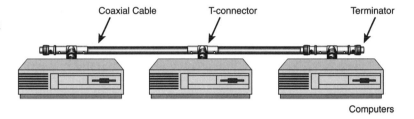

Coaxial Cable T-connector Terminator

Computers

Some coaxial cable is still around, but it's almost never used for new network installations, having been supplanted by the much less-expensive twisted-pair system.

UNSHIELDED TWISTED-PAIR (UTP)

Unshielded Twisted-Pair, or UTP, has become the most common network carrier, and is so called because like-colored pairs of wires in the cable are gently twisted together for better immunity to electrical interference from fluorescent lights, radio signals, and so on. This inexpensive type of cable is also used for telephone connections, although the network variety is of a higher quality and is certified for its capability to carry high data rates. UTP cables are terminated with eight-wire RJ45 connectors, which are wider versions of the ubiquitous modular telephone connectors.

UTP cable quality is categorized by the highest data rate it's been designed and certified to carry reliably. The most common cable types are shown in Table 15.1.

TABLE 15.1 UTP CABLE CATEGORIES

Designation	Highest Data Rate	Application
CAT-1	Less than 1Mbps	Telephone (voice)
CAT-2	4Mbps	IBM Token Ring
CAT-3	16Mbps	10Mbps Ethernet (10BASE-T)

continues

15

TABLE 15.1   CONTINUED

Designation	Highest Data Rate	Application
CAT-4	20Mbps	16Mbps Token Ring
CAT-5	100Mbps	100Mbps Ethernet (100BASE-T), ATM, others
CAT-5E or -5x	250Mbps	Gigabit Ethernet* (1000BASE-T)
CAT-6	250Mbps	Gigabit Ethernet*

Gigabit Ethernet uses four pairs of wire each carrying 250Mbps

The thing to remember here is that you can't use just any old wiring you find in your walls to carry a network signal: You have to look for the appropriate "CAT-something" designation, which will be printed on the cable jacket every foot or so.

UTP cabling can carry token ring signals but is most commonly used for Ethernet networking. Unlike ThinNet's all-in-a-row bus wiring pattern, UTP Ethernet devices are connected to a central device called a *hub* in what is called a *star* network, as shown in Figure 15.3. Star networks are reliable: If any cable in a bus network breaks, the whole network fails. If a cable in a star network fails, only the computer connected by that cable goes offline.

Figure 15.3
Unshielded twisted-pair network with a hub, forming a star pattern.

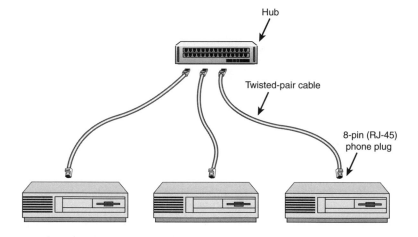

You can buy three varieties of UTP-based Ethernet hardware, denoted 10BASE-T, 10/100BASE-T, and 1000BASE-T in order of increasing speed. I'll discuss the 10BASE-T variety first.

10BASE-T

If you've been paying attention, you might guess that the *10BASE* part means 10Mbps, but *T*? The *T* stands for twisted pair, and you just have to *know* that the maximum permitted cable length is 100 meters, or 330 feet.

15

The maximum cable distance from hub to computer of only 100 meters or 330 feet limits 10BASE-T's usefulness in a large building or campus LAN. Hubs can solve this problem by serving to connect several close-by computers. The hubs can then be connected to each either other with ThinNet or fiber-optic cable, which forms a "backbone" connecting groups of computers, as shown in Figure 15.4.

Figure 15.4
In larger LANs, hubs are connected together to span larger distances. Hubs can be connected using UTP, ThinNet, or fiber-optic cabling.

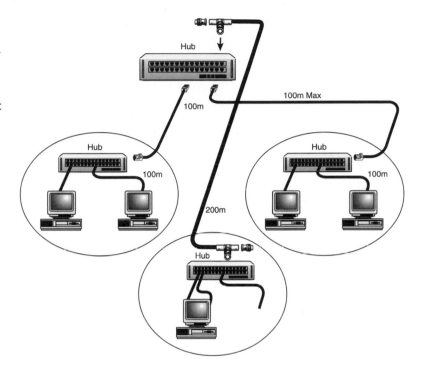

TIP FROM

Bob
& Brian

> Because thin Ethernet cable has only one wire, like our tin can network, only one device at a time can "speak." In networking parlance, this is called a *half-duplex* network. 10BASE-T is usually half-duplex, too. 10BASE-T cards from some manufacturers can operate in full-duplex mode—two network cards can "speak" to each other simultaneously—if all the cards and hubs in the network are so capable.
>
> Operating this way can help boost communication rates somewhat, but it does not necessarily double them. Most computer-to-computer conversations are just like the ones you dread being trapped in at parties: One person does most of the talking, while you just nod and say "uh huh" every so often. In a full-duplex network, the "uh huhs" don't have to interrupt the nonstop talker, so the conversation goes a little bit faster—but not much.
>
> Full-duplex network cards are labeled (something)BASE-Tx by their manufacturers. Paying extra for this feature is generally not worthwhile for the average office network, but it's nice if it comes standard with the network hardware you end up buying. Fast Ethernet adapters, which we'll discuss in the next section, are almost always full-duplex capable.

100BASE-T OR FAST ETHERNET

Fast Ethernet is a 100Mbps version of Ethernet over UTP cable. It is also called 100BASE-T or 100BASE-Tx. (The x stands for full-duplex, which is standard with 100BASE-T networking hardware.)

This hardware is 10 times faster than 10BASE-T hardware. However, the CAT-5 cable required to carry this high-speed signal is a bit more expensive and requires more care in its installation. Hubs and network cards cost a bit more, too.

TIP FROM

Bob & Brian

> The price difference between 10BASE-T and 100BASE-T equipment is so low that it doesn't make sense to buy new 10BASE-T parts now. Most new network cards work at either speed and are labeled 10/100 BASE-T. For new networks, or if you're adding on to an existing 10BASE-T network, these dual-speed network cards are the way to go.

1000BASE-T OR GIGABIT ETHERNET

Gigabit Ethernet is a fairly new technology whose standards have not yet stabilized. It's expensive (now), but a hundredfold increase in speed is nothing to sneeze at if you're involved in high-speed videoconferencing or other such intensive communication work. It's also used for the backbones of large networks and for fast server-to-server connections.

OPTICAL FIBER

Optical fiber is capable of gigabit (1000Mbps) and higher speeds and can also carry data over runs of several miles, quite a bit farther than standard Ethernet. Optical fiber is not generally run directly to individual computers, but between hubs and routers between buildings, to form the "backbone" of a campus network, as shown in Figure 15.5. Optical fiber cables can carry multiple 10 or 100Mbps Ethernet data signals, as well as more advanced, even higher-speed data formats called *Fiber Distributed Date Interface (FDDI)* and *Asynchronous Transfer Mode (ATM)*.

Figure 15.5
Optical fiber cable linking two 100BASE-T hubs via a fiber "uplink" port. Cables contain pairs of fibers because each fiber can carry information in only one direction.

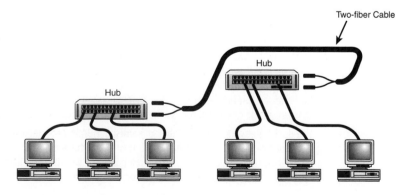

802.11B WIRELESS ETHERNET

It always seemed silly to me to have a portable computer tied down by network and power wires. Now, it doesn't have to be. A standardized wireless Ethernet system called 802.11b is becoming commonly available and reasonably priced. Using wireless network adapters, you can connect computers in a small area (such as a home or office) via radio, as illustrated in Figure 15.6. With modern equipment, the data rate can reach a respectable 11Mbps. Even at around $150 per computer, wireless networking can be a good deal when the cost of wiring and maintenance are factored in. For convenience, wireless probably can't be beat.

Figure 15.6
Wireless Access Point connecting computers to a standard twisted-pair network.

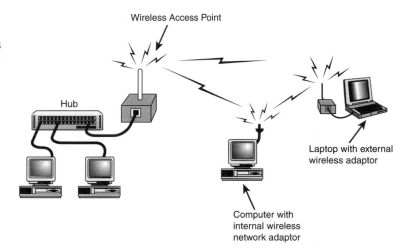

Wireless Access Point

Hub

Laptop with external wireless adaptor

Computer with internal wireless network adaptor

Wireless access is especially handy for users of laptop computers, Palm Pilots, and other mobile users who visit several offices in the course of a day. A device called an *access point* can be installed at each location to make the connection between wireless devices and a standard wired network or the Internet. Then, to quote Buckaroo Banzai, "wherever you go, there you are."

Wireless technology has become so inexpensive that it's now the hip new thing in coffee shops. In fact, a certain big coffee chain from Seattle is rolling this out nationwide—they'll connect you to the Internet for a small hourly fee while you sip a latte! (Your humble authors would never set foot in one of these places, of course, preferring to patronize locally-owned establishments and the original Peet's Coffee & Tea. But I digress.)

In summary, there are several different network technologies involved in any network: data transmission format standards like Ethernet and Token Ring, and electrical wiring standards like 10BASE-T and ThinNet. Networks depend on an agreement to use several specific technologies, each of which relies on another to help it do its job. For example, a file-sharing standard relies on a network protocol, which depends on a data transmission format, which requires a wiring standard.

15

In fact, there's even a standardized way of talking about the way these standards interrelate. In case you haven't guessed already, engineers like nothing more than forming committees to create standards.

THE OSI MODEL

If you've read about networks in any other computer book, you've probably seen a diagram similar to the one in Figure 15.7, the OSI Standard Network Model. The International Organization for Standardization (ISO) and Institute of Electrical and Electronic Engineers (IEEE) developed this model—I think to help computer book authors fill lots of pages trying to explain it. It's in every computer book I've ever seen.

Figure 15.7
The OSI Standard Model for Computer Networks–a required figure in every computer book. Networks are built from components, each of which performs a job for a higher-level component in the "stack."

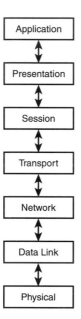

I will spare you the usual long explanation of this diagram because I don't think it's very helpful as an introduction to networking. But I do think it helps illustrate that networks are composed of modular components, *conceptually* stacked one on top of the other, each performing a job for the component above it, using the components below. The parts are interchangeable in that you may often choose one of several available technologies to do a given job. As long as the job is done correctly, the higher layers don't really care how it's done.

The components in this "stack" communicate with their corresponding components in the other computers on the network. As you go down in these stacks, the layers are less concerned with *interpreting* the data they handle and more with simply *moving* it somewhere. The higher level components interpret and communicate with each other to reassure each other that the data they have sent was correctly received, and they rely on the lower levels to actually transport that data from one computer to another.

That's the OSI network model in two paragraphs.

In the real world—at least in the Windows world—the "stack" of components that make up Windows networking isn't just a concept, it really does exist. Figure 15.8 shows the Windows network model. When you want to access a remote network resource somewhere inside the operating system, the following actions occur:

- A *network client* composes data messages to communicate these desires to the remote computer, using an agreed-upon file sharing protocol.

Figure 15.8
A practical Windows network model, with actual Windows network components.

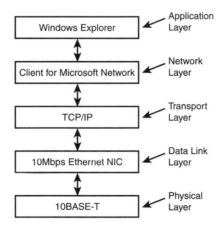

- These messages are packaged according to a *transport protocol*, which specifies how messages are to be broken into manageable pieces, how the pieces are to be addressed to member computers, and how to re-request missing or garbled pieces as they are received.

- The packaged message pieces are called *packets* and are physically carried by a *data link or framing protocol* that determines how to arrange the bits of information in each packet for transmission.

- The bits are converted into electrical pulses, radio signals or flashes of light and carried from one computer to another through a *physical medium* that carries the pulses or flashes to another computer.

- The pulses or flashes work their way up the network components on the other side and are finally delivered to a *server* component that satisfies the request by sending data back through the same system to the client.

The Data Link level is handled entirely by the hardware in a *network interface card (NIC)*, When you buy a network card, you're buying a data link protocol and the attachment to the physical medium. Because the card is what you'll actually see and have to describe to Windows, from this point on, I'll talk about adapters rather than data link protocols.

NETWORK CLIENTS

A network client is one of the most important top-level parts of Windows networking. The *client* is responsible for making remote files, folders, and printers available to your computer. To do this, it communicates with a corresponding server component on another computer, whose job it is to deliver file and printer information to client computers. Your Windows XP computer actually has both components built in, because it can both share files and printers and use shared files and printers.

Microsoft provides two network clients with Windows XP Professional: the Client for Microsoft Networks and a Client for Novell NetWare networks. Novell supplies its own version of the NetWare client, downloadable from their Web site, so you actually have a choice of three.

These client components, at the top of their network stacks, communicate with their corresponding top-level server components in other computers to read and write files, queue printer data, read the contents of folders for display in Explorer, and so on. The Client for Microsoft Networks uses the *Server Message Block (SMB)* and *NetBT (NetBIOS over TCP/IP)* protocols to speak to other Windows computers, Windows 2000 Servers, and IBM OS/2 LAN Manager Servers. You won't ever encounter SMB or NetBIOS directly in your dealings with Windows Networking; they're part of the client and server software.

The Novell client can communicate with Novell NetWare-based file servers using the built-in *NetWare Core Protocol (NCP)*, or with a Windows XP or Windows 2000 Server network service called File Services for Novell Networks.

> **NOTE**
>
> File Services for Novell and File Services for Macintosh are available only with Windows .NET/2000 Server and their more advanced versions. These services allow a Windows Server to share files and printers with Novell workstations and Apple Macintosh computers, respectively.

Each of these client packages uses a transport protocol to carry messages between your workstation and a remote computer's sharing service.

PROTOCOLS

As you learned previously, transport protocols define how data is arranged and sent in a coordinated fashion between computers. There are three transport protocols commonly used on Windows-based computers:

- *TCP/IP (Transport Control Protocol/Internet Protocol)* is one such transport protocol which forms the basis of the Internet. TCP/IP is actually a set of many protocols that are used to provide the services that higher-level network components need: resolving computer names into network card and IP addresses, guaranteed transmission, and internetwork routing. The *TCP* part, or *Transmission Control Protocol*, is the method an IP-based network uses to guarantee that data is sent end-to-end without errors. I'll go into more detail about TCP/IP in a little bit.

- *IPX/SPX (Internetwork Packet Exchange/Sequenced Packet Exchange)* was developed by Novell for its NetWare network software. Windows can use IPX/SPX for its file sharing services as well. Like TCP/IP, IPX/SPX is really a set of protocols that provide many services, including name resolution, guaranteed transport, and Internetwork routing.

- *NetBEUI (NetBIOS Enhanced User Interface)* was developed by IBM for its original IBM PC Network; it provides similar services to TCP/IP and IPX/SPX, except that it doesn't have a mechanism to route data to remote networks. NetBEUI can transport data between computers only on the same physical LAN. NetBEUI was supported by previous versions of Windows, but has been dropped in Windows XP.

The Client for Microsoft Network can use either TCP/IP or IPX/SPX to send its messages to a file server; all that's required is that both the client computer and server computer have at least one of the same protocols installed.

Similarly, Novell's client package communicates with Novell NetWare-based file servers using IPX/SPX, or for recent versions of NetWare, TCP/IP.

The following are some other protocols you might hear about:

- *AppleTalk* and its Ethernet-based counterpart *LocalTalk* are used in Apple Macintosh networking. Windows 2000 Professional provided LocalTalk to facilitate using LAN-connected Apple printers, but it's been dropped from Windows XP.

- *DLC (Data Link Control)* is an IBM networking protocol, but you won't run into it directly unless you're working on a corporate network with IBM mainframes. In that case, if it's used, your company's network management staff will want to take care of this task for you. DLC is also used by some network-connected printers. Like AppleTalk, support for DLC has been dropped by Microsoft.

- *Point-to-Point Protocol*, or *PPP*, is used to carry Internet Protocol data packets across a modem connection. This protocol is used to establish almost all modem connections to Internet service providers. PPP is part of the TCP/IP suite and a standard part of Windows's Dial-Up Networking support.

- *Point-to-Point Protocol over Ethernet*, or *PPPoE*, is used by some DSL and cable modem Internet service providers to link your computer to the ISP's routing equipment. For previous versions of Windows, ISPs provided their own PPPoE software. PPPoE is now built into Windows XP as part of its Broadband Connection support.

- *Universal Plug and Play*, or *UPnP*, lets networked computers and networked devices such as printers and household appliances automatically configure themselves to join whatever network they find themselves plugged into. It can, for example, automatically configure your computer to use an Internet connection shared by another computer on the LAN.

■ *Point-to-Point Tunneling Protocol*, or *PPTP*, is used to create *Virtual Private Networks*, or *VPNs*. PPTP takes data destined for a private, remote network, repackages the data for transmission across the Internet, and at the other end unpackages the data to be released into the private, protected network. I'll go into greater detail explaining VPNs in Chapter 18, "Windows Unplugged: Remote and Mobile Networking."

Network Adapters

Earlier in the chapter, when I described UTP and coaxial cable media, I described the popular physical media and data link protocols used in LANs, and mentioned the Ethernet and Token Ring data link protocols. When you buy a network adapter, they come lumped together: You're buying a piece of hardware that performs both data-link and physical transport functions.

At the physical level, network cards send packets of data through their physical medium from one card to another. Network cards have two ways of sending data: *unicast*, which sends data directly from one card to another specific card, and *multicast* or *broadcast*, which sends the same data packet to *every* card on the network. Each network card has an address (like a phone number) that is actually built right into the hardware of the network card. It is called the *physical network address* or *media access control (MAC)* address.

When a unicast data packet is addressed directly to a MAC address, only the one intended computer receives and examines the data. When a broadcast is made, every computer receives the packet. When a packet arrives by either means, the network adapter uses a hardware interrupt to inform Windows that data has arrived. Windows reads the data out of the network card and passes it up to the next higher layer in the protocol stack to be examined and acted upon.

Resolving Computer Names

The preceding sections pretty much cover the technology for sending data from computer to computer. Next, let's look at how networks find computers by name. (I'll describe the process for TCP/IP. Networks based on the IPX/SPX protocol work in a similar fashion.)

My computer's physical network address is 00-C0-CA-14-09-2F, but I certainly don't want to know that. I want to view files on the computer named Java. It's up to the network software to *resolve* the name Java into its MAC address 00-C0-CA-14-09-2F. How this is accomplished depends on the transport protocol in use: the now-retired NetBEUI, or TCP/IP. The difference between the two is significant.

NetBEUI

I'm sure you've tried to find a friend in a crowded airport lobby. The quickest way to find him or her is to stand up on a chair and shout out his or her name. Works like a charm, even though it momentarily interrupts everyone around you. The old NetBEUI protocol resolved names this way. It broadcast a request to every computer on the network: "Will the computer named Java please send me a message with your MAC address!"

This approach is fine when the desired computer is on the same physical LAN wire; in fact, it's great because it works without any configuration at all. But when two LANs are separated by a WAN link, NetBEUI's technique would require that the broadcast message be sent across the WAN. The WAN link would *have* to transmit every broadcast on every connected LAN to every other connected LAN to be sure that every computer could be found. Remember that WAN links were historically slow, on the order of 64Kbps, and with a few hundred computers sending a broadcast every minute or so, the WAN link would be fully occupied, carrying only broadcast messages and no useful data.

So, NetBEUI was a bad choice for networks with wide area links, and in fact, Microsoft has dropped support for NetBEUI in Windows XP as better ways have been developed.

IP NAME SERVICES AND ROUTING

An *Internet Protocol*, or *IP*, based network takes a more sophisticated approach to finding computers by name. To avoid relying completely on broadcasts for name lookups, IP networks rely on a *directory service* much like the 411 Directory Assistance service for telephones. IP-based protocols send requests for name-to-number lookups to a specific computer, which replies with the required address information. Microsoft supports two name-lookup services: WINS and DNS, which I'll discuss in more detail later on in this chapter.

But this just raises the question of how an IP-based computer can reach the computer hosting the naming service, which might be on a remote network far away. The MAC addresses built into network adapters are essentially random numbers, so knowing a remote computer's MAC address doesn't help you find it—you'd have to broadcast to every computer in the world to locate the destination!

The solution to this problem is that each computer in an IP network is given an *IP address*, which I'm sure you've seen before; it's a number like 63.69.110.193. These are like street addresses, and can be interpreted by routers all over the world to get data packets where they need to go. As the postal service first sends mail to a given state, then a city, then a street, then your house, so a router only has to know where to deliver data for all IP addresses starting with 63. Once it gets there, the 63 router sends the packet to the router responsible for all addresses starting with 63.69, which sends it to the router for 63.69.110, which finally sends it to computer 63.69.110.193. (I'm way oversimplifying this, but it should give you the picture).

When data is sent using IP, the sending computer first determines whether the destination computer is on the same physical LAN. If the destination computer is on the same physical LAN, the sending computer uses the old stand-up-and-shout approach: It broadcasts a request for computer number 63.69.110.193 to please identify itself (in IP lingo, it *ARPs*). The other computer responds with its MAC address, and with that information the network adapter can deliver the packet to its destination.

When the IP address is *not* a local address, the sending computer forwards the packet to a *router*, which forwards the packet out across the WAN or the Internet, which is just a *very large* IP WAN. Routers along the way relay the packet from one router to the next by examining the IP address. The backbone routers of an IP WAN or the Internet know exactly

15

where to send every IP packet, based on its IP address. Eventually, the packet finds its way to a router on the destination LAN, where the router ARPs and sends the packet to its intended computer.

IP ADDRESSES AND NETWORK MASKS

How does a router or computer tell whether an IP address is local? The answer is in the *subnet mask*, that mysterious 255.255.255.something number that you've probably entered into at least one home computer to connect to the Internet.

An IP address is a series of four numbers between 0 and 255. It can be written in binary as a 32-bit binary number, as in this example:

```
11000110 01000110 10010010 01000110
```

A network mask can also be written in binary; for example, 255.255.255.240 is

```
11111111 11111111 11111111 11110000
```

The part of an IP address that lines up with the ones in its subnet mask is called the *subnet number*, and the remainder is the *node number* or node address.

IP address	11000110 01000110 10010010 01000110
subnet mask	11111111 11111111 11111111 11110000
subnet number	11000110 01000110 10010010 01000
node number	110

Every computer on an IP LAN must have the same subnet number. If the subnet number of a destination IP address matches the sender's subnet number, the address is local: shout, get the MAC address, send directly. If the subnet number differs, the computer simply punts: It sends the packet to a designated *gateway*, a router whose job it is to ultimately deliver the packet.

TIP FROM

Bob
& Brian

> You probably suspect that this description is an oversimplification. It's not, actually, for the simple case I've described. What I've left out are details about how routers decide which of several possible directions to send a given packet and how they communicate new routes and traffic reports to each other. For a detailed look at the IP protocol and network technology, you might check out the following books:
>
> *Practical Cisco Routers*, ISBN: 0-7987-2103-1, Que
>
> *Upgrading and Repairing Networks, Third Edition*, ISBN 0-7897-2557-6, Que

NOTE

> If you're interested in the nitty-gritty details of Microsoft's implementation of network protocols, including TCP/IP timing, tuning, and Registry entry details, you might want to dig into the technical whitepapers at `http://www.microsoft.com/Windows2000/techinfo`.

DHCP AND IP ADDRESSING

As I mentioned earlier, a network card's MAC address is physically "burned in" to the adapter's hardware. But IP addressing must somehow be set up in software. We can't just pull a number out of a hat, because each computer on a LAN must use a number with the same network mask, but a different node address than others on its local network. Also, it needs to know the address of its local gateway router, and the addresses of any name-resolving servers.

There's no simple automatic way for a computer to determine this information. It can be assigned and entered manually, but on large networks, this is a cumbersome and difficult task.

To solve this problem the Internet community developed a protocol called BootP. Microsoft "embraced and extended" the BootP protocol and called the result *DHCP (Dynamic Host Configuration Protocol)*. DHCP services are provided by Windows XP Server (as well as Windows 2000 and NT Server) and the Internet Connection Sharing service, as well as many routers and hardware Internet connection sharing devices.

When a computer using DHCP is started (booted) up, it broadcasts a request for an IP address on its local network. A computer running a DHCP server responds to this request with a reply packet that specifies an appropriate IP address, network mask, and other setup information. Since broadcasts aren't passed by routers to other connected networks, only the local DHCP server hears the request and responds with an appropriate local network address. Each DHCP server keeps track of which IP addresses it has assigned to local computers, to avoid handing out the same number twice. It's also responsible for recycling addresses when a computer leaves the network and stops using an address it's been given.

NOTE

Just when you thought things couldn't get more complex . . . they do. Small IP-based LANs with only Windows computers don't even really need a DHCP server. If Windows is set up for automatic (DHCP) IP configuration, and no DHCP server responds to the request for configuration information within 30 seconds or so, it *does* pull an IP address out of a hat. It picks a random IP address in the range 169.254.0.0 through 169.254.255.255.

Windows continues to ask for DHCP service every three minutes, and if a DHCP response does eventually arrive, Windows reconfigures itself accordingly.

Although this works, it's ugly: The boot process is delayed by 30 seconds, and every three minutes the network will seem to "lock up" for 30 seconds, over and over. The fix is to manually assign IP addresses in each computer.

Some people move their computers between networks with DHCP and static setups. This is especially common with laptop computers that commute between home and office. Older versions of Windows could be configured for one network and then had to be completely reconfigured for the other every time they were moved. If you're a commuter, you'll be happy to know that Windows XP Professional has a feature called Alternate Configuration, which lets you set up static IP information to be used when DHCP isn't present. This lets you more easily move between multiple networks, as long as only one has a static IP setup.

15

WINDOWS NETWORKING AND TCP/IP

To return the discussion to name resolution, let me describe how a TCP/IP network turns names into addresses. Two name resolution systems can be involved: WINS and DNS.

WINS

The *Windows Internet Naming Service*, or *WINS*, was introduced with Windows NT, which was the first Microsoft operating system that allowed Microsoft File Sharing to operate over the TCP/IP protocol. Windows users are used to using one-word names to identify computers, and networks can contain computers using NetBIOS and IPX/SPX as well as the TCP/IP protocol. Microsoft developed WINS as an integrated address resolution system. It learns the names of all the computers connected to each network connected to the server running WINS and makes these names available to TCP/IP-based computers on those networks. When a new computer appears on the network, the computer registers itself with the WINS server so that other computers can find it by name.

More importantly, WINS servers trade information across a WAN or the Internet, making name service available out of the reach of NetBEUI-based computers. The addition of WINS and TCP/IP to Microsoft networking made file sharing across a WAN a much more efficient operation, as it removed the requirement for bridging NetBEUI packets across a WAN link.

It works like this: A WINS server can respond to broadcasts ("Will a WINS server please tell me the address of the computer named Java?"), but on a large network, you can also tell Windows to direct its request to a specific WINS server at a particular IP address. This way, a TCP/IP-based client can find computers across a WAN link, through TCP/IP's capability to efficiently route directly addressed packets from network to network, without the need to send broadcast packets across the link as well.

TIP FROM

Bob
& Brian

> Windows XP supports WINS, but it's no longer really necessary. When you use Windows XP or Windows 2000 Server to manage the network, Windows can use the standard Internet-style DNS system to locate network resources.

DNS

Domain name service, or *DNS*, is the name resolution system used by all Internet-based software. The domain name service is a sort of distributed database system that looks up names like www.quepublishing.com and returns IP addresses like 198.70.146.70. It also provides *Inverse DNS* information, which tells you that IP address 63.69.110.193 is http://www.quepublishing.com.

You can use DNS-based naming with Microsoft Networking, too. For example, you can tell Windows Explorer to view \\server.mycompany.com. Windows tries WINS first, if it's set up, and then attempts to resolve the name using DNS. If DNS fails, Windows broadcasts a request to the local LAN. If one of these methods succeeds, Windows can go ahead and use Microsoft File Sharing to connect to the computer.

CAUTION

> I will warn you many times that you must somehow put up a barrier between the Internet access and Microsoft Networking on your computer, even if you only use a modem to connect to the Internet. When you're connected, your shared files are vulnerable to attack by hackers if you're not adequately prepared.

15

On Windows .NET/2000 Server-based networks, in fact, Microsoft is encouraging the use of DNS-like names (such as host.region.company.com) even inside a company's network, rather than the old-fashioned single-word computer names. Microsoft is making this use easier by tying the Windows .NET/2000 Server DNS service into the *Active Directory*, which identifies all of the network's computers, networks, users, and resources.

DNS was designed for the original 1970s' Internet with its fairly static database; entering new computers and domains was time-consuming. The DNS server provided with Windows .NET/2000 Server, however, interacts with the Microsoft networking system on a dynamic basis to learn the names of computers as they plug into and leave the network.

THE MANY FACES OF WINDOWS XP

Now you know what makes a network work. I've described how a network is composed of layers of software and hardware whose purpose is to let high-level client and server software provide useful services to you and the operating system. Security is a major concern in networks: We can't have the mailroom staff looking up the executives' salaries.

The Windows approach to network security varies, depending on the type of network community to which it's connected. The following sections describe what these different network types are and how Windows XP changes with each one.

THE WINDOWS PEER-TO-PEER NETWORK

On a peer-to-peer or *workgroup* network, Windows XP Professional is a terrific member workstation, and you can set up shared folders with just the click of a mouse. Professional is also quite friendly with Windows 2000, NT, and 9x, and treats them as peers, too. It can attach to Novell NetWare and Unix/Linux servers as well, if they're part of your network.

The downside of the peer-to-peer network is that each Windows workstation manages its own separate username/password database. Because there's no centralized control over user privileges, obtaining access to shared folders and printers on your LAN can be hit or miss. If you haven't been added as a user of the computer whose shared resources you want to use, you're out of luck. Users might then be tempted to make their shared folders accessible to "Everyone," and that's *very risky* from a security standpoint, especially if you're connected to the Internet. Everyone means *everyone*; even some high school hacker in Hamburg could get at your files.

→ To learn more about shared folder security, **see** "Specific Configuration Steps For Windows XP," **p. 747.**

15

To locate resources on a peer-to-peer network, you might have to hunt around a bit. Either you must know the name of the computer whose resources you want to use, or you have to poke around My Network Places (called Network Neighborhood in earlier versions of Windows). Poking around is fine on small networks but can be cumbersome on large networks with more than a few dozen computers.

Administration of the computers on a peer-to-peer network is handled on an individual basis also. Each computer has its own privileged "Administrator" account, so anyone with his or her computer's administrator password can have at the Windows setup and configuration. Restricting the damage that individual users can inflict on the computers is rather difficult, though possible, but this type of control would itself have to be administered to each computer individually.

THE WINDOWS .NET/2000/NT SERVER NETWORK

When a Windows 2000 Professional computer is part of a network managed by Windows 2003 Server, Windows 2000 Server, or Windows NT Server, something different happens: Windows XP Pro relinquishes the job of identifying users and their passwords to the server. This is a *good* thing. This is called a *domain* network. A domain is a group of computers under the control of a central set of one or more *domain servers*. As part of a domain, when you log in on any member computer, your identity is actually verified by the server, and you are then automatically recognized by every other Windows XP, 2000, and NT computer on the whole network. Permission to view files, of course, can be granted or taken away by the owner of each computer; I'll explain how to manage permissions in Chapter 27. The point is that with a common user database, you can easily maintain good security practices because you can easily control access to resources properly.

When you're part of a domain (or group of domains), locating shared resources is no easier than it is on a peer-to-peer network. Either you need to know the name of the workstation or server you want to use, or you have to burrow through the domains and computers displayed in domain-sized groups on My Network Places.

Finally, as part of a server-based network, the "domain administrator"—that is, the administrator of the server computer—can exercise some serious control over what users of each computer can see and do, thanks to the Windows profile and policy systems. These features have two effects:

- They provide a way to deliver the same desktop, Control Panel, and software settings to a user no matter which computer he or she uses.
- They let the domain administrator individually remove or "lock down" Windows features and Control Panel options that change network, display, hardware, and network settings for individuals or groups of users. Maintenance and support costs are reduced by removing the users' ability to customize (in management's view: mess up) their own computers. Joking aside, this feature can save big companies *serious* money.

Quite a personality change, isn't it? Of course, exercising this kind of control is completely up to the domain administrator.

THE ACTIVE DIRECTORY NETWORK

Finally, when Windows XP Professional is a member of a server network with Active Directory, an even more comprehensive management structure comes into play. With Active Directory, the network administrators can do everything I mentioned in the preceding sections *plus* delegate management responsibilities to lower levels in the chain of command, at just about any level of detail they desire.

For example, a large company with many small branch offices could let branch managers assign users at their branches to departmental groups but not change their passwords. The network administrator could let the San Francisco network manager change network settings but not the Winnemucka manager, and so on. The level of what Microsoft calls *granularity* in control and delegation is nearly unlimited.

This capability could mean one of two things to you, the Windows XP Professional user:

- Nothing at all because you're not part of an Active-Directory based network
- Nothing at all because you are locked out of all this fun stuff by your network manager

I'm only partly kidding. If you're a Windows XP Professional user on an Active Directory network, these management features affect you only when they prevent you from doing something. The only new thing you have to learn is the telephone number of the network manager who's responsible for your computer. (This manager, on the other hand, has so much new to learn that he or she is probably in a class somewhere right now, on the verge of tears.)

Active Directory services also let network managers assign application software to users or groups, so your desktop automatically picks up icons for software you haven't even installed but your organization thinks you need. When you go to use it, Boom, it installs itself (in theory anyway).

Active Directory also lets you search for network resources and organizational information in a very useful, unified way. The Active Directory is designed to contain all kinds of information about the resources on a network, the network's users, and the structure of the organization itself. We're all used to the searching power on the World Wide Web, and Active Directory brings us the same power to search on a company's worldwide network. Want to find the e-mail address of your pal Sal in the Sonoma Sales Center? No problem, Active Directory can find it in a flash. Need to find a printer in your building that can print on both sides in color? One click, and you'll have it.

I'll talk about Active Directory in more detail later in this chapter.

THE WINDOWS OFFLINE/REMOTE NETWORK

Windows XP Professional can also exhibit multiple personality disorder: Meet the remote workstation. Windows can behave like a standalone computer when you're working at home or toting your laptop around in the field, and then it can act like a domain member when connected to a server-based network by modem or docking port.

15

NOTE

Active Directory is based on the LDAP (Lightweight Directory Access Protocol) protocol, an Internet standard for querying hierarchical databases. Windows 2003 Server runs an LDAP server on every Active Directory-enabled server computer. Administrative changes to the directory can occur on any member server, and the changes are replicated to all of the other servers. The location of the nearest Active Directory server is found using the standard DNS system. This makes it possible for a computer to join an Active Directory network and find its place in the world without any manual configuration: DHCP gives the computer its IP address and DNS servers, DNS locates Active Directory, and Active Directory delivers the rest of the information the computer needs to deliver any other appropriate services.

An additional feature Windows offers to the remote user is the "offline" file. Windows lets you mark files or folders for offline use and copies them from the network to your hard drive. When you're disconnected from the network, you have access to this copy, even though it still appears to be in a folder on another networked computer. When you reconnect, by modem or by plugging into the office network, Windows automatically synchronizes the offline files, copying anything you changed back to the network and retrieving any updated files from the network to your hard disk.

TIP FROM

Bob

& Brian

Offline files are similar to the My Briefcase function offered by Windows 9x. The advantage to offline files, however, is that they appear to stay in their original locations. Windows invisibly keeps track of the offline copies, so you don't have to worry about dragging files to and from the briefcase folder.

To My Briefcase: Good riddance! I have to admit I never understood My Briefcase anyway, and I suspect few people did.

WINDOWS XP'S NETWORK SERVICES

Besides file and printer sharing, Windows XP provides many other network services. You might never interact with some of these services directly, but their presence makes Windows the amazing application platform it is.

Let's take a tour of Windows network services. I'll describe what each service is, why it's useful, perhaps a bit about how it works, and I'll tell you where to find out how to install, configure, or use it, if appropriate.

FILE AND PRINTER SHARING

Networking software was developed to share and transfer files between computers. (America Online Buddy Chat came later, if you can believe that!) Windows XP comes with the following features:

- Client for Microsoft Networks, which gives access to files and printers shared by other Windows computers as well as OS/2, Unix, Linux, and so on.

- File and Printer Sharing for Microsoft Networks, which lets Windows XP Professional share files and printers with users of those same operating systems. Windows XP Pro is limited to 10 simultaneous connections from other computers; the Server version is required for larger LANs.

- Web Sharing, which is a new technology that provides secure file copying to and from shared folders over the Internet, using the Web's Hypertext Transfer Protocol. The "new" part is that it uses full Windows security and the Windows Explorer user interface, while the underlying technology is based on the World Wide Web and Microsoft's Internet Information Server.

- Client for Novell Networks, which gives access to files and printers shared by Novell NetWare file servers.

- Unix Print Services, which lets you use and share printers with computers using the Unix operating system's LPR protocol.

Unlike Windows 2003 Server, however, Pro has no tools to share files with Apple Macintosh computers or to use Macintosh shared folders.

→ For information about installing, configuring, and using Microsoft network software, **see** Chapters 15 through 18.

→ For information about interacting with Novell and Unix servers, see Chapter 20, "Networking Mix and Match."

ROAMING USER PROFILES

When Windows XP Professional is connected to a Windows Server domain, besides simply validating usernames and passwords, Server can supply Pro computers with a *profile* for each user as he or she logs in.

A profile contains information that helps Windows XP Professional make its desktop and folders look the same no matter which physical computer you use. User profiles contain the following:

- Desktop icons and shortcuts
- The contents of your My Files and Documents folder
- Your configuration and preference settings for all the software you use, from your Word preferences to your choice of screen savers
- Management settings that control, for example, whether you are allowed to change Control Panel entries

Roaming user profiles are covered in more depth in Chapter 28, "Managing Users."

DISTRIBUTED APPLICATIONS

Windows XP provides network protocols that let software application developers write programs that interact across a network. You will probably never have to install, configure, or even know such protocols exist; you'll just use the programs that use them and

15

happily go about your business. But someone may mention them, so you should be familiar with their names: RPC and COM+.

RPC

Microsoft's remote procedure call (RPC) network protocol allows software to be split into pieces that run on different computers and interact across a network. The RPC mechanism is used, for instance, when a user on one Windows computer pauses print spooling on another. It's the basis of most of Windows's remote management capabilities; these are more sophisticated things than the authors of the basic file sharing protocols made allowances for.

COM+ (FORMERLY COM AND DCOM)

The former Component Object Model (COM) and Distributed COM (DCOM) services have been combined in Windows 2000 and XP to the upgraded COM+ service. COM+ provides software developers tools to build highly modular software in a variety of languages. You should be happy it exists and happier still if you never hear about it again.

To learn more about COM and DCOM, pick up a copy of *COM/DCOM Unleashed*, published by Sams Publishing.

.NET

The .NET (pronounced "dot net") initiative is Microsoft's most recent replacement for COM, DCOM, and RPC. .NET is an entire software framework for Internet-enabled software application development. Again, it's something that you will probably never interact with directly, but it will make possible a whole new generation of software applications.

VIRTUAL PRIVATE NETWORKING

Windows XP Professional can connect to remote LANs through the Internet using *Virtual Private Networking (VPN)*. This very secure technology makes it safe to use Microsoft networking over the Internet.

→ If you're interested in learning more about Virtual Private Networking, **see** "Virtual Private Networking," **p. 633**.

REMOTE ACCESS

If you travel with a laptop or often work from a location outside your physical LAN, you can still use RAS (Remote Access Service, also called *dial-up networking*) to interact with people and files on your network.

→ For more detailed information about RAS, **see** "Dial-Up Networking," **p. 607**.

CONNECTION BY MODEM

Windows XP Professional allows you to configure a modem for incoming connections as well as outgoing. You can provide access to your LAN via modem, for example, to retrieve files from your office while you are at home or in the field. At most, two incoming connections are permitted with Pro.

➔ To configure Remote Access, **see** "Setting Up Dial-Up Networking," **p. 607**.

INCOMING VPN

Windows XP Professional also allows you to connect to your LAN via the Point-to-Point Tunneling Protocol (PPTP); that is, it lets you create a Virtual Private Network. If your LAN has a full-time Internet connection, it will (or it should) have a firewall installed, thus preventing you from using file sharing directly from the outside world. A VPN connection lets you safely penetrate the firewall to gain access to your LAN over the Internet.

REMOTE DESKTOP AND WINDOWS TERMINAL SERVICES

Windows XP Professional and Windows 2000 Server/Windows 2003 Server provide a sort of remote-control system called, variously, Windows Terminal Services, Remote Desktop, and Remote Assistance. Terminal Services let you use a computer remotely. Your applications run on the remote computer, while you use your local computer's display, keyboard, and mouse. There are three names for what is basically the same piece of software, because it's used three different ways:

- **Terminal Services**—A Windows 2000 Server/Windows 2003 Server can be set up to host applications used by remote clients. For example, one beefy computer can run complex software, while the remote computers, which only need to provide a display and keyboard, can be relative lightweights. Terminal services is also great for remote administration of a server—a manager can sit in front of one computer, but can control and configure servers anywhere in the world.

  Although the service is provided only by Windows 2000 Server/Windows 2003 Server, the client software is available for Windows XP, 2000, 9x, and NT.

- **Remote Desktop**—Windows XP Professional has a Remote Desktop feature, which is a copy of the Terminal Services server limited to *one* incoming connection. It's intended, for example, to enable an employee to access his or her Windows XP Pro computer at the office from home. When a remote user is connected, the XP computer's screen blanks out, so only one person at a time can use the computer.

- **Remote Assistance**—Windows XP Professional and Home Editions' Remote Assistance feature is based on—you guessed it—Terminal Services again, also limited to one connection. In this case, however, the desktop is *not* blanked out when the remote user attaches: It's intended for the remote and local user to work together to resolve a problem. Also, the remote connection can only occur when the computer owner e-mails the remote user an electronic invitation, which is good for one connection only. This makes the service useless for general remote-employee-type work, but handy for one-time assistance.

CONNECTION SHARING

Windows XP Professional has a handy feature that first appeared in the Windows 98 Second Edition: Internet Connection Sharing. This feature lets one XP Pro computer with a modem or high-speed Internet connection provide Internet access to all users of a LAN.

This access is somewhat limited, however. It requires that the LAN use the Windows built-in automatic IP address configuration system, so it's incompatible with WAN configurations. It also requires that the computer with the modem or high-speed connection be left turned on all the time.

Connection sharing is described in more detail in Chapter 19, "Connecting Your LAN to the Internet."

ACTIVE DIRECTORY

As discussed earlier in this chapter, Windows 2000 and Windows XP can take advantage of a service called the *Active Directory (AD)*. Active Directory combines a name/address directory, management and security services, and wide-area replicated database technologies to provide a foundation for all of Windows' networking functions. If your network is managed by a Windows .NET or 2000 Server with AD installed, this service is automatically and transparently made available to you. AD is entirely based on TCP/IP technology, and for this reason, all Windows XP computers should use TCP/IP as their primary, if not only, network protocol.

→ To learn how to use Active Directory services, **see** "Exploring and Searching the Network," **p. 552**.

Active Directory is a *distributed database*. "Distributed" means that information about separate parts of a geographically dispersed network are automatically copied from region to region, from server to server, so that the same information is available at all locations. Any of the information can be managed from any location, and the changes made automatically propagate throughout the network. This might not matter or make sense to the user of an eight-person network, but to the manager of a corporate network that spans several continents, the ability to manage a given computer just as easily from Canada as from Canberra is *very* appealing indeed.

Active Directory is a true database: It can store any sort of information. Out of the box, it's used to store usernames, passwords, group membership, privileges and other security information, and feature-limiting controls called Group Policies, as well as the names and locations of computers and network printers. But it can also be used by software developers to store arbitrary information about software applications, such as the location and names of the nearest database servers—anything that would be useful to have spread throughout an organization's network.

The most significant part of AD is that it's hierarchical: It arranges information in user-defined groups called *containers*, which can be nested to any depth. The purpose of this hierarchy is to let AD represent the real structure of an organization. AD lets a network manager define groups by geographical region, department, workgroup, function, or whatever categories make sense to the organization. Each grouping can contain other groups, until finally actual users and/or their computers, printers, and other resources are entered.

The purpose of this feature is to enable network managers to assign usage and management privileges like the right to access certain files or the right to manage user accounts to these containers at appropriate levels, rather than to individuals. A network manager therefore can grant access to users based on the organization's own structure rather than on a user-by-user basis or through "flat" enterprise-wide groups.

For example, let's say a company has East Coast and West Coast divisions and an accounting department in each (see Figure 15.9).

Figure 15.9
Active Directory lets network managers define groups based on actual organizational structure. These groupings model the organization's chains of command. The resulting structure can then be used to sensibly control access privileges and to delegate management rights.

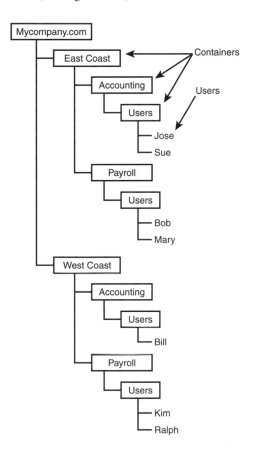

If the network manager grants read and write privileges to a shared network folder to the East Coast container, then all users anywhere in the East Coast structure (Jose, Sue, Bob, and Mary) get access rights to the folder. If Jose is granted "manager" rights to the East Coast Accounting group, then he can control the user accounts for Sue and himself.

Management of all East Coast printers could be granted to a network manager by granting him management rights to the East Coast container. He then would get the right to manage any printers within the entire container, across all its subdivisions.

Active Directory can be integrated into the domain name system for a company's network so that, for example, a computer in the East Coast accounting division could be named big-box.accounting.eastcost.mycompany.com.

Active Directory is used internally by Windows tools such as Explorer, My Network Places, and the Printer Manager. User-written programs can get access to the directory's contents through a programming interface called Active Directory Services Interface (ADSI) or more generally through an Internet protocol called Lightweight Directory Access Protocol (LDAP), which is an industry standard for directory queries and responses. E-mail programs, for example, can be designed to use LDAP to search for e-mail addresses, regardless of the underlying network system, whether it's based on Windows, Novell NetWare, or other networking systems.

INTELLIMIRROR

You might hear the term IntelliMirror and wonder what sort of network feature it is. IntelliMirror actually is just Microsoft's name for several features and services provided by its domain networks based on Active Directory. These are

- **Remote Installation**—Windows XP can be installed from scratch onto an empty hard drive over a network.

- **Roaming User Profiles**—Your My Documents folder and your preferences settings are stored on the network servers and copied to the computers you use, so they're available anywhere on your enterprise network.

- **Group Policy**—Windows's capability to "force" preferences settings and restrict access to system configuration dialog boxes is based on Registry entries defined by the network administrators and copied to your computer when you log in.

- **Application Publication**—Application software such as Word and Excel can be installed automatically across the network, based again on Group policy settings.

Together, these features let network administrators give you the experience of walking up to any computer in your organization and having it be "your" computer with all your files, settings, and applications. You should, in theory, even be able to log off, throw your computer out the window, and replace it with a brand new, empty one, and in short order pick up your work where you left off. In theory, anyway.

INTRANET/INTERNET SERVICES AND TOOLS

Finally, Windows XP comes with a full complement of applications and tools that Internet and Unix users expect on a TCP/IP-based computer. They're not part of Windows Networking, technically speaking, because they don't use the Networking Clients. They communicate with other computers using TCP/IP directly. These tools include the following:

- Internet Explorer (Web browser)
- SNMP Agents
- Telnet
- Ping
- FTP
- NetMeeting
- nslookup
- pathping

- tracert
- Outlook Express (SMTP/POP mail client)
- Internet Information Server (Web server)

These programs are discussed in Part III of this book, "Windows XP and the Internet."

SECURITY

Finally, Windows XP Professional, when it's part of a Windows Server-based network, supports the use of two very sophisticated network security systems to encrypt network traffic and to communicate passwords and information about user rights between computers.

Windows XP Professional supports the IPSec TCP/IP data encryption standard. IPSec provides a means for each of the data packets sent across a network to be encrypted—scrambled—so that an eavesdropper with a wiretapping device can't glean passwords or other sensitive information from your data while it flows through the wires of your building, through airwaves in a wireless network, or across the Internet.

Windows XP also supports the Kerberos network authentication protocol, which was developed at to the Massachusetts Institute of Technology (MIT) and is now widely used in secure distributed network operating systems. Kerberos manages the identification of computer users on a network to eliminate many network security risks, such as the recording and playback of passwords.

TIP FROM

Bob
& Brian

> Both IPSec TCP/IP data encryption and Kerberos network authentication protocol are activated under the control of the administrator of Windows .NET/2000 Server and are invisible to you as a Windows XP Professional user.

NOTE

> If you're really into security—and I mean really into security—I recommend that you grab a copy of *Microsoft Windows 2000 Security Handbook*, published by Que (ISBN: 0-7897-1999-1). Better hang on to your hat, though. . . .

TIPS FROM THE WINDOWS PROS: BECOMING A NETWORKING PROFESSIONAL

I've found that modern network software works perfectly the first time about 99 percent of the time. When things go wrong, however, you quickly find that the diagnostic tools are nowhere near as sophisticated, automated, or helpful as the installation tools. You often need a more complete understanding of network technology and structure to diagnose a broken network than you do to install one, and more to the point, a more complete understanding than I can give you in a general-purpose book like this.

So, the big tip for this chapter is this: If you're planning to set up a network for more than a few computers, or you're setting up a network in a business situation, you should have some pretty solid expertise at hand for the times when problems arise. You might have a consultant install and maintain your network, or you might at least establish a relationship with a consultant or technician whom you can call if you run into trouble.

If you want to become a networking professional yourself, I recommend the following books as places to continue your training:

Upgrading and Repairing Networks, Third Edition, ISBN: 0-7897-2557-6, Que

Practical Network Cabling, ISBN: 0-7897-2233-X, Que

Practical Network Peer Networking, ISBN: 0-7897-2247-X, Que

Practical Firewalls, ISBN: 0-7897-2416-2, Que

CHAPTER 16

CREATING A WINDOWS XP PRO NETWORK

In this chapter

CREATING OR JOINING A NETWORK

In the previous chapter, I discussed the benefits of having a network, whether it's between two computers in your home, ten in your office, or thousands spanning the globe. In this chapter, I'll show you what you'll need to buy in order to install your own home or small-office network using Windows XP Professional. Later in the chapter, I'll cover the actual network installation.

This chapter is directed primarily toward a small group of users, at home or at work, who want to set up a LAN for themselves. This type of LAN is called a *peer-to-peer network* because no one computer has a central role in managing the network. This type of network doesn't take full advantage of all of Windows XP Professional's networking capabilities, but unless you have more than 10 computers to network, you probably don't *need* all those capabilities. For you, a peer-to-peer network may be just the thing to let you share files and printers with your co-workers or housemates. Creating a speedy, useful network isn't nearly as hard or expensive as you might think. In fact, once you've done the planning and shopping, you should be able to get a network up and running in an hour or two.

If you're adding a computer to an existing network, you can skip ahead to the section titled "Installing Network Adapters." If you're on a corporate network, you probably won't have to handle any of the installation details yourself at all—your end-user support department will likely take care of all of this for you and you can just skip ahead to the next chapter.

NOTE

> If you are part of a Windows .NET/2000 Domain network, or if your company uses Remote Installation Services and Management features, you probably won't need to, and might not even be able to, view or change any of the network settings or control panels described in this chapter.

If you're setting up a new network, though, just read on. This chapter should give you all the information you need.

NOTE

> Windows has a feature called a Direct Network Connection that lets you use a serial, parallel, or infrared port to connect two computers without requiring a network adapter. It's not very fast, but it's adequate for one-time file transfers. I'll cover Direct Connection in Chapter 18, "Windows Unplugged: Remote and Portable Networking."

PLANNING YOUR NETWORK

You must plan your network around your own particular needs. What do you expect from a network? The following are some tasks you might want it to perform:

- Share printers, files, and CD-ROM drives
- Share an Internet connection

- Receive faxes directly in one computer and print or route them to individuals
- Provide access to a wide area network (WAN) or other remote site
- Provide access to your LAN via modem or the Internet from remote locations
- Host a Web site
- Operate a database server
- Play multiuser games

You should make a list of your goals for installing a network. You have to provide adequate capacity to meet these and future needs, but you also don't need to overbuild.

16

Instant Networking

If your goal is to share printers, files, and maybe an Internet connection between a few computers that are fairly close together, and you don't want to make any decisions, here's a recipe for instant networking. Get the following items at your local computer store, or at an online shop like www.buy.com:

- One 10/100BASE-T network adapter for each computer that doesn't already have a network interface. These cost about $15 for internal PCI cards, and $40 for PCMCIA or USB adapters. (The buy.com category is Computers-Networking-NIC Cards, PC Cards, or USB Networks. Choose one of the featured or sale items).
- A 10/100BASE-T hub with four or more ports for about $40, *or*, if you want to share an Internet connection, a DSL/Cable-sharing or a dial-up gateway router with a built-in four switch/hub, for under $129. (The buy.com category is Computers-Networking-Hubs or Cable/DSL).
- One CAT-5 patch cable for each computer. You'll place the hub next to one of the computers, so you'll need one short four-foot cable. The other cables need to be long enough to reach from the other computers to the hub. (The buy.com category is Computers-Accessories-Cables).

When you have these parts, skip ahead to the "Installing Network Adapters" section later in this chapter. By the way: I'm not getting a kickback from buy.com! I've just found that buying from them is a no-brainer. Their prices are low enough that it's hardly worth the time to shop around, and more importantly, their service is ultra-reliable and fast.

On the other hand, if you need access to large databases, want fast Internet connectivity, and require centralized backup of all workstations, you'll need to plan and invest more carefully. I'll discuss some of the issues you should consider in the next section.

ARE YOU BEING SERVED?

If you're planning a network of more than a few computers, you have to make the Big Decision: whether or not to use Windows 2000 Server/Windows 2003 Server. The differences between Windows Professional and Windows 2000 Server/Windows 2003 Server are discussed in Chapter 1, "Introducing Windows XP Professional," and again in Chapter 15, "Overview of Windows XP Networking." Windows 2000 Server/Windows 2003 Server provides a raft of networking services that Professional doesn't have, but you must learn how to configure and support them.

The primary trade-offs between Professional and Server boil down to those shown in Table 16.1.

16

TABLE 16.1 PRIMARY DIFFERENCES BETWEEN WINDOWS XP PRO AND WINDOWS 2000 SERVER/WINDOWS 2003 SERVER

Network with Windows XP Professional Only	Network with Windows 2000 Server/Windows 2003 Server
This network provides at most 10 connections to other computers.	Connections to the server are unlimited.
The cost is low.	This network costs a few hundred dollars more, plus additional fees for Client Access Licenses.
Configuration is simple (relatively, anyway!).	This network is complex to configure and administer.
Each machine must be administered independently.	Administration is centralized.
Provides rudimentary remote access, connection sharing, and WAN support.	The features are more sophisticated.
Managing file security is difficult when you have more than one user per computer.	Centralized user management eases the task of managing security.
A given computer can host at most one Web site (domain).	A single server can host multiple Web sites.
This network works with Windows peers only but can use Novell servers.	Internetworks with Windows, Macintosh, and Novell clients.

For me, the 10-connection limit with Windows XP Professional is the main dividing line. You can work around the limit by not having a "main machine" that all users look to for shared files. But this is exactly what you'll find you need as your network grows to this size or larger! So, if you have a network of more than 10 computers, I encourage using at least one copy of Windows 2003/2000 Server.

You can certainly use Server with smaller networks, too. Reasons for doing so include

- You want to connect your LAN through a WAN or through the Internet to another LAN at another location; that is, you want to join your network to a Server domain somewhere else.
- You want to support multiple, simultaneous remote dial-in or Virtual Private Network (VPN) users.
- You want to exercise strict security controls, restrict your users' ability to change system settings, or use automatic application installation.
- You want to share files and printers with Apple Macintosh computers on your LAN.
- You want to host multiple Web sites (domains) on one computer.

If you decide you need or want Windows 2003 Server, you should get a copy of *Special Edition Using Microsoft Windows .NET Server* (published by Que) and a big box of Alka Seltzer before you go any further.

WHEN TO HIRE A PROFESSIONAL

You've probably heard this old adage: "If you want something done right, do it yourself!" It is true to a point. At some point, though, the benefit of hiring someone else outweighs the pleasure of doing it yourself.

For a home network, you should definitely try setting it up yourself. Call it a learning experience, get friends to help, and if things still don't work, treat yourself to a truly humbling experience and watch a high-school-aged neighbor get it all working in 15 minutes. As long as you don't have to run wires through the wall or construct your own cables, you should be able to manage this job even with no prior networking experience. When something is called "Plug and Play" now, it really is.

For a business, however, the balance tips the other way. If you depend on your computers to get your work done, getting them set up should be your first concern, but keeping them working should be your second, third, and fourth. If you have solid experience in network installation, installing a Windows XP network will be a snap. But your business is hanging in the balance, and you should consider the cost of computer failure when you're deciding whether it's worth spending money on setup and installation. Hiring a good consultant and/or contractor will give you the following:

- An established relationship. If something goes wrong, you'll already know whom to call, and that person will already know the details of your system.
- A professional installation job.
- The benefit of full-time experience in network and system design without having to pay a full-time salary.
- Time to spend doing something more productive than installing a network.

If you do want to hire someone, it's important to choose your consultant or contractor very carefully. The following are some tips:

- Ask friends and business associates for referrals before you go to the yellow pages.
- Ask a consultant or contractor for references, and check them out.
- Find out what the contractor's guaranteed response time is, should problems or failures occur in the future.
- Be sure that documentation is one of the contractor's "deliverables." You should get written documentation describing your system's installation, setup, and configuration, as well as written procedures for routine maintenance, such as making backups, adding users, and so on.

16

Even if you do hire someone else to build your network, you should stay involved in the process and understand the choices and decisions that are made.

PLANNING FOR ADEQUATE CAPACITY

After you've looked at your requirements and considered your work habits, make a diagram of your office or home, showing computer locations, and indicate where you want to place your computers and special shared resources, such as modems, printers, and so on. Remember that shared resources and the computers they're attached to need to be *turned on* to be used. So, for example, your main printer should probably be connected to a computer that will be on and accessible when it's needed by others. Likewise, if you use Internet Connection sharing, the computer that makes your Internet connection needs to be turned on in order for others to access the Internet. It may make sense to designate one computer to be your "main machine", leave it turned on, and locate most of your shared resources there.

You can use your designated "main machine" as an ordinary workstation, but it should be one of your fastest computers with lots of memory. If you're planning to have this computer host a Web site using Internet Information Services (IIS), it should have at least 256MB of memory.

PRINTERS

You'll be able to share any printer connected to any of your Windows computers, and use it from any of your other computers. The printer cable will force you to locate the printer within 6 to 10 feet from the computer to which it's connected.

For an office network, remember that you can purchase printers that connect directly to your network so that they can be located farther away from your workstations. You'll pay up to several hundred dollars extra for this capability, but you'll get added flexibility and printing speed. Networked printers still need to use a Windows computer as a "print spooler," so you'll still need to leave their controlling computer on all the time. On the other hand, one Windows XP computer can manage quite a few networked printers.

BACKUP SYSTEM

You must include at least one tape backup system on your network if it's for business use. Your tape backup system should ideally be large enough to back up the entire hard drive of your "main machine" on one tape. I recommend getting a Travan tape storage system and a better backup software package than the Microsoft Backup utility included with Windows XP Professional. The Windows Backup utility is almost adequate, but for business purposes, you should have something that is convenient, that lets you save different backup configurations, and that lends itself to automatic scheduling.

Some backup software can be configured to back up not only the machine with the tape drive, but also other machines, via your network. This type of backup works only when the computers are left turned on, but it can be a real boon in a business environment. A system that performs automatic daily backups of every computer in the office is a valuable insurance policy.

I've used Computer Associates's Arcserve for this purpose; it's rather difficult to install and set up, but it's really a first-class system. Veritas Software's Backup Exec is another good bet.

→ To learn more about network backups, **see** "Install and Configure Backup Software," **p. 536**.

POWER SURPRISE

One of the last things people think about when planning a network is the fact that every computer and external device has to be powered. You might be surprised how often people plan a network and get all their hardware together, only to realize that they have no power outlet near their computer or have placed 10 devices next to one outlet. The result can be a tangle of extension cords and a reprimand from the fire marshal.

Furthermore, your file server(s) or "main machine(s)" should be protected with an *Uninterruptible Power Supply*, or *UPS*. These devices contain rechargeable batteries and instantly step in if the AC power to your building should fail. When a power failure occurs during the exact instant that your computer is writing data to its hard disk, without a UPS you're almost guaranteed some sort of data corruption: lost data, missing files, corrupted database index files, or worse.

TIP FROM

Bob & Brian

> I find it helpful to plug a power strip into a UPS when connecting several low-consumption devices like modems or hub power supplies. I write "UPS" all over these power strips with a red marker so that nobody uses them for laser printers or other devices that should not be plugged into the UPS.

Finally, in an office situation, if you clump your Server or "central" computer, laser printers, office copiers, and fax machine together as many people do, *please* call in an electrician to ensure that you have adequate power circuits to run all these energy-sucking devices.

CHOOSING A NETWORK AND CABLING SYSTEM

For a simple home or small office network, there are three main choices for the type of network connection you'll use:

- 10BASE-T Ethernet over unshielded twisted pair (UTP) wiring
- 100BASE-T or Fast Ethernet, over high-quality CAT-5 UTP wiring
- Wireless networking using radio signals transmitted through antennas or carried through your telephone wiring
- 1000BASE-T or Gigabit Ethernet, over very high-quality CAT-5E or CAT-6 wiring

I described how these systems work in Chapter 15, "Overview of Windows XP Networking." For the average small office or home network, the first three options I listed will provide about the same apparent performance. In the next sections, I'll go over the pros and cons of each type.

The Gigabit Ethernet option is attractive if you edit video on your PC and want to copy multi-gigabyte files around a network, but it's overkill and too expensive for almost any other application. If you want it, you'll need to do some research on the available adapters, hubs, cabling and connector systems. I won't discuss it further in this chapter.

TIP FROM

Bob & Brian

If your network is small and/or temporary, you can run network cables along walls and desks. Otherwise, you probably should keep them out of the way and protect them from accidental damage by installing them in the walls of your home or office. As you survey your site and plan your network, consider how the network cabling is to be routed.

⚠ *If you can't or aren't allowed to drill through your location's walls, see "Can't Drill Through Walls or Ceilings" in the "Troubleshooting" section at the end of this chapter.*

10BASE-T ETHERNET

10BASE-T Ethernet networks use *unshielded twisted-pair cabling*, commonly called *UTP*, *twisted-pair*, or *phone wire*. This last name is a little dangerous because I'm not talking about the thin, flat, ribbon-like cable used to connect a phone to a wall jack, nor is it likely that phone wire installed in the 1930s will work either. 10BASE-T networks require a higher quality cable designated "CAT-3" or better. You can buy premade network cables in lengths from 3 to 50 feet, or you can buy bulk cable and attach the connectors yourself. I'll discuss this more in the "Installing Network Wiring" section later in this chapter.

→ To learn more about UTP wiring, **see** "Unshielded Twisted-Pair (UTP)," **p. 471**.

A cable is run from each computer to a *hub*, which is a small connecting box that routes the signals between each computer. You'll need to get a hub that has at least as many *ports* (sockets) as you have computers, plus a spare or two. 10BASE-T hubs cost roughly $5 to 10 per port. A typical setup is shown in Figure 16.1.

TIP FROM

Bob & Brian

Multiple hubs can be connected together if your network grows beyond the capacity of your first hub. You can just add on rather than replace your original equipment.

TIP FROM

Bob & Brian

If you're planning on using a shared DSL or cable broadband Internet connection, see Chapter 19, "Connecting Your LAN to the Internet," for some advice about hardware connection sharing devices. Some of these devices have a built-in hub, sparing you the expense of buying a separate one.

Figure 16.1
A 10BASE-T network connects each computer to a hub with UTP cabling. It sounds sophisticated, but remember, you can buy this stuff at WalMart.

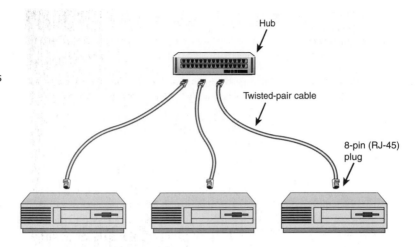

10BASE-T network interface cards (NICs) are available for as little as $5 each, as either ISA or PCI cards, and are made by companies such as Intel, 3COM, NetGear, Farallon, SMC, Kingston, D-Link, Linksys, Boca, and Cnet. Most "nameless" cheap-o cards are based on one of a handful of standard chipsets, so they'll usually work, but your best bet is to only buy cards listed on the Windows Hardware Compatibility List at www.microsoft.com/hcl.

NOTE

> Adapters come in four styles: external adapters that you connect with a USB cable, thin credit-card sized PCMCIA adapters for laptops, and internal PCI or ISA adapters for desktop computers. Be sure to buy a card with the right type of connector for your computer. Newer desktop computers may not have ISA sockets at all, so be careful to check your computer's manual and inspect the inside of the computer for available empty sockets before you purchase an adapter. When buying a new internal NIC, you're best off just getting a PCI version.

I should point out that 10/100BASE-T equipment is so inexpensive now that there's little reason for using 10BASE-T.

TIP FROM

Bob & Brian

> If you do decide to use 10BASE-T network adapters and hubs, I recommend installing CAT-5 cable and connectors for all new wiring. That way, you'll be able to upgrade later to 100BASE-T just by adding new network cards and a hub.

If you want to use existing in-wall wiring for your network, you should be sure it's at least CAT-3 certified. If the cable has eight or more wires with striped color-matched pairs twisted together, it's *probably* CAT-3 compliant.

When you're shopping for a hub, you might see devices called *switches*. Switches are hubs on steroids. Whereas a hub is a simple repeater that forwards received data to every device on the LAN, a switch can route data between several pairs of computers simultaneously, if all are transmitting at once. Switches are important in big corporate networks. If you have one, it's nice, but for a small network, it's not worth paying a premium price to get one.

Overall, 10BASE-T networking is as inexpensive as it gets—hooking up three computers should set you back under $75. It's easy to set up, and it's very reliable. On the down side, though, there is *no* "coolness" factor. This is your father's Oldsmobile. 100BASE-T networks perform somewhat faster, and are just barely more expensive. But for either of these, you must still run cables around, so it's less convenient than wireless solutions.

100BASE-Tx ETHERNET

100BASE-Tx is a supercharged twisted-pair Ethernet network, and although it's 10 times faster than its 10BASE-T predecessor, it's only slightly more expensive. In actual use, it's not quite 10 times faster, but it does help if you're transporting large files. Network cards cost roughly $15 to $75, and hubs cost about $15 per port.

Almost all modern 100Mbps network cards will also operate at 10Mbps if they find themselves connected to a 10Mbps hub, so they are labeled *10/100 cards*. Likewise, most new 100BASE-T hubs are 10/100 compatible. This is a boon, because a 10/100 hub lets you plug in computers with either speed network card, and each computer will communicate as fast as possible.

10/100 network adapters come in three flavors: Internal PCI cards, plug-in PCMCIA cards for laptops, or USB-based adapters for either desktops or portables.

100BASE-T networking is more than fast enough for any home or office. This type of equipment is the current standard for networking, so it's plentiful in stores and nearly guaranteed to work with Windows XP. Many new computers come with 10/100 network cards or plugs built-in. A disadvantage 100BASE-T shares with 10BASE-T networking is the need to string wires between your computers and a hub. Also, 100BASE-T networks really do require high-quality CAT-5 cabling, and any connectors and wall data jacks used have to be CAT-5 certified as well. If you use in-wall wiring, the work has to be done by someone with professional-level skills.

1000BASE-T ETHERNET

At this point in time, I think Gigabit networking is massive overkill for the home and small office network. Yet, as surprising as it may seem, Gigabit Ethernet has come down in price to the point where new Apple Macintosh computers come with 10/100/1000 Mbps Ethernet adapters as standard equipment, and adapters for PCs can cost as little as $75.

If you choose to use Gigabit Ethernet, you'll need to use ultra high-quality Category 6 (CAT-6) wiring, cables, and connectors throughout, and a Gigabit hub that will set you back more than $500. You should use only commercially manufactured patch cables or professionally-installed in-the-wall wiring for gigabit networks.

PHONELINE NETWORKING

HPNA (Home Phoneline Networking Association) devices send network data by transmitting radio signals over your existing telephone wiring, using a network adapter that plugs into a telephone jack (see Figure 16.2). These devices don't interfere at all with the normal operation of your telephones; the extra signal just hitchhikes along the wires.

Figure 16.2
Phoneline networking uses existing household telephone wiring to carry a radio frequency signal between networked computers.

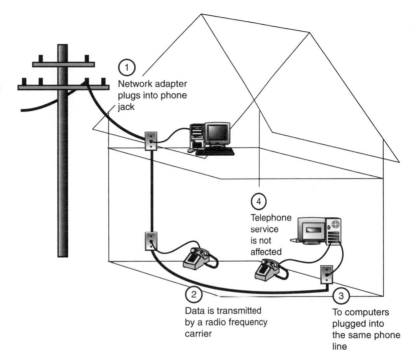

① Network adapter plugs into phone jack

④ Telephone service is not affected

② Data is transmitted by a radio frequency carrier

③ To computers plugged into the same phone line

TIP FROM

Bob & Brian

If you use Phoneline networking, be certain to get only HPNA 2.0 compatible adapters, or better. This will ensure that your equipment will operate at at least 10Mbps, and will work with other manufacturers' products. Don't get any device that connects through your computer's parallel port: It's too slow!

Phoneline networking is intended primarily for home use. The products are relatively inexpensive—about $70 per computer—and don't require you to string cables around the house. However, they have some significant disadvantages:

■ All of your adapters must be plugged into the same telephone line. So, the same extension must be present at a phone outlet near each of your computers. If you have to call in a wiring contractor to add a phone extension, you haven't saved much over a wired network.

■ "Access Point" devices, used to link a standard wired- networked computers to your phoneline network, are relatively rare.

16

Without a hardware access point it's difficult to use a hardware Internet connection sharing device, or to add standard wired computers to your network. However, Windows XP can manage it in software, if necessary. I'll discuss this later in this chapter under "Bridging Two Network Types with Windows XP."

WIRELESS NETWORKING

One way to build a network without hubs, cables, connectors, drills, swearing, tools, or outside contractors is to go wireless. They *call* it Ethernet. Why not really transmit data right through the proverbial ether? A block of radio frequencies in the 2.4GHz (802.11b) and 5GHz (802.11a) bands are reserved for close-range data communications, and standardized products are now available to take advantage of this. Prices have fallen to the point that wireless connectivity is now competitive with wired networks, when installation cost savings are factored in. Because the 802.11b and 802.11a networking standards operate in different frequency ranges, they are not compatible with each other. A newer standard, 802.11g, is in the final stages of approval that will allow 802.11g-compliant devices to work in both frequency ranges and thus bridge the gap between existing 802.11b and 802.11a hardware.

Wireless networking products typically

- Operate at an advertised speed of 11Mbps (802.11b) and 54Mbps (802.11a), with actual transfer rates somewhere around 50 percent of the maximum.

- Can transmit data about 100' indoors and up to 300' outdoors

- Are available for both desktop and laptop computers, in PCI, PCMCIA, or USB formats

- Cost $70 to $250 per adapter

- Can be bridged to a wired LAN through an optional device called an *Access Point*, bridge, or base unit, costing $200 and up

Figure 16.3 shows a typical family of wireless products: a twisted-pair to wireless access point, an access point/gateway router that can also share a DSL or Cable Internet connection, an internal wireless network card, and a PC network card for laptops.

TIP FROM

Bob
& Brian

I recommend researching the current state of the art before you make any decisions because these products are evolving quickly. Check current computer magazines and Web sites for product reviews. Online stores and reviews may help you discover new products and manufacturers you hadn't heard of before.

In any event, don't touch any product that doesn't advertise itself as 802.11a or 802.11b (also called *Wi-Fi*) certified, or doesn't mention that it's Windows XP/2000 compatible.

Figure 16.3
Typical wireless networking equipment. Clockwise from upper left: Access Point, Access Point with Internet Connection Sharing router, PCI adapter, PC card adapter. (Photo used by permission of D-Link.)

TIP FROM

Bob & Brian

If you use a dedicated Internet connection service such as DSL, cable modem, or frame relay, be sure to read Chapter 19 before making any purchasing decisions. At least two companies offer Internet connection sharing, wireless access, and network printer sharing in a single box for under $250. (This is an amazing technological advance. Please pause for a moment and feel mind-boggled before proceeding).

IEEE-1394 (FIREWIRE) NETWORKING

IEEE-1394 is a very high-speed connection technology used primarily to connect portable hard disks and video cameras to computers. This technology is also called FireWire by Apple, and i.LINK by Sony. By any name, it's fast—up to 400Mbps. If two or more of your computers are outfitted with IEEE-1394 (FireWire) ports, you can simply attach your computers together with 1394 cables and forgo the use of network adapters entirely, as Windows XP supports IEEE-1394 for networking use.

With 1394, you don't have to worry about hubs and you can connect your computers together in any fashion as long as each computer is connected to at least one other, and as long as there's only one cable connecting any two given computers. Figure 16.4 shows a typical 1394 wiring setup. Connecting computers to computers rather than accessories requires the use of special cables with six pins on each end, called "6-6" cables.

If you want to add computers without IEEE-1394 adapters to this sort of network, you'll have to have one computer with both a 1394 port and a standard network adapter. Use the Bridging feature, described later in this chapter, to connect the two network types.

16

Figure 16.4
Computers networked with IEEE-1394 (FireWire) can be connected in any convenient way. The maximum cable length of 15 feet limits the usefulness of 1394 for networking, however, and the price of the cables could bring tears to your eyes.

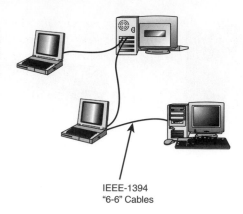

IEEE-1394
"6-6" Cables

IEEE-1394 is fast and convenient. However, the computers have to be within 15 feet (4.5 meters) of each other, as this is the maximum permitted length of IEEE-1394 cables. And the price of those cables—ouch! I found 15 foot 6-6 cables online at buy.com for $15, but at the local CompUSA, I had to pay $25 for a *three foot* cable! Adding an IEEE-1394 adapter to a computer can cost you an additional $60 or more. With these limitations and prices, I wouldn't buy this stuff just to build a network, or to connect more than two or three computers.

If your computer does have an IEEE-1394 adapter, you'll find an icon for it in the Network Connections page, which we'll discuss later in the chapter. Wherever I mention using an icon for a network adapter, you can use the 1394 Connection icon.

MIXED NETWORKING

If you are updating an existing network or are connecting two separate types of networks, you should consider several things.

If you have some existing 10Mbps devices and want to add new 100Mbps devices without upgrading the old, you can buy a dual-speed hub, which connects to each computer at the maximum speed it permits.

You should be wary of some so-called *Autosensing 10/100Mbps Hubs*, which purport to let you connect both 10 and 100Mbps devices. Some of these hubs force the entire network to run at 10Mbps if any one device runs this lower speed. Read the specifications carefully. You want a device called *N-way autosensing*.

Switching hubs, as I mentioned before, don't add a whole lot to a small network, so I wouldn't make a big point of buying one, except in one particular situation: when you have a heavily-used existing 10BASE-T network with a primary file server or "main machine" that everyone uses to store files.

TIP FROM

Bob
& Brian

To speed up a 10Mbps network, instead of replacing all the wiring and network cards in all your computers, upgrade just the network card in your file server to a 100Mbps device. Use a *10/100 switching hub* to connect the server to the workstations. This effectively gives every computer its own full 10Mbps channel to the file server at a minimal cost.

Finally, if you want to mix standard Ethernet, wireless, and/or IEEE-1394 devices on your network, you can use the Bridge feature built into Windows XP, or you'll need one of the access points I mentioned in the previous section. I'll discuss bridging in the section "Bridging Two Network Types with Windows XP," later in this chapter.

PRINTING AND FAXING

Shared printers simply need to be connected their host Windows XP computers with a standard USB or parallel printer cable. If the printer needs to be farther than 10 feet away from a computer, you have three choices:

1. Get a really long cable, and take your chances. The electrical signal for printers is not supposed to be stretched more then 10 feet, but I've gotten away with 25 feet in the past. Buy a high-quality shielded cable. You may get data errors (bad printed characters) with this approach.

2. Use a network-capable printer. You can buy special network printer modules for some printers, or you can buy special third-party "print server" modules, which connect to the printer port and to a network cable. Network supply catalogs list a myriad of these devices. Some of the newer DSL/cable sharing routers and wireless access points have a print server built in. These are great for small offices.

3. Use a printer-extender device. These devices turn the high-speed parallel data signal into a serial data connection somewhat as a modem does. I don't like these as they result in very slow printing.

If your network includes Windows 95, 98, NT 3 or 4, or Windows 3.1 computers, collect the CDs or floppy disks containing the printer drivers for these operating systems for each of your printers. Windows XP Professional lets you load in the printer drivers for the older operating systems and lets these computers automatically download the proper printer driver when they use the shared printer. We'll cover this slick feature in Chapter 17, "Using a Windows XP Network."

Windows XP also lets you share a fax modem installed in any of your Windows XP computers with any other Windows XP computer, which you use as if you were selecting a networked printer. Incoming faxes can be stored in a shared network directory for viewing by any workstation, and/or can be automatically printed on arrival.

Of course, the computer with the printer or modem has to be turned on if the user of another computer wants to print or send a fax.

PROVIDING INTERNET CONNECTIVITY

You'll probably want to have Internet access on your LAN, and it's far better to have one connection to the Net for the entire LAN than to let each user fend for himself or herself.

Windows XP has a built-in connection-sharing feature that lets a single computer use a dial-up, cable, or DSL modem and make the connection on behalf of any user or users on your

LAN. You can also use external hardware devices to make the connection. This topic is important enough that it gets its own chapter. I recommend that you read Chapter 19, "Connecting Your LAN to the Internet," before you buy any equipment.

You also must be sure to study Chapter 21, "Network Security," to build in proper safeguards against hacking and abuse. This is especially important with full-time cable/DSL connections.

PROVIDING REMOTE ACCESS

You also can provide connectivity *in* to your network from the outside world, either through the Internet or via modem. This connectivity lets you get at your LAN resources from home or out in the field, with full assurance that your network is safe from outside attacks. Chapter 18, "Windows Unplugged: Remote and Mobile Networking," covers remote access.

If you need to get to your network from outside and you aren't planning to have a permanent direct Internet connection, you might want to plan for the installation of a telephone line near one of your Windows XP computers so that you can set up a dedicated modem line for incoming access.

INSTALLING NETWORK ADAPTERS

I've made this point before, but it's worth repeating: Before you purchase a network card, be sure to check the Windows XP Hardware Compatibility List (HCL). You should purchase cards that appear on the HCL or that are marked by the manufacturer certifying their compatibility with Windows XP or 2000. You can find the HCL at `http://www.microsoft.com/hcl`.

CHECKING EXISTING ADAPTERS

If your adapter was already installed when you set up Windows XP, it may already be ready to go, in which case you can skip this section and jump down to "Installing Network Wiring." Follow these steps to see whether the adapter is already set up:

1. Right-click My Computer and select Manage.
2. Select Device Manager in the left pane, and open the Network Adapters list in the right pane.
3. Look for an entry for your network card. If it appears and does not have a yellow exclamation point (!) icon to the left of its name, the card is installed and correctly configured. In this case, you can skip ahead to "Installing Network Wiring."

   If an entry appears but has an exclamation point icon by its name (see the example in Figure 16.5), the card is not correctly configured.
4. If no entry exists for the card, the adapter is not fully plugged into the motherboard, it's broken, or it is not "plug and play" capable. Be sure the card is installed correctly. If the card is broken or non–plug-and-play, you should replace it. Check out Chapter 30, "Installing and Replacing Hardware," for troubleshooting tips.

NOTE

> If you see an exclamation point icon in the Network Adapters list, skip ahead to Chapter 22, "Troubleshooting Your Network," for tips on getting the card to work before proceeding.

Figure 16.5
The Device Manager indicates trouble with a network adapter by displaying an exclamation point icon next to its name.

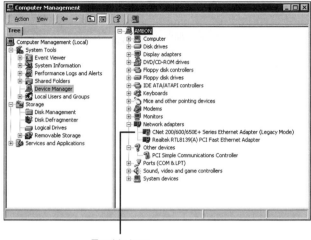

Trouble icon

INSTALLING A NEW NETWORK ADAPTER

If you're installing a new network adapter, follow the manufacturer's instructions for installing with Windows XP or Windows 2000. Even if it does not come with specific Windows XP instructions, the installation should be a snap. Just follow these steps:

1. If you have purchased an internal card, shut down Windows, shut off the computer, unplug it, open the case, install the card in an empty slot, close the case, and restart Windows. (Chapter 30 has some advice on installing adapter cards.)

TIP FROM

Bob
& Brian

> If you've never worked inside your computer, jump ahead to Chapter 30, "Installing and Replacing Hardware," for advice and handy tips.

If you are adding a PCMCIA or USB adapter, be sure you're logged on with a "Computer Administrator" account, and then just plug it in while Windows is running.

If you're using your computer's IEEE-1394 port, there's nothing to install or configure.

2. When you're back at the Windows log in screen, log in as an Administrator user. Windows displays the New Hardware Detected dialog when you log in.

3. The New Hardware Detected dialog might instruct you to insert your Windows XP CD-ROM. If Windows cannot find a suitable driver for your adapter from this CD, it may ask you to insert a driver disk that your network card's manufacturer should have provided (either a CD-ROM or floppy disk).

If you are asked, insert the manufacturer's disk and click OK. If Windows says that it cannot locate an appropriate device driver, try again, and this time click the Browse button. Locate a folder named WindowsXP, Windows2000 (or some reasonable approximation), W2K, or NT5 on the floppy, and click OK.

NOTE

The exact name of the folder containing your device driver varies from vendor to vendor. You might have to poke around a little on the disk to find it.

4. After Windows has installed the card's driver software, it automatically configures and uses the card. Check the Device Manager to see whether the card is installed and functioning. Then you can proceed to "Installing Network Wiring" later in this chapter.

→ For more detailed instructions about installing drivers, **see** Chapter 25, "Maintaining and Optimizing System Performance."

INSTALLING MULTIPLE NETWORK ADAPTERS

You might want to install multiple network adapters in your computer if

- You simultaneously connect to two or more different networks with different IP addresses or protocols. You'd use a separate adapter to connect to each network.

- You want to share a broadband cable or DSL Internet connection with your LAN without using a hardware sharing router. I prefer the hardware solution, as I'll discuss in Chapter 19, but you can do it using one adapter to connect to your LAN and another to connect to your cable or DSL modem.

- You have two different network types, such as Phoneline and Ethernet, and want the computers on both LAN types to be able to communicate. You could use a hardware Access Point, but you could also install both types of adapters in one of your computers, and use the Bridging feature to connect the networks. I'll discuss bridging later in this chapter.

I suggest that you use the following procedure to install multiple adapters:

1. Install and configure the first adapter. If you're doing this to share an Internet connection, install and configure the one you'll use for the Internet connection first.

2. Click Start, Control Panel, Network and Internet Connections, Network Connections. Select the icon named Local Area Connection and choose Rename This Connection in Network Tasks. Change the connection's name to something that indicates what it's used for, such as "Connection to Cable Modem" or "Office Ethernet Network."

3. Write the connection name on a piece of tape or a sticky label and apply it to the back of your computer above the network adapter, or to the edge plate of the network card.

4. Shut down Windows and install the second adapter. Configure it and repeat steps 2 and 3 with the new Local Area Connection icon. Name this connection appropriately, for example, "LAN" or "Wireless Net," and put a tape or paper label on the computer too.

If you follow these steps, you'll be able to distinguish the two connections easily in the future, instead of having to remember which "Local Area Connection" icon is which.

INSTALLING NETWORK WIRING

When your network adapters are installed, the next step is to get your computers connected together. Installing the wiring can be the most difficult task of setting up a network. How you proceed depends on the type of networking adapters you have:

- If you're using wireless adapters, of course you don't have to worry about wiring at all. Just follow the manufacturer's instructions for configuring the wireless network adapters.

- If you're using Phoneline networking, plug a standard modular telephone cable into each Phoneline network adapter and connect them to the appropriate wall jacks. The adapter must be plugged directly into the wall jack, and then additional devices such as modems, telephones, and answering machines can be connected to the adapter.

- If you're using IEEE-1394 networking, buy certified IEEE-1394 cables and plug your computers together as shown in Figure 16.4.

If you're using any of these three network types, get the connections made and skip ahead to the "Configuring a Peer-to-Peer Network" or "Joining a Windows XP/2000 Domain Network" section.

Otherwise, you're using UTP Ethernet adapters and you have to decide how to route your wiring and what type of cables to use. The remainder of this section discusses UTP wiring.

If your computers are close together, you can use pre-built *patch cables* to connect your computers to a hub. (The term patch cable originated in the telephone industry—in the old days, switchboard operators used patch cables to temporarily connect, or patch, one phone circuit to another. In networking, the term refers to cables that are simply plugged in and not permanently wired.) You can run these cables through the habitable area of your home or office by routing them behind furniture, around partitions, and so on. Just don't put them where they'll be crushed, walked on, tripped over, or run over by desk chair wheels.

If the cables need to run through walls or stretch long distances, you should consider having them installed inside the walls with plug-in jacks, just like your telephone wiring. I'll discuss this later in this section. Hardware stores sell special cable covers you can use if you need to run a cable where it's exposed to foot traffic, as well as covers for wires that need to run up walls or over doorways.

GENERAL CABLING TIPS

You can determine how much cable you need by measuring the distance between computers and your hub location(s). Remember to account for vertical distances, too, where cables run from the floor up to a desktop, or go up and over a partition or wall.

CAUTION

> If you have to run cables through the ceiling space of an office building, you should check with your building management to see whether the ceiling is listed as a *plenum* or air-conditioning air return. You may be required by law to use certified *plenum cable* and follow all applicable electrical codes. Plenum cable is specially formulated not to emit toxic smoke in a fire.

Keep in mind the following points:

- Existing household telephone wire probably won't work. If the wires are red, green, black, and yellow: no way. The cable must have color-matched twisted pairs of wires, each with one wire in a solid color and the other white with colored stripes. This type of wiring probably will work for 10BASE-T networking, but not 100BASE-T.

- For 100BASE-Tx networking, you *must* use CAT-5 quality wiring and components throughout: cables, jacks, plugs, connectors, terminal blocks, patch cables, and so on. The cable jacket will usually have this printed every foot or so.

- Even for 10BASE-T networks, I suggest that you keep future upgrades and compatibility in mind by using CAT-5 components for any new cabling and components you buy.

- If you're installing in-wall wiring, follow professional CAT-5 wiring practices throughout. Be sure not to untwist more than half an inch of any pair of wires when attaching cables to connectors. Don't solder or splice the wires.

- When you're installing cables, be gentle. Don't pull, kink, or stretch them. Don't bend them sharply around corners; you should allow at least a one-inch radius for bends. And don't staple or crimp them. To attach cables to a wall or baseboard, use rigid cable clips that don't squeeze the cable, as shown in Figure 16.6. Your local electronics store can sell you the right kind of clips.

- Keep network cables away from AC power wiring and away from electrically noisy devices such as arc welders, diathermy machines, and the like.

Figure 16.6
Use rigid cable clips or staples that don't squeeze the cable if you nail it to a wall or baseboard.

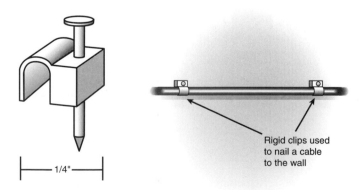

1/4"

Rigid clips used to nail a cable to the wall

16

NOTE

If you really want to get into the nuts and bolts, so to speak, of pulling your own cable, a good starting point is Que's *Practical Network Cabling*, which will help you roll up your shirtsleeves and get dirty (literally, if you have to crawl around through your attic or wrestle with dust bunnies under too many desks at the office).

WIRING WITH PATCH CABLES

If your computers are close together and you can simply run prefabricated cables between your computers and hub, you've got it made! Buy CAT-5 cables of the appropriate length online or at your local computer store. Just plug (click!), and you're finished. Figure 16.1 shows how to connect your computers to the hub.

If you have the desire and patience, you can build custom-length cables from crimp-on connectors and bulk cable stock. Making your own cables requires about $75 worth of tools, though, and more detailed instructions than I can give here. Making just a few cables certainly doesn't make buying the tools worthwhile. Factory-assembled cables are also more reliable than homemade ones because the connectors are attached by machine. They're worth the extra few dollars.

For the ambitious or parsimonious reader, Figure 16.7 shows the correct way to order the wires in the connector.

Figure 16.7
Standard wiring order for UTP network cables.

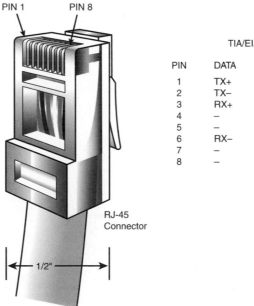

PIN 1   PIN 8

RJ-45
Connector

1/2"

TIA/EIA 568A Standard

PIN	DATA	WIRE COLOR
1	TX+	White/Green
2	TX–	Green
3	RX+	White/Orange
4	–	Blue
5	–	White/Blue
6	RX–	Orange
7	–	White/Brown
8	–	Brown

INSTALLING IN-WALL WIRING

In-wall wiring is the most professional and permanent way to go. However, this often involves climbing around in the attic or under a building, drilling through walls, or working in an office telephone closet. If this is the case, calling in a professional is probably best. Personally, I find it a frustrating task and one I would rather watch someone else do while I sip coffee and eat pastries. Hiring someone to get the job done might cost $30 to $75 per computer, but you'll get a professional job, and if you consider that the price of network cards has gone down at least this much in the last few years, you can pretend that you're getting the wiring thrown in for free.

TIP FROM

Bob & Brian

Look in the yellow pages under Telephone Wiring, and ask the contractors you call whether they have experience with network wiring. The following are some points to check out when you shop for a wiring contractor:

- Ask for references, and check them out.
- Ask for billing details up front: Do they charge by the hour or at a fixed rate? Do they sell equipment themselves, or do you have to supply cables, connectors, and so on?
- Ask for prices for parts and labor separately so that you know whether you're getting a good deal and can comparison-shop.
- Find out what their guaranteed response time is, should problems or failures occur in the future.
- Ask what the warranty terms are. How long are parts and labor covered?

In-wall wiring is brought out to special network-style modular jacks mounted to the baseboard of your wall. These "RJ-45" jacks look like telephone modular jacks but are wider. You'll need patch cables to connect the jacks to your computers and hub, as shown in Figure 16.8.

Figure 16.8
Connect your computers and hub to the network jacks using short patch cables.

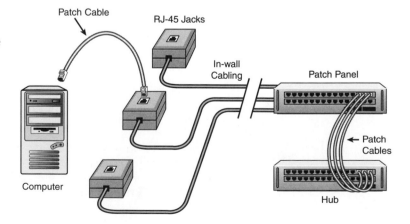

OUT OF THE (PHONE) CLOSET

If you're wiring an office, running all your network wiring alongside the office's phone system wiring to a central location may be most sensible. You might be able to put your hub near the phone equipment in this case. For 10BASE-T, you might even find that your phone wiring is already CAT-3 certified, and you can use spare pairs on the phone system wiring for at least some of your network connections.

But this might require you to enter the phone closet for the first time. In most office buildings, telephone and data wiring are run to a central location on each floor or in each office suite. Connector blocks called *punchdown blocks* are bolted to the wall, where your individual telephone extension wires are joined to thick distribution cables maintained by the phone company or the building management.

These commercial wiring systems are a little bit daunting, and if you aren't familiar with them, it's best to hire a wiring contractor to install your network wiring.

CONNECTING JUST TWO COMPUTERS

If you're making a network of just two computers, you may be able to take a shortcut and eliminate the need for a network hub or additional special hardware. If you want to add on to your network later, you can always add the extra gear then.

If you're connecting two computers with IEEE-1394, you have the simplest possible cabling setup: Just plug one end of a "6-6" cable into a free IEEE-1394 socket on each computer.

If you are connecting two computers with Ethernet, yours is the second easiest possible network installation: Simply run a special cable called a *crossover cable* from one computer's network adapter to the other, and you're finished. This special type of cable reverses the send and receive signals between the two ends, and eliminates the need for a hub. You can purchase a crossover cable from a computer store or network supply shop, or make one as shown in Figure 16.9.

TIP FROM

Bob
& Brian

> Be sure that your crossover cable is labeled as such, as it won't work to connect a computer to a hub and you'll go nuts wondering what's wrong if you try. Factory-made models usually have yellow ends. When I make them myself, I draw three rings around each end of the cable with a permanent-ink marker.

NOTE

> Windows has a feature called a "Direct Network Connection" that lets you use a serial, parallel, or infrared port to connect two computers without a network adapter. This type of connection lets you copy files but isn't as convenient as a full-fledged network setup. I'll cover Direct Network Connection in Chapter 18.

16

Figure 16.9
Wiring for a UTP
crossover cable. The
cable reverses the
send and receive
wires so that two net-
work cards can be
directly connected
without a hub. Note
that the green pair
and orange pairs are
reversed across
the cable.

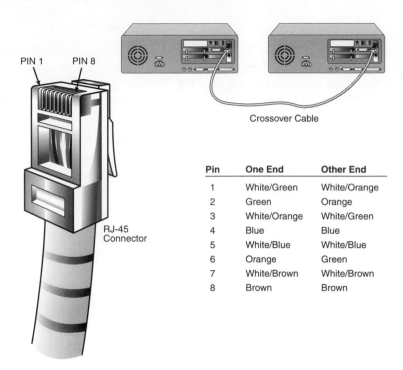

PIN 1   PIN 8

RJ-45
Connector

Crossover Cable

Pin	One End	Other End
1	White/Green	White/Orange
2	Green	Orange
3	White/Orange	White/Green
4	Blue	Blue
5	White/Blue	White/Blue
6	Orange	Green
7	White/Brown	White/Brown
8	Brown	Brown

ADDING NETWORK-CAPABLE PRINTERS

If you have a printer that can directly attach to your network hub, by all means, plug it into your network. You may also use a device called a *print server* to make a printer available on the network without requiring a controlling computer to be turned on. Either type of device will require a patch cable and a free port on your hub.

The printer's manual will tell you how to configure your network to use this type of printer.

CONNECTING MULTIPLE HUBS

You might want to use more than one hub to reduce the number of long network cables you need if you have groups of computers in two or more locations. For example, you can connect the computers on each "end" of the network to the nearest hub, and then connect the hubs to a main hub. Figure 16.10 shows a typical arrangement using this technique.

NOTE

A cascade port is a hub connector designed to be connected to another hub. Some hubs have a separate connector for this purpose, whereas others make one of the hub's regular ports do double-duty by providing a switch that turns the last hub port into a cascade port. Refer to your hub's manual to see what to do with your particular hardware.

Figure 16.10
You can connect groups of computers with multiple hubs to reduce the number of long cables needed. Use the cascade port on the remote hubs to connect to the central hub.

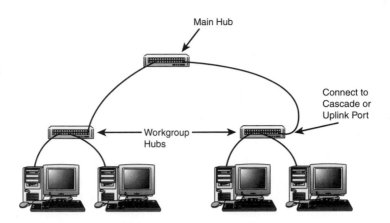

Main Hub

Connect to Cascade or Uplink Port

Workgroup Hubs

16

If you have to add a computer to your LAN and your hub has no unused connectors, you don't need to replace the hub. You can just add an additional hub. To add a computer to a fully-loaded hub, you must unplug one cable from the original hub to free up a port. Connect this cable and your new computer to the new hub. Finally, connect the new hub's *cascade port* to the original hub's free port, as shown in Figure 16.11.

Figure 16.11
You can expand your 10BASE-T or 100BASE-T network by cascading hubs. The instructions included with your hub describe how to connect two hubs using a patch cable. Some hubs have a special cascade port, whereas others have a switch that turns a regular port into a cascade port.

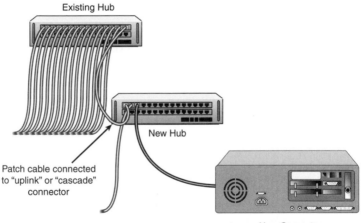

Existing Hub

New Hub

Patch cable connected to "uplink" or "cascade" connector

New Computer

CONFIGURING A PEER-TO-PEER NETWORK

If you're using a UTP network, as you install network cards and plug them into the cables running to your hub, you should see a green light come on at the hub, and possibly on the back of the network card as well, for each computer you connect. These lights indicate that the network wiring is correct.

⚠️ *If you don't get green lights, stop immediately and get the wiring fixed. Check out "Hub Lights Do Not Come On" in the "Troubleshooting" section at the end of this chapter.*

When you're sure that the physical connection between your computers is set up correctly, you're ready to configure Windows XP. With today's Plug and Play network cards and with all the needed software built into Windows, this configuration is a snap.

If your computer is part of a Windows XP/2000 Domain network, which will often be the case in a corporate setting, skip ahead to "Joining a Windows XP/2000 Domain Network." Otherwise, you have two choices for configuring your network software: You can make the settings manually, or you can let the Networking Setup Wizard do the work for you.

NOTE

On a peer-to-peer network, if you want to share or use shared files or printers, you *must* run the Network Setup Wizard at least once. Windows XP's networking features are initially disabled in order to protect you from Internet hacking. The wizard enables networking after ensuring that your Internet connection is secure.

If you want to set up your network manually, you must run the wizard first, and then go through the network settings.

USING THE NETWORKING SETUP WIZARD

Windows XP comes with a Networking Setup Wizard program that can automatically configure each of the computers on your network. The wizard lets you make a few basic choices, but otherwise takes care of all of the technical details for you.

If you want to manage all of the details yourself, skip ahead to "Manually Configuring Your Network," later in this chapter. You might want to do this if you're adding your computer to an existing network that wasn't set up by the wizard to begin with. If you are just setting up a small office or home network, though, the wizard can make quick work of getting your network going.

NOTE

If you're going to use Microsoft's Internet Connection Sharing, configure the computer that will be sharing its Internet connection first. Establish its Internet connection, and then configure the other computers. I'll describe this procedure in detail in Chapter 19. Otherwise, you can configure your computers in any order.

To start the wizard, click Start, Control Panel, Network and Internet Connections, and Set up or change your home or small office network. Read the "checklist for creating a network" if you wish, and then click Next. Follow the wizard through the following steps.

SELECT A CONNECTION METHOD

The wizard asks you to select a statement that best describes your computer. The choices can be confusing, so consider them each carefully. They are

- **This computer connects directly to the Internet. The other computers . . . connect . . . through this computer.** Choose this if your computer will be sharing its Internet connection with the rest of your LAN. This computer will connect to the Internet with its own dial-up modem, or through a cable/DSL modem that's either installed inside or connected directly to a USB port or network adapter. In the last case, you'll have installed two network adapters in this computer: one for the LAN connection and one for the Internet connection. In either case, be sure that you've already configured and tested your Internet connection.

- **This computer connects to the Internet through another computer on my network or through a residential gateway.** Choose this if this computer will be using another computer's shared Internet connection, or if your network has a hardware Internet connection sharing router.

- **Other.** This choice (and a click on Next) leads you to three more alternatives:

  - **This computer connects to the Internet directly or through a network hub. Other computers on my network also connect [this way].** Select this if your computer uses a dial-up or direct DSL/cable connection but you are *not* using Windows's Internet Connection Sharing to share this connection with your LAN. Also, use this choice if your LAN has a routed Internet connection, such as a DSL, cable, or Frame Relay router connected to your network hub.

  - **This computer connects directly to the Internet. I do not have a network yet.** This strange choice would be used if you have a direct Internet connection but no network—the wizard will just make some settings to protect your non-networked computer from Internet hackers.

  - **This computer belongs to a network that does not have an Internet connection.** Select this if none of the computers will ever connect to the Internet, either directly or through the LAN.

NOTE

> If you choose **This computer connects to the Internet directly or through a network hub . . .** above, you need to take special precautions to avoid attacks from Internet hackers. Please read Chapters 19 and 21 for more details. The other configurations are not as great a risk because Windows file sharing will be isolated from the Internet by the Internet Connection Firewall, or by the Network Address Translation function of Internet Connection Sharing or the residential gateway.
>
> If you make this choice, the wizard will enable the Internet Firewall on your LAN adapter, and file sharing will be blocked between your computer and the other computers on your own LAN. You will not be able to share files or access shared files from your computer. If you know that the Internet connection on your LAN has adequate firewall protection installed in its router, you can disable the firewall in your own computer as discussed in Chapter 21.

Make the appropriate selection and click Next.

16

SELECT YOUR INTERNET CONNECTION

If you chose one of the "This computer is directly connected to the Internet" choices, Windows will present a list of options for making that connection, listing your network adapters and your configured dial-up connections. Choose the connection that is used to reach the Internet and click Next. If you use a dial-up or PPPoE connection (a type of DSL service), choose the appropriate dial-up connection. Otherwise choose the network adapter that connects to your Internet service.

GIVE THIS COMPUTER A DESCRIPTION AND NAME

Enter a brief description of the computer (such as its location or primary user) and a name for the computer. Choose a name using just letters and/or numbers with no spaces or punctuation. Each computer on your LAN must have a different name.

If you're hard pressed to come up with names, try the names of gemstones, composers, Impressionist painters, or even Star Wars characters, as long as Mr. Lucas doesn't sue you over them. I use the names of islands in the Indonesian archipelago—with more than 25,000 to choose from there's little chance of running out of unique names!

Some Internet service providers, especially cable providers, require you use a name that they'll provide. (If you have a hardware connection sharing device hooked up to your cable modem, the hardware device will use that name and you can use any names you want on your LAN).

NAME YOUR NETWORK

Choose a name for your network workgroup. This name is used to identify which computers should appear in your list of network choices later on. All computers on your LAN should have the same workgroup name. If you have an existing network, enter the same workgroup name that the other computers use. Otherwise, you could pick a creative name like WORKGROUP.

NOTE

The workgroup name must be different than all of the computer names.

READY TO APPLY NETWORK SETTINGS

Review the list of selections you've made and either click Back to correct them or click Next to proceed.

YOU'RE ALMOST FINISHED

You'll need to run the wizard on the other computers on your LAN. If all the computers use Windows XP, select Just Finish the Wizard, and run the wizard on the other computers. If you have computers running versions of Windows 95, 98, Me, NT, or 2000, you can create a diskette that will let you run the wizard on these older machines, or you can use your Windows XP CD-ROM in these computers.

To use a diskette, choose Create a Network Setup Disk, and insert a blank, formatted floppy disk. If you ran the wizard earlier and just changed some of the settings, choose Use the Network Setup Disk I Already Have, and re-insert the setup disk you created earlier.

CONFIGURE OTHER COMPUTERS

Repeat the wizard procedure on your other computers.

If a computer is running a version of Windows earlier than XP, you'll need the Network Setup Diskette you created earlier, or use the Windows XP CD-ROM. To fire up the wizard from a diskette, insert the diskette into the older computer. Click Start and Run, type `a:setup`, and press Enter.

To use the CD-ROM, insert the CD-ROM in the older computer and wait for it to auto-run the Windows setup program. Choose Perform Additional Tasks, and then Set Up Home or Small Office Networking.

Congratulations—your network is set up! The next chapter will tell you how to start using your network.

MANUALLY CONFIGURING YOUR NETWORK

When it first detects your network card, Windows will install most of the necessary network software components automatically. This can occur during the initial installation of Windows XP or when you later add a network card. I suggest that you go through the installed components, as I'll describe below, to be sure that everything is set up correctly.

ADDING NETWORK CLIENTS, SERVICES, AND PROTOCOLS

When your network card and its drivers are installed, Windows knows the card is there but doesn't have any networking software attached to it. Follow these steps to attach the networking protocols and services you'll need.

Choose Start, Control Panel, Network and Internet Connections, and then Network Connections. Double-click Local Area Connection and select Properties. You should see a Properties dialog with your network card named at the top under Connect Using. The list below Components Checked Are Used By This Connection will probably contain at least four items, as shown in Figure 16.12:

- Client for Microsoft Networks
- File and Printer Sharing for Microsoft Networks
- QoS Packet Scheduler
- Internet Protocol (TCP/IP)

Figure 16.12
Default network components installed with
Windows XP.

These components will suffice for most home or office LANs:

- **Client for Microsoft Networks** lets your computer use files and printers shared by other computers.

- **File and Printer Sharing for Microsoft Networks** lets your computer share files or printers with others. (If you definitely don't need to share files or printers from this computer, you can uncheck this item—this will help protect your computer from unwanted visitors.)

- **QoS Packet Scheduler** is used on some networks to assign varying priorities for different type of network traffic. (It's not necessary for small networks but it doesn't hurt to leave it in.)

- **Internet Protocol (TCP/IP)** is the basic network protocol used for all Internet services, and usually for Microsoft file and printer sharing as well.

There are some additional components required in certain situations:

- If you use Novell NetWare servers, you must add **the Client Service for NetWare** and the **NWLink IPX/SPX** protocol, or their Novell-supplied equivalents. For more information on Novell networking, see Chapter 20, "Networking Mix and Match."

- The **Network Monitor Driver** protocol allows your computer's network communications to be monitored by a network supervisor, for diagnostic purposes. Install this only if requested by your network administrator.

- The **Service Advertising Protocol** service is used on Novell networks; your network administrator will tell you if you need to install it.

If you need to add any of these components, or if any were inadvertently removed, use this procedure to add them:

1. Click Install. From the list shown in the Select Network Component Type dialog box choose Client, Service, or Protocol, and then click Add. (You might need to search

through the list of components under each of these three categories to find the component you're after.)

2. From the list of Network Clients, Services or Protocols, select the desired entry and click OK.

TIP FROM

Bob & Brian

> If Windows asks whether it can restart, select Yes. For previous versions of Windows, I would have suggested selecting No because you would face further restarts as you added other network components. With Windows XP, you're rarely asked to restart more than once, so you might as well get it over with right away.

In addition to these standard components, there are some advanced components available through Windows Setup.

- **Management and Monitoring Tools**
  - **Simple Network Management Protocol** is used on larger networks to monitor computer and router configuration. Install this only if required by your network administrator because it can reveal sensitive information to hackers if no firewall is in place.
  - **WMI SNMP Provider** permits Windows Management Interface application software access to SNMP data.
- **Networking Services**
  - **RIP Listener** lets Windows configure its TCP/IP routing tables to adjust to varying network router availability as broadcast by the Router Information Protocol.
  - **Simple TCP/IP Services** are a set of primitive TCP/IP services such as character stream generation and data echo. They're rarely needed and can make you an easy target for Denial of Service (DOS) attacks by hackers if installed.
  - **Universal Plug and Play** lets your computer automatically discover and connect to networked appliances and other new network devices. UPnP is a new technology that lets network hardware and future network-ready appliances communicate without manual setup.
- **Other Network File and Print Services**
  - **Print Services for Unix** lets Unix/Linux users use your computer's printers (and other shared printers on your network).

In general, you'll need these only if your network is large and your network manager tells you that they are required, or if you have Universal Plug and Play devices. (If you buy a Universal Plug and Play device in the future, its operating instructions will tell you to install the UPnP software.) It's best *not* to install any components unless you're sure you need them. If any are required

1. View the Network Connections window and select Advanced, Optional Networking Components.

2. Select the appropriate category (for example, Networking Services) and click Details.

3. Check the box(es) next to the desired component(s) and click OK.

4. Click Next to complete the installation. Windows may require you to insert your Windows CD-ROM.

CONFIGURING NETWORK COMPONENTS

After adding or checking your network components, you may need to configure them with appropriate network settings.

You need to make configuration settings for only two protocols: NWLink IPX/SPX Compatible Transport and TCP/IP. To configure a protocol, select it from the list of installed network components and click Properties.

NWLINK IPX/SPX COMPATIBLE TRANSPORT

Even if you use a Novell Network server, it is very unlikely that you will need to configure the Novell settings. The Properties page for the NWLink transport has only three settings and the default values should always work. The settings are

- **Internal Network Number.** This must be unique on the network. Windows assigns a random number that will usually work.

- **Frame type.** If you cannot reach the Novell server but other network services function correctly, you may need to manually set the frame type (usually Ethernet 802.2).

- **Network Number.** The system will detect the correct Novell network number if the value entered is 0; otherwise enter the appropriate network number.

TCP/IP

Normally, the TCP/IP protocol is the only one requiring manual configuration. If your network provides a *DHCP (Dynamic Host Configuration Protocol)* server, you can leave the TCP/IP parameters on their default Obtain Automatically setting. DHCP service is provided by most Internet routers, connection sharing devices, and Windows computers providing Internet Connection Sharing.

If you have a small network with no DHCP server and you're not using Internet Connection Sharing or a hardware connection sharing device, you can still leave the TCP/IP settings alone and Windows will choose appropriate automatic-configuration values.

If your computer is part of a network with predetermined IP addresses (such as a corporate LAN or a LAN with routed Internet service), you may have to manually enter IP information. You'll need the following information from your network manager or your Internet service provider:

- IP address
- Subnet mask

- Default gateway
- DNS domain name
- Preferred DNS servers

Automatic Configuration Without DHCP

Dynamic Host Configuration Protocol, or DHCP, is a network service that lets computers receive their TCP/IP configuration automatically over the network. It's great because a network administrator can make all the settings once in a DHCP server configuration program and not have to deal with managing individual setups for tens, hundreds, or even thousands of computers. DHCP service can be provided by Windows XP, 2000 and NT Server, Unix servers, and many network and Internet gateway routers. Computers running Windows Internet Connection Sharing also provide DHCP service for their LAN.

If a computer is set for automatic configuration, it broadcasts a message on the LAN when it boots, basically saying "Help! Who am I?" The LAN's DHCP server responds, assigns an IP address to the computer, and sends other information such as DNS server addresses, the domain name, and so on.

What's interesting is that a Windows TCP/IP network will still work even without a DHCP server.

Here's what happens: When each computer on the LAN is booted up, during its startup, it cries "Help!" as usual. But this time, there's no answer. The computer repeats the request a couple of times, to no avail. So, it picks an IP address at random from the range 169.254.0.1 through 169.254.0.254. (These addresses were reserved by Microsoft for this purpose and will never conflict with other computers on the Internet.) The computer sends a broadcast to the LAN asking whether any other computer is using this address. If none answers, then the computer continues on its merry way. If the address is already in use, the computer tries others until it finds one that is unclaimed.

Each computer on the LAN is able to obtain an IP address this way, but doesn't get network gateways, domain names, or DNS server information. But because this system is only for the simplest of LANs with no server and no permanent outside connections, that's fine. The other information comes if and when these computers dial out to the Internet independently.

Just to be on the safe side, each computer bleats its "Help!" request every five minutes in the hope that there really was a DHCP server that had just been temporarily indisposed. If a DHCP server actually does come online later (perhaps the server computer had been turned off while the others booted up), then the Windows computers discard their made-up IP configurations for the real thing.

When Internet Connection Sharing is in use, the picture is a little different. The sharing computer actually acts as a DHCP server because it has to give the others its own IP address as the gateway and DNS server address for the LAN. This topic is covered in Chapter 19, "Connecting Your LAN to the Internet."

If you are setting up a shared LAN connection to the Internet, see Chapter 19 for a discussion of TCP/IP configuration.

If you have to join your computer to an existing TCP/IP network, you might have to do a little more work. Contact the network manager to obtain instructions for assigning the TCP/IP parameters. If your network has a DHCP server, or if your other computers are already set up for automatic configuration, you can leave the TCP/IP settings on Automatic, and your computer will obtain all its network settings from the DHCP server. (This is *so* slick!)

Otherwise, your network manager will give you the required settings for the five parameters listed above.

16

To configure settings for the TCP/IP protocol, follow these steps:

1. In Local Area Connection Properties, select the Internet Protocol (TCP/IP), and click Properties to open the dialog shown in Figure 16.13.

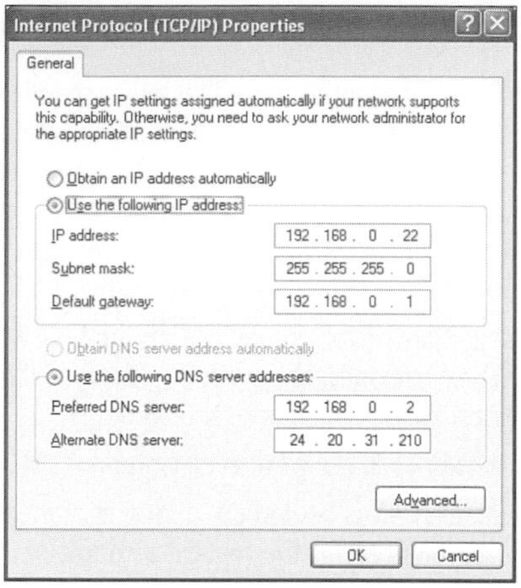

Figure 16.13
To configure TCP/IP parameters, select Internet Protocol and click Properties.

2. Select Use the Following IP Address, and enter the required IP address, subnet mask, and default gateway address, as shown in Figure 16.13. Of course, you need to enter *your* IP address information.

TIP FROM

Bob & Brian

> When you're entering IP addresses, if you enter three digits, the cursor moves to the next part of the address field automatically. If you enter one or two digits, press the period (.) or spacebar to move to the next address field.

3. Select Use the following DNS server addresses and enter one or two DNS server addresses.

4. If your LAN is not connected to the Internet, you're finished, so just click OK. Otherwise, if your LAN has access to the Internet via a direct connection or Connection Sharing, click the Advanced button, and select the DNS tab, as shown in Figure 16.14.

5. Be sure that Append Primary and Connection Specific DNS Suffixes is selected and that Append Parent Suffixes of the Primary DNS Suffix is *not* checked.

6. Under DNS Suffix for This Connection, enter your company's registered domain name, or use your Internet provider's domain. This setting is used only if you use a computer name without a domain name in your Web browser, so it's not terribly important. But this setting is helpful, for example, if you want to refer to your mail server as mail rather than mail.myisp.com. (In a corporate environment, this technique often can be used to automatically reach the nearest mail server on the local connection's domain.)

Figure 16.14
You can enter your LAN's registered Internet domain name here, if you have a permanent connection on your LAN.

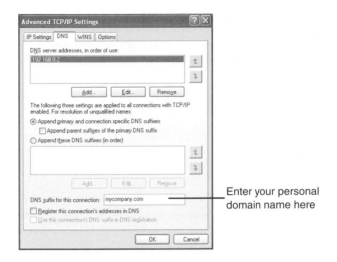

Enter your personal domain name here

7. Click OK when you've made all of the required entries.

The other TCP/IP parameters are used only on larger corporate networks, and when they're appropriate, the network manager will take care of the settings for you—in fact, you probably won't be able to change or even view them.

SETTING YOUR COMPUTER IDENTIFICATION

After you've configured your network, the next step is to make sure that each of the computers on your network is a member of the same domain or workgroup.

If you are part of a Windows domain-type network, your system administrator will give you the information you need to set your computer identification.

NOTE

> Your domain administrator must know about your new computer in advance and must create a *computer account* for it before you try to add your computer to the domain. Just like you have a username and password, so does your computer. Refer to Chapter 3, "Installing Windows XP Professional," for more details.

If you are setting up your own network of Windows computers without Windows 2003 Server, click Start, right-click My Computer, and select Properties. On the Properties dialog, click the Computer Name tab. Check each of the Windows computers on your network. Do they each have a different full computer name and the same workgroup name? If so, you're all set. If not, click the Network ID button, and prepare to answer the wizard's questions.

Click Next on the wizard's first screen, and you are asked to select the option that best describes your computer:

- This computer is part of a business network, and I use it to connect to other computers at work.
- This computer is for home use and is not part of a business network.

Which one you choose makes a significant difference. If you chose the "Home Use" option, the wizard sets up your computer for peer-to-peer networking with the workgroup name "WORKGROUP," and finishes.

NOTE

> If you use the Home Use option, be sure that *all* of your computers are set up the same way, with workgroup name WORKGROUP. Otherwise you'll have trouble working with the other computers on your network.

If you choose the "business" route, Windows configures your computer for a higher standard of security than it will for home use. This choice is described in Chapter 3.

The wizard next asks you to choose from one of the following responses:

- My company uses a network with a domain.
- My company uses a network without a domain.

If you are joining an existing network with a Windows .NET/2000 Server, check With a Domain, but you should consult your network manager first.

Otherwise, if you are building your own network as described in this chapter, select "Without a Domain" and click Next.

The last question asks for a name for the network workgroup. Enter a cute name for your network (using only letters and numbers), such as ACCOUNTING or HOCKEYTOWN, or leave the default setting WORKGROUP in place.

Click Next and then click Finish to complete the setup. You need to let Windows restart your computer if you changed the Workgroup setting.

CAUTION

> You must be sure that every computer on your network uses the same workgroup name if you want them to be able to share files and printers. Be especially careful if you have a mixture of Windows XP Home Edition and XP Professional computers on your network, as the default workgroup names are different for these products.

JOINING A WINDOWS 2003 SERVER/WINDOWS 2000 SERVER DOMAIN NETWORK

This section describes how to add your computer to a Windows 2003 or Windows 2000 domain-type network. If you're lucky, your network administrator will take care of this for you. Alternately, she or he may give you custom-tailored instructions for your network. By all means, use those instructions rather than the generic plan in this section.

Most Windows XP Professional installations will work "out of the box" without the need to install or configure any network components. If your network uses Novell servers, though, you'll need to add either the Microsoft Client for Novell Networks, or the Novell Networks Client software—and unfortunately, only your network administrator can tell you which is appropriate for your organization. Installing additional network components is described earlier in this chapter under "Adding Network Clients, Services, and Protocols."

At the very least, your network administrator will give you three pieces of information:

- The name to be given to your computer.
- The domain name for your network.
- Your network logon name and password.
- Any specific configuration information for the Internet Protocol (TCP/IP). In most cases, it will not be necessary to make any changes in Windows's default settings.

If your computer was connected to the network when you installed Windows XP, and you entered this information then, your network setup is already complete and you can skip ahead to Chapter 17, "Using a Windows XP Network."

If you need to make adjustments to the Internet Protocol settings, at this point you should follow the instructions in under "Manually Configuring Your Network" earlier in this chapter before proceeding.

When you know that the network configuration is correct, use the following procedure to make your computer a member of your network domain:

1. Log on to Windows with a Computer Administrator-type account.
2. Click Start, right-click My Computer, and select Properties. On the Properties dialog, select the Computer Name tab.
3. Click the Network ID button and click Next on the wizard's first screen.
4. Select This computer is part of a business network, and I use it to connect to other computers at work, and then click Next.
5. Select My company uses a network with a domain, and then click Next twice.
6. Enter your network login name, password, and the network domain name, as shown in Figure 16.15. This information will have been supplied by your network administrator. Then, click Next.

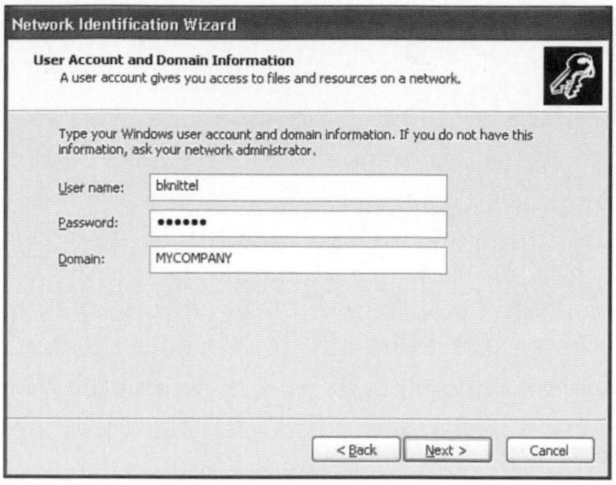

Figure 16.15
To join a domain network, you must enter a domain logon name, password, and the domain name.

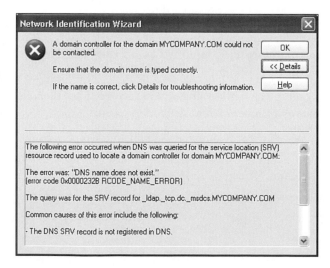

7. You might be asked to enter your computer's name and its domain name. This information will also have been supplied by your network admin. If you're asked, enter the computer and domain names provided, then click Next.

   You also might be prompted for a domain Administrator account name and password. If this occurs the network administrator will have to assist you.

8. You should finally get the message "Welcome to the *xxx* domain." Close the Properties dialog and allow Windows to restart.

   If an error message appears instead, click Details to view the detailed explanation of the problem, as shown in Figure 16.16. Report this information to your network administrator for resolution. The problem could be in your computer or in the network itself.

Figure 16.16
If an error occurs when you attempt to join the domain, this dialog will provide the details you'll need to report to your network administrator.

When your computer has been joined to the domain and restarted, the Windows XP Welcome screen will no longer appear, and you'll need to use the old-style logon system to sign on. To log on, type Ctrl+Alt+Del, and then enter your account name, password, and domain name. You can specify an alternate domain name by entering your user name and account together this way: "*myaccount@domain*".

NOTE

> If your computer is disconnected from the network or you want to install new hardware, you can log on using a *local account.* Select the computer's name rather than your network domain name, and log on using the Administrator account or a Computer Administrator account.
>
> For more information about local accounts, see Chapter 28, "Managing Users."

16

NETWORK SECURITY

Now that you have a LAN—even if it's just a simple peer-to-peer LAN—you should be worried about network security and hackers. Why? Because you'll certainly be connecting to the Internet, even if only intermittently, and when you do, you risk exposing your network to the entire world. These risks are not as far-fetched as you might think.

Refer to Chapter 21, "Network Security," to find out what risks you'll be exposed to and what you can do to protect your LAN. If you use Internet Connection Sharing or a connection sharing router, you're in pretty good shape, but in any case please go through Chapter 21 very carefully. It is *very* important.

CHECKING OUT THE NEIGHBORHOOD

Your network is finally ready to go. After you have configured, connected, and perhaps restarted each of your computers, double-click My Network Places on your Start menu. If you are *not* part of a Windows domain, select View Workgroup Computers. If your network is up and running, you should see one icon for every computer you've connected, as shown in Figure 16.17.

 If you don't see other computers in the View workgroup computers window, see "View Workgroup Computers Shows No Other Computers" in the "Troubleshooting" section at the end of this chapter, and read Chapter 22, "Troubleshooting Your Network."

If you are part of a Windows domain, select Entire Network, Entire Contents, Microsoft Windows Network, and click your own domain's icon to see the list of connected computers.

Congratulations: Your network is up and running! But before you continue on to Chapter 17, "Using a Windows XP Network," there's one unpleasant task left: backups. I really suggest doing this now.

Figure 16.17
When your Workgroup network is up and running, you should see at least one icon for every other computer you've set up.

INSTALL AND CONFIGURE BACKUP SOFTWARE

If you are using your LAN for business purposes, you really should have a good backup system to protect your business data and your investment in setup and configuration. As my friend Richard Katz says, "If you don't back up, you may have to back up a long way."

If you don't already have one, install a tape backup unit and, preferably, a good commercial backup software package on at least one main computer on your network. Follow the instructions on the software to configure it to perform automatic backups.

The Windows backup utility is *almost* adequate for business use, but you really should have something that is convenient, that lets you save different backup configurations, and that lends itself to automatic scheduling.

Backups should ideally be made automatically every day. Typically, I suggest using a schedule that looks something like this:

- Friday: Full backup—entire hard drive, reset "archive" flag. Use at least two different Friday tapes in rotation.

- Monday through Thursday: Differential backups, backing up every file that is new or changed since the last full backup. Use a different tape for each day of the week. A Saturday backup is optional.

Keep your full backup tapes offsite.

Configure the backup software to exclude certain files, if you can:

~*.*   Any file starting with a tilde

*.tmp Any file with extension .tmp

*.bak Any backup file

.ff	Fast-find index files
.ci	IIS Index Server index files

Be sure to test your backup system at least once a month by viewing a tape directory or by restoring a single file from the tape. This will not only ensure that your backup system is functioning properly, but will maintain your skill in operating the backup-and-restore software.

Windows Backup is discussed in more detail in Chapter 29, "Managing the Hard Disk."

BRIDGING TWO NETWORK TYPES WITH WINDOWS XP

Windows XP has a feature new to Windows: the ability to connect or *bridge* two different network types through software. This can eliminate the need for buying a hardware device to connect two disparate networks. Figure 16.18 shows an example of what bridging can do. In the figure, one Windows XP computer serves as a bridge between an Ethernet LAN and a Phoneline LAN.

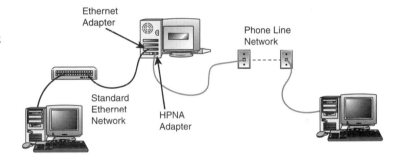

Figure 16.18
Bridging a Phoneline and Ethernet network with Windows XP. Computers on either network can communicate as if they were directly connected.

Bridging is similar to *routing*, but it's more appropriate for small LANs because it's easier to configure and doesn't require different sets of IP addresses on each network segment. Technically, bridging occurs at the physical level of the network protocol stack, so it forwards broadcasts and packets of all protocol types, including TCP/IP, IPX/SPX, AppleTalk, and so on.

→ To learn more about protocol stacks, **see** "The OSI Model," **p. 476**.

To enable bridging in your Windows XP computer, install and configure two or more network adapters, as described under "Installing Multiple Network Adapters" earlier in this chapter. Don't, however, worry about setting up the Internet Protocol (TCP/IP) parameters for either of the adapters. An IEEE-1394 (FireWire) adapter may be bridged as well. Then

1. View the connection icons by clicking Start, Control Panel, Network and Internet Connections, Network Connections.

2. Select the icons you wish to bridge by clicking on the first, holding down the Shift key, and clicking on the second.

3. Right-click on one of the icons and select Bridge Networks.

4. A new icon will appear as in Figure 16.19. Select the new bridge icon, and if you want, rename it appropriately, for example "Ethernet to Phoneline."

Figure 16.19
The Network Bridge icon appears when you have bridged two network connections together.

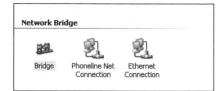

5. Double-click the bridge icon. Select Internet Protocol (TCP/IP) and configure your computer's TCP/IP settings if necessary. You must do this, as any TCP/IP settings for the original two adapters are lost.

When you've created a bridge, your two network adapters function as one and share one IP address, so Microsoft disables the "network properties" of the individual network adapters. You must configure your computer's network properties with the bridge's icon.

Remember that the connection between the two networks depends on the computer with the bridge being powered on.

You can remove the bridge later on by right-clicking the network connections and clicking Remove from Bridge. When you've removed both connections, you can right-click the bridge icon and delete it.

TROUBLESHOOTING

CAN'T DRILL THROUGH WALLS OR CEILINGS

My lease or the physical limitations of my building prevent me from drilling through walls or the ceiling to install network cabling.

In this case, you can install wires along baseboards, around doors, and so on. It's not as pretty, but because network wiring is low voltage, it's not risky to do so as it is with power wiring. (My office has a cable shamefully strung through a skylight, across the ceiling, and into a closet.) You also can use products called *wiring channels* to conceal the wires run along baseboards and rubber guards to protect them where they might be trod upon. You can find these products in the hardware store or in business product catalogs. Of course, you can also consider using a wireless network.

HUB LIGHTS DO NOT COME ON

One or more UTP hub link lights do not come on when the associated computers are connected.

The problem lies in one of the cables between the computer and the hub. Which one is it? To find out, do the following:

1. Move the computer right next to the hub. You can leave the keyboard, mouse, and monitor behind. Just plug in the computer, turn it on, and use a commercially manufactured or known-to-be-working patch cable to connect the computer to the hub. If the light doesn't come on regardless of which hub connection socket you use, you probably have a bad network card.

2. If you were using any patch cables when you first tried to get the computer connected, test them using the same computer and hub socket. This trick may identify a bad cable.

3. If the LAN card, hub, and patch cables are all working, then the problem is in whatever is left, which would be your in-wall wiring. Check the connectors for proper crimping, and check that the wire pairs are correctly wired end-to-end. You might have to use a cable analyzer if you can't spot the problem by eye. These devices cost about $75. You connect a "transmitter" box to one end of your cabling, and a "receiver" at the other. The receiver has four LEDs that blink in a 1-2-3-4 sequence if your wiring is correct.

VIEW WORKGROUP COMPUTERS SHOWS NO OTHER COMPUTERS

The View Workgroup Computers display doesn't show any other computers when I boot up.

If you've eliminated the network card and any UTP wiring as the source of the problem, you can use Windows own built-in diagnostic tools to help. Here's how:

1. The first thing to check is whether the LAN hardware itself is working. Check the Device Manager to be sure that your network card is operating properly. Be sure you're using an approved network card and have up-to-date drivers for it. If the Device Manager gives you a message that reads The Card Is Not Functioning, you almost certainly have the wrong drivers. Check with the vendor to see whether up-to-date Windows XP or Windows 2000 drivers are available for you to download over the Internet.

2. If you have a UTP LAN, make sure all the expected indicators on your hub are lit.

3. On each computer, start a command prompt. Then type the command `ipconfig`.

4. When you see IP addresses listed, be sure each computer has a different IP address. They should all be similar but different. For example, they might look like 209.203.104.x, where the x is different for each computer. If not, check the Internet Protocol properties on each computer to be sure each was correctly configured.

5. Type `ping x.x.x.x`, where x.x.x.x is the computer's own IP address. It should have four "replies," which look like this:

   ```
   Reply from x.x.x.x: bytes=32 time<10msec TTL=128
   ```

   If not, remove, reinstall, and reconfigure the TCP/IP protocol.

6. Type **ping x.x.x.y**, where x.x.x.y is one of the IP addresses of the other computers on your LAN. If the replies don't come back, your network hardware is at fault. Check the wiring as follows:

   On a 10BASE-T or 100BASE-T LAN, see whether an "activity" LED flashes on your network card when you type a ping command. If it doesn't, the problem is your network card. If it does, you might have to get a cable testing device to find out what's wrong with the wiring. (A professional installer will have one—it's time to call for help!)

   Another possibility with combination 10/100BASE-T network cards is that the cards might not have decided to use the correct speed. You can force them to use one speed or the other in the Device Manager by viewing the network card's Properties page and selecting the Advanced tab. This tab usually has a Link Speed/Duplex Mode property. Set all the cards to the appropriate value for the type of hub you are using.

7. If the ping commands work between computers, be sure that each computer's Network Identification has the same workgroup name. This information is on My Computer's Properties page.

8. If none of these steps help, see whether the Event Log has any helpful error messages. To do so, right-click My Computer, select Manage, and view the logs under the System Tool Event Viewer.

9. Finally, you can use a diagnostic provided with Windows. Click Start, Control Panel, Network and Internet Connections. In the Troubleshooters panel, select Network Diagnostics.

For more troubleshooting tips, see Chapter 22, "Troubleshooting Your Win XP Network."

TIPS FROM THE WINDOWS PROS: GRASSROOTS NETWORKING

Despite their becoming so inexpensive and simple to install, networks are extremely complex systems "under the hood." It's hard enough to solve the problems that creep up from time to time in an existing, functional LAN, but new LANs are worse because *everything* is untested, and a little problem in any one part can mess up the whole thing. Where do you start looking for the problem?

The answer is an exercise in delayed gratification! It's exciting to see all the new equipment, parts, and cables all over the place, but as much as I'd like to hook it all up and see what happens when I turn on the switch for the first time, I've found that it's best to start small.

Whenever I build a new network, I put two computers side-by-side on one desk. They can be two regular computers for a peer-to-peer network, or a Windows 2003 Server and a regular workstation for a Server-based network. I wire them together in the simplest possible way, usually with two short patch cables and a hub.

This technique gives me the smallest possible, least complex system to start with. It's much easier to solve a networking problem when you can see both computers' screens at the same time.

When I have these two computers completely configured and tested, I start adding components one at a time: a network printer, an Internet connection, a tape backup system, an uninterruptible power supply, and so on.

When something goes wrong during this technique, I know it must have something to do with the last component I added, and I'm not searching for a needle in a haystack.

Finally, when I have all the parts working, I take the two computers to their final locations and see whether they still work with the real-world wiring. Then I add workstations to the network one at a time. Attaching them this way is not as much fun as assembling the whole thing at once, but I've found that staying up all night diagnosing problems on a new network is even less fun.

16

CHAPTER 17

USING A WINDOWS XP NETWORK

In this chapter

WINDOWS XP WAS MADE TO NETWORK

Aside from finally finding a use for the right button on the mouse, almost all the advancements in the Windows platform over the last 10 years have been made in the area of networking. Back in Windows version 3.1, network software was an expensive add-on product—an afterthought—cumbersome to install and manage. Not so anymore! Networking is built right into the heart of Windows XP, such that Windows is hardly even *happy* without a network attached.

Okay, I'm exaggerating. But the truth is, Windows XP's personality does change for the better when it's connected to a network, and the change depends on the type of network to which it's attached. In this chapter, I'll show you how to use Windows XP networking, and share tips for making the most of whatever type of network you have.

In Windows XP, using files and printers on the network is exactly the same as using files and printers on your own hard drive. The "look and feel" are identical. The only new tasks you have to learn are how to find resources shared by others and how to make your own computer's resources available to others on the network.

I'll use the word *resource* frequently in this chapter. When I say *resource*, I mean a shared folder or printer on someone else's computer, which you can access through the LAN or the Internet. *The American Heritage Dictionary* defines a resource as "an available supply that can be drawn upon when needed." That's actually a perfect description of a network resource: It's there for you to use—provided you can find it, and provided you have permission.

The ways of finding resources and managing permissions change depending on the type of network you have. I talked about these network models in detail in Chapter 15, "Overview of Windows XP Networking," but here's a quick review:

- **Workgroup Network (Peer to Peer)**—A workgroup network, also called a peer-to-peer network, does not have a central server computer to perform user/password verification. On this network, each computer manages its own user list and security system. Home users and small offices usually use workgroup networks. Networks mixing Windows computers with Macintosh, Linux, and Unix computers also fall into this category.

- **Domain Network**—A domain-based network uses Windows .NET/2000/NT Server to provide a centralized user security database. All computers on the network look to a *domain controller*, or primary server, for usernames, group memberships, and passwords.

NOTE

> From now on, I'll write "Windows 2003 Server" when I'm referring to Windows 2003 Server, Windows 2000 Server, or Windows NT 4.0 Server. I know it's confusing. Why Microsoft can't pick a name and stick to it, I'll never understand.

- **Active Directory Network**—Active Directory (AD) adds a distributed, global user directory to a domain network. It not only provides a user and password database, but it also provides a way for management permissions to be delegated and controlled; this capability is very important in large, spread-out organizations.

- **Remote Network**—Windows XP Professional functions very well on a standalone computer, but it also lets you connect to and disconnect from networks, or get remote access by modem, WAN (wide area network), or the Internet. Windows provides special services to help you deal with this "on again/off again" network relationship.

Most network functions are identical regardless of your network type. The following are some notable differences:

- On a domain network, the administrator can set up *roaming profiles* so that your settings, preferences, My Documents folder, and so on are centrally stored on the network, and are available to you on any computer on your LAN or even at other network sites.

- Active Directory gives you added search functions to find users and printers on your network. These search functions appear as added icons and menu choices that non-AD network computers don't have.

- In a domain or Active Directory network, the network administrator may use *policy* functions to restrict the network management features you can use. For example, you might not have the option to map network drives or add network protocols in such a strictly controlled LAN. Rather than rouse up a protest for computer freedom, though, be thankful that you'll have less maintenance and futzing to do yourself.

N O T E

> I'm already tired of typing *Active Directory* over and over, so as I go along, I'll sometimes abbreviate it as *AD*–thought I should warn you!

Members of a Windows network with AD have some options—menu choices and buttons in dialog boxes, for example—that workgroup network users don't have. If you are using a workgroup network, don't feel left out. Because a workgroup typically has fewer than 10 computers, the searching and corporate-style management functions provided by AD simply aren't necessary.

In this chapter, I'll try to point out the differences you may encounter depending on your network type. But it's difficult to generalize about AD networks because AD's policy-based restrictions mean that some options might not appear where I say they will. If you are on a domain or Active Directory network and can't find an option I show you, call your network manager to see whether its use has been restricted.

17

WORKGROUP VERSUS DOMAIN NETWORKING

On a Windows domain-based network (that is, a network managed by a Windows NT, 2000, or 2003 Server), user accounts are set up on the domain servers. Domain users are known by every computer on the network. When you and the network managers are establishing who can and can't have access to files, you can choose users and groups from the entire list of all users in your organization. You can grant access to specific individuals, departments, sites, or other groupings even though those users might be scattered around the globe.

In a workgroup network, however, it's a different story. Each computer in the workgroup has its own separate list of usernames. This makes it more difficult to be sure that a user on one computer can be granted access to another. I'll talk more about managing multiple users on a network in Chapter 28. For now, though, I can offer you this bit of advice:

TIP FROM

Bob & Brian

> You'll find it much easier to set up and use a workgroup network if you set up the same list of users on each your computers. Each user should have a unique password, but it should be the same on every computer.

TRADITIONAL VERSUS WEB SHARING

In Windows XP, you can actually get at shared folders and printers in two ways: through traditional LAN methods or via the World Wide Web. This last method shouldn't come as much of a surprise these days; I think even washing machines come with a Web interface now.

The traditional methods are based on the Microsoft Networking protocol (called NetBT, or NetBIOS over TCP/IP, also called SMB, or Server Message Block).

The new Internet technology for file sharing is called WebDAV (Web Distributed Authoring and Versioning) or Web Sharing, and the new Internet-based printer sharing is called Internet Printing Protocol (IPP). They're both based on the Hypertext Transfer Protocol (HTTP) that most Web sites use, which means that file and print operations can be carried out safely across the Internet, even through corporate firewalls. They require Web server software on the computer that is sharing the files or printers—for example, a computer in your office.

With Web sharing, you can work with files and folders shared by a remote computer just as you would with files found in My Computer, Explorer, or traditional network shared folders. Using IPP Printing, you can connect to a shared printer over the Internet and use it exactly as you would a local or LAN-based printer.

Although the "look and feel" are virtually identical to traditional LAN sharing, the Internet-based methods are not as speedy as ordinary LAN sharing, so they're meant only for remote users who need to get at shared files and printers "at their home base."

There is another significant difference. Traditional networking provides *file and record locking* to mediate access to a file when multiple users try to read and write data at the same time. Database programs like Microsoft Access depend on this. Web Sharing doesn't permit concurrent access, so only one person can modify a given file at a time.

WHAT'S IN A NAME?

Virtually the only difference you'll notice between local and networked files is their names. If you've found the use of the backslash character to be an annoying and peculiar convention, you'd better hang on to your hat because slashes of all persuasions are in your future in a big way.

Let's look at the names of shared network folders and files. Each computer on your network (or on an intranet or the Internet) has a name, and every folder or printer that is offered up for shared use on the network must be given a share name as well. For example, if I want to give officemates the use of my business documents, I might share my hard disk's folder c:\documents and give that folder the share name "docs."

NOTE

> It might seem confusing to use a different name for the share name than for the folder. The reason for this is that whereas folder names can be very long and can contain spaces in them, share names should be 12 characters or less and have no spaces. This isn't very user friendly, but it's the way it is.

Figure 17.1 shows the relationship between my computer named Ambon, its hard disk, and the shared folder, from the point of view of another computer named Bali.

Figure 17.1
Sharing makes a folder, or even a whole hard drive, accessible to the LAN. Ambon shares folder \documents as "docs," and Bali can use this folder by its network name \\\ambon \\docs.

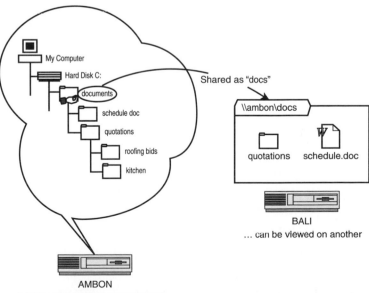

A folder shared from one computer...

THE UNC NAMING CONVENTION

I can specify the location of a file on my hard drive with a drive and path name, like this:

```
c:\documents\roofing bids.xls
```

A user on another computer can refer to this same file using a syntax called the *Universal Naming Convention*, or UNC:

```
\\ambon\docs\roofing bids.xls
```

The double backslash indicates that the name "ambon" is the name of a computer on the LAN rather than the name of a folder in the top directory of the local hard disk. "Docs" is the share name of the folder, and everything past that specifies the path and file relative to that shared folder.

If the computer whose files you want to use is on a LAN using Active Directory, or is part of a distant company network, you may also specify the remote computer name more completely, as in the following:

```
\\ambon.mycompany.com\docs\roofing bids.xls
```

Or, if you know only the remote computer's IP network address (such as if you're connecting to the remote computer with Dial-Up Networking), you can even use a notation like this:

```
\\192.168.0.10\docs\roofing bids.xls
```

No matter which way you specify the remote computer, Windows finds it and locates its shared folder "docs."

NOTE

> Elsewhere in this chapter, I'll use UNC names like **\\server\folder** as a generic sort of name. By "server" I mean the name of a computer that's sharing a folder. It doesn't have to be a Windows 2003 Server—on a peer-to-peer network, there won't usually even be one! It can be any computer on your network. You'll need to use your network's actual computer names and shared folder names.

Shared printers are also given share names and specified by their UNC path. For example, if I share my HP LaserJet 4V printer, I might give it the share name *HPLaser*, and it will be known on the network as \\ambon\HPLaser. Here, it's not a folder, but rather a printer, and Windows keeps track of the type of resource.

NAMING FOR WEB-BASED SHARING

The new Internet-compatible technologies are based on the World Wide Web's Hypertext Transfer Protocol (HTTP) and use the Web's traditional forward slash rather than the backslash.

A Web folder name looks just like a standard Web URL:

```
http://ambon/docs
```

or

```
http://ambon.mycompany.com/docs
```

When you open a Web folder, instead of just displaying a listing of files, as it might if you visited a regular Web page, Windows displays the files in a standard Explorer folder view. You can do anything to the files that you would do in a normal folder: delete, rename, drag files in and out, and open and save files with applications, provided you have the appropriate permissions.

IPP printers shared by Windows 2003 Server and XP Professional use the built-in Web server on those operating systems, and a similar naming scheme, but I'll wait until the section "Using Other IPP Printers" later in this chapter to get into the messy details about that. If you're connecting to a Windows 2000 or XP computer from across the Internet, it's enough to view the "printers" page by typing

```
http://ambon.mycompany.com/printers
```

This allows the Web server software to take care of all the work for you.

MY NETWORK PLACES

How do you find the folders and printers floating around out there somewhere in the Network Twilight Zone? If you've been using Windows for any length of time, you may have guessed by now that you can do the job in several ways.

The most straightforward way is through the My Network Places display. It appears as a choice on the Other Places list of My Computer after you install any network components in Windows XP and it's the starting place for finding network resources.

My Network Places gives you a way to browse, search, and select "favorite" network resources, including shared folders, Web pages, FTP sites, and so on. To open My Network Places, view My Computer, and then select My Network Places from the Other Places menu.

TIP FROM

Bob & Brian

> If you find yourself using My Network Places frequently, you can add it to your Start Menu. Just right-click Start, select Properties, and Customize. Select the Advanced tab and scroll the Start menu items list down to My Network Places. Check it and click OK. You also can drag a shortcut to My Network Places from your Start menu onto the desktop or the quick launch bar.

When you select My Network Places from the My Computer window, you get the "folder" view of My Network Places, as shown in Figure 17.2.

Figure 17.2
My Network Places is the starting point for searching and opening network resources. On a peer-to-peer network, Windows displays icons for all shared folders.

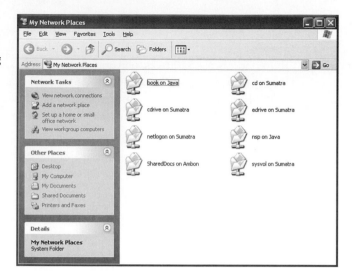

My Network Places is meant to be a place to collect shortcuts to commonly used remote network resources like shared folders, Web Folders, FTP sites, and the like. When you first install Windows, My Network Places doesn't have any of your personalized shortcuts, of course. On a workgroup network, by default it will display an icon for each shared folder on your network. (This is controlled in Explorer by selecting Tools, Folder Options. On the View tab, check Automatically Search For Network Folders and Printers.)

On a domain network, you'll have to browse through the network or ask your network administrator to identify shared network folders for you. I'll show you how to browse later in this chapter under "Exploring and Searching the Network."

My Network Places organizes your network resource shortcuts, and also lists several commonly used tasks:

- **View Network Connections**—Displays and configures your dial-up connections or LAN adapter.

- **Add a network place**—Opens a wizard to create network or Internet shortcuts. I'll discuss the Add Network Place Wizard later in this chapter.

- **Set up a home or small office network**—Runs the Network Setup Wizard. (For more information, see "Using the Network Setup Wizard" in Chapter 16).

On a peer-to-peer-network, there is an additional choice:

- **View Workgroup Computers**—Provides a quick way to view the list of computers in your workgroup.

I suggest that you browse through My Network Places to check out the computers and resources on your network.

TIP FROM

Bob & Brian

> You can drag shortcuts to any of the icons in My Network Places to your desktop for convenience.

USING SHARED FOLDERS

File sharing lets users on a network browse through and use files and folders, no matter on which computer's hard drive the files actually reside. The "look and feel" is exactly the same.

Let's say I want to share a folder named C:\bookstuff. I have to give it a *share name* by which it'll be known on the network. For its share name, I might give the folder the share name "book," as shown in Figure 17.3.

Figure 17.3
Sharing a folder on my computer.

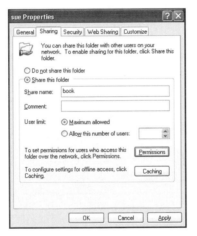

When other network users browse through their My Network Places display, they will see that Book is a shared folder attached to my computer. It looks like any folder on their own computers.

If they open it, they'll see the same folders and file listings I see in c:\bookstuff, as illustrated in Figure 17.4. The information about filenames, dates, and contents is sent over the network. If anyone drags a file into this folder, all other users will see it appear there. If anyone edits a file in this shared folder, the next time another user opens the file, they'll get the changed version. That's network file sharing in a nutshell; the rest is just a matter of details.

On home and small office workgroup networks, you may not even need to go to the trouble to set up shared folders, because Windows automatically makes each computer's "Shared Documents" folder available over the network, as shown in Figure 17.5

Figure 17.4
A network user examining the shared folder (left) sees the same files the owner of the shared folder sees (right).

Figure 17.5
Your computer's Shared Documents folder is shared with the network by default. You can view other computers' Shared Documents in My Network Places.

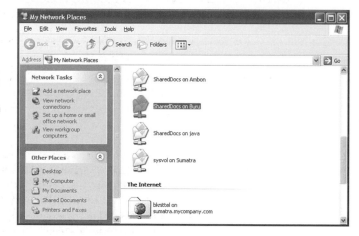

TIP FROM

Bob & Brian

If you put files into your Shared Documents folder, not only will other users of your computer be able to view and use these files, so will other users on your network.

Likewise, you can get to other computers' Shared Documents by looking for folders named "SharedDocs" in My Network Places.

This is a pretty intuitive way to organize things, and you might not need to set up or use any other shared folders.

EXPLORING AND SEARCHING THE NETWORK

Of course, before you can use a network resource, you have to know where to find it. I suggest that you take a moment right now to get familiar with your network.

If you are a member of a workgroup or home network, you can look through your network for shared folders and printers by exploring in the following areas in turn:

- View My Computer and select My Network Places in the Other Places list. On a workgroup network, by default, Windows will automatically display an icon for each shared folder on each of your networked computers. (This can be enabled and disabled by selecting View, Folder Options. On the View tab, check or uncheck Automatically Search for Network Folders and Printers.) You can open these icons to view and use these folders just like the folders on your own hard drive.

- On a workgroup network, you can select View Workgroup Computers in the Network Tasks list to peruse all the computers with the same workgroup name as yours. Opening the computer icons displays any folders and printers they're sharing.

- Select Entire Network or Microsoft Windows Network from the Other Places list to view all the workgroups or domains on your LAN. You can double-click any of these to see the computers in that workgroup. Opening the computer icons displays any folders and printers they're sharing.

If you're on a domain-type network with Active Directory Network, you'll have an additional item in Network Tasks called Search Active Directory.

I'll discuss searching later in this chapter. The network searching tool can help you locate printers, computers, people, and files anywhere in your organization.

If you'll be using any shared folders, Web sites, FTP sites, or Web folders repeatedly, add them to My Network Places for a quick return later. You can use the Add a Network Place Wizard to do so, or you can just drag a shortcut from Explorer's Address bar onto your desktop or other folder, as shown in Figure 17.6.

For example, if you visit a particular FTP site frequently for program or driver updates, highlight the FTP site's name in Explorer and drag the folder icon in the Address bar to your desktop. Release the mouse button when the shortcut arrow appears.

→ To learn how to use the Add A Network Place wizard, **see** "Adding Network Places," **p. 561**.

Figure 17.6
You can drag the icon from Explorer's Address bar to the desktop or to another folder to make an instant shortcut.

You also can explore your network from the Folders view of Explorer, as shown in Figure 17.7. (You can bring up the Folders view in any Explorer window by clicking the Folders button.) This view lets you see that your network is structured like the folders of your hard drive.

Figure 17.7
The Folders view in Explorer lets you browse through your network. This view shows the shared folder "cdrive" on the computer named Sumatra.

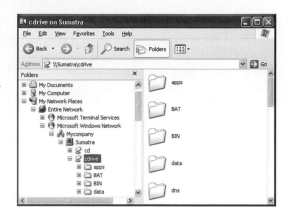

As you can see, within Entire Network is a list of network types, which contain workgroups and domains, which contain computers, which contain shared resources, which contain folders and files.

UNDERSTANDING SHARED RESOURCES

If you do a bit of poking around, you might find that some computers share folders that may not make much sense. Server computers on a domain network, in particular, offer some network resources to member computers that are used by automatic services or for maintenance. Table 17.1 shows some of the shared resources you might see and what they do.

TABLE 17.1   TYPICAL ADMINISTRATIVE FOLDERS SHARED ON A WINDOWS 2003 SERVER

Folder	Description
CertEnroll	Contains data used to provide Security Certificates to member computers, if your network has its own Certificate Authority. This share is used only by the Certificate Wizard.
NETLOGON	Used only by the domain login system.
Published	Contains installation packages for published and assigned application software, which may be available to or forced into your computer. When using the Add/Remove Software Control Panel via the network, files are automatically retrieved from the Published folder.
SYSVOL	Used only by the domain login system.
Printers	Mirrors the computer's Printers folder; can be used by an administrator to install or control printers across the LAN.
Scheduled Tasks	Mirrors the computer's Scheduled Task list; can be used by an administrator for remote maintenance.

TABLE 17.1   CONTINUED

Folder	Description
ADMIN$	Used by remote administration software
IPC$	Used for remote procedure calls, a network software system built into Windows.
print$	Shared folder containing print drivers for the computer's shared printers.
FxsSrvCp$	Shared Fax service data.
C$, D$, and so on	Entire hard drives, shared for administrators' use.

NOTE

> Share names ending with $ usually are hidden from being displayed in Explorer's browsing lists.

17

Of these folders, only Printers and Scheduled Tasks are of interest, and then only to administrators. The operating system uses the others, which should not be modified.

Some computers will have a SharedDocs folder. This is the computer's Shared Documents folder as presented to the network. Any other folders were shared by the computer's users.

SEARCHING THE NETWORK

You can locate shared folders or printers by exploring My Network Places, or you can use the search links under Start, Search. Users with Active Directory at their disposal have more searching choices than those without Active Directory.

You can get to the search tools by clicking Start, Search. Domain network users with Active Directory can also get to the network searching tools by viewing My Network Places and clicking Search Active Directory.

The Search functions let Windows explore resources on your network just as efficiently as it searches your hard disk.

SEARCHING FOR PRINTERS

Active Directory networks provide a very powerful printer search tool. In a large corporate network, hundreds or thousands of network printers may be scattered over a large area. Search for Printers lets an AD network user find just the right type of printer using a powerful query form, which I'll show you in "Finding and Installing a Printer in the Directory" later in this chapter.

SEARCHING FOR COMPUTERS

If you want to quickly locate shared resources on a computer whose name you already know, with or without AD, select Computers or People, A Computer on the Network. You can enter either the full computer name or a fragment of its name. Windows lists the matching computers, as in Figure 17.8.

Figure 17.8
When you're searching for computers by their network names, you can enter full or partial names. Select one of the matching computer icons to explore its shared contents.

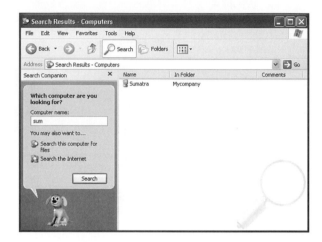

You can explore any of the listed computers to view its shared folders or printers; if you delve into the shared folders, you can open or copy the available files as you find them.

SEARCHING FOR PEOPLE

The Windows search tool lets you locate people by name or by e-mail address. It can look in your personal address book (the one used by Outlook e-mail), in various Internet directories, or, on a domain-type network, in the Active Directory.

To search, click Start, Search, Computers or People, People In Your Address Book. The Find People dialog box will appear, as shown in Figure 17.9

Figure 17.9
Using Find People, you can search by name or e-mail address in the Active Directory or in any of several Internet Directory services.

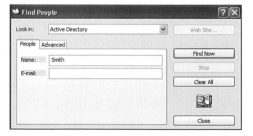

Choose a directory under Look In. You can select from several choices, including Address Book, Active Directory, Bigfoot Internet Directory, and WhoWhere Internet Directory. (I presume that the commercial directory companies have to pay to be placed in the list you see, so the list might change over time.)

Using the Advanced tab of Find People (shown in Figure 17.10), you can perform a more specific search.

Figure 17.10
Advanced searching properties let you specify multiple searching criteria.

To perform an advanced search from the Start menu, follow these steps:

1. Choose Start, Search, Computers or People, People In Your Address Book, and select the Advanced tab.

2. Select the first drop-down list (Name is the default value), and choose a criterion from the list. The searchable attributes include First Name, Last Name, Email, and Organization.

3. Under the second drop-down list (contains is the default value), select a comparison type. The choices are Contains, Is, Starts With, Ends With, or Sounds Like.

4. In the third box, which is empty by default, enter the name or address, or a fragment.

5. Choose Add to add a condition; highlight a condition and click Remove to delete a condition.

6. Enter more filtering items if you want, or select Find Now to begin the search.

The two search tabs on the Find People dialog operate independently of one another, so selections on one tab do not influence searches made with the other.

You can open any entries returned by the search to view comprehensive information about the user, as shown in Figure 17.11. The information is spread out over five tabs:

- **General**—contains name, address and telephone number.

- **Address**—contains complete postal address information.

- **Business**—shows job title, department, the person's manager, and any managed employees.

- **NetMeeting**—indicates direct connection information for NetMeeting chat/voice/videoconferencing, and includes a Call Now button.

- **Digital IDs**—lists any digital e-mail-signing certificates on store for the user; they contain public keys that can be used to encrypt or validate e-mail messages.

Figure 17.11
Find People returns information about the user.

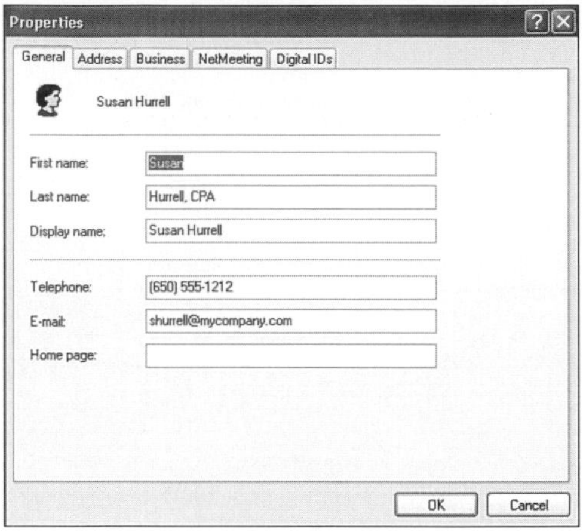

NOTE

You can change and update any of the information for your own account made available for user-level editing by the domain administrator. You also might be able to edit the information for employees you manage, if this is permitted on your network.

SEARCHING FOR FILES OR FOLDERS

When you use Windows Search to look for files and folders, you can tell Windows to look on the network as well as on your own computer.

When entering your search request, under Look In, choose Browse. In the Browse for Folder dialog box, open My Network Places. You can select Entire network if you want Windows to scan every shared folder on every computer of your network. You also can dig down to a specific computer or shared folder to narrow things down. (On the other hand, if you don't know where to look, it's nice to know that Windows can do the schlepping for you.)

As Windows finds matching files, it displays them along with the computer name on which the file was found, as shown in Figure 17.12.

You can view or open the files you've found on the network just as you can files you've found on your own computer.

On an Active Directory network, the domain administrator may choose to list, or *publish*, some shared folders in the directory; they might contain important resources that the company wanted to make widely accessible and easy to find. See "Advanced Active Directory Searching" later in the chapter for more information.

Figure 17.12
When searching the network for files or folders Windows displays the names of the computers on which the matches were found.

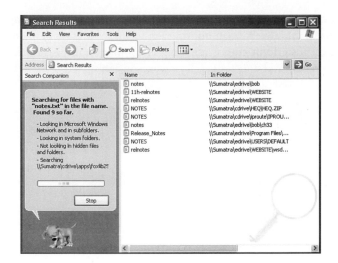

If you are trying to find a particular shared folder, and it has not been explicitly published in the directory, you're out of luck; there's no other way to find it besides browsing.

TIP FROM

Bob
& Brian

> If you have Administrative privileges on a network computer (that is, you are logged in as Administrator, or an equivalent account, and your administrator credentials are valid on the remote computer), you can have Explorer view the special shared folder C$. C$ displays the entire contents of the computer's hard drive. Windows automatically shares a network computer's entire hard disk for use by administrators.

What can you do with the contents of shared folders, assuming you have the appropriate access rights? Just as with folders on your system, you can

- Cut, copy, or paste files and subfolders
- Open documents for viewing, printing, and editing
- Create shortcuts to files and documents on the remote drive or other remote drives

Remember, using Windows XP's Search tools and specifying what you're looking for can be much faster than simply browsing to the location you need, especially if you're not certain where the file or folder is located.

ADVANCED ACTIVE DIRECTORY SEARCHING

I've already shown you how to find users and computers on an Active Directory network, and have promised to talk about finding printers shortly.

I'd like to point out that the Active Directory contains information on many more objects than just users, computers, and printers. It includes shared folders, organizational units, certificate templates, containers (business groupings), foreign security principals, remote storage services, RPC services (used for advanced client/server software applications), and trusted domains. It can also contain information for other objects defined by your own organization. Most of this information is used only by domain administrators to configure Windows networks over vast distances; however, you can search for anything and can specify your qualifications based on more than 100 different criteria.

To make an advanced search, open My Network Places, and select Search Active Directory. The AD search tool will appears, as shown in Figure 17.13. You can select various search categories in the list after the word Find.

Figure 17.13
Using the advanced Active Directory search tool, you can use a simplified form for any of several categories of directory objects, or use the Advanced tab to construct queries using any of the objects fields.

Using the advanced search tool, you can use a quick form-based search for any of the most useful objects, similar to the forms you saw when you searched for users. You can also use the Advanced tab to build specific queries such as "Last Name Starts with xxx." But this is the full-blown search system, and here you'll have 53 fields to choose from when searching for users, everything from Assistant to ZIP code: A to Z, if you need. For example, Figure 17.14 shows what to do if you need to know who belongs to a particular international ISDN telephone number. For advanced searches, you can select various search fields and conditions (such as Last Name, Starts With), and enter values to match. You must click Add to add each search criterion to the search list. Add as many fields as necessary, and then click Find Now.

Figure 17.14
Advanced searches let you dig into the most arcane information imaginable, but where else would you find information like this?

If you choose Custom Search, you have the whole gamut of fields to choose from, and in the Advanced tab, you can enter LDAP (Lightweight Directory Access Protocol) queries directly for submission to the AD service, as shown in Figure 17.15. This is the native query syntax for Active Directory, and it's available here mostly for system debugging. (Strangely, in Custom Search, any qualifiers set in the form-based search are applied along with a manually entered LDAP query; you should be sure to clear out the form if you are not likely to need LDAP directly.)

Figure 17.15
Querying the Active Directory Server directly with its native LDAP query syntax.

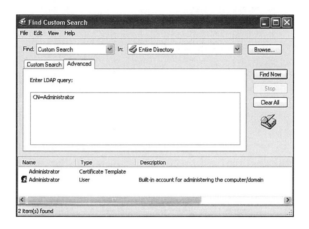

ADDING NETWORK PLACES

By using the Add a Network Place Wizard, you can add shortcuts in My Network Places to network shared folders, for a quick return when you need them in the future. I find Windows a bit hyper-helpful with its Favorites, Histories, Shortcuts, and now Network Places. However, this aid is actually useful because entries in My Network Places appear in the list of choices in every application's Save As dialog, as shown in Figure 17.16. This is very handy for saving files to a remote drive that will be backed up by network administrators, as well as to your applications' default local drive file location, such as My Documents.

NOTE

> The shortcuts in Network Places differ from those in Internet Explorer's "favorites" list. When you open a "favorite" location, you are shown a Web-based *view* of the contents of the location. When you open a "network place," you can actually *manipulate* the files in the remote folder.

17

Figure 17.16
My Network Places is handy because you can select network folders when you're saving files in any application. You can delve deeper into the shared folders, if necessary.

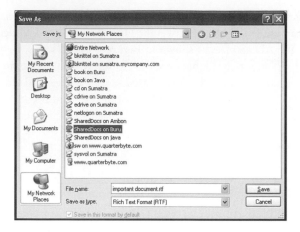

You might find that Windows automatically adds locations to Network Places whenever you open a remote folder by name using Windows Explorer or Internet Explorer's Web Folder view. If you want to add a network place shortcut by hand, do the following:

1. Open My Network Places and select Add a Network Place from the task list.

2. When asked where you want to create the network place, select Choose Another Network Location and click Next.

3. The Add Network Place Wizard asks for the name of the network resource, as shown in Figure 17.17. Enter one of these three types of network resource names:

   - A UNC name for a shared folder, such as `\\server\share`

   - A URL for a Web Sharing folder, such as `http://host/share`

   - The name of an FTP site, such as `ftp://host` or `ftp://host/subfolder`

   You can also choose Browse to search through an Explorer-like view of the Entire Network.

4. Click Next, and enter a name for your Network Place Shortcut. Then select Finish. A shortcut icon appears in My Network Places, and Windows pops up an Explorer window showing the contents of the remote shared folder or site.

TIP FROM

Bob & Brian

> When you're browsing through your network or browsing the Internet using Internet Explorer, you can drag network folders or Web page addresses to My Network Places to instantly make a Network Place shortcut without the Add Network Place Wizard.
>
> Likewise, you can drag the address from the Explorer window's Address bar to your desktop or to a folder to make an instant network shortcut.

Figure 17.17
The Add a Network Place wizard lets you enter a UNC name, a URL for Web folders, or an FTP site.

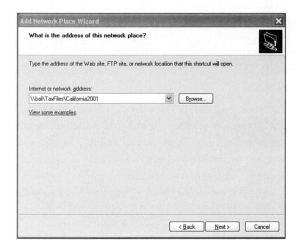

USING A SHARED DISK DRIVE

Shared folders don't have to be subfolders. Computer owners can share the *root folder* of their disk drives, making the entire drive available over the network. This is especially useful with CD-ROM, floppy, and Zip disk drives. If an entire CD-ROM drive is shared, you can access the entire CD from any computer on the network.

Just so you know, Windows automatically shares your entire hard drive with the special name C$. (Any other hard drives would also be shared as D$, E$, and so on.) These shares don't show up when you browse the network—the dollar sign at the end tells Windows to keep the name hidden. But you can enter the share name directly, like `\\ambon\c$`, in Explorer or other programs, to view the entire drive. (You must have Administrator rights on the remote machine to use this feature. On a workgroup network with Simple File Sharing enabled, these administrative shares are never accessible, as all network users are treated as Guest.)

TIP FROM

Bob
& Brian

> If you need to install CD-ROM-based software on a computer with a broken CD-ROM drive but a good network connection, you can put the CD-ROM in another computer's drive, and share the entire drive. See the section, "Mapping Drive Letters," later in this chapter to see how to access the CD from the disabled computer.

USING INTERNET-BASED FILE STORAGE SERVICES

Starting with Windows XP, Microsoft has added the ability to make Network Places shortcuts to commercial services that provide file storage space over the Internet. To use these services, you must first visit the provider's Web site to obtain a username and password (and to take care of small details like payment!). When your account is set up, you can use the Add a Network Place Wizard to create a shortcut to the services.

Then, when you're online, you can easily move files to and from your personal folder on the provider's network, simply by opening the service's Network Place icon. I'll talk more about this type of service in Chapter 18, "Windows Unplugged: Remote and Mobile Networking."

MAPPING DRIVE LETTERS

If you frequently use the same shared network folder, you can make it a "permanent house-guest" of your computer by *mapping* the network shared folder to an unused drive letter on your computer—one of the letters after your hard drive's "C:" and the CD-ROM drive's "D:" (assuming you have one hard drive and one CD-ROM drive and have not already changed your drive mappings). You can give the shared folder \\server\shared the drive letter J:, for example, so that it appears that your computer has a new disk drive J:, whose contents are those of the shared folder.

Mapping gives you several benefits:

- The mapped drive appears along with your computer's other real, physical drives in My Computer for quick browsing, opening, and saving of files.
- Access to the shared folder is faster because Windows maintains an open connection to the sharing computer.
- MS-DOS applications can use the shared folder through its assigned letter. Most legacy DOS applications can't accept UNC-formatted names like \\server\shared\subfolder\file, but they can use j:\subfolder\file.
- If you need to, you can map a shared folder using an alternate username and password to gain access rights you might not have with your current Windows login name.

If you've used Novell or older Windows networks in the past, this may be the only way you've ever used a network! Good news: You still can.

To map a drive, select Tools, Map Network Drive in any Explorer window (such as My Computer). Or you can right-click My Network Places and select Map Network Drive.

Next, select an unused drive letter from the drop-down list, as shown in Figure 17.18. If possible, pick a drive letter that has some association for you with the resource you'll be using: E for Editorial, S for Sales—whatever makes sense to you.

Figure 17.18
You can select an unused drive letter to use for the drive mapping.

Then select the name of the shared folder you want to assign to the drive letter. You can type the UNC-formatted name if you know it already—for example, \\servername\sharename—or you can click Browse to poke through your network's resources and select the shared folder. Find the desired shared folder in the expandable list of workgroups, computers, and share names, as shown in Figure 17.19, and click OK.

Figure 17.19
Browsing for a shared folder. You can open the list view to see network types, work-groups, computers, and shared folders.

After you select the shared folder and click OK, the folder name appears in the dialog, and you have two options:

- If you want this mapping to reappear every time you log in, check Reconnect at login. If you don't check this box, the mapping disappears when you log off.

- If your current Windows username and password don't give you sufficient permissions to use the shared resource, or if your username won't be recognized at the other computer because your account name is different there, select Connect Using a Different User Name. Choosing this option displays a Connect As dialog, as shown in Figure 17.20. Here, you can enter the alternate username and password, and click OK. (On an AD network, you can select Browse to view valid usernames by location if you need help.)

NOTE

You must use the same username for *all* connections to a given computer. If you have other drive letters already mapped to the other computer with your original username, you'll have to unmap those drives before you can make a drive mapping with a different username.

After you map a drive letter, the drive appears in your My Computer list along with your local disk drives. You might notice a couple of funny things with these drives:

- If you haven't accessed the network drive for a while, 20 minutes or so, it might turn gray, indicating that the network connection to the remote computer has been disconnected. When you use the drive again, it will reconnect and turn black.

Figure 17.20

■ If the remote computer (or you) really go offline, a red X appears through the drive.

If you enjoy the more esoteric aspects of networking, there are a couple of nifty features for you—mapping a drive to a subfolder and mapping shared folders with no drive letter.

MAPPING A DRIVE TO A SUBFOLDER

When you're setting up a mapped drive and you browse to find a shared folder, notice that Windows lets you delve into the shared folders themselves. If you drill down into a subfolder and select it as the location to use in mapping a drive letter, you'll find that the mapped drive starts at the subfolder. The subfolder becomes the mapped drive's "root directory," and you can't explore upward into the shared folder that contains it.

NetWare users call this the *map root* function. See Figure 17.21, in which I've selected the subfolder h02\images from the shared folder \\java\book. If I map drive M: to that folder, drive M: will contain the contents of folder \\java\book\h02\images, and it can't be made to see up into \\java\book\h02 or higher. The root, or top-level, directory of M: will be the images folder.

TIP FROM

Bob
& Brian

This feature is most useful to administrators, to set up scripts to map drives based on a user's login name. For example, mail might be stored in subfolders of \\server\mail according to username. Mapping drive M: to folder \\server\mail\%username% lets users get at their mail (directly) via drive M: and discourages users from poking around in other peoples' mail folders.

This way, users can configure their mail programs to get mail from drive M:, and the same configuration will work for everyone.

Figure 17.21
By delving into a shared folder, you can map the root directory of a drive letter to a deeper point in the share.

Mapping a subfolder can be a good thing because it makes any program that uses the mapped drive letter see just that subfolder as the drive's root directory.

MAPPING A SHARED FOLDER WITHOUT A DRIVE LETTER

You can make an established connection to a shared folder, keeping it readily available for quick response without assigning it a drive letter. Follow the procedure shown earlier for mapping a drive letter. When you select the letter to map, go all the way to the bottom of the Drive letter drop-down list, and select (None), the last choice. Continue through the rest of the process as described.

Mapping a shared folder to (None) doesn't add a drive to your My Computer list, but it does make for speedier response from the server when you're accessing that folder. The shared folder will be visible, however, if you choose Map Network Drive, Disconnect Network Drive, or if you use the net use command from the command line.

USING WEB FOLDERS

Windows XP Professional and Windows NT4/2000/2003 Server computers running Internet Information Services (IIS) can share folders using another file sharing system called WebDAV (Web Distributed Authoring and Versioning), or Web Sharing. Because it's based on the standard HTTP protocol, you can access Web folders on your office PC from home, over the Internet, or from another LAN halfway around the world.

Web Folders let you view, use, and manage files and folders over the Internet just as if you were using them on your PC or on your LAN. You get exactly the same look and feel. You can use Microsoft Office 2000 or later, FrontPage, and Internet Explorer version 5 or higher to access Web folders. You don't even have to be using Windows XP; you can use these three applications on earlier versions of Windows as well.

To use a folder that has been shared using Web Sharing, you need to know the folder's URL. It is set by the manager of the Web server you'll be using. In Internet Explorer, you can't use a link in a Web page to pop open a Web Folder. You have to use the following procedure instead:

1. Select File, Open.
2. Enter the Web folder's URL, being sure to start with http:, and check the Open as Web Folder box, as shown in Figure 17.22.
3. Click OK.
4. You might be prompted to enter your login name and password. It's safe to do so, even over the Internet.

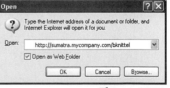

Figure 17.22

An ordinary folder view will appear, as in Figure 17.23. You can treat it in the usual way: view its contents, drag files in and out, create new folders, and rename and delete files if you have the appropriate permissions. These operations take much longer than with LAN file sharing, however.

Figure 17.23
The Web Folder view looks just like an ordinary Explorer folder view.

17

One peculiar thing to note is that after you open a Web Folder from Internet Explorer, the window changes to Windows Explorer view. The "File" menu will no longer have an "Open" choice. If you want to open another Web folder, you'll have to start Internet Explorer again.

Windows will automatically add the Web folder address you used to My Network Places, and the Web Folders list in "other places." This is a convenient way to return to the folder later.

You can also view a Web folder using the Add Network Place Wizard in My Network Places. When you're asked for the location of the network place, enter the Web folder URL starting with http:.

NOTE

> After you open a Web folder, you might be tempted to create a shortcut to it by dragging the address from the Address bar in the Explorer window. This approach doesn't work if you opened the Web folder by choosing File, Open; you get a Web page shortcut instead.
>
> If you opened the Web folder by using the Add Network Places Wizard, however, or by opening an existing Web Folder icon, you get a working folder shortcut. Strange!

 If you see an empty folder, or if you see a plain listing of filenames and dates without icons, see "Web Folder Appears to Be Empty" or "Directory Listing Appears Instead of Web Folder" in the "Troubleshooting" section at the end of the chapter.

USING PRINTERS ON THE NETWORK

Whether you're part of a large corporation or a small workgroup, or even if you're a home user with just two computers, network printing is a great time and money saver. Why connect a printer to each computer, when it will spend most of its time idle? By not having to buy a printer for each user, you can spend the money you save more constructively on faster, higher quality, and more interesting printers. You might add a color photo-quality printer or a transparency maker to give your network users more output choices.

Windows XP really excels at network printing. Here are some of the neat features of Windows XP network printing:

- Windows can print to any of hundreds of printer models, whether they're attached to a computer or connected directly to the LAN.

- It can send printer output to other operating systems. Novell, OS/2, and Linux/Unix printer support is built in to Windows XP Professional. Linux/Unix users can access your shared printers, and users of Novell and Macintosh networks can print to Windows shared printers if your network uses 2003 Server.

- If you select a printer shared by a computer running Windows XP, the necessary printer driver software will be installed on your computer automatically.

- Users of older versions of Windows can attach to a Windows XP network printer, and the correct printer driver for their operating system can be installed for them automatically.

- You can print to and monitor a Windows XP printer over the Internet with new Internet Printer Protocol (IPP) support.

→ To learn more details about monitoring a printer via an Internet connection, **see** "Using Printers Over the Internet with IPP," **p. 575**.

- Printer data is sent to a spooler on the computer that shares the printer. The printer data is stored on the hard disk while the printer catches up, making printing seem faster to user applications. More than one person at a time can send output to the same shared printer; their print requests simply queue up and come out in first-come, first-served order. (You can raise or lower a user's or an individual print job's priority, though, to give preference to some print jobs over others.)

Because the software to do all this comes with Windows XP Professional, and you can hook computers together for as little as $25 each, printer sharing alone is a good reason to install a network.

The best part is that from the user's standpoint, using a network printer is no different than using a local printer. Everything you learned about printing in Chapter 6 applies to network printers; the only difference is in the one-time step of adding the printer to Windows. Later in the chapter, I'll describe how to share a printer attached to your computer; right now, let's look at using a printer that has already been shared elsewhere on the network.

Windows can directly attach to printers shared via Microsoft Networking services, whether from Windows XP, 2000, NT, 95, 98, Windows for Workgroups, OS/2, or even the Samba service from Unix, and also to printers managed by Novell NetWare.

→ To learn how to use Windows with a Novell NetWare network, **see** Chapter 20, "Networking Mix and Match."

INSTALLING NETWORK PRINTERS

To use any networked printer, you have to set up an icon for the printer in your Printers window. One way to do this is to browse or search your network for shared printers. If you locate an appropriate printer, right-click its icon and select Open to set it up for your computer.

However, a more straightforward way to prepare to use network printers is to use the Add Printer wizard on your Printers and Faxes as you would to install a locally attached printer. The Wizard will walk you through locating and installing the printer.

To use the wizard, click Start, Printers and Faxes, and select the Add a Printer task. Click Next. Select Network Printer rather than Local Printer, and choose Next.

Now, you have to identify the shared printer. If you know its network name already, click Connect To This Printer, and enter the share name into the Name box in UNC format—for example, **sumatra****laserjet**—as shown in Figure 17.24.

Figure 17.24

You can enter a UNC shared printer name if know it, or you can leave the Name field blank and choose Next to browse the network for a shared printer.

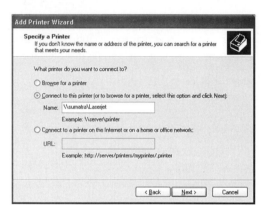

After you've identified the shared printer, click Next to finish installing it. From this point, the installation process proceeds much like the installation of a local printer, as described in Chapter 6.

However, if you don't know the printer's share name, or if you're on a large network, you might need some help identifying the shared printer you want you use. Windows provides a nifty find-a-printer feature for users of an Active Directory network; it lets you find shared printers based on features such as location and capabilities. To use it, select Find a Printer in the Directory, and click Next. I'll describe the process for searching the directory in the next section.

If you don't have an Active Directory network, skip ahead to the section "Browsing for a Suitable Printer."

SEARCHING FOR PRINTERS IN ACTIVE DIRECTORY

If your computer is connected to a domain-type network, the Active Directory can help you locate networked printers in your organization. This feature is very handy if you're a business traveler using the network in an unfamiliar office, or if you're in such a large office setting that you aren't familiar with all the printing resources on your network.

You can search for printers three ways: by name and location, as shown in Figure 17.25; by printer capabilities; or by more advanced attributes.

Figure 17.25
Using the Printers tab
in Active Directory
printer search tool,
you can search for
printers by printer
name, location,
and model.

You can choose a major organizational unit to begin the search from the In drop-down list; you can search the entire directory, choose a major organizational unit, or select Browse to select a more regional subunit. See what choices In has on your network to see whether restricting the search makes sense for your company; otherwise, let the search use the Entire Directory.

Searching by the printer share name, location, or printer model is straightforward; just type a name or part of a name, and select Find Now. What works best when searching by Location depends on how your organization has set up the Active Directory. Yours may use cities, addresses, floors and room numbers, or another system. At any time, you can change your selection criteria and select Find Now again to update the search listing and refine or expand your search.

You can find all the printers in the directory by entering no information in the Find Printers dialog box: Just click Find Now.

TIP FROM

Bob
& Brian

> View the entire directory the first time you use Find Printers. This will give you an idea of how location and printer names are organized in your company. If too many names are listed, you can click Clear All to clear the search listing and then restrict your search using a location name that makes sense for your network. For example, if your company has put floor and room numbers like "10-123" in the Location column, you might restrict your search to printers on the 10th floor by searching for "10-" in Location.

To search for printers based on capabilities you need, select the Features tab, as shown in Figure 17.26. Here, you can limit the directory display to just printers with required color and finishing capabilities, speed, resolution, and available paper sizes.

NOTE

> The name and location attributes you select on the Printers tab, the capabilities you select on the Features tab, and any advanced search restrictions on the Advanced tab all operate together to limit the final result, even though you can see only one of the tabs at a time.

Figure 17.26
Using the Features tab, you can select printers based on printing capabilities such as speed, resolution, and color capability.

If these selections aren't specific enough for you, you can really nail down what you want on the Advanced tab, as shown in Figure 17.27.

Figure 17.27
Using the Advanced tab, you can select printers based on the full range of information stored in the Active Directory.

This tab lets you list your requirements in no uncertain terms. To perform an advanced search, follow these steps:

1. Select Field, and choose a criterion from the list. The searchable attributes include Asset Number, Input Trays, Installed Memory, and Printer Language; you can choose from 27 different attributes.

2. Under Condition, select an appropriate comparison type: Starts with, Greater than or Equal to, and so on. You can also choose Present and Not Present to test whether an attribute is blank.

3. Under Value, enter the desired asset number, number of trays, megabytes of memory, printer language, and so on. Then click Add.

4. Enter more filtering items, or select Find Now to begin the search.

Remember, anything you entered on the Printers or Features tabs factors into this search as well.

 If your Windows displays No Printers Match the Current Search, *see "Can't Find Any Printers in Active Directory" in the "Troubleshooting" section at the end of this chapter.*

You can adjust the search results by double-clicking any of the filtering items you entered; just change the settings and select Add or Remove, and then click Find Now.

Using any of these three tabs, you should be able to quickly narrow down the possibilities enough to choose a suitable printer.

After you've found a printer, what do you do with it? Right-clicking a printer in the search results list gives you two action options: You can connect to it or open it. Connecting installs the printer on your computer; in other words, it adds the printer to the list of those your computer can use. Open displays the printer's current print jobs without installing it.

BROWSING FOR A SUITABLE PRINTER

If you don't know the name of the printer you want to use, you can browse through the network. In this case, choose Connect To This Printer. Leave the Name field blank, and choose Next.

The network display appears, as shown in Figure 17.28, to let you probe into domains or workgroups, computers, and their shared printers.

Figure 17.28
You can browse your workgroup network for shared printers by opening the list view of networks, domains, workgroups, and computers. Shared printers are found listed under each computer. It helps that the list includes only computers with shared printers.

From here, just select the printer you want, and click Next to finish the installation.

FINISHING THE INSTALLATION

When you've chosen a printer, Windows automatically looks to the computer sharing that printer for the correct software driver for Windows XP. If it finds the driver, that driver is instantly downloaded to your PC, and the installation completes without your having to look up the printer's model number, hunt for the right driver diskettes, or otherwise lift a finger.

You might hit a snag, though, if the sharing computer doesn't have the correct Windows XP printer driver for you. You might have this problem if the remote computer isn't running Windows XP. In this case, Windows pops up a message saying: "The server on which the printer resides does not have the correct printer driver installed. If you want to install the driver on your local computer, click OK."

If you want to use the printer, well, now you will have to lift a finger. Click OK, and Windows displays the Add Printer Wizard with its list of known printer manufacturers and models, as discussed in Chapter 6. Choose the correct make and model from the list, and then click OK.

→ If you can't locate the correct printer model in this list and need more detailed instructions on installing printer drivers, **see** "What To Do if Your Printer Isn't Listed," **p. 192**.

If you are adding a second or subsequent printer, after the printer driver has been down-loaded or installed, Windows will ask whether you want this newly installed printer to be set as your default printer. You can choose Yes or No, as you like; then select Next. You can always change your choice of default printer later by right-clicking a printer icon and selecting Set As Default.

When you click Finish, the wizard adds the printer to your list of printer choices, and you're finished. The network printer is ready to use in any application. The whole process usually takes about 15 seconds from start to finish.

NOTE

> When the new printer appears in your printer window, you might want to verify that you can actually use the printer and that its output is correct. To do so, right-click the printer icon and select Properties. Select Print a Test Page to ensure that the network printer is working correctly.

USING A NETWORK PRINTER

When the network printer is set up, you can use it in exactly the same way as you use a locally attached printer, so all the printer management discussion in Chapter 6 applies to network printers, too. The only difference is that the remote computer's administrator may not have given you management privileges for the printer, so you might not be able to change the printer's properties.

It's probably best that you don't have that capability anyway, as it's considered bad form to change the hardware setup of someone else's printer without permission. If you connect to a computer that doesn't use Simple File Sharing (such as Windows 2000 Server), view the printer's Properties page and have access to all the usual printer configuration tabs—Sharing, Ports, Advanced, Security and Device Settings—don't make any changes without the permission of the printer's owner. Changing the port, for example, will certainly make the printer stop working, and the remote user probably won't figure out why for quite some time (when they do, leave town).

You can view and manage the printer's list of pending documents by double-clicking the printer icon. However, you can't cancel or alter the properties of anyone's print jobs but your own unless you have been granted Manage Documents rights.

USING PRINTERS OVER THE INTERNET WITH IPP

A fairly new feature in Windows is the capability to install and print to a shared printer through the Internet as easily as you can through a LAN. The Internet Printing Protocol (IPP) was developed by a group of network and printer technology companies at the initiative of Novell Corporation and Xerox Corporation. They saw the need for a standardized way to provide reliable, secure, and full-featured print spooling functions over the Internet.

The idea is that business travelers should be able to send reports back to their home offices via the Internet and use the same technology to print reports or presentations in a hotel's business center or a commercial copy service center. I use it myself to print to my office's laser printer from home. IPP is based on the Hypertext Transfer Protocol (HTTP), which runs the World Wide Web, so it's simple and it can passes safely through network firewalls. In Windows, IPP uses Windows's own safely encrypted username and password security, so your printers are protected from abuse by anonymous outsiders.

As with all the shared resources I'm discussing, using and providing these services are really separate things. You can use IPP to reach a printer without providing the service yourself, and vice versa. In this section, I'll talk about *using* the service.

The blessing of IPP is that once you've installed the printer icon, you can use the remote printer in exactly the same way as you use any Windows printer. The printer queue, management tools, and other operations are all exactly the same, as long as you're connected to the Internet or the appropriate intranet LAN.

SELECTING AN IPP PRINTER BY ITS URL

You can connect to a remote printer via IPP in either of two ways.

If you know the URL of the IPP-connected printer, you can use the Add Printer Wizard, as I discussed earlier in this chapter. Your network administrator should supply you with the URL, if the printer is on your company's Intranet, or by a hotel or service bureau, after they've gotten your credit card number.

1. Follow the instructions I gave earlier for adding a network printer.
2. When you are asked to enter the printer name, choose Connect to a Printer on the Internet or on a Home or Office Network instead of browsing the network.
3. Enter the URL provided by your administrator or the service you are using, as shown in Figure 17.29, and select Next.
4. You might be prompted for a username and password. If so, enter the name and password supplied by the vendor or, if the printer is on your own network, your network username and password.
5. Continue with the installation procedure described above; you might need to select a print driver if the remote print server doesn't provide it automatically.

Figure 17.29
Adding an Internet-connected printer using IPP. This URL is fictitious, but the hope is that soon you will be able to send output to a printer at a copy center or service bureau as easily as to a printer in your own home or office.

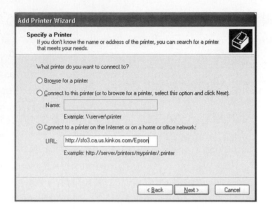

When the new printer icon is installed, you have a fully functional Windows printer. You can view the pending jobs and set your print and page preferences as usual as long as you're connected to the Internet (or the LAN, in a service establishment).

TIP FROM

Bob
& Brian

> If you use a printing service, remember to delete the printer from your Printers folder when you leave town; you don't want to accidentally print reports in Katmandu after you've returned home.
>
> Also, if you are printing to a different brand and model than you normally do, you should select the remote printer and scroll through your document to check for changes in page breaks or other options that could affect your output. If your document's layout has changed because you're about to use a different printer, save your document under a different name before you print it.

SELECTING AN IPP PRINTER VIA THE WEB

If you can reach the Web site of a service bureau or a Windows XP/2000 Professional or Server computer that sports both Internet Information Services (IIS) and a shared printer, Internet printing is a snap.

TIP FROM

Bob
& Brian

> If you use Windows XP Professional or Server at work, and Windows XP Home Edition at home, you can use this feature to print to your office printer from home, as long as the office computer's Web server is reachable over the Internet.

If you view the URL `http://computername/Printers`, replacing *computername* with the actual hostname of the remote computer, you get a display like the one shown in Figure 17.30.

Figure 17.30
Windows XP's Professional and Server versions provide a Web Interface for printer management. The home page gives a quick overview of all shared printers. You can select a printer to view or manage for more detail.

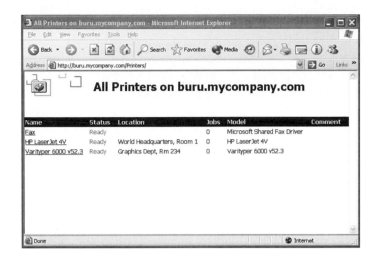

Selecting one of the printers brings up a detailed printer status page, as shown in Figure 17.31. The printer status page lists queued print jobs and current printer status. If you're using Internet Explorer as your Web browser and have IPP printing software installed in Windows, clicking Connect sets this printer up as a network printer on your computer, drivers and all. You can select the printer and use it immediately, right over the Internet.

Figure 17.31
The printer status page shows current print jobs; using it, you can manage the printer and queued documents. The Connect hyperlink installs the printer on your computer.

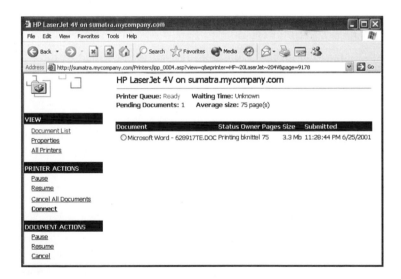

 If you view a Windows XP computer's Printers Web page, and can select printers but don't have the Connect option, see "No Connect Option for Web Printing" in the "Troubleshooting" section at the end of this chapter.

USING OTHER IPP PRINTERS

You can buy an IPP-capable printer and plug it directly into your LAN. An IPP-capable printer will probably provide Web-based management and status, which is a great way to monitor its health from across the country (or across the room).

→ To learn more about installing network-ready printers, **see** "Adding Network-Capable Printers," **p. 520**.

In a workgroup, it might not get a registered hostname, so you might need to refer to it by its assigned IP address, as in `http://192.168.0.24/hplaser4`. The installation instructions for the printer tell you what URL to use.

When you know the URL for the intranet- or Internet-accessible printer, follow the instructions in the section "Installing a Network Printer Without Active Directory" earlier in this chapter. You don't have to search for the printer, though. When you get to the screen shown in Figure 17.27, choose Connect to a Printer on the Internet or on a Home or Office Network. Enter the URL, and then go on installing the printer as instructed earlier.

When it is set up, you can use the printer as if it were directly connected to your PC.

TIP FROM

Bob & Brian

> Connect to the printer this way with just *one* of your Windows XP computers. Share the printer from that computer with the rest of your LAN. This way, you can make installation easier for everyone else.

USING UNIX AND LPR PRINTERS

In the Unix world, most shared printers use a protocol called LPR/LPD, which was developed at the University of California at Berkeley during the early years of Unix and the TCP/IP protocol.

NOTE

> If you have a Unix background, you might be happy to know that the familiar Unix `lpr` and `lpq` utilities are available as command-line programs in Windows XP.

→ For more information about Unix printing, **see** "Internetworking with Unix and Linux," **p. 707**.

Manufacturers such as Hewlett-Packard make direct network-connected printers that accept the LPR protocol, and many companies sell small LPR-based print server devices that can attach to your printer as well. You can connect one of these printers to your LAN, configure its TCP/IP settings to match your LAN, and immediately print without running a cable from a computer to the printer. This way, you can place a printer in a more convenient place than could be reached by a 10-foot printer cable. Better yet, you can use these networked printers without requiring a Windows computer to be left turned on to manage it.

You can install a Windows printer that directs its output to an LPR print queue or device as easily as you can install a directly connected printer. Follow these steps:

1. For the first LPR-based printer you use, you have to install LPR support. Open My Network Places and select View Network Connections. Select Advanced, Optional Networking Components. Check Other Network File and Print Services and click Next. You might need to insert your Windows XP Installation CD-ROM.

2. View Printers and Faxes and select Add a Printer.

3. Select Local Printer. (You choose Local because Network connects only to Windows and IPP shared printers.) Uncheck Automatically Detect and Install My Plug and Play Printer, and click Next.

4. Select the Create a New Port option, and choose LPR Port in the Type of Port box, and click Next.

5. In the Add LPR Compatible Printer dialog, enter the IP address or hostname of the Unix or print server, and the name of the print queue on that server, as shown in Figure 17.32.

Figure 17.32
In this dialog box, enter the IP address or hostname of the LPR print server and the queue or printer name.

6. Select the manufacturer and printer model as usual, and proceed with the rest of the printer installation.

NOTE

> If you enter the wrong IP address, hostname, or print queue name, Windows will not let you change this information. To correct the problem, bring up the printer's Properties page, select the Ports tab, highlight the LPR port, and select Configure Port. If Windows doesn't display a dialog to let you change the IP information, uncheck the LPR port. Delete the port, and add a new LPR port with the correct information. Then check the port to connect your Windows printer to the LPR server.

USING APPLETALK PRINTERS

If your network has AppleTalk printers attached, you probably have Macintosh users on your LAN. If you want to share files with Macintosh users, you need to have Windows 2003 Server on your network because it includes File and Printer Services for Macintosh Networks. These services let Macintosh and Windows users access shared printers and folders on each others' networks as if they were their own.

Windows XP Professional doesn't provide such services, so without the Server version you can't directly use AppleTalk-based printers. Regrettably, Windows XP Professional doesn't come with the AppleTalk Protocol and AppleTalk Printer port monitor components that were provided with previous versions of Windows. You may be able to obtain SMB protocol software to let your Macs use printers shared by Windows.

17

→ To learn more details about internetworking with Macintosh computers, **see** "Internetworking with Macintosh," **p. 713**.

N O T E

> Before giving up, however, check the documentation on your networked printer. Some printers support access via all three standard protocols: AppleTalk, NetBIOS (SMB), and TCP/IP.

USING OTHER NETWORK-CONNECTED PRINTERS

Windows XP can use other types of network-connected printers as well. Some printer models come with a built-in network connection, and others have a network adapter option. You can also buy network printer servers, which are small boxes with a network connector and one to three printer connection ports. These devices let you locate printers in a convenient area, which doesn't need to be near a computer.

The installation procedures for various printer and server models vary. Your networked printer or print server will come with specific installation instructions. When you install it, you have a choice about how the printer will be shared on your network:

- You can install the network-to-printer connection software on *one* of your Windows computers, and then use standard Windows printer sharing to make the printer available to the other computers on your network

- You can install the printer's connection software on *each* of your computers

With the first method, you will guarantee that print jobs will be run first-come-first-served (or you can set priorities for print jobs if you want), because one computer will provide a queue for the printer. Another plus is that you'll only have to do the software setup once; it's much easier to set up the other workstations to use the standard Windows shared printer. The one computer will have to be left on for others to use the printer, however.

With the second method, each computer will contact the printer independently, so there may be contention for the printer. However, no computers need to be left on, since each workstation will contact the printer directly.

You can use either method. The first one is simplest, and is best suited for a busy office. The second method is probably more convenient for home networks and small offices.

USING NETWORK RESOURCES EFFECTIVELY

Tips are scattered throughout this chapter, but I want to collect a few of the best ones here for easy reference. The following tips and strategies will help you make the most of your LAN.

USE MY NETWORK PLACES

My Network Places not only serves as a convenient place to collect shortcuts to network resources, but it also appears under *My Computer* when you open or save files in any application. This feature can save you lots of time when you use the same network folders over and over.

You can make shortcuts in My Network Places for the handful of the network shared folders that you use most frequently.

You can add the names of subfolders when you make these shortcuts, if you find that you always have to drill your way into the main shared folder to get to the folder you actually want.

MAKE FOLDER SHORTCUTS

You can drag the icon appearing in the address field from any shared folder view to your desktop, to My Network Places, or any other convenient place for reuse later. (The Address bar might not appear on your Explorer windows. You might need to right-click the toolbar and check Address Bar. You also might need to uncheck Lock The Toolbars to drag it into a visible position.)

I like to organize projects into folders on my desktop and put related network resources in each. For example, I might have three project folders on my desktop, and in each one, three shortcuts to related shared folders.

Because shortcuts aren't the "real thing," you can have shortcuts to the same network places wherever you need them.

USE OFFLINE NETWORK FOLDERS

If you use network resources from a portable computer or a computer with an intermittent network connection (by design or by accident), you can use the Offline Folders feature to keep local copies of important network folders in your own computer for use when the network is unavailable.

→ If you would like to learn more details about Offline Folders, **see** "Offline Folders," **p. 622**.

PUT TOOLS AND DOCUMENTATION ONLINE

Administrators and power users should put management batch files, Registry installation and setup files, special program utilities, and documentation in a shared network folder, for convenient access from any computer on the network. All your network's users don't need to know it's there unless you want them to.

ORGANIZE YOUR NETWORK TO FIT YOUR USERS

You should organize shared folders to fit the way users actually work. For example, if your organization frequently passes documents back and forth between users, you could make a shared folder named Inbox, containing a subfolder for each user. Co-workers could deliver documents to each other by dropping them into the appropriate network Inbox. Users could each have a shortcut to their Inboxes on their desktops for quick access.

For more suggestions about workgroup management, see Chapter 28, "Managing Users."

SHARING RESOURCES

On a large corporate LAN, most important network resources, shared folders, and printers are set up and tightly controlled by network managers. You might not even be able to share resources from your own computer. This helps control the cost of maintaining and managing the network, but it doesn't help you and your co-workers if you want to share files for a project among yourselves. You might have to plead with your network manager to prepare a common shared folder for you.

On the other hand, you might be able to set up the file sharing yourself. In a workgroup network, it's almost certain you can. Administrators and members of the Administrators and Power Users groups can manage file and printer sharing.

Before deciding to share resources, you should give some thought to just what you want to share, how you want to organize it, and who should have permission to see, use, or change files you've published in the shared folders.

SHARING FOLDERS AND DRIVES

Windows automatically makes your computer's Shared Documents folder available on the network. However, you might want to share other folders with your network cohorts. This capability is built right in to Explorer.

The procedure has some slight differences depending on the type of network you have. If you're using a workgroup-type network with Simple File Sharing enabled, follow the procedure in the next section. If you're on a domain-type network or you've disabled Simple File Sharing, skip ahead to "Sharing Folders on a Domain Network."

NOTE

As you start to select folders to share, you might notice that Windows has automatically already shared your entire hard drive with the name **c$**. Leave this share alone; it lets Administrators manage your computer. You can choose an additional, different name if you want to share your entire hard drive—for example, **cdrive** or **cdrive$**, although Microsoft discourages sharing entire hard disk drives.

SHARING FOLDERS ON A WORKGROUP NETWORK

On workgroup networks, Microsoft provides simplified user interface and security system for file sharing, which is discussed in detail in Chapter 28, "Managing Users." It's the default method, so I'll describe it first. If you've disabled Simple File Sharing, skip head to the next section.

To share a folder with Simple File Sharing, just follow these steps:

1. Select a folder in Explorer, or select the name of the CD-ROM, floppy, Zip, or hard drive itself at the top of the Explorer view, if you want to share the entire disk.

   Microsoft recommends that you only share folders found inside your My Documents folder, but I think that's too restrictive. You can safely share any folder on your hard drive except Documents and Settings, Program Files, and your Windows folder. You should *not* share the entire hard drive that contains your Windows folder.

2. Right-click the folder, and choose Sharing and Security.

3. Select Share This Folder on the Network. Windows fills in the Share Name field with the name of the folder. If the name contains spaces, it may not be accessible to Windows for Workgroups users, so you might want to shorten or abbreviate the name. You also can enter a comment to describe the contents of the shared folder, as shown in Figure 17.33.

Figure 17.33
When sharing a location, be sure to enter a share name. Comments are optional.

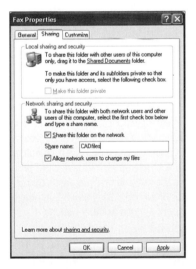

TIP FROM

Bob & Brian

> You can prevent other users from seeing your shared folder when they browse the network by adding a dollar sign to the end of the share name—for example, `mystuff$`. This convention alone does *not* prevent them from seeing your files if they know the share name.

Before clicking OK to make the folder accessible, however, you should consider file security and the ability of other users to access your files. I'll continue this discussion in the next section.

 If you receive a `File Is in Use by Another` *error when attempting to use one of the files in a folder you have shared, see "File Is in Use by Another" in the "Troubleshooting" section at the end of this chapter.*

NOTE

> You must run the Network Setup Wizard at least once to share any of your computer's files, even if you've set up your network manually. The Network Setup Wizard was discussed in Chapter 15.

SHARED FOLDER SECURITY

Sharing security is frequently misunderstood. You can specify the rights of remote users and groups to read or change (that is, write, delete, rename, and so on) the files in your shared folder when you enable sharing, as shown in Figure 17.33. On a workgroup network with Simple File Sharing, it works like this:

- If you check Allow Network Users to Change my Files, remote users will be able to delete, edit, or rename files *only if they would have permission to do so when logged on to computer or connected to your network directly*, using their own account name.

- If you don't check Allow Network Users they'll only be able to view and read files, and then only if they would have permission while logged on directly.

If you are sharing files on a FAT-formatted disk partition, these are the *only controls* you have at your disposal to manage access to your files, because *anybody* can read or write any of your files on a FAT-formatted disk.

CAUTION

> When you are on a LAN, it is not a good idea to share any folders from a FAT-formatted disk because there are no user-level controls to restrict access to your files. It's very easy for someone to enable a Guest account and give a complete outsider or Internet hacker access to your files. If you do enable sharing of a FAT-partition folder, be sure your network is secured by a firewall, and that you aren't concerned about people wandering into your home or office and poking around. Although share-level security is better than no security, it's not as good as other options.

If you have an NTFS formatted hard drive, as long as you pay attention to assigning NTFS permissions to your shared folder, it is not so dangerous to check Allow Network Users to Change My Files.

Network security is a serious matter, and in a business setting, you should be very sure to understand the risks you're exposing your files to and the ways you can protect them.

You should read Chapter 28, "Managing Users," and Chapter 29, "Managing the Hard Disk," for more information about setting User and Group access to folders using NTFS permissions.

After you've chosen whether or not to permit write-access by network users, click OK to make the share available on the network.

 Finally, when you have shared a folder, its icon changes to a hand holding the folder like an offering. This is your cue that the folder is shared. You can right-click the folder later on to select Sharing and Security if you want to stop sharing or change the sharing permissions.

SHARING FOLDERS ON A DOMAIN NETWORK

If your computer is a member of a domain network, or if you've disabled Simple File Sharing, use the following steps to share a folder:

1. Select a folder in Explorer, or select the name of the CD-ROM, floppy, Zip, or hard drive itself at the top of the Explorer view, if you want to share the entire disk.

   Microsoft recommends that you only share folders found inside your My Documents folder, but I think that's too restrictive. You can safely share any folder on your hard drive except Documents and Settings, Program Files, and your Windows folder. You should *not* share the entire hard drive that contains your Windows folder.

2. Right-click the folder, and choose Sharing and Security.

3. Select Share This Folder on the Network. Windows fills in the Share Name field with the name of the folder. If the name contains spaces, it might not be accessible to Windows for Workgroups users, so you might want to shorten or abbreviate the name. You also can enter a comment to describe the contents of the shared folder (refer to Figure 17.3).

TIP FROM

> You can prevent other users from seeing your shared folder when they browse the network by adding a dollar sign to the end of the share name—for example, `mystuff$`. This convention alone does *not* prevent them from seeing your files if they know the share name.

Before clicking OK to make the folder accessible, you should consider file security and the ability of other users to access your files. I'll continue this discussion in the next section.

 If you receive a `File Is in Use by Another` *error when attempting to use one of the files in a folder you have shared, see "File Is in Use by Another" in the "Troubleshooting" section at the end of this chapter.*

SHARED FOLDER SECURITY

By default, other network users will be able to add, delete, and edit files in the shared folder, *if they would have the same permissions with local access.* That is, by default, user-level file security applies to network users as well as local users as long as your hard disk uses NTFS formatting. If your hard disk has FAT formatting, or if you want to restrict access to shared files in *addition* to NTFS security settings, you can specify the rights of remote users and groups to read or change (that is, write, delete, rename, and so on) the files in your shared folder.

On the Sharing properties page (again, refer to Figure 17.3), click Permissions. This displays the Share Permissions page shown in Figure 17.34. Here, you can add or remove entries for Windows users and groups, and allow or deny access in three categories:

Figure 17.34
Sharing Permissions restrict access by network users in addition to any user-level security on the files themselves.

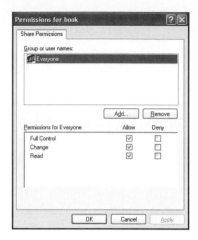

17

- **Read**—The ability to view the list of files in the folder and read files.
- **Change**—The ability to write, edit, delete, and rename files in the folder
- **Full Control**—The ability to read AND Change files, as well as take ownership and change file permissions.

To change sharing permissions, select a user or group name in the upper half of the dialog box, and check or uncheck this user's or group's permissions in the lower half.

If you are sharing files on a FAT-formatted disk partition, these are the only controls you have at your disposal to manage access to your files, because *anybody* can read or write any of your files on a FAT-formatted disk. In this case, you probably should uncheck Fill Control and Change for group Everyone. Then, click Add to add specific users and groups for whom you want to grant Write access.

If your disk is formatted with the NTFS file system, Share Permissions apply in *addition* to the NTFS user-level permission system, so it's generally save to leave the default Share Permissions set to Full Control by Everyone. However, network security is a serious matter, and in a business setting, you should be very sure to understand the risks you're exposing your files to and the ways you can protect them.

You should read Chapter 28, "Managing Users," and Chapter 29, "Managing the Hard Disk," for more information about setting User and Group access to folders using NTFS permissions.

After you've chosen whether or not to permit write-access by network users, click OK twice to make the share available on the network.

Finally, when you have shared a folder, its icon changes to a hand holding the folder like an offering. This is your cue that the folder is shared. You can right-click the folder later on to select Sharing and Security if you want to stop sharing or change the sharing permissions.

SHARING WEB FOLDERS

If you have installed Internet Information Services on your computer, then Web Folder sharing is available by default. When you view a folder's properties, Web Sharing appears as a tab, as shown in Figure 17.35. When you use Web Sharing, you make a folder available to visitors to your computer:

- If there is Internet access to your computer, visitors will be able to see the files—this is an instant way to publish Web pages.

- Visitors using "Open as a Web Folder" will be able to view and modify files in this folder, if they have permission.

→ To learn more about installing the Web services on your computer, **see** Chapter 13, "Hosting Web Pages with Internet Information Server."

Figure 17.35
Web Sharing appears as a folder property when you install IIS and configure the Server Extensions.

⚠ *If Web Sharing does not appear as a tab in a folder's properties, see "Web Sharing Is Not a Choice" in the "Troubleshooting" section at the end of this chapter.*

TIP FROM

> Enabling regular sharing on a folder does not make it available as a shared Web folder, or vice versa.

To make the folder available to Web visitors using Internet Explorer version 5 or higher, Microsoft Office, or FrontPage, select Share This Folder on the Web Sharing tab. A dialog box appears, as shown in Figure 17.36.

Figure 17.36
In this dialog box, you can set up access to the shared folder. To provide read/write access, check Write and set Application Permissions to None.

17

Now you can set a URL name or *alias* for the shared folder; the URL for Web access is `http://hostname/aliasname`, so it's best to enter the name without spaces or punctuation characters.

By default, the folder is set up for read-only access. Remote Web folder users with permission to view the folder will see the folder in a standard Explorer view and can copy and view the files in it, but cannot add or modify the files in it.

To enable read/write access to the shared folder, check Write in the Access Permissions section, *and* set Application Permissions to None.

CAUTION

> If you enable Write access, you must set application permissions to None to prevent outside users from delivering arbitrary programs and scripts to your computer that they could then execute on your computer via the Internet.
>
> By default, Windows *does not* grant anonymous access to Web folders set up using the Web Sharing dialog. If you grant Write access, though, you should confirm this by checking the virtual directory's properties page in the Internet Information Services manager, just to be on the safe side. See "Controlling Access to Web Pages" in Chapter 13 for more information.

These permission settings work in *addition* to NTFS permissions on an NTFS-formatted disk, so the same issues pertain to Web sharing as to standard sharing:

- Don't Web-share a folder on a FAT-formatted partition.
- Carefully check NTFS permissions on any folders you share. For more information on NTFS permissions, see Chapter 28, "Managing Users," and Chapter 29, "Managing the Hard Disk."
- Read Chapters 21, 28, and 29 for important discussions of file and network security.

Bob
& Brian

The most important thing to do after enabling Web sharing is to open a Web browser and attempt to access the shared folder using no username or password, and then with the username and password of a user account that you do not think should have access to the files. If either of these methods works, be sure you want it to. You might not have effective security in place.

SHARING PRINTERS

You can share any local printer on your computer. It can be a printer directly cabled to your computer or one connected via the network using LPR or other network protocols.

To enable printer sharing, do the following:

1. Choose Start and view the Printers and Faxes folder.

2. Right-click the printer icon and choose Sharing, or select Properties and then select the Sharing tab.

3. Select Share This Printer, and enter a network name for the printer, as shown in Figure 17.37. Enter up to 14 characters, using letters, numbers, and hyphens. Avoid spaces if you have Windows 3.x computers on your network. 8.3 naming is recommended if Windows 3.x computers need to access the share.

Figure 17.37
Enabling sharing for a printer.

4. If your network has only Windows XP/2000 computers, click OK, and you're finished. Other network users can now use the shared printer.

Otherwise, continue to the next section to add extra printer drivers for other operating systems.

INSTALLING EXTRA PRINTER DRIVERS

If you have computers running other versions of Windows or other CPU types, you can load the appropriate printer drivers for those operating systems now, and network users will receive them automatically when they connect to your printer. This step is optional, but it's the friendly thing to do.

View the Sharing tab in your printer's Properties dialog box, and select the Additional Drivers button. Windows displays a list of supported operating systems and CPU types, as shown in Figure 17.38. (By the way, "Intel" refers to any Intel or compatible chips like those made by AMD or VIA/Cyrix.)

Figure 17.38
You can install drivers for additional operating systems or CPUs to make it easy for network users to attach to your printer.

Check the boxes for the CPUs and operating systems you want to support, and click OK. Windows then goes through any additional operating systems you chose one-by-one and asks either for your Windows XP CD-ROM, or other operating system installation disks to locate the appropriate drivers, as shown in Figure 17.39.

Figure 17.39
In this dialog box, you are asked to locate the appropriate drivers for each operating system as requested.

You can find these drivers on the original installation disks for the alternative operating system, or often on disks provided with the printer, which might contain support for many operating systems on the same disk.

When installed, the alternative drivers are sequestered in your Windows folder and delivered to users of the other operating systems when necessary.

If one of your network printers stops working, your users have output waiting to print, and you have an alternate printer available, see "Network Printer Has Stopped Working" in the "Troubleshooting" section at the end of this chapter.

SETTING PRINTER PERMISSIONS

If you have a peer-to-peer network and have enabled Simple File Sharing, as discussed in Chapter 28, you don't need to worry about setting permissions for Printers. If you're on a domain network or have chosen to use detailed user-level permissions on your peer-to-peer network you can control access to your shared printers with three security attributes that can be assigned to users or groups, as shown in Figure 17.40:

Permission	Lets User or Group
Print	Send output to the printer
Manage Printers	Change printer configuration settings, and share or unshare a printer
Manage Documents	Cancel or suspend other users' print jobs

You can use the Security tab in the printer's Properties dialog box to alter the groups and users assigned each of these permissions.

Figure 17.40
The Security tab lets you assign printer management permissions for users, groups, and the creator of a networked printer.

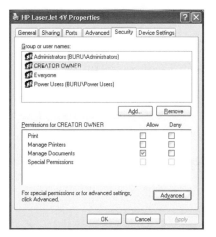

The CREATOR OWNER name applies to the user who submitted a given print job.

You probably don't have to change the default permission settings unless you want to limit use of the printer by outside users in a domain environment only. In this case, delete Everyone, and add specific groups with Print permission.

NOTIFYING USERS WHEN PRINTING IS COMPLETE

You can have Windows send a pop-up message to remote users when print jobs they send to your printer have completed. By default, this feature is turned off when you install Windows XP.

To enable remote user notification, do the following:

1. Open the Printers and Faxes window.

2. Choose File, Server Properties.

3. Select the Advanced tab.

4. Check Notify When Remote Documents Are Printed.

5. If users on your network tend to use more than one computer at a time, check Notify Computer, Not User, When Remote Documents Are Printed. This option sends the notification to the computer where the print job originated rather than to the user who submitted the print job..

6. Click OK.

With remote notification enabled, when a print job has completed, a notification pops up on the sender's desktop, as in Figure 17.41. No message is sent if the print job is canceled, however.

Figure 17.41
Remote Notification tells a user that his or her print job submitted over the network has completed.

TRACKING PRINTER USERS

If you want to track usage patterns of your printer, you can instruct Windows to record print job completion and maintenance alerts in the System Event Log, through settings on the Print Server Properties dialog box. Here's how:

1. Open the Printers and Faxes window.

2. Choose File, Server Properties.

3. Select the Advanced tab.

4. Check Log events to record the degree of login required:

   Log Spooler Error Events records the most severe printer errors.

   Log Spooler Warning Events records less severe errors.

   Log Spooler Information Events records successful print job completion.

5. Click OK.

I generally disable Log Spooler Information Events to prevent the system log from recording print activity, which I don't care to keep track of.

If you do care, though, more detailed recording of printer use and management activity is available through Auditing. Auditing provides a way to record printer activity in the Windows Event Security Log.

The Windows Auditing feature records an event when a specified permission has been either granted or denied. The granting or denying of permission implies that someone completed, or tried to complete, the action that the permission controls.

This situation sounds a little more complex than it is. In practical terms, if you audit success *and* failure of the Print permission, you'll see who submitted print jobs and who tried and was denied. If you audit just failure of the Manage Documents permission, you'll see who tried to delete another user's document and was prohibited.

You can add permissions in the Auditing tab by viewing a printer's Security properties, clicking Advanced, and selecting the Auditing tab. Select Add, choose a user or group of users to select for auditing, and then choose permissions and outcomes to audit, as shown in Figure 17.42.

Figure 17.42
Adding an Audit entry to record when Printing permission has been granted or denied to anyone.

Finally, click OK to add the permission to the Audit list, and add more if desired.

CHANGING THE LOCATION OF THE SPOOL DIRECTORY

When jobs are queued up to print, Windows stores the data it's prepared for the printer in folder of the computer that's sharing the printer. Data for your own print jobs and that for any network users will all end up on your hard drive temporarily. If the drive holding your Windows directory is getting full and you'd rather house this print data on another drive, you can change the location of the spool directory.

To change the location of the Windows print spooler folder

1. View the Printers and Faxes folder.
2. Select File, Server Properties and select the Advanced tab.
3. Enter a new location for the Spool Folder and click OK.

PRINTER POOLING

If your network involves heavy-duty printing, you might find that your printers are the bottleneck in getting your work done. One solution is to get faster printers, and another is to add multiple printers.

If you have two printers shared separately, you'll have to choose one or the other for your printing, and you'll probably encounter bank-line syndrome: The other line always seems to move faster.

The way around this problem is to use printer pooling. You can set up one shared printer queue that sends its output to multiple printers. The documents line up in one list, and multiple printers take jobs from the front of the line, first-come, first served.

To set up pooled printers, follow these steps:

1. Buy identical printers; at least, they must be identical from the software point of view.
2. Set up and test one printer, and configure network sharing for it.
3. Install the extra printer(s) on the same computer as the first. If you use network-connected printers, you need to add the necessary additional network ports.
4. View the printer's Properties, and select the Ports tab. Mark Enable Printer Pooling, and mark the Ports for the additional printers.

That's all there is to it; Windows passes print jobs to as many printers as you select on the Ports pages.

SEPARATOR PAGES

Windows XP has a feature that lets you add a cover page to each print job sent to given printer. The cover page can be configured to show the name of the user who sent the print job, his or her computer name, and so on. On a network with dozens of users sharing a given printer, these cover pages can be very helpful in sorting out whose printouts are whose. On the other hand, using cover pages is wasteful of paper and isn't a good "green" practice unless the confusion around your printers is really significant.

Separator pages have another very important use: They can be used to switch "multiple personality" printers into one language mode or another. For example, some Hewlett-Packard printers accept input in both the PostScript and PCL page description languages. These printers normally detect which format is being used and adjust automatically. They don't always, however, so setup information stored in separator page files can be used to force the issue.

You can set up the pages like this: Create two Windows shared printer icons in the Printers folder, both pointing to the same physical printer on the same LPT port. Configure one with the PostScript driver, and the other with the standard PCL driver. Name the printers appropriately—for example, LaserJet-PS and LaserJet-PCL. Configure each printer with a separator page that forces the printer into the correct mode. This way, you can select the printer driver you want, and the printer will never mistake the language being used. This is really handy if Unix or Macintosh users are sending output to your printers.

Windows ships with four predefined separator files:

pcl.sep	Forces a LaserJet printer into PCL mode and prints a separator page
sysprint.sep	Forces a LaserJet printer into PostScript mode and prints a separator page
pscript.sep	Forces a LaserJet printer into PostScript mode but doesn't print a separator page
sysprtj.sep	Contains a Japanese font version of sysprint.sep

Separator files are stored in your \winnt\system32 folder. You can use one of the predefined files, or you can create one of your own. These plain text files can be edited with Notepad. To assign a separator page to a given printer, follow these steps:

1. Open the printer's Properties box, and select the Advanced tab.
2. Click the Separator Page button and enter the desired filename, or click Browse to find the file manually.
3. Click OK.

The first line of a *.sep file contains only one character, which sets the "escape character" for the rest of the file. Subsequent lines are sent to the printer. Sequences starting with the escape character are interpreted as substitution commands; the sequence is replaced with other text before being sent to the printer. The command substitutions are shown in Table 17.2. In the table, I assume that backslash (\) is the escape character.

TABLE 17.2   SEPARATOR PAGE SUBSTITUTIONS

Sequence	Is Replaced With
\N	Name of the user who submitted the print job.
\I	Print job number.
\D	Date the job was printed.
\T	Time the job was printed.
\Lxxxxxx	Text *xxxxxx* up to the next escape.
\Ffilename	Contents of file *filename*. This file is copied literally with no substitution. It can be used for a "message of the day."
\Hxx	Hexadecimal value *xx*. Particularly useful is \H1B, which emits the ASCII <esc> character used in printer control commands.
\Wnn	Limits the width of the page to *nn* columns.

You can create or modify separator page files using the predefined files as examples. Table 17.2 can help you interpret these files.

TIP FROM

Bob
& Brian

> If you have a two-bin printer, you can put colored paper in the second bin and print the separator pages on it so they really stand out. To do so, add the appropriate printer control sequences to the .sep file. At the beginning of the file, have the sep file reset the printer and switch to bin two, print the separator page stuff, and then switch back to bin one.

SHARING PRINTERS ON THE WEB VIA IPP

If you have installed Internet Information Services on Windows XP, IPP printing is installed by default. Simply view the Web page `http://hostname/printers`.

NOTE

> The built-in Web page support for IPP printing is installed only if you check the Printers Subfolder option when you install Internet Information Services; see Chapter 15 for details.

The Web pages are generated by a set of nearly two dozen ASP script files that are installed in \Windows\Web\printers. (They make fascinating reading, if you want to learn serious ASP programming!)

Windows XP users can access the shared printer across the Internet by viewing the /printers page, if your computer is reachable. Microsoft has made IPP printer drivers available for Windows 9x and Windows NT4 as well as Windows XP/2000, so you can print to an IPP printer from computers running any of these operating systems. The add-on software is available at `http://www.windowsupdate.com`.

You can print to the Windows IPP service from any other operating systems that support IPP. You need to know the correct URL for the printer, which is `http://`*computername*`/printers/`*sharename*`/.printer`. For example, my shared printer \\bali\laserjet is accessible over the Internet as `http://bali.mycompany.com/printers/Laserjet/.printer`. You also can specify the share name for the printer, such as `http://bali.mycompany.com/sharedlaserjet`. This URL can't be browsed as a Web page; it's meant to be used as the target of IPP software only.

You don't have to remember this URL, either; you can view the /printers Web page and select Properties. The resulting page lists the IPP network name and the printer's other printing capabilities.

MANAGING NETWORK USE OF YOUR COMPUTER

If you've shared folders on your LAN, you might want to know who's using them. You could need to know this information if, for example, someone were editing a file in your shared folder. If you tried to edit the same file, you'd be told by your word processor that the file was "in use by another." But by whom?

Computer Management can help you out. Open the Start menu, right-click My Computer, select Manage, and open the Shared Folders system tool. It displays the shared folders that your computer offers and the number of users attached to them.

You can add new shared folders using the Shares tool with a right-click.

You can also view the current users (sessions) and the files they have in use with the Sessions and Open Files views. This will let you know whom to ask to close a file, or, in an emergency, you can disconnect a user or close an open file with the Delete key. (This is a drastic measure and is sure to mess up the remote user, so use it only when absolutely necessary.)

MANAGING NETWORK RESOURCES USING THE COMMAND LINE

If you find yourself repeating certain network and file operations over and over, day after day, it makes sense to try to automate the processes. You may get so used to the graphical interface that you forget the command line, but it's still there, and you can perform drive mappings and printer selections with the command line almost as easily as from the GUI. Batch files, which were so familiar in the old DOS days, are still around and are a great way to perform repetitive administrative tasks.

I use batch files to perform simple computer-to-computer backups of important files. Let's say I want to back up the folder c:\book on my computer to a shared folder of the same name on another computer named abalone. Here's what a batch file to do this might look like:

```
@echo off
net use q: /delete 1>nul 2>nul
net use q: \\abalone\book
xcopy c:/book q: /e /r /c /y
net use q: /delete
exit
```

Of course, I could bring up Explorer, locate my c:\book folder and the abalone book folder, drag the folder from one computer to the other, and repeat this process every time I want to make a copy of my files. But a shortcut to the above batch file on my desktop will do the same job with a double-click, and I can add the batch file as a Scheduled Task to run automatically every night. *Now* which seems more convenient—that nifty GUI or the humble command-line batch file? Knowing the net utilities gives you an extra set of tools to work with, and their ancient origins shouldn't make them seem less worthy!

The net command comes to us virtually unchanged since the original PC network software developed by Microsoft and IBM back in the early 1980s. There are so many variations of the net command that I think of them as separate commands: net view, net use, net *whatever*. Each net command contains a word that selects a subcommand or operation type.

You can get online help listing all the net subcommands by typing **net /?**, and detailed help by typing or **net *command* /?**, where *command* is any one of the net subcommands.

17

MAPPING DRIVES WITH `net use`

The `net use` command is the most useful of the command-line network functions. `net use` makes and disconnects drive mappings, and establishes printer redirection for command-line programs. The basic command is as follows:

```
net use drive sharename
```

The following example

```
net use q: \\abalone\book
```

maps drive letter q to the shared folder \\abalone\book. You can't replace the shared folder attached to an already mapped drive, so it's best to place commands in the batch file to delete any previous mapping before trying to make a new one:

```
net use q: /delete
net use q: \\abalone\book
```

The /delete command prints an error message if there was no previous message. An elegant solution to this is to redirect the output of the first net command to NUL, which discards any output. I usually redirect both standard output and standard error output with

```
net use q: /delete 1>nul 2>nul
```

to ensure that this command will do its work silently.

You can add the /persistent:yes option to a `net use` command to make the drive mapping return when you log off and back on, matching the function of the Reconnect at Login check box in the graphical drive mapping tool.

You can also map a drive to a subfolder of a shared folder—mimicking the "map root" function familiar to Novell NetWare veterans. Subfolder mapping lets you run legacy DOS applications that require that certain files or directories to be placed in the root directory of a hard disk. You can fool them into running with data on a shared network folder. I like to do this because it lets me store data in a centralized place where it will get backed up regularly.

For example, suppose the hypothetical program runit needs to see its data files in the current root directory, and runs from directory \startdir. I want all the files to reside in a shared network folder, in a subdirectory oldprog of a shared folder named \\server\officedata. This batch file does the trick:

```
@echo off
net use e: /delete 1>nul 2>nul
net use e: \\server\officedata\oldprog
e:
cd \startdir
runit
c:
net use e: /delete
exit
```

Creating a shortcut to this batch file in Windows XP lets me run the old program with a double-click.

net use also maps network printers to the legacy DOS printer devices LPT1, LPT2, and LPT3. The capture printer setting found in Windows 9x is not available, and the only way to redirect DOS program output to a network printer is through net use.

The following command directs DOS application LPT1 printer output to the network printer:

```
net use lpt1: \\server\printername
```

The following command cancels it:

```
net use lpt1: /delete
```

THE DISTRIBUTED FILE SYSTEM

One of the features in Windows 2000 Server/Windows 2003 Server is the Distributed File System. This feature lets a domain manager take shared folders from other computers and "graft" them onto the server's own file system. I think a picture might explain this best. Figure 17.43 shows how a server has had shared folders grafted onto C:\Documents\public. The server now appears to have a folder at C:\Documents\public\brochures even though that directory resides in a shared folder on another computer. The Distributed File System detects that access to anything in folder C:\Documents\public\brochures really refers to \\sales\brochures.

This becomes really interesting if this administrator shares the C:\documents folder, say, as \\bigserver\documents. Now, anyone on the network can access \\bigserver\documents\public\brochures. The server will invisibly have a remote user retrieve the file from the "grafted" folders without the user even knowing it.

Figure 17.43
The Distributed File System lets a Windows 2003 Server administrator graft shared folders from elsewhere in the network into the server's own file system, building one virtual file system from several computers.

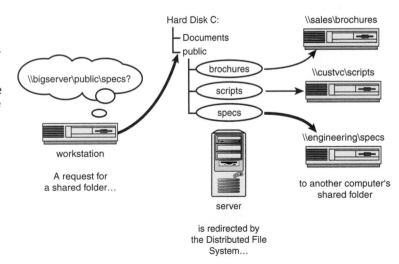

Why is this capability useful? Well, it lets a network administrator build a server that is constructed of interchangeable parts. Bigserver could be the central server of a huge network, sharing millions of files—with none of them actually stored on bigserver! Users would be able to come to one place to find resources, but the workload of serving all these files would be distributed among all the grafted file servers. And if one hard disk failed, it wouldn't take down the whole network. The administrator could simply graft in a replacement file server, instantly restoring service.

Finally, consider this: If every computer on your LAN shared its entire hard drive, and the network administrator grafted every one of these shares into a master folder, you would have a virtual file system containing every single file from every computer in your LAN.

TROUBLESHOOTING

CAN'T FIND ANY PRINTERS IN ACTIVE DIRECTORY

When I use Find Printers, no printers appear in the results list.

You might have selected criteria that no printers match, or you might be specifying the criteria too closely and missing some near but inexact matches. Remove a criterion or two and repeat the search. If your search reveals more printers than you want to look at, try narrowing the search more slowly. Instead of specifying Postscript Level 2 as a Printer Language, for example, try searching for "Post." You might be missing a printer that was entered PostScript Lvl 2.

NO CONNECT OPTION FOR WEB PRINTING

I can view a Windows XP computers/printers Web page and select a printer, but Connect is not shown as an option.

This problem should only occur when you're trying to establish the connection using an older version of Windows. This won't be a problem with Windows XP or Windows 2000. If you are using an older version of Windows, first of all, you must be using Internet Explorer version 5 or higher. Then, you need to have IPP software installed on the computer that is viewing the Web page, and you must be using Internet Explorer as your Web browser. Windows 95, 98, and NT 4 can get IPP software from `http://www.windowsupdate.com`. Download the Internet Printing update. Then, when you view the Web page with IE, you can connect and use the printer.

WEB FOLDER APPEARS TO BE EMPTY

When I view a Web folder known to contain files, it appears to be empty. What's wrong?

The Web server that is sharing the folder does not have Directory Listing enabled on the shared folder. The manager of this Web server (who could be you) needs to set this property in the Web Sharing Properties dialog box for the folder.

DIRECTORY LISTING APPEARS INSTEAD OF WEB FOLDER

When I view a Web folder, I see a columnar text listing of filenames, sizes, and dates instead of the expected folder view with icons.

You did not view the folder using the Open dialog box with Open as Web Folder checked, or the Web site you visited does not have WebDAV, FrontPage, or Office server extensions installed. This can also happen if you opened the folder using a shortcut you created by dragging the Address icon from Explorer when you first viewed this Web folder. Get your shortcut from My Network Places instead.

WEB SHARING IS NOT A CHOICE

When I view a folder or hard drive's Properties, Web Sharing is not available as a choice.

Internet Information Services must be installed, as well as the (FrontPage) Server Extensions. Check to see that these services are properly installed, as explained in Chapter 13. If the Web Sharing tab is still not available, uninstall the Server Extensions and reinstall them.

NETWORK PRINTER HAS STOPPED WORKING

There are documents waiting to be printed on a networked printer, but the printer has stopped working.

If a shared network printer stops working with important documents in its queue, you still might be able to get the documents out by redirecting the output of a stalled printer queue to another printer of the same make and model.

To do this, at the computer that sharing the printer, log on as a Computer Administrator. Open the Printers and Faxes folder, right-click the disabled printer, and select Properties. View the Ports tab. Here, you can direct the queued print output to

- A printer on a different port on the same computer—check the alternative LPT or USB port name.
- A printer on a different network server—Click Add Port, select Local Port, and enter the alternative printer's share name in UNC format, such as **sumatra****laserjet**.

This will send output to the alternative printer, and network users won't have to make any changes to their printer setup. This only works, though, when the alternative printer is completely compatible with the original.

FILE IS IN USE BY ANOTHER

When I attempt to edit a file in a folder I've shared on the network, I receive an error message indicating that the file is in use by another user.

You can find out which remote user has the file open by using the Shared Folder tool in Computer Management, as I described earlier in this chapter under "Managing Network Use of Your Computer."

You can wait for the remote user to finish using your file, or you can ask that person to quit. Only in a dire emergency should you use the Shared Folder tool to disconnect the remote user or close the file. The only reasons I can think of to do this would be that the remote user's computer has crashed, but your computer thinks the connection is still established, or that the remote user is an intruder.

TIPS FROM THE WINDOWS PROS: USING COMMAND-LINE UTILITIES

Setting up a new network can be a grueling task. If you've ever set up a dozen computers in a day, you know what I mean. Think how long it took you to set up Windows, install applications, set up printers and network information, and get the desktop just so . . . then multiply that work by 10 or more. Then repeat the process anytime a new computer is installed, or repaired and reformatted.

Network managers do anything they can to minimize the amount of work they need to do to set up and maintain computers. Windows 2003 Server offers a remote installation service that can set up a completely outfitted Windows XP workstation in a virgin computer, over the LAN, without laying a finger on it. This is a blessing for them, but what about those of us with peer-to-peer workgroup LANs?

The rest of us rely on whatever handy labor-saving tricks we can find to minimize the amount of work needed. Batch files can go a long way to help ease the pain of installing, and they also have two other benefits: They let you make more consistent installations, and they serve as a sort of documentation of whatever configuration they're performing.

My first tip to a workgroup manager is to learn the Windows XP command-line utilities; you can set up batch files to make some consistent settings on new computers. It doesn't hurt to learn how to use Windows Scripting Host. And, the Windows XP Resource Kit offers a big pile of extra command line utilities. Every network manager should have a copy of the resource kit.

Put any batch files and scripts you develop in a shared network folder, and you'll have an installation and configuration toolkit. If a user accidentally disconnects a mapped network drive, that person can visit your folder of handy icons, click MAPDRIVES, and everything can be reset. This can be done with `net use` commands in a batch file.

You can also install printers with the command line. The entire functionality of the Install Printer Wizard is available at the command line; you can pop up graphical utilities like the queue manager, and you even can perform installations and configure printers in a batch file.

Type the following at the command prompt for a full listing of the printer configuration utility's commands:

```
rundll32 printui.dll,PrintUIEntry /?
```

Scroll to the bottom of the list for an eye-popping list of examples. (I warn you, it's ugly. Some experimentation is required to get some of the commands to work, even with the examples given here.)

One really handy use of this command is to install a connection to a network shared printer. This example sets up the local computer to use the shared printer \\bali\laserjet:

```
rundll32 printui.dll,PrintUIEntry /n "\\bali\laserjet" /in
rundll32 printui.dll,PrintUIEntry /n "\\bali\laserjet" /y
```

The first command installs the printer, and the second makes it the default printer.

If you put commands like these in a batch file (using your network's printer names, of course) and put the batch file in a shared network folder, you can add the printer(s) to any computer just by double-clicking the batch file icon. This capability can be a real time-saver when you're configuring many workstations. You could also put these commands in a common login script batch file on your network so that they are executed when your users log in.

17

WINDOWS UNPLUGGED: REMOTE AND MOBILE NETWORKING

In this chapter

GOING UNPLUGGED

LANs were once so expensive and difficult to manage that they were found only in big corporations. Now, networks are found in most businesses and many homes. Internet access is available nearly everywhere, even in coffee shops and airports. We're becoming more and more used to being connected. In fact, with the advent of wireless networking, some people believe that the Internet is going to evolve into the *Evernet*: a global network that's available everywhere, all the time.

We don't have an Evernet yet, but it's become easy—and even expected—that we should be able to connect to our office and home LANs and work wherever we are. Windows XP has several features to help make this possible:

- Dial-Up Networking lets you connect by modem to a remote network and use it as if you were directly connected. File sharing, Active Directory, and network printing are available just as if you were wired right to the LAN.

- Virtual Private Networking lets you exploit the Internet or a wide area network to get from a computer to your own LAN, with a high degree of security.

- Roaming profiles let you have access to your "global" My Documents folder and desktop, even from your mobile computer. (Roaming profiles are available only if you're connecting to a Windows domain-type network, though.)

- Offline Folders let you view and use shared network folders you've designated as important, even when you're not connected or dialed up. Windows gives you this capability by keeping copies of network files stashed away on your own hard drive and invisibly keeping them up-to-date. From your point of view, the network folder is just always there and available.

- Offline Web pages let you mark Web pages and sites for perusal when you're disconnected from the Net.

- Remote Desktop lets you use your Windows XP Professional computer from afar as if you were there.

- Remote Assistance lets you remotely see and control another user's desktop to render assistance or to work cooperatively.

- Built-in support for secure wireless and infrared connectivity lets you walk into remote offices (or coffee shops) and just start surfing and working . . . no wires.

Going "unplugged" is not perfectly effortless, but it's very close, and you'll find you take to it very quickly. You learned about Offline Web pages in Chapter 9, "Browsing the World Wide Web with Internet Explorer." Now it's time to tackle the network features.

DIAL-UP NETWORKING

Windows XP can connect to a remote Windows network via modem. All file sharing, printing, and directory services are available just as if you were directly connected, including any Novell, OS/2, and Unix file and print services provided on the network. Just dial up, open shared folders, transfer files, and e-mail as if you were there, and disconnect when you're finished.

The receiving end of Dial-Up Networking can be handled by the Remote Access Services (RAS) in Windows .NET/2000/NT4 Server or by third-party remote connection hardware devices manufactured by networking companies such as Cisco and Lucent.

Windows XP Professional and Home Edition come with a stripped-down version of RAS, so you can also set up your own Windows XP computer to receive a single incoming modem connection. You can do so, for example, to get access to your office computer and LAN from home, provided your company permits this access.

I'll discuss incoming calls later in the chapter. First, though, let me tell you how to connect to a remote Windows network.

SETTING UP DIAL-UP NETWORKING

To create a dial-up connection to a remote network or computer, you need an installed modem. You learned how to install modems in Chapter 8, "Internet and TCP/IP Connection Options," so start there to install and configure your modem.

You also must get or confirm the information shown in Table 18.1 with the remote network's or computer's manager.

TABLE 18.1   INFORMATION NEEDED FOR A RAS CONNECTION

Information	Reason
Telephone number	You must know the receiving modem's telephone number, including area code.
Modem compatibility	You must confirm that your modem is compatible with the modems used by the remote network; check which modem protocols are supported (V.90, V.32, and so on).
Protocols in use	The remote network must use TCP/IP and/or IPX/SPX. Windows XP does not support the NetBEUI protocol.
TCP/IP configuration	You should confirm that the Remote Access Server assigns TCP/IP information automatically (dynamically) via DHCP. Usually, the answer is yes.

continues

18

TABLE 18.1   CONTINUED

Information	Reason
Mail servers	You might need to obtain the IP addresses or names of SMTP, POP, Exchange, Lotus Notes, or Microsoft Mail servers if you want to use these applications while connected to the remote network.
User ID and password	You must be ready to supply a username and password to the remote dial-up server. If you're calling a Windows .NET, XP, 2000 or NT RAS server, then use the same Windows username and password you use on that remote network.

Armed with this information, you're ready to create a dial-up connection to the remote network. To do so, just follow these steps:

1. Choose Start, My Computer, My Network Places and select View Network Connections. (Note: You might need to close the left Folders pane to see the Task list.)

2. Select Create a New Connection, and click Next.

3. Select Connect to the Network At My Workplace (see Figure 18.1) and then click Next. Choose Dial-Up Connection, and then click Next.

4. Enter a name for the connection, for example, Office LAN, and click Next.

5. On the Phone Number To Dial dialog box, enter the telephone number of the remote dial-in server. You can enter the number directly, including any necessary prefixes or area codes. Select Next. The final page asks if you want Windows to put a shortcut to this connection on your desktop. Check this if you wish, and select Finish.

NOTE

You can delete a connection shortcut later if you don't want it and can drag the connection icon from Network Connections to your desktop later if you do.

Figure 18.1
Choose Connect to the Network At My Workplace from the New Connection Type selections.

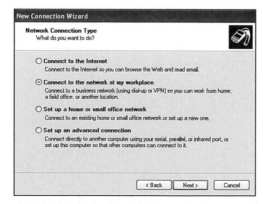

6. After you've clicked Finish, Windows immediately wants to open the connection. You must check the connection properties, so click the Properties button.

SETTING A DIAL-UP CONNECTION'S PROPERTIES

There are two ways you can edit the properties for a dial-up connection from the Network Connections window: You can open the connection icon and click the Properties button, or you can right-click the icon and select Properties.

The Dial-Up Connection's properties page has five tabs and a heap o' parameters. Most of the time, the default settings will work correctly, but you might need to change some of them. I'll walk you through the most important parameters.

→ For detailed instructions on establishing locations and dialing rules, **see** "Phone and Modem Options," **p. 829**.

GENERAL

On the General tab of the Properties dialog (see Figure 18.2), you can set your choice of modems if you have more than one installed. You also can set telephone numbers and dialing rules.

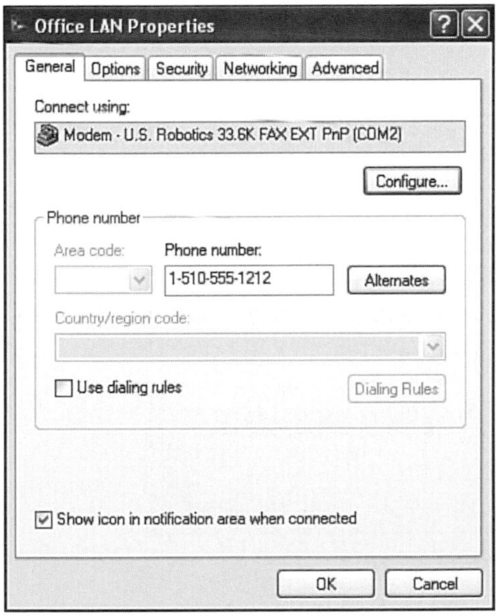

Figure 18.2
General Properties include dialing and modem settings.

The following are the significant parameters:

- **Connect Using**—If you have more than one modem installed, choose which modem to use for this connection. The Configure button lets you set the maximum speed (data rate) to use between the computer and the modem, and other modem properties.

- **Area Code, Phone Number, and Country/Region code**—If the remote server has more than one phone number (or more than one hunt group), you can specify alternate telephone numbers. It's a neat feature if your company has several access points or provides emergency-use-only toll-free numbers.

- **Use Dialing Rules**—Check to have Windows determine when to send prefixes and area codes. If you want to use this, enter the area code and phone number in their separate fields. This feature is useful if you call the same number from several locations with different dialing properties.

- **Show Icon in Notification Area**—This option lets you keep a small connection monitor icon in your task tray when you're connected to the remote network. Opening it lets you quickly disconnect the remote connection, so it's best to leave Show Icon checked.

OPTIONS

The Options tab of the Properties dialog (see Figure 18.3) includes dialing options, choices for being prompted for phone number and passwords, and redialing settings.

Figure 18.3
The Options tab includes dialing and prompting options.

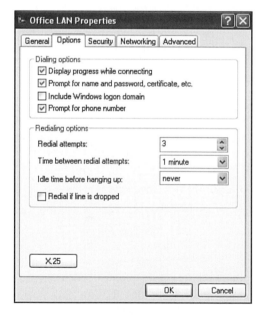

The important options are as follows:

- **Prompt for Name and Password**—If this box is checked, Windows always prompts for your remote connection user ID and password. If it is unchecked, after the first successful connection, Windows stores your password and uses it automatically later on. If you are worried that someone might dial the connection by gaining unauthorized access to your computer, leave this box checked; otherwise, you can uncheck it to skip the password step when connecting.

- **Include Windows Logon Domain**—Be sure to check this box if you are calling a Windows .NET/2000/NT4 domain-type network but your computer is not set up as a member of the same domain. When this box is checked, the dialing dialog box has a space for you to enter the remote domain's name.

- **Prompt for Phone Number**—If this box is checked, Windows displays the phone number it's about to dial. Leave it checked if you don't trust Windows to use the correct area code, prefixes, and so on. It's best to leave it checked until you're convinced.

- **Redialing Options**—If the remote server frequently gives you a busy signal, increase the number of attempts from 3 to, say, 20, and lower the delay from 1 minute to 15 seconds to get quicker redialing action.

- **Idle Time Before Hanging Up**—If you tend to wander off for hours with your modem still online, you can set this option to a reasonable time, and Windows will automatically disconnect you if no network traffic occurs for the specified time.

- **Redial If Line Is Dropped**—This option makes Windows redial immediately if your modem connection fails. It's good if you have lousy phone connections but bad if the remote computer disconnects you because its "idle time" runs out before yours does.

SECURITY

On the Security tab, you can select which encryption methods are required or permitted when you're logging on to the remote connection server.

- **Security Options**—If you are connecting to a Windows .NET, 2000, or NT Remote Access Server, select Typical and set Validate My Identity to Require Secured Password. If the Windows domain name, username, and password you'll use for the remote network are the same as those you use to sign in to your own computer, check Automatically Use My Windows Logon.

- **Advanced (Custom Settings)**—Select Advanced if you are calling a Shiva Remote Access Server. Click the Settings button, and then select Shiva Password Authentication Protocol (SPAP).

> **NOTE**
>
> *Shiva* is shorthand for a user account/password verification system manufactured by Shiva Corporation (now owned by Intel). The Shiva system only validates a caller's right to connect to the modem; it doesn't grant rights to resources (like file servers) on the network.

NETWORKING

The Networking tab of the Properties dialog (see Figure 18.4) defines which network protocols and network services are connected through the dial-up connection.

Figure 18.4
On the Networking tab, you can choose which network protocols and services are enabled for the dial-up connection. Check everything, and set the TCP/IP protocol's properties if necessary.

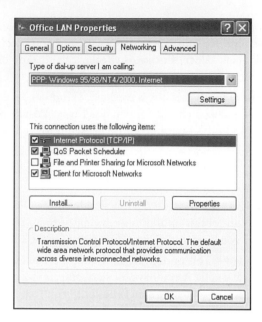

18

Usually, all protocols and services should be checked except File and Printer Sharing. This option should be disabled so remote network users cannot use your computer's shared folders and printers. If you want to let the remote network's users see them, check File and Printer Sharing.

Normally, a Remote Access Server automatically assigns your connection the proper IP address, DNS addresses, and other TCP/IP settings through DHCP, so you don't need to alter the Internet Protocol properties. In the very unlikely event that the network administrator tells you that you must set TCP/IP parameters yourself, select Internet Protocol from the Components list, and click Properties. Enter the supplied IP address and DNS addresses there.

ADVANCED

The Advanced tab configures Internet Connection Sharing and the Internet Connection Firewall. These utilities aren't used when you're connecting to a remote network.

Finally, after you've finished making any changes to the connection's options, select OK. The connection icon is then installed in Network Connections for use anytime.

MANAGING DIAL-UP CONNECTIONS FROM MULTIPLE LOCATIONS

As you've seen already, Windows lets you enter your current telephone area code and dialing prefix requirements so that it can make modem calls using the customs appropriate for your local phone system. This capability is great if you use a portable computer. For example, at home, you might be in area code 415. At the office, you might be in area code 707 and have to dial 9 to get an outside telephone line. When you're visiting Indianapolis, you're in area code 317 and might need to use a telephone company calling card when making long-distance calls.

Windows offers great support for these variations by letting you define "locations," each with a separate local area code and dialing rules. When you use one of your Network Connections icons, as long as you've told Windows your current location, it can automatically apply the correct set of rules when making a dial-up connection.

→ For detailed instructions on establishing locations and dialing rules, **see** "Phone and Modem Options," **p. 829**.

However, if you use an ISP with access points in various cities, or your company has different access numbers in various regions, you'll find that this Locations system does not let you associate a different dial-up number with each location. It would be great if it did, but no such luck.

If you want to use different "local" dial-up numbers for the various locations you visit with your computer, you must set up a separate Network Connections icon for each access number and use the appropriate icon when making a connection at each location.

TIP FROM

Bob & Brian

Set up and test the first access number you need. Then, when you need to add a new access number, right-click the first one, select Create Copy, rename it, and change its telephone number. I name my icons based on the location of the local number: Office-Berkeley, My Office Seattle, and so on.

When you travel and want to make a dial-up connection, select the appropriate dial-up icon, and set your location before you click Dial.

TIP FROM

Bob & Brian

If you travel, you'll find that having your Internet Options set to dial a particular connection automatically is not a great idea. It would dial the chosen connection no matter where you were (and remember, if there's a 50-50 chance of things going wrong, 9 times out of 10 they will). So, if you travel with your computer, you might want to open Internet Explorer and click Tools, Internet Options. Select the Connections tab, and choose Never Dial a Connection. This way, you won't be blind-sided by an inadvertent call to Indiana while you're in India.

MAKING A DIAL-UP CONNECTION

Making a remote network dial-up connection is no more difficult than connecting to the Internet. If you're a mobile user who moves between area codes, check your current location first, and then dial.

18

CHAPTER 18   WINDOWS UNPLUGGED: REMOTE AND MOBILE NETWORKING

CHECK YOUR CURRENT LOCATION

If you've changed area codes or phone systems since the last time you made a modem connection, check your location setting by following these steps before dialing into the network:

1. Open the Control Panel, and select Printers and Other Hardware, then Phone and Modem Options.

2. Check your current location in the list of configured dialing locations using the Dialing Rules tab.

3. Click OK to close the dialog.

Windows should now use the correct area code and dialing prefixes.

CHOOSE A PROFILE OPTION

If your computer is a member of a Windows XP domain network that offers roaming user profiles, you can decide whether to connect using your current local profile or use your remote "roaming" profile. Your network manager will tell you if the network provides roaming profiles. You have two options for making the connection:

- If you connect while you're already logged on to your computer, you'll have access to the files, printers, and all other network resources on the remote network, but the My Documents folder and desktop will remain as they were before you made the connection. You'll be "here."

- If you log off from Windows and then log on again using the Log On Using Dial-Up Connection option, you'll be connected with your user profile on the remote network. Your My Documents folder, home directory, desktop layout, and other preferences will be copied from the server to your mobile computer, and you'll be "there."

If you're not connecting to a Windows domain-type network, if don't have a roaming profile, or if you don't need to use it, use the steps under "Connect to a Remote Network Without a Roaming Profile."

If you have an account with a roaming profile on the remote network, and you want to have access to the My Documents folder and settings you use on that network, follow the steps under "Connect to a Remote Network with a Roaming Profile."

CONNECT TO A REMOTE NETWORK WITHOUT A ROAMING PROFILE

To connect to a remote network using the profile you're already using in your own computer, make the connection directly, without logging out. Just follow these steps:

1. Open the connection from the Start Menu "Connect To" list, from Network Connections, or from a shortcut to the connection.

18

Windows puts a "Connect to" menu on the Start menu when you've defined a dial-up connection. You can select a connection to dial, or right-click it to edit its properties. This is a real timesaver.

2. Windows will open the connection dialog, as shown in Figure 18.5. Enter your login name, password, and domain (if any). You can also select Properties to adjust the connection's telephone number or dialing properties. (The Dialing From choice appears only if you checked Use Dialing Rules and have defined more than one dialing location.)

If you're connecting to a remote Windows .NET/2000 domain, you can enter DOMAIN\username or username@domain in the User name field.

3. You can choose to let Windows remember your password, if you're not worried that other people might use your computer to gain inappropriate access to the remote network. (Giving access to "anyone who uses this computer" is usually used only for a shared ISP connection, not remote networks.)

4. Select Dial. Windows shows you the progress of your connection as it are dials, verifies your username and password, and registers your computer on the remote network.

Figure 18.5
In the Connect dialog box, you can enter your username and password for the remote network. If you're logged in, you can also tell Windows to remember your password and change the dialing properties.

18

If the connection fails, unless you dialed the wrong number, you'll most likely get a reasonable explanation: The password or account name was invalid, the remote system is not accepting calls, and so on. If you entered an incorrect username or password, you are usually given two more chances to re-enter the information before the other end hangs up on you.

If the connection completes successfully, a new connection icon appears in your taskbar, indicating the established connection speed, as in Figure 18.6.

Figure 18.6

You can now use the remote network's resources, as discussed next.

CONNECT TO A REMOTE NETWORK WITH A ROAMING PROFILE

To use the remote network under your user profile on that network, you must log in using the remote connection, using these steps:

1. Log off Windows if you are currently logged on. Choose Start and select Log off.

2. Press Ctrl+Alt+Del to display the logon dialog. Enter your network username, password, and domain. If Log on Using Dial-Up Connection isn't displayed, click the Options button. Check Log On Using Dial-Up Connection, and select OK.

3. Choose a network connection by selecting the name of the remote connection from the drop-down list, and select Dial. You can select VPN or modem dial-up connections.

⚡ *If the connection you need to use isn't shown in the list of connection choices, see "Can't Choose Dial-Up Connection at Login" in the "Troubleshooting" section at the end of this chapter.*

4. When the Connect dialog appears, enter your remote access username and password and logon domain, as previously shown in Figure 18.5. This usually is the same as your network logon information. (You won't have the option to save your password or change the connection properties here, because you're not logged in.) Select Dial.

Windows then dials the remote network connection and logs in. After your profile settings have been copied, you're online and ready to use the network.

> **NOTE**
>
> If the connection fails because the telephone number was wrong, you may need to log on locally to change the number in the connections' properties dialog.

CALLBACKS

For security purposes, some networks don't permit you to just call in; they want to call you, so you not only need the right login name and password, but you also must be at the right location to gain access to the network. This type of access also generates an audit trail through phone company records.

When this type of security is in force, your network manager will contact you to arrange the predetermined telephone number to use to call you. You cannot access the network from any other location unless you arrange for call forwarding from the original number.

Callbacks can also be used to make the remote host pay for a long phone call. Some businesses use callbacks so that employees can dial in from the field at the company's expense.

When callbacks are in effect, you'll dial up the remote network as I described earlier, but as soon as the network accepts your password it will hang up. Within 30 seconds it will call back, and your modem will pick up the line and establish a connection.

If your network manager says that callbacks are optional, you can tell Windows how you want to exercise the option. In Network Connections, select the Advanced menu, choose Dial-Up Preferences, and select the Callback tab. You can indicate that you want callbacks on or off, or that you want to be asked each time you make a connection.

USING REMOTE NETWORK RESOURCES

When you're connected, you can use network resources exactly as if you were on the network. My Network Places, shared folders, and network printers all function as if you were directly connected.

The following are some tips for effective remote networking by modem:

- Don't try to run application software that is installed on the remote network itself. Starting it could take hours!

- If you get disconnected while using a remote network, it's a bummer to have to stop what you're doing and reconnect. You can tell Windows to automatically redial if you're disconnected while you're working. In Network Connections, from the Advanced menu, choose Dial-up Preferences, and select the Autodial tab. Check any locations you work from where you would like Windows to automatically reconnect you.

- You can use My Network Places to record frequently visited remote network folders. You can also place shortcuts to network folders on your desktop or in other folders.

- If the remote LAN has Internet access, you can browse the Internet while you're connected to the LAN. You don't need to disconnect and switch to your ISP. You might need to make a change in your personal e-mail program, though, as I'll note later under "E-mail and Network Connections."

- If you use several different remote networks, you can create a folder for each. In them, put shortcuts to the appropriate connection and to frequently used folders on those networks. Put all these folders in a folder named, for example, Remote Networks on your desktop. This way you can open one folder and be working within seconds.

E-MAIL AND NETWORK CONNECTIONS

If you use your computer with remote LANs as well as an ISP, you might need to be careful with the e-mail programs you use. Most e-mail programs don't make it easy for you to associate different mail servers with different connections.

Although most e-mail servers allow you to retrieve your mail from anywhere on the Internet, most are very picky about whom they let send e-mail. Generally, to use an SMTP server to send mail out, you must be using a computer whose IP address is known by the server to belong to its network. That is, you can usually pick up mail from any servers you use, but you can only send mail out through the server that serves your current connection.

See if your favorite e-mail program can configure separate "identities", each with associated incoming and outgoing servers. If you send mail, be sure you're using the identity that's set up to use the outgoing (SMTP) server that belongs to your current dial-up connection.

MONITORING AND ENDING A DIAL-UP CONNECTION

While you're connected, note that the System Tray connection icon flashes to indicate incoming and outgoing data activity. It's a true Windows tool, which means you can have it do pretty much the same thing in about five different ways.

> **NOTE**
>
> If the connection icon is missing, open Network Connections. Right-click the connection you're using, select Properties, and check Show Icon in Notification Area When Connected.

- If you hover your mouse cursor over the connection icon, a box appears, listing the connection name, speed, and number of bytes sent and received.

- If you double-click it, the connection status dialog box appears, as shown in Figure 18.7. From the status dialog, you can get to the connection properties or disconnect.

- If you right-click it, you can select Disconnect, Status, or Open Network Connections. This is the way to go.

Figure 18.7
The connection status dialog box displays current connection statistics and lets you disconnect or change connection properties. Right-clicking the connection icon in the taskbar is a quicker way to disconnect.

Truthfully, all I ever do with the taskbar icon is make sure it blinks while I'm working and right-click Disconnect when I'm finished.

When you disconnect a remote network connection, the taskbar icon disappears. If you logged in using a remote network profile, you remain logged in using the local copy of this profile until you log out.

ENABLING DIAL-IN AND VPN ACCESS TO YOUR COMPUTER

Windows XP Professional has a stripped-down Remote Access Server built in, and you can take advantage of it to get access to your work computer from home or from the field, or vice versa. You can also enable remote access temporarily so that a system administrator can maintain your computer.

CAUTION

> RAS is not too difficult to set up, but beware: Permitting remote access opens up security risks. Before you enable dial-in access on a computer at work, be sure that your company permits it. In some companies, you could be fired for violating the security policies.

To enable dial-in access, you must be logged on as a computer administrator. Then follow these steps:

1. In Network Connections, select the Create a New Connection Task in the New Connection Wizard. Click Next.
2. Choose Set Up An Advanced Connection, and click Next. Choose Accept Incoming Connections, and click Next.
3. Check the modem to be used for incoming connections.

TIP FROM

Bob & Brian

> Despite what the wizard dialog box seems to say, you can choose at most one modem. You *can* choose one of each different type of connection: modem and direct parallel port.

4. If you want to disconnect incoming connections that sit idle (unused) for too long, click the Properties button and check Disconnect a Call If Idle More Than XXX Minutes, and then click OK.
5. You then are asked whether you want to additionally permit Virtual Private Network connections to your computer. I'll discuss Virtual Private Networking later in this chapter. You can read ahead to decide whether you want it or check Do Not Allow Virtual Private Connections now. You can always repeat this process to enable it later. It's best to not allow virtual private connections now if you're not sure.

18

6. Windows then displays a list of your computer's or domain's users. Select the ones who will be permitted to access your computer remotely, as shown in Figure 18.8. This step is very important: Check only the names of those users whom you really want and need to give access. The fewer accounts you enable, the less likely that someone might accidentally break into your computer.

Figure 18.8
Here, you can choose users who will be granted the right to remote access of your computer. Check only the names of those users really needing access, and don't check Guest.

CAUTION

Under no circumstances should you enable Guest, IUSR_*xxx*, or IWAM_*xxx* (where *xxx* is the name of your computer—for example, IUSR_AMBON) for remote access. The IUSR and IWAM accounts are used exclusively by Internet Information Server for access by Web site visitors, and Guest is used for general network access. There's no way you would ever want to give unprotected access to your network via modem or VPN!

Check only the names of users who need access and who have good (long, complex) passwords.

7. You can enable or enforce callbacks for individual users if you like. Select the username, click Properties, then select the Callback tab. If you do enable callbacks, you must enter any required dialing prefixes and area codes. Windows doesn't use dialing rules when making callbacks.

8. Windows displays a list of network protocols and services that will be made available to the dial-up connection. Generally, you can leave all protocols and services checked.

View the properties page for each checked protocol to specify whether callers have access only to your computer or have access to the LAN via your computer. Unless you have a reason to ban a remote caller (usually you) from reaching the rest of your LAN, you have no reason to disable these services.

NOTE

If you use Internet Connection Sharing or a connection sharing router between the Internet and your computer, you'll have to forward incoming VPN connections to your computer. For details, see "Making Services Available" in Chapter 18.

Access to Windows and NetWare servers through the IPX/SPX protocol is handled without difficulty.

However, the TCP/IP protocol presents a significant problem. Incoming callers must be assigned IP addresses valid on your LAN to be able to communicate with computers other than your own.

If your network has a DHCP server, or if you are using Internet connection sharing or a gateway device, then a caller will automatically receive a valid IP address. You don't have to worry about setting the TCP/IP address.

If your network does not have a true DHCP server on the network, you must manually assign a valid subnet of at least four IP addresses taken from the IP address range of your network. If you don't, incoming callers can access only your computer. (And if that's sufficient, you don't need to worry about this.)

NOTE

You must provide a subnet with one IP address for the RAS server component on your computer and one for each incoming connection. Subnets have an overhead of two addresses, so the minimum subnet size is four addresses (two overhead, one for the server on your computer, and one for a caller). With an eight-address subnet, you could have five incoming connections (two overhead, one for the server, five for callers), although XP limits you to two or three incoming connections total.

Unfortunately, the process of assigning subnet addresses is more complex than I can go into here in any detail, and the articles on this topic in Windows XP's online help are worse than useless. You'll have to get a network manager to assign the subnet for you.

NOTE

You also can read more about TCP/IP networking in *Upgrading and Repairing Networks, 3rd Edition*, published by Que.

TIP FROM

Bob & Brian

Look up your LAN adapter's IP address. If it starts with 192.168, you might try this trick for assigning IP addresses for incoming connections. For the starting and ending addresses, use the first three numbers of your IP address followed by 220 and 223, respectively. For example, my IP address is 192.168.0.34. I'd enter 192.168.0.220 and 192.168.0.223 as the From and To addresses.

When the incoming connection information has been entered, a new icon appears in your Network Connections window. You can edit its properties later or delete it to cancel incoming access. When someone connects to your computer, yet another icon appears in Network Connections showing their username. If necessary you can right-click this to disconnect them.

18

WIRELESS NETWORKING

One great way to work "unplugged" is to maintain your network or Internet connection with wireless networking. Radio-based networking technology has advanced rapidly in recent years, and it's being deployed in schools, universities, corporations and, oddly enough, coffee houses. Whether you're at a client's desk or in an overstuffed chair sipping a *cafe latte*, as long as you're within hundred feet or so of a network access point, you're online.

For a portable computer, what you'll need is a PC-card based radio transmitter/receiver. Windows XP has built-in support for the 802.11 security and signaling protocol used in Wireless networking. The protocol ensures that the data rate is adjusted up and down as the quality of the radio signal reception varies.

However, data sent on a wireless network isn't confined to a network cable. It can be received by any other wireless-equipped computer up to several hundred feet away. The current generation of 802.11b wireless network cards employ an encryption technique called WEP (Wired-Equivalent Privacy), but the word "equivalent" has proven to be over-optimistic: researchers have found that the encryption can be fairly easily broken by a determined eavesdropper. And if WEP encryption isn't enabled, your data is available to anyone nearby.

Most e-mail programs, web sites and FTP servers send passwords without additional encryption, so your account information could be obtained by hackers and other unscrupulous types. So, while wireless networking is a great idea, you should think carefully before using it. For the average home user, the risk is probably not too great. Businesses should be more concerned about the possibility of eavesdroppers monitoring their network data. Still, you should research the issue for yourself before you buy into this technology. It could be some time before manufacturers can alter their hardware and software to improve security.

→ For details on installing and configuring wireless networking, **see** "Wireless Networking," in Chapter 16, **p. 508**.

OFFLINE FOLDERS

You might recognize the "Offline" problem: You'll eventually want to have copies of a remote computer's files on your own computer. If you make changes to your copies, the network's copy will be out of date. If someone changes the originals on the remote computer, your copies will be out of date. And trying to remember where the originals came from and where the most recent copies are located is a painful job. The answer to the offline problem, of course, is automation. Computers can do anything, right?

I don't know if you ever tried to use My Briefcase in previous versions of Windows, but the answer to that question is "not always." My Briefcase was a tool that let you transfer files between computers by copying them to and from a special folder. Or something like that—the whole thing was so confusing I never really understood it. Whenever I tried to use it, it froze, lost files, or crashed my computer. Well, as the saying goes, "It's the thought that counts."

Windows's Offline Folders feature takes care of these problems. Here's the skinny: When you mark a network folder for offline use, Windows stashes away a copy or *caches* the folder's files somewhere on your hard drive, but all you see is the original shared folder on your screen. When you disconnect, the shared file folder remains on your screen, with its files intact. You can still add, delete and edit the files. Meanwhile, network users can do the same with the original copies. When you reconnect later, Windows will set everything right again.

"Right," I can hear you say, "and if you believe that, I have this bridge to sell you." Okay, I was skeptical too at first, but this time, Microsoft really did it right. You'll find that this feature works, and it's more powerful than it seems at first glance. The following are some of the applications of Offline Folders:

- Maintaining an up-to-date copy of a set of shared files on a server (or desktop computer) and a remote or portable computer. If you keep a project's files in an offline folder, Windows keeps the copies on all your computers up-to-date.

- "Pushing" application software or data from a network to a portable computer. If software or data is kept in an offline folder, your portable can update itself whenever you connect or dock to the LAN.

- Automatically backing up important files from your computer to an alternate location. Your computer can connect to a dial-up or network computer on a timer and refresh your offline folders automatically.

After I describe all the functions and settings for Offline Folders, I'll give you some scenarios and show how you can set up Offline Folders to help.

NOTE

> To use Offline Folders, you must disable Fast User Switching. To do this, click Start, Control Panel, and User Accounts. Select Change the Way Users Log On or Off, and uncheck Use Fast User Switching.
>
> Then, you must enable Offline Folders. Open any Explorer window or My Computer. Select Tools, Folder Options. View the Offline Files tab, and check Enable Offline Files.

IDENTIFYING FILES AND FOLDERS FOR OFFLINE USE

You can mark specific files, subfolders, or even entire shared folders from a "remote" server for offline use.

NOTE

> The server I'm talking about might be in the next room, which isn't very "remote" at all, but that's what I'll call it for simplicity's sake. In this section, a "remote" server refers to some other computer that you access via networking.

While you're connected to the remote network, view the desired items in Explorer, My Network Places, or, if you've mapped a drive letter to the shared folder, you can select it under My Computer.

NOTE

> The Offline Folders feature works with folders shared by any network server using Microsoft's standard SMB networking protocol, so you can use shares from Windows, OS/2, Samba, and so on, but not NetWare.
>
> However, you cannot take offline any folder whose full pathname is longer than 64 characters. Windows caches only files whose pathnames are shorter than 64 characters.

When you find the folder or folders you want, select them, and right-click Make Available Offline. Be cautious about marking entire shared drives or folders available offline, though, unless you're sure how much data they contain, and you're sure you want it all. You could end up with a gigabytes of stuff you don't need!

 If Make Available Offline isn't displayed as an option, see "Can't Make File Available Offline" in the "Troubleshooting" section at the end of this chapter.

You might run into a bit of glitch. If you choose a shared folder listed under My Network Places, Make Available Offline isn't a choice. You can select a subfolder, but not the whole shared folder. To make an entire shared folder available offline, select it in Explorer or My Computer.

The first time you mark a folder for offline use, Windows starts the Offline Files Wizard. The wizard then asks you to make choices for three options:

- **Automatically synchronize the Offline Files when I log on and off my computer**—Check this to have Windows automatically update or *synchronize* your cached copies with the network. If unchecked, you need to tell Windows to sync-up files manually.

- **Enable Reminders**—Check this to have Windows periodically pop-up a reminder when you're offline and using cached files.

- **Create a shortcut for the desktop**—Check this to put an Offline Files icon on your desktop. You can use this to see what you've made available offline.

NOTE

> If you select a shortcut to a file and mark it Make Available Offline, Windows does you a favor: It gets the file to which the shortcut points and makes it available offline, too. But Windows doesn't do this with a shortcut to a folder.

 If you get the error Files of This Type Cannot Be Made Available Offline, *see "Can't Make File Available Offline" in the "Troubleshooting" section at the end of the chapter.*

When you've marked a folder for offline use, Windows immediately makes a local copy of it, and when the synchronization is finished, the network folder or file icon appears with a special "roundtrip" marker to indicate that it is available offline.

USING FILES WHILE OFFLINE

When you disconnect from the network by undocking or disconnecting a remote connection, only the offline files and folders remain in the Explorer display, as shown in Figure 18.9.

Figure 18.9
When you disconnect from the network, only offline folders and files remain.

While offline, you can still use the remote folder. You can add, delete, or edit files in it. If you have a drive letter mapped to the offline folder, the drive letter still functions.

This process works so well that it's disconcerting at first because the effect is . . . well, because there is no effect at all. You can happily copy files to a network folder, and it seems to happen, except they don't show up on the remote server until you reconnect.

When you reconnect, you should synchronize your offline folders with the network folders so that both sets will be up-to-date.

THE SYNCHRONIZATION MANAGER

You can synchronize files anytime you are connected to the network containing the original shared folder, whether by LAN, modem, or VPN network connection. You can start a synchronization in five ways (of course):

- Manually, from Explorer's Tools menu or by choosing Start, All Programs, Accessories. This method lets you synchronize any offline folders whose remote server is available.
- Manually, by right-clicking a specific shared file or folder and choosing Synchronize. This method synchronizes just that file or folder.
- Automatically, when your computer is connected and idle.

- Automatically, when you log on, off, or both.
- Automatically, at specified times and days of the week. For a scheduled synchronization, Windows can even automatically makes a dial-up connection.

As wonderful as the Offline Folder system is, it can't help you if two people modify the same file from two different locations. Windows helps you avoid this problem while you're connected by using the online copy of the file whenever available (see the following tip for one teensy exception). This way, everyone uses the same copy, and Windows can use its standard file and record locking mechanism to control access to the file by multiple users.

TIP FROM

Bob & Brian

> Although Windows uses the online copy of the file whenever possible, there is one exception: If the person who shared the files made them available for offline use as "applications," Windows doesn't let you change them, and it uses the local copy when possible. I'll talk about this topic under "Making Your Shared Folders Available for Offline Use" later in this chapter.

During offline use, though, it's possible for both the original and your copy to be changed. When you synchronize, you must pick the "winner," and one set of changes will be lost. If you are keeping copies only of your own files, shared from your own computer, losing one set probably won't be a big problem. You can't work in two places at the same time anyway. If you're dealing with shared files used by many people, though, offline folders can't save you from collisions in editing.

TIP FROM

Bob & Brian

> If you're collaborating with others on a project and editing files offline, the way to avoid problems is to coordinate with each other before editing and synchronize frequently.

MANUAL SYNCHRONIZATION

You can start synchronization manually after you've reconnected to a network whose files you took offline. You must synchronize manually if you connect to the remote server with a dial-up or VPN connection.

In Windows Explorer, choose Tools, Synchronize. Select the shared folders whose files you want to update, as shown in Figure 18.10, and select Synchronize.

Windows copies updated files as necessary and then asks you to resolve any conflicts it encounters. The three types of conflict for any given file are as follows:

- A file on the server was deleted. Windows asks whether you want to delete your local copy, too, or put your copy back on the server.
- You deleted your copy of the file. Windows asks whether you want to pick up another copy or delete the original file on the server.

Figure 18.10
For manual synchro-
nization, check the
network shares
whose folders you
want to update.

- Your copy of the file and the server's copy were both edited since you last synchronized. Windows asks who wins: Do you want to copy your file to the server, the server's copy to your computer, or keep both files under two different names. This dialog box is pretty nicely done; you can view either version with the click of a button. You can check a box to apply the same decision to all file conflicts.

I can't tell you a right or wrong answer for any of these situations. You'll have to determine which is the appropriate answer in each case.

 If you get the error Unable to connect to server, *see "Offline Synchronization Gives* Unable to connect to server *Error" in the "Troubleshooting" section at the end of the chapter.*

After all files have been checked, Windows displays a summary. This synchronization summary indicates any significant problems encountered. If any problems occur synchronizing a folder, Windows stops updating that folder and continues with the next network share.

NOTE

> If the process fails because a file is in use, you should repeat the synchronization when no one is editing files in the shared folder; otherwise, you might lose changes to some files.

AUTOMATIC SYNCHRONIZATION

You can tell Windows to perform synchronization automatically upon logon, logoff, or when your computer is sitting idle while you are connected to the remote network. This feature is good for dockable mobile computers that spend a good deal of their time directly connected to a LAN.

If you bring up the Synchronization Manager (in Windows Explorer, by choosing Tools, Synchronize), you can select the Setup button to display the Synchronization Settings dialog, which is shown in Figure 18.11.

You can specify that Windows is to synchronize selected folders each time you log on or log off while connected to a network. You can check which offline files are to be updated (and which offline Web pages too, by the way; I've been ignoring them, but they are updated with the Synchronization Manager, too). You can also select different folders to update, depending on which connection is active, using the When I Am Using This Network Connection selection.

→ For information on updating offline Web pages, **see** "Browsing Offline," **p. 299**.

Figure 18.11
On the Synchronization Settings dialog, you can specify when automatic synchronization should occur.

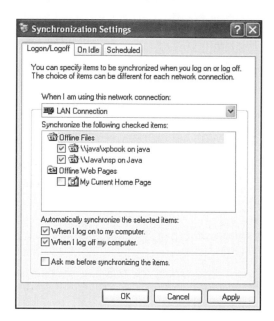

UPDATE ON IDLE

You can instruct Windows to synchronize offline folders and cached Web pages when your computer is sitting idle by using the On Idle tab of the Synchronization Settings dialog. Here, you can also choose which folders to update, depending on which connection is in use. By default, Windows waits for 15 minutes of inactivity before starting an update, and it updates again every 60 minutes. You can change these times by choosing the Advanced button.

Updating when idle is useful for computers that spend a lot of time connected to a LAN, but it is less useful for a portable computer dialed in by modem.

SCHEDULED SYNCHRONIZATION

Finally, you can instruct Windows to begin synchronizations on a timed schedule. Enabling this feature makes sense only if your computer is *on* at the time of the scheduled update. It would be useful to get copies of large files from a LAN server or from a distant server through a VPN connection. The Scheduler can automatically establish a dial-up or VPN connection before synchronizing.

You can view scheduled synchronizations on the Synchronization Manager's Scheduled tab. The Synchronization Settings dialog lists any currently scheduled updates. To add a new entry, click Add, and the Scheduled Synchronization Wizard will walk you through the process.

Once configured, you can manage the scheduling information for scheduled synchronizations just like any other scheduled task. It's a rather complex system with many options (for example, don't synchronize while the computer is running on battery power).

MAKING YOUR SHARED FOLDERS AVAILABLE FOR OFFLINE USE BY OTHERS

When you've marked a network file for offline use, Windows makes a copy of the file on your hard disk. While you're still connected to the network, it's faster to use the local copy when you want to access the file. On the other hand, this would not be appropriate for files that change frequently or for database files that are used by multiple users concurrently.

Windows has to know whether or not it's appropriate to serve up the cached copy for online use, and leaves the choice up to the person who shares the network folder. When *you* share folders on your computer, you should specify the way Windows will make this folder available for offline use by others.

Normally, Windows will *not* give users a cached file when the network copy is available. This is appropriate for database files and editable documents. It's only useful to change the default settings when you are sharing a folder with read-only documents and application programs. In this case, you may be able to give users faster access by following these steps:

1. Simple File Sharing must be disabled. If you are using Simple File Sharing on a workgroup LAN, open Explorer or My Computer and select Tools, Folder Options. Select the View tab and uncheck Simple File Sharing in the Advanced Settings List. Click OK, and then log off and back on.

2. Use Explorer or My Computer to locate the folder you're sharing. Right-click it and select Properties. View the Sharing tab and click the Caching button.

3. Select Automatic Caching of Programs and Documents, and click OK. Close the Properties window.

4. If you disabled Simple File Sharing in step 1, re-enable it, and then log off and back on.

18

You also can force Windows to make files available for offline use by specifying Automatic Caching. With automatic caching, when a network user accesses any file in your shared folder Windows automatically marks it as available for offline use and makes a copy on the user's computer.

The complete list of caching options are described in Table 18.2.

TABLE 18.2   CACHING SETTINGS

Option	Description
Allow Caching of Files in This Shared Folder	If this box is unchecked, the files cannot be copied for offline use. Use this setting to protect sensitive or fast-changing data.
Manual Caching of Documents	Users can select files and folders for offline use and are responsible for synchronizing them. This is the default setting and is appropriate for most cases.
Automatic Caching of Programs and Documents	Windows automatically makes any file accessed by the user available offline and uses the cached copy if it can. You should use this setting if your files are programs or are documents that cannot be modified by the remote users.
Automatic Caching of Documents	Windows automatically makes any opened file available offline, but Windows uses the network copy if it can. You should use this setting to "push" documents to the other user's computer for offline use.

The amount of disk space allocated to "automatically" available offline files is limited to an amount set in the Offline Files properties page.

OFFLINE FILES PROPERTIES

You can control your computer's overall treatment of offline files from Windows Explorer. Select Tools, Folder Options, and then select the Offline Files tab, as shown in Figure 18.12.

Figure 18.12
The Offline Files properties page makes global settings for the handling of offline files.

The settings are described in Table 18.3.

TABLE 18.3   OFFLINE FILES OPTIONS

Option	Description
Enable Offline Files	Uncheck to disable the entire Offline Files system.
Synchronize All Offline Files When Logging On, Synchronize All Offline Files Before Logging Off	Check to force Windows to run the Synchronization Manager when you log on and off. These options also can be set individually for each folder.
Display a Reminder	Uncheck to disable the annoying balloon that pops up on the taskbar to remind you that you're offline. You can also set the time between annoyances.
Create an Offline Files Shortcut on the Desktop	The shortcut can let you view the cached file list; not too useful.
Encrypt Offline Files to Secure Data	Check to have Windows encrypt the cached files. Check this if the files you use are sensitive.
Amount of Disk Space to Use	Limits disk space used to cache temporary ("Automatic") offline files. Manually chosen offline files are *not* counted against this amount.
Delete Files	Deletes temporary and/or manually chosen offline files from the cache. Network copies are *not* deleted. Use this feature to force a refreshed copy of all files
View Files	Displays the Offline Files folder, a listing of all cached files. It provides the same view as given by the desktop icon.
Advanced	Allows you to specify computers whose connection can be lost without triggering Offline mode.

You don't need to change any of these options to use Offline folders. However, after you've been using Offline Folders a while you might find that some of these settings will save you some time or trouble.

USING OFFLINE FOLDERS

Earlier, I listed three uses of offline folders. Now that you've read all the details, you should be able to see how the Offline system handles these tasks:

- Maintaining an up-to-date copy of a set of shared files on a server (or desktop computer) and a remote or portable computer. If you manually select a network folder to be available offline, your computer will always have up-to-date files. If you typically connect to the LAN with a docking portable computer, you can synchronize automatically on logon and logoff. If you connect to the network by a dial-up or VPN connection, you must synchronize manually.

- "Pushing" application software or data from a network to a portable computer. If you put application software or seldom-changed read-only data on a shared network folder and mark it Automatic Caching for Applications, remote users must copy the file across a slow network connection only once. The trick is to have the users always refer to the files by their network shared folder name, even when offline. Windows gives them the cached copy automatically. This capability is a boon for modem users.

- Automatically backing up important files from your computer to an alternate location. You can make a shared folder on a server or computer at your office and create an offline copy of it at home or in your portable. If you do all your work in the offline folder, the synchronization process really is an intelligent backup process. You can even schedule it automatically.

I don't get too enthusiastic about these things usually, but after struggling and suffering with My Briefcase and then working with offline folders, I'd say that they're probably one of the three neatest features I've found in Windows XP.

Remember, after you've marked folders for offline use, continue to use them in the normal way, referring to them using their full network path filenames or through mapped network drives.

 If you can't find a file that was marked for offline use, see "Offline Files Are Missing" in the "Troubleshooting" section at the end of this chapter.

Finally, you can uncheck Make Available Offline on a file or folder at any time to remove it from the cached file list.

WEB FOLDERS AND WEB PRINTING

If a remote computer has Internet Information Services (IIS) installed, has enabled Web Sharing on any folders, and is accessible over the Internet or a corporate Internet, you can access its shared files through Internet Explorer version 5 or higher. This technology lets you copy files to and from a remote computer with a high degree of security, through firewalls that normally block access to file sharing protocols.

When IIS is installed, the computer's shared printers may also be used through the Internet using the Internet Printing Protocol, or IPP. IPP lets remote computers print to shared printers across the Internet, again through firewalls.

You can use these technologies to great advantage if your office or home computer has dedicated Internet access because you access its shared folders over the Internet without using a modem or VPN connection.

These applications are all described elsewhere in this book; I just wanted to be sure they were mentioned here as they're great resources for the "unplugged" user.

Installing IIS is covered in detail in Chapter 13, "Hosting Web Pages with Internet Information Services." Using Web Folders and Web Printing is covered in Chapter 16, "Creating a Windows XP Pro Network."

VIRTUAL PRIVATE NETWORKING

You know that you can use dial-up networking to connect to your office LAN or home computer from afar. But, with the Internet providing network connections and local modem access nearly all over the world, why can't you reach your network through the Internet instead of placing a possibly expensive long-distance call?

Well, in fact, you can. Microsoft networking can use the Internet's TCP protocol to conduct its business, so you can use an Internet connection to access shared files and printers, if the computer you want to reach has an Internet connection up and running.

But the Internet is not a friendly place. With tens of millions of people using it every day, you must expect that some percentage of them are up to no good. Network break-ins are everyday news now. If your computer's file sharing services are exposed to the Internet, any number of people thousands of miles away could just try password after password in the hope of guessing one that will give them access to your files. How do you take advantage of the convenience of accessing network services over the Internet without, figuratively speaking, putting out a big welcome mat that says "Please Rob Me?"

The answer is by the use of firewalls and Virtual Private Networking. I'll describe these concepts in detail in Chapter 21, but in a nutshell, a Virtual Private Network (VPN) lets you connect to a remote network in a secure way. Access by random hackers is blocked by a network firewall, but an authorized user can penetrate the firewall. Authorized data is *encapsulated* in special packets that are passed through the firewall and inspected by a VPN server before being released to the protected network. VPNs create what is effectively a *tunnel* between your computer and a remote network, a tunnel that can pass data freely and securely through potentially hostile intermediate territory.

Figure 18.13 illustrates the concept, showing a Virtual Private Network connection between a computer out on the Internet and a server on a protected network. The figure shows how the computer sends data (1) through a VPN connection which encapsulates it (2) and transmits it over the Internet (3). A firewall (4) passes VPN packets but blocks all others. The VPN Server (5) verifies the authenticity of your data and transmits the original packet (6) on to the desired remote server. The encapsulation process allows for encryption of your data, and allows "private" IP addresses to be used as the endpoints of the network connection.

On Windows XP, VPN connections work like dial-up connections. Once you have an Internet connection established (via modem or a dedicated service), a dial-up connection icon establishes the link between your computer and a VPN server on the remote network. Once connected, the VPN service transmits data between your computer. In effect, you are part of the distant LAN.

You can use Windows XP's VPN service to allow incoming connections to your computer as well. You can use the Internet Connection Firewall or a firewall on your LAN to protect against hackers, yet still connect to your computer through the Internet to retrieve files from afar.

18

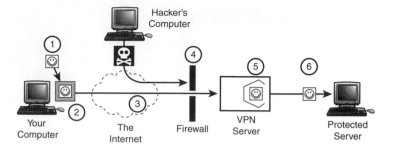

Figure 18.13
A Virtual Private Network encapsulates and encrypts data that is passed over the Internet.

Windows XP supports two VPN encapsulation or repackaging technologies. The *Point-to-Point Tunneling Protocol*, or *PPTP*, was developed by Microsoft and was provided with previous versions of Windows. The *Layer Two Tunneling Protocol*, or *L2TP*, is an industry standard technology, and is faster and better than PPTP. L2TP requires a certificate for its IPSec-based encryption, so if you don't have Windows .NET or 2000 Server, Windows will automatically use PPTP for VPN connections.

SETTING UP FOR VIRTUAL PRIVATE NETWORKING

To establish a VPN connection from your computer to another network, you must know the hostname or IP address of the remote VPN server. This information corresponds to the telephone number in a dial-up connection; it lets you specify the endpoint of the tunnel. VPN connections are set up by the New Connection Wizard. Just follow these steps:

1. Open Network Connections. You can view My Network Places and select the View Network Connections task, or, if Connect To appears on your Start menu, choose Connect To, Show All Connections.

2. Select Create A New Connection from Network Tasks.

3. Select Connect To The Network At My Workplace and click Next. (This is a poorly named choice—you might be connecting to your home computer!)

4. Select Virtual Private Network Connection, and click Next.

5. Enter a name for the connection, such as "VPN to Office."

6. If you use a dial-up connection to connect this computer to the Internet, you can select Automatically Dial This Initial Connection to ensure that your Internet connection is up before attempting the VPN connection, as shown in Figure 18.14. If you have a dedicated Internet connection, use a shared connection from another computer, or want to make a dial-up connection manually, choose Do Not Dial, and click Next.

7. Enter the hostname or IP address of the remote dial-in server—for example, vpn.mycompany.com—and select Next.

8. Click Finish to close the wizard.

NOTE

You can delete a connection shortcut later if you don't want it and can drag the connection icon from Network Connections to your desktop later if you do.

Figure 18.14
You can have Windows automatically dial a selected Internet connection before making a VPN connection.

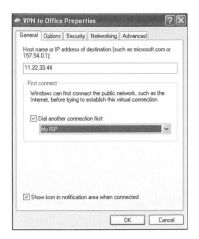

Windows immediately opens the Dialer dialog. Before establishing the connection for the first time, verify the connections properties pages.

VPN CONNECTION PROPERTIES

To modify a VPN connection's properties, click the Properties button on the dialer dialog, or right-click the connection icon in Network Connections and select Properties.

The properties page has five tabs. Most of the time, the default settings will work correctly, but you should check some of them. In this section, I'll walk you through the most important parameters.

GENERAL PROPERTIES

The General tab of the Properties dialog holds the hostname or IP address of your VPN connection server, and if needed, the name of a dial-up connection to use to carry the VPN connection. If you are establishing the VPN connection over a LAN or dedicated Internet connection, you can uncheck Dial Another Connection First.

OPTIONS

The Options tab includes dialing and redialing options. The two important options are

- **Prompt for name and password**—If you tell Windows to remember your username and password when dialing, and after you've made a successful connection once, you can uncheck this option to bypass the Dialing dialog. When you select the connection icon, Windows will just make the connection.

- **Include Windows logon domain**—If the VPN server is a Windows 2003, NT, or 2000 server, you may need to provide your login domain name with your username. You can also enter *domain\username* or, with Windows 2000/.NET servers only, *username@domain*.

SECURITY

It's unlikely that you will need to change any security settings. The data in a VPN connection is usually carried across the Internet, and a high level of security is required. Your password and data should be encrypted in the strongest fashion possible. Be sure that Require Secured Password and Require Data Encryption are set on the Security tab.

If you use the same logon name, password, and domain name on your local computer as you use on the remote network, you can check Automatically Use My Windows Logon Name and Password so that you don't have to enter it whenever you use the connection.

NETWORKING

It's likely that you want to participate as a full member of the remote network, so leave all Components checked on the Networking tab of the Properties dialog.

As I mentioned, Windows XP and 2000 use two types of VPN protocols. Generally, you can leave the Type of VPN server set to Automatic, and Windows will determine to which type it's connected when it makes each call.

If the remote network is a complex, multi-subnet network, or if you want to browse the Internet while you're using the VPN, you also must deal with the gateway issue, which I'll discus later in this chapter under "Routing Issues." To change the gateway setting

1. Select Internet Protocol, and choose Properties. Leave the IP address and DNS information set to Obtain Automatically, and click Advanced.

2. If the remote network has only one subnet, *or* you will set routes to multiple subnets manually, uncheck Use Default Gateway On Remote Network.

DIALING A VPN CONNECTION

Making a VPN connection follows the same procedure as making a dial-up connection:

1. Select the desired VPN connection icon from Network Connections.

2. If this VPN connection requires a dial-up connection, you are prompted with the username and password for your dial-up connection to your ISP. Check for the proper location and dialing rules, and then select Dial. After the connection has been made, Windows proceeds to make the VPN connection.

3. Enter the username and password for access to the remote network. Select Connect.

   Windows then contacts the remote VPN server, verifies your username and password, registers your computer on the network, and creates a connection status icon in the notification area, just as for a standard dial-up connection.

You can use the remote network now, access shared files and folders, access printers, synchronize offline folders, and so on.

When you're finished, right-click the connection icon, and select Disconnect.

ROUTING ISSUES

If the remote network you want to use is a simple, small network with only one subnet or range of IP addresses, you can skip this section. Otherwise, I must address an issue with TCP/IP routing here, as much as I fear it's a real can of worms.

When you establish a VPN connection to another network, your computer is assigned an IP address from that other network for the duration of your connection. This address might be a private, non-Internet-routable address like 192.168.1.100. All data destined for the remote network is packaged up in PPTP or L2TP packets and sent to the remote host. But what happens if you want to communicate with two servers—a private server through the tunnel and a public Web site on the Internet—at the same time?

When you send data to an IP address that doesn't clearly belong to the private network's range, Windows has two choices: It can pass the data through the tunnel and let the network on the other end route it on, or it can pass the data without encapsulation and let it travel directly to the Internet host.

It would seem sensible that Windows should always use the second approach because any IP address other than, say, 192.168.1.xxx obviously doesn't belong to the private network and doesn't need protection. That's right as long as the remote network has only one such subnet. Some complex corporate networks have many, with different addresses, so Windows can't always know just from the address of the VPN connection which addresses belong to the private network and which go direct.

If you plan to use a VPN connection and the Internet at the same time, you must find out whether your remote network has more than one subnet. Then follow this advice:

- If the remote network has only one subnet, tell Windows not to use the remote network as the gateway address for unknown locations. This is the easy case.

- If the remote network has more than one subnet, tell Windows to use the remote network as its gateway, so you can connect to all servers on the remote network. But Internet access goes through the tunnel, too, and from there to the Internet. It slows things down.

- Alternatively, you can tell Windows not to use the remote network gateway and you can manually set routes to other subnets while you're connected. It's tricky and inconvenient. I'll show you how I do it at the end of the chapter, under "Tips from the Windows Pros."

When you know how you'll resolve the gateway issue, refer to the VPN Connection Properties earlier in this chapter to make the appropriate settings on the connection's Networking properties tab.

ENABLING VPN ACCESS TO YOUR COMPUTER

You can enable incoming VPN connections to your computer if it has a dedicated Internet connection. Your Windows XP computer can act as a VPN server for one incoming connection at a time. You can connect to your computer through the Internet from home or in the field from a computer running Windows 9x, NT, 2000, or of course, XP.

To function correctly, however, your computer must have a known IP address, and if its Internet connection is made through a router, Internet Connection Sharing or a connecting sharing device, then PPTP packets must be forwarded to your computer. I'll discuss this in more detail shortly, under "Enabling Incoming VPN Connections with NAT."

The process for enabling VPN access is exactly the same as for enabling dial-in access, so see the section "Enabling Dial-In Access to Your Computer" earlier in this chapter. Follow those instructions, being sure to enable an incoming VPN connection. You don't need to choose any modems to receive incoming modem calls.

When Incoming Calls is configured, your computer can be contacted as the host of a VPN connection. To connect to it, establish a VPN connection as you learned in the preceding section, using your computer's public IP address or hostname as the number to dial.

NOTE

You must configure the Internet protocol to assign valid IP addresses for incoming connections. This topic, which was discussed in "Enabling Dial-Up Access to Your Computer," applies to VPN access, too.

ENABLING INCOMING VPN CONNECTIONS WITH NAT

Microsoft's Internet Connection Sharing and the commercial DSL/cable sharing routers known as Residential Gateways use an IP addressing trick called Network Address Translation or NAT to serve an entire LAN with only one public IP address. Incoming requests, as from a VPN client to a VPN server, have to be directed to a single host computer on the internal network.

This means if you use a shared Internet connection, only one computer can be designated as the recipient of incoming VPN connections. If you use Microsoft's Internet Connection Sharing, that computer should be the one sharing its connection. It will receive and properly handle VPN requests.

If you use a hardware sharing router, the VPN server can be any computer you wish to designate. (Remember that once the VPN connection is established, you can communicate with any of the computers on the LAN). Your router must be set up to forward the following packet types to the designated computer:

TCP port 1723

GRE (protocol 47 . . . this is not the same as port 47!)

Unfortunately, many of the inexpensive commercial DSL/cable connection sharing routers (residential gateways) don't have a way to explicitly forward GRE packets. If you use one of these devices you will need to designate the VPN target computer as a DMZ host, which will receive *all* unrecognized incoming packets.

CAUTION

> If you designate a computer as a DMZ host, that computer can be vulnerable to hacker attacks. You *must* also configure your router to block Microsoft File Sharing packets, at the very least. Set up filtering to block TCP and UDP ports 137 through 139.

→ To learn more about forwarding network requests on a shared Internet connection, **see** "Enabling Access with a Sharing Router," **p. 687**.

REMOTE DESKTOP

Windows XP Professional has a spiffy feature called Remote Desktop that lets you connect to and use your computer from another location. You'll be able to see your computer's screen, move the mouse and type on the keyboard just as if you were there. This is just what you need when you're out of town and need to read a file you left on the computer back home, or if you have to catch up on work at the office while you're at home changing Alexa Marie's diapers. I've been using this feature a lot while writing this book, and I love it.

You also can use the Remote Desktop client program to attach to computers running Windows NT Terminal Server Version and Windows 2003 and 2000 Server's Terminal Services. The client program lets you log on to these computers to access special applications or for administration and maintenance.

NOTE

> You don't have to be miles and miles away to take advantage of Remote Desktop, either. You can also use it to access other computers on your own LAN. For instance, you could use it to start a lengthy computing job on someone else's computer without leaving your own desk.

Third-party programs such as Carbon Copy, PC Anywhere, Timbuktu, and Close-Up have been doing this for years, and they have some more sophisticated features, but Remote Desktop is built into Windows XP and it's essentially free. It's a scaled-down version of Windows Terminal Services, a component of the Windows NT/2000/2003 Server version that lets multiple users run programs on one central server. By stripped down, I mean that only one person can connect to Windows XP Professional at a time, and it forces a local user off.

You can use any Windows-based computer to reach your computer with Remote Desktop. While the host computer (the computer you'll take control of) has to be running Windows XP Professional, the Remote Desktop Client software (that you use to view your XP computer) can run on 16- and 32-bit versions of Windows from 3.1 up to XP. Figure 18.15 shows how this works.

18

Figure 18.15
You can use any Windows-based computer to connect to and control your Windows XP Professional computer.

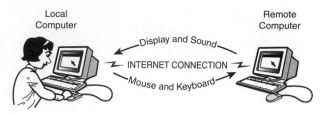

Local Computer

Remote Computer

Display and Sound

INTERNET CONNECTION

Mouse and Keyboard

To use Remote Desktop, the host computer must be reachable over the Internet, and this means that it will need a dedicated Internet connection with a known IP address (or, you'll need someone to make an Internet connection at the computer and tell you what the IP address is). Furthermore, if your computer gets its Internet connection through a shared connection or a residential gateway, your sharing computer or router will have to be set up to forward incoming requests on TCP port 3389 to the computer you want to reach by Remote Desktop.

→ To learn more about forwarding network requests on a shared Internet connection, **see** "Enabling Access with a Sharing Router," **p. 687**.

ENABLING REMOTE DESKTOP ACCESS TO YOUR COMPUTER

To enable Remote Desktop connections to your computer, follow these steps:

1. Right-click My Computer and select Properties. Or, open the old-style System control panel applet.
2. Select the Remote tab and check Allow Users to Connect Remotely to This Computer.
3. If you want to grant Remote Desktop access to any Limited Access users, click Select Remote Users and check the boxes next to their user names. Computer Administrator users can connect without explicit permission.

   In any case, however, only accounts with passwords can be reached. Windows will not grant Remote Desktop access to any user account without a password.
4. Click OK to close the dialogs.

If you want to reach your computer through the Internet, and you use Internet Connection Sharing or a connection sharing router, you'll have to instruct your sharing computer or router to forward Remote Desktop data through to your computer, and you'll only be able to contact one selected computer from outside your network.

You'll have to set up your sharing computer or router to forward incoming requests on TCP port 3389 to the computer you want to reach by Remote Desktop.

→ For a discussion on how to do this, **see** "Making Services Available," **p. 684**.

CONNECTING TO OTHER COMPUTERS WITH REMOTE DESKTOP

To establish a connection to your computer (or another Remote Desktop server) from somewhere else, you'll need a copy of the Remote Desktop Client, also called the Terminal Services Client. There are several ways you can get this program:

- It's preinstalled on Windows XP computers. Select Start, All Programs, Accessories, Communications, Remote Desktop Connection.

- It's on your Windows XP CD-ROM. Insert it in another computer, and from the setup program select Perform Additional Tasks, then Set Up Remote Desktop Connection. This will run the installation program.

- You can download a slightly less-capable version from www.microsoft.com. Search for "Terminal Services Advanced Client". This is handy if you're traveling and don't have an XP disc with you.

When you run the Remote Desktop Client, you'll see the Remote Desktop Connection dialog, as shown in Figure 18.16.

Figure 18.16
The Remote Desktop Connection dialog lets you configure the connection and select the remote computer to use.

Enter the IP address or register DNS name of the computer you'd like to use. Entering a username and password is optional. If you don't enter them now, you'll be asked for them when the connection is established. Click Connect to establish the connection immediately, or click Options to adjust the connection properties first. The properties tabs are described in Table 18.4

When you establish the connection, you'll see a standard Windows logon dialog. Enter your username and password to sign on. It may take a while for the logon process to complete, if Windows has to shut down a logged-on user.

TABLE 18.4   REMOTE DESKTOP CONNECTION PROPERTIES

Tab	Properties
General	*Connection Settings* saves the configuration for a particular remote computer as a shortcut for quick access later.
Display	Sets the size and color depth of the window used for your remote connection's desktop. Display size can be set to a fixed window size or Full Screen.
Local Resources	Connects devices on the local computer so that you may use them as if they were part of the remote computer. (This feature does not work when connecting to Windows NT and Windows 2000 Terminal Services.)
	The Keyboard setting determines whether special Windows key commands like Alt+Tab apply to your local computer or the remote computer.
Programs	Lets you automatically run a program on the remote computer upon logging on.
Experience	Lets you indicate your connection speed, so that Windows can appropriately limit display-intense features like menu animation.

When you're logged on, you'll see the remote computer's desktop, as shown in Figure 18.17, and can use it as if you were actually sitting in front of it. Keyboard, mouse, display and sound should be fully functional. If you maximize the window, the remote desktop will fill your screen. It all works quite well—it can even be difficult to remember which computer you're actually using!

Figure 18.17
When connected to Windows XP via Remote Desktop, your local computer's drives and printers are available for use.

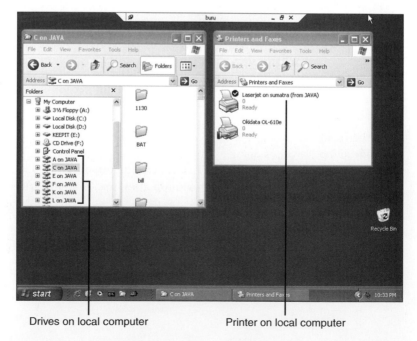

Drives on local computer   Printer on local computer

In addition, any printers attached to your local computer will appear as choices if you print from applications on the remote computer, and the local computer's drives will appear in the list in My Computer. You can take advantage of this to copy files between the local and remote computers.

Finally, your local computer's serial (COM) ports will also be available to the remote computer. (My friend Norm syncs his Palm Pilot to his Windows XP Professional computer from remote locations using this feature).

While you're connected, you might want to use keyboard shortcuts like Alt+Tab to switch between applications. This can confuse Windows, which won't know whether to switch applications on the local computer or the remote computer. You can specify where special key combinations should be interpreted on the Local Resources properties page, as I described earlier, or you can use alternate key combinations to ensure that the desired actions take place on the remote computer. The alternate keyboard shortcuts are shown in Table 18.5.

TABLE 18.5   SOME OF THE REMOTE DESKTOP KEYBOARD SHORTCUTS

Use These Keys:	To Transmit This to the Remote Computer:
Alt+PgUp, Alt+PgDn	Alt+Tab (switch programs)
Alt+End	Ctrl+Alt+Del (task monitor)
Alt+Home	(Displays the Start menu)
Ctrl+Alt+Break	Alt+Enter (toggle full screen)
Ctrl+Alt+Plus	Alt+PrntScrn (screen to clipboard)

18

When you've finished using the remote computer, choose Start, Log Off to end the connection. If you want the remote computer to continue running an application, though, you can simply close the Remote Desktop window or select Disconnect. Your account will stay active on the remote computer until you reconnect and log off, or until a user at that computer logs on.

NOTE

Windows XP Professional only permits one person to use each computer. If you attempt to connect to a computer with Remote Desktop while another user is logged on, you'll have the choice of disconnecting or forcing them off. If Quick User Switch is enabled, they'll be switched out; otherwise they're summarily logged off. This is somewhat brutal; the other user might lose work in progress. If you log on using the same username as the local user, though, you simply take over the desktop without forcing a logoff.

If someone logs on to the remote computer while you're connected from afar, you'll be disconnected. If Quick User Switch is enabled, you can reconnect later and pick up where you left off. Otherwise, the same deal applies: If it is a different user, your applications will be shut down.

REMOTE ASSISTANCE

Remote Assistance lets two people work collaboratively on one Windows XP computer—one at the computer and one remotely, over the Internet. The feature is intended to let people get technical assistance from someone at a remote location, and it's based the same technology as the Remote Desktop feature I described in the previous section. There are several significant differences, however:

- With Remote Assistance, both the local and remote users see the same screen at the same time, and both can move the mouse, type on the keyboard, and so forth.

- Remote Assistance doesn't make the local computer's drives appear in the drive list, nor does it transmit sound back, as Remote Desktop does.

- Remote Assistance connections can't be made *ad lib*. One Windows XP user must invite another through e-mail or Windows Messenger. Or, one user can offer assistance to another using Messenger. In any case, the procedure requires the simultaneous cooperation of users at both ends of the connection.

- Remote Assistance can be used to connect to Windows XP Home Edition. Users of any version of Windows XP can assist each other.

- Remote Assistance allows you to use text chat or to establish voice communication while the desktop session is active.

If you're familiar with NetMeeting's Desktop Sharing function, this may all sound familiar. The difference is that Remote Assistance is based on the more modern Terminal Services technology that powers Remote Desktop, so it's only available to Windows XP users. Also, it just plain works better than Desktop Sharing.

NOTE

> If your computer gets its Internet connection through a shared connection on another computer, or a through a residential gateway (sharing router), your friend won't be able to connect to you unless the router or the computer with the shared connection is set up to forward incoming requests on TCP port 3389 to the computer you want to reach by Remote Assistance.

REQUESTING REMOTE ASSISTANCE

To invite a friend or colleague to work with you on your computer, first contact your friend and confirm that they have Windows XP and are ready to work with you. If you want help making system or network settings, or installing software, you should log in with a Computer Administrator user account before going any further. Then, follow these steps:

1. Select Start, Help and Support.
2. Click Invite A Friend To Connect To Your Computer with Remote Assistance.

3. Select Invite Someone To Help You.

4. You can issue an invitation via Windows Messenger, if you and your friend both have accounts, or via e-mail. Select your friend's name from the Messenger Online list, or enter her e-mail address, as shown in Figure 18.18. Then, click Invite This Person.

5. If you have chosen to send the invitation by e-mail, Windows will pop up a rather alarming message warning you that a program is attempting to send e-mail. Choose Send (and thank the guy who wrote the Melissa virus for making this necessary).

Figure 18.18
Select a Windows Messenger user ID or enter an e-mail address to invite someone to connect to your computer.

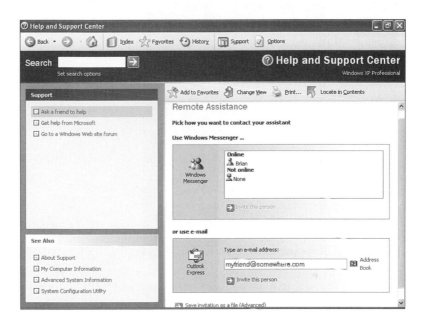

NOTE

If you use a dial-up Internet connection or a DSL service that requires you to sign on, your Internet IP address changes every time you connect. Remote Assistance invitations use this address to tell the other person's computer how to contact you, so they will only work if you stay connected from the time you send the invitation to the time your friend responds. If you have a fixed (static) IP address, this won't be a problem.

If you sent your request via Windows Messenger, you should get a response within a few seconds. If you sent the request by e-mail, it could be some time before the other party reads and receives it.

You also can select Save Invitation as a File to transfer the invitation by other means such as a network or floppy disk. The invitation, whether sent by Messenger, e-mail, or file is actually an XML file containing the IP address of your computer and some encrypted information that specifies how long the invitation remains valid.

If you want to view the list of invitations you've sent by e-mail, select View Invitation Status on the Remote Assistance page. You can then select invitations to delete, expire (disallow), or resend.

When someone responds to your request for assistance, a dialog will appear on your screen asking if it's okay for them to connect. Click Yes, and after a minute or so a window will appear with which you can control the Remote Assistance session, as shown in Figure 18.19.

Figure 18.19
When your Remote Assistant has connected, you can use this window to chat and control the connection.

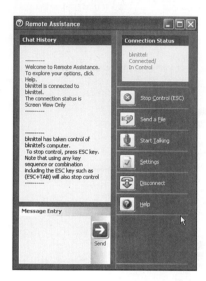

You can use this dialog to type text messages back and forth, initiate a voice connection or a file transfer, or terminate the connection. When the remote user wants to take control of your mouse and keyboard, you'll be asked and can permit or deny this. Even then you can still type and move the mouse yourself, and can end the remote user's control by pressing the Esc key or by clicking End Control on the Remote Assistance window.

RESPONDING TO AN ASSISTANCE REQUEST

When someone invites you to connect by Remote Assistance, you'll either see a popup box in Windows Messenger, or you'll receive an e-mail, as shown in Figure 18.20.

You can directly respond to an instant message invitation as indicated in the message window. To accept an e-mail invitation, open the attachment. (How you do that depends on your e-mail program—in Outlook Express 6, click on the paperclip icon, and select the attachment labeled rcBuddy.MsRcIncident. When the Attachment Warning dialog appears, select Open It.) Opening the attachment should activate the Remote Assistance connection.

Figure 18.20
You might receive an instant message or e-mail invitation requesting Remote Assistance. To accept an e-mail invitation, open the attachment.

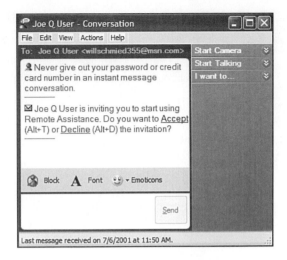

NOTE

You can absolutely prevent others from manipulating your computer when they connect using Remote Assistance—they'll be able to see your screen but not control it. To do this, right-click My Computer and select Properties. View the Remote tab and click Advanced. Uncheck Allow This Computer To Be Controlled Remotely and click OK. In any case, you have to grant the other user permission to manipulate your computer each time a connection is made.

18

You will be asked if you wish to proceed with the connection, and when it's been established, the remote user will be asked if they want to permit you to connect. Assuming you both say yes, at this point patience is called for as it can take more than a minute for the required software to load up and for the other user's desktop to appear on your screen, as shown in Figure 18.21.

The Remote Assistance window has several sections. On the left is a text chat window through which you and the other party can type to each other. Enter messages in the Message Entry window.

Across the top is a menu of controls. The choices are

- **Take Control**—Click this to begin using the other computer's mouse and keyboard. The remote user will be asked to grant permission. Once you have control of the other computer, both of you can use your mouse and keyboard. The remote user can cancel your control at any time by pressing the Esc key.

- **Send A File**—Brings up a dialog to let you transfer a file to the remote computer. You can select a file to send, and the remote use must select a place to store it, as shown in Figure 18.22.

- **Start Talking**—Establishes a voice connection. If both of you have a microphone, speakers, and a sound card, you will be able to speak to each other over your Internet or LAN connection.

Figure 18.21
The Remote Assistance screen has a control panel on the left, and a view of the remote user's screen on the right. Click Take Control if you want to manipulate the remote computer.

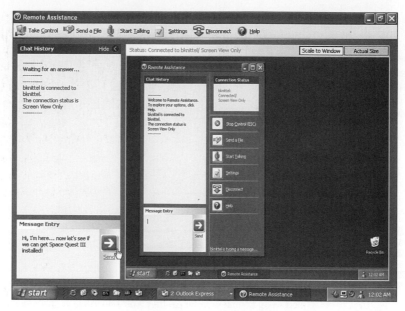

Figure 18.22
File Transfers during Remote Assistance require the sender to select the file and the recipient to select a destination folder.

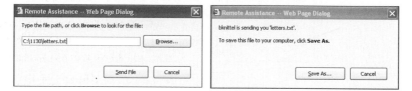

- **Settings**—Lets you change the audio settings for voice communication and the default screen scaling setting.

- **Disconnect**—Ends the Remote Assistance connection.

Most of the window is devoted to a view of your friend's screen. You can click Scale To Window to fit his entire screen in this window, or click Actual Size to see a normal size view which you'll probably have to scroll up and down from time to time.

COPYING FILES BETWEEN TWO COMPUTERS

If you need to transfer files between two computers but you don't already have a LAN in place, you may think you'll have shuttle a floppy disk back and forth 50 times. You do have some other options:

- Use an external high-capacity drive such as a USB-connected hard drive or a Zip disk.

- Install network adapters in the two computers and connect them with a *crossover cable*, as described in Chapter 16. The cable will cost about $7.50, and if you need to buy network adapters, this might set you back another $20 to $50. You'll eventually want the network hardware anyway, though, and with this mini-LAN you can copy mega-files in minutes.

- If both computers have FireWire (IEEE-1394) ports, you can get a so-called "6-6" cable to directly connect the computers, and use the IEEE-1394 ports to set up a LAN. (The price of the cable might bring tears to your eyes, though.)

- You can use the "Direct Connection" networking feature to connect two computers through their parallel, serial or Infrared ports. Parallel or serial connections require special "Direct Connection" parallel or serial data crossover cables—these cables are needed to hook input wires to output wires on each computer and vice versa.

To establish a Direct Connection, connect the cable or point the infrared ports at each other. Then, on the computer that has the files you want to copy, called the Host computer, follow these steps:

1. Open the Network Connections window and select the Create a New Connection task to start the New Connection Wizard. Click Next to get going.
2. Select Set Up an Advanced Connection and click Next.
3. Choose Connect Directly to Another Computer and click Next.
4. Choose Host and click Next.
5. Choose the device for the connection: a parallel, serial or infrared port. If you're using a serial connection, click the Properties button, select a reasonable serial port speed (19200, 38400, or 57600 bps), and click OK. Click Next to proceed.
6. Check the boxes next to the user or users who should be permitted access and click Next.
7. Click Finish. An Incoming Connections icon will appear in your Network Connections window.

Then, on the computer you wish to transfer files to, called the Guest computer, follow these steps:

1. Open the Network Connections window and select the Create a New Connection task to start the New Connection Wizard. Click Next to get going.
2. Select Set Up an Advanced Connection and click Next.
3. Choose Connect Directly to Another Computer and click Next.
4. Choose Guest and click Next.
5. Choose the device for the connection: a parallel, serial or infrared port, then click Next, then Finish. A Direct Connection icon will appear, and the connection dialog will open.
6. If you're using a serial cable connection, click the Properties button, click Configure, and select the same serial port speed you chose on the Host (19200, 38400, or 57600 bps). Click OK twice.
7. Enter a username and password that is valid on the Host computer. You have to use one of the usernames you selected when setting up the Host. Then, click Connect.

18

When the connection is established, you can use Windows Explorer to browse the Host computer's shared network folders and copy files, as described in Chapter 17.

When you're finished, close the connection by right-clicking on the connection icon in the notification area on the Guest computer. On the Host computer, you can disable incoming connections by opening the properties page for the Incoming Connection icon and unchecking the device you chose earlier.

If you can add an infrared adapter to your desktop, you can also use Windows's built-in support for quick wireless infrared file transfers. This technique isn't as involved as the networking approach I've just described. I'll explain it in the next section.

Finally, if you want to move both your files and your preferences and settings, see "Moving Profiles with the Files and Settings Transfer Wizard" in Chapter 28.

INFRARED FILE TRANSFERS

Most portable computers include an infrared data transmission device similar to that used on TV remote controls. Using a data transmission standard called IrDA (after the Infrared Data Association), computers, printers, and handheld organizers can communicate with each other without LAN wiring. Just point them at each other. LAN connections are much faster, so I recommend using them over IrDA any day, but if you don't have a LAN connection, IrDA can give "point and shoot" a whole new meaning.

IrDA comes in two flavors: SIR (Serial InfraRed), which tops out at 112Kbps, and FIR (Fast Infrared), which runs up to 4Mbps. Most new portables support both protocols. The advantage of using SIR is that you can attach an (expensive) adapter to a standard serial port on a desktop computer and give it infrared capability.

NOTE
> An FIR adapter connects to an SIR adapter by automatically lowering its transfer rate. The two standards interoperate quite nicely.

Windows XP includes support for IRDA file transfers between two capable devices such as laptops, digital cameras, and so on. Because most laptop computers have IrDA hardware, you can transfer files between two Windows XP/2000 laptops just by bringing them near each other.

SETTING UP AN INFRARED DEVICE

If your computer has IrDA-compatible hardware installed, Windows detected it and installed support for it during installation. You can tell by checking for a Wireless Link applet in the Control Panel under Printers and Other Hardware.

If you've added an external serial port IrDA adapter, choose Add/Remove Hardware in the Control Panel, select Add Hardware, choose the device manually, and select Infrared Devices. Finally, choose the proper IrDA device type and serial port information.

If the Wireless Link icon is not present in the Control Panel, see "Wireless Link Is Not Present in Control Panel" in the "Troubleshooting" section at the end of this chapter.

Open the applet, and view the Hardware tab to confirm that Windows thinks the device is operating properly (see Figure 18.23). If it's not, select Troubleshoot to diagnose and fix the problem.

The applet has three tabs. On the first two, you can enable transfers of files and images, and select the destination folder for files and images received from other computers and digital cameras. The default folder for received files is your desktop. The default folder for received images is the My Pictures folder inside your My Documents folder. You can change these defaults by clicking Properties and selecting a different folder.

On the Hardware tab, you can set the maximum speed for wireless transfers. If you experience a high error rate, click Properties and try changing the speed from the default 115200bps to 57600 or lower.

Figure 18.23
Using the Wireless Link Control Panel applet, you can configure file transfer directories and the transfer speed.

INFRARED FILE TRANSFER

When another infrared-capable computer is in range of your computer's beam, your computer makes an interesting sound, a Send Files to Another Computer icon appears on the desktop, and a small control icon appears in the notification area (see Figure 18.24). You can instantly send files to the other computer by dragging files to the Send Files icon. Pretty neat!

 If the Send Files icon doesn't appear when you think it should, see "Send Files Icon Doesn't Appear" in the "Troubleshooting" section at the end of this chapter.

To send files to another computer, you can use any of these three methods:

- Drag and drop the files onto the Send Files to Another Computer icon on the desktop.
- Select and right-click a file, choose Send To, and select Infrared Recipient.
- Open the Send Files icon, or select Transfer Files from the control icon in the taskbar to bring up the Wireless Link dialog. This lets you browse for and select the files to transfer. Click Send to transfer the files.

Figure 18.24
When another infrared file transfer device is in range, the Send Files icon (left) appears on the desktop, and the Wireless control icon (right) appears in the notification area.

The Send Files icon appears when another infrared file transfer device is in range

The Wireless control icon appears in the notification area

> **NOTE**
>
> The Wireless Link dialog box is a standard Open File dialog box; it's really a little Explorer window. If you drag a file into this dialog, you're moving it to the displayed folder on your own computer. To transfer a file via drag and drop, you must drag it to the Send Files icon.

After you've selected files to transfer via drag and drop, Send To, or the dialog, progress dialogs appear on both computers, indicating that a file transfer is taking place.

> **NOTE**
>
> When infrared file transfers are enabled, anyone with an IrDA-equipped Windows XP or 2000 computer can zap files onto your computer's desktop. Don't worry, though, because files are never overwritten. If someone sends you a file with the same name as an existing file on your desktop, it's named something like Copy 1 of XXXXXX.

DIGITAL CAMERA IMAGE TRANSFER

When you bring a digital camera with a compatible IrDA interface near your computer, the image transfer utility appears. Follow your camera manufacturer's instructions to copy images from the camera to your computer.

You can specify the directory for image transfers in the Wireless Link properties, from the Control Panel, or from the Wireless Link task tray icon. The default is the My Pictures folder inside your My Documents folder.

INFRARED PRINTING

When your computer has an IrDA interface, you can print to infrared-connected printers. To make a connection to an infrared printer, follow these steps:

1. Power up the printer and point your computer's IR beam at it. Windows may detect and install the printer automatically. If it doesn't, proceed with step 2.

2. In Printers, select Add Printer. Choose Local Printer, and uncheck Automatically Detect.

3. Under Use the Following Port, choose IR (Local Port).

4. Select the printer's manufacturer and model. If it's not listed, and you have a disk from the manufacturer, select Have Disk and locate the Windows XP printer drivers.

5. Supply a name for the printer, choose whether it will be the default printer, and choose whether to share the printer to your LAN.

Now you can use the printer whenever it's in visible range of your computer.

MULTIPLE LAN CONNECTIONS

Most desktop computers sit where they are installed, gathering dust until they're obsolete, and participate in only one LAN. But portable computer users often carry their computers from office to office, docking or plugging into several different local LANs. While Microsoft has made it easy for you to manage several different dial-up and VPN connections, it's difficult to manage connections to several different LANs if the network configuration settings are manually set.

Internet Protocol settings are the difficult ones. If your computer is set to use automatic TCP/IP configuration, you won't encounter any problems; your computer will absorb the local information each time you connect.

If your TCP/IP settings are set manually, things aren't so simple. Microsoft has come up with a partial solution called Alternate Configuration. You can configure your computer for automatic IP address assignment on most networks, and manual assignment on one. The way this works is that Windows looks for a DHCP server when it boots up, and if it doesn't find one it uses the Alternate Configuration. This can be a static IP address, or the default setting of Automatic Private IP address assignment, whereby Windows chooses a random address in the 169.254 subnet. (The automatic technique was the only option in Windows 98, Me, 2000 and XP).

This means that your computer can automatically adjust itself to multiple networks, at most one of which requires manual IP address settings.

To set up Alternate Configuration, open Network Connections, view Local Area Connection's properties, and double-click Internet Protocol. Be sure the General tab uses the Obtain and IP Address Automatically setting. View the Alternate Configuration tab and choose User Configured to enter the static LAN's information.

If you need to commute between multiple networks that require manual configuration, you'll have to change the General settings each time you connect to a different network. I suggest that you stick a 3-by-5-inch card with the settings for each network in your laptop carrying case for handy reference.

18

NOTE

> Although it appears that Microsoft isn't going to solve this problem for us, we can hope that third-party software developers will come up with a tool to manage multiple LAN connections properly. Back on Windows 95 I used a program called Network Hopper that let you choose from a list of multiple network setups. It changed not only the IP address info but even e-mail setups, so that the appropriate mail servers were used on each network. A tool like that for Windows XP would be a real blessing. Developers, care to take this on?

TROUBLESHOOTING

CAN'T CHOOSE DIAL-UP CONNECTION AT LOGIN

When I choose Log On Using Dial-Up Connection, the connection to the remote network is not an available choice.

When you created the connection, you chose For My Use Only rather than For All Users. Because you're now logged out, you don't have access to the connection. You cannot retroactively share the connection. Log on again; then delete and re-create the connection.

VPN CONNECTION FAILS WITHOUT CERTIFICATE

When I attempt to make a VPN connection, I receive the message Unable to negotiate the encryption you requested without a certificate.

You are trying to connect to a VPN server with a higher level of encryption than your computer or the other computer is configured to carry out.

If you are attempting to contact a Windows .NET or 2000 VPN server, contact your network administrator to get the appropriate certificate installed. If you are calling a Windows NT 4 VPN server, this error probably occurred because you enabled IPSec on the Options tab of the Advanced Internet Protocol properties. In this case, disable IPSec.

CAN'T MAKE FILE AVAILABLE OFFLINE

The choice Make File Available Offline doesn't appear when I right-click a file or folder.

To use Offline Folders, you must disable Fast User Switching and enable Offline Folders. See the note in the Offline Folders section, earlier in this chapter.

When I mark files or folders for offline use, I receive the error Files of this Type Cannot Be Made Available Offline.

Microsoft has deemed that some file types (for example, Access's .mdb database files) shouldn't be available offline. They assume that these files are in use by multiple LAN users, and there's no way to reconcile changes made by offline and online users. This can help a lot of people avoid database damage, but it's annoying if you really do want to take the file offline. There is a way to get around this if you are sure you won't take offline any files that might be edited by others while you have them.

If you're on a domain network, ask your domain administrator to modify the Group Policy entry Computer Configuration\Administrative Templates\Network\Offline Files\Files not cached.

If you are on a workgroup network, follow these steps:

1. Log in as a Computer Administrator and start the Microsoft Management Console with Start, Run, mmc.

2. Choose File, Add/Remove Snap-in, Add.

3. Highlight Group Policy and click Add.

4. Leave the Group Policy Object set to Local Computer. Click Finish, Close, and OK.

5. In the left pane, open Local Computer policy and drill down through Computer Configuration, Administrative Templates, and Network to Offline Files.

6. In the right pane, double-click Files Not Cached.

7. Check Enabled, and enter any extensions that should be protected, such as *.dbf. Omit the file types you want to take offline.

8. Click OK and close the MMC console program.

9. Log out, and then log back in.

OFFLINE SYNCHRONIZATION GIVES Unable to connect to server ERROR

When I synchronize offline files, I receive the error Unable to connect to '\\server\file'. The specified network name is no longer available.

The indicated server (actually, any computer sharing a folder you are using offline) might really not be functioning. If you are a mobile user, you also might have checked folders for updating that aren't present in your current LAN or dialed-up network. Windows has no way of knowing which servers should be available and which shouldn't. You must select the servers appropriate to your connection.

OFFLINE FILES ARE MISSING

I can't find files or folders I've clearly marked for offline use.

You might not have synchronized after marking the file, its folder, or a containing folder for offline use. The solution is to go back online and synchronize.

Windows XP also has a strange limitation: The full pathname of an offline file can't be more than 64 characters long. Files with longer pathnames are simply ignored and not copied for offline use. Check the name of the file you've found to be missing; if its full path is more than 64 characters long, this is the problem. The solution is to contact the manager of the computer sharing the original folder and ask him or her to make a network share at a deeper level in the folder tree so that the pathname will be shorter.

WIRELESS LINK IS NOT PRESENT IN CONTROL PANEL

I have a wireless adapter in my desktop [or portable computer], but Wireless Link does not appear in the Control Panel under Printers and Other Hardware.

The IrDA adapter is probably disabled in your computer's BIOS. Shut down and restart your computer. When your BIOS is setting up, press the indicated key to enter its setup utility.

Look at its Built-In Peripherals screen for IrDA options. You must enable IRDA 1.1 support. It might require a DMA and Interrupt port as well, so you might not be able to use infrared and ECP printing at the same time. Save and exit the setup program.

When you restart Windows, it will detect and install support for the infrared connector.

SEND FILES ICON DOESN'T APPEAR

When another computer with an infrared IRDA port is brought near my computer, the Send Files to Another Computer icon doesn't appear.

In this case, the problem could be with either computer. If one of the two computers *can* make a wireless link with at least one other computer, then you know the fault lies with the other.

The following are a few points to check:

- Be sure that the wireless optical ports are within a few feet of each other, are pointed relatively directly at each other, with a clear line of sight between them.
- Check the Device Manager on both computers to be sure that both IrDA ports are working correctly.
- Be sure that both computers have wireless file transfers enabled.
- If all else fails, borrow a handheld video camcorder. These cameras can often "see" the infrared light emitted by IrDA ports. Check to see that the ports on both computers are blinking. If you see one blinking but not the other, you know one computer isn't set up correctly.

TIPS FROM THE WINDOWS PROS: MANUALLY ADDING ROUTING INFORMATION

As I discussed previously (the bit about a can of worms), if you use Virtual Private Networking to connect to a remote network with more than one subnet, you can let Windows set the default gateway to be the remote network. This way, you can contact all the hosts on the remote network and its subnets. Unfortunately, all of your Internet traffic will travel through the tunnel, too, slowing you down. The remote network might not even permit outgoing Internet access.

The alternative is to disable the use of the default gateway and manually add routes to any subnets known to belong to the private network. You can do so at the command line by using the route command, which looks like this:

```
route add subnet mask netmask gateway
```

The *subnet* and *netmask* arguments are the addresses for additional networks that can be reached through the gateway address *gateway*. To add a route, you must know the IP address information for the remote subnets and your gateway address through the VPN.

You must get the subnet numbers from the network administrator on the remote end. You can find the gateway address from your own computer. Connect to the remote VPN, open a command prompt, and type ipconfig. One of the connections printed will be labeled PPP Adapter or L2TP Adapter. Note the IP address listed. This address can be used as the gateway address to send packets destined for other remote subnets.

Suppose you're connecting to a VPN host through a connection named VPN to Client and find these connection addresses:

```
PPP adapter VPN to Client:
        IP Address. . . . . . . 192.168.005.226
        Subnet Mask . . . . . . 255.255.255.255
        Default Gateway . . . . 192.168.005.226
```

Now, suppose you know that there are two other subnets on the remote network: 192.168.10.0 mask 255.255.255.0, and 192.168.15.0 mask 255.255.255.0. You can reach these two networks by typing two route commands:

```
route add 192.168.10.0 mask 255.255.255.0 192.168.005.226
route add 192.168.15.0 mask 255.255.255.0 192.168.005.226
```

Each route command ends with the IP address of the remote gateway address (it's called the *next hop*).

Check your work by typing route print and looking at its output. You should see only one destination labeled 0.0.0.0; if you see two, you forgot to disable the use of the remote network as the default gateway. See that the two routes you added are shown.

To avoid having to type all this every time, you can use another neat trick. You can put a rasdial command and route commands in a batch file, like this:

```
@echo off
rasphone -d "VPN to Client"
route add 192.168.10.0 mask 255.255.255.0 192.168.005.225
route add 192.168.15.0 mask 255.255.255.0 192.168.005.225
```

The rasphone command pops up the connection dialer. When the connection is made, the two routes are added, and you're all set. With this setup, you'll need the network administrator to give you real RAS gateway address of the remote VPN server to use as the "next hop" of the route commands. With a shortcut to this batch file you can connect and set up the routes with just a click.

When you disconnect the VPN connection, Windows removes the added routes automatically.

For more information about rasdial and route, click Start, Help and Support, and search for the commands by name.

18

CHAPTER 19

CONNECTING YOUR LAN TO THE INTERNET

In this chapter

IT'S A GREAT TIME TO CONNECT YOUR LAN TO THE INTERNET

In the 1980s, only big corporations and universities had Internet connections, and then, a single 64Kbps connection was probably shared by hundreds of users. Now, accessing the Internet is as much a daily requirement as the morning paper. We expect to have instant access from any keyboard we can get our fingers on, and personally, I get grumpy using anything less than a 400Kbps connection. That's progress, I suppose.

Because you now have your computers all tied together with a nifty local area network (LAN), it seems silly that each user should have to use a modem to gain Internet access individually. No worries: You have a host of options for shared Internet connections. You can use a high-speed connection to serve the entire LAN, or you can share a modem connection made from one designated Windows XP computer. Either way, shared access makes online life simpler for everyone on the network.

In this chapter, I'll show you what your Internet connection options are and give you some of the pros and cons for each.

CAUTION

> Combining a LAN with an Internet connection also exposes you to some risks from hackers who have nothing better to do than try to break into your computers. In this chapter I'll show you how to minimize the risk, but you should also read Chapter 21, "Network Security," for more details.

THE NUTS AND BOLTS OF THE CONNECTION

19

You're probably familiar with using a modem to connect your own PC to an Internet service provider and thence to the Internet. When you're connecting an entire network of computers, the process is a little more involved. We'll address five main issues, starting with the physical connection itself. We'll discuss the pros and cons of each of the most common and reasonable alternatives.

THE NEED FOR SPEED

Of the several connection technologies, each has advantages and disadvantages in reliability, speed, and cost.

Speed is everything on the Internet now, and the need for raw speed will become even more important in the future. Remember that everyone on the LAN will be sharing a single connection, so you have to consider the speed requirements for the applications you'll be using over the network and multiply that requirement by the number of *simultaneous* users you'll want to support at that speed. If you have eight users checking e-mail and occasionally browsing the Web, your speed requirements might be met by a single modem, but if you have just two users who want to use voice and videoconferencing at the same time, you might need a very high-speed connection indeed.

If you can get it, high-speed DSL, cable, or satellite service will provide a much better experience than a dial-up setup. It costs a bit more per month, but if you take into the account that it can replace several dial-up accounts and free up several phone lines, it might turn out to be the least expensive alternative as well as the most fun.

WAYS TO MAKE THE CONNECTION

When you're using a single computer, you use its analog modem or broadband cable, DSL, or satellite modem to connect to your ISP as needed.

On a LAN, no matter what connection technology you use, you'll want the connection process to be automatic. The connection either needs to be "on" all the time or must be made automatically whenever someone on the network wants to use it. So, you need to use a *dedicated* connection, or you must use *demand-dialing*—that is, a modem that automatically connects whenever a user on the network needs it.

Fortunately, most of the fast, new Internet connection technologies use dedicated, always-on connections. And if you use an analog or ISDN modem to make your connection, Windows XP has built-in software called *Internet Connection Sharing*, which does exactly what you need. Third-party hardware and software devices that can tackle this job are also available.

As an overview, Figure 19.1 shows five ways you can hook up your LAN to an Internet service provider. They are

- Microsoft Internet Connection Sharing (ICS) with an analog or ISDN dial-up connection. In this scenario, the built-in software in Windows automatically dials your ISP from one computer whenever anyone on the LAN wants to connect to the Internet. This is called *demand-dialing*. (By the way, the modem doesn't have to be an external one; I just wanted it to show up in the figure).

- ICS with a broadband DSL or cable modem. The computer that hosts the shared connection uses a LAN adapter or USB port to connect to a broadband modem. This type of connection might be always-on, or, if your ISP uses a connection-based setup called PPPoE, Windows will establish the link whenever anyone wants to use the Internet.

→ To learn more about PPPoE, **see** "Configuring a High-Speed Connection," **p. 280.**

- Connection Sharing Router with a broadband, analog, or IDSN modem. You can use a small hardware device that costs about $100-150 to do the same job as Internet Connection Sharing. The advantage of this is that you don't have to leave a particular Windows XP computer turned on for other users to reach the Internet. It may also be more secure.

- Routed Service with a router. Some ISPs provide *routed* Internet service through DSL, cable, Frame Relay or other technologies. There's an extra charge for this type of service as it provides a separate public IP address to each computer on the LAN. This has some advantages that I'll discuss below, but it also incurs a risk of exposing your network to hackers, unless you're vigilant in setting it up.

19

Figure 19.1
Five ways to connect your LAN to the Internet.

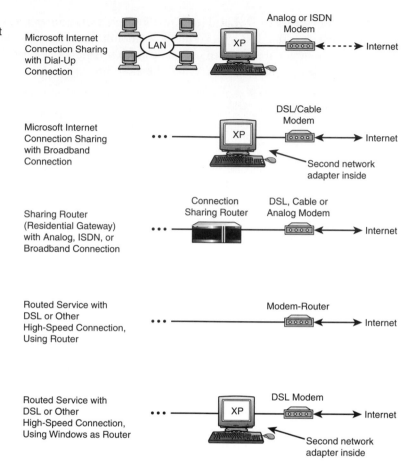

- Routed Service with Windows serving as a router. Some DSL providers can provide routed service with a DSL modem rather than a DSL router. You can use an extra LAN adapter to provide the routing service in Windows XP. This can save you a few hundred dollars, but it may be even less secure than the previous approach.

I discussed the pros and cons of dial-up, ISDN, and broadband connections themselves in Chapter 8, "Internet and TCP/IP Connection Options," so I won't repeat that discussion. Here, I'll discuss the costs and benefits of these five connection-sharing strategies.

NOTE

> Although I really prefer using the shared connection strategies—the first three schemes in Figure 19.1—they have a drawback: It's hard to enable incoming access to your computer. In particular, it makes it hard to reach your computer with Remote Desktop, and difficult for someone to work with you using Remote Assistance. These are some of the niftiest new features in Windows XP, and it's a shame to give them up. I'll show you how to make them work at the end of the chapter, under "Making Services Available."

Now, let's look at the issues involved in having a single ISP connection serve multiple computers.

MANAGING IP ADDRESSES

Connecting a LAN to the Internet requires you to delve into some issues about how computers are identified on your LAN and on the Internet. You'll find some background on this topic in Chapter 15 under "IP Name Services and Routing." In this chapter, we'll focus on how your LAN relates to the Internet as a whole.

As I discussed in Chapter 15, "Overview of Windows XP Networking," each computer on your LAN uses a unique network identification number called an *IP address* that is used to route data to the correct computer. As long as the data stays on your LAN, it doesn't matter what numbers are used; your LAN is essentially a private affair. On LANs with no shared Internet connection, in fact, Windows just makes up random IP address numbers for each computer and that's good enough.

When you connect to the Internet, though, those random numbers can't be used to direct data to you; *public* IP addresses have to be assigned to you by your ISP so that the Internet can properly route data to your ISP and then to you.

Now, when you establish a solo dial-up connection from your computer to the Internet, this isn't a big problem. When you dial up, your ISP assigns your connection a temporary public IP address. Any computer on the entire Internet can send data to you using this number. When you want to connect a LAN, though, it's not quite as easy. There are two approaches:

- You can get a valid public IP address for each of your computers, so they can each participate in the Internet at large
- You can use *one* public IP address and share it among all the users of your LAN

The first approach is called *routed* Internet service, because your ISP assigns a fixed block of IP addresses for your LAN and routes all data for these addresses to your site. The second approach uses a technique called *Network Address Translation* or NAT, in which all of the computers on your LAN share one IP address and connection.

NAT AND INTERNET CONNECTION SHARING

Microsoft's Internet Connection Sharing system and the popular devices called Residential Gateways or Connection Sharing Routers all use Network Address Translation to carry out all Internet connections using one public IP address. The computer or device running the NAT service mediates all connections between computers on your LAN the Internet (see Figure 19.2).

To explain NAT, it's helpful to make an analogy to postal mail service. Normally, mail is delivered to each house according to its address, and the mail delivery person stops at each separate house on a given block. This is analogous to routed Internet service where each of your computers has its own public IP address. Data is routed to your LAN, and then delivered to each computer independently.

Figure 19.2
A NAT device or program carries on all Internet communications using one IP address. NAT keeps track of outgoing data from your LAN to determine where to send responses from the outside.

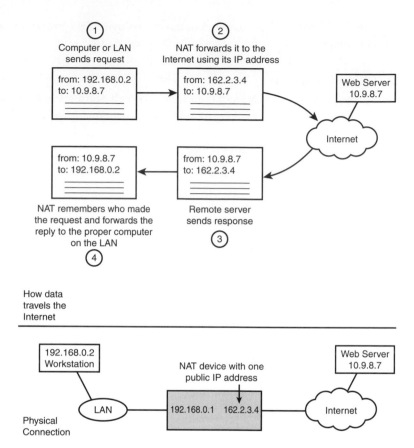

NAT works more like a large commercial office building, where there's one address for many people. Mail is delivered to the mail room, which sorts it out and delivers it internally to the correct recipient. With NAT, you are assigned one public IP address, and all communication between your LAN and the Internet uses this address. The NAT service takes care of changing or translating the IP addresses in data packets from the private, internal IP addresses used on your LAN to the one public address used on the Internet.

Using NAT has several significant consequences:

- You can hook up as many computers on your LAN as you wish. Your ISP won't care, or even know, that more than one computer is using the connection. You will save money because you only need to pay for a single-user connection.

- You can assign IP addresses inside your LAN however you wish. In fact, all of the NAT setups I've seen provide DHCP, an automatic IP address service, so that there's virtually no configuration needed on the computers you add to your LAN.

- If you want to host a Web site, VPN, or other service on your LAN and make it available from the Internet, you'll have some additional setup work to do. When you contact

a remote Web site, NAT knows to send the returned data to you, but when an unsolicited request comes from outside, NAT has to be told where to send the incoming
connection. I'll discuss this later in the chapter.

■ NAT serves as a sort of firewall to protect your LAN from probing by Internet hackers.
Incoming requests, to read your shared folders for example, are simply ignored if you
haven't specifically set up your connection sharing service to forward request to a particular computer.

■ Some network services can't be made to work with NAT. For example, you won't
receive video if you use NetMeeting to communicate with users on the Internet.
NetMeeting tells its private, not public, IP address to the computer on the other end of
the connection. The Internet doesn't know how to route the return video stream back
to you using the private address. (If you use a hardware connection-sharing device,
there's a way around this, although it adds a security risk. I'll discuss this more later in
the chapter.)

All in all, I strongly encourage you to use a NAT service for your shared Internet connection. Unless you use the workaround I mention above, you'll lose the ability to use
NetMeeting video but you'll gain security and convenience, and save money to boot. You
can use the Internet Connection Sharing service provided with Windows XP, or you can use
a hardware device called a Connection Sharing Router or a Residential Gateway. (You could
also use a computer running the Linux operating system with the IP Masquerading service,
but that's beyond the scope of this chapter.)

Starting with Windows 98, Microsoft has provided a NAT service through its Internet
Connection Sharing feature. In addition, Windows XP introduces the Internet Connection
Firewall, an additional security feature that prevents outside people from accessing your
LAN. I'll talk more about the Internet Connection Firewall in Chapter 21.

However, given the choice between Microsoft's Internet Connection Sharing (ICS) service
and an external hardware device, I still strongly prefer the hardware devices, for two reasons:

■ First, to use ICS, you have to leave one of your Windows computers turned on so that
other computers can reach the Internet. Connection sharing routers have to be left on
too, but they consume very little power compared to what a PC sucks up.

■ But more importantly, connection sharing routers provide better security than
Windows. These little boxes have very little going on inside them, so it's more likely
that any security flaws have been noticed and fixed. Windows, on the other hand, is
hugely complex, and Microsoft finds security flaws at the rate of one or two a week. If
you use ICS and host a Web site on the connection-sharing computer, you're inviting
outside people to run complex software on the same computer that's protecting your
network. What if they find a way to circumvent NAT or the Windows Internet
Firewall? And, if you use this computer for Web browsing, e-mail, or any Internet-
related work, you might accidentally receive a Trojan horse or virus program that
undoes your security setup. You'd probably never even know it happened.

19

I won't go so far as to say that you shouldn't trust ICS, and I will show you how to hook up your LAN using all five of the methods I described earlier. I'll just put in as my final word on this issue that I use DSL/Cable Sharing Routers at my home and office.

If you do decide to use an external sharing router, look at the products made by Linksys, D-Link, SMC, and Netgear. They're commonly on sale at office supply stores and online (check www.buy.com), for around $100. Some top-of-the line DSL modem-router combination devices can also provide NAT service. I've seen models made by Flowpoint and Netopia. These can cost about $600, however; more than the cost of a simple DSL modem and a separate connection-sharing router. Your ISP will tell you what kind of hardware is compatible with your particular service.

By the way, while most connection sharing routers on the market are designed for use with cable or DSL Internet service, some can connect with an analog or IDSN modem. If you use dial-up service, you're not left out. Netgear and SMC make devices that can be hooked up to a modem.

On the LAN side, most of the connection sharing devices have an Ethernet port to plug into your LAN, and many have a built-in hub, which is a real convenience. Some products provide phoneline and/or wireless 802.11b networking as well. I recently saw a pretty neat device: the D-Link DI-713P Wireless Broadband Router with 3-port switch. This cool little box provides Internet Connection Sharing, a 3-port switching hub, a print server, and a wireless access point all in one box, and it was on sale for only $220. Wow!

So, whatever type of Internet connection you use and whatever type of LAN you have, you can choose between a hardware device and Microsoft ICS.

Running Your Own Web Servers

If you want to host your own public Web or e-mail servers on your LAN, or if you want to reach your LAN through Remote Desktop or a VPN connection, your network should use an always-on connection so that the network can be reached from the outside. A demand-dialing connection is not a good choice for this use because the connection is established only when you try to reach out. Because the connection has to be on all the time, dial-up service is not very attractive if you have to pay per-minute connection charges to the telephone company. There are 43,200 minutes in a 30-day month and the charges add up fast.

And, whether you use NAT or a routed Internet service, you'll need your ISP to assign you a permanent, or *static*, IP address so that your computers' IP addresses don't change from day to day as a dial-up connection's does. Static IP addressing is not available with every connection technology or ISP, so you have to ask when shopping for your service provider.

Finally, you need a domain name service (DNS), which lets users around the world type http://www.yoursitename.com into their Web browsers to reach you. This service is provided as part of Windows 2003 Server, but not XP Professional. You can have your ISP provide domain name service, but it will probably cost you an extra $5 to $20 a month.

You also might check out the free public DNS service hosted by www.granitecanyon.com. They'll provide name service for free, although you will still have to find and probably pay for a domain registry service.

Inverse DNS

If you go for dedicated Internet access, and your ISP assigns you a block of IP addresses, you might want to ask your ISP to enter *Inverse DNS* information for you as well as register your domain name.

The domain name service (DNS) is called into play whenever you use an Internet address like www.microsoft.com. DNS looks up this name in a directory and returns some computer's IP address—for example, 207.46.131.137. The DNS system can also work in reverse and return the name of a computer given its IP address. For example, the name 4.3.2.1 turns out to be durham2-001.dsl.gtei.net.

When you get routed Internet access, the "inverse" lookup names for the IP addresses assigned to you either are left undefined or are set to some generic names like cust137.dsl131.someISP.com. If you ask, your ISP can set up names that identify your computers and domain so that anyone on the Internet to whom you connect can find out the name of your computer.

Using inverse DNS has some pros and cons. One pro is that some e-mail servers on the Internet don't accept e-mail from systems without a valid inverse DNS entry. If you run an e-mail server on your network, at least that computer should have an inverse DNS entry. One con is that Web site managers can tell the name of your computer and domain when you visit Web sites, so you give up some privacy.

The choice is up to you. If you want to register your computers, talk to your ISP.

The next two sections discuss issues important to business users. If you're setting up an Internet for your home, you can skip ahead to "Getting Your Service Installed," later in the chapter.

A WARNING FOR BUSINESS USERS

My enthusiasm notwithstanding, cable and DSL Internet service are based on new technologies, and the businesses delivering them are new and growing extremely rapidly. I can tell you from direct experience that they can give you a painful, bumpy ride. Some DSL ISPs (two of mine, for example) have already gone bankrupt and stranded their customers.

Customer support ranges from okay to incredibly bad, installation appointments are routinely missed, and even billing can be a terrible mess. Ask a provider for a service level agreement (a guaranteed percentage of uptime and throughput), and the likely reply will be hysterical laughter. If your business truly depends on your Internet connection for survival, DSL and cable are probably not for you.

It will cost lots more in the short term to set up Frame Relay or dedicated ISDN service, but if you lose business when your connection fails, you probably can't afford the risks that come with DSL and cable Internet access in these early years.

FRAME RELAY

I talked about dial-up, DSL, cable, ISDN, wireless, and satellite Internet connectivity in Chapter 8. For serious business use, Frame Relay is one more option to consider. Frame Relay is an older technology that was primarily designed for private, dedicated, long-distance connections for the corporate world. It's connected using hardware very similar to DSL, but it requires its own dedicated telephone line from your office to the phone company and some expensive equipment.

Although installing and setting up frame relay Internet hardware is tough, after the equipment is in, it just plugs into your LAN and virtually no setup is involved with Windows itself. (In Figure 19.1 it falls into the fourth category, Routed Service.)

Frame relay connections are extremely reliable and run at data rates similar to DSL, but have a severe disadvantage in price. Table 19.1 compares the costs for 128Kbps Frame Relay to DSL service.

TABLE 19.1   128KBPS FRAME RELAY VERSUS 128KBPS DSL

	128Kbps Frame Relay	128Kbps DSL
Installation by telephone company	$1,000	$0–100
Setup by ISP	$400	0
Required hardware (modem and so on)	$1,200–1,800	$100–600
Monthly data line fee	$325	$40
Monthly Internet service provider fee	$400	$10

It's pricey, but frame relay users might expect service interruptions of no more than three minutes per month versus perhaps three hours per month with DSL service. If this sounds good to you, you should contact a telecommunications consultant or a networking pro for more information.

GETTING YOUR INTERNET SERVICE INSTALLED

You've done your research, you've found out what connection technologies are available to you, and you've checked prices and asked a few selected ISPs for references. Now what? The following sections describe the steps you need to take to get your network connected.

WHEN THE PHONE COMPANY IS INVOLVED—DSL AND ISDN

If you choose DSL, ISDN, or frame relay service, you have to get a phone line installed and have to deal with the phone company. Now, if you remember her, conjure up a picture of Lily Tomlin's character "Ernestine" taking your order. Got the picture?

Telephone companies are old, big businesses with their own language. In many countries, they're state-owned monopolies, and in most, they're slow, bureaucratic, and highly regulated. The first lesson you have to learn is that you do it their way or not at all. I'll describe the way things are done in the United States to give you a feel for what needs to happen. If you're dealing with Internet service in another country, you'll probably have to make some adjustments to what follows; check with your local ISPs for expert advice on dealing with your telephone company.

If you're lucky, your Internet service provider will manage all aspects of your order, including provisioning, outside and inside wiring, and equipment setup. If you have to deal with the "telcos" directly, you should be familiar with the terminology they'll throw your way. Table 19.2 should arm you with the verbal weaponry you need.

TABLE 19.2   STANDARD "TELCO" TERMINOLOGY

POTS	We've talked all about high-tech services. Did you know that the name for just plain old telephone service is . . . exactly that? *POTS* is a real telephone company acronym. It's used this way: "DSL service can run on top of a standard POTS line."
T1	T1 is a fairly old-fashioned data carrier technology that lets a single pair of wires carry data at 1.5Mbps, which can carry 64 digitized telephone conversations. Telcos use T1 lines to carry phone calls between their offices, and ISDN and frame relay service can also "ride on" T1 lines.
T3	This technology makes a T1 line look like a drinking straw; it runs at 45Mbps.
CO	The *central office* is a phone company switching center. All the telephone wires in your neighborhood—whether they're carrying POTS, ISDN, DSL, or private data service—funnel into a CO, where they connect to the telephone company's switching equipment. From there, T1 and fiber-optic lines connect the central offices.
Switch	This device in a CO cross-connects the telephone lines of subscribers when they call each other or connects them to *trunk lines*, which connect the switches. Switches were designed to interlink only a certain number of lines at once, so lengthy modem calls to ISPs tie up the switches' capacity and give fits to the telephone company.
Demarc	In the U.S., the telephone company is responsible for the wiring and proper operation of any service from its office up to the point the wires enter your building. This point is called the *demarcation point*, or just *demarc*. At this point, the telephone company installs a box with screw terminals, where its wires end and yours are attached.
Outside wiring	The phone company installs *outside wiring* between its street boxes, telephone poles, and so on, and the demarc. The price for this service is included in your installation fee.
Inside wiring	The wiring between the demarc and your networking equipment or telephones is *inside wiring*. This wiring is your responsibility, although the phone company will wire you for a fee if you ask. You can also hire a wiring contractor or do it yourself. Some service providers include inside wiring in the setup fee. The DSL services I've installed all included free inside wiring.

continues

TABLE 19.2 CONTINUED	
Provisioning	The job of determining which wires to use of the thousands installed in the cables running around town, which IP addresses you'll be assigned, and which options to program into the central office's hardware is called *provisioning*. In a company with millions of such resources to track, the process is handled by a separate department. (Judging by how many DSL orders I've seen lost, I suspect that most DSL companies' sales and provisioning departments communicate by carrier pigeon.) If and when your order is eventually processed, you might have to speak to a provisioning specialist to select or confirm some options for your service.

ORDERING THE SERVICE

Ordering the service is the most treacherous part of the whole process. I've been involved in dozens of telephone and network service installations, and by far, most of the problems I have encountered are not technical but administrative: Details get lost or left out, orders get lost or set aside, equipment is not shipped, and due dates slip. I could tell you stories that would curl your hair. So, my two most important tips are as follows:

- For a business installation, if you're the least bit unsure about this process, hire a consultant to help get set up. Or, at least, have your ISP work with you to order any part of the service that involves the telephone company.

- Don't take anyone's word for granted. Take responsibility for knowing whether the ordering and installation process is progressing. Whenever you talk to someone, write down the date, time, their telephone number and name. I'm not kidding about this! Get the information you need to follow your order through the system. Internet service providers, especially DSL and cable providers, are frenzied right now, and the chances are they'll drop the ball somewhere along the way. Keep on top of them.

I recommend that you keep the following list, which I'll call "talking points" (Thank you, Monica), in front of you when you are ordering your service. Keeping a list may sound fussy, but I have been tripped up at various times by forgetting to ask even just one of these questions.

- Is my location qualified for this service? If you only *think so*, how will you find out for sure and when will you let me know?

- What are the setup, installation, equipment, and monthly service costs?

- Do you offer any discounts for longer-term contracts?

- What equipment is included in the price you quoted?

- Do I need to order service from the telephone company, or do you do that?

- When will the service be installed? At what time of day?

- What sort of inside wiring is needed?

- Do you do inside wiring, and is the cost included in your quote?

- Will you waive your setup fee? (It's worth a try).

- What is my order number?

- Who in your organization is responsible for the next step in getting my order completed? What is that person's phone number? When will I hear from him or her?

- Could you please read back my name, address, phone number, e-mail address, and the details of the order as you've taken them down?

SPECIAL NOTES FOR CABLE SERVICE

Although some cable Internet providers can provide you with multiple IP addresses so you can connect multiple computers, I strongly urge you *not* to use this type of service. Instead, you should order service for *one* computer, and use Internet Connection Sharing with two network adapters, or a connection sharing router to provide service for your other computers. There are two reasons for this.

First, when you order more than one IP address on cable service, some providers assign IP addresses that have different IP subnet addresses. This is like giving you telephone extensions with different area codes, and it makes it very difficult to use Microsoft Networking (file sharing) on your LAN. Your computers would not appear in My Network Places.

But more importantly, this type of setup requires you to connect your cable modem directly to your LAN, without any way of putting firewall protection between the Internet and your computers. For protection, you would have to enable the Internet Connection Firewall on each computer, and this means networking wouldn't work. If you didn't enable the firewall, you would expose all of your computers to a *severe security risk*.

CAUTION

> Do not connect a cable modem directly to your LAN. Anyone on the Internet would be able to read and change your shared files and folders.

The solution to this dilemma is to use a single cable connection and share it with your network. You'll have a safe network and will still get cable's fast download speeds.

SPECIAL NOTES FOR ISDN SERVICE

If you are ordering ISDN service, you should know what kind of ISDN modem or router you will be using before you order an ISDN line from the phone company. ISDN provisioning is complex, and most telephone companies can determine the options you need if you tell them the brand of equipment you're using. Also, your ISDN equipment manual may list a special "quick order" code to give your telephone company. You will probably order "2B+D, Data and voice, 64K data" service with no special call functions.

When your ISDN line is installed, be sure to ask the installer for the following information:

- Switch type
- SPID (Service Profile Identifiers) numbers
- Directory numbers

You'll need these when you install your ISDN modem.

CONFIGURING YOUR LAN

You waited weeks for installation day, and the installer finally came. Now all you can think of is all those bits, just waiting to blast their way onto your network. Hang on; we're almost done.

The last step is to set up your network's TCP/IP software to let your computers talk through the Internet connection in a coordinated way. This step depends not so much on the connection type you chose but on the sharing system and the IP address system you'll use.

In the next five sections, I'll describe how to set up each of the five connection schemes diagrammed in Figure 19.1. If you're still in the planning stages for your network, you might want to read all five sections to see what's involved. If your LAN is already set up and your Internet service is ready to go now, just skip ahead to the appropriate section.

CONFIGURING MICROSOFT INTERNET CONNECTION SHARING WITH A DIAL-UP CONNECTION

This section shows how to set up the first Internet connection method illustrated in Figure 19.1.

The Internet Connection Sharing feature provided with Windows XP can share modem, ISDN or broadband connections that require a sign-on procedure. The connection is made automatically whenever any user on the network tries to access the Internet; this is called demand-dialing. The following section describes how to set it up.

SETTING UP THE SHARED CONNECTION

To set up a shared connection, first install and test your modem and ISP information on one computer on the network by configuring a standard dial-up connection. You learned this process in Chapter 8. Be sure that you can access the Internet properly by viewing at least one Web page. When you know this is working, you're ready to set up Internet Connection Sharing. You can do this with the Network Setup Wizard, or set it up manually. To use the Wizard, follow these steps:

1. Click Start, My Computer, select My Network Places, and then select Set Up a Home or Small Office Network.

2. In the Network Setup Wizard, click Next twice. Select This Computer Connects Directly to the Internet as the connection method, and then click Next.

3. In the list of network connections, select the listing for the connection to your ISP as shown in Figure 19.3 and click Next. Your display will not look exactly like the one in the Figure, as it will list the dial-up connections you've defined. Choose the dial-up connection entry you use to reach your own ISP.

4. Complete the rest of the Network Setup Wizard as described in Chapter 8. If you have an existing LAN, be sure to enter the same Workgroup name you used originally, as the Wizard wants to change the setting to WORKGROUP every time you run it.

Figure 19.3
In this dialog box, select the ISP Internet Connection that you want to share.

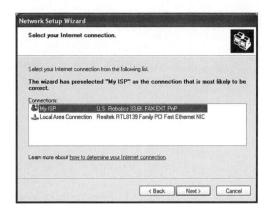

If you have older Windows 95 or 98 computers on your network, you might want to create a diskette with the Network Setup Wizard for these computers by following the instructions you'll encounter in the wizard.

5. When the wizard completes, you might want to restart your computer.

6. Log on again, and try to view any Web page (such as www.google.com). If it appears, proceed to step 7. If it doesn't, you'll have to resolve the problem.

7. When the sharing computer can connect properly, repeat these steps on your other computers, except for one detail: When you run the wizard, select This Computer Connects to the Internet Through Another Computer on My Network or Through a Residential Gateway.

 If your modem doesn't dial up when you try to view a Web page, see "Shared Connection Doesn't Happen" in the "Troubleshooting" section at the end of this chapter.

Connection sharing is now set up. You might want to walk through the manual process described next, just to confirm that all of the settings were made correctly. Otherwise you may skip ahead to the section titled "Configuring the Rest of the Network."

If you don't want to or can't use the Network Setup Wizard on the connection-sharing computer, you can use the manual configuration process described next. Here is the procedure:

1. Click Start, My Computer, and select My Network Places. Select View Network Connections. Right-click the icon for the connection to your ISP, and select Properties.

2. Choose the Advanced tab. Check all the boxes, as shown in Figure 19.4.

3. Select the Options tab. Uncheck Prompt For Name And Password and Prompt for Phone Number. This will let the connection start up without user intervention.

4. If you want a dedicated, always-on connection, check Redial If Line Is Dropped. Set the number of Redial Attempts to 99, the Time Between Redial Attempts to 10 seconds, and Idle Time Before Hanging Up to Never.

19

Figure 19.4
On the computer that is going to share its connection, enable Internet Connection Firewall and Internet Connection Sharing.

CAUTION

Remember, this will keep your analog or ISDN line connected 24/7. Be sure this is what you want!

Usually, though, you'll want a demand-dialing connection. Uncheck redial if Line Is Dropped. Set the number of Redial Attempts to 10, the Time Between Redial Attempts to 10 seconds, and Idle Time Before Hanging Up to 10 minutes. (I recommend using this time; you can increase it later if you find that the line disconnects too frequently while you're working.)

5. Select the Networking tab. In the list of Components used by the connection, be sure that *only* Internet Protocol (TCP/IP) and QoS Packet Scheduler are checked. (This will prevent file sharing from being exposed to the Internet. The Firewall will do that too, but it doesn't hurt to be extra safe.)

6. Click OK. Windows then warns you that it is changing the network address of your LAN adapter to 192.168.0.1. This is now the IP address for this computer on your LAN.

I suggest restarting your computer and confirming that your computer connects to your ISP when you try to view a Web page. Then, proceed by configuring the other computers on your LAN.

CONFIGURING THE REST OF THE NETWORK

When the shared connection is set up, configuring the rest of your LAN should be easy. The computer sharing its Internet connection is now

- A DHCP server, which parcels out IP addresses and setup information
- The network gateway, which forwards to the Internet any network traffic that isn't directed at local computers
- A DNS server, which assists the other computers in converting domain names into IP addresses

Its IP address is 192.168.0.1 and all your other computers simply refer to it for network services.

To configure the other computers on the network, you can use the Network Setup Wizard, or configure manually. First, I'll give the steps for using the wizard. On each of your other computers (all except the connections-sharing computer), follow these steps:

1. Open My Computer from the Start Menu, and select My Network Places. Select Set Up a Home or Small Office Network. If you are setting up older Windows 95/98/2000 computers that don't have a Network Setup Wizard, you can use the diskette you prepared when you setup connection sharing.

2. When the wizard starts, click Next twice. Select This Computer Connects to the Internet Through Another Computer as the connection method, and then select Next.

3. Complete the rest of the Network Setup Wizard as described in Chapter 16, under "Give This Computer a Description and Name." If you have an existing LAN, be sure to enter the same Workgroup name you used originally, because the wizard wants to change the setting to WORKGROUP every time you run it.

4. When the wizard finishes, you might want to restart your computer. Then, you should be able to open Internet Explorer and view a Web site. When you try, the connection-sharing computer should dial out.

NOTE

When you're using a shared dial-up connection, it takes a while for the dialer to go through its paces if the connection wasn't already up, and before it can finish you might get an error from Internet Explorer saying it can't open the page. If this happens, just wait a few seconds and click Refresh to try again.

19

If you're a networking hotshot and want to configure other computers manually, you can use this procedure:

1. Open My Network Places and select View Network Connections. Open Local Area Connection's Properties. (On versions of Windows before XP, you may have to use different selections to get to your network adapter's settings; check online help or your *Special Edition Using* copy for that particular version.)

2. Select Internet Protocol (TCP/IP), and then select Properties.

3. Check Obtain an IP Address Automatically and Obtain DNS Server Address Automatically.

4. Click OK. The computer should reconfigure itself with a new IP address obtained from the computer with the shared dial-up connection.

Now test the shared connection from a computer on your LAN by trying to browse a Web page.

 If the computer can't browse Web pages, see "Can't Access a Shared Modem Connection from the LAN" in the "Troubleshooting" section at the end of this chapter.

CONFIGURING MICROSOFT INTERNET CONNECTION SHARING WITH A BROADBAND CONNECTION

This section shows how to set up the second Internet connection method illustrated in Figure 19.1.

The procedure for configuring a shared high-speed cable or DSL Internet connection with Microsoft ICS is very similar to that for setting up a shared dial-up connection. To prepare, be sure to install and test your DSL or cable connection on the computer you'll use to host the shared connection, as described in Chapter 8. It's essential that you have this working before you proceed to set up your LAN for a shared connection.

TIP FROM

Bob & Brian

> If your broadband service uses a LAN adapter rather than USB to connect your computer to the modem, you'll be installing two LAN adapters in this computer: one for the LAN, and one used to connect to the modem. I suggest that you install them one at a time. After installing the first one, view the adapter's icon in Network Connections, right-click it, and rename it to indicate what it's used for, as shown in Figure 19.5. Repeat this step when you install the second adapter. This will help you later on in the setup process when you need to know which connection goes to your ISP.

Figure 19.5
Install and rename your network adapters one at a time, indicating what purpose they'll serve. "DSL Connection" or "Public Connection" is much more informative than "Local Area Connection #2."

When your broadband connection is working, follow these steps:

1. Click Start, My Computer. Select My Network Places, then select Set Up a Home or Small Office Network.

2. In the Network Setup Wizard, click Next twice. Select This Computer Connects Directly to the Internet as the connection method, and then click Next.

3. In the list of network connections, select the listing for the connection to your ISP as shown in Figure 19.6 and click Next. (Now you see why it's helpful to have renamed the connection icons. Also, note that your list of connections might not look exactly like mine.)

4. Complete the rest of the Network Setup Wizard as described in Chapter 8. If you have an existing LAN, be sure to enter the same Workgroup name you used originally, because the wizard wants to change the setting to WORKGROUP every time you run it.

Figure 19.6
In this dialog box, select the ISP Internet connection that you want to share.

If you have older Windows 95 or 98 computers on your network, you might want to create a diskette with the Network Setup Wizard for these computers by following the instructions you'll encounter in the wizard.

5. When the wizard completes, you might want to restart your computer.

6. Log on again, and try to view any web page (such as www.google.com). If it appears, proceed to step 7. If it doesn't, you'll have to resolve the problem before proceeding. You should check the appropriate connection icon to be sure it's still configured correctly for your ISP.

7. When the sharing computer can connect properly, repeat these steps on your other computers, except for one detail: when you run the wizard, select This Computer Connects to the Internet Through Another Computer on My Network or Through a Residential Gateway.

When Connection Sharing has been set up, follow the instructions under "Configuring the Rest of the Network" in the section immediately preceding this one.

Because it's so important with these always-on broadband connections that the Internet Connection Firewall is actually working, I suggest that you view the icons in Network Connections to be sure that the shared connection says "Firewalled," as shown in Figure 19.7. If it doesn't, use the following manual configuration steps to set it up.

If you want to confirm that the wizard did its job properly, or if you want to configure Connection Sharing manually, rather than using the wizard, you can follow these steps on the computer with the broadband connection:

1. Locate the icon for the broadband connection in Network Connections. Right-click it and select Properties.

2. Choose the Advanced tab. Check all of the boxes, as shown in Figure 19.4.

19

Figure 19.7
Be sure that your
shared broadband
connection says
Firewalled.

The connection
says Firewalled

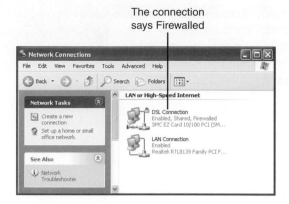

CAUTION

Be sure that Protect My Computer is checked, so that the Internet Connection Firewall is enabled. This is an extremely important line of defense against Internet hackers who'd love nothing more than to get into your computer and LAN. Even if you have no useful information for them to steal, they could still wreak havoc on your computer and use your computer as a base of operations to attack other people.

3. Select the General tab. In the list of Components used by the connection, be sure that *only* Internet Protocol (TCP/IP) and QoS Packet Scheduler are checked. (This will prevent file sharing from being exposed to the Internet. The Firewall will do that too, but it doesn't hurt to be extra safe.)

4. Click OK. Windows then warns you that it is changing the network address of your LAN adapter to 192.168.0.1. This is now the IP address for this computer on your LAN.

I suggest restarting your computer and confirming that your computer connects to your ISP when you try to view a Web page. Now, skip back to the section titled "Configuring the Rest of the Network."

CONFIGURING A SHARING ROUTER WITH AN ANALOG, ISDN, OR BROADBAND CONNECTION

This section shows how to set up the third Internet connection method illustrated in Figure 19.1.

If you are using a hardware connection-sharing device, you're replacing the Windows XP computer in the first or second illustration in Figure 19.1 with a small hardware device. The hardware device serves as your network's gateway.

Your router's manufacturer will provide instructions for installing and configuring it. If you're using cable or DSL Internet service, you'll connect your broadband modem to the router using a short Ethernet patch cable. If you're using a dial-up or ISDN account, you'll need to set up the router and a modem. Then, you'll connect the router to your LAN using one of the two methods shown in Figure 19.8.

Figure 19.8
Connecting a connection sharing router to your LAN.

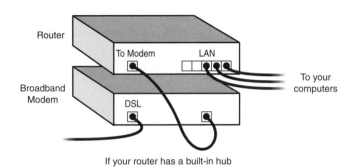

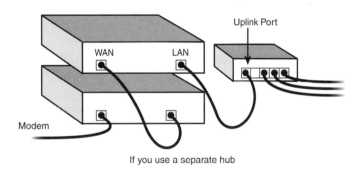

If you connect your router to a separate hub, be sure that the "Link" indicators come on at both the hub and the router. If they don't you might need to switch the hub cable from a regular port to an uplink port or *vice versa*.

You'll then configure the router, telling it how to contact your ISP, and what range of IP addresses to serve up to your LAN. Every device will use a different procedure, but I can show you the basic steps used by the Linksys Cable/DSL Sharing Routers that I have been so happy with.

The procedure will go something like this: When the router is attached to your network, you'll set up one of your computers' LAN adapter to obtain its IP address information automatically. Then you will use Internet Explorer to connect to the router by viewing http://192.168.1.1. (The address may be different for your router). A password is required; on my router the factory default value was admin.

You'll fill in your ISP's IP and sign-on information, if any, on a Web page similar to the one shown in Figure 19.9.

You might need to enter a static IP address, if one is assigned by your ISP. If your ISP uses DHCP to assign IP addresses dynamically, the router may need to be assigned the host and domain name expected by your provider. This is common with cable Internet setups.

If your ISP uses PPPoE to establish a connection, you'll need to enable PPPoE and enter your logon and password. This is common with DSL services. If your DSL provider does use PPPoE, you should enable auto-signon, and you can optionally set up a "keep-alive" value that will tell the modem to periodically send network traffic even if you don't, in order to keep your connection active all the time. (This might violate your service agreement with the DSL provider—better check before you do this.)

When the router is set up, go to each of your computers and follow the instructions under "Configuring the Rest of the Network," earlier in the chapter. You won't have a computer that shares its connection, in this case. You can configure all of the computers manually, or you can use the Network Setup Wizard. Choose My Computer Connects Through Another Computer or a Residential Gateway if you use the wizard, or select both Obtain an IP Address Automatically, and Obtain DNS Information Automatically if you use the manual method.

Figure 19.9
Sample setup page for a cable/DSL connection sharing router.

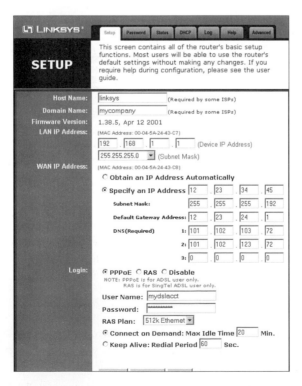

Also, be sure that the Internet Connection Firewall is *not* enabled on any of your computers' LAN adapters. Protection is being provided by the router, and enabling the Firewall will only prevent you from sharing files and printers on your LAN.

CAUTION

> Be sure to change the factory-supplied password of your router after you install it. Also, be sure to disable outside (Internet) access to the router's management screens.

CONFIGURING ROUTED SERVICE USING A ROUTER

This section shows how to set up the fourth Internet connection method illustrated in Figure 19.1.

Some Internet service providers will sell you service that provides multiple, fixed IP addresses. This is the case for all frame relay service, and higher-priced business-class DSL service. You should really have a good reason for going this way, beyond just wanting to connect multiple computers—it's not as secure as a single shared connection. Good reasons might be that you need to use NetMeeting videoconferencing (NAT can't handle this without special workarounds that compromise security), you want the reliabililty of frame-relay service, or you need fixed IP addresses in order to host Web, e-mail, or other Internet-based services.

For this type of service, if you are using a cable, DSL, satellite, or Frame Relay modem with a built-in router, your ISP will help you configure your network. In this setup, you will be provided with a fixed set of IP addresses, which you'll have to parcel out to your computers. Your ISP should help you install all of this, but I can give you some pointers.

First of all, it is *absolutely essential* that your router be set up to block Microsoft file sharing service (NetBIOS or NetBT) packets from entering or leaving your LAN. In technical terms, the router must be set up to block TCP and UDP on port 137, UDP on port 138, and TCP on port 139. It should "drop" rather than "reject" packets, if possible. (This helps prevent hackers from discovering that these services are present but blocked. Better to let them think they're not there at all.)

CAUTION

> If your router is not properly configured to filter out NetBIOS traffic, your network will be completely exposed to hackers. This is absolutely unacceptable. If you're in doubt, have your ISP help you configure the router. Also, visit http://www.grc.com and use the "Shields Up!" pages there to be sure your computers are properly protected.
>
> Even with filtering enabled, this setup is the least secure of the five options discussed in this chapter.
>
> Also, be *absolutely* sure to change your router's administration password from the factory default value to something hard to guess. Don't let your ISP talk you out of this. If your router gets hacked into, the filtering setup can be removed instantly.
>
> For more information about network security please see Chapter 21.

19

Second, if you use the Network Setup Wizard on any of your computers, when asked to choose a connection method, select Other, and on the next page, choose This Computer Connects to the Internet Directly or Through a Network Hub.

The wizard will give you some grief about the security risk involved in your Internet setup and will enable the Internet Connection Firewall on your LAN adapter. This will prevent your computer from sharing files with the rest of the LAN. Since you set up protection in your router and want to share files, you'll need to manually disable the firewall. To do this

1. View Network Connections by opening My Computer or My Network Places.

2. Right-click the Local Area Connection icon (it will say "firewalled" below its name), and select Properties.

3. Select the Advanced tab, and uncheck Protect My Computer. . . . Click OK to close the dialogs.

Third, you'll need to set up an IP address for each computer, plus the network mask, gateway IP address, and DNS server addresses supplied by your ISP, on each of your computers. Keep a list of which IP address you assign to each computer. To set this information

1. View My Network Places and select View Network Connections.

2. Right-click the Local Area Connection icon and select Properties.

3. Select the General tab, select Internet Protocol (TCP/IP), and then click Properties.

4. Enter one of your IP addresses and other assigned information. Figure 19.10 shows an example; you'll have to use the information provided by your ISP.

Figure 19.10
Setting up static assigned IP address information.

19

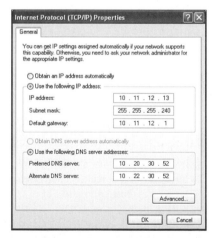

CONFIGURING ROUTED SERVICE USING WINDOWS AS A ROUTER

This section shows how to set up the fifth Internet connection method illustrated in Figure 19.1.

Some DSL Internet service providers can install routed, multiple-IP-address DSL service using only an inexpensive modem, rather than a full-featured router. You might want this sort of service for the same reasons that I listed above under "Configuring Routed Service Using a Router."

You'll have to provide your own router. Windows XP can do the job very nicely and it provides a good firewall feature to boot. Whether this setup is safer than using a hardware router or not, I can't tell you. The Windows Firewall is more sophisticated, but Windows is more likely than a router to get hacked into. If it happens, the hacker will disable the Firewall feature . . . and then you're in trouble.

If you use this setup, I do suggest that you follow these precautions to help protect your network:

- If possible, don't use the Windows XP computer that will serve as your router for day-to-day work. Leave it alone if you can. (Using a DSL modem rather than a hardware DSL router only saves you $400, so this approach doesn't seem very attractive any more, does it?)

- If you must use this computer for day-to-day work, create only "Limited" user accounts, and do not use Computer Administrator accounts except when you must to set up new hardware or software.

- Don't install Internet Information Services, FTP, or other Internet service software on this computer. There's just too great a risk that they have a bug that might compromise this computer that's providing all of your security.

Collect the IP address information provided by your ISP—you'll get one set of information for the router connection, and another set for the LAN computers. Then follow these steps:

1. You'll need to install two LAN adapters in the computer that will serve as your router. If possible, install them one at a time, and rename the resulting Network Connections icons to indicate the purpose of each connection, for example "DSL Connection" and "LAN Connection". Do not run the Network Setup Wizard on this computer. You must configure it manually.

2. Right-click the DSL Connection icon and select Properties. Uncheck both Client for Microsoft Networks and File and Printer Sharing for Microsoft Networks to block access to these services from the Internet.

3. Select the General tab and configure the Internet Protocol properties with the "WAN" port settings provided by your ISP.

4. Select the Advanced tab, and check Protect My Computer . . . to enable the Internet Connection Firewall. Do not check Internet Connection Sharing.

5. Click the Advanced button and select any network services you'll be *providing* from your LAN to the outside world. I'll discuss the Firewall in more detail in the next section.

6. Close this connection's properties, and open the LAN Connection icon's properties.

19

7. Configure the Internet Protocol properties as I discussed in the previous section. Use the first of the allocated LAN IP addresses you were assigned, and the assigned network mask, gateway IP address, and DNS addresses.

8. When you configure the *other* computers on the LAN, use a different assigned IP address for each. Enter the same setup information you used on the routing computer, except for the gateway address: enter the IP address you assigned to the routing computer's LAN connection in step 7.

MAKING SERVICES AVAILABLE

You might want to make some internal network services available to the outside world through your Internet connection. You would want to do this if

- You want to host a Web server using Internet Information Services
- You want to enable incoming VPN access to your LAN so you can securely connect from home or afield
- You want to enable incoming Remote Desktop access to your computer, or have someone help you through Remote Assistance

If you have set up routed Internet service with a router (as in the fourth setup in Figure 19.1), you don't have to worry about this because your network connection is wide open and doesn't use Network Address Translation. As long as the outside users know the IP address of the computer hosting your service, or its DNS name if you have this set up, you're on the air already.

Otherwise, you have either the Internet Connection Firewall, Network Address Translation, or both in the way of incoming access. In order to make specific services accessible, you'll need to follow one of the sets of specific instructions in the next few sections, depending on the type of Internet connection setup you've used. Skip ahead to the appropriate section.

ENABLING ACCESS WITH INTERNET CONNECTION SHARING

When you are using Microsoft's Internet Connection Sharing feature, the Internet Connection Firewall, or both, your network is protected from outside access. This is a good thing when it blocks attempts by hackers to get to your shared files and folders. It also blocks access to some of the neat services you might *want* the outside world to have access to: Virtual Private Networking, Remote Desktop, Remote Assistance, Web and FTP service, and so on.

Access to these services can be granted on a case-by-case basis by configuring the computer hosting ICS or the Firewall. To enable services, follow these steps:

1. On the computer that physically connects to the Internet, click Start, select My Network Places, and then select View Network Connections.

2. Right-click the icon for the external Internet connection and select Properties. View the Advanced tab, and click Settings.

3. On the Advanced Settings dialog, view the Services tab (shown in Figure 19.11).

Figure 19.11
The Services tab lets you specify which services are to be permitted through Internet Connection Sharing and/or the Internet Connection Firewall.

4. Check the Service entry for each service for which you want to permit access and for which you have servers on your LAN. The most common ones to select are FTP Server and Web Server, if you have set up IIS; Internet Mail Server if you have a mail server set up to receive mail; and Remote Desktop if you want to permit access to a computer with Remote Desktop or Remote Assistance.

NOTE

> You don't have to enable items in the firewall list to use these services on computers outside your LAN, just to let outside computers reach *you*.

19

5. When you select a check box, a dialog appears, as shown in Figure 19.12.

6. Enter the IP address of the computer that is hosting this service, if your LAN uses fixed IP addresses. If your LAN uses automatically-assigned addresses from Internet Connection Sharing, this gets stickier; you can enter the computer's name and the software will still locate the correct computer and send requests its way.

7. If you want to use an incoming VPN connection, you must set it up on the computer that hosts the Internet Connection Sharing or Firewall service; the firewall will automatically be opened for it. You can't forward VPN connections to other computers.

Figure 19.12

8. If the service you want to use isn't listed, you'll need to find out what TCP and/or UDP ports the service communicates with. You'll have to search through the service software's documentation or the Internet to find these port values. For example, Symantec PC Anywhere uses TCP Port 5631 and UDP Port 5632.

9. To add an unlisted service, click Add. Enter the name of the service, the IP address or host name of the computer which is running this service, and the port number, as shown in Figure 19.13. Generally, you'll want to use the same number for the port number the public sees (external port) and the port number used on the LAN (internal port). Check TCP or UDP, and then click OK.

   In the PC Anywhere example I'm using, after creating an entry for TCP Port 5631, I'll have to add a second entry to permit UDP Port 5632.

When you've enabled the desired services, incoming requests using the selected service ports will be forwarded through the Firewall to the appropriate computer on your LAN.

Figure 19.13
Enter port information for a new service in this dialog.

19

CAUTION

With the exception of incoming VPN connection service, I suggest that you don't run any other services on the computer that manages your Firewall and/or Internet Connection Sharing, especially IIS. There's too great a risk that a security flaw in the service might let hackers compromise the Firewall.

TIP FROM

Bob & Brian

If you're not sure which port a given service uses, you can use the Firewall's logging feature to find out what ports are used. To do this, open the Advanced Settings page again, click Settings, and view the Security Logging tab. Check Log Dropped Packets and click OK. Then attempt to connect to the sharing computer from outside on the Internet using the service of interest. View the log file (by default, c:\windows\pfirewall.log). The eighth column in this file lists the "destination port" that you tried to use. This is the port your service needs to have forwarded.

ENABLING ACCESS WITH A SHARING ROUTER

If you use a connection-sharing router on your LAN, you'll use a manufacturer-specific procedure to set up forwarding for services you want to expose to the Internet.

One difficulty with these devices is that they usually pass out automatic IP addresses to your LAN's computers, and these may change from day to day. This doesn't mix well with wanting to forward incoming requests to specific computers as their automatic IP address is a moving target.

In this case, you'll have to make special arrangements for the computers on your LAN that you want to host services, including machines that you want friends to be able to connect to with Remote Assistance. This is basically a pain in the . . . but it can be dealt with. There are two ways you can set up forwarding. One is appropriate for services that use standard, well-known TCP or UDP protocol ports (like a Web server or Remote Desktop), and the other is appropriate for access to services that use non-standard protocols (like Microsoft VPN connections).

FORWARDING STANDARD TCP AND UDP SERVICES

For services that you want to host on a permanent basis, the solution is to set up a permanent, static IP address on each computer that you want to use to host services. To do this, go to the computer that hosts the service and follow these steps:

1. Open Network Connections and view the Local Area Connection Icon. Right-click it and select Properties.

2. Select Internet Protocol (TCP) and select Properties. View the General tab.

3. Check Use The Following IP address. Use the router's setup screen to find the IP address of your router, and enter the following information into the IP address fields:

   IP Address: x.x.x.250

   Subnet Mask: 255.255.255.0

   Default Gateway: x.x.x.x

   where x.x.x.x is the IP address of your router. For this computer's IP address, use the same first three numbers, and assign a fixed last number of 250. For example, my router's IP address is 192.168.1.1. I'd enter the following on a computer I want to use to host a Web server:

   IP Address: 192.168.1.250

   Subnet Mask: 255.255.255.0

   Default Gateway: 192.168.1.1

   If you have other computers you'd like to use to host services, assign them IP addresses ending in 249, 248, and so on. Be sure to record which IP address you assign to each computer.

19

4. View the Forwarding setup page on your router's internal configuration screen. For example, Figure 19.14 shows a router set up to forward a whole slew of services into computers on my LAN. Table 19.3 shows what is being forwarded here.

Of course, your gateway router might use different configuration screens—you'll have to check its documentation for examples appropriate for your setup.

Figure 19.14
Service Forwarding configuration for a typical connection sharing router.

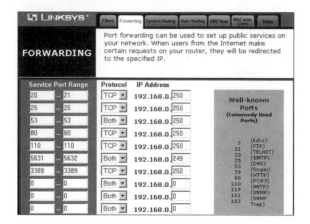

TABLE 19.3   SERVICES BEING FORWARDED IN FIGURE 19.14

Port	Service
20–21	FTP (file transfer protocol)
25	SMTP (simple mail transfer protocol)
53	DNS (domain name service)
80	HTTP (web server)
110	POP3 (mailbox server)
3389	Remote Desktop and Remote Assistance
5631–5632	Symantec PC Anywhere

FORWARDING NON-STANDARD SERVICES

For services that use non-standard protocols or use TCP/UDP in unpredictable ways, you'll have to use another approach to forwarding on your LAN. Incoming Microsoft VPN connections fall into this category. The Point-to-Point-Tunneling Protocol used by the VPN service uses the non-standard GRE protocol. If your particular gateway router can be configured to forward GRE packets (protocol #47), you can use standard forwarding, but most of the inexpensive home gateways can't.

To support this sort of connection, you'll have to open the firewall to *all* incoming requests and forward them to the computer you'd like to reach. This in effect exposes that computer to the Internet, so it's a fairly significant security risk. In fact, most routers call this operation "designating a DMZ host," referring to the notorious Korean no-man's-land called the Demilitarized Zone.

To enable a DMZ host, you'll want to use a fixed IP address on this computer, as described in the previous section. Use your router's configuration screen to specify this selected IP address. The configuration screen for my particular router is shown in Figure 19.15; yours may differ.

Figure 19.15
Enabling a DMZ host to receive all unrecognized incoming connection requests.

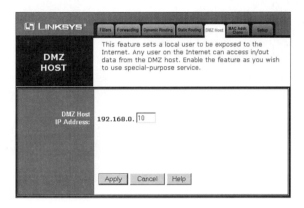

Now, designating a DMZ host means that this computer is now exposed to the Internet, so you must protect it with a firewall of some sort. You could enable Internet Connection Firewall on this computer's LAN Connection, but that would prevent it from using file and printer sharing. Instead, you should enable filtering in the connection sharing router to block access to Microsoft file sharing protocols on ports 137–139 and 445. Figure 19.16 shows how this is done on the Linksys router; your router might use a different method.

It's not a bad idea to enable filtering for these ports even if you're not using a DMZ host. It's *essential* to do so if you set up a DMZ host.

ENABLING ACCESS WITH ROUTED SERVICE USING WINDOWS AS A ROUTER

If you're using routed Internet service but using Windows as the router, you don't have NAT in the way of incoming service requests. Each computer has its own IP address and the incoming requests will be delivered directly to them. However the Internet Connection Firewall is set up to block most incoming access, as it should.

To open up specific ports for incoming services such as Remote Desktop and Remote Assistance, or any other servers you're hosting, see the instructions under "Enabling Access with Internet Connection Sharing." The same properties page is used to specify the services that should be allowed through both Firewall and ICS, no matter which is enabled.

19

Figure 19.16
Configuring filters to block Microsoft file sharing services.

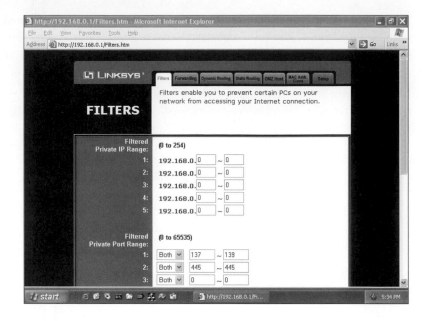

TROUBLESHOOTING

CAN'T ACCESS A SHARED MODEM CONNECTION FROM THE LAN

When I attempt to view an Internet page from a LAN computer, my Web browser doesn't get past "Looking up host www.somewhere.com."

A delay of 30 seconds or so is normal while the dial-up connection is established when you first start using the Internet.

If the connection doesn't progress after 30 seconds, be sure of the following: The sharing computer was turned on when you booted up your computer, the sharing computer is logged in, and your computer is set to obtain its IP address automatically.

Try to make the connection from the sharing computer to be sure the modem is connecting properly. If it's not, see the "Troubleshooting" section at the end of Chapter 8, "Internet and TCP/IP Connection Options," to diagnose the dial-up connection problem.

CAN'T ACCESS A SHARED DSL OR CABLE CONNECTION FROM THE LAN

When I attempt to view an Internet page from a LAN computer, my Web browser doesn't get past "Looking up host www.somewhere.com."

Be sure that the sharing computer was turned on when you booted up your computer, that the connection to the DSL or cable modem is the one marked as "shared," and that your computer is set to obtain its IP address automatically.

Try to view Web pages from the sharing computer to be sure the high-speed connection is functioning. If it's not, see the "Troubleshooting" section at the end of Chapter 14, "Troubleshooting Your Internet Connection," to diagnose the Internet connectivity problem.

Shared Connection Doesn't Happen

When I attempt to view a Web page on a network with a shared connection, no Internet connection is established.

If you are using a modem to establish the shared connection, listen to the modem to see whether it's trying to establish the connection. If it is, you might just need to wait a bit and try to view the page again. Sometimes, Internet Explorer gives an error message before the modem has had enough time to make the connection.

If the modem is making a connection but Web browsing still fails, the dial-up connection on the shared computer might not be set up with a saved password. On that computer, open My Network Places, select View Network Connections, and attempt to make the connection manually. Be sure that you've checked Save This User Name and Password and selected Anyone Who Uses This Computer.

If the modem isn't attempting to make the connection at all, run the Network Setup Wizard again on the sharing computer.

Tips from the Windows Pros: Squeezing Top Speed from Your High-Speed Connection

If you're using a high-speed connection such as DSL or cable, you can make an adjustment to your computer's networking software to get the best speed from your new connection.

Internet TCP/IP software sends data in chunks called *packets*, which are sent in a stream from, say, a Web server to your computer. The receiving computer sends acknowledgments every so often to indicate that the data has been received correctly or to indicate that something was lost or garbled during transmission.

A server sends only a limited amount of data before it expects to receive an acknowledgment. If the limit is reached before an acknowledgment is received, the sender has to stop and wait for one.

Ideally, for the fastest possible transfers, the sender should never have to stop sending because acknowledgments for earlier data arrive before this limit has been reached. Then the sender can go on sending, again hoping that the data will be acknowledged before the limit is reached.

For cable and DSL modems, the data rate is so high and the cross-country travel times so long that a considerable amount of data can be "in flight" before an acknowledgment could possibly be returned. So, to get the maximum use of your DSL or cable connection, you must tell Windows to make the limit larger than normal for a LAN connection.

19

This limit, called the *receive window*, should be larger than the data rate times the roundtrip time for data traveling back and forth between the two computers. This number is the maximum amount of data "in flight." A typical round trip time is .100 seconds for interstate Internet traffic, so for various data rates, the receive window should be at least

At 100Kbps * 0.100 sec / bits per byte   = 1.2KB

500Kbps   6KB

1.5Mbps   19KB

4Mbps   75KB

The default value used by Windows 9x, NT, and 2000 is only about 4KB! This means that Windows sends or lets a remote server send only 4KB and then sits and waits while your connection sits idle.

Windows 2000 and XP slowly boost the window size all by themselves during long file transfers, but when you're browsing Web pages with lots of small graphic images, they never get a chance to boost the window size enough for you to realize the full potential of your fast connection.

The maximum that you can specify the window size in Windows 2000 and XP is greater than 64KB, but 64KB is a practical maximum for DSL or cable service. To set the receive window, you must use the Registry Editor, which is described in Chapter 32, "The Registry." You must add a Registry value to a key that contains TCP/IP software parameters.

CAUTION

> Before adding a Registry value, be sure to read Chapter 32, with its dire warnings about the risks of editing the Registry and its urgings for you to back up the Registry before making a change of this sort.

SETTING THE RECEIVE WINDOW IN WINDOWS XP AND 2000

To set the receive window in Windows XP and 2000, do the following:

1. Open Registry key HKEY_LOCAL_MACHINE\System \CurrentControlSet\ Services\Tcpip\Parameters.
2. Select Edit, New, DWORD value, and name it GlobalMaxTCPWindowSize. Set its value to 20000 (hexadecimal). See Figure 19.17 to see this entry in the Registry Editor.

You must restart your computer for the setting to take effect.

Figure 19.17
You set the Global MaxTCPWindowSize value in this dialog box. Note that Hexadecimal must be checked.

CHAPTER 20

NETWORKING MIX AND MATCH

In this chapter

NETWORKING WITH OTHER OPERATING SYSTEMS

In the previous chapters, you learned about basic peer-to-peer and Active Directory networking, but these chapters considered only "vanilla" Windows networks. Real-life networks are seldom so simple. Often these networks have a mix of operating systems, and Windows must get along with them. Also, some optional networking components are not necessary in most environments, but some network managers do use them for maintenance and monitoring. This chapter covers internetworking and these more obscure parts of the Windows network puzzle.

On a real-life LAN with multiple operating systems, it's not enough that computers be able to coexist on the same network cable. Interoperation, or *internetworking*, is necessary so that users of these various systems can share files and printers. At best, this sharing can occur without anyone even knowing that alternate platforms are involved. Achieving this kind of seamlessness can range from effortless to excruciating.

TIP FROM

Bob & Brian

One way to avoid *all* the hassles of internetworking is to buy a *network appliance*, a small server computer that "speaks" all the networking languages you need: Windows, Unix, Macintosh, or whatever. These devices can cost as little as $1,000 and can put several GB of storage on your network that anyone can access. They tend to be very easy to set up, and some even provide Internet connection sharing, e-mail, and Web server in the same box. Examples include the Sun Cobalt Qube (www.cobalt.com) and the Celestix Aries Appliance Server (www.celestix.com).

If a network appliance isn't in the cards, and you need to get your computers to interoperate directly, you'll find that the ease of internetworking between Windows and another operating systems appears to be directly proportional to Microsoft's interest in capturing the other operating systems' existing customer base. Therefore, you'll find that Novell NetWare access is fully supported, whereas Linux interoperation is entirely absent and left up to you.

NOTE

NetBEUI was the original protocol used for networking in DOS, Windows, and IBM's OS/2. Microsoft has removed support for NetBEUI in Windows XP. Internetworking with DOS and OS/2 is no longer officially supported, although unsupported software makes it possible—at least, in the first version of Windows XP. I'll discuss this later in the chapter under "Internetworking with DOS and OS/2."

INTERNETWORKING WITH NOVELL NETWARE

Novell NetWare was the first PC-based network operating system and for many years was virtually unchallenged as the LAN platform for the business world. It's still arguably the fastest and most efficient file sharing service available for PC networks. NetWare and Windows have been tightly integrated from the start, and Microsoft has made sure that it's virtually effortless to add Windows servers and workstations to a NetWare network.

Behind the scenes, internetworking with NetWare is fairly complex. Windows networking and NetWare use different protocols to communicate with the file sharing computer and possibly a different network transport protocol, as shown in Table 20.1.

TABLE 20.1 COMPARISON OF COMPONENTS USED BY WINDOWS NETWORKING AND NETWARE

Network	Client/Server Protocol	Transport Protocol
Windows Networking	SMB (Server Message Block)	TCP/IP, NetBEUI, and/or IPX/SPX
NetWare 5	NCP (NetWare Core Protocol)	TCP/IP and/or IPX/SPX
NetWare 2 to 4	NCP	IPX/SPX

To simultaneously use files and printers shared by both Windows and NetWare servers, you must reconcile these differences.

To resolve the transport protocol issue, you can use TCP/IP as the protocol for all networking, or you can simply install IPX/SPX as an additional protocol. In this case, connections to NetWare servers will use IPX/SPX, and Windows networking can use TCP/IP or IPX or both protocols.

The differences in the fundamental server protocol can be addressed in one of two ways. You can install in each of your Windows computers a separate network client that communicates directly with NetWare servers, or, if you have a Windows .NET/2000 Server network, you can install Gateway Service for NetWare (GSNW) on the Server computer. The gateway service makes NetWare-based shared resources visible to Microsoft Networking clients. Another Server component, File and Print Services for NetWare (FPNW), works in the opposite direction, making resources from Microsoft Networking servers visible to NetWare users. These aren't choices that you'll have to make as a network user. Your network administrator will choose and install the network services.

In most cases, if your LAN has NetWare servers, your network manager will probably have you install (or will install for you) the Client for NetWare Networks so you can access NetWare servers without any sort of translation. Nowadays, having two network clients doesn't place any significant burden on memory or your computer.

NOTE

Interoperability with NetWare is not available in the 64-bit (Itanium) version of Windows XP Professional.

USING A NETWARE CLIENT

The Client for NetWare is a network driver that adds NCP-based networking support to Windows. It's really so well integrated with Windows that after it's installed, you don't have to treat NetWare servers as any different than Windows servers.

20

NetWare client software has two functions:

- First, it provides the underlying mechanism Windows uses to recognize that filenames like \\server\volume\file indicate that data is stored on a different computer.

- Second, the client provides support for legacy DOS applications that access network services directly through the NetWare Application Program Interface. These programs include NetWare system configuration utilities such as SYSCON and PCONSOLE, and some application software such as chat, e-mail, database, and client/server programs. When you install a NetWare client in Windows, a driver is added to Windows XP's MS-DOS subsystem to perform the functions that the IPXODI, NETX, and VLM programs performed in the DOS days of old.

You do have to decide whose client package to install because both Microsoft and Novell Corporation provide clients. The decision of which to use comes down mainly to compatibility and reliability. Historically, Microsoft's client package has been the most reliable and bug free. The Novell client has better compatibility with those old DOS programs, and some NetWare-specific programs absolutely require it.

NOTE

> Microsoft's Client Service for NetWare does *not* operate with NetWare version 5. If you use NetWare 5, you must download and use Novell's client. I'll discuss Novell's client later in the chapter.

If you need to access shared files and printers only from NetWare servers, you're probably better off with the Microsoft standard client. If your company uses NetWare-specific programs, your network manager can tell you whether you must use the Novell client. If you need it, you can download Novell's client from www.novell.com. I'll talk more about Novell's client later in the chapter. In the following discussion, I'll refer to the Microsoft client as it's the standard offering supplied with Windows XP.

TIP FROM

Bob & Brian

> One other issue that might affect your decision is security. Microsoft's NetWare client can't encrypt passwords sent to NetWare servers. If wire-level security is a concern, and you must protect yourself from people using network monitors to sniff out passwords on your LAN, use the Novell client.

CHOOSING NETWORK PROTOCOLS

You also must decide whether to allow Windows networking to use IPX/SPX as a transport protocol. With more than one protocol installed, you can select which ones are used by the File Sharing service and File Services client software in your computer through a process called *binding*. Bindings have the same sort of purpose as the cords and plugs on an old telephone switchboard, letting you select which higher-level services connect to which transport protocols, and which protocols can be used on each network adapter and dial-up connection.

Windows' SMB file services can use more than one protocol. When connecting to a remote machine, it uses any available protocol that your and the other computer have in common. However, this can cause problems if not every computer on the network has the exact same set of protocols bound to the file services. Windows finds other computers by name using the browser service that runs on just one computer on the LAN. The choice of browser is made by a random process called an *election*, and the browser learns only the names of computers with which it has protocols in common. If the random choice of the browser server happens to pick one that doesn't have a particular protocol bound to Windows file sharing, because that server doesn't see all the computers on the LAN, the rest of the network cannot find those computers by name.

TIP FROM

Bob & Brian

> This information sounds very complicated, but in practical terms, it comes down to one simple point: If you use more than one network protocol for Windows networking, install the *same* set of protocols on *every* computer.

If you have a Windows .NET/2000 Server-based network, your network manager will make this decision. If you have a peer-to-peer network and must make the decision yourself, here's my advice:

- If you're using NetWare version 5, use TCP/IP only, on all computers.
- If you're using NetWare version 3 or 4 without TCP/IP support, install both TCP/IP and IPX/SPX on *every* computer. If you can't install IPX/SPX on some of your Windows computers for some reason, unbind IPX/SPX from Windows file services on every computer, using the procedure covered later in the chapter under "Setting Network Bindings."

Microsoft has suggested that it will phase out support for IPX/SPX in the next version of Windows XP, so I suggest that you make the switch to TCP/IP-only networking now, if you can.

INSTALLING MICROSOFT CLIENT SERVICE FOR NETWARE

After you've done the background research, you can install the Microsoft client, as follows:

1. Log on as Administrator or a Computer Administrator. Click Start, My Computer, My Network Places, View Network Connections. Right-click Local Area Connection, and select Properties.
2. Select Install, highlight Client, and select Add.
3. Highlight Client Service for NetWare, and click OK. This will install the client, NWLink NetBIOS, and NWLink IPX/SPX/NetBIOS Compatible Transport.
4. When the setup process is complete, Windows will ask to restart your computer. Let it.

20

5. When Windows restarts and you log on, the Select NetWare Logon dialog will appear. You must select a primary NetWare logon server if you're going to use a login script:

   - On a NetWare 3 network (also called a *bindery security* network), check Preferred Server and select your default logon server from the drop-down list, or select None.

   - On a NetWare NDS network, check Default Tree and Context, and enter the name and context of the NDS tree you've been assigned by your NetWare administrator.

   You can change the default tree and context or preferred server later on using the Client Service for NetWare control panel applet.

6. If your NetWare administrator has configured Windows XP–compatible login scripts, check Run Login Script. Otherwise, if your NetWare login scripts were designed for a DOS environment, it's best not to run them.

After you've installed the client, it's best to proceed directly to the Control Panel to double-check the client's configuration settings. I'll describe this in the next section.

CONFIGURING MICROSOFT CLIENT SERVICE FOR NETWARE (CSNW)

Both Microsoft's and Novell's NetWare clients have configuration settings that are made from the Control Panel using the "CSNW" applet. To run the configuration applet, select Start, Control Panel. From the See Also list, select Other Control Panel Options and open the CSNW icon.

You should examine the CSNW (Client Service for NetWare) applet as soon as you install the NetWare client to get familiar with its options. The CSNW applet dialog is shown in Figure 20.1.

Figure 20.1
Client Service for NetWare Control Panel applet.

Your NetWare administrator will provide the Preferred Server, Default Tree, and Login Script Options settings. They select the NetWare logon server or context (domain).

Table 20.2 shows an additional set of printing options that you should set before using the network.

TABLE 20.2   ADDITIONAL PRINTING OPTIONS

Option	Description
Add Form Feed	Adds a form feed (page eject) at the end of each print job sent to any Novell print queue. This option dates back to the days of dot-matrix line printers and is undesirable with laser printers.
Notify When Printed	Displays a pop-up message on your screen whenever a print job sent to a Novell print queue has completed. I find it annoying.
Print Banner	Prints a cover page with your username before every print job sent to a Novell printer. It might help you locate your output in a busy office, but mostly it just wastes paper.

TIP FROM

By default, Notify When Printed and Print Banner are checked when you install Client Service for NetWare. I recommend unchecking both of them immediately unless your organization really requires them.

After the Client has been configured, when you log on to Windows, you will also be logged on to the NetWare network. Your network administrator usually will be sure your username and password are the same for Windows XP and for NetWare, so you should not need to specify any additional information after you log on to Windows. If your NetWare username or password are different, however, Windows will prompt you for the required information when you attempt to use a NetWare resource for the first time. You should keep your Windows and NetWare passwords synchronized to avoid this annoyance. I'll discuss passwords later in this chapter.

When you've made any necessary changes to the NetWare configuration, close the dialog box and skip ahead to "Setting Provider Order" later in this chapter.

INSTALLING AND USING NOVELL'S CLIENT SOFTWARE

If your needs or network manager dictate, you can use the Novell network client instead of the Microsoft-supplied client. To download Novell's client software, visit their Web site at www.novell.com.

20

When you've acquired the Novell client software, be sure to study the README file or any release notes supplied with it. Novell updates the client software from time to time, so you should be sure you're using the most up-to-date instructions.

Before you install Novell's client, be sure you have removed the Microsoft client. Open Network Connections, view Properties for the Local Area Connection, and be sure that Client Service for NetWare isn't listed. If it is, select it and choose Uninstall. You must restart your computer before proceeding.

To install the Novell client, follow the instructions provided. The procedure will look something like this:

1. Download the Novell client software for Windows XP and execute the downloaded file by double-clicking it. Unzip the contents into a folder—this can be a temporary folder or one you'll share on the network for repeated installations.

2. Open the selected folder and browse into subfolder NOVELL*language*\\WINNT\\I386. Run setupnw to begin the installation process.

> **NOTE**
>
> When you install the Novell client, choose the Typical installation unless you are certain you need to use Custom. If do you use Custom, don't choose the Select All components button. Doing so might inadvertently install conflicting software components and render your network inoperative.

3. The installation reboots your computer after it's finished copying files.

When Windows restarts, the Windows login dialog box is replaced with a Novell login dialog. This dialog contains options to log in to a Novell NDS tree, a bindery-mode Novell server, or just the Windows workstation. The Novell client also installs a sophisticated, full-featured Novell utility icon in the task tray.

> **NOTE**
>
> If your network uses Microsoft's File and Print Services for NetWare (FPNW) on a Windows .NET/2000 Server, the Novell client can't use the *simulated* NetWare resources shared by the FPNW server because of software incompatibilities.

SETTING PROVIDER ORDER

Provider order determines which computer name service, Novell's or Microsoft's, is queried first to find a given named file or print server. For example, if you choose a shared printer named \\munich\laserjet, Windows has to locate the machine named munich. It might need to query both the Windows computer name service (Active Directory or the browser service) and the NetWare naming service before it finds the name. When you use a mix of Microsoft and NetWare servers, you might be able to speed up network operations by setting the provider order so that the most likely name service is examined first.

In most cases, you won't need to make any changes to Windows's Provider Order list. If your network administrator suggests that you do, just follow these steps:

1. Open Network Connections by selecting Start, My Computer, My Network Place, View Network Connections.

2. From the Advanced menu, select Advanced Settings, and select the Provider Order tab, as shown in Figure 20.2. The dialog lists services used to find access to file servers and print servers, respectively.

Figure 20.2
Provider Order settings let you choose which file or printer service is examined first to find a named remote server.

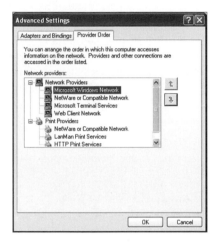

3. Arrange the services so that the type you use most frequently is listed on top, followed by less-often-used services. Highlight a service type, and click the up- or down-arrow button to rearrange the types. In the figure, I've indicated that I most frequently use Windows servers for shared files and Novell servers for printing.

USING NETWARE RESOURCES

After a NetWare client has been installed, you can access NetWare services in the same ways as Windows servers. The only difference, if you're used to the Novell way of naming resources, is that remote folders and files must be specified using standard Windows UNC format.

- NetWare users are familiar with the server\volume:path\file format—for example, `MUNICH\SYS:PUBLIC\SYSCON.EXE`.

- From Windows, the same file would be `\\MUNICH\SYS\PUBLIC\SYSCON.EXE`.

This format takes a bit of getting used to, and you must make some changes to existing batch files and programs. But beyond this small difference, you can treat NetWare resources just like Windows resources and therefore can do the following:

- Browse the network from My Network Places.
- Specify remote files or directories using standard UNC names.

20

- Make drive mappings using the Explorer's Tools menu.

- Make drive mappings from the command line by using the command net use.

- Print to Novell print queues by adding network printers with the Add Printer Wizard in the Printers and Faxes folder.

 If print job banner pages or extra blank sheets appear in print jobs sent to Novell queues, see "Banner and/or Blank Pages Are Printed on NetWare Printers" in the "Troubleshooting" section at the end of this chapter.

BROWSING THE NETWORK

When locating a file, mapping a network drive, or just exploring the network, you can find a NetWare server in My Network Places or any other network browsing dialog. Expand Entire Network, and you'll notice two network branches: Microsoft Windows Network and NetWare or Compatible Network. Expanding the NetWare branch, you can see any available NDS trees or individual NetWare bindery servers, as shown in Figure 20.3.

 If no Novell servers appear in the browsing list, see "Novell NetWare Servers Can't Be Found" in the "Troubleshooting" section at the end of this chapter.

 If some Windows computers are missing from the list, see "Some Computers Are Missing from Entire Network" in the "Troubleshooting" section.

Figure 20.3
NetWare trees and servers appear under the NetWare branch of Entire Network.

You can drill down into shared volumes (for example, sys), folders, and files if you wish.

When you attach to a NetWare server, by default, your Windows login name and password are used to make the connection. You can use an alternate login name and password if you use the Map Network Drive Wizard, which is available from the Explorer's Tools menu. Having different account names and passwords on your Windows and Novell servers can be a bit confusing, however, so your network manager will probably try to make them match. You might need to manually update your passwords to keep them identical on the two server types, which I'll discuss in the next section.

 If you get a Logon Failed error while attempting to attach to a NetWare server, see "Can't Attach to NetWare Servers" in the "Troubleshooting" section at the end of this chapter.

SYNCHRONIZING NETWARE PASSWORDS

If you use the same account name for both Windows and NetWare, as most people do, you should change your password on both systems to the same thing at the same time. That way, your name and password will work for both networks, and you won't be bothered with entering them by hand every time you attach to a NetWare resource.

TIP FROM

Bob
& Brian

> Be sure to connect to your Novell server or servers or trees before changing your Windows password so that the password is updated on all servers. You can simply view any NetWare resource on a server in My Network Places to establish a connection.

If your Novell servers use the NDS directory system for security, you're in luck. When you change your Windows password by pressing Ctrl+Alt+Del and selecting Change Password, your Novell password is set as well for any NDS trees you're currently connected to.

If you use older bindery-based NetWare servers, you must use the old `setpass` DOS utility to update NetWare passwords after changing your Windows password. To do so, follow these steps:

1. Make attachments to any NetWare servers you use by opening My Network Places and browsing into any of their shared volumes.

2. Open a command prompt, and type **pushd *server*\sys\public**, replacing *server* with the name of your primary NetWare server.

3. Change your Windows password by pressing Ctrl+Alt+Del and selecting Change Password (or, if this option doesn't appear, through the User Accounts control panel applet).

4. In the command prompt, type **setpass** and press Enter. Follow the instructions to change your NetWare password.

These steps synchronize all bindery-based NetWare servers.

LISTING YOUR NETWARE CONNECTIONS

On a DOS-based Novell network, you use the `whoami` command to keep track of your current NetWare connections. This function is available in Windows as well: Open My Computer, right-click My Network Places, and select Who Am I.

Who Am I displays a list of attached file servers and NDS trees, as shown in Figure 20.4. If necessary, you can disconnect from a server by selecting it in the connection list and clicking Detach.

20

Figure 20.4
Who Am I displays
currently connected
NetWare servers.

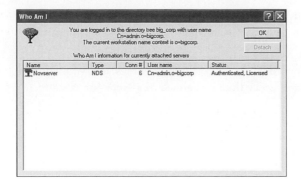

NETWARE AND THE COMMAND PROMPT

NetWare's DOS origins show most clearly in the set of management and operating utilities it uses to control drive mappings and monitor and configure the network. Its beloved utilities, such as MAP, SYSCON, and PCONSOLE, have very limited usefulness under Windows because many of them interacted directly with DOS to change its drive listing and printer configuration. These functions simply don't work with Windows XP because it's based on Windows NT, not DOS.

If you were a command-line aficionado on your Novell network, you'll have to learn a new way of doing things. You'll probably grumble about it for a while (I sure did!), but eventually the new way will become familiar. Table 20.3 shows some key differences between common NetWare and Windows commands.

TABLE 20.3   COMPARING NETWARE AND WINDOWS COMMANDS

NetWare Command	Windows Command
capture lpt1:=server\queue	net use lpt1: \\server\queue
endcap	net use lpt1: /delete
login	(n/a)
logout	(n/a)
map	net use
map f:=server\vol	net use f: \\server\vol
map root f:=server\vol\folder	net use f: \\server\vol\folder
map del f:	net use f: /delete
pconsole	(Use the Windows Printer controls.)
slist	new view /network:nw

Most of the NetWare utilities listed in this table cannot be used on Windows XP if you're using the Microsoft Client Service for NetWare; they simply don't work or don't work correctly.

You can still use many old DOS NetWare utilities to manage your NetWare servers themselves. Many but not all NetWare management programs run correctly in a Windows Command Prompt window. Some NetWare utilities cannot be used in Windows because the operating system management functions they use were designed for DOS, not Windows XP.

NOTE

> Windows-based NetWare 4.0 and 5.0 management utilities do *not* work with the Microsoft Client. These utilities run only with the Novell Client.

TIP FROM

Bob
& Brian

> The easiest way to use a NetWare utility is to open a command prompt and type `pushd \\`*`server`*`\sys\public` to change the current directory to the NetWare server's utility directory. You can also make shortcuts to any often-used utilities.

The MS-DOS environment is simulated in Windows using two drivers loaded in AUTOEXEC.NT: nw16 and vwipxspx. They provide some but not all the services that the old DOS programs IPX and NETX or VLM shell programs did.

TROUBLESHOOTING A NOVELL NETWORK CONNECTION

If you have problems establishing a connection to a Novell server using the Microsoft client, you can use the built-in Windows Troubleshooter to help diagnose the problem.

To use it, choose Start, Help. On the Search tab, search for NetWare, and select Troubleshooter in the left pane. Then select Client Service for NetWare in the right pane.

INTERNETWORKING WITH DOS AND OS/2

DOS and IBM's OS/2 operating system use the same fundamental networking functions as Windows. This fact shouldn't be a surprise, as Microsoft developed the networking software used on the original IBM PC, and its relationship with IBM lasted through the release of the first few versions of OS/2. IBM's LAN Server evolved directly from Microsoft's original LAN Manager product, whose name still appears here and there in Windows XP. You'll see the letters *LM* and the phrase *LanMan* used in some Windows networking components.

However, Microsoft has dropped support for the NetBEUI transport protocol on which the old DOS and OS/2 networking software depended. Ostensibly this is due to NetBEUI's archaic nature (although one might speculate that it's to force the remaining OS/2 holdouts to give up, or as retaliation for IBM's support for Linux). Whatever the reason, this is bad news for those who still depend on OS/2 or DOS-based computers.

If you're using OS/2 Warp, you might be okay because OS/2 Warp offers the option of using NetBIOS over TCP/IP. Check with the OS/2 system manager to see whether this option is enabled on your system. If this is the case, there will be no internetworking difficulties.

20

If you must use NetBEUI, you're in a precarious situation. In the initial release of Windows XP, the NetBEUI protocol *is* supplied on the installation CD-ROM but its use not supported. That is, if it causes problems or doesn't work, Microsoft will tell you to uninstall it, and that's the end of the story. You'll have to give up on internetworking between Windows XP and your older computers. Even if it does work, you're on borrowed time.

CAUTION

> There is no guarantee that Microsoft will continue to supply NetBEUI in the future. It might disappear from future releases of Windows XP. You should begin now to find a way out of using it.

If it's absolutely necessary to continue using NetBEUI in your Windows XP computer, you can install NetBEUI with the following disagreeable procedure. The first seven steps copy the two omitted files into subfolders of your Windows directory.

1. Insert your Windows XP Installation CD-ROM into your CD drive.

2. Open Windows Explorer and select Tools, Folder Options. Select the View tab. Scroll down through the Advanced Settings and if it isn't already checked, check Show Hidden Files and Folders. Click OK. If you don't see the folder view in the left pane, click the Folders button.

3. Browse into your CD-ROM drive into folder \VALUEADD\MSFT\NET\NETBEUI.

4. Right-click NBF.SYS and select Copy.

5. Browse into your hard drive's \WINDOWS\SYSTEM\DRIVERS folder. Select Edit, Paste from the menu.

6. Browse back to the NETBEUI folder on the CD-ROM, right-click NETNBF.INF, and select Copy.

7. Browse into your hard drive's \WINDOWS\INF folder (this folder is normally hidden). Select Edit, Paste from the menu. Close Windows Explorer.

8. Open Network Connections by clicking Start, My Computer, My Network Places, View Network Connections. Right-click Local Area Connection, and select Properties.

9. Select Install, highlight Protocol, and select Add. Select NetBEUI Protocol from the list and click OK. Then you may close Local Area Connection Properties.

After NetBEUI is installed, internetworking with DOS and OS/2 is quite transparent. Just be sure of two things:

■ Install the NetBEUI protocol on *all* computers on your network. (I discussed the reasoning for installing the same protocols on every computer on your network earlier in this chapter under "Choosing Network Protocols.")

■ Do not apply a Windows XP security policy that prohibits the use of the LMHASH password encryption protocol. LMHASH is an old encryption system used to encode passwords stored on servers and transmitted across networks. It was designed for LAN

Manager and hence is used by OS/2 LAN Server. The encryption scheme used by Windows NT, 2000, and XP is more secure, so some network managers prevent the network from using LMHASH to gain protection. Doing so, unfortunately, makes it impossible to internetwork with DOS and OS/2.

 If some Windows or OS/2 computers are missing from the list of all LAN computers in Computers Near Me or Entire Network in My Network Places, see "Some Computers Are Missing from Entire Network" in the "Troubleshooting" section at the end of this chapter.

INTERNETWORKING WITH UNIX AND LINUX

The Unix operating system, originally developed in the 1970s at AT&T's Bell Laboratories as a platform for internal software development, is still evolving and growing. Unix was a commercial operating system distributed at no cost to academic institutions, so a generation of computer scientists learned their art on Unix systems in college. Most Internet software you're familiar with today was developed on Unix systems, and it's the most common operating system for high-end graphics and engineering workstations manufactured by Sun Microsystems, Hewlett-Packard, and many other companies. The Open Source phenomenon has also produced the no-cost GNU and Linux Unix clones, ensuring that a new generation of programmers will continue the tradition of openness, cooperation, and sharing that typify the Unix community.

This section looks at ways to network Windows XP with Unix-type operating systems. Although many of the examples involve Linux (Red Hat Linux 6.0), most of the examples can be translated to almost any Unix-type operating system.

THE SMB/CIFS PROTOCOL

The Server Message Block (SMB) protocol is the high-level network protocol used for Windows and LAN Manager file and printer sharing. To promote interoperation, Microsoft, the Santa Cruz Operation (SCO), Intel, and other companies began the Common Internet File System (CIFS) initiative to extend SMB networking to other operating systems. CIFS-compatible software packages can be obtained for many varieties of Unix and Linux. For this chapter, I'll concentrate on just one: the Samba package. And, because typing Linux/Unix is already getting tiresome, I'll just write Unix from now on, but I mean "Unix and/or Linux."

SAMBA

Certainly the most popular Unix-to-Windows networking package, Samba can be a lifesaver for integrated networks. Samba is an open source (read: free) software suite based on the SMB/CIFS protocol. The Samba server program makes it possible for Unix/Linux computers to share folders and printers that Windows users can access, while the Samba client tools lets Unix/Linux users access folders and printers shared by Windows computers.

20

> **NOTE**
>
> You can get more information about Samba and download a version for your Unix system from www.samba.org. Most Linux distributions include a version of Samba and install it by default.
>
> For a good introduction to Samba, visit www.informit.com and search for samba. Skip down to the "Free Library" results, and select *Sams Teach Yourself Samba in 24 Hours*. After you register or log on, you can purchase the book or read it online for free. (By the way, InformIT is run by one of Que's sister companies.)

SAMBA CLIENT TOOLS

To access file services on a Windows server from Unix, you must know exactly what resources are available from a given host on the network. Samba includes a command-line program called smbclient for just that purpose. This application enables you to list available Windows shares and printers from within Unix. The command

```
smbclient -L \\lombok
```

for example, lists all the folders and printers shared by the computer named lombok.

When you know the name of the desired shared folder, the smbmount command allows you to mount the Windows share on the local Linux file system. The command

```
smbmount //lombok/shareddocs /mnt/winshare -U brian
```

mounts the SharedDocs folder on computer lombok to the local directory /mnt/winshare. The -U switch tells smbclient what username to use when trying to mount the share. You'll be prompted for a password.

> **NOTE**
>
> If the Windows computer is running Windows XP with Simple File Sharing enabled, you can use any username and password. With Simple File Sharing, all network access is made using Guest credentials.

You also can use a Windows printer from a Unix client. The easiest way to configure a Windows printer on a Red Hat Linux system is to use the Red Hat GUI-based print tool while logged on as root. This way, you can set up an SMB-based printer with a minimal amount of hassle. If you are not using Red Hat Linux, you must edit your /etc/printcap file manually. The number of options involved are beyond the scope of this chapter. A thorough reading of the SMB How-To, available from www.linuxdoc.org/HOWTO/SMB-HOWTO.html, is recommended.

SAMBA SERVER TOOLS

Samba also includes tools and servers to make your Unix system look just like a Windows-based network server; this capability lets your Windows computers use files and printers shared by Unix systems.

The parameters for configuring Samba in a server capacity are contained in the file /etc/smb.conf on the Unix host. The default file included with Samba has comments for every parameter to explain what each one is. Configuring the Samba server is beyond the scope of this book. However, I can offer a few pointers:

- Samba is complex. You should read the documentation and FAQs for your Samba version before starting the setup procedure. A good place to start is `www.linuxdoc.org/HOWTO/SMB-HOWTO.html`.

- You can configure Samba for share-level passwords (à la Windows 9x sharing) or user-specific passwords with the `security` option. User security is the usual way to go, although you'll have to set up Unix user accounts for each of your Windows users.

- If you do use user security, you should set `encrypt passwords = yes` in smb.conf, as Windows will not transmit unencrypted passwords without special configuration. You'll also need to set up a user and password file for Samba's use, which is usually specified as `smb passwd file = /etc/smbpasswd`. Your Samba documentation will explain how to do this.

- You can mimic Windows's Simple File Sharing by using share-level security without a password. However, in this case you *must* take care to prevent SMB access to your Unix computer over the Internet.

When you have finished editing the smb.conf file, you can test to see that the syntax is correct by using the Samba program `testparm`. `testparm` checks smb.conf for internal "correctness" before you actually use it in a production environment. By running

```
/usr/bin/testparm
```

you get a printout like the following if all goes well:

```
Load smb config files from /etc/smb.conf
Processing section "[homes]"
Processing section "[printers]"
Processing section "[storage]"
Loaded services file OK.
Press enter to see a dump of your service definitions
```

You can press Enter to see a dump of all the parameters the server uses to configure itself. When the configuration file is complete and correct, you must stop and restart the smbd service to make the changes take effect.

PRINTING TO UNIX QUEUES FROM WINDOWS

You can configure Samba to offer standard Windows shared printer service. As an alternative, Windows XP has built-in support to send output to Unix-based printers using the `lpr` protocol. You can install a standard Windows printer whose output is directed to a Unix system and can use this printer just as you would any local or networked Windows printer.

→ For instruction on connecting to an `lpr`-based printer, **see** "Using Unix and LPR Printers," **p. 578**.

20

PRINTING TO WINDOWS PRINTERS FROM UNIX

You can also install an LPD server on Windows XP Professional to let Unix users print to any local printers shared by your computer. (It can print only to local printers shared by your computer, not to network printers from other machines used by your computer.)

To install this service, log on as Administrator (or as a Computer Administrator) and follow these steps:

1. Open Network Connections by clicking Start, My Computer, My Network Places, View Network Connections.
2. From the menu, select Advanced, Optional Networking Components.
3. Select Other Network File and Print Services and click Details.
4. Check Print Services for Unix and click OK.
5. Click Next. You may need to insert your Windows XP Installation CD-ROM.

These steps install the service but, because of an installer glitch, don't make the service start when you boot your computer. You might have to finish the job manually, like this:

1. Click Start, right-click My Computer, and select Manage.
2. In the left pane, open Services and Applications; then select Services.
3. In the right pane, locate TCP/IP Print Server. Double-click this entry.
4. If the service's Status is not shown as Started, click the Start button.
5. If its Startup Type is not shown as Automatic, select Automatic from the Type drop-down list, and click OK.
6. Close Computer Management.

Now, Unix users can send print jobs to your computer by using the command

```
lpr -S computername -P sharename
```

where *computername* is the DNS name or IP address of your computer, and *sharename* is the share name of any of your printers.

TIP FROM

> By default, Windows treats incoming print jobs as ASCII text that must be formatted and printed. If the Unix machine is sending, say, a PostScript file, Windows will print the PostScript source code rather than the document the file represents. Unix users must use the appropriate -o option to send a "binary" print job in this case. For example, you can enter the following:
>
> ```
> lpr -S ambon -P Laserjet -o l filename.ps
> ```

⚠ *If text files are printed with line feeds inserted where just carriage returns were expected, see "Carriage Returns and Line Feeds Are Mangled" in the "Troubleshooting" section at the end of this chapter.*

TELNET

The `telnet` command is perhaps one of the most well-known Unix network tools. Telnet provides a remote terminal function and on a Unix system lets you use a shell or command prompt environment on a remote system across a LAN or the Internet. Windows XP Professional includes a Telnet client for connecting to other systems running a Telnet server.

Windows XP supplies a Telnet application, but there's a surprise! This version is a Windows console program, meaning it looks like a Command Prompt window rather than a regular graphical Windows program. It also supports built-in NTLM authentication, so it can securely connect to the Telnet host service provided with Windows XP Professional and Server. To connect to a remote server with Telnet—say `amber.somewhere.edu`—you can issue the command by choosing Start, Run, or in a command prompt, as follows:

```
telnet amber.somewhere.edu
```

Alternatively, you can simply run the Telnet program without naming a remote host to start it in its "prompt" mode. Type **help** in prompt mode to see the list of valid commands.

To terminate a Telnet session, you can press Ctrl+] and enter the `quit` command, or simply close the Telnet console window.

TIP FROM

Bob
& Brian

> Microsoft's Telnet client is less than wonderful. You can use the supplied Hyperterminal application or download a free SSH (secure shell) Telnet client from `www.chiark.greenend.org.uk/~sgtatham/putty`. There are commercial SSH clients as well—see `www.ssh.com` and `www.datafellows.com`.
>
> These alternatives don't support NTLM encryption, so they're not secure for connecting to Windows Telnet hosts over the Internet, but the SSH clients are safer for connecting to Unix hosts over the Internet.

THE TELNET HOST SERVICE

Windows XP comes equipped with a Telnet server as well as a client. Having both a server and a client sounds like a boon for network managers, as it theoretically lets a remote user connect to and run programs on your Windows XP computer. It could conceivably also let a Unix user connect to and run programs on a Windows XP computer.

However, I don't recommend using the Telnet Host Service for several reasons. First, it's strictly a command-line service, and few Windows applications are terribly useful without a graphical user interface. You could use some command-line management utilities, I grant you. Second, as I've mentioned, Telnet is an insecure protocol. The Windows XP Telnet server does use the NTLM password encryption protocol to authenticate users, but this feature can be disabled by hacking into the Registry. The result is that, in the end, using it is more of a risk than a benefit, and you can accomplish the same results by using Windows graphical interface management tools, such as Remote Desktop. Third, the Windows XP Professional version is limited to two connections from outside users.

20

CAUTION

> If you're a system administrator, I *really* caution you against using the Telnet service or client to manage your LAN. Administrators will be the prime target of network snoops and Trojan horse authors; you have the passwords they want, and they'll be after you and your computer.

If you *really* want to try it, you must activate it manually:

1. Right-click My Computer and select Manage.

2. Open Services and Applications, and select Services.

3. Select Telnet in the right pane, and right-click Start. If you want the service to run when you boot up Windows, select Automatic under Startup Type.

4. Test the service by opening a Command Prompt window and typing `telnet localhost`.

5. Type `exit` to disconnect. If you want to stop the service, go back to the Services Manager, right-click Telnet, and select Stop.

The Berkeley r Commands

Most Unix operating systems also come equipped with a suite of programs collectively referred to as the "Berkeley r commands." Windows XP includes many of these tools, which are available from the Command Prompt. If you're a Unix user, you're probably already familiar with these commands. Table 20.4 provides a brief list and description of the r commands provided with Windows XP.

TABLE 20.4   BERKELEY r COMMANDS PROVIDED WITH WINDOWS XP

Command	Description
rsh	Remote shell, or rsh, executes a single command on another network system. rsh copies its standard output to the remote system's standard input and redirects the remote system's standard output to the local standard input.
rexec	Remote execute, or rexec, executes a single command on a remote system. This command is similar to rsh, except that it works with a different host service.
rcp	Remote copy, or rcp, is a command for copying files between two systems. rcp can even do third-party copies in which neither the source nor the destination reside on the system executing rcp.

20

TIP FROM

Bob
& Brian

The Berkeley r commands, although very useful, are also inherently insecure because the commands used by these programs are usually passed in plain text through the network. Additionally, these commands are designed to be run in a trusted network where clients are not always required to reauthenticate themselves. This might not always be the case where today's networks are concerned. Because of these inherent vulnerabilities, it's best not to use these commands across the Internet. You might use the Secure Shell package, which replaces all the r commands as well as adds a greater degree of security via strong encryption. SSH also replaces the very insecure Telnet protocol and offers X11-encrypted forwarding.

For information on obtaining a free Windows-based client version of SSH, see the tip on page 711.

INTERNETWORKING WITH MACINTOSH

The Apple Macintosh is arguably *the* computer of choice in the graphic arts, design and publishing worlds. Teetering on the edge of extinction a few years ago, Apple has staged an impressive comeback, and its recent product releases show it's back to stay. So, seamless internetworking with the Mac will remain an important part of the Windows XP network.

Windows NT 4.0 Server brought AppleTalk file and printer sharing to the Windows world and with it a few headaches because of some significant glitches. The situation has improved in the Windows XP version.

The following sections examine some of the problems of having Macs and Windows machines coexist on the same network.

MAC FILES AND NETWORKING

Macintosh files actually consist of two separate parts, or *forks*:

- The data fork, which contains data, document text, program code, and so on
- The resource fork, which contains language-specific strings and dialog box layouts for programs, as well as the association information to link a document with the application that created it

The two parts can be read and written independently on the Macintosh; it's as if each file is composed of two bundled but separate files. Right away, this is a big problem: Windows programs aren't aware of a two-part structure, which can lead to conflicts when Windows users and Mac users write to the same file, as you'll soon learn.

20

A more fundamental problem is that Macintoshes use a proprietary file sharing system called AppleTalk File Protocol (AFP), which runs over Ethernet, as well as a slower serial-port version called LocalTalk. In contrast, PCs use the Server Message Block, or SMB, protocol for file sharing.

To link Macs and PCs on a network, then, either the Macs must learn to "speak" SMB, or the Windows computers must speak AFP. Both solutions are possible. If you have a Windows 2000/2003 Server computer on your network, it comes with Services for Macintosh (dubbed SFM), which speaks AFP to make Windows-based resources to Macs. Mac OS X comes with SMB software built in. You can also install SMB software for older Mac OSs. I'll go into these solutions in a little bit. First, let's look at some of the differences between the Mac and Windows worlds that have an impact on peaceful coexistence on a LAN.

PLANNING FOR COMPATIBILITY

Before getting to the details of *how* to share files between Macintoshes and Windows computers, let's look at what you must do to be sure that the files—however shared—are going to make sense to both platforms.

FILENAME COMPATIBILITY

Mac filenames cannot exceed 31 characters, including the extension (for example, .doc). Mac filenames can contain any character except the colon (:).

> **NOTE**
>
> A second-generation disk formatting system called HFS+ is available as an add-on for users of Mac OS 8 or higher. HFS+ solves many of HFS's limitations; for example, filenames can have up to 255 characters.

Windows permits filenames up to 256 characters in length but has a longer list of unacceptable characters: the colon (:), backslash (\), forward slash (/), question mark (?), asterisk (*), quotation mark ("), greater-than symbol (>), less-than symbol (<), and pipe symbol (|).

Therefore, you must be careful when naming files that are to be visible to users in both camps. It's best to stick with shorter names using characters legal on *both* operating systems.

A more subtle difference between the MacOS and Windows is the way that document/application associations are made. Windows matches up documents to their application programs with the file extension. For example, Windows associates the .doc extension with Microsoft Word, so you can double-click on a .doc file, and Windows launches Word to display the file.

Macs, on the other hand, store this information in each document file's resource fork. Each file notes its document type (for example, WDBN for a Word document) and its application type through what's called the *Creator code* (MSWD for Microsoft Word). Windows applications don't acknowledge the resource fork and generally remove it when writing a new version of a document file on disk. When it detects that this is about to happen (which isn't always), Windows warns you and gives you the option of preserving the resource data. You should always say Yes. Sometimes, though, the document/application link is lost.

Mac users must get used to this, as double-clicking an edited document doesn't automatically launch the appropriate application. They either must search for the application manually or drag the file and drop it onto the application's icon. (They'll probably exact their revenge by removing the .doc extension from Word document filenames.)

 If Macintosh users discover that the Finder can't find the correct application to open a document that has been edited by Windows users, see "Macintosh Files Have Lost Application Associations" in the "Troubleshooting" section at the end of this chapter.

FILE AND VOLUME SIZE LIMITATIONS

Macintosh computers running the Mac operating system (MacOS) versions prior to 7.6.1 can't see further than 2GB into any disk drive, local or networked. If your Windows network shares files from volumes larger than 2GB, your Macs must run OS 7.6.1 or higher.

OS COMPATIBILITY

Before starting to internetwork, you should upgrade your Macs to at least version 7.5.5, or if you'll be sharing volumes larger than 2GB, to version 7.6.1 or higher. If you want to use HFS+ disk formatting, you must upgrade to MacOS 8 or higher.

Also, some Macintosh applications don't properly install themselves when they're installed into a Windows shared folder. An error occurs when more than one user tries to run the application at the same time.

 If Macintosh users get a network error when more than one Mac accesses an application, see "Can't Run Macintosh Application Concurrently" in the "Troubleshooting" section at the end of this chapter.

PRINTING

With a Windows .NET/2000 server with Services for Macintosh in place, Windows and Mac users alike can fully utilize any available PostScript printers. Services for Macintosh can also make non-PostScript printers available to Mac users. However, due to Windows printer driver limitations, Mac users can't print at greater than 300dpi resolution on these printers.

INTERNETWORKING OPTIONS

Macintosh and Windows network users can share files in several ways. Windows .NET/2000 Server provides a "gateway" system that lets Macs use files and printers shared by Windows computers as if the shares came from other Macs, and similarly letting Windows users see and use Mac shares. The process of installing and configuring SFM is not complicated, but it has to be done by the administrator of a Windows Server computer, and as such, it's beyond the scope of this book.

If your network doesn't have Windows .NET/2000 Server, some other options are available.

APPLESHARE IP ON MACINTOSH

Instead of providing the networking gateway on a Windows machine, you can also buy gateway software from Apple to run on one of your Macintoshes.

AppleShare IP (ASIP) is an industry favorite from Apple. ASIP provides file and printer sharing services for both Macintoshes *and* Windows, each in its native file sharing protocol format, using the TCP/IP network transport protocol throughout. ASIP provides an almost complete set of TCP/IP-based services to meet all the basic needs of a workgroup or even large-scale environment with hundreds of users. Services included are Web, e-mail (SMTP, POP, and IMAP), file and printer sharing in both SMB and AFP formats, and FTP.

Its powerful capabilities, easy administration, native SMB support for Windows clients, and relatively low price have made it quite popular. The application is mature, solid, and stable. For small, mixed-platform workgroups, ASIP is an excellent server with a proven track record. It does, however, have one significant limitation: security. Although password and other types of security are built in to ASIP, it's not nearly as robust or deep as Windows XP/2000. This point isn't so critical in a workgroup environment where strong security isn't necessary, but when documents and information need to be strongly protected, ASIP, in its raw form, does not have the capabilities.

MAC OS X

Mac's OS X comes with Windows-compatible Server Message Block (SMB) networking support built in. This means that Macs running OS X can connect directly to drives and folders shared by Windows computers right out of the box.

To connect to a shared Windows folder from the Mac, select the Finder and choose Go, Connect to Server. The dialog box shown in Figure 20.5 will appear.

Figure 20.5
The Connect to Server dialog lets a Mac OS X computer connect directly to a folder shared by Windows. In the Address field, enter smb: followed by the share's UNC name.

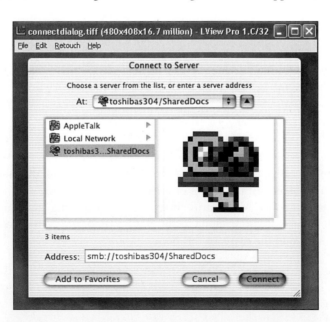

The browser display will not show your network's Windows computers. Instead, you'll have to enter the UNC name of the shared folder directly, in the format smb://computername/sharename, where computername is the name of the Windows computer, and sharename is the name of the shared folder. Click OK to proceed.

The Mac will then prompt you to enter the user name, password, and the workgroup or domain name to use for the connection to the Windows computer. If you're connecting to Windows XP Home Edition or to Windows XP Professional with Simple File Sharing enabled, you don't need to enter any account information, as Simple File Sharing uses the Guest account for all network access. Just click OK. However, if you're connecting to a Windows domain member or server, or XP Pro with Simple File Sharing disabled, enter the appropriate username and password.

When the Mac has made the network connection, the shared folder will appear as a drive icon on the Mac desktop. If you open it, you'll see the Windows files and folders in the Finder display, as shown in Figure 20.6.

Figure 20.6
The Windows computer's files and folders will appear in a standard Finder window.

Remember the point I made earlier about Mac files having two parts or forks? If you copy files from a Mac to a shared Windows folder, Windows creates an extra file to contain the resource information for each file. These files have the same name as the main file, but their names start with a period, as shown in Figure 20.7. Windows users will have to take care to move and rename these files together; otherwise Mac users will receive errors when they try to access the files. Also, as you can see in Figure 20.7, when a Mac user opens a Window share, the Finder creates a .Trashes folder to temporarily hold deleted files. Windows users should ignore this folder.

You can also share folders files from Mac OS X computers to the network using the free Samba file server software.

One potential advantage in using Samba on a Mac over Windows .NET or 2000 server is that Apple licenses the server for unlimited users while Microsoft charges per-computer. If you're only after the Macintosh capability, the Mac approach could let you sidestep the need buy a Windows server product.

NOTE

> For more information about using Windows file shares from OS X, and for instructions on using Samba to share files from your Mac, see
>
> www.opensource.apple.com/projects/documentation/howto/html/
> osxsmb.html

Figure 20.7
When Windows users view the shared folder, each file added by a Mac user will appear as two files, one for the data fork and one for the resource fork. If moved and renamed, they must be moved or renamed together.

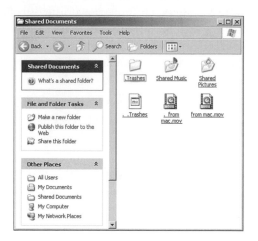

VIRTUAL PC

Virtual PC for Mac OS from Connectix (www.connectix.com) allows you to run Windows operating systems on your Macintosh. Don't laugh! This emulation software makes a Macintosh look like a PC and runs Windows in a window (how ironic). The Windows environment has no idea that it's running on a software emulator, so you can feel free to install all your Windows applications. The connectivity boon here is two-fold. One, you can drag and drop files between the Windows desktop and the Mac desktop. Two, if you plug into the Ethernet network and configure Windows properly, your Windows network will see Virtual PC as a real PC, and networking will be in effect. You can use this virtual Windows computer to share a Mac volume to the network as a Windows share.

Another benefit to VPC is that it enables you to have several different operating systems at hand almost immediately. Because VPC uses files as drive containers, you're limited only to hard drive space on hand (and the 2GB/container limit that VPC imposes). VPC lets you run DOS, Windows 9x, Me, and 2000 (and soon, XP) on your Mac. By the way, I'll sing the praises of another Connectix product, Virtual PC for Windows, in Chapter 31.

DAVE

DAVE, from Thursby Software Systems at www.thursby.com, is a NetBIOS (SMB) client for Mac OS 8.6 through X. It allows a Macintosh to appear on a Windows network as if it were a Windows client connecting via NetBIOS. The sharing is seamless—if not slightly difficult to configure and slow when it's working. (NetBIOS is not exactly a speed demon, even over Ethernet.) Still, it's a feasible solution for a network with a relatively small number of Macintoshes, with mostly Windows computers.

Thursby Software Systems also sells TSStalk (formerly COPSTalk), an AppleShare client for Windows machines. TSStalk allows Windows users to directly and natively access AppleShare IP 5.x and 6.x networks over AppleTalk as if they were using, what else, a Macintosh. Because this is AFP over TCP/IP and not NetBIOS, it's faster. This solution is a decent approach for a network with a relatively small number of Windows computers and mostly Macintoshes.

Both of the preceding solutions can be a great help in an environment that is dominated by one platform or the other. However, there is nothing like a dedicated server that can handle requests from a number of platforms as each new widget on a workstation reduces its over-all capabilities by draining its resources. So, despite their excellent capabilities, it's better to avoid them when a server can be put to use, especially when that server already has the capability to do so built-in.

INTERNETWORKING OVER DIAL-UP AND VPN CONNECTIONS

When you use a dial-up or Virtual Private Networking (VPN) connection to reach a remote network with non-Windows servers, you must be sure that the remote servers' protocols are carried over the connection. In this section, I'll refer to dial-up connections, but whatever I say applies to VPN connections as well.

The AppleTalk protocol is not transmitted over a Windows dial-up connection. You can reach Macintosh file servers only if the remote network uses the file and print services for Macintosh gateway service on a Windows .NET, 2000 or NT server, or, if the Macintosh computers use a Windows-compatible TCP/IP-based protocol.

Unix, and NetWare servers can be reached as long as the appropriate protocol (TCP/IP and IPX/SPX, respectively) is enabled across the dial-up connection. To confirm whether the protocols are enabled, do the following:

1. Click Start, Connect To, right-click the connection name, and select Properties. You can also open the connection properties from the View Network Connections window.

2. Select the Networking tab, and verify that the required protocols are checked under This Connection Uses The Following Items.

The protocols must also be enabled on the Dial-Up Networking server at the remote end. If you enable incoming connections on your own Windows XP Professional computer, verify that the protocols are enabled for your Incoming Connections icon.

NOTE

For more information about enabling incoming connections to your computer, see Chapter 18, "Windows Unplugged: Remote and Mobile Networking."

20

To enable alternative protocols for incoming connections, follow these steps:

1. View Network Connections by clicking Start, My Computer, My Network Places, View Network Connections.

2. Right-click the Incoming Connection icon, and select Properties.

3. Select the Networking tab, and verify that the required protocols are checked under Network Components.

4. Select the name of each protocol in turn. Click Properties, and confirm that Allow Callers to Access My Local Area Network is checked.

These steps ensure that all protocols are routed through your computer when you dial in by modem or through a VPN connection.

ADVANCED NETWORKING SERVICES

Several Windows networking options and settings are difficult to categorize. These topics must be covered somewhere, so I've collected them here.

SETTING NETWORK BINDINGS

Windows lets you specify how network components are connected. As you learned in Chapter 15, "Overview of Windows XP Networking," a network uses many layers of components. Bindings are the connections between these components. Through bindings, you can control whether the file and printer sharing service can be reached by each installed protocol and through which network and/or dial-up adapters.

You'll find step-by-step instructions for setting bindings elsewhere in this book where necessary. Let me give you the general picture here, in case you're arriving at this topic through the index.

To set network bindings, open the Network Connections window, and select Advanced, Advanced Settings from the menu. Select the Adapters and Bindings tab, as shown in Figure 20.8.

Select a network adapter (such as Local Area Connection) in the upper part of the dialog. In the bottom, you can check and uncheck services and individual transport protocols to connect or disconnect these services from the selected network adapter.

To set bindings for dial-up connections, you must view the Properties pages of the individual dial-up connections. On the Networking tab, you can check which services and protocols are to be used across the connection.

INSTALLING OPTIONAL NETWORK COMPONENTS

Windows XP Professional comes with a few networking components that are not used in most networks but can be essential in others. I won't cover these components in great detail because your network manager will probably install them for you if they're used on your LAN.

Figure 20.8
On the Adapters and Bindings tab, you can sever the connection between specific network components.

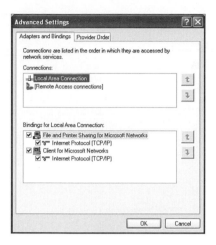

The optional components are listed in Table 20.5. The individual components can be selected for installation by following these steps:

1. Open Network Connections by clicking Start, My Computer, My Network Places, View Network Connections.
2. From the menu, select Advanced, Optional Networking Components.
3. Highlight one of the three components categories listed in the Table and click Details.
4. Check the box next to the desired component(s).

TABLE 20.5   WINDOWS XP OPTIONAL NETWORK COMPONENTS

Category/Component	Description
Management and Monitoring Tools	
Simple Network Management Protocol	A remote monitoring and measurement tool used by some network management systems. This protocol is discussed next.
WMI SNMP Provider	Allows Windows Management Instrumentation applications to access SNMP data.
Networking Services	
RIP Listener	A service to receive network routing information in large networks. Your network manager will indicate whether you need to install it. Don't install unless it's required.
Simple TCP/IP Services	A suite of services that perform simple functions for testing purposes, such as echoing data to a remote computer or generating a stream of data. Don't install these services unless you're instructed to do so by a network manager. They don't do anything useful but can be used by hackers to tie up your network with pointless traffic.

continues

TABLE 20.5 CONTINUED	
Category/Component	**Description**
Universal Plug and Play	Allows Windows to automatically discover and connect to an upcoming generation of new networked devices and appliances.
	Other Network File and Print Services
Print Services for Unix	Printer services for Unix hosts. These services were covered earlier in this chapter under "Printing to Windows Printers from Unix."

Of these services, only SNMP is both useful and not covered elsewhere.

SNMP

The Simple Network Management Protocol, or SNMP, is used by large corporate networks to monitor, measure, and configure network equipment from a central location. It can be used, for example, by monitoring software to detect whether servers or WAN connections have gone offline to alert staff or sound an alarm.

Windows XP Professional doesn't come with a tool to *use* the information SNMP can reveal, but it does come with an optional networking component that lets an SNMP monitor measure network activity in your computer.

SNMP should not be installed unless your network administrator requires its use, as there are some security risks attached to it. If you do choose to install SNMP, you should immediately configure the SNMP monitor to protect your computer's information with a secret "community name." This name is like a password that remote monitors need to supply before they can extract information from your computer. The default community name is public. Your network manager might supply you with an alternate community name. To set it, do the following:

1. Click Start, right-click My Computer, and select Manage.

2. Open Services and Applications, select Services, and locate SNMP Service in the right pane. Double-click it to open its Properties page.

3. Select the Security tab. Select Public, and then click Remove. Next, click Add to enter any community names provided by your network manager. Generally, assign only read-only community rights unless your network manager specifies otherwise.

4. You can additionally restrict SNMP access to specific network hosts (namely, management computers) by selecting Accept SNMP Packets From These Hosts and adding the appropriate IP addresses.

20

NOTE

> SNMP can be a security risk because it reveals the names of user accounts on your computer and your computer's network routing information. A community name with write or create permission can alter network routing tables. For this reason, SNMP should be blocked by your network's firewall, and you should *not* install it unless it's necessary.

TIP FROM

Bob & Brian

> If you're a network manager and use SNMP to monitor equipment health, you might find it valuable to know that Windows XP and 2000's Professional and Server versions come with a utility that can turn specified Windows Event Log entries into SNMP traps (messages) as they happen. This feature is configured by the undocumented program `evntwin`. This utility can let your network monitor detect and report on full hard drives, security violations, and other significant events.
>
> `evntwin` can save a list of event-to-trap mappings to a file. Another undocumented utility, `evntcmd`, can instantly install this file on another Windows XP or 2000 computer, even remotely.

TROUBLESHOOTING

NOVELL NETWARE SERVERS CAN'T BE FOUND

I have installed a NetWare client, but version 2.x NetWare servers do not appear under Entire Network in My Network Places.

Windows might not have correctly identified the Ethernet frame type used by these earlier NetWare versions. In Network and Dial-Up Connections, open the Local Area Connection properties. Select NWLink IPX/SPX Compatible Protocol, and open Properties. Under Frame Type, change the setting from Auto to 802.3.

If you have NetWare version 3 or higher servers on the network, you should configure them to use 802.3 framing in addition to the default Ethernet_II.

CAN'T ATTACH TO NETWARE SERVERS

I'm using the Microsoft Client but can't connect to some NetWare servers running version 3 or higher; my password is rejected.

Have the NetWare administrator enable unencrypted passwords on these servers. The Microsoft client can't send encrypted passwords to NetWare servers. (The Novell client does not have this problem.)

BANNER AND/OR BLANK PAGES ARE PRINTED ON NETWARE PRINTERS

When I send printer output to Novell printers, banner pages are printed at the beginning of my print jobs, and/or blank sheets are printed at the end.

Open the CNSW Control Panel applet, and uncheck Print Banner Pages and Add Form Feed.

SOME COMPUTERS ARE MISSING FROM ENTIRE NETWORK

My list of Computers Near Me is incomplete under Entire Network in My Network Places.

The network has elected a browser master that doesn't have all the protocols used by Windows networking computers on your LAN. This is a random selection, so be sure to install and bind the same set of protocols on every workstation in your LAN.

CARRIAGE RETURNS AND LINE FEEDS ARE MANGLED

When plain-text files are sent from Unix machines to my printers using lpr *and Print Services for Unix, carriage returns and line feeds are mangled. Line feeds are inserted where just carriage returns were present.*

When it's receiving plain ASCII text for printing, the TCP/IP Print Server replaces both LF (line feed or newline) and CR (carriage return) characters with a carriage return/line feed pair. This messes up print jobs that wanted to overprint lines using just a carriage return.

You can disable the translation of both newlines and carriage returns, or just of carriage returns, by adding a value to the Registry.

→ For instructions and warnings about using the Registry Editor, **see** "Using Regedit," **p. 1138**.

Use the Registry Editor called Regedit to find the key HKEY_LOCAL_MACHINE\System\CurrentControlSet\Control\Print\Printers*printername*\PrinterDriverData, where *printername* is the name of the shared printer the Unix user is using.

To prevent the TCP/IP Print Server from replacing either CR or NL with CR+LF, follow these steps:

1. Select key PrinterDriverData and choose Edit, New, DWORD Value. Enter the name Winprint_TextNoTranslation, and set the value to 1.
2. To prevent the server from replacing CR with CR+LF but still replace LF with CR+LF, add the DWORD value Winprint_TextNoCRTranslation with the value 1.
3. After making either of these additions, go to Computer Management, view Services, right-click TCP/IP Print Server, and select Restart.

Some Windows XP printer drivers do not correctly implement overprinted lines. You might find that the lines are now correctly stacked on top of each other, but only the text from the topmost line is visible. You might need to use the binary mode flag (-o l) in your lpr command and add a form feed to the end of your file.

If you later decide to undo the Registry change, you can remove the value item or set its value to 0, and then restart the service.

CAN'T RUN MACINTOSH APPLICATION CONCURRENTLY

When a Macintosh application is installed on a shared folder stored on a Windows XP, NT, or 2003server, an Unable to Open File *error occurs on Macintoshes when more than one Macintosh user attempts to run the application concurrently.*

Some Macintosh programs fail to open their application executable files in the proper file sharing mode. You can patch the problem by using a resource editor program on the Macintosh; just follow these steps:

1. Obtain a copy of ResEdit. An excellent resource (pun intended) for all things resource related is ResExcellence (www.resexcellence.com). There, you can download a copy of ResEdit as well as gain helpful resource editing skills through the huge collection of step-by-step projects. For novice users, a better program is FileBuddy from SkyTag (www.skytag.com).

2. Start ResEdit or FileBuddy. Select Get Info from the File menu. In the dialog that appears, you can select the application.

3. Put a check in the Shared check box.

4. If you're using ResEdit, quit the application and choose Yes to save the changes. In FileBuddy, click OK.

CAUTION

> Resource editing on a Macintosh is as risky as Registry editing in Windows. Always make a copy of whatever file you're going to edit before making changes, and *never* throw out an original, even if it seems that your modified version works like a charm.

MACINTOSH FILES HAVE LOST APPLICATION ASSOCIATIONS

After a shared file has been edited by a Windows user, when Macintosh users open the file, the Macintosh Finder says it can't find the application required to open the document.

The file's resource fork was stripped out when the file was edited in Windows, so the file's Type and Creator codes are missing. The Macintosh user can drag the file and drop it onto the application's icon or manually locate the application. When the Macintosh user saves the file, the association will be restored for future edits.

The Type and Creator codes can also be set using a Macintosh resource editor, as described previously. However, resource editing is tricky and best not done unless it's an emergency.

NOTE

> Type and Creator codes are case sensitive. MSWD is not the same as MsWd or mswd. Case can often cause confusion if you must restore the codes if they were stripped on a trip through Windows or DOS.

TIPS FROM THE WINDOWS PROS: THE HOSTS FILE

If you have an office LAN, especially one with mixed and matched computers, you're probably like me and have a chart of computer names and IP addresses posted on your wall—not just computers, but routers, firewalls, monitored devices, and all manner of devices. Who knows? Soon the espresso machine might be wired in, too.

On a corporate or enterprise LAN, the LAN administrators will probably enter each device into the organization's Domain Name Service system, under your own default domain, so that you can type a command like ping firewall instead of having to type ping firewall.mycompany.com or, worse, something like ping 192.168.56.102.

On a workgroup LAN, you probably don't have your own domain name server. Or your network manager hasn't entered names for the devices you use most frequently (for example, ping espresso). On a heterogeneous network, your Macintosh and testbed Linux machines probably aren't in any domain name list anywhere.

The hosts file is the answer to this annoying situation. You can add entries to the file \windows\system32\drivers\etc\hosts to associate names with IP addresses. The Windows domain-name lookup system looks first in the hosts file before consulting the network, so you can add entries for your own workgroup's computers and devices, regardless of operating system.

The format is simple. Edit the file in Notepad. Add lines to the file, listing IP addresses at the left margin, followed by some whitespace (tabs or spaces), followed by one or more names. You can enter simple names or full domain names. Simple names are assumed to belong to your own domain.

My hosts file looks like this:

```
127.0.0.0 localhost lh
192.168.56.102 firewall fw
192.168.56.45 macone
```

The first entry is the default entry shipped with Windows. localhost stands for "my own computer" and is used for internal testing of the network software. I've added a second name, lh, because I'm lazy and would rather type ping lh than ping localhost.

I added the second entry myself to give a name to my network's firewall. I can now configure the firewall by typing **telnet firewall** or, better yet, **telnet fw** rather than having to look up at that sheet on the wall and type a bunch of numbers.

Finally, there's an entry for my Macintosh computer, macone. This way, I can view its Web server's home page from Internet Explorer using http://macone rather than having to remember its IP address.

This file also serves as a sort of documentation of my network, as it records important IP addresses. One thing you must watch out for, though, is that Windows checks this file before using the real DNS system to look up names. If you put a name in your LAN's (or the Internet's) DNS system, and the computer's IP address later changes, your hosts file will be incorrect. It's best to use this file only for machines that are in nobody's DNS system.

CHAPTER **21**

NETWORK SECURITY

In this chapter

IT'S A COLD, CRUEL WORLD

You might be considering connecting your LAN to the Internet, or you might have done so already. Connecting will probably be more work than you expect (even with, or due to, my advice), but the achievement will be gratifying. After you make just a few keystrokes, a friend in Italy will be able to log on to your network. Millions of potential customers can reach you. You'll be one with the world.

I don't want to spoil your day, but the cruel fact is that, besides your customers, friends, mother, and curious, benign strangers, your computer and your LAN will also be exposed to pranksters, hackers, information bandits, thieves, and a variety of other bad guys who, like anyone else, can probe, prod, and test your system. Will your network be up to the task? Even if you have a single computer only occasionally connected to the Internet by modem, you're still at risk.

By this point in the book, you are aware that network design is foremost a task of planning. It's especially true in this case: *Before* you connect to the Internet, you must plan for security, whether you have a single computer or a large local area network (LAN).

Explaining everything that you can and should do would be impossible. What I want to do in this chapter is give you an idea of what network security entails. I'll talk about the types of risks you'll be exposed to and the means people use to minimize this exposure; then I'll end with some tips and to-do lists. If you want to have a network or security consultant take care of implementation for you, that's great. This chapter will give you the background to understand what the consultant is doing. If you want to go it on your own, then consider this chapter to be a survey course, and your assignment is to continue to research, write, and implement a security plan.

WHO WOULD BE INTERESTED IN MY COMPUTER?

Most of us don't give security risks a second thought. After all, who is a data thief going to target: me or the Pentagon? Who'd be interested in my computer? Well, the sad truth is that there are thousands of people out there who'd be delighted to find that they could connect to your computer. They might be looking for your credit card information, passwords for computers and Web sites, or a way to get to other computers on your LAN. Even more, they would love to find that they could install software on your computer, which they could then use to probe other peoples' computers. They might even use your computer to launch attacks against corporate or governmental networks. Don't doubt that this could happen to you.

With the advent of high-speed, always-on Internet connections, the risks are increasing, because your computer is connected and exposed for longer periods of time. And because operating systems (like Windows XP) are including more and more complex and relatively untested networking software, even if you only use a dial-up modem to link up to the Internet, you're not immune from getting hacked.

In this chapter, I'll explain a bit about how network attacks and defenses work. I'll tell you ways to prevent and prepare for recovery from a hacker attack. And most importantly, I'll show you what to do to make your Windows XP system secure.

NOTE

> If you don't have a local area network installed in your home or office or attached to your computer, you're not off the hook! If you use the Internet, you're part of a huge network, and all the risks and protection measures I'll discuss here apply to you.
>
> On the other hand, if your computer is connected to a Windows Domain-type network, your network administrators probably have taken care of all this for you. In fact, you might not even be able to make any changes in your computer's network or security settings. If this is the case, you might find it frustrating, but it's in the best interest of your organization.

Even if you're not too interested in this, if you don't read any other part of this chapter, you should read and carry out the steps in the section titled "Specific Configuration Steps for Windows XP."

Think You're Safe? Think Again.

I want to give you a practical example of what can happen over the Internet. Just to see how easy it might be, one night at 1 a.m., I scanned the Internet for computers with unprotected Windows File Sharing. I picked a block of IP addresses near mine and used common, completely legal programs to find computers that were turned on and connected. Within a few minutes, I had found 20. I went through these 20 to see whether they had shared files or folders. My efforts didn't take long; on the fourth try, I was presented with the contents of someone's entire hard drive. Of course, I immediately closed the display, but not before noticing that one of the folders on the hard drive was named Quicken and probably contained all this person's checking and savings account information.

Within 10 minutes I had hacked into someone's computer, and I wasn't trying very hard or using one of the many sophisticated tools available. I didn't even have to attempt to break a password. But even if I'd had to, would that person have noticed his or her computer's hard disk light flickering at 1 a.m.? Would you?

To make matters worse, in a business environment, security risks can come from *inside* a network environment as well as from outside. Inside, you might be subject to highly sophisticated eavesdropping techniques or even simple theft. I know of a company whose entire customer list and confidential pricing database walked out the door one night with the receptionist, whose significant other worked for the competition. The theft was easy; any employee could read and print any file on the company's network. Computer security is a real and serious issue. And it only helps to think about it *before* things go wrong.

21

TYPES OF ATTACK

Before I talk about how to defend your computer against attack, let's briefly go through the types of attacks you're facing. Hackers can work their way into your computer and network using several methods. Here are some of them:

- **Password Cracking**—Given a user account name, so-called "cracking" software can tirelessly try dictionary words, proper names, and random combinations in the hope of guessing a correct password. This doesn't take a modern fast processor very long to accomplish.

- **Address Spoofing**—If you've seen the Caller ID service used on telephones, you know that it can be used to screen calls: You only answer the phone if you recognize the caller. But what if telemarketers could make the device say "Mom's calling"? There's an analogy to this in networking. Hackers can send "spoofed" network commands into a network with a trusted IP address.

- **Impersonation**—By tricking Internet routers and the domain name registry system, hackers can have Internet or network data traffic routed to their own computers rather than the legitimate Web site server. With a fake Web site in operation, they can collect credit card numbers and other valuable data.

- **Eavesdropping**—Wiretaps on your telephone or network cable, or monitoring of the radio emissions from your computer and monitor can let the more sophisticated hackers and spies see what you're seeing and record what you're typing.

- **Exploits**—It's a given that complex software has bugs. Some bugs make programs fail in such a way that part of the program itself gets replaced by data from the user. Exploiting this sort of bug, hackers can run their own programs on your computer. It sounds farfetched and unlikely, but exploits in Microsoft's products alone are reported about once a week. The hacker community usually hears about them a few weeks before anyone else does, so even on the most up-to-date copy of Windows, there are a few available for use.

- **Back Doors**—Some software developers put special features into programs intended for their use only, usually to help in debugging. These back doors sometimes circumvent security features. Hackers discover and trade information on these, and are only too happy to use the Internet to see if they work on your computer.

- **Open Doors**—All of the attack methods I described up to here involve direct and malicious actions to try to break into your system. But this isn't always necessary: Sometimes a computer can be left open in such a way that it just offers itself to the public. Like leaving your front door wide open might invite burglary, leaving a computer unsecured by passwords and without proper controls on network access allows hackers to read and write your files by the simplest means. Simple File Sharing, which I'll discuss later in the chapter, mitigates this risk somewhat.

- **Viruses and Trojan Horses**—The ancient Greeks came up with it 3200 years ago, and the Trojan Horse trick is still alive and well today. Shareware programs used to be the favored way to distribute disguised attack software, but today e-mail attachments are the favored method. (I get phony "Happy 99" and "Click here to see Britney nude!" messages about once a week.)

- **Social Engineering**—A more subtle approach than brute force hacking is to simply call or e-mail someone who has useful information and ask for it. One variation on this approach is the e-mail that purports to come from a service provider like AOL, saying there was some sort of account glitch and could the user please reply with their password and social security number so the glitch can be fixed. P.T. Barnum said there's a sucker born every minute. Sadly, this works out to 1,440 suckers per day, or over half a million per year, and it's not too hard to reach a lot of them with one bulk e-mail.

- **Denial of Service**—Finally, not every hacker is interested in your credit cards or business secrets. Some are just plain vandals, and it's enough for them to know that you can't get your work done. They may erase your hard drive, or more subtly, crash your server or tie up your Internet connection with a torrent of meaningless data. In any case, you're inconvenienced. For an interesting write-up on one such attack, see www.grc.com/dos.

If all this makes you nervous about hooking your LAN up to the Internet, I've done my job well. Before you pull the plug, though, read on.

YOUR LINES OF DEFENSE

Making your computer and network completely impervious to all these forms of attack is quite impossible, if for no other reason than there is always a human element that you cannot control, and there are always bugs and exploits not yet anticipated.

You *can* do a great deal, however, if you plan ahead. Furthermore, as new software introduces new features and risks, and as existing flaws are identified and repaired, you'll have to keep on top of things to maintain your defenses. The most important part of the process is that you spend some time thinking about security.

The following sections delve into the four main lines of computer defense. They are

- Preparation
- Active defense
- Testing, logging, and monitoring
- Disaster planning

You can omit any of these measures, of course, if you weigh what you have at risk against what these efforts will cost you, and decide that the benefit isn't worth the effort.

What I'm describing sounds like a lot of work, and it can be if you take full-fledged measures in a business environment. Nevertheless, even if you're a home user, I encourage you to consider each of the following steps and to put them into effect with as much diligence as you can muster. Just think of that poor sleeping soul whose hard disk I could have erased that morning at 1 a.m. (If you missed this poignant example, see the sidebar titled "Think You're Safe? Think Again," earlier in the chapter.)

21

PREPARATION

Preparation involves eliminating unnecessary sources of risk before they can be attacked. You should take the following steps:

■ Invest time in planning and policies. If you want to be really diligent about security, for each of strategies I describe in this chapter, outline how you plan to implement each one.

■ Structure your network to restrict unauthorized access. Do you really need to allow users to use their own modems to connect to the Internet? Do you want to permit access from the Internet directly in to your network, indirectly via a Virtual Private Network (VPN), or not at all? Eliminating points of access reduces risk, but also convenience. You'll have to decide where to strike the balance.

If you're concerned about unauthorized in-house access to your computers, be sure that every user account is set up with a good password—one with letters and numbers or punctuation. Unauthorized network access is less of a problem with Simple File Sharing, as *all* network users are treated the same, but you must ensure that an effective firewall is in place between your LAN and the Internet. I'll show you how to use the Windows firewall later in this chapter.

→ To learn more about simple file sharing, **see** "Simple File Sharing," **p. 972**.

■ Install only needed services. The less network software you have installed, the less you'll have to maintain through updates, and the fewer potential openings you'll offer to attackers.

For example, don't install SMTP or Internet Information Services unless you really need them.

The optional "Simple TCP Services" network service provides no useful function, only archaic services that make great denial of service attack targets. Don't install it.

■ Use software known to be secure and (relatively) bug free. Update your software promptly when fixes become available. Be very wary of shareware and free software, unless you can be sure of its pedigree and safety.

■ Properly configure your computers, file systems, software, and user accounts to maintain appropriate access control. We'll discuss this in detail later in the chapter.

■ Hide from the outside world as much information about your systems as possible. Don't give hackers any assistance by revealing user account or computer names, if you can help it. For example, if you set up your own Internet domain, put as little information into DNS as you can get away with. Don't install SNMP unless you need it, and be sure to block it at your Internet firewall.

TIP FROM

Bob & Brian

> The most important program to keep up-to-date is Windows XP itself. I suggest that you keep up-to-date on Windows XP bugs and fixes through Microsoft's update program *and* through independent watchdogs. Configure Windows to notify you of critical updates. Subscribe to the security bulletin mailing lists at `www.microsoft.com/security`, `www.ntbugtraq.com`, and `www.sans.org`.
>
> If you use Internet Information Services to host a Web site, pay particular attention to announcements regarding IIS. Of all Microsoft products, IIS has had the lion's share of security problems.

Security is partly a technical issue and partly a matter of organizational policy. No matter how you've configured your computers and network, one user with a modem and a lack of responsibility can open a door into the best-protected network.

You should decide which security-related issues you want to leave to your users' discretion, and which you want to mandate as a matter of policy. On a Windows 2000/.NET domain network, the operating system enforces some of these points, but if you don't have a domain server, you might need to rely on communication and trust alone. The following are some issues to ponder:

- Do you trust users to create and protect their own shared folders, or should this be done by management only?
- Do you want to let users run a Web server, FTP server, or other network services, each of which provides benefits but also increases risk?
- Are your users allowed to create simple alphabetic passwords without numbers or punctuation?
- Are users allowed to send and receive personal e-mail from the network?
- Are users allowed to install software they obtain themselves?
- Are users allowed to share access to their desktops with Remote Desktop, Remote Assistance, NetMeeting, Carbon Copy, PCAnywhere, or other remote-control software?

Make public your management and personnel policies regarding network security and appropriate use of computer resources.

If your own users don't respect the integrity of your network, you don't stand a chance against the outside world. A crucial part of any effective security strategy is making up the rules in advance and ensuring that everyone knows.

ACTIVE DEFENSES: BLOCKING KNOWN METHODS OF ATTACK

Active defense means actively resisting known methods of attack. Active defenses include

- Firewalls and gateways to block dangerous or inappropriate Internet traffic as it passes between your network and the Internet at large

- Encryption and authentication to limit access based on some sort of credentials (such as a password)

- Keeping up-to-date on security and risks, especially with respect to Windows XP

When your network is in place, your next job is to configure it to restrict access as much as possible. This task involves blocking network traffic known to be dangerous and configuring network protocols to use the most secure communications protocols possible.

SET UP FIREWALLS AND NAT (CONNECTION SHARING) DEVICES

Using a firewall is an effective way to secure your network. From the viewpoint of design and maintenance, it is also the most efficient tool because you can focus your efforts on one critical place, the interface between your internal network and the Internet.

A firewall is a program or piece of hardware that intercepts all data passing between two networks, for example between your computer or LAN and the Internet. The firewall inspects each incoming and outgoing data packet and only permits certain packets to pass through. Generally, a firewall is set up to permit traffic for safe protocols like those used for e-mail and Web browsing. It blocks packets that carry file sharing or computer administration commands.

NAT (Network Address Translation), the technology behind Internet Connection Sharing, insulates your network from the Internet by funneling all of your LAN's network traffic through one IP address—the Internet analogue of a telephone number. Like an office's switchboard operator, NAT lets all of your computers place outgoing connections at will, but intercepts all incoming connection attempts. If an incoming data request was anticipated, it's forwarded to one of your computers, but all other incoming network requests are rejected or ignored. Microsoft's Internet Connection Sharing and hardware Internet connection sharing routers all use a NAT scheme.

→ To learn more about this topic, **see** "NAT and Internet Connection Sharing," **p. 663**.

The use of either NAT or a firewall, or both, can protect your network by letting you specify exactly how much of your network's resources you'll expose to the Internet.

WINDOWS INTERNET CONNECTION FIREWALL

One of Windows XP's new features is the built-in Internet Connection Firewall (ICF) software. It's designed in such a way that it can be enabled, or attached, on any network adapter or dial-up connection that directly connects to the Internet. Its purpose is to block any traffic that carries networking-related data, so it prevents computers on the Internet from accessing shared files, Remote Desktop, Remote Administration, and other "sensitive" functions. You can deploy the Internet Connection Firewall as illustrated in Figure 21.1.

This figure shows three different ways you might connect to the Internet: with a standard dial-up or DSL/cable connection (Computer A), with a shared dial-up connection (Computers B and C), or a shared DSL/cable connection (Computers D and E). In each case, the Internet Connection Firewall is enabled only on the connection icon that goes directly to the Internet. It wouldn't be enabled on any of the "inside" connections, because there it would block the computer's ability to share files on the LAN.

ICF is enabled by simply checking a box on the properties page of a network or Internet connection. (I'll tell you how to do this later in the chapter under "Specific Configuration Steps for Windows XP.") You also can tell the firewall whether you want it to permit incoming requests for specific services. If you have a Web server, for example, you'd need to tell ICF to permit incoming HTTP data.

Figure 21.1
Three ways you might connect to the Internet. Internet Connection Firewall is used on the connections that go directly to the Internet.

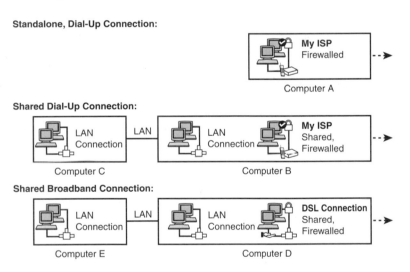

NOTE

Internet Connection Firewall isn't perfect. Amazingly, according to Microsoft, ICF doesn't protect your system while Windows is booting up and shutting down. It's unlikely that a hacker could use an opening of a few seconds to attack you, but you should know that this possibility is there. On the other hand, ICF has the advantage that it automatically opens up to permit incoming Remote Assistance and Windows Messenger connections, so there's a definite trade-off either way.

If I had the choice between using ICF and an external firewall device such as a router with filter rules, personally, I'd forgo Remote Assistance and use the external firewall. But ICF is definitely better than no firewall at all.

21

SIMPLE FILE SHARING

Windows XP introduces a new network security model called Simple File Sharing. Before I explain this, I'll give you some background. In the original Windows NT/2000 workgroup network security model, when you attempted to use a shared network resource, Windows would see if your username and password matched an account on the remote computer. One of four things would happen:

- If the username and password exactly matched an account defined on the remote computer, you'd get that user's privileges on the remote machine for reading and writing files.
- If the username matched but the password didn't, you'd be prompted to enter the correct password.
- If the username didn't match any predefined account, or if you failed to supply the correct password, then you'd get the privileges accorded to the Guest account, if the Guest account was enabled.
- If the Guest account was disabled, and it usually was, you would be denied access.

The problem with this system is that it required you to create user accounts on each computer you wanted to reach over the network. Multiply say 5 users times 5 computers, and you had 25 user accounts to configure. What a pain! (People pay big bucks for a Windows Server-based domain network to eliminate just this hassle.) Because it was so much trouble, people usually would enable the Guest account.

The problem is that Guest is a member of the group Everyone, and usually Everyone has read/write or at least read privileges on the entire hard drive; and full privileges on FAT-formatted disks which have no user-level security at all. This means the user account headache invited people to make their entire computers vulnerable to abuse over their LAN and the Internet.

Enter Simple File Sharing. On all Windows XP Home Edition computers, and as the default option on XP Professional, Simple File Sharing does four things:

- It treats anyone who attempts to use shared resources over the network as Guest.
- The Guest account is enabled by default for network use. You can separately choose whether Guest can log on at your keyboard. This is disabled by default on both Home and Pro.
- Windows removes Everyone from the permission lists for access to the Windows directory. This means that only authorized locally logged-on users can access the Windows directory.
- When you share folders, Windows in most cases automatically applies the correct permissions to the shared folder so that Everyone (that is, Guest) can read and optionally write to the folder. For folders it knows aren't safe to share, it doesn't do this.

This means that it's now very easy to set up shared files and folders for your LAN. You won't be called upon or able to select which individual users get access and which don't. If you share a folder, you share it with read-only or read/write access. It's very simple indeed, and it's perfectly appropriate for home and small office LANs. Microsoft's reasoning here is that it's better to configure a somewhat looser LAN correctly than a stricter LAN poorly. For tight user control, corporations use Server-based networks.

There are two down sides to Simple File Sharing: First, and most important, it's *crucial* that you have a firewall in place. Otherwise, everyone on the Internet will have the same rights in your shared folders as you. That's one of the reasons for the Internet Connection Firewall, and why the Network Setup Wizard is so adamant about either installing the Firewall or disabling file sharing.

The second down side is less troublesome and probably less noticeable to most people: If you attempt to use a shared folder from another computer on which you have the same username and password, you won't get the full rights that you'd have locally. You'll be a guest like anyone else.

On Windows XP Professional, if you want to use the old per-user permission scheme, you can disable Simple File Sharing. You'll have more control over permissions at the cost of lots more work in configuration.

PACKET FILTERING

If you use a hardware Internet connection sharing router (also called a residential gateway) or a full-fledged network router for your Internet service, you can instruct it to block data that carries services you don't want exposed to the Internet. This is called *packet filtering*. You can set this up in addition to NAT to provide extra protection.

Filtering works like this: Each Internet data packet contains identifying numbers that indicate the protocol type (such as TCP or UDP) and the IP address for the source and destination computers. Some protocols also have an additional number called a port, which identifies the program that is to receive the packet. The WWW service, for example, expects TCP protocol packets addressed to port 80. A domain name server listens for UDP packets on port 53.

A packet arriving at the firewall from either side is examined; then it is either passed on or discarded, according to a set of rules that list the protocols and ports permitted or prohibited for each direction. A prohibited packet can be dropped silently, or the router can reject the packet with an error message indicating the requested network service is unavailable. (If possible, I prefer to specify the silent treatment. Why tell hackers that a desired service is present even if it's unavailable to them?) Some routers can also make a log entry or send an alert indicating that an unwanted connection was attempted.

NOTE

> For a good introduction to firewalls and Internet security in general, I recommend *Practical Firewalls*, published by Que; *Maximum Security, Third Edition*, published by Sams; and *Firewalls and Internet Security: Repelling the Wily Hacker* published by Addison & Wesley.

21

Configuring routers for filtering is beyond the scope of this book, but I'll list some relevant protocols and ports in Table 21.1. If your router lets you block incoming requests separately from outgoing requests, you should block any of these for which you don't want to provide a public service. If you have a basic gateway router that would block both incoming and outgoing use of these protocols, you probably only want to filter those that I've marked with an asterisk (*).

TABLE 21.1   SERVICES THAT YOU MIGHT WANT TO BLOCK

Protocol	Port	Associated Service
TCP	20–21	FTP—File Transfer Protocol.
TCP *	23	TELNET—Clear-text passwords are sent by this remote terminal service, which also is used to configure routers.
TCP	53	DNS—Domain Name Service. Block TCP mode "zone" transfers, which reveal machine names.
TCP+UDP	67	BOOTP—Bootstrap Protocol (similar to DHCP). Unnecessary.
TCP+UDP	69	TFTP—Trivial File Transfer Protocol. No security.
TCP	110	POP3—Post Office Protocol.
UDP * TCP *	137–8 139	NetBIOS—Three ports are used by Microsoft File Sharing.
UDP *	161–2	SNMP—Simple Network Monitoring Protocol. Reveals too much information.
TCP *	445	SMB—Windows XP and 2000 File Sharing can use Port 445 as well as 137–139.
TCP	515	LPD—Unix printer sharing protocol supported by Windows XP.

As I said, if you use a hardware router to connect to the Internet, I can't show you the specifics for your device. I can give you a couple of examples, though. My Linksys Cable/DSL Sharing Router uses a Web browser for configuration, and there's a page for setting up filters, as shown in Figure 21.2. In this figure, I've blocked the ports for Microsoft file sharing services.

If you use routed DSL Internet service, your ISP might have provided a router manufactured by Flowpoint, Netopia, or other manufacturers. As an example, filtering is set up in a Flowpoint router through a command line interface, as shown below:

```
remote ipfilter append input drop -p udp -dp 137:138 internet
remote ipfilter append input drop -p tcp -dp 139 internet
```

These are complex devices and your ISP will help you set yours up. Insist that they install filters for ports 137, 138, 139, and 445 at the very least.

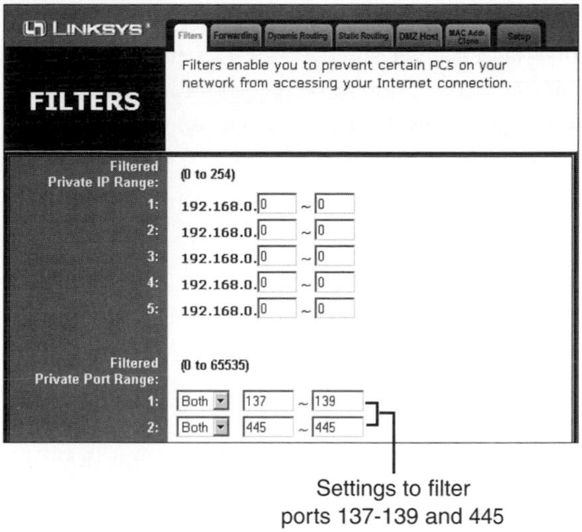

Figure 21.2
Configuring packet filters in a typical Internet connection sharing router.

Settings to filter
ports 137-139 and 445

USING NAT OR INTERNET CONNECTION SHARING

By either name, Network Address Translation (NAT) has two big security benefits. First, it can be used to hide an entire network behind one IP address. Then, while it transparently passes connections from you out to the Internet, it rejects all incoming connection attempts except those that you explicitly direct to waiting servers inside your LAN. Packet filtering isn't necessary with NAT, although it can't hurt to add it.

→ To learn more about NAT, **see** "NAT and Internet Connection Sharing," **p. 663**.

You learned how to configure Windows Internet Connection Sharing in Chapter 19, so I won't repeat that information here.

CAUTION

> Microsoft's Internet Connection Sharing (ICS) blocks incoming access to other computers on the LAN but unless Internet Connection Firewall is also enabled, it does *not* protect the computer that is sharing the Internet connection. If you use ICS you must enable the Internet Connection Firewall on the same connection. Together, they provide adequate protection for all of your computers.

If you have built a network with another type of router or connection sharing device, you must follow the manufacturer's instructions or get help from your ISP to set it up.

TIP FROM

Bob & Brian

> Not all ISPs will help you set up a connection-sharing router. These devices just cut into their revenues. Your ISP may even forbid their use. Better check first, before asking for help in installing one.

21

ADD-ON PRODUCTS FOR WINDOWS

There are now commercial products called *Personal Firewalls*, designed for use on PCs. Products such as Zone Alarm Pro (www.zonelabs.com) can cost under $50. Now that Windows includes an integral firewall, these add-on products may no longer be necessary, but you may still want to investigate them.

I suggest you check www.grc.com and click on the LeakTest link. I expect that by the time this book is in your hands this site will have a review comparing the performance of the Windows XP firewall to the commercial products. This Web site also has a nifty Web-based tool called ShieldsUp that will test your computer for Internet hacking vulnerabilities. I'll talk about this later in the chapter.

SECURE YOUR ROUTER

If you use a router for your Internet connection and rely on it to provide network protection, you *must* make it require a secure password. If your router doesn't require a password, *anyone* could connect to it across the Internet and delete the filters you've set up. Most routers as configured by the manufacturers and ISPs *do not* require a password.

To lock down your router, you'll have to follow procedures for your specific router. You want to do the following:

- Change the router's administrative password to a combination of letters, numbers, and punctuation. Be sure to write it down somewhere!
- Change the SNMP community name (which is in effect a password) to a secret word.
- Prohibit Write access via SNMP or disable SNMP entirely.
- Change all Telnet login passwords, whether administrative or informational.

If you don't want to attempt to lock down your router, your ISP should do it for you. If your ISP supplied your router and you change the password yourself, be sure to give the new password to your ISP.

SET UP RESTRICTIVE ACCESS CONTROLS

Possibly the most important and difficult step you can take is to limit access to shared files, folders, and printers. You can use the guidelines shown in Table 21.2 to help organize a security review of every machine on your network. I've put some crucial items in boldface.

TABLE 21.2   RESTRICTING ACCESS CONTROLS

Access Point	Controls
File Sharing	Don't share your computers' entire hard drives. Share only folders that need to be shared, and if possible choose only folders in your My Documents folder (for simplicity).
Passwords	Set up all accounts with passwords. You can configure your computers to require long passwords if you want to enforce good internal security. I'll show you how to do this later in the chapter.

TABLE 21.2   CONTINUED

Access Point	Controls
Partitions	If you install IIS and want to make a Web site or FTP site available to the Internet, you *must* set up a separate NTFS partition on your hard drive *just* for Web site files. I discussed this in Chapter 13, "Hosting Web Pages with Internet Information Server."
Access Control	Don't use Administrator or any other Computer Administrator account for your day-to-day work. If you accidentally run a Trojan horse or virus program using an Administrator account, the nasty program has full access to your computer. Instead, create and use Limited User accounts to the greatest extent possible.
FTP	If you install a public FTP server, do not let FTP share a FAT-formatted drive or partition. In addition, you must prevent anonymous FTP users from writing to your hard drive. I discussed this in Chapter 13.
SMTP	Configuring an e-mail system is beyond the scope of this book. But if you operate an e-mail server, consider storing incoming mail in a separate partition to avoid getting overrun with too much mail. Also, you *must* prohibit "relaying" from outside SMTP servers to outside domains, lest your server be used as a spam relay site.
HTTP (Web)	*Don't enable both Script/Execute permission and Write permission on the same folder.* Enabling both permissions would permit outside users to install and run arbitrary programs on your computer. You should manually install any needed scripts or CGI programs. (The FrontPage extensions can publish scripts to protected directories, but they perform strong user authentication before doing so.)
SNMP	This network monitoring option is a useful tool for large networks but it also poses a security risk. If installed, it could be used to modify your computer's network settings and, at the very least, will happily reveal the names of all the user accounts on your computer. Don't install SNMP unless you need it, and if you do, change the "community name" from `public` to something confidential and difficult to guess.

KEEP UP-TO-DATE

New bugs in major operating systems and applications software are found every week, and patches and updates are issued almost as frequently. Even Microsoft's own public servers have been taken out by virus software!

Software manufacturers including Microsoft have recently become quite forthcoming with information about security risks, bugs, and the like. It wasn't always the case, as they mostly figured if they kept the problems a secret, fewer bad guys would find out about them, and so their customers would be better off. (That, and it saved them the embarrassment of admitting the seriousness of their bugs.) Information is shared so quickly among the bad guys now that it has become essential for companies to inform users of security problems as soon as a defensive strategy can be devised.

21

You can subscribe to the Microsoft Security Bulletin service at `http://www.microsoft.com/security`. The following are some other places to check out:

`http://www.ntbugtraq.com`

`http://www.sans.org`

`http://www.cert.org`

`http://www.first.org`

`http://www.cs.purdue.edu/coast/coast.html`

`http://www.greatcircle.com`

`newsgroups: comp.security.*, comp.risks`

Some of these sites point you toward security-related mailing lists. You should subscribe to Microsoft Security Advisor Bulletins and the SANS and CERT advisories at least, and perhaps other lists in digest form. Forewarned is forearmed!

TESTING, LOGGING, AND MONITORING

Testing, logging, and monitoring involve testing your defense strategies and detecting breaches. It's tedious, but who would you rather have be first to find out that your system is hackable: you or "them"? Your testing steps should include

- Testing your defenses before you connect to the Internet
- Monitoring Internet traffic on your network and on the connection to your Internet service provider or other networks
- Detecting and recording suspicious activity on the network and in application software

You can't second-guess what 100 million potential "visitors" might do to your computer or network, but you should at least be sure that all your roadblocks stop the traffic you were expecting them to stop.

TEST YOUR DEFENSES

Some companies have hired expert hackers to attempt to break into their networks. You can do this too, or you can try to be your own hacker. Before you connect to the Internet, and periodically thereafter, try to break into your own system. Find its weaknesses.

Go through each of your defenses and each of the security policy changes you made, and try each of the things you thought they should prevent.

First, connect to the Internet, visit www.grc.com, and view the Shields Up page. This web site attempts to connect to Microsoft Networking and TCP/IP services on your computer to see whether any are accessible from the outside world. Click the Test My Shields! and Probe My Ports! buttons to see whether this testing system exposes any vulnerabilities. This is a great tool! (However, if you're on a corporate network, contact your network manager before trying this. If your company uses intrusion monitoring, this probe might set off alarms and get you in hot water.)

As a second test, find out what your public IP address is. If you use a dial-up connection or Internet Connection Sharing, go to the computer that actually connects to the Internet, open a Command Prompt window, and type `ipconfig`. Write down the IP address of your actual Internet connection (this number will change every time you dial in, by the way). If you use a sharing router, you'll need to get the actual IP address from your router.

Then, enlist the help of a friend, or go to a computer *not* on your site but out on the Internet. Open Windows Explorer (*not* Internet Explorer) and in the Address box, type \\1.2.3.4, \\1.2.3.4, except you'll need to use the actual IP address you recorded earlier in place of 1.2.3.4. This will attempt to connect to your computer for file sharing. You should not be able to see any shared folders, and you shouldn't even be prompted for a username and/or password. If you have more than one public IP address, test *all* of them.

 If you are able to view your computer's shared folders, see "Shared Folders Are Visible to the Internet" in the "Troubleshooting" section at the end of this chapter.

If you have installed a Web or FTP server, attempt to view any protected pages *without* using the correct username or password. With FTP, try using the login name anonymous and the password guest.

 If you are able to view your computer's shared folders, see "Sensitive Web Pages or FTP Folders Are Visible to the Internet" in the "Troubleshooting" section at the end of this chapter.

 If you are not able to view protected Web pages or folders even after providing the correct password, see "Can't View Protected Web Pages" in the "Troubleshooting" section at the end of this chapter.

Use network testing utilities to attempt to connect to any of the network services you think you have blocked—for example, SNMP.

 If sensitive network services are found to be accessible, see "Network Services Are Not Being Blocked" in the "Troubleshooting" section at the end of this chapter.

Attempt to use Telnet to connect to your router, if you have one. If you are prompted for a login, try the factory default login name and password listed in the router's manual. If you've blocked telnet with a packet filter setting, you should not be prompted for a password. If you are prompted, be sure the factory default password does not work, because you should have changed it.

 If you can access your router, see "Router Is Accessible via Telnet" in the "Troubleshooting" section at the end of this chapter.

Port scanning tools are available to perform many of these tests automatically. For an example, see the Shields Up Web page at `http://www.grc.com`. I caution you to use this sort of tool in addition to, not instead of, the other tests I listed here.

MONITOR SUSPICIOUS ACTIVITY

If you use Internet Connection Firewall, you can configure it to keep a record of rejected connection attempts. Open the properties page of the firewalled connection, select the Advanced tab, click Settings, and then select the Security Logging tab, shown in Figure 21.3.

Inspect the log file periodically by viewing it with Notepad.

21

Figure 21.3
Enable logging to see what Internet Connection Firewall is turning away.

NOTE

If you use a dial-up connection, the firewall log is less useful. It will accrue lots of entries caused by packets left over from connections made by the dial-up customer who had your temporary IP address before you got it. They'll continue to arrive for a while, just as junk mail does after a tenant moves out.

DISASTER PLANNING: PREPARATION FOR RECOVERY AFTER AN ATTACK

Disaster planning should be a key part of your security strategy. The old saying "Hope for the best, and prepare for the worst" certainly applies to network security. Murphy's law predicts that if you don't have a way to recover from a network or security disaster, you'll need one. If you're prepared, you can recover quickly and may even be able to learn something useful from the experience. Here are some suggestions to help you prepare for the worst:

- Make permanent, archived "baseline" backups of exposed computers *before* they're connected to the Internet and anytime system software is changed
- Make frequent backups once online
- Prepare written, thorough, and tested computer restore procedures
- Write and maintain documentation of your software and network configuration
- Prepare an incident plan

21

A little planning now will go a long way toward helping you through this situation. The key is having a good backup of all critical software. Each of the points discussed in the preceding list is covered in more detail in the following sections.

MAKE A BASELINE BACKUP BEFORE YOU GO ONLINE

You should make a permanent "baseline" backup of your computer before you connect with the Internet for the first time, so you know it doesn't have any virus infections. This backup should be kept permanently. You can use it as a starting point for recovery if your system is compromised.

→ To learn more about making backups, **see** "Backup Tools and Strategies," **p. 1023**.

MAKE FREQUENT BACKUPS WHEN YOU'RE ONLINE

I hate to sound like a broken record on this point, but you should have a backup plan and stick to it. Make backups at some sensible interval and always after a session of extensive or significant changes (for example, after installing new software or adding users). In a business setting, you might want to have your backup program schedule a backup every day automatically. (You *do* have to remember to change the backup tapes, even if the backups are automatic, however!)

WRITE AND TEST SERVER RESTORE PROCEDURES

I can tell you from personal experience that the only feeling more sickening than losing your system is finding out that the backups you've been diligently making are unreadable. Whatever your backup scheme is, be sure it works!

This step is really difficult to take, but I really urge you to try to completely rebuild a system after an imaginary break-in or disk failure. Use a sacrificial computer, of course, not your main computer, and allow yourself a whole day for this exercise. Go through all the steps: Reformat hard disks, reinstall Windows or use the Automated System Recovery feature, reinstall tape software, and restore the most recent backups. You will find this a very enlightening experience, well worth the cost in time and effort. Finding the problem with your system before you need the backups is much better than finding it after.

Also, be sure to document the whole restoration process so that you can repeat it later. After a disaster, you'll be under considerable stress, so you might forget a step or make a mistake. Having a clear, written, tested procedure goes a long way toward making the recovery process easier and more likely to succeed.

WRITE AND MAINTAIN DOCUMENTATION

It's in your own best interest to maintain a log of all software installed on your computers, along with software settings, hardware types and settings, configuration choices, network number information, and so on. (Do you vaguely remember some sort of ordeal with a DMA conflict when you installed the tape software last year? How *did* you resolve that problem, anyway?)

In businesses, this information is often part of the "oral tradition," but a written record is an important insurance policy against loss due to memory lapses or personnel changes. Record all installation and configuration details.

21

TIP FROM

Bob

& Brian

> Windows has no utilities to print out the configuration settings for software and network systems. I use Alt+PrntScrn to record the configurations for each program and network component and then paste the images into WordPad or Microsoft Word.

Then, *print out a copy* of this documentation, so you'll be able to refer to it if your computer crashes.

Make a library of CD-ROMs, repair disks, startup disks, utility disks, backup CDs, ZIP disks, tapes, manuals, and notebooks that record your configurations and observations. Keep them all in one place and locked up if possible.

PREPARE AN INCIDENT PLAN

A system crash or intrusion is a highly stressful event. A written plan of action made now will help you keep a clear head when things go wrong. The actual event probably won't go as you imagined, but at least you'll have some good first steps to follow while you get your wits about you.

If you know a break-in has been successful, you must take immediate action. First, disconnect your network from the Internet. Then find out what happened.

Unless you have an exact understanding of what happened and can fix the problem, you should clean out your system entirely. This means that you should reformat your hard drive, install Windows and all applications from CDs or pristine disks, and make a clean start. Then you can look at recent backups to see whether you have any you know aren't compromised, restore them, and then go on.

But most off all, have a plan. The following are some steps to include in your incident plan:

- Write down exactly how to properly shut down computers and servers.
- Make a list of people to notify, including company officials, your computer support staff, your ISP, an incident response team, your therapist, and anyone else who will be involved in dealing with the aftermath.
- Check http://www.first.org to see whether you are eligible for assistance from one of the many FIRST response teams around the world. FIRST (the Forum of Incident Response and Security Teams) can tell you which agencies might best be able to help you in the event of a security incident; call 1-301-975-3359.
- The CERT-CC (the Computer Emergency Response Team Coordination Center) may also be able to help you, or at least get information from your break-in to help protect others. Check http://www.cert.org. In an emergency, call 1-412-268-7090.

  You can find a great deal of general information on effective incident response planning at http://www.cert.org. CERT offers training seminars, libraries, security (bug) advisories, and technical tips as well.

Specific Configuration Steps for Windows XP

Many of the points I've mentioned so far in this chapter are general, conceptual ideas that should be helpful in planning a security strategy, but perhaps not specific enough to directly implement. The following sections provide some specific instructions to tighten security on your Windows XP computer or LAN. These instructions are for a single Windows XP computer or a workgroup without a Windows .NET/2000 Server. Server offers more powerful and integrated security tools than are available with Windows XP Professional alone (and happily, it's the domain administrator's job to set it all up).

If You Have a Standalone Windows XP Professional Computer

If you have a standalone system without a LAN, you need to take only a few steps to be sure you're safe when browsing the Internet:

- Enable Macro Virus Protection in your Microsoft Office applications.

- Be very wary of viruses and Trojan horses in e-mail attachments and downloaded software. Install a virus scan program, and discard unsolicited e-mail with attachments without opening it. If you use Outlook or Outlook Express, you can disable the "preview" pane that automatically displays e-mail. Several viruses have exploited this open-without-asking feature.

- Keep your system up-to-date with Automatic Updates (see the Automatic Update tab on the System control panel applet), Windows Update, service packs, application software updates, and virus scanner updates. Check for updates every couple of weeks at least.

- Make the Security Policy changes I suggest later in this chapter under "Tightening Local Security Policy."

- Use strong passwords on each of your accounts including the Administrator account. (Sign on as Administrator by typing Ctrl+Alt+Del twice at the Welcome screen. Then change the password and make a password reset diskette.) For all passwords use letters and numbers or punctuation; don't use your name or other simple words.

- Be absolutely certain that the Internet Connection Firewall is enabled on any icon in your Network Connections folder that connects directly to the Internet, as shown in Figure 21.1. To enable the Internet Connection Firewall, use the steps shown later in this chapter under "Configuring Internet Connection Firewall."

If You Have a LAN

If your computer is connected to others through a LAN, follow the first five suggestions from the list in the preceding section. Make the Security Policy changes on *each* computer.

If you are using the Simple File Sharing system option, which I discussed earlier in this chapter, the security situation is quite different than it was in any previous version of Windows. Since *all* access to shared files over any network or Internet connection is granted or denied access without a password, your one and only line of defense is having a firewall in place between the Internet and your computer.

21

It's *absolutely essential* that you have a firewall in place. I've said this before and will repeat it again in the next sections, but this is so important that it can't be over-emphasized:

- If your LAN connects to the Internet by modem, enable the Internet Connection Firewall on the dial-up connection only, on the computer that shares its connection and on any individual ISP dial-up connection icons.

- If your LAN connects to the Internet using Internet Connection Sharing and a DSL or cable modem, enable the Internet Connection Firewall on the LAN adapter that goes to the broadband modem, on the computer that shares its connection.

- If your LAN connects to the Internet using a hardware connection sharing device like a router, you can get additional safety if you configure filters to block the Microsoft file sharing protocols. Block TCP and UDP ports 137–139 and 445.

- If you use a DSL connection with multiple IP addresses and a router, configure packet filtering in your router. Your ISP will help you do this. Block ports 137–139 and 445. (You might have to remind your ISP that Windows XP also uses port 445 for file sharing.)

- If you use cable Internet service with multiple IP addresses provided by your ISP, but have no hardware firewall device in place, **you cannot share files on your LAN**. For this reason, I urge you *NOT* to use this type of Internet service. See Chapter 19, "Connecting Your LAN to the Internet," for details.

ENABLING THE INTERNET CONNECTION FIREWALL

If you use the Internet, whether directly from your computer or through a network connection, you must be sure that some sort of firewall is in place to prevent Internet denizens from reaching into your computer. If you use a hardware Internet connection sharing device, that will protect you, and I gave specific tips for adding additional protection in the previous section.

If you use a direct connection, or if you use Microsoft's Internet Connection Sharing, you must be sure that the Windows Internet Connection Firewall feature is enabled on the connection that actually touches the Internet. Figure 19.1 illustrates this point—the Internet connection is firewalled. (Any local area network connections in your home network should *not* be firewalled; otherwise, file and printer sharing will not work).

Microsoft's Network Setup Wizard should take care of properly enabling the firewall on the proper connections. You can use the following procedure to verify or manually set up the firewall:

1. Go to the computer that directly connects to the Internet.

2. Click Start, Connect To, and select View All Connections. If Connect To doesn't appear, view My Computer, select My Network Places, and then View Network Connections.

3. Find the icon that represents the actual connection to the Internet. This could be a dial-up connection or a local area connection that is used to connect to a broadband DSL cable or satellite modem.

4. The icon for this connection should have the word Firewalled next to it. If it does, you're all set.

5. If it doesn't say Firewalled, right-click the icon and select Properties. View the Advanced tab.

6. Check Protect My Computer and click OK. The icon should now say Firewalled next to it.

Then, if you want to run a Web server, e-mail system, or other network services that you want to be made available to the outside world, see "Making Services Available" in Chapter 18.

TIGHTENING LOCAL SECURITY POLICY

You should set your machine's own (local) security policy whether your have a standalone computer or are on a LAN. Local Security Policy lets Windows enforce some common-sense security rules, like requiring a password of a certain minimum length.

If your computer is part of a Windows domain-type network, your local security policy settings *may* be superseded by policies set by your domain administrator, but you should set them anyway so that you're protected if your domain administrator doesn't specify a so-called global policy.

To configure local security policy, log in as a Computer Administrator, and choose Start, All Programs, Administrative Tools, Local Security Policy. (If the Administrative Tools icon doesn't appear on the menu, the Administrative Tools Control Panel applet can get you there.)

A familiar Explorer view then appears with several main security policy categories in the left pane, as shown in Figure 21.4. I'll list several policy items you may want to change.

Figure 21.4
The Local Policy Editor lets you tighten security by restricting unsafe configuration options.

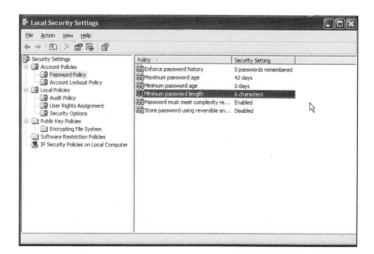

21

To change the settings, select the policy categories from the left pane, and double-click the policy names in the right pane. Appropriate Properties dialogs appear for each; an example is shown in Figure 21.5.

Figure 21.5
Each security policy item has a Properties dialog. You can enter the settings shown in the tables in the following sections.

You don't need to change all the policies. I'll list the important ones in the following sections.

ACCOUNT POLICIES

Account policies can be used to require long, difficult, frequently changed passwords, and make it hard for users to recycle the same passwords over and over when forced to change. You should lock out accounts that fail several login attempts, locally or over the LAN. Table 21.3 shows the password policies and recommended altered settings, and Table 21.4 show the options at your disposal for locking out an account.

TABLE 21.3   PASSWORD POLICY SETTINGS

Password Policy	Local Setting
Enforce password history	10 passwords remembered
Minimum password length	8 characters
Passwords must meet complexity requirements	Enabled
Store password using reversible encryption	Disabled

TABLE 21.4   ACCOUNT LOCKOUT POLICY SETTINGS

Account Lockout Policy	Local Setting
Account lockout duration	30 minutes
Account lockout threshold	5 invalid logon attempts
Reset account lockout counter after	30 minutes

LOCAL POLICIES

You should have an entry in the Event Log whenever someone oversteps his or her bounds. (However, you should not audit Privilege Use because hundreds of spurious entries appear for no apparent reason.) Security options are used to restrict what users can do with system options. Table 21.5 shows the audit policies and recommended settings.

> **NOTE**
>
> If you're interested in how Windows regulates the operation of your computer, take a look at the settings under User Rights Assignment and Security Options. You'll probably never need to change any of these settings, but these two sections are the heart of Windows' security controls.

TABLE 21.5   AUDIT POLICY SETTINGS

Audit Policy	Local Setting
Audit account logon events	Failure
Audit account management	Failure
Audit directory service access	Failure
Audit logon events	Failure
Audit object access	Failure
Audit policy change	Success, Failure
Audit privilege use	No auditing
Audit system events	Failure

No changes are necessary in the User Rights assignments section, but you might want to view these entries to see what sorts of permission restrictions Windows uses. Finally, go through the security options, as listed in Table 21.6.

TABLE 21.6   SECURITY OPTIONS SETTINGS

Security Option	Local Setting
Interactive logon: Do not require Ctrl+Alt+Del	Enabled *
Interactive logon: Log-in Message text	You can display a sort of "Posted: No Trespassing" warning with this entry.
Devices: Prevent users from installing printer drivers	Disabled. If you want to prevent users from installing potentially untested printer and hardware drivers, check out the options for these settings.

continues

TABLE 21.6   CONTINUED

Security Option	Local Setting
Shut down system immediately if unable to log security audits	A common hacker trick is to fill up audit logs with junk messages and then break in. If you want to, you can have Windows shut down when the Security Event Log fills. The downside is that it makes your security system a denial of service risk! (Microsoft's public "hack me if you can" Windows 2000 Server was shut down just this way.)
Devices: Unsigned driver installation behavior	Warn but allow. If you want to prevent users from installing potentially untested printer and hardware drivers, check out the options for these settings.

When you log out and back in, the new restrictive security policies will take effect. You still must export and delete the recovery agent certificate to finish beefing up the security on each computer.

MORE ABOUT SECURITY

This chapter just barely scratched the surface of what there is to know and do about network security. There are lots of great books on the topic, and I've mentioned several of them in this chapter.

You also can get lots of information on the Web. First, www.sans.org and www.cert.org are great places to start looking into the security community. Steve Gibson has plenty to say about security at www.grc.com—it's educational and entertaining.

Finally, you might look into additional measures you can take to protect your computer and your network. There are many ways to configure networks. It's common, for example, to keep any public Web or e-mail servers you have separate from the rest of your LAN. For additional security, you even can buy or build special-purpose firewall routers to place between your LAN and the Internet. One nifty way to do this is shown at http://www.linux-firewall-tools.com/linux/.

In any case, I'm glad you're interested enough in security to have read this far down in the chapter!

TROUBLESHOOTING

SHARED FOLDERS ARE VISIBLE TO THE INTERNET

When I use Explorer to view my computer across the Internet, I am prompted for a username and password, and/or shared folders are visible.

If you have this problem, Microsoft file sharing services are being exposed to the Internet. If you have a shared connection to the Internet, you need to enable the Internet Connection

Firewall, or enable filtering on your Internet connection. At the very least you must block TCP/UDP ports 137 through 139 and 445. Don't leave this unfixed!

If you have several computers connected to a cable modem with just a hub, and not a connection sharing router, you should read Chapter 19 for alternate ways to share your cable Internet connection.

Sensitive Web Pages or FTP Folders Are Visible to the Internet

When I access my Web site from the Internet using a Web browser or anonymous FTP, I can view folders that I thought were private and protected.

First, you must be sure that the shared folders are not on a FAT-formatted disk partition. FAT disks don't support user-level file protection. Share only folders from NTFS-formatted disks.

You must restrict access on the shared folders using NTFS permissions. View the folders in Windows Explorer on the computer running IIS. View the folders' Securities Properties tab. Be sure neither Everyone nor IUSR_XXXX (where XXXX is your computer name) is granted access. On these protected folders, grant Read and Write privileges only to authorized users. In the Internet Information Services management console, you can also disable Anonymous access on the Web site's security page.

Can't View Protected Web Pages

When I try to view protected Web pages or change to a protected directory in FTP, I can't view the pages or folders.

View the virtual folder's Properties page in the Internet Information Services management applet. On the Directory Security tab, click Edit under Anonymous Access and Authentication Control. Be sure that Digest Authentication and Integrated Windows Authentication are checked. If they were checked already, view the folder's Security settings in Windows Explorer as described in the previous troubleshooting tip. Make sure that the desired users or groups are granted appropriate NTFS access permissions on the folder and its files and subfolders.

Network Services Are Not Being Blocked

I can connect to my computer across the Internet with remote administration tools such as the Registry Editor, with SNMP viewers, or with other tools that use network services. How do I prevent this access?

Look up the protocol type (for example, UDP or TCP) and port numbers of the unblocked services, and configure filters in your router to block these services. Your ISP might be able to help you with this problem. You might have disabled the Internet Connection Firewall by mistake.

ROUTER IS ACCESSIBLE VIA TELNET

I can connect to my Internet service router through Telnet across the Internet without providing a secret administrative password. How do I prevent this access?

Configure your router to require a sensible password for access. Choose a password with letters and numbers. Be sure you write it down, and also give it to the technical support department of your ISP. The ISP might even be able to help you change the password.

CHAPTER 22

TROUBLESHOOTING YOUR NETWORK

In this chapter

WHEN GOOD NETWORKS GO BAD

Today's networks are so easy to install and configure that you can just Plug and Pray, er, I mean Play. But when good networks go bad, it's another story, one with all the makings of a Fox Network special.

Every time I get a call from a client with a network problem, I cringe. I never know whether it's going to take 10 minutes or a week to fix. Sometimes the problem isn't so bad; I've fixed more than one "broken" computer by turning it on. If such an easy fix doesn't present itself immediately, though, a bit of a cold sweat breaks out on my forehead. The problem could be anything. How do you even start to find a nasty problem in the maze of cards, wires, drivers, and hidden, inexplicable system services?

Well, if you work for a corporation with a network support staff, of course, the answer to that question is "Call the Help Desk!" or "Call Bob!" or call whatever or whoever is responsible for network problems in your organization. That's clearly the best way to go! Take a refreshing walk around the block while someone else sweats over your network. (If you're on your own, taking that walk might help anyway, before coming back to the job of discovering what the problem might be.) If you want or need to go it alone, though, the good news is that there are some tools provided with Windows that can help you find the problem. After talking about troubleshooting in general, I'll show you how to use them.

I will tell you that, in reading this chapter, you won't find the solution to any network problem you're having. I can't solve your problem here, but I can show you some of the tools available to help you identify the source of a problem you might have.

GETTING STARTED

As a consultant, I've spent many years helping clients with hardware, software, and network problems. The most common—and frustrating—way people report a problem is to say "I can't . . ." or "The computer won't . . ." Usually, knowing what *doesn't* happen isn't very helpful at all. To solve a mystery, you have to start with what you *do* know. I always have to ask "What happens when you try . . . ?" The answer to that question usually gets me well on the way to solving the problem. The original report usually leaves out important error messages and symptoms that might immediately identify the problem.

Also, as you work on a problem, pay as much attention to what *does* work as to what doesn't. Knowing what *isn't* broken lets you eliminate whole categories of problems. It also helps you to see whether a problem affects just one computer or all the computers on your local area network (LAN).

The following are some other questions I ask:

- Does the problem occur all the time or just sometimes?
- Can you reproduce the problem consistently? If you can define a procedure to reproduce the problem, try to reduce it to the shortest, most direct procedure possible.
- Has the system ever worked, even once? If so, when did it stop working, and what happened just before that? What changed?

These questions can help you determine whether the problem is fundamental (for example, due to a nonfunctioning network card) or interactive (that is, due to a conflict with other users, with new software, or confined to a particular subsystem of the network). You might be able to spot the problem right off the bat if you look at the scene this way. If you can't, you can use some tools to help narrow down the problem.

Generally, network problems fall into one or more of these categories:

- Application software
- Network clients
- Name-resolving services
- Network protocols
- Addressing and network configuration
- Driver software
- Network cards and hardware configuration
- Wiring/hubs

→ To learn more information about networks and network components, **see** Chapter 15, "Overview of Windows XP Networking."

If you can determine which category a problem falls in, you're halfway there. At this point, diagnostic tools and good, old-fashioned deductive reasoning come into play.

You might be able to eliminate one or more categories right away. For example, if your computer can communicate with some other computers but not all, and your network uses a central hub, you can deduce that at least your computer's network card and the wiring from your computer to the hub are working properly.

Windows comes with some diagnostic tools to further help you narrow down the cause of a network problem. In the rest of this chapter, I'll outline the tools and suggest how to use them. (You might also peruse Chapter 14, "Troubleshooting Your Internet Connection," for tips on diagnosing network problems specific to the Internet [TCP/IP] protocol.)

DIAGNOSTIC TOOLS

Each diagnostic tool I'll describe serves to test the operation of one or more of the categories I mentioned in the preceding section. I'll go through this toolkit in roughly the order you should try them.

Some tools can be used to find problems in any of the many networking components. These tools quickly identify many problems.

MY NETWORK PLACES

You might not think of it as a diagnostic tool, but My Network Places can be one. It can quickly tell you whether your computer can communicate with any other computers on your LAN using Windows's file and printer sharing client services. If at least one other computer is visible and online, then you can be pretty sure that your computer's network card and cabling are okay.

To use it, open My Network Places, and then open View Workgroup Computers or View Entire Network from the Network Tasks list. Delve into either of these folders to see if you can find any computers listed.

> **NOTE**
>
> View Workgroup Computers appears only if your computer is configured for a workgroup LAN. It is discussed in more detail in Chapter 17, "Using a Windows XP Network."

If you see at least one other computer displayed here, your network cabling and network card are probably okay, and you need to check to be sure that each computer on your network has the same set of network protocols installed. If no computers appear, My Network Places doesn't tell why, so you have to begin the process of diagnosing connectivity and/or higher-level problems. The next place to go is the Event Viewer, which might have recorded informative error messages from network components.

EVENT VIEWER

The Event Viewer is another very important diagnostic tool, one of the first to check, as Windows often silently records very useful information about problems with hardware and software in its Event Log. To display the Event Log, click Start, right-click My Computer, select Manage, and select the Event Viewer system tool. (Alternatively, if you've added Administrative Tools to your Start Menu, you can choose Start, All Programs, Administrative Tools, Event Viewer.)

On the left pane, select the System, Application, and Security logs in turn. The Event Viewer displays Event Log entries, most recent first, on the right (see Figure 22.1).

Figure 22.1
The Event Viewer might display important diagnostic information when you have network problems. View the System, Application, and Security logs in turn.

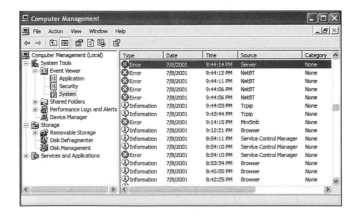

Log entries for serious errors are displayed with a red X circle; warnings appear with a yellow ! triangle. Informational entries (marked with a blue *i*) usually don't relate to problems. Double-click any error or warning entries in the log to view the detailed description and any associated data recorded with the entry. (The Error entries in Figure 22.1 told me that my computer had the same name as another computer on the network: problem solved!)

These messages are usually quite significant and informative to help diagnose network problems; they may indicate that a network card is malfunctioning, that a domain controller for authentication or a DHCP server for configuration can't be found, and so on. The Source column in the error log indicates which Windows component or service recorded the event. These names are usually fairly cryptic. A few of the more common nonobvious ones are listed in Table 22.1.

TABLE 22.1 NETWORK SOURCES OF EVENT LOG ENTRIES

Source	Description
NetBT	Client for Microsoft Networks
MrxSmb	Client for Microsoft Networks
Browser	Name resolution system for Client for Microsoft Networks
Application Popup	(Can come from any system utility; these warning messages are usually significant.)
RemoteAccess	Dial-Up Networking
SMTPSVC	The SMTP mail transport service, part of Internet Information Services (IIS)
W3SVC	The WWW server component of IIS
SNMP	Simple Networking Monitoring Protocol, an optional networking component
IPNATHLP	Internet Connection Sharing
NWCWorkstation	Client for Novell Networks
NwlnkIpx	SPX/IPX Network transport layer
W32Time	Computer clock synchronization service
Dnsapi	DNS client component
Dnscache	DNS client component
atapi	IDE hard disk/CDROM controller

If you're at a loss to solve the problem even with the information given, check the configuration of the indicated component, or remove and reinstall it to see whether you can clear up the problem.

→ To learn more details about the Event Log, **see** "Event Viewer," **p. 922**.

22

TIP FROM

Bob & Brian

> A problem with one network system usually causes other problems. Therefore, the oldest error message in a sequence of errors is usually the most significant; subsequent errors are just a result of the first failure. Because the Event Log is ordered most-recent-first, you might get the most useful information down a bit from the top of the list.

TIP FROM

Bob & Brian

> The real cause of your problem might reveal itself at system startup time rather than when you observe the problem. Reboot your system, and note the time. Then reproduce the problem. Check the Event Log for messages starting at the reboot time.

DEVICE MANAGER

Hardware problems with your network card will most likely be recorded in the Event Log. If you suspect that your network card is the culprit, and nothing is recorded in the Event Log, check the Device Manager.

To use it, click Start, right-click My Computer, select Manage, and choose the Device Manager system tool. Any devices with detectable hardware problems or configuration conflicts appear with a yellow ! icon when you display the Device Manager. If no yellow icons appear, you don't have a *detected* hardware problem. This doesn't mean that you don't have any, but the odds are slim that your network card is the problem.

If devices are shown with ! icons, double-click the device name to see the Windows explanation of the device status and any problems. A device that you've told Windows not to use (disabled) will have a red X on it; this is generally not a problem.

→ For more detailed instructions and tips on device troubleshooting, **see** Chapter 30, "Installing and Replacing Hardware," **p. 1043**.

TESTING NETWORK CABLES

If your computer can't communicate with any other on your LAN, and the Device Manager doesn't indicate a faulty network card, you might have a wiring problem. Wiring problems can be the most difficult to solve, as it's quite difficult to prove that data is leaving one computer but not arriving at another. The ping program, which I'll discuss later in this chapter, can help with this problem.

→ To learn how you can use the ping command to diagnose Internet-related network problems, **see** "ping," **p. 455**.

If your computer is not properly wired into the LAN, in many cases, Windows displays an offline icon right on the system tray and indicates that your network card is disconnected. It might not, though, so you shouldn't take a lack of this kind of message to mean that no wiring problems exist.

22

If your network uses UTP (10 or 100BaseT) cabling plugged into a hub, there's usually a green LED indicator on each network card and at each port on the hub. Be sure that the lights are on at each end of your network cable and those for the other computers on your LAN.

You also can use inexpensive (about $75) cable test devices that check for continuity and correct pin-to-pin wiring order for UTP wiring. They come as a set of two boxes. One gets plugged into each end of a given cable run, and a set of blinking lights tells you whether all four wire pairs are connected and in the correct order. (If you install your own network cabling and/or make your own patch cables, these tools are quite handy to have to check your work.)

With a coaxial (also called ThinNet or 10BASE-2) network, if none of your computers can send data (for example, pings) to any another, a wiring problem is the most likely culprit because a wiring fault usually takes out the whole network. Unfortunately, the network cards don't have any indicator lights to help! You can get a coaxial cable continuity tester, or you might need to manually check each computer's connection.

NOTE

> A *continuity tester* is a small box with two wire probes and a beeper or light. When a sound electrical connection exists between the two probes, the beeper beeps or the light comes on.
>
> To test a coaxial cable with such a tester, you disconnect the cable from the network at both ends. At either end of the cable, you touch one probe to the center pin and the other to the BNC connector's metal outer shell. You should not hear a beep. A beep indicates that the cable is shorted out. Next, have someone at the other end of the cable use a wire to short the other end's center pin to the shell. Now, you should get a beep. No beep indicates that the cable is broken.

TIP FROM

Bob & Brian

> I've cured more than one ailing coaxial network by just walking along the chain of computers, from one end to the other, giving each BNC connector a little twist to make sure its little Frankenstein-neck pins are fully locked. Each T-connector has three connections, so be sure to check all three at each computer. This tour has sometimes also revealed missing terminators and improper rearrangements in the network cable made by untrained users.

NOTE

> If you really want to get into the guts of your network cabling or are planning a major installation and want to learn more details so that you can oversee a professional installation, I recommend that you read *Upgrading and Repairing Networks, Third Edition*, published by Que.

22

CHECKING NETWORK CONFIGURATION

If hardware isn't at fault, you may have a fundamental network configuration problem. Often the Event Log or Device Manager gives these problems away, but if they don't, you can use another batch of tools to check the computer's network configuration.

ipconfig

If your computer can't communicate with other computers on your LAN, after you check the Event Log and Device Manager, you can use the `ipconfig` command-line utility to see whether your computer has a valid IP address. Check others on the LAN, too, to ensure that they do as well.

At the command prompt (which you open by choosing Start, All Programs, Accessories, Command Prompt), type the following command:

>ipconfig /all

The results should look something like this:

```
Windows IP Configuration
        Host Name . . . . . . . . . . . . : AMBON
        Primary DNS Suffix  . . . . . . . : mycompany.com
        Node Type . . . . . . . . . . . . : Broadcast
        IP Routing Enabled. . . . . . . . : Yes
        WINS Proxy Enabled. . . . . . . . : No
        DNS Suffix Search List. . . . . . : mycompany.com

Ethernet adapter Local Area Connection:
        Connection-specific DNS Suffix  . : mycompany.com
        Description . . . . . . . . . . . : Realtek RTL8139(A)
                        PCI Fast Ethernet Adapter
        Physical Address. . . . . . . . . : 00-C0-CA-14-09-7F
        DHCP Enabled. . . . . . . . . . . : No
        IP Address. . . . . . . . . . . . : 202.201.200.166
        Subnet Mask . . . . . . . . . . . : 255.255.255.224
        Default Gateway . . . . . . . . . : 202.201.200.190
        DNS Servers . . . . . . . . . . . : 201.202.203.72
                                            201.202.213.72
```

The most important items to look for are the following:

- **Hostname**—It should be set to the desired name for each computer. If you just can't correspond with a particular computer, be sure it's turned on and correctly named.

- **IP address**—It should be set appropriately for your network. If your LAN uses Internet Connection Sharing, the address will be a number in the range 192.168.0.1 through 192.168.0.254. If your LAN uses DHCP for automatic configuration, your network manager can tell you whether the IP address is correct.

  If you see a number in the range 169.254.0.1 through 169.254.255.254, your computer is set for automatic configuration but no DHCP server was found, so Windows has chosen an IP address by itself. This is fine if your LAN uses this automatic configuration system. However, if there should have been a DHCP server, or if you use Internet Connection Sharing or a hardware Internet Connection router, this is a problem. Restart the ICS computer or the router, and then restart your computer and try again.

- **Network mask**—It usually looks like 255.255.255.0, but other settings are possible. At the very least, all computers on the same LAN should have the same network mask.

Each computer on the same LAN should have a similar valid IP address and the same network mask. If they don't, check your network configuration.

→ To learn more details about IP addressing, network masks, and configuration, **see** "IP Name Services and Routing," **p. 481**, and "Configuring Network Components," **p. 528**.

NETWORK TROUBLESHOOTER

Windows XP features a Network Troubleshooting Wizard that can check for some common network setup problems. Sadly, it holds more promise than good advice. I suggest that you do give it a try, because one of these days it might surprise us all and propose a solution that actually fixes the problem.

To run it, click Start, My Network Places. From the Network Tasks list select View Network Connections. Then, under See Also, select Network Troubleshooter. The troubleshooter is shown in Figure 22.2. At the very least, it will walk you through some helpful, if generic steps to diagnose your network.

Figure 22.2
The Network Troubleshooter can be reached from the Network Connections window.

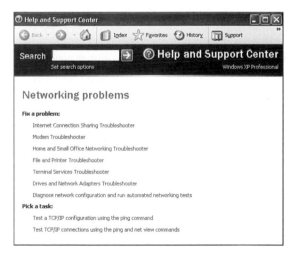

netdiag

netdiag is a comprehensive network connectivity and configuration diagnosis tool included with the Windows XP Professional Resource Kit, a set of extra utility programs and diagnostic tools sold by Microsoft.

At the time this book was published, it wasn't clear whether or not Microsoft would provide these tools on the Windows XP Professional CD. Browse your Windows XP installation CD, and look for a folder named \SUPPORT\TOOLS. If this folder is present, see whether a setup program is inside. If so, good! Run it. It installs a small subset of the Windows XP Resource Kit, including the `netdiag` program I'm about to describe.

If it isn't on your CD (or even if it is), get a copy of the Windows XP Professional Resource Kit. It costs a few bucks, but every organization with a LAN should have a copy, period. Besides `netdiag`, it has enough nifty tools and utilities to keep the most tweak-happy computer user satisfied for weeks.

To use this program, issue the command

```
> netdiag | more
```

to run the diagnostics, and page them through the `more` utility a screenful at a time. Press Enter to see each successive screen.

The output of `netdiag` is long—over 180 lines on my computer—because it tests quite a number of network subcomponents. Scroll through the output looking for tests marked `Failed`. They help point you toward fixing a network problem.

If you have a Windows .NET/2000 Server-based domain network, you should refer any failed tests in the Global Results section to your network administrator because they indicate problems with your computer's domain membership.

> **NOTE**
>
> I've avoided talking about nonstandard (that is, extra money) Windows XP components in this book with this one exception: `netdiag` is an important tool, and one a network maven shouldn't be without.

MY COMPUTER

You can check your computer's identification and domain membership setup by using My Computer. To do so, right-click My Computer, select Properties, and view the Computer Name tab.

On a Windows Workgroup network, you should see your computer's name and the name of your workgroup. The workgroup name should be the same on all computers on your workgroup LAN. All of the computer names *must* be different.

> **NOTE**
>
> None of your computers can use the workgroup or domain name as its computer name. For example, if your workgroup is MSHOME, you can't also name a computer MSHOME. If you find this on one of your computers, change the computer name.

On a Windows domain network, you should see your computer's name displayed as part of a Windows domain name (for example, my computer AMBON would be called `AMBON.mycompany.com` on a domain network) and the domain name. Your domain name might not include `.com`; in any case, though, all computers on the LAN should have the same domain name.

NETWORK CONNECTIONS

You can manually check all installed network protocols and services and their configuration by viewing Network Connections and viewing the properties for Local Area Connection. Confirm that each required protocol is installed and correctly configured. In general, the settings on each computer on your LAN should match, except that the IP address differs usually only in the last of its four dot-separated numbers. If your LAN uses Automatic IP address configuration, you need to use the `ipconfig` command, which I described earlier, to check the settings.

TESTING NETWORK CONNECTIVITY

A few tools can help you determine whether the network can send data between computers; these tools test the network protocols as well as low-level network hardware layers.

ping

`ping` is a fundamental tool for testing TCP/IP network connectivity. Because most Windows XP Professional networks use the Internet (TCP/IP) protocol for file and printer sharing services, as well as for Internet access, most Windows XP Professional users can use the `ping` test to confirm that their network cabling, hardware, and the TCP/IP protocol are all functioning correctly. `ping` sends several data packets to a specified computer and waits for the other computer to send the packets back. By default, it sends four packets and prints the results of the four tests.

To see whether the network can carry data between a pair of computers, use the `ipconfig` command (described previously) to find the IP address of the two computers. Then, on one computer, open a Command Prompt window by choosing Start, All Programs, Accessories, Command Prompt.

Next, type the following command:

```
> ping 127.0.0.1
```

This command tests the networking software of the computer itself, by sending packets to the special internal IP address 127.0.0.1; this test has the computer send data to itself. It should print the following:

```
Reply from 127.0.0.1: bytes=32 time<10ms TTL=128
Reply from 127.0.0.1: bytes=32 time<10ms TTL=128
Reply from 127.0.0.1: bytes=32 time<10ms TTL=128
Reply from 127.0.0.1: bytes=32 time<10ms TTL=128
```

If it doesn't, the TCP/IP protocol itself is incorrectly installed or configured; check the computer's IP address configuration, or, if that seems correct, remove and reinstall the Internet Protocol from Local Area Connection in Network Connections. (I have to say, in more than 10 years of working with PC networks, I've never seen this test fail.)

If your computer can send data to itself, try another computer on your LAN. Issue the `ping` command again, as in this example:

```
> ping 192.168.0.23
```

Of course, you should use the other computer's real IP address in place of 192.168.0.23. You should get four replies as before:

```
Reply from 192.168.0.23: bytes=32 time<10ms TTL=32
Reply from 192.168.0.23: bytes=32 time<10ms TTL=32
Reply from 192.168.0.23: bytes=32 time<10ms TTL=32
Reply from 192.168.0.23: bytes=32 time<10ms TTL=32
```

These replies indicate that you have successfully sent data to the other machine and received it back.

If, on the other hand, the `ping` command returns `Request timed out`, the packets either didn't make it to the other computer or were not returned. In either case, you have problem with your cabling, network adapter or the TCP/IP protocol setup.

You can use `ping` to determine which computers can send to which other computers on your LAN or across wide area networks (WANs) or the Internet. `ping` works when given a computer's IP address or its network name.

NOTE

If you enter a computer name, and ping can't determine the computer's IP address, the problem isn't necessarily a wiring problem—it could be that the DNS or WINS name lookup systems are not working correctly. Try using an IP address with ping in this case to help determine what the problem really is.

DIAGNOSING FILE AND PRINTER SHARING PROBLEMS

If the tests in the previous section don't point to a problem, that is, if basic network connectivity is fine but you're still having problems with file or printer sharing, the next step depends on whether you have a workgroup or domain-type network.

If you're on a domain network, it's time to call your network administrator for assistance. They've had more training and experience in network troubleshooting than I can impart in the space allowed here.

If you're on a home or small office workgroup network, there are a few things you might try. Here are some tips:

- Did you run the Network Setup Wizard on each of your computers? To ensure that you don't inadvertently expose your network to the Internet before it's correctly configured, file and printer sharing is disabled until you've run the Network Setup Wizard at least once. You can change your configuration however you like after it's run, but Microsoft wants the first shot at giving you a secure network.

- If you use Internet Connection Sharing, restart the computer that's sharing your Internet connection and wait a minute or two after it's booted up. Then, restart your other computers. This may help. The ICS computer needs to be up and running *before* any other computers on your LAN start up.

- If you don't see other computers in the View Workgroup Computers window, wait 10 to 20 minutes (really) and then select View, Refresh. Sometimes it takes up to 20 minutes for the list of online computers to be updated.

- If you're used to seeing shared folders and printers appear in My Network Places and Printers and Faxes automatically but they're missing now, again, wait a few minutes, and then select View, Refresh. You might also want to make sure that the "network crawler" is enabled. Select Tools, Folder Options, then select the View tab. Be sure that Automatically Search for Network Folders and Printers is checked. If it wasn't, check it, log off, and back on. Wait a few minutes, and then view My Network Places again.

TESTING NETWORK THROUGHPUT

If your network works but works slowly, you may have a problem with your network cabling or hubs. First of all, if you are 10/100Mbps Ethernet adapters, you'll only get full speed if you your network hub is also 100Mbps capable. If you are using a 10Mbps hub, your network will run at the slower speed. In this case, if you can't live with it, you'll have to update your hub to a 100Mbps or dual-speed unit.

If that's not the problem you can diagnose slow network throughput with the Windows Performance monitor tool. The Performance Monitor can display utilization statistics collected from your network card and its drivers. You must first install the Network Monitor Driver to enable the collection of network driver performance statistics. Do this on the most-used computer on your network:

1. In Network Connections, open Local Area Connections, and select Properties.
2. Select Install, choose Protocol, click Add, and select the Network Monitor Driver.
3. Click OK to close the Properties dialog.

Now run the Performance Monitor by choosing Start, All Programs, Administrative Tools, Performance. You can use the Performance Monitor to measure network utilization and other network statistics.

(If Administrative Tools doesn't appear, right-click the Start button and select Properties. Click Customize and view the Advanced tab. Find System Administrative Tools in the Start Menu Items list and check Display on the All Programs Menu. Then run the Performance Monitor as described above.)

22

MEASURING NETWORK UTILIZATION

In the right pane of the Performance console, you can add an item to the graph of performance statistics like this:

1. Right-click in the graph pane, and select Add Counters.
2. Check Use Local Computer Counters.
3. Select the performance object named Network Interface.
4. Select a counter such as Bytes Received/Sec, Packets Received Errors, and so on.
5. Check Select Instances From List, highlight your LAN adapter interface name and click Add.
6. Select Close.

The Performance Monitor then graphs the amount of data traffic on your network connection or connections and the plot is updated as you watch. Now you can visually monitor the traffic on your network.

→ To learn more details about this nifty system-monitoring application, **see** "Measuring System Performance with Performance Monitor," **p. 848**.

NOTE

> To learn more information about network design and maintenance, take a look at *Upgrading and Repairing Networks, Third Edition* (ISBN: 0-7897-2557-6), from Que.

To remove counters from the Performance graph, you can select the items in the legend below the graph and click the X icon at the top of the graph. Alternatively, you can right-click the graph and select Properties; next, select the Data tab, select Counters, and then click Remove.

TIPS FROM THE WINDOWS PROS: MONITORING YOUR LAN

As businesses increasingly rely on computers by the thousands, flung far and wide around the globe, the job of managing them—that is, monitoring, identifying, and correcting problems—has become an industry of its own. *Enterprise management* is a hot expression in the computer industry now. *Very* pricey software systems have been developed to centrally monitor computers, networks, hubs, routing hardware, UPSs, and even computer room fire alarms. These systems detect problems and can notify staff via pager, e-mail, printouts, or, who knows, probably even carrier pigeon.

22

The purpose of these systems is to catch problems as they develop, with any luck, before they disrupt people trying to do their work.

Instrumentation is the key here: Equipment has to be designed to be monitored. A TCP/IP-based protocol called Simple Network Management Protocol (SNMP) has been around for years, and "managed" network equipment is capable of being probed and reconfigured via SNMP. Along with this capability comes a hefty price tag, but the net cost of maintaining and dispatching staff to fix problems is much greater.

My small LAN with four users and a handful of development and online servers doesn't need a $20,000 management system, managed hubs, and the like. But, even in my little office, I find myself constantly checking to make sure the servers are up, that they have plenty of disk space, and that the Internet connection is working. What I really want is something to check these things periodically and let me know whether something's amiss.

I guess plenty of other people do, too. Free enterprise is a wonderful thing. I searched the Web and found a handful of packages targeted for small LANs just like mine. If you have a LAN you depend on for your business, you might want to check them out. Hearing about a problem from your pager is a lot nicer than hearing about it from a client or an employee!

Using these products, you can specify a series of computers or devices to be periodically tested. The tests can include `ping`, SNMP, file sharing services, Windows Service activity, disk space availability, server responsiveness, and so on. Failures can be announced to a list of alert recipients via pager, e-mail, or printout. (Different problems may call for different announcement methods, of course. If your LAN is down, an e-mail alert won't get delivered.) Some products can even send announcements to selected employees based on their work schedules.

Using these tools, you can enter a list of your most important network servers and other resources, and rest assured that if something goes wrong with any of them, you'll be notified immediately.

The following are a few products worth investigating. Each of these programs can detect whether a remote server is active, can test various types of network services (for example, file sharing, Web services, and so on), and can send a message to a pager if a failure occurs.

- ipMonitor

  www.mediahouse.com/ipmonitor

  (Runs as a Windows Service.)

- Whatsup

  www.ipswitch.com/Products/WhatsUp/whatsup.html

- XperTrak Net
  know-it.com/xtnet.htm
- IPSentry
  www.ipsentry.com
- Servers Alive
  www.woodstone.nu/salive/
- AutoPing
  www.jordan.com/AutoPing/default.asp

Reviewing these products, I found that the product quality is roughly proportional to the price, and it's best, if possible, to use one that runs as a Windows service so that it can do its job even while nobody is logged in to the monitoring computer.

These products are not quite as sophisticated or well designed as their $20,000 cousins, but they might be just the ticket for a small business.

SYSTEM CONFIGURATION AND CUSTOMIZATION

CHAPTER 23

TWEAKING THE GUI

In this chapter

GUI: To Tweak or Not to Tweak

I wanted to start this chapter with something cute or meaningful, but all I could think was that, if you know what this title means, you qualify for the Geek-of-the-Year award. For the rest of you, let's get our minds out of the gutter; tweaking the GUI doesn't mean anything lascivious. This chapter describes the graphical user interface and some interesting, useful, and fun stuff you can do with it—changes to help increase your computing efficiency and perhaps even make your computer more fun to use.

As you know, the GUI is the translator that interprets human input into commands the computer can interpret. It's also responsible for displaying output from computer programs and the operating system so that you can understand the results. The Windows XP GUI is set up with factory defaults that 90 percent of users will never touch, despite its being highly programmable and easily modifiable through the Control Panel, Folder Options, Properties sheets, and so on. If you're a GUI hacker, you know who you are, and if all you want to do is get your work done, well, more power to you because you're the one who's going to get the raise. But playing with the GUI can be fun.

Most folks won't modify their GUIs, but it's a shame they don't. Often, not even knowing there is a recourse, users develop headaches from screen flicker, come down with eyestrain from tiny screen fonts, or they live with color schemes they detest. With a little effort, they can rectify these problems. Likewise, means for managing zip archives, altering the right-click Send To options, and handling numerous other functions users have to deal with every day are just a few clicks, Net downloads, Registry hacks, or Properties sheet settings away. Just for fun, you can choose from hundreds of desktop themes, screen savers, wallpaper images, and so on.

Some of this chapter deals with standard display options. Other portions deal with deeper GUI tweaks and tricks. Just skim for the part that interests you.

→ This chapter doesn't cover multimonitor support because it's related more to hardware upgrades than the GUI. **See** "Installing and Using Multiple Monitors," **p. 1068** for coverage of multiple monitors.

Start Menu Pizzazz!

The default Start menu of Windows XP is much improved over the classic style (in my opinion). I dread returning to Windows 2000 or earlier OSes for whatever reason simply because of the now-old-fashioned Start menu. For those of you who like the classic view, you can get back to it in a flash. But, for those willing to give the new look and feel a solid go, there are many nifty improvements you can take advantage of and even customize.

Accessing properties for the Start menu involves a right-click over the Start button to select the Properties command from the pop-up menu. This reveals the Taskbar and Start Menu Properties dialog box. The Start Menu tab is selected by default (which is strange since it's not the first tab of the dialog box). This tab offers the selections of Start menu and Classic Start menu. The Start menu option is the new Luna visual stylings of Windows XP. The

Classic Start menu is that of Windows 2000. A quick click and you can be back in the land of Windows 2000 out-of-date fashion before you can say baggy jeans.

For those of you sticking with Windows XP's new classy stylings, slam the Customize button to see all the options available to you. From the Customize Start Menu dialog box, you can choose between large (default) and small icons, the number of recently accessed applications to be displayed (5 by default), and which Internet (IE by default) and e-mail (Outlook Express by default) application shortcuts to display.

The Advanced tab (see Figure 23.1) of the Customize Start Menu dialog box controls the following:

- Whether to open submenus on mouseover (default) or only when clicked.
- Whether to highlight newly installed programs (enabled by default).

Figure 23.1
The Advanced tab of the Customize Start Menu dialog box.

- Which items to include on the Start menu: Control Panel (enabled by default), Favorites menu, Help and Support (enabled by default), My Computer (enabled by default), My Documents (enabled by default), My Music (enabled by default), My Network Places, My Pictures (enabled by default), Network Connections, Printers and Faxes, and Run command (enabled by default). Some of these can be normal links or displayed as submenus themselves (see "Cascading Elements Off the Start Menu" earlier this chapter).
- Whether to list the most recently opened documents (and to clear out this list).

With a bit of experimentation, you'll find the combination of features that best suits your preferred Start menu population and function.

WORKING WITH THE TASKBAR

The taskbar itself has configurable options; these are contained on the Taskbar tab of the Taskbar and Start Menu Properties dialog box. The taskbar can be locked so stray mouse actions won't alter its placement or configuration; it can be auto-hidden to maximize

23

desktop area; and it can be set to always appear on top of other maximized windows. You'll probably recall these controls from previous Windows OSes. The latest taskbar feature is the automatic grouping of similar taskbar items. Instead of listing task buttons in their order of launch, they are grouped by similar interface. For example, if you have Control Panel, My Computer, and Windows Explorer open, they can appear as a single button. This single button displays a number indicating how many applications are accessed through it (I just love the grouping feature). You can elect to show or hide the clock and even hide inactive system tray icons.

If you're experienced with previous Windows OSes you might be familiar with how quickly the system tray (next to the clock) can fill up with icons. I've had systems with more than a dozen. Windows XP manages its system tray much more intelligently by allowing inactive icons to be hidden. Plus, instead of displaying a long stream of active icons, only two or so are displayed with a double-arrow button, which can be used to access the hidden icons. By enabling Hide inactive icons (which is the default) you can also customize which icons are hidden or displayed.

As with previous versions of Windows, you can still drag the taskbar to any edge of your desktop: top, bottom, or sides. You can also still expand the thickness of the taskbar to allow multiple rows of task buttons. Just hover the mouse pointer near the edge of the taskbar so that it turns into a double arrow, and drag it up or down.

CUSTOMIZING THE START MENU

As new applications are installed, the All Programs section of the Windows XP Start menu can become horribly cluttered. Almost every application will create its own Start menu submenu and propagate it with numerous shortcuts—often to worthless documentation or sales promotions. I rarely let an installed application dictate the state of my Start menu, and I'll tell you how you can take control too.

The Start menu is little more than a folder hierarchy full of shortcuts. Changing the layout of the Start menu (or at least the All Programs section) is just a matter of folder and shortcut manipulation—easy. Just right-click over the Start button and select Open or Explorer. You'll be dropped into a My Computer or Windows Explorer interface pointing to the . . . \Documents and Settings\<username>\Start Menu folder. Any item you add to this folder (that is, at the same level as the Programs folder) will be displayed above the dividing line within the All Programs submenu. Any item you add within the Programs folder or any of its subfolders will appear as you expect in the Start menu hierarchy. Be sure only to create shortcuts within this folder hierarchy.

You also should be aware that there are actually two Start menus for every user. There is the Start menu which is associated with your user profile (the one stored in the . . . \Documents and Settings\<username>\ folder, where <username> is your user account name), and there is the Start menu stored in the . . . \Documents and Settings\All Users\Start menu folder. The latter Start menu includes items that appear in every users' Start menu. When you need to make a change for everyone on this system, make it within the All Users area. If it is for only one user, make that change within their personal Start menu.

DISPLAY PROPERTIES

The most obvious means for altering your GUI display settings is the Display Properties dialog box. From there, you can reach a multitude of GUI settings, mostly affecting visual stylings rather than GUI functionality per se:

- Screen saver settings
- Desktop background
- Colors and fonts for GUI elements
- Active Desktop setting
- Color depth and resolution
- Special GUI effects such as menu sliding
- Energy-saving settings
- Device drivers
- Advanced properties such as hardware acceleration

You can most easily reach the display properties by right-clicking the desktop and choosing Properties. The resulting dialog box is shown in Figure 23.2.

Figure 23.2
You can alter a multitude of display attributes from the Display Properties dialog box (Themes tab shown). Programs such as virus protectors or video drivers may introduce additional tabs to this dialog box.

NOTE

> You also can get to the display properties from the Control Panel. Click Start, Control Panel, Appearance and Themes, and Display.

I'll briefly describe this dialog box tab by tab. You've probably used it before, so I won't belabor it; however, I will point out the basics and mention any specifics you should be aware of.

THEMES TAB

To quote the dialog box itself, "A theme is a background plus a set of sounds, icons, and other elements to help you personalize your computer with one click." That just about sums it up, I think. All the settings you make on the other tabs of the Display Properties dialog box can be saved to a theme file on the Themes tab (see Figure 23.2). Windows XP includes a few themes, such as the default Windows XP scheme (a.k.a. Luna) and the classic theme (similar to the default theme of Windows 2000). Microsoft offers several other themes for download, and many third parties have created themes for Windows XP as well. To download additional themes from Microsoft, select the Mode Themes Online option from the Theme pull-down list, and Windows XP will take you to the online theme stash.

DESKTOP TAB

The desktop is used to express your inner personality. "Hanging wallpaper" (a picture of your kids, your car, a sunset, a nebula, and so forth) on your desktop gives the environment a more personalized feeling. Microsoft includes dozens of options for you. These include small tiles (a.k.a. patterns) that are repeated across and down your screen to make a pattern as well as larger single images centered on the screen (some of which are quite stunningly beautiful). If the image is too small to fill up your desktop, you can always set the Position control to Stretch.

NOTE

> Stretching takes a picture smaller than your screen resolution and enlarges it so that it fills the screen. Stretching can distort the picture or cause it to pixelate, so if you want it to look good, make sure to shoot the picture at, or convert it to, a size roughly matching the resolution setting of your display. Then choose the Center option.

TIP FROM

Bob & Brian

> If the image is larger than the screen's resolution, stretching actually shrinks the image to fully fit on the desktop. If stretching is turned off, and the image is larger than the screen, you'll only be able to see the center portion of the image that fits within your display.

By the way, if you don't want a pretty picture (or you need to hide the image of the sultry pin-up before your spouse returns), you can select None in the list of backgrounds to view a solid background color. That solid color can be altered on this tab, using the Color button on the Desktop tab, or via the Appearance tab's Advanced button. The color setting will be hidden if you use a tiled image or a full-screen size image. But it will show up as the background color for the names of shortcuts populating your desktop.

If you don't like the images offered by default, you can always add your own spicy image. Just click the Browse button to find images elsewhere. You can select .BMP, .JPG, .GIF, .DIB, and .PNG images, or even entire .HTM Web pages. In addition to files already on your local system (or accessible over your local network), you can grab any image from a Web site by right-clicking over it and selecting Set as Background from the pop-up menu.

 If you've used a photo as a background for your desktop, but it appears blocky, see "Stretched a Bit Thin" in the "Troubleshooting" section at the end of this chapter.

Clicking on the Customize Desktop button at the bottom of the Desktop tab opens the Desktop Item dialog box (Figure 23.3). On the General tab of this dialog box, you can select from four common shortcut icons to appear on the desktop: My Documents, My Computer, My Network Places, and Recycle Bin. You can also manage the icons used for these desktop shortcuts using the Change Icon and Restore Default buttons.

Figure 23.3
The Desktop Item dialog box, Desktop tab.

Another interesting feature of Windows XP's new user experience is the Desktop Cleanup Wizard. By default it is launched every 60 days to prompt you to remove items you've not been using. If you elect to remove items from the desktop, they are moved into an Unused Desktop Items folder which is added to the desktop by this wizard. You can disable the 60 day launch by clearing the check box (that's one of the first settings I change!). You can also force a desktop cleanup by clicking the Clean Desktop Now button.

The Web tab of the Desktop Items dialog box is used to configure the Web components on the desktop (this used to be called Active Desktop). From here you can add new Web components or remove existing ones. Desktop Web components are miniature Web browsers which can be resized and moved around, plus they actively update their content as long as an Internet connection is available. To add a new Web page item, click the New button. From the New Desktop Item dialog box, click Visit Gallery to see a collection of Microsoft pre-selections, enter your own URL, or click Browse to add a locally stored image or HTML document. After you've added all the items you wish, you can close this dialog box and drag the components around on the desktop to arrange them as you desire. Once you have the components arranged as you please, reopen the Desktop Items dialog box to lock the desktop items so a stray mouse click won't re-arrange them.

After you've added a Web component (via a URL) to the available items to display on your desktop, you can customize the schedule and download restrictions through their Properties dialog box. Desktop Web components can be synchronized automatically on a custom defined schedule or manually. You can also specify what to download, such as everything, only the front page, or only up to a specific number of kilobytes. All of these configuration settings are very self-explanatory, so take a few minutes and explore them.

SCREEN SAVER TAB

We all know what screen savers are. On the Screen Saver tab of the Display Properties dialog box, you can choose from several supplied screen savers and perhaps others that you have installed from other sources. In the old days when phosphors would "burn," screen savers actually did something useful. They prevented a ghost of the image on the screen from being burned into the screen for all time, no matter what is being displayed. Most modern CRTs don't actually need a screen saver to save anything because the phosphors are more durable. Also, LCD monitors don't need them either because they don't have any phosphors on the screen at all.

So, what good is a screen saver nowadays, you ask? Well, some older monitor/card combinations go into low-power states when the screen is blanked, so if you choose Blank Screen, there could be some advantage.

The SETI@home Screen Saver

Interested in space exploration? Think life might exist on other planets? If you want to become part of the largest global experiment in massive parallel processing, you can download the SETI@home screen saver to harness your computer's otherwise wasted CPU cycles to sift through signals from outer space, searching for signs of intelligent life out there. (Go to `http://setiathome.ssl.berkeley.edu/` if you're interested in participating.)

SETI@home is a scientific experiment that harnesses the power of hundreds of thousands of Internet-connected computers in the Search for Extraterrestrial Intelligence (SETI). The screen saver downloads and analyzes radio telescope data captured at the world's largest radio telescope in Arecibo, Puerto Rico. There's a small but captivating possibility that your computer will detect the faint murmur of a civilization beyond Earth.

Your computer gets a "work unit" of interstellar noise which it analyses when the screen saver comes up. A work unit requires approximately 20 hours of computing time on most computers. If an unnatural noise is detected, you and the people back at the University of California will be alerted. The scientists will attempt to confirm the finding by doing their own analysis and ruling out man-made radio sources such as radar and such. If it is finally confirmed, you and the team can pack up and head for Sweden to pick up your Nobel Prize. If nothing is found (which is somewhat more likely), your system moves on to the next work unit.

As of this writing, almost four million computers were participating. This huge, collective-computing model has set the standard by which massively parallel-processing experiments using small computers are based. There are dozens of sites which use this scenario to perform calculations on encryption codes, calculating PI, and even performing Internet searching and indexing.

Now that beats the old days of screen savers featuring flying toasters, doesn't it?

Because far too many people leave their computers on all the time (it's not really true that they will last longer that way), efforts have been made by power regulators and electronics manufacturers to devise computer energy-conservation schemes. Some screen savers will turn off the video card instead of displaying cute graphics. And, of course, some screen savers are fun to watch. The 3D-Pipes screen saver that comes with Windows XP is pretty mesmerizing actually.

Some screen savers are mindless; others are more interesting. Some, such as the Marquee, have additional options, such as font, size, and color. You can check out each one as the spirit moves you. Just highlight it on this tab, and click Preview. Don't move the mouse until you're ready to stop the preview. If a particular screen saver has configuration elements, click on the Settings button.

If you're looking to find the actual screen saver files on your hard drive, most of them have an .scr extension and are stored in the windows\system32 folder. Most files are 100KB or smaller in size. Double-clicking a screen saver runs it. Just press a key or click the mouse to stop it from running.

The Web is littered with screen savers. Just do a search. The following are some sources:

- Screen Saver Heaven:
  `http://www.galttech.com/ssheaven.shtml`

- Screensaver.com:
  `http://www.screensaver.com`

Between those two sources alone, you have access to more than 2,500 screen savers. Plus, most of the screen savers designed for Windows 3.x, Windows 9x/Me, Windows NT, and Windows 2000 will work on Windows XP.

In addition to selecting the screen saver du jour, you should also define the length of time the system must be idle before the screen saver is launched, as well as whether to display Welcome screen or return to the desktop when the system is resumed (that is, when the keyboard or mouse is activated by a user).

→ The Energy Star settings for monitors are covered under the Power applet discussion. **See** "Working with Power," **p. 786**.

If you are working from a portable system or are an energy conservationist (why do you have a computer in the first place?), the Screen Saver tab also offers quick access to the power saving properties of Windows XP via the Power button. This opens the Power Options Properties dialog box, which is a Control Panel applet in its own right. The Power Options applet is discussed a bit later in this chapter.

APPEARANCE TAB

From the Appearance tab (see Figure 23.4), you can radically alter the look of your entire Windows machine. You can do some serious mischief here, creating some egregious color schemes that will attract the fashion police. Or you can design or choose schemes that improve readability on screens (or eyes) with certain limitations. If, perchance, you're using a monochrome monitor (no color), altering the colors may still have some effect (the amount depends on how you installed Windows), so these settings are not just for systems with color screens.

In most cases your desktop is set to the Windows XP style by default, which is fine for most screens and users. If you prefer the stylings of Windows 2000, you can go retro by selecting Windows Classic style from the Windows and buttons pull-down list.

Figure 23.4
The Display
Properties dialog box,
Appearance tab.

The Windows Classic style offers all of the color scheme pre-defined options you remember, such as Desert, Eggplant, and Wheat. But even if you stick with the new XP styling, there is the default, Olive Green, and Silver color schemes, and even these can be customized through the Advanced button.

The final pull-down selection box on this tab is Font size. I bet you can guess what it's for. So, if you have trouble reading the names of icons or dialog boxes, increase the size of the font!

The Effects button opens the Effects dialog box. From here, you can set the following:

- Whether menus and ToolTips are animated or not, and whether the animation is fade or scroll. Set to Fade effect by default.

- Whether screen fonts are smoothed using the standard Windows method, or using ClearType. ClearType often improves the visibility range on older LCD displays. The Standard method is selected by default.

- Whether to use large icons. Not selected by default.

- Whether to show shadows under menus. Enabled by default.

- Whether to show the contents of a window while dragging. Enabled by default.

- Whether to hide the underlined letters for keyboard shortcuts until the Alt key is pressed. Enabled by default.

The Advanced button opens the Advanced Appearance dialog box, which is used to alter the color settings, component size, and fonts of each individual component of a windowed display. By using the various pull-down lists or clicking in the preview area, you can fine-tune the color and font scheme.

TIP FROM

Bob & Brian

> If you spend considerable time creating a color, component, and font styling, be sure to save it as a theme on the Themes tab. Otherwise, if you switch to another view, even for a second, you'll lose all of your previous settings.

Choosing a color called Other brings up the Color Refiner dialog box (this is true on the Desktop tab as well). You work with two color mix controls here. One is the *luminosity bar* (which looks like a triangle arrow pointing left), and the other is the *color refiner cursor* (which looks like a set of crosshairs).

You simply drag around these cursors one at a time until the color in the box at the lower left is the shade you want. As you do so, the numbers in the boxes below the color refiner change.

- *Luminosity* is the amount of brightness in the color.
- *Hue* is the actual shade or color. All colors are composed of red, green, and blue.
- *Saturation* is the degree of purity of the color; it is decreased by adding gray to the color and increased by subtracting gray.

You also can type in the numbers or click the arrows next to the numbers if you want, but using the cursors is easier. When you like the color, you can save a color for future use by clicking Add to Custom Colors.

SETTINGS TAB

On the Settings tab (see Figure 23.5) of the Display Properties dialog box, you can tweak the video driver's most basic settings—screen resolution (desktop size) and color quality (color depth).

TIP FROM

Bob & Brian

> Unless you have a very fast computer or an intelligent co-processed AGP video card, you will find that running in true color at a high resolution, such as 1280×1024, can be annoying if you have Show window contents while dragging turned on. When you move a window, it moves jerkily across the screen. If you play videos such as QuickTime, MPEG, or RealPlayer movies, you'll also notice that these higher color depths can slow down the movies or make them play jerkily. Try using a setting of 16-bit color depth (aka "high color") for movies and photos. If you don't view movies and photos but only do non-photographic tasks such as word processing, spreadsheet work, and so forth, you might even want to try 256 colors.

23

Figure 23.5
The Display Properties dialog box, Settings tab.

Assuming that Windows XP has properly identified your video display card and that the correct driver is installed, the Color quality drop-down list box should include all the legitimate options your card is capable of. Your color depth options are limited by the amount of video RAM on the card and the resolution you choose. The higher the resolution, the more memory is used for pixel addressing, limiting the pixel depth (number of colors that can be displayed per pixel). With many modern cards, this limitation is no biggie, and it's likely that many Windows XP users will not have to worry about it except in cases when they have large monitors displaying 1600×1200 and want 32-bit color *and* a high refresh rate. If you find that setting the color scheme up to high color or true color causes the resolution slider to move left, this is the reason. All modern analog color monitors for PCs are capable of displaying 16 million colors, which is dubbed true color.

 If you've changed the screen area only to find that you can no longer see some icons or open windows on the desktop, see "Where Did Those Icons Go?" in the "Troubleshooting" section at the end of this chapter.

You must click the Apply button before the changes are made. When you do, you are warned about the possible effects. The good thing about the no-reboot video subsystem, first introduced with Windows 98, is that the driver settings should revert within 15 seconds unless you accept them. So, if the screen goes blank or otherwise goes bananas, just wait. It should return to the previous setting.

 If, after toying with the screen resolution, you notice that your once-speedy computer seems to have lost its zip, see "Moving in Slow Motion" in the "Troubleshooting" section at the end of this chapter.

The Screen resolution setting makes resizing your desktop a breeze. Obviously, we all want to cram as much on the screen as possible without going blind. This setting lets you experiment and even change resolution on-the-fly to best display whatever you're working on. Some jobs, such as working with large spreadsheets, databases, CAD, or typesetting, are much more efficient with more data displayed on the screen. Because higher resolutions require a trade-off in clarity and make onscreen objects smaller, you can minimize eyestrain by going to a lower resolution, such as 800×600 pixels (a pixel is essentially one dot on the screen). If you find the dialog box doesn't let you choose the resolution you want, drop the color palette setting down a notch and try again.

All laptop and notebook computers have LCD monitors, which have screens that are optimized for one resolution, called the *native* resolution. Unless a laptop computer is hooked up to an external monitor, don't bother changing the setting from the native, sometimes called *suggested*, resolution. Choosing a lower one results in blocky display (though still usable in some cases because of intelligent engineering that provides anti-aliasing). Trying a higher resolution definitely does not work. Check the computer's or monitor's manual if you're in doubt about which external monitor resolutions are supported.

23

If you've connected an external TV monitor to your computer but cannot read the fonts on the screen, see "What Does That Say?" in the "Troubleshooting" section at the end of this chapter.

If you are experiencing any problems with your video system, from pop-up errors blaming the video system, to a flickering display, to even trouble resetting the resolution and color, click on the Troubleshoot button. This button launches the Video Display Troubleshooter. It's a Q&A type of wizard that helps you discover solutions to problems. Overall, I've found the Windows XP troubleshooters worth their weight in gold.

If the screen flicker really annoys you, see "Reducing Screen Flicker" in the "Troubleshooting" section at the end of the chapter.

Windows XP boasts the Dual View feature. Dual View allows Windows XP to display the same desktop view on two or more monitors. On a notebook where it was common to display the desktop both on the LCD panel and an external monitor, this is nothing new. But, on desktop PCs equipped with multiple video cards, you can now use multiple monitors. The screen resolution of each monitor is controlled from the Settings tab. Just select the monitor to set the context for the screen resolution and color quality controls.

The Advanced button on the Settings tab opens the Monitor and Adapter Properties dialog box. This dialog box has five tabs—General, Adapter, Monitor, Troubleshoot, and Color Management.

Contrary to some advertising accompanying new flat-panel monitors, LCDs don't give a hoot about high refresh speed. In fact, they don't like high speeds. LCDs use a completely different technology, typically with a transistor for each pixel. The dots don't have to be refreshed as they do in a CRT. I noticed a blurry display on a desktop LCD screen once and tracked down the problem to a 72Hz refresh rate on the video card. I lowered it to 60Hz, and the image cleared up. This advice applies only to LCDs that are attached to analog display cards. Some outboard LCD monitors are driven by their own digital adapter cards, and refresh settings don't affect those cards.

The General tab is used to alter the display's DPI setting and how display changes are handled. The DPI or Dots Per Inch changes the size of items displayed on your screen. The Handling of display changes option simply sets the system to restart before applying, apply without restarting, or ask about restarting whenever changes are made to the display settings.

C A U T I O N

> If you specify a refresh rate that is too high for your monitor, it could damage the monitor. Also, trying to expand the desktop area to a larger size might not work. You just get a mess on the screen. If you have this problem, try using a setting with a lower refresh rate, such as 60Hz or "interlaced." The image may flicker a bit more, but at least it will be visible.

The Adapter tab displays information about the video card and offers access to configure, uninstall, update, or rollback the video driver through the Properties button. The List All Modes button is used to view the color, resolution, and refresh rate combinations supported by this video adapter.

 If, while you're tinkering with the refresh rates for your monitor, the monitor goes blank, don't panic; instead, see "Uh-Oh, My Monitor Died" in the "Troubleshooting" section at the end of this chapter.

The Monitor tab offers access to configure, install, upgrade, or rollback the monitor driver and to set the screen refresh rate. Use the screen refresh rate with caution as it can damage older monitors or render your desktop unviewable. Higher refresh rates reduce the flickering of the display.

 If, after you install a new LCD monitor, you discover that the image is blurry, see "Blurry Images in LCD" in the "Troubleshooting" section at the end of this chapter.

The Troubleshoot tab is used to set the hardware acceleration rate, anywhere between None and Full. Basically this indicates how much video processing is offloaded to the video adapter instead of being performed by Windows XP on the CPU. The more you can offload processing to the video card, the more smoothly your system will function. If you have problems with jitters or lockups, you may need to reduce the amount of hardware acceleration.

The Color Management tab is used to set the color profile used to manage colors for your adapter and monitor. If you are performing high-end image processing you may want to investigate this feature in the Windows XP Resource Kit.

→ If you have a new driver for your display card or monitor and want to install it, **see** or "Add Hardware," **p. 816**.

WORKING WITH POWER

The Power Options applet is the tree-hugger's dream. Well, it's at least a necessary feature for users of portable systems, and increasingly handy for desktop users over the last few years as those larger machines have evolved to become more miserly with electricity. This applet is designed to help the computer consume electricity at a more modest pace. This conservation is accomplished by powering down the monitor and hard drives after periods of inactivity. Several pre-defined power schemes are included, but with just two controls (one for the monitor and one for the hard disks) its not hard to define your own.

In addition to turning off the energy guzzling components, the Power Options applet also manages standby, hibernation, APM, and UPS.

Standby is a feature of most notebook systems that allows the system's state to be saved to RAM and the monitor and hard drives to be powered off. A system can return to fully active state from standby at any point before the batteries are drained. Once power is lost, the system state is lost as well, because it is only stored in RAM. The Power Options applet's Advanced tab offers a single control relative to standby—whether to require a password to resume from standby.

Hibernation is a feature that is a cross between standby mode and shutting down a system. With hibernation, the system state is saved to the hard drive, and then the system is powered down. Once the system is powered back on, the system state is restored. Since the system state data is stored on the hard drive, it is not dependent on constant power to be maintained, and you can return days later and jump back into working right where you left off. The Power Options applet's Hibernate tab offers a single control to enable or disable hibernation. Keep in mind that no passwords are required to resume from hibernation, so it is not a secure feature. Also, take note that this tab displays the amount of drive space required to save the system state. If the required space approaches your available free space, you might lose data or be completely unable to reboot from hibernation.

23

If your system supports APM (Advanced Power Management), the APM tab allows you to enable or disable APM. APM allows for finer tuning of power consumption by your system and its components. It also supplies battery power status information so you can keep track of your portable juice. APM is typically available on portable systems and some "green" desktops or server systems.

The UPS tab offers control and interface configuration for uninterruptible power supplies. These wonderful tools are an essential part of any production environment where computers are used. The nation's power grid is not always up to par. Blackouts, brownouts, spikes, dips, and even noisy electricity can damage or destroy computer equipment. Just ask residents of California! A UPS conditions the incoming electricity so a consistent regulated flow reaches its delicate circuits. You may already know that a shock from static electricity can destroy your system; just think what a surge from a nearby lightning strike will do. UPSes can be integrated into Windows XP by a serial or USB cable. These connections feed data about the power levels of the UPS's battery to the computer and allow the UPS to inform the system when the power is out. When the city electricity goes out, the UPS will supply the computer with power from its battery. If properly configured, the UPS can instruct the system to automatically shut down or hibernate after so many minutes of battery supplied life force. That way, the system will have a graceful shutdown instead of an abrupt loss of power.

NOTE

> When no one is logged into the system, what power saving settings does Windows XP use? When no one is logged in, Windows XP automatically uses the power saving options set for the last user who logged in with computer administrator privileges. So, when the next computer administrator level user logs in, their power options settings are stored as the global defaults on the log in screen, overwriting any previous settings.

If you can't reduce your power consumption through the Power Options applet to suit your needs, then you need to turn off the computer and go chop some wood instead.

TWEAK UI

Many Windows experts have become fond of an unsupported Microsoft product called Tweak UI, which is available and freely downloadable from the Microsoft site. Tweak UI is one of the Microsoft "Power Toys" developed by programmers at Camp Bill in Redmond, Washington. Tweak UI works fine on Windows XP as it did on Windows 2000 and Windows 98. Version 2.00.1.0 of Tweak UI is the newest available for download as of the time of this writing, and it has been fully optimized for usage on Windows XP.

Tweak UI enables you to make more than 100 changes to the Windows XP user environment. For example, you can do the following:

- Scroll smoothly in Windows Explorer
- Enable the mouse wheel for scrolling
- Speed up the display rate of menus
- Add special folders to your operating system that have mouse setting refinements
- Add more types of "New" documents when you right-click a folder and choose New
- Add or remove installed programs from the list of available programs through the Add or Remove Programs applet.
- Repair Start menu and desktop hotkeys, font folders, and icons
- Cover your tracks by erasing temp files, document lists, and history files
- Control whether CDs play automatically when you insert a disk
- Add or remove drives from being displayed in My Computer
- Configure auto-logon

You can download the Tweak UI Power Toy from the Power Toys home page at http://www.microsoft.com/WINDOWSXP/home/downloads/powertoys.asp.

1. Double-click on the TweakUiPowertoySetup.exe file.
2. Click Next to dismiss the opening page, acknowledging that you are about to install the Tweak UI power toy.
3. Accept the licensing agreement and click Next to continue.
4. Provide your user name and organization information, and then click Next to continue.
5. The default installation type is Complete (which is really the only type since there are no installation options); click Next to continue.
6. Click Install to start the installation.
7. Click Finish to end the installation process.
8. You can now access the Tweak UI power toy from the Power Toys for Windows XP folder located on your Start menu.

When you run it, you see the dialog box displayed in Figure 23.6.

Figure 23.6
Tweak UI offers lots of fun stuff to play with here!

NOTE

If you want to uninstall Tweak UI, be sure to read its Help file under "How to Uninstall."

The following are issues with Tweak UI as it pertains to Windows XP:

- If you do not have permission to alter the list of drives that appear in My Computer, the My Computer tab is not shown.
- Depending on the security permissions granted to the current user, some Tweak UI features may not have any effect. For example, if the current user doesn't have permission to edit the part of the Registry that contains the desktop, then changes to the desktop don't have any result.

You might want to check out the other Power Toys too, not just Tweak UI. The following tools that tweak the user interface are available:

Open Command Window Here	This PowerToy adds an "Open Command Window Here" context menu option on file system folders, giving you a quick way to open a command window (cmd.exe) pointing at the selected folder.
Alt-Tab Replacement	With this PowerToy, in addition to seeing the icon of the application window you are switching to, you will also see a preview of the page. This helps particularly when multiple sessions of an application are open. (See Figure 23.7.)

| Virtual Desktop Manager | Manage up to four desktops from the Windows taskbar with this PowerToy. |
| Taskbar Magnifier | Use this PowerToy to magnify part of the screen from the taskbar. |

Figure 23.7
The Alt-Tab replacement in the XP Power Toys shows the page you are switching to, in a thumbnail. This is useful especially when switching between a large number of similar applications or documents, or images.

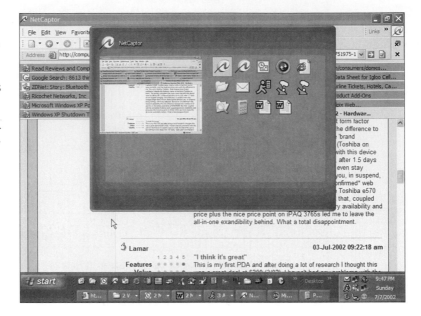

MISCELLANEOUS GUI TIPS

Windows XP offers lots of new features and capabilities. But you don't have to settle for the out of the box defaults; you can customize to your heart's content. In the following sections, we provide you with several tips to help you soup up your Windows XP installation.

 If you've become really frustrated because single clicks are interpreted by Windows as double-clicks (and you can't seem to find any mention of the problem in this chapter), never fear; there's an easy solution. See "Single- or Double-Click?" in the "Troubleshooting" section at the end of this chapter.

FONTS PREVIEW TRICK

If you've ever tried to see what a font looked like before you printed it, you know how frustrating it can be. But, getting a preview of a font is now easier than ever before. There are actually two ways to view the output of a font through the OS itself. The first method is enabled by default on the system. Just open the Fonts applet through the Control Panel, and then double-click on any listed font. A dialog box displays details about the font, a sample of most characters, and several sizes of characters (see Figure 23.8).

The second method for viewing a font sample requires that your system be configured for single-click mode. This is done through the Folder Options applet from the Control Panel. Once single-click mode is enabled, open the Fonts applet. The View menu will now have a Preview command. When Preview is selected, you will see a small sample of each font as you position your mouse cursor over its icon. It only displays the line "The quick brown fox" in the selected font. I don't like the single-click mode, so I don't use this feature.

Figure 23.8
A font sampling dialog box.

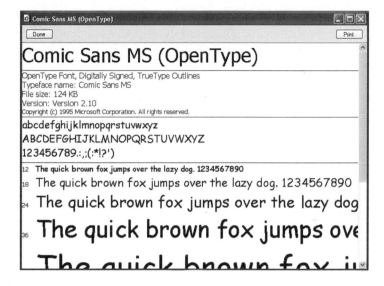

WHICH WINDOWS ARE YOU USING?

If you're dual- or multi-booting between Windows XP (using the classic interface style) and other Windows products, you may sometimes wonder which operating system you're running at any given time because the GUIs of the post-Windows 95 OSes are often virtually indistinguishable. Yes, you'll see a few giveaways, such as My Network Places versus Network Neighborhood (assuming your desktop is visible), but in essential look and feel, the similarities easily outweigh the differences.

To determine what's running, you could open the Control Panel, open the System applet, and read the dialog box. But that's a pain. Instead, you can use these techniques to remind yourself.

- Although many people like to turn off large icons on the first level of the Start menu, leaving them on displays the operating system name when you click Start. You can locate this option by right-clicking the taskbar and clicking Properties. Then select the Start Menu tab and click Customize.

- Executing winver from the Run command or a Command Prompt opens a dialog box that displays the OS name, version, applied Service Packs, and the amount of physical RAM installed in the system.

- Click Start and right-click the My Computer icon. From the menu that appears, click Properties. The first set of information on the General tab is labeled System, and names the version of Windows you're currently using.

23

TWEAKING THE CLOCK TO ADD YOUR COMPANY NAME

You can put your company's name or abbreviation on the taskbar next to the clock, or even an identifier if you have different machines, different operating systems, or different departments. Here's how you do it:

1. Select the Date, Time, Language, and Regional Options applet in the Control Panel and select the Regional and Language Options icon.

2. On the Region Options tab, click Customize.

3. Click the Time tab.

4. Set the time format as h:mm:ss ttttttt (each t is a placeholder for one character in your message, with eight characters max).

5. Set both AM and PM symbols to your message (leave the AM/PM text in place if you want them to remain in the clock display).

For example, I have mine set to AM- LANW and PM- LANW respectively, because LANW is the name of my company (see Figure 23.9). Because you have only eight characters to work with, you might end up obliterating the display of AM or PM, so you might want to change your time code to 24-hour format. Don't worry about time stamps being messed up in other programs, however. Windows internally uses 24-hour time codes, and even though Outlook Express mail might appear to go out stamped 8:07 LANW, for example, it really goes out with 24-hour time. The options you are setting on the Time tab of the Regional Options really affect only the display.

Because this tag also affects programs that have an "insert time stamp" function, you could use it to your benefit, for example, to track not only when a file was opened or edited, but from what department.

Figure 23.9
You can embed a message in the system clock to identify a machine or operating system.

ADMINISTRATOR TOOLS NOT SHOWING UP

Windows XP is designed as an end-user operating system. Thus, most of the system-level management tools are not made readily accessible by being placed in plain sight on the Start menu. Instead, they all are contained within a subfolder of the Control Panel known as Administrative Tools. Open the Control Panel, click Performance and Maintenance, and choose Administrative Tools to open a folder containing these management tools.

Other than manually creating a shortcut to the Administrative Tools folder, there is no easy way to add this item to the Start menu's top level. Well, that's true as long as you are using the new Luna display styling. If you revert to the Classic Start menu, you'll be able to enable the display of the Administrative Tools item within the Start menu through the Start menu's Properties, Start menu tab, Customize button.

However, there is a bit of a back-road method which can allow you to gain access to Administrative Tools without having to open the Control Panel first. By setting the Control Panel to Display as a menu (Start menu's Properties, Start menu tab, Customize button, Advanced tab), whenever you select the Control Panel item in the Start menu, it will display a fly-open menu of all the applets it contains, thus offering you quick access to all of the tools there, including Administrative Tools.

CHANGING THE LOCATION OF THE MY DOCUMENTS FOLDER

This is a very cool tip. As you know, many applications default to saving or opening files in the My Documents folder. If you are like me, you employ your own organizational scheme for saving documents and files, which does not include the My Documents element. Having every Save dialog box default to My Documents is a huge annoyance! It's almost enough to make you throw up your hands and surrender to saving your documents where Microsoft wants you to. In fact, that location may be pretty well hidden. In a multi-user system, XP creates the My Documents folder under the user's name, like this

        C:\documents and settings\bob\my documents

If you're the only person using the computer, this is particularly annoying, since having to "drill down" through those folders every time you want to open a document is a pain. Well, fret no more. In earlier versions of Windows, you had to hack the Registry to change the location of the My Documents folder, but now changing the location is much simpler.

All you have to do is the following:

1. Right-click the My Documents icon on the desktop or through My Computer or Windows Explorer.
2. Choose Properties.
3. Click Move, then select the new destination.

This action doesn't move the original My Documents folder; it just redefines where the My Documents variable actually points to. In other words, it lets you declare another pre-existing folder as the default Save As and Open folder. If you already have documents stored in the original location, you'll need to copy or move them to the new location of the My Documents folder.

CASCADING ELEMENTS OFF THE START MENU

Cascading is the ability to expand certain folders right off of the Start menu. These expanded menus are also called *fly-open menus*. The native Windows XP interface can be configured to add cascading menus for the Control Panel, My Computer, My Documents, My Music, My Pictures, and Network Connections. This is the same feature we discussed earlier to gain direct Start menu access to Administrative Tools.

The process is simple: Just open the Properties for the Start menu (right-click over the Start menu button and then select the Properties command from the pop-up menu). Select the Start Menu tab, click Customize, and then select the Advanced tab. Scroll down the list of Start menu items and change the settings for the desired items to Display as a menu.

VIRTUAL DESKTOP

If you find yourself running out of space on your sole monitor and you've already maxed out the resolution, there is still more room to be had. Cool Desk from ShellToys Inc. brings the acreage of nine virtual desktops to your fingertips. Switching between virtual desktops occurs with a mouse click. You can even move applications from one virtual desktop to another. This simple tool can greatly expand your workspace. It's like having nine monitors stacked on your computer desk.

You can grab this nifty tool from `http://www.shelltoys.com/`.

AUTOPLAY

AutoPlay is the feature of Windows which automatically launches or plays a CD once it is inserted into the CD-ROM drive. Under Windows XP, you have more control than ever over AutoPlay. By opening the Properties dialog box of a CD-ROM drive from Windows Explorer or My Computer, you'll be able to access the AutoPlay tab. From here, you can define for each type of CD (music files, pictures, video files, mixed content, or music CD) whether to take no action, play, open folder to view files, print, launch slide show, and more.

SWITCH CONTROL AND CAPS LOCK KEYS

If you are frustrated by the location of the Ctrl and Caps Lock keys, there is a way to move them. Microsoft has created a document which describes the complex process of editing the Registry to alter the locations of keys on the keyboard. They provide an example of switching the left Ctrl and Caps Lock keys, but they provide instructions on how to switch around any key on the keyboard. Since Microsoft did such a great job of writing this one out, I'll leave it up to them to explain it: `http://www.microsoft.com/HWDEV/input/W2kscan-map.htm`.

AUTO SCROLLING WITH A THREE-BUTTON MOUSE

Do you have a three-button mouse and wish you had a wheel mouse to make it easier to scroll your Web pages? Don't bother coveting your neighbor's wheel mouse because Internet Explorer and your three-button mouse can do the next best thing. When you're working in an Internet Explorer window, just click the center mouse button. The cursor changes to a two-headed arrow shape. Now move the mouse away or toward you, and the page scrolls. Click again or click another mouse button, and the scrolling function is terminated.

CUSTOMIZING FOLDER VIEWS

Windows XP offers a wide range of options for customizing how files are displayed through the My Computer and Windows Explorer utilities. The View menu (see Figure 23.10) offers the following controls:

- **Toolbars**—This control is used to display or hide the standard buttons, address bar, and links bar. You can also lock the bars (so stray clicks don't alter your layout) or fully customize the button toolbar.

- **Status bar**—This control enables the display of an information bar at the bottom of the utility which shows object details, file size, free space, and so on.

- **Explorer bar**—This control sets the folder item to be displayed in the right-hand pane. No selection displays the context-sensitive quick access menus of File and Folder Tasks, Other Places, and Details. Selections in this control include: search, favorites, history, contacts, and folders.

- **Views**—This section allows quick change of the view used to display file objects: thumbnails, tiles (default), icons, list, and details.

- **Arrange Icons by**—This command is used to sort file objects by name, size, type, or modification date. There are also settings for show in groups, auto arrange (maximize layout starting from upper left corner), or align to grid.

- **Choose Details**—This command sets the details that appear in ToolTips, details, and Tile view. The defaults are name, size, type, and modification date. Among the 33 options included are attributes, owner, subject, company, and file version.

- **Customize this Folder**—This command is used to define custom attributes for the selected folder (see next section).

- **Go to**—This menu is used to navigate back, forward, up one level, to the home page, or to recently visited locations.

23

Figure 23.10
The View menu of
Windows Explorer.

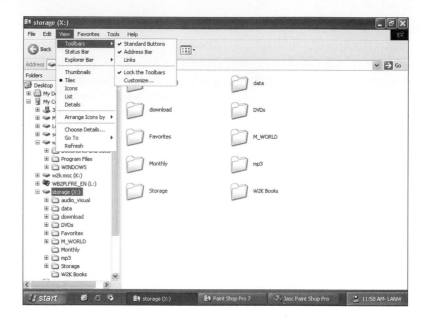

Figure 23.10
The View menu of
Windows Explorer.

CUSTOMIZE THIS FOLDER

If you have a complex organizational structure to your personal files, you might find this feature quite intriguing. Customizing folders allows you to select from six templates designed for a specific type of file (document, image, or music) or collection of files (all, one artist, one album). These templates set how the contents of these folders are displayed as well as the context for the menu commands. Additionally, you can define a custom image for thumbnails and a unique icon for the folder. All these customizations can help you keep track of what you've got stored where.

SETTING FOLDER OPTIONS

Folder Options should be seen as more of a superset of controls over all folders on a system, while folder customization is on an individual or parent and sub-folder basis. Folder Options is a Control Panel applet that can also be accessed from the Tools menu of My Computer and Windows Explorer. This applet is used to set a wide range of file system features.

The General tab of the Folder Options dialog box defines whether common tasks are shown in folders or whether only classic Windows folders are displayed; whether folders are opened in the same or a new window; and whether single-clicks or double-clicks are used to open items. If you make changes to this tab, you can always return to the default by clicking the Restore Default button.

The View tab (see Figure 23.11) performs two major functions—folder view management and advanced settings management. For folder view management, all folders can be reset to their default views, or the currently selected folder's view can be applied to all folders. Advanced settings management contains a long checklist of settings.

NOTE

The common tasks view or the view which displays the File and Folder Tasks, Other Places, and Details context panels is an interesting and useful feature of Windows XP. However, in the releases since Beta 2 of Windows XP, the common tasks pane disappears whenever you select any other item from View menu's Explorer Bar submenu. I find this highly frustrating because I want both the common tasks pane and the Folders pane. Hopefully Microsoft will release an update to Windows XP that re-enables this functionality.

Figure 23.11
The View tab of Folder Options.

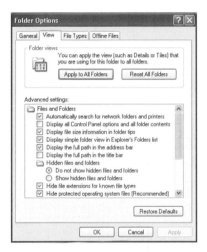

Because I like seeing every file on my system, I always enable Show hidden files and folders, and disable the Hide file extensions and Hide protected OS files. You need to make your own choice on what you want the OS to show you and hide from you. If you want to return to the defaults, just click the Restore Defaults button.

NOTE

If you've tried to delete a folder that looked like it was empty but an error message states the folder still contains files, you are probably dealing with hidden files. To see what's not being shown, go change the Hidden files and folders Advanced setting. I've run into this issue a few times with downloaded applications that must be extracted to a temporary folder before being installed. They sometimes include files pre-marked as hidden.

The File Types tab (see Figure 23.12) is where the registration of file extensions or file types is managed. All registered file types are listed. Because changing a file type is just defining which application is used to open or view the file type, you can alter these settings as you see fit. The Advanced button is used to manipulate more advanced features of file type registration, such as displayed file type name, icon, and actions (such as open, play, display, install, and so on). New file types can be created manually. Existing file types can be deleted. In most cases, the registration of file types is managed by the OS and byapplications as they are installed.

Figure 23.12
The File Types tab of Folder Options.

In some instances you'll discover that one file type can be opened or accessed by more than one application. And nine times out of ten, the application you don't want will be the one launched when you double-click on the file. To associate the file with the tool of your choice, modify the file type's application association through the Change button.

If you want to learn more about file type management, consult the Windows XP Resource Kit.

The Offline Files tab configures the caching of network content on the local system in order to maintain access to cached files while disconnected. This feature is discussed in Part IV of this book.

CONFIGURING THE RECYCLE BIN

The Recycle Bin holds recently deleted files to provide you with a reasonable opportunity to recover them. As we talked about in Chapter 4, the Recycle Bin will hold the last deleted files that fit within its size restriction. That restriction by default is 10% of the drive space for each partition or volume on the system. However, you can and should customize the Recycle Bin for your specific needs.

The Recycle Bin's Properties dialog box (accessed by right-clicking over the icon, and then selecting Properties) has a Global tab and a tab for each partition/volume on the system. The Global tab offers a control that allows you to configure your drives independently or to use one setting for all drives (the default). If you've never deleted a file by mistake and don't think you ever will, you can elect to delete files immediately without storing them in the Recycle Bin. If you'd rather just limit how much space Windows uses to store deleted files, you can set a maximum size for the Recycle Bin as a percentage of drive space. A final control on the Global tab enables a deletion confirmation dialog box—I think this should be left enabled.

Remember, if you select to configure the properties for each drive independently, you must use the provided tabs labeled for each drive on your system. Each drive will display the size of the drive and the space reserved for the Recycle Bin along with the other controls we just discussed.

When limiting the amount of space to use for deleted files, the default percentage is 10%. This is usually a good size, but as hard disk sizes increase, you may want to reduce this to 5%. Keep in mind that files moved to the Recycle Bin are not actually deleted. Instead, their path information is removed from the normal interfaces and moved into the Recycle Bin. Deleted files still remain on the drive exactly where they were before the deletion operation. This means they take up space on the drive. So, if you leave the default percentage setting at 10% on a 20GB hard drive, you can have up to 2GB of deleted files still sitting on the drive slowing down the drive's seek time.

23

TUNING VISUAL EFFECTS

In addition to the controls we've already mentioned in the Display applet, there are additional visual effect controls in the System applet from the Control Panel. On the System applet's Advanced tab, click on the Settings button in the Performance area. This opens the Performance Options dialog box. The Visual Effects tab (see Figure 23.13) can be set to allow Windows to manage effects, set for best appearance, set for best performance, or set with your own custom settings.

Figure 23.13
The Visual Effects tab of Performance Options.

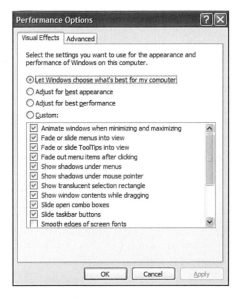

When Custom settings is selected, you can then enable or disable a long list of effects. These effects include animate resizing of windows, fade ToolTips, show shadows under menus, and use visual styles on windows and buttons.

Unless your system is low on physical RAM, uses an old non-AGP video card, or uses a video card with less than 8MB of native RAM, there is little need to modify the default settings for these controls in respect to performance. However, if you think no shadows or no animation looks better, you can customize the look and feel of the user environment all you want.

TROUBLESHOOTING

REDUCING SCREEN FLICKER

My CRT is flickering and annoying me. How can I change it?

Increase the refresh rate of the display subsystem to at least 70Hz. Right-click the desktop, choose Properties, and then choose Settings, Advanced, Monitor. Finally, change the refresh rate.

WHERE DID THOSE ICONS GO?

I changed the screen resolution, and now I can't find items off the edge of the screen and I have windows I can't close.

You might have this problem when you switch to a lower resolution from a higher one. Theoretically, Windows is good about relocating desktop icons, but some applications might not do the same. For example, the small AOL Instant Messenger dialog can be off the edge of the screen somewhere, and when it is, you can't get to it. Closing and rerunning the program doesn't help. One trick is to switch to the application by pressing Alt+Tab. Then press Alt+spacebar, and press M. This key combination invokes the Move command for the window. Then you can use the arrow keys on the keyboard to move the window (typically to the left and/or up). When you have the title bar of the window in view, press Enter. If this trick doesn't work, switch back to the previous higher resolution, reposition the application window in question closer to the upper-left corner of the screen, and then switch back to the lower resolution. It may help to remember that your screen is always decreased or increased in size starting from the lower-right corner and moving up or down diagonally.

WHAT DOES THAT SAY?

I want to use an external TV monitor, but the output text is illegible.

Some video cards and laptops can be plugged into a TV monitor or regular TV that has video input. But displaying computer output on a TV monitor is problematic for a couple of reasons. For starters, some video display cards don't let you run the TV at anything higher than 640×480 resolution. Also, TV sets (as opposed to professional TV monitors) often *overscan*, pushing the edges of the image off the edge of the screen. The following are a few points to remember when you're using a TV or video projector; whether you're doing presentations, playing games, or giving your eyes a break by moving your focal plane back a bit:

- If your computer and TV have "S" (Super VHS) inputs, use them. They increase the clarity a bit. Don't expect miracles, though.
- Use Display Properties to switch to 640×480 resolution.

- Check to see whether your Display Properties dialog has buttons to center the image on the TV. It's most likely off center or needs resizing when you first try it. Some ATI drivers have advanced properties for fine-tuning TV display.

- Your application may have a "zoom" control for easily increasing the size of text onscreen, without the hassle of reformatting the entire document. MS Office tools such as Excel and Word, for example, have such a feature. Try bumping up the zoom size to increase legibility.

SINGLE- OR DOUBLE-CLICK?

I seem to accidentally run programs and open documents with a slip of the finger.

You probably have Single-Click selection turned on. As a result, one click (or tap, if you're using a touch pad) runs the program or opens the document that is highlighted. Change to Double-Click selection mode by opening a folder window, choosing Tools, Folder Options, and selecting Double Click to Open an Item.

UH-OH, MY MONITOR DIED

I changed my resolution or refresh rate, and now the screen is blank.

Normally, you shouldn't have this problem because Windows XP asks you to confirm that a screen resolution works properly and switches back to the previous resolution if you don't confirm. If somehow you changed color depth and resolution, and the system is stuck with a blank screen, you can reboot, press F8 during boot, and choose Safe Mode. Access the Device Manager on the Hardware tab of the System applet. The System applet is accessed either through the Control Panel or by opening the Properties dialog for My Computer. Select the video display, and reset the properties to what the computer was running at before the change. Be sure to reset both the screen resolution *and* the color depth. In the worst case scenario, start with 640×480 and 16 colors. After you've booted successfully, then right-click the desktop, choose Properties, click Settings, and increase the settings one step at a time. Don't change resolution *and* color depth at the same time, though. Increase one first and then the other.

MOVING IN SLOW MOTION

I increased the resolution, but now the screen updates slowly when I drag windows around.

Unless you're doing high-resolution photographic-quality work, you don't need the high-resolution 24-bit or 32-bit color depth settings. These settings just serve to slow down screen redraws when you move windows about. On the Settings tab of the Display Properties dialog, try dropping to 16-bit color or even 256 colors, and enjoy the speed increase.

BLURRY IMAGES IN LCD

I switched to an LCD screen, and the image is blurrier than I expected.

Unlike CRTs, LCDs do not benefit from higher refresh rates. Don't try to use anything above a 60Hz refresh rate for an LCD monitor. Also, check the LCD monitor's internal settings (check its manual) for a "phase adjustment" or focus adjustment to help clear up fuzziness on small text.

STRETCHED A BIT THIN

I set up a picture for my desktop wallpaper, but it looks blocky.

You're stretching a small bitmap. Either use a larger image, or turn off the Stretch setting for the image. See the Display Properties, Background, Picture Display option.

CHAPTER 24

CONFIGURATION VIA CONTROL PANEL APPLETS

In this chapter

SIZING UP THE CONTROL PANEL

As most experienced Windows users know, the Control Panel is the central location for making systemwide modifications to everything from accessibility options to user profiles. Microsoft has moved some features around in Windows XP from where you might expect them from your experience with Windows 2000, NT, 98, and so on. Most of these movements have resulted in new or expanded applets in the Control Panel. So, before throwing up your hands in frustration, check there (and Table 24.1 in the next section). The Help system also has a "Where is it now?" feature, which will help you locate seemingly vanished items.

Not all the settings the Control Panel handles are pivotal to effective or reliable operation of the system. In fact, many of the adjustments you can make from the Control Panel applets are interface improvements rather than related to system reliability and functionality. For example, the Display applet, among other things, can be used to make Windows a little easier to use or tolerate. Other applets are more imperative, such as applets for setting user rights, installing new hardware, or running system diagnostics.

The preference settings you make via the Control Panel applets are stored in the Registry. Some are systemwide, whereas others are made on a per-user basis and go into effect when you log in. Many Control Panel applets can be accessed through other utilities. For example, Printers and Faxes can be added to your Start menu, the Display applet can be accessed by right-clicking the desktop and clicking Properties, Folder Options can be accessed through the Tools menu of My Computer and Windows Explorer, and Internet Options can be accessed through Internet Explorer's Tools menu. Although the paths may be multifarious, the results are the same; you usually end up running a Control Panel extension (files with .CPL extensions) to do your bidding.

Keep in mind that you must have high-level permissions to modify many of the settings in the Control Panel. User-level settings such as display appearances are not a big deal. However, systemwide settings such as addition and removal of hardware are governed by the security monitor, and you must have the requisite permissions to successfully make modifications.

TIP FROM

Bob
& Brian

> As you learned in Chapter 4, "Using the Windows XP Interface," you can opt to "expand" the Control Panel, making the applets appear in a fly-out window (by choosing Start, Control Panel), thus allowing you to avoid opening the whole Control Panel as a window. Using this fly-out window is worthwhile if you use the Control Panel a lot. To make this your default setting, right-click the Start menu and select Properties. In the dialog box that appears, click Customize, select the Advanced Tab, and then select the Display As A Menu radio button under Control Panel in the list of Start menu items.
>
> If you use a particular applet a lot, you can drag it into the Start menu or the Quick Launch bar for even faster access.

Not all the Control Panel settings are discussed in detail in this chapter. Because a few of the Control Panel options pertain to other topics, such as networking or printing, or fall under the umbrella of system management, performance tweaking, or system applications, you'll find them in later chapters. Table 24.2, in the next section, lists each applet and where to look in this book for coverage of those not discussed here. Also, I won't bore you by covering each and every option in the dialog boxes. Many of the settings are intuitively obvious.

OPENING THE CONTROL PANEL

One of the most common ways to access the Control Panel is to click Start, Control Panel. But there are several other ways, such as using the Control Panel link in the Other Places quick access menu or, in Windows Explorer folder view, clicking on the Control Panel sub-element of My Computer. If you have opted to expand the Control Panel in your Start menu, you can still right-click over the Control Panel name and select Open from the pop-up menu to open the regular Control Panel window.

THE NEW CONTROL PANEL

No matter how you get there, the Control Panel in Windows XP is displayed by default in category view. Category view organizes the most commonly accessed functions of Control Panel applets into groups. In Windows XP, the Category view is the default method of navigating the Control Panel applets. If you are new to configuring a Windows OS, the Category view offers a natural language guide to finding the right location to make an intended change. Within each category is a list of tasks and related Control Panel icons. As you can see from Figure 24.1, this view is much different from the Control Panel that appeared in previous versions of Windows (which is now referred to as the Classic view).

Selecting a task or its icon in Category view takes you to another Control Panel screen containing either a more specific breakdown of tasks you can select or a screen where the configuration setting described by the selected task must be performed (see Figure 24.2).

If you need to make a change within the category but the task is not listed in the task list, you can open one of the offered Control Panel icons to open the applet and find the correct tab for your desired setting change.

BREAKING DOWN THE CATEGORY VIEW

There are nine categories in the category view. Tables 24.1 through 24.7 list the tasks for each category, the applet tab or application the task opens, and the page number in this chapter where that exact tab is discussed. Table 24.8 lists the Control Panel icons displayed within or related to a category.

NOTE

> The Add or Remove Programs category does not display a task list, instead it opens the Add or Remote Programs applet directly. The User Accounts category opens the multi-function task User Accounts utility. Please see Chapter 29, "Managing the Hard Disk," for a discussion of this tool.

Figure 24.1
The Control Panel in the default Category view (top), and in the Classic view (bottom).

Click to change to Classic view

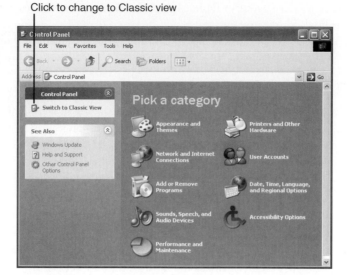

Click to change to Category view

TABLE 24.1   APPEARANCE AND THEMES CATEGORY VIEW

Task	Applet	Tab
Change the computer's theme	Display	Themes
Change the desktop background	Display	Desktop
Choose a screen saver	Display	Screen Saver
Change the screen resolution	Display	Settings

Figure 24.2
Clicking the Appearance and Themes category takes you to this screen.

More tasks from which to choose

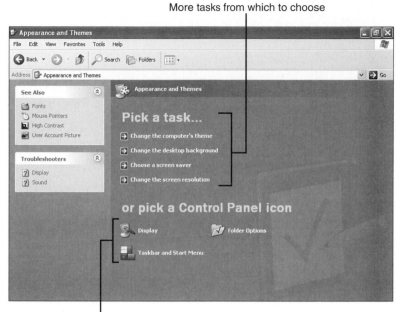

These icons open specific Control Panel applets

TABLE 24.2 NETWORK AND INTERNET CONNECTIONS CATEGORY VIEW

Task	Applet	Tab/Wizard
Setup or change your Internet Connection	Internet Options	Connection
Create a connection to the network at your workplace	Network Connections	New Connection
Set up or change your home or small office network	Network Connections	Network Setup

TABLE 24.3 SOUNDS, SPEECH, AND AUDIO DEVICES CATEGORY VIEW

Task	Applet	Tab
Adjust the system volume	Sounds and Audio Devices	Volume
Change the sound scheme	Sounds and Audio Devices	Sounds
Change the speaker settings	Sounds and Audio Devices	Volume

TABLE 24.4   PERFORMANCE AND MAINTENANCE CATEGORY VIEW

Task	Applet	Tab
See basic information about your computer	System	General
Adjust visual effects	Performance Options	Visual Effects
Free up space on your hard disk	Disk Cleanup	(application)
Back up your data	Backup or Restore Wizard	(application)
Rearrange items on your hard disk to make programs run faster.	Disk Defragmenter	(application)

TABLE 24.5   PRINTERS AND OTHER HARDWARE CATEGORY VIEW

Task	Applet	Wizard
View installed printers or fax printers	Printers and Faxes	(none)
Add a printer	Printers and Faxes	Add Printer

TABLE 24.6   DATE, TIME, LANGUAGE, AND REGIONAL OPTIONS CATEGORY VIEW

Task	Applet	Tab
Change the date and time	Date and Time	Date & Time
Change the format of numbers, dates, and times	Regional and Language Options	Regional Options
Add other languages	Regional and Language Options	Languages

TABLE 24.7   ACCESSIBILITY OPTIONS CATEGORY VIEW

Task	Applet	Tab
Adjust the contrast for text and colors on your screen	Accessibility Options	Display
Configure Windows to work for your vision, hearing, and mobility needs	Accessibility Options	(wizard)

TABLE 24.8   CONTROL PANEL ICONS WITHIN CATEGORIES

Category Wizard	Related Applets
Appearance and Themes	Taskbar and Start menu, Folder Options, Display
Network and Internet Connections	Network Connections, Internet Options
Add or Remove Programs	Add or Remove Programs
Sounds, Speech, and Audio Devices	Sounds and Audio Devices, Speech
Performance and Maintenance	Administrative Tools, Scheduled Tasks, Power Options, System
Printers and Other Hardware	Printers and Faxes, Scanners and Cameras, Game Controllers, Mouse, Keyboard, Phone and Modem Options
User Accounts	User Accounts
Date, Time, Language, and Regional Options	Regional and Language Options, Date and Time
Accessibility Options	Accessibility Options

As you can see, the category view offers an alternate route to the Control Panel applets and several other useful utilities. Windows XP defaults to category view, so it is important to be familiar with how to navigate through this new mechanism.

For those who prefer the old Control Panel display, Windows XP does offer a classic view where all of the applets are displayed as they were in previous versions of Windows (refer to Figure 24.1). To access the Classic view, click on the Switch to Classic View command in the Quick List to the left the categories within Control Panel. Then, to return to the category view, click on the Switch to Category View command in the Quick List.

As you can see, Windows XP often offers multiple means to access a control, setting, application, or display of information. Understanding by what means Windows XP provides these paths by default (such as with Category View of the Control Panel) and the alternates (such as the Classic View of the Control Panel or direct access through an object's Properties), will aid you in extracting the most productivity out of the OS as possible.

WHAT SHOULD YOU USE?

Working with the Control Panel in category view may simplify access to common configuration controls. However, not all of the controls for Windows XP can be accessed through category view (at least not directly). So, in order to provide an exhaustive discussion of the applets, this chapter focuses on reviewing each applet as listed in the Classic View. If you want to use the Category view, refer to the tables we just presented.

Table 24.9 shows a list of all the standard Control Panel applets and what they accomplish.

Your Control Panel may include other applets which are installed by other products from Microsoft and third parties. For example, in the Classic view portion of Figure 24.1 an additional applet of Tweak UI appears. This is not a native applet, but is added to the Control Panel when the Tweak UI program is installed (see Chapter 23 for more information on Tweak UI). Following the table, I'll cover each of the included applets (the ones not covered in other chapters) in alphabetical order.

TABLE 24.9 CONTROL PANEL APPLETS

Applet	Description
Accessibility Options	Sets keyboard, mouse, sound, display, and other options for increasing ease of use by those who are visually, aurally, or motor impaired.
Add Hardware	Installs or troubleshoots a wide variety of hardware devices such as sound, video, CD-ROM, hard and floppy disk controllers, SCSI controllers, display adapters, keyboard, mouse, and ports. Installation of printers is covered in Chapter 6, "Printing and Faxing."
Add or Remove Programs	Adds, removes, or modifies applications or Windows XP components from Microsoft or a third-party. It supports remote application installation over the LAN.
Administrative Tools	Provides shortcuts to the administrative tools—Component Services, Computer Management, ODBC settings, Event Viewer, Local Security Policy, Performance, and Services. Administrative Tools is covered in Chapter 27, "System Utilities." Component Services are not covered in this book.
Date and Time	Sets the current date, time, and time zone for the computer. It can also synchronize system time with an Internet time server.
Display	Sets colors of various parts of Windows display elements, as well as other display-related adjustments, such as desktop background, screen saver, display driver, screen color depth and resolution, refresh rate, energy-saving modes, and color schemes or themes. The Display applet is covered in detail in Chapter 23, "Tweaking the GUI."
Folder Options	Sets systemwide folder view options, file associations, and offline files. The Folder Options applet is covered in detail in Chapter 23.
Fonts	Adds and deletes typefaces, and displays examples of system-installed typefaces for screen display and printer output. Fonts are covered in Chapter 26, "Font Management."

24

TABLE 24.9   CONTINUED

Applet	Description
Game Controllers	Adds, removes, and configures game controller hardware, such as joysticks and gamepads.
Internet Options	Sets Internet Explorer options.
	Internet Options are covered in Chapter 9, "Browsing the World Wide Web with Internet Explorer."
Keyboard	Sets key repeat rate, cursor blink rate, language of your keyboard, keyboard type, and drivers, and includes keyboard troubleshooting wizards.
Mouse	Alters mouse properties such as motion speed, double-click, button orientation, cursor shapes, and other proprietary settings dependent on your mouse driver.
Network Connections	Manages all network connections, including LAN, dial-up WAN, and VPN. Networking components (clients, services, and protocols) are configured. These connections are covered throughout Part IV, "Networking."
Phone and Modem Options	Adds, removes, and sets the properties of the modem(s) connected to your system. Using this applet, you can declare dialing rules (long-distance numbers, call waiting, credit card calling, and so on). You also can add and remove telephony drivers.
	Installing and configuring a modem are covered in Chapter 8, "Internet and TCP/IP Connection Options." The other features of this applet are discussed here.
Power Options	Provides options for setting the Advanced Power Management (APM) and Advanced Configuration and Power Management (ACPM) functions. Using this applet, you can set timeouts for monitor, hard disk, system standby, and hibernation. The Power Options applet is covered in detail in Chapter 23.
Printers and Faxes	Adds, modifies, removes, and manages printer and fax devices. Using this applet, you can manage the print queue for each printer and enable direct faxing from applications.
	The Printers and Faxes applet is covered in Chapter 6.
Regional and Language Options	Sets how Windows displays times, dates, numbers, and currency through region/country settings and language preferences.
Scanners and Cameras	Adds, removes, sets properties for, and troubleshoots scanners and digital cameras.
Scheduled Tasks	Sets up automatic execution of applications, utilities, disk cleanup, and so on. Task scheduling is covered in Chapter 27.

24

continues

TABLE 24.9   CONTINUED

Applet	Description
Sound and Audio Devices	Assigns sounds to system events and manages sound devices.
Speech	Sets voice options for text-to-speech translation.
System	Examines and changes your identification (workgroup name, domain name, computer name), installed devices, amount of RAM, type of processor, and so on. Using this applet, you can add, disable, and remove specific devices using the Device Manager; set up hardware profiles; set up user profiles; optimize some parameters of system performance; set environment variables; and set emergency startup options.
	The use of the System applet is rather complex and thus is partially covered in this chapter and partially in Chapter 27.
Taskbar and Start Menu	Sets the properties for the taskbar and Start menu. This was covered in Chapters 4 and 23.
Users Accounts	Adds, deletes, or alters users. Using this applet, you can assign groups, manage passwords, and set logon mode.
	Passwords and security are covered in Chapter 28, "Managing Users."

TIP FROM

Bob & Brian

Windows NT 4 and 9x included a PCMCIA applet in the Control Panel. That applet was dropped in Windows 2000 and was not included in Windows XP. It didn't do much anyway, other than let you control whether PC cards beeped when installed and removed. If your system has PC card slot services installed, the system tray contains an icon for PC card control and for starting and stopping PC card devices. See Chapter 25, "Maintaining and Optimizing System Performance," for details.

NOTE

Many Control Panel dialog boxes have a question mark button in their upper-right corners. You can click this button and then click an item in the dialog box that you have a question about. Windows then shows some relevant explanation about the item.

In those dialog boxes where no question mark appears in the title bar, click F1 to open the Help system. The Help window will include information relevant to the applet in use.

ACCESSIBILITY OPTIONS

Microsoft has made a point of increasing computer accessibility for people who are physically challenged in one way or another. Over the last half decade, Microsoft has increasingly included accessibility options in its operating systems, with features that allow many handicapped people to use Windows without major machine or software modifications.

Many people have difficulty seeing characters on the screen, and others have trouble typing on the keyboard or controlling the mouse. People who are partially paralyzed or who have muscle-coordination problems have been at a disadvantage with computers for a long time. Now, with these accessibility options, the playing field is being leveled at least somewhat. Even if you are not disabled, some of the Accessibility options may prove useful for you.

Accessibility options are broken down into several categories, with their respective tabs: Keyboard, Sounds, Display, Mouse, and a few others on the General tab.

ACCESSIBILITY KEYBOARD SETTINGS

The keyboard settings deal with such problems as accidentally repeating keys or pressing combinations of keys. These options fall into three categories: *Sticky keys*, *Filter keys*, and *Toggle keys*.

Sticky keys are settings that, in effect, stay "down" when you press them once. They are good for controlling the function of the Alt, Ctrl, and Shift keys if you have trouble pressing two keys at the same time. To use them, set the Sticky keys option on; then choose the sub-options as you see fit. For some users, the shortcut of pressing the Shift key five times is a good way to activate Sticky keys. If you turn on this activation method, note that pressing the Shift key five times again turns off Sticky keys. This trick isn't explained clearly in the dialogs. Also, if you choose the Press Modifier Key Twice to Lock option, that means you press, for example, Shift twice to lock it. You can then press Shift twice again to unlock it.

Filter keys let you "filter" (remove) accidental repeated keystrokes in case you have trouble pressing a key cleanly once and letting it up. This feature prevents you from typing multiple keystrokes. The shortcut key for turning on this feature works like the one for Sticky keys; it's a toggle.

TIP FROM

Bob
& Brian

> Filter keys, when activated, can make it seem that your keyboard has ceased working unless you are very deliberate with keypresses. You have to press a key and keep it down for several seconds for the key to register. If you activate this setting and want to turn it off, the easiest solution is to use the mouse to run or switch to the Control Panel (via the taskbar), run the Accessibility Options applet, turn off Filter Keys, and click Apply or OK.

24

The Toggle keys option, when turned on, sounds a high-pitched tone when Caps Lock, Scroll Lock, and Num Lock keys are activated and a low-pitched tone when they're turned off again.

Each of these three keyboard features can be used independently or together. Note that a slowdown in performance occurs at the keyboard if sounds are used, because the sound is generated by playing a WAV file that briefly eats up your system resources. Processing of keypresses doesn't commence until after the keyboard sound finishes, which can result in jerky performance.

When Sticky keys or Filter keys are turned on, a symbol appears in the system tray. The Sticky keys feature is indicated by the three small boxes, representative of the Ctrl, Alt, and Shift keys. The Filter keys feature is represented by the stopwatch, which is representative of the different key timing that goes into effect when the option is enabled.

ACCESSIBILITY SOUND SETTINGS

The two Accessibility sound settings— Sound Sentry and ShowSounds—are for those with hearing impairments. Instead of playing a sound when an error message or other event that causes a sound occurs, some type of visual display appears onscreen.

With Sound Sentry, a portion of the normal Windows screen blinks, typically the window or application that is generating the error. With ShowSounds turned on, a text caption or special icon will pop up over a window or dialog box when a sound is played. The information in the pop-up window will inform you of the sound played and whether the audio clue as a warning, error, and so on.

If you choose Sound Sentry, you have a choice of the visual warning to use. The options are offered in a pull-down list which includes: Flash active caption bar, Flash active windows, and Flash desktop. Typically, you'll want the window of the application or at least its title bar to flash. Don't make the desktop flash because it won't indicate which program is producing the warning.

TIP FROM

Bob & Brian

> Some programs are finicky about the sound options, especially ShowSounds. If they're not programmed correctly, they don't display a sound. Think of it like closed captioning for TV. Not all shows have it.

ACCESSIBILITY DISPLAY SETTINGS

Special display settings in the Accessibility Options applet increase the screen contrast by altering the display scheme. Using this applet really is just an easy way to set the display color scheme and font selection for easier reading, just as you could do from the Display applet, as discussed in Chapter 23. The big plus of setting the contrast here is that you can quickly call it up with a shortcut key combination when you need it. Just press Left-Alt, Left-Shift, Prnt Scrn, and the settings go into effect. I have found this feature useful for when my eyes are tired or in imperfect lighting situations. Figure 24.3 shows the effect it had while I was writing this chapter.

Figure 24.3
The effect of turning on the default high-contrast setting.

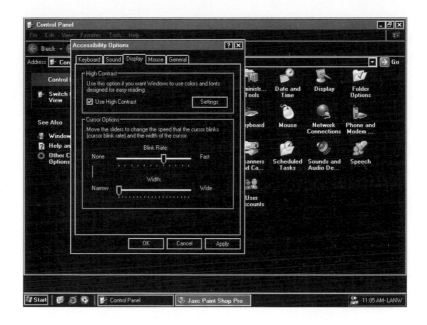

TIP FROM

You get to select which predefined color scheme (both Windows provided and ones you've created through the Display applet) will be used as the high contrast scheme. It's easier to observe the look of the schemes using the Display applet than in the Accessibility Options applet. Do it there, and then decide which one you like best. Then come back to the Accessibility dialog and make your choice.

ACCESSIBILITY MOUSE SETTINGS

Using the Mouse Settings tab, you can control the mouse with the keypad, in case you have problems controlling your mouse's movements. This feature can bail you out in case your mouse dies for some reason, too, or if you simply don't like using the mouse. As is covered in Chapter 4, you can execute many Windows and Windows application commands using the keyboard shortcut keys. But sometimes an application still responds only to mouse movements and clicks. Graphics programs are a case in point. When you use this Accessibility option, your arrow keys do double duty, acting like pointer control keys.

To use this option, simply turn on Mouse Keys from the dialog box, and apply the change. Then, to activate the keys, press Left-Alt, Left-Shift, and Num Lock at the same time. The system tray should show a new icon. If the icon has a red line through it, Mouse keys are disabled, so press the Num Lock key to enable them.

Now you can move the pointer around the screen using the arrow keys on the numeric number pad. If you're using a laptop, you'll have to consult its manual to determine how to activate the numeric keypad. The normal arrow keys won't cut it.

Click the Settings button if you need to adjust the speed settings for the arrow keys. Turn on the Ctrl and Shift options for speeding up or slowing down the mouse, assuming you can press two keys simultaneously. This setting really speeds things up.

If you adjust the configuration on the Settings dialog box, you have to click OK and then click Apply before the changes register. Then you can go back and adjust as necessary.

OTHER ACCESSIBILITY SETTINGS (GENERAL TAB)

The final Accessibility tab is General, which is divided into four sections, each of which is described in Table 24.10.

TABLE 24.10   OTHER ACCESSIBILITY SETTINGS

Setting	Description
Automatic Reset	If multiple people are using the same computer, it's a good idea to have the Accessibility features time out if they're not used for a while. If you turn off this option, the settings stay in operation until you manually turn them off, even surviving reboots.
Notification	This setting determines how you're alerted to a feature being turned on or off. By default, a little dialog box appears, but you can change it to a sound.
Serial Key Devices	You can opt to use special input devices designed for the disabled. Just connect such a device to a free serial port, and choose the port (COM1 through COM4) and baud rate.
Administrative Options	The first option applies your Accessibility settings (such as high contrast, and so on) to the *logon desktop*. The logon desktop is what you see when a user is logging on or when you press Ctrl+Alt+Del. It is a different desktop than the user desktop. If you choose this option, all users of the machine have the benefit (or annoyance) of seeing the settings when they are logging on.
	The second option, when activated, copies the current Accessibility settings for each new user an administrator adds to the computer.

ADD HARDWARE

The Add Hardware applet is used to install new devices as well as troubleshoot hardware-related problems. The ability to disable or remove a hardware devices has been relegated to the Device Manager (see the System applet later this chapter).

In general, Windows XP detects new hardware during bootup. If drivers are not located automatically (typically only for non-Plug-and-Play devices), you'll be prompted for a location to search (such as floppy, CD, or the Windows Update site). Once drivers are located, they are installed and the device is activated. In some cases, you'll be prompted to reboot the system for the new hardware to be fully functional. Sorry, even under Windows XP, hardware level device drivers often require a reboot. Think of it as changing a rung on the ladder you are climbing; it's always a good idea to step off of it while the repair is being made.

The Add Hardware applet is for use when the manufacturer does not supply an installation tool and when the installed device is not automatically detected during bootup. If you meet these criteria, you can use the Add Hardware applet to install the device drivers for your new equipment.

When you first launch the applet, it attempts to locate new hardware by performing a system scan for yet unidentified devices. If none are found, you'll be asked if the hardware has already been installed or is it still outside the computer (in other words, not installed). If you select that the hardware is not yet installed, the wizard informs you that you must install the hardware to continue with the installation. I always knew Microsoft could develop a sense of humor.

TIP FROM

Bob
& Brian

> The System applet is used to fine-tune device settings (such as IRQ and port) and updating devices and drivers. The Add Hardware applet is only for adding hardware. Also, note that there are other locations throughout Windows for installing some devices, such as printers—which can be installed from the Printers folder—or modems—which can be installed from Phone and Modem Options—even though the effect is the same as using this applet.

It is always a very good idea to read the manufacturer supplied manual for installation and operational procedures. If none were provided, check the vendor's Web site. If you still can't find any guides for installation, go ahead and try the Add Hardware applet.

It's always a good idea to save your work and stop any applications when performing driver installations or upgrades, or when making configuration changes to hardware. It is possible for a new driver to crash the system, but under Windows XP this is a rare occurrence.

For non-Plug and Play hardware or for Plug and Play stuff that, for some reason, isn't detected or doesn't install automatically, you need to run the applet. The typical scenario is as follows:

1. Launch the Add Hardware applet.
2. Click Next. A search is performed for new hardware.
3. If none are found, you are asked whether the hardware is already installed. If not, you'll be asked to install the hardware in order to proceed.
4. A list of installed hardware is presented. To install new equipment, scroll down and select Add a new hardware device. Otherwise, select an existing item to troubleshoot. Click Next.
5. If you elected to troubleshoot an existing item, you'll see a status report and a message stating that clicking Finish will launch the troubleshooter for this device.

6. If you selected the Add a new hardware device item, you'll be asked where the system should search again for the device, or you may manually select the device from a list.

7. There is only a slight chance that the second automated search will detect the new device. In most cases, you'll have to proceed with the manual method.

8. The manual installation method requests that you select a general type of hardware or the Show All Devices item. Click Next.

9. A list of manufacturers and device models is displayed. If your product is listed, select it, and then click Next. Otherwise, click the Have Disk button.

10. The Have Disk button opens a dialog box where you provide the path to the new device drivers.

11. From this point you'll need to follow the prompts as they appear, because each type of device has different requirements. Some need no additional settings while others require the defining of ports, IRQs, and so on. You may also be prompted to provide the Windows XP distribution CD, so keep it handy.

TIP FROM

Bob & Brian

In some cases, you are given the option of adjusting settings after the hardware is installed and possibly adjusting your hardware to match. (Some legacy cards have hardware settings [via dip switches or jumpers] or software adjustments that can be made to them to control the I/O port, DMA address, and so forth.) You may be told which settings to use in order to avoid conflicts with other hardware in the system.

If, for some reason, you don't want to use the settings the wizard suggests, you can manually set your own. You can do so using the Device Manager (from the System applet). See "System: Device Manager" later in this chapter for coverage of the Device Manager.

CAUTION

In general, be cautious about configuring resource settings manually. When you change settings manually, the settings become fixed, and Windows XP's built-in device contention resolution is less likely to work. Also, if you install too many devices with manually configured settings, you might not be able to install new Plug and Play devices because no more settings are available. In the worst-case scenario, the system might not even boot if conflicts occur with primary hardware devices such as hard disk controllers or video cards. If you decide to use manual configuration, make sure you know what you're doing, and have in hand the specs for the hardware in question.

In cases in which the wizard detects a conflict, you are alerted upon finishing the wizard. You then have the option of bailing or continuing despite the conflict. You could also back up and choose a different model of hardware, one you think is compatible with what you're attempting to install.

ADD OR REMOVE PROGRAMS

As you know, many programs come with their own installation (Setup) programs that handle all the details of installation, such as file copying, making Registry additions, making file associations, and adding items to the Start menus. An ever-growing number of applications even provide their own uninstall routine, which appears as a unique icon within their Start menu folder. You'll rarely add programs through the Add or Remove Programs applet. Most of what you'll use this applet for is to remove applications or portions thereof when a dedicated tool is not provided by the vendor.

CHANGE OR REMOVE PROGRAMS

You've probably noticed that not all programs show up in the Add or Remove Programs applet. They don't appear because only programs complying with the 32-bit Windows API standard for installation get their filenames and locations recorded in the system database, allowing them to be reliably erased without adversely affecting the operation of Windows. Many older or less-sophisticated applications simply install in their own way and don't bother registering with the operating system.

Most modern applications are written in compliance with the Microsoft Windows standards for installation and removal. Thus, you see them in your installed applications list in the Add or Remove Programs applet. This list is mainly the result of the PC software industry's response to kvetching from users and critics about tenacious programs that are hard to root out after they're installed. Some ambitious programs spread themselves out all over your hard disk like oil on your garage floor with no easy way of reversing the process. Users complained about the loss of precious disk space, unexplained system slowdowns, and so forth.

 If you need help removing a program because it doesn't show up in the Add or Remove Programs list, see "Program Doesn't Show Up" in the "Troubleshooting" section at the end of this chapter.

This problem was the inspiration for such programs as Uninstaller, CleanSweep, and other utilities that monitor and keep a database of the files a program installs; they wipe out these files effectively when you decide to remove the program, also returning any modified Windows settings to their previous state with any luck. This process is better relegated to those writing the operating system, I feel, and Microsoft rightly set up standards for installation and removal of applications, overseen by this applet. Even if an application isn't installed via the Add or Remove Programs applet per se, if well behaved, it should still make itself known to the operating system and register changes it makes, enabling you to make changes and/or uninstall it from there.

TIP FROM

Bob

& Brian

> Never attempt to remove an application from your system by deleting its files from the \Program Files folders (or wherever). Actually, never may be too strong. Removal through manual deletion should only be as a last resort. Always attempt to use the Add or Remove Programs applet or the uninstall utility from the application first. For tips on manually removing programs, see "Program Doesn't Show Up" under the "Troubleshooting" section at the end of this chapter.

24

What's more, the built-in uninstaller lets you make changes to applications, such as adding or removing suboptions (assuming the application supports that feature).

Use of the uninstall feature of the applet is simple:

1. Run the Add or Remove Programs applet from the Control Panel.

2. Check the list of installed applications. A typical list appears in Figure 24.4. Note that you can sort the applications by some interesting criteria in the sort box, such as frequency of use. (That one helps weed out stuff you almost never use.)

Figure 24.4
Choosing the program to uninstall or change.

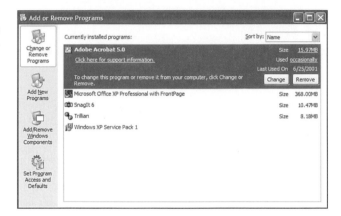

3. Select the program you want to change or uninstall.

4. Click the Change/Remove button.

5. Answer any warnings about removing an application as appropriate.

TIP FROM

Bob & Brian

> Obviously, removing an application can't easily be reversed by, say, restoring files from the Recycle Bin because settings from the Start menu and possibly the Registry are deleted.

Some applications (for example, Microsoft Office) prompt you to insert the program CD when you attempt to change or remove the app. These prompts can be annoying, but what can you do? The setup, change, and uninstall programs for some large suites are stored on their CDs, not on your hard disk. So, just insert the disc when prompted.

ADD NEW PROGRAMS

As you know, installation of new programs is usually as simple as inserting a CD into the drive. The autorun program on most application CDs does the rest. Or, when it doesn't, you can run the Setup file on the disk, and the rest is automatic. Ditto for programs you download off the Net. Still, you can install from the Add or Remove Programs applet if you want or if the program's instructions suggest it. This part of the applet provides a front end for running an application's Setup program. Big Whoop. But, what launching a setup through the applet does is gather uninstall data for applications that otherwise don't properly register with the OS for uninstallation. Here's what you do:

1. Click Add New Programs in the left panel of the opened Add or Remove Programs applet.

2. Choose the source:

   - CD or Floppy—Choose this option for CD, floppy, or hard disk folder. You have to browse through your hard disk to get to the right folder.

   - Windows Update—This option runs Internet Explorer, connects to the Microsoft site, and runs Windows Update just as though you had started that process from the Start menu. Don't choose this option unless you're trying to update your Windows installation.

3. The wizard is looking for any file named setup.exe or install. If it finds this file on the CD or floppy, just choose the desired file, and follow the instructions you see. If the setup program you're looking for isn't called setup.exe or install, then you have a little more work to do. Change the Files of Type drop-down list to Program Files or All Files, and poke around a bit more. But make sure you choose a file that's actually a setup file. If you point to a regular old application, it will just run normally. Nothing weird will happen; you just won't be installing anything.

4. Click Finish to complete the task and make the new software's installation or setup procedure run. Instructions vary depending on the program. If your program's setup routine isn't compatible with the applet, you are advised of this fact. After installation, the new program appears in the list of removable programs only if it's compatible with Windows XP's install/remove scheme.

INSTALLING PROGRAMS FROM THE NETWORK

As you learned in Chapter 1, "Introducing Windows XP Professional," an administrator of a Windows 2000 or Windows 2003 Server domain can "publish" or "push" applications to workstations. When an application is published over the LAN, it usually is automatic. In other words, the software is installed without the knowledge of the user or the necessity for user input. However, some applications can be marked as optional instead of mandatory. An optional application can be installed over the network from Add New Programs.

When you choose Add New Programs, you have another option, showing applications that are available on the network.

Push Technology Meets the LAN

You might have heard the term *push* used in relation to the Web over the past couple of years. But how does this technology apply to the LAN and to applications? The idea of push is that it's a bit like television or radio. You turn on your TV, and there's the show. You don't have to do anything except choose the channel. Push technology on the Web works the same way. When you're connected, information is sent to your computer on a regular basis—for example, displaying stock prices in a ticker window on your desktop.

The push I'm talking about here with the LAN works much the same way, except that instead of being sent a Web page or stock ticker, you're sent an entire application that gets installed automatically on your computer, according to your system administrator's wishes.

Next, open the box called Category, which you use to narrow down the class of application you want to install. (The system administrator makes up the categories.) When you select such an application for installation, note that the administrator who set it up for publishing may have turned off the possibility for you to make installation choices such as which portions, add-ins, or other options to install.

The capability for a server system to push applications to clients is part of IntelliMirror. For more information on IntelliMirror and pushing applications to client systems, please consult the Windows XP Resource Kit and documentation on Windows 2000 Server or Windows 2003 Server.

24

NOTE

> In the case of "pushed" (or *assigned*) applications, when you log on to the machine or network, the applications assigned to you are added to your machine across the network automatically. In fact, if you accidentally or intentionally delete the application from your computer, it reinstalls itself.

ADD/REMOVE WINDOWS COMPONENTS

In addition to managing add-on products and applications through the Add or Remove Programs applet, the components of Windows XP itself are installed and removed here. Clicking the Add/Remove Windows Components button opens the Windows Components Wizard dialog box (Figure 24.5). From here, you can install additional Windows XP components by marking their check boxes. Plus, you can remove existing components by clearing their check boxes. However, be careful since there are often many sub-levels of selections. Click on the name of an item, not its check box, and then click the Details button to view its sub-components. Marking or clearing a top-level item will install or remove all of its subcomponents.

Figure 24.5
The Windows
Components Wizard
dialog box.

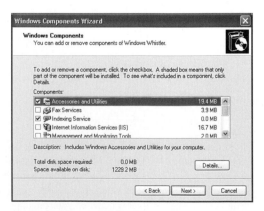

After you've made your selections and clicked Next, the system will install or remove components based on your instructions. You may be prompted for the Windows XP distribution CD, so be prepared.

SET PROGRAM ACCESS AND DEFAULTS

This new feature in Windows XP, added with Service Pack 1, enables you to choose your own default middleware applications. For more on how to do this, see the section "Department of Justice Consent Decree Compliance" in Appendix B.

DATE AND TIME

Date and Time is a simple applet you're sure to have used in the past to adjust the system date and time. That is, it adjusts the hardware clock in the computer, which is maintained by a battery on the motherboard. The system date and time are used for myriad purposes, including date- and time-stamping the files you create and modify, stamping e-mail, controlling the scheduler program for automatic application running, and so on.

24

NOTE

> The Date and Time applet doesn't change the format of the date and time, only the actual date and time stored on your computer's clock. To change formats, see the description of the Regional applet later in this chapter.

When you're a member of a Microsoft network domain, you should never need to set the clock. It is kept synchronized to the domain controller (a Windows 2000, Windows NT, or Windows 2003 Server). Many network services, including authentication protocols and replication, require exact or close synchronization of all systems within the network.

If your system is part of a workgroup or just a standalone, you can sync your clocks with an Internet time server. The Date and Time applet includes a new third tab for doing just that. However, this capability is not available on domain clients. The ability to sync with an Internet time server through the Date and Time applet is reserved for workgroup members, standalone systems, and domain controllers.

The Date and Time applet can also be accessed by double-clicking on the clock on the taskbar or right-clicking over the clock and selecting Adjust Date/Time. To set the date and time, follow these steps:

1. Run the Date/Time applet.
2. Alter the time and date by typing in the corrections or by clicking the arrows. The trick is to click directly on the hours, minutes, seconds, or AM/PM area first, then use the little arrows to the right of them to set the correct value. So, to adjust the a.m. or p.m., click AM or PM, and then click the little up or down arrow. After setting the month and year, you can click the day in the displayed calendar.

3. Click the Time Zone tab to adjust the zone. Why? It's good practice to have your time zone set correctly for programs such as client managers, faxing programs, time synchronizing programs, or phone dialing programs. They may need to figure out where you are in relation to others and what the time differential is. Also, if you want your computer's clock to be adjusted automatically when daylight saving time changes, make sure the Automatically Adjust Clock for Daylight Saving Changes check box is selected.

4. Click the Internet Time tab. On this tab you can enable clock synchronization with an Internet time server. Two known time servers are provided in the pull-down list, but you can type in others. If you want to force a sync, click the Update Now button.

5. Click OK to save changes and close the applet.

When Internet synchronization is enabled, your clock is reset to match the time servers once each week. Internet synchronization should only be configured on systems with an active Internet connection. Clock synchronization will not initiate a dial-up connection. Plus, if there is a firewall or proxy server between your client and the Internet, the clock synchronization packets may be blocked.

TIP

> You can also adjust the time and date using the TIME and DATE commands from a DOS command prompt. For example, open a DOS box (click Start, All Programs, Accessories, Command Prompt), type **time**, and press Enter. This command displays the current time and a prompt to enter the new time, as shown here:
>
> ```
> The current time is: 21:39:31.78
> Enter the new time:
> ```
>
> Enter the new time or press Enter to leave the time as it is. The same process applies to the date. Type **date** and press Enter. The current date is displayed with a prompt to enter the new date, as shown here:
>
> ```
> The current date is: Thu 11/04/2001
> Enter the new date: (mm-dd-yy)
> ```

GAME CONTROLLERS

If you're serious about playing games on your computer, you need a game controller (and often more than one); that means something more than a mouse. Typical controllers include joysticks, flightsticks, gamepads, driving wheels, and other hardware devices designed specifically for the games of your choice. If you're an extreme gamer, the type of controller you need can vary greatly with the types of games you play. High-tech gaming these days requires high-tech controls. Game controllers have reached the point at which serious flight simulator enthusiasts hook up a flightstick, throttle, and separate rudder foot pedals to more accurately simulate the flying experience. Sports gamers usually go for handheld digital gamepads for fast response times. And fans of racing games just aren't getting the full experience without a force feedback steering wheel with its own set of foot pedals for the gas and break (and possibly even a clutch).

This book doesn't cover gaming to any extent, but if you are a gamer, and you buy a game controller, it likely comes with an installation program. If not, Windows XP may detect it automatically or you may need to run the Add Hardware applet. If that doesn't seem to work, you can try adding it through the Game Controllers applet. In most cases, USB devices have no-brainer installations. Just plug it in and you are good to go.

For the last several years, heavy gamers have opted for Windows 95 and 98 as their platforms because of their more extensive support for games. The kinds of direct hardware access and the display driver optimizations that games expect have traditionally been unsupported on the NT platform. The DirectX support on Windows 9x has been superior in this regard.

With Windows 2000, the NT platform began to change this legacy. As a result, options such as game controller settings in the Control Panel have appeared. There has been some migration to the Windows 2000 platform for gaming, but Windows XP is even more gamer friendly and promises a solid following.

Windows XP supports DirectX 8.0, including accelerated video card and sound card drivers that provide better playback for different types of games, full-color graphics and video, and 3D animation. DirectX automatically determines the hardware capabilities of your computer and then sets your programs' parameters to match. This allows multimedia applications to run on any Windows-based computer and at the same time ensures that the multimedia applications take full advantage of high-performance hardware.

Low-level functions of DirectX 8.0 are supported by the components that make up the DirectX Foundation layer—namely the following:

- DirectDraw
- Direct3D
- DirectSound
- DirectMusic
- DirectInput
- DirectPlay
- DirectShow

Of particular interest to gamers are DirectDraw (which provides extremely fast, direct access to the accelerated hardware capabilities of a computer's video adapter), DirectInput (for quick processing of game controller input), Direct3D (which supports advanced, real-time, three-dimensional graphics), and DirectPlay (which supports game connections over a modem, the Internet, or a LAN).

TIP FROM

Bob & Brian

When you upgrade to Windows XP, the system doesn't always automatically set up previously installed game devices. You need to manually add your devices through the Control Panel.

24

NOTE

> If you want to optimize your computer for gaming or want to build one from the ground up, I suggest you pick up a copy of *The AnandTech Guide to PC Gaming Hardware*, published by Que. This book will walk you through the building, configuring, and optimizing of a high-powered gaming PC that can squeeze every drop of performance from Windows, DirectX, and DirectSound.

After you install a game controller, you can click the Advanced button if you need to alter the controller ID and/or the port to which it's connected. Each game controller should be assigned a different ID. You can share the same game port for a number of controllers by disconnecting one and connecting another. You might be prompted to remove a game controller from the list before a new one can be connected, however, depending on the kind of controller and the port to which it's connected.

- For a custom controller (one not listed in the Add list), click Add, and then click Custom. Fill in the settings for controller type, axes, and number of buttons; then give the controller a name.

- To choose from a list of brand-name controllers, click Add Other, and choose a manufacturer and model. (Some of the devices that show up in this list aren't game controllers, but many are.) If you have a disk for your game port or game controllers, click Have Disk, insert the diskette if necessary, or browse to the appropriate folder location.

KEYBOARD

The Keyboard applet (see Figure 24.6) lets you fine-tune the way the keyboard behaves, check the keyboard driver, and perform some keyboard troubleshooting. The Input Locales tab has been removed from this applet; to change your language settings, you must use the Regional and Language Options applet (later in this chapter.)

Figure 24.6
Adjusting key-repeat speed and delay can be useful for avoiding unwanted characters.

The main attractions here are the repeat rate, the repeat delay, and the cursor blink rate. By altering the key-repeat delay (the time after pressing a key before it starts to repeat) and the repeat speed, you can calm down an ill-behaved keyboard or improve usability for someone with a mobility impairment. Altering the delay before the repeat sets in might be helpful if you use applications that require extensive use of, say, the PgUp and PgDn, Enter, or the arrow keys (perhaps in a point-of-sale situation).

You also might want to change the cursor blink rate if the standard blinking cursor annoys you for some reason. You can even stop it altogether (the setting is "none"). I prefer a non-blinking one myself.

The defaults for these keyboard settings are adequate for most users and keyboards.

MOUSE

With each passing year, it seems that the mouse, trackpad, roller, graphics tablet, or pointing stick has become more and more the means through which users interact with the computer. I remember when the mouse was an option. Nowadays, you can barely shut down a computer without a mouse, much less use it effectively.

Obviously, then, the mouse being a major means of interface with your computer, it behooves you to optimize its functioning. The Control Panel's Mouse applet (located under the Printers and Other Hardware option in the Control Panel) lets you do just that, with many aspects of your mouse's operation being adjustable (see Figure 24.7):

- Left/right button reversal
- Double-click speed
- ClickLock
- Look of the pointers
- Pointer scheme
- Pointer speed
- Enhance pointer precision
- Snap to the default button of dialog boxes
- Display pointer trails and length
- Hide pointer while typing
- Show location of pointer when Ctrl is pressed
- Set wheel scroll to number of lines or screen at a time
- Troubleshooting
- Access device properties (same controls as through Device Manager)

The options vary based on pointing device type, and sometimes you are supplied with even fancier options if your pointing device comes with a custom driver. For example, the Synaptics touchpads let you scroll a window by sliding your finger down the right side of the trackpad.

24

Figure 24.7
Setting mouse properties can help you get your work done more efficiently, though the defaults usually work fine without modification.

Poor lefties never get a fair shake in life, what with all the right-handed scissors and tools around. Well, they get one here (except for some types of weird, ergonomically shaped mouse devices that don't work well in the left hand). If you're left handed, you can move the mouse to the left side of the keyboard and then reverse the function of the buttons on the Buttons tab of the Mouse applet. Right-clicks then become left-clicks. Of course, DOS programs don't know squat about this mouse setting, but for Windows and Windows programs, the button reverse will work.

On the same tab, you can set the double-click speed. A middle-range setting is appropriate for most folks. Double-click the folder icon to try out the new double-click speed. The folder opens or closes if the double-click registered. If you're not faring well, try adjusting the slider, and then try again. You don't have to click Apply to test the slider settings. Just moving the slider instantly affects the mouse's double-click speed.

If all else fails and you just can't find a double-click speed to suit your needs or abilities, forget double-clicks altogether. Instead, click on an icon or any selectable object in the Windows XP environment. A single click usually will highlight the option. Think of this as getting the object's attention. Then, press Enter on the keyboard to launch, open, or execute the selected object.

As you know, the pointer cursor changes based on the task at hand. For example, when you're editing text, it becomes an I-beam. You can customize your cursors for the fun of it or to increase visibility. You can even install animated cursors to amuse yourself while you wait for some process to complete. Just as with icons and screen savers, the Web is littered with Windows cursors, in case you would like to collect a few thousand. Windows XP comes with enough to keep me happy, organized into schemes. You can change individual cursors or change a set of them in one fell swoop by using the *cursor schemes.*

Like color schemes and sound schemes, cursor schemes are collections of cursor shapes. When you select a scheme, all the cursors in the scheme go into effect at once. You can choose from about 20 canned schemes.

NOTE

Use one of the Extra Large cursor schemes if you have trouble seeing the pointer. Also, some of the schemes change the pointer into things that don't resemble pointers and can make selecting or clicking small objects difficult because the pointer's hotspot is difficult to locate. Sometimes the cursor is very distracting and can obscure the very item you want to select or click.

You can change individual cursors in a scheme, if you like. To change a cursor assignment, click a cursor in the list. Then click Browse. The default location is . . . \windows\cursors. Animated cursors move for you in the Browse box (a thoughtful feature). After you custom tailor a set of cursors to your liking, you can save the scheme for later recall. Click Save As, and name it.

TIP FROM

Bob
& Brian

In the olden days of Windows, if you used DOS programs that required the mouse, they required DOS mouse drivers. If the DOS mouse driver and the Windows mouse driver's speed settings were different, using the mouse could be annoying because your body would learn hand-eye coordination with one environment that didn't match the other. Some DOS mouse drivers let you adjust the speed in that environment, so you could match the two. In Windows XP, DOS-environment mouse support is provided by Windows. As my co-author Brian says, DOS support under Windows XP is one of the marvels of the modern world because it is so well thought out and extensive.

If you're frustrated because the mouse pointer still appears on the screen while you're in DOS, see "Using DOS Programs with a Mouse" in the "Troubleshooting" section at the end of the chapter.

TIP FROM

Bob
& Brian

If you use an external serial mouse on your laptop, it might not wake up after your laptop goes into a suspended state. For example, if you close the lid to a laptop running Windows XP, it will probably go into Standby or Hibernate, depending on your laptop and Windows settings. When you wake it up, your external mouse might not wake up along with it because the mouse driver may not know to reinitialize the mouse. Here's a way around that problem, short of rebooting: Choose Control Panel, System, Hardware, Device Manager. Next, click Computer. Then choose Action, Scan for Hardware Changes to do a search for new hardware. Because the mouse was not initialized, it fell off the list of current hardware. Doing the scan finds it and reinitializes it. The mouse should now work.

PHONE AND MODEM OPTIONS

The Phone and Modem Options applet lets you add, remove, and set the properties of the modems connected to your system. You can also declare dialing rules (long-distance numbers, call waiting, credit card calls, and so on), and add and remove telephony drivers.

If you can't get your modem to connect, see "Cannot Connect" in the "Troubleshooting" section at the end of this chapter.

The Windows Telephony Interface

Windows XP has a *telephony* interface, essentially an API that provides the means (hooks) for communications applications to work through the operating system. In fact, this interface is called TAPI. Through TAPI, the operating system provides a standard way for communications applications to access COM ports and devices such as modems and telephone sets when handling data, fax, and voice transmissions.

TAPI empowers applications to make, answer, and hang up calls; put calls on hold; perform call transfer; record voice mail; and make conference calls. Fully TAPI-compliant applications should be able to work with conventional telephone lines, PBX and Centrex systems, and with specialized services such as cellular, ISDN, and DSL.

Much like the way process contention is handled by TCP/IP for network transmission or by the process scheduler for CPU usage, TAPI allows multiple communications to request the same resources, without a data collision occurring. The advantage to the end user is that you don't have to shut down a program that's waiting for incoming calls before you use a different program to send a fax, for example. Nor do you have to keep entering modem, phone number, dialing options, and COM port settings into each new communications program installed. These settings, just like printer settings, are stored in the system and are available for every communications program, such as HyperTerminal or dial-up connections through Network Connections.

The Phone and Modems applet in the Control Panel offers a central location for altering some TAPI settings, as well as for installing and configuring modems and telephone devices. Installing and configuring a modem were covered in Chapter 8, "Internet and TCP/IP Connection Options," so I'll dispense with the basics of modem installation here. Refer to that chapter if you're hooking up a new modem.

TIP FROM

Bob & Brian

You can use cell phones for data communications, for example, from a laptop in the field. Remember two points, though. The phone must be set to run in analog mode. Also, in the best of circumstances, you will get only 9600bps throughput because of limitations in the cellular transmission channel.

To set up cellular communications, you need a modem that is compatible with the cell phone you have and a cable designed specifically for connecting your model of phone to that modem. I use a standard Motorola "flip phone" with a Megahertz cellular-ready modem. With this combo, not much fiddling is required, but I made sure *before* I purchased the modem that it would work with my make and model phone.

As for settings, I did drop down the transfer rate to 9600 baud, and because my phone is analog/digital, I have to force it into analog mode for each call. This extra step is a bit of an annoyance, but I'll survive. Then I connect the cell phone to the modem, power up the phone, and initiate the dialing sequence. With any luck, I get on the Internet. Don't forget the per-minute cost of cellular connections! The charges can add up. If you do a lot of on-the-road connecting, check out one of the wireless connection options such as Ricochet's or Hughes's service, which are typically offered at a reasonable flat rate for a full 24×7 connection.

TIP FROM

Bob & Brian

> Windows XP supports *modem aggregation*, which is also called *PPP multilink dialing*. It essentially allows you to group modems together to increase the connection bandwidth. This process is a little tricky and requires multiple phone lines and multiple ISP accounts to work, as well as an ISP that supports synchronization of multiple modems.

In general, your default TAPI and modem properties will probably work fine and won't need to be changed. If you do need to change them, remember that changes affect all applications that use the modem whose properties you modify. To change the modem properties after installation is complete, open the Control Panel, and double-click the Phone and Modem Options icon.

DIALING RULES

On the Dialing Rules tab of the Phone and Modem Options dialog, you can set up your dialing locations and rules pertaining to those locations, such as phone number prefixes for outside lines, calling card access codes, and so on. If you move around (road-warrior style), you can add some new locations to the default one that's already set up for you as the current user.

You can either edit or add a dialing location from this tab. Table 24.11 describes the settings.

TABLE 24.11   SETTING DIALING RULES FOR EACH LOCATION

Option	Description
Location Name	This field specifies the name of each configuration set. To create a new configuration, use the New button and type a name in the Create New Location dialog box.
Country/Region	This field contains a drop-down menu that lists the international dialing codes for most countries of the world. Choose the name of the country from which you will be originating calls. The United States, Canada, and many Caribbean countries all use the same Country Code.
Area Code	Type your own area code in this field.
To Access an Outside Line for Local Calls	If your modem line is in an office where you must dial 9 for an outside line or some other code for long distance, type that number here. If you have a direct outside line, leave this field blank.
To Access an Outside Line for Long-Distance Calls	If you have to dial 9 or 8 for long-distance calls, enter that number. Remember that you need to use this field only when your modem is connected to a PBX or other telephone system that uses a special code for toll calls. Do *not* use this field for the 1 prefix that you dial before making long-distance calls. The dialer adds that code automatically.

continues

TABLE 24.11   SETTING DIALING RULES FOR EACH LOCATION

Option	Description
Use this carrier code to make long-distance calls	If you use one of the long distance services which require a carrier code to be dialed, such as 10-10-811 or 10-10-220, use this field to provide it. The dialer adds that code automatically.
Use this carrier code to make international calls	If you use one of the international calling services which require a carrier code, use this field to provide it. The dialer adds that code automatically.
To Disable Call Waiting, Dial	If your phone service has call waiting, it can be a nuisance and cause your data connection to fail when a phone call comes in while you're online. Most call waiting services let you turn off the service for the duration of the current call by entering *70, 70#, or 1170 before making the call. If you have call waiting, you should turn on this option and enter the code your phone company tells you, or choose the correct code. Often your local telephone directory has the necessary code listed. The comma after the code causes a 1- or 2-second pause after dialing the special code, often necessary before dialing the actual phone number.
Tone or Pulse Dialing	Most pushbutton telephones use tone dialing (known in the United States as TouchTone dialing). However, older dial telephones and some cheap pushbutton phones use pulse signaling instead. Chances are good that your telephone circuit will accept tone dialing even if a dial telephone is connected to it. Try it if in doubt. Change to pulse if it doesn't make a connection.

AREA CODE RULES TAB

On the Area Code Rules tab, you can set details about the use of an area code, specifically the use of the 1 prefix for certain exchanges. If you have to dial 1 (but no area code) for certain areas, you can add those prefixes here.

Click New to create a new rule, and fill in the resulting dialog box.

CALLING CARD TAB

You might not need to worry about calling cards at all if you travel using an ISP that has many points of presence. The larger ISPs such as Mindspring, CompuServe, and AOL have local dial-up numbers from most major cities. Some also have 800 numbers that you can use when connecting phones from remote locations. If you need to bill your connection to a telephone company (or long-distance service) calling card, though, you set those options on the Calling Card tab.

TIP FROM

Bob

& Brian

If you use more than one calling card, you can create a different location for each one. Telephony programs, such as Phone Dialer or the Send Fax Wizard, normally let you change the location before dialing.

As you probably know from using a calling card for voice calls, to place and charge a call with a calling card, you dial a special string of numbers that includes a carrier access code, your account number, and the number you're calling. In some cases, you have to call a service provider, enter your account number, and wait for a second dial tone before you can actually enter the number you want to call.

To assign a calling card, follow these steps:

1. Click the location you are assigning it to on the Dialing Rules tab of the Phone and Modem Options dialog.
2. Click Edit.
3. Fill in the general information and any area code rules.
4. Click the Calling Card tab.
5. Choose the card type you have. If it's not listed, click New and fill in the resulting dialog box, using the ? (question mark) button for assistance. If your service is one of the presets, all the necessary settings, such as pauses and dialing codes, are made for you.
6. Enter your Account Number and Personal ID Number (PIN) if necessary. Not all calling card options require them, so these options may be grayed out.

SETTING OR EDITING CALLING CARD SCRIPTS

If you get into editing the calling card rules for a location, you're in pretty deep. There's not enough room here to walk you through a description of every setting and how the dialog box works, but I can give you a few tips. For more details, consult the Windows XP Resource Kit.

Basically, you can set up and edit a sequence of events, like a script, in the Edit Calling Card dialog. You can not only change the sequence of events, but you can also enter any specific numbers or other codes. When you make the call, the events progress from the top of the box to the bottom. You can set up a script for each kind of call: local, long distance, and international.

You can use the Edit Calling Card dialog box when you have to fine-tune a calling card's dialing script. Do so only if the presets for your calling card service don't already work. The six buttons below the steps list insert new steps into the script.

24

Some services require you to wait for a "bing" tone before continuing with the dialing. If the tone your carrier plays isn't detected by your modem, try experimenting with different pause lengths instead. You typically are allowed a few seconds to enter the remainder of the sequence, so the pause amount may not be critical as long as you have waited for the bing.

If a connection isn't working, and you're fine-tuning these events, it sometimes helps to lift the receiver of a phone on the same line and listen (or turn on the modem's speaker), monitoring the sounds. You'll be better able to figure out where a sequence is bombing out.

SETTING MODEM PROPERTIES

So much for dialing rules. The second tab in the Phone and Modem Options dialog—Modems—is for setting modem properties. Accessing a modem's properties opens the same dialog box as when accessing a device's properties through the Device Manager. Typically, you don't need to change your modem properties, so unless you're having difficulty, remember this old adage: If it ain't broke, don't fix it.

To alter a modem's properties, follow these steps:

1. Click the Modems tab.
2. Choose the modem.
3. Click Properties.

TIP FROM

Bob

& Brian

Notice that you can add and remove modems from this Properties dialog box, too, although you can do so just as easily from the Add Hardware applet.

You can dig pretty deeply into the tabs on a modem's Properties dialog box, especially the Advanced one. As per usual Microsoft strategy on its communications stuff, if you're used to pre-Windows XP dialogs, you'll find things have shifted around, and you'll have to do a little hunting. Table 24.12 lists a few notes about some of the more salient settings.

TABLE 24.12   MODEM PROPERTIES SETTINGS

Setting	Description
Port	You can use the drop-down Port menu to specify the COM port to which your modem is connected. If you don't have a drop-down list box, you don't have a choice of ports.
Speaker Volume	The Speaker Volume control is a slide setting that sets the loudness of the speaker inside your modem. In some cases, you will have only Off and On as options rather than a variable speaker volume.

TABLE 24.12 CONTINUED

Setting	Description
Maximum Port Speed	When your modem makes a connection, it tries to use the maximum speed to exchange data with the modem at the other end of the link. As a rule, if you have a 38400bps or faster modem, the maximum speed should be three or four time the rated modem speed (for example, set your modem speed to 115200) to take advantage of the modem's built-in data compression. Note that the Advanced settings' Port Speed setting interacts with this one.
Dial Control	You can choose whether the dialer should wait to detect a dial tone before proceeding.
Extra Initialization Commands	The Extra Settings section is a place to send additional AT commands to your modem. In most cases, you don't need to add any special commands. Because different modem manufacturers use slightly different command sets, you'll have to consult your modem manual for specific commands.
Data Protocol	If you're using a cellular phone with the modem, choose Cellular Protocol in the default settings page's Data Protocol drop-down list. Cell phones use special data error compression and correction protocols to increase connection speed. The modem still works with this setting turned off, but the connection may improve if it's turned on. Don't use Cellular Protocol if your cell phone service doesn't support it.
Change Default Preferences	The Data bits, Parity, and Stop bits settings must be the same at both ends of a data link. The most common settings are 8 data bits, no parity, and one stop bit. These are set on the Advanced tab of the Default Preferences dialog box. On the General tab of this dialog box, call preferences options control when idle calls are disconnected and how long to attempt a connection before canceling. Also on this tab are settings for port speed, data/protocol, compression, and flow control—consult the modem's manual for specifics on these settings.
Advanced Port Settings	Clicking this button brings up the Advanced Port Settings dialog box. These settings determine how incoming and outgoing data is buffered by the COM port UARTS. Leave them alone unless you have information from your ISP or modem manufacturer, or you suspect that dropping them will help with connection success. Before you change these settings, drop the maximum port speed, which controls the data transmission speed between the modem and the port. If you do experiment with them, and your throughput drops significantly, return to this screen, and click Defaults to set the sliders and check box back to the original suggested settings.

24

continues

TABLE 24.12   CONTINUED

Setting	Description
Distinctive Ring	A tab for this option appears only if your modem supports the feature. "Distinctive ring" is a service from your phone company that provides different ring patterns for different kinds of incoming calls. Depending on the kind of modem you have, you can have between three and six numbers, or addresses, for one telephone line. Each number can have a distinctive ring pattern. You can also assign each ring pattern to a specific type of program. For exam- ple, if you have two rings assigned for fax calls, any call received with that ring pattern could be automatically sent to your fax program. Some phone companies have distinctive ring patterns based on the duration of the ring rather than the number of rings. Some modems support this scenario. In general, you should choose the desired number of rings for each kind of incoming call based on settings you get from your phone company. Then check your modem's manual for details on using this feature. You'll have to enable the distinctive ring feature first by clicking the check box before you can alter the ring settings.

DIAGNOSTIC PROPERTIES

You can click the Diagnostics tab in the original Modem Properties dialog box to make it active. The Diagnostics tab asks the modem to identify itself. It can further test the modem's capability to respond to the standard AT command set, display the contents of its internal registers, and display its settings. Click Query Modem to make it so. The results of the diagnostics query will make sense only if you compare them to the expected results in the modem's manual. If things don't look square, you should look for troubleshooting information in the manual or contact the vendor for modem-specific repair options.

REGIONAL AND LANGUAGE OPTIONS

The Regional and Language Options settings affect the way Windows displays times, dates, numbers, and currency. When you install Windows, chances are good that the Regional settings are already set for your locale. This will certainly be true if you purchase a computer with Windows XP preinstalled on it, from a vender in your country or area.

Running this applet from the Control Panel displays the dialog box you see in Figure 24.8.

To change the settings, simply click the appropriate tab, and then click the drop-down list box for the setting in question. Examples of the current settings are shown in each section, so you don't need to change them unless they look wrong. The predefined standards are organized by language, then by country. If you can't find a standard to your liking, you can always create a customized format.

Figure 24.8
Making changes to the Regional settings affects the display of date, time, and currency in Windows applications that use the internal Windows settings for such functions.

Scanners and Cameras

Using the Scanners and Cameras applet, you can add, remove, set properties for, and troubleshoot your connection to scanners and digital cameras. As scanners and digital cameras become as omnipresent as the trusty printer, provisions are being made to assist in the transfer of documents and images from them into the computer. Especially with the advent of the digital still camera, many new convenient methods for facilitating the transfer of captured images are being made available. This is a must if the digital camera is to become as prevalent as the standard film camera.

The Scanners and Cameras applet is used to install scanners, digital still cameras, digital video cameras, and image-capturing devices.

After a device is installed, Scanners and Cameras can link it to a program on your computer. For example, when you press Scan on your scanner, you can have the scanned picture automatically open in the program you want.

With some cameras and scanners, you can create linked events that execute when you do something on the camera or the scanner. Typically, this means pressing a button on the scanner or camera.

In the best of all worlds, detection of your scanner or camera will occur automatically as Windows Plug and Play detection notices the device. But as you know, sometimes running the Add Hardware wizard is required to force a search. To do that, use this applet to install a scanner device like this:

1. Run the Scanners and Cameras applet, and click Add an imaging device. (Ideally, you should hook up the device before doing so.) Follow the wizard, and choose the make and model if necessary.

2. Choose the port the device is connected to. You can use the option Automatic Port Select if you don't intend to be consistent with which port you use for this connection, or you don't want to bother guessing which port it's on.

3. When an item is installed, the drivers are added to the boot list at startup, and appropriate features in the operating system are modified for gaining access to the device.

You can check and test a scanner or camera by selecting it and clicking the Properties button. The Properties dialog for the device appears. Here, you can alter the port number if you need to and check other settings as applicable. If color profiles are available for the device, you can add or remove them using the Color Management tab.

 If your camera or scanner doesn't show up in the installed devices list, see "It's Not Here" in the "Troubleshooting" section at the end of this chapter.

GETTING IMAGES INTO THE COMPUTER

How you acquire images from the device into the computer varies depending on the product. Some cameras use a USB connection, some use a serial cable, and some use FireWire, while others use PC Card memory sticks or even high-density floppies.

When the physical connection is made, it's a matter of triggering the correct "event" to initiate communication between the system and the digital imaging device for image transfer. To link a program to a scanner or digital camera event, follow these steps:

1. Open the Scanners and Cameras applet.

2. Click the scanner or camera you want to use, click Properties, and then click the Events tab.

3. In Scanner Events or Camera Events, click the event you want to link to a program.

4. In Send to This Application, click the program you want to receive the image from the scanner or camera. If the Events tab isn't displayed, you're out of luck; the feature isn't available for the selected scanner or digital camera. Also, at this point, most applications don't support linking to scanners and digital cameras using this new technique. It may take some time for software makers to incorporate it, just as it took awhile for *TWAIN* to be supported by the PC industry at large. Also, note that linking is available only with the programs that appear in Send to This Application.

SOUNDS AND AUDIO DEVICES

The Sounds and Audio Devices applet is your stopping place when it comes to adjustments to your sound system and the sounds the computer makes to alert you of errors, new mail, and so on.

NOTE

> As you might know, you adjust the volume of your computer speakers (and other inputs and outputs) by choosing Start, All Programs, Accessories, Entertainment, Volume Control. Alternatively, you can simply double-click the little speaker next to the clock in the system tray. By single-clicking the same little speaker, you can quickly adjust the master volume control. The Volume Controls are covered in Chapter 5, "Using the Simple Supplied Applications."

There's a bunch of fun to be had from this applet, should you like to twiddle with your sounds. Most of what people do with this applet is change the goofy sounds their computers make in response to specific events.

If your computer had a sound card (or motherboard-based sound chip set) when you installed Windows XP, it's likely Windows established a default set of rather boring sounds for your system, most of which you've probably grown tired of already. Aside from making life more interesting, having different sounds for different types of events is also more informative. You know when you've made an error as opposed to when an application is acknowledging your actions, for example.

The sounds the system uses are stored on disk in the .WAV format. You can create, purchase, or download just about any sound you can think of from the Internet. I downloaded the sound of Homer Simpson saying "Doh!" and the theme from the original TV show *Star Trek* the other day, for example.

→ You can use the Sound Recorder accessory program to create your own WAV files, if you care to. To learn more about it, **see** "Volume Control," **p. 171**.

THE VOLUME TAB

The Volume tab is used to set the master volume. This is the same master volume control which appears in the Volume Control tool and when you single-click the speaker in the system tray. Clicking the Advanced button opens the Volume Control tool so you can access all of the input and output audio controls.

Also on this tab are speaker controls. If you have a special speaker system, such as surround sound or 3-D audio, these controls help you fine tune your settings.

THE SOUNDS TAB

The Sounds tab is used to associate Windows events with sounds. Windows XP comes with tons of sound files, a big improvement over the measly assemblage of WAV files supplied with some earlier versions of Windows. In fact, just as with the color schemes, you can create and save sound schemes by using the Control Panel's Display applet (covered in Chapter 23); you can set up and save personalized schemes to suit your mood. Microsoft supplies a fairly rich variety of sounds for your auditory pleasure.

24

Despite the diverse selection, I still use a few of the sounds I've put together using the Sound Recorder. I have one, for example, that says "New Mail" when I receive e-mail. Sometimes I didn't notice the generic "boop" sound when new mail arrived, so I changed it.

If you want to get fancy, you can record from a CD or tape recorder rather than from a microphone. This way, you can sample bits and pieces from your favorite artists by popping the audio CD into the computer and tapping directly into it rather than by sticking a microphone up in front of your boom box and accidentally recording the telephone when it rings. Just check out the Volume Control applet, and figure out which slider on the mixer panel controls the input volume of the CD. Then use the Sound Recorder applet to make the recording. I have a few good ones, such as James Brown's incomparable "Ow!" for an error message sound.

TIP

> You should make sure that WAV files you intend for system sounds aren't too large. Sound files *can* be super large, especially if they are recorded in 16-bit stereo. As a rule, you should keep the size to a minimum for system sounds because it takes a few seconds for a larger sound to load and play.

You assign sounds to specific Windows "events" like this:

1. Open the Control Panel, and run the Sounds and Audio Devices applet. Select the Sounds tab, as shown in Figure 24.9.

Figure 24.9
The Sounds and Audio Devices Properties dialog box, Sounds tab.

2. The Program Events section lists the events that can have sounds associated with them. Several classes of events are listed on a typical computer, such as Windows, NetMeeting, Windows Explorer, and so on. As you purchase and install new programs in the future, those programs may add their own events to your list. An event with a speaker icon next to it already has a sound associated with it. You can click it and then

click the play button (the one with the triangle pointing right, just like the play button on a VCR or stereo) to hear the sound. The sound file that's associated with the event is listed in the Sounds box.

3. Click any event for which you want to assign a sound or change the assigned sound.

4. Open the drop-down Sounds list, and choose the WAV file you want to use for that event. Some of the event names may not make sense to you, such as Asterisk, Critical Stop, or Exclamation. These names are for the various classes of dialog boxes that Windows XP displays from time to time. The sounds you're most likely to hear often will be Default Beep, Menu Command, New Mail Notification, Question, Open Program, Close Program, Minimize, Maximize, and Close program. You might want to start by assigning sounds to them and then add others as you feel like it.

5. Repeat these steps for each item you want to assign or reassign a sound to. Then click OK to close the dialog box.

TIP FROM

Bob & Brian

> The default folder for sounds is \windows\media. If you have a WAV file stored in another folder and want to assign it to an event, use the Browse button to locate it. You don't have to move your sound files to the \windows\media folder for it to work. However, if you're planning on reassigning sounds regularly, you'll find that the process is easier if you move your WAV files into the media folder first.

At the top of the list of available sounds is an option called <none>, which has the obvious effect: No sound will occur for that event. Assigning all events to <none> effectively silences your laptop for use in a library or other silent setting. You can also silence all sounds easily by choosing the No Sounds sound scheme as explained next.

In the same way that the Display Properties page lets you save color schemes, the Sounds and Audio Devices applet lets you save sound schemes. You can set up goofy sounds for your humorous moods and somber ones for those gloomy days. I often tire of a sound scheme, so I have a few setups that I can easily switch to. The ones supplied with Windows XP are pretty decent, actually, and considering the amount of work required to set up your own schemes, you'll probably make out best just trying a scheme to see if you like it. To choose an existing sound scheme, just use the Sound scheme pull-down list and select one.

You can set up your own sound schemes by assigning or reassigning individual sounds, as I've already explained. But unless you *save* the scheme with the Save As button, it'll be lost the next time you change to a new one. So, the moral is that after you get your favorite sounds assigned to system events, save the scheme. Then you can call it up any time you like.

THE AUDIO AND VOICE TABS

On both the Audio and Voice tabs, you can declare the default hardware you want to use for audio playback, recording, MIDI playback, voice playback, and voice recording. Most systems offer minimal choices in these departments because typical computers have only a single sound system. You might find something strange in the sound playback and recording settings, such as the option to use your modem for these purposes (if your modem has voice messaging capability). Don't bother trying to use your modem for voice messaging unless you have multiple sound cards in the computer.

The Advanced buttons for these categories could be useful, however, depending on your sound system's chipset. Some offer options to adjust bass and treble; expanded stereo (sort of a wider sound based on adjustment of the "phase" of the signal going to the amplifier); sample-rate conversion options; equalization optimization based on the kind of speakers you have; and hardware acceleration (use full acceleration if you're a gamer because it affects DirectSound used in some games).

The Use only default devices option determines which sound card or cards your programs will use. If you use programs that require a specific type of sound card, and that sound card is selected as a default device on this tab, select this check box. That way, if for some reason your preferred devices aren't available, the program doesn't bomb or freak out by trying to use a sound card that Windows thinks is a reasonable replacement. For any situation I've been in, leaving the check box cleared has never been a problem.

THE HARDWARE TAB

The Hardware tab of the Sounds and Audio Devices Properties dialog simply lists all the sound, video, DVD, and other multimedia hardware items currently installed. You can check their properties and current status, as well as troubleshoot them. You can get to the same properties dialog boxes offered here via the Device Manager, but this tab limits the device list only to multimedia-related hardware.

SPEECH

The Speech applet is used to configure the voice that you'll hear whenever the text-to-speech translation feature is used. Now, the voice offered is still too jerky and coarse for my taste. I remember my first voice-enabled computer game "Parsec" for the TI; that was nearly 20 years ago. And the voice it used is just about the same as what is offered here in Windows XP. I can't wait until the sultry voice of the *Star Trek: The Next Generation* computer becomes the standard.

The Microsoft SAM voice is limited in its configurability. But, Windows XP will accept third-party voices which may offer greater end-user control.

Currently, text-to-speech or TTS is only available through Microsoft Office XP. To use it, you must enable the Speak Text command in the Language bar under Options. Once enabled, highlight the section of the document you want read to you, then issue the Speak Text command from the Language bar.

SYSTEM: DEVICE MANAGER

The System applet is covered in Chapter 27, "System Utilities," but we wanted to mention an important element accessed through the System applet here—the Device Manager. The Device Manager is accessed from the System applet's Hardware tab by clicking on its name-sake button. When launched, you are presented with a category list of the devices installed in the system (see Figure 24.10). When there are no problems, the display is a bit bland. To see the individual devices, expand any of the listed categories. Then, to access a device's Properties dialog box, just double-click on it.

Figure 24.10
The Device Manager.

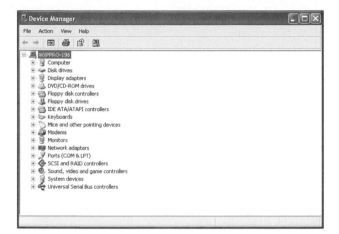

The Device Manager serves several functions, the foremost of which is to aid in the resolution of hardware problems. When any device fails to function as expected it will be highlighted with a yellow triangle or a red stop sign. The yellow triangle indicates a warning or a possible problem. A red stop sign indicates a device conflict or other serious error. When the Device Manager is launched and a device has an outstanding issue, its category will be expanded so you can easily see the warning or error icon.

When a device's Properties dialog box is opened, the General tab displays basic information about the device, plus details on the device's current status. In most cases, the status report will point out exactly what is preventing the device from functioning normally. You may be able to correct the issue on your own, or if you need help or guidance, click the Troubleshoot button for a wizard. You'll be amazed how useful these wizards are! Merlin would be proud.

Depending on the device, there can be many other tabs in addition to the General tab. In most cases, you'll see a Driver tab, and almost as frequently you'll see a Resources tab. The Driver tab offers details about the currently installed driver for this device and enables you to update, roll back, or uninstall the driver.

Device driver roll back is a new feature to the Windows product line. Roll back will remove the current driver and restore the previous driver (assuming there was one). The ability to remove the current or newly installed driver to return to the previously used driver is often a lifesaver. I can't remember how many times I've had to remove a new driver, then had to go through the process of re-installing the hardware just to get the old driver back. The Roll Back Driver button now performs this operation with a simple click. No muss, no fuss.

→ For more information on Device Driver rollback, **see** "Device Driver Rollback," **p. 1060**.

The Resources tab specifies the system resources to which the device is assigned. These include IRQ, I/O ranges, DMA, and more. On PnP devices, you can switch the settings from automatic to either a predefined configuration set or a fully customized setting. On legacy cards, you may need to alter the physical device settings (such as dip switches or jumpers) first, and then set the Resources tab to match. For some PnP cards, the settings on the Resources page are read-only. Meaning you must use a vendor-supplied configuration utility to change the settings away from automatic control.

As for any other tabs that may appear in a device's Properties dialog box, be sure to consult the respective user manual.

From the main Device Manager view, you can perform a few helpful actions:

- Change views between devices by type, devices by connection, resources by type, and resources by connection
- Force a scan for hardware changes
- Update the driver for the selected device
- Disable the device in the current hardware profile
- Uninstall the device from the system
- Eject or unplug a device

NOTE

A hardware profile is similar to a user profile except it focuses on the presence or absence of devices. Hardware profiles are typically used on portable systems that have interchangeable PC card devices or which use a docking station or other transient external devices. Each hardware profile contains active device drivers for a specific set of devices. Upon bootup, the system attempts to match the located device set with a known hardware profile. Hardware profiles are discussed in Chapter 25, "Maintaining and Optimizing System Performance."

TROUBLESHOOTING

PROGRAM DOESN'T SHOW UP

A program I'm trying to kill doesn't show up in the Add or Remove Programs applet. How can I remove it?

This often is the case with programs that don't announce themselves thoroughly to Windows as they are being installed. You have to find the program on the hard disk and eliminate it using the Windows Explorer. Finding a program is often as simple as browsing to the Program Files folder, opening it, and looking around for a folder holding the program in question. Often, deleting the folder is all you have to do. Look for an "uninstall" application there first because it will do a more complete job of removal than just killing the folder, most likely, because some stray DLLs and other support files may be scattered about, not to mention shortcuts in your Start menus that you'll want axed.

As a second (and possibly quicker) means of discovering the location of an unlisted program, you can use its Start menu shortcut to lead you to the application's source. Open the Start menu, and click your way to the application. When you see it, *right-click* it. Now choose Properties from the context menu. Then click Find Target to go directly to the folder where the program resides. Then you can start your dirty work.

If you're trying to kill a program that seems to start up all on its own when you boot up, choose Start, Programs, Startup. Anything in this group autoexecutes upon bootup. Right-click the offending item, and choose Delete. This trick doesn't remove the program from your hard disk, but it prevents the program from starting at boot time.

No Battery Icon in System Tray

I don't see a battery icon in the system tray. My laptop seems to be brain dead about batteries and power conservation.

Be sure APM is enabled for the computer via the Power Options applet in the Control Panel. Also, make sure the computer complies with APM (check your BIOS settings).

Cannot Connect

My modem isn't connecting for some reason.

More often than not, modem problems are caused by incorrect phone numbers and/or a bad phone line connection. Assuming Windows detected and installed your modem, don't get esoteric in your troubleshooting. Just as you're most likely to find a lost item where you think it should be, it's the silly things that keep modems from working—a bad or incompletely inserted phone wire, bad wall jack, or splitter; or a phone number that's missing an area code (or has an unnecessary area code) being dialed. Another typical goof is to specify an external access number (typically 9), which might be necessary at the office but not on the road. Check the properties for the dial-up networking connection you're trying to use. Also, of course, double-check the user ID and password. You might be dialing in and physically connecting just fine, but the remote server is kicking you off because of incorrect user ID or password.

Finally, recall that a number of troubleshooters are built into Windows XP. One of them is for modems. Choose Start, Help, and in the right pane, click Troubleshooting.

It's Not Here

My camera or scanner doesn't show up.

Sometimes starting with the obvious is easiest. Does the device have power? Is your scanner or camera plugged in and turned on? Check the power cables and the data connection. Does the camera have a good power source? Digital cameras eat up batteries at a ravenous rate. Either use fresh batteries or an external power source. (I recommend getting nickel-metal hydride batteries for digital cameras. They work much longer than normal alkalines or Ni-Cad batteries.) If the connection is an infrared one, make sure the camera and computer IR sensor are lined up properly.

Some devices don't connect correctly unless they're turned on. See your device documentation if you need more information.

As per my usual admonition, check your cables! Make sure you have the correct type of cable plugged into the correct ports on both the device and your computer. See your scanner or camera documentation for more information. Your device may be connected to a port that is disabled. A serial port, for example, is often disabled to allow an internal modem to work.

Next, check to see whether the driver for your device is installed. Virtually all cameras and scanners are Plug and Play these days, so Windows XP should install the drivers for them automatically. However, you might need to install drivers for some devices manually. See the section in the this chapter covering the Scanners and Cameras applet for details on installing a driver. If that doesn't help, and the device is listed as installed (in Control Panel, Scanners and Cameras), try removing it and reinstalling it via that applet and then reinstalling it (by clicking Remove and then Add).

Using DOS Programs with a Mouse

Why is the mouse pointer still on the screen while I'm in DOS?

Lots of folks still run DOS programs, even under Windows 9x, NT, 2000, and now XP. Most DOS programs are keyboard driven and don't require a mouse. Normally, however, when you run DOS programs in a window, the mouse pointer sits annoyingly on the screen, even though it's useless.

You can hide the mouse pointer when running an MS-DOS program, assuming you don't need it. To hide it, right-click the title bar of the MS-DOS window to display the menu, and then click Hide Mouse Pointer. (If the program switches between character-based and graphics modes, you might need to hide the mouse pointer again.) When the mouse pointer is hidden, you can't see it inside or outside the program's window. To display the mouse pointer, press Alt+Spacebar, and choose Display Mouse Pointer from the resulting menu.

CHAPTER 25

MAINTAINING AND OPTIMIZING SYSTEM PERFORMANCE

In this chapter

RUNNING A TIGHT SHIP

If you're reading this chapter, you probably are the kind of user or administrator who is interested in keeping your Windows workstation spinning like a top. Or maybe you are responsible for maintaining a myriad of computers on the company LAN, and your charges insist that you do the same for them. You're also likely to be looking for ways to boost the performance of your system by tweaking system software.

In this chapter, I'll start by discussing some of the techniques that will best serve you in the process of improving system stability and performance. The rest of the chapter deals with configuration of the various program application subsystems—Win32, Win16, DOS, and a bit on OS/2.

MEASURING SYSTEM PERFORMANCE WITH PERFORMANCE MONITOR

Before you can improve your system's performance, you need to find out how well it's currently performing. Use Windows XP's integrated Performance Monitor to learn what's happening inside your system in much more detail than is available from the Task Manager's Performance tab (press Ctrl+Alt+Del to bring up the Task Manager).

Performance Monitor creates a graphical or numeric display of essential system information, such as memory use, status of hard disk use, CPU activity, network traffic, and many other quantifiable aspects of your computer's real-time operations. You can display the gathered information in graph, histogram, or numeric format. Displaying this information is useful for trying to get a handle on what's happening with your computer, particularly when you're troubleshooting or tracking down bottlenecks.

Not only does Performance Monitor put up a real-time display, it also interacts with Performance Logs and Alerts (another administrative tool). Using a combination of the two, you can record performance data for later analysis, set up system alerts to send a message, run a program, or start a log specifying whether a counter's value is above, below, or equal to a defined threshold.

To start the Performance Monitor, click Start, Control Panel, Performance and Maintenance, Administrative Tools, and finally, double-click Performance.

When you start the Performance Monitor, the default display shows three counters, as shown in Figure 25.1. These counters are

- **Memory Pages/second**—This counter indicates how many times per second Windows has to move programs or data between memory and the hard disk. Much of the activity measured by this counter is the swapping of data between memory and the hard disk's page file, which holds active programs and data that currently can't fit into memory. If this value frequently rises above 20, your system might have a memory bottleneck; add more RAM to the system to improve performance.

Figure 25.1
The Performance Monitor displays operating system and hardware performance measurements in a chart format.

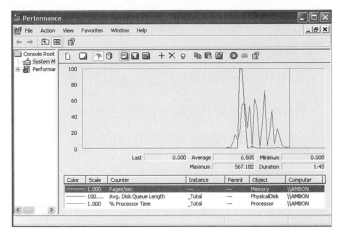

- **Average Disk Queue Length**—This is the number of blocks of data waiting to be written to your hard disk, and generally should be no higher than 2 plus the physical number of hard drives on your system. If it frequently rises higher, your disk's transfer speed is too low.

- **% Processor Time**—This is the percentage of time that your processor is actually busy doing your work. If this value frequently exceeds 85%, consider adding a faster processor.

Each measurement is color-coded, and the default graph of current activity uses a moving vertical red stripe to indicate where the latest information is displayed.

To add additional counters, click the + (plus) button on the toolbar. From the resulting dialog box, choose a computer to measure, the performance object (the choices include various system components such as Memory, Network Interface, and Processor), and then the specific performance counter.

What can you measure with the Performance Monitor?

- Processor activity, including the percentages of time the processor handles many different types of activities.

- Network activity, including data transfer rates to and from the specified computer.

- Pagefile activity, including what percentage of your pagefile is in use at a given time.

All together, there are more than 40 different performance objects whose activity can be tracked with the Performance Monitor, and many offer 10 or more counters that measure different aspects of the object's performance. It's almost overwhelming what you can measure. Performance Monitor is a hugely flexible tool. If you're responsible for managing a computer network, you can mix and match counters and objects from different computers on the same graph. Therefore, you could, for example, compare some interesting statistics such as disk hits, print jobs, or network requests from different computers on the same graphical display to help you get a sense of bottlenecks in data throughput.

As you add counters to your display, the list at the bottom of the window grows, and each new counter is added to the chart and assigned a color. You can sort the list by clicking the column heads. If you wonder what a given counter is actually measuring, click Explain. You then see a description of the counter, as shown in Figure 25.2.

TIP FROM

Bob and Brian

You can keep the Explain window open and click around on counter names to quickly learn about them, without clicking the Explain button each time.

Figure 25.2
This dialog box contains an overwhelming array of possible counters to display. Click Explain to read a description of a selected counter.

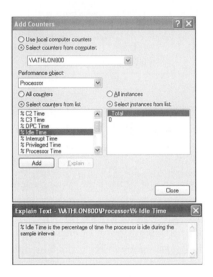

To change the format of the display, click the toolbar buttons indicating bar graph (which Microsoft incorrectly calls a histogram), line graph (the default), or textual display.

TIP FROM

Bob & Brian

To single out one counter in a chart, click the Highlight button in the toolbar, and then click the object's name in the list at the bottom of the window.

Modify your charts or histograms by using various properties available from the Properties button on the toolbar. You can add a background grid; add x- and y-axis titles; change the scaling, fonts, and colors; and much more. Click the red-and-white X button to freeze the display for analysis, and click it again to capture new data. Click the Source tab to locate a log file to display rather than display current events. By changing the display, you can analyze logs you might have stored in the past (see the "Event Viewer" section in Chapter 27). If, at any point, you want to store a snapshot of your display, right-click in the display area, and choose Save As. Give it a name, and it is then stored as an HTML file. Clicking its filename in the Explorer brings it up in Internet Explorer, complete with graphics. This file is basically just a screen shot.

Tuning Windows Performance with the System Applet

When you discover how your system is performing, it's time to consider ways to speed up your system if you're not satisfied.

First of all, if your system has less than 128MB of RAM, your first move to increase performance should be to upgrade your system's RAM to at least 128MB or more. Windows XP really, *really* likes to have lots of memory, and with today's prices, you can add an additional 128MB for as little as $20. Memory modules come in 256MB and 512MB increments as well, if your computer is designed for them. You'll notice a big improvement in performance when you step up to 128MB. You probably won't notice much more improvement past 256MB unless you use memory-hungry applications such as Adobe Photoshop and Microsoft Access.

TIP FROM

Bob & Brian

> If you're using a computer with its video built in to the motherboard (rather than located on a separate card), your effective memory is reduced by as much as 10MB or more because your system's memory is shared with the video card. For example, a system with 64MB of RAM that uses shared video memory (sometimes referred to as Unified Memory Architecture or UMA) can have as little as 54MB of available RAM, or even less! This is another good reason to consider a memory upgrade, or at least stay away from chipsets with integrated video (except those that use nVIDIA's nForce chipset).

25

However, if you already have at least 128MB of memory, or if you're looking for ways to fine-tune Windows to find more performance, the System Applet provides several ways you can improve your system's performance without wielding a screwdriver or opening up your system.

To open the System applet, click Start, Control Panel, Performance and Maintenance and System, or just right-click My Computer and select Properties.

The System properties sheet's General tab appears in Figure 25.3. The General tab lists the processor type, processor speed (a big improvement over older Windows versions), and the physical RAM (memory) installed. If you are running with less than 128MB of RAM or with a processor running at less than 300MHz, your system performance will be very slow when using Windows XP.

To adjust the performance of your system, click the Advanced tab. It has five sections:

- Performance
- User Profiles
- Startup and Recovery
- Environmental Variables
- Error Reporting

Click the Settings button in the Performance section to get started.

Figure 25.3
This system has just enough RAM and processor speed to run Windows XP Professional comfortably.

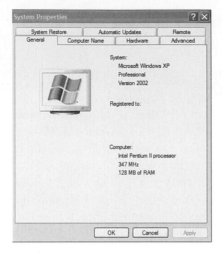

ADJUSTING VISUAL EFFECTS FOR PERFORMANCE

If you have a fast PC (the one I'm using for this chapter has an 800MHz Athlon processor with 256MB of RAM), you can take full advantage of all the visual niceties provided by Windows XP's Visual Effects menu (see Figure 25.4).

Figure 25.4
Windows XP Professional's Visual Effects menu offers many animation and effects settings you can adjust.

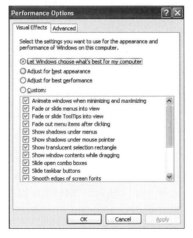

However, if you're running with less than 128KB of RAM, have a processor under 500MHz, or have a slow video card (such as a PCI-based video card or typical motherboard-integrated video circuits), you might want to adjust Windows XP's defaults.

If you select Adjust for Best Performance, all the animations and effects shown in Figure 25.4 are turned off. If you select Adjust for Best Appearance, all the animations and effects are turned on. If you use Let Windows Choose What's Best for My Computer, none, some, or all of the animations and effects will be enabled, depending on the speed of your hardware. For example, on my 800MHz system with a fast AGP video card, all features were turned on except Smooth Edges of Screen Fonts. Select Custom to choose the options you want turned off or on. You can speed up screen displays by turning off options in the Visual Effects menu.

TIP FROM

Bob & Brian

> If you enable Smooth Edges of Screen Fonts, you can further fine-tune its behavior through the Appearance tab of the Display properties sheet. Click Effects and select either Standard or ClearType for the smoothing method, or disable it if you prefer. ClearType is a better choice for LCD displays, while Standard or disabled works better for CRT displays and many presentation projectors.

ADJUSTING PROCESSOR, MEMORY, AND VIRTUAL MEMORY USAGE

To improve the performance of your computer by adjusting processor, memory, and virtual memory usage, click the Advanced tab of the Performance Options sheet (see Figure 25.5). The Advanced tab provides three ways to affect the performance of your system:

- **Processor Scheduling**—Adjusts the balance of processor time between programs and background processes.

- **Memory Usage**—Adjusts the balance of memory usage between programs and system cache.

- **Virtual Memory**—Adjusts the size and location of the paging file, which uses the hard disk to hold active applications and data that can't currently fit into memory.

Each option is covered in the following sections.

Figure 25.5
The Advanced dialog box enables you to adjust three factors to improve system performance.

OPTIMIZING VIRTUAL MEMORY (PAGING) FILE SIZE

Windows XP Professional—like Windows 2000, Windows NT, Windows Me, Windows 9x, and Windows 3.x—incorporates a virtual memory scheme. As you might know already, virtual memory is a method for tricking the operating system into thinking it has more apparent RAM for use by applications than is physically present in the computer. Windows XP Home Edition uses a hard disk file called pagefile.sys to simulate RAM. Windows XP Home Edition's Virtual Memory Manager (VMM) constantly tracks the amount of free RAM, and when the available RAM is exhausted, the VMM begins swapping out 4KB chunks of data and instruction code to pagefile.sys. As portions of the data or code are needed, they are swapped back into RAM chips, where they can be used by the CPU. This activity is called *paging*. The upshot is that more applications and services can run simultaneously than would normally be the case. On the other hand, CPU access to the page file on your hard drive is monumentally slower than to your physical system memory.

The default VMM settings applied when you install Windows XP Professional are based on your hard disk space and partition designations. One swap file is created in the root of the partition containing the operating system. Each partition can have its own pagefile.sys, and the size of the file is dynamic. Windows 9x and Me allow only a single swapfile, although its size can vary. So, if you have several disks or partitions, Windows XP Professional might decrease the size of a pagefile on one partition and shift paging onto another one as available hard disk space decreases.

TIP FROM

Bob & Brian

> The automatic adjustment of paging file locations is a huge advantage for Windows XP over older Windows versions, and provides yet another reason for adding one of today's bigger, faster hard drives to your system. However, for best performance, you might prefer to move all of your pagefile to a newer, faster drive with more space than your old one, as described in the following paragraphs.

Because Windows XP Professional is such a huge operating system and today's office suites, games, movies, and graphics editors are bigger than ever before, it's imperative that paging be intelligent and plentiful. This is especially important if your system barely exceeds the minimum RAM recommendation, as you learned in Chapter 2, "Getting Your Hardware and Software Ready for Windows XP."

If you want to ensure that your hard disk doesn't thrash itself to death and that the system runs efficiently, not making you wait every time you switch between windows or move something around on the screen, you should install at *least* 128MB of RAM, let Windows manage the pagefile size, and keep lots of free space on your drive.

The default pagefile size is equal to the amount of RAM in your computer plus 12MB. As disk space dwindles, the file can shrink. The minimum can be no less than about 2MB. Usually, you should leave the pagefile at its recommended size, although you might increase its size if you routinely use programs that require a lot of memory. You can check with the software maker for information about how demanding applications might benefit from increasing the allocation.

You can optimize virtual memory use by dividing the space between multiple drives and especially by removing it from slower or heavily accessed drives. To best optimize your virtual memory space, you should divide it across as many physical hard drives as possible. When you're selecting drives, keep the following guidelines in mind:

- Try to avoid having a large pagefile on the same drive as the system files. You should have at least a 2MB pagefile on the boot volume. The system requires this to write events to the system log, send an administrative alert, or automatically restart after a system Stop error occurs in the event of a system failure.

- Avoid putting a pagefile on a fault-tolerant drive, such as a mirrored volume; some of today's high-performance systems come with mirrored IDE drives (the second drive immediately reflects changes to the first drive). Pagefiles don't need fault tolerance, and some fault-tolerant systems suffer from slow data writes because they must write data to multiple locations.

- Don't place multiple pagefiles on different partitions on the same physical disk drive. This only makes your hard drive work even harder. Most systems have only one physical drive, so this is not usually a problem. If you have split the drive into more than one drive letter, be careful where you place pagefiles.

TIP FROM

Bob & Brian

If you have multiple drive letters, it can be difficult to tell whether drive letters above C: are located on a second physical drive or are partitions of your first hard drive. Use the Microsoft Computer Management program (which you can access from the Administrative Tools folder in the Control Panel) and run the Disk Management tool to view local drives and their drive letters.

25

The following are some other points to consider when you're adjusting the pagefile:

- Setting the pagefile's initial size and maximum size to the same value increases efficiency because the operating system does not need to expand the file during processing. Setting different values for initial and maximum size can contribute to disk fragmentation. Expanding the default size of the pagefile can increase performance if applications are consuming virtual memory and the full capacity of the existing file is being used. To determine how large your pagefile should be based on your system workload, you should monitor the Process (_Total)\Page File Bytes counter in the Performance Monitor. This counter indicates, in bytes, how much of the pagefile is being used.

- Don't put a large pagefile on a disk that is used a lot, such as one used for serving applications and databases. It slows down overall performance.

- The operating system always needs 5MB free on its partition. Be sure you don't use up the whole system boot drive.

- Change the file size a little at a time, and test the performance.

TIP FROM

Bob
& Brian

> For additional speed improvements, consider defragmenting your hard disk and upgrading your hard disk, hard disk controller, or motherboard for faster disk performance. Before installing a new IDE hard drive, find out which transfer protocol it uses. If the new drive uses Ultra DMA/66 or Ultra DMA/100, and your present IDE controller doesn't, you could have booting problems. See whether the drive manufacturer has provided a method of reverting to an Ultra DMA level supported by your system. If not, you might have to turn off DMA support completely in your system BIOS and suffer a large performance hit. Sometimes when you're upgrading a hard drive, upgrading the motherboard at the same time will serve you well, for just this reason.

To change the initial and maximum size of the workstation's pagefile, the file locations, and the number of pagefiles, follow these steps:

1. Open the Control Panel, and run the System applet, or right-click My Computer and select Properties.

2. View the Advanced tab; then click Settings under Performance Options. View the Advanced tab and in the Virtual Memory area, click Change, and then Custom Size. You then see the dialog box shown in Figure 25.6.

Figure 25.6
You can set Pagefile sizes and locations in this dialog box.

3. Edit the initial size and maximum size if you want to change them, and click Set.

TIP FROM

Bob
& Brian

Short on disk space? If you're seriously short on space, you can turn off the VMM and then delete the pagefile. You can't delete it while it's in use, though. So, first, you have to turn it off. Next, you can just remove the pagefile using the Control Panel's System applet, reboot, and then delete the inactive file from the Windows Explorer.

You can use the Performance Monitor discussed earlier in this chapter to get a sense of how much virtual memory is being used. To get started, open the Performance Monitor and click the + (plus) button on the toolbar. Choose Paging File from the Performance Object drop-down list. Then add Usage and Usage peak. View the statistics in whatever way you like. Figure 25.7 shows an example. In this figure, you can see that even with 15 programs running, I'm still only at 3.354 percent usage, with a peak of 6.212%.

Figure 25.7
You can check virtual memory usage via the Performance Monitor by adding paging file monitoring for display in the chart.

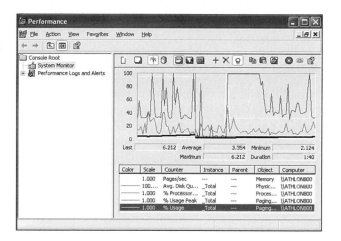

25

SETTING MULTITASKING PRIORITIES

As you know, Windows XP Professional is a multithreaded, preemptive multitasking operating system. Left to its own devices, it does an extremely good job of balancing user requests with the need for internal system operations and control. The result from the user's point of view is performance that appears to be highly responsive, even though some internal sleight of hand and task juggling might be going on under the hood. You'll really appreciate Windows XP's excellent multitasking capabilities when your system is juggling multiple browser windows, an e-mail client, two or three word-processing documents, a spreadsheet, and a photo editor. Sound like *your* office?

As well as it works by default, one setting can slightly improve overall smoothness of Windows XP Professional's multitasking, depending on what you use your computer for. To set it, do the following:

1. Click Start, right-click My Computer, and select Properties.
2. Select the Advanced tab and click the Settings button in the Performance section.

3. View the Advanced tab, shown earlier in Figure 25.5. In this dialog box, you can set the tasking priority for your applications.

4. Click either Background Services or Programs, and save the change by clicking OK.

Normally, Programs is selected, ensuring that the foreground application (the window you're currently working with) gets more CPU time slices than programs running in the background. Time slices are also shorter and variably sized, which results in more responsive action from an application as you work in it. Unless you have CPU-intensive applications running in the background, though, you won't notice a difference in foreground performance.

If you're running something important in the background that bogs down too much when you're doing other foreground work on the computer, choose the Background Services option. Examples might be data acquisition programs, communications programs, Internet Connection sharing, a Web server, or a backup utility. The time slices are doled out in longer portions with this setting.

SETTING MEMORY USAGE

By default, Windows XP devotes more memory to running programs than to the system cache (the memory used for disk caching and handing background operations). If your computer is used entirely as a workstation and doesn't share folders, drives, or its Internet connection with other computers on a network, this setting should be left alone. However, if your computer is used as a server, and particularly if you have 256MB of RAM or more, change the default for Memory Usage (see Figure 25.5) from Programs to System Cache to improve performance for shared resources.

When you're finished customizing Performance settings, click OK to close the Performance Options dialog box and return to the Advanced tab of the System Properties window.

SETTING ENVIRONMENT VARIABLES

Settings that you're not likely to use but could still prove handy are the environment variables. What do environmental variables do? They indicate where temporary files are stored, what folder contains Windows program files, and other settings that affect system performance.

In DOS and Windows 9x, environment variables were usually set up in the AUTOEXEC.BAT file, using lines like this:

```
SET PROMPT=$P$G
```

In Windows XP, environment variables for Windows applications are set up using a nifty graphical user interface. In addition, old DOS and Windows 3.x applications will see any environment variables set up by the AUTOEXEC.NT file, which we'll discuss later in this chapter, under "Configuring the DOS Environment."

NOTE

The environment variables defined here are used by every Windows application, and are the initial environment variables set for each command prompt window. If you change environment variables in the command prompt window (say, in a batch file), the changes apply only to that window and will disappear when the window is closed.

By clicking the Environment Variables button on the System applet's Advanced tab, you can change the environment variables in the resulting dialog box (see Figure 25.8).

Figure 25.8
Examining the Environmental Variables for the current user (top) and for all users of the system (bottom).

In this dialog box, you can create new variables, delete a variable, or edit a variable using the corresponding buttons. Notice that this dialog box lists systemwide variables as well as per-user ones (for the currently logged-on user account). Setting a variable in the System Variables area alters the defaults for all users.

If you need to alter a variable, you must understand what happens if there's a conflict between system variables named in different places or commands in the operating system. As a rule, the last value declared for a variable overrides all previous declarations: The last one in wins! Windows XP sets variables in the following order:

1. System-level variables.

2. User-level variables.

3. AUTOEXEC.NT-declared variables (seen only by MS-DOS or Windows 3.x applications). AUTOEXEC.NT contains commands similar to those used in the AUTOEXEC.BAT file used by older versions of Windows. We'll discuss AUTOEXEC.NT later in this chapter.

4. Anything subsequent, issued by a user or command-line program, utility, or batch file.

NOTE

> I need to make an important distinction here. AUTOEXEC.NT variable settings go into effect only when the execution of an MS-DOS or Windows 3.x program triggers a VDM to be created, such as if you run a program that runs in MS-DOS. AUTOEXEC.NT settings (such as the SET BLASTER command, which sets up sound support) do not affect variables in the standard command prompt window. Of course, if you run a command prompt window, set environment variables from the prompt, and then run a program, that program inherits the variables from that box. When you close the box, though, those settings are discarded. The next command prompt window you open will have only the systemwide and user-level variables as declared by the System dialog box discussed in the preceding paragraphs.

Why modify system variables? Good question. Not many people need to. Probably the most likely reason to modify these variables is to add directories to the system's search path. Or you might have particular applications that require environment variables set. Some command-line utilities also look for environment variables. For example, copy has an environmental variable which determines whether it prompts before overwriting files.

Chances are that you'll never need to adjust environmental variables, but if you want to send temporary files to a drive besides C:, this is where you do it.

TIP FROM

Bob & Brian

> If you have two or more physical hard drives, you really ought to adjust the TEMP and TMP variables to take advantage of the additional drive. Although Windows XP Professional can automatically adjust its paging file to use an additional drive with more space, it still uses the \Windows\Temp folder on the boot drive (usually C:) no matter how much faster another drive is or how little space you have on the C: drive. Because print jobs and other temporary files are stored in the folder specified by these variables (and can cause you to run out of space on the C: drive in some cases), you should create a folder called TEMP on the new drive and change these variables to use it. After you make this change, delete the temporary files in \WINDOWS\TEMP and get back lost space.

PROGRAM COMPATIBILITY WIZARD

One of the biggest concerns any user of a new Windows version is, "Will it run my software?" This fear goes all the way back to the birth of Windows, when Windows 386 was unable to run some programs designed for Windows 286, and Windows 3.x couldn't run all Windows 3.0 programs.

Fortunately, Windows XP Professional includes a Program Compatibility Wizard that can help you run your "golden oldie" Windows 95, Windows 98/Me, Windows NT 4.0, or Windows 2000 program under Windows XP. Because many corporations upgrade software far less often than home or small-business users (imagine $100 for an upgrade times 10,000 users), this feature can be critical to your company's successful deployment of Windows XP.

By default, Program Compatibility is turned off for all the programs you install, because many 32-bit Windows programs will run with Windows XP without any problems. If you have problems with a particular program (game and education programs are the most common culprits), start the wizard by clicking Start, All Programs, Accessories, Program Compatibility Wizard.

When the wizard (which is part of Windows XP's Help and Support Center) starts, click Next after you read the introduction.

You can select the program that needs compatibility help from a list of programs already installed, by choosing the program currently in the CD-ROM drive, or by locating the program manually. After you select a program and click Next, choose the version of Windows you want Windows XP to emulate (note that Windows NT 4.0 compatibility is for NT 4.0 with Service Pack 5 installed) as shown in Figure 25.9.

Figure 25.9
The Program Compatibility Wizard lets you run your program in any of four modes compatible with recent Windows versions.

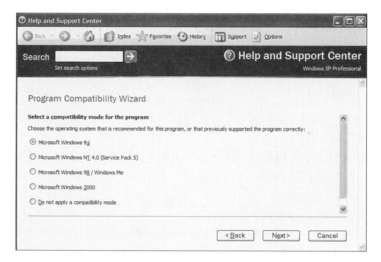

After you select the compatibility mode, select any special display options needed by the program. For example, you can run the program in 256-color mode, 640 × 480 screen resolution, or without Windows XP visual themes without resetting your normal screen settings (see Figure 25.10). This is a great benefit if you have programs that normally require you to change these options before they'll work correctly.

After you choose the display options, click Next to test the program. If you chose display options, the screen might blank briefly as the monitor resets to the color depth and resolution you selected. When you close the program, you have the option to save the compatibility settings, discard them, or stop the process.

Figure 25.10
Select color depth and resolution needed for your game, or disable the Windows XP visual themes if your program requires these special settings.

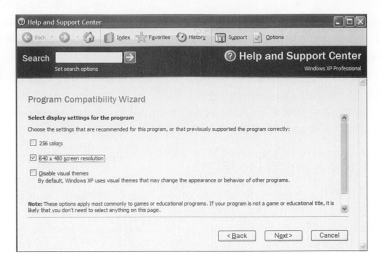

NOTE

There are still some application incompatibilities that the wizard can't fix. I've found a few older Windows programs that simply won't run under Windows XP under any setting of the Program Compatibility Wizard. There's nothing to be done in this case but contact the manufacturer. Some manufacturers are eager to hear bug reports and gracious about providing updates, but others—Epson Corporation is notable for this—basically tell you to go jump in a lake. That's life, I guess.

CONFIGURING THE PROGRAM ENVIRONMENTS

Chapter 23, "Tweaking the GUI," and Chapter 24, "Configuration via Control Panel Applets," covered quite a few of the adjustments that you can make to the Windows XP user environment. Those chapters also addressed a variety of settings that affect the operation of Windows on a more rudimentary level, such as Properties sheets for printers and other devices you might have installed on a typical system or network. In addition to all these settings and properties, Windows XP allows for fine-tuning of program and system handling under the various operating system environments that Windows XP can control: 32-bit Windows, 16-bit Windows, and DOS.

As discussed in Chapter 1, "Introducing Windows XP Professional," and Chapter 2, "Getting Your Hardware and Software Ready for Windows XP," Windows XP runs non–NT-based applications that fall into four classes: MS-DOS, Windows 3.x, OS/2 1.x character-based, and POSIX character-based.

How does Windows XP handle programs written for different operating systems? Windows XP has a feature called *environment subsystems*, which enables Windows XP to emulate a particular operating system's operation and translate a program's request for services into Windows XP commands. Each subsystem basically is an emulator responsible for providing the API for each operating system and then translating the API calls to the 32-bit Windows subsystem, which passes the commands onto Windows XP for processing.

Some optimization and configuration of the various environments are possible, typically to allow for higher compatibility with non–Windows XP programs. Or, in some cases, the adjustments possible are purely aesthetic or convenience factors. The following sections describe options for configuring applications and subsystems. They also describe some specific programs or classes of programs (such as DOS-based TSRs) and how best to run them under Windows XP.

In the following sections, you'll learn about settings for the following:

- Windows 16-bit
- DOS

32-bit Windows tuning was covered earlier in this chapter in the section, "Tuning Windows Performance with the System Applet."

VDM—THE VIRTUAL DOS MACHINE

Windows XP provides support for old MS-DOS and Windows 3.x applications through a program subsystem called the Virtual DOS Machine, or VDM. VDM is a program that mimics the hardware and software of a computer running MS-DOS. This program then loads and executes MS-DOS and Windows 3.x programs in a controlled environment. The "virtual" part signifies that an old program running in the VDM thinks it can directly control hardware like the video card and keyboard, when in fact, the VDM intercepts all hardware control attempts and uses Windows XP to carry out the desired operations safely. An illegal or dangerous hardware operation can simply be rejected. No user application program can directly manipulate hardware on Windows XP—that's why it's so sturdy. When you run a Windows 3.x application or an MS-DOS program, Windows XP runs it through the VDM where it can do whatever it wants without the risk of actually crashing the computer.

The Virtual DOS Machine can be configured by several settings and setup files, which I'll discuss in the following sections.

CONFIGURING THE WINDOWS 3.X ENVIRONMENT

Windows XP runs Windows 3.x programs without a hitch thanks to its "Windows-on-Windows" or WOW system that lets these older Windows programs see the 16-bit Windows operating system environment that they expect. WOW in turn depends on the Virtual DOS Machine to provide emulated hardware support. This sounds complex, and it is, but from the user's point of view, you can just run an older Windows application and it just plain works.

One significant thing that WOW does is monitor the old configuration files WIN.INI and SYTEM.INI. Old Windows programs expect to see Windows's system settings in these files in the Windows directory. Windows XP therefore keeps copies of these files up-to-date with your system's current settings. It also tries to detect changes made to these old configuration files made by legacy programs which are attempting to signal Windows to make changes.

One thing that WOW can't completely fix is the filename length limitation that hearkens back to DOS.

25

If you run Windows 3.x applications on Windows XP, as discussed in Chapter 4, "Using the Windows XP Interface," you'll see truncated file and folder names in any program that looks at the hard disk directory. You see these shortened names because Windows 3.x applications were hostage to the limitation of DOS's 8.3 file-naming conventions. This limitation can be annoying, especially in a Browse box, but there's absolutely nothing you can do about it. The best thing you can do is upgrade to a 32-bit Windows version of the program.

If you can't upgrade, at least understanding how the truncated names are generated helps a bit. Following are some of the rules governing truncated NTFS and DOS file-naming rules and some hints for using them.

First, consider the rules of Windows 9x, NT 4, Windows 2000, and Windows XP long filenames:

- Files and directory names can be up to 256 characters in length.
- You can include a file type or extension, separated from the rest of the name by a period, such as *2002 Sales Reports.WKS*. (If associated file extensions are hidden via the Folder Options, the extension is invisible in listings, however.) Windows XP doesn't care how many periods are in a name, and only considers the last one when looking for the file type: Sales.Reports.xls and Salesreports.xls are both taken to be Excel files.
- Special characters not allowed are as follows:
  ?, ", \, /, <, >, *, |, and :
- Spaces can be included. No problem.
- Uppercase and lowercase are both allowed, and they appear in listings. However, they aren't interpreted by Windows XP or its applications as being different from one another. In other words, you can't store a file called mybudget.xls and another one called MYBUDGET.XLS in the same folder, because Windows XP interprets both files as having the same name. If you tried to copy or move one file into the folder containing the other file, you would be asked if you wanted to replace the original file.

Windows XP automatically generates shorter DOS-compatible filenames when needed by a Windows 3.x program by doing the following:

- Removing illegal characters and replacing them with _ (an underscore).
- Removing any spaces in the name.
- Using only the last period that has three consecutive letters after it as the extension.
- Truncating the first name to six letters and adding a tilde (~) and a single-digit number as the last two characters of the first name. Consider these examples:

Windows XP Name	DOS/Windows 3.x Name
Quarterly Sales Reports.WK3	QUARTE~1.WK3
Quarterly Sales Reports. Atlanta.Georgia.WK3	QUARTE~1.WK3
Qrtr[Sales]Reports from Atlanta,Georgia.WK3	QRTR_S~1.WK3

When you use any programs that generate documents you're going to use with DOS and Windows 3.x applications, you might want to adopt a naming convention that makes sense to you when the longer names are converted to shorter DOS names. Try to use only one period, and use the extension that the application expects. Because the first six letters are retained, pack as much description into them as possible. If you use the same first eight letters for several filenames, they'll look almost identical under the Windows 3.x and DOS applications.

ALLOTTING INDEPENDENT MEMORY SPACE FOR WINDOWS 3.X APPLICATIONS

Windows XP creates a separate instance of the virtual DOS machine (VDM) program for each MS-DOS program that you run, but normally all 16-bit Windows 3.x applications are run by one VDM. This is necessary because the old Windows depended on being able to directly transfer data back and forth between programs in ways that modern Windows programs aren't allowed (again, for reliability's sake). The result is that, just like in a real Windows 3.x machine, a Windows 3.x application that crashes can take down the whole VDM, crashing any other Windows 3.x programs (but not, thankfully, Windows XP itself).

Well, unlike death and taxes, this isn't necessarily a fact of life. The one adjustment you can make to the Windows 3.x subsystem is to prevent this all-or-nothing situation.

Technically, you're not actually making an adjustment to the subsystem; instead, you're making a setting for individual Windows 3.x applications. Through a simple setting, you can cause an application to request its own VDM. The memory space that it runs in is then totally isolated, protected from other applications that might run amok. The upside is that one errant Windows 3.x application can't take down another. The downside is that any Windows 3.x applications running in their own memory space can't communicate with other Windows 3.x applications as they would in a true Windows 3.x computer. DLL services, for example, are not running or functional, so data passing between applications is quashed. However, this isn't a big problem for most Windows XP users, because you'll probably seldom use more than one or two Windows 3.x applications at once anyway.

You make the setting to the properties for the Windows 3.x program. As an example, I'll use a Windows 3.x version of the popular Pretty Good Solitaire shareware program. To change the setting, follow these steps:

1. Create a shortcut for the program in question; to make a shortcut, right-click the program icon in Windows Explorer and select Create Shortcut.
2. Right-click the shortcut, and choose Properties. In the Shortcut Properties dialog box, choose the Shortcut tab, and then click Advanced. You then see the dialog box shown in Figure 25.11.

TIP FROM

Bob

& Brian

> Many Windows 3.x programs were developed for 256-color displays, and might not function properly with the 65, 536, or 16.8 million color displays now used by Windows. If necessary, you can also use the Compatibility tab to select 256-color or other display settings, or to choose compatibility mode settings described earlier in this chapter in "Program Compatibility Wizard."

25

Figure 25.11
You can set this option to give a Windows 3.x application its own memory space. You can do so only from a shortcut for the application.

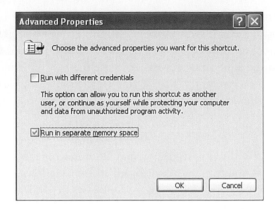

From this dialog box, you have only to put a check in the Run In Separate Memory Space check box.

The other option, Run with Different Credentials, allows you to select which user name should be used to run the program. This is useful if a program was installed by a particular user, not by the system administrator, but you want all users of the computer to be able to run the program. Select the user who installed the program when prompted by the system.

CONFIGURING THE DOS ENVIRONMENT

If you still use DOS programs, you'll be glad to know that the DOS environment that Windows XP uses is highly configurable. I discussed the Virtual DOS Machine or VDM in the previous section. It provides a simulated MS-DOS computer environment in which your old DOS applications run. You can configure it in several ways:

- By configuring the user variables in the System dialog box, as discussed in the section "Setting Environment Variables."
- By making selections from the DOS window's Control menu.
- By making settings in the Properties sheet for a shortcut to the DOS application.
- By setting up custom AUTOEXEC.NT and CONFIG.NT configuration files you can address most special memory or environment setting requirements a DOS program might have.
- By entering environment-altering commands at the command prompt.

You can choose from a great number of settings, including the following, all of which can be set for an individual program or as defaults to be used any time a command prompt window or DOS program is run. You can make the following settings:

- Set the window font (including TrueType and bitmapped font styles)
- Set the background and foreground colors for normal text
- Set the background and foreground colors for pop-up boxes
- Choose window or full-screen viewing

- Set the default window position on the screen
- Use or turn off the QuickEdit mode
- Use or hide the Windows XP mouse pointer in the application

In addition to these settings, you can set environment variables, specify memory requirements (for EMS and XMS), and set other nitty-gritty options using Program Information Files (PIF files) and the System option in the Control Panel. Unless specified otherwise, Windows XP uses the file _DEFAULT.PIF, stored in the default Windows folder (either \WINDOWS or \WINNT), as the basis for MS-DOS sessions and running applications that don't have a PIF. When you alter the "properties" for DOS applications by right-clicking the application and making settings, you create a customized PIF file for that application. The result of running any DOS application, however, is that Windows XP Professional creates a PIF on-the-fly and assigns the default settings to it unless other settings are specified.

 If your MS-DOS program gives error messages when it tires to open files, see "MS-DOS Program Can't Open Enough Files" in the "Troubleshooting" section at the end of this chapter.

 If your older MS-DOS application displays lots of strange characters on the screen, especially the combination "← [", see "MS-DOS Application Displays Garbage Characters" in the Troubleshooting section at the end of this chapter.

SETTING THE COMMAND PROMPT WINDOW PROPERTIES FROM A WINDOW

The command prompt window displays a text-mode window that looks a lot like a DOS computer's screen. This window is actually a true 32-bit Windows application, although it can also execute old MS-DOS applications. Settings you make in to the command prompt window affect both the Window itself, and any DOS programs run it. In fact, by far the simplest means for altering the DOS environment is via the Properties dialog box of a DOS window. If you need to fine-tune the DOS environment, this is most likely the way you will do it.

When you open a command prompt window or run a DOS-based program, the window defaults to a standard size, background color, and font. Configuration options on the window's Control menu allow you to alter settings for the specific session. Options in the dialog boxes also let you save the settings to establish new defaults. You can set the properties like this:

1. Choose Start, Run.
2. Enter **cmd**, and press Enter. This runs the Windows XP command prompt, a true 32-bit Windows program. The settings you'll make here are applied to the VDM as well.
3. On the resulting command prompt window, click the upper-left corner to open the Control menu, and choose either Properties or Default.
   - Properties sets the properties for this box and optionally all other boxes with the same title (as seen in the box's title bar) in the future.
   - Default applies the settings to all DOS-based programs and command prompt windows from here on out (even with other programs running in them).

25

The resulting dialog box is the same in either case; only the window title is different. You can see it in Figure 25.12.

Figure 25.12
Here, you can set the properties for all command prompt windows.

4. Click through the four tabs, and notice the settings. You can click the ? (question mark) button in the dialog box and then click any of the settings to learn more about them.

5. Make changes as necessary, and click OK.

If you're changing the properties for a specific window, the default is to change the properties for this window only. If you want to use these settings every time you launch this program, select Modify Shortcut That Started This Window, and then click OK.

When you make this choice, Windows edits the PIF for the DOS application in question (or the _DEFAULT.PIF in the case of a CMD window), storing the settings.

NOTE

> The Control menu's Edit command and its associated cascading menu options are covered in Chapter 5, "Using the Simple Supplied Applications," which describes the use of the Clipboard and OLE.

TIP FROM

Bob
& Brian

> Setting a large buffer size can be a real boon if you run batch files or other programs that normally cause text to scroll off the top of the screen. A large buffer enables you to scroll back the screen and check program flow and error messages.

EDITING ADVANCED SETTINGS FOR A DOS APPLICATION FROM ITS PROPERTIES SHEET

If you're experiencing difficulties while running specific DOS programs, you should read this section to learn about making deeper changes to the properties settings for them. When you manipulate the properties (via the PIF) for a program, Windows XP Professional fine-tunes the VDM environment for the particular application, allowing it to run more smoothly, or in some cases simply allowing it to run at all.

MS-DOS applications were designed to run in solitude. They assume that they are the only applications running and usually are memory hogs. Often they want at least 640KB of RAM and perhaps even extended (XMS) or expanded (EMS) memory. Running several non-Windows programs simultaneously—especially DOS programs—is just asking for territorial conflict.

To successfully accommodate the DOS-based applications still in use, Windows XP Professional must be ingenious in managing computer resources such as RAM, printers, modems, mouse devices, and display I/O. Significant sleight of hand is required to pull off this task smoothly, but Microsoft has done this fairly well, partly due to the use of PIFs.

PIFs (program information files) are small files stored on disk, usually in the default Windows folder (\WINDOWS or \WINNT) or in the same folder as the application. They contain settings Windows XP Professional uses when it runs a related application. When you modify the properties of a DOS executable or shortcut, Windows XP, in turn, edits the associated PIF. With the correct settings, the program runs properly, sparing you the aggravation caused by program crashes, sluggish performance, memory shortages, and other annoying anomalies. PIFs have the same initial name as the application but use .PIF as the extension (123.PIF, for example). When you run an MS-DOS application (using any technique), Windows XP searches the application's directory and the system search path for a PIF with the same name as the application. If one is found, this file's settings are applied to the DOS environment by the DOS environment subsystem before running the application. If no PIF is found, Windows XP uses the default settings stored in a file named _DEFAULT.PIF, stored in the \WINNT or \WINDOWS folder. These settings work for most DOS applications, but not all; games and educational programs are likely to need the most modifications.

25

TIP FROM

Bob
& Brian

> In earlier versions of Windows, you had to edit a PIF using the PIF Editor. You no longer need to do so. For all intents and purposes, you can forget about the existence of PIFs and focus on a DOS application's properties instead by right-clicking the application and choosing Properties. However, if you have specific instructions provided with an older application for making PIF file settings, follow the advice provided for the program in configuring the application's properties.

DOS property settings can affect many aspects of an application's operation, such as (but not limited to) the following:

- The folder (directory) that becomes active when an application starts
- Full-screen or windowed operation upon launch
- Conventional memory usage
- Expanded or extended memory usage
- The application's multitasking priority level

- The application's shortcut keys
- Foreground and background processing

Some DOS programs come with PIFs, knowing you might run them under Windows. PIF settings from a Windows 3.x computer work under the Windows XP environment, so you can copy them to the appropriate directory, or take note of the settings on the Windows 3.x machine and reenter them on the Windows XP machine.

Earlier versions of Windows (namely Windows 3.x) sported more settings for DOS programs, but because Windows XP Professional is more intelligent than its now-obsolete sibling, many of them are history.

To edit these properties for a DOS program, do the following:

1. Find the program file or a shortcut to it.
2. Right-click and choose Properties. You then see a dialog box like the one shown in Figure 25.13. (In this example, I adjusted the properties for a DOS shareware game.)

Figure 25.13
Setting the property settings for a DOS application.

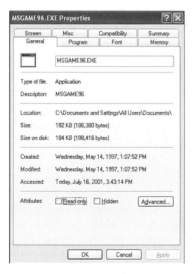

Poke through each tab, and use the ? (question mark) button for help on the settings. Educational and game programs will most often require you to adjust the Memory and Compatibility settings.

TIP FROM

Bob & Brian

> You can check the Program tab's Close On Exit setting if you want the program's window to close when the application exits. In most cases, you'll want this checkbox enabled. However, you might want to keep this check box cleared when you run an application such as tracert or ping or a dir listing, in which you want to read the program's screen output after it completes execution. If the program is not executing properly, you'll also want to be able to see the error output it generates before closing the window.

TIP FROM

*Bob
& Brian*

> The Screen tab's Usage options determine whether the application initially comes up windowed or full-screen. You still can toggle between views by pressing Alt+Enter. Of course, in full-screen display, the mouse is surrendered to the application. When you use a mouse with a windowed application, the mouse works within the window on its menus, and with Windows once you move the mouse back to the Windows desktop. No DOS-based mouse driver is needed; the Windows XP driver works in either case.

CUSTOM STARTUP FILES

The Program tab from a DOS program's Properties dialog box has an Advanced button. You can choose it to further configure the MS-DOS environment with what amounts to the old CONFIG.SYS and AUTOEXEC.BAT commands. In Windows XP, as in Windows NT and Windows 2000, these files are called CONFIG.NT and AUTOEXEC.NT; they are the default files loaded into each DOS VDM. This is a point I really want to make clear:

- The files CONFIG.SYS and AUTOEXEC.BAT in your hard drive's root folder are *ignored* by Windows XP.

- The files CONFIG.NT and AUTOEXEC.NT in \WINDOWS\SYSTEM32 *are* used but only when Windows needs to start up an old MS-DOS or Windows 3.x application. The settings in these files affect *only* the one application you're running at the time, because they're read by the VDM program before it starts up the old application.

If you don't want every application's VDM to use these settings, you can control it. You can specify alternative AUTOEXEC and CONFIG files to be used instead.

From the application's Program tab, click the Advanced button. You then see the dialog box shown in Figure 25.14; here, you can name alternative files to be used. Just enter the names of the files. You should create your own modified files for this use. Start by copying CONFIG.NT and AUTOEXEC.NT to a new folder (the folder of the DOS application in question is a good spot) and then editing them with a plain text editor such as Notepad. You can find the files in the \WINDOWS\SYSTEM32 directory.

Figure 25.14
You can further fine-tune the DOS environment by using CONFIG.NT and AUTOEXEC.NT or similar files of your choice.

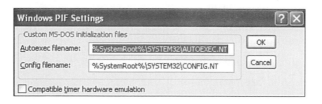

When you run a DOS application, Windows XP Professional creates a DOS VDM by loading the DOS environment subsystem and sort of "booting up" DOS. In the process, it reads in settings from CONFIG.NT and AUTOEXEC.NT in just the same way real DOS read CONFIG.SYS and AUTOEXEC.BAT when it booted. The only difference is the filenames and the file locations. In this case, the files are in the SYSTEM32 directory (usually

\WINDOWS\SYSTEM32 or \WINNT\SYSTEM32) instead of the root directory. Each time you run a DOS application in a new window (each time a VDM is created), Windows XP Professional reads the CONFIG.NT and AUTOEXEC.NT files. The great thing about this capability is that you can change the settings and rerun a program, and the new settings get read and go into effect immediately. It's like rebooting DOS after fine-tuning CONFIG.SYS and AUTOEXEC.BAT—except faster.

TIP FROM

Bob
& Brian

> Editing these files properly is no piece of cake. I suggest you have at hand a good DOS reference like Que's *Special Edition Using DOS 6.22, Third Edition*.

Microsoft, for some reason, chose not to provide a comprehensive list of the settings permitted in CONFIG.NT in the online Help and Support, so I've listed them in Table 25.1.

TABLE 25.1   COMMANDS AVAILABLE FOR CONFIG.NT

Command	Description
country=	Sets the language conventions for the session.
device=	Installs loadable device drivers. Be careful with drivers that attempt to address hardware directly; they don't work. You can load display drivers such as ANSI.SYS and memory managers such as EMM.SYS and HIMEM.SYS.
dos=	Tells Windows 2000 what to do with the Upper Memory Area (where to load DOS, as in dos=high).
dosonly	Allows only DOS programs to be loaded from a COMMAND.COM prompt. POSIX, OS/2, and Windows programs don't run. Note that a COMMAND.COM prompt and a Windows XP command prompt window's prompt are not the same. If you run COMMAND.COM, you get a DOS VDM window running the DOS command interpreter. Command Prompt windows run Windows XP's command interpreter (CMD.EXE), whose command set differs and expands on MS-DOS's.
echoconfig	Activates the display of CONFIG and AUTOEXEC commands as they are executed from the files.
EMM	Lets you configure EMM (Expanded Memory Manager) support when the program's properties specify the value for EMS memory as greater than 0.
fcbs=	Sets the maximum number of file control blocks (FCBs).
files=	Sets the maximum number of open files.
install=	Loads a memory-resident (TSR) program into memory before the window comes up or an application loads.
loadhigh=	Loads device drivers into the High Memory Area (HMA).
ntcmdprompt	Replaces the COMMAND.COM interpreter with the Windows XP interpreter, CMD.EXE. After you load a TSR or when you shell out of an application to DOS, you get CMD.EXE instead, from which you have the added benefits of the Windows XP interpreter.

TABLE 25.1	CONTINUED
Command	**Description**
rem	Marks a line as a comment, causing the system to ignore it when "booting" the file.
stacks=	Indicates the amount of RAM set aside for stacking up hardware interrupts as they come in.

TIP FROM

Bob & Brian

> If you run DOS programs which require different CONFIG.NT and AUTOEXEC.NT files, store each program's CONFIG.NT and AUTOEXEC.NT files in the program's own folder and specify their location in the dialog box shown in Figure 25.13.

If you enter CONFIG.NT into the Search box in Windows XP Professional's Help and Support Center, some of the terms above are listed under the Full-Text Search Matches section of Search Results. Click on the the individual terms for more information.

THE WINDOWS XP COMMAND LINE

Despite the ease of use of the Windows graphical user interface, using the command-line interface remains a useful way to perform many maintenance, configuration, and diagnostic tasks. Many of the most important diagnostic tools such as ping, tracert, and nslookup are only available from the command line, unless you purchase third-party graphical add-ons to perform these functions. Using batch files remains a useful way to encapsulate common management functions; batch files (or shortcuts to batch files) can be placed in shared folders as a way of distributing management functions on a network. Together, command-line utilities and scripts run with either Windows Scripting Host (wscript.exe) or the command-line-based scripting host (cscript.exe) provide a complete set of building blocks from which you can build very high-level utilities if normal Windows commands aren't sufficient for your needs.

The Windows XP Professional command-line utilities include many of the same programs found in DOS and earlier versions of Windows. In many cases, the programs have been enhanced considerably. Utilities not found in DOS or Windows 9x are also available.

Command-line programs fall into five categories, as shown in Table 25.2.

TABLE 25.2	CATEGORIES OF COMMAND-LINE PROGRAMS
Types of Commands	**Description**
Built-in	These commands are built in to the command interpreter; for example, dir, copy, and rename.
Native	These commands call .EXE files; for example, sort.exe, net.exe, and more.exe.

25

Table 25.2   Continued

Types of Commands	Description
Subsystem	These commands are .EXE files from older operating systems that were designed to adjust the environment or interface. They run inside the virtual DOS machine. Examples are `DOSKEY`, `SETVER`, `himem.sys`, and `dosx.exe`.
Batch file	These commands direct the flow of batch files; for example, `for`, `goto`, `if`, and `else`.
Configuration	These commands go in AUTOEXEC.NT, CONFIG.NT, and CONFIG.SYS in the root drive. They tune the subsystem during startup.

The command interpreter (the DOS shell) in Windows XP is, by default, CMD.EXE. The CMD.EXE command interpreter is similar to DOS's old COMMAND.COM shell but has enhanced batch file functions and also has built-in command-line editing and a command history function similar to that provided by `DOSKEY` in DOS and Windows 9x. You don't need `DOSKEY` in Windows XP, unless you want to use its command aliasing feature.

Many of the built-in commands are significantly enhanced since Windows 9x and NT 4. To see a complete list of command-line utilities along with syntax and usage examples, open the Help and Support Center and search for Command-line reference A-Z. Click each command for use, syntax, and examples.

What's New or Different from MS-DOS

Windows XP retains and enhances almost all the functionality of MS-DOS. The following sections explain new Windows XP commands not found in MS-DOS, changes to MS-DOS commands, and unavailable MS-DOS commands.

TIP FROM

Bob
& Brian

> You can see the command line syntax and options for most commands by typing the command name followed by `/?` in a command prompt window. For example, `rasdial /?` lists the options for the rasdial command.
>
> The online command line reference provides more detail. See the previous tip to find out how to view the command line reference.
>
> Also, try typing `help xxxx`, where *xxxx* is the name of the program you're interested in. Some commands are documented this way.

Windows XP Commands

Table 25.3 explains Windows XP system commands not found in MS-DOS. Commands marked with an asterisk (*) can be used only in CONFIG.NT.

TABLE 25.3 WINDOWS XP COMMANDS

Command	Function
arp	Displays and modifies entries in the Address Routing Protocol cache, which stores IP addresses matched to Ethernet or Token Ring network cards.
assoc	Displays or modifies file name associations.
at	Schedules commands and programs to run on a computer at a specified time and date.
atmadm	Monitors connections and addresses registered by the ATM Call Manager on an ATM (asynchronous transfer mode) network.
bootcfg	Configures, queries, and changes Boot.ini settings to change how the system starts.
cacls	Displays or modifies discretionary access control lists (DACLs) of files.
chkntfs	Displays and sets automatic drive checking on FAT16, FAT32, and NTFS volumes when the system starts up.
cipher	Displays or changes encryption settings for files and folders on NTFS drives.
cmstp	Installs or removes a Connection Manager service profile.
compact	Displays or alters compression settings for files and folders on NTFS drives.
cprofile	Removes wasted space from specified user profiles and can also remove user-specific file associations.
convert	Converts filesystems from FAT or FAT32 to NTFS.
cscript	Windows Script Host; use to run .VBS (Visual Basic Script) programs and other scripts.
diskpart	Manages drive and disk partitions.
Dosonly*	Prevents starting applications other than MS-DOS–based applications from the COMMAND.COM prompt.
driverquery	Displays all installed device drivers and properties.
Echoconfig*	Displays messages when reading the MS-DOS subsystem CONFIG.NT file.
endlocal	Ends localization of environment variables.
eventcreate	Administrator-only tool for creating a custom event in a specified event log.
eventquery	List events and properties from specified event logs.
eventtrigger	Displays and configures event triggers on networked or local systems.
eventcommand	Configures trapping of events.

25

continues

TABLE 25.3   CONTINUED

Command	Function
expand	Expands and displays location of compressed files stored on distribution disks or CDs.
findstr	Searches for text in files using regular expressions.
finger	Displays information about remote computers running Finger (usually Unix-based systems).
flattemp	Enables or disables flat temporary folders; use as an alternative to the normal nested temporary folders within the default \Temp folder.
fsutil	Administrator-only tool for managing FAT and NTFS file systems.
ftp	Simple file transfer protocol program.
ftype	Displays and modifies file types used with filename extensions and the default command strings.
getmac	Displays the Media Access Control (MAC) or physical address and network protocol for the network cards used by the local computer and computers on the networks.
gpresult	Displays Group Policy settings and Resultant Set of Policy (RSOP) settings for the specified user or computer.
gpupdate	Refreshes local and network (if based on Active Directory) Group Policy and security settings; replaces secedit/refreshpolicy option.
helpctr	Opens and configures Help and Support Center.
hostname	Displays hostname used by a computer running TCP/IP.
ipconfig	Displays IP configuration for the system and can refresh DHCP and DNS settings.
ipseccmd	Configures IPSec (Internet Protocol Security) policies for local registries, remote registries, or a directory service.
ipxroute	Displays and modifies the routing tables used by the IPX protocol used with some versions of Novell NetWare.
irftp	File transfer program for infrared ports.
lodctr	Registers, saves, and restores specified performance counter names and Explain text.
logman	Schedules and manages performance counter and event trace log collections on both local and specified remote systems.
lpq	Displays status of Line Printer Daemon print queues.
lpr	Sends commands to the Line Printer Daemon to prepare for printing.
macfile	Manages File Server for Macintosh servers and drives.
mmc	Opens Microsoft Management Console.

TABLE 25.3   CONTINUED

Command	Function
mountvol	Creates, deletes, and lists volume mount points; enables user to link volumes without using a drive letter.
msiexec	Installs, modifies, and performs operations on Windows Installer.
msinfo32	Opens Microsoft System Information.
nbtstat	Displays statistics for NetBIOS over TCP/IP (NetBT) protocol.
net	When used with keywords, performs a wide variety of network usage and management tasks.
netsh	Scripting utility for displaying or modifying the network configuration of a local or remote computer.
netstat	Displays details about active TCP/IP connections.
nslookup	Diagnostic tool for Domain Name System (DNS) infrastructure; requires that TCP/IP be running.
ntbackup	Starts Ntbackup program with specified options for backing up data or system state.
ntcmdprompt*	Runs the Windows 2000 command interpreter, CMD.EXE, rather than COMMAND.COM after running a TSR or after starting the command prompt from within an MS-DOS application.
ntsd	Tool for software developers.
openfiles	Displays or queries open files; can also disconnect files opened by network users.
Pagefileconfig.vbs	Administrator-only tool to display and configure paging file/virtual memory settings. Run with Cscript.
pathping	Diagnostic tool for checking network latency and packet loss.
pbadmin	Administers phone books.
pentnt	Detects floating-point errors in early Pentium chips and can also disable the hardware and enable floating-point emulation.
perfmon	Runs Windows XP Performance console with setting files used by the Windows NT version of Performance Monitor.
popd	Changes to the directory last set with the pushd command.
prncfg.vbs	Configures or displays printer configuration information. Run with Cscript.
prndrvr.vbs	Lists, adds, and deletes printer drivers. Run with Cscript.
prnjobs.vbs	Manages print jobs. Run with Cscript.
prnmngr.vbs	Manages printers and printer connections. Run with Cscript.
prnport.vbs	Manages TCP/IP printer ports.

25

continues

TABLE 25.3   CONTINUED

Command	Function
prnqctl.vbs	Prints test pages and controls print queues (pause, resume, clear).
pushd	Saves the current directory for use by the popd command and then changes to the specified directory.
query	Runs specified Terminal Server query commands.
rasdial	Automates connection process for Microsoft clients using specified domain and phone number data or phonebook data.
rcp	Copies files between a computer running rshd (the Unix/Linux remote shell daemon/service) and a Windows XP computer.
reg	Adds, changes, and displays Registry subkeys and values.
regsvr32	Registers specified .dll files.
relog	Exports performance counter data into specified formats for import into database and spreadsheet programs.
replace	Replaces files in destination folder with same-named files in source folder; can also add files to destination folder.
reset session	Delete a session from Terminal Server.
rexec	Runs commands on remote Unix/Linux computers which are running the Rexec daemon (service).
route	Displays and modifies the local IP routing table.
rsh	Runs commands on remote computers running the rsh daemon (service), such as the Rshsvc.exe program included with the Windows 2000 Server Resource Kit.
rsm	Manages removable-storage media such as tape libraries and others.
runas	Allows user to run specified commands with different permissions than their current login provides.
sc	Controls services with the Service Controller.
schtasks	Schedules tasks.
secedit	Manages system security settings.
setlocal	Begins localization of environmental variables.
shutdown	Shuts down specified local or remote computers.
start	Runs a specified program or command in a secondary window and in its own memory space.
systeminfo	Displays detailed technical information about specified local or remote computers.
sfc	System File Checker; configures protection for system files.
taskkill	Ends specified tasks or processes.

TABLE 25.3   CONTINUED

Command	Function
tasklist	Displays programs and services running on remote or local computers.
tcmsetup	Configures or disables TAPI client.
telnet	Runs Telnet service and issues specified commands.
tlntadm	Remotely manages computers running Telnet Server.
tftp	Transfers files to and from Unix/Linux computers running the Trivial File Transfer Protocol (tftp) daemon (service).
title	Sets the title of the command prompt window.
tracerpt	Processes trace logs or data from event trace providers and generate reports.
tracert	Trace Route command; traces routing to specified IP address or URL.
typeperf	Displays performance counter data onscreen or exports it to a data file you can import with a spreadsheet or database program.
unlodctr	Removes the Performance counter names and Explain text for a service or device driver from the Registry of a local or remote computer.
vssadmin	Displays the current volume snapshot backups and snapshot writing programs.
w32tm	Diagnoses problems with Windows Time.
winnt	Starts Windows XP upgrade from an MS-DOS command prompt.
winnt32	Starts Windows XP upgrade from a command prompt in a 32-bit version of Windows (9x/Me/NT/2000/XP).
wmic	Controls Windows Management Instrumentation (WMI) and WMI-managed systems.
&&	Command following this symbol runs only if the command preceding the symbol succeeds.
||	Command following this symbol runs only if the command preceding the symbol fails.
&	Separates multiple commands on the command line.
( )	Groups commands.
^	(Escape character.) Allows you to type command symbols &, |, and so on, as text.
; or ,	Separates parameters.

CHANGES TO MS-DOS COMMANDS

Table 25.4 lists changes and improvements to MS-DOS commands.

TABLE 25.4 CHANGES TO MS-DOS COMMANDS IN WINDOWS XP

Command	Changed Features
chcp	This command changes code pages for full-screen mode only.
cmd	CMD.EXE replaces COMMAND.COM.
del	New switches provide many more functions.
dir	New switches provide many more functions.
diskcomp	Switches /1 and /8 are not supported.
diskcopy	Switch /1 is not supported.
doskey	This command is available for all character-based programs that accept buffered input. DOSKEY has been improved by a series of enhancements.
format	Switches /b, /s, and /u are not supported. Adds new filesystem and cluster-size switches.
label	The symbols ^ and & can be used in a volume label.
mode	This command has had extensive changes.
more	New switches provide many more functions.
path	The %PATH% environment variable appends the current path to a new setting at the command prompt.
print	Switches /b, /c, /m, /p, /q, /s, /t, and /u are not supported.
prompt	New character combinations allow you to add ampersands ($a), parentheses ($c and $f), and spaces ($s) to your prompt.
recover	This command recovers files only.
rmdir	The new /s switch deletes directories containing files and subdirectories.
sort	This command does not require the TEMP environment variable. File size is unlimited.
xcopy	New switches provide many more functions.

I'll talk a bit more about some enhanced commands at the end of this chapter, under "Tips from the Windows Pros."

UNAVAILABLE MS-DOS COMMANDS

The MS-DOS commands in Table 25.5 are not available at the Windows XP Home Edition command prompt.

TABLE 25.5   MS-DOS COMMANDS NOT AVAILABLE IN WINDOWS XP HOME EDITION

Command	New Procedure or Reason for Obsolescence
assign	Not supported in Windows XP.
backup	Not currently supported.
choice	Not currently supported.
ctty	Not currently supported.
dblspace	Not supported.
defrag	Windows XP automatically optimizes disk use. To optimize a disk manually, right-click it in My Computer, click Properties, and then, on the Tools tab, click Defragment Now.
deltree	The rmdir /s command deletes directories containing files and subdirectories.
dosshell	Unnecessary with Windows XP.
drvspace	Not currently supported.
emm386	Unnecessary with Windows XP. Note: emm386 is not used, but an EMM control does appear in CONFIG.NT for CMD.EXE.
fasthelp	This MS-DOS 6.0 command is the same as the Windows XP command help. Windows XP also provides an online command reference.
fdisk	Disk Management prepares hard disks for use with Windows XP.
include	Multiple configurations of the MS-DOS subsystem are not supported.
interlnk	Not supported. Use the Network Connections Wizard to configure a direct connection via parallel, serial, or infrared (IR) ports.
intersrv	Not supported. Use the Network Connections wizard to configure a direct connection via parallel, serial, or infrared (IR) ports.
join	Increased partition size and an improved filesystem eliminate the need to join drives.
memmaker	Windows XP automatically optimizes the MS-DOS subsystem's memory use.
menucolor	Multiple configurations of the MS-DOS subsystem are not supported.
menudefault	Multiple configurations of the MS-DOS subsystem are not supported.
menuitem	Multiple configurations of the MS-DOS subsystem are not supported.
mirror	Not supported in Windows XP.
msav	Not supported.
msbackup	Windows XP provides the optional NTBackup utility (under the Administrative Tools in the Control Panel) for computers with tape drives or the xcopy command for computers without tape drives. Install NTBackup from the \3RDPARTY\MSFT\NTBACKUP folder of the Windows XP CD-ROM.

25

continues

TABLE 25.5 CONTINUED

Command	New Procedure or Reason for Obsolescence
mscdex	You don't need to configure the MS-DOS subsystem to use CD-ROM drives. Windows XP provides access to CD-ROM drives for the MS-DOS subsystem. Actually, mscdexnt is the Windows 2000 replacement for mscdex and is run in AUTOEXEC.NT.
msd	You can use the System Information snap-in instead. To start System Information, choose Start, Run, and then type msinfo32. System Information is much more accurate and much more complete than msd.
numlock	Not currently supported.
power	Not supported.
restore	Not currently supported.
scandisk	Not supported.
smartdrv	Windows XP automatically provides disk caching for the MS-DOS subsystem.
submenu	Multiple configurations of the MS-DOS subsystem are not supported.
sys	Windows XP does not fit on a standard 1.2MB or 1.44MB floppy disk.
undelete	Not supported in Windows XP.
unformat	Not supported in Windows XP.
vsafe	Not supported.

Speeding Up Legacy Programs

Read on if you want to learn how to monitor a 16-bit Windows-based program or an MS-DOS–based program. In Windows XP Professional, 16-bit Windows-based programs run as separate threads in a multithreaded process called Windows Virtual DOS Machine (NTVDM). The NTVDM process simulates a 16-bit Windows environment.

An MS-DOS–based program runs in its own NTVDM process. You can monitor a 16-bit program or an MS-DOS–based program running on your computer with System Monitor by monitoring the NTVDM instance of the Process performance object. Note that 16-bit programs running in an NTVDM appear only if they are started in a separate memory space. If you find that your 16-bit programs are not performing well under Windows XP Professional, you can access some of the program's properties by right-clicking the name of the program in Windows Explorer and configuring the properties as follows:

- If the program is in a window, and the display performance is slow, on the Screen tab, click Full-Screen.
- If the program is in a window and seems to pause periodically, click the Misc tab, and set the Idle Sensitivity slider to Low.

You can turn off Compatible Timer Hardware Emulation for the program if performance does not improve by changing the previously described settings. To do so, right-click _DEFAULT.PIF or the program name, select Properties, point to Program, and click Advanced. In the dialog box that appears, clear the Compatible Timer Hardware Emulation check box. This change typically causes a decrease in performance and should be made only if other efforts fail.

KEEPING A COMMAND PROMPT WINDOW OPEN AFTER EXECUTION OF A PROGRAM

To keep a command prompt window open after a program has executed, you can open the window first and then run the program manually. When the program is terminated, the window will stay open. However, if you run the program by entering its name into the Run box or from a shortcut in the Windows GUI, it will close automatically by default. To keep the window open, follow these steps:

1. Create a shortcut to the DOS program or batch file.
2. Right-click the shortcut, and choose Properties.
3. Select the Program tab.
4. Uncheck Close on Exit. The window should now be kept open after the program finishes.

TROUBLESHOOTING

ADJUSTING PROGRAM SETTINGS

I can't get my Windows 95 program to work, even if I use the Program Compatibility Wizard.

The Program Compatibility Wizard isn't a cure-all for program compatibility problems, although it can help many otherwise-incompatible programs to run.

Before you decide you simply can't use the program at all with Windows XP, try the following:

1. Try using additional compatibility settings—When Windows 95 was first introduced, many system still used standard VGA (640 × 480) resolution with only 256 colors. If you didn't select these options before, or didn't disable the visual themes, try running the wizard again and make these additional settings.
2. Try using a different Windows version when you run the compatibility wizard—If your program specifies "Windows 95 or Windows NT 4.0", for example, try both compatibility mode settings before you give up.
3. Reinstall the program—it's possible that when Windows XP was installed that your program's installation was damaged.
4. Be sure you have installed the latest patches and updates from the program vendor.

These same steps will help you with any program compatibility problem you encounter.

MS-DOS PROGRAM CAN'T OPEN ENOUGH FILES

When I run my MS-DOS application, I get the error "Too Many Files Open" or a similar message

By default, MS-DOS applications run by the VDM are allowed to open only 20 files. Some older programs, especially database programs, want to open more. In DOS or Windows 9x, you'd have added the line

```
FILES=99
```

to your config.sys file. In Windows XP, you must add this line to your CONFIG.NT file. Use Search to find this file on your computer, or look in \WINDOWS\SYSTEM32. Of course, if you specified an alternate setup file for this application, you'll want to change that file rather than CONFIG.NT.

MS-DOS APPLICATION DISPLAYS GARBAGE CHARACTERS

When I run an old MS-DOS application, I see lots of junk characters on the screen, and many occurences of "← [".

Some older programs that displayed text on the computer screen depended on the assistance of a display driver program called ansi.sys. Ansi.sys isn't installed by default in CONFIG.NT, so you're seeing the control message that your program was intending for ansi.sys to interpret; these should have resulted in color changes or cursor movements.

You need to add the line

```
device=ansi.sys
```

to your CONFIG.NT file. Use Search to find this file on your computer, or look in \WINDOWS\SYSTEM32. Of course, if you specified an alternate setup file for this application, you'll want to change that file rather than CONFIG.NT.

TIPS FROM THE WINDOWS PROS: GETTING MORE OUT OF THE COMMAND PROMPT WITH COMMAND EXTENSIONS

If you grew up with MS-DOS, like I did, you might find that even Windows XP's many enhancements to Windows aren't enough to keep you out of command-prompt-land permanently.

Believe it or not, you still can't make a printout of the files and folders stored in a given folder from Windows Explorer. And, when it comes to switching drives and folders, the command is quicker than the mouse.

If you want to move around your system faster than Explorer can do it, take advantage of the enhancements to Prompt provided by the Command Extensions activated by default with Windows XP Professional.

Command Extensions make lots of your favorite command-line utilities a lot more powerful in Windows XP Professional than they were in Windows 9x/Me.

Command extensions can be turned off by typing the command **CMD /Y** and pressing Enter at a command prompt. To turn them back on again, type **CMD /X** and press Enter.

COMMANDS AFFECTED BY COMMAND EXTENSIONS

When command extensions are enabled, the following commands have new features or are available for use:

- ASSOC *
- CALL
- CD or CHDIR
- COLOR *
- DEL or ERASE
- ENDLOCAL
- FOR
- FTYPE *
- GOTO
- IF
- MD or MKDIR
- POPD
- PROMPT
- PUSHD
- SET
- SETLOCAL
- SHIFT
- START

commands available only when command extensions are enabled.

If you like to write batch files, you'll find that changes to the FOR command alone will make your head spin with possibilities. Type **help for >x & notepad x** to read all about it.

In the following sections, you'll see how to use some of the other enhanced commands to get more done at the command-prompt level.

TIP FROM

Bob

& Brian

> For a list of valid commands at the command prompt, type HELP|MORE and press Enter.

USING COMMAND EXTENSIONS TO MAKE CD (CHANGE DIRECTORY) EASIER

The CD (Change Directory) and MD (Make Directory) commands allow you to change to a different folder and make a new folder from the command prompt as an alternative to using the Windows Explorer.

When command extensions are enabled, you can change to a long directory (folder) without putting quote marks around the name:

CD \My Documents\My Music\My MP3s

25

Without command extensions, you'd need to enter the following command:

```
CD "\My Documents\My Music\My MP3s"
```

Forget the quotes, and you'd see an error message.

Normally, MD (Make Directory) can create just one folder (directory) at a time. When command extensions are enabled, you can create a nested series of folders with a single command. For example, this single command creates a series of folders below your current folder. You could use a command like this within the \My Documents folder to create folders for your home budget:

```
MD "My Budget\4th Quarter\Travel"
```

(Yes, you need the quote marks!)

USING COMMAND EXTENSIONS TO MAKE PROMPT MORE POWERFUL

When you open a command-prompt session in Windows XP, the default prompt uses the $p (current drive and path) $g (greater-than) sign to display your current location:

```
C:\Documents and Settings\All Users>
```

But, if you've mapped a network drive to a drive letter, either with Windows Explorer or the command-prompt NET USE command, all you normally see is a drive letter when you change to the network drive:

```
S:\>
```

When command extensions are enabled, you can use the following PROMPT command to display the server name (if any):

```
PROMPT $M$P$G
```

Now, you will be reminded of the true network path and the drive letter you're using to access it.

Figure 25.15 shows you how this special prompt command makes life easier for you when you work with network drives.

Figure 25.15
Using the MP$G PROMPT to display the actual path to a mapped network drive.

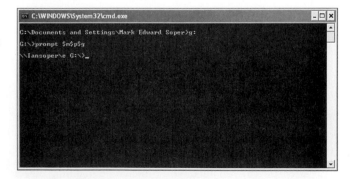

USING COMMAND EXTENSIONS TO CHANGE THE COLOR OF THE COMMAND PROMPT WINDOW

Very experienced DOS users might remember when the ANSI.SYS device driver and complex batch file commands were needed to change the screen color in a command-prompt session. When command extensions are enabled, you can use the COLOR command to do the same thing. And, if you want to use more than one command-line session at the same time, you can color-code each one.

To see a complete list of the color codes you can use, type `color /?` and press Enter.

Here are two examples:

To change the color of the screen to light blue and the text to light aqua (very easy on the eyes), enter **COLOR 9B**.

To reset the screen color to its original colors, enter **COLOR**.

When you close the command-prompt window, the colors are reset to the ordinary black background, white text display.

25

CHAPTER 26

FONT MANAGEMENT

In this chapter

A LITTLE WINDOWS FONT HISTORY

In this chapter, I'll explain a bit about font technology, how to add and remove fonts from your system, how to choose and use fonts wisely, how to procure new fonts, how to create fonts of your own, and how fonts interact with Internet Explorer.

Microsoft continues the move toward improved font management in Windows XP. As in Windows 9x, NT, and 2000, when you open the Control Panel and choose Fonts, a Fonts folder opens. (In reality, it's the folder X:\winnt\fonts; just replace X with your startup drive letter.) It is one of those specially treated system folders that magically has its own unique menu and right-click commands with options to let you do the following:

- Add and remove fonts
- View fonts in various ways
- List fonts by similarity of looks
- List only the basic font family name and hide variations such as bold and italic to make selection easier

Since the days of Windows 3.0, one of the big attractions to Windows was that it included a unified system for displaying and printing text across all Windows applications and printers.

The Macintosh had it all over the PC in the desktop publishing arena in the late 80s and early 90s, and had the PC not caught up, I think Apple would be the frontrunner in personal computers today.

Not to be outdone of course, Gates and his team caught on fast enough, developing their own font system and building it into the then quickly evolving Windows. With Windows 3.1 came TrueType fonts, and things began to work just about as well as the Macintosh. A user with only a single printer driver and one pool of fonts could effectively lay out and print complex documents across a broad spectrum of applications. Each new version of Windows has improved on the Microsoft font technology.

Windows XP benefits from all the developments of previous versions of Windows. Plus, the unstoppable march of printer technology has brought the price of full-color printing in the 1200dpi range down to below $100.

A LITTLE FONT PRIMER

Anyone interested in fonts should first become acquainted with basic typographic nomenclature. Let's start at the top.

The word *font*, as used in Windows, really refers to a typeface. Those people in typesetting circles believe the term is misused in PC jargon, and you should really be calling, say, Arial a typeface. But, oh well. There goes the language (again). Fonts are specified by size as well as by name. The size of a font is measured in *points*. A point is 1/72 of an inch.

Windows XP comes with a basic stock of fonts (about 60). The exact number of fonts depends on the printer or printers you have installed and the screen fonts you have chosen to install.

→ To learn more about installing printers, **see** "Printing and Faxing," **p. 183**.

 If your screen fonts (such as text under icons on the desktop) seem too large or too small, see "Icon Fonts Too Large or Small" in the "Troubleshooting" section at the end of this chapter.

FONT SUBSTITUTIONS

Fonts are readily available on the Internet these days, so finding fonts you might need is no biggie. You just download them and drop them into the Fonts folder (see the section later on adding fonts). Also, OpenType makes it easier to compress and incorporate fonts into your documents so that, when you share them with others, they are displayed correctly even if the recipient doesn't have the fonts installed in his or her system.

NOTE

> From this point on, I'll use the terms *OpenType* and *TrueType* interchangeably because they are so closely related.

But what if you have older documents that were formatted with fonts not in your system and that you can't acquire? Some word processors, such as Microsoft Word, have an option to substitute missing fonts with present fonts. In Word, choose Tools, Options, Compatibility, Font Substitutions. If all the fonts you need to print the document are installed in the system, you are told that everything is hunky dory. If not, you can make changes. Check the help file for the word processing program for details.

Another kind of font substitution pertains only to PostScript printers. Because PostScript printers have internal fonts, printing is faster using them than forcing Windows to download a similar font file into the PostScript rasterizer and then commence printing. For example, the Windows Arial font and the PostScript Helvetica font are virtually identical. So, you can tell your PostScript printer driver to just use the Helvetica font in the printer whenever you print a document formatted with Arial. Likewise, Times can be substituted for Windows's Times New Roman.

A font substitution table is responsible for setting the relationship of the screen and printer fonts. In Windows NT, 2000, and XP, you can find this table on the Device Settings tab of a Printer's Properties dialog box.

26

Microsoft's Special LCD Font Technology: ClearType

Remember the eight-track tape player? (Oops, there I go dating myself again.) Okay, how about an LP record? Well, add to the list of soon-to-be-landfill items those fat, heavy, heat-producing old CRT (Cathode Ray Tube) monitors. Yup, soon you're going to have more room on your desk for paper-clip organizers and pen holders. In a year or two, having a CRT will stigmatize you as a relic of the past. You won't want any part of it. And the likes of NEC, Mag, Sony, and the rest will see to it, gently "encouraging" us all to shell out fairly big time for the privilege of reading LCD (liquid crystal displays) instead of glowing phosphor ones.

But technology marches on. We're being quickly converted to LCDs regardless of what's on our desktops. Wrist watches and calculators have used LCDs for years. Now PalmPilots, cash registers, ATMs, pay phones, and even gas pumps are using them. And, of course, all laptop computer displays are LCD in one form or another. Soon to proliferate the market will be *ebooks*—electronic gadgets you can read plug-in or downloadable books on, complete with text, graphics, hot links, and more.

Realizing the increasing popularity of the LCD for text display, the folks at Microsoft who were working on TrueType and OpenType got to thinking about improving that technology. Because the pixels on an LCD are square rather than round, and because their focus is perfect (there is no bleeding between dots, which tends to smooth out the look a tad), low-to-medium resolution LCDs tend to display text with a choppy look. To worsen the matter, pixels in LCDs are typically on or off. Microsoft came up with ClearType, which it claims will make words on your LCD screens look as smooth as the words on a piece of paper.

Essentially, ClearType is not dissimilar from the font smoothing in TrueType screen fonts. It's just tailored to LCD technology, using shades of gray (or color) to fill in the tiny gaps between and around the pixels that construct onscreen characters.

Although ClearType font technology works with existing systems such as CRT monitors or LCD panels being driven by analog video display boards, you're going to see noticeable improvements only on color LCDs driven by digital control boards, such as those found in laptops and high-quality flat panel desktop displays.

The advantages gleaned from ClearType are less obvious as the resolution of the LCD panel increases. Low-resolution LCDs form blockier characters because they have fewer pixels to work with. On high-resolution LCDs, pixels are smaller, so pixelation is less obvious to the eye.

26

Building a Font Collection

Windows XP comes with a set of trustworthy TrueType fonts that will meet your needs for many occasions. Most folks get by just fine with Times New Roman, Courier New, and Arial, with maybe an occasional character from Symbol or WingDings. What else could you need? Why should you purchase or download freeware or shareware fonts? And how do you install them and choose which fonts to use in your documents? Let's look at these topics in order.

The prime reason to expand your collection of fonts is simply to make your documents look spiffier, express your message with more alacrity, or convey a specific mood such as formal, festive, or casual.

After you've settled on the font format you're going to use, your next task is to decide how to acquire the fonts. Will you pay for them or download freebies over the Net? The number of typeface designs available for Windows totals in the thousands and is still growing. With that much variety, selecting a set of fonts that's right for you can be a daunting proposition.

CLASSES OF FONTS

Having a basic understanding of font classifications is a good idea before you start purchasing fonts and designing your own documents.

The two primary categories of fonts are *serif* and *sans-serif* designs. Serifs are the little embellishments that extend from the main *strokes* of the character. Serifs often are added to improve readability. As the name implies, sans-serif fonts lack these embellishments, making for a cleaner look. Sans-serif fonts tend to work well for headlines (most newspapers use them), whereas serif fonts are traditionally used for body text (this book is a good example). Combining one serif and one sans-serif font in this way will look good together, but two sans-serif or two serif fonts will clash.

The next major classification of fonts has to do with the spacing between characters. In *monospaced* fonts, every character occupies the same amount of horizontal line space. For example, *l* and *W* get the same amount of linear space. In the following sentence you can see an example of a monospaced font:

```
This text is set in a monospaced font called MacmillanUSAdigital.
```

By contrast, *proportionally spaced* fonts give differing amounts of line space, depending on the character. A *W* gets more space than an *l* or an *i*. The body text in this book uses proportionally spaced fonts, making it easier to read. The advantage of using monospaced fonts is that they allow you to easily align columns of text or numbers when you're using a simple word processor such as Notepad or sending e-mail. You can use the spacebar to align the items in the columns, as you would on a typewriter.

TIP FROM

Bob & Brian

For easier alignment, numerals in most proportionally spaced fonts are monospaced. But in proportionally spaced fonts, you still have the problem with the spacebar. A press of the spacebar in a monospaced font advances the cursor one full block, just as any character does. In a proportional font, the spacebar moves the cursor only a small increment. So, it's still difficult to align rows of characters using the spacebar. If your word processing program has tab stops, setting them and then using the Tab key can help overcome this problem. Using tabs can be problematic when you're reading a document in a program other than the one it was created in, because not all programs translate tabs identically. Aligning columns in e-mail, for example, is a dicey proposition at best because e-mail programs use different fonts and often give users the option of choosing the display font on their own. It might or might not be a monospaced font. Using HTML-based (rich-text) e-mail is one solution to this problem, though not all e-mail client programs can handle it properly. See Chapter 10, "Sending E-mail with Outlook Express," for more details about HTML mail.

26

 If you can't get columns of text or numbers to align in a document someone has sent you, see "Text Columns Out of Alignment" in the "Troubleshooting" section at the end of this chapter.

Two other categories of fonts (after headline and body text) are ornamental and nonalpha-betic symbols. *Ornamental* (sometimes called *display)* fonts have limited application. They are often fun in the short term, or for a one-shot deal such as a poster or a gag. They often attract attention but are too highly stylized to be suitable for body text, and they can distract the readers' attention from your message. Windows doesn't come stocked with any decora-tive fonts. One that was popular a few years ago (and overused!) was Zapf Chancery. You should use ornamental fonts sparingly and only when you want to set a special mood.

Symbol or pi fonts contain special symbols such as musical notes, map symbols, or decora-tions instead of letters, numbers, and punctuation marks. Good examples are Symbol, Zapf Dingbats, and WingDings.

→ To learn more about symbol and other non-keyboard characters, **see** "Character Map," **p. 168**.

PROCURING FONTS

Due to increased interest in typography generated by desktop publishing technology and now with the Web, the number of font designers and vendors has exploded. Fonts are included as part of cheesy applications packages, as well as in the better word processing programs. And the Web is riddled with sites pushing everything from high-class fonts from respected foundries down to $2 fonts.

Many leading font vendors, including Bitstream, Monotype, SoftKey, and others, are pro-ducing TrueType font collections. Although you can find these collections in most software stores, Web downloads are easier. Quite charitably, Microsoft has a site that lists all the type foundries known to it, with descriptions and links. Check out this very helpful site:

```
http://www.microsoft.com/typography/links/links.asp?type=foundries&part=1
```

If that link dies for some reason, check back at the primary Microsoft fonts site and click around the following:

```
http://www.microsoft.com/typography/default.asp
```

Other sites you might find of interest are as follows:

- Agfa/Monotype's site:
  ```
  http://www.monotype.com/
  ```
- Bitstream:
  ```
  http://www.bitstream.com
  ```
- Adobe Systems:
  ```
  www.adobe.com
  ```
- And for some cheapie (and free) fonts, check the following:
  ```
  www.buyfonts.com
  http://www.fontcraft.com/scriptorium/index.html
  ```

I've also seen numerous cheapie CD-ROMs in several computer stores that pack hundreds of TrueType fonts on them.

NOTE

Although shareware and freeware TrueType fonts are plentiful, be aware that not all TrueType fonts have sophisticated hinting built in. Therefore, they might not look as good as fonts from the more respectable font foundries. Some reports from users indicate that funky font files can make your system freak out a bit. In general, though, even the free TrueType (OpenType) fonts will look very good, and you'll be hard pressed to notice the difference.

MANAGING A SYSTEM'S FONT COLLECTION

Windows XP's font management allows you to

- Add new fonts to the system
- Remove unnecessary fonts, freeing disk space
- View fonts onscreen or print out samples of each font you have
- Display groups of fonts that are similar in style

To perform any of these functions, you need to use the Fonts applet found in the Windows XP control panel. Specifically, open the Control Panel through the Start menu, select Appearance and Themes, and then click the Fonts options located in the See Also pane. This opens the windows shown in Figure 26.1.

Figure 26.1
The Fonts folder displaying icons and names for installed fonts.

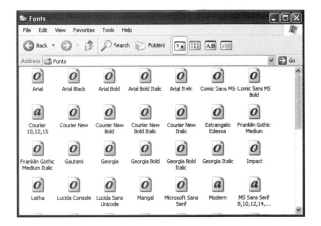

ADDING FONTS

Some font sets come with an installer. In that case, you can just run it as instructed. The fonts are dumped into the Fonts directory, and the system adds them to the Font Registry, whereupon they can be used from your applications. If no installation program came with your fonts, or if you want to add some fonts to your system that you downloaded from the Internet or otherwise acquired, just follow these steps:

1. Open the Control Panel as described in the previous section. The resulting folder window appears, looking much like any other folder. All fonts currently installed in the system appear in this folder, with each font style being a separate file.

2. Choose File, Install New Font. The Add Fonts dialog then appears. Browse to the location of the font files you want to install. Use the Network button if the files are across the LAN. It runs the Map Network Drive Wizard. After you target the source folder, all the fonts in that location are listed in the dialog box.

→ To learn how to map a network drive, **see** "Mapping Drive Letters," **p. 564**.

3. Select the fonts you want to install. Note that if you want an entire font family, you have to select all similarly named files. If you try to install a font that's already in your system, the installer won't let you, so don't worry about accidentally loading one you already have.

4. Choose whether you want the font files *copied* into the Fonts folder as part of the installation process. They work either way. Copying into the Fonts folder keeps things tidier, though it does make a copy of the file, using up more disk space. I like to copy them into the Fonts folder so that I know where all my fonts are. If you use this approach, you can later erase any duplicate source files to save disk space. (Fonts range from about 80 to 400KB each, averaging about 200KB.) If you choose not to copy the files, shortcut icons appear in your Fonts folder instead of normal font icons.

TIP FROM

Bob & Brian

> Don't turn off the Copy check box unless you know that the source files will be available when you want to use the font. If the source files are on a CD-ROM, a floppy, or a workstation on the LAN, you'll probably be better off if you copy them onto the local hard disk.

5. Click OK to finalize the operation. After the installation process is complete, all newly added fonts are added to your font list and are visible in Windows applications that offer font selection.

TIP FROM

Bob & Brian

> You can copy fonts into the system by dragging the font files into the Fonts folder. This one-step process is quick and dirty.

DISPLAYING AND PRINTING FONT EXAMPLES

You can quickly acquire a large selection of fonts, thus easily forgetting what you have on hand. Several utility programs are available to help you keep track of fonts or show a little example of them in font selection lists within applications and such. Check the Web for such programs, by searching for "font," "font tool," or "font view." A few examples of tools to look for include FontShow, LogotypeMaker, and FontShowcase.

The Fonts folder has a few tricks of its own to make font management a bit easier. For starters, you can view and/or print the characters of a font easily by following these steps:

1. Open the Fonts folder.

2. Double-click any icon in the folder. The font then opens in the font viewer (Figure 26.2).

Figure 26.2
The Font Viewer displaying Arial.

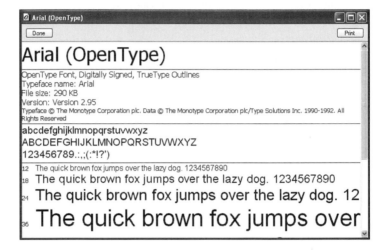

3. If you need printouts, just right-click a font and choose Print, or open the font as per above and click the Print button. To print multiple fonts in one fell swoop, select them first, and then choose File, Print. You get a one-page printout for each font.

TIP FROM

Bob & Brian

> The font viewer displays a font's character set regardless of the location of the font. So, if you want to check out the font's look before installing it, just open the floppy disk or other folder containing the font, and double-click it.

HIDDEN SYSTEM FONTS

Some fonts are normally hidden because they are required by the system. If a user accidentally deleted them, the system wouldn't work. For example, dialog boxes wouldn't have text in them. Unless you turn on viewing of hidden files via the Folder options in an Explorer window, you won't see these fonts. If you do turn on viewing of hidden files and then view the Fonts folder in Details view, you'll see an H in the Attributes column. Make sure not to delete or move these files.

→ File viewing options are covered in "Setting Folder Options," **p. 796**.

TIP FROM

Bob & Brian

> Programs that are multilingual-aware automatically use a font that contains multiple character sets. If you are using a program that is not multilingual-aware, such as Notepad, the font might appear as black boxes or lines. To make the text appear correctly, you might need to manually select a font that contains multiple character sets. Both Tahoma and Microsoft Sans Serif font support multiple character sets.

REMOVING FONTS

Fonts consume space on your hard disk. A typical TrueType font consumes between 50 and 200KB of disk space. If you're a font monger, you could easily chew up a gigabyte or two with fonts you end up never using.

TIP FROM

Bob & Brian

> A little-known fact is that even if an italic or bold font has been removed, most word processing applications for Windows, such as Microsoft Word, can still emulate it on-the-fly. It won't look as good as the real thing, but it will work.

If you get on a spring-cleaning jag and decide to remove some fonts, follow these steps:

1. Open the Fonts folder.
2. To remove an entire font family (normal, Bold, Italic, and Bold Italic), turn on the View, Hide Variations setting. If you want to remove individual styles, turn off this setting so you can see them.
3. Select the font or fonts you want to remove.
4. Press the Del key; choose File, Delete; or right-click one of the selected fonts and choose Delete.
5. When a dialog box asks you to confirm the removal, choose the Yes button. The font is then moved to the Recycle Bin.

TIP FROM

Bob & Brian

> You also can drag a font file to another folder, but the default is for that operation to create a copy of the font and not remove it from your arsenal of system fonts. If your aim is to organize your seldom-used fonts into folders, the easiest way would be to right-click and drag them into the new folders, and then choose Move from the resulting context menu.

TROUBLESHOOTING

FOREIGN-LANGUAGE FONTS DON'T APPEAR

When I'm running a specific program, I can't see the correct foreign-language fonts in dialog boxes, display menus, and within my documents.

You might have this problem if the program you are using doesn't understand how to use Unicode fonts. Unicode fonts are extended fonts that have support for the multiple languages built in to them. To work around this problem, you can try the following procedure:

1. Open the Control Panel, select Date, Time, Language and Regional Options, and then choose Regional and Language Options.

2. Select the Advanced tab.

3. Under Language for non-Unicode programs, select the language version of non-Unicode programs that you want to use.

Note that only non-Unicode programs are affected by alterations to the system locale, and you might be prevented from altering the locale setting if you don't have administrative privileges or if the network policy settings conflict.

TEXT COLUMNS OUT OF ALIGNMENT

Sometimes when I read e-mail or another document that contains columns of text or numbers, they are out of alignment.

You can have this problem if the document was formatted with a monospaced font and you're viewing it in a proportionally spaced font. Select the text in question, and change the font to Courier, Courier New, or some other monospaced font. If your program doesn't allow altering the font of selected text, it might allow you to change the font of all displayed text. E-mail programs often fall into this category. Look for the relevant option setting within the application. For example, in Outlook Express, you choose Tools, Options, Read, Fonts.

DOCUMENT FROM ANOTHER USER IS DISPLAYED IMPROPERLY

I received a complex document that doesn't look right at all. I suspect something is wrong. The text is readable, but I suspect either the author of the document must have had too many drinks or some technical glitch must have happened.

This problem is yet another symptom of the document's font or fonts not being installed in the system that's displaying it. The document probably looks just fine on the computer that its author was using. If you're not going to be printing it or proofing it for layout but care only about the textual content, don't worry about it. If you need to print the document or proof it for line breaks, layout, page arrangement, and so forth, it's imperative that you have the document's font or fonts on your computer. Have the author send you the fonts, or purchase them if they are not free. Then install them as explained in this chapter. Finally, reopen the document.

Another option is to have the author send you another version of the document with embedded fonts. Many fonts can be embedded in your documents so that they will be available on other machines, even if the typeface was not installed originally. Not all Fonts allow this. To find out about this feature plus a myriad of other pieces data, download the Microsoft Font properties extension from http://www.microsoft.com/typography/property/property.htm. This fonts extension tool adds a number of tabs to a font's properties dialog box, including whether or not the font can be embedded (permanently and/or temporarily) and whether the document can be edited or opened read-only.

Note that even if the correct fonts are not available in the system, most layout programs indicate what they are *supposed* to be. To find out, click any text in question, and look at the program's toolbar. For example, Microsoft Word indicates in the Standard toolbar the name of the font in which the text is formatted. That's the font you're going to need to have in your system to see the text displayed properly.

DIALOG BOX FONTS ARE UNREADABLE

Fonts in all my dialog boxes look very weird or unreadable.

You can have this problem for a couple of reasons. First, ensure that the regional settings are correct for your area (see "Document From Another User Is Displayed Improperly"). Next, choose Control Panel, Display, Appearance and click Message Text. Look to see what font size you have chosen for dialog box messages, and change it if necessary.

Dialog boxes that programs display can also get weird if you have removed necessary system fonts such as MS Sans Serif and MS Serif. Check the Fonts folder to see that they are available. Replace them from another system if necessary.

ICON FONTS TOO LARGE OR SMALL

My icon fonts are too small (or too large).

If your screen fonts (such as text under icons on the desktop or in Explorer windows) are the wrong size, you can change the system fonts to another size. Choose Control Panel, Display Properties, Settings, General, and look for the fonts setting. Then choose another size. You might have to reboot. Also see the note in Chapter 23, "Tweaking the GUI," about LiquidView from Portrait Displays (http://www.portrait.com), which can increase the size of many of the smaller fonts, icons, and graphic elements that make up the User Interface.

SYSTEM ADMINISTRATION AND MAINTENANCE

CHAPTER 27

SYSTEM UTILITIES

In this chapter

GETTING UNDER THE HOOD

Windows XP is rife with system management and administrative utility programs—so many, in fact, that you can easily become overwhelmed by the number of tools and the multitudinous paths for reaching those tools. As writers who have pounded on Windows systems since the days of version 1.1, my co-author and I can easily report that the mandate of effectively discussing the administrator tools for Windows XP was a bit daunting, even to us.

If you're the kind of user who likes to pop the hood, see what's inside, and do a little tinkering, or if you're an administrator who has the job of managing computers in a corporation, this is the chapter for you. You'll want to read through the descriptions of the various tools covered here and learn a bit about how to use them.

So far, you've learned about the basic Control Panel utilities and many of the configuration and maintenance tools and applets. Dividing the tools into clearly delineated chapters was somewhat difficult, as many do not fall neatly into a category. The following is how it all shook out in the end:

- Chapter 23, "Tweaking the GUI," discusses most of the user environment alteration tools, most of which are display or formatting oriented Control Panel applets.

- Chapter 24, "Configuration via Control Panel Applets," discusses a majority of the Control Panel applets not already covered in Chapter 23.

- Chapter 25, "Maintaining and Optimizing System Performance," discusses a number of primarily hardware-related tools.

- This chapter discusses the balance of the computer management tools, some of which are very powerful, especially the Microsoft Management Console (MMC), which is a highly customizable toolbox you can build for your own sleuthing purposes. If you did not find a tool you were looking for by skimming the other chapters, it is likely here. See the "Microsoft Management Console (MMC)" section in this chapter or the Windows XP Resource Kit for more information on this tool interface.

If you're a Windows 9x or NT maven, some tools that you are likely familiar with in those interfaces have changed names and locations in Windows XP. But, if you are stepping over from Windows 2000, you'll find things reassuringly familiar. Most of the system-level control tools, with the exception of the System applet, are Microsoft Management Console (MMC) tools.

Table 27.1 describes each of the system management tools. With the exception of the Recovery tool (which is described in Chapter 29, "Managing the Hard Disk"), each of these tools is discussed later in this chapter.

TABLE 27.1   SYSTEM MANAGEMENT TOOLS

Tool	Description
Task Manager	A tool for killing crashed applications, listing currently running processes, and checking system performance.

TABLE 27.1 CONTINUED

Tool	Description
Computer Management	A subset of Microsoft Management Console, for extensive control of the local machine.
Windows Update	Online tool for ensuring your system is running the latest software additions and bug fixes.
Scheduled Tasks	A utility program for automating execution of programs.
File Signature Verification tool	A tool that prevents critical system files from being altered.
System File Checker	A command-line executable that verifies system file versions are aligned properly.
System Monitor	(a.k.a. Performance) A tool that creates a graphical and/or numeric display of essential system information, such as memory usage, status of the hard disk usage, CPU activity, and network traffic. This tool is discussed in Chapter 25, "Maintaining and Optimizing System Performance."
Event Viewer	A tool for viewing system-generated log files.
Recovery Console	A tool that attempts to recover a broken or otherwise non-booting system. This tool is discussed in Chapter 29, "Managing the Hard Disk."
System applet	This applet offers access to controls for system name, network membership, hardware management, system restoration, automatic updates, working remotely, and more.
Local Security Policy	Defines Group Policy for the local system. This item is discussed in Chapter 21, "Network Security."
Services	Manages how services are launched within the XP environment.
System Tools	A section of the Start menu used to access several tools: Files and Settings Transfer Wizard, Backup, Disk Cleanup, Disk Defragmenter, System Restore, Activate Windows, and System Information.
System Information	This tool provides a detailed view into the configuration and status of the systems hardware and software.
Accessibility	This section of the Start menu contains tools for the visual and mobility impaired.

These tools are scattered throughout the Windows XP environment. To stick to some semblance of order, we will try to discuss these tools in the following order based on their location or execute/access point: Control Panel applets, Administrative Tools, Start menu items, and then Run command/Command Prompt utilities. However, most of these tools can be accessed through more than one of these means.

27

SCHEDULED TASKS

Scheduled Tasks is found in the Control Panel and in the Start menu (All Programs, Accessories, System Tools, and Scheduled Tasks). Using the Scheduled Tasks, you can set up any program or script (or even open a document) to be run automatically at predetermined times. This utility is very useful for running system maintenance programs or your own scripts and programs when you can't be around to execute them manually.

TIP FROM

Bob & Brian

You could even use the Scheduled Tasks to run a script that starts or stops a specific system service. The `net` command can be used to start and stop services using simple syntax:

```
net start "service name here"
```

or

```
net stop "service name here"
```

Most folks don't even need to think about this capability, but if you are a software developer and use a special debugging or testing service, this capability might be handy to start it up when you log in. Remember that there is no "when I log off" scheduler entry, so you can't automate shutting off the process when someone logs out.

You also can cause a specific script or program to run (1) when the system boots, (2) when a user (any user) logs on, or (3) when the system is idle. Why is this different from putting the script or program in the Startup group for All Users? Well, the Scheduled Tasks lets you specify the security context to use for this login task. For example, whenever a user logs on, you can have the Scheduled Tasks run a program with Administrative privileges to record information in a protected file. Using the Scheduled Tasks this way is similar to using the Run As option. (See Chapter 28, "Managing Users," for more details about Run As.)

NOTE

When the Scheduled Tasks runs a task as a different user, the logged-on user cannot see or interact with the program. Be sure that scheduled tasks can operate without user input and exit cleanly when they've done their work. And keep in mind that once an application or service is running, even if it was launched through a scheduled task, it still will affect system performance as if you ran it manually.

After you declare tasks to run, the Scheduled Tasks sits in the background, checking the computer's system clock, and when a predetermined time for a task rolls around, the Scheduled Tasks runs it as though executed from the specified user.

After you've defined a task to be executed, the Scheduled Tasks service automatically will launch at startup each time the computer boots. The Scheduled Tasks service does not significantly affect system performance. The service is required to monitor the time and other system events that are defined as triggers to launch applications, scripts, and so on. The Scheduled Task service cannot be configured to load based on the logged-on user because it is a systemwide service. Even if a user without scheduled tasks is logged in, a scheduled task from another user can execute in the background.

NOTE

Obviously, the computer has to be alive to run a task, so if you expect to do a disk cleanup at 4 a.m., be sure you've left the computer on. If you turn on the system at 4:01 a.m., you missed the execution. The scheduler will not inform you of missed launchings; you'll have to view the information in the Last Run Time column within the Scheduled Tasks window to figure it out for yourself.

TIP FROM

Bob
& Brian

If you upgraded from Windows 98/SE/Me/NT/2000 and had automated tasks assigned there, they should have been converted or imported to the Windows XP Scheduled Tasks automatically.

To assign tasks to the Scheduled Tasks, follow these steps:

1. Run the Scheduled Tasks by choosing Start, All Programs, Accessories, System Tools, Scheduled Tasks. If you have any scheduled tasks, they appear in the list already.

2. Click Add Scheduled Task to invoke a wizard that walks you though adding a new task. Click Next to see a list of programs (see Figure 27.1). If the program isn't listed in the resulting list, click the Browse button to find it. (For system-related applications, the most likely browse locations are in the \windows or \windows\system32 folders. For programs you've installed, try the Program Files subfolders.)

Figure 27.1
The Scheduled Task Wizard's program selection page.

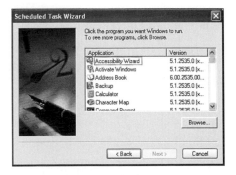

3. Click Next, and choose how often you want the program to run (see Figure 27.2). Click Next again, and then specify applicable time options, such as time of day, as required.

4. Click Next, and you are prompted to enter the user's name and password so that the task can be executed as though the user (typically, you) were there to run it. (It may already be entered for you, using the current user's name, preceded by the computer

name.) After a username and password are set, another user cannot cancel or delete the task unless that user has the correct permissions. If you are working with a user account without a password, don't type in anything in the password field.

Figure 27.2
The Scheduled Task Wizard's execution schedule page.

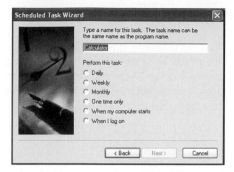

The computer name is technically necessary only if you are on a network but want to run the task with local authentication. I cannot think of any reason to do so, unless your domain account doesn't have the correct local rights.

5. Click Next. If you want to set advanced options such as idle time, what to do if the computer is running on batteries, and what to do after the task completes, mark Open Advanced Properties For This Task When I Click Finish.

6. Click Finish to close the wizard. The task is then added to the list and will execute at the preassigned time.

If you chose to open the task's advanced properties upon clicking Finish, its dialog box now opens. To open this same dialog box manually, open the Scheduled Tasks applet, right-click the task in question, and choose Properties. The three tabs on this dialog box enable you to modify it as follows:

■ From the Task tab on the Properties dialog, you can disable the task temporarily, without having to delete it, by clearing the Enabled check box.

■ Use the Schedule tab to change the task's timing. You can change the scheduled time using the options present, or use the Advanced button to access more advanced scheduling options. There is also a check box that allows you to enable multiple schedules for the task.

When you're finished, click OK to save any changes made to the properties sheet. Now that you've established a task, though, there are still more issues to consider.

If you want to remove a task from the Scheduled Tasks list, right-click it, and choose Delete. Choosing Delete here doesn't remove the executed application from your hard disk, it just removes the task from the list of tasks to be executed.

To use controls that affect all tasks in the Scheduled Tasks applet, use the commands on the Advanced menu from the main Scheduled Tasks window's menu bar. You'll see a number of useful items there, as shown in Table 27.2.

TABLE 27.2   ADVANCED SETTINGS FOR THE SCHEDULED TASKS

Option	Description
Stop Using Scheduled Tasks	This option turns off the scheduler, preventing it from running any added tasks. The scheduler won't start automatically the next time you start Windows XP. To reactivate it, you have to open the Scheduled Tasks and choose Start Using Scheduled Tasks.
Pause Scheduled Tasks	This option temporarily suspends added tasks in the task list. This capability is useful if you are running a program whose operation could be slowed down or otherwise influenced by a scheduled task. To resume the schedules for all tasks, choose Advanced, Continue Scheduled Tasks. If a task's execution time is now past, it will run at the next scheduled time.
Notify Me of Missed Tasks	If a task can't complete for some reason, a dialog box pops up, letting you know what was missed. For example, if the computer was turned off when a task should have been run, you'll be told of this situation when you boot up next.
AT Service Account	The Scheduled Tasks runs any commands scheduled using the at command-line utility, which is a carryover from Windows NT. By design, commands scheduled by at all run under the same login account. This option lets you specify which account is to be used. You can leave it set to the default LocalSystem setting, or you can turn on This Account to specify a user account.
View Log	This option brings up a text file in Notepad, listing tasks completed, date, and other information about the tasks. Note that some tasks listed in the log might not appear in the Scheduled Tasks list. This omission can result from system tasks initiated by other services such as synchronization (such as Web page subscriptions and offline folders). For coverage of these issues, see Chapter 9, "Browsing the World Wide Web with Internet Explorer," and Chapter 18, "Windows Unplugged: Remote and Mobile Networking."

TIP FROM

Bob
& Brian

You can run one of your tasks immediately by right-clicking the task in question and choosing Run. You also can reach Scheduled Tasks tasks through the Explorer by going to the \windows\tasks folder.

 If the Scheduled Tasks fails to activate properly, see "The Scheduled Tasks Doesn't Activate Correctly" in the "Troubleshooting" section at the end of this chapter.

27

You can view scheduled tasks on a remote computer by opening My Network Places, opening the computer in question, and then opening the Scheduled Tasks folder. You need administrative privileges if you want to view the settings on a remote machine. If you want to edit remote settings, the requirements are greater; you can edit tasks on a remote computer running Windows 95 or later, Windows NT 4.0, Windows 2000, or Windows XP only if that remote computer has remote Registry software installed and shares the *x$* share, where *x* is the hard disk on which the Scheduled Tasks folder resides. That is, it must be shared with an "Administrative Share."

Unlike under Windows 2000, Windows XP tasks do not have task-level ACLs. However, if the user account defined as the "run as" account does not have access to the executable, the task will not be able to run.

NOTE

> If you are familiar with the old at command-line utility from Windows NT, you'll be happy to know that it still works in Windows XP. Commands scheduled with at appear in the Scheduled Tasks's list, as well as the list of commands that at displays. It's one and the same list. However, if you modify the command within Scheduled Tasks, it will no longer appear in the list displayed by at. at is the command-line tool used to schedule tasks on a Windows NT system. The at command is still supported by Windows XP (as it was under Windows 2000). You can see the correct syntax for this command-line tool by entering **at ?** at a command prompt. at stands for "at time" and was originally found on Unix systems.

SYSTEM APPLET

The System applet offers a wide range of functions through its multi-tabbed interface. You access the System applet through the Control Panel. When the Control Panel is in Classic view, double-click on the System icon to open the System applet. When the Control Panel is in Category view, open the Performance and Maintenance category, and then click on the System icon. Let's take a look at each tab and the options on each.

The General tab (see Figure 27.3) displays the system OS version, registration details, and basic computer info (CPU type, speed, and RAM).

SETTING THE COMPUTER NAME

The Computer Name tab is the same interface as is accessed through the Network Identification command of the Network Connections applet's Advanced menu. This interface is used to change the computer name and manage domain and workgroup membership. The Network ID button launches a wizard that guides you through configuring the computer for standalone use, workgroup membership, or domain membership. The Change button opens the Computer Name Changes dialog box where the computer name and domain or workgroup membership is defined with simple radio buttons and text fields. Altering network configuration is discussed in greater detail in Chapter 17, "Using a Windows XP Network."

Figure 27.3
The System applet (or System Properties) dialog box, General tab.

Adding a system to an existing domain will require that you know the name and password of an administrator account in that domain OR that a computer account for the client has already been defined in the domain. For more information on this, see Part IV, "Networking."

MANAGING AND CONTROLLING HARDWARE

The Hardware Tab has four buttons. The Add Hardware Wizard button launches the Add Hardware wizard just as the Add Hardware applet does. This is discussed in Chapter 24. The Device Manager button launches the Device Manager; this is also discussed in Chapter 24. The Hardware Profiles button opens the Hardware Profiles dialog box where hardware profiles are managed. This is discussed in Chapter 25. The Driver Signing button opens the Driver Signing Options dialog box.

Driver Signing is a security feature that aids in preventing malicious rogue or Trojan horse drivers from being installed onto a mission-critical system. By enabling driver signing, you can configure a system to refuse all device drivers except those that are "signed" by Microsoft or other MS-approved vendors. This dialog box offers three settings: Ignore, Warn, and Block. Ignore allows the installation of any driver. Warn prompts you each time you attempt to install a non-signed driver. Block only allows signed drivers to be installed.

The default setting of Driver Signing is Warn. Keep in mind that this safety feature is designed from the Microsoft perspective. In their eyes, the only legitimate and safe drivers are those that have been approved by their labs. In many cases, drivers that Microsoft has not preapproved are perfectly safe and legitimate. However, ignore this security at your own risk. If you don't trust the vendor or fully trust the distribution method, don't install unsigned drivers.

27

ADVANCED SYSTEM PROPERTIES

The Advanced Tab of the System applet has five buttons. Three of these buttons are labeled Settings and are contained within sections titled Performance, User Profiles, and Startup and Recovery. The other two buttons are below these sections; they are labeled Environmental Variables and Error Reporting.

The Settings button under the Performance heading opens the Performance Options dialog box. The Visual Effects tab of this dialog box is discussed in Chapter 23. The Advanced tab of this dialog box is used to set memory usage parameters and is discussed in Chapter 25.

The Settings button under the User Profiles heading opens the User Profiles dialog box. This interface is used to manage local and roaming profiles stored on the local computer. This is discussed in Chapter 28.

The Settings button under the Startup and Recovery heading opens the Startup and Recovery dialog box. This interface is used to configure multibooting actions and how system failures are handled. This is discussed in Chapter 31 and 33.

The Environmental Variables button opens the Environmental Variables dialog box. This interface is used to define user and system variables. These include TEMP and TMP, which point to storage locations where Windows can create temporary files. In most cases you should not edit the system variables. There are some application installations that may require this activity, but specific details should be included in that application's installation instructions.

TIP

> If the storage volume where your main Windows directory resides is becoming full, you can perform three operations to improve performance and keep the risk of insufficient drive space to a minimum. First, move the paging file to a different volume on a different hard drive (see Chapter 25 for details on this). Second, define the TEMP and TMP variables to point to a \Temp folder you create on a different volume on a different hard drive. Third, through Internet Options, define a location for the temporary Internet files within the alternate \Temp folder. After rebooting, the new locations will be in use. However, you may need to delete the old files from the previous temporary file locations (typically \Documents and Settings\<username>\Local Settings\Temp and \Documents and Settings\<username>\Local Settings\Temporary Internet Files\).

The Error Reporting button opens the Error Reporting dialog box. On this interface you can define whether Windows XP automatically reports system problems to Microsoft. This information is submitted anonymously and is used to help Microsoft fine tune the system and to create fixes and patches. It is enabled by default. You can select just to submit OS related issues or to include (all or some) Program issues as well.

CONTROLLING SYSTEM RESTORE SETTINGS

The System Restore tab is used to track and reverse damaging changes made to your system, and it enables you to set the defined space usage for the System Restore feature. This feature is discussed in Chapter 33. The System Restore command is also found in the Start menu under All Programs, Accessories, and System Tools.

SETTING AUTOMATIC UPDATES

The Automatic Updates tab defines how Windows XP handles Windows Update downloadable modules. Windows Update is an online OS fixing and patching tool. Windows XP, by default, automatically checks for new updates periodically and at each new logon. System updates can be set to automatic install, prompt to install, or manual only. If you elect to decline an update, an additional control to restore declined updates becomes available.

I've found that allowing Windows to download and install updates automatically keeps me up-to-date without having to remember to initiate an update check. Of course, it's possible that an update could damage your system. Microsoft can't control all the variables that might appear on Joe Q. Public's system, and updates, although they often fix bugs, can introduce new ones.

If this should happen, you can always roll back a system to its state before the update (see "Using Rollback to Uninstall a Windows Update," later in this chapter), or use the System Restore feature (see Chapter 33), so using automatic updates is not necessarily a poor choice. But I prefer to at least know whether an update is being performed by choosing the Notify Me Before Downloading Any Updates And Notify Me Again Before Installing Them On My Computer option. This way I am then more likely to correlate some strange new system behavior with an update that just took place.

USING THE REMOTE TAB

The Remote tab controls whether Remote Assistance and Remote Desktop are enabled. Remote Assistance allows you to grant dual control over your desktop with another computer over a network or the Internet. When enabled, the other client can see your desktop, conduct a real-time chat with you, and even use their mouse and keyboard to make changes and operate your system. Remote Assistance was designed to allow a system administrator, tech support specialist, instructor, or even a knowledgeable computer buddy to aid end-users with tasks without having to leave their workspace.

Remote Desktop allows you to access your current desktop or logon environment from a remote system. This allows an employee to access their work system from their home computer and have full access to their files and applications.

Both of these features are discussed in the following sections.

27

REMOTE ASSISTANCE

Remote Assistance works through the exchange of time-sensitive invitation scripts via e-mail. To initiate an invitation

1. Click the Start menu, All Programs, then Remote Assistance.

TIP FROM

Bob & Brian

> You also can access this page through Help and Support by clicking on the Invite a Friend to Connect to Your Computer with Remote Assistance link under Ask for Assistance.

2. The Remote Assistance help page opens (see Figure 27.4).

Figure 27.4
The Remote Assistance page of the Help and Support Center.

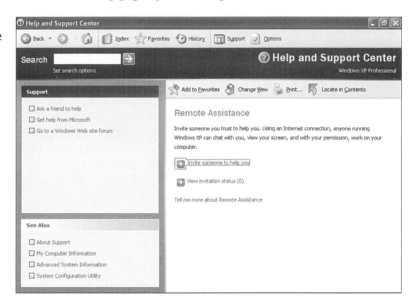

3. Click Invite someone to help you. The invite page opens (see Figure 27.5).

NOTE

> Remote Assistance requires a compatible OS on the remote system (currently only Windows XP is compatible), with either Windows Messenger Service or a MAPI-compliant e-mail utility (such as Microsoft Outlook or Outlook Express). Remote Assistance also requires that both systems have Internet access.

4. If you have MSN Messenger installed and a contact list defined, you can select an invitee from Messenger. Or, you can provide an e-mail address to send an invitation. Since Outlook Express (OE) is installed by default and MSN Messenger is not, we'll use OE.

Type in an e-mail address to send a Remote Assistance initiation, and then click Invite this person. The e-mail invitation page opens.

Figure 27.5
The invite page for
Remote Assistance.

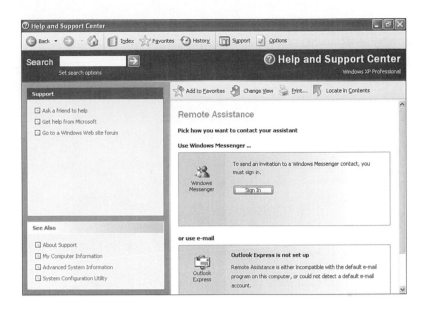

NOTE

The invitation can also be saved as a file. When saved as a file or included as an e-mail attachment, the invitation is a 900KB file named rcBuddy.MsRcIncident.

5. Provide a From name and a message to include in the e-mail invitation. Then click Continue.

6. Define the invitations expiration period in minutes, hours, or days.

7. Select whether to require a password to connect, and then provide the password. Click Send invitation.

8. A warning prompt appears, stating that another application is attempting to send an e-mail message on your behalf, click Send.

When the invitation appears in the invitee's inbox, they only need to execute the attachment.

CAUTION

Microsoft warns to only execute attachments from people you trust or from whom you are expecting an attachment. It is very easy to create a malicious utility masquerading as a valid Remote Assistance invitation.

When it's executed, you'll be prompted for a password (if required) and whether you want to initiate a Remote Assistance connection. Once you click Yes, the connection attempt commences. If a connection is started, the invitor is prompted whether to allow the connection

27

to continue. After clicking Yes, the Remote Assistance floating tool window appears on the original system (Figure 27.6) and the Remote Assistance remote desktop utility (Figure 27.7) appears on the invited system.

Figure 27.6
The Remote Assistance floating tool window as it appears on the original or host system.

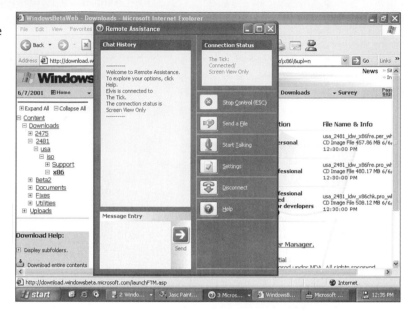

Figure 27.7
The Remote Assistance remote desktop utility as it appears on the invited or remote system. Notice that the host's desktop can be seen in the background of the invitee's screen.

From either system, you can send chat text, stop the session, transmit a file, initiate voice chat, or disconnect the session. From the remote system, you can request full control of the original desktop and control it with the remote system's mouse and keyboard. This is a great tool for walking someone through a complex task or training them on software usage.

Remote Assistance should only be used when both systems are connected by a fairly high-bandwidth link, such as over a 10+MB LAN or via ISDN, DSL, or Cable modem Internet link. It will work over slow modem connections, but you are more likely to experience significant performance delays and disconnects. The faster the connection, the more responsive the remote assistance will be and the higher resolution the remote visuals. Unless blocked by a firewall, proxy, or other security screen between the two systems, Remote Assistance can link two systems on a LAN or over the Internet.

REMOTE DESKTOP

Remote Desktop is basically a remote control feature built right into Windows XP. It enables a remote system to connect to the session as a host client. The host client is the system where user sessions are paused (such as via Fast Switching) for remote connection. Remote systems establish connections via an IIS subcomponent—Remote Desktop Web Connection—which must be installed on the IIS server in the same network as the host client.

An additional benefit of Remote Desktop is that, when your host system is configured, you can use either Remote Desktop or a valid Terminal Services client on a remote system to connect to your host.

Configuring a network to support Remote Desktop is a bit of a challenge. Consult the Windows XP Resource Kit for exhaustive details on the installation and configuration of this amazing feature.

Fortunately, the use of Remote Desktop is quite simple. However, there is one caveat: You must plan ahead for Remote Desktop to work. You must leave an active logon session running to which Remote Desktop will connect from your remote system. It is not possible to connect into a system with Remote Desktop without an active session. To set up Remote Desktop, follow these easy steps:

1. Log on to the host system.
2. Use the Start, Log Off command, and then click Switch User (remember, switching users is not the same as logging off).
3. Log on to the remote system.
4. Launch Internet Explorer.
5. Open the URL `http://<servername>/tsweb/` where `<servername>` is the name or IP address of the IIS server on the network.
6. You might be prompted to provide logon credentials for the domain or IIS server system. In most cases, you must provide them in the form `<domainname>\<username>` or `<systemname>\<username>`.

27

7. After logon, you are presented with the Remote Desktop Web Connection screen where you must provide the computer name or IP address of the host client and what sized screen to open (options include 640×480, 800×600, 1024×768, and Full Screen). Click Connect.

When connected, you'll have complete control over the host client session from the remote system. Once properly configured, this could be an extremely versatile tool for telecommuters.

Remote Assistance and Remote Desktop offer useful features that are new to the Microsoft Windows product. However, they are poor imitations of full-featured third-party products such as PCAnywhere, Carbon Copy, and Timbuktu. If you are on a tight budget, these new Windows XP features might be of some use. However, if you need true versatility, security, and a broader range of control over remote control types of access, grab a true remote control product.

Administrative Tools

The Administrative Tools are a collection of system control and configuration utilities which Microsoft deemed powerful and technical enough to separate into its own category from the Control Panel applets. The Administrative Tools include Component Services, Computer Management, ODBC Sources, Event Viewer, Local Security Policy, Performance, and Services. Each of these is discussed in the following sections (with the exception of Component Services and ODBC Sources which are not discussed in this book; please consult the Windows XP Resource Kit for details on these items). These two tools are fairly complex and are used by program developers and network database integrators. In most cases, these controls are beyond what most end users or administrators will need or use.

Computer Management

In addition to the Task Manager and Control Panel, another tool named Computer Management (Figure 27.8) is probably the most likely candidate for configuring and administering your PC. To get to it, open the Control Panel (in Category view), select Performance and Maintenance, then Administrative Tools, and finally, double-click Computer Management. A simpler method is to right-click your My Computer icon (on your desktop or in your Start menu) and select Manage from the pop-up menu.

27

> **N O T E**
>
> The Computer Management utility is just one of many MMC (Microsoft Management Center) tools. The MMC is a powerful programming infrastructure for creating system control utilities. You can even create your own custom tool sets using MMC consoles. The MMC is discussed in the "Microsoft Management Console (MMC)" section later in this chapter as well as in the Windows XP Resource Kit.

Figure 27.8
The Computer
Management utility
from Administrative
Tools. Shared Folders
node selected

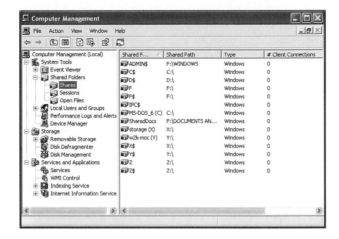

Computer Management provides easy access to the following tasks:

- Managing local users and groups
- Managing shared devices and drives
- Checking system event logs containing information such as logon times and application errors
- Seeing which remote users are logged in to the system
- Viewing currently running system services, starting and stopping them, and setting automatic startup times for them
- Managing server applications and services such as the Indexing service and IIS

The Computer Management tool looks similar to the familiar Windows Explorer. It uses a two-pane view, with the *console tree* (for navigation and tool selection) in the left pane and details of the active item shown the right pane.

Items in the tree are called *nodes* (akin to folders in Explorer). The three nodes in Computer Management are as follows:

- System Tools
- Storage
- Services and Applications

As you would expect, you can conduct administrative chores by selecting a tool in the console tree and then clicking items in the right pane. When you select an item in the right pane, toolbar and menu options change as appropriate for that item, typically displaying attributes of the item or tool you selected. For example, the System Information branch can show you which IRQs are assigned already, and the Local Users and Groups branch can display the names and properties of all the users on the machine.

27

In previous versions of Windows NT, you had to hunt around through Control Panel applets to discover properties and settings that are now conveniently grouped together in Computer Management. I'll be honest; things are still a little confusing just because some of the properties available from Computer Management can also be reached via the Control Panel. An example is the Device Manager, which can be reached from the System applet in the Control Panel as well as the System Tools node in Computer Management. It's the same tool, and having multiple paths to the same destination is nothing new in Windows.

TIP FROM

Bob & Brian

> You must be assigned Administrator privileges to fully utilize the Computer Management tools. If you have lesser privileges, you'll have limited access to system properties and are locked out of making certain administrative changes to the system.

Explore with the interface to uncover all that is available from these three "little" nodes in the left pane. However, avoid making any changes or modifications (where possible) unless you know what affects your alterations will have. You'll be surprised. Open each node by clicking the boxed + (plus) sign. If you choose View, Details, some helpful information about various items in the right pane is displayed along with the items.

By default, you manage the local computer. To manage a remote computer (assuming you have permission), right-click the topmost item in the tree (Computer Management), and choose Connect to Another Computer.

Also by default, the view is set to Basic. To gain access to more advanced settings in the console, choose View, Advanced.

A few points about each node are listed in the following sections.

SYSTEM TOOLS NODE

This node includes five subnodes:

- **Event Viewer**—used to view the event details contained in the Application, Security, and System logs. This tool is discussed later as an Administrative Tools utility in its own right.

- **Shared Folders**—used to manage shared folders and remote users accessing shared folders.

- **Local Users and Groups**—used to manage local user accounts and groups. This tool is discussed in Chapter 28.

- **Performance Logs and Alerts**—used to define logs and alerts related to system performance. This tool is identical to that accessed through the Performance tool (a.k.a. System Monitor interface). This tool is discussed in Chapter 25.

- **Device Manager**—used to troubleshoot device problems and configure device and drivers settings. This is identical to the Device Manager accessed through the System applet. This tool is discussed in Chapter 24.

The Shared Folders node (refer to Figure 27.8) amounts to what used to be NetWatcher in previous Windows versions. The three folders under the Shared Folders node are as follows:

■ **Shares**—Allows you to manage the properties of each shared resource. For example, you can alter the access rights for a shared resource so that certain users have read-only access. You can also change share permissions for a resource in the Properties dialog box of any shared resource by right-clicking the resource and clicking Properties.

■ **Sessions**—Allows you to see which users are connected to a share and optionally disconnect them.

■ **Open Files**—Allows you to see which files and resources are open on a share. You also can close files that are open.

STORAGE NODE

This node includes three subnodes:

■ Removable Storage
■ Disk Defragmenter
■ Disk Management

The Removable Storage is used to check the physical location of removable storage devices (such as CD-ROM, DVD-ROM, JAZ, Zip, tapes, and optical disks), check the existence of media pools (typically robot-controlled multidisk gadgets), and check properties of offline media. This node also provides a means for labeling, cataloging, and tracking all your removable media; controls library drives, slots, and doors; and provides drive-cleaning operations.

This node can work together with data management or backup programs like the one supplied with Windows XP (the Backup program is covered in Chapter 29, "Managing the Hard Disk"), conveying information about storage properties.

The Disk Defragmenter node runs the disk defragmenter program. This is the same tool with a slightly different interface as the Disk Defragmenter on the Tools tab of a drive's Properties dialog box.

The Disk Management node runs Disk Management (known as Disk Administrator under Windows NT). This tool is used to define new drives as Basic or Dynamic, create/delete/manage partitions and volumes, format, assign drive letters, and so on.

All three of these nodal tools are discussed in Chapter 29.

SERVICES AND APPLICATIONS

Through the Services and Application node, you can view and manage the properties of any server service or application that is installed on the computer, such as the file indexing service, and IIS (Internet Information Server). If this were Windows 2003 Server, you'd also have access to networking services such as DNS (domain name service) and DHCP (Domain Host Configuration Protocol).

TIP FROM

Bob & Brian

> Sometimes you might want to incorporate a list of displayed items into another document. You can export the list as a text file for this purpose. To do so, display the list in question, with the columns arranged as you like. Then choose Action, Export List. You can name the file in the resulting Save As dialog box.

EVENT VIEWER

The Event Viewer is an administrative application used to view the log files which record hardware, software, and system problems and security events. You can think of an event as any occurrence of significance to the operating system. Logs are very useful because, like a seismograph in earthquake country or a black box in an airplane, they provide a historical record of when events occurred. For example, you can see when services were started, stopped, paused, and resumed; or when hardware failed to start properly; when a user attempts to access protected files; or an attempt to remove a printer over which he or she doesn't have control. The logs report the level of danger to the system, as you can see in Figure 27.9. For a shortcut to the Event Viewer, you can choose Start, Control Panel (in Category view), Performance and Maintenance, Administrative Tools, Event Viewer.

Figure 27.9
The System log viewed through the Event Viewer.

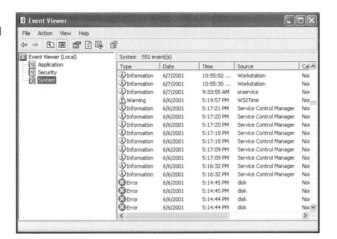

As you know, Windows XP has an intelligent internal security design. So, as you might expect, numerous more subtle events than those described here can generate messages internal to the operating system that are not directly reported to the user. Events such as applications being run, drivers being loaded, or files being copied between directories are common examples. Though kept out of sight, these events are monitored and recorded in log files available for later examination by the system administrator. Many events are stored in the log by default. Others are optional and can be set within dialog boxes pertaining to specific operations.

TYPES OF LOG FILES

Windows XP generates three primary logs (files), though others are possible. These logs are explained in Table 27.3.

TABLE 27.3   WINDOWS LOG FILES

Type of Log	Description
Application log	The application log contains events logged by applications or programs. For example, a database program might record a file error in the application log. The program developer decides which events to record.
Security log	The security log can record security events such as valid and invalid logon attempts, as well as events related to resource use such as creating, opening, or deleting files. An administrator can specify which events are recorded in the security log. For example, if you have enabled logon auditing, attempts to log on to the system are recorded in the security log.
System log	The system log contains numerous entries pertaining to system events such as booting up, shutting down, loading drivers, and errors with hardware conflicts such as conflicts between ports, CD-ROMs, SCSI cards, or sound cards. For example, the failure of a driver or other system component to load during startup is recorded in the system log. The event types logged by system components are predetermined by Windows XP and cannot be altered by the user or administrator.

Now that you have a basic understanding, let's consider the Event Viewer. The Event Viewer is an application that displays each of the log files. Aside from simply displaying a log file, the Event Viewer also lets you do the following:

- Apply sorting, searching, and filtering that make it easier to look for specific events
- Control settings that affect future log entries, such as maximum log size and the time old entries should be deleted
- Clear all log entries to start a log from scratch
- Archive logs on disk for later examination and load those files when needed

27

NOTE

Only a user with Administrative privileges can work with the security log. Other users can view the application and system logs, however. By default, security logging is turned off. You can use Group Policy to enable security logging. The administrator can also set auditing policies in the Registry that cause the system to halt when the security log is full.

WORKING WITH EVENT VIEWER LOGS

The following steps explain how you can use the Event Viewer to open the three available logs and more easily view specific events:

1. Open the Event Viewer program in Administrative Tools via the Control Panel. When you run it, the basic Event Viewer window comes up. (The meaning of each column is explained in the following section.)

2. Choose the log you want to view by clicking it in the left pane.

3. Just as with the File Manager, changes to the log that occur while you're examining it are not always immediately reflected. Press F5 to update the log if you suspect that some system activity has occurred while you've been running the program.

4. Normally, the list is sorted with the most recent events at the top of the list. You can reverse this order if you want by choosing View, Oldest First.

5. You can optionally filter out events that you don't want to wade through. For example, you can show events that occurred only during certain times of the day, events pertaining to a specific user or event ID, or only a certain event type (such as only errors or warnings). Just choose View, Filter, and fill in the dialog box. (The options are explained in the section titled "Filtering Events.")

6. You might want to search for a specific event. To do so, choose View, Find, and enter the relevant information in the resulting dialog box.

7. If you want to see more information about an event, double-click it. Another dialog box then appears, listing details. An example is shown in Figure 27.10.

Figure 27.10
An Event Properties or event details properties dialog box.

Details of your security log won't make much sense if you're not a programmer. Even then, the messages are cryptic. The system and application logs offer more in the way of understandable English. Most useful is information about drivers failing to load (often leading you to IRQ and port conflict resolutions).

VIEWING A REMOTE COMPUTER'S LOGS

By default, the local computer's log is displayed. If you want to examine a networked computer's log, just right-click over the Event Viewer (local) node and select Connect to another computer from the pop-up menu.

LOG INTERPRETATION

Careful monitoring of event logs can help you predict and identify the sources of system problems. For example, if log warnings show that a disk driver can read or write to a sector only after several retries, this information could be a foreshadowing that the hard disk sector may die eventually. Logs can also confirm problems with software. If a program crashes, a program event log can provide a record of activity leading up to the event. When a program does crash, you often see a system message informing you that a log entry is being made.

Essentially, each log file consists of a database table with eight columns, which are described in Table 27.4.

TABLE 27.4 DECIPHERING EVENT LOGS

Column Name	Meaning
Type	Indicates the type of event. The five types of events are described in Table 27.5.
Date	Reports the date the event was logged (according to the system clock).
Time	Reports the time that the event occurred.
Source	Lists the name of the application software or device driver that reported the problem.
Category	Shows the general classification this event falls under. Each of the three logs has different categories of events.
Event	Lists an event number. Event numbers are assigned to events based on a coding system Microsoft has designed. The event ID matches a message file. The message is displayed in the details box for the event.
User	Indicates the specific user for whom the event applies. Many events are related to a specific user.
Computer	Specifies the computer where the event happened.

27

As mentioned in Table 27.4, five different icons characterize an event type, as shown in Table 27.5.

TABLE 27.5   EVENT TYPES

Type of Event	Meaning
Error	Indicates serious trouble of some sort, such as the device driver not loading, IRQ or other hardware conflicts, missing network cards, and so forth.
Warning	Indicates non-serious trouble, but worthy of attention soon, such as being low on hard disk space (which could bring down the system).
Information	Indicates a non-serious situation. Typically, these notices concern successful operations achieved by applications, drivers, or services. For example, when a network driver loads successfully, an Information event is logged.
Success Audit	Indicates success of a procedure.
Failure Audit	Similar to a success audit but reversed; indicates that failed attempts are logged. Failures typically occur because the user making the attempt doesn't have the correct privileges.

TIP FROM

Bob
& Brian

> Many typical hardware problems—such as conflicting protocols, network card conflicts, and IRQ conflicts—are reported in the system log. The Event Viewer can help you sleuth out possible entries explaining the problem.

FILTERING EVENTS

One way of seeing several similar events you're interested in (for example, to see how many times the same event occurred) is to click the relevant column head in the Event Viewer. Clicking the head sorts the listing according to the column's data. As in Windows Explorer and other Windows programs, the column sorter toggles between ascending and descending order.

A more powerful approach for culling out the items you're interested in is to use filtering. When logs get quite large or if you have a server that supports a high density of workstation activity, this approach might be the most effective technique for ferreting out what you need to examine. The System Log Properties dialog box you use for filtering is shown in Figure 27.11.

After you set up a filter, don't be alarmed if all your entries suddenly seem to have disappeared; they're probably just being filtered. Check the View menu, and you'll see the Filter option selected. Choose it again to eliminate the filter.

SETTING LOGGING OPTIONS

You can stipulate a few settings that affect how log entries are recorded. These settings are most useful in managing the size of your logs so that they don't eat up too much disk space. There are potentially so many loggable events that even a typical day on a busy network server could produce far larger log files than you would want to wade through, or that you would want to devote disk space to.

Figure 27.11
On the Filter tab of the System Properties dialog box, you can limit the listing to specific conditions.

To view or change options for a log file, right-click the log file in question, and choose Properties. Then click the General tab to see the dialog box shown in Figure 27.12.

Figure 27.12
Setting a log's options.

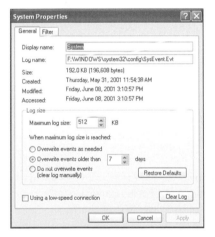

If you don't archive the log (see the next section), then you should probably have the log "wrap" around after it reaches the maximum log size. The Overwrite Events as Needed option ensures that, when the log fills up, a new event takes the place of the oldest preexisting log entry.

If you really want to ensure that you get to see the log entries, choose the Do Not Overwrite Events option. After the maximum size is reached, subsequent events are not written, and thus lost. If so, you have to use the Action, Clear All Events command to make room for new entries.

27

USING ARCHIVED LOG FILES

A final option in the Event Viewer lets you create archives of log files and to reload those files for later examination. As a rule, archiving log files isn't of much use unless you're running a very secure operation in which extensive background records of system or network usage are mandated by the government or the corporation where you work. Most likely, in such a secure operation, you'll be doing regular tape or other forms of backup, which might include backups of the log files anyway. In this case, this regimen might meet your security requirements, depending on your tape rotation scheme. If it doesn't, you can archive your event logs. Archiving is a relatively simple process.

TIP FROM

*Bob
& Brian*

> One case to be made for archiving is this: Logs can be useful in isolating network or machine failures. By keeping copies of past logs, you have something to compare with current versions that list new failures. By comparing logs, you can perhaps notice how and when the errors began to accumulate. Generally speaking, a network failure starts simple and then increases in frequency until a catastrophic failure occurs. Old logs can help here.

You can store archives as text files, comma-delimited files (text files with a comma between each field for use in database or spreadsheet programs that can import this format), or binary files with the .EVT extension. Only the .EVT files retain all the property information for each event. If you want to reload the file for later use, save it as an .EVT file.

Note that the file created by the archiving process isn't affected by any filtering active at the time. That is, all events in the log are written into the archive file. The Action, Save Log File As command can save the log as a .EVT, .TXT, or .CSV file. The Action, Export List command can save into .TXT or .CSV as plain text or Unicode text.

NOTE

> After you save, the log is archived, but the current log isn't cleared. Its contents are unaffected. If your log is full, you have to clear it manually.

To recall an archived log for later examination, open it using the Open Log File command from the Action menu.

⚡ *If your security log file is empty, see "No Events in Security Log" in the "Troubleshooting" section.*

SERVICES

As you learned in Chapters 1 and 2, Windows XP is highly modular. Many of the inner housekeeping chores of the operating system are broken down into services that can be added, removed, started, and stopped at any time, without requiring a reboot. A typical Windows XP system has 80 or more services running at any one time. You can view which services are running by using the Services tool. Use this tool to start and stop services. Figure 27.13 shows a typical Services listing. To start, stop, pause, or restart a service, you can use the context menu or the VCR-like buttons on the toolbar. For deeper control of a service, such as to declare what automatic recovery steps should be taken in the case of the service crashing, which hardware profiles it should run in, and more, open its Properties dialog box.

Figure 27.13
While you're checking the status of services, you can start, stop, and pause system services from this screen.

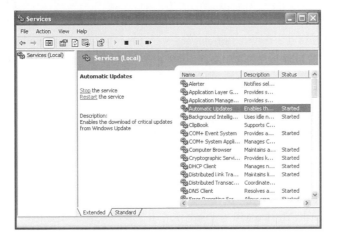

Within the Properties dialog box, you'll find controls to set a service's startup type (automatic, manual, or disabled), start/stop/pause/resume buttons, and a startup parameters field. You also can set the account under which the service is executed (Log On tab), define how a service recovers from failures (for example, restart, run a program, or reboot the system) (Recovery tab), and view a list of service, program, and driver dependencies (Dependencies tab).

SYSTEM TOOLS

The System Tools section of the Start menu (All Programs, Accessories, System Tools) includes several interesting tools. Most of these are discussed in other chapters (such as Chapter 28, "Managing Users" [Files and Settings Transfer Wizard], and Chapter 29, "Managing the Hard Disk" [Backup, Disk Cleanup, Disk Defragmenter, and System Restore]). But, two tools from this menu are discussed in the following sections: Activate Windows and System Information.

ACTIVATE WINDOWS

You might recall from Chapter 3, I discussed the issue of Windows activation. If you failed to activate your system during installation, for whatever reason, you can use this tool to activate Windows XP. Keep in mind that you have 30 days to activate your system after the installation before it will no longer function. Also remember that if you try to activate the same copy of Windows XP on multiple computers, Microsoft's storm troopers may come a knockin' at your e-door.

27

Just be sure to have Internet access when you start this tool if you want to activate online. You can also activate over the phone. This wizard will walk you through the simple but necessary process of activating Windows XP. It will even provide you with the phone number to call if you don't have Internet access for online activation.

SYSTEM INFORMATION

System Information is a simple but elegant tool. Opening this tool reveals a complex hierarchy of four folders, which in turn lead to a zillion lower folders containing an exact blueprint of your system, hardware, system components, and software environment. (You might have additional nodes in your system because some software you install may add nodes of their own.)

This tool is the first place I go whenever I have to install new hardware, especially when it's a legacy device that requires manual configuration of its system resources. Even for PnP devices, you may discover that they are not infinitely configurable. Instead, many devices have only three or four system resource combination sets (these include IRQ, memory address space, I/O, DMA, etc). If your system does not have available resources to match one of these sets, the device will not function. If a device is limited to certain configuration sets, this will be detailed in the user manual and will appear as options on the Resource tab of the device's Properties dialog box.

The top level, labeled "System Summary," shows you basic information about your computer, operating system revision number, CPU, RAM, virtual memory, pagefile size, BIOS revision, and so on (see Figure 27.14).

Figure 27.14
See a summary of your system properties easily from the System Summary node.

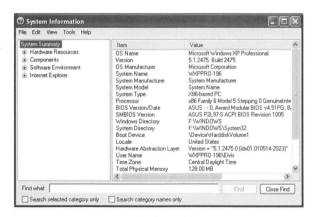

Four nodes appear in the right pane of this figure:

- Hardware Resources displays hardware-specific settings, such as DMA, IRQs, I/O addresses, and memory addresses. The Conflicts/Sharing node identifies devices that are sharing resources or are in conflict. This information can help you identify problems with a device. Some IRQs can be shared between devices successfully.

- The Components node provides a truly powerful view of all the major devices in your system. Open any subfolder and click an item. In a few seconds, information pertaining to the item is displayed, such as drive IDs, modem settings, and video display settings. In some cases, you can also see driver details. Check the folder called Problem Devices to see a list of all devices not loading or initializing properly.

- The Software Environment node is like a super Task Manager. It displays details of twelve categories of software settings. You can see the system drivers, certified drivers, environmental variables, print jobs, network connections, running tasks, loaded modules, services, program groups, startup programs, OLE registration, and Windows error reporting.

TIP FROM

Bob & Brian

> Ever wonder why some darned program starts up when you boot, even though it's not in your Startup group? It's probably hiding the Software Environment, Startup Programs folder. Travel down the path from System Information, Software Environment, Startup Programs, and take a look. I just checked mine and found RealTray and RealJukeboxSystray there. Hey, I don't want these things slowing down my bootup process. Office Startup is there, too. Unfortunately, you can't remove these startup utilities by right-clicking and choosing Delete. You have to use their related Setup programs. For example, to disable RealJukeboxSystray, I had to right-click its icon in the system tray and choose Disable Start Center.
>
> There also is a helpful tool within Help and Support that can be used to enable or disable startup items. It's called the System Configuration Utility. To get to it, open Help and Support, click Use Tools to View Your Computer Information and Diagnose Problems under the Pick a Task section, scroll down in the Tools menu, and then click System Configuration Utility. Then click Open System Configuration Utility in the right pane, and then select the Startup tab.

ACCESSIBILITY

The Accessibility section of the Start menu (All Programs, Accessories, Accessibility) includes several tools to ease, simplify, improve, or enable computer interaction for those users who are visually, audibly, or mobility impaired. These tools are in addition to the system settings available through the Accessibility Options applet in the Control Panel.

The Accessibility wizard is a great tool to help you quickly configure the system so it is at its most beneficial to you, no matter what disability affects you. This wizard walks you step-by-step through a decision making tree to determine fonts, screen size, colors, sounds, mouse actions, keyboard responsiveness, and so on. The results from this wizard make changes to the environment. These are the same changes you could manually adjust through the Accessibility Options applet in the Control Panel.

The Magnifier is a desktop looking glass that magnifies portions of the display by two times or more. When launched, a view window is created at the top of the desktop. The Magnifier

27

can follow the mouse cursor, or focus on keyboard activities for text editing. This tool is a must for those with a slight visual impairment who need just a bit of magnification to read displayed text.

The Narrator is a text-to-speech program design to aid computer usage for the visually impaired. The Narrator will read aloud English text from most programs. Just highlight the text and then press Ctrl+Shift+Spacebar. It can also be set to read screen events (that is, read everything on the active window) and typed characters. The voice is the same controlled through the Speech applet. It's a bit coarse, but you can understand it.

The On-Screen Keyboard is just that, a point-and-click keyboard. It is designed to aid those with mobility impairments whose computer control is restricted to a joystick-type mouse. With just a mouse, the On-Screen Keyboard can be used to "type" out text or perform key-sequences.

The Utility Manager is used to manage the three accessibility tools (Magnifier, Narrator, and On-Screen Keyboard). These tools can be set to launch at login, at desktop lock, or when Utility Manager is launched.

These tools provide basic functionality for those with visual or mobility impairments. However, Microsoft warns that these tools should only be used as stop-gap measures. Those needing consistent aid in interacting with their computers should employ a dedicated specialty solution. Microsoft maintains a Web site with information on accessibility solutions at http://www.microsoft.com/enable/.

WINDOWS UPDATE

Windows Update serves to synchronize your operating system files with the newest developments for it at Microsoft. These can include free programs, security updates, bug fixes, drivers, or other extensions to the operating system. Using the Internet and Web technologies for updating your operating system means you don't have to wait for the next release of the operating system or install service packs to get interim updates.

OBTAINING NEW UPDATES

The Windows Update command is found in several places, including the top of the All Programs section of the Start menu and on the Tools menu of Internet Explorer. Manually launching Windows Update gives you the ability to selectively download offered updates. However, you can easily configure Windows XP to download all relevant updates automatically. This setting is made on the Automatic Updates tab of the System applet (see earlier this chapter).

NOTE

> Another Start menu item in the same category as Windows Update is Windows Catalog. This tool opens an Internet Explorer window to the Windows Catalog Web site. This site maintains a database of products made for Windows, including applications, devices, and complete PCs.

Microsoft is very keen on having you visiting the update Web site regularly. To do so, you can simply connect to the Net, and choose Start, All Programs, Windows Update. A typical page at the Web site looks like the one shown in Figure 27.15. The look of the pages and the list of updates obviously change from week to week, so what you see there might differ slightly from what you see here.

Figure 27.15
Visit the Windows Update site regularly to keep Windows XP up-to-date.

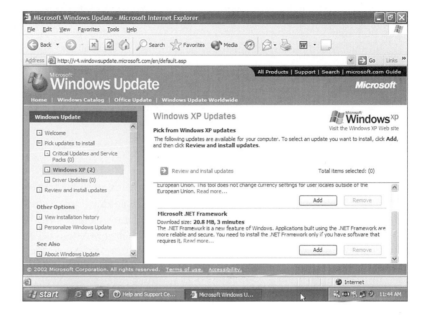

The ActiveX components that run when you visit the site scan your computer to determine what updates have been made in the past and which ones are outstanding. According to Microsoft, no corporate espionage or personal eavesdropping ensues during the process of system analysis. This is accomplished by downloading a master list of available updates and allowing a client-side component to determine which items are applicable to your system. Other than making requests for the master list of updates and for downloading the selected updates, no information is sent to Microsoft.

 If you're seeing Windows Update in the wrong language, see "Wrong Language" in the "Troubleshooting" section at the end of this chapter.

The first time you run it, the update tool creates a database of consummated updates on your computer. This information allows the installer to do the following:

- More quickly determine which updates you haven't installed the next time you visit the site
- Remove items you no longer want
- Roll back the system to its previous state in case an update causes troubles

Look for a History button on the Web page (not the History button on the Internet Explorer toolbar, obviously) to see what you installed and when.

USING ROLLBACK TO UNINSTALL A WINDOWS UPDATE

If you notice unruly system behavior after updating drivers, patches, or system files from Windows Update, you'll probably want to roll back your system to its previous state. You can remove such items by using the Update site. Look for instructions about uninstalling items there. You might have to display past updates by clicking the View Installation History button on the Web page. Then you can scroll down to the update and click Uninstall.

If you don't have Web access, are you sunk? No. Good thing, because you could conceivably make an update only to find it kills your networking or Web access. Some items, such as standalone programs, can be removed via the Control Panel's Add/Remove Programs applet, so check there to remove something such as FrontPage Express or non-Microsoft applications. Of course, you can't use this approach to roll back system files, patches, or drivers. To do that, you can use System Restore capability of Windows XP. Please see Chapter 33 for details.

TASK MANAGER

The Task Manager is one tool you're bound to frequent, perhaps more than any other. Whenever an application crashes, you believe you're running some suspect process that you want to kill, or you want to check on the state of system resources (for example, RAM usage), you can use the Task Manager. Even as nothing more than an educational tool, the Task Manager is informative.

The Task Manager is always available, with a simple press of the "three-finger salute" (Ctrl+Alt+Del), and up pops the Task Manager (Figure 27.16). Note that this is different from Windows NT and Windows 2000 where the Windows Security dialog box appeared following this keystroke pattern. You can also launch the Task Manager by pressing Ctrl+Shift+Esc or right-clicking over an empty area on the Taskbar and selecting Task Manager from the pop-up menu.

Figure 27.16
The Task Manager shows you which applications and processes are running and lets you terminate hung programs. It also indicates some important aspects of system performance.

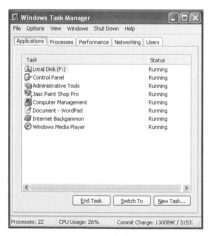

The Task Manager of Windows XP has five tabs, two more than that of Windows NT and Windows 2000. Plus, there is a new menu—Shut Down. The Shut Down menu performs many of the same operations that the Windows Security dialog box performed under Windows NT/2000 when you pressed Ctrl+Alt+Del. This menu offers quick access to Stand By, Hibernate, Turn Off, Restart, Log Off current user, and Switch User. You'll note that all of these functions can also be accessed through the Start menu's Log Off and Turn Off Computer commands.

The other menus of File, Options, View, Windows, and Help all contain the items you've become accustomed to. These menus are somewhat context sensitive, meaning they have different elements depending on which tab is selected. You are smart enough to figure out what most of these commands do, so take the time to explore each menu from each tab. However, I will point out a few interesting commands when appropriate.

APPLICATIONS TAB

You can click the Applications tab of the Task Manager to see a list of the programs currently running on the computer. Not a lot of information is displayed, only the application name and the status (running or not responding). However, this tab does provide a more complete report than you'll get by glancing at the taskbar buttons or via the dialog box you see if you press Alt+Tab.

You can sort the list by clicking the column heads. If an application has multiple documents open, the application appears only once in the list, probably with the name of the document that is foremost at the time (has the focus). Some applications don't comply with this single-document interface (SDI) approach, listing each new document as a separate application. Some examples of non-SDI applications are MS Office programs such as Word, Excel, and PowerPoint.

From this list, you can kill a hung application. If an application has hung, it is probably reported in the list as Not responding (although this is not always true). Click the End Task button to terminate the task. If a document is open and unsaved, and if, for some unexpected reason, the program responds gracefully to Windows's attempt to shut it down (which is unlikely), you might see a dialog asking whether you want to save. More likely, Windows XP will just ask for confirmation to kill the application.

⚠ *If you have killed applications and they still appear in the Applications tab listing, see "The Task Manager Is Stalled" in the "Troubleshooting" section at the end of this chapter.*

TIP FROM

Before you give an application its last rites, pause for a bit. In general, it's not a good idea to kill an application if you can avoid doing so. Terminating an application can cause instability in the operating system (even though it shouldn't in most cases because of the kernel design). Or at the least, you can lose data. Try "jiggling" the application in various ways, in hopes of being able to close it gracefully first. Switch to it and back a few times. Give it a little time. Maybe even do some work in another application for a few minutes, or take a trip to the water cooler. Try pressing Esc while the application is open.

27

> When executing some macros in Word, for example, I noticed that one of my macros hangs for no apparent reason. It seems to crash Word. So, I killed it from the Task Manager, losing some work. I later realized the solution was to press Esc, which terminated the macro. Having slow network connections and attempting to link to nonexistent Web pages, printers, or removable media can also cause apparent hangs. Try opening a drive door, removing a network cable, or performing some other trick to break a loop a program might be in before resorting to killing the program from the Task Manager. This is especially true if you've been working on a document and you might potentially lose data.
>
> Some applications will so intensely perform calculations that the Task Manager will list them as Not Responding. If you suspect this, give the program five minutes or so to complete its thinking, I've learned the hard way to be patient with some applications.

Dr. Watson, Come Quick!

You might want to know about a debugging program called Dr. Watson which is supplied with Windows XP. It's primarily designed for programmers or for technical support people who might be helping you resolve a software conflict on the workstation. The program sits in memory, keeping an eagle eye on applications as they run. If one bombs or breaches security, Windows XP shuts down the errant program, and Dr. Watson creates an entry in a special log file named Drwtsn32.log found in the \Documents and Settings\All Users\ Application Data\Microsoft\Dr Watson folder by default. The entry contains key information about what the application did wrong, and some other details of your computer's operation at the time of the error. If you are getting application crashes on a specific program, you can contact the vendor and ask whether the tech support people want to see the log. To start the Dr. Watson program to set up preferences, you can choose Start, Run, and enter `drwtsn32`. The default settings are fine under most circumstances.

Incidentally, two Dr. Watson programs are actually included with Windows XP. You'll find both 32-bit and 16-bit versions for the corresponding Windows applications. The programs are named drwtsn32.exe (for 32-bit programs) and drwatson.exe (for 16-bit programs).

By default, drwtsn32.exe creates a Crash Dump file for each error that is generated. It is a binary file that can be opened and examined in a debugger program. These files can be quite large, however. They take up space on your disk and cause a bit of a system slowdown while writing the files to disk. The last time I checked one of these files on one of my machines, it was 45MB. If you don't expect to be debugging a program, you can turn off this feature by running drwtsn32.exe and turning off the Create Crash Dump File option.

Notice that you can also switch to an application in the list or run a new one. Just double-click the application you want to switch to (or click Switch To). Similarly, to run a new application, click New Task, and enter the executable name or use the Browse dialog box to find it. This dialog is no different from the Start, Run dialog box, even though its name is different.

 If you're frustrated because you cannot send the Task Manager to the background, see "Sending the Task Manager to the Background" in the "Troubleshooting" section at the end of this chapter.

Processes Tab

Whereas the Application tab displays only the full-fledged applications you're running, the Processes tab shows *all* running processes, including programs (for example, Photoshop), services (for example, Event Log), or subsystems (for example, wowexec.exe for running

Windows 3.x applications). In addition to just listing active processes, Windows XP displays the user or security context (that is, the user, service, or system object under which the process is executing) for each process—a great new feature not present in previous OSes. Also by default, the percentage of CPU utilization and memory utilization in bytes is listed. You can change the displayed information through the View, Columns command.

Almost any listed process can be terminated by selecting it and then clicking the End Process button. There are some system-level processes which even you as administrator don't have sufficient privileges to kill. You might also discover at times that an application will fail to be killed, typically due to a programming error or a memory glitch. In those cases, you should reboot the system. You might find that sometimes a hung application also will prevent a normal shutdown. If your attempt to reboot fails, you'll have to resort to manually turning the power off and then back on. Hopefully, you saved often and didn't lose too much work.

TIP FROM

Bob & Brian

> At the bottom of the Processes tab is a check box labeled Show processes from all users. If you've switched users, you can see not just the processes under your user account and those of the system, but also those of other active users. Plus, once displayed, you can also terminate them using the End Process button.

By studying the entries in the process list, you can learn some interesting facts about the operating system. For starters, you might be shocked to see just how many separate processes the operating system has to multitask just to keep going (see Figure 27.17). Notice that the highlighted process is ntvdm (NT Virtual DOS Machine); also, notice that wowexec.exe is running in it and is indented a bit (it appears just above ntvdm). The processes running along with the wowexec (three instances of Alarm, listed below wowexec) are also indented. All Windows 3.x processes run in the same VDM (by default), with wowexec.exe (WOW means "Windows on Windows") being the process that emulates Windows 3.x. Terminating the ntvdm or wowexec process will terminate all three Windows 3.x applications.

For more details on managing DOS and Windows 3.x environments, please jump to Chapter 25, "Maintaining and Optimizing System Performance."

If the true identity of some of the processes is something you're dedicated to uncovering, check the Services snap-in described later in this chapter. Many of the entries in the processes list are system services, the bulk of which load during bootup.

ALTERING THE PRIORITY OF A TASK

In the beginning, all tasks are created equal. Well, most of them, at least. All of the processes under your user account's security context will have Normal priority by default. Most kernel or system processes will have High priority. You might want to increase or decrease the priority of a process, though changing the priority typically isn't necessary. To do so, right-click the task and choose the new priority through the Set Priority sub-menu.

27

Figure 27.17
Examining running processes. Notice the wowexec.exe process, which is the Windows 3.x subsystem, and the three Windows 3.x programs.

Avoid altering the priority of any task listed with a user name of SYSTEM. This indicates the process is in use by the kernel. Altering the execution priority of such processes can render your system nonfunctional. Fortunately, process priority settings are not preserved across a reboot, so if you do change something and the system stops responding, you can reboot and return to normal. In some cases, raising the priority of an application can improve its performance. However, increase the priority in single steps instead of automatically setting it to the maximum. Throwing another top-priority application into the mix of kernel-level activities can render the system dead too.

There are six priority levels you can assign to processes: Realtime, High, AboveNormal, Normal, BelowNormal, and Low. Realtime is restricted for use by administrators. You should keep away from High since it can interfere with essential OS operations (especially if you have several user processes set to High). More details about process priorities is discussed in Chapter 25, "Maintaining and Optimizing System Performance."

TIP FROM

> If you have a multiprocessor computer, and you want to assign a task to a given processor, right-click the process and choose the Set Affinity command. Choosing this command guarantees that the process receives CPU time only from the CPU you choose.

PERFORMANCE TAB

The Performance tab of the Task Manager indicates important conditions of your operating system. It shows a dynamic overview of your computer's performance, including CPU usage; memory usage; and totals of handles, threads, and processes (see Figure 27.18).

From the Performance tab, the View menu includes CPU History and Show Kernel Times. The former command is used to show different graphs for each CPU (only useful on multiple CPU systems). The latter command sets the display to show kernel activity in red and user activity in green on the CPU and Page file usage graphs. You should also notice that paging file usage is shown instead of memory usage.

Figure 27.18
The Performance tab displays some interesting statistics and a chart of CPU and page file usage over time.

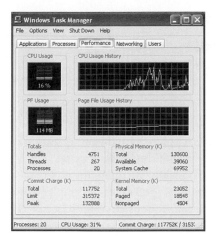

Although CPU usage is interesting, the most important of these numbers is memory usage. You can easily check in the Physical Memory area to see how much memory is installed in your system, how much is available for use by applications before disk caching begins, and how much the system is using for caching.

NOTE

> System cache is the total current swap and RAM area allocated for system operations. When your computer has to go to a disk cache to access information it significantly slows down overall system performance, which is why having more system RAM is almost always better.

The Kernel Memory area reports the memory in use strictly by the operating system for running the operating system internals. Nonpaged kernel memory is available only to the operating system. This memory is in physical RAM and can't be paged out to the hard disk because the operating system always needs fast access to it, and it needs to be highly protected. Paged memory can be used by other programs when necessary. Commit memory is memory allocated to programs and the system. Because virtual memory increases the amount of actual memory available, the Commit Peak memory can exceed the maximum physical memory.

In the Totals section, you can see the number of handles, threads, and processes. Threads are discussed in more detail in Chapter 2. Handles are tokens or pointers that let the operating system uniquely identify a resource, such as a file or Registry key, so that a program can access it.

Most of these size reports are of use only to programmers. However, the charts can offer strong, telltale signs of system overstressing. If you see, for example, that your page file usage is consistently nearing the top of its range, you are running too many programs. If the CPU is topped out most of the time, you also could be in trouble. Perhaps you have a background task running that is consuming way too much CPU time. An example could be a background program doing statistical analysis or data gathering.

27

TIP FROM

*Bob
& Brian*

When the Task Manager is running, even if minimized, a green box appears in the system tray, indicating CPU usage. It's a miniature bar graph.

NETWORKING TAB

The Networking tab (see Figure 27.19) displays a bandwidth consumption history graph. As network operations occur, this graph will plot the levels of usage. The View menu includes a Network Adapter History submenu. This submenu offers the ability to include bytes sent (red), bytes received (yellow), and bytes total (green) on the graph (shown by default). At the bottom of this tab, a list of all network connections along with details is displayed. The Columns command from the View menu is used to add or remove data columns from this display. This tab can give you a quick heads up if you suspect a network slowdown.

Figure 27.19
The Networking tab shows network traffic activity.

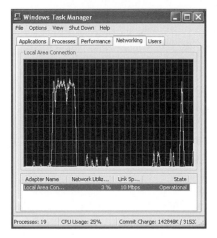

USERS TAB

The Users tab shows a list of all active users on this system or connected via the network. From here you can disconnect a network user, log a local user off, or send a user a text message. The Users tab will only be visible if you are not participating in a Windows 2000/Windows 2003 Server Active Directory–based network, or have not disabled Fast User Switching if participating in a workgroup.

PROTECTING THE SYSTEM FILES

We are all familiar with the problem of an operating system becoming suspiciously unstable after the installation of a new application or a driver or after a system crash. Microsoft has been painfully aware of this problem for some time, and many a technician (whether a Microsoft employee or not) has been forced to instruct a PC user to "reinstall Windows" as the only solution. We all know how much fun that is. If you think Windows operating systems sometimes seem like a house of cards stacked level upon level, waiting for a single *.DLL or other system file to fail, well, you're right. This kind of vulnerability is wholly unacceptable in mission-critical settings, so Microsoft had to come up with preventive measures.

NOTE

> Windows XP also supports a new side-by-side DLL feature. This automatic feature keeps track of the DLL versions used by installed applications. If a system update or an application install attempts to change the version of a DLL that is needed by a service or application, XP automatically places a copy of these necessary DLLs in the \Windows\WinSxS folder. Each time an application is launched, XP checks its list to see what version of each required DLL is needed and loads those DLLs into that application's virtual machine. No more "DLL hell." This feature is completely automatic and invisible to the user.

Windows has means for setting up options that prevent the often-unintentional destabilization of the operating system from applications or driver installations or, in the worst case, the introduction of viruses that intentionally alter or overwrite system files. Windows XP's Security Manager and file system work in symphony to help protect critical system files and drivers. Several areas of system functionality help prevent damage from the installation of untested drivers or from modification of system executables such as dynamic link libraries (DLLs). They are as follows:

- **Windows File Protection service**—This service is a function of the operating system that continually monitors protected system files, standing guard against attack.

- **System File Signature Verification tool**—You can use this command-line executable to check the signatures on your essential system components.

- **System File Checker tool**—You can use this command-line executable to verify that system file versions align properly.

The essential (and automatic) portion of this trio is the first one. Windows XP's file protection system is enabled by default, and it prevents the replacement of the protected system. Windows File Protection runs in the background and protects all files installed by the Windows XP setup program—.SYS, .DLL, .OCX, .TTF, .FON, and .EXE files. If one is replaced or altered, by default, a dialog box alerts you that a program is attempting to alter a system file.

In Chapter 25, you learned about setting up the three levels of overwrite protection for Windows File Protection: ignoring, warning, or preventing modification of all system files. Here, I'll talk a bit about a standalone utility supplied with Windows XP that you can use to scan for modified files that may have slipped through the detection process.

RUNNING THE FILE SIGNATURE VERIFICATION TOOL

To verify that system files have a digital signature, follow these steps:

1. Choose Start, Run, and then enter **sigverif** to launch the File Signature Verification tool.

2. Normally, the program searches for any system files not signed, and when you close the program, the results are saved in SIGVERIF.TXT. If you want to search for nonsystem

files as well or append to an existing log of found items, click the Advanced button and set up the log file's name, append option, and other related options.

3. Back in the File Signature Verification dialog, choose Start. The tool then checks to see which system files are digitally signed and displays its findings. Typically, you see the message displayed stating that files have been scanned and verified as digitally signed. Otherwise, you'll see a list of files that have not been digitally signed. If you have logging enabled, these search results are also written to SIGVERIF.TXT in the <system root>\Windows directory (by default).

USING THE SYSTEM FILE CHECKER

Another program, closely related to the File Signature Verification tool, is the System File Checker. This tool looks for protected system files and verifies that their version numbers link up with the operating system and that they haven't been replaced or trashed accidentally. The System File Checker is a command-line program that you set up using a keyboard-entered command. It then runs the next time you boot.

> **NOTE**
> You must be logged in as a system administrator to run this program.

If the System File Checker discovers that a protected file has been overwritten, it retrieves the correct version of the file from the <systemroot>\system32\dllcache folder and then replaces the incorrect file. It uses the following syntax for program execution:

`sfc [/scanonce] [/scanboot] [/cancel] [/quiet]`

The details for these parameters are as follows:

`/scanonce`

The preceding syntax scans all protected system files once.

`/scanboot`

The preceding command scans all protected system files every time the computer is restarted.

`/cancel`

The preceding command cancels all pending scans of protected system files.

`/quiet`

This command replaces all incorrect file versions without prompting the user.

> **NOTE**
> What if something or someone has trashed the \system32\dllcache folder? No problem. The `sfc /scanonce` or `sfc /scanboot` commands repair the contents of dllcache if it's unreadable.

27

Windows File Protection, if turned on, normally prevents any kind of intrusion that might result in a corrupted file, at least from an outside source such as a third-party program installation. If all is working as planned, you don't have to worry about running this program or the File Signature Verification program with any regularity. If you want to play it super safe, though, protecting also against microscopic bit loss on the hard disk or crafty hacking, you can use the /scanboot option to check each time you boot. The verification process doesn't take very long to complete.

MICROSOFT MANAGEMENT CONSOLE (MMC)

As mentioned previously, the Computer Management tool actually is a subset of something much larger and more extensible—the Microsoft Management Console (MMC). I suppose what happened is that Microsoft finally understood that PC administrators were frustrated by the myriad convoluted means for managing their computers. Managing local or remote machines by hopping around between Control Panel applets, Explorer Properties sheets, and icons such as Network Neighborhood just didn't cut the mustard. Administrators and power users wanted one unified tool, a so-called *single-seat* solution for computer management. They also demanded the capability to construct personalized toolkits to delegate specific administrative tasks to users or groups without jeopardizing the health of the system by giving away the farm.

The Microsoft Management Console does just this. It's a highly extensible tool interface based on modules called snap-ins that perform specialized services. In turn, snap-ins also can be made up of additional extension snap-ins.

When a customized set of snap-ins and extensions is put together, you can save it as an MMC console for later use. Consoles are saved as .MSC files that are small and easily transportable because, basically, they're just a list of objects and properties. So, you can create an MMC console for, say, co-workers, and e-mail it to them, post it on the Web, or make it available in a shared folder on the LAN. Consoles can be exclusively assigned to a specific user or group of users using system policy settings. Because MMC files are editable, you can change them after the fact, adding or removing snap-ins and extensions at will.

Putting together your own MMC consoles is as easy as pie. As when you build a Web page or a brochure, you can start with an existing template of tools and then add or remove snap-ins and extensions. Microsoft supplies a broad selection of tools for futzing with the operating system, and other snap-ins are available from third parties.

The following steps show you how to create a personalized console:

1. To open the base Microsoft Management Console application, choose Start, Run and enter **mmc**. The empty console is nonfunctional until you add some snap-ins. Also, the menu commands apply to the entire console because no individual snap-ins are yet loaded.

27

2. Choose Console, Add/Remove Snap-in. On the resulting Add/Remove Snap-in dialog box, click the Standalone tab. Choose the insertion point for the snap-in from the drop-down list. Use Console Root because there probably isn't another choice, anyway.

3. Click the Add button. You see a list of standalone snap-ins, as shown in Figure 27.20.

Figure 27.20
The Add Standalone Snap-in dialog box.

4. For this example, suppose you want to add Computer Management to your console. Click it, and then click Add. A dialog box comes up asking whether changes you make with this console will apply to the local computer or a remote one. Typically, you choose local. Then, click Finish.

5. When you return to the Add/Remove Snap-in dialog box (which might require closing the Add Standalone Snap-in dialog box), click the Extensions tab. Now you get to choose the details of the standalone snap-in that you want available in your console. This step is similar to clicking the Details button when you do a custom installation of programs such as Office.

NOTE

Not all snap-ins have extensions.

6. Check the extensions you want included in your console. Uncheck the ones you don't want included.

7. Repeat the process to add and set the details for other snap-ins. For example, you might want to add Certificates Management to your console.

TIP FROM

Bob
& Brian

You can open a second console window by right-clicking a service in the left pane and then choosing New Window from Here. Then choose Window, Tile Horizontally to arrange the windows.

To save your console, choose Console, Save, and save it in the usual fashion. It is given an .MSC extension. You can later run it by double-clicking it.

In summary, understand that the Microsoft Management Console is a powerful tool, complex enough to write an entire book about. For more information about the Microsoft Management Console, check the following site:

`http://www.microsoft.com/management/mmc/default.htm`

NOTE

You can find a growing gallery of snap-ins for the MMC by clicking Help, Microsoft on the Web, Snap-in Gallery. You also can find a FAQ about the MMC there.

TROUBLESHOOTING

THE TASK MANAGER IS STALLED

My Task Manager seems stuck. It doesn't reflect newly opened or closed applications.

You might have this problem if you've paused the Task Manager. Choose View, Update Speed, and then choose any setting other than Paused. Another approach, if you want to keep it paused, is to choose View, Refresh Now.

SENDING THE TASK MANAGER TO THE BACKGROUND

My Task Manager doesn't drop into the background when I click another program.

Like some Help files, the Task Manager has an Always on Top option. Choose Options, and turn off this setting.

WRONG LANGUAGE

I'm seeing Windows Update in the wrong language. Why?

You're probably having this problem because of settings in Windows and Internet Explorer. But let's start at the beginning. The first thing to know is that every copy of Windows has a language tag associated with it. If you're running an English version of Windows XP, then Windows Update is only going to offer to download English-based add-ins for the operating system.

Now with that said, yes, you can change the language in which you view the Windows Update pages. If you have the wrong Regional settings in Windows and/or in Internet Explorer, you might be dishing up Greek or Italian when you want English. Here's the order in which Windows Update checks for your language preference:

1. Language tag of your copy of Windows and Internet Explorer
2. Your system's Regional Settings
3. Internet Explorer's auxiliary language preferences setting

The catch is that Internet Explorer has a feature called Accept Language, which supersedes the Windows Regional Settings. If you are viewing Windows Update (which is available in multiple languages), Internet Explorer looks to the list of languages in your language preference settings to determine which language to display. This list is prioritized, so if you have Greek as the first language and English as the second, Windows Update is displayed in Greek.

To see the Windows Update site in a different language, you can adjust your Internet Explorer's language preference settings as shown here. Note that changes here affect other multilanguage sites that you view.

1. In Internet Explorer, choose Tools, Internet Options.

2. On the General tab, click the Languages button.

3. Select the language you want, and then use the Move Up button to place your selection at the top of the list of languages. Click OK.

4. Click OK in the Internet Options dialog, and restart your browser.

5. Reload the Windows Update page

THE SCHEDULED TASKS DOESN'T ACTIVATE CORRECTLY

My Scheduled Tasks doesn't seem to activate correctly. What's the problem?

You can check several things when a Scheduled Tasks job doesn't activate correctly. Here's the rundown; check these steps in order:

1. Open the Scheduled Tasks window, and then open the properties for the task. Make sure the task is actually enabled via the Enabled check box on the Task tab.

2. On the Schedule tab, verify that the schedule is set correctly.

3. Check the permissions for all the items involved in running the task, such as scripts, executables, and so on. Make sure the permissions for those items match those of the user account assigned to the task.

4. If a user whose account a task is set to run in is not logged on at the time the task is scheduled to run, the task runs but is not visible. Check the task log file to see whether the task was running but you didn't know it.

5. Some commands hang, waiting for user input, unless launched with command-line arguments. Research the command or executable you are trying to run. Check the Help file for the program or issue the command from a command prompt window, followed by /?, -?, or just ? to see a display of options.

6. Check or ask your administrator to check that Scheduled Tasks service is turned on (by choosing My Computer, Manage).

7. Check the Status column in the Scheduled Tasks window, and look for the task in question. (Use the Details view.) Table 27.6 describes the status types.

TABLE 27.6   SCHEDULED TASK STATUS TYPES

Status	Description
Blank	The task isn't current running, or it already ran and encountered no obstacles.
Running	The task is currently being run.
Missed	One or more attempts to run this task was missed, possibly because the computer was not turned on, or the scheduler was paused at the time.
Could not start	The most recent attempt to start the task failed for some reason. Check the log file if you care to investigate further. The log file, named schedlgu.txt, is stored in the \Windows folder. This file is used to record the activity of scheduled tasks.

NO EVENTS IN SECURITY LOG

No events are showing in my security log.

By default, security logging is turned off in Windows XP. Therefore, no security events are monitored or recorded, and your security log is devoid of entries even if you *do* have the administrative rights required to view them. See Chapter 21 for details on auditing and the recording or logging of security events into the Security log.

TIPS FROM THE WINDOWS PROS: POWER USER TRICKS

The following tricks are two of my personal favorites. The first is helpful if you frequently work with a laptop computer and want to add a serial mouse without closing all your applications and rebooting.

The second tip is especially helpful if you want to deter workgroup users from using the Windows Update feature without first checking with the system administrator.

ADDING A SERIAL MOUSE WITHOUT REBOOTING

Due to the cramped or otherwise uncomfortable position I have to assume to use my laptop keyboard, I very often plug in an external, ergonomic keyboard with a trackpad on it. Then I can sit back in my chair, keyboard on my lap, or even stand the computer up sideways. In any case, I don't always want to power down and then reboot just to plug in the keyboard and mouse.

Now, if the mouse and keyboard were USB devices, this wouldn't be a problem because USB supports hot docking. Keyboards, mouse devices, graphics tablets, and many other external devices such as cameras, printers, scanners, and PDAs are available in a USB-enabled version, but that doesn't mean you own them.

My keyboard plugs into the PS/2 port, which is no problem. Although making PS/2 connections with a computer turned on is not advisable (it can blow the driver chip for the port), I do it anyway, and on my Dell 7000, it hasn't posed a problem. The keyboard is immediately recognized and works fine. But the rub is that the trackpad, which connects to

27

the serial port (a second PS/2 port for a mouse is not available on my machine), isn't recognized. Connecting the mouse doesn't result in anything at all, functionally. For a while, I resorted to rebooting Windows XP. Hibernating or suspending didn't force a hardware redetection. Another approach was to run Add/Remove Hardware, but that's a pain because it takes too long.

I discovered that the Device Manager can scan hardware and see whether anything new is lying around, without its driver. After I had installed the trackpad software, it was part of the Device Manager's list for the computer. But when the mouse is sensed as unplugged, the operating system marks it as not functioning (with an exclamation mark in the Device Manager). To get it going again, no reboot is necessary. I just had to do the following:

1. Reconnect the mouse.

2. Get to the Device Manager (you can do so from Control Panel, System, Hardware tab).

3. Click somewhere on the computer's tree, such as the top level, the icon showing the computer name. (This step is imperative, or the next step isn't possible.)

4. Choose Action, Scan for Hardware Changes.

5. Wait about 10 seconds while Windows does its thing. Now the external mouse should work.

This trick works on desktop systems too!

REMOVING WINDOWS UPDATE FROM THE START MENU

As good an idea as Windows Update is, unauthorized use of it could be annoying to a system administrator. Corporate system administrators who are responsible for hundreds of PCs need to control what goes on their machines, especially in the way of core operating system updates. It is possible to remove the Windows Update icons that appear in the Start menu, and even prevent the users from accessing the Windows Update site (http://windowsupdate.microsoft.com) from anywhere within Windows.

By using the Windows XP Microsoft Management Console's snap-in called Local Computer Policy, you can disable Windows Update on the Start menu. Although you can modify and configure MMC to view policies in many ways, the most generic way to configure a new console root is as follows:

1. Choose Start, Run. Then enter MMC and click OK.

2. From the console, choose Add/Remove Snap-in.

3. Choose Add, Choose Group Policy. Then click Add, Close, and finally OK.

4. Navigate down by expanding the Local Computer Policy by expanding User Configuration, then expand Administrative Templates, then select Start Menu and Taskbar.

5. Double-click Remove Links to Windows Update.

6. Select the Disabled radio button.

7. Click OK.

8. Click File, Exit. If prompted to save settings to the Console, click No.

CHAPTER 28

MANAGING USERS

In this chapter

MULTIPLE USERS ON ONE MACHINE

In many instances, a single computer is used by more than one user, which creates some challenges. While we sometimes use computers to share information, we often want to keep information confidential. We want to customize our desktop settings, and want the computer to look and behave the same way every time we use it, no matter who has used it in between. Furthermore, we might want to prevent other users and network visitors from seeing or changing our files. These issues can make sharing a computer troublesome, and the Windows 9x product line addressed them poorly. Windows XP is a great improvement thanks to the following features:

- *User Accounts* let you set up access for each individual who wants to use the computer. Each account has its own name and optional password.

- *User Profiles* let users configure their own personalized desktop scheme, icons, preferences, and settings, and give users their own personal My Documents folder.

- *Access control* or *file permissions* let users specify just who is permitted to have access to which of their files.

In this chapter, we'll go over these features so you can decide how much control you want to exercise over your computer. Using these features is optional—you can make your system as secure or as open as you wish.

First, though, there is a bit of background on accounts that we need to cover. If you already know about user accounts (or don't care to know about them), you can skip ahead to the section "Working with Passwords."

USER ACCOUNT TYPES

Each user identifies him- or herself to Windows with a username and an optional password (or in high-tech environments, perhaps with a smart card or a fingerprint scanner). Windows keeps track of each user in its list of *accounts*, or known users. For each user, Windows associates information such as whether the user has Administrative privileges, the user's desktop and sound preferences, and the location of the user's My Documents file folder.

A list of valid users is stored in each Windows XP computer. These are called *local accounts* because the information about the user is stored on the computer itself, and the username and password are recognized only on this one computer. If the computer is a member of a domain-type network, the network's domain controller holds a master list of all accounts for the entire domain, for example the entire corporation. These are called *global accounts*, because the account information is accessible anywhere on the network, and any member computer can validate the user's name and password.

Whether this matters to you depends on what kind of network your computer is connected to:

- If your computer is not connected to a network, all the users of your computer are local users and you don't need to worry about this distinction. You will be interested in reading about User Profiles, however, later in this chapter.

- If you're a member of peer-to-peer workgroup network, each of your computers will have its own separate list of local users. This can be inconvenient, because users of one computer won't necessarily be recognized by your other computers. We'll talk more about this later on in the Simple File Sharing section.

- If you're a member of a domain network, your computer can have both local and global users. You can define local accounts that only have access to the individual computer, if you want. There is also a local Administrator account for each computer, with its own password. This lets you maintain and update your computer without knowing the master domain Administrator's password. Your domain administrator may prevent you from creating or using local accounts, however.

GUEST AND ADMINISTRATOR ACCOUNTS

If you installed Windows XP Professional yourself, during the installation process you had the opportunity to enter the names of several users. In addition to any individual users you specified, two special user accounts were automatically created on your machine: Administrator and Guest.

The Guest user account provides access to your computer by people who don't have a predefined username and password, without you needing to set up a new account for them. This account is disabled by default, to prevent unauthorized local or network access to your computer. I strongly urge you to leave this account turned off. Even though the Guest account has lower privileges than a normal user account and can't modify system settings or install software, it's still risky to let random people have access to a computer, especially in a business setting.

The Administrator user account is the opposite of the Guest account. Logging on using the Administrator account (or any account with Administrator privileges) gives you the power to read or modify any file on your computer, change any local user's password, install or remove software, or anything else you please. The Administrator account can bypass all security measures.

As I'll discuss in the next section, by default, Windows XP Professional gives *all* additional user accounts Administrator privileges unless your computer is a member of a domain-type network. I don't think giving such high privilege is a good idea because any programs you run will have full access to the computer—and virus software takes advantage of this. I recommend that you remove the Administrator privileges from your regular user accounts, and use the Administrator account directly only when you

- Don't have permission to access a file you need
- Need to create or change the password of another user account
- Need to install new hardware or software

Microsoft gave all users Administrator privileges to make these actions easier for you, but I think they're needed seldom enough that it's not worth the added risk. I'll tell you how to remove the default Administrator privileges later in this chapter under Assigning Permissions to Groups.

28

⚠️ *If you are told your user account doesn't have permission to accomplish some necessary maintenance task, see "Can't Install Hardware or Software" in the "Troubleshooting" section at the end of this chapter.*

When you do want to log on using the actual Administrator account, if you use the Welcome screen, you will notice that Administrator doesn't appear as a choice. Pressing Ctrl+Alt+Del twice while viewing the login screen displays the old-style login dialog. In it, you can type "Administrator" and enter the password, as shown in Figure 28.1.

Figure 28.1
To log on as Administrator, press Ctrl+Alt+Del twice to switch from the graphical XP login screen to the old-style Windows logon dialog.

> **TIP FROM**
>
> *Bob & Brian*
>
> I strongly suggest that you do not use the Administrator account or an account with Administrator privileges on a day-to-day basis. Running Windows XP as Administrator makes you especially susceptible to Trojan horses and viruses because the Trojan horse code then runs with full privileges to your machine. If you are logged on as a normal user, the virus is limited in what it can damage.

THE RUN AS COMMAND

If you find that you are logging in and out frequently to do administrative tasks, try using the Run As command. You can do so by opening the Start Menu or Windows Explorer and locating the program that you want to run as a different user. (It could be a Control Panel item, the Microsoft Management Console, or any other application.) Right-click the program name, and select Run As, as shown in Figure 28.2. (If Run As doesn't appear, try pressing the Shift key while you right-click.) You then can type the username and password of the privileged account you want to use. If you need to, you can enter a domain account using the *username@domain* format.

> **NOTE**
>
> Run As doesn't work with Windows Explorer, the Printers folder, or desktop icons. Run As also doesn't work with user accounts that are set up with SmartCard authentication systems.

> **CAUTION**
>
> Be sure the Administrator password is kept secure. Remember that the Administrator password is the master key to your computer.

28

Figure 28.2
You can choose to run selected applications in the security context of a different user.

WHY USE SEPARATE USER ACCOUNTS?

Windows XP requires that you add a separate user account for each person that uses your computer. Using separate accounts makes good sense:

- Each user can set their desktop, color, sound, and application preferences separately.

- Each user has their own "desktop" so downloads and icons won't accumulate from other users (I know some people whose desktop is completely covered with icons. This would drive me crazy!)

- E-mail, My Documents and other files are stored separately, so each user has some measure of privacy.

When you create accounts, you should consider what kind of privileges to grant the users. As I mentioned earlier, Windows XP provides three types of account privilege levels:

- Computer Administrators have privileges equal to the Administrator account.

- Power Users can add and remove software but can't modify information for other users' accounts.

- Limited Users can't install programs or make changes to important system settings.

Children and non-technical users, for example, probably should have Limited privileges, so they don't accidentally erase files or programs. In a business setting, *no* regular day-to-day user account should have Administrator privileges—the risk of someone running virus-infected software from a highly privileged account is too great.

Windows asks for one or more account names when it's first installed. These are all created with Administrator privileges. If you set up accounts when you installed Windows, you can

28

change their status as I'll describe in the next few sections. When you're creating new accounts, you can set their privilege level as you go.

TIP FROM

Bob
& Brian

> Microsoft's basic User Accounts control panel only lets you choose between Computer Administrator and Limited privileges. That should be okay for home use, but in business settings I recommend that you read on down to the User Groups section to see how to set up users with the Power Users setting. I would use that category for most users.

WORKING WITH PASSWORDS

By default, Windows does not create passwords for user accounts when they're created. You really should create a password for every account on your computer. Not only do passwords prevent people from using your computer without permission, but Windows disables some features on accounts without passwords. For example, the Remote Desktop feature isn't available to you if your account doesn't have a password.

So, to get the most out of Windows *and* for safety's sake, create a password on every account on your computer.

You can create or change your own password at any time. Computer Administrator users also can change the passwords for other local users' accounts. The procedure depends on whether your computer is a member of a domain network.

If you are a member of a domain network

1. Press Ctrl+Alt+Del to bring up the Windows Security dialog box.
2. Click the Change Password button.
3. Enter your current password and desired new password twice, as indicated.
4. Click OK.

You also can edit account passwords using the User Accounts Control Panel applet, as described later in this chapter under "User Management for Domain Networks."

If your computer is not part of a domain network, or is not part of any network

1. Click Start, Control Panel, User Accounts.
2. Select your account if necessary, and choose Create a Password or Change My Password.
3. If you're adding a password for the first time, you'll be asked to enter the password twice, to be sure of the spelling. You also should enter a password hint, something that will remind you (and *only* you) what your password is. The hint will be displayed on the Welcome screen if you mistype you password when you try to log on. Remember that anyone can see the hint, so "My husband's name" is not a good choice. Then, click Create Password.

If you're changing your password, you'll have to enter your current password, and then type in your desired new password twice as indicated. Then click Change Password.

4. If you're entering a password for your own account for the first time, you'll be asked if you want to make your My Documents folder private. (This privacy feature works only if your hard disk was formatted with or updated to use the NTFS file system, as discussed in Chapter 29.) If you choose to make it private, other users will not be able to see into it or view its files.

If you change your mind about this later, open My Computer, right click your My Documents folder, select the Sharing tab, and check or uncheck Make This Folder Private. Click OK to confirm the change.

Because passwords aren't created when you first installed Windows, you'll probably want to change your password the first time you log on. That's a good time to go ahead and make a password reset disk, as described later in this chapter.

CHANGING OTHER USERS' PASSWORDS

To the greatest extent possible, users should change their own passwords. If a user forgets his or her password, it can be recovered with a Password Reset disk. If that's not available, the password can be changed by the Administrator or a Computer Administrator user, but at a significant cost: As a security measure, Windows will erase any other passwords it has associated with that user, *including the key needed to read encrypted files and e-mail.*

> **NOTE**
> Computer Administrator users can change any local user account's password through the User Accounts control panel—just select the desired account's icon and click Change Password or Create Password. However, the actual "Administrator" account doesn't appear in the User Accounts list. You can change the Administrator account password with the Local Users and Groups computer management tool, which I'll discuss later in this chapter.

CHANGING NETWORK PASSWORDS

You also can change passwords that Windows has stored for other computer networks. Whenever you access a network resource on network or workgroup you're not a member of or don't have an account on, Windows will prompt you for a username and password to use while accessing just that resource. Windows stores the passwords in a list for reuse later on.

> **NOTE**
> You will rarely need to view or modify this list, but you may wish to delete entries in it if you've accessed sensitive network resources and you're worried that someone else might use your account to get access to them.

To modify or delete stored passwords for other computers, open Control Panel and select User Accounts. Then

- If you don't have administrator privileges, Windows will display a dialog box with a link titled Manage Your Passwords. Choose this.

- On a domain network, select the Advanced tab and click Manage Passwords.

- If you have a workgroup network, select Manage My Network Passwords on the Related Tasks list.

Any stored passwords will be displayed in the dialog box shown in Figure 28.3. You can select and remove entries, or click Properties to change the username and password used to access the listed server.

Figure 28.3
This dialog box lets you delete or alter the list of passwords that Windows stores for use on remote computers.

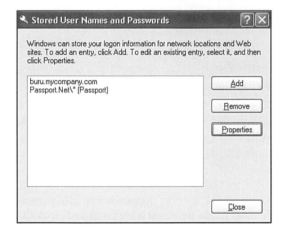

PREVENTING PASSWORD DISASTERS

Your password is the key to all the information you have stored in the computer. This includes not only private files and e-mail, but also additional security information such as your Microsoft .NET Passport, Wallet, network passwords, and the access key for any files you've encrypted. The use of passwords to protect this information is essential. Then again, people tend to forget passwords or to leave jobs, so there has to be a way to gain access to a user's files without the password.

To this end, a Computer Administrator can reset any other user's password. But a security system wouldn't be worth much if the administrator could go in and read any user's "encrypted" files or get at their credit card information. The compromise reached in Windows XP is that the Administrator can change a user's password to regain access to an account, but there is a cost: as a security measure, Windows will erase any other passwords it has associated with that user, *including the key needed to read encrypted files and e-mail*. Why? Because Windows offers to remember the passwords you type for Web sites, network computers, e-mail, and other protected resources, these would become available to anyone who was able to change your Windows password. Erasing them after a forced password change eliminates this risk.

On a domain-type network, you'll have to contact a network administrator if you lose or forget your password. That's your only recourse. However, if you have a non-networked Windows XP computer, or you have a workgroup-type network, users can protect themselves from all this by creating password reset disks before a password emergency occurs. With a reset disk, you can change even a forgotten password without the risk of losing your encrypted files and your .NET Passport.

To create a password reset disk, you will need a blank, formatted floppy disk. Follow these steps:

1. Click Start, Control Panel, User Accounts.

2. Select your own account and, from Related Tasks, choose Prevent a Forgotten Password.

Then, follow the wizard's instructions. When the wizard has finished, be sure to label the disk clearly, like "Mary's password disk for Computer XYZ." It's as good as your password for gaining access to your computer, so store the reset disk in a secure place.

You don't have to re-create the disk if you change your password in the future. The disk will still work regardless of your password at the time. However, a password disk works only to get into the account that created it, so each user should create one for him or herself.

IF YOU FORGOT YOUR PASSWORD . . .

Forgetting the password to your computer account is an extremely unpleasant experience. It's definitely no fun to have your own computer thumb its proverbial nose at you and tell you it's not going to let you in to get your own files. If this happens to you, take a deep breath. You might be able to recover from this. Here are the steps to try, in order of preference:

1. If you created a password reset disk, as I described in the previous section, you're in good shape. Follow the instructions below under "Using a Password Recovery Disk."

2. If you are a member of a domain network, contact the network administrator to have her or him reset your password. The administrator *might* be able to recover any encrypted files you created.

3. Log on as Administrator or with any Computer Administrator user account and follow the procedure outlined under "Creating and Managing User Accounts," later in this chapter, to reset your account's password. (If your computer uses the Welcome screen, you can sign on as Administrator by typing Ctrl+Alt+Del twice. This brings up the standard Windows logon dialog.)

4. If you don't remember the password to any Administrator account, or you can't find someone else who does, you're in big trouble. There are programs available that can break into Windows XP and reset the Guest or Administrator account password. It's a gamble—there's a chance these programs might blow out your Windows installation. Still, if you're in this situation, you probably will want to risk it. Here are some programs you might look into:

Locksmith from Sysinternals.com and Winternals.com is able to replace the Administrator or Guest passwords. The system works by booting the target system

28

from a floppy and then controlling it from another system over a serial cable. From the remote system, passwords are changed through an easy-to-use GUI interface.

Windows 2000/NT Key from LostPasswords.com works just as well on Windows XP as it does on Windows NT and Windows 2000. In fact, this little guy saved my own you-know-what just recently. It creates a Linux boot disk, which pokes through an NTFS or FAT volume, finds the Windows security registry file, and replaces the administrator's password so you can reboot and log on.

5. If you only need to retrieve files, you can remove the hard drive and install it in another Windows XP or 2000 computer as a *secondary* drive. Boot it up, log on as a Computer Administrator, and browse into the drive.

6. If you get this far, things are pretty grim. You'll need to reinstall Windows using the Clean Install option, which will erase all your user settings. Then, as Administrator, you can browse into the Documents and Settings folder to retrieve files from the old user account folders.

If you are not a member of a domain network, I hope you can avoid all this by creating a password reset disk ahead of time. (I've had to go as far as step 4 myself, so I know how frustrating this can be.)

USING A PASSWORD RECOVERY DISK

If you have lost your password and have a password reset disk, you can use it to log on and reset your password. Just attempt to sign on using the Welcome screen. Click Did You Forget Your Password when the logon fails, and then click Use Your Password Reset Disk.

Then, follow the Password Reset Wizard's instructions to change your password, and store the password reset disk away for another day. You don't need to make another recovery disk after using it.

CREATING AND MANAGING USER ACCOUNTS

To create new local user accounts or to modify an existing account, log on as Administrator or with a Computer Administrator account. Keep in mind that you don't need to log on as Administrator to manage your own account.

CAUTION

> Every user account in Windows XP has a unique *security identifier*, called an *SID*. This unique identifier ties all security settings to the user account. If you delete a user account, you also delete its SID, and it can never be used again. Even if you create a new user account with the same username and properties, the SID will be different for the new account. The new account will not be able to view the old account's My Documents files. You will be forced to regenerate all security data, such as group information, set file ownership and access permissions, and so on. As a general rule, you should delete user accounts only when absolutely necessary for organizational purposes.

28

Two programs are used to manage user accounts: the User Accounts control panel applet, and the Local Users and Groups management tool. I'll discuss both.

USER ACCOUNTS CONTROL PANEL

The easiest way to administer user accounts is with the Control Panel tool. Select Start, Control Panel, User Accounts.

NOTE
If your computer is a member of a domain network, you probably don't need to, and might not be permitted to add local user accounts. Check with your domain administrator.

What you'll see depends on whether your computer is a member of a Windows domain-type network. I'll cover standalone and workgroup computers first, and the domain version in the subsequent section.

USER MANAGEMENT FOR WORKGROUP NETWORKS

On a standalone or workgroup network computer, the User Accounts program is shown in Figure 28.4. You can perform three tasks here:

Figure 28.4
The User Accounts control panel applet lets you create, delete, and modify user accounts on a workgroup computer.

- To modify the password, name, picture, or security level of an account, or to delete an account, select Change an Account or click on one of the account icons.
- To create a new account, (no surprise here) click Create a New Account.
- To choose between the new graphical Windows XP login screen and the older Windows logon dialog box, choose Change the Way Users Log On or Off.

28

Microsoft has done a good job of designing the Windows XP account management tool, and most of the dialog boxes are self-explanatory. I'll go through them here to show you what's possible.

CHANGING AND DELETING ACCOUNTS

You can alter an account's settings at any time using the User Accounts control panel. You can always change your own account settings. In addition, Computer Administrator users can adjust any user's account.

Selecting Change an Account or clicking on an account icon displays the Change Account task list, as shown in Figure 28.5. Here you can

- Change the name of a login account.

Figure 28.5
Manage account settings with the Change User Account screen.

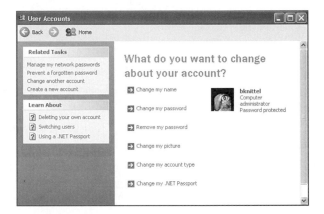

- Add, change, or remove an account's password. Changing another account's password has consequences—please see the section "Working with Passwords," earlier in this chapter.

- Change the picture associated with an account. These pictures appear on the Welcome screen. You can select one of the several provided by Microsoft, or choose Browse to select one of your own digital photographs. You can use any image file in .BMP, .GIF, .JPG, or .PNG format. The picture will be displayed at about postage stamp size, so it's best to choose fairly small images of an object or person that fills the picture.

- Change the account type from Computer Administrator to Limited or vice versa. (To set the accounts to the intermediate Power Users setting, see the "User Groups" section.)

- Delete the account. (This option is available only when you're logged on with a different, Administrator-level account. You can't delete the account you're currently using, and you can't delete a Computer Administrator account if it's the only one.) When you delete an account, you have the option of retaining or deleting the user's personal files stored in their My Documents and Desktop folders. If you want to keep them, they'll be put into a folder on your desktop.

- Change your Microsoft .NET Passport. This is where your user account is matched up with a Passport e-mail address. You can use this task to assign a Passport or change your Passport settings. (This task is only available when you're changing your own account.)
- Modify passwords stored for access to other network resources, by clicking the Related Tasks option.

You cannot view or alter the Administrator account from the User Accounts control panel. Nor can you set user accounts to the Power Users privilege level. To do that, you need to use the more powerful Local Users and Groups management tool, discussed later in this chapter.

NOTE

> Although Microsoft doesn't seem to encourage you to, I recommend that you assign passwords to *all* the accounts on your computer. To set the password for the real Administrator account, you'll have to follow the procedure in the next section.

ENABLING AND DISABLING THE WELCOME SCREEN

One of Windows XP's new features is the friendly graphical logon system called the Welcome Screen. There are actually three options for the Windows sign-on process:

- The Welcome Screen allows users to choose their account names and passwords from a list. It's fast and user-friendly.
- The Windows Logon dialog box requires users to enter a username, password, and optional network domain name. This enhances security by not presenting potential hackers with a visible list of logon names to try.
- A higher-security option requires users to type Ctrl+Alt+Del before seeing the Logon dialog box. Ctrl+Alt+Del forces Windows to suspend any programs (including a virus that might be masquerading as the logon program) and to run the real logon system.

Unless your network administrator has prevented your changing these options, you can control which logon procedure is used on your computer. As a Computer Administrator user, run the User Manager by clicking Start, Control Panel, User Accounts. Under Pick A Task, select Change the Way Users Log On or Off.

Then, you can check or uncheck Use the Welcome Screen. When the Welcome Screen is enabled, you can enable or disable the Fast User Switching feature.

NOTE

> You can enable Fast User Switching or the Offline Files feature, but not both at the same time. Offline Files was described in Chapter 18. To use one feature, you'll have to disable the other.

28

By the way, the Welcome Screen is not available if your computer is a member of a domain network: You'll always be presented with the old tried-and-true Windows logon dialog box when you go to sign on.

USER MANAGEMENT FOR DOMAIN NETWORKS

If your computer is a member of a domain network, Windows displays a different set of user management dialog boxes. To manage local users you must be logged on as the local or domain Administrator. Click Start, Control Panel, User Accounts. Windows displays the local user list as shown in Figure 28.6.

Figure 28.6
Local User Management control panel applet for domain member computers.

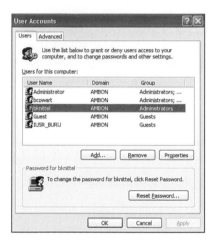

ADDING USER ACCOUNTS

On a domain member computer, you can create new local accounts for local users, and also let members of other domains log on to your computer. (Anyone in your own domain can log on without doing anything extra.) There are different procedures for setting up each type of user.

To let an existing user from another domain log on to your computer, follow these steps:

1. Open the User Accounts control panel applet.
2. Click Add. Enter the user's logon name and domain name. You can click Browse to locate a user by searching Active Directory. When you have identified the user, click Next.
3. Select the desired privilege level for this user; this will assign the account to one of three groups: Power Users, Users or Administrators, as shown in Figure 28.7. Click Finish. If you want this user to be prevented from installing or configuring software, select Users; otherwise you would generally want to select Power Users.

Figure 28.7
The Group
Membership dialog
box lets you assign a
user account to one of
three security levels.

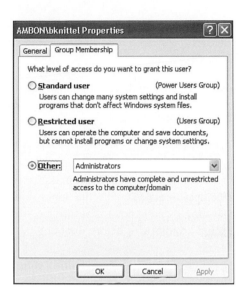

To create a new local account (one that will be able to use your computer but not other resources on your network), follow these steps:

1. Open the User Accounts control panel applet and select the Advanced tab.
2. Click Advanced to view the Local Users and Groups management tool.
3. Select the Users folder in the left pane.
4. Select Action, New User, or right-click User and select New User.
5. Fill in the new user information.

I'll discuss the Local Users and Groups management tool later in this chapter.

CHANGING USER ACCOUNTS

To edit an existing account, open the User Accounts Control Panel applet, and highlight the appropriate user entry.

If you have Administrator privileges, you can click Reset Password to change the account's password.

Select Properties to modify the account's user name or security privileges. Change the user's basic security level by selecting the Group Membership tab (refer to Figure 28.7).

For more detailed control of user privileges and group membership, you can use the Local Users and Groups management tool.

28

ADVANCED SETTINGS

The Advanced tab on the User Accounts control panel applet has three unrelated security management tools:

- **Passwords and .NET Passports**—Lets you delete or change passwords for other computer systems that Windows has remembered for you. For more information on maintaining other passwords, see "Changing Network Passwords" earlier in this chapter.

- **Advanced User Management**—Opens the Local Users and Groups computer management tool, which I'll discuss in the next section.

- **Secure logon**—Lets you determine whether users must press Ctrl+Alt+Del before logging on. This is a good idea because it eliminates the opportunity for Trojan horse virus programs to present a fake login dialog box to capture passwords. This feature is enabled by default, and you should think twice before disabling it.

LOCAL USERS AND GROUPS MANAGEMENT TOOL

The basic User Accounts control panel is adequate for most situations, but if you want to alter the Administrator account, or if you want to assign accounts to your own user groups, you must use the Local Users and Groups management tool.

To run Local Users and Groups on a domain member computer, open the User Accounts control panel. Select the Advanced tab and click the Advanced button. On a workgroup or standalone computer, click Start and right-click My Computer. Select Manage, and open the Local Users and Groups entry.

The utility appears in Figure 28.8.

Figure 28.8
The Local Users and Groups management tool lets you manage group membership and change settings for all user accounts.

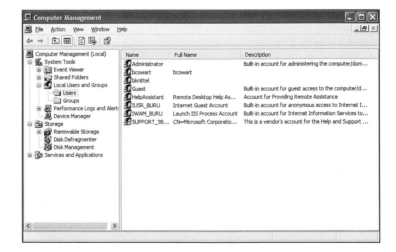

TIP FROM

If you can't get to the Local Users and Groups tool any other way, try this trick: click Start, Run, and enter mmc. Click File, Add/Remove Snap-In. Click Add. Select Local Users and Groups. Click Add, Finish, Close, and OK.

If you view Local Users and Groups on your own computer you will see your user accounts plus a few others, as listed in Table 28.1.

TABLE 28.1   PREDEFINED USER ACCOUNTS

Account Name	Description
Administrator	The "real" administrator account; can read or change any file on the computer and can alter any user account.
Guest	Used by people without local accounts, also used for network file access by unknown remote users.
HelpAssistant	Used by remote users when you invite them to take control of your computer for Remote Assistance.
IUSR_*xxxx*	Used to access files if Internet Information Services is installed. Anonymous Web surfers can only see files that IUSR_xxxx is permitted to access.
IWAM_*xxxx*	Used by Internet Information Services as the user context for CGI programs it runs.
SUPPORT_*xxxx*	Used by Microsoft to provide online support using the Remote Assistance feature (and probably for a hefty fee).

You should not modify the settings or passwords for HelpAssistant, IUSR_*xxxx*, IWAM_*xxxx* or SUPPORT_*xxxx*. Windows manages access to these accounts.

CREATING ACCOUNTS

To create a new local user account, follow these steps:

1. Navigate to the Users folder in the left pane, click the Action button, and select New User. The New User dialog box then appears, as shown in Figure 28.9.

2. Enter the desired logon name and other information requested in the form. You may uncheck User Must Change Password if the new user doesn't mind that you know his or her password. You can check Password Never Expires if you don't want to enforce the good practice of frequent password changes.

3. Click Create to finish. The dialog will stay up and you can continue adding more new accounts, or click Close to remove the dialog.

28

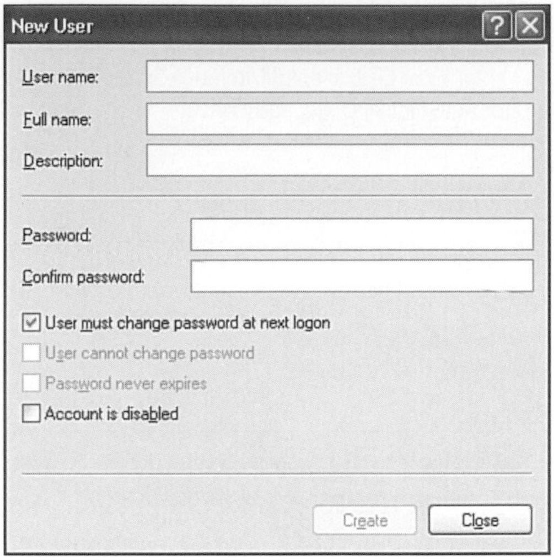

Figure 28.9
You can use the
New User dialog
box in Computer
Management to
create new
user accounts.

CHANGING PASSWORDS

You can change account passwords with this tool. Right-click an account name in the Users list and select Set Password. If you're changing another user's password, you'll be warned that doing this will erase any stored passwords they have, *including the key needed to read encrypted files and e-mail.* Be sure the other user doesn't have a password reset diskette and can't change his or her own password before using this technique to change it.

(By the way, this is the only way another Computer Administrator can change the Administrator account's password, as Administrator doesn't appear in User Accounts control panel applet).

USER ACCOUNT PROPERTIES

To edit the properties of a user account, do the following:

1. Select the Users folder in the left pane.
2. Double-click the user account that you want to edit in the right pane to bring up the properties of the selected user.

In the Properties dialog box, you have the option of adding users to groups, editing logon scripts and profiles, and specifying password options.

There are three tabs on the User Properties dialog box:

- General, shown in Figure 28.10, lets you configure the account's password properties. You can make it impossible for the user to change the password, or require frequent password changes. You can also disable the account, and remove the "Account is locked out" check mark that appears for period of time after a user has failed to supply the correct password three times.

Figure 28.10
The properties interface of a Windows XP Professional user account contains three main tabs that you can configure.

- Member Of lets you add and remove the user from User Groups, which I'll discuss in the next section.
- Profile lets you assign a User Profile folder, home folder, and logon script. These are described later in the chapter as well.

ASSIGNING GROUP MEMBERSHIPS

On the Member Of tab of the Properties dialog, you can add the user to any security groups necessary. By default, all user accounts are made members of the Users or Administrators group. I'll discuss groups and group privileges in more detail later in this chapter.

To add a user to a group, follow these steps:

1. Select the Member Of tab and click Add.
2. Select the local computer or the user's domain in the Look In drop-down box.
3. Select a group, click Add, then OK.

CAUTION

Do not add any user accounts to the Administrators group unless the account will be used only to perform administrative tasks. Adding a user account to this group and using it for day-to-day activities would expose you to the same risks as using the Administrator account.

ASSIGNING USER PROFILES

On the Profile tab of the Properties dialog (see Figure 28.11), you can specify the location in which to store the account's *user profile*. A user profile is a folder in which a user's My Documents folder, Registry data (hive), temporary Internet files, and other personal folders and settings are kept. I'll discuss user profiles in more detail later in this chapter.

28

Figure 28.11
Profile properties let you specify an alternate path for the user profile, as well as a logon script and a home (default) folder or drive.

User profiles are normally kept in C:\Documents and Settings, in subfolders with the same name as the user's account. On a domain-member computer, users can have *roaming user profiles* that are normally kept on a central server, and copied to and from local computers when the user logs in and out.

The following is the procedure to change an account's default profile path, although this is rarely necessary:

1. View the account's properties in the User Accounts control panel. Select the Profile tab.

2. Enter an alternative path in the Profile Path text box. You may enter "%USERNAME%" in place of the account name if you are changing multiple accounts at once.

SETTING LOGON SCRIPTS

You can specify a logon script that runs automatically each time the user logs on. The logon script file is a batch file containing commands to set up the user's environment. One of the primary uses of logon scripts is to map network drives and printers. You can use other start-up commands as necessary, though.

If you want to create logon scripts for your local users, you must save them in the local %SYSTEMROOT%\System32\Repl\Import\Scripts directory, where %SYSTEMROOT% is normally \windows or \winnt. Be sure that all users have at least Read and Execute permissions to this directory, or their logon scripts will not run. The script files should have a .BAT or .CMD extension.

→ If you want to learn more details about setting file permissions, **see** "NTFS File Permissions," **p. 974**.

TIP FROM

Bob
& Brian

I have found that the directory %SYSTEMROOT%\System32\Repl\Import\Scripts does not exist by default on Windows XP Professional computers. You might have to create the subdirectory Repl\Import\Scripts manually. After you do so, you can create and specify logon scripts to run.

Then follow these steps:

1. Move your cursor to the Logon Script field (see Figure 28.11).

2. Type just the name of the logon script file that you want to execute. Do not type the path; it is assumed to be %SYSTEMROOT%\System32\Repl\Import\Scripts.

3. Click OK or Apply.

If a logon script is specified but does not run, see "Logon Scripts Won't Run" in the "Troubleshooting" section at the end of the chapter.

SETTING UP HOME DIRECTORIES

On the Profile tab of the user accounts Properties dialog, you also can specify the user's home directory. A home directory is a default directory that applications can use as a starting point for Save As dialog boxes.

On a LAN environment, it's very useful to locate the home directory on a network server, rather than on the local computer. This way, the same folder is always available every time the user logs in. Roaming User Profiles accomplish this by copying the My Documents folder to and from the server, but the Home Directory mechanism is available on workgroup networks, not just domain networks.

Home directories are very useful in a LAN environment because they allow you to access your files from any computer that you log in to during the course of your day. The Home Directory entry on the Profile tab gives you the option either to

■ Specify a directory path on the local computer.

■ Connect a given drive letter to a specified network share name, in UNC format. You can use the string "%USERNAME"% in this field to stand for the user's logon name.

As an example, on a workgroup network you might create a shared folder named \\AMBON\HOME, with a subfolder for each user on your network. You can then set each user's profile to use drive H and path \\AMBON\HOME\%USERNAME% as the home directory. When any user logs in, drive H is automatically set up to use the correct shared folder. You'll have to do this for each user on each of your computers. On a workgroup network, however, all users have access to the other users' home directories, if you use Windows' default Simple File Sharing scheme.

28

SHARING FILES AMONG USERS

When you set up multiple users on your computer, you'll notice that every user gets his or her own clean desktop and My Documents folder. In fact, if your hard drive is formatted using the NTFS file system, users have the option of making their My Documents folder private when they create a password, so that other users can't see into them.

That's great for keeping everyone's stuff separate, but what do you do when you want to have files that anyone can get to? This might come up when different people are working on a collaborative project, or when one you want to keep common non-confidential information in a shared place.

Windows provides a simple solution to this with the Shared Documents folder. In Figure 28.12, you can see that My Computer shows each user's My Documents folder, and the common Shared Documents folder. Shared Documents is a place to put files and folders that you want to make available to each user on the computer. (This folder is also automatically made available to your other computers, if you have installed a home or office network.)

Figure 28.12
My Computer shows each user's My Documents folder, plus the common Shared Documents folder.

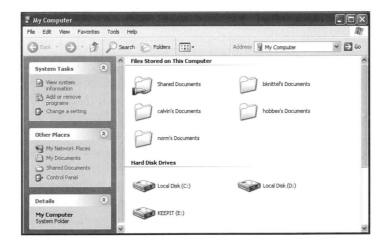

Inside Shared Documents are folders named Shared Music and Shared Pictures, to help you start organizing your common files. You can create other folders in there as well, as you see fit.

Computer Administrator users can browse into other users' personal My Documents folder as long as they didn't choose to make them private when they created their password. In Figure 28.12 you can see the personal My Documents folders for several other users, along with my own. Limited Users can't view any other user's My Documents folder, so they are limited to using their own folder or Shared Documents.

For more information about making your My Documents folder private, see "Working With Passwords" earlier in this chapter.

Of course, you can also create other folders anywhere on your computer's hard drive, and any user can view and use these folders. The advantage of Shared Folders is that it appears on everybody's My Computer display, so it's quite convenient.

WORKING WITH PRIVATE FILES

If your hard drive is formatted using the NTFS (New Technology File System) directory structure, Windows can let you prevent or allow others to access your My Documents folder. The first time you create or change the password for your own account using the User Accounts control panel applet, Windows asks: Do you want to make your files and folders private?

If you say yes, other users will not be able to browse into your My Documents folder (more precisely, they will not be able to get into your User Profile folder, which will be discussed later in this chapter). You can still share documents with other users and with network users using the Shared Documents folder, by creating new folders on the hard drive, or by using the other network shared folders.

You can change the Private/Public setting of your My Documents folder at any time. Just open My Computer, right-click your My Documents folder, select the Sharing tab, and check or uncheck Make This Folder Private. Click OK to confirm the change.

If your hard drive is formatted with the FAT file system, private folders will not be available. Any user can read any file on a FAT-formatted hard drive.

→ To learn more about NTFS, **see** "Choosing a File System: FAT, FAT32, or NTFS," **p. 80**. To see how to convert a FAT-formatted disk to NTFS, **see** "Convert", **p. 1009**.

There are a couple of things you should consider, though, if you are counting on this feature for privacy.

First, remember that any Computer Administrator user can change your account's password, and log on as you. Then they'll have the ability to see your files without any problems. Folder privacy doesn't make your files completely inaccessible to everyone else, only a bit more difficult to get to.

Second, Windows XP Professional manages private folder security with the industrial-strength file protection system used by Windows NT and 2000 and their various server versions.

NOTE

> Users of XP Home Edition don't have access to the settings and controls that let the users of these other, pricier operating systems adjust and manage file security. For Home users, however, that's fine because these features are complex and easy to mess up.

28

However, there is one confounding situation that could arise as a result of this. When you create files in a private My Documents folder and then move them to the Shared Documents folder or another public folder, the "privacy" attribute is moved along with the files. If you move the files with Windows Explorer (or My Computer or any of Explorer's other guises), you're okay because Explorer will care of adjusting the files' security settings, and other users will then be able to read the files.

However, if you move the files using the command line (that is, with the Move command), the files' security settings will not be reset and other users will be see these files listed, but will not be able to open, edit or delete them.

 If you have files that can't be opened because they were moved out of a private My Documents folder, see "Access Is Denied Opening a File" in the "Troubleshooting" section at the end of this chapter.

SIMPLE FILE SHARING

While home users are typically happy letting anyone at any computer read or modify any file, business users usually need to restrict access to files with payroll, personnel, and proprietary information. Windows XP and its predecessors, Windows NT and Windows 2000, were designed for business use, so they require usernames and passwords for identification, and have a security system that lets computer owners restrict access to sensitive files on a user-by-user basis.

Unfortunately, on a Windows peer-to-peer or workgroup network, there is no centralized list of authorized usernames. This makes maintaining control of who is and isn't permitted to access network files on each computer difficult. Here's why: When you attempt to use a file or printer shared by another computer, Windows sends your username and password to the other computer. In versions of Windows prior to XP

- If the username and password match a user account already set up on the other computer, Windows uses that account's permission settings to determine whether to grant you access to the file.

- If the user information doesn't match, Windows prompts you to enter a username and password that the other computer will recognize.

- If you do fail to provide a valid password, the remote Windows computer gives you the permissions assigned to the "Guest" account, which is usually disabled or does not have permission to access the resource you want.

An advantage of this system is that users can determine precisely which users could access files and folders. The disadvantage is that it would require you to set up identical user accounts for each network user on every computer, and then grant these users permissions to modify shared files and folders.

Smaller business and home users found the security setup cumbersome to use and difficult to set up properly. This pushed people into eliminating security restrictions completely, just to get the network to work. That's a risky approach, so Microsoft gave Windows XP Professional a new option called "Simple File Sharing."

N O T E

> Simple File Sharing applies *only* on a peer-to-peer network. Domain network users must live with the full, more complex security system.

The Simple File Sharing feature can be enabled or disabled from the Tools, Folder Options, View tab in any Windows Explorer window, as shown in Figure 28.13.

Figure 28.13
Simple File Sharing is enabled by default; disable it to use the old Windows NT/2000 access control system on a peer-to-peer network.

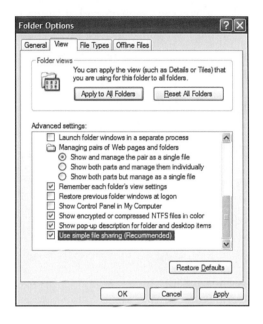

When you first install Windows XP Professional, it is enabled. (By the way, XP Home Edition users have Simple File Sharing too, but can't disable it.)

When Simple File Sharing is enabled

- Network users are not prompted for a username or password. Instead they are automatically granted access using the permissions granted to the Guest account, even if Guest is disabled for direct logins.

- The Security properties tab that is normally used to assign per-user permissions to files and printers is not displayed.

- Windows automatically assigns appropriate security permissions to folders and printers when you share them. If you check Allow Network Users to Change My Files, network users can read, write, rename, or delete the contents of the shared folder. If you don't check this option, network users can view but not modify the contents.

If you disable Simple File Sharing, or if your computer is a member of a domain network, your computer will display different dialog boxes when you go to share a folder, and you'll have access to the Security properties page on folders and printers.

28

It's generally not necessary to disable Simple File Sharing but it *is* important to protect your computer and your network from Internet hacking. Be sure to read Chapters 19, "Connecting Your LAN to the Internet," and 21, "Network Security," to be sure your network is protected.

NTFS FILE PERMISSIONS

If your hard drive is formatted using the NTFS (NT File System) directory structure, and you're not using Simple File Sharing, you can assign control of who is permitted to access files and folders on a per-user or per-group basis.

To display or modify NTFS permissions, select a file or folder in Windows Explorer, right-click Properties, and select the Security tab, as shown in Figure 28.14.

Figure 28.14
You can use the NTFS Permissions dialog box to a folder to restrict access to both network and local users.

 If the Security tab doesn't appear, see "Security Tab Is Not Present" in the "Troubleshooting" section at the end of this chapter.

In the top part of the dialog box is the list of users or user groups with access to the file or folder. You can select any of the names in the list to view their associated permissions in the bottom half of the dialog.

The permission properties can each be granted or revoked individually. The permissions are Full Control, Modify, Read & Execute, List Folder Contents, Read, and Write. Their properties are listed in Table 28.2.

TABLE 28.2 NTFS FILE PERMISSION SETTINGS AND THEIR FUNCTIONS

Permission	Properties
Full Control	Gives all the rights listed below, plus lets the user change the file's security and ownership settings.
Modify	Lets a user modify a file's contents or delete a file.

Permission	Properties
TABLE 28.2	CONTINUED
Read & Execute	Allows a user to read a file's contents and/or run an executable file as a program.
Read	Lets a user read a file's contents only.
Write	Lets a user create a new file, or write data in an existing file, but not read a file's contents. For a folder, lets users add new files to the folder but not view the folder's contents.

Note that each permission has both Allow and Deny check boxes. To get access to a given resource, a user must be explicitly listed with Allow checked or must belong to a listed group that has Allow checked, and must not be listed with Deny access or belong to any group with Deny marked. Deny preempts Allow.

All these permissions are additive. In other words, Read and Write can both be checked to combine the properties of both. Full Control could be marked Allow but Write marked Deny to give all access rights except writing. (This permission would be strange but possible.)

The most productive use of NTFS file permissions is to assign most rights by group membership. One exception is with user home directories or profile directories, to which you usually grant access only to the Administrators group and the individual owner.

TIP FROM

> If you edit Permissions, before you click OK or Apply, click the Advanced button and view the Effective Permissions tab, as discussed later in this chapter. Enter a few user-names to see that the permissions work out as you expected. If they do, only then should you click OK.

 If you find that even Administrator can't gain the rights to delete a file or folder, see "Administrator Can't Delete File or Folder" in the "Troubleshooting" section at the end of this chapter.

INHERITANCE OF PERMISSIONS

Normally, permissions are assigned to a folder (or drive), and all the folders and files within it *inherit* the permissions of the top-level folder. This makes it possible for you set permissions on just one object (folder), to manage possibly hundreds of other files and folders contained within. If necessary, explicit permissions can be set on a file or subfolder to add to or override the inherited permissions. Permissions displayed in the Security tab (as in Figure 28.13) will be grayed out if they have been inherited from a containing folder.

You can view or change the inheritance setting for a file or folder by clicking the Advanced button on the Security properties page. In Figure 28.15, the folder has a check in Inherit from Parent the Permission Entries that Apply to Child Objects. That's the usual case.

28

Figure 28.15
The Advanced Permissions dialog box lets you control the inheritance of permissions, and set detailed permissions for user and groups.

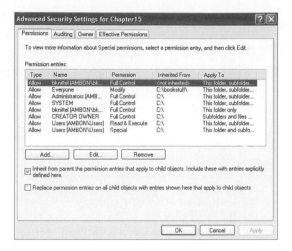

If you uncheck the box, Windows gives you the option of starting with a blank permissions list (Remove) or keeping a copy of the settings it had before (Copy). In either case, the item now has its own independent list of access rights, which you can edit at will.

When you change permissions on a folder, you may want to cancel any manually added permissions set on the files and folders it contains. Checking the Replace Permission Entries on All Child Objects box will reset the permissions on all files in this folder and in subfolders, and will force all subfolders to inherit permissions from this folder.

NOTE

> Changing the permissions of the root folder of the drive containing Windows may make your system unusable. It's best not to mess with the permissions of your C (or boot) drive.

ADVANCED SECURITY SETTINGS

If you edit access permissions in the Advanced Security Settings dialog, you can exercise more "fine grained" control over permissions. It's rarely necessary, but for your reference, Table 28.3 lists the available permission settings.

TABLE 28.3   NTFS ADVANCED FILE PERMISSION SETTINGS AND THEIR FUNCTIONS

Permission	Properties
Traverse Folder/Execute File	For folders, this special permission allows a user the right to move through a folder to which he or she doesn't have List access, to reach a file or folder to which he or she does have access. For files, this permission allows the running of applications. (This permission is necessary only if the user wasn't granted the Group policy "Bypass Traverse Checking".)

TABLE 28.3   CONTINUED

Permission	Properties
List Folder/Read Data	For folders, allows the user to view the names of files or sub-folders inside a folder. For files, allows the user to read the data in a file.
Read Attributes	Allows the user to view the attributes of the file or folder (that is, Hidden, Read-Only, or System).
Read Extended Attributes	Allows the user to view extended attributes of files or folders as defined by another program. (These attributes vary depending on the program.)
Create Files/Write Data	For folders, allows the user to create new files inside the folder. For files, allows the user to add new data or overwrite data inside existing files.
Create Folders/Append Data	For folders, allows the user to create new subfolders. For files, allows the user to append data to the end of an existing file. This permission does not pertain to deleting or overwriting existing data.
Write Attributes	Allows the user to change the attributes of the file or folder.
Write Extended Attributes	Allows the user to change the extended attributes of a file or folder.
Delete Subfolders and Files	For a folder, allows the user to delete subfolders and their contents. This permission applies even if the Delete permission has not been expressly granted on the individual subfolders or their files.
Delete	Allows or denies the user to delete the file. Even if Delete is denied, a user can still delete a file if he or she has Delete Subfolders and Files permission on the parent folder.
Read Permissions	Allows the user to view the file's or folder's permissions assigned to a file or folder.
Change Permissions	Allows the user to change the file's or folder's permissions.
Take Ownership	Allows the user to take ownership of a file or folder.

VIEWING EFFECTIVE PERMISSIONS

The Effective Permissions tab on the Advanced Security page lets you enter a username and see what privileges the user will have as a result of the current security settings on the file or folder, as shown in Figure 28.16.

This dialog box displays the effective permissions *as edited*, before they are applied to the file folder. This lets you verify that the permissions you have set operate as desired before committing them to the file by clicking OK or Apply.

28

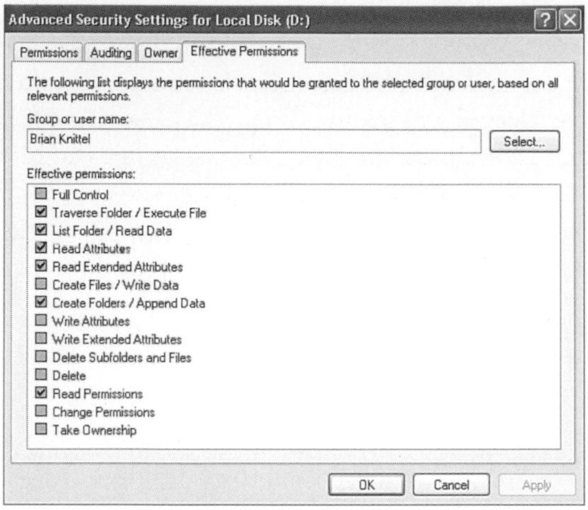

Figure 28.16
Effective Permissions shows you how edited Permissions settings will work before they're actually applied to the file.

ACCESS AUDITING

The Advanced Security Settings dialog provides a way for you to monitor access to files and folders through the Event Log. The Auditing tab (see Figure 28.17) lets you specify users and access types to monitor, and whether to record log entries for successful access, failure to access, or both. Auditing can be set for the use of each access attribute that you can set with Permissions: List Folder, Write Data, and so on.

Figure 28.17
Auditing properties record events in the Security Event log whenever the selected access privileges succeed and/or fail.

Auditing is useful in several situations:

- To determine what files and folders an errant application program is attempting to use
- To monitor users for attempts to circumvent security
- To keep a record of access to important documents

To enable auditing, locate the folder or file you want to monitor, view its Security properties, click Advanced, view the Auditing page, and click Add. Select a specific user or group (or Everyone), and check the desired events to audit. You can prevent a new audit setting from propagating into subfolders by checking Apply These Auditing Entries to Objects and/or Containers Within This Container Only. You can enable the resetting of audit properties of all subfolders and files by checking "Replace Auditing Entries on All Child Objects . . ."

An entry is made in the Security Event log for each audited access, so be careful if you are enabling auditing on the entire hard drive!

TAKING OWNERSHIP OF FILES

Sometimes files or folders have security attributes set so stringently that even Administrator can't read or modify them. Usually this occurs when the file has permissions set only for its owner and not the usual list: Owner, Administrator, System, and Backup Operators, as when a user account is deleted. In this case, no user is able to access the files in that user's My Documents folder.

If you absolutely need to access such files, you can take ownership of the file or folder, and then assign permissions to read and write as appropriate. To take ownership of a file or folder

1. Log on as Administrator.
2. View the file or folder in Explorer, right-click it, and choose Properties.
3. View the Security tab and click Advanced.
4. View the Owner tab, and select Administrator (the user) or Administrators (the group) from the list. You may want to check the Replace Owner on Subcontainers box to change subfolders as well.
5. Click OK.
6. Add privileges as necessary to grant access to the desired user(s).

ASSIGNING PERMISSIONS TO GROUPS

It's common in an office environment to want shared folders that are accessible by some users and not by others. For instance, you may wish to put payroll information in a shared folder and grant access only to certain administrative employees. In a school environment, you might want some folders that are accessible only by teachers, and others accessible only by members of a particular class. If you're using Simple File Sharing, this isn't possible, but if you are using manual permissions, it's fairly straightforward.

The best practice in this case is to create local *user groups*, which are collections of users that can be given privileges that carry over to the group's members. You can add the group and assign permissions for specific folders and files without having to list each of the qualified users separately. Another benefit is that you can add and remove users from the group later on without having to modify the settings of the various folders.

28

To create local user groups, follow these steps:

1. Right click My Computer, click Manage, and open Local Users and Groups; or, on a domain computer, click the Advanced button on the Advanced tab of the User Accounts control panel applet.

2. Right-click the Group entry in the left pane.

3. Select Actions, New Group.

4. Enter a name for the new group, such as Accounting.

5. Click Add and select users to add to the group.

To grant the group permissions to specific folders

1. Highlight the folder or file in Windows Explorer.

2. Right-click and select Sharing and Security.

3. Select the Security tab and click Add.

4. Select the group name (on a domain computer you may select domain groups or local groups by selecting Location and choosing a domain name or the local computer name).

5. Click OK, and then check the appropriate permissions for the group to have.

6. If Everyone or other groups are listed as having rights to this folder, you may want to select the group(s) and uncheck any undesired privileges. If the entry is grayed out, the privileges are inherited from a containing folder. In this case, select Advanced, uncheck Inherit from Parent, and choose Copy to retain copies of the current settings. You can then remove the entries you don't want.

7. **Important:** Before you click OK to commit the changes, use the Effective Permissions tab on the Advanced Properties dialog to check the effective rights of a few different users to be sure that the rights are what you intend. Be sure that Administrator has at least taken ownership privileges.

 If you find that a user has access to something he or she shouldn't, see "A User Has Access to a Restricted Object" in the "Troubleshooting" section at the end of the chapter.

REMOVING USERS FROM THE ADMINISTRATORS GROUP

For reasons that I can't quite fathom, Microsoft decided to make all local users members of the Administrators group in Windows XP. This may have been to reduce the number of support calls from people who said "My computer won't let me install this new hardware," but I think it's a *very bad* idea to have users operate with Administrator privileges on a day-to-day-basis.

The Microsoft Users Accounts tool lets you assign users to either the Administrators group or the Users group, which has very restricted privileges. It also forces you to keep one regular user in the Administrators group, even though the Administrator account is still present (although usually hidden).

I suggest that you either

- Set up one account to use as the additional Administrator, use it only for installing software and hardware, and make all of your regular user accounts Limited users
- Use the Local Users and Groups utility to remove your regular user accounts from the Administrators group, and add them to the Power Users group

SECURING YOUR PRINTERS

Printers can be secured in the same way that access is controlled for files and folders: through user and group privileges. In the case of printers, the privileges allow users to add jobs to the printer, delete other people's jobs, and so on.

On a domain network, the network manager usually takes care of this. And on a workgroup it's generally not important to restrict access to printers. If you are using Simple File Sharing, it's not even possible to set up specific printer access privileges.

If you decide to, however, you can set printer access permissions by right-clicking a printer in your Printers folder and selecting Properties. The Security properties tab resembles the properties tab of files and folders, and can be modified in the same way.

USER PROFILES

User profiles contain all the information that the computer needs to personalize your system's look and feel. Your user profile contains your desktop icons, shortcuts, personalized Start menu, and your personal file folders such as My Documents and My Pictures. The profile also contains your network settings, network printer definitions, and desktop settings, which are stored in a Registry file named NTUSER.DAT. This file is accessed as part of the Windows Registry when you are logged in.

Normally, user profiles are stored under C:\Documents and Settings, in folders with the same name as the user account. For example, the user profiles for Administrator is stored in C:\Documents and Settings\Administrator. When accounts are deleted and re-created, when Windows is reinstalled, or when users log on to domain accounts with the same name as local accounts, Windows may append something to the user name—usually the name of the local computer, the domain, and/or a number.

A profile is really just an ordinary folder. It just contains some important stuff and it's used in a special way—the contents of its Desktop subfolder, for instance, appear on your desktop when you log on, and the contents of its Start Menu subfolder appear when you click the Start button. The contents of a user profile are shown in Table 28.4.

28

Table 28.4   Contents of a User Profile Folder

Item	Contains
Application Data *	User-specific files needed by application programs such as Explorer and Outlook Express
Cookies	Internet Explorer (IE) data
Desktop	Icons and files displayed on the desktop. This is where desktop stuff is actually stored
Favorites	Lists of shortcuts used by the Favorites menu in IE
Local Settings	Like Application Data; includes temporary files
Documents **	User's actual My Documents folder
NTUSER.DAT	User's Registry data (HKEY_CURRENT_USER)
NetHood	Shortcut icons used by My Network Places
PrintHood	Shortcut icons used by Printers and Faxes
Recent **	Shortcuts to recently accessed documents
SendTo	Shortcuts used to fill the "Send To" context menu
Start Menu	Shortcuts displayed on the user's Start menu
Templates	Templates used by various applications to create blank documents

Some of these folders are hidden. You must select Tools, Folder Options, View, Show Hidden Files and Folders to see them.

*** Explorer plays games with the names it shows you. This table lists the folders' actual names, but Explorer displays "My Documents" when viewing your profile, and "So and So's Documents" when viewing someone else's. It always lists the "Recent" folder as "My Recent Documents".*

You might hear the phrase "user profile" used in four different contexts. They are

■ Local user profiles, which are stored on each computer's hard drive as I mentioned earlier.

■ Roaming user profiles, which are stored on a domain network file server, and are copied to and from individual computers as needed when you log on and off. This is how your personal settings "follow" you from one location to another. You should know that the copies—including potentially sensitive files—stay on each computer after you log out.

■ Mandatory profiles, which are set up by the network administrator and can't be modified by the user. They're copied *to* local computers for use when you log on, but aren't copied *back* to the server when you log off, as a roaming profile is.

■ The default profile, which is stored on your computer (or domain server) and is copied for a user the first time he or she logs on. The default profile settings are stored in C:\Documents and Settings\Default User, a hidden folder.

You can't set up roaming or mandatory profiles as a Windows XP Professional user—you have to leave that to your network administrator. However, if you intend to set up several user accounts on your computer, and find that you have to make a lot of configuration changes for each, you can do some useful work ahead of time by modifying the default pro-file—I'll talk about that at the end of the chapter under "Tips from the Windows Pros."

THE PROFILE MANAGER

The Profile Manager will let you copy profile data from one account to another, as well as change an account's roaming/local profile status.

NOTE

> The User Profile Manager only lists profiles for accounts that have logged on to the computer at least once. When a new account is created, its profile folder is *not* created at that time. When the user logs on for the first time, the user's profile is created by copying the contents of the Default User profile, which is stored in \Documents and Settings\Default User.

To start the Profile Manager, click Start, right-click My Computer, and select Properties. View the Advanced tab, and in the User Profiles section, click Settings. The Profile Manager lists all profiles for the local computer, as shown in Figure 28.18.

Figure 28.18
User profile folders contain the user's Registry settings, My Documents, desktop, and so on. They can be copied using the User Profiles tool.

Select a profile from the list and select one of the three action buttons. (Not all options may be available. You can't delete or copy the profile of an account that is currently logged on). The buttons are

- **Change Type**—Lets you choose between a Local and Roaming profile. The Roaming option is available only when your computer is a member of a domain network.

28

- **Delete**—Deletes the profile from \Documents and Settings. This does not delete the account itself, just the user's profile folder and Registry entries. You can use this button to remove an account's settings, files, and Registry entries if for some reason they have become corrupt. When the user logs back on, their profile will be copied from the Default User profile. However, deleting the profile deletes the user's My Documents file. You should make a copy of the user's My Documents folder and everything in it before deleting the original profile.

- **Copy To**—Lets you copy one user's profile to another. At the end of the chapter, I'll show you how to use this to set up the default profile given to newly added users.

  When you use Copy To, the Copy dialog lets you select who is permitted to use the profile folder. You'll need to manually select the user accounts that will be using the profile in its copied location.

> **NOTE**
>
> You can't just manually copy the files and subfolders from one user profile to another. The files have exclusive security permissions, and the Registry file has security data inside it that makes the profile unusable by other users. The Profile Manager works because it changes the security data as it copies the profile.

You can configure several user accounts to use the same profile folder—in essence they'll share a common desktop, permissions, preferences, and so on. To do this, use the Profile Manager to copy an existing profile to a new directory, say C:\Documents and Settings\ Shared. Be sure to click the Change button under Permitted to Use to select which accounts will use the new profile. (You may select Everyone to allow all users to access the profile.) Then use the Local Users and Groups management tool to change the profile directory for the user accounts to refer to this directory.

> **NOTE**
>
> On a workgroup LAN, you might be tempted to mimic the domain's roaming user profile feature by storing each user's profile on a shared network folder. This doesn't work because the user will have a different SID (security identifier) on each computer, even if she or he has the same login name on each computer. The registry file NTUSER.DAT is tied to the SID, so the profile will not function on machines other than the one that created it. This is one of the essential attributes of a domain LAN: Users have a global SID that follows them from computer to computer, and this makes roaming profiles possible.

MOVING PROFILES WITH THE FILES AND SETTINGS TRANSFER WIZARD

You can copy your user profiles between computers using the Files and Settings Transfer Wizard. You might want to do this if you

- Upgrade computers or operating systems
- Switch between your home computer and a portable computer rented for a trip
- Decide to erase your hard drive and start over with a fresh copy of Windows

The wizard can copy your user profile (My Documents folder, Registry settings, and so on) to a floppy disk, but it's best to store the wizard's data on a zip drive, CD-RW, or a shared network folder because the amount of information can be quite large. You can also use a direct serial cable connection between two computers, but this requires you to purchase a "Serial PC to PC File Transfer Cable" from a computer store or other vendor.

Run the wizard first on the "old" computer, the one whose settings you want to move or save. The older computer can be running Windows 95, 98, 98SE, ME, NT, 2000, or XP. If it's running older versions of Windows, insert your Windows XP CD-ROM, and run the wizard from the Setup menu. On Windows XP, click Start, All Programs, Accessories, System Tools, Files and Settings Transfer Wizard. The wizard will give clear instructions as you go.

You can choose to copy settings only, files only, or both files and settings. Windows will display the list of file types and settings it will copy. You can choose Let Me Select a Custom List if you want to modify the list of files or directories to transfer.

Then, run the wizard on the "new" computer to transfer the documents and settings into your Windows XP user account.

TROUBLESHOOTING

CAN'T INSTALL HARDWARE OR SOFTWARE

When I try to install new software, use a Control Panel or Computer Management tool, or set up hardware like a printer or network adapter, I get an error message telling me I don't have sufficient privilege to perform the operation.

Limited User accounts are not allowed to perform many management functions, or to make changes to the Windows software folder. In general this is a good thing because it prevents unauthorized people (like young children, visitors, or meddlesome in-laws) from making changes to your computer setup. More subtly, it can help prevent rogue software from taking over your computer without your knowledge.

If you are using a Limited User account and run into a roadblock because of this, you can either get a Computer Administrator user to perform the task for you, or you can have them change your account to make you a Computer Administrator as well.

ACCESS IS DENIED OPENING A FILE

When I attempt to open a document, I get the message Access is Denied.

This can occur if you are using Fast User Switching and the document is in use by another logged-on user, or if the document was in use by a crashed application. If this is the case, have the other user close the application, or use the Task Manager to kill the errant application.

This can also occur if you move files from a private My Documents folder to a public folder using the command line move command. In this case, the file's security attributes have been moved with the file, so it's still "private." One way to fix this is for the original owner of the file to locate the file in Windows Explorer. She or he needs to drag the file to her or his My Documents folder, and then drag it back to the shared location. Explorer will then fix the security settings.

A Computer Administrator user can also use the `cacls` command to change the file's security settings. In a command prompt window, change to the directory containing the file, and type the following command

```
cacls filename /G Everyone:F
```

where *filename* is the name of the file you're trying to fix.

USERS CANNOT ACCESS SHARED RESOURCE

Share permissions are set up with Everyone to have Full Control. The users get a message telling them they don't have permission to access the folder.

If you are not using Simple File Sharing, check to be sure that NTFS permissions are not overriding share permissions on the shared resource. Remember that between the two types of permissions, the most restrictive permission is applied.

LOGON SCRIPTS WON'T RUN

I have set up logon scripts for the all users of my machine, but they run only when I log on.

Make certain that you have specified the logon script properly in the Profile tab of each user account. Enter just the name of the script file (for example, MYLOGON.BAT).

Make certain that the logon scripts are stored in the proper directory (%SYSTEMROOT%\ System32\Repl\Import\Scripts), and make certain that all users have at least Read and Execute permission to the directory.

A USER HAS ACCESS TO A RESTRICTED OBJECT

A user in the Users local group has access to an object that the Users local group is not assigned permissions for.

Check to see whether the user belongs to any other groups that have been assigned permissions. Remember that permissions accumulate through groups.

SECURITY TAB IS NOT PRESENT

When I select a file, folder, or printer's properties, there is no Security tab.

On a domain network, this can occur if the disk drive containing the folder is not formatted with the NTFS file format. If the disk drive is NTFS-formatted, your domain administrator may have disabled your access to the Security dialog.

On a standalone computer or workgroup LAN, the Security tab will not appear if the disk was not formatted with NTFS, or if you are using Simple File Sharing. In this case Windows manages the security settings for all folders so that it can successfully manage access to shared folders. You can temporarily disable Simple File Sharing while you make access-control changes to non-shared folders, if necessary.

To find out if the hard drive is NTFS-formatted, select the drive icon in My Computer. The format type is displayed under Details.

Administrator Can't Delete File or Folder

I have found some files or folders that can't be deleted even by Administrator. They don't have the Read-Only attribute set, but Windows informs me that access is denied.

Sometimes a file or more often a folder is set with access controls such that even Administrator can't access or delete it. To erase such a folder, take ownership of it as described earlier in this chapter. Give Administrator full access rights. Use the Advanced security button to view Advanced Permissions, and check Replace Permission Entries on All Child Objects. Click OK and Apply, and then try to delete the folder again.

If you are using Simple File Sharing you will need to disable it temporarily to view the Security properties dialog boxes.

Tips from the Windows Pros: Setting up for Multiple Users

I have a lot of (quirky, I'm told) preferences that I like to make when I set up a new computer: Start menu settings, application settings, icon placement, and so forth. If you are setting up multiple users for your computer, you can save everyone a lot of configuration-tweaking time by setting up the default user profiles before the users log on for the first time. To do this

1. Log on to the computer as one of the new users.
2. Make the changes to the computer that you want all users to have, such as power management settings, desktop icons, Start menu, wallpaper, and so on. Install application software, load up shortcuts, whatever you want each user to have.
3. Log off, and log back on as Administrator.
4. Open My Computer, select Tools, Folder Options, select the View tab and check Show hidden files and folders. Click OK.
5. Open the Start menu, right-click My Computer, and select Properties (or select View System Information from the System Tasks list). View the Advanced tab and click User Profile settings, to bring up the dialog previously shown in Figure 28.18.
6. Select the profile for the user you just configured and click Copy To.
7. Click Browse, and browse to \Documents and Settings\Default User. Click OK.
8. Under Permitted to Use, check Change and select Everyone.
9. Click OK.

Now, when users log on for the first time, they will start out with a nicely configured computer.

Unfortunately, on a domain network, default profiles are taken from the domain server. Only the domain administrator can change the default profile there.

28

MANAGING THE HARD DISK

In this chapter

29

HARD DISK MANAGEMENT

For many users and system administrators, intelligent hard disk management really forms the core of efficient system management. Until a new technology evolves to replace the hard disk, we're stuck with the problems and limitations created by what is, in a sense, a crude system of motors, spinning platters, and very delicate parts, such as read/write heads floating just microns above a flying surface that can be easily ruined by particles as small as those found in a puff of cigarette smoke. Perhaps some day hard disks will be relics of the past, bookends, like the 5MB drives I have on my bookshelf. (They make good doorstops, too.) Until that time, though, we're stuck with the peculiar vagaries of hard disks. The good news is that high-capacity drives are cheap and plentiful these days.

No doubt, the vast majority of Windows XP users will never set up RAID arrays, multiple-booting arrangements, or dynamic disks; use encryption; or need to do any remote disk administration. Perhaps they will perform occasional disk cleanups and defragmenting as well as learn to share folders over the network. These tasks are enough to get by with. Yet, with a bit more knowledge gleaned by reading through this chapter, you will learn how extensive Windows XP's hard disk configuration capabilities are.

> **NOTE**
>
> *RAID* is short for *redundant array of independent* (or *inexpensive*) *disks*. In this hard disk scheme, two or more drives are connected together in combination for higher fault tolerance and performance. RAID arrangements are used frequently on servers but aren't generally necessary for personal or client computers.

This chapter describes the following:

- Using Windows XP's disk management tools
- Learning organizational strategies for arranging files and partitions on your hard disk
- Working with the supplied Disk Management utility
- Managing removable storage
- Cleaning up your drives
- Defragmenting and repairing your drives
- Converting to NTFS
- Compressing files
- Encrypting files
- Freeing up space
- Backing up your data
- Zipping files
- Using third-party file system tools
- Troubleshooting hard disk problems

WINDOWS XP FILE AND STORAGE SYSTEMS

The following sections describe this new dynamic storage model, its benefits, and its draw-backs. You'll also learn about the features and advantages of NTFS v.5.

Windows XP uses a new concept in storage models (introduced by Windows 2000), which Microsoft terms *dynamic storage*. Although Windows XP still supports the old, familiar models of partitions and drives, upgrading your hard disk to this new storage type brings with it a new way of thinking about partitions and how they are organized.

CAUTION

> Converting a hard disk to dynamic storage is a one-way process. To change a dynamic disk back to a basic disk, all volumes must be deleted before converting the drive back to basic storage. Also, note that dynamic disks can be read by Windows XP Pro, Windows 2003 Server, and all version of Windows 2000. Windows XP Home, Windows NT, Windows 98/SE/Me, and all earlier versions of Windows cannot access dynamic storage volumes. When you change the boot disk to dynamic, you can no longer multi-boot into another operating system because the familiar boot loader screen disappears for good.
>
> One last point of concern when dealing with Dynamic Disks is that they absolutely can-not be used on a multi-booting computer system. Only one installation of Windows can own a set of Dynamic Disks, so if you are planning on using Dynamic Disks as your RAID solution on a multi-boot computer, think about investing in a hardware-based (SCSI) RAID solution.

DYNAMIC STORAGE

I can best explain dynamic storage by comparing it to previous methods of structuring a hard disk.

The traditional storage model of disk structure used partition tables. Each hard drive could hold up to four *primary partitions* or up to three primary partitions and one *extended (sec-ondary) partition*. Within this extended partition, you created logical drives. The total num-ber of primary partitions and logical drives cannot exceed 32 per hard drive. This disk structure is understood and can be accessed by MS-DOS, Windows, and all versions of Windows NT up to release 4.0. The annoyances and limitations of this partition table methodology are artifacts of Microsoft operating systems, incidentally, not something imposed by hard disks themselves or their manufacturers. Some other operating systems don't suffer the same peculiarities.

NOTE

> Storage types are separate from the file systems they contain. Both basic and dynamic disks can contain any combination of FAT16, FAT32, NTFS v4, or NTFS v5 partitions or volumes. All drives are either basic or dynamic.

29

With dynamic storage, the restraints of primary and extended partitions are gone. Under this storage model, free space on a hard drive is divided into volumes instead of partitions, and these volumes can be noncontiguous and span one or more disks. In addition, volumes on a dynamic disk can be configured as simple, spanned, mirrored, striped, or RAID-5. Basic storage partitions can only be configured as simple partitions unless they are remnants from a previous OS retained during an upgrade.

- A *simple* volume uses free space available on a single disk. This space can be a single contiguous region or multiple concatenated regions. Under the basic storage model, each partition or logical drive is assigned a separate and distinct drive letter and functions as a distinct region of disk space. Dynamic storage can be configured to see multiple regions of a disk as a single volume, accessed with a single assigned drive letter.

- A *spanned* volume takes the concept of a simple volume and extends it across multiple disks (up to a maximum of 32). All joined regions on these disks are seen as a single volume to programs accessing them. However, if a single unit in a spanned volume fails, the entire set is lost.

- A *mirrored* volume is a volume in which data from one disk is mirrored or duplicated on a second disk. This process provides for data redundancy, often called *fault tolerance*. If one disk fails, the data can be accessed from the second disk. A mirrored volume cannot be spanned; each volume must be contained on a single disk. Programs see only one volume, and Windows ensures that both disks are kept in sync. *Mirroring* is also known as *RAID-1*.

- A *striped* volume is a volume in which data is stored across two or more physical disks. When data is written to a striped volume space, it is allocated alternately and evenly to each of the physical disks. A striped volume cannot be mirrored or spanned via Windows XP (it is possible on hardware-based RAID). *Striping*, often termed *RAID-0*, is used to increase storage system throughput. If a single unit in a striped volume fails, the entire set is lost.

- A *RAID-5* volume is a fault-tolerant version of a striped volume. When data is written to a RAID-5 volume, it is striped across an array of three or more disks, and a parity value is added. If a hard disk belonging to a RAID-5 volume fails, the data can be re-created by the remaining drives using this parity value. Note the difference here between a mirrored volume and a RAID-5 volume.

NOTE

A mirrored volume contains two disks; if either one fails, the operating system goes to the other for data access.

A RAID-5 volume contains three or more disks, any of which can fail without the system halting. The operating system then reconstructs the missing data from the information contained on the remaining disks.

So, what are the advantages of dynamic storage?

- First and foremost, noncontiguous regions of multiple disks can be linked so that they appear as one large region of disk space to any program. By linking them, you can increase the size of a disk volume on-the-fly, without reformatting or having to cope with multiple drive letters.

- Second, and perhaps more important from an administrator's point of view, is that disk and volume management can be performed without restarting the operating system.

The catch to all this is that on a multiboot system, non-Windows 2000, non-Windows XP Pro, or non-.NET Server systems cannot even see dynamic storage drives. Unlike NTFS which only applies to the formatted partition, dynamic storage affects the entire hard drive. Only Windows XP Pro, Windows 2003 Server, and Windows 2000 can see drives configured as dynamic storage. So, if you plan on using dynamic storage, plan ahead and keep other OSes on different hard drives. Plus, you must ensure the boot drive is a basic storage drive as well so the boot menu will function.

ORGANIZATIONAL STRATEGIES

Although the disk systems described in the preceding section are interesting, especially to power users and system administrators who have multiple drives available, most Windows XP users will end up setting up their systems with standard partitions (that is, basic storage) and the NTFS file format. But what about other file systems? How should you organize multiple disks? What about preparing your disks, and what kinds of strategies should you consider?

If you're not going to stick with the straight and narrow of running only NTFS on your hard disk, consider these alternative strategies and rules to follow:

- Whenever possible, create a separate partition for your data files. This tip has particular relevance to users who test new software or operating systems. If you store your data on a separate partition, reinstalling an operating system is a simple matter of formatting your system partition and starting from scratch. Although you still have to reinstall your programs, using a separate data partition eliminates the need to fuss and ensures you didn't miss a data file somewhere along the line. It also makes backups simple and straightforward. You can do one backup of your system partition; you then need to update this backup only when you add a new device or software program. Data backups can be run on a daily or weekly basis (as determined by how often your data changes) and set to run on your data partition.

TIP FROM

Bob & Brian

> When you have a data partition in place, right-click the My Documents icon on your desktop, select Properties, and reset the target folder location to your data partition. Resetting it ensures that all your favorites, application settings, and history files are also kept separate from the system partition. (Windows domain network users with roaming user profiles have less to worry about on this score, as their My Documents files are copied to the domain server as well as their local computer.)

29

29

- Buy a disk image program (such programs are discussed toward the end of this chapter). You can purchase one for less than $75, and it is worth its weight in gold if you like to "tinker" with your system and program configurations. After you have your operating system set up, your principal applications installed, and everything tweaked and configured to perfection, you can create an image of your system on a separate drive or partition. If you need to reinstall your operating system for whatever reason, the complete process—from beginning to end—should take no more than 20 minutes. Couple this program with the separate data partition discussed in the preceding bullet, and you have a system that you can rebuild from scratch with minimal effort or time loss.

  When you add, delete, or reconfigure a program, or make changes to the hardware configuration of your disk subsystem, be sure to update your disk image.

  Some clients I know have gone so far as to buy and install a separate hard drive just for image storage. At $150 or less for a 10GB drive, a hard drive is probably one of the best investments in crash protection you can buy. As a matter of fact, I'm considering making dedicated image drives a standard system configuration for all computers I maintain.

- If you have more than two IDE hard drives, put both drives on your primary IDE controller and your CD-ROM on the secondary controller. Configuring a system this way puts all the strain on one IDE bus when copying data from drive to drive, but mixing a CD-ROM drive and a hard disk on the same channel is worse. CD-ROM drives transfer data at a much slower rate than hard disks. Mixing fast and slow devices on the same controller forces the controller to run at the slower of the two rates. If you really want good performance with complex drive scenarios (multiple hard disks and CD-R or CD-RW), I suggest that you look into SCSI controllers.

- If you want to install Windows XP in a dual-boot configuration with other OSes, please jump over to Chapter 31, "Multibooting Windows XP with Other Operating Systems." There, all the ins and outs of multibooting are discussed along with all the necessary steps.

WINDOWS XP'S DISK MANAGEMENT TOOLS

Windows XP comes equipped with a handful of disk management tools, ranging from very powerful ones that can create hard disk stripe sets, create mirror disks, and/or beat a disk into submission, to a couple that are simply convenience items.

The most often-used tools are available right off the Tools tab of a drive's Properties sheet. To reach the Properties sheet, right-click a drive in Explorer. Figure 29.1 shows the Properties tabs for both a FAT drive and an NTFS drive. Notice the difference in the number of tabs. NTFS has more options because of its support for security and quota management.

The following sections explain the use of the bulk of hard disk management tools included in Windows XP.

Figure 29.1
Properties sheets
for FAT and NTFS
volumes.

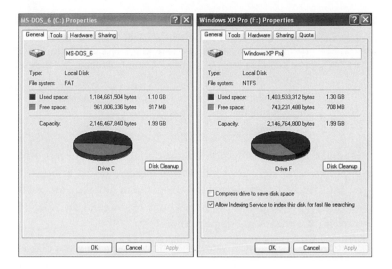

DISK MANAGEMENT

The Disk Management utility (see Figure 29.2) is responsible for the creation, deletion, alteration, and maintenance of storage volumes in a system. This tool is located within the Computer Management interface of Administrative Tools (accessed through Start, Control Panel, Administrative Tools, Computer Management, Disk Management). Another means is by right-clicking My Computer and choosing Manage. Using the Disk Management utility, you also can assign the drive letters used by your CD and hard disk drives.

Figure 29.2
The Disk
Management tool as
part of Computer
Management.

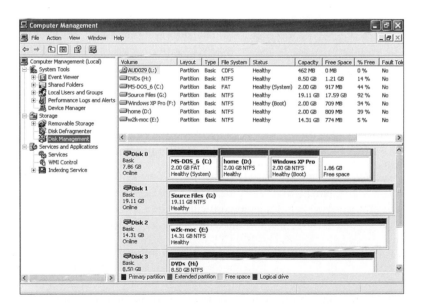

TIP FROM

Bob
& Brian

> If the Administrative Tools menu selection is not displayed on the Start menu, right-click over the Start menu and select Properties, click Customize, click the Advanced tab, scroll down to the System Administrative Tools items, and then select the appropriate radio button.
>
> If you enable the Control Panel to act as a menu, Administrative Tools can be accessed through it off the Start menu as well.

As discussed in Chapter 27, "System Utilities," this single interface lets you manage both local and remote computers using the various administration utilities shown in the left pane. Using this interface, I will show you how to perform different procedures on your existing and new hard disks. The process is quite simple for most of the operations because you will be presented with a wizard to complete them.

Most operations on disks can be performed by right-clicking the disk or volume you want to affect. As usual, you are presented with a context-sensitive menu from which you can perform any actions relating to the volume or disk you clicked. You can also see, from the graphical layout in the Disk Management, just what is going on with your disks at any given time. As always, you can select the Help option from within any menu to get an explanation of the operations available to you.

TIP FROM

Bob
& Brian

> You can change the way specific types of volumes are displayed in Disk Management. To do this, click the Settings button at the end of the button bar. From there, you can select the color you would like to use to represent any of the various disk states that will be shown by the Disk Management. By selecting the Scaling tab from the Settings dialog box, you can also change the way in which the Disk Management shows the scaling of each disk. This capability is particularly useful if you would like the scale display to be more representative of the actual physical sizes of your disks.

ASSIGNING DRIVE LETTERS AND JOINING VOLUMES

Using the Disk Management, you can easily assign logical drive letters to your hard disks and removable drives such as CD-ROMs. You can't change the drive letter of your boot drive (usually the C: drive), but you can change any of the others.

To change the letter, right-click the disk volume or drive in the bottom-right pane of the Disk Management, and select Change Drive Letter and Paths. A dialog box appears, listing the current drive letter assignment. Click Change. Under Assign a Drive Letter, choose the desired new letter. Click OK and confirm that you really do want to make the change.

In addition to or instead of assigning a drive letter to a disk drive or partition, you can "graft" the disk volume onto another. Windows lets you specify a folder that will become the mount point for the new drive. For example, I might create a folder named C:\TEMP. Because I want lots of space for it, I can install a new hard drive and, instead of assigning it a drive letter, tell Windows to access it through C:\TEMP. My C:\TEMP files and subfolders are then stored on the alternate drive.

TIP FROM

Bob & Brian

> By using a mount point, you can add space to the folders under the mount point folder using an available drive. This is a good way to add space in a controlled fashion for a specific purpose, such as storing scratch files or Web page images.

GRAFTING VERSUS DYNAMIC DISKS

Assigning mount points is different from what happens when you aggregate dynamic disks into one large volume. Although dynamic disks and regular disks (simple disks) both support the use of mount points, dynamic disks can create one large, apparently contiguous disk space. Mount points graft subsequently added drives at a folder, sort of like grafting two trees by tying together a branch from each tree. Figures 29.3 and 29.4 illustrate the differences between the two approaches. In Figure 29.4, I've grated my music files from drive G:\MUSIC into the mount point on drive H:\MP3.

Figure 29.3
You can join drives two different ways. Using mount points is one way, and using dynamic disk aggregation is another.

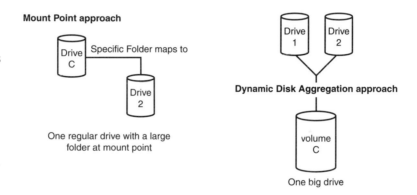

Figure 29.4
Assigning a partition or volume to a folder rather than a drive letter joins the volume to an existing volume. The contents of the added volume appear as subdirectories of the mount point folder.

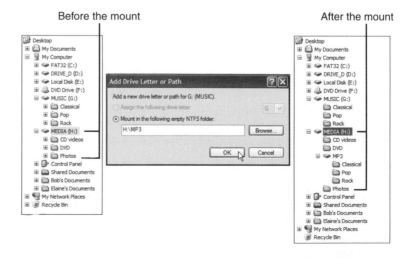

29

NOTE

> You can graft new volumes or disks onto a folder only on an NTFS-formatted drive. The new volume can have any format, however.

NOTE

> If the folder you specify as the mount point already contains files, they are inaccessible as long as the drive-to-path mapping exists because that folder is now remapped into the new location. The original files reappear if you delete the drive path. Therefore, it's usually a good idea to create a new folder as a mount point or delete all of the contents of an existing folder before establishing the mount point.

Even if you have several hard drives and CD-ROM drives, you can graft them all together onto your C: drive, making it look like one big file system. It's a great management concept: You can add space to your file system by attaching new disk volumes right into the original folder structure. (Unix users are probably smirking at this point because the Unix operating system has worked this way since it was written in the 1970s.)

If you mount a drive and assign it a drive letter, you can gain access to it through both pathways.

To graft a disk volume to an existing file system, follow these steps:

1. Create the folder that is to serve as the mount point for the new drive or volume.
2. Highlight the new drive or volume in Disk Management.
3. Right-click, select Change Drive Letter and Paths, and click Add.
4. Select Mount in the Following Empty NTFS Folder.
5. Enter the folder's pathname, or click Browse to locate it.
6. Click OK to save the path.

TIP FROM

Bob & Brian

> When Explorer shows you free disk space on the original drive, it measures only the space on the physical drive, not space on any grafted drives. You'll actually have more space than you think because files on the grafted folders are stored on another volume. If you want, you can also assign a drive letter to the added volume so that you can view and monitor its free space directly.
>
> Alternatively, you can use the command prompt, change to the folder in the grafted volume, and use the DIR command. The DIR command lists free space on the actual current volume.

You can assign a given drive or volume to at most one drive letter, but an arbitrary number of paths. (It's a little bit strange to see the same files appear in several different places, so I recommend that you not go nuts with this feature.)

TIP FROM

Bob & Brian

> If you're running out of room on your C: drive, see whether it makes sense in your situation to add lots of space to just one folder (for example, My Documents). If it does, install and format a new hard drive, and assign it a letter. Copy the original folder to the new drive. Then add a path to the new hard drive using the name of the original folder. This way, you can preserve your original data and have lots of room for growth.

By the way, this "grafting" technique works with both basic and dynamic NTFS disks. Only Windows dynamic disks can be "grown" by changing their partition size on-the-fly. If you use a basic-formatted disk, as most users do, the grafting trick is a good one to know.

TIP FROM

Bob & Brian

> Another really good time to use this feature is when you've backed up application data onto a CD-R or CD-RW. If you want to use the backed-up data in an emergency, you can add a path for your CD-ROM drive to make its files appear in the original data location expected by your application. That way, you can use the data off the CD-R without restoring it to disk or reconfiguring your application. Later, you can delete the path to regain access to the "real" folder.

DYNAMIC DISK MANAGEMENT

If you are using only Windows XP on a system, upgrading your storage devices to dynamic disks is usually the best way to go because of the many advantages of the new dynamic disk storage system. Remember, though, that you can't boot into or read your dynamic disks from any other operating system after you upgrade them. You can upgrade a disk through Disk Management, right-clicking the drive's icon in the bottom pane (click the part of the graphical display that reads "Disk 0," "Disk 1," and so on, not on the volume), and choosing Upgrade to Dynamic Disk. Then choose the disk and click OK. Next, just follow the wizard, and you'll be set.

CAUTION

> Don't upgrade to dynamic disks until you read all the material here on the topic and review the Help system's coverage of it in Disk Management. As you learned earlier in this chapter, dynamic disks cannot be changed back to basic disks without completely destroying any partitions and reformatting the disk. If you have to do that, right-click the volume and select Delete Volume. From there, you can just re-create your simple volume by right-clicking a disk and going through the applicable wizard. Also, remember that other operating systems such as Windows XP Home, Windows 9x, and DOS can't use dynamic disks, so if you intend to multiboot your machine, you should not upgrade the drive. Whether a drive is basic or dynamic has no bearing on network client access to shared folders.

If you don't seem to have the option of upgrading to dynamic disks, one of two possible reasons might be the cause. First, the disks may have already been upgraded to dynamic disks. Second, the disk is not a hard drive but rather a CD device or removable media device.

N O T E

> You cannot install Windows XP onto a dynamic disk volume that you've added to a dynamic disk from another instance of Windows XP or Windows 2000. This is a limitation of the Windows XP Setup program in that it needs to see a partition table in order to install onto the disk. Disk partitions created from a dynamic disk do not contain partition tables and as such cannot be utilized by Setup. The only types of disks that contain partition tables are simple disks and dynamic disks that were upgraded from simple disks. However, you can convert the boot drive to a dynamic volume after installation has completed.

EXTENDING A DISK

One of the really cool options available in the Disk Management is the option to extend a volume on a dynamic storage drive. Extending is really just another way of "stretching" a simple volume to a specified size when unallocated space is present on the disk. Sometimes you might want to rearrange the way you've set up your disks, so this option can come in very handy.

To perform the actual extend operation on a disk, you need to have an area of the disk that is unallocated. From there, you simply right-click an existing partition and select Extend Volume to bring up the Extend Volume Wizard. The wizard allows you to specify the size that you would like to extend the volume to. Finishing the operation leaves you with a disk that is now larger than before. This operation is not limited to volumes that are mounted as drive letters. You can also perform this task on volumes that are mounted into directories.

When Disk Management extends a disk, it is really just creating a new partition and mapping it to the same drive letter as the partition to be extended. It is, in effect, a spanned volume. Although this approach is a bit different from the traditional method performed by disk utilities such as Partition Magic, the upside of the Disk Management approach is that you can extend your disk without having to wait for the volume to be resized and data to be shuffled around. The Disk Management approach happens very quickly without even rebooting your system.

CREATING A SPANNED VOLUME

A spanned volume is a volume in which the disk space spans across multiple partitions and/or disks. Using a spanned volume is a very handy way of taking a couple of small disks and turning them into one large disk, mounted under one drive letter or folder. Simple volumes can also be extended using spanned volumes, as shown in the previous section. Spanned volumes can be created only on dynamic disks. A spanned volume basically is the same as an extended volume, except the former adds drive space from other hard drives while the latter adds drive space from the same drive.

Creating a spanned volume is just a matter of right-clicking an empty partition and selecting New Volume, which opens the New Volume Wizard. This wizard enables you to select the spanned volume option. Next, you are given the option to select which disks to include in your spanned volume. At this point, you also can select the amount of space to use for each disk. The total size of your spanned volume is the cumulative total of the space you select on each disk.

Finally, you are prompted for the mount point and the format for your new spanned volume.

CREATING A STRIPED VOLUME

One of the procedures you can perform with Disk Management is creating a striped volume. Creating such a volume is often desirable simply because of the ease of administration as well as the substantial gain in speed. Creating a striped volume is really practical only if you're using more than one disk. In fact, you must have more than one disk. For the definition of a striped volume, see "Dynamic Storage" earlier in this chapter.

NOTE

Unfortunately for users, Microsoft decided to leave out the option to create RAID sets from Windows XP. This option, as well as mirroring, is included only in the Server and Advanced Server versions of what Microsoft is calling Windows .NET. You are not precluded from using a hardware-based RAID controller with Windows XP Professional and Home, however. In devices such as these, the BIOS is used to set up the RAID options, thereby bypassing the operating system.

When you're creating a striped volume, you are creating partitions of the same size across two or more disks. Bear this point in mind as you plan your implementation because you need to have the same amount of space available on each disk that you want to use for your set.

To create a striped volume, just follow these steps:

1. Right-click one of the disks to be used in the striped volume set, and select New Volume. The New Volume Wizard then opens.

2. Select Striped. Then select Next.

3. Select the disks you want to include as part of a striped volume. The New Volume Wizard automatically selects the first free disk as the first in the striped volume. The remaining two disks can be selected from the left column and added to the right column for the set. When you are done adding disks, click Next.

NOTE

Notice that the wizard automatically sets the size for all selected disks to the largest amount of free space that is equally available on each disk.

4. You then are prompted for the mount point of your new striped set. The three options here bear further explanation:

- **Assign the Following Drive Letter**—This option assigns your set one drive letter like any normal drive. Selecting this option is the most common method of mounting a striped set, and it will suffice for most purposes.

- **Mount in the Following Empty NTFS Folder**—This option is a bit different from anything previously offered in Windows. By mounting a striped set to a folder, you are effectively creating a mount point within another disk. The mount point isn't actually on another disk in the physical sense. The folder you use just has the amount of storage equal to the size of your striped set. This approach is more closely related to the Unix approach, where the actual drive letter is not used but the folder is referred to as the mount point. (Mount points were discussed earlier in this chapter.)

- **Do Not Assign a Drive Letter or Drive Path**—Selecting this option creates the striped set and leaves it for you to allocate at a later time using either of the two methods mentioned previously.

5. Select the volume format options.

6. When you are presented with a summary of the actions to be performed by the wizard, choose the Finish button so that your new striped volume will be created and mounted under the path you chose in step 4.

> **NOTE**
>
> In Explorer, notice that the icon for the folder mount point shows up as a hard disk. This icon appears simply so that you can differentiate between a mounted folder and a plain folder.

RAID and Dynamic Disk Information Storage

When a basic disk is made a member of a mirror, stripe, or RAID set, it's marked (or "signed") with a tiny hidden partition at the end of the disk drive. This partition tells Windows that the disk is a member of a fault-tolerant disk set. The information about the configuration itself—for example, whether a given disk is the primary or secondary disk in a mirror set—is stored in the Registry. If you think about it, you can see that this is not a great place to store this kind of information: If a disk is damaged, Windows might not be able to read the Registry to find the configuration information. That's why you were always exhorted to update your Emergency Boot Disks when you made changes in the old Windows NT Disk Management; the disk configuration was stored on the emergency disks, too.

For dynamic disks, Windows creates a 4MB partition at the end of each disk drive in which it stores all the configuration information for all the dynamic drives in your computer. This redundant information helps Windows reconstruct a picture of the whole system if any drives are damaged or replaced, and it's another good reason to use dynamic disks over basic when you're building a Windows XP or 2000 system.

REMOVABLE STORAGE

Removable Storage is another tool within Computer Management. Its job is to track and catalog the data stored on removable storage devices. These devices can take the form of tape backup drives, MO drives, JAZ drives, or the changers that control many removable storage devices. The Removable Storage Manager works by allowing you to create *media pools*—collections of media to which the same management properties (such as security permissions or backup routines) apply.

Removable Storage is another of those "buried" Windows XP features that you're not likely to know about unless you know where to look. Open the Control Panel, click Administrative Tools, and then click Computer Management. In the right pane, expand Storage and click Removable Storage. From here, you can create and manage media pools and also get information about the physical locations for media.

NOTE

> If you're not certain whether a given removable device is compatible with Windows XP, check the Hardware Compatibility List (HCL) at the Microsoft Web site (www.microsoft.com/hcl).

As implemented, Removable Storage is limited to the small scope of hardware supported under it. But like many other Windows XP features (the Indexing Service, for example), it has tremendous potential when third-party vendors develop hooks to its functions and interface. At the moment, it stands as a useful tool to catalog backup media, such as tapes and optical cartridges, but little else.

See "Backup," later in this chapter, for more details about using removable storage management features as an adjunct to your backup strategies.

DISK DEFRAGMENTER

When an operating system stores data on a hard disk, it places that information in the first available "hole" it can find that isn't already occupied by another file. If the disk already contains several other files, however, that location might not be large enough for the complete file. When this happens, the operating system places as much of the file as it can in the space available and then searches for another open hole for the balance of the file. This process continues until the entire file has been written to disk. Any files not written to a contiguous disk location are considered "fragmented."

The problem with fragmentation is that it slows down the rate at which your hard disk can retrieve information and supply it to the requesting program. Hard disks remain largely mechanical devices and are governed by the laws of physics. To access files stored on a disk, the drive must physically move a small arm to the correct location on a spinning platter. These movements are measured in milliseconds, but milliseconds add up, especially when a file is spread over a hundred unique locations.

29

Fragmentation is not always a bad thing. If an operating system had to find a contiguous section of disk space for each and every file it stored, as your drive filled, your system would slow. Eventually, your system would reach a point where the disk still had ample free space, but none of this space would be in contiguous blocks big enough to hold a file.

Disk Defragmenter addresses this fragmentation problem by reorganizing all the files on your hard disk so that they are stored as complete units on a single area of the disk. To do so, it identifies any remaining free areas, moves small files there to open up more space, and uses this newly opened space to consolidate larger files. This shuffling process repeats until all the files are shuffled around in this manner and the entire disk is defragmented.

The MFT

NTFS contains, at its core, a file called the *master file table (MFT)*. It is similar to the file allocation table in the FAT system. At least one entry exists in the MFT for every file on an NTFS volume, including the MFT itself. The MFT also contains extended information about each file, such as its size, time and date stamps, permissions, data content, and so forth.

As you add more files to an NTFS volume, the number of entries to the MFT grows. When files are deleted from an NTFS volume, their MFT entries are marked as free and may be reused, but the MFT does not shrink. Thus, space used by these entries is not reclaimed from the disk.

NTFS preallocates a specific amount of the volume for storage of the MFT and, in an effort to ensure high performance, tries not to fragment it. NTFS also does its best to allocate free space on the disk intelligently. If you are running low on disk space, it relinquishes reserved and unused MFT areas for your files. If the MFT is running low, it grabs space from the file area for more entries. As you would expect, if you have a large number of files, the MFT becomes larger. If you have a small number of files, the MFT is smaller.

Here's the rub: If you try to pack a zillion files onto an NTFS volume (I can't give you an exact number because it will vary based on volume and file size), and you run out of disk space, you could exhaust the MFT, which can result in a major bummer when the directory table for the volume blows up. You get no warning. If you intend to store a huge number of small files on an NTFS partition, and you think you might unexpectedly run out of room on the volume, you should consider a Registry hack that preallocates more room for the MFT by adding a value to the Registry.

Caution: This procedure modifies the Registry. Do I have to remind you to back up the Registry first? If you aren't a Registry whiz already, be sure to read Chapter 32, "The Registry," before trying this operation.

To add this value, perform the following steps:

1. Run the Registry Editor (Regedt32.exe), and go to the following subkey:

   HKEY_LOCAL_MACHINE\System\CurrentControlSet\Control\FileSystem

2. From the Edit menu, choose New, DWORD value.

3. Type the name of the new value entry as **NtfsMftZoneReservation**.

4. Double-click on this new value entry to open the Edit DWORD Value dialog box. Provide value data for this new value entry.

   NtfsMftZoneReservation is a REG_DWORD value that can take on a value between 1 and 4, where 1 corresponds to the minimum MFT zone size and 4 corresponds to the maximum. The sizes are not absolute. You might have to experiment with the sizing to determine what is best for you. Microsoft supplies no specific details about the number of file entries available under each size.

5. Close the Registry Editor, and restart your computer.

Keep in mind that this is a runtime parameter and it does not affect the format of a volume. Rather, it affects the way NTFS allocates space on all volumes on a given system. Therefore, to be completely effective, the parameter must be in effect from the time a volume is formatted throughout the life of the volume.

For more information, check the following URL:

`http://support.microsoft.com/support/kb/articles/Q174/6/19.ASP`

> **NOTE**
>
> Defragmenting a large drive with many files on it can take a lot of time. Let the Task Scheduler handle it because it can run at night when you're not around and don't need access to your hard disk drive. However, the defragmenter included with Windows XP cannot be automated. You'll need to purchase a full-blown commercial defragmenter to take advantage of automated scheduling. I've had great success with Symantec's Norton Speed Disk (`www.symantec.com`) and Executive Software's Disk Keeper (`www.execsoft.com`). By the way, the native Windows XP defragmenter is a limited version of Disk Keeper.

When should you defragment your drive? In reality, because today's drives are so fast, you're not likely to notice slowdowns unless you're using very large data files, or you use the same files and/or applications regularly, which can fragment them. For typical users who are hopping around between programs, creating new files, and deleting files on a regular basis, the average access times they experience with a drive will be acceptable, even when fragmented.

If you start to notice a general hard disk access slowdown, the first thing to suspect is a RAM shortage, or that you have too many files open and your drive's pagefile is being hit too much (that is, swapping is going on). After ruling that out, however, take a trip down defrag lane. Run the program, and it will tell you whether your drive is fragmented enough to make it worth your time to defragment.

RUNNING DEFRAG

To run Disk Defragmenter, follow these steps:

1. Select Disk Defragmenter from the Storage section of Computer Management.

2. Click to select a drive in the list of volumes.

3. Click the Analyze button. In a few minutes, the result of the analysis will appear. You'll see a screen like the one shown in Figure 29.5.

Figure 29.5
Running Defrag's analysis on a drive indicates whether you would net any advantage from defragmenting.

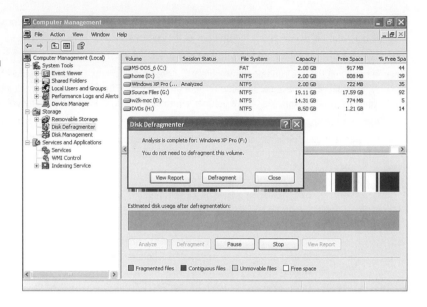

4. Click the View Report button if you're the curious type. You can really get into the numbers here, viewing statistics about the drive, and checking to see where the maximum fragmentation is occurring, the number of fragments, the file sizes, and so on. Figure 29.6 shows an example from my hard disk. You can save the report or print it, if you like.

Figure 29.6
Details of a defrag analysis can be helpful in determining where most of your fragmentation is occurring. Scroll the top pane, and check to see whether your pagefile is fragmented. Typically, it won't be, but if it is, this is a good reason to defragment.

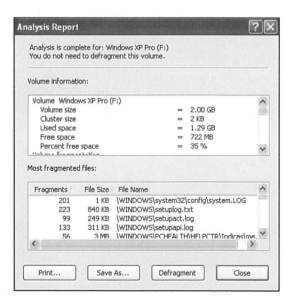

5. If you decide to go ahead and defragment, click the Defragment button and get ready to wait. As the defragmenting progresses, you'll see the progress reported across the bottom graph in the window. The graphic display slowly becomes primarily blue, indicating that most files are now contiguous. You will see some areas of green, indicating system files (possibly a large area if a pagefile is on the drive). You might have some small areas of fragmentation left over as well. The leftover fragmentation is due to this being a free defragmentation tool, which does not include high-level defragmentation techniques, or due to the files being open and locked, thus unable to be moved by the tool.

DETECTING AND REPAIRING DISK ERRORS

NTFS was introduced and billed as a "robust and self-healing" file system. All in all, I would have to agree with Microsoft on this one. I have yet to have an NTFS partition go "sour" on me in any way, shape, or form. I've had NTFS partitions that would not boot and key system files that would not run, but for the most part, these errors were self-inflicted and usually brought on by playing with fire.

Some other versions of Windows have the ScanDisk program whose job it is to detect and repair the file allocation table (FAT) when you shut down improperly. You also can run it manually from time to time. This program hearkens back to DOS days. From within the Windows XP GUI, the replacement program for ScanDisk is called Error Checking.

TIP FROM

Bob & Brian

> If you dig a little deeper, you'll find command-line hard disk volume checkers in the %SystemRoot%\System32 directory. They are not called ScanDisk, as they were in some previous versions of Windows. Look for chkntfs.exe (for NTFS partitions) and chkdsk.exe (for FAT/FAT32 partitions). For a description of how each works, just add the normal /? switch, or see Windows online help. The available commands enable you to turn on or off automatic checking and repair a "dirty" (improperly shut down) drive at bootup.

Error Checking checks the file system for errors and the drive for bad sectors (bad spots). To run the program, do the following:

1. In My Computer or the Explorer, right-click the drive you want to check.
2. On the context menu, choose Properties.
3. Click the Tools tab.
4. In the Error-Checking section, click Check Now. A dialog box appears, as shown in Figure 29.7.

29

Figure 29.7
Checking a disk for errors in the file system and bad spots on the disk.

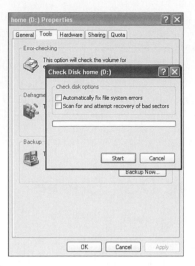

You can run the error check with neither of the option boxes turned on. You are not required to close all open files and programs. However, if you check either of the boxes, you are told that all files must be closed for this process to run. You are given the option of deferring the check until the time you restart your system, however.

The meaning of the options is as follows:

Automatically Fix File System Errors	If file directory errors (for example, lost clusters, files without end-of-file markers, and so on) are found, this option specifies whether the program should fix them.
Scan for and Attempt Recovery of Bad Sectors	This option specifies whether the program should attempt to locate bad sectors, mark them as bad, and recover data from them, writing it in a known good area of the disk. If you select this option, you do not need to select Automatically Fix File System Errors; Windows fixes any errors on the disk.

TIP FROM

Bob & Brian

If your volume is formatted as NTFS, Windows automatically logs all file transactions, replaces bad clusters automatically, and stores copies of key information for all files on the NTFS volume.

29

CONVERT

Convert is a command-line program that converts an existing FAT16 or FAT32 partition to NTFS.

CAUTION

This conversion process is a one-way street. The only way to revert an NTFS partition back to a FAT partition with the native tools is to reformat the drive. To revert and not lose your data, you have to use a program such as PartitionMagic.

The command-line syntax for the Convert program is as follows:

```
CONVERT volume /FS:NTFS [/V]
```

The arguments are as follows:

volume	Specifies the drive letter (followed by a colon), mount point, or volume name
/FS:NTFS	Specifies that the volume be converted to NTFS
/V	Specifies that Convert should be run in Verbose mode

Considering the work the Convert program has to do, it's surprisingly fast, even on a well-populated disk.

NOTE

If the Recovery Console was installed on the disk partition you're converting to NTFS, you'll have to reinstall the Recovery Console after the conversion has completed. For more information about the Recovery Console, see "Recovery Console," page 1157 .

ENCRYPTION

The Encrypting File System (EFS) provides the core file encryption technology used to store encrypted files on NTFS volumes. When a file is encrypted, the data stored on the hard disk is scrambled in a very secure way. Encryption is transparent to the user who encrypted the file; you do not have to "decrypt" an encrypted file before you can use it. You can work with an encrypted file just as you would any other file; you can open and change the file as necessary. However, any other user or an intruder who tries to access your encrypted files is prevented from doing so. Only the original owner and the computer's designated recovery agent can get into encrypted files. Anyone else receives an `Access Denied` message when trying to open or copy your encrypted file.

Folders can be marked as encrypted, too. What this means is that any file created in or copied to an encrypted folder is automatically encrypted. The folder itself isn't encrypted, though. Anyone with the proper file access permissions can see the names of the files in it.

→ To learn more details about recovery agents and how to recover and decrypt files when the username and password of the encryptor have been lost, **see** "Protecting and Recovering Encrypted Files," **p. 1014**.

> NOTE
>
> EFS encryption only protects the files while they reside on the NTFS volume. Once they are accessed for use by an application, they are decrypted by the file system drivers. This means that files that are encrypted on the drive are not encrypted in memory while being used by an application. This also means that transferring files over the network is done without encryption. Any file action that performs a copy (which includes moves across partitions or volumes) will inherit the settings of its new container. In other words, if the new container is not encrypted, the new file will not be encrypted either, even if it was encrypted in its previous location. If you back up EFS-protected files, they are stored on the backup media in their normal form, not encrypted. EFS only protects files on the hard drive, no where else. Use EFS only when expressly needed. EFS will cause significant performance reduction if a significant number of commonly accessed files are encrypted, due to the CPU processing required to decrypt them for use.

You encrypt or decrypt a folder or file by setting the encryption property for the folder or file just as you set any other attribute, such as read-only, compressed, or hidden (see Figure 29.8).

Figure 29.8
Setting encryption for a specific folder.

After you set the option to encrypt a folder and click OK on a folder's Properties dialog, you are prompted to confirm the attribute change. From this dialog, you can set the option to encrypt all the subfolders and files within the folder you are encrypting.

29

It is recommended that you encrypt at the folder level rather than mark individual files so that new files added to the folder will also be encrypted. This point is crucial because most editing programs write a new copy of the file each time you save changes and then delete the original. If the folder containing an encrypted file isn't marked for encryption, too, editing an encrypted file would result in your saving an unencrypted version.

How File Encryption Works

As a kid, you probably played around with simple codes and ciphers in which you exchanged the letters of a message: D for A, E for B, and so on. You might look at this as the process of "adding three" to each letter in your message: Each letter gets bumped to the third next letter in the alphabet. To decode a message, you subtracted three from every letter to get the original message back. In this code, you could say that the "key" is the number three. Anyone knowing the technique and possessing the key could read and write these secret messages.

Although this example is very simplistic, it illustrates the basic idea of numeric encryption. The cryptographic system used by Windows for the Encrypted File System also uses a numeric technique, but it's extremely complex and uses a key that is 128 digits long. Such a large number means many possible choices, and that means it would take someone a very long time to guess a key and read an encrypted file.

When you mark a file for encryption, Windows randomly generates such a large number, called a unique *file encryption key (FEK)*, which is used to scramble the contents of just that one file. This unique key is itself scrambled with your own personal file encryption key, an even longer number stored in the Windows Certificate database. The encrypted unique key is then stored along with the file.

When you're logged in and try to open an encrypted file, Windows retrieves your personal key, decodes the unique key, and uses that key to decode the contents of the file as it's read off the hard disk.

The reason for the two-step process is to let Windows use a different and unique key for each file. Using different keys provides added security. Even if an attacker managed to guess the key to one file, he or she would have to start afresh to find the key to other files. Yet your personal key can unscramble the unique key to any file you've encrypted. It's a valuable thing, this key, and I'll tell you how to back it up in a certificate file for safekeeping.

As a backup in case your personal key gets lost, Windows lets each computer or domain administrator designate recovery agents, users who are allowed to decode other people's encrypted files. Windows also encrypts the unique FEK for each of the recovery agents. It, too, is stored along with the file, and anyone possessing a recovery key can also read your encrypted files. You'll learn about the benefits and risks of this system in "Protecting and Recovering Encrypted Files" later in this chapter.

You can use EFS to keep your documents safe from intruders who might gain unauthorized physical access to your sensitive stored data (by stealing your laptop, for example).

You also can encrypt or decrypt a file or folder using the command line and the following syntax (the following is not an exhaustive list of the cipher syntax; execute **cipher /?** at a command prompt for the complete list of parameters and syntax):

```
CIPHER [/E | /D] [/S:dir] [/I] [/F] [/Q] [dirname [...]]
```

The arguments are as follows:

/E	Encrypts the specified directories. Directories are marked so that files added afterward will be encrypted.
/D	Decrypts the folder and halts any further encryption on that folder until reactivated.
/S	Forces the CIPHER command to be recursive; that is, it encrypts all files and folders in the specified folder and all subfolders below it.
/I	By default, the CIPHER command stops when an error is encountered. This parameter forces the encryption process to continue even if errors occur.
/F	Forces the encryption operation on all specified directories, even those already encrypted. Already-encrypted directories are skipped by default.
/Q	Reports only the most essential information about a file or folder's encrypted status.
Dirname	Specifies a pattern or directory.

Used without parameters, CIPHER displays the encryption state of the current directory and any files it contains. You can use multiple directory names and wildcards, but you must place spaces between parameters.

RULES FOR USING ENCRYPTED FILES

When you work with encrypted files and folders, keep in mind the following points:

- Only files and folders on NTFS volumes can be encrypted.

- You cannot encrypt files or folders that are compressed. Compression and encryption are mutually exclusive file attributes. If you want to encrypt a compressed file or folder, you must decompress it first.

- Only the user who encrypted the file and the designated recovery agent(s) can open it. (You'll learn more about recovery agents shortly.)

- If you encrypt a file in a shared directory, it is inaccessible to others. Windows XP will display encrypted files in green, just like compressed files are displayed in blue.

- Encrypted files become decrypted if you copy or move the file to a volume or partition that is not formatted with NTFS.

- You should use Cut and Paste to move files into an encrypted folder. If you use the drag-and-drop method to move files, they are not automatically encrypted in the new folder.

- System files cannot be encrypted.

- Encrypting folders or files does not protect them against being deleted, moved, or renamed. Anyone with the appropriate permission level can manipulate encrypted folders or files. (These users just can't open them.)

- Temporary files, which are created by some programs when documents are edited, are also encrypted as long as all the files are on an NTFS volume and in an encrypted folder. I recommend that you encrypt the Temp folder on your hard disk for this reason. Encrypting your original files keeps them safe from prying eyes, but programs often leave temp files behind—usually in the Temp folder—and these files remain vulnerable.

NOTE

> The paging file is also a problem in this regard and unfortunately cannot be protected directly, as far as I know. However, you can configure the Local Security Policy to clear the pagefile when you shutdown the system. Just enable the "Shutdown: Clear virtual memory pagefile" policy under the Local Policies, Security Option section.

- On a domain network, you can encrypt or decrypt files and folders located on a remote computer that has been enabled for remote encryption. Check with your system administrator to see whether your company's servers support this capability. Keep in mind, however, that opening an encrypted file over a network still exposes the contents of that file while it is being transmitted. A network administrator should implement a security protocol such as IPSec to safeguard data during transmission.

- You should encrypt folders instead of individual files so that if a program creates temporary files and/or saves new copies during editing, they will be encrypted as well.

- Encrypted files, like compressed folders, perform more slowly than unencrypted ones. If you want maximum performance when folders or files in the folders are being used extensively (for example, by database programs), think twice before encrypting them.

SUGGESTED FOLDERS TO ENCRYPT

I recommend that you encrypt the following folders:

- Encrypt the My Documents folder if you save most of your documents there. Encrypting this folder ensures that any personal documents saved there are automatically encrypted. However, a better alternative would be to create a subfolder under My Document for personal files and encrypt just this folder. This approach relieves you from having to track which files are encrypted and which are not.

- Encrypt your Temp folder so that any temporary files created by programs are automatically encrypted.

CAUTION

> If someone steals your laptop computer or gains physical access to your desktop computer, it's possible that even with all of Windows XP's file access security and file encryption, that person can gain access to your files. How? There is a trick that allows this to happen, and you should guard against it. Here's how it works: By reinstalling the operating system from a CD-ROM, a thief can set up himself or herself as the system administrator. If the default file recovery certificate is still on the computer at this point, the intruder can view encrypted files. To guard against this situation, you should export the file recovery certificate to a floppy disk and remove it from the computer. I'll show you how in the next section.

PROTECTING AND RECOVERING ENCRYPTED FILES

Encrypted files are supposed to be very secure; only the user who creates an encrypted file can unscramble it. But this security hangs on your own personal file encryption key, which is stored in the Windows Certificate database (see the sidebar "How File Encryption Works" earlier in this chapter). Where would you be if you accidentally deleted your file encryption certificate, or if your user account was deleted from the system? Could the secret recipe for Aunt Dottie's Zucchini Fritters be lost forever this way? Probably not. The Encrypted File System has a "back door" that lets designated recovery agents open any encrypted file.

The availability of this back door is both good news and bad news. The good news is that encrypted files can be recovered when necessary. The bad news is that this capability opens up a potential security risk, and you need to be sure you take measures to protect yourself against it.

SECURING THE RECOVERY CERTIFICATE

Your ability to recover encrypted files hinges on two factors:

- Being listed by the Windows Local or Group Security Policy as a designated recovery agent
- Possessing the file recovery certificate that holds the recovery key data

With a few dirty tricks, it's possible for someone who steals your computer to get himself or herself in as administrator and pose as the recovery agent. So, if you really want to ensure the privacy of your files with the Encrypted File System, you have to save the file recovery certificate on a floppy disk or other removable medium and remove the certificate from your computer.

To back up and remove the recovery certificate, do the following:

1. Be sure that at least one file on your computer has been marked Encrypted by any user.
2. Log in as the local administrator (*XXXX*\Administrator, where *XXXX* is the name of your computer).

3. Start the Microsoft Management Console by choosing Start, Run. Then type `mmc` and press Enter.

4. Choose File, Add/Remove Snap-In. Then select Add. Next, highlight the Certificates snap-in and click Add. Select My User Account and click Finish. Finally, click Close and then click OK.

5. In the left pane, expand the Certificates node, Current User, Personal, Certificates.

6. In the right pane, you should see a certificate listed with its Intended Purposes shown as `Encrypting File System`, as shown in Figure 29.9. If this certificate is not present, and you're on a domain network, your domain administrator has done this job for you, and you don't need to proceed any further.

Figure 29.9
Certificate Manager showing the Administrator's file recovery certificate.

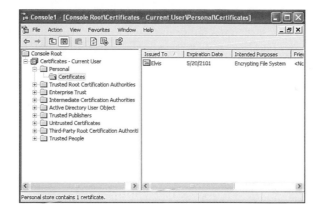

7. Right-click the EFS certificate entry, and select All Tasks, Export to launch the Certificate Export Wizard.

8. Click Next, then select Yes, Export the Private Key, and click Next. Select Personal Information Exchange, uncheck Enable Strong Protection, and uncheck Delete the Private Key if Export Is Successful. Then click Next.

9. Enter a password twice to protect this key. (You must remember this password!) Then click Next.

10. Specify a path and filename to be used to save the key. Insert a blank, formatted floppy disk, and type the path and filename, such as `A:\RECOVERY.PFX` (not case sensitive). Click Next and then Finish. A dialog box appears stating the export was successful; click OK.

11. Right-click the certificate entry again, and select Delete.

12. Label the floppy disk clearly "EFS Recovery Key for *XXX*", where *XXX* is the name of your computer. Store this diskette in a safe place away from your computer.

13. Restart your computer. After it's restarted, log on as Administrator again, and confirm that you can't view the file you encrypted as another user.

CAUTION

> You should back up and delete the Administrator's recovery certificate (that's the procedure you just performed), but don't delete Administrator as the recovery agent from the Local Security Policy. Leave the Local Security Policy alone. If you delete the entries there, you'll disable EFS.

PROTECTING YOUR OWN FILE ENCRYPTION CERTIFICATE

If your user account is lost, or if you accidentally delete your own file encryption certificate some day, you might lose access to your own files. The recovery agent could still help out, but you can protect yourself by exporting your own personal EFS certificate. Basically, follow the same procedure as for the local administrator while logged in as a user. Just be sure to have at least one encrypted file before starting the process. Once complete, label the disk "EFS for *UUU* on *XXX*," where *UUU* is your user account name and *XXX* is your computer name. Store it in a safe place.

RECOVERING ENCRYPTED FILES ON YOUR OWN COMPUTER

If your user account is deleted, or you end up reinstalling Windows from scratch, you'll lose access to your encrypted files because the Encryption database will be lost. You can log on as Administrator and reinstall the encrypted file recovery certificate, or you can log on as yourself and reinstall your file encryption certificate to get the files back with the following procedure:

1. Choose Console, Add/Remove Snap-In, and then select Add. Next, highlight the Certificates snap-in and click Add. Select My User Account and click Finish. Finally, click Close, and then click OK.

2. In the left pane, expand the Certificates node, Current User, Personal, Certificates.

3. In the right pane, right-click and select All Tasks, Import to start the Certificate Import Wizard.

4. Click Next. Enter the name of the certificate file—for example, `a:\recovery.pfx`—and click Next.

5. Enter the password for the certificate, and check Mark the Private Key as Exportable. Click Next twice, and then click Finish.

You should now be able to access the encrypted files. I suggest that you remove the Encrypted check mark from these files. Log on again as the Normal user of these files and re-encrypt them if you want.

COMPRESSION: HOW IT WORKS, HOW TO USE IT

Windows XP ships with built-in provisions for file compression that is implemented via NTFS. It's not strictly true that only NTFS files and folders can be compressed, because a command-line program called `compress` can compress FAT-based files and folders. However, you must, in turn, use the expand command to decompress the resulting files and folders before you can use them. This procedure is awkward. So, for practical purposes, compression is implemented seamlessly into the operating system only on NTFS-formatted volumes.

File compression works by encoding data to take up less storage space. Digital data is compressed by finding repeatable patterns of binary 0s and 1s. The more patterns found, the more the data can be compressed. Text can generally be compressed to about 40 percent of its original size and graphics files from 20 to 90 percent. Some files (namely .EXE files) compress very little because of the lack of repeating data patterns within the program. The amount of compression depends entirely on the type of file and compression algorithm used.

Compressing a file or folder in Windows is a simple and straightforward process:

1. Open Windows Explorer, and select the file or folder you want.

2. Right-click, and select Properties from the context menu.

3. Select the Advanced button at the bottom of the Properties dialog.

4. In the Advanced Attributes dialog that appears, put a check mark in front of the Compress Contents to Save Disk Space option (refer to Figure 29.8).

5. When you click OK, you are prompted to choose whether you want to compress files and folders, if you're compressing a folder, recursively. Doing so is generally desirable and a safe bet.

Two caveats are in order with compression:

■ A file or folder can be compressed or encrypted, but not both. These options are mutually exclusive.

■ By default, compressed files are shown in blue, while encrypted files are shown in green. If you choose Control Panel, Folder Options and select the View tab, you can find an option to display compressed and encrypted files or folders in an alternate color.

CAUTION

You should keep in mind some disk space requirements when using compression. If you try to compress a volume that's running extremely low on free space, you might see this error message:

```
Compression Error
File Manager/Explorer cannot change compress attributes
for:
"path\filename"
```

These error messages indicate that the system needs additional free space to perform compression. The system is not designed to manipulate the data in place on the disk. Additional space is needed to buffer the user data and to possibly hold additional file system metadata. The amount of additional free space required depends on the cluster size, file size, and available space.

Use compression only when expressly needed. Compression will cause significant performance reduction if a significant number of commonly accessed files are compressed, due to the CPU processing required to decompress them for use.

INDEXING

Windows XP comes with a text-search system called the Indexing Service. This system scans files and folders on your hard disk and builds a database of the words it finds in them. This database helps speed up the Search for Files and Directories option when you're looking for words within files or keywords in file descriptions and helps the Internet Information Services Web server perform Web site searches. You can also query the index directly.

NOTE

> Right off the bat, I should reassure you that the Indexing Service pays attention to file privileges when it displays results of searches. It never reports a match for a file the person searching doesn't have permission to view.

MANAGING THE INDEXING SERVICE

To view the Indexing Service Manager, open Computer Management from Administration Tools, expand Services and Applications, and then select Indexing Service (as shown in Figure 29.10). Under Indexing Service, the manager displays any *catalogs* defined on your system. A catalog is a self-contained index for a folder or group of folders. By default, a System catalog is defined for use by Search for Files and Folders. If you've installed Internet Information Services, you also have a Web index, which can be used by scripts to let visitors to your Web site search its pages.

Figure 29.10
The Indexing Service Manager displays all defined index catalogs.

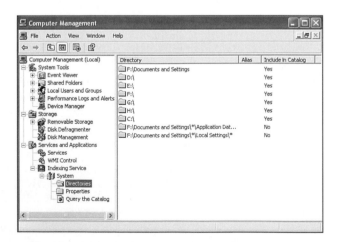

If you want to use the Indexing Service, select Indexing Service in the left pane, and choose Action, Start from the menu. Answer Yes to Do You Want the Indexing Service to Start Whenever You Boot Your Computer?

Choosing Yes starts the service, which immediately begins its job of cataloguing files on your hard drive. It does its job of scanning files periodically from now on, as long as the computer is turned on.

INDEXING SERVICE PROPERTIES

You can right-click the Indexing Service entry in Computer Management to adjust the service's global properties. The Generation tab has some useful settings, as shown in Table 29.1.

TABLE 29.1 GENERATION TAB OPTIONS

Option	Description
Index Files with Unknown Extensions	If this option is checked, the Indexing Service includes all files in the index, regardless of file type. If it is unchecked, only registered file types are indexed. It's probably best to leave the box checked.
Generate Abstracts	If this option is checked, for each indexed file, the Indexing Service extracts and stores the first few sentences of each matching file and displays them on the search results. Check this box with caution because it can consume an enormous amount of disk space. I recommend that you leave it unchecked on the Service's Properties sheet.
Maximum Size	This option sets the maximum length in characters of abstracts. If you choose to generate abstracts, keep them short. I suggest going no higher than the default 320 characters.

CATALOG PROPERTIES

By default, the Indexing Service Properties settings apply to each catalog managed by the Indexing Service. However, you can select the Properties sheet for each individual catalog by right-clicking the catalog name in the left pane and selecting Properties (in Figure 29.10, the catalog is named "System"). Then you can uncheck Inherit Above Settings from Service on the Generation tab and customize them on a catalog-by-catalog basis.

A good use of this capability would be to enable abstracts for the Web index if you have installed Internet Information Services and use searching on your Web site.

NOTE

Under each catalog is an entry named Properties, but it is a display page only. To change the catalog's properties, you have to right-click its name in the left pane.

29

CATALOG DIRECTORIES

You can control which directories (drives and folders) are included in and excluded from a catalog by using the Directories folder. Under any catalog name in the left pane, select the Directories entry, and view the cataloged folders in the right pane.

Here, you can add any additional drives to include in your index and add any folders you want to exclude from the index. To add an Include or Exclude entry, right-click in the right pane, and select New, Directory.

In the resulting dialog, enter the full path to the folder to be indexed, or use `X:\` to add the entire drive *X:*. Check Yes or No under Include in Index. If you want to add a directory on a remote computer, enter its full *UNC* network name—for example, `\\machine\sharename\folder`—and a username and password to be used to access the shared folder.

CONTROLLING INDEXING OF INDIVIDUAL FILES

You can also remove files or folders from all catalogs by using the files' or folders' Properties sheets.

To exclude a file from any catalogs, right-click the file or folder, and select Properties, Advanced. Under Archive and Index attributes on the resulting dialog, you can uncheck For Fast Searching, Allow Indexing Service to Index This File or Folder. Unchecking this box prevents the Indexing Service from ever scanning the file. However, just checking the box is not enough to put the file into an index; the folder must be listed in the catalog's Directories list or in a subfolder of a listed folder.

USING THE INDEXING SERVICE

The System catalog is used automatically by the All Files and Folders search option accessed through the Search item on the Start menu, and it's especially handy when you're searching for a keyword or specific file type. The index is used to hasten the search of any cataloged folder.

The Web folder is used by scripts or FrontPage extensions on the Internet Information Server, which is described in Chapter 13, "Hosting Web Pages with Internet Information Server."

You also can search any catalog directly from the Indexing Service Manager. Select Query the Catalog in the left pane, and a search form appears in the right. Enter any desired keywords, and click Search to begin a query. I was surprised to find that my system's temporary Internet files are included in the catalog, as test queries returned matches based on words in Web pages I had recently visited.

DISK CLEANUP UTILITY

In the course of daily use, Windows XP generates thousands of temporary files to aid in system operation. These files are critical to the operation of the programs that use them when the programs are being used. As most people are well aware, though, temporary files have a habit of being much more persistent than their name implies. And over the course of time, these files add up in a hurry and consume large amounts of valuable disk space. The Disk Cleanup utility provides you with a safe and reliable way to delete these temporary files from all their various hiding spots and thus free up disk space on your hard drive.

To access this utility, do the following:

1. Choose Start, All Programs, Accessories, System Tools, Disk Cleanup. In the resulting dialog, choose the drive to analyze. Alternatively, you can right-click a drive in the Explorer, and then choose Properties, General, Disk Cleanup.

2. The program then searches this drive for files that can be safely deleted or compressed. The details of this analysis are then displayed in a dialog similar to the one shown in Figure 29.11.

Figure 29.11
Report of a disk cleanup analysis.

Near the top of the dialog box is the total amount of disk space you can free on this drive by accepting the selected recommendations listed below. You can exclude or include file groups from the cleanup process by placing a check mark in front of the types listed. When you select an entry, you see a description of which files that group contains and what their purpose is. By selecting a group and then the View Files button, you can see exactly which files are slated for death in the resulting folder window. Use this option if you have any doubts about a group of files, where they reside, or what they do.

The following file groupings might be listed:

■ **Downloaded Program Files**—These files are ActiveX controls and Java applets used by Web pages you have visited. If you delete them, they will simply be reloaded the next time you visit the pages.

■ **Temporary Internet Files**—This one is a biggie. Every time you access a Web page, your browser stores or caches the various elements of that page on the hard disk. When you revisit a page, any elements that have not changed since your last visit are reloaded from the hard disk, rather than the site itself, to speed the rendering process.

Deleting these temporary Internet files frees the largest amount of disk space of any of the group lists. If you use a modem to access the Internet, however, you will notice longer rendering times the next time you return to one of your favorite sites.

NOTE

> Agreeing to delete temporary Internet files does not delete your *cookies* (personalized settings for Web sites), so don't worry about having to reenter user ID information or other such information for sites you visit a lot. Cookies are stored in x:\Documents and Settings*<username>*\Cookies. Temporary Internet files are stored by default in x:\Documents and Settings*<username>*\Local Settings\Temporary Internet Files (where x: is the volume the system is installed on).

- **Recycle Bin**—Clearing this folder is the same as manually clearing your Recycle Bin. It is a good idea to have a quick look at the files stored there before choosing this option. Select this option, and click the View Files button under the group description; a folder window then opens, listing the contents.

- **Temporary Offline Files**—Similar to cached Web pages, when you connect to a network location and access a read-only file, a temporary copy is sometimes stored on your hard drive. Clearing these temporary copies does not erase the files you explicitly marked as available for offline use, so this is a safe choice.

- **Offline Files**—If you use the Synchronization features of Windows XP (see Chapter 18, "Windows Unplugged: Remote and Mobile Networking"), selected files and folders from a network connection are stored locally for access while you are disconnected. Do not delete these files unless you're sure you can work without the local copies. You'll lose any changes you made to offline files if you delete them here, so don't make this choice without synchronizing first.

- **Compress Old Files**—Windows can compress files not accessed within a specified period. To configure this period, select this group and click the More Options button.

- **Catalog File for the Content Indexer**—The Windows Indexing Service (see the description earlier in this chapter) speeds file searches by building and maintaining indexes on your hard disk. Selecting this option removes any old index files not in use but does not delete any current indexes.

On the Disk Cleanup dialog, also notice the second tab marked More Options. The Windows Components option provides a quick access shortcut to the Windows Components Wizard. From this wizard, you can select major system components (such as IIS and Indexing Services) to add or remove. Also on this tab is a shortcut to Add/Remove Programs under the section labeled Installed Programs. The System Restore Clean up button is used to delete all but the most recent restore points. This may free up a significant amount of drive space, but it will eliminate your ability to rollback to previous states of the system. (See Chapter 33 "Troubleshooting and Repairing Windows XP" for information in System Restore.)

TIP FROM

Bob
& Brian

> Running Disk Cleanup weekly does wonders to improve a system's performance. The first time you run it, the program might take quite awhile to run, but with regular exercise, this program speeds up because the disk stays cleaner. Once a month—after you check the contents of the individual folder groups carefully—you should empty all folders of all temporary files. Then follow up by running a defragmentation utility.

USING INTERNET EXPLORER'S CACHE CLEANUP

If you would prefer not to use the Disk Cleanup utility, you can choose a second option for clearing out those disk-hogging cached Internet files.

To access it, open the Control Panel, and select the Internet Options icon. On the Internet Properties dialog, you will find a section titled Temporary Internet Files. The Delete Files button works exactly as advertised. The Settings button allows you to configure options for how often cached files are checked against their original counterparts, how much disk space these cached files are allowed to take up, and in which folder they are stored.

When the disk space setting is exceeded, files are removed on a "First In, First Out" basis; that is, the oldest files are deleted to create space for newer ones.

The Move Folder option lets you specify a location where these temporary files will be stored. I think it's a great idea to change this path to a temporary folder or a drive with lots of free space. I usually redirect Internet Explorer to deposit its temporary Internet files into a \temp folder I've created on one of my drives. If you do a lot of Web surfing, you'll want to map this temp location to a fast volume that is not on the same hard drive as your main Windows partition.

TIP FROM

Bob
& Brian

> Changing the location for the storage of temporary Internet files is especially a good idea if the system is a client on a domain network and roaming profiles are in use. By storing the temporary files outside of your profile, it will take less time to log in and log out, plus your profile will consume less space on the network server.

BACKUP TOOLS AND STRATEGIES

Nobody plans to lose or corrupt an important file. But then again, no one I know gets up in the morning and plans to crash his car either. Things happen, though, and for all the same reasons you buy car insurance, you should also be taking all the necessary steps to safeguard all those bits and bytes that reside on your system's hard drive.

WINDOWS BACKUP PROGRAM

Windows is installed with a backup utility that should meet the needs of most individual users. With it, you can back up folders or files—both local and remote—to a Windows recognized tape device, to a removable storage device (JAZ drive, MO drive, Zip drive,

29

and so on), or to a file on a local or remote drive. If Windows XP can read the file (FAT16, FAT32, or NTFS natively), then it can be backed up.

NOTE

> Windows XP's Backup program is acceptable for an individual user's computer, but it's not really adequate for LAN or server backups because it can't fully back up remote computers. If you're setting up a LAN, you might look into more sophisticated programs, such as the server versions of Arcserve or Backup-Exec. If your computer is on a LAN, your system administrator might have a more sophisticated centralized backup system available to you.

NOTE

> Windows XP offers versatile removable storage services used to manage groups of removable media (a.k.a. media pools). Windows keeps track of what media can be overwritten, which can be deleted, and which media need to be retired. However, in many situations, especially for individual users, managing media pools is too much work for too little benefit. For the most part, you can more than adequately manage your own media manually through proper labeling.
>
> An easy to follow scheme for tape management (or any medium for that matter) is to have 5 or 6 tapes. Rotate each tape after each full backup (in many cases this occurs once a week). Keep track of the uses of each tape. For example, label the tapes "My Stuff 1/5", ". . . 2/5", and so on. Then each time you insert the next tape, write the date on the label. Keep in mind that tape media usually are designed for 6 to 10 uses before they need to be replaced. You can use them dozens of times, but as the use numbers add up, the reliability of the recorded data, as well as the physical integrity of the tape itself, degrades. Once you've reached the reliable use lifetime (6 to 10) of a medium, replace it. By this process (one week full backup rotation with 5 tapes for 6 uses), you'll need to buy new tapes about every seven months.
>
> If you'd like to learn more about media management, there is plenty of coverage in the Help and Support of Windows XP as well as in the Windows XP Resource Kit.

The first time backup is launched (Start, All Programs, Accessories, System Tools, Backup), the Backup or Restore Wizard is launched. The first page of this wizard has a check box which controls whether the wizard is launched every time. The wizard can be used to backup or restore files. These wizards offer few options; they mainly ask whether you want to back up or restore, what types of documents to manage (My Documents and settings only, everyone's documents and settings, or all data), and where to put the backup. If that's all you need, then you don't need me.

However, there is lots more to explore in the Backup utility if you switch to Advanced Mode. You can do so by clicking on the link. Plus, you can choose to always open Backup in Advanced Mode by de-selecting the Always Start in Wizard Mode check box.

When you reach Advanced Mode, you'll actually be seeing the Backup utility proper (see Figure 29.12). I think its humorous that Microsoft labeled using the utility directly "advanced." From the Welcome tab of the Backup utility, you can launch more advanced wizards which offer a broader range of activities and settings. There is a wizard for backing up, restoring, and Automated System Recovery (ASR).

Figure 29.12
The Welcome tab of the Backup program.

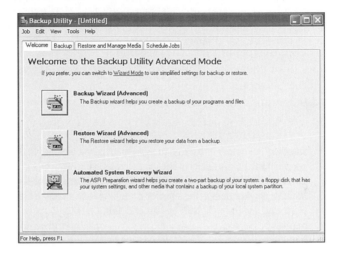

ASR is a two-part backup solution which creates a backup set that can be used to fully restore your system. It creates a boot floppy and a media set. The ASR backup can restore your system even if you can no longer boot into Windows XP or you replace your hard drive. Just boot with the floppy and follow the prompts to restore your entire system from the backup media.

NOTE

Emergency Repair Disks are a thing of the past. Windows XP does not offer a facility to create and ERD. In fact, the recovery and restoration tools included with Windows XP don't need an ERD. Instead, Windows XP uses other mechanisms to protect its Registry, SAM, and configuration settings. First, the Registry actively maintains its own backup copies. Second, the native backup utility can save System State. This includes the Registry and all essential system configuration settings. If your system is just damaged, the repair capabilities of Disaster Recovery are able to rebuild the system. In the case of a complete system loss, a full backup can restore your system. In either case, the ERD is no longer required.

In addition to the Welcome tab's wizards, there are three other tabs of control. The Backup tab is used to manually configure a backup operation. The Restore and Manage Media tab is used to manually configure a restore operation and perform basic media management tasks. The Schedule Jobs tab is used to view and alter scheduled backup jobs.

29

If you are completely new to backing up, use either default wizard or the advanced wizard to walk you through the process. You'll get the hang of it very quickly. If you are a backup veteran, I don't even need to tell you how to perform a backup.

The Backup tab's interface is very straightforward. Just mark the check box beside each item you want to include in the backup. Keep in mind that marking a parent box will automatically include all sub-folders and file contents. And don't forget to mark the System State check box to protect your Registry and system configuration.

Backups can be stored to tapes or files. The tape option is only available if you have a tape device installed locally. Otherwise, all other storage locations are accessible through the File option. Through the File option, you can define the destination path to a file on a local hard drive, on a Zip disk, on floppies, or even across the network to a network share.

TIP FROM

Bob
& Brian

> Selecting the option to back up to a file is actually a blessing in disguise. Because many people don't have traditional backup devices such as DAT tapes or DLT drives, backing up to a file facilitates backup to other common removable media such as CD-Rs. Backing up your data in this manner is preferable to simply writing files to a CD-R. Normally, if you simply back up files and directories to your CD-R drive, you lose your permissions as well as make all the files read-only by virtue of the fact that they are backed up to read-only media. By backing up to a single file from Backup, you retain these settings and can restore with all of them intact. You can even compress this file before you write it to your CD-R by using your favorite zip program.

After you made your file selections and defined the destination, click the Start Backup button. This reveals the Backup Job Information dialog box (see Figure 29.13). From this dialog box, the following items can be configured:

- Description
- Append or overwrite/replace media
- Allow only the owner and administrator access to the backup
- Schedule the backup (via Schedule button)
- Set Advanced options (via Advanced button)
- Cancel backup (via Cancel button)
- Start backup (via Start Backup button)

Figure 29.13
The Backup Job Information dialog box.

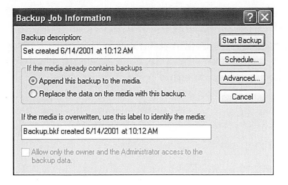

Scheduling a backup is not difficult; just follow the prompts. You'll need to save your backup selections, and then provide the username and password under which you want the backup job to execute. Once you are presented with the Scheduled Job Options dialog box, be sure to click the Properties button to define the schedule you need. A thorough discussion of the scheduling options is included later in this chapter.

The Advanced options include

- Backup data in Remote Storage

NOTE

> Remote Storage is an optimization mechanism where unused or infrequently accessed files are moved off to a remote storage location, such as a network share or a tape device. If the user requests a migrated file, it is automatically retrieved and returned to its original location, invisible to the user. Remote Storage is supported by Windows XP via NTFS. However, no details are included in Windows XP's Help system on how to configure it so you'll need to consult the Windows XP Resource Kit for details.

- Verify data after backup
- Compress data to save space
- Include system protected files with System State
- Disable volume snapshot

NOTE

> A volume snapshot allows most open and locked files to be included in the backup. If this feature is disabled, open and locked files will most likely not be included in the backup.

- Set backup type

29

There are five types of backup supported by Windows XP's Backup utility. It is a good idea to consider the different types of backups available before initiating your backup. As you probably know, the operating system provides a means for keeping track of which files have been changed since the last backup—the archive bit. Based on whether a file's archive bit is turned on or off, the backup program either backs it up or skips over it. Your job is to set the correct options so the Backup program is relative to this bit. You can find these options through the Advanced button as discussed or by opening the Tools, Options dialog and selecting the Backup Type tab. Here, you can set how your files are backed up to your media, with the following options:

- **Normal**—The Normal backup does a backup of every file you've selected while also clearing, or turning off, the archive bit on each file. This type of backup sets each file's attribute to signify that it does not need to be backed up again until it has changed.

- **Copy**—The Copy type of backup simply copies the files to your backup media and leaves the archive bit alone. Using this option, you can have several backups happening on the same files without each of them stepping on each other's toes. In other words, if you use the Copy backup option, using the Normal option still backs up every file because the archive bit is still set on them.

- **Differential**—This option backs up only the files that have been changed since the last normal or incremental backup, while leaving the archive bit set for each file. With this option, any file backed up looks as though it has not been backed up.

- **Incremental**—The Incremental option is the same as the Differential option, with the exception that it does, in fact, clear the archive bit on files that it backs up.

- **Daily**—The Daily option backs up all files that have been modified only on the day that the backup is performed. Be careful with this one because you could end up not backing up everything you want if you do not run nightly backups.

Differential Versus Incremental Backups

Let me give you a bit more explanation of the differences between *differential* and *incremental* backups. You can use the differential and incremental options to save time and tapes when backing up frequently. Keep in mind that full backups can take a lot of time and can fill more than one tape or disk.

If you do a full backup and then successive differential backups, each differential backup includes any files changed or added since the full backup. The successive backups do grow in size, but not by much, and you need only two backup sets to fully restore a system: the full backup and the most recent differential.

With incremental backups, only files changed since the last full or incremental backup are saved. With incrementals, the individual backup sets are indeed smaller, but you would need to restore the full and all subsequent incremental backups, in date order, to fully recover all your files. This situation is rather dangerous, in my opinion. I can hardly find my own head some days, let alone a dozen backup tapes.

For a LAN server or business computer, I recommend that you do a full backup weekly and a differential backup daily. For a home computer, you might try a monthly full backup and weekly differential backups.

All the backup options have their places in certain situations. I personally leave the backup type at Normal so that all my files are always backed up, no matter what. You might find that another option suits you better, so feel free to experiment with all these options to find the best one for you.

RESTORING DATA FROM A BACKUP

"The best laid plans of mice and men oft gang a-glay," as the saying goes. When you've lost data and had enough foresight to have backed it up, you're in luck. Or you hope you are, at least. Backing up is the first half of recovering your data. With any luck, you'll be able to get it back the way it was before whatever bolt of lightning hit your PC. The Restore tab of the Backup dialog comes in at this point. Restoring from a backup is a very simple process, which you can execute in three essential steps:

1. Run the Backup program (by choosing Start, All Programs, Accessories, System Tools, Backup).

2. Use the Restore Wizard from the Welcome tab if you want a walkthrough. Alternatively, select the Restore and Manage Media tab, and adjust a few simple parameters.

3. Begin the restore, and insert media if and when prompted.

Of course, you might want to understand a few option and parameter details, for better control of your restorations. The following sections discuss the options. You should probably read along before doing your first couple of data recoveries. After you have the theories under your belt, then you can proceed.

Notice the left pane of the Restore tab. Here, you can view all the available Backup media pools. You can expand these nodes to display all possible source media and pools. They're displayed in a familiar tree view of the directories and files backed up to each related medium. As with the process of Backup, you simply select the files or folders you want to restore. And, of course, by selecting a top node of the tree, you include everything beneath it.

Next, it's a good idea to look at the settings on the Restore tab of the Options dialog box (Tools menu, Options). Here, you can choose from options that dictate how files will be handled if you are restoring one that already exists in your restore destination. The safest bet here is to not replace any file with a restored version. This is generally the best bet unless you have a specific reason to do so. Reasons for overwriting existing files do crop up, though. For example, if know that you somehow trashed, misedited, or otherwise mangled the file you currently have on disk, you can revert to the last-backed-up one. In that case, you need to enable replacement.

Other than the general restore options, the only real option for the restore portion of the Backup program is the option to specify the location in which you want to restore the files. You choose this option from the drop-down list at the bottom of the Restore tab. Three options are available:

29

■ **Original Location**—This option restores the files to the exact place from which they were backed up. Be careful with this one; it could cause you problems with files that are open. You should make sure you're not trying to restore over a file that may be in use by another application or the system.

■ **Alternate Location**—This option gives you the opportunity to restore the files to a destination of your choosing. If this option is selected, you are prompted for the location to which you want to restore via an entry box beneath the location options. From there, you can use the Browse button to find your restore destination. If you use this option, the directory structure of your backed-up files will be retained in the new destination.

■ **Single Folder**—Selecting this option dumps all the files from your backup to a single folder. Be aware that using this option does not preserve the directory structure of your backed-up data. It simply ignores the structure and restores all the files to the directory you choose.

After you've selected your restore destination, you can click the Start Restore button to begin. If you selected Alternate Location or Single Folder, you're given the option to configure Restore options via the Advanced button on the Confirm Restore dialog box. The options in the Advanced Restore Options dialog are as follows:

■ **Restore Security**—This option enables you to restore the same permissions for the files and folders you're restoring to their original settings. In most cases, choosing this option is best because you don't want to have to set them one-by-one after the restore has finished.

■ **Restore Junction Points, and Restore File and Folder Data Under Junction Points to the Original Location**—Turn on this check box if you've created junction points using the linkd command, and you're trying to restore the junction points and the data that the junction points point to. If you don't, only the pointers are restored, not the data. You also should turn on this box if you are restoring a mounted drive's data.

■ **When Restoring Replicated Data Sets, Mark the Restored Data as the Primary Data for All Replicas**—This option is relevant only to Windows 2003 Server and should be grayed out on any machine running Windows XP Professional or Home.

■ **Restore the Cluster Registry to the quorum disk and all other nodes**—This option is relevant only to Windows 2003 Server and should be grayed out on any machine running Windows XP Professional or Home.

■ **Preserve Existing Volume Mount Points**—This option most often applies when you're restoring the data for an entire drive, such as when you're replacing a drive. Typically, you put in a formatted drive, re-create the mount points, and then restore the data. You don't want to overwrite the mount points, so you turn on this option. If you have not re-created the mount points, and you want to restore the entire data and mount points as stored in the backup set, then uncheck this box.

Finally, by selecting the OK button, you can then select OK on the Confirm Restore dialog to start the restore.

SCHEDULING JOBS

Finally, we come to my personal favorite, the Schedule Jobs tab of the Backup dialog. This feature is a great addition to an already very capable backup program. There should really be no reason for most people not to have a reasonably current backup of their system at any given time if they use this tool.

Strategies for scheduling backups vary from person to person or machine to machine. Some people, myself included, are extremely paranoid and go for the "back up every single night" method. As you can guess, backing up this frequently saves a great deal of heartache in the event of a total system meltdown. I can't tell you how many times backing up has saved my neck. On the other hand, say you have a machine at your home or business that rarely gets used or is just acting as a proxy server. This kind of machine really only needs backups at much longer intervals than your personal workstation. In this case, it's usually safe to back up a system like this only every week or so. In the end, it's up to you how you feel you need to schedule your backups. Just remember, your system will probably go down at some point. Being prepared is the best insurance around for this nasty inevitability.

To use the scheduling features of backup, you simply double-click any date using the provided calendar or click the Add Job button. This gives you a chance to use the Backup Wizard. The options for it are very straightforward. In fact, if you read the previous section on backing up, you should have no problem whatsoever using this wizard.

> **NOTE**
>
> You will be prompted to set the account information for the backup because it may end up running when another logged-in user doesn't have the rights to initiate the backup. When you're prompted, you can specify a "Run As" user and password.

> **NOTE**
>
> The Schedule Job dialog is actually the same one used when scheduling any common task via Scheduled Tasks, a system tool covered in Chapter 27. You might want to refer to that chapter for some more details on the options.

The Settings tab on the Schedule Job dialog offers somewhat lower-priority options. You should take a gander at them, though, if you're intending to get serious about automated backups. Among the settings are those that affect idle time and power management. You should consider power settings if you're doing a backup from a laptop running on batteries. The Idle Time options could be useful if there is a possibility that someone will be using the computer when backup begins. If good computer responsiveness is important, you can ensure the backup process stops if someone sits down to the keyboard and begins work. Check the Stop the Task If the Computer Ceases to Be Idle check box.

29

ALTERNATIVE AND CREATIVE BACKUP STRATEGIES

The following sections provide a few alternative ideas for doing your backups. You can choose from many other possible ideas because of the proliferation of device types and off-site backup services (for example, CD-R, CD-RW, Internet-based services, LAN-based backups, and so on). However, you might find one of these ideas interesting and potentially very helpful in your work setting.

USING OFFLINE FILES AND FOLDERS

Windows XP has a little-known feature called Offline Files and Folders. The implementation of this tool is aimed at notebook users who connect to the corporate network, update files, and then journey off with their laptops on another adventure.

Here's how it works: The user logs on to the server and marks a network folder as available while offline. This folder and its contents are then replicated to the user's system. While on the road, the user adds new files to the folder and modifies or deletes existing ones. When the user returns and logs back on the network, Windows XP automatically synchronizes all changed files—in both directions. For example, if the user deleted a file from the offline folder on his or her notebook, the synchronization process notes the discrepancy and asks whether this file should also be deleted from the server. A similar process takes place for new or modified files.

→ Offline folders are also discussed in the chapter on mobile network users. To learn more about these folders, **see** "Offline Folders," **p. 622**.

"This is all well and good for mobile users," you say. "But why is this topic described under backup strategies?" Because the synchronization process does not give a nit whether you physically disconnect your machine from the network; it can automatically update changed files every time you log off or on. In addition, you can easily force synchronization at any time by using a simple menu command.

TIP FROM

Bob
& Brian

> Let me describe precisely how I ensure I have a recent backup of my working files throughout the course of a day. Both my main working system and my notebook have network cards, connected by a $10 twisted-pair crossover cable. The notebook has a shortcut to the folders containing all my critical data (book chapters, contact files, business correspondence, and so on), and these folders are enabled for offline access. Whenever I need a break or a distraction arises, I manually force a synchronization between the notebook and my working system. This way, if disaster strikes, I can quickly restore a damaged file by forcing another synchronization. The notebook detects whether something is amiss and offers to right the error.

MAKING INACCESSIBLE DEVICES ACCESSIBLE

The backup strategy described here, at first glance, looks a bit convoluted, but if you apply a little thought and creativity, you will be amazed at the range of possibilities that unfold from it.

Every power user has at least one device in his or her computer stable that won't play nice with another. In my case, it happens to be my USB Zip drive. The device works flawlessly on my IBM ThinkPad, but the USB port on my main working machine will not work under Windows XP until Epox comes out with a BIOS update.

This minor irritation would have remained minor had I not developed such a high regard for my trusty little Zip drive. It is fast, convenient, and flexible. It addition, it is a perfect place to copy chapter versions and backups as they evolve. In short, I wanted the same back-up flexibility I had on my notebook available to me on my main machine. And being the doggedly persistent person I am, I finally found a way.

Do you remember that crossover cable I talked about earlier? If you have more than one computer in your house, or if you work on computers for a living, go buy one. It has to be the handiest item in my arsenal, and it costs only $10. A crossover cable lets you connect the LAN cards of two computers together into a mini-network without hubs or any other hardware.

As I noted previously, my notebook and my main system "talk" to each other via network cards and my crossover cable. Janus (my working system) can see Penelope (my notebook). Penelope can see and utilize the Zip; Janus cannot. But if A can see B, and B can utilize C, then why don't I give A access to C?

Here's how to make it so:

- Computer A can talk to B.
- Computer B has a device attached that A cannot use directly, for whatever reason.
- On computer B, select the device from Windows Explorer and share it (select the device, right-click, and select Share from the pop-up menu displayed). Give it a share name to reflect its function or purpose.
- Now go back to computer A and map a drive to that device (via Windows Explorer, Tools, Map Network Drive). In the folder box, you have to specify both the computer name and the device's share name. In my case, it is \\penelope\zip.

I created a shortcut on my desktop for this drive mapping and added it to my Send To menu. Now I can quickly back up a file from Windows Explorer with a single right-click.

GUARDING YOUR PROFILE

Windows XP stores your user profile in the folder \Documents and Settings\<*youruser-name*>. The subfolders contained here contain all the tweaks, configurations, and data files that make up what you see and access while working under Windows XP. Guard this folder tree with your life! With a little manipulation, this information can be copied to a safe haven and slipped back into place should the unforeseen occur, and you have to reinstall your operating system.

NOTE

If your computer is a member of a Windows domain network, and you're set up with a Roaming User Profile, your profile folder is automatically copied from the domain server to your computer when you log in and back again when you log out. It is an automatic backup, of sorts, so you can be a little more relaxed about it.

If you need to restore a profile copy in this environment, you should contact your network administrator because this task is fairly tricky.

The following are some of the invaluable goodies contained on the profile tree:

- Your Favorites folder
- Your History folder
- All the configuration settings and program templates for MS Office
- Your Desktop settings
- The default folder for data files (My Documents)
- Your most recently accessed files list
- The folder your cookies are stored in
- Your SendTo folder
- Your Start menu configuration
- Your section of the Windows Registry
- A bevy of application settings, temp files, and IE history files, in a folder called Local Settings

As you can see, all this stuff is very good, and it's tailored specifically to your computing experience under Windows XP.

The root folder of your profile (in my case, C:\Documents and Settings\Bob) contains two key files: NTUSER.DAT and a backup of this file, NTUSER. They are your user Registry settings and are locked by the operating system in such a way as to forbid any other program from accessing them directly. Therefore, you cannot copy either of these files while logged on as *yourusername* (even if you have administrative rights under *yourusername*). An attempted copy operation will fail. The problem is that the rest of the tree structure is useless without these key files because they tell the operating system (and indirectly, the programs that use them) which files can be found where.

Ah, grasshopper, but this problem is not insurmountable. The following steps illustrate how you can wrestle a copy of your profile away from the arms of Windows XP.

NOTE

> The following example uses a network drive as a copy point for simplicity. Realistically, the place you copy your profile is dependent on the resources at hand. The key here is to get it off your system volume and somewhere safe. This location can be a Zip drive (if it will fit), a CD-R drive, or at the very least, a separate partition. Personally, I keep my profile backed up to both another partition on my main system and a backup partition on my notebook. I tend to be a bit protective of my data, and for good reason, as you will read shortly.

1. Log off from *yourusername* and log on as Administrator. This is a key step; as noted previously, you cannot properly copy your profile tree while logged on as yourself.

2. In Windows Explorer, create a folder on a network drive you have access to, and name it—for example, `Profile Backup`.

3. Go to your user profile (in my case, C:\Documents and Settings\Bob), select the highest folder in your profile tree (Bob), and drop it on the network folder you just created (Profile Backup). Go have a cup of coffee; this process could take awhile if you have several data files stored here.

4. Last but not least, make sure you keep this backup profile updated on a routine basis. Most users can generally afford to lose a day or so of work; losing some work is unpleasant, but it is tolerable. But if you're like me, by the end of a busy week, you've probably added 10 or more "gems" to your Favorites list, messed with your NORMAL.DOT template three or four times, and shuffled your Start menu at least once.

The preceding routine is not about protecting your data; that is a separate routine which should be done on a level that reflects the value you place on the data you create every day. What it is about is protecting the configuration settings that represent your daily working environment under Windows XP.

So, you follow this sage advice and dutifully copy your profile somewhere safe on a routine basis. How is this effort going to reward you? Well, should you need to reinstall your operating system, your efforts are going to reward you by allowing you to re-create your desktop, its shortcuts, and most of your program configurations quickly and painlessly.

Trust Me, It Happens to Everyone

What follows is a personal experience I had right in the midst of writing this very chapter.

Some hard drives run for 10 years; some die an untimely death when they are only a month old—hence the term *Mean* Time Between Failure (MTBF), which is an average estimate of how long the drive manufacturer expects its product to run before it fails. Unfortunately, I ended up on the low end of the bell curve the other day when my three-month old hard drive died a prompt and dramatic death. Luckily, I had made a profile backup the night before onto a partition on my notebook reserved solely for machine-to-machine backups.

I borrowed a spare hard drive from a friend, partitioned it in two (*always, always* make a data partition on your drive), installed Windows XP on the boot partition, and installed the base productivity programs I use every day (Office 2000 and a smattering of "can't live without" utilities). This last step is an important one. To slide an alternative profile into an existing installation, you must restore your system to a point that closely mirrors when you backed up your earlier profile. In my case, this necessitates installing Office. You do not have to configure or tweak anything; just install it to ensure the Windows XP Registry knows it exists.

With all key applications installed, I connected my trusty crossover cable to my notebook, logged off as Bob, and logged back on as Administrator. I connected to the notebook's backup partition and copied my saved profile to my main system. I logged off as Administrator, logged on as Bob, and presto-pocus: My desktop returned, Word found all my tweaked document templates, my Favorites were right where I left them, and Outlook knew exactly where to find my data files. I often find myself cursing as I watch a progress bar tick away at 3 a.m. as I store my day's profile onto my notebook for safekeeping, but when I'm going the other way and fixing a disaster, that progress bar is a lovely sight indeed.

ZIPPING FILES

If you've been on the Internet for any length of time, you've run into zipped files (a.k.a. *filename*.zip). Zipping files is a way to combine multiple files and even a directory structure into one single file that is compressed. Zipped files make the transfer of data files and programs not just simpler, but faster, too. PKZip 2.04g was a command-line utility which was used to create zip files. As zipping became popular, many third-parties created utilities to perform zipping operations through GUI interfaces. My favorite utility of these is WinZip. But with Windows XP, I may never use it again.

Windows XP includes built-in zipping capabilities—viewing, creating, and extracting. Viewing zip files is easy. Windows XP treats .zip files as a compressed folder, no matter what utility was used to create them. They appear as folders with a zipper. You can view and access the contents just as if they were stored in any typical folder on the file system.

Zip files are created by issuing the New, Compressed (zipped) Folder command from either the File menu or the right-click menu in Windows Explorer or My Computer. After naming the folder (be sure to retain the .zip extension), you can drag and drop files or folder structures into it. Once your files are inside the "compressed folder", the .zip file can be manipulated like any other file, including attaching to e-mails or uploaded via FTP.

Extracting files from a .zip file via Windows XP is no different than moving or copying files from normal folders; just drag and drop. Or, while viewing the contents of a .zip file, issue the Extract command. This launches the Compressed (zipped) Folders Extraction Wizard, which walks you through the process of locating a destination for the contents and initiating the extraction.

It has taken a bit of getting used to. I'm so in the habit of viewing and extracting the contents of zip files through WinZip that I can't seem to remember that Windows XP will perform the tasks for me. I've had to uninstall WinZip, but now that it's gone I don't miss it.

THIRD-PARTY MANAGEMENT TOOLS

Table 29.2 provides a list of tools that you should not be without if you are serious about hard disk tweaking, backup, and recovery. By searching on the Web, you can find any of these programs easily because they are so popular.

TABLE 29.2 THIRD-PARTY TOOLS

Type of Program	Vendor	Product Name
Defragmentation Programs	Executive Software	Diskeeper
	Symantec	Norton Speed Disk
Undelete Programs	Executive Software	Undelete
	Symantec	Norton Utilities
Disk Management Tools	PowerQuest	Drive Image
	PowerQuest	Drive Copy
	PowerQuest	PartitionMagic
	V Communications	System Commander
	Symantec	Norton Ghost
Compression Programs	Nico Mak Computing	WinZip
	PKWare	PKZip
	Pacific Gold Coast Corp.	TurboZIP
	Info-Zip	Info-Zip

HARD DISK TROUBLESHOOTING

Eventually, if you work with computers long enough, you are going to face some form of hard disk problem. It's not a matter of *if*; it's a matter of *when*. The laws of statistics apply to everyone and everything—and that includes hard drives. In the following sections, when I speak of hard drive problems, I'm not referring to a software program that is acting petulantly or a DLL that has been overwritten by a poorly designed installation routine. I'm talking about the inability to access a critical file, a hard drive that will not boot, or one of those cryptic `Fatal Error - Cannot access hard disk` messages that cause the blood to drain from the face of even the hardiest administrator.

These sections are not meant to be comprehensive. Full books have been written on solving hardware problems, and thousands of individual chapters on hard drives and the multitude of problems they can exhibit. What these sections will do, however, is give you some tried-and-true directions to head in if your hard drive starts to give you grief.

Hard drive problems range from file system structures that have been twisted out of shape to catastrophic, dead-in-the-water hard drive failures. And as any seasoned administrator will tell you, the catastrophic failures are the easy ones to diagnose and fix. More often than not, the inconsistent "what the heck?" problems are the real "head-scratchers."

29

To keep it simple, let's begin with the most important factor in troubleshooting problems of all shapes and sizes—be it a car that will not start or a computer that will not boot. And that is . . .

TAKE THE MENTAL APPROACH FIRST

I come from a long line of tradesmen who made a living getting their hands dirty and solving mechanical problems. As a writer and computer consultant, I rarely get my hands dirty anymore, but I have discovered that the principles of problem-solving I learned when I was young are the same across all fields. You need to be methodical, and if you are going to make assumptions, they had better be good ones; otherwise, you just might steer yourself down the wrong garden path.

The very first step to take when you have a disk access problem is to stop, sit down, and think. Although this advice might seem obvious, it is seldom realized in practice. People experience what they conclude is a hard drive problem, open their case, and start ripping out components when, in fact, they have a file system problem that could have been easily resolved by running Error Checking on their drive. Similarly, others start reinstalling operating systems when the problem is not software at all, but a failing CMOS battery that is causing the motherboard to lose sight of the hard drive.

None of this exposition is meant to imply that I'm smarter or better at diagnosing problems than the next guy, and in the end, I might come to the same conclusion as the person who leapt in and started ripping his or her case apart. What separates us, in my humble opinion, is that the steps I use to solve a problem today will apply equally well to a completely different problem I encounter a week from now.

So, when you have a hard drive problem—or what you think is a hard drive problem—before you pick up a CD-ROM or a screwdriver, get yourself a cup of coffee, and take a few minutes to get a clear picture of the nature of the problem in front of you. The following are some questions you might want to ask yourself:

- When did the problem start?
- What was I doing when I first noticed the problem?
- Is the problem consistent? If so, how? If not, what is missing from the puzzle?

This last point bears some elaboration. Computers, as a whole, are extraordinarily consistent devices. Input goes in here; output comes out over there. In the case of hard drives, you lay out structures on them, and the operating system uses these structures to tell programs where their data is located. When you have inconsistencies, one of two forces is at work:

- You're not seeing or you're overlooking something.
- You could have more than one problem on your hands.

The key of this forced reflection is to have a "plan" before you react. And the cornerstone of that plan must be to do no further harm and to figure out what the problem is without complicating matters further.

So, the next highly recommended tools to pick up, after you've pondered and had a cup of coffee, are a notepad and a pencil. Begin by jotting down some notes on what happened, what you think the problem is, and what might be a good course of action to solve that problem. Use your notepad to reason out the problem; more often than not, eliminating a piece of flawed logic with an eraser is easier than restoring all the programs to your hard drive.

PROBLEMS AND SOLUTIONS

Hard drive problems fall into two general categories:

- Hardware
- File structure

Hardware-related problems involve the hard drive itself, cabling, power, connections, and the motherboard.

File structure problems involve the tracks and partitions on the hard disk, the boot records, and the files the operating system uses to initialize itself.

If you power up your computer, and the BIOS cannot find the attached hard drive, chances are you have a hardware problem. On the other hand, if the BIOS finds and recognizes your hard drive but fails to boot, you likely have a file structure problem. Note the *chances are* and *likely* qualifiers. As you read through the following scenarios, bear in mind the complications that can be brought on by compounded problems. In other words, file structure problems and hardware problems can, at times, overlap. For example, a damaged master boot record (MBR) may be the result of a failing hard drive; repairing the MBR might fix a consequence of the problem but not the problem itself.

SCSI Disk Boot Problems

A boot problem can sometimes be caused by SCSI settings that have changed since you installed Windows XP. The state of the SCSI BIOS at the time you installed Windows XP becomes part of the setup of the operating system and is stored in the BOOT.INI file. If you subsequently make a change in the SCSI BIOS after NT is installed, that alone can contradict the stored BOOT.INI file settings and can prevent the operating system from finding the system files and booting up. Don't change the SCSI BIOS settings after you install Windows XP, or if you do, you should edit BOOT.INI in a text editor (carefully!) to reflect the changes. The BOOT.INI file uses the following syntax:

```
scsi(A)disk(B)rdiskpartition\<winnt_dir>
```

Here are the specifics for the parameters in the ARC path when you use the `scsi()` syntax on an X86 computer:

- A is the ordinal number for the adapter linked to the Ntbootdd.sys driver.
- B is the SCSI ID for the target disk.
- C is always 0 when SCSI drives are used.
- D is the partition.

When an IDE ATA drive is in use, this line will have multi(A) as its front item. Then, B remains 0 and C indicates the drive used.

Take note that A, B, and C are all ordinal numbers; that means you should start counting with zero. So, the second drive is 1, the third is 2, and so on. But, D is a cardinal number, so the first partition is 1, the second is 2, and so on.

29

SYSTEM STARTS BUT CANNOT FIND THE HARD DRIVE

If the computer fires up (the BIOS information appears and the floppy drive is accessed but nothing more), you have some sleuthing to do. Just follow these steps:

1. Turn off the computer, open it, and check the cables. Are the power and data cables attached to the drive? Is the wide, flat data cable flipped over backward on end? Check to see that pin #1 on the motherboard connects to pin #1 on the drive.

2. Check the settings on the drive to make sure they are correct. If you have a SCSI drive, check the ID number and termination as per the instruction manual for the drive. If you have an IDE drive, check the master/slave settings and channel assignment. If you have two devices on the same IDE channel, both set to master or both set to slave, there will be a conflict. You can have only one master and one slave per IDE channel. You typically change the setting by using a little jumper on the back of the hard drive next to the data and power connectors (ditto for IDE-based CD-ROM drives).

3. Check the BIOS settings by pressing the appropriate key during POST (Power-On Self Test) and having the computer autodetect the drive type. Make sure the drive is listed and/or recognized.

TIP FROM

Bob

& Brian

> Most modern PCs and BIOSes autodetect the hard drive that's connected to the data cable after the drive gets power. You no longer have to enter all the explicit information about the drive, such as number of heads, sectors, the landing zone, and so on. Just set the BIOS to Autodetect.

HARD DRIVE INITIALIZES BUT WILL NOT BOOT

Windows XP offers several features that allow you to repair a system that will not start or will not load Windows XP. These features are useful if some of your system files become corrupted or are accidentally erased, or if you have installed software or device drivers that cause your system to not work properly. However, these features are used more to restore a system with a damaged Registry or destroyed system files rather than hard drive–specific problems. If you've already tried the actions listed in this section to no avail, flip over to Chapter 33, for details on numerous other recovery techniques that may be of benefit to you. Be sure to check out Safe Mode, Recovery Console, and parallel installations.

TIPS FROM THE WINDOWS PROS: QUIETING A NOISY SYSTEM

Hard drives vary in the noise output they produce. Sometimes the stepper motors are annoyingly loud. Other drives have loud spindle motors. When a drive is coupled to the body of the computer housing, motor noises can be effectively amplified, increasing the aggravation you experience using a system. If your computer sounds like a garbage disposal from time to time, chances are good that the stepper is not a quiet one, and as the head dances around on the platters, the drive shakes just enough to get the computer chassis rattling a bit, too. It's a bit like the relationship between the strings and the body of a violin.

Spindle motors (the motor that turns the platters at high speed) often start out life quietly, only to get noisy over time as the bearings wear in (or out). This noise is particularly annoying in laptop computers if you happen to use them in a quiet place, such as a library or in a home office. I actually replaced my 8GB IBM 3.5-inch drive once this year (Dell laptop, free of charge thanks to Dell), only to find that within a few months it developed the same annoying whine again, so I gave up and accepted it.

Some environments, such as recording studios, require that a computer be seen and not heard. For desktop systems, there are a couple solutions. One is to get some long wires for the keyboard monitor, pointing device, and so on, and relegate the computer to a closet. A more practical approach is to buy an after-market kit that quiets your PC's power supply and hard disk. Check the Web for information about such kits, such as at www.quietpc.com.

The bottom line here is to check out the specs on drive noise, if you care about that. Or you can listen for a quiet computer, find out what kind of drive it has, and then order that brand and model the next time you're shopping.

In the case of serious noise (you turn on the computer, and it really does sound like a garbage disposal), well, you're in trouble. This noise is a sign of your hard disk after crashing (the heads are actually rubbing on the surface of the platters) or in the process of crashing. Get out while the getting is good. Back up your data and/or whole drive, and replace it as soon as possible. Then restore the data.

In some cases, the noise you hear is not from your hard drive, but from the fans on the case or the power supply. These plastic fan blades collect dust. The dustier your environment and the higher your average humidity, the faster these fans become caked with crud. In many cases you can use a can of compressed air to clean off the fans. But when that doesn't work, you can attempt to remove the fan's protective screen and wipe the blades clean with a slightly moist paper towel. *DON'T* spray or drip any liquids into the system.

If you find that you are cleaning off your fan every month or so, you should consider getting a room filter to clean your air or attach part of an A/C filter over the air intake holes on your system. Just be sure that the airflow is not restricted or you'll end up overheating the system. Keep in mind your CPU and hard drives are air cooled; that's why there are fans in the case. If you restrict the airflow too much, the heat will build up and cause problems. If you hear a beeping sound much like that of European police cars, that's the warning sign that the CPU is too hot.

INSTALLING AND REPLACING HARDWARE

In this chapter

30

UPGRADING YOUR HARDWARE

No matter how high the performance of your office computer, sooner or later it will start to slow down as newer programs demanding faster and faster hardware show up on your desktop. And, chances are you'll run out of performance before your company's computer replacement time has come. This chapter will help you make the hardware changes—large or small—you need to get the most work and useful life out of your computer. We'll discuss how to upgrade and install hardware, how to add a second monitor, how to connect new and old hard drives, and how to add memory.

The single most helpful thing you can do to make your Windows XP computer run at peak speed is give it enough system memory (or *RAM*, short for Random Access Memory). Just as a reminder, there are two types of memory in your computer: hard disk space and RAM. RAM is used to hold Windows and the programs you're actually using, and Windows XP wants *lots* more than any previous version of Windows. As we discussed in the early chapters of this book, XP can run with as little as 64MB of RAM, but it will run *very* slowly and you'll find the experience unpleasant. Memory is very inexpensive these days, and boosting your RAM up to at least 256 MB will make a huge difference. I'll discuss adding RAM later in this chapter.

Now, if you're already running Windows XP Professional on a full-bore, state-of-the-art system such as a 2 Gigahertz-plus Pentium 4 or 1GHz-plus AMD Athlon system, and your computer has a fast video accelerator and lots of memory, you don't have much more to do in the way of actual hardware optimizing. You might just adjust the pagefile sizes, or convert as many partitions to NTFS as you can. Some of the settings you can make are discussed in Chapter 24, "Configuration via Control Panel Applets," and Chapter 25, "Maintaining and Optimizing System Performance," and the remainder are discussed in Chapter 27, "System Utilities."

By the same token, if you're doing common, everyday tasks such as word processing, and you're already satisfied with the performance of your computer as a whole, you probably don't need to worry about performance boosters anyway. Your system is probably running just fine, and the time you'd spend trying to fine-tune it might be better spent doing whatever it is you use your computer for (like earning a living).

If you're anywhere between these two extremes, however, you may want to look at the tune-ups and hardware upgrades we'll discuss in this chapter.

TIP FROM

Bob & Brian

> This chapter just scratches the surface of the ins and outs of hardware installation and updates. If you want all the details, and I mean *all* the details, you should get a copy of the best-selling book *Upgrading and Repairing PC's, 13th Edition*, by Scott Mueller, published by Que.

BIOS SETTINGS

Windows XP depends upon proper BIOS settings to enable it to detect and use hardware correctly. At a minimum, your drives should be properly configured in the system BIOS, and your CPU type and speed should be properly set (either in the BIOS or on the motherboard, depending upon the system). Windows XP boots much faster than other recent flavors of Windows, but you can improve boot speed even more with these tips:

- Set up your BIOS boot order to start with drive C: so that you can skip the floppy stepper motor test.
- Disable the floppy drive seek.
- Enable BIOS and video shadowing.

 If, after tinkering with your BIOS settings, you find that your computer will no longer boot up, see "Altered BIOS Settings Prevent Computer from Booting" in the "Troubleshooting" section at the end of this chapter. Remember, too, that if you're looking at BIOS settings, most systems give you the option of exiting the BIOS without saving the settings. If you think you made a mistake, exit without saving and try again.

UPGRADING YOUR HARD DISK

One of the most effective improvements you can make to a system is to get a faster or larger hard drive, or add another drive. SCSI hard disks used to seriously one-up IDE drives, but the new breed of Ultra DMA EIDE drives (which I call Old MacDonald Disks—EIEIO!) are quite speedy and a whole lot cheaper than SCSI. An EIDE bus supports four drives (two each on the primary and secondary channels) and is almost always built in to your motherboard. Adding a CD-ROM (or CD-RW or DVD-ROM) drive claims one, leaving you with a maximum of three EIDE hard drives unless you install a separate add-on EIDE host adapter or have a motherboard with RAID support.

TIP FROM

> Many recent motherboards feature on-board IDE RAID, which can perform either mirroring (which makes an immediate backup copy of one drive to another) or striping (which treats both drives as part of a single drive for speed). While the RAID features on these motherboards don't support RAID 5, the safest (and most expensive!) form of RAID, they work well and are much less expensive than any SCSI form of RAID. Just remember that mirroring gives you extra reliability at the expense of speed, because everything has to be written twice, and striping with only two disks gives you extra speed at the expense of reliability–if one hard disk fails you lose everything.

The following are some essential considerations for upgrading your hard disk system:

- Don't put a hard drive and a CD-ROM drive on the same channel unless necessary (put the hard drive on the primary IDE1 channel and the CD-ROM on the secondary IDE2 channel). On some computers, the IDE channel negotiates down to the slowest device on a channel, slowing down the hard disk's effective transfer rate. Make sure the hard drive containing Windows is designated as the Primary Master drive.

- Defragment the hard disk with the Defragmenter utility, which you can reach through Start, Control Panel, Performance and Maintenance, Rearrange Items on your Hard Disk. Do this every week, and the process will take just a few minutes. But, if you wait months before you try this the first time, be prepared to wait a long time for your system to finish.

- Upgrade the disk controller (more properly called a *host adapter*). If you're using an Ultra Wide SCSI or later hard disk, for example, make sure you have a controller that takes maximum advantage of it. If you're using IDE, your host adapter is most likely built in to the motherboard on any Pentium-class or better system. If your drives support UDMA/33 (Ultra DMA) or faster UDMA modes but your motherboard supports only the slower PIO modes, install a replacement UDMA host adapter or upgrade your motherboard. Most modern motherboards, I should point out, do support UDMA, so you're probably okay on this score.

- Get a faster disk drive: UDMA/33 or faster for IDE; Ultra2Wide or faster for SCSI (but remember, you need to match the drive to the SCSI host adapter you have or plan to buy). 7,200RPM IDE drives are now common, and the faster spin rate compared to the previous 5,400RPM standard makes most of them transfer data a bit quicker than their slower siblings.

ADDING RAM

Perhaps the most cost-effective upgrade you can make to any Windows-based system is to add RAM. If your disk is heavily thrashing each time you switch between running applications or documents, you probably need RAM. While Microsoft says Windows XP can run with as little as 64MB of RAM, we've found that it only really runs at full speed with 128MB, and 256MB is even better.

Windows automatically recognizes newly added RAM and adapts internal settings, such as when to swap to disk, to take best advantage of any RAM you throw its way. Upgrade beyond 128MB of RAM if you can afford it, especially if your system uses the economical SDRAM or DDR SDRAM DIMM modules. Memory prices fluctuate constantly, but these days 256MB memory modules are selling for about $40. This is a very cost-effective upgrade indeed.

TIP FROM

Bob & Brian

> If you run very disk and memory-intensive applications such as high-resolution scanning, image processing, video editing, or databases, consider adding memory beyond 128MB. Windows XP isn't crippled by the 512MB limit found in Windows 9x and Me, and many systems on the market today can use as much as 1.5GB of RAM. Although, depending on how you use your system, more than 256MB–512MB of RAM may be overkill.

ADDING HARDWARE

One of the tasks that is most common for anyone responsible for configuring and maintaining PCs is adding and removing hardware. The Control Panel contains an applet designed for that purpose; it's called the Add Hardware applet. You can use it in cases in which the operating system doesn't automatically recognize that you've swiped something or added something new, whether it's a peripheral such as a printer or an internal device such as a DVD-ROM, additional hard disk, or whatever.

If you're a hardware maven, you'll be visiting this applet a lot, especially if you're working with non–Plug and Play hardware. Plug and Play hardware installation is pretty much a no-brainer because Windows XP Professional is good at detection and should install items fairly automatically, along with any necessary device drivers that tell Windows how to access the new hardware.

TIP FROM

Bob & Brian

> You use the System applet or the Computer Management "Device Manager" Console, not Add Hardware, for fine-tuning device settings, such as IRQ and port, updating devices and drivers, and removing hardware. You use Add Hardware only for adding or troubleshooting hardware.
>
> A quick way to get to either utility is to click Start, and right-click My Computer. Select Properties, and then select the Hardware tab. From there you can open the Device Manager.

If you've purchased a board or other hardware add-in, you should first read the supplied manual for details about installation procedures. Installation tips and an install program may be supplied with the hardware. However, if no instructions are included, you can physically install the hardware and keep reading. You should close any programs you have running, just in case the installation process hangs the computer. The computer doesn't hang very often in NT-based Windows, such as Windows XP Professional , but it can. Save your work, and close your applications before you plug in the new device.

For non-Plug and Play hardware, or for Plug and Play stuff that isn't detected or doesn't install automatically for some reason, you need to run the Add Hardware applet. The wizard starts by searching for new Plug and Play hardware. If nothing is found, Windows asks whether the device is installed already. If you select "Yes, I have already connected the hardware," Windows assumes you're having some trouble with a device or need to install it manually (see Figure 30.1). Your currently installed devices are listed with an option to troubleshoot or to add something new. For veterans, the combination option of adding new hardware or troubleshooting installed hardware seems a bit weird until you get used to it. I guess Microsoft wanted the wizard to perform double-duty. If you select "No, I have not added the hardware yet," the wizard closes.

30

30

Figure 30.1
When a new Plug and Play device isn't found, you see this dialog box. Scroll down and choose Add a New Hardware Device.

Next, you're asked whether you want the wizard to attempt to detect and install the hardware automatically or specify the item yourself. (Legacy hardware interrogation is a science all its own, and I'm always amazed when some old job like an ISA sound card is detected properly.) If you select Search, you'll see a "gas gauge" apprising you of the progress for each category and the overall progress, and you'll hear lots of hard disk activity.

If a new device is found that doesn't require any user configuration, a help balloon appears onscreen near the system tray, supplying the details of what was located (see Figure 30.2). Windows displays the device at the end of the search process.

Figure 30.2
During the search process, any new hardware located is displayed near the system tray/clock.

In case the item isn't detected properly, click Next and a list of common hardware types is displayed (Figure 30.3). If you don't see a category that matches your hardware, select Show All Devices. Just choose the applicable category, and click Next.

Figure 30.3
Common hardware types are listed in alphabetical order. Select the type, or Show All Devices to install your device manually.

Be sure you choose the precise brand name and model number/name of the item you're installing. You might be prompted to insert your Windows XP CD-ROM so that the appropriate driver file(s) can be loaded. If your hardware came with a driver disk, use the Have Disk button to directly install the driver from the manufacturer's driver disk or downloaded file.

Early in the wizard's steps, you have the option of specifying the hardware yourself and skipping the legacy scan. Choosing this option can save you time and, in some cases, is the surer path to installing new hardware. It also lets you physically install the hardware later, should you want to. The wizard doesn't bother to authenticate the existence of the hardware; it simply installs the new driver.

If the device plugs into an external serial, parallel, or SCSI port, you might want to connect it, turn it on, and restart your system to install it. Some of these devices can't be installed via the Add Hardware Wizard if they're not present when the system is started.

TIP FROM

Bob
& Brian

> In some cases, you are given the option of adjusting settings after the hardware is installed and possibly adjusting your hardware to match. (Some legacy cards have switches or software adjustments that can be made to them to control the I/O port, DMA address, and so forth.) You may be told which settings to use to avoid conflicts with other hardware in the system.
>
> If, for some reason, you don't want to use the settings that the wizard suggests, you can use your own settings and manually configure them. You can do so from the Add Hardware Wizard or via the Device Manager (from the System applet). See "The Device Manager" later in this chapter.

CAUTION

> In general, be cautious about configuring resource settings manually. When you change settings manually, the settings become fixed, and Windows XP's built-in device contention resolution is less likely to work. Also, if you install too many devices with manually configured settings, you might not be able to install new Plug and Play devices because none will be available. In the worst-case scenario, the system might not even boot if conflicts occur with primary hardware devices such as hard disk controllers or video cards. If you decide to use manual configuration, make sure you know what you're doing, and have the specs for the hardware in question at hand.

In cases in which the wizard detects a conflict, you are alerted when you finish walking through the wizard steps. You then have the option of bailing out or continuing despite the conflict. You can also back up and choose a different model of hardware, such as one you think is compatible with what you're attempting to install. Figure 30.4 shows a typical message when a conflict is detected.

30

Figure 30.4
When a hardware conflict is detected, it's reported by the wizard at the end of the installation process.

You now have the choice of setting the hardware resources for this device manually. Click View or change resources for this hardware (Advanced) to change the settings. On the next screen, click Set Configuration Manually. You'll see something similar to the dialog box in Figure 30.5, displaying the conflicting setting and the other device that uses the same setting.

Figure 30.5
Use caution when manually changing resources for a device. You may end up choosing an unavailable resource. In this dialog box, the I/O range is not available because of a conflict with another COM port.

Click Change Setting to change the settings; if the system displays an error message, use the Setting Based On scroll box to try a different Basic configuration, or change the manual settings you made to alternative values. Keep trying configurations until the conflicting device listing is clear. Then, click OK and restart your computer if prompted.

If you're unable to select a non-conflicting setting with the device you're installing, change the settings for the conflicting device with the Device Manager as discussed later in this chapter. In some cases, particularly with ISA cards, you may not be able to resolve a conflict and will need to remove one of the cards or disable the conflicting device on one of the cards with the Device Manager. PCI and AGP cards can share IRQ settings and fully support Windows XP's Plug and Play feature, making them a much better choice for installation in today's crowded systems.

PROVIDING DRIVERS FOR HARDWARE NOT IN THE LIST

When the hardware you're attempting to install isn't on the device list, the problem is one of the following:

- The hardware is newer than Windows XP
- The hardware is really old and Microsoft decided not to include support for it
- The hardware must be configured with a special setup program, as with some removable-media drives such as the Iomega Zip drive

In these cases, you need to obtain the driver from the manufacturer (or Microsoft; check Web sites) and get it ready on floppy disk, CD-ROM, or on the hard disk (either locally or across an available network). If the manufacturer supplies a setup disk, forget my advice, and follow the manufacturer's instructions. However, if the manufacturer supplies a driver disk and no instructions, follow along with these steps:

1. Run the Add Hardware applet and click Next.
2. Select Yes, I Have Already Connected the Hardware, and click Next.
3. Scroll to the bottom of the list and select Add a New Hardware Device. Click Next.
4. Select Install the Hardware that I Manually Select From a List and click Next.
5. Select the appropriate device category and click Next.
6. Click the Have Disk button. Enter the location of the driver (you can enter any path, such as a directory on the hard disk or network path). Typically, you insert a disk in your floppy or CD-ROM drive. If you downloaded the driver software from a Web site, locate it on your hard drive. In either case you can use the Browse button if you don't know the exact path or drive. If you do use the Browse option, look for a directory where an .INF file appears in the dialog box.
7. Assuming the wizard finds a suitable driver file, choose the correct hardware item from the resulting dialog box, and follow the onscreen directions.

TIP FROM

Bob

& Brian

> If you're not sure which ports and interrupts your other boards are using, you can use the Device Manager to locate available and used IRQs, ports, DMA, and so on.

⚠ *If you've added some hardware and it doesn't work, see "New Hardware Doesn't Work" in the "Troubleshooting" section at the end of this chapter.*

REMOVING HARDWARE

One major change from Windows 2000 to Windows XP is that the Add Hardware wizard in Windows XP doesn't double as the Remove Hardware wizard, as the Add/Remove Hardware wizard in Windows 2000 did. To remove hardware, you need to use the Device Manager portion of the System applet.

→ For details about the Device Manager, **see** "The Device Manager," **p. 1055**.

TIP FROM

Bob & Brian

> You can stop PC Cards (PCMCIA cards) by clicking the PC Card icon in the system tray, which has the same effect as disabling the item from this applet. You can remove the PC Card after you stop it.

USING THE SYSTEM APPLET

One of the tools you're more than likely to rely on frequently for management of the computer's hardware is the Control Panel's System applet. Although there are a few others we'll mention here and in other chapters, the System applet's Hardware tab is most likely to be of use to you when managing hardware. To open the System applet, click Start, right-click the My Computer icon and choose Properties. You can also choose the Performance and Maintenance option in the Control Panel and click the System button.

The General tab tells you what operating system you're running, the registered user's name, the type and speed of the processor, and the amount of RAM. Checking this tab is a relatively quick way to find out the amount of RAM Windows is detecting—which is particularly useful if you've just added some and you're wondering whether you installed it correctly. Also, if you're considering adding more RAM and don't recall how well the computer is currently endowed this is the place to look.

TIP FROM

Bob & Brian

> The addition of processor speed to Windows XP's General tab is a long-needed improvement to Windows. However, if you need more detailed technical information (such as the exact type of memory modules your system is using, the amount of RAM on your video card, and so forth), the best hardware reporting utility we know of is SiSoftware's Sandra. The Professional version with all the bells and whistles plus free updates is just $29. Get more than a taste of Sandra's power with the free Standard version, available from the SiSoftware Web site at
>
> www.sisoftware.demon.co.uk/sandra/

The other tabs and settings in this applet deal more with network and system repair issues and are discussed in other chapters. So, let's start with the Hardware tab. Figure 30.6 shows the Hardware tab of the Control Panel's System applet.

Figure 30.6
The Hardware tab of the System applet is a control center for examining and modifying hardware.

The Hardware tab's first option is the Add Hardware Wizard button. This button runs the same Add Hardware Wizard covered earlier in this chapter.

TIP FROM

Bob & Brian

> You must be logged on as an administrator or a member of the Administrators group to make alterations to the hardware devices, driver signing settings, and drivers. If your computer is connected to a network, network policy settings may also prevent you from completing this procedure.

When your hardware is installed, the other buttons on the Hardware tab (Driver Signing, Device Manager, and Hardware Profiles) are used to manage hardware and resolve problems.

The two buttons we're going to focus in the next two section are the Driver Signing and Device Manager buttons. The fact that these two buttons are grouped together on the Hardware tab is no accident. Drivers make hardware work with Windows, and Microsoft has gone to great lengths to make sure that Windows XP Professional users have reliable drivers for their hardware.

While you work with hardware and its drivers through the Device Manager, how well your hardware works with Windows depends on the settings in Driver Signing.

DRIVER SIGNING

If you go to the hardware manufacturer's Web site for drivers, you might see both signed and unsigned drivers. If you want to block the use of any unsigned drivers, or turn off the warning that an attempt to install unsigned drivers will display, click the Driver Signing button and select the option you want to use.

30

The first button in this section, Driver Signing, a safety feature first developed by Microsoft for Windows 2000 and Windows Me, helps prevent bogus files and drivers from invading your operating system and potentially crashing it. Signed drivers are drivers which have passed testing standards established by the Windows Hardware Quality Labs (WHQL), and are the preferred drivers for use with Windows XP. All drivers supplied on the Windows XP CD-ROM and provided through Windows Update bear a digital signature indicating they've passed WHQL testing.

You or your administrator can configure three levels of protection on a computer. Clicking the Driver Signing button brings up a dialog for doing just that, as shown in Figure 30.7.

Figure 30.7
Setting the digital signature protection level for a machine can protect against the addition of bogus drivers and system files.

Based on the settings you choose, Windows XP either ignores device drivers that have no signature, warns you when it detects device drivers that are not digitally signed (the default), or prevents you from installing device drivers without digital signatures. Table 30.1 lists the options.

TABLE 30.1   CODE SIGNING OPTIONS

Setting	Meaning
Ignore	Any and all device drivers will be installed, without checking for a valid digital signature.
Warn	If you try to install a driver that doesn't have a valid signature, you'll be alerted with a dialog box (see Figure 30.8) during the installation process. You can then cancel or continue.
Block	Drivers are always checked for signature. If one valid signature is missing, the installation process stops dead in its tracks.
Apply Setting as System Default	Only if you're logged in as a member of the Administrator group can you alter this setting, because it affects all users. When it is set on, it applies the settings above to all users who log on.

→ An additional tool for verifying the signature of files, including all the system files, is called the File Signature Verification tool (sigverif). To learn more about it, **see** "Running the File Signature Verification Tool," **p. 941**.

You can use non-signed (non-WHQL approved) drivers with Windows XP, but the default Driver Signing setting listed in Table 30.1 will warn you if you do; see Figure 30.8 for a typical warning. Generally, you should use signed drivers for your hardware; use unsigned drivers only if signed drivers are unavailable or you need to fix an urgent hardware problem with a driver that hasn't had time to go through WHQL testing.

Figure 30.8
Windows XP's warning when you attempt to install an unsigned driver.

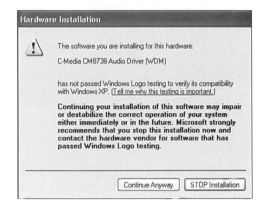

Leaving the default Warn setting for signature verification is probably the wisest choice for general usage. You should instruct users of the computer to check with you or the administrator if a warning pops up during installation of a program. Then a decision can be made on an ad hoc basis. Using the highest level of protection can be annoying because an installation will simply terminate mysteriously if the signature isn't found. Of course, in certain mission-critical settings, that result may be just what you want.

THE DEVICE MANAGER

The Device Manager provides a one-stop solution for checking device settings, reinstalling and updating drivers for existing drivers, and removing devices.

You can get to the Device Manager in two main ways:

■ Choose Start, Control Panel, Printers and Other Hardware, System, Hardware, Device Manager.

■ Choose Start, Control Panel, Performance and Maintenance, Administrative Tools, and then double-click Computer Management. Open the System Tools branch, and then click Device Manager. While more tedious to get to, you do get quicker access to the other administrative tools from this view (see Figure 30.9).

Figure 30.9
The Device Manager
through the eyes of
the Computer
Management Console.

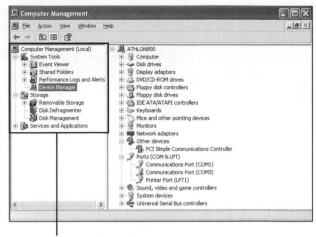

When you choose Device Manager from
the Hardware tab of the System applet,
you don't see this list of other administrative tools.

By default, the Device Manager displays Devices by Type, as seen in Figure 30.9. Click View
to change to different views such as View Devices by Connection, by Resources (IRQ, I/O
Port address, DMA channels, and memory addresses) by Type, Resources by Connection,
and to view Hidden devices.

In the Device Manager listing, you can click a + (plus) sign to expand a device category to
investigate the installed components in the category. Note that problematic items are
marked with a yellow exclamation mark. You can check on any item's status by right-clicking
it and choosing Properties.

Choosing this option opens a Properties dialog box, like the one shown in Figure 30.10. You
can do some serious device tweaking from this dialog box.

Figure 30.10
A Properties dialog
box for a malfunction-
ing hardware device
(left) and for a nor-
mally functioning
device (right).

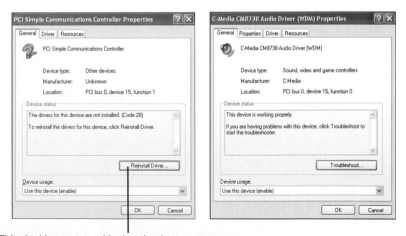

This doubles as a troubleshooting button as necessary.

Choices on the dialog box vary from device to device, but almost all devices use the General, Driver, and Resources tabs as shown in Figure 30.10. The most important items are discussed in Table30.2.

TABLE 30.2 PROPERTIES DIALOG BOX TABS

Tab	Options and Notes
General	Device Status: Displays whether the device is reported as working properly or indicates device problems. Troubleshoot: If the device is not working, you can click the troubleshooter to walk through a wizard. The drivers for the device must already be installed for this button to appear. Reinstall Driver: Click this button to reinstall the driver for the device; not shown if the device is working properly. Device Usage: You can check the hardware configurations that are available on your computer. You also can disable a device in a hardware configuration by selecting Disable from this scroll box.
Settings	The options on this tab vary with the device.
Driver	Driver Details: This section of the Driver tab displays the author of the driver, version, and location on the hard disk. It's worth checking. Most of the drivers will be from Microsoft, unless you installed one from another manufacturer. Update Driver: This button runs the Upgrade Device Driver Wizard, which walks you through the process of adding a driver. Refer to the "Adding and Removing Hardware" section earlier in the chapter if you have questions about the process of changing a driver. Roll Back Driver: Restores the previously installed driver. Very useful if a new driver causes the system to fail. Uninstall: You can use this tab to remove the device drivers for this device. Removing the drivers effectively kills the device. You might have to reboot afterward, but in many cases, it's not required. You can add the device manually later if you change your mind. Sometimes removing and reinstalling a device can clear up problems you were having with it.
Resources	Set Configuration Manually: If you suspect that the device is conflicting with other devices and this is why it's not working, you may be allowed to configure it manually.

30

In the following sections we'll take a closer look at some of the functions found on the various tabs described in the preceding table.

USING THE TROUBLESHOOTER

The Windows XP troubleshooters have been mentioned several times in this book, beginning in Chapter 1, "Introducing Windows XP Professional." The hardware-related troubleshooters included with Windows XP Professional include

- Games and Multimedia Troubleshooter
- Display Troubleshooter
- Sound Troubleshooter
- DVD Troubleshooter
- Internet Connection Sharing Troubleshooter
- Modem Troubleshooter
- Home and Small Office Network Troubleshooter
- Hardware Troubleshooter
- Input Device Troubleshooter (keyboard, mouse, camera, scanner)
- Drives and Network Adapters Troubleshooter
- USB Troubleshooter
- Printing Troubleshooter

Although these troubleshooters won't always solve your problems, they'll at least walk you through a logical train of investigation for your malady, possibly leading you to a conclusion or avenue of thought you hadn't previously tried.

You can start troubleshooters from various points within Windows, such as Display properties and Device Manager, but you can access most of them through the Help and Support Center:

1. Choose Start, Help and Support.
2. Type List of Troubleshooters into the search box and click the arrow to start the search.
3. You then see a list of troubleshooter wizards similar to the list above.
4. Run the troubleshooter that applies. You may be asked some questions that require running the Device Manager to determine the status of your hardware.

TIP FROM

Bob & Brian

If a USB controller doesn't install properly, especially if the controller doesn't show up in the Device Manager, the problem might be in your system BIOS. Most BIOSes have a setting that can enable or disable the USB ports. Shut down and restart. Do whatever your computer requires for you to check the BIOS settings during system startup (usually hitting the Del or Esc keys on the initial boot screen). Then enter the BIOS setup and enable USB support.

When that is done, if the USB controller still doesn't appear in the Device Manager, it's possible that the computer's BIOS might be outdated. Check with the computer's or motherboard's manufacturer for a possible update to support USB under Windows XP Professional Edition.

Note that you can attempt to troubleshoot a specific installed device by running the Add Hardware applet from the Control Panel and highlighting the afflicted item. Also, the properties sheet for some devices offers a troubleshooter as well.

UPDATING DEVICE DRIVERS

At some point, you'll need to get the latest driver for a device. Before you download and install the new driver, use this checklist:

1. Do you have permission to upgrade drivers? You need to be logged in as Administrator.
2. Is it really the latest driver? Check the manufacturer's site and the Microsoft site to see what you can find. The following sites are good places to start:

   www.microsoft.com/hcl

   www.windrivers.com

NOTE

> You might want to try running Start, All Programs, Windows Update, choosing Product Updates, and then choosing Device Drivers. Microsoft may have listed updated device drivers for your system.

3. Does the "new" driver work with Windows XP? In a pinch, you might be able to use Windows 2000 drivers for some types of devices.

After you've downloaded the new driver, open the Device Manager using either of the methods described earlier in the section "The Device Manager." You can install your new driver using these steps:

1. Open the Device Manager (if you're using the Computer Management approach, choose Device Manager in the left pane).
2. Click the device in question, and open its Properties dialog box.
3. In the Properties dialog box, select the Driver tab, and click Details if you want to see what version of the driver you are currently using, or just click Update Driver to proceed with updating the driver.
4. When the Update Wizard starts running, select Install From a List and click Next.
5. On the second page, choose the second option, Don't Search, and click Next.
6. Click Have Disk. Browse to the location of the driver. If the driver isn't found on the disk, you might have a problem. The .INF file on the disk and the accompanying driver files must meet the requirements of Windows XP to be deemed acceptable for installation. Return to the manufacturer's Web site and look for another driver.

30

> Downloadable drivers are usually stored in compressed form on the manufacturer's Web site. If the file is an .EXE (executable) file, you will need to open it in Windows Explorer before you can use its contents; opening it might also install the driver for you. If the driver is in a .ZIP archive file, you will need to uncompress it. Fortunately, Windows Explorer in Windows XP Professional can uncompress .ZIP files for you. You won't need to download a separate unzipping utility.

DEVICE DRIVER ROLLBACK

Device driver rollback allows you to "roll back the clock" and use the previous driver you installed for a device if the newly installed driver doesn't work. When Windows XP installs a new driver for a device, it backs up the old driver, rather than simply replacing it as with previous versions of Windows.

To start the process, click the Roll Back Driver button on the Driver tab discussed in the previous section. If there are no previous driver versions, you are given the opportunity to run the Troubleshooter instead to help solve problems with your device.

If a previous driver version is available, click Yes to roll back to that driver. The Driver display changes to show the driver release date and information for the previous driver. Restart the computer if prompted.

THE RESOURCES TAB

If you decide to change the resources for a device using the Resource tab that appears when you view a device's properties in Device Manager, be cautious. Manually setting a device's resource assignment can result in conflicts with other installed devices, and doing so imposes restrictions on the Plug and Play system's capability to dynamically allocate resources in the future.

To reassign a resource, click the resource in question on the Resources tab, and choose Change Setting. In an attempt to prevent folks from inadvertently doing damage, the manual resource assignment dialog box keeps an eye on what you're doing. If you attempt to reassign to a resource that is already in use, you'll be warned about the conflict as you saw in Figure 30.5, earlier in this chapter.

Some drivers don't have resources that can be reassigned. Others have an option button called Reinstall Driver that's useful if the system thinks that would solve a nonfunctioning-device problem. Most PCI cards don't permit their resources to be reassigned, because they obtain their resource settings from Windows or from the system BIOS. Some systems allocate resources depending upon which slot you use for a particular card.

CAUTION

> Notice the Setting Based On drop-down list on the Resources tab. It lists the hardware configurations in which the currently selected device is enabled. If you choose a hardware configuration other than the default, and you change any resource settings, resource conflicts may occur when you use the default hardware configuration. Resource conflicts can disable your hardware and cause your computer to malfunction or to be inoperable.
>
> If you have multiple hardware configurations (see later in this chapter), the moral of the story is to try to keep the same configurations for hardware between them. It's okay to totally *turn off* specific pieces of hardware for a given saved hardware configuration, but when you start changing the resource allocations for each one, you could end up with a mess.

UNDERSTANDING AND RESOLVING HARDWARE CONFLICTS

Windows, together with its Plug and Play technology, has grown far better at detecting and preventing hardware conflicts over the past few years. Still, system conflicts do arise, especially when you're using ISA cards and other legacy hardware. More often than not, configuration and installation problems are due to incorrect settings on an ISA network, I/O, sound, modem, and SCSI cards. The result is cards that conflict with one another for the same IRQ (interrupt request line), base I/O port address, DMA, or base memory address. Usually, these settings are made by changing jumpers or DIP switches on the board.

NOTE

> Some legacy cards can be configured via software settings rather than DIP switches and jumpers. For example, 3Com's popular 3C509B Ethernet adapter card uses its own utility program to set the IRQ and port address. You might have to run such a configuration program (typically using a DOS command prompt) to set up the card before it will run correctly under Windows XP.
>
> Some ISA cards can also be switched into a true Plug-and-Play mode by flipping a switch or moving a jumper block on the actual card or running a software configuration program.

As I mentioned earlier, you can force Windows XP to use manually selected system resources, such as IRQ, for a given piece of gear. In the Device Manager, choose the item, open its Properties dialog box, click the Resources tab, turn off Use Automatic Settings, and enter the resource or resources you want to assign. If the card uses manual configuration, you will need to set the board to the settings you select in the Device Manager.

CAUTION

Don't manually assign resources unless you know what you're doing. The result can be an operating system that won't boot or a bunch of other components in your system that no longer work.

Hardware uses four major resources:

- IRQ
- DMA
- I/O Port Addresses
- DMA channel

If you install Plug and Play cards (which configure themselves automatically), you seldom need to be concerned about these settings, especially if the cards use the PCI expansion slot (virtually any current card does). If your system originally ran Windows 98 or newer versions, it probably supports a feature called IRQ steering or IRQ sharing, which eliminates the major cause for hardware conflicts when you use PCI cards.

However, if your system uses ISA cards, or you still use legacy ports such as serial (COM), parallel (LPT), and PS/2 mouse ports, IRQ and other resource conflicts can still be a problem.

IRQs

PC architecture includes a means for a piece of hardware to quickly gain the attention of the CPU through a message called an *interrupt request*, or *IRQ*. Interrupts are sent over one of the 15 IRQ wires on the computer's bus. Such a request is a direct line to the CPU, which then services the request accordingly. A common example occurs when data comes in to your system's modem or LAN card. The modem or LAN card triggers the predetermined interrupt line (IRQ), and the CPU then begins to execute the program code that is appropriate for handling that interrupt. In fact, a part of the operating system called the *interrupt handler* is responsible for making it so.

Table 30.3 lists the common IRQs in an Intel-based computer. This information, in conjunction with the IRQ and the Conflicts/Sharing nodes of the Computer Management application, might help you to assign boards effectively. But remember, it's always best to let Windows make hardware assignments unless you are really stuck and something important just won't work. Also, remember that if hardware isn't on the Hardware Compatibility List (HCL), you're better off just going shopping than wasting a day tinkering with settings.

TABLE 30.3   TYPICAL IRQ ASSIGNMENTS IN 80286-BASED OR LATER x86 SYSTEMS

IRQ	Typical Assignment
0	System Timer (used by system; not available)
1	Keyboard (used by system; not available)
2	Redirected to IRQ 9; not available
3	COM2:, COM4: (can be shared *only* if COM 2/COM 4 are *not* used at the same time)
4	COM1:, COM3: (can be shared *only* if COM 1/COM 3 are *not* used at the same time)
5	LPT2: or Sound Blaster/compatible sound card
6	Floppy disk controller (used by system; never available)
7	LPT1: (printer port) can be shared only if used on a PCI card; the built-in parallel port's IRQ can't be shared
8	System clock (used by system; never available)
9	Old EGA/VGA cards or available
10	Often available
11	Often available
12	PS/2 mouse (available only on systems that don't have a PS/2-style mouse or have the port disabled)
13	Math coprocessor (not available; all modern CPUs have a built-in math co-processor)
14	IDE hard disk controller (never available)
15	Secondary IDE hard disk controller (never available on 1995 or later systems)

Common add-on devices which use an IRQ include

- Modern PCI and AGP video cards
- SCSI host adapter cards
- IDE host adapter cards
- Fax/modem cards
- Network interface cards

With only IRQ 9, 10, and 11 to choose from on many systems, it would be impossible to install all of these cards unless

- An existing device is disabled
- IRQ sharing is possible

30

If two ISA devices (or an ISA and a PCI device) try to share an IRQ, a system lockup will usually take place, or at best, neither device will work. A common cause of this a few years ago was when a serial mouse was attached to COM 1 and a fax/modem was assigned to COM 3. As you can see from the IRQ table, both of these ports use IRQ 4. The system worked until the user tried to operate the modem; then, the system locked up.

MS-DOS and old versions of Windows didn't always use the printer (LPT) ports' IRQs, enabling IRQ 7 (LPT1) and IRQ 5 (LPT2) to be used by other devices. However, Windows XP uses the IRQs assigned to a device, so that sharing can only take place under these circumstances:

- Both devices using the IRQ are PCI devices; on most recent systems, this enables the PCI cards and any built-in PCI devices to share IRQs, as in Figure 30.11.

- When two ISA cards or an ISA and a PCI card are set to the same IRQ, Windows XP shifts to a "polling" mode, wherein the CPU regularly checks for and services I/O requests rather than waits for IRQ lines to be activated. Obviously, this process can slow down overall system performance because it creates another software loop that the operating system has to service.

Figure 30.11
IRQ sharing enables this PC to use IRQ 10 for both a USB card and the onboard Fast Ethernet network adapter.

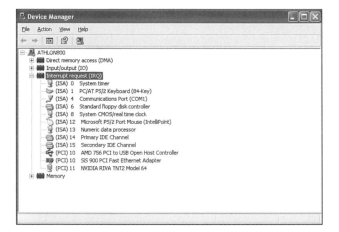

As shown Figure 30.11, IRQ steering is enabled automatically by Windows XP when the system supports it. In some cases, however, some motherboards might not permit IRQs to be shared, even by PCI devices.

If you find yourself short on IRQs or if you have two devices attempting to use the same IRQ and creating a conflict, you can try these possible solutions:

- One solution with PCI cards causing conflicts is to try moving the PCI card to another slot. On some machines, each PCI slot's PCI Interrupt (A through D) is mapped to an ISA-type IRQ. By simply moving a card to a neighboring slot, you may be able to get your hardware working.

- Another solution for IRQ cram is to set up multiple hardware profiles. You might not get all items to work under one profile, but you can have a couple of profiles and at least not have to throw anything away. You just reboot in another profile when you need access to a specific piece of gear.

- Another workaround is to use USB, IEEE-1394, and SCSI devices. As you probably know, all of these port types support multiple devices on the same wire. No IRQs are required other than for the controller, which typically takes only one, and most recent systems already have USB ports onboard and enabled. Yet USB supports up to 127 devices, IEEE-1394 up to 63 devices, and SCSI typically 7 (or 15 if your card supports Wide SCSI). If you're struggling with where to put a scanner, printer, digital camera, or additional external hard drive, consider these buses. While you can daisy-chain devices from the parallel port, it's difficult to get more than two devices (printer and another one) working correctly. And, even the "high-speed" EPP and ECP parallel port modes are scarcely faster than USB, and are considerably slower than any form of SCSI or IEEE-1394.

DMA CHANNELS

A typical PC has eight DMA channels, labeled 0 to 7. DMA channels are used for rapidly transferring data between memory and peripherals without the help of the CPU. Some cards even use several of these channels at once. (For example, the SoundBlaster 16 WaveEffects sound card uses two DMA channels.) Typical users of DMA channels are

- Memory access controllers
- ECP printer ports
- Floppy disk controllers
- ISA Network cards
- ISA Scanner cards
- ISA SCSI host adapters
- ISA sound cards

While recent EIDE hard drives use a variation of DMA called Ultra DMA (UDMA) for fast data transfer, DMA transfers performed by PCI-based devices don't use specific DMA channels. The only time a PCI device ever needs to use a DMA channel is if it's emulating an ISA device that uses one, such as a PCI-based sound card emulating an ISA-based sound card.

Sharing DMA channels is even worse than sharing IRQs. Because DMA channels are used to transfer data, not simply activate devices, you should *never* share DMA channels used by network cards, scanners, or SCSI host adapters, as a DMA conflict could result in data loss. Fortunately, with relatively few devices requiring DMA channels today, it's normally quite easy to avoid sharing a DMA channel.

Table 30.4 shows the typical assignments.

30

TABLE 30.4 TYPICAL DMA CONTROLLER ASSIGNMENTS

Channel	Typical Assignment
0	Generally used for DMA refresh
1	Available; may be used by ISA sound cards or by PCI sound cards emulating ISA sound cards
2	Floppy disk controller
3	ECP printer ports; some may use DMA 1 instead
4	DMA controller; used by system and not available
5	Available; may be used by ISA sound cards or by PCI sound cards emulating ISA sound cards
6	Available
7	Available

TIP FROM

Bob & Brian

> Some devices are hidden from view in the Device Manager. Hidden devices include non-Plug and Play devices (devices with earlier Windows 2000 device drivers) and devices that have been physically removed from the computer but have not had their drivers uninstalled. To see hidden devices in the Device Manager list, choose View, Show Hidden Devices. A check mark should appear on the menu, indicating that hidden devices are showing. Click it again to hide them.

I/O PORT ASSIGNMENTS

Using DMA is the fastest way to transfer data between components in the PC. However, an older technology called *memory-mapped I/O* is still in use today. (*I/O* means *input/output*.) In PC architecture, I/O ports are mapped into system memory and therefore are accessed by the CPU using memory addresses. As you might expect, each device that uses an I/O port must have a different port address, or data intended for one device will end up at another.

Check out the I/O folder off the Hardware Resources node in Computer Management, as shown in Figure 30.12, to see a sample list of I/O addresses and assignments. As you can see, this folder contains quite a few assignments. Note that the addresses are in standard memory-mapping parlance—hexadecimal.

NOTE

> A common source of I/O contention occurs among video cards, SCSI devices, and network cards. However, most devices can use a choice of several I/O port address ranges to avoid conflicts.

Figure 30.12
Typical I/O assignments in a Windows XP machine are numerous. Notice the scrollbar. Only about half the assignments are visible in this figure.

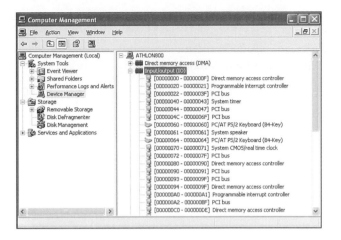

30

Memory Addresses

Similar to the I/O port address, the base memory address is the beginning memory address that some cards or motherboard hardware use to communicate with the CPU. Sometimes this setting is called the *RAM starting address* (or *start address*).

Some older cards (you'll notice this often with network adapters or SCSI cards which have an onboard BIOS) must have their base memory address set by a jumper or software. Then the device driver for that component needs its software setting to match the jumper. A typical base memory address reads like this: 0xA0000 or just A0000. Sometimes the last digit is dropped, like this: A000.

If you open Computer Management and go to System Information, Hardware Resources, Memory, you'll see memory addresses such as the following:

```
0xA0000-0xBFFFF   PCI bus
```

This address means the memory area between A0000 and BFFFF is assigned to the PCI bus. (The 0x indicates that it is a hexadecimal address.) So, when setting memory addressing, you need to consider not only the base addresses, but also the amount of RAM space the addresses will occupy. Some cards use 16KB of space, and others use 32KB or more. Check the card's manual for options. Using more memory can, in some cases, improve the operation of the card, but it decreases your system's memory availability because that space will be occupied. The end result depends on the type of card.

When you specify a memory address for a card, the operating system reserves that memory area for it. Regular RAM in that area is not used by the CPU, to prevent conflicts that could result from trying to write data or program code into system RAM at that address. Instead, the reserved area is used only by the device driver for your piece of hardware.

Most older ISA cards use an upper memory address that falls somewhere between A000 and FFFF. However, many VL-Bus, PCI, and some ISA cards can use address space above 1MB, or even above 16MB in the case of 32-bit cards. If your card can utilize a high address, it's better to do so because it minimizes the chances of conflicting with the operating system.

30

INSTALLING AND USING MULTIPLE MONITORS

Windows XP Professional supports multiple monitors, a great feature first developed for Windows 98. You can run up to ten monitors with Windows XP, but most commonly, you will probably run just two or three. By using multiple monitors, you can place a large amount of information on your screens at once. Use one screen for working on video editing, Web design, or graphics and the other for toolbars. Leave a Web or e-mail display on at all times while you use the other monitor for current tasks. Display huge spreadsheets across both screens.

The following are some rules and tips to know about using multiple monitors:

- Some new laptops support attaching an external monitor and can display different view on the internal LCD screen and on the external monitor. This feature is called DualView, and if your laptop supports it, your user's manual will show you how to enable the feature. You can ignore this section's instructions on installing a device adapter and just follow the instructions for setting the Display properties to use the second monitor.

- Because most computers don't have more than one or two PCI slots open, if you want to max out your video system, look into the new breed of multimonitor video cards available from Matrox, ATI, and various vendors which use nVidia GeForce 2 MX video chipsets. In a single slot, you can drive two or four monitors with these cards. With only two slots, you can drive four to eight monitors. Multimonitor video cards are available for either AGP or PCI slots.

- Most multimonitor situations consist of two cards: either two PCIs or a mix of one PCI and one AGP.

- If you mix AGP and PCI, older BIOSes sometimes have a strange habit of forcing one or the other to become the "primary" display. It is the display that Windows first boots on and the one you use for logging on. You might be annoyed if your better monitor or better card isn't the primary display because most programs are initially displayed on the primary monitor when you launch them. Therefore, you might want to flash-upgrade your BIOS if the maker of your computer or motherboard indicates that such an upgrade will improve the multiple-monitor support for your computer by letting you choose which monitor or card you want to make the primary display.

- If you're unhappy with your system's choice of the primary display, you can adjust it with Display properties once both displays are running.

 If you aren't having luck assigning the primary display, and your secondary card is taking over the role of primary display, see "Setting the Primary Display" in the "Troubleshooting" section at the end of this chapter.

- The operating system always needs a VGA device, which becomes the primary display. The BIOS detects the VGA device based on slot order, unless the BIOS offers an option for choosing which device is to be treated as the VGA device. Check your BIOS settings to see whether any special settings might affect multimonitor display, such as whether the AGP or PCI card will default to primary display, or the PCI slot order. Slot 1 is typically the slot nearest the power supply connector.

■ The design of the card itself is what makes it capable of operating on multiple monitors with Windows XP, not the driver. Don't expect any vendors to be able to add multiple monitor support simply by implementing a driver update. Either the card can support multimonitoring, or it can't. Some cards should technically be able to do so but are not stable enough to handle the capability at this time.

■ Some motherboards with onboard I/O such as sound, modem, and LAN may have difficulties with multiple monitor configurations, especially if the devices share an IRQ with a particular PCI slot. You might want to disable any onboard devices you're not using to free up resources that can be used for additional video cards.

■ Just because a set of cards supports multimonitoring under Windows 98 doesn't mean it can under Windows XP. These two operating systems have completely different video architectures.

TIP FROM

Bob
& Brian

> Microsoft doesn't provide much specific information on which video cards/chipsets work in multimonitor mode, perhaps because BIOS and motherboard issues can affect the results different users will have with the same video cards. The RealTimeSoft Web site contains a searchable database of thousands of working combinations as well as links to other multiple monitor resources, including RealTimeSoft's own UltraMon multi-monitor utility. Check it out at
>
> `www.realtimesoft.com`

Follow these steps to install a secondary display adapter for use with multiple monitors:

1. Boot up your system into Windows XP Professional, and right-click a blank area of your desktop. From the resulting pop-up menu, select Properties.

2. Go to the Settings tab. Confirm that your primary display adapter is listed correctly (that is, if you have an ATI Rage Pro, then ATI Rage Pro should be listed under Display). Your display adapter *should not* be listed as VGA, or multimonitoring will not work. If this is the case, you need to find and install correct Windows XP drivers, or consult your display manufacturer's Web site.

3. Be sure you are using at least 65636 colors (the 16-bit setting [also known as Medium] is recommended). Then click OK, and when prompted, select Apply Without Restarting.

4. After you've confirmed that you have drivers loaded for your display adapter and that you are in a compatible color depth, shut down and then power off your system.

30

5. Disconnect the power cable leading to the back of your system, and remove the case cover. Confirm that you have an available PCI slot. Before inserting your secondary display adapter, disable its VGA mode if possible by adjusting a jumper block or DIP switch on the card. Newer cards use the software driver or BIOS settings to enable or disable VGA mode.

 If you have problems setting up your monitor, see "Setting the Primary Display" in the "Troubleshooting" section at the end of this chapter.

6. Insert your secondary display adapter, secure it properly with a screw, reassemble your system, and reconnect the power. Next, connect a second monitor to the secondary display adapter.

7. Turn on both the monitors, and power up the system. Allow the system to boot into Windows XP.

8. After you log in, Windows XP detects your new display adapter and brings up the Hardware Wizard. Confirm that it detects the correct display adapter and, when prompted, tell Windows XP to search for a suitable driver. Then click Next.

9. Windows XP then finds information on the display adapter. When you are prompted, insert your Windows XP installation CD or the driver disk that came with your adapter, and click OK.

10. Windows XP then copies files. When the process is completed, click Finish. Windows XP then also detects your secondary monitor (if it is a PnP monitor). When you are prompted, click Finish again.

11. Now that all appropriate drivers are installed, right-click a blank portion of your desktop, and select Properties again. Next, go to the Settings tab. You will notice that two Monitor icons now appear in the center window of the display applet representing your two monitors (look ahead to Figure 30.13). Left-click the Monitor icon labeled 2, and it is highlighted in blue.

12. Under Display, your secondary adapter should be displayed. In the lower-left corner below the Colors section, check the box labeled Extend My Windows Desktop into This Monitor.

13. When Windows XP gives you a warning concerning compatibility, click Yes.

14. While the Monitor icon labeled 2 is highlighted, adjust the color depth and resolution for the new monitor.

15. You might want to change the way your monitors are positioned by left-clicking and holding down the mouse button while you drag the Monitor icons. (Note that the displays must touch along one edge.) When you find a desirable position, just release the mouse button, and the Monitor icon is aligned adjacent to the first Monitor icon. Also note that wherever the two displays meet is the location your mouse will be able to pass from one display to the next, so a horizontal alignment is preferred for a standard desktop monitor arrangement (see Figure 30.11).

16. Click OK. Windows XP then asks whether you want to restart or apply your changes. Select Restart to allow Windows XP to reboot your system.

17. After the system is rebooted and you log on to your system, multimonitoring should be functional, and you should have an extended desktop displayed on your second monitor. You also should be able to move your mouse into this extended desktop.

Figure 30.13
A system running dual monitors. The relative size of monitors 1 and 2 reflects the resolution (monitor 1 has a higher resolution than monitor 2).

30

NOTE

You can set up Windows XP with more than one secondary display adapter, up to a maximum of nine additional displays. To do so, just select another supported secondary display adapter with VGA disabled, and repeat the preceding steps with another monitor attached to the additional secondary adapter.

After you finish these steps, you can drag items across your screen onto alternate monitors. Better yet, you can resize a window to stretch it across more than one monitor. Things get a little weird at the gap, though. You have to get used to the idea of the mouse cursor jumping from one screen into the next, too.

TIP FROM

If you're not sure which monitor is which, click the Identify button shown in Figure 30.13 to display a large number across each monitor for a few seconds.

⚡ *If you're having trouble getting your multimonitor setup to work, see "Setting the Primary Display" in the "Troubleshooting" section at the end of this chapter.*

⚡ *If you don't have enough open slots for multiple monitors, see "Not Enough Slots" in the "Troubleshooting" section at the end of the chapter.*

INSTALLING A UPS

While power outages in California have received a lot of press in recent months, blackouts and power outages (and the data loss they can cause) can happen anywhere. While Windows XP Professional contains a backup utility that can be used to protect your data, and you may use a network drive that's backed up every night for your data, you should also be concerned about keeping power going to your PC during its normal operation between backups.

A battery backup unit (also called a *UPS*, which is short for *Uninterruptible Power Supply*) can provide battery power to your system for as much as ten to fifteen minutes, which is long enough for you to save your data and shut down your system. The UPS plugs into the wall (and can act as a surge suppressor) and your computer and monitor plug into outlets on the rear of the UPS.

Electronic circuitry in the UPS continually monitors the AC line voltages, and should the voltage rise above or dip below predefined limits or fail entirely, the UPS takes over, powering the computer with its built-in battery and cutting off the computer from the AC wall outlet.

As you might imagine, to prevent data loss, the system's response time has to be very fast. As soon as the AC power gets flaky, the UPS has to take over within a few milliseconds, at most. Many (but not all) UPS models feature a serial (COM) or USB cable, which attaches to the appropriate port on your system. The cable sends signals to your computer to inform it when the battery backup has taken over and to start the shutdown process; some units may also broadcast a warning message over the network to other computers. UPS units with this feature are often called *intelligent UPS* units.

TIP FROM

Bob
& Brian

> If the UPS you purchase (or already own) doesn't come with Windows XP-specific drivers for the shutdown and warning features, contact the vendor of the UPS for a software update.

The Power Options applet in Control Panel can be found by clicking Start, Control Panel, Performance and Maintenance, Power Options. Figure 30.14 shows the UPS tab, which enables you to select the model of UPS that's connected to your system, set up signaling for models which support automatic shutdown, and inform you of the battery's condition and how long you can expect the system to work from battery (a factor often called the *UPS runtime*).

If your UPS doesn't have provisions for automatic shutdown, its alarm will notify you when the power has failed. Shut down the computer yourself after saving any open files, grab a flashlight, and relax until the power comes back on.

Figure 30.14
The UPS tab in Power Options after a UPS model has been selected, but before the UPS has been connected.

UPS Considerations for Windows XP Professional

Ideally, all your workstations assigned to serious tasks (what work isn't serious?) should have UPS protection of some sort. Although it's true that well-designed programs such as Microsoft Office XP have auto-backup options that help to restore files in progress if the power goes out, they are not always reliable. Crashes and weird performance of applications and operating systems are enough to worry about, without adding power loss on top. And if the power fails during a disk write, you might have a rude awakening because the hard disk's filesystem could be corrupted, which is far worse than having a lost file or two.

My advice is that you guard against the ravages of power outages at all reasonable costs. With the ever-increasing power and plummeting cost of notebook computers, one of the most economically sensible solutions is to purchase notebook computers instead of desktop computers, especially for users who change locations frequently. They take up little space, they are easier to configure because the hardware complement cannot be easily altered, and they have UPSs built in. When the power fails, the battery takes over.

TIP FROM

Bob & Brian

When you're using laptops, be sure your batteries are still working, though. With time, they can lose their capacity to hold a charge. You should cycle them once in a while to check out how long they will run. If necessary, replace them. Also, you should set up the power options on a laptop to save to disk (hibernate) in case of impending power loss. You'll typically want to set hibernation to kick in when 5 to 10 percent of battery power is remaining, just to ensure that the hard disk can start up (if sleeping) and write out the system state onto disk.

30

If you are using Windows XP Professional systems as servers, you'll certainly want UPS support, as discussed in the networking section of this book. Windows XP Professional can alert any connected workstation users of impending system shutdown as the UPS battery begins to drain if their UPS units are equipped with suitable software drivers. Users are warned to save their work and shut down (assuming they are running on a power source that is also functional, of course).

Before shelling out your hard-earned dough for UPS systems, you should check to see which ones are supported by Windows XP Professional. Consult the Hardware Compatibility List on the Microsoft site. Also, consider this checklist of questions:

- Do you want to purchase a separate UPS for every workstation or one larger UPS that can power a number of computers from a single location?

- What UPS capacity do you need for each computer? The answer depends on the power draw of the computer box, the size of the monitor, and whether you want peripherals to work on battery, too. To fully protect your network, you should also install a UPS on network devices such as routers, hubs, bridges, modems, telephones, printers, and any other network equipment. Check the real-world specs for the UPS. The capacity is also determined by how long you want the UPS to be able to operate after a complete power outage. If you just want enough time for you or another user to save work, a relatively small UPS will do. If you want to be able to get through a day's work doing stock trades, you'll need a hefty unit.

TIP FROM

Bob & Brian

> Network hardware and modems should be powered by the UPS, but printers should not be. Laser printers, in particular, have such high power requirements that your actual runtime for a given UPS unit will be just a fraction of what it would be if the laser printer were left off the UPS circuit. Because systems can store print jobs as temporary files until a printer is available to take them, there's no need to waste precious battery power to keep any type of printer running through a blackout.

- What software support do you want? Do you need to keep a log of UPS activity during the day for later analysis? What about utilities that test the UPS on a regular basis to ensure it's working?

- As I mentioned previously, Windows XP Professional has services built in for responding to a UPS's signal that an outage has occurred. They can be configured to alert users, automatically shut down the system, and/or execute a program of your choice. Automatic and graceful shutdown of the system is important in case a power failure lasts long enough to deplete the UPS batteries. In addition to connected users being warned of an impending shutdown, new users can be prevented from connecting to such a server.

TIP FROM

Bob

& Brian

> In some cases, UPS vendors provide software for configuring their devices. You can use them instead of the one provided in Windows XP.

INSTALLING AND CONFIGURING THE WINDOWS XP UPS SERVICE

If you are going to use a UPS that doesn't support signaling to the computer via a data cable, you don't have to worry about installing or configuring the Windows XP UPS service. It won't make any difference and isn't needed.

You can install the UPS according the manufacturer's instructions or, if it's a Plug and Play device, follow standard procedures for installing new hardware. Typically, you connect the UPS to the power source, the computer to the UPS, and the serial cable between the UPS and the computer.

NOTE

> Be aware that normal serial cables do not cut the mustard for connecting a UPS to a Windows XP Professional machine. UPS serial cables, even between models from the same manufacturer, use different pin assignments. You're best off using the cable supplied by the maker of the UPS.

Another way to install the driver for a particular UPS model is to go to the Control Panel and run the Power Options applet, as shown in Figure 30.14. Click Select, and choose the UPS make and model you have and the COM port the UPS data cable is on, if any. The COM port is used to receive signals from the UPS about its charge level and the state of the AC power source.

If your UPS isn't listed, choose Generic Make, select Custom, and make sure to check the signal polarity settings in Table 30.3. For listed UPS devices, the polarities are preset for you.

After you select the type of UPS, return to the UPS tab of the Power Options Properties dialog, and click Configure to set up what you want Windows XP Professional to do in the event of a power interruption. The UPS Configuration dialog is shown in Figure 30.15.

Editable items on the tab differ, depending on what UPS you have installed, but they fall into the following categories:

- The conditions that trigger the UPS device to send a signal, such as regular power supply failure, low battery power, and remote shutdown by the UPS device
- The time intervals for maintaining battery power, recharging the battery, and sending warning messages after power failure
- An optional executable program specified to run when power outage is sensed
- Final behavior of Windows in case of complete discharge of the UPS backup battery (typically a graceful shutdown)

Figure 30.15
Here, you can set the UPS and system behavior for cases of power outage.

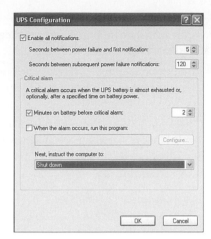

30

You can use Table 30.5 when you're considering the settings.

TABLE 30.5   THE UPS CONFIGURATION DIALOG BOX

Option	Description
Enable All Notifications	Check this box if you want notifications of impending power failure to appear on the users' screens and sent to users currently connected to the computer over the LAN. The message is broadcast over the local node. It doesn't cross a router.
Seconds Between Power Failure and First Notification	Set how much time elapses between the power failure and when the power failure signal is sent to the computer. This figure is subtracted from the total expected battery life to determine when the system should begin shutdown. The range is 0 to 120 seconds.
Time Between Subsequent Power Failure Notifications	If the UPS can keep the system messages going for some time, set this time to determine how often (5 to 300 seconds) the user should be notified of impending doom. Too-frequent messages can be annoying and can unnecessarily alarm users in the case of regularly occurring power fluctuations. Messages sent too seldom can be overlooked.
Minutes on Battery Before Critical Alarm	Set how long after the UPS kicks in a critical notification and/or alarm should sound be issued, warning of imminent system shutdown. Base this setting on the capacity of the UPS and the power load of your system complement. A smart UPS might be able to signal the computer to indicate a critical state. If not, estimate on the conservative side, based on the manufacturer's manual.

TABLE 30.5   CONTINUED

Option	Description
When the Alarm Occurs, Run This Program	When the critical alarm goes off, you can optionally choose to run a program of no more than 30 seconds in execution time. (See the next option.)
Next, Instruct the Computer To	Set what should happen after a critical alarm goes off and an optional program runs. You can choose Shutdown or Hibernate. Hibernate allows the machine to return to the previous state after resumption of power.

30

SETTING POLARITIES FOR A GENERIC UPS

For a smart UPS, serial data lines are used to communicate with the UPS. For a generic UPS, though, the data lines are ignored, and Windows uses the COM port's modem-status signaling lines. AC and battery status are received from the UPS using two of these lines, and a third line, the DTR signal, goes from the computer to the UPS. This signal can tell the UPS to turn itself off when Windows XP Professional has finished shutting down. This capability helps extend the life of the UPS batteries by avoiding a full discharge.

If your UPS isn't listed among those supported and you don't have Windows XP-compatible drivers you can install, Windows XP Professional doesn't know what your UPS is capable of and how it sends signals to the computer, if at all. When you choose Generic and then choose Custom, you see a Next button. Clicking it brings up the dialog box shown in Figure 30.16.

Figure 30.16
Here, you can set custom polarities for a UPS that Windows 2000 Professional doesn't know how to preconfigure.

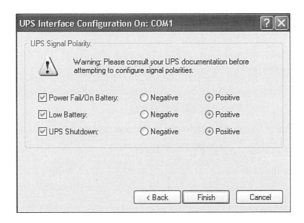

Assuming the UPS has a serial link to the computer, you can set the port and fill in the blanks as necessary. Turn off all the options if the UPS has no serial link to a COM port. As the dialog box warns, you should consult the manufacturer or manual to ensure the settings are correct.

Table 30.6 describes the salient settings in the UPS polarities.

TABLE 30.6   UPS POLARITIES

Setting	Description
Power Fail/On Battery	Can the UPS send a power failure signal on the CTS (clear-to-send) pin of the serial link? If so, check this box, and indicate which voltage polarity (+ or –) signals the failure. These interface voltages indicate the active state for the signal. For example, if you select a negative interface voltage for the power failure signal, the normally positive signal becomes negative when a power failure occurs.
Low Battery	Can the UPS send a low-battery signal on the DCD (data-carrier-detect) pin of the serial link? If so, check this box and set the polarity.
UPS Shutdown	Can the UPS receive a signal from the Windows XP machine on the DTR (data-terminal-ready) pin of the serial link? (This signal is used to tell the UPS when the battery power is no longer needed either because the AC source was revived or because the computer shuts off.) If so, check the box, and indicate which voltage polarity (+ or –) signals the cessation of battery power need.

RUNNING A COMMAND FILE WHEN THE POWER FAILS

The UPS Configuration dialog box has an option for running an executable file when a power failure is detected. It is an option only. Warning messages are sent out (assuming those options are supported and turned on) regardless of whether you choose this option. However, you might want to run a specific executable before the computer is shut down.

If you use this option, make sure the program or script you choose can execute in 30 seconds or less. Failure to complete execution in 30 seconds jeopardizes the safe shutdown of your Windows computer.

Do the following to declare and set up the executable file:

1. In the UPS Configuration dialog box, select the When the Alarm Occurs, Run This Program check box, and then click Configure.
2. In the resulting UPS System Shutdown Program dialog box, select the Task tab.
3. Type the name of the file in the Run field.
4. If you want the scheduled task to run at a specified time, select the Enabled (Scheduled Task Runs at Specified Time) check box, and continue this procedure.
5. Select the Schedule tab, and then select the frequency and start time of the task.
6. You can make additional schedule settings by clicking the Settings tab.
7. Set any additional options you want in the Scheduled Task Completed, Idle Time, and Power Management areas of the Settings tab; then click OK.
8. In the Set Account Information dialog box, type the Run As and password information, and then click OK.

> The command file must reside in your %SystemRoot%\System32 folder and have a file-name extension, such as .EXE, .COM, .BAT, or .CMD.

→ To learn more details about the Run As setting, **see** "Guest and Administrator Accounts," **p. 951**.

TESTING YOUR UPS CONFIGURATION

Testing your UPS configuration from time to time is wise, just to make sure you aren't let down when a real emergency occurs. Follow these steps to do so:

1. Close any open documents or programs.
2. Simulate a power failure by disconnecting the power to the UPS device. Check to see that, after disconnecting the power to the UPS device, the computer and peripherals connected to the UPS device continue operating and that a warning message appears on the screen.
3. Wait until the UPS battery reaches a low level, at which point a system shutdown should occur.
4. If the UPS service is configured to run a command file, check to see that it executes in under 30 seconds.
5. Restore power to the UPS device.
6. Check the system log in the Event Viewer to ensure that all actions were logged and that no errors occurred.

USING HARDWARE PROFILES

Windows has a feature called Hardware Profiles that lets you boot up Windows with different sets of hardware devices enabled. Profiles grew out of the need for docking laptops to be able to boot with a different set of driver settings based on whether the laptop was on the road or connected to a docking station with its own external monitor, additional CD-ROM drive, and so on. Profiles have become more capable with Plug and Play, sensing when the computer is "hot-docked" and kicking in the appropriate profile when needed. Also, for complex arrangements such as on a desktop computer stuffed to the gills with devices, it is sometimes necessary to disable some devices so that others can have access to certain limited resources such as interrupt requests (IRQs). I should add that hot-dockable ports such as USB, IEEE-1394, and PC Cards have reduced the need for hardware profiles somewhat, since their hardware can be attached and removed on-the-fly without rebooting.

In addition to allowing different combinations of hardware, Hardware Profiles allow the same hardware to be configured with different resource settings. In essence, you can have almost a different computer with each hardware profile.

30

Hardware profiles are set up on the System applet, which you can view by clicking Start, right-clicking My Computer, and selecting Properties. View the Hardware tab and click the Hardware Profiles to bring up the Hardware Profile manager.

> **N O T E**
>
> Windows enables or disables devices by simply installing or not installing their drivers at boot time.

Windows XP creates one hardware profile called Profile 1 automatically whenever it's installed on any type of computer. As additional devices are installed, they're automatically added to Profile 1.

To create an additional hardware profile, open the System properties sheet, click the Hardware tab, click Hardware Profiles, and copy Profile 1 to another profile (see Figure 30.17).

> **N O T E**
>
> You must be logged on with Administrator privileges to alter the hardware profiles.

To change the hardware in any profile, select that profile when you reboot and disable or change the settings for devices through the Device Manager. The Properties button on the Hardware Profiles screen lets you adjust profiles for portable computer use and select whether the profile is displayed as a startup option. Table 30.7 shows a typical laptop scenario after creating two profiles and enabling and disabling some devices.

TABLE 30.7   TYPICAL LAPTOP HARDWARE PROFILES

Example	Description
Profile 1: "On the Road"	Use when traveling. Contains enabled modem and printer.
Profile 2: "At the Office"	Use when docked to the docking station or port replicator. Enables LAN card, external monitor, and CD-ROM drive.

To switch between hardware profiles, reboot your computer and select the hardware profile you want to use at boot time.

After you've copied a profile, you can begin to modify it to meet your needs. Click the profile, and then click Properties. You can declare some aspects of the profile at this stage. You can indicate, for example, whether it's a profile on a laptop computer. Table 30.8 lists some of the options and their meanings.

Figure 30.17
User Profiles on a system with two profiles available.

TABLE 30.8	HARDWARE PROFILE OPTIONS
Option	**Description**
Delete	Use this option to eliminate a profile. You can't delete the currently active profile.
Wait Until I Select a Hardware Profile	When you boot the computer, you are presented with a list of profiles early in the boot process. If this option is on, the computer will wait forever for you to select the profile to boot into.
Select the First Profile If I Don't Select a Profile in x Seconds	Profiles appear in the list above this setting. The order determines the first profile. You can organize the profiles using the arrow buttons so that the first one is the default profile you want to boot in case you don't intervene. I like to change the default for x Seconds from 30 to 10 to save time when booting.
This Is a Portable Computer	If you're on a desktop, don't check this box. If you're on a laptop that is going to be alternately docked and undocked, check it, and choose the appropriate radio button. The Unknown button is selected by default if Windows can't figure out the docking status at the current time. You can help clear up the confusion by clicking one of the other options.
Include This Profile as an Option When Windows Starts	You can opt to have a profile not appear in the bootup list if you want to keep it on hand for future use but don't want it to show up in the list of profiles to choose from when you boot up.

ALTERING A HARDWARE PROFILE'S DEVICE COMPLEMENT

Windows XP Professional is pretty good about detecting and setting up separate hardware profiles for popular docking stations and port replicators. However, if yours isn't detected, you can use the technique presented here to alter what drivers will load with each profile. You can use this technique for personalizing profiles on any kind of computer, be it desktop or portable, for that matter.

The way you differentiate hardware profiles is to first create multiple copies of the same profile, then turn off or on devices in each to suit your needs, and resave them. After settings are made, you reboot. During bootup, you are prompted to choose between them.

TIP FROM

Bob

& Brian

> You should use different hardware profiles for any computer where you alter the physical setup regularly in a predictable manner, such as switching between two monitors.

The following is the basic game plan for modifying existing profiles:

1. Get your system running with a superset of the hardware you're going to want to use. That is, use as much external stuff—such as hard drives—as possible. This step may require your using the Control Panel's Add/Remove Hardware applet as well (see earlier in this chapter).

2. Choose Control Panel, System. Then click Hardware Profiles.

3. Select the profile you want to use as a basis for your scaled-down (undocked) profile, and click Copy.

4. Name the new profile something meaningful, such as `Undocked Laptop`.

5. Click the Properties button, and look at the options there. If you're modifying a portable computer, check the appropriate box, and indicate the current state (docked or undocked) and whether you want the new hardware profile to be presented as an option for the user to choose when Windows boots. (Normally, you would want it to show, but you could disable this option if you, for example, were loaning the computer to someone and didn't want to confuse him or her with boot options.) Click OK to close that dialog box.

6. Now comes the tricky part. You have to boot up in a specific profile before you can modify the settings therein. Do so, and pick the profile you want to modify.

7. Choose Control Panel, System, and click the Device Manager button.

8. In the Device Manager window, click the + (plus) sign next to any piece of hardware whose inclusion/exclusion in one of your profiles you want to alter. Highlight the specific item, and click Properties.

9. At the bottom of the resulting Properties dialog, use the Device Usage drop-down list to choose whether you want to enable or disable the specific piece of hardware in your current profile.

10. Repeat for each device whose usage will be affected by a given profile.

11. Repeat steps 6 through 10 for each profile you want to adjust.

TROUBLESHOOTING

NOT ENOUGH SLOTS

I don't have enough slots for multiple monitors. What should I do?

Some video display cards support more than one monitor; they have a connector for each monitor. If you need single-slot support for two monitors, try ATI's RADEON VE (www.ati.com), Appian Graphics' Appian Hurricanc (based on the RADEON VE chipset—www.appian.com), Matrox's Millennium G450 and G550 (www.matrox.com/mga), nVidia's GeForce2 MX-based cards such as the ELSA GLADIAC 511PCI and 511TWIN (www.elsa.com), and Hercules 3D Prophet II MX Dual Display (www.Hercules.com). If you need support for up to four monitors, Matrox G200's Multi-Monitor cards are available in versions that handle two or four monitors per card. Appian Technology's 2-port and 4-port Jeronimo Pro cards (www.appiantech.com) are also available. With two 4-port and one 2-port card, you could get 10 monitors in three PCI slots or an AGP slot and two PCI slots. Check the Windows Hardware Compatibility List for details of the latest cards that support multiple monitors all in one card.

SETTING THE PRIMARY DISPLAY

I can't get my multimonitor system to choose the primary display properly.

As discussed in the section about multimonitor arrangements earlier in the chapter, it can be tricky to force Windows XP to use a particular video display card as the secondary display. If a display card isn't disabled from running in VGA mode, the computer runs the card's Power-On Self Test (POST). When that happens, Windows XP assigns it primary display status; if the other card's VGA mode can't be disabled, you will not be able to use the secondary card. Most users will want to keep their first video card as the primary display, so they need to know how to prevent the POST from happening.

Generally, dual-display works best when one video card is AGP and one is PCI. However, this doesn't guarantee that the faster AGP video card will wind up being your primary display. You may need to set the system BIOS option for default video to PCI to enable an AGP+PCI dual display to work properly.

If your video card has a jumper block or switch that can be used to disable VGA mode, this option will make it easier to use the card as a secondary card, since only the primary card needs VGA mode. VGA mode is used for the system's power-on self-test (POST) and to display startup options before the Windows GUI is initialized.

Many desktop systems with onboard video automatically disable the on-board video when you install a PCI or AGP video card, making it necessary to install two video cards (or a multi-monitor video card) if you want multiple monitor support.

Generally, you can't tell if a secondary card will work until after you boot Windows XP with the secondary card in place, the system detects it and installs the drivers, and the system tries to initialize the card. If the card is initialized successfully, you should see the Windows desktop on both screens. If the secondary monitor's screen stays black, check the Device Manager listing for the video card. If the card is listed with a yellow exclamation mark, it's not working properly. A Code 10 error on the card's properties sheet's General tab indicates the card was unable to start. Restart the system and change the default display setting in the BIOS and retry it. If necessary, try a different slot for the card.

ALTERED BIOS SETTINGS PREVENT COMPUTER FROM BOOTING

I've altered my BIOS settings, and now the computer won't start.

Today's computer BIOSes have *so* many arcane settings that it's quite possible to alter one that will prevent proper booting. Before you futz with the advanced CMOS settings (not just the simple stuff like time, date, boot order, power settings, ports, and such), read the manual that came with the computer or motherboard. If you decide to change something, write down the old value before doing so. When in doubt, don't alter advanced CMOS settings that affect how the chip set works, whether and where the BIOS and video shadowing is done, and so on. The default settings are designed by the motherboard maker to work under most situations and operating systems. Because Windows is the most popular operating system, you can bet it was already tested and configured for Windows 9x, NT, 2000 or XP (unless you have a very old motherboard).

That said, what do you do if you've changed something in the CMOS and now the computer won't boot? You can try the computer's or motherboard's manual or Web site for information about settings for Windows XP. If you find nothing, then you should wind back the settings to the factory defaults. Most CMOS setups have a "Set to Default" or similar command you can issue.

The Set to Default option might also be a good course to take if you make CMOS settings that prevent your computer from booting and you can't remember how to undo the changes. The Default settings are usually conservative enough to work under most circumstances. The BIOS in some systems may also have a "Fail-Safe Defaults" option that sets your BIOS to its most conservative settings.

If what you've done has changed the hard disk "Type," or if you manually entered the number of sectors, tracks, platters, and so on, and now it won't boot, use the Auto Detect Hard Disk BIOS setting to discover and enter those numbers automatically (this is known as *drive autotyping*).

New Hardware Doesn't Work

I've added some hardware, but it doesn't work.

Try these steps, in this order:

1. Try the troubleshooters included in the Help system, assuming the hardware fits into one of the neatly packaged categories. Open them through the Help and Support page as described previously.

2. Try rebooting Windows XP.

3. Use the Computer Management Console and the Device Manager to check resources assigned to the hardware to be sure that it's not conflicting. Check the hardware's manual to determine whether you should be setting some DIP switches or jumpers on it to avoid conflicts if the device isn't a Plug and Play device.

4. Remove the item and reboot. Then use the Device Manager to make sure the item is truly removed from the operating system. If it isn't, remove it manually in the Device Manager (by right-clicking and choosing Uninstall), and reboot until it's gone.

5. Power down, add the hardware again (running the Add Hardware applet if the hardware isn't detected at bootup), and configure as necessary.

6. Contact the manufacturer.

Tips from the Windows Pros: Upgrading and Optimizing Your Computer

Following are several tips I've learned over the years that will help save you hours of headaches.

Make the Move to PCI Cards

Even if your system still has one or more ISA slots and you have cards to match, it's time to retire this 1984-vintage technology and switch to PCI cards. Here are a few of the reasons why:

- Most recent systems support PCI IRQ steering, which enables multiple PCI devices to share a single IRQ without conflicts. However, if an ISA card uses an IRQ, it usually can't be shared with any other card, ISA or PCI. A single ISA sound card, for example, might use two IRQs, preventing any other device from using those IRQs. The ISA cards in your system could literally prevent you from installing other cards, no matter how many free slots you have.

- ISA cards are much slower than PCI cards, and require much more CPU attention. The result? Your system is a lot slower than it needs to be.

- ISA cards don't support recent technologies that are now common with PCI cards. Here are just a couple of examples: If you want Fast Ethernet's 100Mbps network speed, you can't achieve it with an ISA card. Want Dolby Digital 5.1 sound for your DVD movies? Forget that old ISA sound card; only some top-of-the-line PCI sound cards support it.

Use the Device Manager to uninstall your old card, shut down your machine, and remove it before you install a PCI card to replace it. If you're changing motherboards, keep in mind that many recent motherboards have on-board sound, and some also have built-in modems and even Fast Ethernet 10/100 ports built-in.

KEEP YOUR EYES ON THE HARDWARE COMPATIBILITY LIST

If you've been accustomed to thumbing your nose at Microsoft's Hardware Compatibility Listing because you've been using Windows 9x, it's time to reform your behavior. In a pinch, Windows 9x could use older Windows drivers and could even load MS-DOS device drivers to make older hardware work correctly. Windows XP, like other NT-based versions of Windows, has done away with AUTOEXEC.BAT and CONFIG.SYS, so you can't use DOS-based drivers anymore. And, while Windows XP can use some Windows 2000 drivers in an emergency, you're much better off with drivers made especially for Windows XP.

You can view the online version of the HCL by setting your browser to

www.microsoft.com/hcl

The HCL also offers links to let you download drivers from either Microsoft or the manufacturer's Web site.

TIP FROM

Bob & Brian

> Hardware failures, power failures, and human errors can prevent Windows XP from starting successfully. Recovery is easier if you know the configuration of each computer and its history and if you back up critical system files when making changes to your Windows XP configuration.
>
> A good hedge against this problem is to create a technical reference library for all your hardware and software documentation. Your reference library should include the history of software changes and upgrades for each machine, as well as hardware settings such as those described here.

SLEUTHING OUT CONFLICTS

When you're hunting down potential IRQ, memory, and I/O conflicts, try using the Device Manager to help out. Yes, Computer Management, System Information, Hardware Resources, Conflicts Sharing will show you potential conflicts, so that's a good place to look, too. But let me share a trick with the Device Manager that isn't readily apparent.

Normally, a class of devices called Hidden Devices isn't shown. To show them, open the Device Manager (either via Control Panel, System or from Computer Management). Then, on the View menu, click Show Hidden Devices. A check mark next to Show Hidden Devices indicates that hidden devices are showing. Click it again to clear the check mark. Hidden devices include non-Plug and Play devices (devices with earlier Windows 2000 device drivers) and devices that have been physically removed from the computer but have not had their drivers uninstalled.

OPTIMIZING YOUR COMPUTER FOR WINDOWS XP

Finally, here's my biggest tip. . . .

Optimizing your computer for Windows XP is actually pretty easy. I'm very impressed with this operating system's capability to keep on chugging. It doesn't cough or die easily if you mind your manners.

- If you're buying new stuff for an upgrade, consider only hardware that's on the HCL.
- When you're buying a new machine, get it with Windows XP Professional preinstalled and from a reputable maker with decent technical support, not just a reputable dealer. The dealer might not be able to solve complex technical problems. Brand-name manu-facturers such as Dell, Compaq, Gateway, IBM, and so on have teams of engineers devoted to testing new operating systems and ironing out kinks in their hardware, with help from engineers at Microsoft.

  If you love to upgrade and experiment, more power to you. I used to build PCs from scratch, even soldering them together from parts. Then again, you can also build your own car. (I used to just about do that myself, too.) Or you can buy it preassembled from some company in Detroit. It really isn't worth spending much time fiddling with PC hardware unless you are putting together systems for a specific purpose. With the amazingly low price of computers these days, don't waste your time. And don't cut cor-ners in configuring a new machine. For an extra 50 bucks, you can get goodies such as a modem, network card, and faster video card thrown in. Do it up front, and save the hassle down the road.

- Run Windows Update frequently.
- Keep the hard disks defragmented (see Chapter 29), and make sure you have a decent amount of free space on your drives, especially your boot drive.

NOTE

Chapter 2 contains a lot of discussion about computer upgrades. This is a good starting point whenever you are considering a computer hardware or software upgrade.

30

CHAPTER 31

MULTIBOOTING WINDOWS XP WITH OTHER OPERATING SYSTEMS

In this chapter

WHY MULTIBOOT?

In today's world of advanced operating systems and low hard disk prices, it certainly is not uncommon for many users to want to experiment with different operating systems. The world of consumer computing is ripe with many different options. With the proliferation of the Internet and its accompanying high-bandwidth needs, whole operating systems are available for free download via many commercial distributors' FTP sites.

Along with just plain curiosity and experimentation, there are good solid reasons for needing to switch between operating systems:

- Many users use two or more operating systems because of application compatibility issues. Hardware support issues arise too: Windows 98 might have drivers for old hardware that Windows XP doesn't support.

- Some users want to run specific applications or games in the most well-suited environment possible.

- A developer might swap between Windows XP Professional and NT 4.0 to test application compatibility.

- Web site developers need to use different OS versions to see how their pages look with the corresponding different Web browser versions.

- As an author, I need several operating systems functioning on a single computer to meet my testing and writing needs.

Other than buying multiple computers, multibooting—selecting one operating system at bootup time—is the most sensible way to handle these needs.

> **NOTE**
>
> You should read, or at least skim, this entire chapter before beginning to implement a complex multiboot arrangement. We have not reiterated some considerations under each scenario. Pay particular attention to the issues of file formats, as well as applications and data sharing between operating systems. Then be sure to see "Tips from the Windows Pros: Living with More Than One OS" at the end of the chapter, which covers third-party multiboot solutions.

Windows XP Professional directly supports multibooting with the following operating systems:

- Windows XP Home Edition
- Windows 2000 Professional
- Windows NT 3.51 or Windows NT 4.0
- Windows 95, Windows 98 and Me
- Windows 3.1 or Windows for Workgroups 3.11
- MS-DOS
- OS/2

Multibooting with Linux is also possible, although it takes some extra effort.

In this chapter, we'll tell you how to set up a multi-booting computer. And later in the chapter, we'll show a way to run multiple OSes without the need to reboot at all.

> **NOTE**
>
> Although this chapter provides some solid fundamentals for dual-booting operating systems, an in-depth discussion of the topic could—and in fact does—fill an entire book. For additional details on setting up multiboot scenarios, we recommend that you pick up a copy of *The Multi-Boot Configuration Handbook*, published by Que.

PREPARATION

As discussed in Chapter 2, "Getting Your Hardware and Software Ready for Windows XP" and Chapter 3, "Installing Windows XP Professional," it is certainly possible, with a bit of work, to run multiple operating systems on your Windows XP Professional computer. Whatever the operating system on your machine at the moment, you've no doubt spent hours and hours fine-tuning it and learning all the little quirks, and you probably have all the settings, applications, and data files arranged to your liking. Well, take heart—you can probably make it live harmoniously with Windows XP Professional.

> **CAUTION**
>
> Installing a new operating system is not always a smooth procedure, as you probably know. I strongly recommend that you create a backup, or at least an emergency repair disk before you install another operating system on your computer. That way, you can revert to it in case of catastrophe.

Depending on your current or planned system, running multiple operating systems can be as simple as installing your new copy of Windows XP alongside your current operating system. But if you're like me, that will not be the perfect choice. Either way, I'll try to cover all the common methods so you can make the choice that's right for you. After all, if you were the type who settles for things the way they were, you would skip this chapter because a single operating system is all you need.

FILE SYSTEM SPECIFICS

Your goal in creating a multiboot system is to have all the operating systems coexist in such a manner that they will be capable of sharing files with each other. Nothing is more frustrating than realizing that you must reboot to retrieve a file, copy it to a floppy, and reboot again to copy into your other operating system. A little bit of knowledge about file systems can save you many headaches down the road.

Not all operating systems use hard disks in the same manner. There are several different *file system* formats out there, which determine how file space is allocated, where directory information is stored, and so forth. The problem is that each operating system has its own list of supported file system types. Table 31.1 lists the various file systems supported by the operating systems discussed in this chapter. Note that in the table, RO stands for read-only, RW stands for read/write, and NS stands for not supported. Be sure to read the footnotes for any operating system you want to use.

TABLE 31.1 RELATIONSHIPS BETWEEN FILE SYSTEMS AND OPERATING SYSTEMS

OS	Fat16	Fat32	NTFS4	NTFS5	Extended2
Windows 95	RW	NS	RO[1]	RO[1]	RO[2]
Windows 95b	RW	RW	RO[1]	RO[1]	RO[2]
Windows 98	RW	RW	RO[1]	RO[1]	RO[2]
Windows NT 4.0	RW	NS[3]	RW[4]	RW[4]	RO[6]
Windows 2000	RW	RW	RW[7]	RW	RO[6]
Windows XP	RW[5]	RW	RW[7]	RW	RO[6]
Linux	RW	RW	RO[8]	RO[8]	RW

1. Windows Me/9x can read the NTFS file system via a free utility called NTFS For Windows 98. Although NTFSWIN98 is read-only, it works very well and is highly recommended. A version with limited write capability can be purchased. You can obtain these products from http://www.sysinternals.com.

2. Windows Me/9x can gain read-only access to Linux's extended2 file system by using the free utility FSDEXT2. This utility can be found at http://www.yipton.demon.co.uk.

3. You can use the FAT32 utility for Windows NT 4.0 to read and write to FAT32 file systems from Windows NT 4.0. This utility can be obtained from http://www.sysinternals.com. *This utility is not free.*

4. If an NTFS partition is to be shared with Windows 2000 or XP, you must use Windows NT 4.0 Service Pack 4 or later.

5. You can't format a new partition with FAT16 during XP's installation process or disk manager. Another OS must create it.

6. Windows NT 4.0, Windows 2000 and Windows XP can read extended2 file systems by using the free utility Explore2FS. This utility can be found at http://uranus.it.swin.edu.au/~jn/linux/explore2fs.

7. Windows 2000 and XP automatically convert NTFS version 4 volumes to NTFS version 5.

8. Although the 2.2.x Linux kernel does contain a read/write driver for NTFS, you should use the driver only in read-only mode. The write portion of the NTFS driver is still in the very early stages of development and might damage your partition. You can enable read-only support when recompiling your kernel for NTFS support.

Understanding the interplay between these various file systems is key in creating an efficient multiboot system. To the greatest extent possible, you should choose a format that's compatible with all the operating systems you'll want to use, on at least one disk partition. This will give a place to store files that can be read no matter which OS you're using.

Where you have the choice of several different candidate file systems, you must decide which is best, based on your hardware and the application for which you are creating your multiboot system. The following sections quickly recap file system descriptions, with an eye toward multibooting issues.

FAT16

FAT16 is the oldest file system mentioned in this chapter. It was originally intended for file systems based on the DOS operating system. As such, it is quite antiquated and not often used today. FAT16 might be your only choice in some situations due to its two major advantages:

- FAT16 is supported by almost all operating systems, including all versions of Windows, OS/2, MS-DOS, and Linux.
- The structure of the FAT16 file system is much simpler than the others, giving it much less software overhead. This gives FAT16 increased speed on volumes less than 1GB in size.

One big limitation of FAT16 is the fact that it cannot be installed in primary partitions greater than 2GB in size with MS-DOS and Windows 9x/Me; 4GB is the limit for FAT16 with Windows NT/2000/XP. To use the full capacity of a disk beyond those limits, an extended partition can be created, but it must be broken into non-bootable logical drives of no more than 2GB/4GB in size each. For example, a 10GB drive prepared as a FAT16 drive for use with both Windows Me and Windows XP would need to be divided into five drive letters, C: through G:. Also, the larger the partition, the less efficient FAT16 is in allocating space to small files—more disk space is wasted. As explained later in the chapter, this limitation has been overcome by FAT16's new brother, FAT32.

> **NOTE**
>
> If you are using the first edition of Windows 95, you can use only the FAT16 file system. Versions of Windows 95 prior to Windows 95 OSR2 cannot read FAT32 partitions. A prompt upgrade to Windows 98 is recommended for this as well as for many other reasons.
>
> Also, keep in mind that Microsoft frequently uses the term FAT to refer to both FAT16 and FAT32 file systems.

FAT32

The FAT32 file system was introduced with Windows 95 OSR2. FAT32 was essentially the answer to most of the shortcomings of FAT16. The following are among FAT32's strengths:

- FAT32 supports partitions up to 2TB in size (that's 2,048GB to you and me).
- FAT32 increased the number of clusters (decreasing the cluster size) on the hard disk, making the storage of small files take up less room than it did previously with FAT16.
- The structure of FAT32 remains very small, providing a notable speed increase over FAT16.

31

Of course, with all changes come pain and compatibility issues. To this day, Windows NT 4.0 does not natively support FAT32. The addition of FAT32 file support into Windows 2000 and XP is a welcome one, especially for multibooting users. However, neither FAT versions support the advanced security and reliability features of NTFS, as explained in the following section.

NTFS

The New Technology File System, or NTFS, brought with it many welcome additions to the world of Microsoft computing, including the following:

- Permissions—NTFS brought with it a concept used in the Novell and Unix worlds for quite some time. Permissions enable you to configure files and folders to be accessible only by specific users, user groups, or both. This is imperative for networked multiuser operating systems.

- Compression—You can transparently compress folders or files on an NTFS volume.

- Reliability—NTFS is much more reliable, and as such is suited to a server environment. Disk repair applications seldom need to be run on an NTFS file system.

- Large volumes are accessed much quicker with NTFS—Although FAT still rules the below-1GB world, NTFS excels at accessing files and folders in very large disk partitions.

- Encryption came with the version of NTFS supplied with Windows 2000 and XP (also known as NTFS 5). Now you can lock individual files or folders for high levels of security.

- Dynamic disk arrangements enable you to group separate physical drives into one large virtual drive (see Chapter 29, "Managing the Hard Disk," for a full discussion). However, be careful with dynamic disks—only Windows 2000 and XP Professional support it, and other operating systems can't boot from a drive that's been set up for dynamic disk partitions.

A disadvantage of NTFS, however, is that it can't be read directly by DOS, OS/2, Unix, or Windows Me/9x. You can download a free utility to read NTFS disks from http://www.sysinternals.com, and you can purchase a program with limited writing ability. Still, this isn't as straightforward as having support built into the operating system. Likewise, Linux has only limited support for NTFS—reading works but writing is dangerous. So, NTFS is not a generally useful format for a *shared* partition on multiboot systems.

By the way, there are now two versions of NTFS: versions 4 and 5. Version 4 was used by Windows NT version 4.0. The updated version 5 is used by Windows 2000 and XP and supports additional capabilities such as encrypted files and dynamic disk partitions that can be rearranged while Windows is running. These capabilities aren't available with XP Home Edition, but Home Edition still uses the newer disk format.

The version difference will only affect you if you share an NTFS-formatted disk volume between Windows NT 4.0 and Windows XP or 2000. The newer OSes will update your NTFS partitions to version 5, so you must update Windows NT 4.0 to Service Pack 4 or later so that it can read the new format.

APPLICATION CONSIDERATIONS

Along with all the file system considerations of a multiboot system, application installation problems also can arise unless you install each operating system and its applications in a separate partition. This is particularly true of Microsoft operating systems because some of them share the same installed directory names ("Program Files" is a notable example). Because of these potential problems, the following list of precautions is particularly useful:

- It's good practice to isolate operating systems whenever possible to minimize the impact of any catastrophic events such as system crashes, crunched file allocation tables, or applications that run amok. In other words, good disk partitioning is one way to increase protection for all the operating systems you run.

- Putting different OSes on separate partitions minimizes the chances that applications running on the different platforms will dump on one another's settings in unexpected ways.

- Many applications install files in the Windows or other common folders, and it's necessary to reinstall these applications under each OS to make sure that all files are copied where necessary. If you can tolerate the trouble, it's best to install the application into a different folder (on a different partition) each time. A common "Program Files" folder shared by multiple OSes brings the chance that OS-specific settings might give you trouble with other OSes.

That last bit of advice is a contentious one. Even your authors disagree. Bob thinks it's usually safe to use a single folder for an application's common files, and saves disk space, while Brian thinks that disk space is cheap, and having to chase down installation conflicts is an expensive waste of time. You may have to decide on a case-by-case basis after some experimentation.

If you find that an application acts erratically when installed into the same folder on several different OSes, reinstall it into a separate directory from each operating system. That is, install it onto the separate OS-specific partitions, or create a special application folder for each operating system (for example, \program files\win98\badapp or \program files\winXP\badapp, and so on) and install the problem apps there.

THE WINDOWS XP BOOT LOADER

As mentioned earlier in this chapter, one of the great advantages of the approaches we're advocating in this chapter is that we're using the Windows XP boot loader. The primary asset it gives us is a menuing system that lets you choose which OS to start every time you boot up your computer. The following sections explain the functioning of the boot loader.

THE MASTER BOOT RECORD

The *master boot record* (MBR) is the portion of the disk that tells your computer where to find the partition boot sector. All operating systems must be started up by some type of master boot record, whether this contains the system's native code or a multiboot utility. When

31

your system is booted, a chain of events ensues, based on your currently installed operating systems. The following is a simplified version of this chain of events for an installation containing Windows XP:

1. After POST (power on self test), the system BIOS reads the master boot record (MBR).

2. Control is passed to the master boot record, which then looks for the partition listed as the "active partition" in the partition table of the startup disk, as defined in your BIOS.

3. After the active partition is found, the master boot record loads sector 0, the partition's boot sector, into memory and executes it.

4. The partition boot sector points to NTLDR (NT loader) in the root of the partition and executes that.

5. NTLDR reads the contents of BOOT.INI, located in the partition's root folder. BOOT.INI lists the locations and names of the computer's bootable operating systems. If more than one OS is listed, NTLDR displays a menu of OS choices. If only one is listed, which is the usual case, NTLDR fires it up directly.

At this point, the user can select the operating system to boot up. Windows 2000 and NT use this same system. In the next few sections, we'll explain how to set up multiple operating systems so that they all end up as choices in BOOT.INI.

 If you are having problems with the Windows boot loader, see "Boot Menu Isn't Displayed" in the "Troubleshooting" section at the end of this chapter.

 If you want to remove the Windows boot loader, see "Removing the Windows XP Boot Loader" in the "Troubleshooting" section at the end of this chapter.

THE BOOT.INI SETTINGS FILE

BOOT.INI handles many options for booting your system. For now, you can see your current BOOT.INI by selecting Start, Run and entering `C:\boot.ini`, which opens the BOOT.INI with Notepad.

The BOOT.INI file has two sections.

THE [BOOT LOADER] SECTION

This section defines two specific settings:

- **Timeout**—This setting defines how long the system will wait until it boots into the default operating system. This value is in seconds. A value of -1 makes the system wait indefinitely until you make a manual selection. A value of 0 makes the system boot immediately into the default operating system.

- **Default**—This is the default operating system that will boot up, unless there is user intervention. The value of the Default entry must match the *location* part of one of the operating systems entries, which are described in the next section.

THE [OPERATING SYSTEMS] SECTION

This section contains a list of operating systems installed on your computer. You can see the option for Windows XP your BOOT.INI file if you've successfully completed an installation.

Each entry in this section is of the form

```
location="OS Name" /options
```

where *location* specifies the drive and folder on which the operating system is stored, "*OS Name*" is a text description of the OS, and *options* is an optional list of operating system load modifiers. For Windows NT, 2000, HP Home Edition and the 32-bit version of Windows XP, an entry might look like this:

```
multi(0)disk(0)rdisk(0)partition(1)\WINDOWS="Windows XP Professional"
```

(This strange format is a throwback from the days when Windows NT ran on the Alpha and MIPS processors. The format for the 64-bit Itanium processor version of Windows XP Professional is different, and equally obtuse.) In most setups, the rdisk number indicates the physical hard drive (0 = first), and partition indicates the partition number on the drive (1 = first). The entry is followed by a folder name.

TIP FROM

Bob & Brian

> For a listing of the options permitted in boot.ini, check out
> `http://www.labmice.net/install/bootini.htm` and
> `http://appdeploy.com/tips/bootiniswitches.shtml`

Non-NT–based operating systems are loaded through files that contain images of the master boot record that the OS is usually loaded by. For example, when you install Windows XP on a system that was previously running MS-DOS, the original MS-DOS boot sector is saved in a file, and the resulting BOOT.INI entry is

```
C:\ ="MS-DOS"
```

MULTIBOOT SCENARIOS

The possibilities for multibooting are nearly endless when you consider that a system can have multiple drives, each drive can have multiple partitions, and each partition can have an operating system on it. However, the scenarios discussed next represent the most common and usable configurations. When you understand the scenarios offered here, you should be able to effectively conquer any multiboot setup.

We recommend that you at least read through the first scenario fully, regardless of your own designs. This will give you a better understanding of the overall process. We'll also refer to that scenario so we can reduce repetition. All these configurations assume that you already have a working computer with at least a CD-ROM drive and hard disk.

31

NOTE

> Always be careful to consider file system compatibility between all these operating systems. Use Table 31.1 as a reference before forging ahead with your installations. This will save you many of the common problems associated with setting up a multiboot system.

NOTE

> All the following scenarios work on the assumption that you are able to boot from your CD-ROM drive. Most modern computers have this capability. A little-known fact is that some of the older operating systems in these examples are capable of booting from their respective CD-ROM installation disks. Windows NT 4.0, 2000, and XP can and will boot from your CD-ROM drive, as will OEM versions of Windows 98 and most modern versions of Linux. This method is much quicker and less error prone than the traditional method of booting from a floppy disk.
>
> Booting from the CD-ROM is usually enabled simply by changing the boot sequence from within your system's BIOS so that it checks the CD for an operating system before checking the hard drive. Consult your computer's operating manual for the proper method to enable this feature for your specific system BIOS. Chapter 3 has more ideas on how to boot from a CD-ROM in case you're having trouble in this department. Look for the troubleshooting tip at the end of the chapter titled "DOS Won't Recognize the CD-ROM Drive."

DUAL-BOOTING WINDOWS XP PROFESSIONAL AND WINDOWS ME/9X

Many people want or need to run Windows XP and Windows Me, 95, or 98 in the same computer. Because Windows 95, 98, and Me behave almost identically in this situation, for the remainder of this section, I'll use 9x to refer to all three of these older versions.

The following sections discuss two ways of dual booting:

- In the same partition
- In separate partitions

PUTTING WINDOWS XP PROFESSIONAL AND WINDOWS 9X IN THE SAME PARTITION

If you already have a Windows 95/98 installation, you can simply install Windows XP beside it for a dual-boot arrangement from the same partition. I don't recommend this setup, however. Because this arrangement will mix Windows XP and Windows 9x programs in one \Program Files folder, you could end up with serious software version conflicts.

Despite this, if it's absolutely necessary, you can follow these steps to install both Windows XP and 9x on the same partition:

1. Assuming you have successfully installed Windows 9xon your system, begin the Windows XP Professional installation wizard by inserting the CD-ROM.

2. If the wizard does not autorun, you can initialize it by choosing Start, Run and then typing **D:\i386\winnt32**, where D: is the letter of your CD-ROM drive.

3. After Windows Setup has launched, choose New Installation as the Installation Type. This will install Windows XP into a new system folder called \WINNT. From here, simply continue the Windows XP installation as usual.

4. When asked if you want to update your hard drive to use the NTFS format, choose No (leave the partition alone). If you upgraded to NTFS, Windows 9x would not be able to read the disk.

5. When the Windows XP installation has concluded, you should be able to successfully boot into either Windows XP or Windows 9x via the Windows XP boot menu presented at system startup.

Although this configuration is common, it can have its pitfalls. The following are some important things to keep in mind with this configuration:

- Dual-booting Windows XP and Windows 9x from the same partition is ill advised. In this configuration, for example, both operating systems will use the same Program Files folder, which can result in version conflicts.

- Be aware, also, that Registry settings for an application on Windows 9x will not follow you into the Registry of Windows XP, and vice versa. You might have to reinstall some applications in order for them to function correctly in both operating systems. In some instances, you might even have to purchase separate Windows 9x- or Windows XP-specific versions of some applications. Finding out which ones you need to do this with is simply a matter of experimenting with each respective operating system.

TIP FROM

Bob & Brian

> Don't worry about the Registries from the two OSes stepping on each other. Windows 9x stores user Registry info in \Windows or \windows\profiles, while Windows XP stores user Registry data in \Documents and Settings\<username>.

PUTTING WINDOWS XP PROFESSIONAL AND WINDOWS 9X IN SEPARATE PARTITIONS

As you have no doubt gathered by now, the preferred approach uses separate partitions. This arrangement is more flexible and foolproof in the long run.

First, you must plan the installation from a file system standpoint. This will give you a better foundation from which to proceed:

- The Windows 9x partition should be a FAT32 file system with C:\WINDOWS (the system directory), along with C:\Program Files contained in it.

- Windows XP will reside on the second partition, containing the Windows XP %SystemRoot% directory (typically D:\WINNT), along with D:\Program Files. You can format this partition with NTFS or FAT32.

■ You might want to reserve a third and final FAT32 partition solely for sharing data between the two operating systems. You can use drive C for this, too, of course.

> **NOTE**
>
> Wherever I suggest that you might want multiple partitions, remember they don't all need to be placed on the same drive. You can add additional hard drives and install partitions there. The setup procedure remains the same, however. Just select the additional drive when you're choosing a partition to set up, format or install.

If you format the Windows XP partition with NTFS during installation, remember that it will not be visible to Windows 9x. Any FAT16 or FAT32 partitions located *after* the NTFS partition *will* be visible to Win9x. This can have the odd effect of making these extra partitions appear with different drive letters in the different operating systems, as each OS assigns letters to the partitions it recognizes, in order. I'll give you a concrete example of this later in the chapter under "Avoiding Drive Letter Madness."

USING FDISK TO DEFINE PARTITIONS

Chapter 3 covered the fact that Setup will enable you to use unpartitioned free space to create a second partition (either NTFS or not) for installing Windows XP. You also learned about using a third-party program such as PartitionMagic to more flexibly help in that process, especially if you don't have any "free" (meaning unpartitioned) space on your hard disk, which is likely the case. If you already have a free partition or two for installing Windows XP after Windows 9x/Me, you can skip ahead to the section titled "Installing Windows XP Professional into the Second Partition." If you need to define partitions before starting the Windows XP setup process (for example, to set up versions of Windows 9x or other operating systems), this section will give you an overview of the FDISK partitioning program that comes with DOS and Windows 9x.

> **CAUTION**
>
> Using the FDISK editor is a permanent process. If you have any disk partitions currently defined on your system, be sure to have a backup of all your important data because it might be damaged in this process. Unless you are partitioning your disk for the first time, you might find PartitionMagic more suited to the task of configuring your disk partitions. PartitionMagic also has the added advantage of being able to actually resize your existing partitions for a maximum amount of flexibility. More information on PartitionMagic can be found at
>
> `http://www.powerquest.com/partitionmagic/index.html`

If you need to set up partitions on a new disk, in lieu of using PartitionMagic (for whatever reason), you can opt to use the trusty old Microsoft-supplied FDISK program to do the job. It works okay in a pinch (especially on an unpopulated drive or one you're going to wipe), and a knowledge of FDISK can sometimes come in handy.

The following discussion shows how to start with a blank hard disk, use FDISK to create the partitions, and then install Windows 9x and Windows XP. The following explains how to define partitions for each operating system:

1. First, boot from the Windows 9x CD-ROM and select the second option, Boot from CD-ROM. If you are booting from a Windows 9x installation floppy, just proceed to step 2.

2. Select Start Computer with CD-ROM Support.

3. After finally booting into DOS, run the FDISK program, which will give you the opportunity to partition your disk so that each operating system can occupy a different partition. This is simply done by typing `fdisk` at the prompt:

   `A:>fdisk`

4. When FDISK is loaded, you are asked whether to enable large disk support. Select Yes, which enables you to later format the disk with the FAT32 file system. (If you selected No here, you would only be able to create a partition of 2048MB or less using the FAT16 file system.)

5. Next, you will be presented with a menu of options for partitioning your hard disk, as shown in Figure 31.1. For the purposes of this installation, select option 1, Create DOS Partition or Logical DOS Drive. This option enables you to create the first partition for installing Windows 9x.

Figure 31.1
The FDISK main menu screen.

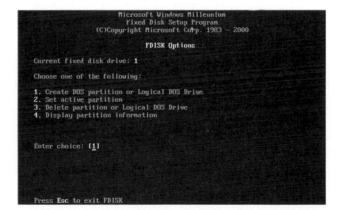

6. Select Create Primary DOS Partition to create a bootable primary partition.

NOTE

All Microsoft operating systems must be bootable from the first primary partition on the primary IDE bus. The only exclusion to this is a SCSI-based system, which must be bootable from the first primary partition of the SCSI controller-assigned boot disk. This does not mean the system and other files must be installed here; it only means that the Windows boot information must be installed in the MBR (master boot record) of this partition.

7. When asked whether you would like to use the maximum available size for this partition, select No. You will need additional space to be left on the disk for the other two partitions that will house the Windows XP system and the shared data partition.

8. Next you are asked for the size of the first partition. This particular setting will vary depending on the operating systems involved and the amount of disk space available.

    Table 31.2 (immediately following this set of steps) shows the minimum and recommended sizes for each operating system. You can make the partition larger than the recommended size, if you have the space.

9. Use the backspace key to erase the size that FDISK has filled in. Using the information in Table 31.2, enter the desired size for your first primary partition, in MB. For a 2GB partition, enter 2048.

10. Next, you must define the first partition as being the active partition so that the computer knows from which partition it should try to boot from. Press Esc to return to the main FDISK menu. Select option 2, Set Active Partition, to pick the first partition and set it as active.

31

CAUTION

> If more than one primary partition is listed (as might be the case with some Compaq models that use a special diagnostic partition for their BIOS setup program and testing software), make sure you select the partition you just created.

11. If you want to create the XP and data sharing partitions during the XP install procedure, you can leave the remainder of the disk unpartitioned and skip ahead to step 15.

    Otherwise, you may now create the logical partitions to house your remaining two file systems. This can be done by selecting option 1, Create a DOS Partition or Logical DOS Drive, and then selecting option 2, Create Extended DOS Partition.

12. FDISK adds all addition FAT partition entries inside what it calls an Extended DOS partition. Therefore, you should allocate enough space for the Extended DOS Partition to hold your Windows XP volume *and* your shared data volume. If you need no other partitions, you can allocate all remaining space to the Extended Partition. Select a size, press Enter, and then Esc.

13. FDISK will prompt you for the size of the first FAT partition to create inside the extended partition—FDISK calls this a Logical DOS Drive. Select a size in MB for the Windows XP partition, and then press Enter and Esc.

14. FDISK will prompt you for the size of the next Logical DOS Drive. Allocate the remaining space to your data drive and press Enter.

15. Press Esc to exit FDISK. Finally, press Ctrl+Alt+Delete to restart the computer.

TABLE 31.2   RECOMMENDED HARD DRIVE CAPACITY FOR EACH OPERATING SYSTEM

Operating System	Minimum Size	Recommended Size
Windows 98	225MB to 400MB	2048MB
Windows NT 4.0	124MB	1024MB
Windows 2000 Professional	650MB	2000MB
Windows XP Home Edition	1500MB	2000MB
Windows XP Professional	1500MB	2048MB
Linux (Red Hat 6.1)	135MB to 1.2GB	2048MB

NOTE

Microsoft and others' discussions of disk space requirements in particular and hard disk storage in general are often confusing because MB (Megabyte) and GB (Gigabyte) have two different meanings. Hard drives and similar storage devices are normally rated in decimal MB, in which 1MB equals one million bytes, and decimal GB, in which 1GB equals one billion bytes. However, disk utilities such as FDISK and most system BIOSes rate drives in binary MB/GB; a binary MB is $1,024 \times 1,024$ (the value of a kilobyte times a kilobyte), for a total of 1,048,576 bytes, and a binary GB is $1024 \times 1024 \times 1024$, for a total of 1,073,741,824 bytes. Thus, there are substantial differences in the size of decimal versus binary MB/GB. Recently, the term Mebibyte (Mi) has been developed to refer to binary MB and Gibibyte (Gi) to binary GB, but this usage is not yet widespread.

31

INSTALLING WINDOWS 9X INTO THE FIRST PARTITION

After you've defined at least two partitions, you are ready to install Windows 9x into the first one. After that we'll install Windows XP in the second one.

1. If you are installing Windows 9x (and you have a bootable version of the installation CD) you can install it by booting from its installation CD-ROM. Select Start Windows 9x Setup from CD-ROM.

NOTE

If you're having trouble accessing the CD-ROM drive, check the BIOS settings, or as a good little trick, many systems will boot up from a Windows 9x emergency startup disk with CD-ROM support (even one made on another machine). You can boot into DOS this way, with CD-ROM drivers loaded. Then run the Setup program located on the CD.

2. When you're in the Windows 9x installation program, you will be given the option to format drive C: and continue with the installation. Setup may also require that you format partition D:. It's okay to do this.

3. Continue with the Windows 9x installation, making sure that Windows is placed in the \WINDOWS folder on the C: partition by accepting the default.

CAUTION

> If you've been booting from your CD-ROM installation disc, be sure to change the boot sequence in your BIOS so that your hard disk boots before your CD-ROM. This is essential for a successful installation.

TIP FROM

Bob & Brian

> Windows 9x is installed first for a very important reason. Windows 9x will always write its own master boot record to make the system boot into it after an installation. You'll want to make sure that Windows XP has the last say in what gets installed at the master boot level so that you can take advantage of its versatile boot loader.

INSTALLING WINDOWS XP PROFESSIONAL INTO THE SECOND PARTITION

Continue your multiboot pursuit with the installation of Windows XP. Per Microsoft's recommendations, you should run the Windows XP installation program from within Windows 9x.

1. Insert the Windows XP disc. The Windows XP Installer should auto-run. If it doesn't, select Start, Run, and type **D:SETUP**, where D: is your CD-ROM drive letter.

2. Select Install Windows XP. When asked what type of installation you want to perform, select New Installation (Advanced) and click Next, as shown in Figure 31.2.

Figure 31.2
Choose New Installation here to install XP into a separate partition.

3. Proceed through the License Agreement and Product Key pages to the Setup Options page. Click Advanced Options and check I Want To Choose The Install Drive Letter And Partition During Setup. This gives you the opportunity to select the D: partition as well as convert it to the NTFS file system later on in the setup. Click OK, and then Next.

4. After the Windows Setup Wizard copies some files to your hard disk, it will reboot your system and continue the installation from a text-based setup. From this setup, you will have the option to select where you'd like to install your Windows XP system, as

shown in Figure 31.3. If you didn't create the XP and data partitions earlier, you can use this menu to create new partitions by pressing C. Finally, select the second partition as the Windows XP install procedure and press Enter.

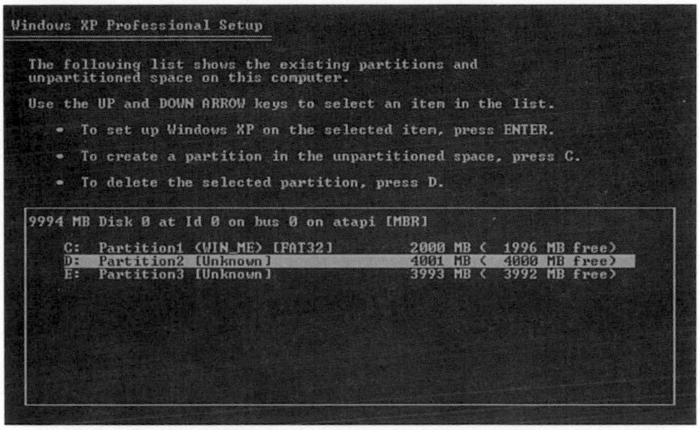

Figure 31.3
Selecting the location of the \WINDOWS install directory from within the text-mode Windows XP Setup. Windows 2000 and NT Setup offer a similar choice.

5. Next, you will be given the option to select the type of file system to use. You can keep your already formatted partition intact, select a new file system format, as shown in Figure 31.4.

Figure 31.4
Here, you can choose to leave the original file system intact, or select a different file system for the Windows XP partition.

The "Quick" versions of these choices do not test the drive as it formats. Testing takes some time but it's worthwhile, so I recommend that you not use the Quick format options.

TIP FROM

Bob & Brian

> Remember, you can convert a FAT partition to NTFS at any later time using a Windows command-line utility. Windows can't convert NTFS back to FAT, however. If in doubt, use FAT for now.

6. After making your choice, Setup will proceed to do its thing and install Windows XP. During setup, there will be one or two restarts and you'll see the multiboot menu. Ignore it and let the default "Windows XP Setup" choice start up. This choice will be removed when Setup has completed successfully.

7. When you subsequently restart your computer, you should see the options shown in Figure 31.5.

Figure 31.5
The final result—The Windows XP boot loader now shows both operating systems at boot time.

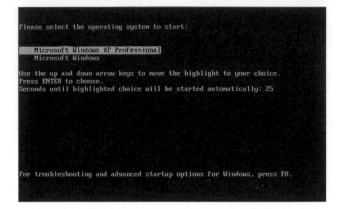

FORMATTING THE DATA-SHARING PARTITION

On some of our machines, we're quite content with two partitions only, with data placed either on the Windows 9x partition if it is nonsensitive, or on the Windows XP NTFS partition (and optionally in an encrypted folder) if it is sensitive. However, I recommend using a third partition to give you a place to store files that you want to keep whilst installing and uninstalling operating systems on the other two. I used such a partition while writing this book to hold my screen-capture program and notes; the main OS partitions needed to be erased and reinstalled dozens of times.

If you did create an extra data partition as I described in the previous section, the final installation step is to format this remaining partition. This can be done by using the Windows XP Disk Administration program, or the FORMAT command from a Command Prompt window in either OS.

→ **See** Chapter 29, "Managing the Hard Disk," for more about formatting partitions with Disk Management.

AVOIDING DRIVE LETTER MADNESS

As I mentioned earlier, when you use file formats that are not compatible among all the operating systems you're using, logical drive letters will likely shift around based on which operating system you're booting.

The reason for this is that on bootup, Windows scans your disk controllers in the following order looking for fixed or removable hard disks:

1. Primary IDE Controller, Master Drive
2. Primary IDE Controller, Slave Drive
3. Secondary IDE Controller, Master Drive
4. Secondary IDE Controller, Slave Drive
5. SCSI Controllers, in SCSI ID order
6. Additional controllers (such as USB, IEEE-1394 drives)

(If your computer boots from a SCSI drive, the SCSI drives are scanned first.) Only the compatible partitions on these drives are scanned and assigned drive letters in the order found. This means that Windows 9x will skip over NTFS partitions, and will assign different drive letters to any subsequent FAT partitions it finds than Windows XP, 2000 or NT will.

For example, if I had one hard drive with three partitions, defined as follows:

#1 FAT32, Windows 98 Boot partition

#2 NTFS, Windows XP Boot partition

#3 FAT32, Data only

and a CD-ROM drive, Windows 98 and Windows XP will assign the default drive letters shown in Table 31.3.

TABLE 31.3   LOGICAL DRIVE LETTER ASSIGNMENTS

Drive	Partition	Drive Letter assigned by Windows 98	Drive Letter assigned by Windows XP
Hard Drive	#1, FAT32	C:	C:
	#2, NTFS	(none)	D:
	#3, FAT32	D:	E:
CDROM	CDFS	E:	F:

Notice that under Windows 98 the data partition is D:, whereas under Windows XP it is E:. This is not a problem if you store only data on the drive. However, it becomes more complicated if your applications expect to find support files on a given drive under any OS.

You might have already thought about using Windows XP Disk Management to reassign the drive letters while Windows XP is running. Although it is true that Disk Management can set drive letters in any way you please, you can't change the boot drive's letter. In our example, this means that we can't reverse the D and E drives letters to match Windows 98.

31

However, there is another way. Retail copies of PartitionMagic include a program called DriveMapper that can remap the drive letters under Windows 98. You can run PartitionMagic in Windows 98, use the DriveMapper option, and reassign the data drive to E:, skipping D: altogether when you're running Windows 98. Then make your CD-ROM drive F:. Now, you can have the same logical drive assignment in both operating systems.

CAUTION

> If possible, reassign letters before you install applications; otherwise, Registry settings, shortcuts, and support files can point to the wrong drive. Consult the PartitionMagic user's guide or Help file for more about considerations when reassigning drive letters.

WINDOWS XP HOME EDITION AND WINDOWS XP PROFESSIONAL

Installing both the Home Edition and Professional version of Windows XP on the same system is popular for many people who need to test applications in both environments.

Because both operating systems use the same boot loader and compatible file systems, installation and setup are simple. However, you *must* ensure that the two versions are installed onto different partitions or hard drives.

To set up dual-booting of Windows XP Home Edition and XP Professional, simply install them both one after the other, taking care to select the Advanced Options button on the Special Options page during setup. Check I Want To Choose The Install Drive Letter And Partition During Setup, and then click OK. This will let you select the partition on which each version gets installed.

WINDOWS XP PROFESSIONAL AND WINDOWS 2000 OR NT

Installing both Windows XP and earlier NT versions on the same system is also something you might want to do. This configuration is popular for many people already running Windows NT 4.0 who want to try Windows XP before completely canning their previous installation. This is a worthwhile pursuit and can be obtained with a little care and planning.

If you already have Windows NT 4.0 installed, you are probably using either the FAT16 file system or NTFS. Looking at Table 31.1, you can see that Windows XP supports both of the file systems supported by Windows NT 4.0. When installing Windows XP Professional, you simply select a new installation, as opposed to an upgrade, and the installer will handle the rest. As with the previous configuration, Windows XP will save your Windows NT 4.0 installation and give you the choice of selecting it at boot time.

This setup also can suffer from the same sort of problems as the Windows 98/Windows XP configuration. You must be careful to not overlap your new and old installation directories. And although you can have them coexist on the same partition, you'd be installing files from two different versions of Windows into the same "Program Files" folder. It's much more prudent to have them occupy separate partitions or drives.

CAUTION

> Windows XP uses an updated version of the NTFS file system: NTFS5. Before installing Windows XP, you must be sure that you've first updated your installed version of Windows NT 4.0 with service pack 4 or greater. This will ensure that your NT 4.0 installation will be capable of reading your NTFS disk after adding Windows XP to your system. Service pack 6a is the current (and final) version.
>
> Even with the service pack, however, NT Version 4 won't be able to read XP's encrypted or compressed files.

31

If you want to test or use Windows XP's advanced file system features, or if the NTFS version issue worries you, you can use this setup on a dual Windows XP/Windows NT installation.

Partition 1   Windows NT, NTFS version 4

Partition 2   Windows XP, NFTS version 5

Partition 3   Shared files, FAT16

Because Windows NT can't read FAT32 disks, you have use a FAT16 partition as a shared file volume.

To dual-boot NT and XP, do the following:

1. Install Windows NT 4.0. Chances are good that you already have it installed, in which case this portion of the job is already complete.

2. You're going to want to have another partition to house Windows XP. Unless you have free, unpartitioned space available, you'll need to install an additional disk drive, or use PartitionMagic to insert a new partition on an existing drive. If you do have unpartitioned space, you can install Windows XP directly into that. You can leave the new partition unformatted.

3. Boot up Windows NT, insert the Windows XP setup disc, and choose Install Windows XP from the menu. (If the menu doesn't start automatically, look on the CD's root directory for Setup.exe and run it.)

4. Choose New Installation from the wizard's first page; otherwise, you'll wipe out Windows NT 4.0.

5. Accept the agreement, enter the serial number, and follow the wizard.

6. From the Select Special Options page of the Windows XP Setup Wizard, select the Advanced Options button. Check I Want To Choose The Install Drive Letter And Partition During Setup, and then click OK.

7. After the Windows Setup Wizard copies some files to your hard disk, it will reboot your system and continue the installation from a text-based setup. From this setup, you will have the option to select where you'd like to install Windows XP. Choose the partition you created in step 2, or choose any unformatted free space (if you have any).

8. Next, you will be given the option to select how you want the target partition formatted. Select Format as NTFS or Convert to NTFS.

9. The Setup process will continue normally. When it's finished, you'll be able to choose either Windows NT 4.0 or Windows XP when your computer boots up.

TIP FROM

Bob
& Brian

> See the earlier section titled "Formatting the Data-Sharing Partition" for some thoughts about creating a third partition to store data that can be shared between the two operating systems.

WINDOWS XP, WINDOWS NT 4.0, AND WINDOWS 9X/ME

Although it might be uncommon, it is possible to create a setup using all three of these operating systems. Take the following approach:

1. Create three partitions (or four if you want a separate data partition). You can create these partitions on one or two hard drives.

2. If you decide you want a data partition, make it FAT16 because NT 4.0 can't see FAT32. FAT16 is the one common denominator. See Table 31.4 for a suggested layout. As you can see from the table, we're suggesting using FAT16 for all the partitions to ensure maximum compatibility and the least amount of drive letter shifting.

3. Install Windows 9x/Me in the first partition. If asked whether you want to upgrade to FAT32, say no unless you don't mind having the first partition invisible to Windows NT 4.0.

4. Install Windows NT in the third partition and upgrade it to at least Service Pack 4. This system will dual-boot. Check it to see that it works acceptably.

5. Install Windows XP in New Installation mode, into the last partition. This should add the third operating system to the boot loader.

6. Format the data partition however you like. Remember that for maximum compatibility between all three operating systems, you'll want to use FAT16.

When you're finished, the Windows XP boot loader will give you the option of booting into each of the three operating systems. Remember to heed the cautions explained earlier in this chapter regarding sharing data and applications between operating systems.

TABLE 31.4 BOOTING WINDOWS XP, NT 4.0, AND WINDOWS 9X

Partition #	Operating System	Format	Notes
Partition 1	Windows 95 OSR2 Windows 98 or Windows Me	FAT16	Can use FAT32 if you don't mind this partition not being seen by NT 4.0.
Partition 2	Optional Data Partition	FAT16	We've put it second so its drive letter says the same under all 3 OSes.
Partition 3	Windows NT 4.0 SP4 or later	FAT16	Can use NTFS if you are aware of the consequences.
Partition 4	Windows XP	NTFS	

31

NOTE

> You can't multiboot more than one version of Windows 95, 98, and Me even if they're on different partitions. The only way to have more than one Windows 9x on a single machine is with a third-party boot manager such as BootMagic or System Commander. (See the section "Tips from the Windows Pros: Living with More Than One OS," at the end of this chapter.)

WINDOWS XP AND LINUX

Using both Windows XP and Linux on the same system is a very rewarding multiboot scenario. This gives you two very powerful operating systems that can work in harmony on the same system. Linux can be booted from any type of partition on any installed disk, be it primary or logical. This enables you to create a Linux partition anywhere you have enough space to put it.

One of the great advantages of this configuration is Linux's capability to read, and sometimes write, nearly every file system under the sun. You'll be able to share files between your two systems with a minimal amount of hassle. Be sure to see Table 31.1 (earlier in this chapter) to properly plan for file sharing between both operating systems.

NOTE

> Linux can read NTFS partitions quite well. But with the current level of NTFS support, when Linux writes to an NTFS partition, it causes some repairable damage to the file system that Windows XP has to fix the next time it boots. This makes me nervous, so I'd suggest that you avoid the need to have Linux write to an NTFS disk. Install Windows XP in a FAT32 partition, or use a third FAT16 or FAT32 partition to store common files.

LILO, THE LINUX LOADER

Just as Windows XP uses the Windows loader to select an operating system and boot up, Linux uses LILO—the LInux LOader. LILO has a comparable ability to select among several OSes in different locations. It's possible to use LILO as your primary boot program and to configure it to select between Linux and Windows XP.

However, configuring LILO is beyond the scope of this book. I'll only discuss how to set up multibooting with the Windows loader, so if you're following these instructions it's important that whatever process you use to set up your system, you end up with the Windows loader on your primary disk's Master Boot Record, rather than LILO.

There are two ways to make sure this happens:

- If you install Linux first, and then Windows XP, the XP loader will replace LILO. Then you can use the procedure described later in this section to create a Linux boot file for the Windows loader.

- If you install XP first, then Linux, you'll have to take care to tell the Linux installation system not put LILO on your computer's Master Boot Record (MBR). If it does, the XP loader will be overwritten. How you specify this differs from one Linux distribution to another, and may even differ between versions of the same distribution. In the instructions later in this section, I'll describe how to do this for Red Hat Linux version 7.1, but the procedure may be different for your copy of Linux. If the XP boot loader does get overwritten, you'll find out quickly: You won't get a boot choice menu. You'll have to follow the procedure under "Boot Menu Isn't Displayed" in the Troubleshooting section at the end of this chapter.

Clearly, it easiest and safest if you can install Linux first. If you can't, please read your Linux distribution's installation instructions carefully, and select an installation mode that does not automatically put LILO on the Master Boot Record. The scenario we discuss in the next section assumes that you've already installed Windows XP before installing Linux.

 If you do accidentally overwrite the Windows Loader with LILO, see "Boot Menu Isn't Displayed" in the "Troubleshooting" section at the end of this chapter.

INSTALLING LINUX

This section deals with the task of installing Linux in a multiboot situation with Windows XP. Although a complete tutorial on the installation of Linux is out of the scope of this chapter, we will try to cover the essential points needed to make your system multibootable.

The procedures in this chapter assume that you are using the current version of Red Hat Linux, which is 7.1 at the time of this writing. For the purposes of this example, you will be installing Linux onto a separate partition on the same disk as your Windows XP installation. Refer to Table 31.2 to be sure you have enough free space to install both Windows XP and Linux.

TIP FROM

Bob
& Brian

> If you do not have enough space in your hard drive, consider adding a second disk or using the PartitionMagic program to shrink an existing partition.

NOTE

Although the following information provides the basics for dual-booting Windows XP with Linux, you'll find much more detailed coverage in *The Multi-Boot Configuration Handbook*, published by Que. You should also search the Web for information. Check out `http://www.linuxdoc.org/HOWTO/mini/Linux+NT-Loader.html` and `www.linuxdoc.org/HOWTO/mini/Multiboot-with-LILO.html`.

You can install Linux and Windows XP in either order. Just be sure to read the previous section titled "LILO, the Linux Loader." If you want to use NTFS for Windows XP, be sure to leave additional room for a FAT32 partition on which to store files you want to share between the two operating systems. Refer to Table 31.2 to find the minimum amounts of space needed. If you can, allow 3 or more GB for each partition.

Now, let's cover some of the important aspects of the Red Hat Linux installation procedure.

1. Boot from the Red Hat Linux installation CD-ROM. This will bring you to the Red Hat Linux installation program. Press Enter to begin a graphical-interface installation.

2. After some preliminary questions about your keyboard and mouse, you will be prompted for what type of installation you would like. In the examples shown here, I chose the Custom class (see Figure 31.6) so that I could specify that LILO not overwrite the Master Boot Record. This is very important if you're installing Linux after Windows XP! If you're installing Linux first, you can select a Workstation install, which will simplify your choices during the setup.

Figure 31.6
Selecting the Custom installation type from within the Red Hat installation program.

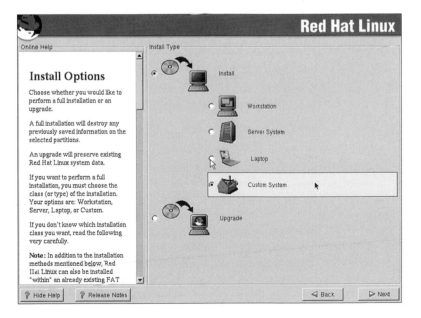

3. The next option offered by the Red Hat installation is whether you'd like automatic partitioning. Select the option to manually partition with Disk Druid and click Next. This step is necessary to create a multiboot system with Windows XP, using the Windows boot loader.

4. On the following screen, the Disk Druid tool gives you the option of creating your Linux partitions. Although there are many options for partitioning and mounting Linux partitions, you can make it much easier on yourself simply by creating a root and swap partition. These are all that is needed to successfully install Linux. On the bottom pane, you can see a representation of your disk, as well as the used and free space available on it (see Figure 31.7).

Figure 31.7
The Red Hat Disk Druid disk partition-ing tool.

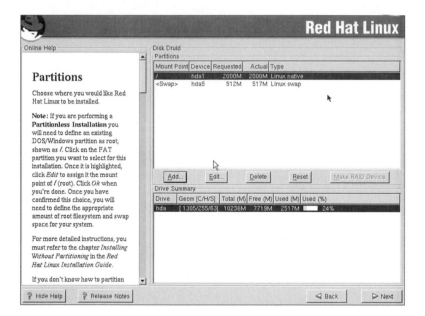

5. Click the Add button, and you can now add a partition for your Linux system. (If you have already installed Windows XP, you'll add the Linux partitions in addition to any already used for XP.) Because you will need to create two partitions, one each for / (or root) and swap, you must plan the sizes of each beforehand.

TIP FROM

Bob & Brian

A good rule of thumb is to create a swap file that is at least the size of your installed memory. Twice the size is even better. This will be enough for most workstation applications. For example, if you're allowing 2GB (2048MB) for Linux on a system with 128MB of RAM, you could create a 1920MB root partition and a 128MB swap partition.

6. First, click the Add button to define the / (root) partition.

7. Type / into the Mount Point field and make sure the Partition Type is the default Linux Native.

8. In the size field, add the size in megabytes for your root partition.

9. Select OK to create the partition. Notice now that the Free column on the second pane has changed to reflect the remaining space on the partition. This is the space left for your swap partition.

10. Next, click Add and define the swap partition. In the size field, enter the desired size in MB for the swap partition.

11. For the partition Type, select Linux Swap, and the Mount Point field will automatically change to reflect that you are creating a swap partition.

    Click OK to create the partition. At this point, if you haven't yet installed Windows XP, there should be a big chunk of unpartitioned space still available, as shown in Figure 31.8. Otherwise, you should end up with little or no unused space left.

12. After you have created these two partitions, click Next to continue the installation.

Figure 31.8
Root and swap partitions as defined in the Red Hat Disk Druid tool.

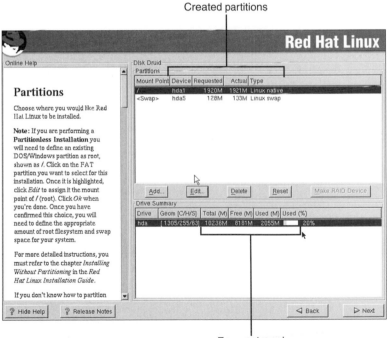

Created partitions

Free and used space totals

13. You will be asked whether you'd like to format your Linux root partition. This is perfectly safe so leave the option checked and continue by clicking Next.

14. On the next screen, Under LILO Configuration, check Create Boot Disk and Install LILO. Under Install LILO Boot Record On, select On First Record of Boot Partition, as shown in Figure 31.9. (If you've installed Windows XP already, it's important that you make these choices no matter which Linux distribution you are using.)

Figure 31.9
Boot disk and LILO configuration from the Red Hat Linux installer.

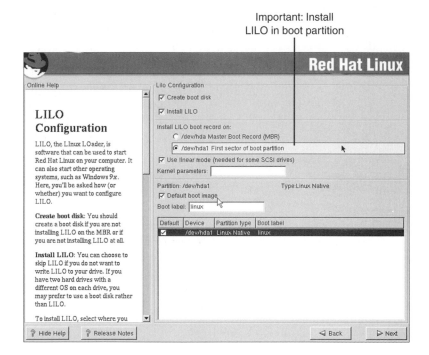

Write down the name of the partition that contains LILO. It will be named something like /dev/hda1. You'll need to know this later when I discuss locating the Linux boot sector.

15. The bottom part of this screen sets which partitions show up in LILO's boot menu, as well as how you want to label the partitions. If you've already installed Windows XP, LILO will add an entry for your Windows XP partition and label it dos. This will actually enable you to boot into Windows XP's boot sector from within LILO by simply typing dos at the LILO prompt. Most likely, you'll want to leave this at its default setting.

16. Click Next and proceed through the setup menus to configure networking and other peripherals, user accounts, and so on. Follow the instructions in your Linux distribution manual because this will vary from version to version.

17. The installation will finally create and format your Linux file system and install system packages to complete the installation.

18. When prompted, insert your disk and the installer will create the boot disk for you. This boot disk will enable you to boot into Linux in case of an emergency (such as in case the Windows XP loader fails you!).

19. After LILO is installed, the Red Hat installation will finish and you may reboot your system.

GETTING THE LINUX BOOT SECTOR

After you install Linux, you'll need to create an image or file dump of the Linux boot sector. You need this to configure the Windows XP boot loader to boot into Linux. Here's how to get it:

1. Get a blank, formatted 1.44MB floppy disk.

2. Shut down and reboot your computer with the Linux boot disk discussed in the previous section.

3. When Linux has finished booting, log in as root using the password you supplied during installation. All the following steps must be performed as root.

4. Remove the boot disk, insert the formatted MS-DOS floppy into your disk drive and type the following command:
   ```
   mount -t msdos /dev/fd0 /mnt/floppy
   ```
   This will make the disk available to you by mounting it in the directory /mnt/floppy.

TIP FROM

Bob & Brian

> If you need to format the floppy from within Linux, you may do so by typing the following command from the prompt:
> ```
> fdformat /dev/fd0; /sbin/mkfs -t msdos
> ```
> This command will give you a freshly formatted MS-DOS disk in Linux. From there you can simply mount the disk to get access to it.

5. The next step is to write the Linux boot sector to the disk. The most important part of this step is to make sure you take the boot sector from the correct partition. This partition is the one that was installed in LILO during the Linux installation. If you're unsure which partition contains the Linux boot sector, issue the following command:
   ```
   more /etc/lilo.conf
   ```
   which will give you output similar to the following:
   ```
   boot=/dev/hda1
   map=/boot/map
   install=/boot/boot.b
   prompt
   timeout=50
   image=/boot/vmlinuz-2.4.2-2
       label=linux
       root=/dev/hda1
       read-only
   ```

31

6. The "boot=" entry at the top of the file tells us that LILO is installed in /dev/hda1. Using the dd program, issue the following command:

```
/bin/dd if=/dev/hda1 of=/mnt/floppy/bootsect.lnx bs=512 count=1
```

This command will copy the Linux boot sector at /dev/hda1 to a file called bootsect.lnx on your disk.

7. Next, unmount the floppy disk using the following command:

```
umount /dev/fd0
```

8. Finally, remove the floppy disk from your computer and reboot the system:

```
/sbin/reboot
```

If you haven't already installed Windows XP, do this now. If you created an extra partition to use for shared file storage, you can create and it now as well.

Adding Linux to the Windows XP Boot Loader

After both Linux and Windows XP are both installed, you can add Linux to the Windows XP boot loader from any version of Windows you have installed. The steps are exactly the same and are not operating system-dependent.

1. First, copy the bootsect.lnx file, which you created in the previous section, from your floppy disk to the root of your C: drive. This can be done from a command prompt or from the Windows Explorer. This file must be located in the root folder.

2. Modify the BOOT.INI file to add an entry for Linux. The easiest way is to open the System control panel applet, view the Advanced tab, select Settings under Startup and Recovery, and click Edit.

3. Next, add the following line at the end of the BOOT.INI file:

```
C:\bootsect.lnx="Red Hat Linux 7.1"
```

4. You can now save BOOT.INI, reboot, and select Red Hat Linux 7.1 as one of your boot menu options. It's a long and complex procedure, but that's one of the reasons we love Linux!

Mounting Windows Disks Within Linux

Next, you'll want Linux to mount your Windows disks so that you can share files between both operating systems. This will enable you to copy files back and forth without using external media such as floppy disks. All the following steps must be performed as root because they are system-sensitive procedures:

1. First, create the directories within which you will mount the Windows file systems. The normal Linux convention is to create these directories in the /mnt tree.

2. Issue commands to create the directories for your Windows FAT16 or FAT32 partitions:

```
mkdir /mnt/windisk1
mkdir /mnt/windisk2
(etc).
```

NOTE

These directory names are a matter of taste. You can use whatever name you feel comfortable with at this point. As long as these directories exist, your Windows partitions should mount easily.

3. To test the first mount point, attempt to mount the first FAT32 partition using this command:

`mnt -t vfat /dev/hda1 /mnt/windisk1`

4. You can examine the contents of this partition by simply executing

`ls /mnt/windisk1`

5. If the mount was successful, you will see a familiar list of files and directories found on your first Windows partition.

6. Likewise, you can mount an NTFS partition with the following command:

`mount -t ntfs /dev/hda2 /mnt/windisk2`

using the correct hard drive number, of course.

NOTE

By default, the NTFS file system driver is not enabled in Red Hat Linux. You must consult your documentation to enable this driver. As stated previously, if you use this driver, it is recommended that you use the read-only version. The current read/write version of the NTFS driver is still in the alpha stages as of this writing.

Enabling these file systems to automatically mount in Linux involves a procedure that is out of the scope of this discussion. Although it is possible, only experienced Linux users should attempt to modify the system's boot time mount parameters. Typically, the changes needed to auto-mount foreign file systems are made in /etc/fstab. Red Hat Linux includes a GUI utility, called linuxconf, that makes this task much more simple. Consult the documentation that came with your Linux distribution.

THE VIRTUAL MACHINE APPROACH

If you need access to multiple operating systems primarily for testing purposes, rather than for long periods of work, there's a way to enjoy the use of multiple operating systems without any of the hassle of multiboot setups. In fact, you can even use multiple operating systems simultaneously on the same computer. It's done with a setup called a *virtual machine*. It's an old concept (IBM used it on its mainframes back in the 1970s) that's making a big comeback thanks to today's fast processors and huge hard disks.

A virtual machine program emulates (simulates) in software all of the hardware functions of a PC. It lets an entire operating system (called a *guest* operating system) run as an ordinary application program on a *host* operating system like Windows XP. Since all of the hardware functions are emulated, the guest OS doesn't "know" it's not in complete control of a computer. When it attempts to physically access a hard disk, display card, network adapter or serial port, the virtual machine program calls upon the host operating system to actually carry out the operation.

Even though the software may need to execute several hundred instructions to emulate one hardware operation, the speed penalty is only 5 to 10 percent. And if a guest OS crashes, it doesn't take down your system. You can simply click a Reset menu choice and "reboot" the virtual machine. Check out Figure 31.10, where I have DOS, Linux, and Windows Me running in separate virtual machines.

Figure 31.10
Virtual PC running Windows Me, Linux, and DOS on three virtual machines.

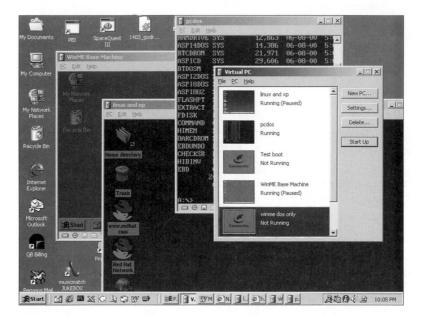

Another advantage of the virtual machine programs currently on the market is that they don't allow the guest OS unfettered access to your real disk drives. Instead, you create a *virtual disk*, a single large file on your host operating system that contains the contents of what the virtual machine sees as a hard drive. With today's large hard drives, it's no big deal to create a 1 or 2GB file to serve as a virtual hard drive to host Windows 95, and another for Windows NT, and another for Linux . . . you get the picture.

If you make a backup copy of the file after installing a guest operating system on one of these virtual disk drives, you can return the guest OS to its original, pristine state just by copying the backup over the virtual disk file. You can even boot up a guest OS, start a bunch of applications, and save the virtual machine in this exact state. When you want to use it again, you can just fire up the whole system starting right from this point. If you're a tester or experimenter, a virtual computer can save you hours of time installing, reinstalling, and rebooting.

Of course, you still need separate licenses for all of the extra operating systems you install, but the virtual machine can let you run as many OSes and as many configurations of these OSes as you like, separately or simultaneously. And all of this comes without the need to hassle with BOOT.INI or worry about partitions.

NOTE

> Have you wondered how operating system book authors get screen pictures of the bootup and installation process? In the old days, we had to use film cameras or video recorders. Now, we just use virtual PC programs, and use screen capture software to get images of our desktop. It's a walk in the proverbial park.

If this sounds interesting, there are two products you should check into:

- VMWare, sold by VMWare. Check out `www.vmware.com`. VMWare was the first commercial system to emulate a PC on a PC. (Previous PC emulators ran on other computing platforms.)
- Virtual PC, sold by Connectix. These folks created Virtual PC for the Macintosh some time ago, and recently released Virtual PC for the PC. Check out `www.connectix.com/products/vpc4w.html`.

Both vendors have trial versions that you can download and test before buying. Both also support networking, device and file sharing, and cut-and-paste capability between the host OS and several types of guest OS.

MACINTOSH AND WINDOWS

Has a friend ever given you a Macintosh disk and asked if you can read it, or have you wanted to run a particularly cool Mac program and been bummed that you can't? Well, think again.

Actually, the Mac can read and write PC disks, so that is one way around this hassle. Just give the colleague a formatted PC disk and ask him to copy the files you want onto the floppy. Or, you might try a program called Mac-In-DOS made by Pacific Micro. We've tried that and like it. It works in the PC and reads, formats, and writes Mac disks in the PC floppy drive. Search for it on the Web. It's about $100 to buy, and you can download a free demo.

But if you want to actually run Mac programs on the PC, can you? Well, believe it or not, the answer is yes. Sort of.

Just as there are PC-on-a-PC virtual machine programs, as we discussed in the previous section, and PC-on-a-Mac programs such as VirtualPC, SoftPC, and SoftWindows, several Mac emulators can run Mac programs on your PC. One such program we've been experimenting with and are impressed with is called Executor, from ARDI. Executor is a virtual

Macintosh machine program for reading and writing Macintosh formatted media and running Macintosh programs.

ARDI has implemented the core of the Macintosh operating system independently from Apple Computer, Inc. As such, Executor requires no software (or ROM chip) from Apple, which makes it the only solution for many customers who need to run Macintosh programs who don't already have a Macintosh. (Some of the other emulators require you to have an Apple ROM chip from one of their computers.)

Executor runs as a native Windows application, either in full-screen mode or in a window (see Figure 31.11). You can print from Executor to any printer that your system can talk to (local printers, remote printers, faxes if you have the right software, and so on). You can cut and paste text and graphics between Executor and other applications. You can create shortcuts for a Macintosh application so that Executor will start up and run that application.

Figure 31.11
Executor runs many Mac programs on the PC under Windows 9x, NT, 2000, and XP.

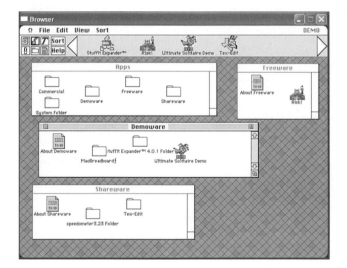

Unfortunately, Executor will not support applications that are "PowerPC-only," which is an increasing proportion. Additionally, although ARDI supports most core operating system services, newer services are not supported. Macintosh programs are capable of querying the operating system to determine which services are supported and which aren't, but programmers often make assumptions that are valid for real Macintoshes but that are not valid under Executor. Executor doesn't yet support the system services that were added after Macintosh System 7.0 (Apple is now shipping 9.0 and X), nor does it yet support networking or system software extensions (known as INITs and CDEVs). ARDI has a compatibility database on its Web site at `http://www.ardi.com`, which you should check if you're interested in running a particular program.

TROUBLESHOOTING

BOOT MENU ISN'T DISPLAYED

When I start up my PC, I don't get a choice of operating systems. Instead, an operating system boots up directly.

What has happened is that an installation program overwrote the normal XP boot loader (for example, Linux may have installed the Linux Loader LILO). To restore the Windows loader, boot your computer from your Windows XP installation CD and follow the instructions to repair a damaged Windows XP installation. The only repair options you need to select at this point are the options to repair the startup environment and the boot sector. Your emergency disk will come in handy as the repair mechanism uses it to find your Windows XP partition.

REMOVING THE WINDOWS XP BOOT LOADER

I want to remove the Windows XP Boot Loader.

This might be needed if you have incorrectly installed an operating system and want to remove it to start over. The same process of removing the Windows XP boot loader is applicable to the Windows NT 4.0 boot loader. If you choose to perform this step, however, you must be sure that you have an operating system to boot into. For this example, assume you have Windows 98/95 installed and want to return to a state in which it is the only operating system available.

First, while you are booted into Windows 98/95, you must create a bootable system disk. This can be accomplished by selecting the Add/Remove Programs control panel. Then select the Startup Disk tab.

After creating a startup disk, reboot your system using the new disk. After you have fully booted into MS-DOS, simply enter the following command from the command prompt:

```
sys C:
```

This will install the Windows 98 startup boot sector onto drive C: and remove the Windows XP boot loader. Now that you're able to boot back into Windows 9x, simply remove the Windows XP directories.

You can optionally remove the following files to clean up the rest of the Windows XP boot loader files:

```
C:\boot.ini
C:\ntldr
C:\ntdetect.com
```

TIPS FROM THE WINDOWS PROS: LIVING WITH MORE THAN ONE OS

Even with all the advice in this chapter, managing more than one operating system on the same machine at the same time can be a daunting task. Fortunately, some special tools can save you at your darkest moments. (You never expected to find purple prose in a computer book, did you?)

The Windows XP multiboot loader is capable of supporting a large number of multiboot situations—probably more than will fit on the screen in a list. Still, editing the BOOT.INI file is an intimidating process, and you must remember quirky rules about the order of operating system installation.

If you're interested in loading up a killer system with three or more operating systems, we recommend using a program designed specifically for the job. I'll describe a couple of them for your consideration.

Once again, the PowerQuest people come toq the rescue with their offering, called BootMagic, which is bundled with PartitionMagic. This program uses a graphical interface to help you set up and run multiple operating systems in the same machine, with a minimum of compatibility problems. You can run the setup interface from DOS, Windows 9x, or Windows NT/2000/XP. The program supports Windows XP/2000, Windows 95/98, Windows NT 4.0 (server and workstation), Windows NT 3.51 (server and workstation), Windows 3.x (must be installed with DOS 5 or later), MS-DOS 5.0 or later, PC-DOS 6.1 or later, Open DOS, OS/2 3.0 or later, Linux, BeOS, and most other versions of DOS and PC-compatible OSes (check their site at www.powerquest.com for more info).

Another similar program is System Commander Deluxe, from V Communications. This product has received rave reviews from some magazines. System Commander Deluxe enables you to install and run any combination of PC-compatible operating systems, including Windows 95/98, Windows 3.x, Windows NT, DOS, OS/2, and all of the PC-compatible Unixes including Linux. Like BootMagic, this program also has a graphical user interface. In addition, it does partition management such as resizing, creation, and deletion. It's available from V Communications, Inc. (check their site at www.v-com.com).

31

CHAPTER 32

THE REGISTRY

In this chapter

WHAT IS THE REGISTRY?

The Windows XP *Registry* is a database in which Windows and application programs store startup information, hardware settings, user preferences, file locations, license and registration information, last-viewed file lists, and so on. In addition, the Registry stores the *associations* between file types and the applications that use them. For example, the Registry holds the information that tells Windows to use Media Player when you click on an MPG movie file. In the early days of DOS and Windows, programs stored this kind of information in a random collection of hundreds of files scattered all over your hard disk. (Remember CONFIG.SYS?) Thankfully, those days are now only a dim memory.

Most of the time, you can get by without giving the Registry a second thought, because almost every useful Registry entry is set from a Control Panel applet, an application's preferences dialog, or Windows Setup. From time to time, though, you might have to roll up your sleeves to find the location of an errant device driver, you might need to remove an unwanted startup program, or you might just be curious what kind of information Microsoft Office keeps on file about you. This chapter tells you how to go on these kinds of missions.

Two Different Views

One of the advantages of having two authors for this book is that you get two viewpoints. I (Brian) must confess I am a card-carrying Registryphobe; I think Registry tweaking is dangerous and minimally useful. As far as I'm concerned, the Registry is best left alone. I make my living programming with my computer, and the less fancy and more stable it is, the better. "Stock" is the way for me.

For my co-author Bob, who also makes his living with his computer, the Registry is a tweaker's paradise of undocumented adjustments and fascinating Windows trivia. He can change file locations, tune up networking performance, and generally adjust his computer to be "just so." To each his own! We'll both have our say here in telling you how to be careful with the Registry and in showing you how to work with it effectively.

HOW THE REGISTRY IS ORGANIZED

The Registry leaves the plain text files of AUTOEXEC.BAT and WIN.INI far, far behind. It is a specialized database organized a lot like the files and folders on a hard disk. In fact, the Registry Editor navigates through the Registry using the same expandable list display that Windows Explorer uses to display a disk.

Just as a hard disk contains partitions, the Registry contains separate sections called *hives*. (The reason Microsoft chose the word hive is unclear. It had something to do with busy bees, but more than that, the folks there won't say.) In each hive is a list of named keys that correspond to the folders on a hard disk. Just as a file folder can contain files and yet more folders, a Registry key can contain values, which hold information such as numbers or text strings, and yet more keys. Even the naming of file folders and *keys* are similar: A folder might be named \Documents and Settings\brian\chapter32, and a Registry key might be named \HKEY_CURRENT_USER\Software\Microsoft. Let's look at the Registry starting with its top-level keys.

The two main "top-level" keys are as follows:

- HKEY_LOCAL_MACHINE contains all the hardware and machine-specific setup information for your computer. For example, it lists every device driver to load and all your hardware's interrupt settings. It also holds software setup information that is common to all users.

- HKEY_USERS has a subkey for each user of the computer. Under each user's key, Windows stores user-specific information, such as color preferences, sounds, and the location of e-mail files.

The Registry Editor also presents three other sections that look like separate top-level keys:

- HKEY_CURRENT_USER is the subsection of HKEY_USERS corresponding to the logged-on user. It holds preferences and software setup information specific to the current user, such the choice of screen saver and Office's default language.

- HKEY_CURRENT_CONFIG, which is a shortcut to HKEY_LOCAL_MACHINE\System\CurrentControlSet\Hardware Profiles\ Current, contains the hardware settings specific to the hardware profile chosen when Windows was started.

- HKEY_CLASSES_ROOT is a strange beast. This Registry section stores file associations, linking file types to applications. It's a combined view of two other Registry keys: HKEY_LOCAL_MACHINE\Software\Classes, which holds settings for all users, with the addition of HKEY_CURRENT_USER\Software\Classes, which holds any personal settings stored for the current user. If the same value is defined in both HKEY_CURRENT_USER\ . . . and HKEY_LOCAL_MACHINE, the HKEY_CURRENT_USER value is used.

32

In reality, these keys are views into subkeys of the first two, as illustrated in Figure 32.1.

These three "virtual" top-level keys are there for convenience—it's easier to look in HKEY_CURRENT_USER than to try to remember where to find user entries under the ugly numbered keys inside HKEY_USERS.

Within each of the top-level keys, there are several subkeys holding related information. HKEY_CURRENT_CONFIG, for example, contains two keys: Software and System. Software in turn contains two keys: Fonts and Microsoft. (By the way, with keys, just as with folders, you can spell out the full path—HKEY_CURRENT_CONFIG\Display\Settings— or just refer to Settings, if you know you're discussing HKEY_CURRENT_CONFIG\Display).

All this might seem a little daunting, but remember that the purpose of the Registry keys is to organize setup information sensibly. Instead of having this information in many mysteriously named and randomly located files, it's all here, filed away in the Registry.

Figure 32.1
The Registry is composed of two true top-level keys and three "virtual" top-level keys.

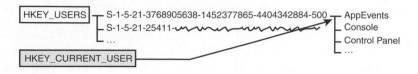

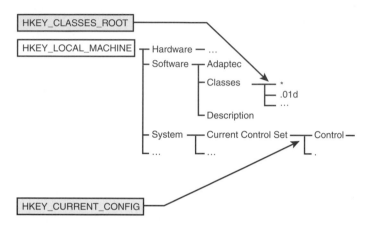

CAUTION

> Another similarity between Registry keys and file folders is that both can have "access permissions" set to prevent unauthorized users from examining or modifying them. I won't go further into this topic, except to recommend that you *don't* attempt to set or modify the default permissions in the Registry. It's too easy to make a mistake that will prevent even Windows itself from having access to the information it needs. If you implement Group Policies, the *Policy Editor* will adjust Registry permissions as necessary.

The Registry database itself is stored in several separate files, called *hives,* which I mentioned earlier. HKEY_LOCAL_MACHINE is stored in the folder \windows\system32\config, in several hive files: SAM, SECURITY, SOFTWARE, and SYSTEM. HKEY_USERS is stored with each user's subkey in a separate hive file. These are kept in each user's profile folder (\Documents and Settings*username*) as a file named NTUSER.DAT, except the "Default User" key, which is in \windows\system32\config\DEFAULT. Finally, each user has a list of keys used to add to or override HKEY_CLASSES_ROOT, which is stored in \Documents and Settings*username*\Local Settings\Application Data\Microsoft\Windows\UsrClass.dat. (If you're interested, you can see that even this information is maintained in the Registry, under the key HKEY_LOCAL_MACHINE\SYSTEM\ControlSet001\Control\hivelist. Just don't try to change these values!)

You generally can't examine or modify these files directly while Windows is running because Windows maintains exclusive control of them. Backup software uses special Windows program functions to get access to back up or restore them. The exception, though, is that the NTUSER.DAT files for users not currently logged in are not locked, so they can be copied and backed up as normal files.

REGISTRY CONTENTS

What's in the Registry, anyway? There's a lot to it; many entire books have been written about it. If you want a full-blown guide to the Windows XP Registry, you might look for Microsoft's *Windows XP Resource Kit*, or check your local bookstore for other weighty tomes. Short of that (way short) I can still do a quick overview of the Registry to give you some idea of its organization and contents.

You just learned about the five main sections of the Registry. Let's go through them one by one now, and hit on some of each section's highlights.

HKEY_LOCAL_MACHINE

As you might expect, HKEY_LOCAL_MACHINE contains information specific to your computer, settings that aren't user-specific. They include hardware settings and software information that is global for all users.

The main keys in HKEY_LOCAL_MACHINE are shown in Table 32.1.

TABLE 32.1   MAIN KEYS IN HKEY_LOCAL_MACHINE

HARDWARE	Contains information about the computer's hardware platform and Plug and Play devices, discovered afresh each time the system is booted. No configurable settings are located here.
SAM and SECURITY	Contain the Windows Security Account Manager databases. These keys always appear to be empty because only Windows itself is allowed to read or edit the information.
SOFTWARE	Contains system-wide software settings for applications and Windows itself. This key contains many subkeys. The Classes subkey is special and is given its own virtual view as HKEY_CLASSES_ROOT. The other entries are generally named after software manufacturers. I'll describe some of the more interesting keys in a moment.
SYSTEM	Contains a series of numbered ControlSet entries, each of which contains the settings for hardware and system services. One of them is chosen as the CurrentControlSet subkey. As you install or remove hardware, Windows rotates through the ControlSet entries, using one as the "current control set." This way, it can keep previous versions to use as a backup.

The fun bits are in the SOFTWARE keys under HKEY_LOCAL_MACHINE. Under SOFTWARE is the special Classes subkey, which I'll describe in the HKEY_CLASSES_ROOT section of this chapter. Also, there are subkeys named after software manufacturers that contain systemwide settings for these companies' various programs.

Under Microsoft, naturally, is a slew of subkeys for the software systems provided with Windows and for any add-ons you've purchased, such as Office. You'll have more than 100 subkeys in HKEY_LOCAL_MACHINE\Software\Microsoft just after installation and more when you start adding your own software.

Most of the juicy settings that control Windows itself are found in HKEY_LOCAL_MACHINE\Software\Microsoft\Windows\CurrentVersion.

I'll discuss just one of these juicy keys. When you log in to your computer, you know that Windows can start up some programs automatically. You can actually set a program to be started up at login in any of five ways:

- A shortcut in the Startup folder of your Start menu (in \Documents and Settings\ *yourloginname*\Start Menu\Programs\Startup)

- A shortcut in \Documents and Settings\All Users\Start Menu\Programs\Startup

- A key named Run, RunOnce, or RunOnceEx in \HKEY_LOCAL_MACHINE\Software\Microsoft\Windows\CurrentVersion

- A key named Run, RunOnce, or RunOnceEx in \HKEY_CURRENT_USER\Software\Microsoft\Windows\CurrentVersion

- A run= or load= entry in WIN.INI in the Windows directory (usually \windows or \winnt. Yes, WIN.INI is still around, because some older programs count on it being there.)

> **NOTE**
>
> To maintain compatibility with older 16-bit Windows software (and even some new software that should know better), the original Windows SYSTEM.INI and WIN.INI files still exist, and Windows XP keeps a few of their entries up-to-date with information copied from the Registry. This lets older software that really depends on the old INI file system still function. It's too bad that this old stuff is still around, but compatibility has turned out to be more important than neatness.

The Run keys are often set by software manufacturers who want their software to run automatically when you log on. Sometimes this is a good thing—as when Windows uses it to start the taskbar program. But this technique is sometimes used to install annoying programs you really don't want to run. If the programs don't have configuration or preference settings that will disable the run-on-logon behavior, you can delete their value entries under these keys.

The RunOnce and RunOnceEx keys are used mostly by installation programs that need to complete their work after you restart your computer. Windows normally deletes these entries after you've logged in once and these programs have run, but they are sometimes not properly removed.

 If you're plagued by unwanted or buggy programs when you log in, see "Tracking Down Errant Startup Programs" in the "Troubleshooting" section at the end of this chapter.

HKEY_CURRENT_CONFIG

HKEY_CURRENT_CONFIG is a virtual top-level key containing information Windows uses to initialize during its bootup phase, and very little else. Despite its important-sounding name, you'll find virtually nothing of interest to humans in here. The information is all set up automatically when you create Hardware Profiles.

By *virtual*, I mean that the keys in HKEY_CURRENT_CONFIG are really contained in other parts of the Registry, and using HKEY_CURRENT_CONFIG is just a convenient way to get at them. A curious feature of this one is that its subkeys come from several different parts of the Registry. Its System\CurrentControlSet subkey comes from one of the HKEY_LOCAL_MACHINE\SYSTEM\ControlSet### keys, and various parts of its Software subkey come from other parts of HKEY_LOCAL_MACHINE. The Registry presents the information from these various keys again under HKEY_CURRENT_CONFIG as a matter of convenience.

HKEY_CLASSES_ROOT

HKEY_CLASSES_ROOT is another of these virtual keys, provided to give programmers quick access to information from other places in the Registry. What you see under HKEY_CLASSES_ROOT are the contents of HKEY_LOCAL_MACHINE\Software\ Classes, plus any additional user-specific settings stored under HKEY_CURRENT_USER\ Software\Classes, whose entries add to or override the HKEY_LOCAL_MACHINE entries.

A large part of the Classes section is devoted to the associations the Explorer makes between file types (or filename extensions, like .doc) and the programs that are used to open, display, or edit them. This is the information you're editing when you change associations in the Explorer by choosing Tools, Folder Options, File Types, as discussed in Chapter 21.

These entries contain the nitty-gritty linkage information that Windows uses to locate software components based on ActiveX Controls, OLE, and the COM+ interprocess communication system. These entries are confusing, complex, and best left completely alone.

Table 32.2 gives an overview of the structure of HKEY_CLASSES_ROOT.

TABLE 32.2 THE STRUCTURE OF HKEY_CLASSES_ROOT

Entry	Description
. through .zip	For each listed file extension, the default value assigns a name to the file type. Each of these file type names appears later as a subkey of its own. File types that have OLE handlers have a subkey PersistentHandler, which gives a Class ID (a string of numbers like {098f2570-b . . . -03f3}). They are listed under the CLSID subkey, where the program file for the handler is named. Files that have associated programs to edit or display them also have shell or shellx subkeys, which contain the commands Explorer uses when you attempt to open a file using a double-click.

32

continues

TABLE 32.2   CONTINUED

Entry	Description
filetype	Each named file type (for example, VBScript) contains the CLSID number of the associated handler for the file type. Windows looks up this information through the CLSID subkey to find the associated program.
CLSID	Contains a subkey for each registered Active-(*something*) handler; the sub-keys and values name the handler and point to the file containing its program code.

HKEY_USERS

HKEY_USERS contains a subkey for each authorized user of the computer and an entry named .DEFAULT. The .DEFAULT section contains just that—the basic settings given to each new local user added to the computer. (I say *local* because, on a Windows .NET or 2000 Server domain-based network, when a user logs in for the first time using a domain login name, his or her default Registry entries are obtained from the domain's server, not the local computer.)

The user subkeys of HKEY_USERS have long numeric names. These names are the GUID or Globally Unique User Identification numbers generated by Windows as a computer-friendly representation of the user's name. It's by these numbers that Windows tracks users, whether local or domain-based.

Nothing else is in HKEY_USERS besides these per-user subkeys. They appear as the contents of HKEY_CURRENT_USER and HKEY_CLASSES_ROOT when the associated user is logged in.

HKEY_CURRENT_USER

HKEY_CURRENT_USER contains settings, preferences, and other information specific to the currently logged-in user. This whole "section" is actually a subkey of HKEY_USERS, as discussed previously, but is provided this way as an easy way to get to the information.

The Software keys in HKEY_CURRENT_USER are similar to the Software subkeys in HKEY_LOCAL_MACHINE. They're grouped by software manufacturer, and Windows entries are stored in HKEY_CURRENT_USER\Software\Microsoft\Windows \CurrentVersion.

BACKING UP AND RESTORING THE REGISTRY

Because the Registry is now the *one* place where all the Windows hardware and software settings are stored, it's also the one thing that Windows absolutely needs to run. You will hear dire warnings from Microsoft, other computer books, installation manuals, and now me: It's very important to back up the Registry before you edit it. If a critical entry is lost or changed incorrectly (for example, one that holds the name of a driver file for your graphics display adapter), Windows may not be able to start at all.

If you have a Registry problem, before attempting any drastic measures, see "Recovering from a Suspected Registry Problem" in the "Troubleshooting" section at the end of this chapter.

Make it a habit to back up the Registry every time you back up your hard disk and before you install new hardware or software. I can tell you from personal experience that without a Registry backup, something as common as a bad graphics card installation program can cost you a whole day of trying to get your system to boot again! Windows XP Professional has some built-in protection to help avoid this type of disaster, but you should still take your own precautions.

BACKING UP THE REGISTRY

You can back up the Registry in Windows XP in three main ways: You can back it up as part of a regular disk backup, you can use the Registry Editor to save a key to a disk file, or you can use a special-purpose Registry backup program.

I suggest that you set your favorite disk backup program to back up the Registry files every time you back up your hard disk. Before you install a piece of new hardware or a significant software package, do a full disk backup, including the Registry. Before you manually edit the Registry for other purposes, back up the Registry by any of the means I'll discuss in the next few sections.

TIP FROM

> An Automated System Recovery backup is a fourth Registry backup of sorts—it saves the most critical, hardware-related information from the Registry on the Emergency Repair Diskette (ERD), then puts *everything* in the larger backup set. An up-to-date ERD can help you get Windows back on its feet if you have a Registry or other disaster. If you really want to get a gold star for preparedness, update your ERD every time you've added new hardware, *after* it has proven to be stable and work correctly.

32

→ To learn how to make an Emergency Repair Disk, **see** "Backup Tools and Strategies," **p. 1023**.

BACKING UP WITH WINDOWS BACKUP

To run the Backup utility included with Windows XP Professional,

1. Open the Start menu and choose More Programs, Accessories, System Tools, Backup.
2. Click Advanced mode, and select the Backup tab.
3. Check System State as shown in Figure 32.2. If you want to back up more than just the Registry, select any other drives and/or folders you wish to back up.
4. Select a destination for the Registry backup. You can save to a tape drive, network drive, Zip disk, or to a file on your hard drive (you could enter "C:\regback.bkf"). Select the desired backup destination (for example, "File"), and enter the desired location under Backup media or file name. Click Start Backup.
5. Click Advanced and uncheck Automatically back up System Protected Files with the System State. (This will cut the backup from more than 1GB of data down to around 10MB). Click OK.
6. Check Replace the data on the media with this backup, then click Start Backup.

The System State backup option backs up the Registry along with boot files, Active Directory files, and Certificates. For this reason, it is a good idea to select System State every time you make a backup, to disk or tape.

Now, with this backup on hand, if Registry problems occur after your installation, you can use the Backup utility again to restore the Registry to its previous state.

Figure 32.2
Check System State to add the Registry to your backup set.

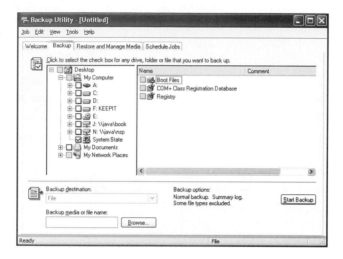

Although it's best to perform a full backup to tape, disk, or other high-capacity storage media, you can perform a quick System State backup to a local disk file in preparation for adding new hardware or software.

NOTE

With Backup, you cannot save the System State of a remote computer, only the local computer. For remote or centralized backup services—to back up the Registries of all the computers on your network—you need to buy a third-party backup program. If you're managing a large network of computers, you should definitely investigate centralized backup systems.

BACKING UP WITH THIRD-PARTY DISK BACKUP SOFTWARE

Third-party disk backup software made for Windows XP Professional will include an option to back up the Registry. Be sure to check this option whenever you are backing up your hard disk. It may have options like the Windows Backup program to back up just the Registry and to back up to a disk file, so you can make a quick backup before attempting Registry edits.

You should check your backup software's manual for instructions on saving Registry and system information when you back up. I suggest that you *always* include the Registry in your backups.

BACKING UP WITH THIRD-PARTY REGISTRY BACKUP SOFTWARE

There are third-party programs specifically designed to backup and restore the Registry and other critical Windows files. For example, SuperWin's WinRescue program (www.superwin.com) can not only back up and restore the Registry, but can defragment the Registry's files and work magic to revive a non-bootable Windows system. If you're a Registry hacker, it would be worth buying a Registry backup tool.

These programs will come with their own extensive instructions on backing up, restoring, repairing, and maintaining the Registry.

BACKING UP WITH REGEDIT

The Registry Editor, called Regedit, has a mechanism to export a set of Registry keys and values to a text file. If you can't or won't use a more comprehensive backup system before you manually edit the Registry, at least use this editor to select and back up the key that contains all the subkeys and values you plan to modify. This way, you can back up all the sections you plan to edit in one backup.

That way, if it's necessary later, you can restore these exported files, recovering any changed or deleted keys and values. Remember, though, that Regedit cannot remove entries you added that were not in the Registry before the backup! So, if an entry you add causes problems, the Registry Editor backup will not help you recover.

To back up a key and its subkeys and values, follow these steps:

1. To run Regedit, choose Start, Run. Type regedit and click OK.
2. Select the key you plan to modify, or a key containing all the keys you plan to modify, in the left pane.
3. Select File, Export (see Figure 32.3).

Figure 32.3
You can save a Registry key and any keys and values it contains with Regedit.

32

4. Choose a location and filename to use to store the Registry keys. I usually use the desktop for temporary files like this, so I'll see them and delete them later.

> I recommend *not* using the default extension .REG. This extension is associated with Registry entries in the Windows Explorer, and selecting a REG file in Explorer instantly and silently restores it to the Registry. This operation is far too serious to have happen with just a mouse click or two.

5. Select All Files from the Save As Type list, and enter a name with an extension other than .REG—for example, `c:\before.sav`.

6. Click Save. The chosen key or keys are then saved as a text file.

> You can use this technique to copy a set of keys and values from one section of the Registry to another. First, export the desired key and values to a file. Edit the file with Notepad, and use the Edit/Replace menu to change all of the key names to the desired new location. Then import the file back into the Registry. I have used this method to copy a group of Registry entries under HKEY_CURRENT_USER to HKEY_USERS\.Default, for example, so that all newly created user accounts will have the desired setting.

RESTORING THE REGISTRY

If you've made Registry changes that cause problems, you can try to remember each and every change you made, re-enter the original information, delete any keys you added, and thus undo the changes manually. Good luck! If you were diligent and made a backup before you started, however, you can simply restore the backup and have confidence that the recovery is complete and accurate.

 If you think you have Registry problems, see "Signs of Registry Problems" in the "Troubleshooting" section at the end of this chapter.

To restore a Registry backup you made, follow the steps described in the following sections.

RESTORING THE REGISTRY WITH DRIVER ROLLBACK

If you encounter problems immediately after installing or updating a device driver, you might be lucky enough not to need to manually restore the Registry. Windows XP may be able to help you automatically. Use the Device Manager's "Roll Back Driver" feature to see if this fixes your problem.

→ To see detailed instructions on updating device drivers, **see** "Updating Device Drivers," **p. 1059**.

RESTORING THE REGISTRY FROM WINDOWS BACKUP

The Windows Backup utility's Restore feature lets you replace Registry and other System files saved before a failed installation or change. This step is fairly drastic, so be sure you've exhausted the less invasive procedures before you resort to this method. If you did a full backup, you're fairly safe because all program files will be restored along with the Registry. If you backed up only the Registry itself, there's a chance that the old Registry entries won't solve any problems created by replaced system programs.

Follow these steps to restore the backup:

1. Click Start, More Programs, Accessories, System Tools, Backup (or choose Backup if it's on your Start menu).

2. Click Advanced Mode, and select the Restore and Manage Media tab.

3. Select Tools, Options. Choose Always Replace the File on My Computer. (You must choose this option because you're replacing files that exist but contain the wrong information.) Then click OK.

4. Expand the list of cataloged backups (see Figure 32.4). Then locate the backup you want to restore, and check System State. If you want to restore other files and/or volumes backed up at the same time, check them as well.

Figure 32.4
You can restore the Registry by restoring a System State backup.

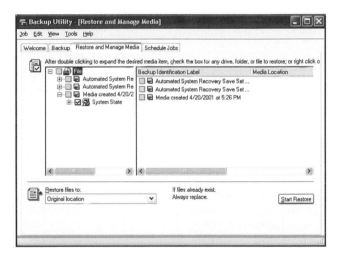

5. Select Start Restore. A dialog box then warns you that System State is always restored to the current location. Click OK.

6. When a dialog box offers you Advanced options, just click OK to proceed.

7. A dialog box appears to let you enter the name of the backup set file you're restoring. Enter the name you used when you made the backup—for example, `c:\before.bkf`. Correct the name if necessary, and click OK.

8. When the backup is complete, Backup asks you to restart the system. You really must reboot now because the Registry files have not actually been restored. The recovered Registry data has been set aside and will only be installed the next time Windows starts. If you make any other Registry changes before restarting, they will be lost when the restored files are installed.

Restoring the Registry from Regedit

If a Registry editing session has gone awry, and you need to restore the Registry from a Regedit backup, follow these steps:

1. In Regedit, select File, Import.
2. Select All Files from the Files of Type list.
3. Locate the file you used to back up the Registry key or keys—for example, `c:\before.sav`.
4. Select Open.

The saved Registry keys are then imported, replacing any changes or deletions. However, any keys or values you've added to the Registry will not be removed. If they are the cause of the problem, this restore will *not* help.

If the Registry problems persist, you can try a rather drastic measure: You can use Regedit to delete the key or keys that were changed and then import the backup file again. This time, any added keys or values are removed. I suggest you try this approach only with keys related to add-on software, *not* for any of the Microsoft software or hardware keys.

TIP FROM

Bob
& Brian

My final word on Registry repair: If you encounter problems with the Registry entries for hardware or for Windows itself, and restoring the Registry doesn't help, you are probably better off reinstalling Windows or using the Emergency Recovery procedure than trying any further desperate measures to fix the Registry.

TIP FROM

Bob
& Brian

If you encounter what you think are Registry problems with add-on software, your best bet is to uninstall the software, if possible, and reinstall it before attempting *any* Registry restores or repairs.

Using Regedit

You might never need to edit the Registry by hand. Most Registry keys are set by the software that uses them. For example, Office XP sets its own preference values, and the Control Panel applets set the appropriate Display, Sound, and Networking Registry entries. In a way, the Control Panel is mostly just a Registry Editor in disguise.

You might need to edit the Registry by hand if directed by a technical support person who's helping you fix a problem, or when you're following a published procedure to make an adjustment for which there is no Control Panel setting.

In the latter case, before going any further, I need to say this one last time, to make it absolutely clear: Few circumstances really require you to edit the Registry by hand. Be sure you really need to before you do. And, if so, back up the Registry, or at least the section you want to change, before making any changes.

In the next few sections, I'll cover the basics of the Registry Editor.

VIEWING THE REGISTRY

The Registry Editor doesn't have a Start menu item. You must run it from the Start, Run dialog. Enter regedit and click OK.

Regedit displays a two-pane display much like Explorer, as shown in Figure 32.5. The top-level keys, which are listed below My Computer, can be expanded just like drives and folders in the Explorer. In the pane on the right are the values for each key. The name of the current selected key is shown in the status bar.

Figure 32.5
The Regedit screen shows keys on the left and values on the right.

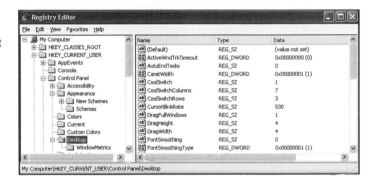

Values have names, just as the files in a folder do, and it's here that configuration information is finally stored. Each key has a (Default) value, which is the value of the key itself, and any number of named values. For example, in Figure 32.5, key HKEY_CURRENT_USER\Desktop is shown. The value of HKEY_CURRENT_USER\Desktop itself is undefined (blank), and the value HKEY_CURRENT_USER\Control Panel\Desktop\CoolSwitch is 1.

Registry values have a data type, which is usually one of the types shown in Table 32.3.

TABLE 32.3	DATA TYPES SUPPORTED BY REGEDIT
REG_SZ	Textual information, a simple string of letters
REG_DWORD	A single number displayed in hexadecimal or decimal
REG_BINARY	Binary data, displayed as an arbitrary number of hexadecimal digits
REG_MULTI_SZ	A string that can contain more than one line of text
REG_EXPAND_SZ	Text that can contain environment variables (such as %TEMP%)

*Other data types such as REG_DWORD,_BIG_ENDIAN, and REG_FULL_RESOURCE_
DESCRIPTOR exist, but they are obscure, rare, and can't be edited with Regedit.*

SEARCHING IN THE REGISTRY

You can search for a Registry entry by key name, value name, or the contents of a value string. First, select a starting point for the search in the left pane. You can select My Computer to select the entire Registry, or you can limit your search to one of the top-level keys or any subordinate key. Next, select Find from the menu, and enter a search string into the Find dialog. The Find feature is not case sensitive, so upper- and lowercase don't matter. You can check any of the Look At boxes, as shown in Figure 32.6, to designate where in the Registry you expect to find the desired text: in the name of a key, in the name of a value, or in the data, the value itself.

Figure 32.6
In the Find dialog, you can select whether to search key names, value names, or value data.

Check Match Whole String Only to search only for items whose whole name or value is the desired string.

> **NOTE**
>
> Most of the time I check all the Look At boxes but not Match Whole String Only.

Select Find Next to start the search. The Regedit display indicates the first match to your string, and by pressing F3, you can repeat the search to look for other instances.

TIP FROM

Bob & Brian

> The search function has two limitations:
>
> • You can't enter a backslash (\) in the search string when looking for a key or value name; Regedit won't complain, but it won't find anything either.
>
> • You can't search for the initial HKEY_*xxx* part of a key name. That's not actually part of the name; it's just the section of the Registry in which the key resides.
>
> So, to find a key named, for example, HKEY_CLASSES_ROOT\MIDFile\shell\Play\ Command, you can't type all that in and have Find jump right to the key. If you already know the full pathname of a key, use the left pane of Regedit to browse for the key directly.

EDITING KEYS AND VALUES

Regedit has no Save or Undo menu items. Changes to the Registry happen *immediately* and *permanently*. Additions, deletions, and changes are for real. This is the reason for all the warnings to back up before you poke into the Registry.

ADDING A VALUE

To add a value to a key, select the key in the left pane, and choose Edit, New. Select the type of value to add; you can select any of the supported Registry data types: String, Binary, DWORD, Multi-String, or Expandable String. (The instructions you're following will indicate which type of value to add.) A new value entry then appears in the right pane, as shown in Figure 32.7.

Figure 32.7
New value adds an entry in "Rename" mode.

Enter the new value's name, and press Enter to edit the value.

- For string values, enter the text of the desired string.
- For DWORD values, choose Decimal or Hexadecimal, and enter the desired value in the chosen format (see Figure 32.8).
- For binary values, enter pairs of hexadecimal characters as instructed. (You'll never be asked to do this, I promise.)

Figure 32.8
You can choose to enter a DWORD value in either decimal or hexadecimal notation.

CHANGING A VALUE

If you want to change a value, double-click it in the right-hand pane to bring up the Edit Value dialog. Alternatively, you can select it and choose Edit, Modify from the menu, or right-click and select Modify from the context menu. Then make the desired change, and click OK.

That is all you will likely ever need to do with Regedit. However, in the extremely unlikely case that you would want to delete a value or add or remove a key, the following sections can help see you through these processes.

32

DELETING A VALUE

If you've added a Registry value in the hope of fixing some problem and found that the change wasn't needed, or if you're instructed to delete a value by a Microsoft Knowledge Base article or other special procedure, you can delete the entry by viewing its key and locating the value on the right-hand pane.

Select the value and choose Edit, Delete from the menu, or right-click and select Delete from the context menu. Confirm by clicking OK.

CAUTION

There is no Undo command in the Registry Editor—when you delete a value, it's gone for good. Be sure you've made a Registry backup before editing or deleting Registry keys and values.

ADDING OR DELETING A KEY

Keys must be added as subkeys to existing keys; you can't add a top-level key. To add a key, select an existing key in the left pane, and select Edit, New, Key from the menu. Alternatively, right-click the existing key, and select New, Key from the context menu. A new key appears in the left pane, where you can edit its name, as shown in Figure 32.9. Press Enter after you enter the name.

32

Figure 32.9
A new key appears in "Rename" mode.

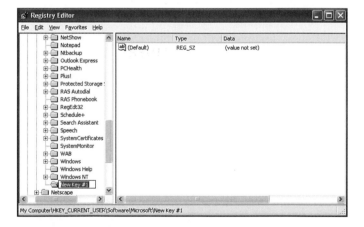

You can delete a key by selecting it in the left pane and choosing Edit, Delete from the drop-down menu, or by right-clicking it and selecting Delete from the context menu. Click OK to confirm that you do intend to delete the key. Deleting a key deletes its values and all its subkeys as well, so without the protection of Undo (or a Registry Recycling Bin), this action is serious.

RENAMING A KEY

As you have probably guessed, the pattern for renaming a key follows the Explorer exactly: Choose the key in the left pane and select Edit, Rename, or right-click the key and select Rename. Finally, enter a new name, and press Enter.

CAUTION

> Don't attempt to rename keys without a *very good* reason, such as you mistyped the name of the key you were adding. If Windows can't find specific Registry keys it needs, Windows may not boot or operate correctly.

USING COPY KEY NAME

As you have probably noticed by now, Registry keys can be pretty long, tortuous things to type. The Registry Editor offers a bit of help to finger-fatigued Registry editors (and authors): Choosing Edit, Copy Key Name puts the name of the currently selected key into the Clipboard, so you can paste it elsewhere, should the need arise. For example, when you've found a neat Registry trick, you might want to e-mail your friends about it.

ADVANCED REGISTRY EDITING

The Registry Editor has some advanced features you'll need only if you're managing a network of Windows XP computers or if you run into really serious problems with your Windows installation.

EDITING THE REGISTRY OF A REMOTE COMPUTER

The Registry Editor permits administrators to edit the Registry of other computers on a network. Of course, this operation is highly privileged, and you must have administrator privileges on the computer whose Registry you want to edit. To edit a remote computer's Registry, choose File, Connect Network Registry. Next, enter the name of the remote computer, or choose Browse to select one graphically; then click OK. (Interestingly, Browse doesn't let you use Active Directory to select a computer to manage, only the basic Network Neighborhood list.)

When you've connected, the computer's Registry keys appear in the list along with your own, as shown in Figure 32.10.

NOTE

> For you to be able to connect to the Registry on a Windows 95 or 98 computer, it must have Remote Management installed. This option must be installed as part of the computer's Network Services through the Network Control Panel. Windows Me is not supposed to support remote Registry editing but you can install the Remote Management feature from a Windows 98 CD-ROM. On Windows NT, 2000, and XP, the Remote Registry service is installed automatically.

32

Host Computer   Remote Computer

Figure 32.10
Viewing and editing a
remote computer's
Registry.

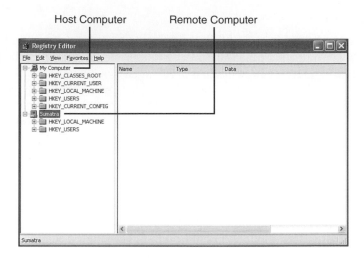

Note that only the two main "real" top-level keys will appear: HKEY_LOCAL_MACHINE
and HKEY_USERS—the virtual keys will not. When you have finished editing the remote
computer's Registry, right click its name in the left-hand pane and select Disconnect.

NOTE

> You can't use File, Export or File, Import to save or load a remote Registry's values. These
> commands might appear to work, but they operate only on the local computer's Registry.

EDITING REGISTRY ENTRIES FOR ANOTHER USER

If you open a Registry Editor and look under HKEY_USERS, you will find that the only
available subkeys are .DEFAULT, four entries for system services, and your own subkey,
which is also accessible as HKEY_CURRENT_USER. As I mentioned earlier, Windows
stores various parts of the Registry in data files called hives, and loads the hive containing
your part of HKEY_USER only when you are currently logged on. When you log out, your
subkey is unloaded from the Registry, and the hive file is left in your user profile folder.
(And if you have a roaming user profile, your profile folder is copied back to the domain
server. That's how your settings are able to follow you from one computer to another.)

As an administrator, you might find it necessary to edit Registry HKEY_USER entries for
another user. For example, a startup program in HKEY_CURRENT_USER\Software\
Windows\CurrentVersion\Run might be causing such trouble that the user can't log on.
(Can you tell this is a pet peeve of mine?) If you can't log on as that user, you can edit his or
her HKEY_CURRENT_USER Registry keys in another way:

1. Log on as Administrator and run Regedit

2. Select the HKEY_USERS window.

3. Highlight the top-level key HKEY_USERS.

4. Select File, Load Hive.

5. Browse to the profile folder for the desired user. It is in \Documents and Settings\ *username* for a local machine user in a workgroup, or for a Windows Server domain, in the folder used for user profiles on the domain controller.

6. Type the filename NTUSER.DAT. (The file does not appear in the browse dialog because it's "super hidden": a hidden system file). Then click Open.

7. A dialog then appears, asking you to enter a name for the hive. While HKEY_USERS normally loads user hives with a long numeric name, I suggest that you type the user's logon name. Click OK. The user's Registry data is then loaded and can be edited, as shown in Figure 32.11.

Figure 32.11
An offline user's Registry hive is now loaded and can be edited.

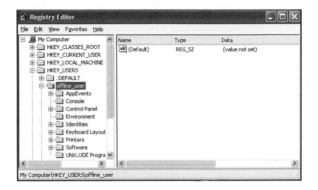

8. When you're finished editing, unload the hive. Select the key you added under HKEY_USERS (for example, the offline user key in Figure 32.11), and select File, Unload Hive. Confirm by clicking Yes on the warning dialog.

EDITING REGISTRY ENTRIES FOR ANOTHER WINDOWS INSTALLATION

If you need to retrieve Registry entries from an installation of Windows 2000 or XP on another hard disk or partition, you can load any of that installation's hive files for editing or exporting. This might happen when you

- install a new hard disk and install Windows XP on the new disk.
- have a severe Registry error that prevents Windows from booting at all. If you can't use the Emergency Recovery procedure to fix the problem, you can install Windows onto another drive, partition, or folder on your computer. When you boot up that copy of Windows, you can load the original installation's Registry files for editing. Then you can try to boot up the original installation.

To edit the other installation's Registry, you will need to locate its hive files. They are usually found in the locations shown in Table 32.4.

TABLE 32.4   USUAL LOCATION OF HIVE FILES

Key	Hive File
HKEY_LOCAL_MACHINE\SAM	\winnt\system32\config\sam
HKEY_LOCAL_MACHINE\Security	\winnt\system32\config\security
HKEY_LOCAL_MACHINE\Software	\winnt\system32\config\software
HKEY_LOCAL_MACHINE\System	\winnt\system32\config\system
HKEY_USERS\.Default	\winnt\system32\config\default

To edit another Windows installation's Registry, use the technique I described under "Editing Registry Entries for Another User." But instead of locating a user's NTUSER.DAT file, locate the desired hive file on the other hard drive or partition. Unload it after you've exported or corrected the desired information.

EDITING REGISTRY SECURITY

Just as files and folders have security attributes to control access based on user and group identity, Registry keys and values have a complete set of Access Control attributes that determine who has rights to read, write, and modify each entry. For example, the Registry keys that control system services can't be modified by non-Administrator users; otherwise they could conceivably make the entries refer to their own programs which would then run at a high privilege level. Access controls on the Registry is thus a key part of Windows security.

If you absolutely must change permissions or auditing controls, locate the desired key or value, right-click it, and select Edit, Permissions. The Permissions dialog looks just like the comparable dialog for files and folders (see Figure 32.12), and lets you set read, write, and modify rights for specific groups and users. There is a corresponding set of audit settings.

Figure 32.12
Registry Key
Permissions control
which users or groups
are allowed to see or
modify the Registry
key and its values.

Needless to say, incorrectly changing Registry key access rights can cause profound problems with Windows, so I encourage you not to make any changes to Registry access settings unless you're explicitly instructed to do so. (This occasionally happens: Microsoft periodically issues security bulletins that tell how to eliminate newly discovered security holes in Windows. Sometimes the procedure involves limiting access to Registry keys.) Other than this, however, I recommend that you not attempt to change Registry security settings.

OTHER REGISTRY TOOLS

I've said that, although most Windows functions are controlled by Registry entries, most of these settings are made using Control Panel applets, Computer Management tools, and application preferences menus. There are some settings, however, that can't be made using any standard Windows program.

Making these changes used to require you to directly edit the Registry. Now, however, you'll find a raft of third-party add-on tools to make these changes more safely via a nice graphical user interface. Let's go through a couple of the more popular utilities.

TweakUI

Microsoft produced a tool called TweakUI. If you don't geek-speak, its name means "adjust the user interface in cool and arcane ways." You can download TweakUI from Microsoft's Web site at http://www.microsoft.com/WINDOWSXP/home/downloads/powertoys.asp. This version works with Windows 2000 and Windows XP. TweakUI is definitely worth having.

Using TweakUI, you can adjust mouse sensitivity, window movement, animation effects, the appearance of icons in the Explorer views, the visibility of desktop icons such as Internet Explorer, the visibility of local and network drives in the Explorer, and some security features such as hiding the name of the last-logged-on user. Tweak UI is covered in more detail in Chapter 23.

X-Setup

X-Setup, by Xteq, is like TweakUI on steroids. This shareware program presents more than 750 Registry-only settings and tweaks using a slick graphical Explorer-like interface. It includes wizards for some of the more complex tasks like mapping file types to Explorer icons. One of its niftiest features is its ability to record a series of changes to a log file that it can then play back on other computers. It's free for home, nonprofit, and governmental users, or $199 per 10 copies for commercial users, at www.xteq.com.

Registry Toolkit

Registry Toolkit is a shareware Registry Editor made by Funduc software with a nifty search-and-replace system. You can scan the Registry, changing all occurrences of one string to another, which is great for some nasty jobs. It also keeps a log of changes made so that edits can be undone. Its user interface isn't very comfortable or slick, but if you need to manage a lot of identical changes in the Registry, this is one tool to check out. It's free to try; $25 to register, at www.funduc.com.

RESPLENDENT REGISTRAR

Resplendent Registrar is a powerful Registry editing tool produced by Resplendence Software Projects (www.resplendence.com) with a drag and drop interface. Other features include a Registry defragmentation tool, a Registry compare tool, support for volatile Registry keys, and the option to edit Registry hive files on disk, allowing power users and administrators to edit Registry images of broken Windows installations. It's also shareware ($44.95), and there's a free "lite" version.

REGISTRY PRIVILEGES AND POLICIES

In Windows NT, 2000, and XP Professional, Registry keys and values can have permissions set to define who has permission to view and edit them, just like folders and files. The Windows Policies system, which allows administrators to restrict users' ability to change their computer configuration, is based on Registry access control.

In a nutshell, Policies install Registry keys and values that tell Windows administrative programs such as Control Panel to hide certain controls and settings. For example, a policy entry might make the Display Control Panel hide the Power Management settings. These restricting Registry entries are then locked into place with permission settings that prevent the users from seeing or changing them.

You don't usually manage these entries using Regedit, but by using the Policy Editor and Manager, which is described in Chapter 28, "Managing Users."

CAUTION

> I gave this warning before, but it bears repeating: Trying to manually change Registry privileges is very dangerous. Don't do it! You could easily render your system not only inoperative, but also out of your own ability to repair.

NOTE

> I have one more tip that's so cool, I put it at the end of the chapter under "Tips from the Windows Pros."

TROUBLESHOOTING

SIGNS OF REGISTRY PROBLEMS

How can I determine whether Windows problems are caused by the Registry?

Registry corruption can take two forms: either the Registry's database files can be damaged by an errant disk operation, or information can be entered incorrectly, by hand or by a buggy program. No matter what the cause, the result can be a system that won't run. (I have encountered this problem myself. A bad display driver entry caused Windows to reboot over and over.)

Other signs of Registry corruption or errors could be as follows:

- Drivers aren't loaded, or they give errors while Windows is booting.
- Software complains about components that aren't registered or cannot be located.
- Undesirable programs attempt to run when you log in.
- Windows does not boot, or it starts up only in Safe mode.

RECOVERING FROM A SUSPECTED REGISTRY PROBLEM

How do I recover from a Registry problem?

If any of the signs of a Registry problem occur just after you install new software or hardware, after you've edited the Registry manually, or after an unexpected and unprotected power loss to the computer, then you might have a Registry problem. Try these fixes in turn, checking after each step to see whether the problem is resolved:

1. If the problem occurred right after you installed new software, see whether the software manufacturer has released any updates for the software (especially during the first six months or so after Windows XP is released). If an update is available, install the updated software before proceeding. In any case, try reinstalling the software. If that doesn't fix the problem, *uninstall* it and then reinstall it again.

2. If the problem occurred right after installing a new piece of hardware or updating a device driver, try updating the device driver or using the Driver Rollback feature.

→ For information on the Device Rollback, **see** "Device Driver Rollback," **p. 1060**.

3. Restart Windows, and just before Windows startup screen would appear, or when the "Please select the operating system to start" appears, press the F8 key. Select Last Known Good Configuration. Last Known Good uses the previous boot's version of HKEY_LOCAL_CONFIG, so good hardware settings might be preserved there.

4. If you get to this point, get professional technical help if it is available. If that's not an option, continue to step 5.

5. Use System Restore to try to return to an earlier saved system configuration.

→ For information on the System Restore, **see** "System Restore," **p. 1162**.

6. If none of these fixes solve the problem, or if you can't get Windows started, try starting Windows in Safe mode. Starting this way circumvents many display driver setup problems. If you suspect the problem is caused by the display driver, set Windows to use the Standard VGA driver and restart. Then reinstall your normal graphics adapter (using the most recent updated driver).

7. If you have a backup containing the Registry (System State), restore it. This fix should return you to a state where you had a working system.

8. Use the Emergency Repair Disk to repair Windows (Repair mode).

9. Reinstall Windows in Repair mode.

→ For more information about reinstalling Windows, **see** "As a Last Resort," **p. 1160**.

10. Reinstall Windows in Clean Install mode. This will require you to reinstall all of your applications and reconfigure users, so it's an absolute last resort.

TRACKING DOWN ERRANT STARTUP PROGRAMS

How do I track down and eliminate startup programs that don't appear in the Start menu but start anyway when I launch Windows?

When you log on, Windows examines the Startup folder in your personal Start Menu\ Programs folder as well as in the corresponding folder under \Documents and Settings\ All Users.

In addition, Windows examines the Startup folder in the Start Menu Programs folders of both the user logging in and the All Users folder.

Windows also looks in the Registry for values in the following keys:

> HKEY_LOCAL_MACHINE\Software\Microsoft\Windows\CurrentVersion\Run
>
> HKEY_LOCAL_MACHINE\Software\Microsoft\Windows\CurrentVersion\RunOnce
>
> HKEY_CURRENT_USER\Software\Microsoft\Windows\CurrentVersion\Run
>
> HKEY_CURRENT_USER\Software\Microsoft\Windows\CurrentVersion\RunOnce

The LOCAL_MACHINE entries are run for all users, and the CURRENT_USER entries are, of course, specific to each individual user.

If you're trying to eliminate a Startup program and can't find it in your own Startup folder, look in the following places:

1. Look for a shortcut or program in the folder \Documents and Settings\Default User\ Start Menu\Programs\Startup.

2. Examine SYSTEM.INI in C:\windows. Look for `load=` or `run=` lines in the `[boot]` section. The program might be run from here.

3. Examine the Startup folders under Programs in both your Start menu and in the All Users Start menu folder. Right-click your Start button, and select Explore to examine these folders. Note: You must have administrator privileges to delete an entry from the All Users Startup folder.

4. Run Regedit, and browse to key HKEY_CURRENT_USER\Software\Microsoft\Windows\CurrentVersion. Look for Run, RunOnce, or RunOnceEx subkeys. Check their values for entries that are starting the undesired program. The RunOnce entries are often set by installer programs to complete an installation process after rebooting and are sometimes not eliminated properly.

5. Repeat the same process with HKEY_LOCAL_MACHINE\Software\Microsoft\Windows\CurrentVersion, looking for Run, RunOnce, or RunOnceEx keys.

NOTE

> If you can't log in as the affected user, and you suspect that the startup program is run from the HKEY_CURRENT_USER Registry entry, see "Editing Registry Entries for Another User" earlier in this chapter.

TIPS FROM THE WINDOWS PROS: REGISTRY TIPS ON THE WEB

As I've said repeatedly in this chapter, I don't much like the idea of fooling with the Registry. While I like to set up my desktop with a familiar set of icons, I don't like to customize things much beyond that because I want a computer to behave the way the documentation says it will. (And if something doesn't work, I like to be able to just blame Microsoft and not worry that I might have caused the problem.)

But that's just me. Many people are interested in knowing what you can alter through Registry settings, and whole Web sites have sprung up to share Windows Registry tips and tricks. If you're interested, you might check out these three:

```
www.regedit.com
www.jsiinc.com/reghack.htm
http://is-it-true.org/nt/nt2000/utips/index.shtml
```

To be honest, I don't find much of the listed tips to be helpful, and the TweakUI program I discussed earlier provides an easy way to do the same things. I have found one tip, though, that's useful enough to pass on.

If you're a big Command Prompt user, you probably are used to opening a Command Prompt window and then having to change directories to get to the folder you want to work in. There's a neat Registry trick that will let you open a Command Prompt window in any folder using the right-click menu in Explorer. Here are the steps:

1. Click Start and Run. Type **regedit** and press Enter.
2. Open key HKEY_CLASSES_ROOT\Directory\shell.
3. Add a new key under shell named **CmdHere**.
4. Edit its (Default) value, and change the value to **CMD &Prompt Here**. This text will appear on the right-click menu.
5. Add a new key under CmdHere named **command**.
6. Set its (Default) value data to **cmd /k pushd "%1"** taking care to add the quotation marks exactly as shown.

Now, in the Explorer, you can right-click any folder, and CMD Prompt Here will appear on the menu. If you select it, a command prompt window will open with this folder as the current directory. (You can even select a shared folder on another networked computer. Windows prints a grumpy error message but it still works).

Here's one final tip: If you do find a Registry tweak that you find useful, I suggest that you use the Registry Editor's "Export Registry File" function to save the altered key in a file. Edit the resulting .REG file with Notepad so that it lists only the key(s) and/or value(s) that need to be changed. This way, you can install it on other computers or on other users' accounts without having to use the Registry Editor. Just locate the .REG file in Explorer and double-click.

32

CHAPTER 33

TROUBLESHOOTING AND REPAIRING WINDOWS XP

In this chapter

TROUBLESHOOTING 101

Inevitably, the only time you'll ever have a problem with your computer system is the exact moment when it's not convenient. Or more specifically, the moment when any delay would be severely detrimental to the continuation of your job or life. Fortunately, Windows XP has benefited from the failures of its preceding OSes and as a result is more stable than any other Microsoft OS.

That is not to say that Windows XP will never experience a failure. However, the frequency of such failures is greatly reduced and in many cases Windows XP can self-heal.

In this chapter, I discuss many of the fault-tolerant features of Windows XP, along with specific tools you can employ to resolve problems.

Windows XP is chock full of helpful troubleshooting information. In many locations throughout the user experience, you'll see a button labeled "Troubleshooter." This button is most common when viewing the Properties dialog box of a device. This button launches a troubleshooting wizard that walks you through common resolution techniques for the problems you are encountering. You also can locate troubleshooting links within the Help and Support Center. Just search on a topic and look for the link to launch the troubleshooting wizard.

While I'm discussing device Properties dialog boxes, I should also mention that you can gain access to these (among a few others, such as Computer Management for drives and Phone and Modem options for modems) through the Device Manager. Within the Device Manager you can look for devices with problems by looking for the yellow exclamation point or the red stop sign over the device's icon. See Chapter 30's section titled "System: Device Manager."

BOOT OPTIONS

Windows XP offers several alternate boot methods which can be used to bypass a problem or boot into a reduced environment so you can solve the problem. If you can't boot the system, this is the time to start considering the boot options. For example, if you've recently installed a new device driver that caused a serious system failure (you can't boot), you can use a boot option to boot without that driver (this is called the "Last Known Good Configuration," to be exact).

TIP FROM

Bob & Brian

> If you *can* boot, but you're being plagued by other strange system anomalies, read the "System Restore" section later in this chapter. It might be a better choice for a simple repair. If you can boot, but a device isn't working after having just installed a new driver, check the section on "Driver Rollback," in Chapter 30.

The boot options of Windows XP are accessed during the early stages of system startup. If you have more than one OS on your system, the boot menu will be displayed. You'll have until the counter reaches zero to press F8. If you have only Windows XP Pro on your computer, you'll see a message about pressing F8 after the computer's own Power-On Self Test and the display of the graphical booting screen. You'll have only a few seconds, so keep your finger over the F8 button and press it when the message appears. Pressing F8 at the correct moment reveals the Advanced Options Menu which contains several boot options. These options are listed in Table 33.1.

TABLE 33.1   SAFE MODE STARTUP OPTIONS

Option	Description
Safe Mode	Starts Windows XP using only basic files and drivers (mouse, except serial mouse devices; monitor; keyboard; mass storage; basic video; default system services; and no network connections).
Safe Mode with Networking	Starts Windows XP using only basic files and drivers, plus network connections.
Safe Mode with Command Prompt	Starts Windows XP using only basic files and drivers. After you log on, the command prompt is displayed instead of the Windows desktop.
Enable Boot Logging	Starts Windows XP while logging all the drivers and services that were loaded (or not loaded) by the system to a file. This file, called ntbtlog.txt, is located in the %windir% directory. Safe Mode, Safe Mode with Networking, and Safe Mode with Command Prompt add to the boot log a list of all the drivers and services that are loaded. The boot log is useful in determining the exact cause of system startup problems.
Enable VGA Mode	Starts Windows XP using the basic VGA driver. This mode is useful when you have installed a new driver for your video card that is causing Windows XP to hang or start and lock up half-way into the initialization process. The basic video driver is always used when you start Windows XP in Safe mode (Safe Mode, Safe Mode with Networking, or Safe Mode with Command Prompt).
Last Known Good Configuration	Starts Windows XP using the Registry information that Windows saved at the last shutdown. Use this option only in cases in which you strongly suspect a program has written incorrect or damaging information to the Registry. The last known good configuration does not solve problems caused by corrupted or missing drivers or files. Also, any changes made since the last successful startup are lost.

33

continues

TABLE 33.1 CONTINUED	
Option	**Description**
Directory Services Restore Mode	This option is only valid for domain controllers.
Debugging Mode	Starts Windows XP while sending debug information through a serial cable to another computer.
Start Windows Normally	This option boots the system without altering the normal boot operation. Use this selection to return to normal booting after you've made any other selection from the advanced menu. Selecting this option causes the normal boot to occur immediately; you will not be returned to the boot menu.
Reboot	This command reboots the system immediately, without first booting into Windows XP or even returning to the boot menu.
Return to OS Choices Menu	This command returns to the boot menu without making an alternate boot selection.

After you've made a selection from the Advanced Options Menu, you are returned to the boot menu (Unless Reboot or Start Normally is chosen, of course). Notice your selected option is listed in blue at the bottom of the screen. From this point, you can select an OS from the list and continue with booting based on your selections.

TIP FROM

Bob & Brian

> If a symptom does not reappear when you start in Safe mode, you can eliminate the default settings and minimum device drivers as possible causes.

Using Safe mode, you can start your system with a minimal set of device drivers and services. For example, if newly installed device drivers or software is preventing your computer from starting, you might be able to start your computer in Safe mode and then remove the software or device drivers from your system. Safe mode does not work in all circumstances, especially if your system files are corrupted or missing, or your hard disk is damaged or has failed.

In general, if you've just performed some operation that caused a system failure, the best first reboot action is to use the Last Known Good Configuration. If that fails to resolve the issue, use Safe Mode. If the problem is specific to the video drivers (or suspect that it is), you might want to use Enable VGA Mode instead of Safe Mode. If you've just recently changed video drivers or the video card itself, you may want to use the Enable VGA mode if things don't act normally during the reboot.

When you are able to access the system through Safe Mode, you need to resolve the issue causing the boot problem. In most cases, this will require you to reverse your last system alteration, application install, driver update, and so on. If your system stops booting properly and you did not make any changes, then you should probably call Microsoft tech support. They may be able to help track down the culprit and get things back on track.

If none of these boot options results in a repaired system or offers you the ability to boot the system, you'll need to move on to the Recovery Console.

RECOVERY CONSOLE

The Recovery Console feature provides you with a command-line interface that enables you to repair system problems via a limited set of commands. For example, you could use the Recovery Console to enable and disable services, repair a corrupted master boot record, or copy system files from a floppy disk or a CD-ROM. The Recovery Console gives you complete control over the repair process but can be dangerous if not used with caution. If you're not an advanced user, you should stay away from this set of commands. If you do plan to pursue use of the Recovery Console, I highly recommend consulting the Windows XP Resource Kit.

The Recovery Console can be used in two ways. It can be installed so that it always appears on the boot menu as an alternate OS. Or, you can use it by initiating a repair via the setup routine. Both of these methods are discussed in this section.

To run the Recovery Console on a system that will not start, do the following:

1. Insert the Windows XP Setup Disk into your floppy drive or, if you have a bootable CD-ROM drive, insert the Windows XP CD into your CD-ROM drive.

2. Restart your computer.

3. Follow the directions on the screen. If you're using the Setup disks, you are prompted to insert the other Setup disks into the disk drive. Loading files might take several minutes. Choose the options to repair your Windows XP installation when prompted (press R for repair instead of Enter to install) and finally to start the Recovery Console when prompted.

N O T E

> To see the commands available on the Recovery Console, type `help` at its command prompt. You can also find useful information at `www.microsoft.com/technet/prodtechnol/winxppro/reskit/prmb_tol_ezjh.asp`.

To install the Recovery Console on your computer so that it is always available, you must be logged on to Windows XP as a user with an Computer Administrator account type to be able to complete this procedure.

1. Log on to Windows as a Computer Administrator user.

2. With Windows running, insert the Windows XP CD into your CD-ROM drive.

3. If you're prompted to upgrade to Windows XP, choose No.

33

4. At the command prompt (Start, All Programs, Command Prompt), switch to your CD-ROM drive, and then type the following:

   `\i386\winnt32.exe /cmdcons`

5. A dialog box appears, explaining what the Recovery Console is for, telling you it requires about 7MB of hard disk space, and asking whether you want to proceed. Click Yes.

6. A wizard starts and copies the files onto your hard disk. That's it.

Now that the Recovery Console is installed, it is listed as a selection on the boot menu—not on the Advanced Options Menu.

The following are some notes on installing the Recovery Console:

■ To run the Recovery Console after it has been installed, you must restart your computer and select the Recovery Console option from the boot menu.

■ You must be logged on as a Computer Administrator user to be able to install the Recovery Console. If your computer is connected to a network, network policy settings may also prevent you from completing this procedure.

■ To see the commands available on the Recovery Console, type **help** at the command prompt.

■ You can allow a user to run the Recovery Console without logging on by enabling the Auto Admin Logon attribute in the Security Configuration Editor. The AutoAdminLogin attribute is located in the Console tree under Local Computer Policy, Computer Configuration, Windows Settings, Security Settings, Local Policies, Security Options. Otherwise, once the Recovery Console is started, you'll be prompted for the Computer Administrator user account's password.

■ If your computer does not start, you can run the Recovery Console from the Windows XP CD (if you have a bootable CD-ROM drive) or the Setup disks.

■ If you install the Recovery Console on a hard disk drive or partition formatted with the FAT file system and later convert the partition to NTFS, you'll need to reinstall the Recovery Console.

In many cases, the Recovery Console offers you enough reach to repair most problems. However, in the event that the Recovery Console fails to support necessary system alterations, you'll need to attempt a parallel installation.

PARALLEL COPIES OF WINDOWS XP

Before you resort to doing a fresh installation over the top of a dead system, or wiping out the disk and starting over, you might want to try one other approach. This trick can sometimes get you up and running again, assuming you have enough disk space—and some patience. The following procedure creates a back door into a broken installation so that you can remove or change offending drivers, disable some offending services, tweak the Registry, and so on in hopes of getting it back up again. If nothing else, you can do a clean installation and pull in your settings from the old installation.

The basic idea is that you do a clean installation of Windows XP into a fresh directory. Then you can use Regedt32 either to alter the Registry of the dead system or pull what you can out of it (such as user settings) into the new one so that you can trash the old installation.

Here are the basic steps:

1. Install Windows XP into a fresh directory (a clean installation). For example, if your Windows directory is C:\Windows, you might use C:\Windows2 for this new installation.

2. Boot up Windows using the newly installed system. This should occur by default.

3. Try to repair the old copy by deleting or replacing defective driver files in the original Windows installation directory structure.

If you suspect that a system service is crashing on bootup and that's what's crashing your computer, you can try editing the old system's Registry to disable the service. Here's how:

1. Run Regedt32.exe from the newly installed version of Windows XP and select the following key:

HKEY_LOCAL_MACHINE

N O T E

> If you need help running Regedt32, see Chapter 32, "The Registry." Don't tinker with the Registry unless you know what you're doing. Improper editing of the Registry can result in a dead computer.

2. Click Load Hive on the File menu, and open the following Registry file on the original Windows XP installation folder

oldwindowsfolder\System32\Config\System

where *oldwindowsfolder* is the name of the folder of your original Windows installation.

3. Assign this hive a name such as OldSystem. This key contains the old HKEY_LOCAL_MACHINE\System data from your old setup.

4. Browse into the subkey CurrentControlSet if it's displayed. If it's not, look in key Select at Value Current. It will be a number such as 1, 2, or 3. Back in OldSystem, open key ControlSet00x, where x is the number you found under Current.

5. Browse into the Services key, and look for the likely offending service. Under each service's key is a value named Start, with one of the following values:

    1. Starts in the first phase of bootup (these services are usually used to access file systems)

    2. Starts automatically, just after booting

    3. Starts manually

    4. Disabled

33

Services with a Start value of 1 are used to boot Windows, and you shouldn't touch them. Services with a Start value of 2 are started just about the same time as the Login dialog appears in Windows. If your Windows system boots and then promptly crashes without your help, try setting the Start value of any suspected service(s) to 3 or 4. Be sure to write down the names of the services and their original Start values before you change anything!

6. Select the OldSystem key, and select the File menu, Unload Hive.

7. Use Notepad to view file the C:\BOOT.INI. You should see two entries for Windows XP, one using the original directory and one using the new directory. Note the order in which they're listed.

8. Shut down Windows and reboot. You have to select a Windows installation from the two Windows XP entries listed. Refer to your notes made in step 7 to determine which entry is which. Select the old (original) installation to boot.

You might need to repeat this process a few times, disabling a different service or two each time. If you can manage to reboot the old system with some system services disabled, uninstall and reinstall those services to recover your installation.

This procedure is a little bit like performing brain surgery with a shovel, but it has resurrected systems for me before.

As a Last Resort

You can reinstall Windows XP over a damaged Windows XP system. Doing so might be time-consuming, but reinstalling is useful if other repair attempts do not solve your problem. You should attempt an upgrade install first. If this works, you will have repaired your OS and retained your installed applications and most system configuration settings. If upgrading fails, you must perform a fresh install, which means you'll have to re-install all of your applications and remake all of your settings changes. Unless you format the drive, your data files will remain unaffected by the upgrade or fresh install process.

TIP FROM

Bob
& Brian

If you do a fresh install, you don't have to worry that your documents and settings will get wiped out. They won't. During a re-install, Windows XP setup checks to see if there are pre-existing Documents and Settings for each user account you create, and uses a modification of that name to create the new account settings. For example, my account name is Bob. So, under D:\Documents and Settings, there is a sub-folder called D:\Documents and Settings\Bob. When I did a fresh reinstallation on the same drive, and set up my user account again (using the name "Bob" once again), XP did not overwrite the existing Bob folder. Instead it created a new folder called D:\Documents and Settings\Bob.HP-Laptop. XP appended the name of my computer onto my username. Now all I had to do was fish around in files and folders under Bob (such as Desktop, Favorites, Cookies, Application Data, and so on) and copy those over to the new Bob.HP-Laptop folder. Then I'm back in business.

However, it is always a good idea to back up your data. Go back and check out the "Backup Tools and Strategies" section in Chapter 29 for ideas on performing that activity. Keep in mind that if your system fails to boot, you can't get access to the Windows backup tool to create a backup. So, you must be proactive by backing up your important files on a regular basis. You might get lucky and be able to use the Safe Mode Command Prompt or the Recovery Console to access a command prompt where you can copy files to a floppy, removable medium, or other drives. But relying on this is not smart.

TIP FROM

Bob
& Brian

> If data recovery is what you are after, there are ways to reclaim your data from the hard drive. These techniques assume that the files or folders you want to reclaim did not use NTFS encryption. There are several approaches you could consider. First, if you have a dual-boot system, look for the Documents and Settings folder on the XP boot drive. Drill down until you find the files you want. This assumes the OS you boot into can read the file system that your user files are stored under, of course. Second, you can try connecting the drive to another computer that boots an OS capable of reading the volumes and folders in question. Then go looking for the files. Find them, and copy them where you'd like.

NOTE

> In cases where the lost data files were encrypted under NTFS, you will need a *recovery key* to gain access to them. See Chapter 29 for more about managing the hard disk, and Chapter 28 for details about managing users and passwords.

PREVENTING PROBLEMS

I have never believed that having to re-install and re-configure an OS is a true recovery method. Its more of a start-over-from-scratch method. There are some system failures which require such far reaching procedures, but in many cases you can prevent them. The most successful preventative measure is backing up. In fact, the only insurance you have from one moment to the next that your system and your data will even be accessible is a back up. Backups should be performed automatically and frequently. But just backing up is not enough; you must also verify that your backups are working properly and periodically walk through the process of restoring your system in the event of a failure.

Backups are the key to a long life of your data. In fact, most of the repair capabilities of Windows XP are based around backups. Many repair functions don't correct problems directly; instead they restore saved functioning files over problematic ones. This includes the Last Known Good Configuration, many functions within Recovery Console, and the System Restore capability (discussed later in this chapter). But all of these restore or repair functions focus on the OS, not on your data. Only a backup you configure and execute will protect your data.

Flip back to Chapter 29, "Managing the Hard Disk," for more details about backups.

33

Backups are not the only preventative measures you should take. You should also regularly check your system's performance. This process was discussed in Chapter 25, "Maintaining and Optimizing System Performance."

It is also a good idea to use a UPS (Uninterruptible Power Supply). A UPS conditions the power being fed to the computer and can provide several minutes of power in the event of a blackout. A UPS will prolong the life of your computer by protecting its sensitive components from electric fluctuations.

Regularly check the Event Viewer for device, driver, and service problems. Problems of this nature usually appear in the System log. They are usually indicated by a yellow triangle or a red stop sign as the event detail's icon. If you see problems related to key components of the system, you need to investigate the situation and resolve the problem. Unfortunately, the event details do not always provide enough information. You'll need to use the Help and Support Center, the Microsoft online knowledge base (`support.microsoft.com`), or Microsoft technical support over the phone to decipher what cryptic information is presented. In many cases, the Windows XP troubleshooter will provide a workable solution. Otherwise, you should consult the vendor's Web site for updated drivers and troubleshooting instructions.

> **NOTE**
>
> The Event Viewer is discussed in Chapter 27, "System Utilities." The hardware troubleshooter (both through the Add Hardware applet and the Device Manager) is discussed in Chapter 24, "Configuration via Control Panel Applets."

You should also endeavor to regularly perform drive maintenance on your system. Maintaining healthy drives reduces the number of drive and file system related problems. Drive maintenance involves the following:

- Manually removing old data files, either via deletion or backup
- Use Disk Cleanup to remove unnecessary files
- Use Error-checking to verify the volume is supporting its file system properly
- Use Defragmenter to consolidate files and aggregate free space

> **NOTE**
>
> These drive tools are discussed in Chapter 29, "Managing the Hard Disk."

SYSTEM RESTORE

System Restore is a fabulous mechanism which first appeared with Windows Me. Now Windows XP incorporates it, too. System Restore enables you to restore the computer to a previously saved state. So, you can "roll back" your computer to the way it was working before your dog jumped on the keyboard, or before you installed that stupid program or device driver that lunched your system. Here's how it works.

Performing a system restore does not affect personal files, such as documents, Internet favorites, or e-mail. It simply reverses system configuration changes and removes installed files to return the system to a stored state. System Restore automatically monitors your system for changes. Periodically easily identifiable restoration points are created. Plus, you can create your own restoration points manually.

It should be obvious, but I'll state it anyway: System Restore is only accessible if you can boot Windows XP. If your system does not boot, you must use one of the previously mentioned system recovery techniques.

There are two control interfaces for System Restore. One is on the System Restore tab of the System applet. The other is the System Restore utility itself accessed through Start, All Programs, Accessories, System Tools, System Restore.

The System Restore tab (see Figure 33.1) of the System applet is where System Restore is enabled or disabled for all drives in the computer. It is enabled by default.

Figure 33.1
The System Restore tab of the System applet where drive by drive settings are defined to enable storage of system restore archives.

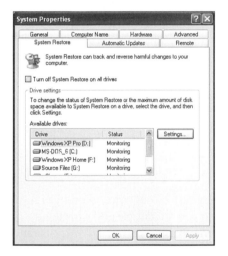

While enabled, you can define on a drive-by-drive basis how much space can be consumed by System Restore to maintain restoration points. You can choose to turn off System Restore for individual drives or set the percentage of the drive usable by System Restore. Each drive has either 20% or 12% of its total size set as the default and maximum allowed usage levels (see Figure 33.2). (It seems that if the 20% level results in a value over 400 MB, then the 12% level is used.) Keep in mind that if you disable System Restore on a drive, no changes to that drive are retained in restore points.

The number of restore points retained by System Restore will depend on the amount of allowed drive space usage as well as the rate and significance of changes to the system.

Figure 33.2
Drive settings dialog
box for System
Restore.

Restore points are created by Windows XP automatically whenever any one of several specific events occurs:

- On first boot after installation
- Every 24 hours of calendar time or every 24 hours of computer uptime
- When a program is installed using InstallShield or Windows Installer
- Automatic updates via Windows Update
- Any restore operation
- Installation of unsigned device drivers
- At any restore operation using Backup

Keep in mind that not all program installations use InstallShield or Windows Installer. Thus, you should always manually create a restore point before installing applications.

The creation of a restore point at any restore operation allows you to reverse a restoration. Thus, if after a successful restoration you are not pleased with the outcome, you can reverse the restoration. The system automatically removes any failed or incomplete restoration operations.

System Restore does not replace the uninstallation process for removing an application. System Restore only monitors and protects against changes to the OS. It does not track the addition of new files to the system. Use the Add or Remove Programs utility or a vendor provided uninstall routine to remove applications.

The System Restore tool (see Figure 33.3) in the System Tools section of the Start menu is actually a wizard accessed by clicking its icon in the Start menu under All Programs, Accessories, System Tools. This wizard walks you through the process of restoring the system to a previous saved state or to manually create a restore point. Just make a radio button selection and then click Next.

Figure 33.3
The System Restore tool.

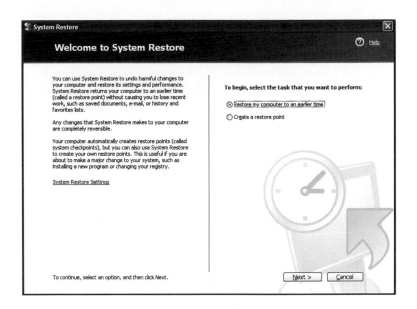

When restoring a system, the list of available restoration points is displayed along with a calendar to help in time-lining and identifying. Once you've selected a restore point, you'll be asked to confirm your wish to restore the system to the saved state and informed that the system will reboot to perform the action. Once the restore is complete, a new third radio button option for Undo My Last Restoration will appear on the first page of the System Restore Wizard.

Creating a restore point is even simpler. All you need to do is provide a name for the restore point and click Create. The system state data will be saved.

BLACK MAGIC OF TROUBLESHOOTING

It often seems like many professional technophiles have some sort of black magic they use when resolving problems. If you blink, you miss whatever it is they do to get the system back in working order. It's often as if you are working with a techno-mage.

Yes, it is true that some of our skills at resolving problems do seem like hocus pocus. But in reality, it's a mixture of experience and knowledge. Both of which you can gain with time and effort.

In my experience, I've found that most computer problems are physical in nature. Meaning some component is not connected properly or has become damaged. Of the remaining 5%, more than 4.99% is caused directly the user—whether through deliberate or accidental activity. User caused problems are typically configuration changes, installation of new drivers, or deletion of important files and folders.

When I troubleshoot a problem on my own systems, I try to mentally walk backwards through whatever I've done to the system over the last few days or weeks. In many cases, I'll remember installing some downloaded application or changing some Control Panel setting that I meant to uninstall or reverse, but never got around to do it. If the brainstorming fails to highlight any suspects, I check for physical issues. Is everything powered on? Are cooling fans still spinning? Are all the right cables still firmly connected?

If I don't discover anything obvious physically, I try a power-off reboot. The power-off reboot will reset all hardware devices, and in many cases resolve the problem (if it was device related). If possible, shut down the system gracefully. Then keep the power off for about 10 seconds before switching the system back on. You'll be amazed at how often this works.

My next steps always include a walk through the Event Viewer and any other types of log files I can find. Let the problem guide you in this process. For example, if the video system is failing, you probably don't need to look through the modem logs.

For me, every problem is unique. Often requiring a different resolution than any other problem I've tackled in the past. However, there are some general rules or guidelines I try to follow:

- Try only one change at a time
- Reboot twice after each change
- Test each change for success
- Try the least invasive first
- Keep a log of your changes, you may need to undo them to produce a result, or you may need the resolution process again in the future
- Consult vendor Web sites for possible solutions, if the problem seems to be specific to one device or software component
- Be patient and take your time
- After a few attempts at possible solutions, step back and re-evaluate before continuing
- If you get frustrated, take a break. Anger and frustration are counter-productive when you need to be thinking clearly
- Try to undo any recent changes to the system, including new hardware or software patches
- Review areas of the system which have caused problems in the past
- Try to repeat the failure; knowing where, how, or why the failure occurs can lead to a solution

Troubleshooting is both an art and a science. You'll need organized patience and outrageous ingenuity. Plus, knowing where to look stuff up never hurts. Keep in mind that the entire Internet is waiting at your finger tips and mouse clicks. Search groups.google.com as well the regular Web. You'll be amazed at what you find. Be precise in your search techniques to help find the exact messages you need to read. The MS knowledge base is extremely helpful, too. Plus, lots of helpful information is included within the Help and Support system of Windows XP as well as the Windows XP Resource Kit. If all else fails, contact Microsoft technical support over the phone (see support.microsoft.com for contact numbers). In most cases, if the troubleshooting techniques in this book don't resolve the issue, it usually beyond the end-user to correct.

SCATTER-GUN TROUBLESHOOTING

Not all of the troubleshooting techniques applicable to Windows XP are contained within this one chapter. If you've noticed, we've been discussing troubleshooting within every chapter. That organizational decision was intended to group recovery information with the discussion of the related technologies, deployment, usage, and management. So, before you throw your hands up in frustration that your questions are not answered or your problem is not resolved in this chapter, go check out the chapter dedicated to the specific subject earlier in this book.

33

INSTALLING SERVICE PACK 1

In this appendix

ABOUT SERVICE PACKS

Windows XP is part of Microsoft's "New Technology" or NT family of operating systems, along with Windows NT, 2000, and 2003 Server. These operating systems were designed from the ground up for stability, reliability, and security, and to keep them in tip-top shape, Microsoft releases a constant stream of software updates called Critical Updates, Recommended Updates, and Hotfixes:

- Critical Updates are just that: Fixes for bugs that are so severe or involve such serious security risks that you really *have* to install them. As you know, XP can automatically download these and offer to install them, so you don't miss out. You can also find a list of Critical Updates by visiting the Windows Update Web site.

- Recommended Updates are not security fixes, but updates to accessory programs like Messenger and Media Player, new desktop themes and the like. Recommended Updates are also listed on the Windows Update Web site.

- Hotfixes are bug fixes that affect a small enough group of users that Microsoft doesn't send them out to everyone. Instead, you have to hunt for them by researching the Knowledge Base at support.microsoft.com, or hear about them from Microsoft's Tech Support department. They're not widely advertised because (a) if you're running into a serious-enough problem, you'll go looking for the solution, and (b) Hotfixes tend to be released in a hurry without extensive testing, so they sometimes cause new problems of their own. Hotfix users tend to be corporate IT people whose job it is to stay on top of these things.

Periodically—every 12 months or more often—Microsoft gathers all of the Critical Updates, Recommended Updates, and Hotfixes, tests them extensively, and releases them as a Service Pack. Service Packs, then, represent a complete set of fixes and additions made since the initial release of an operating system. Service Packs can be obtained on CD-ROM media, or can be downloaded from Windows Update.

If you're used to Windows 95, 98, and Me, where you were basically left twisting slowly in the wind when it came to bug fixes, this is a really big deal. You have a real operating system now, and you are now get going to get the kind of support you should have been getting all along.

Service Pack 1, or SP1, is the first such release for Windows XP, and it contains not only new features (see Appendix B for that story), but also fixes for hundreds of bugs and security problems that were discovered after XP's initial release. Don't let the "hundreds of bugs" worry you—in a collection of programs as large as XP, there are bound to be *thousands* of bugs. Most of them are very, very obscure, and affect only a few users with specific hardware and software combinations.

You might wonder whether you really need to install Service Packs, since you probably install the Critical Updates that XP downloads and informs you of from time to time. The answer is yes, for two reasons. First, Service Packs fix those annoying bugs that you may not even realize are there—that odd crash every other week, or that weird sound that Media Player makes once in while. Second, application programs will eventually appear that require a certain Service Pack in order to run. Windows evolves, so you need to keep up.

Here are some other things that you should know about Service Packs:

- They're cumulative, so, when Service Pack 2 appears, it will include all of the changes in Service Pack 1.

- If you use Add/Remove Programs to install optional Windows components after installing a service pack, you *don't* have to run the Service Pack procedure again. However, Windows Setup may ask you to insert the Service Pack media, or it may need to download updated files.

- At about the same time that a Service Pack is released, new computers should come with the patches already installed. To check the current service pack level of your Windows XP computer, open Windows Explorer and select Help, About Windows. Or, type winver at the command prompt. Compare that to current Service Pack level listed at windowsupdate.com.

- While this appendix describes the procedure for obtaining and installing Service Pack 1, it's very likely that the procedure will be the same for subsequent service packs as well. You won't need a new copy of this book when SP1 has become obsolete!

Now, let's talk about how to install the Service Pack on your computer.

INSTALLATION OPTIONS

Windows XP Service Pack 1 (SP1) comes in three different flavors for you—depending on what your download tastes are or if you acquire SP1 on CD-ROM. The three means of installing SP1 onto your computer are summarized here and explained in detail throughout the rest of this appendix.

- **Standalone**— The traditional Service Pack, it weighs in about 120MB and includes all files required to deploy SP1 to one or many computers on your network. The XPSP1.EXE file is a self-extracting executable file that will upgrade any Windows XP build 2600 computer to Windows XP SP1. The Standalone version can be used to "slipstream" existing Windows XP installation media—that is, it can update a copy of the Windows XP setup files so that future installations will have SP1 preinstalled—and also has a handful of command-line switches that can be used to modify its behavior at the time of execution.

  At 120MB, the size of this download may be too much for some Internet connections; thus this version is also available from Microsoft as a CD-ROM that can be ordered for a small shipping charge. If the download is too much for your Internet connection to handle, the small shipping charge is a worthwhile investment.

- **Express** —The Patch or Express upgrade works on the specific computer that downloads or executes a small program named SP1EXPRESS.EXE, which runs about 2MB in size. This program downloads from Microsoft just those service pack components needed for your computer. This saves download time. However, you'd only want to use this method if you have a single Windows XP computer, as each custom download can run up to 100MB in size. If you try to update two or more computers this way, you'd spend way too much time downloading files. Also, you cannot install the Express

A

upgrade over the network using Group Policy, nor can you modify its behavior from the command line using switches.

- **Integrated** —The Integrated version is a full installation version of Windows XP that has SP1 included into its code. This can either be a new installation CD-ROM acquired from Microsoft or an OEM, or a slipstreamed installation CD-ROM or network share that you have created locally. Installing an Integrated version performs a full installation of Windows XP SP1 (subject to customization by the installer, as always) without the need to subsequently install the Service Pack.

Regardless of how you choose to install SP1, you should perform the following steps:

- Professional users only: Update your Automated System Recovery disk.
- We recommend that you perform a full backup of the files that you keep on your computer.
- Disable any real-time virus checkers before you install SP1, because they might interfere with your installation. (Be sure to re-enable the virus checkers after you install SP1.)
- Check the space requirements for installing SP1 on your computer. You will need about 320MB of free space on your hard drive if installing from a network folder, or about 575MB if installing from a CD-ROM or downloaded file.

STANDALONE UPGRADE

The Standalone upgrade is the most robust of the three versions of SP1, as previously discussed in the introduction to this appendix. You can opt to install the Standalone upgrade in several different ways, depending on how you acquired the SP1 file and where it is located relative to the computer you are installing it on. You can use the Standalone SP1 upgrade in three different ways:

- To perform a normal upgrade of Windows XP to Windows XP SP1 locally on the computer to be upgraded.
- To perform a network upgrade of Windows XP from a shared folder.
- To create a slipstreamed Windows XP SP1 installation source that can be used to deploy new installation via RIS or with a CD-ROM.

INSTALLING SERVICE PACK 1 LOCALLY

Most home and small office users will want to install SP1 locally. You can use either a CD-ROM–based installation kit, or file downloaded from Microsoft. The procedure is identical once you've determined the location of the installation file. Proceed as outlined:

1. Locate and double-click the xpsp1.exe file, or start the installation from the command line by entering x:\xpsp1.exe, where x is the location of the SP1 file.
2. If installing from a CD-ROM, you will be prompted to run the file from its location or save it to disk. Select Run This Program from its Current Location, and then click OK.

3. The Windows XP Service Pack 1 Setup Wizard appears informing you of some items of concern. After you've read the warnings, click Next to dismiss the opening page of the Wizard.

4. On the *License Agreement* page, you must click I Agree to enable the Next button. Click Next to continue.

5. On the *Select Options* page (see Figure A.1), you will face the single most important decision you need to make during the upgrade process. Select whether or not you want to be able uninstall the SP1 upgrade at a later time by selecting Archive Files or Do Not Archive Files. We recommend that you select the Archive Files option—be aware, however, that this will require about 200MB of additional disk space on your hard drive. After making your selection, click Next to continue.

Figure A.1
Selecting the Archive option lets you remove the Service Pack at a later date, should problems arise.

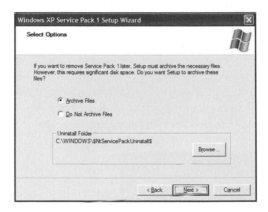

6. The *Updating Your System* page (see Figure A.2) now appears. During this phase of the upgrade, Windows will inspect your current Windows XP files, archive your current Windows files, and lastly, install the SP1 files.

Figure A.2
The Service Pack installer displays a progress dialog as it archives and installs files.

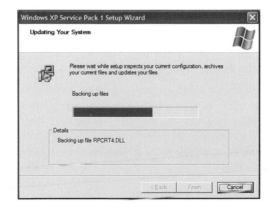

A

7. After some time, you will be presented with a summary page (see Figure A.3) informing you that the installation of SP1 has been completed. Restart your computer to complete the installation of SP1 onto your computer.

Figure A.3
Completing the SP1 installation process.

8. On the subsequent restart, typing winver at the command prompt shows the new (and upgraded) Windows XP status on your computer. See Figure A.4. You can also see this by selecting Help, About Windows in Windows Explorer.

Figure A.4
WINVER shows the version of Windows XP installed on your computer.

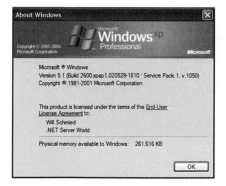

9. If you disabled your anti-virus software, be sure to re-enable it at this time.

10. We suggest that you now create a full system backup or ASR backup of your computer. If you suffer a crash and try to restore a system backup made *before* the Service Pack installation, you will render your computer unable to restart.

→ To learn more about using the Windows Backup utility or the Automated System Recovery Utility, **see** "Backup Tools and Strategies," **p. 1023.**

INSTALLING SERVICE PACK 1 FROM THE NETWORK

Installing SP1 from a network file share is the best option when you have several computers to upgrade. This option works equally well in either a workgroup or domain network environment. The first step is to place the expanded Service Pack files on a shared network drive. For the purposes of this example, I am going to assume that you will want to first extract the files from the XPSP1.EXE file before starting the installation process; if this is not the case, simply skip step 2 of the procedure that follows.

1. On the file server to host the files, create and share a folder to hold the installation files.

2. From the command line, enter the following command to extract the SP1 files to the folder you just created: $x:\spxp1.exe$ /x, where x is the location of the $xpsp1.exe$ file. You will be prompted to specify the location to store the extracted files to (see Figure A.5). Enter the local or network path of the shared folder and click OK.

Figure A.5
Extracting the SP1 files without installing SP1.

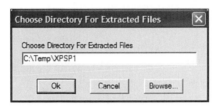

3. Ensure that the network folder has NTFS and/or share permissions that let network users read but not modify the files.

Then, at each computer that you want to update with the Service Pack, browse to the shared network folder you created in the previous steps and

■ run the program update\update.exe if you extracted the files in step 2, or

■ run xpsp1.exe if you did not.

You can run the required setup program from the command prompt using a mapped drive letter or the full UNC pathname, or by double-clicking the program in Windows Explorer.

The rest of the procedure is identical to that outlined in steps 3–10 under "Installing Service Pack 1 Locally."

Modifying Installation Behavior of Service Pack 1 from the Command Line

As with all Service Packs, Windows XP SP1 can be installed from the command line, using switches to modify the behavior of the setup routing. The full list of command line options is

```
xpsp1.exe /f /l /n /q /s:folder /u /z
```

or

```
update.exe /f /l /n /q /s:folder /u /z
```

TABLE A.1   COMMAND LINE OPTIONS FOR SERVICE PACK INSTALLATION

Switch	Description
/f	Forces all open applications to close before the computer is restarted following the installation of the service pack (SP). Cannot be used with /s, /l, or /z.
/l	Lists all hot fixes currently installed on the computer. Does not install anything.
/n	Installs the SP, but does not enable support for uninstalling it later. Cannot be used with /l or /s.
/o	Reserved for future use.
/q	Installs the SP in "quiet" mode, suppressing all user interface screens.
/s:folder	Installs the SP and Windows XP from source files in the specified folder.
/u	Installs the SP in unattended mode. Although the prompts appear, the installation will proceed without waiting for user input. Neither the progress bar nor any errors that might occur will appear during the installation.
/z	Installs the SP, but does not automatically restart the computer upon the completion of the installation. Cannot be used with /l or /s.

NOTE

> The switches described in Table A.1 work with either the XPSP1.EXE self extracting archive or the update.exe file (which actually starts the service pack installation process).

NOTE

> You can precede the switches in Table A.1 with either a slash (/) or a dash (-); it makes no difference to the setup routine. Additionally, the switches are not case sensitive.

The switches outlined in Table A.2 only work with the XPSP1.EXE file.

TABLE A.2   ADDITIONAL XPSP1.EXE SWITCHES

Switch	Description
/x	Extracts Service Pack files without starting update.exe.
/u /x:folder	Extracts Service Pack files and places them in the specified folder without prompting and without starting update.exe.

EXPRESS UPGRADE

Upgrading a single computer using the Express upgrade is a process relatively similar that of using the Standalone upgrade version. The key difference is that instead of already having all of the required files available on the local computer (or elsewhere on the local network), the update program will download the required files to your computer as it needs them. In this way, the upgrade is similar to that you may have experienced in the past when attempting to upgrade Internet Explorer.

To upgrade your Windows XP computer to SP1 using an Express upgrade, proceed as follows:

1. Download the Express upgrade file, SP1EXPRESS.EXE to your computer and execute it. The file can be obtained from the Windows Update Web site.

2. The Windows XP Service Pack 1 Setup Wizard appears, informing you of some items of concern. After you've read the warnings, click Next to dismiss the opening page of the Wizard.

3. On the *License Agreement* page, you must click I Agree to enable the Next button. Click Next to continue.

4. On the *Select Options* page (see Figure A.1), you will face the single most important decision you need to make during the upgrade process. Select whether or not you want to be able uninstall the SP1 upgrade at a later time by selecting Archive Files or Do Not Archive Files. We recommend that you select the Archive Files option—be aware, however, as this will require about 200MB of additional disk space on your hard drive. After making your selection, click Next to continue.

5. The *Updating Your System* page (see Figure A.2) now appears. During this phase of the upgrade, Windows will inspect your current Windows XP files, archive your current Windows files, and lastly, install the SP1 files.

6. After some time, you will be presented with a summary page (see Figure A.3) informing you that the installation of SP1 has been completed. Restart your computer to complete the installation of SP1 onto your computer.

7. If you disabled your anti-virus software, be sure to re-enable it at this time.

8. We suggest that you now create a full system backup or ASR backup of your computer. If you suffer a crash and try to restore a system backup made *before* the Service Pack installation, you will render your computer unable to restart.

→ To learn more about using the Windows Backup utility or the Automated System Recovery Utility, **see** "Backup Tools and Strategies," **p. 1023.**

A

NOTE

You cannot use the Express installation method to install SP1 on Windows XP Professional 64-bit Edition.

All in all, the only difference between the Standalone upgrade and the Express upgrade is when and how you get the SP1 upgrade files onto your computer. When all is said and done, you will have the same result regardless of which method you choose to employ. As discussed previously, the chief advantage to using the Standalone upgrade is that you can easily upgrade more than one computer from the Standalone upgrade file.

INTEGRATED

Installing Windows XP SP1 using Integrated installation media can be done via one of two ways: either using a CD-ROM that you have created via slipstreaming or acquired from a vendor, or by making use of the Remote Installation Service of Windows 2000 Server.

This procedure can be used on an existing Windows XP computer, as well as a new computer with a blank hard drive.

The process to install from an integrated-setup CD-ROM is the same as installing Windows XP from the CD-ROM as discussed in Chapter 3. For more information about deploying Windows XP using RIS, see `http://www.microsoft.com/technet/prodtechnol/winxppro/reskit/prbc_cai_bowe.asp` from Chapter 2 of the Windows XP Professional Resource Kit.

NOTE

> Upgrading an existing, activated Windows XP machine using the integrated version of the service pack *DOES NOT* require a new product key. You should use the same product key the machine was originally activated with if needed.

REMOVING SP1

Should Service Pack 1 not be to your liking, have no fear—you can easily uninstall it from the Add or Remove Programs applet of the Control Panel. To uninstall SP1, you must have enabled support for this during the installation of SP1. See Figure A.1 for details about enabling uninstallation. To remove SP1, proceed as follows:

1. Open the Add or Remove Programs applet by clicking Start, Settings, Control Panel, Add or Remove Programs. Figure A.6 shows what your Add or Remove Programs page might look like, depending on what applications you have installed on your computer.

Figure A.6
Preparing to uninstall Windows XP SP1.

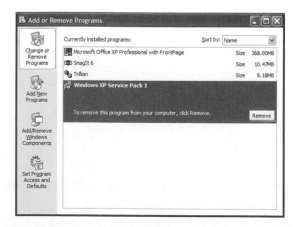

2. Highlight Windows XP Service Pack 1 and click Remove.

3. Click Yes at the warning dialog shown in Figure A.7 and follow the remaining prompts to finish the uninstallation. You may see a dialog box displaying a list of applications that you have installed since installing SP1. These applications may not function properly after the removal of SP1, and thus may require reinstallation.

Figure A.7
Are you sure you want to uninstall Windows XP SP1?

Windows XP Service Pack 1

This program removes Windows XP Service Pack 1 and restores your previous configuration.

Do you want to remove Windows XP Service Pack 1?

Yes   No

A

New Features in Service Pack 1

In this appendix

WHAT'S NEW?

Service Pack 1 (SP1) to Windows XP has a wide variety of included items that will make Windows XP more secure, while at the same time adding great new functionality previously unavailable in a mainstream product such as Windows. Some of the features of SP1 include

- **Windows CE for Smart Displays (Mira)**—Support for smart display devices running Windows CE .NET that interact via 802.11 wireless with a Windows XP base station.

- **Windows XP Media Center Edition**—Support for a new version of Windows XP that will run on a new generation of computers with integrated TV and multimedia hardware. A simplified graphical interface will allow you to interact with these computers with a remote control as well as a mouse.

- **USB 2.0**—An enhancement to USB 1.x that increases maximum transfer rates to 480Mbps.

- **IPv6**—Support for the next version of the IP protocol, created due to the need for more publicly addressable IP addresses.

- **Consent Decree compliance** Allows users to "hide" links to Microsoft middleware products such as Internet Explorer and Outlook Express, and have other options shown instead.

- **Windows .NET Messenger 4.7** New version of Messenger that features enhanced security and compliance with the DOJ Consent Decree.

- **Tablet PC** Support for full-featured "baby" laptop computers with touch screens and handwriting recognition that can be picked up and taken on the go. A new version of Windows XP (Tablet PC Edition) will power these devices, which allow for new and unusual ways to use Windows.

- **Microsoft Product Activation**—Changes Product Activation to disable certain pirated versions of Windows XP. The changes should have no effect on legally obtained copies of Windows.

- **Security Fixes and Improvements**—Includes all patches and hot fixes that have been released for Windows XP since it was released to manufacturing last year.

Bluetooth, Bluetooth...Where Art Thou?
Don't look for Bluetooth in SP1—it's not there.

There may be deeper issues with Bluetooth support for Windows XP than Microsoft wants to discuss: Bluetooth is seen as interference to an 802.11b wireless network, and can completely prevent it from functioning properly. The problem lies in the design of Bluetooth—it hops between frequencies in its 2.4GHz band about 1,600 times per second, which is enough to all but completely disrupt other 2.4GHz-based wireless traffic—such as that of an 802.11b network.

Now let's look at each of Service Pack 1's major features and, in some cases, the gotchas.

WINDOWS CE FOR SMART DISPLAYS (MIRA)

Windows CE for Smart Displays (which was code-named Mira) is a new technology developed jointly between Microsoft and leading PC and peripheral manufacturers. It's a three-pronged system that makes use of your existing Windows XP SP1 computer, new devices that are Mira-enabled and running Windows CE .NET, and a connection between the two using 802.11b (Wi-Fi) technologies. Figure B.1 gives an example of how this works in your home (or office).

Figure B.1
Windows CE for Smart Displays (Mira) connects to your Windows XP SP1 computer and extends its functionality.

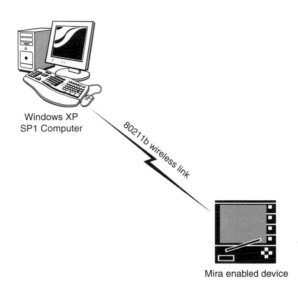

Windows XP
SP1 Computer

802.11b wireless link

Mira enabled device

Windows CE for Smart Displays–enabled devices connect to the Windows XP SP1 computer via Windows Terminal Services (Remote Desktop) running over an 802.11b connection. In essence, they let you carry your computer's screen around the office, house, or yard. These devices promise to be ideal for those tasks that do not require heavy keyboard input, since the stylus is the input method by design. Such activities could include Web browsing or Smart House control, although more uses will undoubtedly come to your mind as you use one.

Windows XP Home users unfortunately will need to upgrade in order to use Windows CE for Smart Displays, as the remote desktop features are not found in the XP Home Edition. Although as of this writing, Mira products were not available for testing, we were advised that Windows CE for Smart Displays will include the following functionality:

- It promises to provide instant-on access to the network, because the operating system will be embedded, as in other Windows CE machines, and won't have to boot from hard disk.
- Promises to support auto logon and auto reconnect to the network.
- Provides support for Universal Plug and Play (UPnP) .

B

What makes Mira different from the way we compute today? Consider the following comparisons between existing technologies and these new devices:

- Windows CE for Smart Displays–enabled devices bear a strong resemblance to standard flat-panel monitors. The resemblance stops at the surface, however, as a flat-panel monitor is only a display device. A Windows CE for Smart Displays device is an input device as well, and acts as a "front-end" to your computer. With Mira, you can take the screen anywhere in your home or office, as long as you can maintain wireless connectivity.

- Windows CE for Smart Displays–enabled devices will look similar to third-party Internet appliances. Windows CE for Smart Displays will initially ship in two form factors: 15-inch detachable displays, and six- to 10-inch remote mobile monitors, which can be placed up to 150 feet away. Such appliances are usually created for a single purpose, such as email or Web browsing, without having the full functionality of a Windows-based computer. Mira-enabled devices promise to deliver full-featured Windows support, flexibility, and capabilities unlike their single-purpose Internet appliance cousins.

- Windows CE for Smart Displays–enabled devices are not meant to be substitutes for standard desktop or laptop computers. They are instead designed to complement the existing desktop or laptop environment by extending its usefulness and range to the entire household or to create an extended office. A full-function PC combined with a touch screen is another animal, and will be sold as a "Tablet PC" running a specialized version of Windows XP.

If you are a PocketPC user, another way to think of Windows CE for Smart Displays is as a grown-up PocketPC sporting a full-size display rather than a dinky one, and connected to the base computer via a wireless LAN card. Remember the Mac Newton? Newton was just a little ahead of its time, and didn't cut the mustard in the marketplace. This is partly because the rest of the supporting technology—such as 802.11b—wasn't in place yet. Now that wireless has matured, something like Mira can emerge again. This time it's Microsoft's turn. I expect Apple will have a second go of it though, too.

NOTE

> Windows CE for Smart Displays is still evolving as a technology. While the Windows XP end of the deal is part of SP1, the hardware end is dependent on the individual hardware manufacturers. To keep up to date on Mira developments, be sure to see `http://www.microsoft.com/windowsxp/mira/default.asp`.

NOTE

> Since its release (and success) of the XBox game console, Microsoft has become emboldened to enter the hardware field more strongly. Later this year they will release their own version of wireless networking products. The Microsoft-branded access point and network cards will aim to correct many security vulnerabilities found in current wireless network setups with an improved security architecture.

WINDOWS XP MEDIA CENTER EDITION

Service Pack 1 incorporates changes designed to make Windows XP compatible with a new generation of PC hardware that will come with an integrated TV tuner, audio and multimedia interfaces, and a TV-like remote control.

This new generation of PC will not only function as a standard computer, but will additionally be… you guessed it, a media center, allowing a user to access music, video and photos at a distance from anywhere in the room. Recording, editing and playback software will make a Media Center computer a combination CD player, DVD player, audio jukebox, and TIVO-like digital television recorder. In media-player mode, the new devices will sport a simplified user interface more suitable for distance viewing.

In the near future, the PC will move from its typically small arena (such as on the desk in your home office) to other places in the house, notably the living room. Rich digital media is the wave of the future, including music, photos, and movies. Since all of these rich media experiences typically rely on a computer, Microsoft hopes that those computers will be running Windows—on the same turf where your TiVo, CD player, DVD player, and VHS deck are now top dogs. Figure B.2 shows a sample Windows Media Center Start screen, available as of this writing.

NOTE

> Unfortunately, Microsoft has indicated that—at least at the present time—they have no plans to make this new version of Windows or the required additional hardware available as an upgrade or aftermarket option; they will be bundled together on new specially-equipped computers only. So, for those of us with standard computers running Windows XP Home Edition or Professional, installing SP1 will not give us Media Center capabilities.

For the rest of us, it's interesting to note that Media Center's basic functionality is already available to some extent. Take a basic PC, install a video capture card with a TV-out jack (many video cards and even laptops have them), and connect the PC to a large monitor or a large-screen TV; connect your sound card to a good amp and speakers; add a wireless mouse and keyboard, and you have the basics of the Media Center. Add TV recording software and you have everything but the slick user interface and the remote control.

NOTE

> Keep an eye on `http://www.microsoft.com/windows/ehome/default.asp` for more information on Windows XP Media Center.

B

Figure B.2
The Windows XP
Media Center Edition
Start screen.

USB 2.0 Support

The Universal Serial Bus (USB) has been a thing of wonder for the computer peripheral market. Now instead of needing a variety of different connector types, one simple connection can be used to connect all types of peripherals to a computer. Typical peripherals include keyboards, mice, printers, scanners, Web cameras, digital cameras, and speakers. The existing USB 1.x standard only specified a 12Mbps transfer rate, which was more than adequate when the standard was initially approved in 1996 (and later amended in 1998), but has since come up short. While the majority of components, such as mice and keyboards, work just fine under USB 1.x standards, other devices require more bandwidth for data transfer suffer. Devices such as scanners, printers, speakers, and external storage (for example hard drives and CD-RW) suffered the most under USB 1.x. USB 2.0 corrects this issue, but only if both your computer and operating system support it.

As you probably know, the standard called *FireWire* has given USB 1.x a real run for its money, and was out of the gate about two years earlier than USB 2.0. FireWire (also known as IEEE 1394 or Sony's "iLink") is found in many laptops and high-end desktop machines (paying Apple Computer commensurate royalties on each installation, by the way).

In short, Intel (who developed USB) was caught with its pants down, with USB looking pretty doggy in comparison to FireWire's fleetness.

In response, Intel went back to the drawing board to supercharge USB. It took several years to iron out the technicalities from what I've heard (tackling problems such as data echoes within USB2 cables)—issues which had already been solved with FireWire. So now we have a supposedly better mouse trap. And perhaps it is. FireWire's top speed is 400Mbps, whereas USB 2.0 is faster, at 480Mbps. Not a huge increase, but still about 20%. The big plus is that

B

USB is backward compatible, so you can mix and match USB 1 and 2 products on the same USB daisychain. This is pretty cool, and might put USB over the top.

Don't forget though, support for USB 2.0 in SP1 doesn't mean you can miraculously plug in your USB 2.0 peripherals and expect them to fly at full throttle. They won't, unless you have a USB 2.0 port on your computer. If you plug a USB 2.0 drive into an older USB (1) connector, it will likely work, but will fall back to 12Mbps, not 480.

Although available for some time now as an update on the Windows Update Web site, support for USB 2.0 has been lacking from Windows XP—until SP1 that is. Microsoft Knowledge Base Article Q312370 addressed the pre-SP1 support for the USB 2.0 standard in Windows XP. With the inclusion of USB 2.0 support in Windows XP SP1, you should now be able to experience reliable, high-speed USB performance from your USB 2.0–compliant devices.

NOTE

> There is no official USB 2.0 support for Windows 2000, but rather a beta offering from Microsoft—although this will probably change with the release of Windows 2000 SP3. USB support for Windows 2000 and 9x is offered by several third-party developers via USB 2.0 add-on adapters.

IPv6

In 1947, AT&T developed a system called the North American Numbering Plan (NANP) which began implementation in 1950. Under that plan, all telephone numbers in World Zone 1 (which covers the United States, Canada, Mexico, and Caribbean countries) would have the format have: XXX-YYY-ZZZZ. The XXX part is what we now call the "area code." This scheme was the result of the increase in popularity of the telephone, and the resultant shortage of available phone numbers. The same problem is happening with the Internet. You may not be aware of it, but there is a shortage in Internet addresses now. According to ZDNet UK News, the EC (European Commission) says 74 percent of IPv4 addresses belong to North American organizations, with the Massachusetts Institute of Technology and Stanford each owning more addresses than the People's Republic of China. Obviously, the Internet is running out of IP addresses under the current IPv4 addressing system. Ipv6 (supported in SP1), aims to solve the shortage.

Under IPv4, IP addresses are 32-bit numbers consisting of four binary octets separated from each other by periods, such as 11000000.10101000.00000000.10011010, which is 192.168.0.154 in decimal notation. This way of providing IP addressed provides for 2^{32} or 4,294,967,296 possible addresses, of which a small amount are reserved for private networks and cannot be routed in the Internet.

The IPv6 addressing system aims to solve this problem by making use of a 128-bit number to represent a unique IP address. Using 128 bits gives you 2^{128} or 340,282,366,920,938,463,463,374,607,431,768,211,456 (3.4×10^{38}) possible addresses.

B

That is enough IP addresses to provide 655,570,793,348,866,943,898,599 (6.5×10^{23}) address-es for every square meter of the Earth's surface. That *should* help solve the shortage of available public IP addresses. Of course, the true power of the IPv6 addressing system is that it allows multiple hierarchical levels of organization and flexibility in design that is currently lacking from the IPv4 Internet of today.

Windows XP (build 2600) shipped with a developer's version of the IPv6 protocol. SP1 provides IPv6 support native to the operating system. In SP1, you can now install IPv6 from the Properties page of your Local Area Connection, just as would you install any other protocol, client, or service.

A 128-bit IPv6 address, as you might suspect, looks different from what you are used to seeing in IPv4. An IPv6 address in binary form looks like

```
0010000111011010 0000000011010011 0000000000000000 0010111100111011
0000001010101010 0000000011111111 1111111000101000 1001110001011010
```

which translates into

```
21DA:00D3:0000:2F3B:02AA:00FF:FE28:9C5A
```

in hexadecimal.

Looks confusing, doesn't it? Well, it certainly can be. Take a look Figure B.3, showing the output of an IPCONFIG/ALL command run on a Windows XP SP1 system.

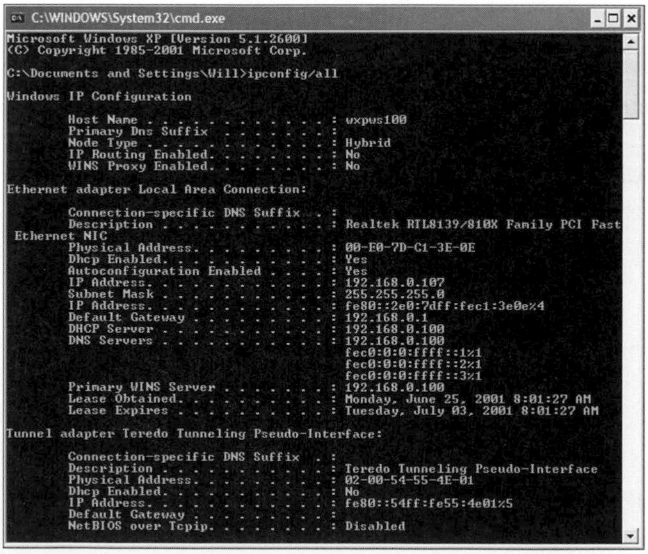

Figure B.3
IPCONFIG under IPv6—much more than meets the eye!

The IPv6 protocol and addressing system should all but put an end to memorizing IP addresses! Using the IPv6 protocol, IP classes and CIDR (Classless Inter-Domain Routing) will be things of the past. The three commonly used Private IP ranges (`10.0.0.0/8`, `172.16.0.0/12`, and `192.168.0.0/16`) will be replaced by one site-local address range (`FEC0::/48`). The familiar loopback address of `127.0.0.1` is replaced by `::1`.

NOTE

Whoa! Hold on just a minute here! What's up the with the :: thing going on in IPv6?

In the interest of making things ever easier, you can use double-colon (::) to represent contiguous strings of zero value. So, the loopback address of 0:0:0:0:0:0:0:1
becomes simply ::1. Of course, you can only use a double-colon once in an IPv6 IP
address—for obvious reasons.

Additionally, you can use leading zero suppression to remove the leading zeros within an
individual 16-bit string. Thus 21DA:00D3:0000:2F3B:02AA:00FF:FE28:9C5A becomes
21DA:D3:0:2F3B:2AA:FF:FE28:9C5A. Of course, the drivers within the operating system and
the infrastructure hardware devices (routers, switches, and so on) will handle all of these
conversions automatically, invisible to you.

For more information on IPv6...
Visit the official IPv6 site, located at http://www.ietf.org/html.charters/ipv6-charter.html, or
visit the Microsoft Web site on IPv6, located at http://www.microsoft.com/ipv6.

DEPARTMENT OF JUSTICE CONSENT DECREE COMPLIANCE

In reaction to the Consent Decree signed by Microsoft, you will now be able to "hide"
Microsoft middleware applications from view. This is a major paradigm shift for Microsoft
and the Windows family.

About the Consent Decree
Read more about the Consent Decree at http://www.microsoft.com/presspass/press/2001/nov01/
11-02SettlementPR.asp and http://www.microsoft.com/presspass/trial/nov01/
11-06revised.asp.

The changes to Windows center around the addition of a new Start menu item and Add or
Remove Programs applet option. The Set Program Access and Defaults shortcut (shown in
Figure B.4) is the first clue you will see that something has changed. Clicking it (or selecting
the same option from the Add or Remove Programs applet) opens the window shown in
Figure B.5.

B

Figure B.4
The Set Program Access and Defaults shortcut—new to SP1.

Figure B.5
The Set Program Access and Defaults page.

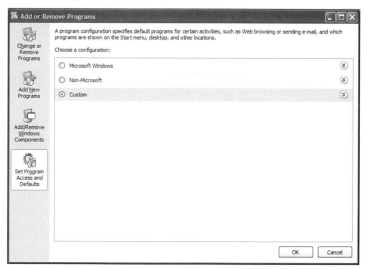

Depending on your computer, you may have three (as in Figure B.5) or four options here. The four available options are

- **Computer Manufacturer**—If your computer is an OEM PC (that is, manufactured by Dell, Gateway, or some other OEM), you will have this option. Choosing this option will return your computer to the middleware configuration chosen by the maker of the PC.

- **Microsoft Windows**—Choosing this configuration restores all Microsoft middleware applications to your Start menu. This will also cause third-party middleware products to become "hidden," assuming they properly support the new feature in SP1.

- **Non-Microsoft**—This choice will cause all of the Microsoft middleware products to be hidden in favor of showing the current configured third-party alternatives you are using.

- **Custom**—The choice allows you to customize how you want each type of middleware application to behave (see Figure B.6). Of course, for this to properly work, each application must be properly coded to allow the third-party application to identify itself to Windows that it should be added to this configuration screen.

Figure B.6
Configuring the Custom option—note that initially only Microsoft products are listed.

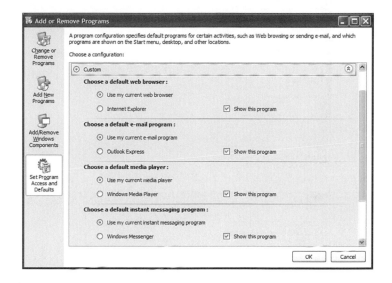

It's interesting to note that until all other middleware manufacturers implement the proper coding in their applications, Microsoft will still reign supreme in the Windows middleware wars. Why? Unless altered after this writing, you'll note that it takes only a click or two to return your settings to Redmond's preferred defaults—the Microsoft middleware products. The user interface makes this all too easy. To install third-party software means (typically) downloading and installing the software, but with the Microsoft products, a click or two will do, even if you had previously chosen to "remove'" them. This is because disabling them actually leaves them on your hard disk, sitting at the ready for quick reinstallation. We think this is out of compliance with the spirit of the Fed's mandate to play fair in the middleware area. To be fairer, there should be equally easy links to install, say, "Netscape" products, or AOL Messenger, Eudora, and so forth.

WINDOWS .NET MESSENGER 4.7

Windows .NET Messenger has received a minor facelift in SP1—one that should catch your attention immediately upon loading: No advertising at the bottom! Figure B.7 shows a typical older Windows .NET Messenger window, in this case version 4.6. As you can see, it has the annoying advertising at the bottom that most of us have grown to ignore.

B

Figure B.7
Windows .NET
Messenger version
4.6–advertising
offered at no extra
charge.

In Messenger version 4.7 (see Figure B.8), you will no longer be subject to the annoyance of advertising at the bottom of the Messenger window.

Figure B.8
I will view Messenger
advertising no more,
forever!

In addition to the removal of the advertising from the bottom of the Messenger window, Messenger also got a code revision to shore up some security weaknesses that it had. Additionally, you can now use the Windows Components Wizard (see Figure B.9) to remove Start menu links to Messenger (and Outlook Express for that matter). Previously this capability existed only for Internet Explorer.

Just the Messenger, Please
Windows. NET Messenger is also be available for download by itself from the Messenger Web site, located at `http://messenger.microsoft.com/`.

Figure B.9
Hiding Messenger
from the Windows
Component Wizard.

Windows Components Wizard

Windows Components
You can add or remove components of Windows XP.

To add or remove a component, click the checkbox. A shaded box means that only part of the component will be installed. To see what's included in a component, click Details.

Components:

☑ 🖳 Outlook Express	0.0 MB
☑ 📇 Update Root Certificates	0.0 MB
☑ ◆ Windows Media Player	0.0 MB
☑ 👤 Windows Messenger	0.0 MB

Description: Includes Windows Accessories and Utilities for your computer.

Total disk space required: 0.0 MB
Space available on disk: 16253.2 MB

Details...

< Back   Next >   Cancel

TABLET PCs

Although not new to the market, Tablet PCs will get a boost with the release of SP1. SP1 includes support specifically designed for the unique computing environment of Tablet PCs. Tablet PCs fit in somewhere between full-featured computers, such as desktop and laptop computers, and the slimmed-down Mira-enabled devices. Whereas Mira-enabled devices require a "base station" to operate, a Tablet PC does not. Tablet PCs can be thought of easier to use, smaller, lighter laptop computers that still offer full functionality. Tablet PCs typically only have USB ports, moving away from the legacy serial and parallel ports of today's Intel-based PC, and also have a docking station that typically contains a CD-ROM drive. A typical Tablet PC is shown in Figure B.10.

Figure B.10
A typical Tablet PC.

B

All I Want for Christmas…Is a Tablet PC.
To keep up to date on the developments in the Tablet PC arena, be sure to visit `http://microsoft.com/windowsxp/tabletpc/`.

PRODUCT ACTIVATION

Although controversial, Microsoft Product Activation (MPA) is not going away anytime soon. In fact, Microsoft has modified MPA in two small ways with the release of SP1; neither of which should have any impact on those legitimately using Windows XP.

It's no surprise that pirated copies of Windows XP are available. Rumor has it that you can buy a pirated, cracked copy of Windows XP for less than $3.00 from "anonymous" East Asian sources. Microsoft has identified the Volume License Key (VLK) that the majority of these pirated copies of Windows XP is tied to, and disabled it for use in SP1 and the Windows Update Web site. What this means, in simple terms, is that copies of Windows XP installed using the pirated VLK will not accept installations of SP1 and cannot access the Windows Update Web site.

The second change to Product Activation is actually a benefit to the typical user. You will now have a three-day grace period if you install Windows XP using the same Product Key on two different systems. In the past, there was no grace period available and an immediate phone call to Microsoft was required to activate the second installation. This will prove to be a great benefit to those users who have a system experience a non-recoverable disaster and need to reinstall Windows XP onto a new computer.

SECURITY FIXES AND OTHER IMPROVEMENTS

It's no surprise that SP1 includes a roll-up of all security patches and hot fixes that have been released for Windows XP since it was sent to manufacturing in 2001. (Hot Fixes are security updates and bug fixes that are important enough to be released before and between service packs. While Windows Update delivers the most critical Hot Fixes, there are hundreds of others that are announced only in the Microsoft Knowledge base and must be downloaded manually. Service Packs like SP1 deliver *all* of collected Hot Fixes). Many of these updates can be attributed to the Trustworthy Computing code review that Microsoft conducted during the early months of 2002.

Trustworthy Computing
To see what Microsoft has to say about its Trustworthy Computing initiative, see
`http://www.microsoft.com/presspass/features/2002/feb02/02-20mundieqa.asp`.

Although there are several hundred security and functionality fixes included in Windows XP SP1, the following lists some of fixes that address the more common and troublesome bugs that you may have come across. To read about any particular item, enter the following into your browser address box:

```
http://support.microsoft.com/default.aspx?scid=kb;EN-US;q######
```

Where ###### is replaced by the six-digit Knowledge Base article number given in the list.

- Q307274 Windows XP Stops Responding (Hangs) During Windows Shutdown
- Q307316 Volume License Product ID Is Revealed During the Sysprep.exe Mini-Setup Wizard
- Q307754 Cannot Print from a Window XP-Based Computer to a Shared Printer on a Windows 95-Based Computer
- Q307869 Files and Settings Are Not Transferred When You Use the Files and Settings Transfer Wizard
- Q308131 You May Not Be Able to Sign Up for the Internet by Using a Modem
- Q308219 Hard Disk Performance Is Slower Than You Expect
- Q308381 Windows XP Application Compatibility Update (October 25, 2001)
- Q308677 Error Message Appears When a Limited User Tries to Stream Media in Windows Media Player
- Q309127 List of Fixes That Are Included in the Windows XP Dynamic Update 1.0 Package
- Q309521 Windows XP Update Package, October 25, 2001
- Q310436 Cannot Play a DVD in Windows XP
- Q310772 PCMCIA Device May Not Work in Windows XP
- Q310869 STOP Error When You Start Windows After You Connect a Scanner
- Q311542 Devices May Not Power Up Properly When Resuming From Standby
- Q311804 Your Computer Hangs When You Log On to a Terminal Services Session
- Q311822 Your Computer May Hang If You Unexpectedly Remove a PC Card Storage Device While the Computer Is in Standby
- Q311889 Cannot Establish a Remote Assistance Connection
- Q312368 Data Loss May Occur After Reinstalling, Repairing, or Upgrading Windows XP
- Q312369 You May Lose Data or Program Settings After Reinstalling, Repairing, or Upgrading Windows XP
- Q312370 Universal Serial Bus 2.0 Support in Windows XP
- Q312401 List of Fixes That Are Included in the Windows XP Dynamic Update 1.1 Package
- Q312505 OpenGL-Based Program Causes Access Violation in Windows XP
- Q313484 Windows XP Application Compatibility Update (December 17, 2001)
- Q313596 Cannot Select a .jpg Image as Your Desktop Background Image

B

- Q313896   DHCP Clients Cannot Obtain an IP Address from the DHCP Server
- Q313910   Backup Now and Defragment Now Buttons Start the Wrong Tools
- Q314293   Computer Does Not Resume When You Press a Key on Your USB Keyboard
- Q314412   The Built-in Administrator Account May Appear in the User Accounts Tool
- Q314448   Msconfig.exe Stops Responding if User Is Not an Administrator
- Q314582   List of Fixes That Are Included in the Windows XP Dynamic Update 1.2 Package
- Q314612   Windows XP Cannot Enter Standby Mode When Window Media Player Is Paused
- Q314634   Windows XP Does Not Detect Your New USB Device
- Q314994   You Cannot Receive DHCP Configuration After Successful Authentication
- Q315000   Unchecked Buffer in Universal Plug and Play Can Lead to System Compromise for Windows XP
- Q315056   Preventing Distributed Denial-of-Service Attacks that Use the Universal Plug-and-Play Service
- Q315502   The USB Keyboard Does Not Work After Your Resume Your Computer from Standby or Suspend
- Q315621   Cannot Add FQDN Web Folders that Require Basic Authentication to "My Network Places"
- Q316309   Windows Installer Error 1619 When You Install from NTFS Protected Directories
- Q316676   "STOP 0x0000000A" Error Message When You Change from AC Power to DC Power
- Q317326   Stop 0x000000D1 Error Message When You Turn Your Computer Off
- Q317751   Explorer.exe Process Uses Many CPU Cycles When Windows Is Idle
- Q317895   MS02-018: Patch Available for Cross-Site Scripting in IIS Help File Search Facility Vulnerability
- Q318159   Damaged Registry Repair and Recovery in Windows XP
- Q318573   Erratic Behavior Occurs If You Create a "Desktop" Folder on the Desktop
- Q319580   Windows XP Application Compatibility Update (April 10, 2002)
- Q320008   You May Not Be Able to Shut Down Your Windows XP Computer
- Q320552   Problems with the InterActual DVD Playback Program
- Q322097   Slow Browsing to Windows 98 or Windows Me Clients from Windows XP
- Q323681   Problems After You Create a Folder That Is Named "Desktop" on the Desktop in Windows XP

B

INDEX

encapsulated PostScript
   files, 206
files, 977
folders, 132, 977
hardware, 1080
media pools, 1003
Outlook Express, 348-349
shortcuts, 550
spanned volumes,
   1000-1001
startup floppies, 99
striped volumes, 1001-1002
swap files, 854
user accounts, 111, 965
user groups, 980
workgroups, 535
zip files, 1036

Creator code, 714, 725

**Credential Manager Key
Ring, 45**

Critical Updates, 1170

**cross-platforming, 718,
1121-1122**

**crossover cables, 519, 648,
1033**

cscript command, 875

**CSNW (Client Service for
NetWare), 698-699**

CSV files, 357

Ctrl key, 123, 794, 814

Ctrl+Alt+Delete, 145-146

**CTS (clear-to-send) pin,
1078**

ctty command, 881

currency, 836

cursors
   blink rate, 827
   schemes, 828

**Customize this Folder (View
menu), 795-796**

customizing
   folders, 121, 796
   Internet Explorer, 310, 315
   Media Player, 254-255

Start menu, 776
toolbars, 21

Cut and Paste, 1012

cutting and pasting
   text, 173-176
   videos, 245

D

daily backups, 1028

data
   backups, 808
   partitions, 84
   pasted, 182
   recovery, 1161
   restoring from backups,
      1029-1031
   storage, 1106
   traceroute test, 461
   writing, 977

data and time, 93

**data-carrier-detect (DCD)
pin, 1078**

**Data Encryption Standard
(DESX), 45**

data files, storing, 140

data forks, 713

**Data Link Control (DLC),
479**

data links, 477

data rates, 692

**data-terminal-ready (DTR)
pin, 1078**

data types, 1139

databases
   Active Directory, 492-494
   distributed, 492
   whois, 460

datatypes, 196

**date and time configuration,
808-810**

**Date and Time applet
(Control Panel), 810,
823-824**

**Date, Time, Language, and
Regional Options category
view (Control Panel), 808**

DAVE, 718-719

Dazzle, 250

dblspace command, 881

**DCD (data-carrier-detect)
pin, 1078**

DCOM, 490

debugging applications, 936

debugging mode, 1156

decompression, 80

decryption, 1010-1012

dedicated connections, 661

default
   configuration
      email, 332
      Logon mode, 109-110
   documents, 418, 432
   gateways, 528, 656-657
   printers, 198
   profiles, 982
   settings
      connections, 288
      homepages, 322
      *Internet Explorer,
         312-313*
      modems, 835
      operating systems, 1096
      power savings, 787
      printer drivers, 574
      programs, 397

defective driver blocking, 63

**defining partitions,
1100-1103**

defrag command, 881

defragmentation
   hard drives, 1003-1007,
      1087
   Registry, 1148

**defragmentation utilities,
1037, 1046**

How can we make this index more useful? Email us at indexes@quepublishing.com

M

How can we make this index more useful? Email us at indexes@quepublishing.com

How can we make this index more useful? Email us at indexes@quepublishing.com

Other Related Titles

Upgrading and Repairing Networks, Third Edition
by Terry W. Ogletree
ISBN: 0-7897-2557-6
$59.99 USA/$89.95 CAN

How Computers Work, Sixth Edition
by Ron White
ISBN: 0-7897-2549-5
$34.99 USA/$52.95 CAN

Special Edition Using DOS 6.22, Third Edition
by Jim Cooper
ISBN: 0-7897-2573-8
$49.99 USA/$74.95 CAN

Special Edition Using the Internet and Web
by Michael Miller
ISBN: 0-7897-2613-0
$29.99 USA/$44.95 CAN

How the Internet Works
by Preston Gralla
ISBN: 0-7897-2582-7
$29.99 USA/$44.95 CAN

How Wireless Works
by Preston Gralla
ISBN: 0-7897-2487-1
$29.99 USA/$44.95 CAN

Absolute Beginner's Guide to Personal Firewalls
by Jerry Lee Ford, Jr.
ISBN: 0-7897-2625-4
$24.99 USA/$37.95 CAN

Absolute Beginner's Guide to Cable Internet Connections
by Mark Edward Soper
ISBN: 0-7897-2705-6
$24.99 USA/$37.95 CAN

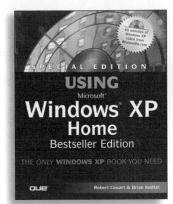

Special Edition Using Microsoft Windows XP Home Edition, Bestseller Edition
by Robert Cowart and Brian Knittel
ISBN: 0-7897-2851-6
$49.99 USA/$74.95 CAN

Special Edition Using Microsoft Office XP
by Ed Bott and Woody Leonhard
ISBN: 0-7897-2513-4
$39.99 USA/$59.95 CAN

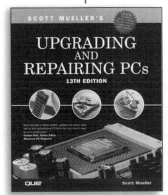

Upgrading and Repairing PCs, 13th Edition
by Scott Mueller
ISBN: 0-7897-2542-8
$59.99 USA/$89.95 CAN

RUNNING THE CD INCLUDED WITH THIS BOOK

This CD-ROM is optimized to run under Windows 95/98/Me/NT/2000/XP using the QuickTime Player version 5 (or greater), from Apple. This CD-ROM is not designed to run on a Mac. If you don't have the QuickTime 5 Player installed, you must install it, either by downloading it from the Internet at http://www.quicktime.com, or by running the Setup program from the CD-ROM. If you install from the Web, it's fine to use the free version of the QuickTime player. You don't need to purchase the full version.

To install the QuickTime player from the CD-ROM, follow these steps:

1. Insert the CD-ROM in the drive.
2. Use Explorer or My Computer to browse to the CD-ROM.
3. Open the QuickTime folder.
4. Double-click on the setup program there.
5. Follow the setup instructions onscreen.

RUNNING THE CD IN WINDOWS 95/98/ME/NT/2000/XP

Minimum Requirements:

- QuickTime 5 Player
- Pentium II P300 (or equivalent)
- 64MB of RAM
- 8X CD-ROM
- Windows 95, Windows 98, Windows 2000, Windows Me, or Windows NT 4.0 with at least Service Pack 4
- 16-bit sound card and speakers

This presentation can run directly from the CD (see below for running it from the hard drive for better performance if necessary) and should start automatically when you insert the CD in the drive. If the program does not start automatically, your system might not be set up to automatically detect CDs. To change this, you can do the following:

1. Choose Settings, Control Panel, and click the System icon.
2. Click the Device Manager tab in the System Properties dialog box.
3. Double-click the Disk drives icon and locate your CD-ROM drive.
4. Double-click the CD-ROM drive icon, and then click the Settings tab in the CD-ROM Properties dialog box. Be sure the Auto Insert Notification box is checked. This specifies that Windows will be notified when you insert a compact disc into the drive.

If you don't care about the auto-start setting for your CD-ROM, and don't mind the manual approach, you can start the lessons manually, this way:

1. Insert the CD-ROM.
2. Double-click the My Computer icon on your Windows desktop.
3. Open the CD-ROM folder.
4. Double-click the startnow.exe icon in the folder.
5. Follow instructions on the screen to start.